Fodor's 96

Mexico

"When it comes to information on regional history, what to see and do, and shopping, these guides are exhaustive."

—*USAir Magazine*

"Usable, sophisticated restaurant coverage, with an emphasis on good value."

—Andy Birsh, *Gourmet Magazine* columnist

"Valuable because of their comprehensiveness."

—*Minneapolis Star-Tribune*

"Fodor's always delivers high quality...thoughtfully presented...thorough."

—*Houston Post*

"An excellent choice for those who want everything under one cover."

—*Washington Post*

Fodor's Travel Publications, Inc.
New York • Toronto • London • Sydney • Auckland

Fodor's Mexico

Editor: Edie Jarolim

Contributors: Dan Goss Anderson, Rob Andrews, Robert Blake, Wendy Luft, Bevin McLaughlin, Maribeth Mellin, "Mexico" Mike Nelson, Tracy Patruno, Peg Rosen, Mary Ellen Schultz, M. T. Schwartzman, Dinah Spritzer.

Creative Director: Fabrizio La Rocca

Cartographer: David Lindroth

Cover Photograph: Peter Guttman

Text Design: Between the Covers

Copyright

Special Sales

CONTENTS

Maps

ON THE ROAD WITH FODOR'S

A GOOD TRAVEL GUIDE is like a wonderful traveling companion. It's charming, it's brimming with sound recommendations and solid ideas, it pulls no punches in describing lodging and dining establishments, and it's consistently full of fascinating facts that make you view what you've traveled to see in a rich new light. In the creation of *Mexico '96,* we at Fodor's have gone to great lengths to provide you with the very best of all possible traveling companions— and to make your trip the best of all posible vacations.

About Our Writers

The information in these pages is a collaboration of a whole roster of extraordinary writers.

A psychologist-turned-journalist and archaeology buff, **Patricia Alisau** updated the Oaxaca, Chiapas and Tabasco, and Mexico City chapters of this book. She was so drawn to the surrealism of Mexico City— "Where in the U.S. can you find pyramids?" she asks—that she moved to the capital some 20 years ago. She spends much of her time in the colorful markets, where fresh fruit is piled high next to stacks of dried batwings, an ancient cure for a faithless lover. She was restaurant and night-club columnist for the *News,* Mexico's English-language daily, worked as a photo stringer for AP during the Nicaragua Revolution, and has written for Mexico's *Vogue* magazine.

Tucson-based freelance writer **Dan Goss Anderson,** who wrote the Sonora chapter, is a born-again convert to the lures of Mexico. He lived within 50 miles of the country for the first 38 years of his life but never had the courage to cross the border. Then one day he came home, gathered his wife and two small sons, and moved south to Hermosillo, Sonora. Knowing only about a dozen words in Spanish when he arrived, he returned to the states two years later with a firm grasp of the language and an abiding appreciation for the country and, especially, its people.

We borrowed **Jessica Blatt** and **Ariana Mohit** from our Berkeley guide series to write about Northeast Mexico and the state of Veracruz. Jessica was the co-editor of *Mexico on the Loose 1995,* and not only survived the experience but was downright enthusiastic about getting the chance to eat her way through Veracruz after attending a wedding in Oaxaca. Ariana, who wrote the Northeast and Veracruz sections of the same book, discovered an affinity for *carne asada* and freak, out-of-nowhere thunderstorms during her months of research. Both writers are unconscionably young and energetic.

Chris Humphrey combed the Copper Canyon, the Heartland, and Guadalajara for us this year before he joined Generation Dos Equis (XX)—as *Newsweek* dubbed the growing group of twentysomethings seeking fame and fortune (well, mostly fortune) south of the border—by moving to Mexico City. He's likely to come closer to fame (or at least respectability) in his new job as an editor/correspondent for the Mexico City *News,* a highly-regarded source of English-language information for much of the country.

When she was fresh out of college, our Acapulco correspondent **Wendy Luft** jumped at the chance to take a job with the Mexican tourist office—for a year or two at most, she figured. Some 25 years later, she and her Mexican husband and their adolescent sons, inveterate travelers all, traverse the country together from their home base in Mexico City. As a writer, editor, and public relations representative, Wendy has written and collaborated on many travel books and articles about her adopted country.

Maribeth Mellin, our long-time Baja California and Yucatán updater, covers Mexico for *San Diego Magazine.* She writes in an office filled with photos and artifacts from Mexico's two isolated peninsulas, including a snapshot of the 140-pound marlin she caught in the Sea of Cortés and a handcarved jaguar from Cobá. She refused to marry her husband (who'd been traveling to Baja for over 20 years) until he rambled through her beloved Yucatán with her in a rented VW bug. She finally said "yes" enroute to Chichén Itzá while humming the Mexican ballad "Amor," which became their wedding song.

It was the quixotic silver jewelry that her aunt brought back from Mazatlán that hooked **Kate Rice,** who wrote the new introduction to this book, on Mexico. During a summer spent in the country in a vain attempt to improve her Spanish, she fell hard for its art and cuisine—especially the mangoes dipped in hot sauce sold on the street corners of Guadalajara. It's been a family affair all along: Her brothers lead mule rides into remote reaches of Baja California's Sierra San Francisco and traced the paths of the Maya along the rivers of Chiapas. For the past few years, Kate has been covering Mexico for publications including *Tour & Travel News* and *Business Traveler International*.

Like many natives of Texas, **Melissa Rivers** spent her youth thinking of Mexico as her personal backyard playground. This never-grow-up writer still looks forward to her yearly trips for Fodor's to Cancún, Cozumel, and Isla Mujeres, where she wiggles her pudgy toes in the warm sand, paddles frantically after rainbow-colored fish among the reefs, chases iguanas, and scampers through the jungle exploring Maya ruins. She also enjoys sleuthing out the best the region has to offer and hopes to reap the fruits of her research by retiring there someday—if she ever grows up, that is.

In other words, you're in good hands. Editor **Edie Jarolim** first got a taste for Mexico in the late 1970s, when she attempted (unsuccessfully) to visit every Maya ruin in the Yucatán on a two week vacation. Her frequent return forays—she wrote the Copper Canyon chapter and updated the Sonora, Cancún, Cozumel, and Isla Mujeres sections of earlier editions of this guide—have been made easier by a recent move to neighboring Arizona. She knows the Spanish conquistadors were a cruel bunch, but can't help but admire the good sense of a group who set out to vanquish Veracruz and Acapulco instead of, say, Saskatchewan.

What's New

We rearranged the chapters a bit this year to make it easier for you to find the places you want to explore (*see* How to Use This Book, *below*). We also beefed up the shopping sections throughout, the better to help you indulge in one of Mexico's great pastimes. And we've greatly expanded our coverage of the state of Veracruz, home to great seafood, outdoor cafés, and little-visited archaeological sites—in short, one of the country's hidden tourist treasures.

A New Design

If this is not the first Fodor's guide you've purchased, you'll immediately notice our new look. More readable than ever? We think so—and we hope you do, too.

Travel Updates

Just before your trip, you may want to order a Fodor's Worldview Travel Update. From local publications all over Mexico, the lively, cosmopolitan editors at Worldview cull information on concerts, plays, dance performanes, opera, gallery and museum shows, sports competitions, and other special events that coincide with your visit. See the order blank in the back of this book for more information, call 800/799–9609, or fax 800/799–9619.

And in Mexico

The big news this year is the **devaluation of the peso,** started at the end of 1994 and continuing through 1995; as we went to press in mid-year, Mexico's currency was worth nearly 60% less than it had been the year before (with an exchange rate of 6.02 pesos to the dollar). On the one hand, this signals increased purchasing power for travelers (though prices of chain hotels, generally calculated in dollars, remain stable); on the other, it means that projects in progress before the devaluation—including many tourist developments—have been put on hold until the dust from the economic bombshell clears.

But even before devaluation, there were signs of a move toward slowing growth. This is especially true in **Cancún,** Mexico's number one tourist destination, fast approaching the saturation point in hotel development. Instead, existing properties are being renovated and, in a surprising trend, many are turning all-inclusive. One of the few deluxe international properties to open recently was the Caesar Park Beach & Golf Resort.

The offshore island of **Cozumel** is taking steps to curb progress' toll on the environment by halting development of several deluxe hotels. At the same time, however, Cozumel has added a new cruise ship pier and expanded the older one to accommodate the growing number of visiting ships; it has also become the home port of the *Regent Star*. And the American influence is more evident than ever. No less than six American fast food chains have opened on or near the waterfront in the last year, and the Hard Rock Cafe joined the ranks on the waterfront across from the municipal pier.

Development continues along the Caribbean Coast, too, especially in the Cancún–Tulum Corridor: An 81-mile-long stretch of coastal Route 307 is gradually being widened to four lanes, and tourist services are sprouting along its sides. The most striking change is still evolving at **Tulum,** the most frequently visited Maya ruin on the Yucatán peninsula: The Mexican government is developing a formal tourist complex and has changed the highway entrance to the site. Cars and buses now park far from the actual ruins, which makes viewing Tulum's temples and altars a much more serene experience.

At the same time, **ecotourism** is on the rise here, thanks to the exotic birds, marine life, and lagoons of the **Sian Ka'an Biosphere Reserve.** Small resorts catering to scuba divers and fishermen are gaining in popularity along the **Xcalak peninsula** at the southern base of the Quintana Roo coast, near the Belize border. The final frontier of this vast, sparsely inhabited, and beautiful region, Xcalak has miles and miles of deserted, undeveloped beaches (though rumors of impending construction abound).

And not far from the Oaxacan coastal town of Puerto Angel, a new ecological museum has opened in tiny **Mazunte,** where sea turtles come annually to lay their eggs. Once the site of mass slaughtering of the turtles for their meat and shells, Mazunte built the aquarium-filled museum following the government ban on turtle hunting.

Nor is the country's culture being neglected. In the magnificent Santo Domingo monastery-church complex in **Oaxaca City,** a new museum has been dedicated to Colonial religious art produced in the area; it's in the former military barracks that occupied part of the monastery until 1994. In addition, road travel to Oaxaca City from Mexico City has been improved with the completion of the Tehuacan–Oaxaca City toll road. Tehuacan now connects with the toll road to Mexico City, and the driving time to the capital has been cut by about one hour.

This new Oaxaca road is just the latest in a series: An ambitious **highway construction program** is rapidly improving driving conditions throughout Mexico. Toll roads now connect Mexico City and Acapulco; Nogales and Mazatlán; León and Monterrey; and more are currently under way. The highways are safe and fast, but take note: Tolls sometimes as high as 40¢ a mile can make using them prohibitively expensive.

Bus travel within Mexico and from the U.S. border has also changed dramatically in recent years. New agreements now allow American tour buses to enter Mexico, thus eliminating the inconvenience of changing carriers at the border. And recently several Mexican bus lines began offering service to destinations within the United States, often at significantly lower rates than U.S. bus lines. Tickets for cities as far from the border as Denver can now be booked in Mexico, and service is expanding rapidly. These changes, and an overall ground travel improvement program, has spurred a dramatic increase in both the quality and frequency of service inn the border region and throughout Mexico. Air-conditioned *gran lujo* (deluxe) vehicles—often called planes on wheels—frequently feature televisions, wet bars, and hostess service.

In contrast, talk about privatizing the rail lines, once widespread, has died down in the current economic crises, so **train transport** in Mexico is unlikely to improve in the near future. First-class schedules have been cut, and dining, sleeping, and club cars are often removed from trains with little, if any, notice to travelers. Service has particularly suffered near the U.S. border, where more profitable motorcoaches are taking over. In addition, maintenance on the popular Chihuahua–Pacific railway has deteriorated, though American tour operators are currently working with Mexico to place luxurious private cars on this train and others that service the Yucatán, colonial cities, and other popular tourist destinations.

How to Use This Book

Organization

Up front is **The Gold Guide,** comprising two sections on gold paper that are chock-full of information about traveling within your destination and traveling in general. Both are in alphabetical order by topic. **Important Contacts A to Z** gives you addresses and telephone numbers of organizations and companies that offer destination-related services and detailed information or publications. Here's where you'll find information about how to get to Mexico from wherever you are. **Smart Travel Tips A to Z,** the Gold Guide's second section, gives specific tips on how to get the most out of your travels, as well as information on how to accomplish what you need to Mexico.

Chapter 1 introduces you to the entire country of Mexico, giving you a capsule overview of the chapters and of the country's favorite pleasures and pastimes. The remaining chapters of the book are arranged geographically: We take you first to Mexico City, the capital and main transportation hub, and then move from the northwest (Baja California) to the southeast (the Yucatán Peninsula), heading roughly north to south along the two coasts. Each chapter covers exploring, shopping, sports, dining, lodging, and arts and nightlife and ends with a section called Essentials, which tells you how to get there and get around and gives you important local addresses and telephone numbers.

At the end of the book, you'll find Portraits, wonderful essays about Mexico, as well as suggestions for pre-trip reading, both fiction and non-fiction.

Stars

Stars in the margin are used to denote highly recommended sights, attractions, hotels, and restaurants.

Restaurant and Hotel Criteria and Price Categories

Restaurants and lodgings are chosen with a view to giving you the cream of the crop in each location and in each price range. Within each chapter, price charts will help you tailor your choices to your purse.

In all restaurant price charts, costs are per person, excluding drinks, tip, and tax. In hotel price charts, rates are for standard double rooms, excluding city and state sales taxes.

Hotel Facilities

Note that in general you incur charges when you use many hotel facilities. We wanted to let you know what facilities a hotel has to offer, but we don't always specify whether or not there's a charge, so when planning a vacation that entails a stay of several days, it's wise to ask what's included in the rate.

Dress Codes in Restaurants

Look for an overview in the Packing for Mexico section of Smart Travel Tips A to Z in the Gold Guide pages at the front of this book. Then, at the beginning of the individual chapters' dining sections we tell you what's most common in that area. In general, we note dress code only when men are required to wear a jacket or jacket and tie.

Credit Cards

The following abbreviations are used: **AE,** American Express; **DC,** Diner's Club; **MC,** MasterCard; and **V,** Visa. Discover is not accepted outside the United States.

Please Write to Us

Everyone who has contributed to *Mexico '96* has worked hard to make the text accurate. All prices and opening times are based on information supplied to us at press time, and the publisher cannot accept responsibility for any errors that may have occurred. The passage of time will bring changes, so it's always a good idea to call ahead and confirm information when it matters—particularly if you're making a detour to visit specific sights or attractions. When making reservations at a hotel or inn, be sure to mention if you have a disability or are traveling with children, if you prefer a private bath or a certain type of bed, or if you have specific dietary needs or any other concerns.

Were the restaurants we recommended as described? Did our hotel picks exceed your expectations? Did you find a museum we recommended a waste of time? We would love your feedback, positive and negative. If you have complaints, we'll look into them and revise our entries when the facts warrant it. If you've happened upon a special place that we haven't included, we'll pass the information along to the writers

so they can check it out. So please send us
a letter or postcard (we're at 201 E. 50th
St., New York, New York 10022). We'll
look forward to hearing from you. And in
the meantime, have a wonderful trip!

Karen Cure
Editorial Director

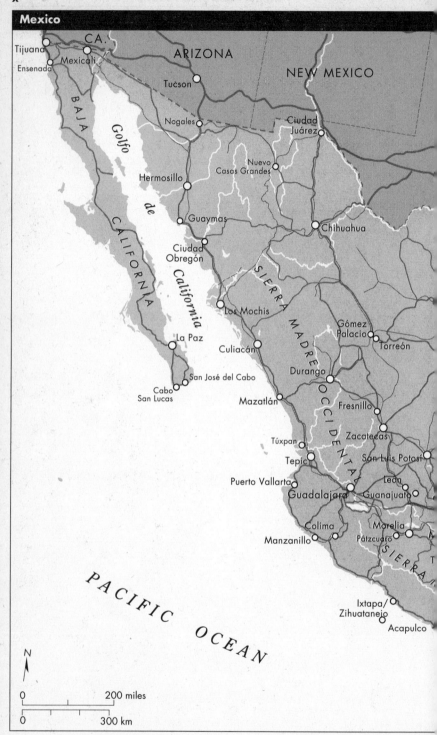

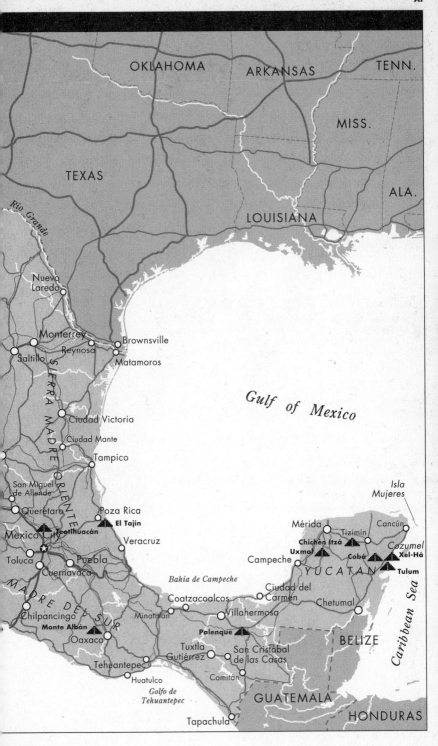

Mexican States and Capitals

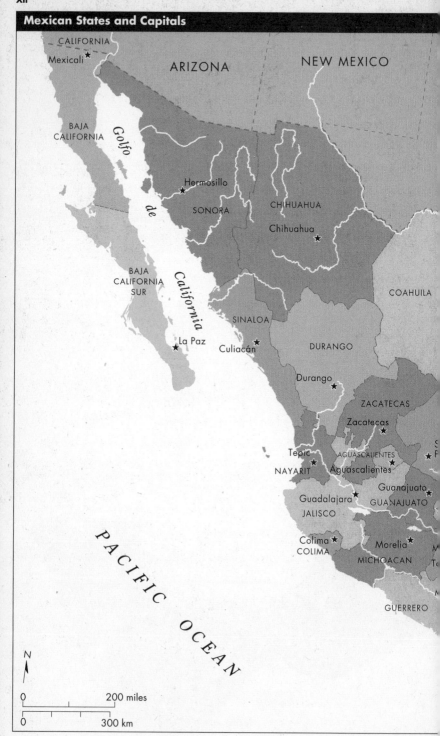

CALIFORNIA
Mexicali ★

ARIZONA

NEW MEXICO

BAJA
CALIFORNIA

Golfo

Hermosillo ★

SONORA

CHIHUAHUA

Chihuahua ★

de

BAJA
CALIFORNIA
SUR

California

COAHUILA

SINALOA

La Paz ★

Culiacán ★

DURANGO

Durango ★

ZACATECAS

Zacatecas ★

Tepic ★

AGUASCALIENTES

NAYARIT

Aguascalientes ★

Guanajuato ★

Guadalajara ★

GUANAJUATO

JALISCO

Colima ★
COLIMA

Morelia ★

MICHOACAN

GUERRERO

PACIFIC OCEAN

N

0   200 miles

0   300 km

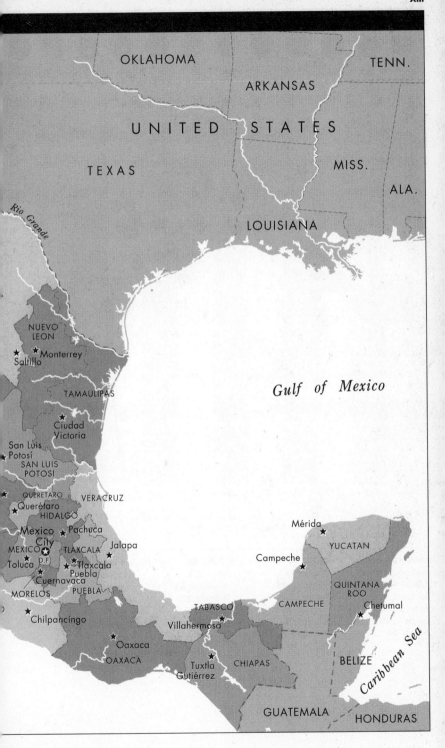

World Time Zones

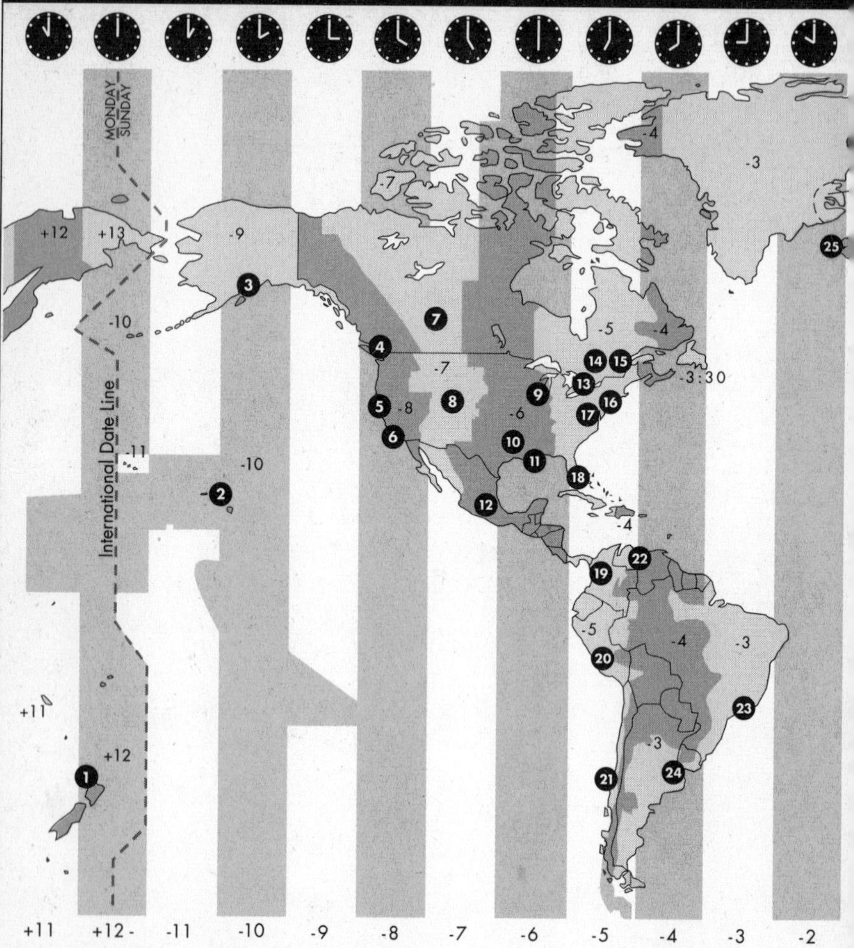

MONDAY
SUNDAY
International Date Line
+12
+13
-9
-10
-11
-7
-4
-3
-5
-3:30
-8
-6
+11
+12
+11 +12 - -11 -10 -9 -8 -7 -6 -5 -4 -3 -2

Numbers below vertical bands relate each zone to Greenwich Mean Time (0 hrs.).
Local times frequently differ from these general indications,
as indicated by light-face numbers on map.

Algiers, **29**
Anchorage, **3**
Athens, **41**
Auckland, **1**
Baghdad, **46**
Bangkok, **50**
Beijing, **54**

Berlin, **34**
Bogotá, **19**
Budapest, **37**
Buenos Aires, **24**
Caracas, **22**
Chicago, **9**
Copenhagen, **33**
Dallas, **10**

Delhi, **48**
Denver, **8**
Djakarta, **53**
Dublin, **26**
Edmonton, **7**
Hong Kong, **56**
Honolulu, **2**

Istanbul, **40**
Jerusalem, **42**
Johannesburg, **44**
Lima, **20**
Lisbon, **28**
London (Greenwich), **27**
Los Angeles, **6**
Madrid, **38**
Manila, **57**

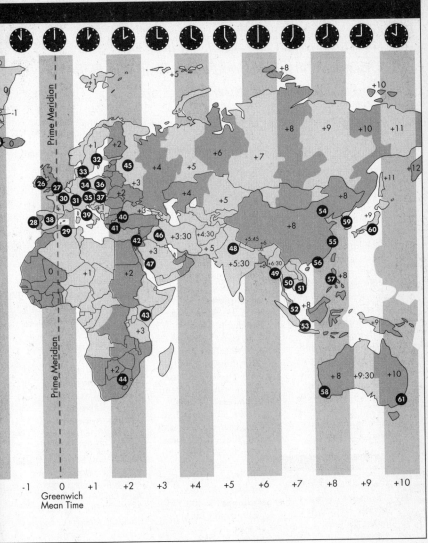

Mecca, **47**
Mexico City, **12**
Miami, **18**
Montréal, **15**
Moscow, **45**
Nairobi, **43**
New Orleans, **11**
New York City, **16**

Ottawa, **14**
Paris, **30**
Perth, **58**
Reykjavík, **25**
Rio de Janeiro, **23**
Rome, **39**
Saigon (Ho Chi Minh City), **51**

San Francisco, **5**
Santiago, **21**
Seoul, **59**
Shanghai, **55**
Singapore, **52**
Stockholm, **32**
Sydney, **61**
Tokyo, **60**

Toronto, **13**
Vancouver, **4**
Vienna, **35**
Warsaw, **36**
Washington, D.C., **17**
Yangon, **49**
Zürich, **31**

IMPORTANT CONTACTS A TO Z

An Alphabetical Listing of Publications, Organizations, and Companies That Will Help You Before, During, and After Your Trip

No single travel resource can give you every detail about every topic that might interest or concern you at the various stages of your journey—when you're planning your trip, while you're on the road, and after you get back home. The following organizations, books, and brochures will supplement the information in Fodor's *Mexico '96*. For related information, including both basic tips on visiting Mexico and background information on many of the topics below, study Smart Travel Tips A to Z, the section that follows Important Contacts A to Z.

A

AIR TRAVEL

The major gateways to Mexico include Acapulco, Cancún, Cozumel, Guadalajara, Ixtapa/Zihuatanejo, Mazatlán, Mérida, Mexico City, Puerto Vallarta, and San José in Los Cabos. Mexico City is 4½ hours from New York, 4 hours from Chicago, 3½ hours from Los Angeles. Cancún is 3½ hours from New York and from Chicago, 4½ hours from Los Angeles. Acapulco is 6 hours from New York, 4 hours from Chicago, and 3½ hours from Los Angeles.

CARRIERS

Carriers serving Mexico include **Aero California** (☎ 800/237–6225) from Los Angeles and Phoenix; **Aeromexico** (☎ 800/237–6639) from Atlanta, Dallas, El Paso, Houston, Los Angeles, McAllen, TX, Miami, New Orleans, New York, Phoenix, San Antonio, San Diego, and Tucson; **America West** (☎ 800/235–9292) from Phoenix to Mexico City, Cabo San Lucas, and Mazatlán; **American** (☎ 800/433–7300) from Chicago, Dallas/Fort Worth, and Miami; **Continental** (☎ 800/525–0280) from Cleveland, Denver, Houston, and Newark, NJ; **Delta** (☎ 800/241–4141) from Atlanta, Dallas/Fort Worth, Los Angeles, and New York; **Mexicana** (☎ 800/531–7921) from Chicago, Denver, Los Angeles, Miami, Newark, San Antonio, San Francisco, and San Jose; **Northwest** (☎ 800/447–4747) from Detroit to Cancún and Cozumel and from Tampa, Memphis, and Minneapolis to Cancún, Cozumel, and Ixtapa; **Taesa** (☎ 800/328–2372) from Chicago, Laredo, TX, and Oakland; **United** (☎ 800/538–2929) from Chicago, Los Angeles, Miami, San Francisco, and Washington/Dulles; and **USAir** (☎ 800/428–

4322) from Philadelphia and Tampa to Mexico City.

Mexicana and Aeromexico provide the bulk of air service within Mexico and regional airlines have filled in most of the gaps. **Aerocaribe** (reserve through Mexicana) serves the Yucatán and the Southeast; **Aeromar** (reserve through Mexicana or Aeromexico) serves central Mexico; **Aerolitoral** (reserve through Aeromexico or Mexicana) serves northeastern Mexico, and **Aeroponiente** (reserve through Aeromexico) serves southwestern Mexico. **Aviacsa** (☎ 961/2–80–81 in Chiapas; ☎ 5/559–1955 in Mexico City) flies between Mexico City and Tuxtla Guttiérez; and **Aero California** (☎ 800/237–6225) serves Colima, Guadalajara, Loreto, Los Mochis, Puebla, Tepic, Tijuana, and several other gateways.

FROM THE U.K.➤ **British Airways** has a direct flight from London to Mexico City. Other airlines flying to Mexico, with brief stops en route, include **Continental** (via Houston), **American** (via Dallas or Miami), **KLM** (via Amsterdam), **Air France** (via Paris), **Delta** (via Atlanta), **United** (via Chicago or Washington, Dulles), **Lufthansa** (via

Frankfurt), and **Iberia** (via Madrid).

COMPLAINTS

To register complaints about charter and scheduled airlines, contact the U.S. Department of Transportation's **Office of Consumer Affairs** (400 7th St. NW, Washington, DC 20590, ☎ 202/366–2220 or 800/322–7873).

CONSOLIDATORS

An established consolidator selling to the public is **TFI Tours International** (34 W. 32nd St., New York, NY 10001, ☎ 212/736–1140 or 800/745–8000).

PUBLICATIONS

For general information about charter carriers, ask for the Office of Consumer Affairs' brochure **"Plane Talk: Public Charter Flights."** The Department of Transportation also publishes a 58-page booklet, **"Fly Rights"** ($1.75; Consumer Information Center, Dept. 133-B, Pueblo, CO 81009).

For other tips and hints, consult the Consumers Union's monthly **"Consumer Reports Travel Letter"** ($39 a year; Box 53629, Boulder CO 80322, ☎ 800/234–1970) and the newsletter **"Travel Smart"** ($37 a year; 40 Beechdale Rd., Dobbs Ferry, NY 10522, ☎ 800/327–3633). Good books on the subject include *The Official Frequent Flyer Guidebook,* by Randy Petersen ($14.99 plus $3 shipping; 4715-C

Town Center Dr., Colorado Springs, CO 80916, ☎ 719/597–8899 or 800/487–8893); *Airfare Secrets Exposed,* by Sharon Tyler and Matthew Wonder (Universal Information Publishing; available for $16.95 plus $3.75 shipping from Sandcastle Publishing, Box 3070-A, South Pasadena, CA 91031, ☎ 213/255–3616 or 800/655–0053); and *202 Tips Even the Best Business Travelers May Not Know,* by Christopher McGinnis ($10 plus $3 shipping from Irwin Professional Publishing, Box 1333, Burr Ridge Parkway, Burr Ridge, IL 60521, ☎ 708/789–4000 or 800/634–3966)..

WITHIN MEXICO

Mexicana (☎ 800/531–7921) and **Aeromexico** (☎ 800/237–6639) provide the bulk of air service inside Mexico, and regional airlines have filled in most of the gaps. **Aerocaribe** (reserve through Mexicana) serves the Yucatán and the Southeast; **Aeromar** (reserve through Mexicana or Aeromexico) serves central Mexico; **Aerolitoral** serves northeastern Mexico, and **Aeroponiente** serves southwestern Mexico (reserve both through Aeromexico). **Aviacsa** (☎ 961/3–50–29 or 961/2–80–81 in Chiapas; ☎ 5/559–1955 or 5/590–9522 in Mexico City) flies between Mexico City and Tuxtla Gutiérrez; and **Aero California** (☎ 800/546–

6017) serves Colima, Guadalajara, Loreto, Los Mochis, Puebla, Tepic, and Tijuana.

B

BETTER BUSINESS BUREAU

For local contacts, consult the **Council of Better Business Bureaus** (4200 Wilson Blvd., Arlington, VA 22203, ☎ 703/276–0100).

BUS TRAVEL

Gateway cities such as El Paso, Del Rio, Laredo, McAllen, Brownsville, and San Antonio, Texas, and Tijuana are served by several small private bus lines as well as by **Greyhound Lines** (☎ 800/231–2222).

WITHIN MEXICO

In Mexico City, the best first-class bus lines include **ADO** (☎ 5/542–7192 or 5/542–7199), serving Yucatán, Cancún, Villahermosa, and Veracruz from the Eastern Bus Terminal, and Matamoros, Oaxaca, and Tampico from the Northern Bus Terminal (☎ 5/587–5700 or 5/567–1577); **Cristóbal Colón** (☎ 5/542–7263), which goes to Chiapas, Oaxaca, and the Guatemala border from the Eastern Bus Terminal; **ETN** (☎ 5/272–8736), which goes to Guadalajara, Querétaro, and Guanajuato from the Northern Bus Terminal; and **Transportes del Norte** (☎ 5/587–5377), which goes up to the U.S. border from the Northern Bus Terminal.

C

CAR INSURANCE

Experienced and reliable sources for Mexican car insurance are **Sanborn's Mexican Insurance** (☎ 210/686–0711), **Instant Mexico Auto Insurance** (☎ 619/428–3583), and **Oscar Padilla Mexican Insurance** (☎ 619/428–2221).

CAR RENTAL

Major car-rental companies represented in Mexico include **Avis** (☎ 800/331–1084, 800/879–2847 in Canada), **Budget** (☎ 800/527–0700, 0800/181–181 in the U.K.), **Hertz** (☎ 800/654–3001, 800/263–0600 in Canada, 0181/679–1799 in the U.K.), and **National Interrent** (☎ 800/227–3876, 800/227–7368 in Canada, 0181/950–5050 in the U.K.). In Mexico, rental prices vary by location, type of car, and travel season. Rates in Mexico City begin at $40 a day or $260 a week for an economy car with unlimited mileage. This does not include tax, which in Mexico is 10%.

RENTAL WHOLESALERS

Contact **Auto Europe** (Box 7006, Portland, ME 04112, ☎ 207/828–2525 or 800/223–5555).

CHILDREN AND TRAVEL

FLYING

Look into **"Flying With Baby"** ($5.95 plus $1 shipping; Third Street Press, Box 261250, Littleton, CO 80126,

☎ 303/595–5959), co-written by a flight attendant. **"Kids and Teens in Flight,"** free from the U.S. Department of Transportation's Office of Consumer Affairs, offers tips for children flying alone. Every two years, the February issue of *Family Travel Times* (*see* Know-How, *below*), published 10 times a year by Travel With Your Children (TWYCH, 45 W. 18th St., New York, NY 10011, ☎ 212/206–0688; annual subscription $55), covers destinations, types of vacations, and modes of travel.

KNOW-HOW

The *Family Travel Guides* catalog ($1 postage; ☎ 510/527–5849) lists about 200 books and articles on family travel. Also check *Take Your Baby and Go! A Guide for Traveling with Babies, Toddlers and Young Children,* by Sheri Andrews, Judy Bordeaux, and Vivian Vasquez ($5.95 plus $1.50 shipping; Bear Creek Publications, 2507 Minor Ave., Seattle, WA 98102, ☎ 206/322–7604 or 800/326–6566). *The 100 Best Family Resorts in North America,* ($12.95) and the two-volume *50 Great Family Vacations in North America,* ($18.95 per volume) both by Jane Wilford with Janet Tice (add $3 shipping; Globe Pequot Press, Box 833, 6 Business Park Rd., Old Saybrook, CT 06475, ☎ 203/395–0440 or 800/243–0495, 800/962–0973 in

CT), help plan your trip with children, from toddlers to teens.

TOUR OPERATORS

Contact **Rascals in Paradise** (650 5th St., Suite 505, San Francisco, CA 94107, ☎ 415/978–9800 or 800/872–7225). If you're outdoorsy, look into **American Wilderness Experience** (Box 1486, Boulder, CO 80306, ☎ 303/444–2622 or 800/444–0099), the **American Museum of Natural History** (79th St. and Central Park W., New York, NY 10024, ☎ 212/769–5700 or 800/462–8687), and **Wildland Adventures** (3516 N.E. 155th St., Seattle, WA 98155, ☎ 206/365–0686 or 800/345–4453).

CRUISING

Among the many cruise lines that ply Mexican waters are **Commodore** (☎ 800/529–3000), **Cunard** (☎ 800/221–4770), **Holland America** (☎ 800/426–0327), **Carnival** (☎ 800/327–2058), **Dolphin/Majesty** (☎ 800/992–4299 or 800/645–8111), **Norwegian** (☎ 800/327–7030), **Princess** (☎ 800/421–0522), **Regency** (☎ 212/972–4499), and **Royal Caribbean** (☎ 305/539–6000).

To find a travel agency that specializes in cruises, contact the **National Association of Cruise Only Travel Agencies (NACOA)** (3191 Coral Way, Suite 630, Miami, FL 33145, ☎ 305/446–7732, FAX 305/446–9732) for a listing of member firms in your state. If writing, enclose a self-addressed stamped envelope.

SPECIAL-INTEREST CRUISES

For whale watching and educational cruises, contact the **Oceanic Society Expeditions** (Fort Mason Center, Bldg. E, San Francisco, CA 94123, ☎ 415/441–1106 or 800/326–7491), **Classical Cruises** (132 E. 70th St., New York, NY 10021, ☎ 800/367–6766, FAX 212/249–6896), or **The Smithsonian Institution**'s Study Tours and Seminars (1100 Jefferson Dr. SW, Room 3045, Washington, DC 20560, ☎ 202/357–4700).

CUSTOMS

U.S. CITIZENS

The **U.S. Customs Service** (Box 7407, Washington, DC 20044, ☎ 202/927–6724) can answer questions on duty-free limits and publishes a helpful brochure, "Know Before You Go." For information on registering foreign-made articles, call ☎ 202/927–0540.

CANADIANS

Contact **Revenue Canada** (2265 St. Laurent Blvd. S, Ottawa, Ontario, K1G 4K3, ☎ 613/993–0534) for a copy of the free brochure **"I Declare/Je Déclare"** and for details on duties that exceed the standard duty-free limit.

U.K. CITIZENS

HM Customs and Excise (Dorset House, Stamford St., London SE1 9PY, ☎ 0171/928–3344) can answer questions about U.K. customs regulations. Ask for **"A Guide for Travellers,"** detailing standard procedures and import rules.

D

FOR TRAVELERS WITH DISABILITIES

COMPLAINTS

To register complaints under the provisions of the Americans With Disabilities Act, contact the U.S. Department of Justice's **Public Access Section** (Box 66738, Washington, DC 20035, ☎ 202/514–0301, TDD 202/514–0383, FAX 202/307–1198).

ORGANIZATIONS

FOR TRAVELERS WITH HEARING IMPAIRMENTS➤ Contact the **American Academy of Otolaryngology** (1 Prince St., Alexandria, VA 22314, ☎ 703/836–4444, FAX 703/683–5100, TTY 703/519–1585).

FOR TRAVELERS WITH MOBILITY PROBLEMS➤ Contact the **Information Center for Individuals with Disabilities** (Fort Point Pl., 27–43 Wormwood St., Boston, MA 02210, ☎ 617/727–5540, 800/462–5015 in MA, TTY 617/345–9743); **Mobility International USA** (Box 10767, Eugene, OR 97440, ☎ and TTY 503/343–1284, FAX 503/343–6812), the U.S. branch of an international organization headquartered in Belgium (*see below*) that has affiliates in 30 countries; **MossRehab Hospital Travel Information Service** (1200 W. Tabor Rd., Philadelphia, PA

19141, ☎ 215/456–9603, TTY 215/456–9602); the **Society for the Advancement of Travel for the Handicapped** (347 5th Ave., Suite 610, New York, NY 10016, ☎ 212/447–7284, FAX 212/725–8253); the **Travel Industry and Disabled Exchange** (TIDE, 5435 Donna Ave., Tarzana, CA 91356, ☎ 818/344–3640, FAX 818/344–0078); and **Travelin' Talk** (Box 3534, Clarksville, TN 37043, ☎ 615/552–6670, FAX 615/552–1182).

FOR TRAVELERS WITH VISION IMPAIRMENTS➤ Contact the **American Council of the Blind** (1155 15th St. NW, Suite 720, Washington, DC 20005, ☎ 202/467–5081, FAX 202/467–5085) or the **American Foundation for the Blind** (15 W. 16th St., New York, NY 10011, ☎ 212/620–2000, TTY 212/620–2158).

IN THE U.K.

Contact the **Royal Association for Disability and Rehabilitation** (RADAR, 12 City Forum, 250 City Rd., London EC1V 8AF, ☎ 0171/250–3222) or **Mobility International** (228 Borough High St., London SE1 1JX, ☎ 0171/403–5688), an international clearinghouse of travel information for people with disabilities.

PUBLICATIONS

Several free publications are available from the U.S. Information Center (Box 100, Pueblo, CO 81009, ☎ 719/948–3334): **"New Horizons**

THE GOLD GUIDE / IMPORTANT CONTACTS

for the Air Traveler with a Disability" (address to Dept. 355A), describing legally mandated changes; the pocket-size **"Fly Smart"** (Dept. 575B), good on flight safety; and the Airport Operators Council's worldwide **"Access Travel: Airports"** (Dept. 575A).

The 500-page **Travelin' Talk Directory** ($35; ☎ 615/552–6670) lists people and organizations who help travelers with disabilities. For specialist travel agents worldwide, consult the **Directory of Travel Agencies for the Disabled** ($19.95 plus $2 shipping; Twin Peaks Press, Box 129, Vancouver, WA 98666, ☎ 206/694–2462 or 800/637–2256).

TRAVEL AGENCIES AND TOUR OPERATORS

The Americans with Disabilities Act requires that travel firms serve the needs of all travelers. However, some agencies and operators specialize in making group and individual arrangements for travelers with disabilities, among them **Access Adventures** (206 Chestnut Ridge Rd., Rochester, NY 14624, ☎ 716/889–9096), run by a former physical-rehab counselor, and, in Canada, **Travel Trends** (2 Allan Plaza, 4922–51 Ave., Box 3581, Leduc, Alberta, T9E 6X2, ☎ 403/986–9000 or 800/661–2109 in Canada), which has group tours and is especially good for cruises.

FOR TRAVELERS WITH DEVELOPMENTAL DISABIL-

ITIES➣ Contact the nonprofit **New Directions** (5276 Hollister Ave., Suite 207, Santa Barbara, CA 93111, ☎ 805/967–2841).

FOR TRAVELERS WITH HEARING IMPAIRMENTS➣ One agency is **International Express** (7319-B Baltimore Ave., College Park, MD 20740, ☎ TDD 301/699–8836, FAX 301/699–8836), which arranges group and independent trips.

FOR TRAVELERS WITH MOBILITY IMPAIRMENTS➣ Try **Hinsdale Travel Service** (201 E. Ogden Ave., Suite 100, Hinsdale, IL 60521, ☎ 708/325–1335 or 800/303–5521), a travel agency that will give you access to the services of wheelchair traveler Janice Perkins; and **Wheelchair Journeys** (16979 Redmond Way, Redmond, WA 98052, ☎ 206/885–2210), which can handle arrangements worldwide.

DISCOUNTS

Clubs include **Entertainment Travel Editions** (fee $28–$53, depending on destination; Box 1068, Trumbull, CT 06611, ☎ 800/445–4137), **Great American Traveler** ($49.95 annually; Box 27965, Salt Lake City, UT 84127, ☎ 800/548–2812), **Moment's Notice Discount Travel Club** ($25 annually, single or family; 163 Amsterdam Ave., Suite 137, New York, NY 10023, ☎ 212/486–0500), **Privilege Card** ($74.95 annually; 3391 Peachtree Rd. NE, Suite 110, Atlanta GA 30326, ☎ 404/262–0222 or 800/236–9732), **Travelers**

Advantage ($49 annually, single or family; CUC Travel Service, 49 Music Sq. W, Nashville, TN 37203, ☎ 800/548–1116 or 800/648–4037), and **Worldwide Discount Travel Club** ($50 annually for family, $40 single; 1674 Meridian Ave., Miami Beach, FL 33139, ☎ 305/534–2082).

G

GAY AND LESBIAN TRAVEL

ORGANIZATION

The **International Gay Travel Association** (Box 4974, Key West, FL 33041, ☎ 800/448–8550), a consortium of 800 businesses, can supply names of travel agents and tour operators.

PUBLICATIONS

The premiere international travel magazine for gays and lesbians is **Our World** ($35 for 10 issues; 1104 N. Nova Rd., Suite 251, Daytona Beach, FL 32117, ☎ 904/441–5367). The 16-page monthly "Out & About" ($49 for 10 issues; ☎ 212/645–6922 or 800/929–2268), covers gay-friendly resorts, hotels, cruise lines, and airlines.

TOUR OPERATORS

Cruises and resort vacations are handled by **R.S.V.P. Travel Productions** (2800 University Ave. SE, Minneapolis, MN 55414, ☎ 800/328–RSVP) for gays, **Olivia** (4400 Market St., Oakland, CA 94608, ☎ 800/631–6277) for lesbian travelers. For mixed gay and lesbian resort vacations, contact **Atlantis Events** (8335 Sunset Blvd., West Hollywood, CA 90069, ☎ 800/628–5268). **Toto Tours** (1326 W. Albion Suite 3W, Chicago, IL 60626, ☎ 312/274–8686 or 800/565–1241) has group tours.

TRAVEL AGENCIES

The largest agencies serving gay travelers are **Advance Travel** (10700 Northwest Freeway, Suite #160, Houston, TX 77092, ☎ 713/682–2002 or 800/695–0880), **Islanders/Kennedy Travel** (183 W. 10th St., New York, NY 10014, ☎ 212/242–3222 or 800/988–1181), **Now Voyager** (4406 18th St., San Francisco, CA 94114, ☎ 415/626–1169 or 800/255–6951), and **Yellowbrick Road** (1500 W. Balmoral Ave., Chicago, IL 60640, ☎ 312/561–1800 or 800/642–2488). **Skylink Women's Travel** (746 Ashland Ave., Santa Monica, CA 90405, ☎ 310/452–0506 or 800/225-5759) is a good resource for lesbians.

H
HEALTH ISSUES

FINDING A DOCTOR

For members, the **International Association for Medical Assistance to Travellers** (IAMAT, 417 Center St., Lewiston, NY 14092, ☎ 716/754–4883; 40 Regal Rd., Guelph, Ontario N1K 1B5, ☎ 519/836–0102; 1287 St. Clair Ave., Toronto, Ontario M6E 1B8, ☎ 416/652–0137;

57 Voirets, 1212 Grand-Lancy, Geneva, Switzerland; membership free) publishes a worldwide directory of English-speaking physicians meeting IAMAT standards.

MEDICAL-ASSISTANCE COMPANIES

Contact **International SOS Assistance** (Box 11568, Philadelphia, PA 19116, ☎ 215/244–1500 or 800/523–8930; Box 466, Pl. Bonaventure, Montréal, Québec H5A 1C1, ☎ 514/874–7674 or 800/363–0263), **Medex Assistance Corporation** (Box 10623, Baltimore, MD 21285, ☎ 410/296–2530 or 800/573-2029), **Near Services** (Box 1339, Calumet City, IL 60409, ☎ 708/868–6700 or 800/654–6700), and **Travel Assistance International** (1133 15th St. NW, Suite 400, Washington, DC 20005, ☎ 202/331–1609 or 800/821–2828). Because these companies also sell death-and-dismemberment, trip-cancellation, and other insurance coverage, there is some overlap with the travel-insurance policies sold by the companies listed under Insurance, *below.*

PUBLICATIONS

The Safe Travel Book, by Peter Savage ($12.95 plus $2 postage; Lexington Books, 866 3rd Ave., 22nd Floor, New York, NY 10022, ☎ 212/702–4771 or 800/223–23485, FAX 212/605–4872), and *Traveler's Medical Resource,* by William W. Forgey ($19.95; ICS Books, Box 10767, Merrillville, IN

45410, ☎ 219/769–0585 or 800/541–7323), are authoritative.

WARNINGS

The **National Centers for Disease Control** (Center for Preventive Services, Division of Quarantine, Traveler's Health Section, 1600 Clifton Rd., MSE03, Atlanta, GA 30333, automated hot line ☎ 404/332–4559) provides information on health risks abroad and vaccination requirements and recommendations.

I
INSURANCE

Travel insurance covering baggage, health, and trip cancellation or interruption is available from **Access America** (Box 90315, Richmond, VA 23286, ☎ 804/285–3300 or 800/284–8300), **Carefree Travel Insurance** (Box 9366, 100 Garden City Plaza, Garden City, NY 11530, ☎ 516/294–0220 or 800/323–3149), **Near** (Box 1339, Calumet City, IL 60409, ☎ 708/868–6700 or 800/654–6700), **Tele-Trip** (Mutual of Omaha Plaza, Box 31716, Omaha, NE 68131, ☎ 800/228–9792), **Travel Insured International** (Box 280568, E. Hartford, CT 06128-0568, ☎ 203/528–7663 or 800/243–3174), **Travel Guard International** (1145 Clark St., Stevens Point, WI 54481, ☎ 715/345–0505 or 800/826–1300), and **Wallach & Company** (107 W. Federal St., Box 480, Middleburg, VA 22117,

☏ 703/687–3166 or 800/237–6615).

IN THE U.K.

The **Association of British Insurers** (51 Gresham St., London EC2V 7HQ, ☏ 0171/600–3333; 30 Gordon St., Glasgow G1 3PU, ☏ 0141/226–3905; Scottish Provident Bldg., Donegall Sq. W, Belfast BT1 6JE, ☏ 01232/249–176; and other locations) gives advice by phone and publishes the free **"Holiday Insurance,"** which sets out typical policy provisions and costs.

L
LODGING

APARTMENT AND VILLA RENTALS

Among the companies to contact are **At Home Abroad** (405 E. 56th St., Suite 6H, New York, NY 10022, ☏ 212/421–9165), **Europa-Let** (92 N. Main St., Ashland, OR 97520, ☏ 503/482–5806 or 800/462–4486), **Property Rentals International** (1008 Mansfield Crossing Rd., Richmond, VA 23236, ☏ 804/378–6054 or 800/220–3332), **Rent-a-Home International** (7200 34th Ave. NW, Seattle, WA 98117, ☏ 206/789–9377 or 800/488–7368), **Vacation Home Rentals Worldwide** (235 Kensington Ave., Norwood, NJ 07648, ☏ 201/767–9393 or 800/633–3284), **Villas and Apartments Abroad** (420 Madison Ave., Suite 1105, New York, NY 10017, ☏ 212/759–1025 or 800/433–3020), and **Villas International** (605 Market

St., Suite 510, San Francisco, CA 94105, ☏ 415/281–0910 or 800/221–2260). Members of the travel club **Hideaways International** ($99 annually; 767 Islington St., Portsmouth, NH 03801, ☏ 603/430–4433 or 800/843–4433) receive two annual guides plus quarterly newsletters and arrange rentals among themselves.

HOME EXCHANGE

Principal clearinghouses include **HomeLink International/Vacation Exchange Club** ($60 annually; Box 650, Key West, FL 33041, ☏ 305/294–1448 or 800/638–3841), which gives members four annual directories, with a listing in one, plus updates; **Intervac International** ($65 annually; Box 590504, San Francisco, CA 94159, ☏ 415/435–3497), which has three annual directories; and **Loan-a-Home** ($35–$45 annually; 2 Park La., Apt. 6E, Mount Vernon, NY 10552-3443, ☏ 914/664–7640), which specializes in long-term exchanges.

HOTELS

International hotel chains with Mexican properties include **Best Western** (☏ 800/528–1234), **Club Med** (☏ 800/CLUB MED), **Hyatt International** (☏ 800/228–9000), **Marriott** (☏ 800/228–9290), **Posadas de México** (Fiesta Americana and Fiesta Inn hotels, ☏ 800/FIESTA–1); **Holiday Inn** (☏ 800/HOLIDAY), **Omni** (800/THE–OMNI), **Princess**

(☏ 800/442–8418, or in NY 800/223–1818), **Quality Inn** (Hoteles Calinda, ☏ 800/228–5151), **Radisson** (☏ 800/333–3333), **Sheraton** (☏ 800/325–3535), **Presidente** (☏ 800/447–6147), and **Westin Regina Hotels** (☏ 800/228–3000). **Grupo Sol's Melia Hotels** (☏ 800/336–3542) are part of a reliable Spanish-owned chain. Good Mexican-owned chains include **Krystal** (☏ 800/231–9860) and **Camino Real** (☏ 800/722–6466).

If you arrive in Mexico City without a reservation, the **Mexican Hotel and Motel Association** operates a booth at the airport that will assist you (☏ 5/571–3268 or 5/571–3262).

M
MAIL

American Express cardholders or traveler's check holders can have mail sent to them at the local American Express office. For a list of the offices worldwide, write for the *Traveler's Companion* from **American Express** (Box 678, Canal Street Station, New York, NY 10013).

MONEY MATTERS

ATMS

For specific **Cirrus** locations in Mexico, call ☏ 800/424–7787; for **Plus** locations, consult the directory at your local bank.

CURRENCY EXCHANGE

If your bank doesn't exchange pesos, contact **Thomas Cook Currency Services** (41 E. 42nd St.,

New York, NY 10017, or 511 Madison Ave., New York, NY 10022, ☎ 212/757–6915 or 800/223–7373 for locations) or **Ruesch International** (☎ 800/424–2923 for locations).

WIRING FUNDS

Funds can be wired via **American Express MoneyGram** (☎ 800/926–9400 from the U.S. and Canada for locations and information) or **Western Union** (☎ 800/325–6000 for agent locations or to send using MasterCard or Visa, 800/321–2923 in Canada).

U.S. CITIZENS

For fees, documentation requirements, and other information, call the **Office of Passport Services** information line (☎ 202/647–0518).

CANADIANS

For fees, documentation requirements, and other information, call the Ministry of Foreign Affairs and International Trade's **Passport Office** (☎ 819/994–3500 or 800/567–6868).

U.K. CITIZENS

For fees, documentation requirements, and emergency passports, call the **London passport office** (☎ 0171/271–3000).

The country code for Mexico is 52. For local access numbers abroad,

contact **AT&T USA Direct** (☎ 800/874–4000), **MCI** Call USA (☎ 800/444–4444), or **Sprint** Express (☎ 800/793–1153).

The **Kodak Information Center** (☎ 800/242–2424) answers consumer questions about film and photography.

Ferrocarriles Nacionales de México (Mexican National Railways, ☎ 5/547–6593) has information on trains throughout Mexico.

From the United States, you can get information on trains and rail-hotel packages by calling **Mexico by Train** (☎ and FAX 210/725–3659 or 800/321–1699). *See also* Train Tours *under* Tour Opeators, *below.*

On the U.S. side, **Amtrak** (☎ 800/USA–RAIL) will get you only as far as San Antonio; **Greyhound** (☎ 800/231–2222) offers bus service from there to Nuevo Laredo, where you can change for the coach to Monterrey.

EDUCATIONAL TRAVEL

The nonprofit **Elderhostel** (75 Federal St., 3rd Floor, Boston, MA 02110, ☎ 617/426–7788) for people 60 and older, has offered inexpensive study programs since 1975. The nearly 2,000 courses cover everything from marine science to myths. Fees

for two- to three-week international trips—including room, board, and transportation from the United States—range from $1,800 to $4,500.

For people 50 and over and their children and grandchildren, **Interhostel** (University of New Hampshire, 6 Garrison Ave., Durham, NH 03824, ☎ 603/862–1147 or 800/733–9753) runs 10-day summer programs involving lectures, field trips, and sightseeing. Most last two weeks and cost $2,125–$3,100, including airfare.

ORGANIZATIONS

Contact the **American Association of Retired Persons** (AARP, 601 E St., NW, Washington, DC 20049, ☎ 202/434–2277; $8 per person or couple annually). Its Purchase Privilege Program gets members discounts on lodging, car rentals, and sightseeing.

For other discounts on lodgings, car rentals, and other travel products, along with magazines and newsletters, contact the **National Council of Senior Citizens** (membership $12 annually; 1331 F St., NW, Washington, DC 20004, ☎ 202/347–8800) and **Mature Outlook** (subscription $9.95 annually; 6001 N. Clark St., Chicago, IL 60660, ☎ 312/465–6466 or 800/336–6330).

PUBLICATIONS

The 50+ Traveler's Guidebook: Where to Go, Where to Stay, What to Do, by Anita Williams and Merrimac Dillon ($12.95; St. Martin's Press, 175 5th Ave., New York, NY 10010, ☎ 212/674–5151 or 800/288–2131), offers many useful tips. **"The Mature Traveler"** ($29.95; Box 50400, Reno, NV 89513; ☎ 702/786–7419), a monthly newsletter, covers travel deals.

SPORTS

TENNIS AND GOLF

For tennis and golf tournament information, contact the **Federación Mexicana de Tenis** (Miguel Angel de Quevedo 953, Mexico D.F. 04330, ☎ 5/689–9733) and the **Federación Mexicana de Golf** (Avenida Lomas de Sotelo 1112, Despacho 103 y 104, Col. Lomas de Sotelo, Mexico, D.F. 11200, ☎ 5/395–8642), respectively.

STUDENTS

HOSTELING

Contact **Hostelling International–American Youth Hostels** (733 15th St., NW, Suite 840, Washington, DC 20005, ☎ 202/783–6161) in the United States, **Hostelling International–Canada** (205 Catherine St., Suite 400, Ottawa, Ontario K2P 1C3, ☎ 613/237–7884) in Canada, and the **Youth Hostel Association of England and Wales** (Trevelyan House, 8 St. Stephen's Hill, St. Albans, Hertfordshire AL1 2DY, ☎ 01727/855–215 and 0727/845–047) in the United Kingdom. Membership ($25 in the U.S., C$26.75 in Canada, and £9 in the U.K.) gets you access to

5,000 hostels worldwide that charge $7–$20 nightly per person.

I.D. CARDS

Get the **International Student Identity Card** (ISIC) if you're a bona fide student or the **International Youth Card** (IYC) if you're under 26. In the United States, the ISIC and IYC cards cost $16 each and include basic travel accident and illness coverage, plus a toll-free travel hot line. Apply through the **Council on International Educational Exchange** (*see* Organizations, *below*). Cards are available for $15 each in Canada from **Travel Cuts** (187 College St., Toronto, Ontario M5T 1P7, ☎ 416/979–2406 or 800/667–2887) and in the United Kingdom for £5 at student unions and student travel companies.

ORGANIZATIONS

A major contact is the **Council on International Educational Exchange** (CIEE): In the United States: 205 E. 42nd St., 16th Floor, New York, NY 10017, ☎ 212/661–1450; 729 Boylston St., Boston, MA 02116, ☎ 617/266–1926; 9100 S. Dadeland Blvd., Miami, FL 33156, ☎ 305/670–9261; 1093 Broxton Ave., Los Angeles, CA 90024, ☎ 310/208–3551; and 43 college towns nationwide. In the United Kingdom: 28A Poland St., London W1V 3DB, ☎ 0171/437–7767. Twice a year, the organization publishes *Student Travels* magazine. The CIEE's Council Travel

Service is the exclusive U.S. agent for several student-discount cards.

Campus Connections (325 Chestnut St., Suite 1101, Philadelphia, PA 19106, ☎ 215/625–8585 or 800/428–3235) specializes in discounted accommodations and airfares for students. The **Educational Travel Centre** (438 N. Frances St., Madison, WI 53703, ☎ 608/256–5551) offers rail passes and low-cost airline tickets, mostly for flights departing from Chicago.

In Canada, also contact **Travel Cuts** (*see above*).

PUBLICATIONS

See the **Berkeley Guide to Mexico** ($17.50; Fodor's Travel Publications, ☎ 800/533–6478, or from bookstores).

T

TOUR OPERATORS

Among the companies selling tours and packages to Mexico, the following have a proven reputation, are nationally known, and have plenty of options to choose from.

GROUP TOURS

For escorted tours to all major destinations in Mexico, contact **Armadillo Tours** (4301 Westbank Dr., Bldg. B, Suite 360, Austin, TX 78746, ☎ 512/328–7800 or 800/284–5678), **Arrow Stage Lines** (4001 South 34th St., Phoenix, AZ 78552, ☎ 602/437–3484 or 800/777–3484), **Gadabout Tours** (700 E. Tahquitz Canyon Way, Palm

Springs, CA 92262, ☎ 619/325–5556 or 800/952–5068), and **Go With Jo** (910 Dixie Land Road, Harlingen, TX 78552, ☎ 210/ 423–1446 or 800/999– 1446).

For tours of Mexico's Copper Canyon, contact **Brennan Tours** (1402 3rd Ave., Suite 717, Seattle, WA 98101, ☎ 206/622– 9155 or 800/237– 7249), **Frontier Tour and Travel** (1923 N. Carson St., Carson City, NV 89706, ☎ 702/882– 2100 or 800/647– 0800), **Globus/Cosmos** (5301 S. Federal Circle, Littleton, CO 80123, ☎ 303/797–2800 or 800/221–0900), **Maupintour** (Box 807, Lawrence, KS 66044, ☎ 913/843–1211 or 800/255–4266), **Mayflower Tours** (1225 Warren Ave., Box 490, Downers Grove, IL 60515, ☎ 708/960– 3793 or 800/323– 7604), and **Tauck Tours** (11 Wilton Rd., Westport, CT 06881, ☎ 203/226–6911 or 800/468–2825).

THEME TRIPS

ADVENTURE➤ Adventure travel in Mexico can mean hiking through the Copper Canyon, volcano climbing outside Mexico City, or river rafting on the Rio Usumancita (known as the "Mayan River of Ruins") and on the Rio Antigua near Veracruz. Baja adventures may include sea kayaking, whale-watching, scuba diving, and natural history crusies. Contact **All Adventure Travel** (5589 Arapahoe #208, Boulder, CO

80303, ☎ 800/537– 4025), **American Wilderness Experience** (Box 1486, Boulder, CO 80306, ☎ 303/ 444–2622 or 800/444– 0099), **Baja Expeditions** (2625 Garnet Ave., San Diego, CA 92109, ☎ 619/581–3311 or 800/843–6967), **Far Flung Adventures** (Box 377, Terlingua, TX 79852, ☎ 915/371– 2489 or 800/359– 4138), **Mountain Travel-Sobek** (6420 Fairmount Ave., El Cerrito, CA 94530, ☎ 510/527–8100 or 800/ 227–2384), **Remarkable Journeys** (Box 31855, Houston, TX 77231, ☎ 713/721– 2517 or 800/856– 1993), and **Trek America** (Box 470, Blairstown, NJ 07825, ☎ 908/362–9198 or 800/221–0596).

ART AND ARCHAEOLOGY➤ The **Archaeological Conservancy** (5301 Central N.E., Suite 1218, Albuquerque, NM 87108, ☎ 505/266–1540) and **Center for Indigenous Studies in the Americas** (1121 N. 2nd St., Phoenix, AZ 85004, ☎ 602/253–0107) are two non-profit organizations that lead archaeological tours to all of the major Mexican ruins. Commercial tour operators that focus on archaeological ruins include **Armadillo** tours (4301 Westbank Dr., Bldg. B360, Austin, TX 78746, ☎ 512/328– 7800 or 800/284– 5678), **Far Horizon's Cultural Discoveries** (Box 1529, 16 Fern La., San Anselmo, CA 94960, ☎ 415/457– 4755), **Maya-Carib** (87

Wolf La., Pelham, NY 10803, ☎ 914/354– 9824 or 800/223– 4084), **M.I.L.A./Peru Tours** (100 S. Greenleaf Ave., Gurnee, IL 60031, ☎ 708/249–2111 or 800/367–7378), **Nature Expeditions International** (Box 11496, Eugene, OR 97440, ☎ 503/484–6529 or 800/869–0639), and **Sanborn Tours** (2015 S. 10th St., McAllen, TX 78505, 210/682–9872 or 800/315–8482).

For tours that emphasize arts and crafts, try **Esplanade Tours** (581 Boylston St., Boston, MA 02116, ☎ 617/ 266–7465 or 800/426– 5492) and **Gadabout Tours** (700 E. Tahquitz Canyon Way, Palm Springs, CA 92262, ☎ 619/325–5556 or 800/ 952–5068). Programs run by the **Smithsonian Institution's Study Tours and Seminars** division (1100 Jefferson Dr. SW, Room 3045, Washington, DC 20560, ☎ 202/ 357–4700) explore the culture and ruins of Mexico's native peoples.

BICYCLING/WALKING➤ For mountain biking and walking tours of the Baja region or road biking tours through the Yucatan try **Backroads** (1516 5th St., Suite L101, Berkeley, CA 94710, ☎ 510/ 527–1555 or 800/462– 2848).

DIVING➤ Packages are available to Cozumel, Cabo San Lucas, and La Paz. Among the leading dive packagers are **Diving Plus** (Box 1320, Detroit Lakes, MN, 56501, ☎ 218/ 847–4441 or 800/552– 3419), **Rothschild Con-**

THE GOLD GUIDE / IMPORTANT CONTACTS

THE GOLD GUIDE / IMPORTANT CONTACTS

sultants (900 West End Ave., Suite 1B, New York, NY 10025, ☎ 212/662–4858 or 800/359–0747), and **Tropical Adventures** (111 2nd Ave., Seattle, WA 98109, ☎ 206/441–3483 or 800/247–3483).

FISHING➤ For boat charters and vacation packages throughout Mexico, contact **Anglers Travel Connections** (1280 Terminal Way, Suite 30, Reno, NV 89502, ☎ 702/324–0580 or 800/624–8429), **Cutting Loose Expeditions** (Box 447, Winter Park, FL 32790, ☎ 407/629–4700, FAX 407/644–9944), **Fishing International** (Box 2132, Santa Rosa, CA 95405, ☎ 800/950–4242), **Mexico Sportsman** (202 Milam Building, San Antonio, TX 78205, ☎ 210/212–4567 or 800/633–3085), and **Rod and Reel Adventures** (3507 Tully Road, Modesto, CA 95356, ☎ 209/524–7775 or 800/356–6982).

HEALTH➤ **Spa-Finders** (91 Fifth Ave., New York, NY 10003, ☎ 800/ALL–SPAS) represents several spas in Mexico.

HORSEBACK RIDING➤ To spend a week in the saddle exploring the Sierra Madre, Mesa Colorada, and Mismalda, contact **FITS Equestrian** (685 Lateen Rd., Solvang, CA 93463, ☎ 805/688–9494 or 800/666–3487).

LANGUAGE INSTITUTES➤ Recommended places to learn Spanish and live with a Mexican family include the **Spanish Language Institute Center for Latin American Studies** (Apdo. Postal 2–3, Cuernavaca, Moreles 62191, ☎ 73/17–52–94 or 73/11–00–63; in the U.S., contact Language Link Inc., Box 3006, Peoria, IL 61612, ☎ 800/552–2051); **Instituto Falcon** (Mora 158, Guanajuato, Guanajuato 36000, ☎ and FAX 473/2–36–94); **Instituto Allende** (Ancha de San Antonio #20, San Miguel de Allende, Guanajuato 37700, ☎ 465/2–01–90, FAX 465/2–45–38); **Centro de Idiomas de la Universidad Autónoma Benito Juárez** (Armenta y López Burgoa, Oaxaca, Oaxaca 68000, ☎ 951/659–22, FAX 951/91–95–1); and **Instituto Jovel, A.C.** (Apdo. Postal 62, Ma. Adelina Flores 21, San Cristóbal de las Casas, Chiapas 29200, ☎ and FAX 967/8–40–69). **AmeriSpan Unlimited** (Box 40513, Philadelphia, PA 19106, ☎ 800/879–6640, FAX 215/986–4524) can arrange for language study and homestay in a number of Mexican cities.

NATURAL HISTORY➤ **Earthwatch** (680 Mount Auburn St., Watertown, MA 02272, ☎ 617/926–8200) recruits volunteers to serve in its EarthCorps as short-term assistants to scientists on research expeditions. **Forum Travel International** (91 Gregory La., #21, Pleasant Hill, CA 94523, ☎ 510/671–2900, FAX 510/671–2993) operates wildlife and bird-watching programs in some of Mexico's less visited natural habitats. The **National Audubon Society** (700 Broadway, New York, NY 10003, ☎ 212/979–3066) charters vessels for its natural history-themed cruises in the Sea of Cortez. **Oceanic Society Expeditions** (Fort Mason Center, Bldg. E, San Francisco, CA 94123, ☎ 415/441–1106 or 800/326–7491), **Ocean Voyages** (1709 Bridgeway, Sausalito, CA 94965, ☎ 415/332–4681, FAX 415/332–7460), and **Pacific Sea-Fari Tours** (2803 Emerson St., San Diego, CA 92106, ☎ 619/226–8224) run whale-watching expeditions on the Sea of Cortez.

SINGLES➤ **Grammercy's Single-World** (401 Theodore Fremd Ave., Rye, NY 10580, ☎ 914/967–3334 or 800/223–6490) has cruises to the Mexican Riviera.

TRAIN TOURS➤ **Copper Canyon Adventures** (Box 781451, San Antonio, TX 78278, ☎ 210/694-0821 or 800/322-4888), **DRC Rail Tours** (16800 Greenspoint Park Dr., Suite 245 N., Houston, TX 77060, ☎ 800/659–7602), **RFD Travel** (5201 Johnson Dr., Mission, KS 66205, teo. 800/365–5389), and **Sierra Madre Express of Tucson** (Box 26381, Tucson, AZ 85726, ☎ 520/747–0346 or 800/666–0346) all run deluxe trains to the spectacular Copper Canyon.

ORGANIZATIONS

The **National Tour Association** (546 E. Main St., Lexington, KY 40508, ☎ 606/226–4444 or 800/682–8886) and **United States Tour Operators Association** (USTOA, 211 E. 51st St., Suite 12B, New York, NY 10022, ☎ 212/750–7371) can provide lists of member operators and information on booking tours.

PACKAGES

Independent vacation packages are available from major tour operators and airline wholesalers. Contact **Aeromexico Vacation Planners** (☎ 800/245–8585), **American Airlines Fly Away Vacations** (☎ 800/321–2121), **Certified Vacations** (Box 1525, Ft. Lauderdale, FL 33302, ☎ 305/522–1414 or 800/233–7260), **Club Med** (40 W. 57th St., New York, NY 10019, ☎ 800/258–2633), **Continental Airlines Grand Destinations** (☎ 800/634–5555), **Delta Dream Vacations** (☎ 800/872–7786), and **United Airlines' Vacation Planning Center** (☎ 800/328–6877). **Gogo Tours,** based in Ramsey, New Jersey, sells Mexico packages exclusively through travel agents.

Large regional operators specialize in putting together Mexico packages for travelers from their local area. Arrangements may be charter or scheduled air. Contact **Apple Vacations** (25 Northwest Point Blvd., Elk Grove Village, IL 60007, ☎ 800/365–2775 or 708/640–1150), **Friendly Holidays** (1983 Marcus Ave., Lake Success, NY 11042, ☎ 800/221–9748 or 516/338–1200), and **Travel Impressions** (465 Smith St., Farmingdale, NY 11735, ☎ 800/224–0022 or 516/845–7000).

FROM THE U.K.➤ Companies with packages to Mexico include **Bales Tours** (Bales House, Junction Rd., Dorking, Surrey RH4 3HB, ☎ 01306/876–881 or 01306/885–991, FAX 0136/740–048), **British Airways** (Astral Towers, Betts Way, London Rd., Crawley, W. Sussex RH10 2XA, ☎ 01293/611–361, FAX 0129/722–704), **Journey Latin America** (14–16 Devonshire Rd., Chiswick, London W4 2HD, ☎ 0181/747–8315, FAX 0181/742–1312), and **Kuoni Travel** (Kuoni House, Dorking, Surrey RH5 4AZ, ☎ 01306/740–888, FAX 01306/740–8640).

For a custom-designed holiday, contact **Steamond Travel** (23 Eccleston St., London SW1 9LX, ☎ 0171/730–8640, FAX 0171/730–3024), or **Trailfinders** (42–50 Earls Court Rd., London W8 6FT, ☎ 0171/937–5400, FAX 0171/938–3305).

PUBLICATIONS

Consult the brochure **"Worldwide Tour & Vacation Package Finder"** from the National Tour Operators Association (*see* Organizations, *above*) and the Better Business Bureau's **"Tips on Travel Packages"** (publication No. 24-195, $2; 4200 Wilson Blvd., Arlington, VA 22203).

For names of reputable agencies in your area, contact the **American Society of Travel Agents** (1101 King St., Suite 200, Alexandria, VA 22314, ☎ 703/739–2782).

U

U.S.
GOVERNMENT
TRAVEL BRIEFINGS

The U.S. Department of State's Overseas Citizens Emergency Center (Room 4811, Washington, DC 20520; enclose SASE) issues **Consular Information Sheets,** which cover crime, security, political climate, and health risks as well as embassy locations, entry requirements, currency regulations, and other routine matters. For the latest information, stop in at any U.S. passport office, consulate, or embassy; call the interactive hot line (☎ 202/647–5225 or FAX 202/647-3000); or, with your PC's modem, tap into the Bureau of Consular Affairs' computer bulletin board (☎ 202/647–9225).

V

VISITOR
INFORMATION

For a current calendar of events, train schedules and fares, brochures and other general information about travel in Mexico, contact the nearest **Mexican Government Tourism Office (MGTO)** or call the Mexico

Ministry of Tourism's information hot line at ☎ 800/44–MEXICO (within Mexico, toll-free 91/800/90–392). If you're planning to drive into Mexico, contact the **Mexico Surface Tourism Office for U.S. and Canada** (2707 N. Loop W, Suite 440, Houston, TX 77008, ☎ 713/880–8772, FAX 713/880–0286).

IN THE U.S.

MGTOs are located at at 405 Park Ave., Suite 1401, New York, NY 10022, ☎ 212/421–6655, FAX 212/753–2874; 1911 Pennsylvania Ave. NW, Washington, DC 20006, ☎ 202/728–1750, FAX 202/728–1758; 128 Aragon Ave., Coral Gables, FL 33134, ☎ 305/443–9160, FAX 305/443–1186; 70 E. Lake St., Suite 1413, Chicago, IL 60601, ☎ 312/565–2786, FAX 312/606-9012; 2707 N. Loop W, Suite 450, Houston, TX 77008, ☎ 713/880–5153, FAX 713/880–1833; 10100 Santa Monica Blvd., Suite 224, Los Angeles, CA 90067, ☎ 310/203–8191, FAX 310/203–8316. If there is no office near you, call 800/446–3942.

IN CANADA

MGTOs are at 1 Place Ville Marie, Suite 1526, Montreal, Quebec H3B 2B5, ☎ 514/871–1052, FAX 514/871-3825; 2 Bloor St. W, Suite 1801, Toronto, Ontario M4W 3E2, ☎ 416/925–0704, FAX 416/925-6061; 1610–999 W. Hastings St., Vancouver, BC, V6C 2W2, ☎ 604/669–2845, FAX 604/669–3498.

IN THE U.K.

The MGTO maintains an office at 60 Trafalgar Sq., London WC2N 5DS, ☎ 0171/734–1058, FAX 0171/930–9202.

W
WEATHER

For current conditions and forecasts, plus the local time and helpful travel tips, call the **Weather Channel Connection** (☎ 900/932–8437; 95¢ per minute) from a touch-tone phone.

SMART TRAVEL TIPS A TO Z

Basic Information on Traveling in Mexico and Savvy Tips to Make Your Trip a Breeze

The more you travel, the more you know about how to make trips run like clockwork. To help make your voyages hassle-free, Fodor's editors have rounded up dozens of tips from our contributors and travel experts all over the world, as well as basic information on visiting Mexico. For names of organizations to contact and publications that can give you more information, *see* Important Contacts A to Z, *above.*

A
ADDRESSES

The Mexican method of naming streets is exasperatingly arbitrary, so **be patient when searching for street addresses.** Streets in the centers of many colonial cities (those built by the Spaniards) are laid out in a grid surrounding the zócalo and often change names on different sides of the square; other streets simply acquire a new name after a certain number of blocks. As in the United States, numbered streets are usually designated "north/south" or "east/west" on either side of a central avenue. Streets with proper names, however, can change mysteriously from Avenida Juárez, for example, to Calle Francisco Madero; one has no way of knowing where one begins and the other ends. On the

other hand, blocks are often labeled numerically, according to distance from a chosen starting point, as in "la Calle de Pachuca," "2a Calle de Pachuca," etc.

Many Mexican addresses have "s/n" for *sin número* (no number) after the street name. This is common in small towns where there are fewer buildings on a block. Similarly, many hotels give their address as "Km 30 a Querétaro," which indicates that the property is on the main highway 30 kilometers from Querétaro.

As in Europe, addresses in Mexico are written with the street name first, followed by the street number. The five-digit zip code (*código postal*) precedes, rather than follows, the name of the city. "Apdo." (*apartado*) means "post office box number."

Veteran travelers to Mexico invariably make one observation about asking directions in the country: Rather than say that they do not know, Mexicans tend to offer guidance that may or may not be correct. This is not out of malice, but out of a desire to please.

AIR TRAVEL

If time is an issue, **always look for nonstop flights,** which require no change of plane and make no stops. If possi-

ble, **avoid connecting flights,** which stop at least once and can involve a change of plane, although the flight number remains the same; if the first leg is late, the second waits.

When traveling within Mexico, remember to **arrive at least one hour before your internal flight,** as overbooking is common. **Collect and recheck your baggage with each plane change** to decrease the chances of loss. Be prepared to pay a departure tax on Mexican domestic flights.

CUTTING COSTS

For significantly lower airfares to Mexico, **consider flying into Tijuana from southern California** and then catching a domestic flight to your final destination. The Sunday travel section of most newspapers is a good source for other discounts.

MAJOR AIRLINES➤ The least-expensive airfares from the major airlines are priced for round-trip travel and are subject to restrictions. You must usually **book in advance and buy the ticket within 24 hours** to get cheaper fares, and you may have to **stay over a Saturday night.** The lowest fare is subject to availability, and only a small percentage of the plane's total seats are sold at that price. It's good to **call a number of airlines—and when you are quoted a good price, book it on the spot**—the same fare on the same flight may not be available the next day. Airlines generally allow you to change your return date for a $25 to $50 fee, but most low-fare tickets are nonrefundable. However, if you don't use it, you can apply the cost toward the purchase price of a new ticket, again for a small charge.

CONSOLIDATORS➤ Consolidators, who buy tickets at reduced rates from scheduled airlines, sell them at prices below the lowest available from the airlines directly—usually without advance restrictions. Sometimes you can even get your money back if you need to return the ticket. Carefully read the fine print detailing penalties for changes and cancellations. If you doubt the reliability of a consolidator, **confirm your reservation with the airline.**

CHARTER FLIGHTS➤ Charters usually have the lowest fares and the most restrictions. Departures are limited and seldom on time, and you can lose all or most of your money if you cancel. (The closer to departure you cancel, the more you lose, although sometimes you will be charged only a small fee if you supply a substitute passenger.) The flight may be canceled for any reason up to 10 days before

departure (after that, only if it is physically impossible to operate). The charterer may also revise the itinerary or increase the price after you have bought the ticket, but only if the new arrangement constitutes a "major change" do you have the right to a refund. Before buying a charter ticket, **read the fine print** about the company's refund policies. Money for charter flights is usually paid into a bank escrow account, the name of which should be on the contract, and if you don't pay by credit card, **make your check payable to the carrier's escrow account** (unless you're dealing with a travel agent, in which case, his or her check should be payable to the escrow account). The U.S. Department of Transportation's Office of Consumer Affairs has jurisdiction.

Charter operators may offer flights alone or with ground arrangements that constitute a charter package. You typically must book charters through your travel agent.

ALOFT

AIRLINE FOOD➤ If you want to improve your chances of getting a good meal on a plane, **ask for special meals when booking.** These can be vegetarian, low cholesterol, or kosher, for example; commonly prepared to order in smaller quantities than standard catered fare, they can be tastier.

SMOKING➤ Smoking is banned on all flights

within the United States of less than six hours' duration and on all Canadian flights; the ban also applies to domestic segments of international flights aboard U.S. and foreign carriers. On U.S. carriers flying to Mexico, a seat in a no-smoking section must be provided for every passenger who requests one, and the section must be enlarged to accommodate such passengers if necessary as long as they have complied with the airline's deadline for check-in and seat assignment. If you are sensitive to smoke, request a seat far from the smoking section to help avoid the thickest fumes, or fly on Delta or Northwest; all flights to Mexico on both carriers have been designated non-smoking. Foreign airlines are exempt from these rules—you're likely to find lots of smokers on Mexican flights—but do provide no-smoking sections, and Aeromexico has recently designated all flights from Dallas, Atlanta, and Phoenix to Mexico as nonsmoking.

B
BUSINESS HOURS

BANKS

Banks are generally open weekdays 9 AM to 1:30 PM. In some larger cities, a few also open weekdays 4 to 6 PM, Saturday 10 AM to 1:30 PM and 4 to 6 PM, and Sunday 10 AM to 1:30 PM; however, the extended hours are often for deposits only. Banks will give you cash advances in pesos (for a fee) if you have a major credit card.

GOVERNMENT OFFICES

Government offices are usually open 8 AM to 3 PM; along with banks and most private offices, they are closed on national holidays.

MUSEUMS

Along with theaters and most archaeological zones, museums close on Monday, with few exceptions.

STORES

Hours are generally weekdays and Saturday from 9 or 10 AM to 7 or 8 PM; in resort areas, shops may also be open on Sunday. Business hours are 9 AM to 7 PM, with a two-hour lunch break (siesta) from about 2 to 4 PM.

BUS TRAVEL

Getting to Mexico by bus is no longer for just the adventurous or budget-conscious. In the past, bus travelers were required to change to Mexican vehicles at the border, and vice versa. Now, however, in an effort to bring more American visitors and their tourist dollars to off-the-beaten-track markets and attractions, the Mexican government has removed this obstacle and a growing number of trans-border bus tours are available.

For travel within Mexico, buses run the gamut from comfortable air-conditioned coaches with bathrooms, televisions, and hostess service (*gran lujo*, deluxe and first-class) to dilapidated

"vintage" buses (second- and third-class) on which pigs and chickens travel and stops are made in the middle of nowhere. While a lower-class bus ride can be interesting if you are not in a hurry and want to see the sights and experience the local culture, these fares are only about 10% to 20% lower than those in the premium categories. Therefore, travelers planning a long-distance haul are well advised to **buy the first-class or *gran lujo* tickets when traveling by bus within Mexico;** unlike tickets for the other classes, these can be reserved in advance.

The Mexican bus network is extensive, far more so than the railroads, as buses are the poor man's transportation. Buses go where trains don't go, service is more frequent, tickets can be purchased on the spot (except during holidays and on long weekends, when advance purchase is crucial), and first-class buses can be almost as comfortable as trains. **Bring something to eat on all overnight bus rides** in case you don't like the restaurant where the bus stops, and **bring toilet tissue,** as rest rooms vary in cleanliness. Smoking is prohibited on a growing number of Mexican buses, though the rule is occasionally ignored.

In large cities, bus stations are a good distance from the center of town. Though there's a trend toward consolidation, some towns

have different stations for each bus line. Bus service in Mexico City is well organized, operating out of four terminals; *see* Bus Travel *in* Important Contacts A to Z, *above*.

C
CAMERAS, CAMCORDERS, AND COMPUTERS

LAPTOPS

Before you depart, **check your portable computer's battery** because you may be asked at security to turn on the computer to prove that it is what it appears to be. At the airport, you may prefer to **request a manual inspection,** although security X-rays do not harm hard-disk or floppy-disk storage. Also, **register your foreign-made laptop with U.S. Customs.** If your laptop is U.S.-made, call the consulate of the country you'll be visiting to find out whether it should be registered with local customs upon arrival. You may want to **find out about repair facilities at your destination** in case you need them.

PHOTOGRAPHY

If your camera is new or if you haven't used it for a while, **shoot and develop a few rolls of film** before you leave. Always **store film in a cool, dry place**—never in the car's glove compartment or on the shelf under the rear window.

Every pass through an X-ray machine increases film's chance of clouding. To protect it, carry

THE GOLD GUIDE / SMART TRAVEL TIPS

it in a clear plastic bag and **ask for hand inspection at security.** Such requests are virtually always honored at U.S. airports, and usually are accommodated abroad. Don't depend on a lead-lined bag to protect film in checked luggage—the airline may increase the radiation to see what's inside.

VIDEO

Before your trip, **test your camcorder, invest in a skylight filter to protect the lens, and charge the batteries.** (Airport security personnel may ask you to turn on the camcorder to prove that it's what it appears to be.) The batteries of most newer camcorders can be recharged with a universal or worldwide AC adapter charger (or multivoltage converter), usable whether the voltage is 110 or 220. All that's needed is the appropriate plug.

Videotape is not damaged by X-rays, but it may be harmed by the magnetic field of a walk-through metal detector, so **ask that videotapes be hand-checked.** Videotape sold in Mexico is based on the PAL standard, which is different than the one used in the United States. You will not be able to view your tapes through the local TV set or view movies bought there in your home VCR. Blank tapes bought in Mexico can be used for camcorder taping, but they are pricey. Some U.S. audiovisual shops convert foreign tapes to U.S.

standards; contact an electronics dealer to find the nearest.

CHILDREN AND TRAVEL

All children, including infants, must have proof of citizenship for travel to Mexico. Children traveling with a single parent must also have a notarized letter from the other parent stating that the child has his or her permission to leave their home country. In addition, parents must now fill out a tourist card for each child traveling with them.

DRIVING

If you are renting a car, **arrange for a car seat when you reserve.** Sometimes they're free.

FLYING

Always **ask about discounted children's fares.** On international flights, the fare for infants under age 2 not occupying a seat is generally either free or 10% of the accompanying adult's fare; children ages 2 through 11 usually pay half to two-thirds of the adult fare. On domestic flights, children under 2 not occupying a seat travel free, and older children currently travel on the "lowest applicable" adult fare. Some routes are considered neither international nor domestic and have still other rules.

BAGGAGE➤ In general, the adult baggage allowance applies for children paying half or more of the adult fare. Before departure, **ask about carry-on allow-**

ances, if you are traveling with an infant. In general, those paying 10% of the adult fare are allowed one carry-on bag, not to exceed 70 pounds or 45 inches (length + width + height) and a collapsible stroller; you may be allowed less if the flight is full.

SAFETY SEATS➤ According to the FAA, it's a good idea to **use safety seats aloft.** Airline policy varies. U.S. carriers allow FAA-approved models, but airlines usually require that you buy a ticket, even if your child would otherwise ride free, because the seats must be strapped into regular passenger seats. Foreign carriers may not allow infant seats, may charge the child's rather than the infant's fare for their use, or may require you to hold your baby during takeoff and landing, thus defeating the seat's purpose.

FACILITIES➤ When making your reservation, **ask for children's meals or a freestanding bassinets** if you need them; the latter are available only to those with seats at the bulkhead, where there's enough legroom. If you don't need the bassinet, **think twice before requesting bulkhead seats**—the only storage for inflight necessities is in the inconveniently distant overhead bins.

LODGING

Most hotels allow children under a certain age to stay in their parents' room at no extra charge, while others charge them as extra adults; be sure to **ask about the cut-off age.**

CRUISES

Cruises that call at ports on the Caribbean coast and Mexican Riviera are available from Miami, Tampa, and Los Angeles. Some ships also call in Mexico as part of a Panama Canal transit. To get the best deal on a cruise, **consult a cruise-only travel agency.**

CUSTOMS AND DUTIES

IN MEXICO

Upon entering Mexico, you will be given a baggage declaration form and asked to itemize what you're bringing into the country. You are allowed to bring in two liters of spirits or wine for personal use; 400 cigarettes, 50 cigars, or 250 grams of tobacco; a reasonable amount of perfume for personal use; one movie camera and one regular camera and 12 rolls of film for each; and gift items not to exceed a total of $300. You are not allowed to bring meat, vegetables, plants, fruit, or flowers into the country.

BACK HOME

IN THE U.S.➤ You may bring home $400 worth of foreign goods duty-free if you've been out of the country for at least 48 hours and haven't already used the $400 exemption, or any part of it, in the past 30 days.

Travelers 21 or older may bring back one liter of alcohol duty-free, provided the beverage laws of the state through which they reenter the United States allow it. In addition, 100 non-Cuban cigars and 200 cigarettes are allowed, regardless of your age. Antiques and works of art more than 100 years old are duty-free.

Duty-free, travelers may mail packages valued at up to $200 to themselves and up to $100 to others, with a limit of one parcel per addressee per day (and no alcohol or tobacco products or perfume valued at more than $5); outside, identify the package as being for personal use or an unsolicited gift, specifying the contents and their retail value. Mailed items do not count as part of your exemption.

IN CANADA➤ Once per calendar year, when you've been out of Canada for at least seven days, you may bring in C$300 worth of goods duty-free. If you've been away less than seven days but more than 48 hours, the duty-free exemption drops to C$100 but can be claimed any number of times (as can a C$20 duty-free exemption for absences of 24 hours or more). You cannot combine the yearly and 48-hour exemptions, use the C$300 exemption only partially (to save the balance for a later trip), or pool exemptions with family members. Goods claimed under the C$300 exemption may follow you by mail; those claimed under the lesser exemptions must accompany you.

Alcohol and tobacco products may be included in the yearly and 48-hour exemptions but not in the 24-hour exemption. If you meet the age requirements of the province through which you reenter Canada, you may bring in, duty-free, 1.14 liters (40 imperial ounces) of wine or liquor *or* two dozen 12-ounce cans or bottles of beer or ale. If you are 16 or older, you may bring in, duty-free, 200 cigarettes, 50 cigars or cigarillos, and 400 tobacco sticks or 400 grams of manufactured tobacco. If you decide to bring in alcohol and tobacco, they must accompany you on your return.

An unlimited number of gifts valued up to C$60 each may be mailed to Canada duty-free. These do not count as part of your exemption. Label the package "Unsolicited Gift— Value under $60." Alcohol and tobacco are excluded.

IN THE U.K.➤ From countries outside the EU, including Mexico, you may import duty-free 200 cigarettes, 100 cigarillos, 50 cigars or 250 grams of tobacco; 1 liter of spirits or 2 liters of fortified or sparkling wine; 2 liters of still table wine; 60 milliliters of perfume; 250 milliliters of toilet water; plus £136 worth of other goods, including gifts and souvenirs.

THE GOLD GUIDE / SMART TRAVEL TIPS

D

DINING

Mexican restaurants run the gamut from humble hole-in-the-wall shacks, street stands, *taquerías*, and American-style fast-food joints to internationally acclaimed gourmet restaurants. Prices, naturally, follow suit. To save money, **look for the fixed-menu lunch known as *comida corrida*,** which is served between 1 and 4 PM almost everywhere in Mexico.

Lunch is the big meal; dinner is rarely served before 8 PM. There is no government rating of restaurants, but you'll know which ones cater to tourists simply by looking at the clientele and the menu (bilingual menus usually mean slightly higher prices than at nontourist restaurants). Credit cards—especially MasterCard (Banamex and Carnet) and Visa (Bancomer)—are increasingly accepted.

FOR TRAVELERS WITH DISABILITIES

When discussing accessibility with an operator or reservationist, **ask hard questions.** Are there any stairs, inside *or* out? Are there grab bars next to the toilet *and* in the shower/tub? How wide is the doorway to the room? To the bathroom? For the greatest accessibility, meeting the latest legal specifications, **opt for newer facilities,** which more often have been designed with access in mind. Older properties

or ships must usually be retrofitted and may offer more limited facilities as a result. Be sure to **discuss your needs before booking.**

DISCOUNT CLUBS

Travel clubs offer members unsold space on airplanes, cruise ships, and package tours at as much as 50% below regular prices. Membership may include a regular bulletin or access to a toll-free hot line giving details of available trips departing from three or four days to several months in the future. Most also offer 50% discounts off hotel rack rates. Before booking with a club, **make sure the hotel or other supplier isn't offering a better deal.**

DRIVING

There are two absolutely essential things to remember about driving in Mexico. First and foremost is to **carry Mexican auto insurance,** which can be purchased near border crossings on either the U.S. or Mexican side. If you injure anyone in an accident, you could well be jailed—whether it was your fault or not—unless you have insurance. Guilty until proven innocent is part of the country's Code Napoléon. **Purchase enough Mexican automobile insurance at the border to cover your estimated trip.** It's sold by the day, and if your trip is shorter than your original estimate, some companies may issue a pro-rated refund for the unused time upon

application after you exit the country.

The second item is that **if you enter Mexico with a car, you must leave with it.** In recent years, the high rate of U.S. vehicles being sold illegally in Mexico has caused the Mexican government to enact stringent regulations for bringing a car into the country—at great inconvenience to motoring American tourists. In order to drive into the country, you must cross the border with the following documents: Title or registration for your vehicle; a birth certificate or passport; a credit card (AE, DC, MC, or V); a valid driver's license with a photo. The title holder, driver, and credit card owner must be one and the same—that is, if your spouse's name is on the title of the car and yours isn't, you cannot be the one to bring the car into the country. For financed cars, leased cars, rental cars, or company cars, a notarized letter of permission from the bank, lien holder, rental agency, or company is required.

When you submit your paperwork at the border and pay a $12 charge on your credit card, you will receive a tourist visa, a car permit, and a sticker to put on your vehicle, all valid for six months. Be sure to turn in the permit and the sticker at the border prior to their expiration date; otherwise you could incur high fines.

One alternative to going through this hassle when you cross is to **have your paperwork done in advance** at a branch of Sanborn's Mexican Insurance; look in the Yellow Pages for an office in almost every town on the U.S.–Mexico border. You'll still have to go through some of the procedures at the border, but all your paperwork will be in order and Sanborn's express window will ensure that you get through relatively quickly. For this service Sanborn's charges $10 to those who buy insurance through the company, $25 to those who don't. The fact that you drove in with a car is stamped on your tourist card, which you must give to immigration authorities at departure. If an emergency arises and you must fly home, there are complicated customs procedures to face.

For day trips and local sightseeing, engaging a car and driver (who often acts as a guide) for a day can be a hassle-free, more economical way to travel than renting a car and driving yourself. Hotel desks will know which taxi companies to call, and you can negotiate a price with the driver.

ROAD AND TRAFFIC CONDITIONS

There are several well-kept toll roads in Mexico—primarily of the two-lane variety—covering mostly the last stretches of major highways (*carreteras*) leading to the capital. (*Cuota* means toll road; *libre* means no toll, and such roads are usually not as smooth.) Some excellent new roads have recently opened, making car travel safer and faster. These include highways connecting Acapulco and Mexico City; Cancún and Mérida; Nogales and Mazatlán; León and Aguascalientes; Guadalajara and Tepic; Puebla, Tehuacán, and Oaxaca; and Nuevo Laredo and Monterrey. However, tolls as high as 40¢ per mile can make using these thoroughfares prohibitively expensive. Approaches to most of the large cities are also in good condition, and the government-sponsored Northern Border Program is cleaning up some of the ubiquitous potholes.

In rural areas, roads are quite poor: **Use caution, especially during the rainy season,** when rock slides are a problem. Driving in Mexico's central highlands may also necessitate adjustments to your carburetor. Generally, driving times are longer than for comparable distances in the United States. *Topes* (road cops, or bumps) are also common; it's best to slow down when approaching a village.

Driving at night is not recommended and should be avoided especially in remote and rural areas because of free-roaming livestock, the difficulty of getting assistance, and the risk of banditry. The last can occur anywhere, though the coast road between Manzanillo and Playa Azul is reported to be particularly risky at present. Common sense goes a long way: If you have a long distance to cover, **start early and fill up on gas;** don't let your tank get below half-full. Allow extra time for unforeseen occurrences as well as for the trucks that seem to be everywhere. By day, **be alert to animals,** especially cattle and dogs. (The number of dead dogs lying beside—and in the middle of—Mexican highways is appalling.)

Traffic can be horrendous in the cities, particularly in Mexico City. As you would in metropolitan areas anywhere, **avoid rush hour** (7–9 AM and 5–7 PM) and lunchtime (1–3 PM). Signage is not always adequate in Mexico, so if you are not sure where you are going, **travel with a companion and a good map.** Always lock your car, and never leave valuable items in the body of the car (the trunk will suffice for daytime outings).

The Mexican Tourism Ministry distributes free road maps from its tourism offices outside the country. Guía Roji puts out current city, regional, and national road maps, which are available in bookstores; gas stations generally do not carry maps.

RULES AND SAFETY REGULATIONS

Illegally parked cars are either towed or their license plates removed, which requires a trip to the traffic police headquarters for payment of a fine. When in doubt, **park in a lot instead of on the street;** your car will probably be safer there, anyway.

If an oncoming vehicle flicks its lights at you in daytime, slow down: it could mean trouble ahead. When approaching a narrow bridge, the first vehicle to flash its lights has right of way. One-way streets are common. One-way traffic is indicated by an arrow; two-way, by a two-pointed arrow. A circle with a diagonal line superimposed on the letter *E* (for *estacionamiento*) means "no parking." Other road signs follow the now widespread system of international symbols, a copy of which will usually be provided when you rent a car in Mexico.

SPEED LIMITS➤ Mileage and speed limits are given in kilometers: 100 kph and 80 kph (62 and 50 mph, respectively) are the most common maximums. A few of the newer toll roads allow 110 kph (68.4 mph). In cities and small towns, **observe the posted speed limits,** which can be as low as 20 kph (12 mph).

NATIONAL ROAD EMERGENCY SERVICES➤ To help motorists on major highways, the Mexican Tourism Ministry operates a fleet of more than 275 pickup trucks, known as the *Angeles Verdes,* or Green Angels. The bilingual drivers provide mechanical help, first aid, radio-telephone communication, basic supplies and small parts, towing, tourist information, and protection. Services are free, and spare parts, fuel, and lubricants are provided at cost. Tips are always appreciated (figure $5 to $10 for big jobs, $1 to $2 for minor repairs).

The Green Angels patrol fixed sections of the major highways twice daily from 8 AM to 8 PM (later on holiday weekends). If you break down, pull off the road as far as possible, lift the hood of your car, hail a passing vehicle, and ask the driver to notify the patrol. Most bus and truck drivers will be quite helpful. To reach the local Green Angels, call their toll-free hot line at 91/800/903–0092. In Mexico City, the number is 5/250–8221.

If you witness an accident, do not stop to help but instead locate the nearest official.

FUEL AVAILABILITY AND COSTS

PEMEX franchises all the gas stations in Mexico. Stations are located at most road junctions, cities, and towns but generally do not accept U.S. credit cards or dollars. Fuel prices are the same at all stations (except near the U.S. border, where they are a bit lower) and run slightly higher than in the United States. Unleaded gas—called Magna Sin—is now available nationwide, but it's still a good idea to fill up whenever you can.

At the gas stations, keep a close eye on the attendants, and if possible, avoid the rest rooms: They're generally filthy.

H
HEALTH CONCERNS

AIR POLLUTION

The air pollution in Mexico City can pose a health risk. The sheer number of people in the capital, thermal inversions, and the inability to process sewage have all contributed to the high levels of lead, carbon monoxide, and other pollutants in the atmosphere in Mexico City. Though the long-term effects are not known, children, the elderly, and those with respiratory problems are advised to avoid jogging, outdoor sports, and being outdoors more than necessary.

HEALTH RISKS, SHOTS, AND MEDICATIONS

According to the Centers for Disease Control and Prevention (CDC), there is a limited risk of malaria and dengue fever in certain rural areas of Mexico. Travelers in most urban or easily accessible areas need not worry. However, if you plan to visit remote regions or stay for more than six weeks, **check with the CDC's International Travelers Hotline.** In areas with malaria and dengue, which are both carried by mosquitoes, take mosquito nets, wear clothing that covers the body, apply repellent containing DEET, and use a spray against flying insects in living and sleeping areas. The hot line recommends chloroquine (analen) as an antimalarial agent; no vaccine exists against dengue.

The major health risk in Mexico is posed by the contamination of drinking water, fresh fruit, and vegetables by fecal matter, which causes the intestinal ailment known as traveler's diarrhea. To prevent it, **watch what you eat and drink.** Stay away from uncooked food and unpasteurized milk and milk products, and **drink only bottled water or water that has been boiled** for at least 20 minutes. When ordering cold drinks at untouristed establishments, skip the ice: *sin hielo.* (You can usually identify ice made commercially from purified water by its uniform shape and the hole in the center.) Hotels with water purification systems will post signs to that effect in the rooms. *Tacos al pastor*—thin pork slices grilled on a spit and garnished with the usual cilantro, onions, and chile—are delicious but dangerous. Be wary of Mexican hamburgers, because you can never be certain what meat they are made with (horsemeat is very common).

If these measures fail, try paregoric, a good antidiarrheal agent that dulls or eliminates abdominal cramps,

which requires a doctor's prescription in Mexico; or in mild cases, Pepto-Bismol or Imodium (loperamide), which can be purchased over the counter. Get plenty of purified water or tea—chamomile is a good folk remedy for diarrhea. In severe cases, rehydrate yourself with a salt-sugar solution (½ tsp. salt and 4 tbsp. sugar per quart/liter of water).

SUN BURN

Caution is advised when venturing out in the Mexican sun. Sunbathers lulled by a slightly overcast sky or the sea breezes can be burned badly in just 20 minutes. To avoid overexposure, **use strong sunscreens and avoid the peak sun hours** of noon to 2 PM.

DIVERS' ALERT

Scuba divers take note: **Do not fly within 24 hours of scuba diving.**

I

INSURANCE

Travel insurance can protect your investment, replace your luggage and its contents, or provide for medical coverage should you fall ill during your trip. Most tour operators, travel agents, and insurance agents sell specialized health-and-accident, flight, trip-cancellation, and luggage insurance as well as comprehensive policies with some or all of these features. Before you make any purchase, **review your existing health and homeowner policies** to find out whether they

cover expenses incurred while traveling.

BAGGAGE

Airline liability for your baggage is limited to $1,250 per person on domestic flights. On international flights, the airlines' liability is $9.07 per pound or $20 per kilogram for checked baggage (roughly $640 per 70-pound bag) and $400 per passenger for unchecked baggage. However, this excludes valuable items such as jewelry and cameras that are listed in your ticket's fine print. You can buy additional insurance from the airline at check-in, but first **find out if your homeowner's policy covers lost luggage.**

FLIGHT

You should **think twice before buying flight insurance.** Often purchased as a last-minute impulse at the airport, it pays a lump sum when a plane crashes, either to a beneficiary if the insured dies or sometimes to a surviving passenger who loses eyesight or a limb. Supplementing the airlines' coverage described in the limits-of-liability paragraphs on your ticket, it's expensive and basically unnecessary. Charging an airline ticket to a major credit card often automatically entitles you to coverage and may also embrace travel by bus, train, and ship.

HEALTH

If your own health insurance policy does not cover you outside the United States,

consider buying supplemental medical coverage. It can provide from $1,000 to $150,000 worth of medical and/or dental expenses incurred as a result of an accident or illness during a trip. These policies also may include a personal-accident, or death-and-dismemberment, provision, which pays a lump sum ranging from $15,000 to $500,000 to your beneficiaries if you die or to you if you lose one or more limbs or your eyesight, and a medical-assistance provision, which may either reimburse you for the cost of referrals, evacuation, or repatriation and other services, or may automatically enroll you as a member of a particular medical-assistance company (*see* Health Issues *in* Important Contacts A to Z, *above*).

For U.K. Travelers➤ You can buy an annual travel-insurance policy valid for most vacations during the year in which it's purchased. If you go this route, make sure you will be covered if you have a preexisting medical condition or are pregnant.

TRIP

Without insurance, you will lose all or most of your money if you must cancel your trip due to illness or any other reason. Especially if your airline ticket, cruise, or package tour is nonrefundable and cannot be changed, it's essential that you **buy trip-cancellation-and-interruption insurance.** When considering how

much coverage you need, look for a policy that will cover the cost of your trip plus the nondiscounted price of a one-way airline ticket should you need to return home early. Read the fine print carefully, especially sections defining "family member" and "preexisting medical conditions." Also **consider default or bankruptcy insurance,** which protects you against a supplier's failure to deliver.

L
LANGUAGE

Spanish is the official language of Mexico, although Indian languages are spoken by approximately 20% of the population, many of whom speak no Spanish at all. Basic English is widely understood by most people employed in tourism, less so in the less developed areas. At the very least, shopkeepers will know the numbers for bargaining purposes.

As in most other foreign countries, knowing the mother tongue has a way of opening doors, so **learn some Spanish words and phrases.** Mexicans are not scornful of visitors' mispronunciations and grammatical errors; on the contrary, they welcome even the most halting attempts to use their language. For a rudimentary vocabulary, featuring many terms travelers are likely to encounter in Mexico, *see* the Spanish Vocabulary section at the end of this guide.

The Spanish most Americans learn in high school is based on Castilian Spanish, which is different from Latin American Spanish. Not only are there differences in pronunciation and grammar but also in vocabulary: Words or phrases that are harmless or everyday in one country can take on offensive meanings in another. Unless you are lucky enough to be briefed on these nuances by a native coach, the only way to learn is by trial and error.

LANGUAGE PROGRAMS

Attending a language institute is an ideal way not only to learn Mexican Spanish but also to acquaint yourself with the customs and the people of the country. For total immersion, most language schools offer boarding with a Mexican family, but your choice of lodgings and of length of stay is generally flexible (*see* Theme Trips *under* Tour Operators *in* Important Contacts A to Z, *above*).

LODGING

The price and quality of accommodations in Mexico vary about as much as the country's restaurants, from super-luxurious, international-class hotels and all-inclusive resorts to modest budget properties, seedy places with shared bathrooms, *casas de huéspedes* (guest houses), youth hostels, and *cabañas* (beach huts). You may find appealing bargains while you're on the road, but if your comfort level is high, **look for an English-speaking staff, guaranteed dollar rates, and toll-free reservation numbers in the United States.**

Hotel rates are subject to the 10% value-added tax, and service charges and meals are generally not included. The Mexican government categorizes hotels, based on qualitative evaluations, into *gran turismo* (super-deluxe hotels, of which there are only about 50 nationwide); five-star down to one-star; and economy class. Keep in mind that many hotels that might otherwise have rated higher have opted for a lower category to avoid higher interest rates on loans and financing.

High- versus low-season rates can vary significantly (*see* When to Go, *below*). Hotels in this guide have air-conditioning and private bathrooms with showers, unless stated otherwise, but bathtubs are not common in inexpensive hotels and properties in smaller towns.

Mexican hotels— particularly those owned or managed by the international chains—are always being expanded. In older properties, travelers may often have to choose between newer annexes with modern amenities and rooms in the original buildings with possibly fewer amenities and—equally possible, but not certain—greater charm.

It's essential to **reserve in advance** if you are traveling during high season or holiday periods. Overbooking is a common practice in some parts of Mexico, such as Cancún. Travelers to remote areas will encounter little difficulty in obtaining rooms on a "walk-in" basis.

One last note of advice: If you are particularly sensitive to noise, you should **call ahead to learn if your hotel of choice is located on a busy street.** Many of the most engaging accommodations in Mexico are on downtown intersections that experience heavy automobile and pedestrian traffic. And large hotels are known to feature lobby bars with live music in the middle of an open-air atrium leading directly to rooms. When you book, **request a room far from the bar.**

APARTMENT AND VILLA RENTALS

If you want a home base that's roomy enough for a family and comes with cooking facilities, **consider a furnished rental.** It's generally cost-wise, too, although not always— some rentals are luxury properties (economical only when your party is large). Home-exchange directories do list rentals—often second homes owned by prospective house swappers—and some services search for a house or apartment for you (even a castle if that's your fancy) and handle the paperwork. Some send an illustrated

catalogue and others send photographs of specific properties, sometimes at a charge; up-front registration fees may apply.

HOME EXCHANGE

If you would like to find a house, an apartment, or other vacation property to exchange for your own while on vacation, **become a member of a home-exchange organization,** which will send you its annual directories listing available exchanges and will include your own listing in at least one of them. Arrangements for the actual exchange are made by the two parties involved, not by the organization.

M
MAIL

The Mexican postal system is notoriously slow and unreliable; **never send packages** or expect to receive them, as they may be stolen (for emergencies, use a courier service or the new express-mail service, with insurance). There are post offices (*oficinas de correos*) even in the smallest villages, and numerous branches in the larger cities. Always **use airmail for overseas correspondence;** it will take anywhere from 10 days to two weeks or more, where surface mail might take three weeks to arrive. Service within Mexico can be equally slow. It costs NP$2 to send a postcard or letter weighing under 20 grams to the United States, Canada, or Great Britain.

RECEIVING MAIL

To receive mail in Mexico, you can have it sent to your hotel or use *poste restante* at the post office. In the latter case, include the words "a/c Lista de Correos" (general delivery), followed by the city, state, postal code, and country. A list of names for whom mail has been received is posted and updated daily by the post office. American Express card members can have mail sent to them at the local American Express office. For a list of locations, ask for a copy of *Traveler's Companion* at any American Express office; or write to American Express (Box 678, Canal Street Station, New York, NY 10013).

MEDICAL ASSISTANCE

No one plans to get sick while traveling, but it happens, so **consider signing up with a medical assistance company.** These outfits provide referrals, emergency evacuation or repatriation, 24-hour telephone hot lines for medical consultation, dispatch of medical personnel, relay of medical records, cash for emergencies, and other personal and legal assistance.

MONEY AND EXPENSES

As of January 1, 1993, the new unit of currency in Mexico became the *nuevo peso*, or new peso, which is subdivided into 100 centavos. At press time (spring 1995), the peso was in flux due to devaluation enacted by the new Zedillo administration. While exchange rates were as favorable as one U.S. dollar to NP$6.02, one Canadian dollar to NP$4.4, and a pound sterling to 9.7, the market and prices are likely to have adjusted themselves by 1996.

The old peso, which had a cumbersome exchange of 3,000 to one U.S. dollar, was to be completely phased out by January 1994, but at press time there was still old currency in circulation, and many public phones and vending machines in rural areas still accepted only the old coins. The new paper currency differs in design and, in some cases, size, from the old and comes in denominations of 10, 20, 50, 100, 200, and 500. The new 10-, 20-, 50-, and 100-peso bills are equal to the old 10,000, 20,000, 50,000 and 100,000 notes, respectively. Newly introduced were the 2-, 5-, 10-, and 20-peso coins. The 1,000-, 500-, 200-, 100-, and 50-peso coins were replaced by the smaller, newly designed 1-peso and 50-, 20-, 10-, and 5-centavo coins. Needless to say, it is somewhat confusing. Travelers should **examine coins carefully before paying and when receiving change.** Note: NP$ generally precedes prices in new pesos. To avoid fraud, it's wise to make sure that "NP" is clearly marked on all credit-card receipts.

Dollars are widely accepted in many parts of Mexico, particularly near the border and in Cozumel. Many tourist shops and market vendors, as well as virtually all hotel service personnel, take them, too.

Traveler's checks and all major U.S. credit cards (except Discover) are accepted in most tourist areas of Mexico. The large hotels, restaurants, and department stores accept cards readily. Some of the smaller restaurants and shops, however, will only take cash. Credit cards are generally not accepted in small towns and villages, except in tourist-oriented hotels. When shopping, you can usually get much better prices if you **bargain with dollars.**

ATMS

Cirrus, Plus and many other networks connecting automated-teller machines operate internationally. Chances are that you can **use your bank card at ATMs** to withdraw money from an account and get cash advances on a credit-card account if your card has been programmed with a personal identification number, or PIN. Before leaving home, **check in on frequency limits** for withdrawals and cash advances. Also **ask whether your card's PIN must be reprogrammed** for use in Mexico. Four digits are commonly used overseas. Note that Discover is accepted only in the United States.

On cash advances you are charged interest from the day you receive the money from ATMs as well as from tellers. Although transaction fees for ATM withdrawals abroad may be higher than fees for withdrawals at home, Cirrus and Plus exchange rates are excellent because they are based on wholesale rates only offered by major banks.

COSTS

Mexico has a reputation for being inexpensive, particularly compared with other North American vacation spots such as the Caribbean; the recent devaluation of the peso has made this particularly true, though prices of the large chain hotels, calculated in dollars, have not gone down, and some restaurant owners and merchants have raised their prices to compensate for the devaluation. In general, costs will vary with the when, where, and how of your travel in Mexico. "When" is discussed in When to Go, *below.* As to "how," tourists seeking a destination as much as possible like home, who travel only by air or package tour, stay at international hotel chain properties, eat at restaurants catering to tourists, and shop at fixed-price tourist-oriented malls may not find Mexico such a bargain. Anyone who wants a closer look at the country and is not wedded to standardized creature comforts can spend as little as $35 a day on room, board,

and local transportation. Speaking Spanish is also helpful in bargaining situations and when asking for dining recommendations. As a rule, the less English is spoken in a region, the cheaper things will be.

Cancún, Puerto Vallarta, Mexico City, Acapulco, and Ixtapa and to a lesser extent Mazatlán, Manzanillo, Huatulco, and southern Baja California are the most expensive places to visit in Mexico. Taxis are supposed to charge fixed rates to and from the airport and between hotels and beaches or downtown, but be sure to **agree upon a price before hiring a cab.** Water sports can cost as much as they do on the Caribbean islands. All the beach towns, however, offer budget accommodations, and the smaller, less accessible ones are often more moderately priced, examples being the Gulf Coast and northern Yucatán, parts of Quintana Roo, Puerto Escondido, and the beaches of Chiapas.

Average costs in the major cities vary, although less than in the past because of the increase in business travelers. A stay in one of Mexico City's top hotels can cost more than $200 (as much or more than at the coastal resorts), but meal prices have gone down with the devaluation of the peso; you can get away with a tab of $45 for two at what was once an expensive restaurant.

Probably the best value for your travel dollar is

found in the smaller inland towns, such as San Cristóbal de las Casas, Mérida, Morelia, Guanajuato, and Oaxaca, where tourism is less developed. Although Oaxaca lodging can run more than $150 a night, simple colonial-style hotels with adequate accommodations for under $40 can be found these days, and tasty, filling meals are rarely more than $15.

EXCHANGING CURRENCY

For the most favorable rates, **change money at banks.** You won't do as well at exchange booths in airports, rail, and bus stations, nor in hotels, restaurants, and stores, although you may find their hours (and lack of bureaucracy) more convenient. To avoid lines at airport exchange booths, **get a small amount of currency before you leave home.**

TAXES

AIRPORT➤ An airport departure tax of U.S. $12 or the peso equivalent must be paid at the airport for international flights from Mexico, and there is a domestic air departure tax of around U.S. $6. Traveler's checks and credit cards are not accepted.

VAT➤ Mexico has a value-added tax of 10% called I.V.A. (*impuesto de valor agregado*), which is occasionally (and illegally) waived for cash purchases. Other taxes and charges apply for phone calls, dining, and lodging.

TRAVELER'S CHECKS

Whether or not to buy traveler's checks depends on where you are headed; **take cash to rural areas and small towns, traveler's checks to cities.** The most widely recognized are American Express, Citicorp, Thomas Cook, and Visa, which are sold by major commercial banks for 1% to 3% of the checks' face value—it pays to **shop around.** Both American Express and Thomas Cook issue checks that can be counter-signed and used by you or your traveling companion. So you won't be left with excess foreign currency, **buy a few checks in small denominations** to cash toward the end of your trip. Record the numbers of the checks, cross them off as you spend them, and keep this information separate from your checks.

WIRING MONEY

You don't have to be a cardholder to send or receive funds through MoneyGram[SM] from American Express. Just go to a MoneyGram agent, located in retail and convenience stores and in American Express Travel Offices. Pay up to $1,000 with cash or a credit card, anything over that in cash. The money can be picked up within 10 minutes in the form of U.S. dollar traveler's checks or local currency at the nearest Money-Gram agent, or, abroad, the nearest American Express Travel Office (in Mexico City, 5/326–3521 or 5/326–2777). There's no limit, and the recipient need only present photo identification. The cost runs from 3% to 10%, depending on the amount sent, the destination, and how you pay.

You can also send money using Western Union. Money sent from the United States or Canada will be available for pickup within 15 minutes. Fees range from 4% to 10%, depending on the amount you send.

P

PACKAGES AND TOURS

A package or tour to Mexico can make your vacation less expensive and more convenient. Firms that sell tours and packages buy airline seats, hotel rooms, and rental cars in bulk and pass some of the savings on to you. In addition, the best operators have local representatives to help you out at your destination.

A GOOD DEAL?

The more your package or tour includes, the better you can predict the ultimate cost of your vacation. Make sure you know exactly what is included, and **beware of hidden costs.** Are taxes, tips, and service charges included? Transfers and baggage handling? Entertainment and excursions? These can add up.

Most packages and tours are rated deluxe, first-class superior, first class, tourist, and budget. The key difference is usually accommodations. Remember, tourist class in the United States might be a comfortable chain hotel, while in Mexico you might share a bath and do without hot water. If the package or tour you are considering is priced lower than in your wildest dreams, **be skeptical.** Also, **make sure your travel agent knows the hotels** and other services. Ask about location, room size, beds, and whether it has a pool, room service, or programs for children, if you care about these. Has your agent been there or sent others you can contact?

BUYER BEWARE

Each year consumers are stranded or lose their money when operators go out of business—even very large ones with excellent reputations. If you can't afford a loss, take the time to **check out the operator**—find out how long the company has been in business, and ask several agents about its reputation. Next, **don't book unless the firm has a con-sumer-protection program.** Members of the United States Tour Operators Association and the National Tour Association are required to set aside funds exclusively to cover your payments and travel arrangements in case of default. Nonmember operators may instead carry insurance; look for the details in the operator's brochure—and the name of an underwriter with a solid reputation. Note: When it comes to tour operators, **don't trust escrow accounts.** Although there are laws governing those of charter-flight operators, no governmental body prevents tour operators from raiding the till.

Next, **contact your local Better Business Bureau and the attorney general's office** in both your own state and the operator's; have any complaints been filed? Last, **pay with a major credit card.** Then you can cancel payment, provided that you can document your complaint. Always **consider trip-cancellation insurance** (*see* Insurance, *above*).

BIG VS. SMALL➤ An operator that handles several hundred thousand travelers annually can use its purchasing power to give you a good price. Its high volume may also indicate financial stability. But some small companies provide more personalized service; because they tend to specialize, they may also be experts on an area.

USING AN AGENT

Travel agents are an excellent resource. In fact, large operators accept bookings only through travel agents. But it's good to **collect brochures from several agencies** because some agents' suggestions may be skewed by promotional relationships with tour and package firms that reward them for volume sales. If you have a special interest, **find an agent with expertise in that area;** the American Society of

Travel Agents can give you leads in the United States. (Don't rely solely on your agent, though; agents may be unaware of small niche operators, and some special-interest travel companies only sell directly to consumers.)

SINGLE TRAVELERS

Prices are usually quoted per person, based on two sharing a room. If traveling solo, you may be required to pay the full double occupany rate. Some operators eliminate this surcharge if you agree to be matched up with a roommate of the same sex, even if one is not found by departure time.

PACKING
FOR MEXICO

Pack light: Though baggage carts are available now at airports, luggage restrictions on international flights are tight, and you'll want to save space for purchases. Mexico is filled with bargains on textiles, leather goods, arts and crafts, and silver jewelry.

What clothing you bring depends on your destination. For the resorts, bring lightweight sports clothes, bathing suits, and cover-ups for the beach. Bathing suits and immodest clothing are inappropriate for shopping and sightseeing, both in cities and beach resorts. Mexico City is a bit more formal than the resorts and because of its high elevation, cooler. Men will want to bring lightweight suits or

slacks and blazers for fancier restaurants; and women should pack tailored dresses. Many restaurants require jacket and tie. Jeans are acceptable for shopping and sightseeing, but shorts are frowned upon for men and women. You'll need a lightweight topcoat for winter and an all-weather coat and umbrella in case of sudden summer rainstorms.

Resorts, such as Cancún and Acapulco, are both casual and elegant; you'll see high-style designer sportswear, tie-dyed T-shirts, cotton slacks and walking shorts, and plenty of colorful sundresses. The sun can be fierce; **bring a sun hat (or buy one locally) and sunscreen for the beach and for sightseeing.** You'll need a sweater or jacket to cope with hotel and restaurant air-conditioning, which can be glacial. Few restaurants require jacket and tie.

Take an extra pair of eyeglasses or contact lenses in your carry-on luggage, and if you have a health problem, **pack enough medication** to last the trip or have your doctor write a prescription using the drug's generic name, because brand names vary from country to country (you'll then need a prescription from a doctor in the country you're visiting). In case your bags go astray, **don't put prescription drugs or valuables in luggage to be checked.** To avoid problems with customs officials, carry medications in original packaging. Also don't forget the addresses of offices that handle refunds of lost traveler's checks.

ELECTRICITY

Electrical converters are not necessary because the country operates on the 60-cycle, 120-volt system; however, many Mexican outlets have not been updated to accommodate three-prong and polarized plugs (those with one larger prong), so you may need an adapter. Hotels sometimes have 110-volt outlets for low-wattage appliances marked "For Shavers Only" near the sink; don't use them for high-wattage appliances like blow-dryers.

LUGGAGE

REGULATIONS➤ Free airline baggage allowances depend on the airline, the route, and the class of your ticket; ask in advance. In general, on domestic flights and on international flights between the United States and foreign destinations, you are entitled to check two bags— neither exceeding 62 inches, or 158 centimeters (length + width + height), or weighing more than 70 pounds (32 kilograms). A third piece may be brought aboard; its total dimensions are generally limited to less than 45 inches (114 centimeters), so it will fit easily under the seat in front of you or in the overhead compartment. In the United States, the Federal Aviation Administration gives airlines broad latitude to limit carry-on allowances and tailor them to different aircraft and operational conditions. Charges for excess, oversize, or overweight pieces vary.

If you are flying between two foreign destinations, note that baggage allowances may be determined not by piece but by weight—generally 88 pounds (40 kilograms) in first class, 66 pounds (30 kilograms) in business class, and 44 pounds (20 kilograms) in economy. If your flight between two cities abroad *connects* with your transatlantic or transpacific flight, the piece method still applies.

SAFEGUARDING YOUR LUGGAGE➤ Before leaving home, **itemize your bags' contents** and their worth, and label them with your name, address, and phone number. (If you use your home address, cover it so that potential thieves can't see it.) Inside your bag, **pack a copy of your itinerary.** At check-in, **make sure that your bag is correctly tagged** with the airport's three-letter destination code. If your bags arrive damaged or not at all, file a written report with the airline before leaving the airport.

PASSPORTS AND VISAS

If you don't already have one, **get a passport.** While traveling, **keep one photocopy of the data page** separate from your wallet and leave another copy with someone at home. If you lose your passport, promptly call the nearest embassy or consulate, and the local police; having the data page can speed replacement.

U.S. CITIZENS

All U.S. citizens, even infants, need a valid passport or a certified birth certificate, notarized affadavit of citizenship, or voter's registration card, plus a photo I.D. to enter Mexico for stays of more than 180 days. New and renewal application forms are available at any of the 13 U.S. Passport Agency offices and at some post offices and courthouses. Passports are usually mailed within four weeks; allow five weeks or more in spring and summer.

CANADIANS

Canadians need a tourist card, birth certificate, or valid passport to enter Mexico for stays of up to six months. Passport application forms are available at 28 regional passport offices as well as post offices and travel agencies. Whether for a first or a subsequent passport, you must apply in person. Children under 16 may be included on a parent's passport but must have their own to travel alone. Passports are valid for five years and are usually mailed within two to three weeks of application.

U.K. CITIZENS

Citizens of the United Kingdom need a tourist

card and a valid passport to enter Mexico for stays of up to three months. Applications for new and renewal passports are available from main post offices as well as at the passport offices, located in Belfast, Glasgow, Liverpool, London, Newport, and Peterborough. You may apply in person at all passport offices, or by mail to all except the London office. Children under 16 may travel on an accompanying parent's passport. All passports are valid for 10 years. Allow a month for processing.

**PERSONAL
SECURITY AND
COMFORT**

Many Americans are aware of Mexico's reputation for corruption. The patronage system is a well-entrenched part of Mexican politics and industry, and workers in the public sector—notably policemen and customs officials—are notoriously underpaid. Everyone has heard, at least secondhand, a horror story about highway assaults, pickpocketing, bribes, or foreigners (not to mention the Mexicans themselves) languishing in Mexican jails.

Just as you would anywhere, **use common sense.** Wear a money belt; put valuables in hotel safes; avoid driving on untraveled streets and roads at night; and carry your own baggage whenever possible. Reporting a crime to the police is

often a frustrating experience unless you speak excellent Spanish and have a great deal of patience.

Women traveling alone are likely to be subjected to *piropos* (catcalls). Don't wear tight clothes. Don't enter street bars or cantinas unaccompanied. On the street, avoid direct eye contact with men, which invites further acquaintance. If you speak Spanish, pretend you don't and ignore would-be suitors or say "no" to whatever they say.

R

RAIL TRAVEL

In recent years, train schedules and first-class service from the U.S.–Mexico border have been cut significantly, in part because of the introduction of good trans-border bus transport (*see* Bus Travel, *above*). At this writing, Mexicali (across from Calexico, CA) was the only city along the border from which first-class rail service into Mexico was available (via the *El Pacífico* into Guadalajara). Currently *El Regiomontano* has only a second-class train that makes trips from Nuevo Laredo at the border. For the best rail service to the capital, **take a bus from Nuevo Laredo to Monterrey, where you can pick up the first-class train to the capital.** *El Regiomontano* makes stops in Saltillo and San Luís Potosi; private rooms with bath and one or two berths are available. The entire train

system is likely to be in flux for the next few years as the Mexican government works toward privatizing it.

WITHIN MEXICO

Although Ferrocarriles Nacionales de México (*see* Rail Travel *in* Important Contacts A to Z, *above*) began upgrading service in 1987 with air-conditioning and dining, club, and sleeping cars, the effort lost its steam. The Mexican government officially announced in 1994 that it was slowly moving out of the luxury rail business and would be looking to privatize this segment of the industry over the next several years. As first-class bus service proliferates throughout the country, first-class rail cars and schedules are being cut, often with little or no advance notice. The *Chihuahua-Pacific Railway* (☎ 14/15–77–56 in Chihuahua), one of Mexico's most popular tourist trains, coasts alongside the Copper Canyon from Chihuahua to Los Mochis on the Pacific coast. At press time, Pullman service was still available on *El Regiomontano* (Mexico City to Monterrey); *El Jarocho* (Mexico City to Veracruz); and *El Tapatío* (Mexico City to Guadalajara). Whichever train you take, **be prepared for a relatively slow ride and bring a snack.** The meals are less than appetizing.

Primera especial (special first-class) tickets on overnight trains

THE GOLD GUIDE / SMART TRAVEL TIPS

entitle passengers to reserved, spacious seats. *Primera regular* (regular first-class) service is also available on many trains. Second-class tickets are not available from U.S. agents, but first-class seats are not expensive and, in terms of comfort, well worth the few extra pesos.

Sleeping accommodations consist of *camarines* (private rooms with bath and a single lower berth), *alcobas* (same as *camarines,* but with an upper and a lower berth), and couchettes.

Train tickets must be purchased at least one day in advance, from Mexico City's Buenavista Station, local stations, or local Mexican travel agents, who will, of course, charge you extra. You can also reserve first-class tickets and rail-hotel packages in advance (10 to 15 days is recommended) from the United States by calling Mexico by Train (*see* Rail Travel *in* Important Contacts A to Z, *above*).

RENTING A CAR

When considering this option, remember that Mexico is still a developing country. Acquiring a driver's license is sometimes more a question of paying someone off than of having tested skill, and the highway system is very uneven: in some regions, modern, well-paved super highways prevail; in others, particularly the mountains, potholes and dangerous, unrailed curves are the rule.

CUTTING COSTS

To get the best deal, **book through a travel agent and shop around.** When pricing cars, **ask where the rental lot is located.** Some off-airport locations offer lower rates—even though their lots are only minutes away from the terminal via complimentary shuttle. You may also want to **price local car-rental companies,** whose rates may be lower still, although service and maintenance standards may not be up to those of a nationally recognized firm. Also **ask your travel agent about a company's customer-service record.** How has it responded to late plane arrivals and vehicle mishaps? Are there often lines at the rental counter, and, if you're traveling during a holiday period, does a confirmed reservation guarantee you a car?

Always **find out what equipment is standard** at your destination before specifying what you want; it often lowers costs considerably to **do without automatic transmission or air-conditioning** if they're optional.

INSURANCE

When you drive a rented car, you are generally responsible for any damage or personal injury that you cause as well as damage to the vehicle. Before you rent, **see what coverage you already have** by means of your personal auto-insurance policy and credit cards. For about $14 a day, rental companies sell insurance,

known as a collision damage waiver (CDW), that eliminates your liability for damage to the car; it's always optional and should never be automatically added to your bill.

When you drive in Mexico, it is necessary at all times to **carry proof of Mexican auto liability insurance,** which is usually provided by car-rental agencies and included in the cost of the rental. If you don't have proof of insurance and happen to injure someone—whether it's your fault or not—you stand the risk of being jailed.

REQUIREMENTS

In Mexico your own driver's license is acceptable. An International Driver's Permit, available from the American or Canadian Automobile Association, is a good idea.

SURCHARGES

Before picking up the car in one city and leaving it in another, **ask about drop-off charges or one-way service fees,** which can be substantial. Note, too, that some rental agencies charge extra if you return the car before the time specified on your contract. To avoid a hefty refueling fee, **fill the tank just before you turn in the car.**

S

SENIOR-CITIZEN DISCOUNTS

To qualify for age-related discounts, **mention your senior-citizen status up front** when booking hotel reservations, not when checking out, and before you're seated in restaurants, not when paying your bill. Note that discounts may be limited to certain menus, days, or hours. When renting a car, **ask about promotional car-rental discounts**—they can net lower costs than your senior-citizen discount.

SHOPPING

At least three varieties of outlets sell Mexican crafts: indoor and outdoor municipal markets, government-run shops (known as *Fonart*), and tourist boutiques in towns, shopping malls, and hotels. If you **buy in the municipal shops or markets** you can avoid the VAT, and you'll be able to pay in pesos or dollars. Boutiques usually accept credit cards if not dollars; although they are overpriced, they are also convenient. (You may be asked to pay up to 10% more on credit card purchases; savvy shoppers have greater bargaining clout.) The 10% tax (I.V.A.) is charged on most purchases but is often disregarded by eager or desperate vendors.

It is not always true that the closer you are to the source of an article, the better the selection and price are likely to be. Mexico City, Oaxaca, and San Miguel de Allende have some of the best selections of crafts from around the country, and if you know where to go, you will find bar-

gains. Prices are usually higher at beach resorts.

Bargaining is accepted in most touristy parts of Mexico and is most common in the markets. Start by offering no more than half the asking price and then come up very slowly, but **pay no more than 70% when bargaining.** Always shop around. In major shopping areas like San Miguel, shops will wrap and send purchases back to the United States via a package delivery company. In some areas you will be able to have items such as *huaraches* (leather sandals), clothing, and blankets tailor-made. If you buy woolens or wood items, it's wise to freeze or microwave them when you return to destroy possible insect infestation. Keep in mind that items made from tortoiseshell and black coral will not be allowed back into the United States.

STUDENTS ON THE ROAD

To save money, **look into deals available through student-oriented travel agencies.** To qualify, you'll need to have a bona fide student I.D. card, which will be useful for getting discounts on transportation and admissions to museums and other attractions as well. Members of international student groups also are eligible. *See* Students *in* Important Contacts A to Z, *above.*

T
TAXIS

AT THE AIRPORT

From the airport, **take a government-subsidized cab;** the driver will accept the taxi vouchers sold at stands outside the airport, which in theory ensure that your fare is established beforehand. However, in practice you may be overcharged, so prepare yourself by locating the taxi originating and destination zones on a map and make sure your ticket is properly zoned; if you only need a ticket from zone three to zone four, don't pay for a ticket from zone one. Even then, the rates for non-government-subsidized cabs routinely exceed the official taxi rate.

IN CITIES AND BEACH RESORTS

In Mexican cities, **take a taxi rather than public transportation,** which, though inexpensive, is frequently slow and sometimes patrolled by pickpockets. Always **establish the fare beforehand,** and **always count your change.** In most of the beach resorts, there are inexpensive fixed-route fares, but if you don't ask, or your Spanish isn't great, you may get taken. In the cities, and especially the capital, meters do not always run, and if they do, their rates have usually been updated by a chart posted somewhere in the cab. For distances more than several kilometers, negotiate a rate in advance; many drivers will start by asking how much you want to pay to get a sense of how street-smart you are. In all cases, if you are unsure of what a fare should be, ask your hotel's front desk personnel or bell captain.

Taxis are available on the street, at taxi stands (*sitios*), and by phone. Street taxis—usually Volkswagen Beetles—are subsidized cabs and are always the cheapest; sedans standing in front of hotels will charge far more. Never leave luggage unattended in a taxi.

In addition to private taxis, many cities operate a bargain-price collective taxi service using VW minibuses (called *combis*) and sedans, both downtown and at the airports. The service is called *colectivo* or *pesero*. Peseros run along fixed routes, and you hail them on the street and tell the driver where you are going. The fare—which you pay before you get out—is based on distance traveled. (For information on taxis in Mexico City, *see* Chapter 2.)

TELEPHONES

Thanks to the privatization of Telefónos de México in 1991, Mexico's phone service, long exasperatingly inefficient, is gradually being overhauled. In the meantime, the variety of public phones that exist in the country can be confusing at best. You'll see traditional black, square phones with push buttons or dials; although they have a coin slot on top, you may make local calls on them for free. Then there are the new blue or ivory push-button phones with digital screens. Some phones in rural areas have coin slots that accept only old peso coins; the large, 1,000-peso coins allow for ample local conversations. Other new phones have both a coin slot and an unmarked slot; the latter are for LADATEL (Spanish acronym for "long-distance direct dialing") cards, handy magnetic-strip debit cards that can be purchased at tourist offices as well as at newsstands and stores with a LADATEL logo. They come in denominations of up to NP$50 and can be used for both local and long-distance calls. Still other phones have two unmarked slots, one for a LADATEL card and the other for a credit card. These are primarily for Mexican bank cards, but some accept U.S. Visa or MasterCard, though *not* U.S. telephone credit cards.

So far, there is still no touch-tone (digital) circuitry in operation in Mexico. Although some hotel, office, and residence phones have a "tone/pulse" switch, if you think you'll need to access an automated phone system or voice mail in the United States, it's a good idea to take along a touch-tone simulator (you can buy them for about $17 at most electronic stores). Nor are multi-line phones that automatically bounce incoming calls to the next available line common in Mexico; this is why there are often many telephone numbers listed for a single place. With the increased installation of new phone and fax lines in major Mexican cities, many phone numbers are in the process of being changed; a recording may offer the new number, so it's useful to learn the Spanish words for numbers 1 through 9.

LONG-DISTANCE

The international services of AT&T, MCI, and Sprint make calling home relatively convenient and let you avoid huge hotel surcharges (though you'll still pay for accessing your long-distance operator). To connect with AT&T's USA DIRECT service, dial 95/800/674–7000; MCI's access number is 95/800/462–4240, and Sprint's is 95/800/877–800. It's wise to **use the LADATEL phones found in many hotel lobbies** if you need to make a long distance call.

TIPPING

When tipping in Mexico, remember that the minimum wage is the equivalent of $6 a day and that the vast majority of workers in the tourist industry live barely above the poverty line. However, there are Mexicans who think in dollars and know, for example, that in the United States porters are tipped about $1 a bag; many of them expect the peso equivalent from foreigners but are happy to accept NP$1 from Mexicans.

They will complain either verbally or with a facial expression if they feel they deserve more—you and your conscience must decide. Overtipping, however, is equally a problem. Following are some general guidelines, in pesos.

Porters and bellboys at airports and at moderate and inexpensive hotels: NP$4 per bag

Porters at expensive hotels: NP$7 per bag

Hotel room service: NP$6 (expensive hotels) or NP$3 (moderate and inexpensive hotels)

Maids: NP$3 per night (all hotels)

Waiters: 10%–15% of the bill, depending on service (make sure a 10%–15% service charge has not already been added to the bill, although this practice is not common in Mexico)

Taxi drivers: a 5%–10% tip is appreciated but not necessary.

Gas station attendants: 50 centavos

Parking attendants and theater ushers: NP$2–NP$3; some theaters have set rates.

W
WHEN TO GO

Mexico is sufficiently large and geographically diverse that you can find a place to visit any time of the year. October through May are generally the driest months; during the peak of the rainy season (June–September), it may rain for a few hours every day. But the sun often shines for the rest of the day, and the reduced off-season rates may well compensate for the reduced tanning time.

From December through February, the Mexican resorts—where the vast majority of tourists go—are the most crowded and therefore the most expensive. To avoid the masses, the highest prices, and the worst rains, **consider visiting Mexico during October, April, or May.** Hotel rates at the beach resorts can be cut by as much as 30% in the shoulder season, 50% in the off-season.

Mexicans travel during traditional holiday periods—Christmas through New Year's, Semana Santa (Holy Week, the week before Easter), and school vacations in the summertime—as well as over extended national holiday weekends, called *puentes* (bridges). Festivals play a big role in Mexican national life. If you plan to travel during a major national event, reserve both lodgings and transportation well in advance (*see* Festivals and Seasonal Events *in* Chapter 1).

CLIMATE
The variations in Mexico's climate are not surprising considering the size of the country. The coasts and low-lying sections of the interior are often very hot if not actually tropical, with temperatures ranging from 24°C to 31°C (75°F to 88°F) in winter and well above 32°C (90°F) in summer. A more temperate area ranging from 16°C to 21°C (60°F to 70°F) is found at altitudes of 1,220–1,830 meters (4,000–6,000 feet). In general, the high central plateau on which Mexico City, Guadalajara, and many of the country's colonial cities are located is springlike year-round.

Climate in Mexico

ACAPULCO

Jan.	88F	31C	May	90F	32C	Sept.	90F	32C
	72	22		77	25		77	25
Feb.	88F	31C	June	90F	32C	Oct.	90F	32C
	72	22		77	25		77	25
Mar.	88F	31C	July	91F	33C	Nov.	90F	32C
	72	22		77	25		75	24
Apr.	88F	31C	Aug.	91F	33C	Dec.	88F	31C
	72	22		77	25		73	23

COZUMEL

Jan.	82F	28C	May	89F	32C	Sept.	89F	32C
	68	20		73	23		75	24
Feb.	84F	29C	June	89F	32C	Oct.	87F	31C
	68	20		75	24		73	23
Mar.	86F	30C	July	89F	32C	Nov.	84F	29C
	69	21		75	24		71	22
Apr.	89F	32C	Aug.	91F	33C	Dec.	84F	29C
	71	22		75	24		68	20

ENSENADA

Jan.	64F	18C	May	70F	21C	Sept.	77F	25C
	45	7		54	12		61	16
Feb.	66F	19C	June	72F	22C	Oct.	73F	23C
	46	8		57	14		55	13
Mar.	66F	19C	July	75F	24C	Nov.	72F	22C
	46	8		61	16		48	9
Apr.	68F	20C	Aug.	75F	24C	Dec.	66F	19C
	52	11		63	17		46	8

GUADALAJARA

Jan.	75F	24C	May	88F	31C	Sept.	79F	26C
	45	7		57	14		59	15
Feb.	77F	25C	June	84F	29C	Oct.	79F	26C
	46	8		61	16		59	15
Mar.	82F	28C	July	79F	26C	Nov.	77F	25C
	48	9		59	15		48	9
Apr.	86F	30C	Aug.	79F	26C	Dec.	75F	24C
	54	12		59	15		46	8

LA PAZ

Jan.	72F	22C	May	88F	31C	Sept.	92F	33C
	57	14		64	18		76	24
Feb.	74F	23C	June	92F	33C	Oct.	89F	32C
	56	13		69	21		71	22
Mar.	80F	27C	July	95F	35C	Nov.	81F	27C
	56	13		75	24		66	19
Apr.	83F	28C	Aug.	93F	34C	Dec.	74F	23C
	60	16		76	24		59	15

MEXICO CITY

Jan.	70F	21C	May	79F	26C	Sept.	72F	22C
	41	5		52	11		52	11
Feb.	73F	23C	June	77F	25C	Oct.	72F	22C
	45	7		54	12		52	11
Mar.	79F	26C	July	73F	23C	Nov.	72F	22C
	48	9		52	11		52	11
Apr.	81F	27C	Aug.	73F	23C	Dec.	70F	21C
	50	10		52	11		43	6

MONTERREY

Jan.	68F	20C	May	88F	31C	Sept.	88F	31C
	48	9		68	20		70	21
Feb.	73F	23F	June	91F	33C	Oct.	81F	27C
	52	11		72	22		63	17
Mar.	79F	26C	July	91F	34C	Nov.	75F	24C
	55	13		72	22		55	13
Apr.	86F	30C	Aug.	93F	34C	Dec.	70F	21C
	64	18		72	22		50	10

PUERTO VALLARTA

Jan.	84F	29C	May	91F	33C	Sept.	93F	34C
	63	17		68	20		73	23
Feb.	86F	30C	June	93F	34C	Oct.	93F	34C
	61	16		73	23		73	23
Mar.	86F	30C	July	95F	35C	Nov.	91F	33C
	63	17		73	23		68	20
Apr.	88F	31C	Aug.	95F	35C	Dec.	86F	30C
	64	18		73	23		64	18

SAN MIGUEL DE ALLENDE

Jan.	79F	26C	May	91F	33C	Sept.	82F	28C
	48	9		61	16		61	16
Feb.	82F	28C	June	91F	31C	Oct.	82F	28C
	52	11		63	17		61	16
Mar.	88F	31C	July	84F	29C	Nov.	81F	27C
	55	13		61	16		52	11
Apr.	90F	32C	Aug.	84F	29C	Dec.	77F	25C
	59	15		61	16		48	9

1 Destination: Mexico

MEXICO: WHERE PAST AND PRESENT MEET

MEXICO IS LIKE *mole,* the complex and uniquely Mexican sauce whose myriad variations appeal to many tastes at once.

It is a nation so diverse that most Americans have only a vague inkling of what it's about. It's a place of ethereal cloud forests and regions so barren they were the setting for *Dune,* the science fiction film about a desert planet; of chill mountain heights and tropical jungles filled with shrill monkeys and a verdant growth of mango, papaya, and avocado. Its dimensions can be mind-boggling: Sections of the Copper Canyon are half again as deep as the Grand Canyon in Arizona.

It is a land of powerful muralists whose works chronicle the struggles of its people, while at the same time its musicians and dancers celebrate their survival.

Worlds collide in Mexico. It can be a bastion of Spanish formality or enclave of California casualness, with business people dressed in flip-flops and shorts, their cellular telephones poking out of their shirt pockets.

It is a vacation mecca of computer-designed resorts—sites chosen for their perfect confluence of white beach and crystal sea, where hotels have sprouted shoulder-to-shoulder for high glitz destinations of sand, sun, and fun.

Yet much of it remains unchanged since the days of the conquistadors. In Chiapas, Maya Indians still work their fields with little more than machetes, smiling with benign amusement at the mountains of gear that adventure-travel outfitters use for rafting the rivers that have served as Maya highways for a millennium.

A past that is still very much a part of the present is central to Mexico's allure. In Mexico City's Zócalo—as the main square of any Mexican town or city is called—the pre-Hispanic Templo Mayor sits in the corner created by the juxtaposition of the 16th-century Cathedral and the 17th-century

National Palace. Nearby, the ruins of another Aztec temple have been incorporated into a subway stop.

Some contrasts verge on the comic. Even as Jack Nicklaus declares an ocean-front hole in one of his new courses in Cabo San Lucas his favorite, drivers on the new four-lane highway nearby must beware of the area's greatest traffic hazard in the cool desert night: cows drawn to the pavement that retains the warmth of the sun hours after sunset. Fences remain a relatively new concept in Cabo, but cows are beginning to sprout Day-Glo collars.

And halfway up the Baja Peninsula from Los Cabos, where bulldozers and construction crews are busily erecting condos for golfers, 1,000-year-old polychrome paintings of men and women, sea turtles, and whales lie hidden in the Sierra San Francisco, mountainous terrain so rough that only adventure travelers willing to travel by burro can see them.

Passengers on private trains crossing Mexico's Copper Canyon in cruise ship–style luxury wander through tiny gems of colonial villages and watch the dances of the Tarahumara, indigenous people who live in caves or stone huts, just one step removed from hunter-gatherers.

An air-conditioned bus ride from the beaches of ultra-modern Cancún stand Maya temples, built with such cunning that on spring and autumn equinoxes the sun's shadows make it appear as though a giant serpent were descending a pyramid's steps, melding with a carved serpent's head at the base. Tent cities of vendors hawking T-shirts and other souvenirs have sprouted outside some temples, yet others remain entwined in the vines of the jungles that surround them, looking much as they did when another era of tourists sought them out a century ago.

In the Pacific resort of Mazatlán, the old city center is a mix of Spanish and French-style buildings carefully restored, while a string of modern, beachfront hotels line the water's edge. Beyond the city limits lie the Sierra Madres and the mountain villages where the veins of gold that first attracted the fortune-seeking, empire-building conquistadors are still mined.

Cities such as Querétaro, San Miguel de Allende, and Morelia were also of major importance in the days of colonial Mexico—at one point, a third of the world's silver came from the mines of Guanajuato. Their architecture—European baroque facades and French doors opening onto wrought-iron balconies—has the feel of a Parisian neighborhood suddenly relocated to the American West.

The colorful colonial capital of Oaxaca is itself a babe compared to the Zapotec pyramids outside the city dating as far back as 500 BC. Villagers living in the ring of settlements that surround Oaxaca like moons still practice crafts honed and perfected by their ancestors centuries before the arrival of the first Europeans.

Mexico, in short, is a land that has blended the legacies and traditions of both conqueror and vanquished and made them so uniquely Mexican that it is hard to see where one ends and the other begins.

T IS A BLEND so distinct that visitors can quite literally taste the difference in seemingly familiar foods. A simple cup of American hot chocolate is pale and insipid next to Mexican hot chocolate, a virile, lusty drink sweetened by honey or sugar, thickened with cornmeal, and spiced with pumpkins and peppers to make a powerful cup of substance.

Certainly, much of Mexico is familiar to many Americans—16 million visit annually. With the advent of the wide-bodied jet and cheap charters, resorts such as Acapulco and Puerto Vallarta, once getaways for movie stars and the super-rich, opened to the masses. More recently, isolated enclaves like Cabo San Lucas, whose private airstrips kept it accessible only to fanatic and idiosyncratic fishermen and their celebrity cronies, opened international airports. The result: a desert-by-the-sea golf mecca.

But for all that Mexico is America's next-door neighbor, it can also seem remote. Only recently has Mexico's Ministry of Tourism sought to deal with the red tape that made it almost impossible for Americans to drive across the border. And to simplify border crossing regulations for motorists, tourism officials had to deal with border crossing guards demanding bribes before agreeing to institute some of the new procedures.

An airline system centered on Mexico City can make domestic travel complicated—often the way to get from one resort to another is only via Mexico City. And despite repeated efforts to privatize and improve Ferrocarriles Nacionales de Mexico (FNM), the federal rail system, Mexican trains make Amtrak look like the Concorde.

Communication with home can be tough, too—even in major resorts. Anyone who has actually tried to use Mexican phones can do nothing but marvel at the popularity of Telmex, the Mexican phone company, on the stock market. Cellular phones abound because they are faster to get and often more reliable.

Still, privatization has greatly improved the quality of the nation's buses. Brazilian-built Mercedes motorcoaches and American imports have replaced smoke-belching recycled inter-city buses used in the past on tours. Moreover, with the new, deluxe service between many cities—plush, reclining seats, hostesses dispensing drinks and snacks, and current movies playing overhead—Mexican bus travel has entered what was once the exclusive realm of the airlines.

And more than 7,000 miles of new roads were built under the Salinas administration. They link major tourist centers such as the megaresort of Cancún with the colonial city of Mérida, which has been a major center in the Yucatán since the days the Maya flourished. The Green Angels, a highway patrol whose mechanics aid motorists in distress, patrol these roads.

Indeed, tying it all together is the great common denominator of Mexico: It is a land of great courtesy. That could be one reason that tourist crime is relatively low. Mexico's vacation destinations are as safe as—if not safer than—major U.S. destinations. A fundamentally Mexican security springs from the innate graciousness of a friendly and hospitable people.

— *Kate Rice*

WHAT'S WHERE

Mexico City

Two volcanoes and a pyramid complex flank Mexico's capital, once the center of Aztec civilization and now the country's cosmopolitan business, art, and culinary hub. From the Alameda, a leafy center of activity since Aztec times, to the Zona Rosa, a chic shopping neighborhood, Mexico City offers endless options to urban adventurers. Day trips might include colonial Puebla, where mole sauce and Talavera tiles originated, or the floating gardens of Xochomilco.

Baja California

Separated from mainland Mexico by the Gulf of California, Baja has a 2,000-mile-long coast that stretches from Tijuana to Los Cabos. The earliest of south-of-the-border retreats for the rich, reclusive, or rebellious against Prohibition, Baja still hosts isolated fishing enclaves and raucous watering holes; nature lovers come to watch the whales migrate in winter.

Sonora

Rancheros continue to ride the range in Mexican cowboy country, but beef has been upstaged by beaches in this northwestern state's economy. Along with relatively unspoiled (and inexpensive) coastal towns such as Kino Bay and Guaymas, Sonora's lures include colonial Alamos, an immaculate former silver mining center, and a sprinkling of Spanish missions.

The Copper Canyon: From Los Mochis to Chihuahua City

The Copper Canyon is actually a series of gorges, some of them deeper than the United States' Grand Canyon; they are home to the Tarahumara Indians, renowned for their running ability. A train trip through this magnificent, largely uncharted region usually begins or ends in Chihuahua, a lively mid-sized city with a museum devoted to Pancho Villa.

Pacific Coast Resorts

Hollywood introduced us to two of the Mexican Riviera's most popular towns: Liz Taylor and Richard Burton's sleepy, steamy Puerta Vallarta in *Night of the Iguana,* and the sparkling Manzanillo coast that served as the backdrop to Bo

Derek in *10.* These days both places are prime cruise ship destinations, as is Mazatlán, a bustling port that attracts sportsfishing enthusiasts and surfers.

Guadalajara

The colonial architecture that dates to Guadalajara's heyday as a silver lode for the Spanish is among the lures of Mexico's second-largest city; Guadalajara also introduced the world to mariachis and tequila. Some of the best arts and crafts in the country can be found at Tlaquepaque, on the outskirts of town, and Tonalá, about 10 minutes away.

The Heartland of Mexico

Rich with the history of Mexico's revolution, the heartland is a treasure of colonial towns—Zacatecas, Guanajuato, Querétaro, Morelia, and Pátzcuaro—whose residents now lead quiet, largely traditional lives. Even in San Miguel de Allende, an American art colony and home to a well-known language institute, women wash their clothes and gossip at the local *lavanderia* as they have for hundreds of years.

Acapulco

If Acapulco no longer tops the glitterati top-ten list, it remains both a sentimental favorite and a party-hearty resort town, boasting some of the glitziest discos this side of the Pacific. The cobblestoned streets of nearby Taxco, the silver city, are lined with master jewelers, while Ixtapa/Zihuatanejo, a few hours away, juxtapose modern shopping malls with pristine beaches.

Oaxaca

The geographic, ethnic, and culinary diversity of Oaxaca has made the state a favorite of Mexico aficionados. Descendents of the Mixtec and Zapotec Indians, who built the Monte Albán and Mitla complexes near Oaxaca City, comprise the majority of residents; their handicrafts and festivals are extremely colorful. Although less exotic, the state's coastal developments of Puerto Escondido and Bahías de Huatulco are beloved by surfers and beach bums.

Chiapas and Tabasco

Much in the news these days because of the rebellion of its indigenous peoples, the state of Chiapas has always been an off-the-beaten-path destination, a gateway to

Guatemala best known for the colonial town of San Cristóbal and for the jungle-covered ruins of Palenque, considered by many to be the most interesting in Mexico.

Northeastern Mexico and Veracruz

Many winter Texans get their first taste of Mexico in the northeastern border towns of Nueva Laredo, Reynosa, and Matamoros; those who venture farther down to Monterrey are rewarded with the far more sophisticated dining and shopping of the country's third-largest city. The little-explored pyramids of El Tajín and the raffish charm of Veracruz, the first European city established on the North American mainland, are among the many reasons to continue south.

The Yucatán Peninsula

Mexico's most visited region, the Yucatán has something for everyone: the high-profile sparkle of Cancún; the spectacular snorkeling of Cozumel; the laid-back beachcombing of Isla Mujeres; the fascinating Spanish–Maya mix of Mérida; and the evocative Maya ruins of Tulum, Chichén Itzá, and Uxmal. The region is an ecotourist's dream, too, from the huge Sian Ka'an Biosphere Reserve on the Caribbean Coast to Río Lagartos National Park on the Gulf of Mexico, migration ground for thousands of flamingos and other birds.

PLEASURES & PASTIMES

Beaches

Beaches are the reason most tourists visit Mexico. Generally speaking, the Pacific is rougher and the waters less clear than the Caribbean; consequently there is better snorkeling and scuba diving at the latter. Cancún, Cozumel, and Isla Mujeres, as well as what has come to be called the Cancún–Tulum Corridor, are among the best and most popular beach destinations on the Caribbean coast. Beaches on the Gulf of Mexico are often covered with tar. The Acapulco waters, though much improved by a recent clean-up effort, are still somewhat polluted, but there is no problem at the other Pacific resorts. All beach resorts offer a variety of water sports, including waterskiing, windsurfing, parasailing, and if the water is clear enough, snorkeling and scuba diving. Surfers favor Puerto Escondido, near Huatulco, and Santa Cruz, near San Blas.

Bullfighting

Of all the imports to Mexico of the Spanish conquest, bullfighting was perhaps the most sympathetic to the character of the native Indian peoples, who took up the stylized, ceremonial contest between man and beast with enthusiasm and skill. The sport was refined and popularized over the centuries, until every major city and most small towns had a bullring or some semblance of an arena. As in Spain, the last few decades have seen some decline of the popularity of the sport in Mexico, where it has been superseded by such modern games as soccer and has been the object of negative publicity by animal-rights' activists. It remains a strong part of the Latin American culture, however, and can be thrilling to watch when performed by a skilled toreador. Ask at your hotel about arenas and schedules; most fights are held on Sunday afternoon.

Charreada

This Mexican rodeo is a colorful event involving elegant flourishes and maneuvers, handsome costumes, mariachi music, and much fanfare. There are charreadas most Sunday mornings at Mexico City's Rancho del Charro; inquire at your hotel or at a travel agency.

Dining

Mexican cooking is developing an international reputation and popularity. It is not subtle. It is spicy, varied, and exotic. The poor subsist on staples of rice, beans, and tortillas, which form the basis for creative variations of sophisticated national dishes.

Seafood is abundant, not just on the coasts but also in the lake regions around Guadalajara and in the state of Michoacán. *Ceviche*—raw fish and shellfish (*mariscos*) marinated in lime juice and topped with *cilantro* (coriander), onion, and chili—is almost a national dish, though it originated in Acapulco. It is worth trying, but make sure it's fresh. Shrimp, lobster, and oysters can be huge and succulent; bear in mind the folk adage about eating oysters only in months with names that contain the letter *r*, and be sure to avoid raw shellfish in any area where cholera or water pollution may be a risk. Other popular seafood includes *huachinango* (red snapper), abalone, crab, and swordfish.

Mexicans consume lots of beef, pork, and barbecued lamb (*barbacoa*), with a variety of sauces. Chicken and other poultry tend to be dry and stringy, but when drenched in sauces or disguised in *enchiladas, tacos,* or *burritos,* they are quite palatable. Chicken *mole* (covered with a spicy, chocolate-based sauce) can be especially tasty. Regional variations are described in the appropriate chapters.

Maize was sacred to the Indians, who invented innumerable ways of preparing cornmeal, from the faithful tortilla to the *tamale* (cornmeal wrapped in banana leaves or corn husks), *tostada* (lightly fried, open tortilla heaped with meat, lettuce, etc.), and simple *taco* (a tortilla briefly heated, filled, and wrapped into a slim cylinder; one variation on this is called *flauta,* or flute).

Fresh fruits and vegetables are another Mexican pleasure. Jicama, papaya, mamey, avocado, mango, guayaba, peanuts, squash, and tomatoes are just some of the produce native to Mexico. (All fresh produce should be washed in purified water, however, because bacteria exist in Mexico to which foreigners may not have been exposed.)

Other Mexican specialities less common abroad are *antojitos* or *botanas* (appetizers), *chilaquiles* (a rich breakfast dish made with chile, tortilla, tomatoes, onions, cream, and cheese), and *chile nogada* (a large poblano chili stuffed with pork, raisins, onion, olives, and almonds and topped with a creamy walnut sauce, and pomegranate seeds). Soups are rich—particularly the pork-based *pozole, sopa azteca* (avocado and tortilla in a broth), and *sopa de flor de calabaza* (squash-flower soup).

But this barely touches on the plenitude and diversity of Mexican cuisine, which also encompasses an astonishing assortment of breads, sweets, beers, wines (which are fast improving), and cactus-based liquors. Freshly squeezed fruit juices and fruit shakes (*licuados*) are safe to drink—

if not diluted with unpurified water—and taste heavenly. Coffee varies from standard American-style and Nescafé to espresso and *café de jarra,* which is laced with chocolate and served in a coarse clay mug. Imported liquor is very expensive; middle-class Mexicans stick with the local rum and tequila.

Horseback Riding

Horseback riding is a sport the Mexicans love. The dry ranchlands of northern Mexico have countless stables and dude ranches, as do San Miguel de Allende and Querétaro in the heartland. Horses can be rented by the hour at most beaches, and horseback expeditions can be arranged to the Copper Canyon in Chihuahua and the forest near San Cristóbal, Chiapas.

Hot Springs

Mexico is renowned for its *balnearios* (mineral bath springs), which today are surrounded by a cluster of spa resorts and hacienda-type hotels. Most of the spas are concentrated in the center of the country, in the states of Aguascalientes, Guanajuato, México, Morelos, Puebla, and Querétaro.

Hunting, Fishing, and Bird-Watching

The best area for these activities is Baja California and the Sea of Cortés. Deep-sea fishing off the northern Pacific and near Cozumel are also renowned. For calendar and permit information for both hunting and fishing, contact your local Mexican consulate.

Jai Alai

Bet on a good time—and also on the winners—if you watch this fast-paced Basque sport, a bit like handball but played with a large scoop called a *fronton*. Tijuana and Mexico City have the largest stadiums, but you'll find smaller arenas in other cities around the country.

Ruins

Amateur archaeologists will find heaven in Mexico, where some of the greatest ancient civilizations—among them, the Aztecs, the Olmecs, and the Maya—left their mark. Pick your period and your preference, whether for well-excavated sites or overgrown, out-of-the-way ruins barely touched by a scholar's shovel. The

Yucatán is, hands down, the greatest source of ancient treasure, with such heavy hitters as Chichén Itzá and Uxmal, but you're unlikely to find any region in the country that doesn't have some interesting vestige of Mexico's Indian past. A visit to Mexico City's archaelogical museum, arguably the best in the world, could ignite the imagination of even those who thought they had no interest in antiquity, and help others focus on the places they'd most like to explore further.

Shopping

Mexico is one of the best countries in the world to purchase *artesanías* (handicrafts), and many items are exempt from duty. The work is varied, original, colorful, and inexpensive, and it supports millions of families who are carrying on ancient traditions. Though cheap, shoddy merchandise masquerading as "native handicraft" is increasingly common, careful shoppers who take their time can come away with real works of art.

Mexican craftspeople excel in ceramics, weaving and textiles, silver, gold, and semiprecious stone jewelry, leather, woodwork, and lacquerware; each region has its specialty.

CERAMICS➤ Blue Talavera–style (Puebla); black (Oaxaca); masks and figurines (Michoacán); also in Jalisco, Taxco, Valle de Bravo, Tlaquepaque, and Chiapas.

JEWELRY➤ Silver (Taxco, San Miguel de Allende, and Oaxaca; be sure purchases are stamped "925," which means 92.5% pure silver); gold filigree (Oaxaca, Guanajuato); semiprecious stones (Puebla, Querétaro).

LEATHER➤ Yucatán, Chiapas, Oaxaca, and Jalisco are key destinations.

METALWORK➤ Look for copper in Santa Clara del Cobre in Michoacán, tin in San Miguel de Allende.

WEAVINGS AND TEXTILES➤ Options are many and varied: shawls and blankets around Oaxaca, Jocotopec, near Guadalajara, and Pátzcuaro; *huipiles, guayaberas,* and other embroidered clothing in the Yucatán and Michoacán; henequen hammocks and baskets in the Yucatán; and reed mats in Oaxaca and Valle de Bravo. The Mezquital region east of Querétaro can also be rewarding.

WOODWORK➤ Best bets include masks (Guerrero, Mexico City), *alebrijes* (painted wooden animals, Oaxaca), furniture (Guadalajara, Michoacán, San Miguel de Allende, and Cuernavaca), lacquerware (Uruapan, Michoacán, and Olinalá, Guerrero), and guitars (Paracho, Michoacán).

Soccer

As in Europe, this is Mexico's national sport (known as *futból*). It is played almost year-round at the *Estadio Azteca* in Mexico City as well as in other large cities.

Tennis and Golf

Most major resorts have lighted tennis courts, and there is an abundance of 18-hole golf courses, many designed by such noteworthies as Percy Clifford, Joe Finger, and Robert Trent Jones. At private golf and tennis clubs, you must be accompanied by a member to gain admission. Hotels that do not have their own facilities will often secure you access to ones in the vicinity.

FODOR'S CHOICE

Archaeological Sites

★ **Chichén Itzá.** The best known Maya ruin, Chichén Itzá was the most important city in the Yucatán from the 11th to 13th centuries. Its eclectic architecture is evidence of a complex intermingling of ancient cultures.

★ **Palenque.** Nestled in a rainforest in Chiapas, these Maya ruins have a magical quality, perhaps because of their intimacy.

★ **Teotihuacan.** Predating the Aztecs and believed by them to be the birthplace of the gods, this pyramid complex outside Mexico City was one of the largest cities in the ancient world.

★ **Tulum.** The spectacular backdrop of the Caribbean and proximity to Cancún explain why Tulum is the most visited archaeological site in the Yucatán.

★ **Uxmal.** Arguably the most beautiful of Mexico's ruins, Uxmal represents Maya style at its purest, including ornate stone friezes, intricate cornices, and soaring arches.

Beaches

★ **Playa de Amor, Cabo San Lucas.** From this secluded cove at the very tip of Baja California you can see the Sea of Cortés on one side, the Pacific Ocean on the other.

★ **Yelapa, near Puerta Vallarta.** Walk from the beach of this small fishing village, accessible only by boat, to stunning waterfalls in the jungle.

★ **Bara Vieja, near Acapulco.** Those tired of being hassled by vendors in Acapulco often retreat to Bara Vieja, a magnificent beach about 16 miles to the east.

★ **Zicatela, Oaxaca Coast.** A long stretch of cream-colored sand, Zacatela is one of the top 10 surfing beaches in the world.

★ **Playa Norte and Playa Cocoteros, Isla Mujeres.** These adjoining beaches on sleepy Isla are ideal for watersports and palapa lounging alike.

Special Moments

★ **The divers at La Quebrada, Acapulco.** It's heart-stopping to see these swimmers take the plunge off 130-foot-high cliffs—after praying at a small cliffside chapel.

★ **Whale-watching at Scammon's and San Ignacio lagoons, Baja.** Go out on a boat for the best views of the great gray mammals, who pass here en route from Alaska each winter.

★ *Los voladores,* **Papantla.** A precursor of bungee jumping, this ancient ceremony involves five "flyers" who hurl themselves from a tiny platform set atop a 100-foot pole.

★ **A** *calesa* **(horse-drawn carriage) ride through Merida.** Discover Old World graciousness by trotting slowly through the wide streets and French-style neighborhoods of Yucatán's capital.

★ **Overlooking the Copper Canyon from Divisadero.** Whether you just get off the train briefly or stop overnight, you'll be blown away by the vista of the grand abyss.

Museums

★ **Museum of Contemporary Art, Monterrey.** The best of post-modern Latin American art is gathered at this gallery, where a chic coffee house attracts the city's intellectuals.

★ **Museo Nacional de Antropología, Mexico City.** There are 100,000 square feet of displays at the greatest museum in the country, which hosts archeological treasures from all of Mesoamerica.

★ **Museo de Frida Kahlo, Mexico City.** The characterful former home of the now-fashionable Kahlo is filled with her disturbing, surrealistic paintings and those of friends such as Klee and Duchamp.

★ **Na-Bolom, San Cristobal de las Casas.** Franz and Gertrude Blom lived in a lovely garden-filled setting; their former residence contains displays reflecting their extensive archaeological, ethnological, and ecological interests.

★ **CICOM Museum of Anthropology, Villahermosa.** Artifacts from the Olmec jaguar cult are among the fascinating exhibits at this museum, part of a research complex.

Shopping

★ **Tlaquepaque, outside Guadalajara.** Crafts-seekers throng to this village where some of the most talented glass-blowers, potters, and jewelers in Mexico gather.

★ **Saturday market, Oaxaca.** At the largest Indian market in Mexico you'll find a wealth of colorful wares, including native *huipiles* (embroidered blouses), hand-carved wooden animals, and black regional pottery.

★ **Zona Rosa, Mexico City.** Antiques, crafts, and the latest fashions are abundant in this tony neighborhood, chockful of galleries, boutiques, and cafes.

★ **Calle Real de Guadalupe, San Cristobal de Las Casas.** This street is lined with shops selling some of the most striking indigenous folk art in Mexico, including multicolored *fajas* (sashes) and beribboned hats.

★ **El Centro (downtown), Puerto Vallarta.** Few Mexican cities have a collection of native crafts, among them clothing and household goods, as representative as that of Puerta Vallarta.

Restaurants

★ **Coyuca 22, Acapulco.** Some diners book a year in advance to ensure a table at this Continental restaurant for high season; it's one of the most expensive dining rooms in town, and one of the most beautiful. *$$$$*

★ **El Centenario, Mexico City.** The setting, in a restored 17th-century mansion, is superb, and the menu is enticing, featuring inventive versions of authentic pre-Hispanic dishes. *$$$$*

★ **La Belle Epoque, Mérida.** Middle Eastern, French, and Yucatecan specialties star in the former ballroom of an elegant mansion, overlooking a pretty urban park. *$$$$*

★ **Nuu-luu, Oaxaca.** Excellent Oaxacan cooking is the draw at this open-air restaurant that lives up to its Mixtec name, "picturesque place." *$$*

★ **Rincón Maya, Cozumel.** This friendly downtown restaurant, decorated with folk art, serves good versions of traditional Maya fare. *$$*

Hotels

★ **La Casa Que Canta, Zihuatenejo.** Perched on a cliff overlooking Zihautenejo Bay, this thatch-roof complex features individualized suites with handcrafted furnishings. *$$$$*

★ **Las Brisas, Acapulco.** Jeeps transport guests around this secluded hillside haven, set on 110 acres that offer every imaginable activity and amenity. *$$$$*

★ **Quinta Real, Guadalajara.** Classical Mexican architecture and Spanish-style furnishings distinguish this luxury hotel in a quiet residential neighborhood. *$$$$*

★ **Chan Kah, Palenque.** A resident monkey is among the charms of this jungle retreat near the Maya ruins; accommodations are in comfortable bungalows. *$$$*

★ **La Mansión del Bosque, San Miguel de Allende.** This renovated hacienda across the street from a park rents moderately priced rooms on a short- or long-term basis. *$$*

After Hours

★ **Fantasy and Extravaganzza discos, Acapulco.** Two standouts in a city where Saturday-night fever still rages, Fantasy is Acapulco's most exclusive disco, while Extravaganzza boasts the best light and sound show as well as a drop-dead view of Acapulco Bay.

★ **Plaza de los Mariachis, Guadalajara.** A personal serenade is expensive, but the price of a beer will let you listen in on the heart-rending songs in the city where they originated.

★ **Gran Café La Parroquia, Veracruz.** People-watch into the wee hours over a cup of *café con leche* at this classic coffeehouse, renowned all over Mexico.

★ **Zona Rosa, Mexico City.** Niza and Florencia streets in the capital's Pink Zone are lined with lively nightclubs, bars, and discos that don't get hopping until after midnight.

★ **Carlos 'n' Charlie's, Cancún.** For raucous, crawl-out-of-the-rafters action, it's hard to beat this link in the ubiquitous Anderson chain.

FESTIVALS AND SEASONAL EVENTS

Mexico has a full calendar of national holidays, saints' days, and special events; below are some of the most important or unusual ones. For further information and dates, contact the Mexican Government Tourism Office (*see* Important Contacts A to Z *in* The Gold Guide) or the Mexico Ministry of Tourism's information hot line at 800/44–MEXICO.

JAN. 1➤ **New Year's Day** is a major celebration throughout the country. Agricultural and livestock fairs are held in the provinces; in Oaxaca, women display traditional *tehuana* costumes.

JAN. 6➤ **Feast of Epiphany** is the day the Three Kings bring gifts to Mexican children.

JAN. 17➤ **Feast of San Antonio Abad** honors animals all over Mexico. Household pets and livestock alike are decked out with flowers and ribbons and taken to a nearby church for a blessing.

JAN.➤ **Feast of the Immaculate Conception** is a religious celebration in which lights and flowers transform Morelia.

FEB. 2➤ **Día de la Candelaria,** or Candlemas Day, means fiestas, parades, bullfights, and lantern-decorated streets. Festivities include a running of the bulls through the streets of Tlacotalpan, Veracruz.

FEB.–MAR.➤ **Carnaval** is celebrated throughout Mexico, but most notably in Mazatlán and Veracruz, where there are parades with floats and bands.

MAR. 21➤ **Benito Juárez's Birthday,** a national holiday, is most popular in Guelatao, Oaxaca, where Juárez, the beloved 19th-century president of Mexico and champion of the people, was born. This is also the day that Fiesta de la Primavera, held in Cuernavaca near Mexico City, marks the beginning of spring with carnivals and agricultural fairs.

MAR.–APR.➤ **Holy Week** or (Semana Santa) is observed throughout the country with special passion plays during this week leading up to Easter Sunday.

APR.–MAY➤ **San Marcos National Fair,** held in Aguascalientes, is one of the country's best fairs. It features lively casino gambling, native *matachnes* (dances performed by grotesque figures), mariachi bands, and bullfights.

MAY 1➤ **Labor Day** is a day for workers to parade through the streets.

MAY 5➤ **Cinco de Mayo** marks the anniversary of the French defeat by Mexican troops in Puebla in 1862 with great fanfare throughout the country.

MAY 15➤ **Feast of San Isidro Labrador** is noted nationwide by the blessing of new seeds and animals.

JUNE 1➤ **Navy Day** is commemorated in all Mexican seaports and is especially colorful in Acapulco, Mazatlán, and Veracruz. The **Feast of Corpus Christi** is celebrated in different ways. In Mexico City, children are dressed in native costumes and taken to the cathedral on the *zócalo* (main square) for a blessing. In Papantla, Veracruz, the Dance of the Flying Birdmen, a pre-Hispanic ritual to the sun, is held throughout the day.

JUNE 24➤ **Saint John the Baptist Day,** a popular national holiday, sees many Mexicans observing a tradition of tossing a "blessing" of water on most anyone within reach.

JULY 16➤ **Our Lady of Mt. Carmel Day** is celebrated with fairs, bullfights, fireworks, sporting competitions, even a major fishing tournament.

JULY 24–31➤ **Guelaguetza Dance Festival,** a Oaxacan affair, dates back to pre-Columbian times.

LATE JULY➤ **Feast of Santiago,** a national holiday, features *charreadas,* Mexican-style rodeos.

AUG. 15➤ **Feast of the Assumption of the Blessed Virgin Mary** is celebrated nationwide with religious processions. In Huamantla, Tlaxcala, the festivities include a running of the bulls down flower-strewn streets.

AUG. 25➤ **San Luis Potosí Patron Saint Fiesta** is the day the town honors its patron, San Luis Rey, with traditional dance, music, and foods.

AUTUMN

SEPT. 15–16➤ **Independence Day** is marked throughout Mexico with fireworks and parties that outblast New Year's Eve. The biggest celebrations take place in Mexico City.

SEPT. 29➤ **San Miguel Day** honors St. Michael, the patron saint of all towns with San Miguel in their names— especially San Miguel de Allende—with bullfights, folk dances, concerts, and fireworks.

OCT.➤ **October Festivals** mean a month of cultural and sporting events in Guadalajara.

OCT. 4➤ **Feast of St. Francis of Assisi** is a day for processions dedicated to St. Francis in various parts of the country.

OCT. 12➤ **Columbus Day** is a national holiday in Mexico.

OCT.–NOV.➤ **International Cervantes Festival,** in Guanajuato, is a top cultural event that attracts dancers, singers, and actors from a number of different countries.

NOV. 2➤ **All Souls' Day,** or **Day of the Dead,** the Mexican version of Halloween, commemorates the departed in a merry way, with candy skulls sold on street corners and picnickers spreading blankets in cemeteries.

NOV. 20➤ **Anniversary of the Mexican Revolution** is a national holiday.

NOV.–DEC.➤ **National Silver Fair,** an annual Taxco event, is an occasion for even more silver selling than usual.

DEC. 12➤ **Feast Day of the Virgin of Guadalupe** is the day on which Mexico's patron saint is feted with processions and native folk dances, particularly at her shrine in Mexico City.

DEC. 23➤ **Feast of the Radishes,** a pre-Christmas tradition in Oaxaca, is one of the most colorful in Mexico: Farmers carve prize radishes into amusing shapes and display them in the city's main plaza, while celebrants devour fritterlike *buñuelos* and smash their ceramic plates in the streets.

DEC. 16–25➤ **The Posadas** and **Christmas** are when candlelight processions that lead to Christmas parties and to *piñatas* (suspended paper animals or figurines) that are broken open to yield gifts. Mexico City is brightly decorated, but don't expect any snow.

2 Mexico City

Two volcanoes and a pyramid complex flank Mexico's capital, once the center of Aztec civilization and now the country's cosmopolitan business, art, and culinary hub. From the Alameda, a leafy center of activity since Aztec times, to the Zona Rosa, a chic shopping neighborhood, Mexico City offers endless options to urban adventurers. Day trips might include colonial Puebla, where mole sauce and Talavera tiles originated, or the floating gardens of Xochomilco.

By Frank
"Pancho" Shiell

Updated by
Patricia Alisau

MEXICO CITY is a city of superlatives: It is both the oldest (670 years) and the highest (2,240 meters, or 7,349 feet) city on the North American continent, and with nearly 24 million inhabitants, it is the most populous city in the world. It is Mexico's cultural, political, and financial core—on the verge of the 21st century but clinging to its deeply entrenched Aztec heritage.

Before the 16th-century arrival of the conquering Spaniards, Mexico City was the flourishing capital of the Aztec civilization. Well over 500 years after the mysterious demise of the great city of Teotihuacan—whose gargantuan pyramids just northeast of the city are a must-see—wandering Aztecs in search of their prophesied promised land would build their city upon encountering an eagle, perched on a prickly pear cactus, holding a snake in his beak. In 1325, the official date of the founding of Mexico City (upon which historians disagree), they discovered it on this very spot. Called Tenochtitlan, even then it was the biggest city in the Western Hemisphere and, according to historians, one of the three largest cities on earth. Tenochtitlan occupied what was then an island in shallow Lake Texcoco, connected to lakeshore satellite towns (now neighborhoods) by a network of *calzadas* (canals and causeways; now freeways). When he first laid eyes on the city, Spanish conquistador Hernán Cortés was dazzled by the glistening metropolis, which reminded him and his men of Venice.

A combination of factors made the conquest possible. The superstitious Aztec emperor Moctezuma II believed the white, bearded Cortés on horseback to be the mighty plumed serpent-god Quetzalcoatl, who, according to a tragically ironic prophesy, was suppose to arrive from the east in the year 1519 to rule the land. Moctezuma therefore welcomed the foreigner with gifts of gold and palatial accommodations.

But in return, Cortés initiated the bloody massacre of Tenochtitlan, which lasted almost two years. Joining forces with him was a massive army of Indian "allies," gathered from other settlements like Cholula and Tlaxcala, who were fed up with the Aztec Empire's domination and taxation. With the strength of their numbers and the European tactical advantages of brigantines built to cross the lake; imported horses, firearms, and armor; and, inadvertently, smallpox and the common cold, Cortés succeeded in devastating Tenochtitlan. Only two centuries after it was founded, the young Aztec capital lay in ruins, about half of its population dead from battle, starvation, and contagious European diseases to which they had no immunity.

Cortés began building the capital of what he patriotically dubbed New Spain, the Spanish Empire's colony that would spread north to cover what is now the United States southwest and south to Panama. Because he had difficulty pronouncing the word Tenochtitlan, he named the city Mexica (Meh-*she*-ka), which was the real name of the Aztecs (the Spaniards were the ones who had originally dubbed the Mexica Indians "Aztecs"). At the site of the demolished Aztec ceremonial center—now the 10-acre Zócalo—he started building a church (the precursor of the gigantic Metropolitan Cathedral), mansions, and government buildings. He utilized the slave labor—and artistry—of the vanquished native Mexicans. On top of the ruins of their city, and using rubble from it, they were forced to build what became the most European-style city in North America, but unlike the random layout of contemporary medieval European cities, it followed the sophisticated grid pattern of the Aztecs. The Spaniards also drained and filled in Lake Texcoco, preferring wheels and horses (which they introduced to Mexico) over canals and canoes for transport. (The filled-in lake bed turned out to be a soggy support for the immense buildings that have been slowly sinking into it ever since they were built.) For much of the construction material they quarried local volcanic porous stone called *tezontle,* which is the color of dried blood and forms the thick walls of many historic downtown buildings.

During the colonial period, the city grew, and the Franciscans converted the Aztecs to Christianity. In 1571 the Spaniards established the Inquisition in New Spain and burned heretics at its headquarter palace, which still stands in Plaza de Santo Domingo.

More than 200 years later, Mexicans rose up against Spain. The historic downtown street 16 de Septiembre commemorates the "declaration" of the War of Independence. On that date in 1810, Father Miguel Hidalgo rang a church bell and cried out his history-making *grito* (shout) to his countrymen "to recover the lands stolen three centuries ago from our forefathers by the hated Spaniards . . . Viva Mexico!" That "liberty bell," which now hangs above the main entrance to the National Palace, is rung on the eve of every September 16 by the president of the republic.

Today, travelers flying into or out of Mexico City get an aerial view of the still-remaining portion of Lake Texcoco on the eastern outskirts of the city; at night the vast expanse of city lights abruptly ends at a black void that appears to be an ocean.

In-flight views also provide a panorama of the vast, flat 1,482-square-kilometer (572-square-mile) Valley of Mexico, the *Meseta de Anahuac,* completely surrounded by mountains, including, on its south side, two supposedly extinct and usually snowcapped volcanoes, both well over 17,000 feet high: Popocatepetl and Iztaccihuatl. ("Popo," as the first volcano is affectionately called, started to bubble and boil in December 1994, and villages surrounding the volcano had to be evacuated temporarily.) The volcanoes are separated by the 2½-mile-high Cortés Pass, from which the arriving conquistador, after a nine-month trek from Veracruz, gazed down for his first astonishing glimpse of Tenochtitlan.

Unfortunately, the single most widely known fact about the capital is that its air is polluted. Many foreigners envision the city as being wrapped in black smog every day; they picture gray skies and streets packed with vehicles. But in reality, although the capital does have a serious pollution problem, it also has some of the clearest, bluest skies anywhere. At 7,349 feet, it often has mild daytime weather perfect for sightseeing and cool evenings comfortable for sleeping. Mornings can be glorious—chilly, and bright with the promise of the warming sun.

Smog is not the only thing Mexico City has in common with Los Angeles: The city lies on a fault similar to the San Andreas in California. In 1957 a major earthquake took a tragic toll, and scars are still visible from the devastating 1985 earthquake (8.1 on the Richter scale); the government reported 7,000 deaths, but according to vox populi the death toll reached 50,000.

Growing nonstop, Mexico City covers about a 1,000-square-kilometer (386-square-mile) area of the valley. The city limits are surrounded on three sides by the state of Mexico and bordered on the south by the state of Morelos. Advertising campaigns and tour packages usually tout Mexico's paradisaical beach resorts and ancient ruins, but cosmopolitan, historic Mexico City is an important destination in itself, more foreign and fascinating than many major capitals on far-away continents. And since so many flights from the United States pass through the capital, visitors should not pass up the opportunity to stop here at least for two days but preferably for five.

EXPLORING

Orientation

Most of Mexico City is aligned around two major intersecting thoroughfares: Paseo de la Reforma and Avenida Insurgentes. Administratively, the city is divided into 16 *delegaciones* (districts) and about 400 colonias each with street names fitting a given theme, such as rivers, philosophers, doctors, or revolutionary heroes. The same street can change names as it goes through different colonias, making it a bit more difficult to find an address. Hence most street addresses include the colonia they are in, and, unless you're going to an obvious place, it is very important to tell your taxi driver the name of the colonia.

The principal sights of Mexico City are organized into three tours. You need a full day to cover each thoroughly, though each can be done at breakneck speed in four or five hours. Tour 1, Zócalo and Alameda Park, concentrates on a relatively compact area that can be seen on foot. Its focus is historical, since the Zócalo, its surrounding Centro Histórico, and Alameda Park were the heart of both the Aztec and the Spanish cities. The second tour, taking in Reforma, Zona Rosa, and Chapultepec Park, will necessitate some form of transportation if done in its entirety, but strong walkers can cover most of it on their own. Exploring San Angel and Coyoacán in southern Mexico City will also require a taxi ride or two. Originally separate colonial towns, both were absorbed by the ever-growing capital, yet they retain their original pueblo charm and tranquility.

Tour 1: Zócalo and Alameda Central

Numbers in the margin correspond to points of interest on the Zócalo and Alameda Central map.

The **Zócalo** (formal name: **Plaza de la Constitución**) of Mexico City was built by the Spaniards on the site of the main temple complex of Tenochtitlan, the capital of the Aztec empire. This enormous paved square, the largest in the Western Hemisphere, was built by Indian slave labor on the site of the Aztec ceremonial center, which once comprised 78 buildings. Throughout the 16th, 17th, and 18th centuries, the Spaniards and their descendants constructed elaborate churches and convents, elegant mansions, and stately public edifices, many of which have long since been converted to other uses. There is an air of Old Europe to this section of the city, which, in its entirety (the Centro Histórico), is a national monument that has been undergoing a major refurbishing; at press time much had already been accomplished and even more was underway. Imposing buildings are constructed with the ubiquitous blood-red volcanic *tezontle* stone and the quarry stones that the Spaniards recycled from the rubble of the Aztec temples they razed. Throngs of small shops, eateries, cantinas, and street vendors contribute to an inimitably Mexican flavor, even an exuberance. Repaved, pedestrian-only streets, such as La Palma and Motolinia, add to the delightful strolling opportunities.

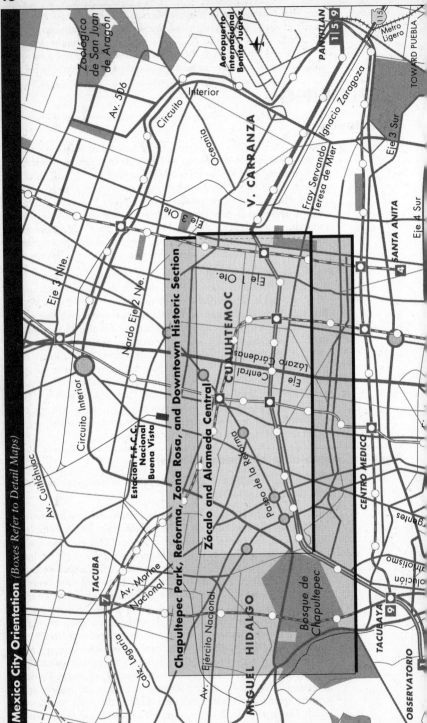

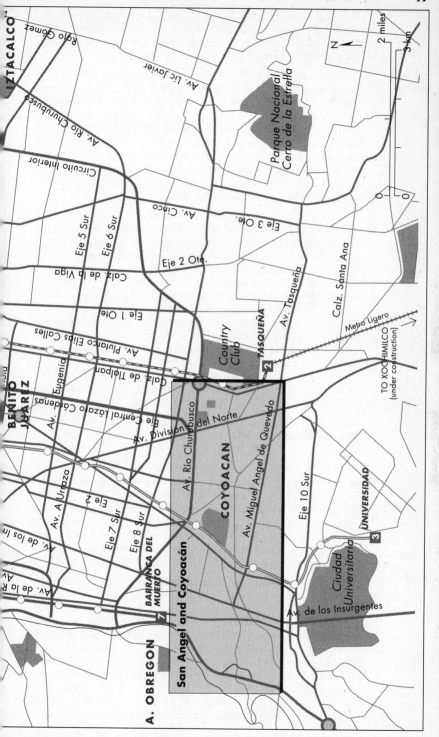

During the daytime, the downtown area is filled with people and vibrant with activity. As in any other big city, travelers should be alert to pickpockets, especially on crowded buses and subways, and avoid dark, deserted streets at night.

Zócalo means "pedestal" or "base": In the mid-19th century an independence monument was envisioned for the square, but it was never built. The term stuck, however, and now the word *zócalo* is applied to the main plazas of most Mexican cities. Mexico City's Zócalo (since it's the original, it is always capitalized) is used for government rallies, protest marches and sit-ins, and festive events. It is also the focal point for Independence Day celebrations on the eve of September 16 and is spectacularly festooned during the Christmas–New Year holiday season. Flag-raising and -lowering ceremonies take place here in the early morning and late afternoon.

Around the square are the two most important symbols of church
❶ and state in Mexico. On the north side is the **Catedral Metropolitana** (Metropolitan Cathedral), which, over the centuries, has sunk noticeably into the spongy subsoil. Its lopsidedness is evident when viewed from across the square, but engineering projects to stabilize the structure are always being undertaken. Construction on this oldest and largest cathedral in Latin America began in 1573 and continued intermittently throughout the next three centuries. The result is a medley of baroque and neoclassical touches. Inside are four identical domes, their airiness made earthbound by rows of supportive columns. There are five altars and 14 chapels, mostly in the fussy, Churrigueresque style, an extremely decorative form of Spanish Baroque from the mid-17th century. Like most Mexican churches, the cathedral is all but overshadowed by the innumerable paintings, altarpieces, and statues—in graphic color—of Christ and the saints.

Adjacent to the cathedral, the comparatively small 18th-century **Sagrario Church,** even more tilted, has an elaborate Churrigueresque facade.

Turn left as you leave the cathedral and walk one block north on Sem-
❷ inario to view the excavated ruins of the **Templo Mayor** (Great Temple of the Aztecs). It was unearthed accidentally in 1978 by telephone repairmen and has since been turned into a vast and historically significant archaeological site and museum. At this temple, dedicated to the Aztec cult of death, captives from rival tribes—as many as 10,000 at a time—were sacrificed to the bloodthirsty god of war, Huitzilopochtli. Seven rows of leering stone skulls adorn one side of the structure.

The adjacent **Museo del Templo Mayor** contains 3,000 pieces unearthed from the site and from other ruins in central Mexico; they include ceramic warriors, stone carvings and knives, skulls of sacrificial victims, a rare gold ingot, models and scale reproductions, and a room on the destruction of Tenochtitlan by the Spaniards. The centerpiece is an eight-ton disk discovered at the Templo Major; it depicts the myth of the goddess Coyolxauhqui (the moon), who was decapitated and dismembered by her brother, Huitzilopochtli, for trying to persuade her 400 other brothers to murder their mother. *Corner of Guatemala and Argentina.* ☛ *$3.* ☼ *Tues.–Sun. 9–6. Call ☎ 5/542–4784 to 4786 to reserve English-language tours.*

As you return to the Zocalo on Seminario, make a quick detour one
❸ block east to Calle Academia and the **Museo José Luis Cuevas.** One of the newest museums in the downtown area, it offers a superb collection of modern art, as well as works by Mexico's enfant terrible, José Luis

Zócalo and Alameda Central

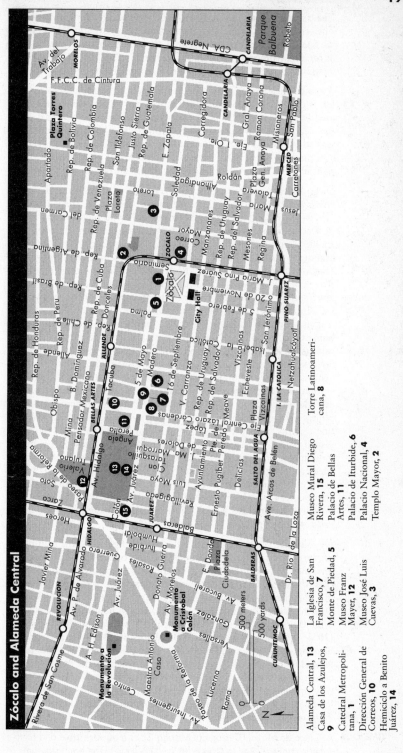

Alameda Central, **13**
Casa de los Azulejos, **7**
Catedral Metropolitana, **1**
Dirección General de Correos, **10**
Hemiciclo a Benito Juárez, **14**

La Iglesia de San Francisco, **7**
Monte de Piedad, **5**
Museo Franz Mayer, **12**
Museo José Luis Cuevas, **3**

Museo Mural Diego Rivera, **15**
Palacio de Bellas Artes, **11**
Palacio de Iturbide, **6**
Palacio Nacional, **4**
Templo Mayor, **2**

Torre Latinoamericana, **8**

Cuevas, who is ranked as one of the country's best contemporary artists. The sensational Sala Picasso contains more than 30 original works by the Spanish master. Up-and-coming Latin American artists may be seen at rotating temporary exhibits. *Academia 13, ☎ 5/542–8959.* ☛ *Small admission fee.* ⊙ *Weekdays noon–8, weekends 10–6. Closed Wed.*

★ ❹ As you return to the Zócalo on Seminario, the first building on your left is the vast **Palacio Nacional,** or National Palace, which was initiated by Cortés on the site of Moctezuma's home and remodeled by the viceroys; its current form dates from 1693, although a third floor was added in 1926. Now the seat of government, it has always served as a public-function site. In fact, during colonial times, the first bullfight in New Spain took place in the inner courtyard.

Diego Rivera's sweeping, epic murals on the second floor of the main courtyard have the power to mesmerize. For more than 16 years (1929–45), he and his assistants mounted the scaffolds day and night, perfecting techniques adapted from Renaissance Italian frescoes. The result, nearly 1,200 square feet of vividly painted wall space, is grandiosely entitled *Epic of the Mexican People in Their Struggle for Freedom and Independence.* The larger-than-life paintings represent two millennia of Mexican history, as seen through the artist's vivid imagination. The innocence of pre-Hispanic times is portrayed by idyllic, almost sugary scenes of Tenochtitlan. Only a few vignettes—a lascivious woman baring her leg in the marketplace, a man offering a human arm for sale, and the carnage of warriors—acknowledge other aspects of ancient life. As you walk around the floor, you'll pass images depicting the savagery of the conquest and the hypocrisy of the Spanish priests, the noble independence movement, and the bloody revolution. Marx appears amid scenes of class struggles, toiling workers, industrialization (which Rivera idealized), the decadence of the bourgeoisie, and nuclear holocaust. The murals are among Rivera's finest works. They are also the most accessible and probably the most visited of the artist's paintings. The palace also houses two minor museums—dealing with 19th-century president Benito Juárez and the Mexican Congress—and the liberty bell rung by Padre Hidalgo to proclaim independence in 1810 hangs high on the central facade. It chimes every eve of September 16, while from the balcony below, the president repeats the historic shout for independence known as *el grito.* ☛ *Free.* ⊙ *Daily 9–5. Closed holidays.*

As you leave the building turn left and then right onto the south side of the Zócalo, which is occupied by the twin buildings of **Ayuntamiento** (City Hall). The one on the west, decorated with colonial tiles of arms of Cortés and other conquistadores, was originally built in 1532, destroyed by fire in 1692, and rebuilt in 1722. In 1935, the Distrito Federal needed more office space; to maintain architectural symmetry in the Zócalo, the "matching" structure across the street (20 de Noviembre) was built. Complete your tour of the square by

❺ heading north, through the arcade, on 5 de Febrero. The **Monte de Piedad** (Mountain of Piety) will be on your left, at the far northwest corner of the Zócalo. It was built to help the poor in the late 18th century on the site of an Aztec palace. It currently houses the National Pawn Shop, which sells jewelry, antiques, and other pawned goods. ⊙ *Mon.–Sat. about 10–7.*

TIME OUT   At Cinco de Mayo 10 is one of Mexico City's most venerable and atmospheric cantinas, **Bar la Opera** (☎ 5/512–8959). The bar-restaurant has two claims to fame: Pancho Villa supposedly rode his horse into the place and demanded service by shooting a hole in the ceiling (you can still see it); and it was one of the first cantinas to allow women. Stop in for a drink, lunch, dinner, or a snack.

There are two notable sites one block north of Cinco de Mayo on Calle Tacuba at the **Plaza Manuel Tolsá:** the **Palacio de Minería,** a 19th-century architectural landmark; and the neo-classical **Museo Nacional de Arte** (National Art Museum), which contains a superb collection of religious and contemporary artwork. *The museum is at Calle Tacuba 8, ☎ 5/512–3224. ☛ $2. ☉ Tues.–Sun. 10–5.*

From Calle Tacuba, walk two blocks south to Calle Madero, one of the city's busiest and most typical streets in terms of its architectural variety. On the south side of Calle Madero, between Bolívar and Gante, is
⑥ the **Palacio de Iturbide** (Emperor Iturbide's Palace), which has been converted into a branch of Banamex (Banco Nacional de México). This handsome Baroque structure—note the imposing door and its carved-stone trimmings—was built in 1780 and became the residence of Iturbide in 1822. One of the heroes of the independence movement, the misguided Iturbide proclaimed himself emperor of a country that had thrown off the imperial yoke of the Hapsburgs only a year before; his empire, needless to say, was short-lived. Major cultural exhibitions are held in the atrium. *Calle Madero 17, ☎ 5/518–2187. ☛ Free. ☉ Inner atrium: weekdays 9–6, and on weekends during exhibitions.*

⑦ **La Iglesia de San Francisco,** built on the site of Mexico's first convent (1524), is located a block west of the palace, on the same side of Calle Madero. Moctezuma's zoo was supposed to have stood on the site in Aztec times. The present 18th-century French Gothic church is one of the newest buildings on the street. The beautiful ceiling paintings are being restored.

⑧ In stark contrast to the church is the **Torre Latinoamericana** (Latin American Tower), once the tallest building in the capital. This 47-story skyscraper was built in 1956, and on clear days the observation deck and restaurant on the top floors afford fine views of the city. *Calle Madero and Eje Central Lázaro Cárdenas. ☛ $3. ☉ Observation deck: daily 10 AM–11:30 PM.*

Three other interesting buildings are off Eje Central Lázaro Cárde-
⑨ nas, a main thoroughfare. The 17th-century **Casa de los Azulejos** (House of Tiles) is catercorner from the tower, on the north side of Calle Madero at the corner of Callejón de la Condesa. Its well-preserved facade of white, blue, and yellow tiles, iron grillwork balconies, and gray stonework make it among the prettiest Baroque structures in the country. Currently occupied by Sanborns, a chain store/restaurant, it was built as the palace of the counts of the Valle de Orizaba, an aristocratic family from early Spanish rule. Reopened in March 1995 following refurbishing, the interior is more dazzling than ever. A Moorish patio, a monumental staircase, and a mural by Orozco are worth seeing. This is a good place to stop for lunch, and the shops upstairs have an excellent selection of jewelry and crafts at fair prices. *Calle Madero 4. ☉ Daily 8 AM–10 PM.*

⑩ Continue north on Callejón de la Condesa to the **Dirección General de Correos** (General Post Office) at the corner of Calle Tacuba and Eje Central Lázaro Cárdenas. This neo-Renaissance building (1908) epitomizes the grand imitations of European architecture common in Mexico during the Porfiriato, or dictatorship of Porfirio Díaz (1876–1910). On the upper floor, the **Museo de la Filatelia** exhibits the postal history of Mexico. ☉ *Mon.–Sat. 8 AM–midnight, Sun. 8–4. Museum: Weekdays 9–7.* ☛ *Free.*

★ ⑪ The most celebrated public building of the Díaz period is the **Palacio de Bellas Artes** (Fine Arts Palace), which is diagonally across from the post office, at the corner of Eje Central Lázaro Cárdenas and Avenida Juárez and across from Alameda Park. This colossal marble palace was constructed as an opera house between 1904 and 1934, with time out for the revolution. Today the theater serves as a handsome venue for international and national artists, including such groups as the Ballet Folklórico de México. It boasts a Tiffany stained-glass curtain depicting the two volcanoes outside Mexico City. In addition, the palace is renowned both for its architecture—by the Italian architect Adamo Boari, who also designed the post office—and for its paintings by several celebrated Mexican artists, including Rufino Tamayo and Mexico's trio of muralists: Rivera, Orozco, and Siqueiros. In the palace Rivera reconstructed his mural *Man at the Crossroads,* which was commissioned for and then torn down from Rockefeller Center in New York City, because of its political message (epitomized by the face of Lenin). Temporary art exhibits are also held at the palace. ☎ *5/510–1388.* ☉ *Tues.–Sun. 10:30–6:30.*

⑫ Aficionados of colonial Spanish decorative and applied arts should detour at this point to visit the **Museo Franz Mayer,** located one block west of the rear of the Palacio de Bellas Artes, facing the north side of Alameda Park. The museum opened in 1986 in the 16th-century Hospital de San Juan de Dios. Exhibits include 16th- and 17th-century antiques such as wooden chests inlaid with ivory, tortoiseshell, and ebony; tapestries, paintings, and lacquerware; Rococo clocks, glassware, architectural ornamentation; and an unusually large assortment of Talavera ceramics and tiles. Wall plaques explain in detail the history of the production of tiles (*azulejos*), a technique carried from Mesopotamia and Egypt to the Persians, Arabs, and Spaniards, who brought it to Mexico. It also has an impressive collection of more than 700 different editions of the book *Don Quixote.* The museum building is faithfully restored, with pieces of the original frescoes peeking through; classical music plays in the background. *Av. Hidalgo 45, at the Plaza Santa Veracruz,* ☎ *5/518–2267.* ☛ *$1.25.* ☉ *Tues.–Sun. 10–5. Call ahead for an English-speaking guide.*

⑬ **Alameda Central** (Alameda Park), across Avenida Hidalgo from the Plaza Santa Veracruz, has been one of the capital's oases of greenery and a center for activities since Aztec times. The Indians held their *tianguis* (market) on the site. In the early days of the Viceroyalty, it was where victims of the Inquisition were burned at the stake. National leaders, from 18th-century viceroys to Emperor Maximilian and President Díaz, clearly envisioned the park as a symbol of civic pride and prosperity: Over the centuries, it has been endowed with fountains, railings, a Moorish kiosk imported from Paris, and ash, willow, and poplar trees. Its most conspicuous man-made structure is the white ⑭ marble semicircular **Hemiciclo a Benito Juárez** (monument to Juárez) on the Avenida Juárez side of the park. It is a fine place for strolling (and resting) and listening to live music on Sundays and holidays.

⑮ **Fonart,** the government-owned handicrafts chain, has a store at Avenida Juárez 89, just west of the park (*see* Shopping, *below*). At the far western side of the Alameda is **Museo Mural Diego Rivera,** built to display Diego Rivera's controversial mural *Sunday Afternoon Dream in the Alameda Park,* originally painted on a lobby wall of the Hotel Del Prado in 1947–48. The controversy was due to Rivera's inscription, "God does not exist," which he later replaced with the bland "Conference of San Juan de Letrán." Following the hotel's destruction in the 1985 earthquake, this gentle and poetic mural, which survived undamaged, was moved in its entirety across the street to the museum built to house it. *Museo Mural Diego Rivera, at Calles Balderas and Colón,* ☎ *5/510–2329.* ☛ *$2.* ☉ *Tues.–Sun. 10–6.*

Tour 2: Reforma, Zona Rosa, and Chapultepec Park

Numbers in the margin correspond to points of interest on the Chapultepec Park, Reforma, Zona Rosa, and Downtown Historic Section map.

The Paseo de la Reforma, modeled after the Champs-Elysées in Paris, was built by Emperor Maximilian in 1865 to connect the Palacio Nacional with his residence, the Castillo de Chapultepec. Reforma is 30 blocks long, so public transportation is recommended if you want to cover all the sights described. Begin at Reforma's northern end, about 2 kilometers (1 mile) north of Bellas Artes, in the area known as **Tlatelolco** (Tla-tel-*ohl*-coh). Before the conquest, Tlatelolco and Tenochtitlan were sister cities, and the domain of Cuauhtémoc, the last Aztec emperor. In modern times its name makes residents shudder, because it was here that several hundred protesting students were massacred by the Mexican army in 1968. The 1985 earthquake destroyed several high-rise apartment buildings in Tlatelolco, in which hundreds perished.

❶ The center of Tlatelolco is the **Plaza de las Tres Culturas,** so named because Mexico's three cultural eras—pre-Hispanic, colonial, and modern—are represented on the plaza in the form of the small ruins of a pre-Hispanic **ceremonial center** (visible from the roadway); the **Iglesia de Santiago Tlatelolco** (1609) and **Colegio de la Santa Cruz de Tlatelolco** (1535–36); and the ultra-contemporary **Ministry of Foreign Affairs** (1970). The church contains the baptismal font of Juan Diego, the Indian to whom the Virgin of Guadalupe appeared in 1531. The Colegio (college), founded by the Franciscans after the Conquest, was once attended by the sons of the Aztec nobility. *The plaza is bounded on the north by Manuel González, on the west by Av. San Juan de Letrán Norte, and on the east by Paseo de la Reforma, between Glorieta de Peralvillo and Glorieta Cuitláhuac.*

❷ The plaza itself can be seen in passing, but nearby are two other points of interest. Between República de Chile and Allende is the **Mercado de la Lagunilla,** known affectionately as the Thieves' Market. Go on Sundays, when it is busiest, and watch your money: Here, along with the usual flea-market fare, you can find antiques (some of them fake), toys, secondhand books and clothes, semiprecious stones, art, and some handicrafts.

❸ Nearby is **Plaza Garibaldi,** Mexico City's mariachi square (*see* Nightlife, *below*). Pass through here during the day, but return at night, when it resounds with music and festivity until the wee hours, especially on weekends. One warning: Late at night things can get a bit raucous. Choose a cantina, order a tequila; the musicians will be around shortly to serenade you (tipping is essential). Late at night, well-to-do Mexicans usually park along the west side of the square to enjoy some "drive-up" mariachi serenading especially for them. On the north side of the square is the Mercado de San Camilito, where typical Mexican food is served. *Just east of Eje Central Lázaro Cárdenas, between República de Honduras and República de Perú.*

Chapultepec Park, Reforma, Zona Rosa, and Downtown Historic Section

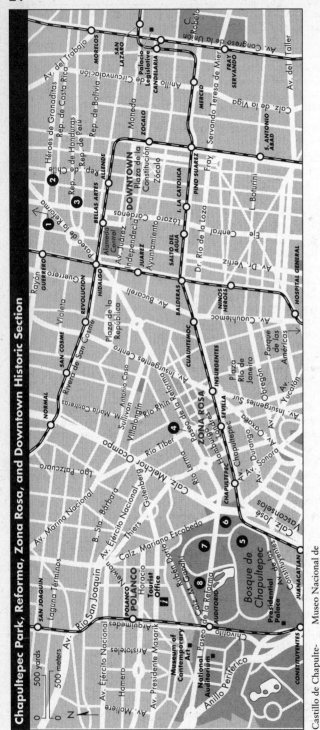

Castillo de Chapultepec, **5**

Mercado de la Lagunilla, **2**

Monumento a la Independencia (El Ángel), **4**

Museo de Arte Moderno, **6**

Museo Nacional de Antropología, **8**

Museo Rufino Tamayo, **7**

Plaza de las Tres Culturas, **1**

Plaza Garibaldi, **3**

From Plaza Garibaldi, return to Paseo de la Reforma and walk west (left). In about 10 minutes you'll reach the junction of Reforma, Avenida Juárez, and Bucareli. Along the stretch of Reforma west of this intersection there are a number of statues erected at the request of Porfirio Díaz to honor illustrious men, including Simón Bolívar, Columbus, Pasteur, and Cuauhtémoc. The most famous of these stat-

❹ ues is used by locals as a geographic point of reference: it is the **Monumento a la Independencia,** a Corinthian column topped by a gold angel (thus the more common "the Angel"). Beneath the pedestal lie the remains of the principal heroes of the independence movement, and an eternal flame burns in their honor.

★ The Angel marks the midpoint of the western edge of the **Zona Rosa** (Pink Zone), which for years has been a favorite part of the city for tourists and locals because of the plethora of restaurants, cafés, art and antiques galleries, hotels, discos, and shops. The architecture in the Zona Rosa is appealing, too. Most buildings, two or three stories high, were originally private homes built in the 1920s for the wealthy. All the streets are wistfully named after European cities; some, such as Genova, are garden-lined pedestrian malls accented with contemporary bronze statuary.

To enjoy the Zona Rosa, just walk the lengths of Hamburgo and Londres and follow some of the side streets, especially Copenhague—a veritable restaurant row. The large handicrafts market on Londres is officially **Mercado Insurgentes,** though most people call it either **Mercado Zona Rosa** or **Mercado Londres** (*see* Shopping, *below*). Just opposite the market's Londres entrance is **Plaza del Angel,** a small shopping mall where a *minitianguis* (native market) specializes in antiques and curios on Saturday and Sunday. Contrasting with the mercado, the sleek new **Plaza La Rosa** shopping mall, with entrances near the northeast corner of Londres and Amberes, is filled with fancy boutiques and shops.

TIME OUT Stop for tea and pastries at one of two tea shops on Hamburgo: **Duca d'Este** on the southeast corner of Florencia (164-B Hamburgo, ☎ 5/525–6374) or **Salón de Té Auseba** (159-B Hamburgo, ☎ 5/511–3769).

The third area of Reforma covers most of the first of three sections of **Bosque de Chapultepec** (Chapultepec Park). The main entrance to the park lies four blocks southwest of the Zona Rosa. The 1,600-acre park functions as a "green space" for families on weekend outings, cyclists, joggers, and museum goers. It is also one of the oldest parts of Mexico City, having been inhabited by the Mexica (Aztec) tribe as early as the 13th century. The Mexica poet-king Nezahualcoyotl had his palace here and ordered construction of the aqueduct that brought water to Tenochtitlan. Ahuehuete trees (Moctezuma cypress) still stand from that era, when the woods were used as hunting preserves.

The entrance to the park is guarded by the **Monumento a los Niños Héroes** (Monument to the Boy Heroes), consisting of six marble columns adorned with eaglets. In it are supposedly buried the six young cadets who wrapped themselves in the Mexican flag and then jumped to their deaths from the ramparts during the U.S. invasion of 1847. (That war may not take up much space in American textbooks, but to the Mexicans it is still a troubling symbol of their neighbor's aggressive dominance: The war cost Mexico almost half of its national territory—the present states of Texas, California, Arizona, New Mexico, and Nevada.)

★ ❺ The **Castillo de Chapultepec,** like the Palacio Nacional, witnessed the turbulence and grandeur of all Mexican history. In its earliest permutations, its home on the Cerro del Chapulín (Grasshopper Hill) was a Mexica palace, where the Indians made one of their last stands against the Spaniards; later it was a Spanish hermitage, gunpowder plant, and military college. Emperor Maximilian used the castle (parts of which date from 1783) as his residence, and his example was followed by various presidents from 1872 to 1940, when Lázaro Cárdenas decreed that it be turned into the **National History Museum.**

Displays on the museum's ground floor cover Mexican history from the conquest to the revolution; the bathroom, bedroom, tea salon, and gardens were used by Maximilian and his wife, Carlotta, during the 19th century. The ground floor also contains works by 20th-century muralists O'Gorman, Orozco, and Siqueiros, whereas the upper floor is devoted to temporary exhibits, Díaz's malachite vases, and religious art. Situated on top of a hill, the Castillo is accessible by car, on foot (10 minutes), or by a free but unreliable shuttle bus and elevator. ☎ 5/553–6242. ☛ $2. ☉ Tues.–Sun. 9:30–5.

Just down the hill from the Castillo is the **Museo Galeria de la Lucha del Pueblo Mexicano por su Liberatad,** which goes by the more fanciful **Museo del Caracol** (Museum of the Snail) because of its spiral shape. The museum concentrates on the 400 years from the Viceroyalty to the Constitution of 1917, using dioramas and light-and-sound displays that children can appreciate. ☎ 5/553–6285. ☛ $1.25. ☉ Tues.–Sun. 9–5.

❻ The **Museo de Arte Moderno** (Museum of Modern Art) is just north of the Castillo on the south side of Reforma. Two rooms are devoted to plastic arts from the 1930s to the 1960s; a third focuses on the past 20 years; and a fourth room and annex house temporary exhibits of contemporary Mexican painting, lithography, sculpture, and photography. ☎ 5/553–6211. ☛ $3. ☉ Tues.–Sun. 10–6.

The private collection of painter Rufino Tamayo now has a permanent
❼ home in the sleek and austere **Museo Rufino Tamayo.** Tamayo's unerring eye for great art is evidenced by paintings and sculptures by such contemporary masters as Picasso, Miró, Warhol, and Henry Moore. *In Chapultepec Park, on the north side of Paseo de la Reforma and west of Gandhi,* ☎ 5/286–6519. ☛ $3. ☉ Tues.–Sun. 10–6.

The greatest museum in the country—and arguably one of the finest
★ ❽ archaeological museums anywhere—is the **Museo Nacional de Antropología** (National Museum of Anthropology), just west of the Museo Rufino Tamayo. Even its architectural design (by Pedro Ramírez Vázquez) is distinguished. The collection is so extensive—covering some 100,000 square feet—that four hours are barely adequate to see it. However, bilingual guides take you through the highlights in two-hour tours. English guidebooks are available in the bookshop.

Begin in the Orientation Room, which traces the course of Mexican prehistory and the pre-Hispanic cultures of Mesoamerica. There are 12 rooms on the ground floor, including preclassical cultures, Teotihuacan, the Toltecs, Oaxaca, the Maya, and the north and west of Mexico. The so-called Aztec calendar stone and profusely feathered Aztec headdresses, reconstructed Mayan temples, and reproductions of the Mayan paintings from the ruins of Bonampak are just some of the highlights. Statuary, jewelry, weapons, clay figurines, and pottery evoke the brilliant, quirky, and frequently bloodthirsty civilizations that peopled Middle America during Europe's Dark Ages. The nine rooms on the upper floor contain faithful ethnographic displays of current indigenous peoples, using maps, photographs, household objects, folk art, clothing, and religious articles. ☎ *5/553–1902.* ✆ *$3.* ⊗ *Tues.–Sat. 9–6, Sun. and holidays 10–6.*

Other sights in the first section of Chapultepec Park include three small boating lakes; the Casa del Lago, a cultural center; a botanical garden; archaeological excavations (visitable by appointment); and the zoo housing Mexico's pandas, gifts from China. **Los Pinos,** the residential palace of the president of Mexico, is located on the park's southern boundary, at Avenida Constituyentes and Parque Lira. It is heavily guarded and cannot be visited. The less crowded second and third sections contain a fancy restaurant, amusement parks (*see* What to See and Do with Children, *below*), the national cemetery, and the **Lienzo Charro** (rodeo).

TIME OUT   After visiting the museums, take a five-minute taxi ride just north of the park to Colonia Polanco, which is quickly upstaging the Zona Rosa as the chic place for shopping and dining. The outdoor tables at **Sanborcito's,** also known as **Restaurante Polanco,** are usually filled by the residents of this well-heeled, tranquil neighborhood. It has a small but moderately priced menu and is especially good for brunch. *Julio Verne and Emilio Castelar, overlooking a lovely park with a statue of Lincoln.*

Reforma wends its leisurely way west into the wealthy neighborhoods of Lomas de Chapultepec, where most of the houses and estates are behind stone walls.

Tour 3: San Angel and Coyoacán

Numbers in the margin correspond to points of interest on the San Angel and Coyoacán map.

To explore the southern part of the city—which until 50 years ago was separate pueblos—take a taxi or pesero down Avenida Insurgentes. At 34 kilometers (21 miles) the longest avenue in the city, Insurgentes did not exist as such before the 1920s.

Get off at Avenida La Paz. On the east side of Insurgentes is a bizarre monument to revolutionary leader and onetime president Alvaro Obregón. The gray granite **Monumento al General Alvaro Obregón** marks the spot where the national hero Obregón was gunned down in a restaurant in 1928. Its main attraction used to be none other than Obregón's hand and forearm—eerily preserved in formaldehyde—which he lost in a 1915 battle. However, it's been removed for burial.

★ Cross Avenida Insurgentes on Avenida La Paz, then take the southern fork off Avenida La Paz (Calle Madero) until you come to the **Plaza San Jacinto.** You are now in San Angel, a little colonial enclave of cobblestoned streets, gardens drenched in bougainvillea, stone walls, and pastel houses.

Plaza San Jacinto is interesting in its own right. In 1847 about 50 Irish soldiers of St. Patrick's Battalion—who had sided with the Mexicans in the Mexican–American War—had their foreheads branded here with the letter *D* (for deserters) and were then hanged by the Americans. These men had been enticed to swim the Rio Grande and desert the ranks of U.S. General Zachary Taylor by pleas to the historic and religious ties between Spain and Ireland; as settlers in Mexican Texas, they felt their allegiance lay with Mexico, and they were among the bravest fighters in the war. They met their end when the

San Angel and Coyoacán

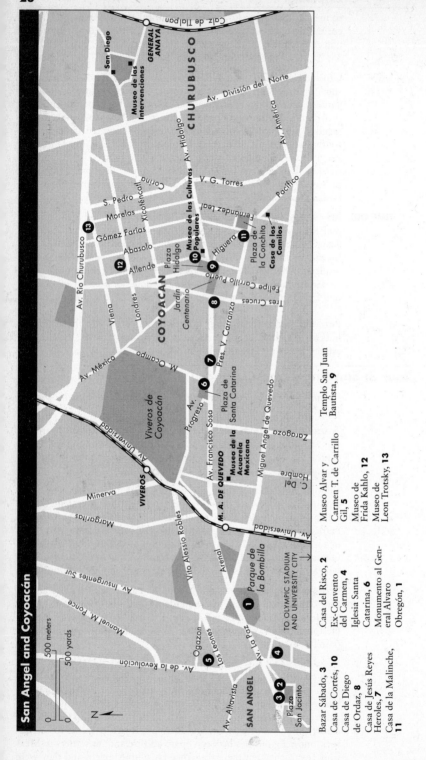

500 meters
500 yards

N

SAN ANGEL

Plaza
San Jacinto

TO OLYMPIC STADIUM
AND UNIVERSITY CITY

Parque de
la Bombilla

VIVEROS

M. A. DE QUEVEDO

Viveros de
Coyoacán

Museo de la
Acuarela
Mexicana

Plaza de
Santa Catarina

COYOACÁN

Jardín
Centenario

Plaza
Hidalgo

Museo de las Culturas
Populares

Casa de los
Camilos

Plaza de
la Conchita

CHURUBUSCO

Museo de las
Intervenciones

GENERAL
ANAYA

San Diego

Av. División del Norte

Av. Río Churubusco

Av. Universidad

Bazar Sábado, **3**
Casa de Cortés, **10**
Casa de Diego
de Ordaz, **8**
Casa de Jesús Reyes
Heroles, **7**
Casa de la Malinche,
11

Casa del Risco, **2**
Ex-Convento
del Carmen, **4**
Iglesia Santa
Catarina, **6**
Monumento al Gen-
eral Alvaro
Obregón, **1**

Museo Alvar y
Carmen T. de Carrillo
Gil, **5**
Museo de
Frida Kahlo, **12**
Museo de
Leon Trotsky, **13**

Templo San Juan
Bautista, **9**

American flag flew over Chapultepec Castle after the death of the *niños héroes* (*see* Tour 2, *above*). A memorial plaque at No. 23 listing their names and expressing Mexico's gratitude for their help in the "unjust North American invasion" now stands in the plaza, where each September a ceremony is conducted in their honor.

❷ One of the prettiest houses facing the plaza—and also open to the public—is the **Casa del Risco.** It was built in 1681, and covering the entire eastern wall of the patio, a huge free-form sculpture explodes with colorful porcelain, tiles, shells, and mosaics. Although it's not ranked among the city's top museums, the **Museo de la Casa del Risco** houses a splendid collection of 14th- to 18th-century European and colonial Mexican paintings as well as period furnishings. *Plaza de San Jacinto 5 and 15,* ☎ *5/616–2711.* ☛ *Free.* ☉ *Tues.–Sun. 10–5.*

❸ Off to one side of the plaza is the **Bazar Sábado,** specializing in unique high-quality handicrafts at excellent prices. Outside, vendors sell embroidered clothing, leather goods, wooden masks, beads, *amates* (bark paintings), and trinkets. Inside the bazaar building, a renovated two-story colonial mansion, are the better-quality—and higher-priced—goods, including *alebrijes* (painted wooden animals from Oaxaca), glassware, pottery, jewelry, and papier-mâché flowers. There is an indoor restaurant as well. ☉ *Sat. 10–7.*

❹ After strolling around San Angel, retrace your steps along Calle Madero to Plaza del Carmen, at the corner of Avenida La Paz and Avenida Revolución. The **Ex-Convento del Carmen** (Carmelite Convent and Church) was erected by Carmelite friars with the help of an Indian chieftain between 1615 and 1628; the tile-covered domes and fountains, gardens, and cloisters make these the most interesting examples of colonial religious architecture in this part of the city. The church still operates, but the convent is now the **Museo Regional del Carmen,** with a fine collection of 18th-century religious paintings, icons and mummified corpses. *Av. Revolución 4 at Monasterio 10.* ☎ *5/616–1254.* ☛ *$2; free Sun.* ☉ *Tues.–Sun. 10–5.*

A large selection of Mexican folk art is on sale at the Fonart branch at Avenida La Paz 17, almost at the corner of Avenida Revolución.

❺ Take Avenida Revolución one block north to the **Museo Alvar y Carmen T. de Carrillo Gil.** This private collection contains early murals by Orozco, Rivera, Siqueiros, and works by modern artists from Europe such as Klee and Picasso. *Av. Revolución 1608 at Desierto de los Leones.* ☎ *5/548–6467.* ☉ *Tues.–Sun. 10–6.*

The next part of the tour is set in Coyoacán, a neighborhood (formerly a village) that extends east of Avenida Insurgentes and about 1 kilometer (less than a mile) from San Angel. Consider taking a taxi to the Plaza de Santa Catarina on Avenida Francisco Sosa, about halfway into the center of Coyoacán, because the tour involves a lot of walking.

Coyoacán means "Place of the Coyotes," and according to local legend, a coyote used to bring chickens to a friar who had saved the coyote from being strangled by a snake. Coyoacán was founded by Toltecs in the 10th century and later settled by the Aztecs, or Mexica. Bernal Díaz Castillo, a Spanish chronicler, wrote that at the time of the conquest there were 6,000 houses. Cortés set up headquarters in Coyoacán during his siege of Tenochtitlan and at one point considered making it his capital. He changed his mind for political reasons, but many of the Spanish buildings left from the two-year period it took to build Mexico City still stand.

Today, Coyoacán still exudes its charm as an old pueblo. The neighborhood has had many illustrious residents from Mexico's rich and intellectual elite, including Miguel de la Madrid, president of Mexico from 1982 to 1988; Orozco, the muralist; Gabriel Figueroa, cinematographer for Luis Buñuel and John Huston; the film star Dolores del Río; El Indio Fernández, a film director; and writers Carlos Monsiváis, Elena Poniatowska, and Jorge Ibargüengoitia.

While superficially it resembles San Angel, Coyoacán has a more animated street life. Most of the houses honor the traditions of colonial Mexican architecture, and the neighborhood is very well kept. As you walk east on Avenida Francisco Sosa, a block to your left is the **Viveros de Coyoacán** (Nurseries of Coyoacán), an expansive, tree-filled park.

6 On one side of the Plaza Santa Catarina is the **Iglesia Santa Catarina,** a pretty 16th-century church; in the plaza there is a bust of Mexican historian Francisco Sosa, who lived here and wrote passionately about **7** Coyoacán. Stop in at Avenida Francisco Sosa 202, the **Casa de Jesús Reyes Heroles,** home of the late minister of culture. It is a fine example of 20th-century architecture on the colonial model and is now used as a cultural center. Continuing along Avenida Francisco Sosa, you **8** will pass the 17th-century **Casa de Diego de Ordaz** at the corner of Tres Cruces, a *mudéjar* (Spanish-Arabic) structure adorned with inlaid mortar. De Ordaz was a Spanish captain in Cortez' army.

You now stand at the entrance to the **Jardín Centenario,** a large park, surrounded by two important colonial buildings and outdoor cafés. Small fairs and amateur musical performances are frequent occur- **9** rences. At the opposite end of the park is the **Templo San Juan Bautista,** one of the first churches to be built in New Spain. It was completed in 1582, and its door is decorated with a Baroque arch. To the left of the church is the heart of Coyoacán, Plaza Hidalgo, the main square. On the north side of the plaza, across from the church, **10** sprawls the **Casa de Cortés,** where Cuauhtémoc was held prisoner. It is supposed to have been rebuilt in the 18th century by one of Cortés's descendants from the stones of his original house; the municipal government now has offices here.

One of the most powerful symbols of the conquest is located in Coyoacán but, significantly perhaps, is not even marked. This is the **11** **Casa de la Malinche,** the somber-looking, fortresslike residence of Malinche, Cortés's Indian mistress and interpreter, whom the Spaniards called Doña María and the Indians called Malintzín. Malinche was instrumental in the conquest by enabling Cortés to communicate with the Nahuatl-speaking tribes he met en route to Tenochtitlan. Today she is a much-reviled Mexican symbol of a traitorous xenophile—hence the term *malinchista,* used to describe a Mexican who prefers things foreign. The legends say that Cortés's wife died in this house, poisoned by the conquistador; they also say he wrote his famous letter to Emperor Charles V here. The house faces a pretty park called Plaza de la Conchita, in the center of which lies an 18th-century church. *Two blocks east of Plaza Hidalgo on Calle Higuera, at the corner of Vallarta.*

TIME OUT Return to Plaza Hidalgo for some refreshments before embarking on the next part of the tour. **La Guadalupana,** on Higuera, between Caballo-calco and San Francisco Figeroca, is a popular refurbished cantina from the 1920s with snacks (such as shrimp broth and *totopos con frijoles,* a kind of corn tortilla with beans); unlike the city's traditional old cantinas,

La Guadalupana welcomes women. The quesadillas served in the little restaurants on Higuera have attained citywide fame.

From the plaza, walk five blocks north on Allende to the corner of Londres. Remodeled in early 1992, the bright blue adobe house—the ★ ⑫ **Museo de Frida Kahlo**—is where the painter Frida Kahlo was born and lived with Diego Rivera almost continuously from 1929 until her death in 1954. Kahlo has become quite a cult figure in recent years, not only because of her paintings—mostly self-portraits in the surrealist tradition—but because of her bohemian lifestyle and flamboyant individualism. As a child Kahlo was crippled by polio, and several years later she was impaled on a tramway rail. She had countless operations, including the amputation of a leg; was addicted to painkillers; had affairs with Leon Trotsky and several women; and married Rivera twice. Kahlo's astounding vitality and originality are reflected in this house, from the giant papier-mâché skeletons outside and the painted tin retablos on the staircase to the gloriously decorated kitchen and the bric-a-brac in her bedroom. Even if you know nothing about Kahlo, a visit to the museum—also filled with letters, diaries, clothes, and paintings by Kahlo and other great moderns, including Klee and Duchamp—will leave you with a strong, visceral impression of this early feminist artist. *Londres 127,* ☎ *5/554–5999.* ☞ *$3.* ☉ *Tues.–Sun. 10–6.*

Leon Trotsky lived, and was murdered, a short walk away. Go three blocks east on Londres and then two blocks north on Morelos; his house is on the northwest corner of Viena. From the outside, the ⑬ **Museo de Leon Trotsky** resembles an anonymous and forbidding fortress, with turrets for armed guards; it is difficult to believe that it is the home and final resting place for the ashes of one of the most important figures of the Russian Revolution. But that fact only adds to the allure of the house, which is owned by Trotsky's grandson.

This is a modest, austere dwelling—anyone taller than five feet must stoop to pass through doorways to Trotsky's bedroom (with bullet holes in the walls from the first assassination attempt, in which the muralist Siqueiros was implicated), his wife's study, the dining room, and the study where Ramón Mercader finally drove an ice ax into Trotsky's head. (On his desk, cluttered with writing paraphernalia and an article he was revising in Russian, the calendar is open to the fateful day of August 20, 1940.) The volunteers will tell you how Trotsky's teeth left a permanent scar on Mercader's hand; how he clung to life for 26 hours; what his last words were; and how his death was sponsored by the United States. Not all of the volunteers, however, speak English. *Viena 45,* ☎ *5/658–8732.* ☞ *$2.* ☉ *Tues.–Sun. 10–5.*

What to See and Do with Children

The best place to take children in Mexico is the parks, particularly Chapultepec. It has a **children's zoo** with a miniature railroad for viewing the animals, picnic grounds, and a boating lake. Youngsters can play with the animals, ride ponies, and climb tree houses. *First section of Chapultepec Park.* ☞ *Free.* ☉ *Daily 8–6.*

Chapultepec Mágico is a children's amusement park with various games and rides, including a *montaña rusa* ("Russian mountain," or roller coaster). *Second section of Chapultepec Park.* ☞ *Small admission charge (under $2) includes 30 free rides or games.* ☉ *Tues.–Sun. 10–6, closed Mon.*

Opened in late 1993, **El Papalote, Museo del Niño** is an interactive museum with five theme sections: *Our World; The Human Body;* the punning *Con-Sciencia,* which has exhibits relating to both consciousness and science; *Communication,* which focuses on topics ranging from language to computers; and *Expression,* which includes art, music, theater, and literature. There are also temporary exhibits, workshops, an IMAX theater, store, and restaurant. *Av. Constituyentes 268, second section of Chapultepec Park,* ☎ *5/224–1259.* ☛ *$3 adults, $2.20 children.* ⊙ *Daily 9–1 and 2–6, and Thurs. nights, 7–11.*

Reino Aventura is a 100-acre theme park on the southern edge of the city, comprising six "villages": Mexican, French, Swiss, Polynesian, American, and Children's World. Shows include performances by trained dolphins. *Carretera Picacho a Ajusco, Km 1.5.* ☛ *About $10, includes entrance and all rides (discounts for senior citizens and children).* ⊙ *Fri–Sun 10–6:30.*

Ripley's Museo de lo Increíble (Museum of the Incredible), for children of all ages, has 14 exhibit rooms chockablock with believe-it-or-not items. *Londres 4 (east of the Zona Rosa),* ☎ *5/546–3784 or 5/546–76700.* ☛ *$4 adults, $3 children.* ⊙ *Weekdays Fri. 11–7, weekends 10–7.*

SHOPPING

Native crafts and specialties from all regions of Mexico are available in the capital, as are designer clothes and modern art. The best, most concentrated shopping area is the **Zona Rosa,** an 18-square-block area bounded by Reforma on the north, Niza on the east, Avenida Chapultepec on the south, and Varsovia on the west. The neighborhood is chock-full of boutiques, jewelry stores, leather-goods shops, antiques stores, and art galleries, as well as dozens of great little restaurants and coffee shops. Day or night, the Zona Rosa is always lively.

Polanco, a choice residential neighborhood along the northeast perimeter of Chapultepec Park, is blossoming with fine shops and boutiques, many of which are branches of Zona Rosa or downtown establishments. Many are located in malls like the huge ultramodern **Plaza Polanco** (Jaime Balmes 11).

There are hundreds of shops with more modest trappings and better prices spread out along the length of Avenida Insurgentes, as well as along Avenida Juárez and in the old downtown area. The major department-store chains are **Liverpool** (at Av. Insurgentes Sur 1310, Mariano Escobedo 425, and in the Plaza Satélite and Perisur shopping centers), **Suburbia** (at Horacio 203, Sonora 180, Av. Insurgentes Sur 1235, and also in Plaza Satélite and Perisur), and **El Palacio de Hierro** (at the corner of Durango and Salamanca), which is noted for fashions by well-known designers at prices now on par with those found in the United States. The posh and pricey shopping mall **Perisur** is out on the southern edge of the city near where the Periférico Expressway meets Avenida Insurgentes. **Plaza Satélite** mall is in a northern suburb called Satellite on the Anillo Periférico. Department stores are generally open Mondays, Tuesdays, Thursdays, and Fridays from 10 AM to 7 PM, and on Wednesdays and Saturdays from 10 AM to 8 PM.

Sanborns is a mini department-store chain with 20 branches in Mexico City alone. Those most convenient for tourists are at Madero 4 (its original store in the House of Tiles, downtown); on the Reforma, one at the Angel monument and another at the Diana Fountain; and in the

Zona Rosa, one at the corner of Niza and Hamburgo and another at Londres 130 (in the Hotel Calinda Geneve). They feature a good selection of quality ceramics and handicrafts (they can ship anywhere), and most have restaurants or coffee shops, a pharmacy, and periodical and book departments carrying English-language publications.

Under the auspices of the National Council for Culture and Arts, **Fonart** (National Fund for Promoting Handicrafts) operates six stores in Mexico City and others around the country. The most convenient locations are at Londres 136, 2nd floor, Zona Rosa (☎ 5/525–2026), and at Juárez 89 (☎ 5/521–0171), downtown just west of Alameda Park. Prices are fixed, and the diverse, top-quality folk art and hand-crafted furnishings from all over Mexico represent the best artisans. Major sales at near wholesale prices are held at the main store-warehouse (Av. Patriotismo 691, Col. Mixcoac) during the second half of March, June, September, and November.

A Saturday "must" for shoppers and browsers is a visit to the **Bazar Sábado** (Saturday Bazaar) at Plaza San Jacinto in the southern San Angel district (*see* Tour 3, *above*). On Sundays, more than 100 artists exhibit and sell their paintings and sculptures at the **Jardín del Arte** (Garden of Art) in Parque Sullivan, just northeast of the Reforma–Insurgentes intersection. Along the west side of the park, a colorful weekend mercado with scores of food stands is also worth a visit.

The following list will get you started. As you explore, you will find hundreds more.

Zona Rosa

Plaza La Rosa, a sparkling modern shopping arcade between Amberes and Génova, houses 72 prestigious shops and boutiques. It spans the entire depth of the block from Londres to Hamburgo with entrances on both streets. The pink neocolonial **Plaza del Angel** (Londres 161) has a *Centro de Antigüedades* (antiques center) with several fine shops. On Saturday, together with other vendors, they set up a flea market in the arcades and patios. On Sunday bibliophiles gather here to sell, peruse, and buy collectors' books and periodicals.

Antiques
Antigues Coloniart (Estocolmo 367, ☎ 5/514–4799), has good-quality antique paintings, furniture, and sculpture. The store is open by appointment only.

Art
The **Juan Martín Gallery** (Dickens 33-B, Polanco, ☎ 5/280–0277) is one of the city's best avant-garde studios. The store and gallery of the renowned **Sergio Bustamante** (Campos Eliseos 204–6, Polanco, ☎ 5/282–2638) displays and sells the artist's wildly surrealistic sculptures and interior-design pieces.

Clothing
Acapulco Joe's (Amberes 19, ☎ 5/533–4774; also in Polanco at Mazaryk 318, ☎ 5/581–3044) has great T-shirts, beachwear, and hip unisex sportsclothes. **Guess** (Amberes 17, ☎ 5/207–2891) features chic denim sportswear for guys and gals.

Designer Items
Cartier (Amberes 9, ☎ 5/207–6104 and Masaryk 438 in Polanco, ☎ 5/545–8064) sells genuine designer jewelry and clothes, under the auspices of the French Cartier. However, **Gucci** (Hamburgo 136, ☎ 5/207–9997) has no connection with the European store of the same

name; nevertheless, it has a fine sellection of shoes, gloves, and handbags. **Ralph Lauren** (Amberes 21, ☎ 5/514–1563) is the home of Polo sportswear made in Mexico under license and sold at Mexican prices.

Jewelry

The owner of **Los Castillo** (Amberes 41, ☎ 5/511–8396) developed a unique method of melding silver, copper, and brass, and is considered by many to be Taxco's top silversmith. Taxco silver of exceptional style is sold at **Arte en Plata** (Amberes 24, ☎ 5/511–1422 and Londres 162, ☎ 5/511–1422), with many designs inspired by pre-Hispanic art. **Pelletier** (Torcuato Caso 237 in Polanco, ☎ 5/250–8600) sells fine jewelry and watches. **Tane** (Amberes 70, ☎ 5/511–9429; Edgar Allan Poe 68, in Polanco, ☎ 5/281–4775; and other locations) is a treasure trove of superb silver works—jewelry, flatware, candelabra, museum-quality reproductions of antique pieces, and bold new designs by young Mexican silversmiths. The **Mexican Opal Company** (Hamburgo 203, ☎ 5/528–9263) is run by Japanese who are very big on opals. They sell set and loose stones as well as a selection of jewelry in silver and gold. Open by appointment only.

Leather

For leather goods, you have more than a few choices in Mexico City. **Gaitán** (Hamburgo 89, ☎ 5/514–8227) features an extensive array of leather coats, luggage, golf bags, and saddles. **Aries** (Florencia 14, ☎ 5/533–2509, and Santa Catarina 207 in San Angel, ☎ 5/616–2248) is Mexico's finest purveyor of leather goods, with a superb selection of clothes, shoes, and accessories for both men and women. The prices are high. Just down the street, **Antil** (Florencia 22, ☎ 5/525–1573) also specializes in high-quality leather goods.

Mexican Handicrafts

Browse for fine works of folk art, sculpture, and handicraft, from silver to ceramics, in the two-story gallery **Manos Mexicanas** (Amberes 57, near Londres, ☎ 5/514–7455). The **Mercado Insurgentes** (also called **Mercado Zona Rosa**) is an entire block deep, with entrances on both Londres and Liverpool (between Florencia and Amberes). This is a typical neighborhood public market with one big difference: Most of the stalls (222 of them) sell crafts. You can find all kinds of handmade items—including serapes and ponchos, baskets, pottery, silver, and onyx, as well as regional Mexican dresses and costumes.

Girasol (Génova 39, ☎ 5/511–5589) has a whimsical selection of hand-loomed fabrics and delightful hand-embroidered gowns and skirts. Handwoven wool rugs, tapestries, and fabrics with original and unusual designs can be found at **Tamacani** (Varsovia 51, ☎ 5/207–3696).

The Unusual

Arte Popular en Miniatura (Hamburgo 130, ☎ 5/514–1405) is a tiny shop filled with tiny things, from dollhouse furniture and lead soldiers to miniature Nativity scenes. **Flamma** (Hamburgo 167, at the corner of Florencia, ☎ 5/511–8499 or 5/511–0266) is a town house that sells a beautiful array of handmade candles.

Downtown

The Zócalo and Alameda Park areas have interesting markets for browsing and buying handicrafts and curios; polite bargaining is customary. The biggest is the **Centro Artesanal Buenavista** (Aldama 187, by the Buenavista Central Train Station). **La Lagunilla** market (on Libertad, just east of Paseo de la Reforma Norte) attracts antiques hunters who know how to determine authenticity, and also coin collectors. The best day is Sunday, when flea-market stands are set up outside, with everything from collectibles to interesting knickknacks to junk. Within the colonial walls of **La Ciudadela** market (Balderas, about four blocks south of Avenida Juárez) are 344 artisans' stalls selling a variety of good handicrafts from all over the country.

Museo de Artes Populares (Museum of Arts and Crafts) could well be a museum but is in fact a large store displaying and selling an array of folk art and handicrafts—pottery, ceramics, glassware, textiles, and more—from practically every region of the country. Housed in an early 18th-century convent (across the street from Alameda Park and the Juárez Monument, at Juárez 44, ☎ 5/518–3058), it is open 7 days a week.

Bazar del Centro (downtown, at Isabel la Católica 30, just below Madero) is a restored late-17th-century noble mansion built around a garden courtyard that houses several chic boutiques, top-quality handicraft shops, and prestigious jewelers such as **Aplijsa** (☎ 5/521–1923 or 5/510–1800), known for its fine gold, silver, pearls, and gemstones. Other shops sell Taxco silver, Tonalá stoneware, and Mexican tequilas and liqueurs. This complex is elegant, and also has a congenial bar.

Portales de los Mercaderes (Merchants' Arcade), extending along the entire west side of the Zócalo between Madero and 16 de Septiembre avenues, has attracted merchants since 1524. Today it is lined with jewelry shops, selling gold (sometimes by the gram) and authentic Taxco silver at prices lower than those in Taxco itself, where the overhead is higher. In the middle of the arcade (Plaza de la Constitución 17) is **Tardán** (no ☎), an unusual shop specializing in fine quality and fashionable men's hats of every imaginable type and style.

Celaya (Cinco de Mayo 13, ☎ 5/521–1787), in the downtown historic section, is a decades-old haven for those with a sweet tooth. It specializes in candied pineapple, papaya, guava, and other exotic fruit, almond-paste, candied walnut rolls, and *cajeta,* a typical Mexican dessert of thick caramelized milk.

Feders (2 locations: the factory at Bufon 25 in Colonia Nueva Anzures, ☎ 5/250–3241, and a booth at Bazar Sábado, Plaza San Jacinto 11, San Angel) has great hand-blown glass, Tiffany-style lamps, and artistic wrought iron.

SPORTS

Bullfights
The main season is the dry season, around November through March, when celebrated *matadores* appear at **Plaza México,** the world's largest bullring, which seats 40,000. Gray Line Tours offers bullfight tour packages (*see* Guided Tours *in* Mexico City Essentials *below*); or tickets, which range from about $6 to $25, can be purchased at hotel travel desks. Try the bullring ticket booths on Saturday between 11 AM and 2 PM or Sunday between 11 AM to 3:30 PM for tickets as well. The ring is located next to the Cuidad de Deportes sports complex, and the show goes on at 4 PM. *Calle A. Rodín and Holbein, Col. Nápoles,* ☎ 5/683–1625.

Golf
All golf courses are private in Mexico City, but you can play if you are a guest of a member. Travelers staying at the Sheraton Maria

Isabel and the Camino Real hotels can have the hotel arrange admittance to the Bella Vista Golf Club, located off the Querétaro Highway (☎ 5/360–3501). Green fees Tuesday through Friday are $50; weekends, $100.

Horse Racing

The season at the beautiful **Hipódromo de las Américas** lasts from mid-January through December, when thoroughbreds run daily. Betting is pari-mutuel. The races are especially enjoyable to watch from the swank Derby or Jockey Club restaurants. Tickets cost about $5 and can be purchased at hotel travel desks or at the track, which is located in the northwest section of the city near the Querétaro Highway. *Av. Industria Militar, Lomas de Sotelo,* ☎ *5/557–4100.*

Jai Alai

You can watch and bet on men playing this lightning-fast Basque-style handball game at the newly remodeled **Frontón México** (Plaza de la Republica 17, ☎ 5/566–9679) Tuesday through Sunday at 8 PM. Women's matches are played at **Frontón Metropolitano** (Bahía de Todos los Santos 190) daily except Sundays, 4 PM–10 PM. Betting, which goes on while the games are being played, is a fascinating skill in itself; instructions on the betting sheets are in Spanish and English. Dress up if you attend a game; jacket and tie for men are customary.

Jogging

There are jogging tracks in Chapultepec Park and at the Villa Olímpica (Olympic Village). Another joggers' favorite is along the pastoral paths of the Coyoacán Nurseries by the Viveros Station of the No. 3 metro line. Early morning runners will probably see young novice bullfighters there going through their training maneuvers. Keep in mind, by the way, that air quality is often poor and this is the highest city in North America—7,349 feet/2,240 meters above sea level—so take it easy until your heart and lungs become accustomed to the altitude.

Tennis

Tennis clubs are private in Mexico so tennis buffs should consider staying at one of the hotels (*see* Lodging, *below*) that have courts on site.

Water Sports

The best place for swimming is your hotel pool. The vast **Cuemanco** sports park (Canal de Cuemanco, on the way to Xochimilco) has an artificial lake for canoeing. Rowers can also ply their sport in the lakes of Chapultepec Park. Rentals are nearby.

DINING

Mexico City has been a culinary capital ever since the time of Moctezuma. Chronicles tell of the daily banquet extravaganzas prepared for the slender Aztec emperor by his palace chefs. Over 300 different kinds of dishes were served for every meal, comprising vast assortments of meats and fowls seasoned in dozens of ways; limitless fruit, vegetables, and herbs; freshwater fish; and fresh seafood that was rushed to Tenochtitlan from both seacoasts by sprinting relay runners.

Until the 15th century, Europeans had never seen indigenous Mexican edibles such as corn, chilies of all varieties, tomatoes, potatoes, pumpkin, squash, avocado, turkey, cacao (chocolate), and vanilla. In turn, the colonization brought European gastronomic influence and ingredients—wheat, onion, garlic, olives, citrus fruit, cattle, sheep, goats, chickens, pigs (and lard for frying)—and ended up broadening the already complex pre-Hispanic cuisine into one of the most multi-faceted and exquisite in the world: traditional Mexican.

Mexico's food, like its art, is as diverse and abundant as its geography. Distinct regional specialties typify each of the republic's 32 states and even the different provinces within the states. Fresh ingredients are bountiful, recipes are passed down through generations, and preparation requires much loving care and a lot of patience. (Mexican gastronomes are dismayed by foreigners' glaring misconceptions of Mexican food as essentially tacos, enchiladas, and burritos; they are bewildered by Tex-Mex, and appalled by Taco Bell.)

Today's cosmopolitan Mexico City, with some 15,000 restaurants, is a gastronomic melting pot. Here you can find establishments ranging from simple family-style eateries to five-star world-class restaurants. In addition, there are fine international restaurants specializing in cuisines of practically every foreign culture. Among them, the most prevalent are Spanish and haute-cuisine French—France also invaded Mexico and influenced its eating traditions.

In the past decade a renaissance of Mexican cooking has brought about a new wave known as *cocina mexicana moderna* (modern Mexican cuisine), which is featured in many Mexico City restaurants. Emphasis is on the back-to-basics, delicate tastes of traditional regional dishes served in smaller portions with refined aesthetic presentation. Also significant in this modern trend is the revival of ancient indigenous cuisine—foods, especially fish, that were baked, grilled, or steamed in leaves.

Mexico City mealtime hours are 7–11 AM for breakfast (*desayuno*), 1–4 PM for lunch (*comida*), and 7 PM–midnight for dinner (*cena*). At deluxe restaurants, dress is generally formal (jacket and tie), and reservations are almost always required; see reviews for details. (Even if a deluxe restaurant doesn't *require* a jacket and tie, diners are likely to feel out-of-place if they're not well dressed.) For tourists on the run there are American-style coffee shops (VIPS, Denny's, Shirley's, and Sanborns) all over the city; some are open 24 hours.

The following selection of recommended restaurants is organized by cuisine and price range.

CATEGORY	COST*
$$$$	over $40
$$$	$25–$40
$$	$15–$25
$	under $15

per person, excluding drinks and service

French

$$$$ **Fouquet's de Paris.** Located in the Camino Real hotel, this is a branch of the renowned Parisian restaurant and an elegant haven of peace and tranquility. The best pâtés in Mexico and tender, juicy lamb chops are part of the diverse and stylish menu. The desserts are in a class all their own. The sorbets, such as the delicately flavored passion fruit, are outstanding, and the cakes, mousses, and pastries are light and delicious. Month-long gastronomic festivals are held here throughout the year, and each October or November chefs from the original Fouquet's in Paris take over the kitchen. ✕ *Hotel Camino Real, Mariano Escobedo 700, ☎ 5/203–2121. Reservations required. Jacket required. AE, DC, MC, V. Closed Sun. No lunch Sat.*

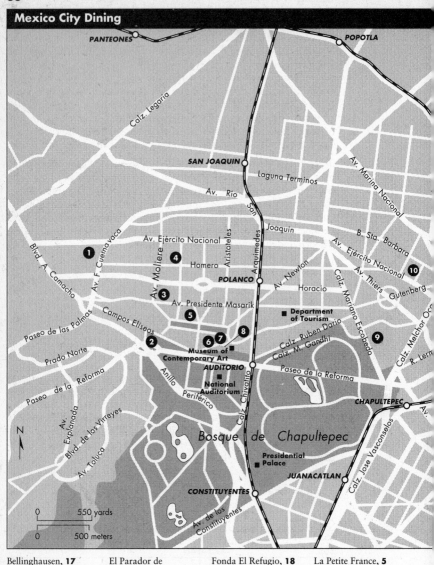

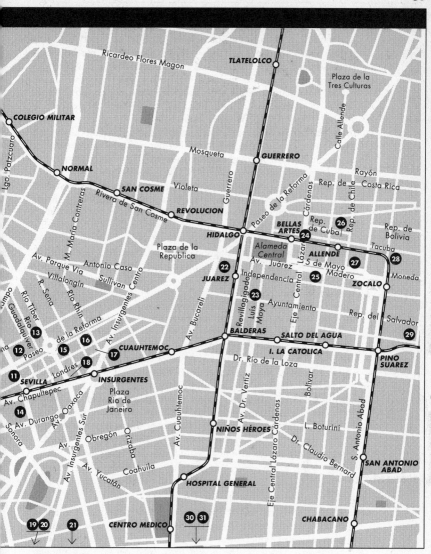

Los Irabien, **31**
Maxim's de Paris, **7**
Meson El Cid, **22**
Prendes, **25**
San Angel Inn, **30**
Suntory, **21**

$$$ **Champs Elysées.** On the corner of Amberes and Reforma, command-
★ ing an impressive view of the Independence (Angel) monument, is one
of the bastions of haute cuisine in Mexico City. The variety of sauces
served with both meat and fish dishes is impressive, with the hol-
landaise sauce over sea bass or red snapper probably taking top hon-
ors. Regulars find either the roast duck (carved at your table) or the
pepper steak hard to resist. Of particular note is the generous cheese
board. ✗ *Amberes 1, Zona Rosa,* ☎ *5/514–0450. Reservations
advised. AE, DC, MC, V. Closed Sun.*

$$ **La Petite France.** This restaurant in the Pasaje de Polanco has a very
Mediterranean feel, with tables spilling out onto the street, hanging
plants, and white wrought-iron furniture. The imaginative menu
includes such specialties as fish soup with Pernod and roast lobster
with basil, along with such typically Mediterranean dishes as stuffed
mushrooms and *moules Provençales* (mussels Provençal). Fish dishes
are popular, with *truite meunière* (trout, lightly fried and served with
lemon), a giant prawn brochette, and deep-fried sea bass claiming
most of the attention. Beautifully garnished and presented, the dishes
catch the eye with a colorful, good selection of steamed vegetables. ✗
Av. Presidente Masaryk 360, Col. Polanco, ☎ *5/280–8851 or 5/280–
9335. Reservations accepted. AE, DC, MC, V. No dinner Sun.*

$ **El Buen Comer.** One of the more original Polanco eating spots, El
Buen Comer ("Eating Well") consists of not more than 20 tables in
the front yard and garage of a private house. The entrance is discreet
and can easily be missed, and the atmosphere inside is that of a large,
private lunch party. Oysters are served with an unusual vinegar and
chopped shallot sauce but are so tasty they can be savored with just a
squeeze of lime. The four house pâtés are excellent. A favorite main
course of the habitués is quiche Lorraine, and the quiche royale with
shrimp is a must for seafood lovers. The fondues are exquisite. Whole
steaks can be served to order with fine herbs, pepper, tartar, or shal-
lots. El Buen Comer makes a great stop after shopping in Polanco. ✗
Edgar Allan Poe 50, Col. Polanco, ☎ *5/281–1094 or 5/282–0325.
Reservations required at lunch. AE, D, MC, V. Closed Sun.*

International

$$$$ **Estoril.** Rosa Martin, who founded this highly successful restaurant in
★ an exquisitely furnished 1930s town house in fashionable Polanco,
runs it with her daughter Diana. It boasts only the very best ingredients
and serves international cuisine with a Mexican flair; its forte, however,
is traditional Mexican. The *perejil frito* (fried parsley) is a popular
starter. The main dishes offer some unusual taste combinations: giant
prawns in Chablis or curry sauce and sea bass in fresh coriander sauce.
To finish, try either the delicious *tarte tatin* (an upside-down apple tart
with caramel) or the homemade sorbets, especially the refreshing mint
flavor. ✗ *Alejandro Dumas 24, Col. Polanco,* ☎ *5/280–9828. Reservations advised. Jacket and tie. AE, DC, MC, V.*

$$$$ **Hacienda de los Morales.** This Mexican institution, set in a former
hacienda that dates back to the 16th century, is grandly colonial in style,
with dark wood beams and huge terra-cotta expanses. The menu combines both international and Mexican cuisines, with some imaginative
variations on both. The walnut soup, served either hot or cold, is a delicate and unusual specialty. Fish is seemingly unlimited, with a rainbow
trout meunière (lightly sautéed in butter, served with lemon juice and
parsley), sea bass *marinière* (in a white-wine sauce), and a mixed
seafood gratin. The charcoal-broiled grain-fed chicken has a distinct flavor, and the paillard is always of the highest quality. The Hacienda de los

Morales is regularly hired for functions, so don't be surprised if there's a lot of activity. ✕ *Vázquez de Mella 525, Col. Los Morales,* ☎ *5/281–4554 or 5/281–4703. Reservations advised. AE, DC, MC, V.*

$$$$ **La Jolla.** This chic, intimate restaurant in the Marquis Reforma is the first in the country to specialize in Belgian cuisine. The menu, which also includes fine Mexican fare, is supervised by Dutch executive-chef Raul Reicharth, who has won many awards for his creative cookery. Some of the most popular entrées are succulent pheasant with pureed celery and warm endive salad, and steamed dorado (sea bass) with a bread-crumb crust. There are scrumptious tarts and mousses for dessert. La Jolla is especially romantic at night, with its candlelit tables, soft piano music, and splendid view of Paseo de la Reforma, the city's grand avenue. Well-heeled Mexican executives pack the place at breakfast. ✕ *Paseo de la Reforma 465,* ☎ *5/211–3600. Reservations advised for dinner. Jacket and tie. AE, DC, MC, V. Closed weekends.*

$$$$ **Les Célébrités.** In addition to offering superb French fare, this elegant
★ restaurant also serves the best in Mexican cuisine. When the Nikko México hotel opened in 1987, chef Joel Roubenchon, one of the creators of nouvelle cuisine in France, came to Mexico to set up this restaurant off the hotel lobby. With him came the ultimate in restaurant technology and a policy of using only the very finest ingredients. The menu features such one-of-a-kind dishes as medallion of lobster in guayaba sauce; salmon roll stuffed with lemon mousse in grapefruit sauce; and, for dessert, pomegranate sherbet or red and green prickly pear sherbet. ✕ *Nikko México, Campos Elíseos 204, Col. Polanco,* ☎ *5/280–1111. Reservations required. Jacket and tie. AE, DC, MC, V.* ☉ *Weekdays 6:30 AM–11 PM. Closed Sun. No lunch Sat.*

$$$$ **Maxim's de Paris.** Here you can enjoy the best French food anywhere and, better yet, nouvelle Mexican cuisine created by Yves Ferrer, the first chef and now the restaurant's manager. His pre-Hispanic *crepas de huitlacoche* (crepes of corn fungus) are a stylish delicacy. Inspired by Mexico's great wealth of foodstuffs, Ferrer conceived original dishes such as fillet of sea bass in jellied sauce of beef bone marrow. Operated under the auspices of the original Maxim's in Paris, this spacious but intimate restaurant is Parisian art deco under a stained-glass ceiling; the wine cellar is nonpareil, and the service impeccable. ✕ *Hotel Presidente InterContinental México, Campos Elíseos 218, Col. Polanco,* ☎ *5/327–7700. Reservations required. Jacket and tie. AE, DC, MC, V. Closed Sun. No lunch Sat.*

$$–$$$ **Bellinghausen.** This is one of the most pleasant lunch spots in the Zona Rosa. The partially covered hacienda-style courtyard at the back, set off by an ivy-laden wall, is a magnet midday for executives and tourists alike. A veritable army of waiters scurry back and forth serving such tried-and-true favorites as *sopa de hongos* (mushroom soup) and *filete chemita* (broiled steak with mashed potatoes). The *higaditos de pollo* (chicken livers) with a side order of sautéed spinach is another winner. Other specials include *cabrito* (baby goat), roast lamb, and Spanish paella; the fish and seafood are also superb. ✕ *Londres 95, Zona Rosa,* ☎ *5/525–8738 or 5/207–4978. Reservations advised. AE, DC, MC, V. Closed Sun.*

Italian

$$ **La Lanterna.** The Petterino family has run this two-story restaurant in the same building for 20 years. The downstairs has the rustic feel of a northern Italian trattoria, with the cramped seating adding to the intimacy. Upstairs is more spacious. All the pastas are made on the premises, and the Bolognese sauce, in particular, is a local favorite. Try the raw artichoke salad, *conejo al Salmi* (rabbit in a wine sauce), *filete*

al burro nero (steak in black butter), and *saltimbocca à la Romana* (veal and ham in Marsala sauce). ✗ *Paseo de la Reforma 458, Col. Juárez,* ☎ *5/207–9969. No reservations. MC, V. Closed Sun.*

Japanese

$$$$ **Suntory.** Suntory's restaurants in Boston, Singapore, Paris, and São Paulo have led its name to become synonymous with the best in Japanese dining. As you enter this one, by way of three rocks in a bed of well-raked sand, you are transported into a small-town patio in a dense green garden. In this enchanted world you are not absolved of the difficulty of choice. Is it the teppanyaki room to watch your fresh meat or fish prepared with a variety of vegetables? Or perhaps the shabu-shabu room beckons with wafer-thin sashimi and a copper pot of steaming vegetable broth in which elegant slices of beef are cooked? If you are a raw-fish enthusiast, perhaps the sushi bar? Prices are high, especially for Mexico, but the ingredients are of the highest quality. ✗ *Torres Adalid 14, Col. del Valle,* ☎ *5/536–9432; also at Montes Urales 555, Lomas Chapultepec,* ☎ *5/202–4711. Reservations advised. AE, DC, MC, V.*

Mexican

$$$$ **El Centenario.** The talk of the town since its inauguration in 1993, this
★ thoroughly Mexican restaurant occupies a restored 17th-century mansion in the heart of the downtown historic center. Elegant colonial antiques are strikingly posed against folk art and pastel walls. The enticing menu includes excellent versions of authentic pre-Hispanic dishes such as *pollo en pipián verde* (chicken in green-pumpkin-seed sauce) and *huachingo mixote* (red snapper steamed in a parchment bag). Try the *chicharrón* (crispy pork rind) or guacamole appetizer, but be sure to leave room for desserts such as cactus-fruit ice cream with tequila. An ebullient street-level cantina features drinks, *botanas* (appetizers), and old-time piano music. ✗ *República de Cuba 79,* ☎ *5/521–2934 or 5/521–7866. Reservations required. AE, MC, V. Closed Sun.*

$$$$ **Isadora.** Some of Mexico City's most inventive and exciting cooking takes place in this converted private house in Polanco. The three smallish dining rooms have a 1920s feel but are uncharacteristically ascetic—pale walls dabbed with modern-art squiggles. The management sponsors "cooking festivals," and virtually every month the kitchen produces dishes from a different country. The basic menu changes six times a year, and over that same period it will include three Mexican foodfests. What might be called the set menu features coarse duck pâté and excellent seafood pasta, with no holding back on the juicy prawns, shellfish, and squid. Ice creams, meringues, and chocolate cake for dessert benefit from the addition of the chef's delicate, pale green mint sauce. ✗ *Molière 50, Col. Polanco,* ☎ *5/280–1586. Reservations advised. Jacket and tie. AE, DC, MC, V. Closed Sun.*

$$$$ **Los Irabien.** This beautiful dining area filled with leafy plants and the owner's impressive art collection is a worthwhile stop for the gourmet and culture hound alike. Chef Enrique Estrada, who trained at the Waldorf Astoria in New York, is one of Mexico's finest exponents of nouvelle cuisine à la Mexicaine. His *ensalada Irabien* triumphs as a mixture of smoked salmon, abalone, prawn, quail eggs, lettuce, and watercress. Two outstanding entrées include the nopal cactus stuffed with fish fillet in garlic and the fillet steak in strawberry sauce *a la pimienta*. Less exotic dishes, such as a juicy prime rib of beef, are also available, and lavish care in preparation and presentation is evident in all courses. Los Irabien is one of the city's breakfast spots par excellence. Where else could one be tempted by *huevos de codorniz* *huitzilopochtli* (quail eggs with tortilla on a bed of *huitlacoche* in a squash-blossom sauce)? ✕ *Av. de la Paz 45, Col. San Angel,* ☎ *5/660–2382. Reservations advised. Jacket and tie. AE, DC, MC, V.*

$$$$ San Angel Inn. In the south of the city, this magnificent old hacienda
★ and ex-convent, with its elegant grounds and immaculately tended gardens, is both a joy to the eye and an inspiration to the palate. The dark mahogany furniture, crisp white table linens, and beautiful blue-and-white Talavera place settings all combine to touch just that right note of restrained opulence. There are many dishes to be recommended, especially the *crepas de huitlacoche* (corn-fungus crepes) and the *sopa de tortilla* (tortilla soup). The *puntas de filete* (sirloin tips) are liberally laced with chili and the *huachinango* (red snapper) is offered in a variety of ways. Desserts—from light and crunchy meringues to pastries bulging with cream—can be rich to the point of decadence. ✕ *Calle Diego Rivera 50, corner Altavista, Col. San Angel Inn,* ☎ *5/616–1527 or 5/616–1402. Reservations advised. Jacket required. AE, DC, MC, V.*

$$$ Lincoln. With its portrait of the great statesman in the entrance and large following of local politicians, Lincoln is reminiscent of a New England club—leather upholstery, discreet dining booths, and plenty of dark wood—but the menu is traditional Mexican, with an emphasis on fish. The salsa verde, with large chunks of cheese, onion, and *perejil* (parsley), is an ideal complement to the appetizers. From there the range and choice are impressive. Soups include such delicacies as *sopa de almejas* (clam soup) and a thick crab soup. Among the main dishes, the *huachinango a la veracruzana* (red snapper Veracruz-style) is notable. The typical *albóndigas en chipotle* (meatballs in spicy chile sauce) is another favorite. ✕ *Revillagigedo 24, Col. Centro,* ☎ *5/510–1468. Reservations accepted. AE, DC, MC, V.*

$$$ Prendes. This downtown institution, first opened in 1892, has an air of history and legend—the president of Mexico comes here, as did his predecessors. Trotsky ate here with Ramón Mercader, who axed him to death two days later. The decor is minimal but is highlighted by the famous Prendes murals, which depict such celebrities as Gary Cooper and Walt Disney who also dined here. Prendes features some traditional Mexican dishes, but emphasis is now on delicate and decorative nouvelle Mexican cuisine. Oysters, *ceviche* (raw fish marinated in lime juice, tomatoes, onions, and chile), or a cream of maize soup are typical starters. The *filete chemita* (fillet of beef) and the fillet of fish meunière with nuts are two popular main courses. ✕ *16 de Septiembre 10, Col. Centro,* ☎ *5/512–7517. Reservations required. Jacket and tie. AE, DC, MC, V. No dinner.*

$$–$$$ El Arroyo. More than just a restaurant, this dining complex is a famous attraction in itself, complete with its own bullring. Located at the south end of town near the beginning of the highway to Cuernavaca, it was founded more than 50 years ago by the Arroyo family and is now run by jovial Jesús ("Chucho") Arroyo. His loyal following includes celebrities, dignitaries, and bullfighters, along with local families, groups, and tourists: More than 2,600 people can dine simultaneously in a labyrinth of 11 picturesque dining areas. Typical Mexican specialties—roast baby lamb wrapped in maguey leaves, chicken mole, a dozen types of tacos, and much more—are prepared in open kitchens. There's mariachi music galore and the full gamut of Mexican drinks, including pulque. The small bullring is the setting for bullfights with *novilleros,* or young bullfighters just beginning their careers, during the bullfight season (from about April through October), as well as for special banquets and lively fiestas. Breakfast starts at 8 AM and lunch is served until 7 PM. ✕ *Insurgentes Sur 4003,*

Col. Tlalpan, ☎ *5/573–4344. Reservations advised; required for groups. AE, DC, MC, V.*

$$–$$$ **Fonda El Refugio.** Since it opened in 1954, this fine Zona Rosa restau-
★ rant has been internationally known for its authentic Mexican cuisine, featuring the best dishes from each major region of the country—for example, the Yucatán, Michoacan, Guerrero, Chihuahua, Sonora, and Veracruz. The first thing you see upon entering this converted two-story town house is a mouth-watering display of homemade cream-pudding desserts. Atmosphere is casual yet classy in the intimate colonial-decor dining rooms. The menu varies daily, with a selection of appetizers, soups, and regional dishes such as chicken mole, assorted *chiles rellenos,* grilled pork chops, and *albóndigas en chile chipotle* (meatballs in chile chipotle sauce). There is also a set house specialty for each day of the week. Whichever day it is, start with a plate of *botanas* (hors d'oeuvres) and try the refreshing *aguas* (fresh-fruit and seed juices) made with *chía* (sage seeds), *jamaica* (hibiscus), or *tamarindo.* The *café de olla* (cinnamon-flavored coffee boiled in a clay pot and sweetened with brown sugar) is perfect after dessert. Ask for a table in the downstairs dining salon; it's the prettiest. ✗ *Liverpool 166, Zona Rosa,* ☎ *5/207–2732 or 5/525–8128. Reservations advised. AE, DC, MC, V. Closed Sun. and holidays.*

$$–$$$ **Las Palomas.** In a residential neighborhood not far from the Zona Rosa, this congenial meeting place is delightfully decorated with colorful hand-painted tiles, wrought-iron grillwork, flowers, and art. Socialite-owner-hostess Lila Briones attends loyal customers, who even include some of her rival restaurateurs and chefs, as well as noted journalists and authors. Lila is faithful to the recipes she inherited from the days of her great-grandmother's country hacienda, such as homemade *tinga* (shreds of beef in a sauce of various chilies) and sensational homemade green chicken mole. Other specialties include huachinango in homemade avocado sauce, *cochinita píbil* (baby pig Yucatecan style), and *bacalao* (codfish Spanish style, with red and green bell peppers). Among desserts: homemade rice pudding and *natillas* (Spanish-style custards). A folkloric trio and guitarist-balladeer add to the milieu. ✗ *Cozumel 37, Col. Roma,* ☎ *5/553–7084. Reservations advised. AE, MC, V.*

$$ **Focolare.** Among the prettiest eateries in the Zona Rosa, Focolare serves fine Mexican regional fare on a covered patio with a fountain in the middle and a blue-tile staircase leading to the second floor. This is a great breakfast spot. The buffet caters to the Mexican taste (red-hot chili first thing in the morning), but it also has less violent ways to start the day. If you wanted to do a gastronomic tour of Mexico, Focolare would be a good guide to the places that should be given priority. From Puerto Angel, for example, comes a delicious *calamares* dish in a delicate mandarin sauce. There's a strong representation of dishes from the Yucatán, such as *conchinita píbil,* and several varieties of mole from Oaxaca. Service is attentive. On Friday and Saturday nights, a *Fiesta Mexicana* features a live mariachi group, local *ranchero* singers, and a huge hot and cold buffet, topped off by a simulated cock fight (the roosters are not armed with razors). Large tour groups invade the place, but the show is lots of fun. There's a cover charge of $8 Friday and $7 Saturday. On Sunday, a healthy brunch is accompanied by a live band. ✗ *Hamburgo 87, Zona Rosa,* ☎ *5/207–8257. Reservations required Fri. and Sat. nights. AE, DC, MC, V.*

$$ **Fonda del Recuerdo.** A popular family restaurant, the *fonda* (inn) also has a solid reputation among tourists. Every day from 2 to 10, five different marimba groups from Veracruz provide music that creates a festive atmosphere. The place made its name with its fish and seafood platters from the Gulf state of Veracruz and the house special is *huachinango a la Veracruzano* (a whole sea bass swimming in a succulent sauce made of tomato, chopped onion, olives, and mild spices). Sharing its fame is the *torito*, a drink made from tequila and exotic tropical fruit juices (be careful: It really packs a punch). The rest of the traditional Mexican menu features meat and *antojitos* (Mexican appetizers). Meat from the kitchen's own *parillas* (grills) is always first-rate. The portions here are huge, but if you have room for dessert, the *crepas de cajeta al tequila* (crepes of caramelized milk with tequila) are worth trying. ✕ *Bahía de las Palmas 39, Col. Anzures,* ☎ *5/260–1290. Reservations advised. AE, DC, MC, V.*

$$ Fonda Don Chón. This simple family-style restaurant, deep in downtown, is famed for its indigenous Mexican dishes. Fonda Don Chón is for the adventurous, although some pre-Hispanic delicacies, such as corn fungus, are featured at some of Mexico's most elegant restaurants. A knowledge of zoology, Spanish, and Nahuatl helps in deciphering the menu, which changes daily. A gamut of products from throughout the republic are prepared fresh every day, and no processed foods are used. *Escamoles de hormiga* (red ant roe), 97% protein, is known as the "caviar of Mexico" for both its deliciousness and its costliness. Among the exotic entrées are armadillo in sesame mole sauce, iguana soup, and snake (boa or rattle) steak. More traditional specialties include *mixiote de carnero* (barbecued lamb in maguey leaves). The coconut cake dessert is excellent, and live music adds to the atmosphere. ✕ *Regina 159, Col. Centro,* ☎ *5/522–1070. No reservations. AE, MC, V.* ☉ *Daily 10 AM–7 PM.*

$$ Las Mercedes. Las Mercedes specializes in traditional Mexican food, with some ancient recipes that have stood the test of time. The decor is modern rustic, with furniture from Michoacán and a pleasant terracotta and coffee color scheme. Both the *sopa de fideos con albondiguitas* (pasta soup with little meatballs) and the *sopa de tortilla* (tortilla soup) make excellent starters. The *lomo de cerdo en salsa de huitlacoche* (pork in a sauce made from the corn fungus) is exceptional. The *plato Mercedes,* a sampling of both the old and the new Mexican cuisines, is highly recommended. Las Mercedes is a good choice for breakfast, when such delicacies as eggs with shrimp, oysters, and asparagus are offered. ✕ *Río Guadalquivir 91, Col. Cuauhtemoc,* ☎ *5/208–7369. Reservations accepted. AE, DC, MC, V. Closed Sat.*

$$ Los Girasoles. This new downtown "in" spot, which has already been staked out by the local yuppies and trendsetters, is owned by two prominent Mexico City society columnists who know how to get their names in print. Los Girasoles (sunflowers) is located on a lovely old square in a restored three-story colonial home and features nouvelle Mexican cuisine—light and tasty and very innovative. Dishes gleaned from the best local cooking masters are offered. For example, the traditional Mexican bean soup is dressed up with a pinch of chile and noodles. Meat, fish, and seafood dishes are blended with exotic herbs and spices; desserts pay homage to the fine fruits found in the country with such creations as *guanabana* and *zapote* mousse. One of the nicest places for dining is the covered terrace outdoors on the street level. ✕ *Plaza Manuel Tolsa on Calle Tacuba,* ☎ *5/510–0630 and 5/510–3281. Reservations recommended for lunch. AE, DC, MC, V.*

$ Café de Tacuba. This typically Mexican restaurant is an essential breakfast, lunch, dinner, or snack stop for those exploring the city's downtown historic district. Since it opened in 1912, in a section of an old convent, it has charmed locals and visitors with its warm colonial decor and traditional Mexican fare. In the rear dining room, huge

18th-century oil paintings depict the historic invention of *mole poblano,* a complex sauce including a variety of chilies and chocolate, created by the nuns in the Santa Rosa Convent of Puebla. Of course, mole poblano is on the menu here, as are delicious tamales made fresh every morning—Oaxaca style with black mole and wrapped in banana leaf, or a fluffy Mexico City version. Enjoy pastries galore. ✕ *Tacuba 28, Col. Centro,* ☎ *5/518–4950. No reservations. MC, V.*

$ **Café la Blanca.** Just west of the Zócalo, this high-ceilinged, turn-of-the-century restaurant is decorated with a series of huge blown-up photos of downtown in the early 1900s. The place is immense—as is the menu, which includes all the favorite Mexican dishes (try the enchiladas *gratinadas,* with green sauce and topped with melted cheese), a selection of tamales, and such staples as broiled chicken, roasted meat, and fish. Meals are served with a platter of bread and pastries; you're charged for whatever you help yourself to. The clientele, primarily local, gathers here for breakfast (from 7 AM on), lunch, and dinner (until 11 PM); the menu, unlike the waiters, is bilingual. ✕ *Cinco de Mayo 40,* ☎ *5/510–0399. No reservations. No credit cards.*

$ **Las Cazuelas.** Traditional Mexican cooking at its best is on tap at one
★ of the most famous of the capital's fondas. The open-view kitchens are kept immaculately clean, and diners often take a peek at the bubbling mole and *pipián* sauces (the latter a *picante,* sesame-flavored Yucatecan specialty) before being seated. The large dining area is brightened by hand-painted chairs from Michoacán and by the crisp green-and-white table linen. Ideal Mexican appetizers to share are *entremés ranchero de carnitas* (pork morsels in red sauce). The tortilla soup, a chicken broth filled with strips of baked tortillas, a dash of *chile pasilla,* and bits of cheese, makes another excellent starter. Main courses center on various moles or pipián sauces with pork or chicken. Finish with a *café de olla* (cinammon coffee in a clay mug) and a domestic brandy, then enjoy some fine mariachi singing from a talented and professional group (from 4 to 6 daily). ✕ *San Antonio 143, corner of Illinois, Col. Napoles,* ☎ *5/563–4118. No reservations. AE, MC, V.*

Spanish

$$$ **El Parador de Manolo.** A period two-story house was remodeled into this Spanish restaurant in fashionable Polanco. The Bar Porrón on the ground floor serves a variety of Spanish tapas, including an excellent prawn mix in a spicy sauce. In the brasserie-style dining room upstairs, choose from a Spanish menu or from the list of the chef's recommendations. The specially cured Serrano ham is possibly the best in the city, while the *calamares fritos* (fried squid) or the *crepas de flor de calabaza al gratin* (squash-blossom crepes) make other fine starters. Fish dishes are the most appealing for a main course, although the chateaubriand Parador for two (in a black, corn fungus sauce) is truly original. Desserts cater to the Spanish sweet tooth and are less notable. Wines are on display downstairs, as are the fresh fish of the day. ✕ *Presidente Masaryk 443, Polanco,* ☎ *5/281–4918 or 5/ 281–1118. Reservations accepted. AE, MC, V.*

$$ **Meson El Cid.** The Meson (tavern), which exudes Old Spain atmosphere, was founded about 15 years ago by a real Spanish emigré. During the week, classic dishes like paella, spring lamb, suckling baby pig, and Cornish hens with truffles keep customers happy, but on Saturday night this place really comes into its own with a unique dining experience: a medieval banquet. The fun unfolds with a procession of costumed waiters carrying huge trays of steaming hot viands. A caged cat (the grandson of the first feline to play this role, the waiters will

tell you) heads the parade as in olden days, when a king's food was tested for poisoning by letting a cat nose around it in first. (The cat was always smart enough not to touch the stuff if it was tampered with.) Entertainment is provided by a student singing group dressed in Spanish medieval capes and hats. ✗ *Humboldt 61, Col. Centro,* ☎ *5/521–1940 or 5/521–1661. Reservations advised for banquet. AE, DC, MC, V. No dinner Sun.*

LODGING

As might be expected of a megalopolis, Mexico City has 24,000 hotel rooms—enough to accommodate every taste and budget. Though the city is huge and spread out, most hotels are located within the districts listed below, which are not far from one another. Chapultepec Park and the swank Polanco neighborhood are on the west side of the city. Paseo de la Reforma runs from Chapultepec, northeast through "midtown," and intersects with Avenida Juárez at the beginning of the downtown area. Juárez becomes Avenida Madero, which continues east to the downtown historic district and its very core, the Zócalo. The Zona Rosa, replete with boutiques, cafés, restaurants, and night spots, is just south of Reforma in the western midtown area. Huge numbers of business travelers tend to fill up deluxe hotels during the week; some major hotels discount their weekend rates. You can expect hotels in the Expensive and Very Expensive categories to have purified water, air-conditioning, cable TV, radio, minibars, and extended (often 24-hour) room service. Note: Not yet ready for us to review when we went to press, the posh Hong Kong–owned Mandarin Hotel should be open in Polanco by the time you read this.

The following selection is organized by the major areas of the city and then by price.

CATEGORY	COST*
$$$$	over $160
$$$	$90–$160
$$	$40–$90
$	under $40

All prices are for a standard double room, excluding service charge and sales tax (10%).

Airport

$$$$ **The Continental Plaza Aeropuerto.** Formerly the Fiesta Americana, this deluxe hotel—with climate control, a satellite color TV, radio, minibar, and purified water in every room—is located over a short covered footbridge from the airport terminal, making it convenient for those who arrive late and have an early morning flight. For this convenience you pay a price. Discounted day rates (7–6) are available. ▦ *Benito Juárez International Airport, 15520,* ☎ *5/785–0505 or 800/88–CONTI, ℻ 5/785–0134. 600 rooms and suites. Restaurant, bar, coffee shop, pool, sauna, health club, nightclub, car rental, free parking. AE, DC, MC, V.*

Chapultepec Park and Polanco

$$$$ **Camino Real.** Super luxurious and immense—about the size of the
★ Pyramid of the Sun in Teotihuacan—this 8-acre city within a city hosts heads of state and celebrities as well as business and pleasure travelers. Impressive works of art embellishing the endless corridors and lounges

Mexico City Lodging

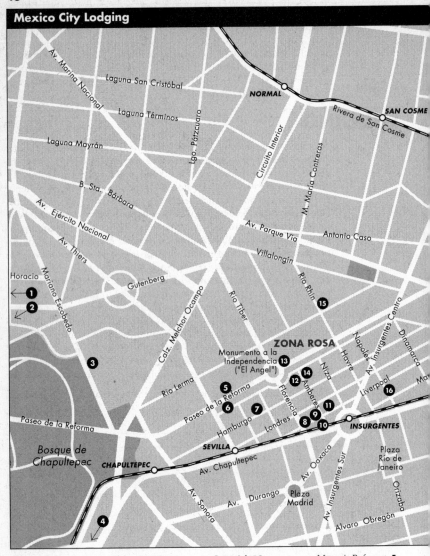

Aristos, **14**
Calinda Geneve, **11**
Camino Real, **3**
Catedral, **21**
Century, **10**
Continental Plaza
Aeropuerto, **24**

Fiesta Americana
Reforma, **18**
Four Seasons Mexico
City, **6**
Galería Plaza, **7**
Gran Hotel Howard
Johnson, **23**
Hotel de Cortés, **20**

Imperial, **19**
Krystal Rosa, **9**
Majestic, **22**
Marco Polo, **12**
María Cristina, **15**
María Isabel Shera-
ton, **13**

Marquis Reforma, **5**
Misión Park Plaza
México, **16**
Nikko México, **1**
Park Villa Motel, **4**
Plaza Florencia, **8**

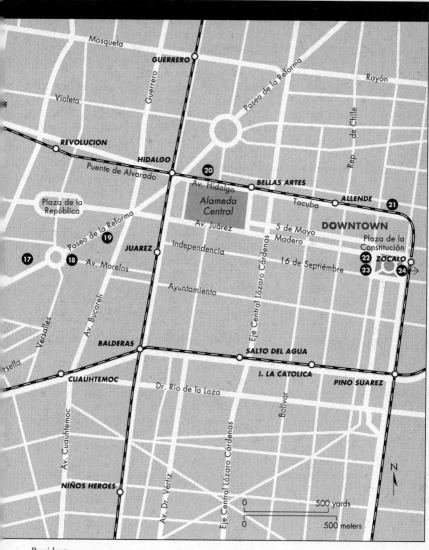

Presidente
Inter-Continental
México, **2**
Sevilla Palace, **17**

include Rufino Tamayo's mural of *Man Confronting the Universe,* and an imposing sculpture by Calder. The fifth-floor executive level features 100 extra-large guest rooms with special amenities. Fouquet's de Paris restaurant (*see* Dining, *above*) holds frequent culinary festivals, and the airy Azulejos features Mexican cuisine and special Sunday buffet brunches. The hotel just finished a complete refurbishing of all its rooms and public areas. The only drawback: Although it's near Chapultepec Park and Polanco, taxi travel to the hotel is almost always necessary. ☎ *Mariano Escobedo 700, 11590,* ☎ *5/203–2121 or 800/722–6466,* ᖴᴬˣ *5/250–6897 or 5/250–6723. 713 rooms and suites. 10 restaurants and bars, sports bar, pool, 4 tennis courts, health club, business services. AE, DC, MC, V.*

$$$$ **Presidente Inter-Continental México.** This 42-story hotel is, like its next-door neighbor, the Nikko, adjacent to Chapultepec Park and the posh Colonia Polanco. The dramatic five-story lobby is a hollow pyramid of balconies, with music presented daily at the lively lobby bar. The rooms are very spacious, and all have minibars and work areas. On clear days, those on the top two floors afford views of two snowcapped volcanoes, Popocatepetl and Iztaccihuatl. Renovations completed in 1994 included the installation of a gym on the 11th floor. There are a number of smart stores and no fewer than six eateries on the premises, including a branch of Maxim's of Paris (*see* Dining, *above*). ☎ *Campos Elíseos 218, 11560,* ☎ *5/327–7700, or 800/327–0200,* ᖴᴬˣ *5/327–7750. 659 rooms and suites. 5 restaurants, coffee shop, lobby lounge, exercise room, baby-sitting, parking. AE, DC, MC, V.*

$$$ **Nikko México.** Part of the Japanese Nikko chain, this glistening, 42-floor high rise occupies a prime position: It's in Polanco and adjacent to Chapultepec Park, just a five-minute walk to the Anthropology Museum. The executive floor has better rooms and extra facilities. Three top restaurants excel in their gastronomic specialties: Les Célébrités (French), Teppan Grill (Japanese), and El Jardín (Mexican). The elegant, cozy Shelty's Pub is also a big hit with locals. ☎ *Campos Elíseos 204, 11560,* ☎ *5/280–1111 or 800/NIKKO–US,* ᖴᴬˣ *5/280–9191. 771 rooms and suites. 3 restaurants, 2 bars, indoor pool, 3 tennis courts, health club, jogging, travel services. AE, DC, MC, V.*

$ **Park Villa Motel.** This two-story colonial hacienda, in a tranquil resi-
★ dential setting, is ideal for travelers with a car. Overlooking its pretty garden is the Restaurant Jardín del Corregidor, which serves authentic Spanish cuisine. If you are driving, you'll need to get directions to its secluded site near the southeast side of Chapultepec Park. The nearest subway stop is Juanacatlán. ☎ *Gómez Pedraza 68 (enter at Constituyentes), 11850,* ☎ *5/515–5245,* ᖴᴬˣ *5/515–4514. 45 rooms. Restaurant. No credit cards.*

Zona Rosa

★ **Galería Plaza.** Part of the Westin Hotel deluxe chain, this ultramodern property is conveniently located on a quiet street in the elegant Zona Rosa, ideal for shopping, nightlife, and dining out. Standard rooms are relatively small, but service and facilities are faultless. Rooms on the Executive Floor, where a special concierge desk provides personalized service and easy checkout, are larger. Other advantages include the 24-hour restaurant, a rooftop heated pool with sun deck, and a secure underground parking lot. ☎ *Hamburgo 195 at Varsovia, 06600,* ☎ *5/211–0014 or 800/228–3000,* ᖴᴬˣ *5/207–5867. 450 rooms and suites. Restaurant, lobby lounge, 24-hr room service, concierge, valet parking. AE, DC, MC, V.*

$$$$ **Aristos.** This 15-story hotel is on the busy Paseo de la Reforma, on the edge of the Zona Rosa, in front of the U.S. Embassy, and near the Mexican Stock Exchange. The rooms are well supplied with all the amenities and are attractively decorated in shades of peach and mauve, with brass and wood accents. The business center has a bilingual staff and a message service. ⌧ *Paseo de la Reforma 276, 06600,* ☎ *5/211–0112,* FAX *5/525–6783. 360 rooms and suites. Restaurant, beauty salon, sauna, exercise room, dance club, travel services. AE, DC, MC, V.*

$$$$ **Century.** This zebra-stripe high-rise stands out in the middle of the Zona Rosa. Rooms have round Roman-style marble baths, round beds, and semicircular private balconies. The rooftop Regine restaurant is romantic, and the street-level Petit Pois serves a good breakfast and luncheon buffet. All rooms have a private balcony. The large penthouse suites are superb. ⌧ *Liverpool 152, 06600,* ☎ *5/726–9911,* FAX *5/525–7475. 143 rooms. 2 restaurants, bar, pool, massage, sauna, dance club, baby-sitting, car rental, parking. AE, DC, MC, V.*

$$$$ **Krystal Rosa.** Part of the Mexican Krystal Hotel chain, this superbly run, recently remodeled high-rise hotel is centrally located in the heart of the Zona Rosa and has an excellent view of the city from the rooftop pool terrace. There's a chic lobby cocktail lounge, a bar with local entertainers, and a restaurant, Kama Kura, that serves superb Japanese cuisine. Three club floors feature VIP check-in and service, complimentary Continental buffet breakfast, and rooms with extra amenities. ⌧ *Liverpool 155, 06600,* ☎ *5/228–9928 or 800/231–9860. 300 rooms and suites. 2 restaurants, 2 bars, pool, business services. AE, DC, MC, V.*

$$$ **Marco Polo.** Posh and right in the center of the Zona Rosa, this inti-
★ mate yet ultramodern all-suite hotel offers the amenities and outstanding personalized service often associated with a small European property. All rooms feature climate control, a color cable TV, FM radio, minibar, and kitchenette. Rooms on the top floor facing north have excellent views of Paseo de la Reforma, and the U.S. Embassy is close by. In the street-level El Bistro de Marco Polo, you can listen to sophisticated jazz at lunch, over cocktails, and at dinner. ⌧ *Amberes 27, 06600,* ☎ *5/207–1893,* FAX *5/533–3727. 60 rooms and 4 penthouse suites with Jacuzzi and terrace. Restaurant, bar, business services, valet parking. AE, DC, MC, V.*

$$ **Calinda Geneve.** A Quality Inn, referred to locally as El Génova, this is an older but continually refurbished five-story hotel in the Zona Rosa. Traditional colonial-style carved wood chairs and tables furnish the pleasant lobby, and guest rooms are smallish but comfortable. The hotel's attraction as a gathering place has always been the Salón Jardín, a striking Belle Epoque gallery with a profusion of plants and a high stained-glass ceiling. It's a popular place for both guests and nonguests for meals and cocktails. The hotel's informal streetfront Café Jardín serves until 11 PM. ⌧ *Londres 130, 06600,* ☎ *5/211–0071 or 800/228–5151,* FAX *5/208–7422. 318 rooms. Restaurant, café, room service, coin laundry, travel services. AE, DC, MC, V.*

$$ **Misión Park Plaza México.** A part of the Misión chain, this very comfortable hotel is well placed for shopping and sightseeing. All rooms are air-conditioned and have a color TV with a VCR and movies courtesy of the house. ⌧ *Nápoles 62, 06600,* ☎ *5/533–0535,* FAX *5/533–1589. 50 rooms. Coffee shop, lobby lounge. AE, MC, V.*

$$ **Plaza Florencia.** This is a modern hotel on a busy avenue that borders the Zona Rosa. Rooms are well furnished, cheerfully decorated, and soundproofed against the location's heavy traffic noise; the higher floors have views of the Angel monument. Some large family suites are available. All rooms have air-conditioning, heat, a color TV, and a phone. ☎ *Florencia 61, 06600,* ☎ *5/211–0064,* FAX *5/511–1572. 130 rooms, 10 suites. Restaurant, bar, coffee shop. AE, DC, MC, V.*

Midtown and along the Reforma

$$$$ **Four Seasons Mexico City.** Inaugurated in 1994, this is one of the newest and—perhaps by definition—one of the most luxurious hotels in the capital. Surrounding a traditional courtyard with a fountain, the stately eight-story building was modeled after the 18th-century Iturbide Palace in downtown Mexico City. A spacious marble lobby is filled with huge bowls of fresh flowers and lovely European furnishings. Definitely geared to the business traveler, rooms have outlets for PCs; there's also a board room on the premises and a business center with computer and cellular phone rentals. Dining and drinking areas have original names: El Restaurant (for breakfast, lunch and dinner), El Bar, El Café, and El Salón. All Four Seasons amenities are featured. ☎ *Paseo de la Reforma 500, 06600,* ☎ *5/286–6020 or 800/332–3442,* FAX *5/286–5588. 240 rooms and suites. 2 restaurants, bar, pool, exercise deck, health club, business services. AE, DC, MC, V.*

$$$$ **María Isabel Sheraton.** Don Antenor Patiño, the Bolivian "Tin King," inaugurated this Mexico City classic in 1969 and named it after his granddaughter, socialite Isabel Goldsmith. The entire hotel was remodeled in 1992, but the glistening brown marble and Art Deco details in the lobby and other public areas remain. All guest and public rooms are impeccably maintained, but penthouse suites in the 22-story Tower Section are extra spacious and exceptionally luxurious. Location is prime: across from the Angel and the Zona Rosa, with Sanborns next door and the U.S. Embassy a half block away. ☎ *Paseo de la Reforma 325, 06500,* ☎ *5/207–3933 or 800/325–3535,* FAX *5/207–0684. 751 rooms and suites. 3 restaurants, bar, room service, pool, massage, sauna, health club, concierge floor, business services, valet parking. AE, DC, MC, V.*

$$$$ **Marquis Reforma.** One of Mexico City's newest and most luxurious,
★ this hotel is within walking distance of the Zona Rosa. It has a striking pink stone and curved glass facade, and its seventh-floor suites have picture-perfect views of Chapultepec Castle. The elegant lobby is done up in classic European style, with paintings, sculpture, and palatial furniture. Guest-room furniture and decor are Art Deco–inspired. The award-winning La Jolla Restaurant specializes in Belgian cuisine (*see* Dining, *above*). The fully staffed Corporate Center offers state-of-the-art computer services, and guest-room phones feature a second plug for computers with fax modem. ☎ *Paseo de la Reforma 465, 06500,* ☎ *5/211–3600 or 800/525–4800,* FAX *5/211–5561. 209 rooms, including 84 suites. 2 restaurants, bar, exercise room, business services, valet parking. AE, DC, MC, V.*

$$$ **Fiesta Americana Reforma.** This immense hotel is well organized for business travelers and large groups. It has an ample selection of bars, restaurants, and entertainment, including a popular nightclub, the Barbarella. There is not much Mexican atmosphere, but you can get a good tan on the sun deck, work out in the gym, listen to live jazz in the lobby bar, or eat in one of the three restaurants. All rooms are equipped with minibars. ☎ *Paseo de la Reforma 80, 06600,* ☎ *5/705–1515 or 800–FIESTA–1,* FAX *5/705–1313. 610 rooms. 3 restaurants, 2 bars, exercise room. AE, DC, MC, V.*

$$$ **Sevilla Palace.** This is a glistening modern showplace with five panoramic elevators to its 23 floors, a covered rooftop pool with Jacuzzi, health club, terraced rooftop lounge with a city view, restaurants, a top-floor supper club with entertainment, and convention halls with capacities of up to 1,000. It's well located near the Columbus traffic circle and attracts lots of tourists from Spain. ⌐ *Paseo de la Reforma 105, 06030,* ☎ *5/566–8877 or 800/732–9488,* FAX *5/535–3842 or 5/703–1521. 414 rooms. 2 restaurants, 3 bars, pool, hot tub, health club, nightclub, meeting rooms, valet parking. AE, DC, MC, V.*

$$ Imperial. Opened in 1990, the Imperial occupies a stately, turn-of-the-century European-style building right on the Reforma alongside the Columbus Monument. Quiet elegance and personal service are keynotes of this privately owned property. The hotel's Restaurant Gaudí has an understated, tony atmosphere and serves fine Continental cuisine with some Spanish selections. All rooms have safes, minibars, cable TV, and air-conditioning. ⌐ *Paseo de la Reforma 64, 06600,* ☎ *5/705–4011,* FAX *5/703–3122. 60 rooms, junior and master suites. Restaurant, bar, café, business services, meeting rooms, travel services. AE, DC, MC, V.*

$$ María Cristina. Full of Old World charm, this Spanish colonial-style
★ gem is a Mexico City classic. Impeccably maintained since it was built in 1937 (it was last refurbished January 1995), the peach-color building surrounds a delightful garden-courtyard that is the setting for its El Retiro bar and Río Nansa restaurant. Three tastefully decorated apartment-style master suites, complete with Jacuzzis, were added in the early '90s. All rooms have color cable TV, a minibar, and a safe. Located in a quiet residential setting near Sullivan Park, the hotel is just a block from the Paseo de la Reforma and close to the Zona Rosa. ⌐ *Río Lerma 31, 06500,* ☎ *5/566–9688,* FAX *5/566–9194. 156 rooms and suites. Room service, beauty salon, travel services, valet parking. DC, MC, V.*

Downtown

$$$ Hotel de Cortés. This delightful small hotel, operated by Best Western,
★ is housed in a colonial building (1780) that has been designated a national monument. A major renovation in 1990 gave luster and luxury to the colonial-decor rooms and added two lovely soundproofed suites overlooking Alameda Park across the busy street. A restaurant also views the park, and a friendly bar opens to the tree-shaded central courtyard and fountain, a lovely setting for tea or cocktails. The Franz Mayer Museum is just a block away, and it's an easy walk to Bellas Artes. Loyal guests make reservations many months in advance. ⌐ *Av. Hidalgo 85, 06000,* ☎ *5/518–2181 or 800/334–7234,* FAX *5/512–1863. 29 rooms and suites. Restaurant, bar. AE, DC, MC, V.*

$$ Gran Hotel Howard Johnson. The name was changed, but locals still refer to this establishment by its original (and more appropriate) name: Gran Hotel de la Ciudad de México. Ensconced in what was formerly a 19th-century department store, this older, more traditional hotel has contemporary rooms with all the amenities. Its central location—adjacent to the Zócalo and near the Templo Mayor—makes it the choice of serious sightseers. And its distinctive Belle Epoque lobby is worth a visit in its own right, with a striking stained-glass Tiffany dome, chandeliers, singing canaries in gilded cages, and 19th-century wrought-iron elevators. The fourth-floor Mirador breakfast restaurant overlooks the Zócalo. The Del Centro restaurant/bar is run by Delmónicos, one of Mexico City's best. The hotel has been undergoing a long-term, gradual refurbishing; be sure to request a renovated room and one that does not look out on a brick wall. ⌐ *16 de Septiembre 82, 06000,* ☎ *5/510–4040, or 800/654–2000,* FAX *5/512–2085. 125 rooms. 2 restaurants, bar, concierge, travel services, parking. AE, DC, MC, V.*

$$ Majestic. The atmospheric, colonial-style Hotel Majestic, built in 1937, is perfectly located for anyone interested in exploring the downtown historic district: It is right on the Zócalo at the corner of Madero. It's also perfect for viewing the Independence Day (September 16) celebrations, which draw hundreds of thousands of people to this square. In fact, many tourists book a room a year in advance of the festivities. Accommodations are comfortable, and the service is efficient and courteous. The seventh-floor dining room and terrace—which feature international and Mexican specialties—have marvelous panoramas of the entire Zócalo. The Sunday buffet (1–5 PM) features live Mexican music. Colorful handpainted ceramic tiles and potted plants decorate the public areas. ☎ *Madero 73, 06000,* ☎ *5/521–8600 or 800/528– 1234,* ☒ *5/512–6262. 85 rooms. Restaurant, air-conditioning, minibar. AE, DC, MC, V.*

$ Catedral. Located right behind the Cathedral and one block from the Templo Mayor, this older seven-story hotel in the heart of the downtown historic district has been completely refurbished inside and out. Public areas and guest rooms are now sparkling, with lots of marble and glass. Rooms are cheerful, and the service is friendly. Two new top-floor garden terraces overlooking historic rooftops and the cathedral are pleasant for cocktails and snacks. The hotel restaurant is excellent, and its El Retiro bar attracts a largely Mexican clientele to hear live Latin music. ☎ *Donceles 95, 06000,* ☎ *5/512–8581,* ☒ *5/ 512–4344. 116 rooms. Bar, coffee shop, room service, nightclub, dry cleaning, laundry service, travel services. AE, MC, V.*

THE ARTS AND NIGHTLIFE

Mexico City has a rich cultural scene and nightlife, with something for virtually every taste. Good places to check for current events are the Friday edition of *The News,* a daily English-language newspaper, and *Tiempo Libre,* a weekly magazine listing activities and events in Spanish. Both are available at newsstands.

The Arts

Dance

The world-renowned **Ballet Folklórico de México,** directed by Amalia Hernández, offers a stylized presentation of Mexican regional folk dances and is one of the most popular shows in Mexico. Performances are given on Sundays at 9:30 AM and Wednesdays at 8 PM at the beautiful Palacio de Bellas Artes (Palace of Fine Arts), at Av. Juarez and Eje Central Lazaro Cardenas; it's a treat to see the Tiffany glass curtain lowered. On Sunday evenings at 8, the troupe performs at the excellent Museum of Anthropology in Chapultapec Park. Call the Palace of Fine Arts box office, ☎ 5/709–3111, or TicketMaster, ☎ 5/325–9000, for information on prices and for reservations. Hotels and travel agencies can also secure tickets.

Not to be confused with the above is the **Ballet Folklórico Nacional de México,** directed and choreographed by Silvia Lozano. The company performs authentic regional folk dances regularly at the Teatro de la Ciudad, also known as the Mexico City Opera House (Donceles 36, ☎ 5/510–2197).

The **National Dance Theater,** a component of the National Auditorium complex in Chapultepec Park, and the **Dance Center** (Campos Elíseos 480, ☎ 5/520–2271) frequently sponsor modern dance performances.

Music

The primary venue for classical music is the **Palace of Fine Arts** (Av. Juárez and Eje Central Lázaro Cárdenas, ☎ 5/709–3111), which has a main auditorium and the smaller Manuel Ponce concert hall. The National Opera has two seasons at the Palace: January–March and August–October. The National Symphony Orchestra stages classic and modern pieces at the palace in the spring and fall.

The top concert hall, often touted as the best in Latin America, is **Ollin Yolitzli** (Periférico Sur 1541, ☎ 5/655–3611), which hosts the Mexico City Philharmonic several times a year. The State of Mexico Symphony performs at **Nezahualcoyotl Hall** in University City (☎ 5/655–6511). The **Teatro de la Ciudad** (Donceles 36, ☎ 5/510–2197) is also a popular site for a number of musical programs, both classical and popular, year-round.

Theater

An amateur theater group called the **Theater Workshop** puts on plays in English at various times of the year at the Universidad de las Americas (University of the Americas), Puebla 223, within walking distance of the Zona Rosa; check *The News* for listings. Visitors with a grasp of Spanish will find a much wider choice of theatrical entertainment, including recent Broadway hits. Prices are reasonable compared with stage productions of similar caliber in the United States. Though Mexico City has no central theater district, most theaters are within a 15- to 30-minute taxi ride from the major hotels. The top theaters include **Hidalgo** (Av. Hidalgo 23, ☎ 5/521–3859), **Insurgentes** (Av. Insurgentes Sur 1587, ☎ 5/660–2304; closed for remodeling at press time), and **Virginia Fabregas** (Velasquez de Leon 29, ☎ 5/535–5948). Theater tickets are available through TicketMaster (☎ 5/325–9000).

Nightlife

Night is the key word to understanding the timing of going out in Mexico City. People generally have cocktails at 7 or 8 PM, take in dinner and a show at 10 or 11, head to the discos at midnight, and then find a spot for a nightcap somewhere around 3 AM. The easiest way for the non-Spanish-speaking visitor to do this is on a nightclub tour (*see* Guided Tours, *in* Mexico City Essentials, *below*). However, those who set off on their own should have no trouble getting around. For starters, Niza and Florencia streets in the Zona Rosa are practically lined with nightclubs, bars, and discos that are especially lively on Friday and Saturday nights. The big hotels offer both bars and places to dance or be entertained, and they are frequented by locals. Outside of the Zona Rosa, Paseo de la Reforma, and Insurgentes Sur have the greatest concentration of night spots. Remember that the capital's high altitude makes liquor extremely potent, even jolting. Imported booze is very expensive, so you may want to stick with what the Mexicans order: tequila, rum, and *cerveza* (beer).

Dinner Theater

The splashiest shows are found in the big hotels and in Zona Rosa clubs. **El Patio** (Atenas 9, ☎ 5/520–4862) is a classic, old-style nightclub with tiny tables; it features Latin American and other international headliners. **El Gran Caruso** (Londres 25, on the edge of the Zona Rosa, ☎ 5/705–1457) is where the waiters sing arias between courses. In the Fiesta Americana Reforma, **Barbarella** (Paseo de la Reforma 80, ☎ 5/705–1515) features top international entertainers Thursday through Saturday nights. **La Veranda** (María Isabel Sheraton, Paseo de la Reforma 325, ☎ 5/207–3933, ext. 3718) serves dinner while international-caliber stars perform; afterward the dance floor is open.

Dancing

Dance emporiums in the capital run the gamut from cheek-to-cheek romantic to throbbing strobe lights and ear-splitting music. Most places have a cover charge, but it is rarely more than $10. **Lipstick** (Hotel Aristos, Paseo de la Reforma 274, ☎ 5/211–0112) is a long-time favorite where the action begins nightly at around 10. **Antillanos** (Francisco Pimentel 78, ☎ 5/592–0439), a short cab ride from the Zona Rosa, is *the* place to go for hot salsa music and dancing to well-known local bands. **Rockotitlan** (Insurgentes Sur 952-202, ☎ 5/687–7893), in the southern part of town, is a noisy, fun place and one of the most popular discos around.

Hotel Bars

The lobby bars in the **María Isabel Sheraton** (Reforma 325), **Presidente InterContinental México** (Campos Elíseos 218, Polanco), **Camino Real** (Mariano Escobedo 700), and **Galería Plaza** (Hamburgo 195, Zona Rosa) are all good bets for a sophisticated crowd and lively music, usually until long after midnight.

After Midnight

Gitanerías (Oaxaca 15, Col. Roma, ☎ 5/208–9066) continues to be an authentic Spanish flamenco nightclub (*tablao*). Now, in addition to a fiery flamenco there is also disco dancing to flamenco and Latin rhythms. Only light supper and drinks are served, and the first show starts at 11:30.

The traditional last stop for nocturnal Mexicans is **Plaza Garibaldi,** where exuberant mariachis gather to unwind after evening performances—by performing even more. They play in the square and inside the cantinas and clubs surrounding it; the better ones are **Guadalajara de Noche** (☎ 5/526–5521) and **Tenampa** (☎ 5/526–6176). If the extroverted singer-musicians focus on you, a friendly smile and a tip are expected. These places stay open Sunday through Thursday until 4 AM, and even later on Friday and Saturday.

EXCURSIONS

Basílica de Guadalupe and Teotihuacan; Tepotzotlán and Tula

Hugging the roads to the north of Mexico City are several of the country's most celebrated pre-Columbian and colonial monuments. The Basílica de Guadalupe, a church dedicated to Mexico's patron saint, and the pyramids of Teotihuacan make an easy day tour, as does the combination of the ex-convent (now a magnificent museum of the viceregal period) at Tepotzotlán and the ruins at Tula, also to the north but in a slightly different direction.

Exploring La Villa de Guadalupe

"La Villa"—more formally known as La Villa de Guadalupe, the site of the two Basilicas of the Virgin of Guadalupe—is Mexico's holiest shrine. Its importance derives from the miracle that the devout believe transpired here on December 12, 1531, when an Indian named Juan Diego received from the Virgin a cloak permanently imprinted with her image so he could prove to the priests that he had indeed had a holy vision. On that date each year, millions of pilgrims arrive, many crawling on their knees for the last few hundred meters, and praying for cures and other divine favors. The **Antigua Basílica** (Old Basilica) dates from 1536, although various additions were made during the intervening centuries; the altar was executed by sculptor Manuel Tolsá. The basilica now houses a museum of ex-votos (votive offerings) and popular religious art, painting, sculpture, and decorative and applied arts from the 15th to the 18th century.

Because the structure of the old church had weakened over the years and the building was no longer large enough, or safe enough, to accommodate all the worshipers, Pedro Ramírez Vázquez, the architect responsible for Mexico City's splendid National Museum of Anthropology, was commissioned to design a new shrine. In this case the architect's inspiration failed him, however: The Nueva Basílica, completed in 1976, is a grotesque and most unspiritual mass of steel, wood, resinous fibers, and polyethylene designs. It holds 10,000 people; the famous cloak is enshrined in its own altar and can be viewed from a moving sidewalk that passes below it.

Exploring Teotihuacan
Most tour buses to the ruins stop briefly in **Acolmán** to see the outstanding Gothic church and ex-convent, now a museum. The original Augustinian church (1539) is noteworthy for its vaulted roof and pointed towers; the ornate cloister and Plateresque facade, set off with candelabralike columns, were added a century later by the monks.

Teotihuacan occupies a monumental place in early Mexican history that is easily matched by the physical grandeur and scale of the site itself. It was, most likely, settled around 100 BC and reached its zenith about four centuries later. At the time of its decline in the 8th century, it was one of the largest cities in the world, with possibly as many as 200,000 people. It was set on fire and destroyed around AD 750 and over the years was completely buried. Its history and even its original name were lost.

Centuries later, the Aztecs arrived in the Valley of Mexico. Because the memory of the grandeur of the city in this area survived the passage of time, these new settlers named the site Teotihuacan, which meant "place where the gods were born!" It was here, the Aztecs believed, that the gods created the universe.

★ The major structures along the mile-long **Calzada de los Muertos** (Avenue of the Dead) are the **pyramids of the Sun and Moon; the Ciudadela** (Citadel) with its **Temple of Quetzalcóatl** (Plumed Serpent) and **Tlaloc** (the goggle-eyed Rain God); and the **palaces of Quetzalpapalotl** (Plumed Butterfly), **Caracoles Emplumados** (Plumed Conch Shells), and **Los Jaguares** (Jaguars).

Climbing one pyramid is probably enough for most people. The Pyramid of the Sun is the largest, standing 210 feet high, and affords a spectacular view of the entire area. Wear comfortable clothes (especially shoes) and bring sunscreen or a visored hat when you visit.

Many of the artifacts uncovered at Teotihuacan are on display at the Museum of Anthropology in Mexico City. The on-site museum contains only scale models and chronological charts. ☉ *Archaeological site: daily; on-site museum closed Mon.* ☛ *$4.25; free Sun.*

Seeing the ruins will take two to four hours, depending on how taken you are with the place (or when your tour bus leaves).

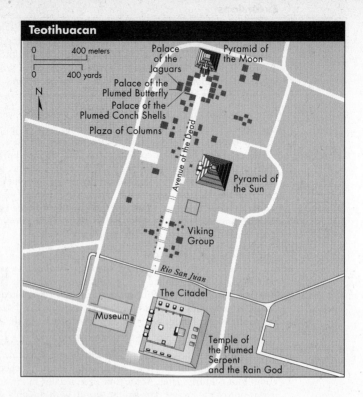

Teotihuacan

- Palace of the Jaguars
- Pyramid of the Moon
- Palace of the Plumed Butterfly
- Palace of the Plumed Conch Shells
- Plaza of Columns
- Avenue of the Dead
- Pyramid of the Sun
- Viking Group
- Río San Juan
- The Citadel
- Museum
- Temple of the Plumed Serpent and the Rain God

0   400 meters
0   400 yards

N

Exploring Tepotztlán

The **Jesuit church** and **school of San Francisco Javier** at Tepotzotlán rank among the masterpieces of Mexican Churrigueresque architecture. The unmitigated Baroque facade of the church (1682) is the first thing to catch the eye, but inside and out, every square inch has been worked over, like an overdressed Christmas tree. Note especially the gilded, bemirrored Chapel of the Virgin of Loreto.

Exploring Tula

Tula, capital of the Toltecs (its original name was Tollán), was founded in about AD 1000 and abandoned two centuries later. The 4.5-meter (15-foot) warrior statues (called *atlantes*), rather than the ruins themselves, give Tula its fame. These basalt figures tower over Pyramid B, their harsh geometric lines looking vaguely like totem poles. Crocodiles, jaguars, coyotes, and eagles are also depicted in the carvings and represent the various warrior orders of the Toltecs.

Visitor Information

There are no tourist offices in the area, but a good English-language guidebook to Teotihuacan is sold at the site.

Getting There

To reach La Villa de Guadalupe by car, take Paseo de la Reforma Norte until it forks into Calzada de Guadalupe, which leads directly to the shrine. Alternatively, you can take the No. 3 metro from downtown to the Basílica stop. Buses run every half hour from the Central de Autobuses del Norte to Teotihuacan, and the trip takes about one hour. In addition, many tour companies offer combination visits to the two sights.

To get to Tepotzotlán from Mexico City, follow Periférico Norte. After 41 kilometers (25 miles), you'll come to the exit for Tepotzotlán. Tula is about 8 kilometers (5 miles) north of Tepotzotlán. Buses to Tula/Tepotzotlán leave Mexico City every 20 minutes.

Xochimilco, Cuernavaca, and Tepoztlán

This excursion to the south and southwest of Mexico City begins in Xochimilco (So-chee-*meel*-co), famous for its floating gardens, where visitors can take rides in gondolalike boats and get a fleeting sense of pre-Hispanic Mexico City. Beyond Xochimilco, in the neighboring state of Morelos, lies Cuernavaca, a weekend retreat for wealthy chilangos (residents of Mexico City) and foreigners. The climate in Cuernavaca, just 85 kilometers (53 miles) and an altitude descent of almost 2,500 feet from Mexico City, changes dramatically to lush semitropical. The city is known for its many Spanish-language schools, some spectacular hotels and restaurants, the beautiful Borda Gardens, and Diego Rivera murals in the Palacio de Cortés (Palace of Cortés). An overnight stay is recommended. From Cuernavaca we suggest a detour to Tepoztlán, which features a 16th-century Dominican convent.

Exploring Xochimilco

When the first nomadic settlers arrived in the Valley of Mexico, they found an enormous lake. As the years went by and their population grew, the land was not sufficient to satisfy their agricultural needs. They solved the problem by devising a system of *chinampas* (floating gardens), rectangular structures something like barges, which they filled with reeds, branches, and mud. They planted them with willows, whose roots anchored the floating gardens to the lake bed, making a labyrinth of small islands and canals on which they carried the flowers and produce grown on the chinampas to market.

Today Xochimilco is the only place in Mexico where the gardens still exist. Go on a Saturday, when the *tianguis* (market) is most active, or on a Sunday. (Note that Xochimilco is a popular destination for families on Sundays.) On weekdays the place is practically deserted, so it loses much of its charm. Hire a *trajinera* (flower-covered launch); an arch over each launch spells out its name—usually a diminutive for a woman's name—in flowers. As you sail through the canals, you'll pass mariachis and women selling tacos from other launches.

Exploring Cuernavaca

Downtown Cuernavaca is fairly compact. The most attractive sights are the mansions of the wealthy weekenders set in the hills on the edge of town, but you must be a guest to get in. There are, however, a number of spectacular hotels and restaurants with equally spectacular gardens—several of them housed in restored colonial mansions and even haciendas—where visitors can get a sampling of life behind the high stone walls. The major sights are located near the main square. The **Palacio de Cortés**—Cortés's palace-cum-fortress—now houses the **Museo de Cuauhnáhuac** (Museum of Cuauhnáhuac, the Indian name for Cuernavaca), which focuses on Mexican history before and after the conquest. On permanent exhibit is a collection of some of Diego Rivera's finest murals, which, like those of Mexico City's National Palace, dramatize the history and the horrors of the conquest, colonialism, and the revolution. The beautiful and spacious **Jardín Borda** (Borda Gardens), three blocks west, was designed in the late 18th century by one member of the Borda family (rich miners of French extraction) for one of his relatives; Maximilian and Carlotta visited the gardens frequently, and novelist Malcolm Lowry turned them into a sinister symbol in *Under the Volcano*. Opposite the gardens is the **Catedral de la Asunción,** an architecturally eclectic structure noteworthy for its 17th-century Japanese wall paintings. Diagonally opposite the cathedral is the **Palacio Municipal;** the paintings inside depict life in the city before the Spaniards. Also near the square is the **Robert Brady Museum** (Netzahuacoyotl 4, ☎ 73/18–8554), a delightful restored colonial mansion housing an eclectic collection of art and artifacts assembled by Brady, an artist, antiquarian, and decorator who hailed from Fort Dodge, Iowa. The museum is open Tuesday through Sunday 10 to 6.

DINING AND LODGING

Cuernavaca has some of the finest hotels and restaurants in all Mexico. Indeed, many people come here just for a sumptuous, relaxed meal in a glorious garden setting. Many Cuernavaca hostelries began as restaurants and added on rooms to satisfy clients who felt too lazy to drive back to Mexico City after a heavy meal. Among the most spectacular—and pricier—places, both for dining and lodging, is **Las Mañanitas** (Ricardo Linares 107, ☎ 73/14–14–66), near the center of town, with 23 exquisite suites and gardens inhabited by flamingos, peacocks, and cranes. About 15 minutes south of town, the home of the late heiress Barbara Hutton was converted into a restaurant, set amidst formal Japanese gardens and contemplation pools; more recently, the posh **Camino Real Sumiya** (take Civac exit on Acapulco Hwy., ☎ 73/19–02–04) was built on the property. Other lodging alternatives are the **Hacienda de Cortes** (☎ 73/15–88–44) in the nearby town of Atlacomulco, a hacienda that dates from the 16th century and actually once belonged to *El Conquistador* himself. A good place just for dining is the **Vienes** (Lerdo de Tejada 302, ☎ 73/18–40–44), one block west of the main plaza. It serves excellent Austrian and Hungarian dishes and irresistible pastries. **La Strada** (Salazar 3, ☎ 73/18–60–85), just around the corner from the Palace of Cortés, offers Italian food on a colonial, candlelit patio.

Exploring Tepoztlán

This tiny village is best known for its pyramid-on-the-mount and for the dances held here during Carnival, when celebrants don bright masks depicting birds, animals, and Christian figures. Anthropologists Robert Redfield and Oscar Lewis both did fieldwork here in the 1950s. The landmark is the multibuttressed Ex-Convent (1559), with fine paneled doors adorned with Indian motifs.

Visitor Information

The **Morelos State Tourist Office** in Cuernavaca is located in Colonia Las Palmas. *Morelos Sur 802,* ☎ 73/14–38–60. ☺ *Weekdays 9–8.*

Getting There

To reach Xochimilco by car, take Periférico Sur to the extension of División del Norte; an alternate route is from Calzada de Tlalpán to Calzada México Xochimilco and then Calzada Guadalupe Ramírez. Xochimilco is 21 kilometers (13 miles) from the Zócalo in Mexico City; the trip should take between 45 minutes and 1 hour, depending on traffic. If Xochimilco is your final destination, you are probably better off taking a taxi. By public transportation, take metro line No. 2 to Taxqueña and then any bus marked Xochimilco.

To continue south by car, return to Periférico Sur, turn left (south) on Viaducto Tlalpán, and watch for signs to Cuernavaca in about a half hour. The *cuota,* or toll road (Rte. 95D), costs about U.S. $7 but is much faster than the *carretera libre,* or free road (Rte. 95). On Route 95D, it will take you about 1½ hours to cover 85 kilometers (53 miles).

Tepoztlán is 26 kilometers (16 miles) east of Cuernavaca via Route 95D. Buses also run every 20 minutes.

Cholula, Puebla, and Tlaxcala

This excursion takes you southeast of Mexico City to Puebla, a well-preserved colonial city and once the center of the Spanish tile industry. Eight kilometers (5 miles) to the west is Cholula, a sacred spot in ancient Mexico and home to an important pyramid and scores of churches. You can detour along the way to see the volcanoes, Popocatepetl (poh-poh-kah-*teh*-petal) and Iztaccihuatl (eez-tah-*see*-waddle), up close. On your return to the capital, leave time—an entire day would be best—to visit the city of Tlaxcala, with its rare church and former convent, and an amazing archaeological site nearby.

Exploring Cholula

As you leave Mexico City—if the smog is not too thick—the **volcanoes** will be visible to the south. "Popo" is 5,455 meters (17,887 feet) high. To see it up close you should exit at either of the main highways at Chalco and follow the signs to the Parque Nacional. Popo last erupted in 1802, but rumblings and bubblings in late 1994 were sufficiently strong to cause nearby villages to be temporarily evacuated. The legend states that Popocatepetl, an Aztec warrior, had been sent by the emperor—father of his beloved Iztacchuatl—to bring back the head of a feared enemy in order to win Iztacchuatl's hand. He returned triumphantly only to find that Iztacchuatl had killed herself, believing him dead. The grief-stricken Popo laid out her body on a small knoll and lit an eternal torch that he watches over, kneeling. Each of the four peaks composing the volcano is named after different parts of her body—hence its nickname "The Sleeping Lady." (In addition, the silhouette of the volcano resembles the figure of a reclining woman.) Climbing Popo or "Izta" is for serious mountaineers, but the park, a verdant pine forest, makes a good spot for a picnic.

Most of the 40 colonial churches in Cholula are in poor condition, but 6½ kilometers (4 miles) south of town, in **San Francisco Acatepec,** is one of the two most stunning and well-preserved churches in the country. Completely covered with Puebla tiles, it has been called the most ornate Poblano Rococo facade in Mexico. Equally unusual is the interior of the church in **Santa María Tonantzintla,** 3 kilometers (2 miles) toward Cholula. Its polychrome wood-and-stucco carvings—inset columns, altarpieces, and the main archway—are the epitome of Churrigueresque. Set off by ornate gold-leaf figures of vegetal forms, angels, and saints, the carvings were done by native craftsmen.

Closer to town, the **Great Pyramid** was the centerpiece of a Toltec and then Aztec religious center and consists of seven superimposed structures connected by tunnels and stairways. The Spaniards, as they often did, built a chapel to **Nuestra Señora de los Remedios** (Our Lady of the Remedies) on top of it. Behind the pyramid is a vast temple complex of 43 acres, once dedicated to Quetzalcóatl. ☛ *About $5.* ☉ *Daily 10–5.*

Exploring Puebla

Maize was first cultivated in the Tehuacán Valley; later, the region was a crossroads for many ancient Mesoamerican cultures, including the Olmecs and Totonacs. The town of Puebla is notable for its idiosyncratic Baroque structures, which are built of red brick, gray stone, white stucco, and the beautiful Talavera tiles produced from local clay.

The Battle of May 5, 1862—resulting in a short-lived victory against French invaders—took place just north of town. The national holiday, Cinco de Mayo, is celebrated yearly on that date in its honor.

While in Puebla, don't miss the **cathedral.** Onyx, marble, and gold adorn the high altar, designed by Mexico's most illustrious colonial architect, Manuel Tolsá. In addition, the **Iglesia de Santo Domingo** (Santo Domingo Church) is especially famous for its Rosary Chapel, where almost every centimeter of the walls, ceilings, and altar are covered with gilded carvings and sculptures. The **Amparo Museum,** filled with the private collection of pre-Hispanic and colonial art of Mexican banker and philanthropist Manuel Espinoza Yglesias, is one of the most beautiful in Mexico.

The colonial **Convento de Santa Rosa,** now a museum of native crafts, contains the intricately tiled kitchen where Puebla's renowned mole sauce was believed to have been invented by the nuns as a surprise for their demanding gourmet bishop. Puebla is also famous for *camote,* a popular candy made from sweet potatoes and fruit. La Calle de las Dulces (Sweet Street) is lined with shops competing to sell a wide variety of freshly made camote.

DINING AND LODGING

Puebla is noted for its cuisine, and two of Mexico's most popular dishes were created here to celebrate special occasions. Already noted above, *mole* is a type of spicy sauce made with about 15 different ingredients; the best known mole includes bitter chocolate. Another Puebla specialty believed to have been initiated by the town's nuns, *chilies en nogada,* is a green poblano chili filled with ground meats, fruits, and nuts, covered with a white sauce of ground walnuts and cheese, and topped with red pomegranate seeds; the colors represent the red, green, and white of the Mexican flag. **Las Bodegas del Molino,** set in a 16th-century hacienda at the edge of town (Molino de San José del Puente, ☎ 22/49–03–99) is truly remarkable, both for the setting and the cuisine. A traditional favorite is **Fonda Santa Clara** (307 Calle 3 Poniente, ☎ 22/42–26–59), just a few blocks from the zócalo.

Fine hotels in Puebla include the 83-room **Camino Real** (7 Poniente 105, ☎ 22/32–89–83), located in a converted 16th-century convent two blocks from the zócalo; and **El Meson del Angel,** at the entrance to the city (Hermanos Serdan 807, ☎ 22/24–30–00). The **Royalty** on the main square (☎ 22/42–47–40) is small, well maintained, and considerably less expensive.

Exploring Tlaxcala

Capital of the tiny state of the same name, Tlaxcala (Tlas-*ca*-la) will interest both archaeology buffs and church lovers. The **monastery complex of San Francisco** (1537–40), which stands atop a hill one block from the handsome main square, was the first permanent Catholic edifice in the New World. The most unusual feature of the church is its wood ceiling beams, carved and gilded after the Moorish fashion. (Moorish, or *mudéjar,* architecture appeared in Mexico only during the very early years after the conquest, when Spain was still close enough in time to the Moorish occupation to be greatly influenced by Arabic architectural styles.) The austere convent, now a museum of history, boasts 18th-century religious paintings and a small collection of pre-Columbian pieces. Near the convent is a beautiful outdoor chapel whose symmetrical rear arches show Moorish and Gothic traces.

The **Palacio de Gobierno** (Government Palace), which occupies the north side of the zócalo, was built in about 1550. Inside are vivid epic murals of Tlaxcala before the conquest, painted in the 1960s by local artist Desiderio Hernández Xochitiotzin.

About 1 kilometer (less than a mile) west of Tlaxcala is the large, ornate **Sanctuary of Ocotlán.** It dates from the 18th century and was built on the site where a miracle was believed to have been performed by the Virgin. (In 1541, during a severe drought, she answered the prayers of an Indian by causing water to flow from the ground.) Noteworthy sights here are the Churrigueresque, white-plaster facade, which conjures up images of a wedding cake; the two Poblano (red-tile) towers; and, inside, the brilliantly painted and gilded Camarín de la Virgen (the Virgin's Dressing Room).

About 22 kilometers (13 miles) southwest of Tlaxcala is the archaeological site of **Cacaxtla.** Accidentally discovered in 1975, it contains a breathtaking series of frescoes, dating back to about AD 100, which depict scenes of a fierce battle between Maya and Central Mexican warriors.

Visitor Information
The **Puebla Tourist Office** can supply information. *5 Oriente 3,* ☎ *22/ 46–12–85.* ⊙ *Mon.–Sat. 9:30–8:30, Sun. 9:30–2.*

Getting There
From Mexico City, head east toward the airport and turn onto Calzada Zaragoza, the last wide boulevard before arriving at the airport; it becomes the Puebla Highway at the toll booth. Route 190D is the toll road straight to Puebla; Route 150 is the more scenic free road (the trip on the former takes about 1½ hours, on the latter approximately 3 hours). To go directly to Cholula, take the exit at San Martín Texmelucan and follow the signs. From Puebla, Cholula is a couple of kilometers west. To stop at the volcanoes, take the free road 33 kilometers (20 miles) to Chalco. From there it is 4 kilometers (2½ miles) to the Amecameca-Chalco sign, from which you continue 22 kilometers (13½ miles) on Route 115 to Amecameca.

Toluca and Valle de Bravo

This excursion to the west of Mexico City encompasses Toluca, capital of the state of Mexico and renowned for its Friday market, and Valle de Bravo, a lovely lakeside village popular with vacationing chilangos; it's often called Mexico's Switzerland because of its green, hilly setting. We suggest a brief stop en route at Desierto de los Leones, a forested national park whose centerpiece is an intriguing Carmelite monastery.

Exploring Toluca
On the way to Toluca, the **Desierto de los Leones** is a 5,000-acre national park. There are several walking trails throughout the pine forest. The focal point is the ruined 17th-century Carmelite exmonastery, strangely isolated amid an abundance of greenery. The park played a significant role during the War of Independence: At a spot called Las Cruces, the troops of Father Hidalgo trounced the Spaniards but resolved not to go on and attack Mexico City, an error that cost the insurgents 10 more years of fighting.

The capital of the state of Mexico, Toluca is an industrial town. Once famous only for its Friday market, Toluca now has much more to offer. Indians still come in from the surrounding villages on Friday to sell their produce and handicrafts at the huge municipal market, but it's hard to find any indigenous goods among the radios and CDs from Asia and the denim jackets and jeans from the United States. For local crafts, your best bet is the **Casa de Artesanías** on Paseo Tolloca. Two sights that shouldn't be missed are the **Jardín Botánico Cosmovitral** (Cosmovitral Botanical Garden), located in a remodeled, turn-of-the-century Art Nouveau structure that once housed the public market, and the **Museo de Artes Populares** (Museum of Popular Arts) in the Centro Cultural (Cultural Center).

TIME OUT If you fancy a picnic and don't mind a bit of a drive, make a 44-kilometer (27-mile) detour south of Toluca on Route 130 to **Nevado de Toluca Park.** At 4,691 meters (15,390 feet), the Nevado de Toluca, a now extinct volcano, is Mexico's fourth-largest mountain; on clear days its crater affords wonderful views of the valley. Picnickers might also enjoy a stop at **Parque de los Venados** (Park of the Deer).

Exploring Valle de Bravo

Valle de Bravo is colonial, with white-stucco houses trimmed with red balconies, tile roofs, and red-potted succulents cluttering the doorways. A hilly town that rises from the shores of Lake Avandaro and is surrounded by pines and mountains, Valle was founded in 1530 but has no historical monuments to speak of. It does, however, offer plenty of diversions: boating, waterskiing, and swimming in the lake and its waterfalls, and the more sociable pleasures of the Sunday market, where exceptionally good pottery is the draw. Although Valle is an enclave for artists and the wealthy, it attracts inhabitants who prefer a low profile.

Visitor Information

The **Mexico State Tourist Office** in Toluca is located at Edificio Plaza Toluca. *Av. 5 Lerdo de Tejada Pte. 101,* ☎ *721/4–10–99.* ☺ *Weekdays 9–3 and 5–8.*

Getting There

By car from Mexico City, follow Paseo de la Reforma all the way west. It eventually merges with the Carretera Libre at Toluca, and after 20 kilometers (12 miles), you'll see signs for the turnoff to the Desierto de los Leones; it's another 10 kilometers (6 miles) to the park. To go straight to Toluca, take the toll highway (expensive, but worth it); alternatively, buses depart Terminal Poniente every 20 minutes. There are two choices for getting to Valle de Bravo: the winding but scenic route, which you pick up 3 kilometers (2 miles) west of Zincantepec, or Route 15. The former takes twice as much time but is worth it if you have the leisure and enjoy unspoiled mountain scenery.

MEXICO CITY ESSENTIALS

Arriving and Departing

By Plane

AIRPORTS AND AIRLINES

All roads (and flights) lead to Mexico City. **Mexicana** (☎ 800/531–7921 in the U.S.; 5/325–0990 in Mexico City) has scheduled service from Chicago, Denver, Los Angeles, Miami, New York, Newark, Philadelphia, Pittsburgh, San Antonio, San Francisco, and San Jose. It has direct or connecting service at 30 locations throughout the country. **Aeromexico** (☎ 800/237–6639 in the U.S.; 5/228–9910 in Mexico City) serves Mexico City daily from Houston, Los Angeles, Miami, New Orleans, New York, Ontario (California), Phoenix, San Diego, Tampa, San Antonio, Tucson, and Washington, D.C. (as well as Tijuana). Aeromexico and Mexicana offer special low joint fares with certain U.S. airlines for connections from throughout the United States to their gateway cities. Aeromexico serves some 35 cities within Mexico and has three commuter subsidiaries that offer connections in Mexico City: **Aeromar,** based in Mexico City, flies to cities in central Mexico and on the Gulf of Mexico and Pacific coasts; **Aeroponiente** serves cities in the central and Pacific regions from its hub in Guadalajara; **Aerolitoral,** based in Monterrey, serves north-central cities as well as San Antonio, Tucson, and McAllen, Texas. **Taesa** (☎ 800/328–2372; 5/227–0700 in Mexico City), a fast-growing Mexican airline, has direct flights (but not nonstop) to Mexico City from Chicago, New York (JFK), and Oakland; directs and nonstops from Tijuana; and nonstops from Laredo, Texas.

U.S. carriers serving Mexico City include **American, Continental, Delta,** and **United. Air France** flies nonstop between Houston and Mexico City.

BETWEEN THE AIRPORT AND CENTER CITY

The spectacular new wing of Mexico City's *Aeropuerto Internacional Benito Juárez,* inaugurated in February 1994, is a high-tech, state-of-the-art elongation of the east end of the existing airport. It is occupied by American, Delta, and United airlines, as well as by all the major car-rental agencies; two banks and five currency exchanges (*casas de cambio*); Cirrus and Plus ATMs that disburse pesos to Visa and MasterCard holders; places to rent cellular phones; and lots of shops. A multilevel parking garage for 2,500 cars has also been added (short-term parking: about $1 per hour).

Porters and free carts are available in the baggage-retrieval areas. Banks and currency exchanges rotate their schedules to provide around-the-clock service. While dollar bills (not coins!) are acceptable at the airport, for convenience, and especially if you prefer a rapid departure from the airport, bring $50–$75 in pesos with you. The Mexico City Tourist Office and the Hotel Association both have stands in the arrival areas that can provide information and find visitors a room for the night, respectively.

If you're taking a taxi, be sure to purchase your ticket at one of the official airport taxi counters marked **Transportación Terrestre** (ground transportation), located in the baggage carousel areas as well as in the concourse area and curbside. (Avoid *pirata,* taxi drivers offering their services.) Government-controlled fares are based on which *colonia* (neighborhood) you are going to and are usually about $7 (per car, not per person) to most hotels. A 10% tip is customary for airport drivers, because they help with baggage. All major car-rental agencies have booths at both arrival areas, but renting a car is not recommended unless you are heading out of town or know Mexico City *very* well.

By Car

Throughout Mexico City, a new and *strictly enforced* law, *Un Día Sin Auto* (One Day Without a Car), applies to all private vehicles, including your own. One of several efforts to reduce smog and traffic congestion, this law prohibits every privately owned vehicle (including out-of-state, foreign, and even rental cars) from being used on one designated weekday. Cars in violation are inevitably impounded by the police. Expect a hefty fine as well. The weekday is specified by the last number or letter of the license plate. To find out which is your day to be without a car, contact the Mexican Government Tourism Office nearest you, and by all means plan your schedule accordingly.

By Train

The train system in Mexico is currently in a state of flux and badly in need of refurbishing. At press time, there was no nonstop train service from the U.S. border to Mexico City; bus service from Nuevo Laredo, across from Laredo, Texas, departed to Monterrey, where passengers could pick up the *Regiomontano* to Mexico City. For the most up-to-date information about schedules and prices, contact **Mexico by Train** (☎ and ℻ 210/725–3659 or 800/321–1699).

By Bus

Greyhound (☎ 800/231–2222) buses make connections to major U.S.-border cities, from which Mexican bus lines depart throughout the day. Reserved seating is available on first-class coaches, which are comfortable but not nearly as plush as the new intercity buses (*see below*). If you plan stopovers en route, make sure in advance that your ticket is written up accordingly. In Mexico, platform announcements are in Spanish only. From Matamoros, the trip to Mexico City takes about 14 hours; from Laredo, 15 hours; from Ciudad Juárez (El Paso), 24 hours; from Nogales, 40 hours; from Tijuana, 44 hours.

Getting Around

By Bus

WITHIN MEXICO CITY

The Mexico City bus system is used by millions of commuters daily because it's cheap—less than 8¢—and goes everywhere. Buses are packed during rush hours, so, as in all big cities, you should be wary of pickpockets. One of the principal bus routes runs along Paseo de la Reforma, Avenida Juárez, and Calle Madero. This west–east route connects Chapultepec Park with the *Zócalo* (main plaza). A southbound bus also may be taken along Avenida Insurgentes Sur to San Angel and University City, or northbound along Avenida Insurgentes Norte to the Guadalupe Basilica. Mexico City Tourism offices provide free bus-route maps.

BETWEEN CITIES

These days, buses are what's happening in Mexican intercity transport, with ultramodern, superdeluxe motorcoaches (which show U.S. movies and serve soft drinks and coffee) becoming the most popular way to travel. ETN (Enlaces Terrestres Nacionales, ☎ 5/368–0212 or 5/368–1188) serves cities to the west and northwest, such as Guadalajara, Morelia, Querétaro, Guanajuato, and Toluca. UNO (☎ 5/542–9628, 5/542–6654, or 5/512–1036) buses depart southeast to such destinations as Puebla, Oaxaca, Veracruz, Merida, and Cancún. Reserved-seat tickets can be purchased at Mexico City travel agencies.

Various other classes of intercity bus tickets can be purchased at **Mexicorama** (☎ 5/525–2050) in the Plaza del Angel arcade in Zona Rosa. Buses depart from four outlying stations (*terminales de autobuses*), where tickets can also be purchased: Central de Autobuses del Norte (going north), Cién Metros 4907; Central de Autobuses del Sur (going south), Taxqueña 1320; Central de Autobuses del Oriente, known as TAPO (going east), Ignacio Zaragoza 200; and Terminal de Autobuses del Poniente (going west), Río Tacubaya and Sur 122.

By Pesero

Originally six-passenger sedans, then vans, and now minibuses, *peseros* operate on a number of fixed routes and charge a flat rate (a peso once upon a time, hence the name). Peseros offer a good alternative to buses and taxis. Likely routes for tourists are along the city's major west–east axis (Chapultepec Park/Reforma/Avenida Juárez/Zócalo) and north–

south along Insurgentes, between the Guadalupe Basilica and San Angel/University City. Just stand on the curb, check the route sign on the oncoming pesero's windshield, hold out your hand, and it will pick you up. Tell the driver where to stop, or press the button by the door. Fares range from less than 20¢ for up to 5 kilometers (3 miles) to about 35¢ for more than 17 kilometers (10.5 miles).

By Subway

Transporting 5 million passengers daily, Mexico City's metro is one of the world's best, busiest, safest, and cheapest transportation systems— the fare is cheaper than for buses, 40 centavos (less than 8¢). The impeccably clean marble-and-onyx stations are brightly lit, and modern French-designed trains run quietly on rubber tires. Some stations, such as Insurgentes, are shopping centers. Even if you don't take a ride, visit the Zócalo station, which has large models of central Mexico City during three historic periods. The Bellas Artes station has replicas of archaeological treasures on exhibit, and inside the Pino Suárez station is a small Aztec pyramid, a surprise discovery during construction.

There are nine intersecting metro lines covering more than 160 kilometers (100 miles). It's a bit confusing: The number 8 had been previously assigned to a line whose construction was canceled because it would have destroyed unearthed Aztec ruins. Line 9 was subsequently built. Now number 8 (which completes the numerical sequence) designates the newest (9th) line, which was approaching completion at press time. Segments of lines 1 and 2 cover the most points of interest to tourists, including the Zona Rosa, Bellas Artes, and the Centro Histórico. At the southern edge of the city, the Taxqueña station (line 2) connects with the electric train (*tren eléctrico*) that continues south to Xochimilco. To the southeast, the new *Metro Ligero* from the Pantitlán station (lines 1, 5, and 9) heads east to Chalco in the state of Mexico. The various lines also serve all four bus stations, the Buenavista train station, and the airport; however, baggage is not allowed on board during rush hours. User-friendly, color-coded maps are available free at metro-station information desks and Mexico City tourism offices, and color-keyed signs and maps are posted all around.

Trains run frequently (about a minute apart) and are least crowded at night and between 10 AM and 4 PM. To reduce discomfort during crowded rush hours, regulations require men to ride separate cars from women and children. Hours vary somewhat according to the line, but service is essentially from 5 or 6 AM to 12:30 AM on weekdays; 6 AM to 1:30 AM on Saturday; 7 AM to 12:30 AM on Sunday and holidays.

By Taxi

The Mexico City variety comes in several colors, types, and sizes. Unmarked *turismo* sedans with hooded meters are usually stationed outside major hotels and in tourist areas; however, they are uneconomical for short trips. Their drivers are almost always English-speaking guides and can be hired for sightseeing on a daily or hourly basis (always negotiate the price in advance). *Sitio* (stationed) taxis operate out of stands, take radio calls, and are authorized to charge a small premium. Among these, **Servi-Taxis** (☎ 5/516–6020) and **Super-Taxis** (☎ 5/566–0077) offer 24-hour service. Taxis that cruise the streets range from sedans to Volkswagen Beetles—the latter with the front passenger seat removed for more legroom. (Some Beetles are green and called *ecologicos* because they use lead-free gas.) They are available either when the *libre* (free) light is on or when the windshield *libre* sign is displayed. Taxi meters are gradually being converted to the Nuevo Peso system; for meters that have not been

Mexico City Subways

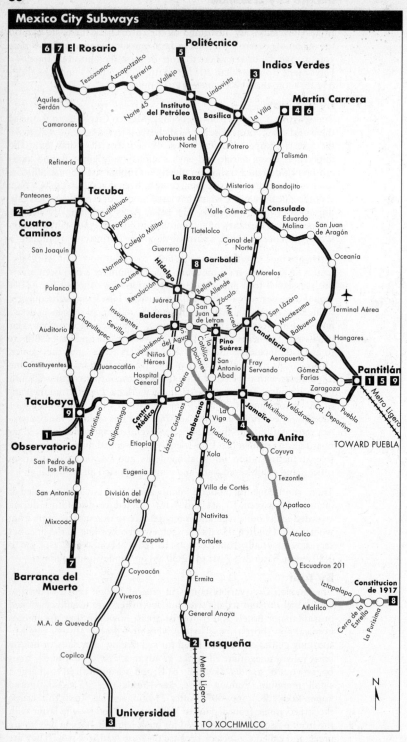

reprogrammed simply lop off three zeros to figure out the fare. Taxi drivers are authorized to charge 10% more at night, usually after 10. Taking a taxi in Mexico City is extremely inexpensive and tips are not expected unless you have luggage—then 10% is sufficient.

By Car

Millions of intrepid drivers brave Mexico City's streets every day and survive, but for out-of-towners the experience can be frazzling. One-way streets are confusing, rush-hour traffic is nightmarish, and parking places can be hard to come by. Police tow trucks haul away illegally parked vehicles, and the owner is heavily fined. As in any large city, getting your car back here is a byzantine process. LOCATEL (☎ 5/658–1111) is an efficient 24-hour service for tracing vehicles that are towed, stolen, or lost (in case you forgot where you parked). There's a chance an operator on duty may speak English, but the service is primarily in Spanish. Visitors can hire a chauffeur for their cars through a hotel concierge or travel service such as American Express. An automobile will come in handy if you plan to explore the nearby communities of Cuernavaca, Puebla, and Toluca (*see* Excursions, *above*), but don't forget the Day Without a Car program (*see* Arriving and Departing by Car, *above*).

Guided Tours

Mexico City has no dearth of tour operators eager to show you around the capital. You can book tours through the travel desk at most hotels or contact the following reputable tour operators, which can arrange half- and full-day tours or one involving a special interest: **American Express** (Paseo de la Reforma 234, ☎ 5/207–7132), **Mexico Travel Advisors** (**MTA**) (Génova 30, ☎ 5/525–7520), and **Gray Line** (Londres 166, ☎ 5/208–1163).

Orientation

The basic city tour ($27) lasts four hours and takes in the Zócalo, Palacio Nacional, Catedral Metropolitana, and Bosque de Chapultepec. A four-hour pyramid tour costs around $30 and covers the Basílica de Nuestra Señora de Guadalupe and the major ruins at Teotihuacán.

A wonderful way to see the downtown historic center is via the **Tren Turístico** (☎ 5/709–5589), which runs charming replicas of 1920s 20-passenger trolleys. The 30-minute narrated tour covers sights including the Zócalo, Colegio de San Idelfonso, Plaza de Santo Domingo, Plaza Manuel Tolsá (location of the Palacio de Minería and Museo Nacional de Arte), Plaza de la Santa Veracruz (Museo Franz Mayer), and the Palacio de Iturbide. The trolleys depart from and return to Pino Suárez 30 (three blocks south of the Zócalo at the corner of República de Salvador). You can get off at any stop you wish and board a subsequent trolley. Departures are every half hour from 10 AM to 5 PM, Tuesday–Sunday; English-language tours depart Tuesday and Sunday at 11 AM. Price: $3.

Special-Interest

CULTURAL

The seven-hour tour ($55) is run on Sunday mornings only and includes a performance of the folkloric dances at the Palacio de Bellas Artes, a gondola ride in the canals of Xochimilco's floating gardens, and a visit to the modern campus of the National University.

BULLFIGHTS

Also on Sundays only are trips to the bullring with a guide who will explain the finer points of this spectacle. This four-hour afternoon tour ($41) can usually be combined with the Ballet Folklórico-Xochimilco trip (*see above*).

These are among the most popular tours of Mexico City. The best are scheduled to last five hours and include transfers by private car rather than bus, dinner at an elegant restaurant (frequently Del Lago), a drink and a show at the Plaza Garibaldi, where mariachis play, and a nightcap at Gitanerías, which features Spanish flamenco performances. Nightlife tours begin at $78.

Walking

Huge as it is, Mexico City is not difficult to negotiate. Both the downtown Centro Histórico and the Zona Rosa are compact and easily walkable. In fact, the best way to see them is on foot.

Important Addresses and Numbers

Consulates and Embassies

The **U.S. Embassy** (Paseo de la Reforma 305, ☎ 5/211–0042) is open weekdays 8:30–5:30 but is closed for American and Mexican holidays; however, there's always a duty officer to take calls on holidays and after closing hours. The **Canadian Embassy** (Schiller 529, ☎ 5/254–3288) is open weekdays 9–4 and is closed for Canadian and Mexican holidays. The **British Embassy** (Lerma 71, ☎ 5/207–2449) is open weekdays 9:30–1 and 4–7.

Emergencies

POLICE

Dial 06 for police, Red Cross, ambulance, fire, or other emergency situations. If you are not able to reach an English-speaking operator, call the SECTUR hot line (*see* Visitor Information, *below*). For missing persons or cars, call LOCATEL (☎ 5/658–1111).

HOSPITAL

American British Cowdray Hospital (Calle Sur 137–201, corner of Observatorio, Col. las Américas; ☎ 5/272–8500 for emergencies, 516–8077 for the switchboard).

English-language Bookstores and Publications

Sanborns—a mini department-store chain with branches all over town, including two along Paseo de la Reforma, two in the Zona Rosa, and one downtown on Calle Madero in the House of Tiles—carries U.S. newspapers and magazines, paperbacks, and guide-books. The **American Book Store** at Calle Madero 25 has an even more extensive selection. *The News,* a daily English-language newspaper, available at hotels and on newsstands in the tourist areas, provides a summary of what is happening in Mexico and the rest of the world with cultural and entertainment listings and daily stock market reports.

Visitor Information

The **Mexico City Tourist Office** (Departamento de Turismo del Distrito Federal, or DDF) maintains information booths at both the international and domestic arrivals areas at the airport, at the Buenavista train station, and inside the Fonart handicraft store at Avenida Juárez 89. In town, information, brochures, and assistance are available in the lobby of its main office at Amberes 54 at the corner of Londres in the Zona Rosa. This office also provides information by phone with its INFO-TUR service (☎ 5/525–9380) from 9 AM to 9 PM daily. Operators are multilingual and have access to an extensive data bank. The **Secretariat of Tourism** (**SECTUR**) operates a 24-hour multilingual hot line that pro-

vides information on both Mexico City and the entire country (☎ 5/
250–0123, 5/250–0493, 5/250–0027, 5/250–0589, 5/250–0151, 5/
250–0292, or 5/250–0741). If the lines are busy, keep trying. You can
also call toll-free from anywhere in Mexico other than Mexico City (☎
91–800/9–03–92 or, from the U.S., 800/482–9832). These numbers
reach SECTUR's Tourist Information Center at Presidente Masaryk
172 (in Polanco), open weekdays, 8 AM–8 PM.

A new city-government entity, **Agencia del Ministerio Público para Tur-
istas,** has been set up exclusively to assist tourists with legal advice. It
has two offices: in the Zona Rosa (Florencia 20, corner of Hamburgo,
☎ 5/625–8761) and in the downtown historic center, near the Templo
Mayor (Argentina corner of San Idelfonso, ☎ 5/789–0833). A central
phone number for both (☎ 5/625–8618) answers 24 hours a day, 365
days a year. However, the service is inefficient and slow.

3 Baja California

Separated from mainland Mexico by the Gulf of California, Baja has a 2,000-mile-long coast that stretches from Tijuana to Los Cabos. The earliest of south-of-the-border retreats for the rich, reclusive, or rebellious against Prohibition, Baja still hosts isolated fishing enclaves and raucous watering holes; nature lovers come to watch the whales migrate in winter.

By Maribeth
Mellin

BAJA (LOWER) CALIFORNIA is a moonscaped finger of land dipping southward from the international boundary that divides California and Mexico. Separated from the Mexican mainland by the 240-kilometer- (150-mile-) wide Sea of Cortés (also called the Gulf of California), Baja extends about 1,300 kilometers (800 miles) into the Pacific. Despite their names, both Baja California and the Gulf of California are part of Mexico.

Although only 21 kilometers (13 miles) across at one point and 193 kilometers (120 miles) at its widest, Baja features one of the most varied and beautiful terrains on the planet. The peninsula's two coasts are separated by soaring mountain ranges, with one peak more than 10,000 feet high. Countless bays and coves with pristine beaches indent both shores, and islands big and small—many inhabited only by sea lions—grace the 3,364 kilometers (2,000 miles) of coastline. There are stretches of desert as empty as the Sahara where only cacti thrive and, in contrast, there are cultivated farmlands and vineyards.

Varied, too, is the demographic makeup of Baja. The border strip of northern Baja is densely populated. Tijuana, Mexico's fourth-largest city, is home to nearly 2 million people, making it more populous than the rest of the entire peninsula. La Paz, with about 170,000 residents, is the only city of any size south of Ensenada. The two towns at Los Cabos (The Capes) have yet to reach city status.

Baja is divided politically into two states—Baja California (also referred to as Baja Norte, or North Baja) and Baja California Sur (South)—at the 25th parallel, about 710 kilometers (440 miles) south of the border. Near the tip of the peninsula, a monument marks the spot where the Tropic of Cancer crosses the Transpeninsular Highway (Mexico Highway 1).

Native Baja Californians will tell you in no uncertain terms that they live in the first California, discovered by pirates, missionaries, and explorers long before the California of the United States. To this day, most of Baja's visitors have that same sense of adventure and the unquenchable desire to discover nature's holdouts. As there are cult films and cult books, perhaps there are cult travel destinations. If so, Baja heads the list. Long before the rich and famous stumbled upon the resorts of mainland Mexico, they found Baja. Back in the days of Prohibition, when Hollywood was new, the movie crowd learned the joy of having an international border so near. John Steinbeck brought attention to La Paz when he made it a setting for his novella *The Pearl*. Erle Stanley Gardner put aside his typewriter in Baja to battle marlin off Los Cabos. Bing Crosby put up some of the money for the first resort hotel in San José del Cabo, when the only way to get there was aboard a yacht or private plane.

Tijuana and Mexicali, the peninsula's border cities, are U.S. suburbs in a sense. Spanish and English are spoken interchangeably, and rock music blares in high-tech discos while mariachi bands blast their horns in corner bars. Manufacturers from throughout the world are setting up *maquiladoras* (factories) to make, among other things, computer chips and televisions.

Today, Tijuana is far more than the bawdy border town it became after Prohibition was enacted in the United States in the 1920s. Upscale shopping centers and gourmet restaurants line the Zona Río. The city has an international airport; a fine cultural center that presents professional music, dance, and theater groups from throughout the world; deluxe high-rise hotels; and a burgeoning population. Although its government would love Tijuana to become a major tourist destination and have visitors stay for days and even weeks, the city is still best known as a place for an intense, somewhat exotic, day-long adventure.

Mexicali, 185 kilometers (115 miles) east of Tijuana, is the capital of Baja California. **Tecate,** located between Tijuana and Mexicali, is a typical village whose main claim to fame is the Tecate brewery, where one of Mexico's most popular beers originates. **San Felipe,** about 200 kilometers (125 miles) south of Mexicali, is the northernmost town on the Sea of Cortés.

On Baja's Pacific Coast, travelers stream down the Transpeninsular Highway to **Rosarito Beach** and **Ensenada.** Before the 1,708-kilometer-long (1,059-mile) Transpeninsular Highway (Mexico Highway 1) was completed in 1973, traveling south of Ensenada was a rough, lonely, and somewhat dangerous adventure. After the paved, four-lane highway was built, thousands of people found their way south, and in 1974 Baja California Sur became Mexico's 30th state. Still, Highway 1 could hardly be called a freeway. It travels through some of the most desolate land imaginable.

From Ensenada, Highway 1 bypasses the Sierra de Juárez Mountains, where alpine meadows blossom in the Parque Nacional Constitución de 1857 east of Ensenada, as well as the Sierra San Pedro Martir range and Picacho del Diablo (Devil's Peak), which, at 10,126 feet, is Baja's highest point. Dirt roads, where even cars with four-wheel drive have trouble much of the year, lead from the highway to secluded ranches and campgrounds in these mountain ranges.

Scattered through these mountains and the Sierra del Gigante in Baja Sur are scores of monumental cave paintings, larger-than-life figures drawn with remarkable skill in red, blue, yellow, and black. They date back some 2,000 years, and no one can say who did them. The caves are difficult to reach and, sadly, tours are discouraged (to keep vandals away), but there are some excellent reproductions of the paintings on the walls of the Twin Dolphin Resort in Los Cabos.

Every January through March thousands of great gray whales migrate 8,000 kilometers (6,000 miles) from the Bering Strait to the waters off southern Baja, where they give birth to their calves. For those few months travelers come from all over the world to **Guerrero Negro** and a few bays and lagoons farther south. On the edge of the Vizcaíno Desert, Guerrero Negro is not a hospitable place. If it weren't for the whales' breeding ground at Scammon's Lagoon and the salt flats between the desert and the sea, no one would be here.

Loreto is the site of the first mission in the Californias, established by Padre Eusebio Kino in 1683. Four Indian tribes—the Kikiwa, Cochimi, Cucapa, and Kumyaii—inhabited the barren lands of Baja at that time. It didn't take long for civilization's wars and diseases to nearly obliterate them. The first mission church, still in use, was built in Loreto by Padre Juan Salvatierra in 1697, and it was from here that Fray Junípero Serra began a chain of missions throughout Baja and what was then Alta California (now California, United States).

La Paz, 354 kilometers (220 miles) south of Loreto, was the first settlement established by the Spaniards in Baja. Hernán Cortés and his followers were drawn to La Paz by stories of the magnificent pearls

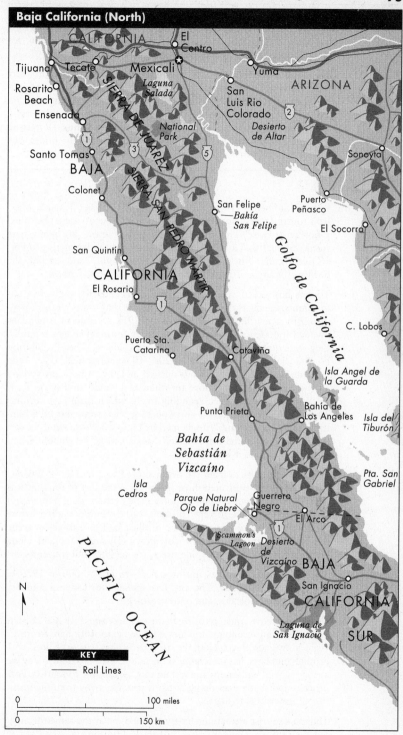

CALIFORNIA

El Centro

Tijuana
Tecate
Mexicali
Yuma
ARIZONA

Rosarito
Beach
Laguna
Salada
San
Luis Rio
Colorado

Ensenada
Desierto
de Altar

SIERRA DE JUAREZ

National
Park

Santo Tomas
BAJA

Sonoyta

Colonet
SIERRA SAN PEDRO MARTIR

San Felipe
—Bahía
San Felipe

Puerto
Peñasco

El Socorro

San Quintín

CALIFORNIA

El Rosario

Golfo de California

C. Lobos

Puerto Sta.
Catarina
Cataviña

Isla Angel de
la Guarda

Punta Prieta
Bahía de
Los Angeles
Isla del
Tiburón

Bahía de
Sebastián
Vizcaíno

Isla
Cedros

Pta. San
Gabriel

Parque Natural
Ojo de Liebre
Guerrero
Negro
El Arco

Scammon's
Lagoon
Desierto
de
Vizcaíno
BAJA

San Ignacio

CALIFORNIA

PACIFIC OCEAN

N

Laguna de
San Ignacio
SUR

KEY
—— Rail Lines

0
100 miles

0
150 km

and beautiful women to be found here. The Jesuits arrived in 1720, and a permanent settlement was established in 1811. Today, La Paz is a busy governmental center and sportfishing city, with plans for resorts, marinas, and increased tourism.

The southernmost tip of the peninsula is a natural rock archway where the Pacific Ocean and the Sea of Cortés merge. Marlin and sailfish leap high above the warm sea waters, glistening in the sun that shines 300 days a year, bringing fishermen and sun worshippers to Cabo San Lucas and San José del Cabo, called **Los Cabos.** Despite all the development that has taken place there, and its steep prices, Los Cabos remains a mysteriously natural hideaway.

TIJUANA

Just 29 kilometers (18 miles) south of San Diego lies Tijuana, Mexico's fourth-largest city. A metropolis, Tijuana can no longer be called a border "town." The official language is Spanish, but many here speak "Spanglish," a mix of Spanish and English. Tijuana's promoters like to call it "the most visited city in the world," and certainly the border crossing at Tijuana is the busiest in the United States.

Tijuana has served as a gigantic recreation center for southern Californians since the turn of the century. Before that it was a ranch, populated by a few hundred Mexicans. In 1911 a group of Americans invaded the area and attempted to set up an independent republic; they were quickly driven out by Mexican soldiers. When Prohibition hit the United States in the 1920s, Tijuana boomed. The Agua Caliente Racetrack and Casino opened in 1929. Americans seeking alcohol, gambling, and more fun than they could find back home flocked across the border, spending freely, which fueled the region's growth. Tijuana became the entry port for what some termed a "sinful, steamy playground," frequented by Hollywood stars and the idle rich. Then Prohibition was repealed, Mexico outlawed gambling, and Tijuana's fortunes dwindled.

The flow of travelers from the north slowed to a trickle for a while, but Tijuana still captivated those in search of the sort of fun that was illegal or just frowned upon at home. The ever-growing numbers of servicemen in San Diego kept Tijuana's sordid reputation alive. Before the toll highway to Ensenada was finished in 1967, travelers going south drove straight through downtown Tijuana, stopping along Avenida Revolución and its side streets for supplies and souvenirs.

The city's population has mushroomed—from 300,000 in 1970 to nearly 2 million today. The city has spread into canyons and dry riverbeds, over hillsides, and onto ocean cliffs.

City leaders have come to realize that tourism creates jobs and bolsters Tijuana's fragile economy, and they have begun to work hard to attract visitors. Avenida Revolución, the main street that was once lined with brothels and bars, has undergone tremendous rehabilitation. Today the avenue is lined with shops and restaurants, all catering to tourists. Park benches and shade trees on brick paths winding away from the traffic encourage visitors to linger.

Tijuana's tourist attractions have remained much the same throughout the century. The impressive El Palacio Frontón (Jai Alai Palace), where betting is allowed, draws crowds of cheering fans to its fast-paced matches. Some of Mexico's greatest bullfighters appear at the oceanfront and downtown bullrings; some of Latin America's most

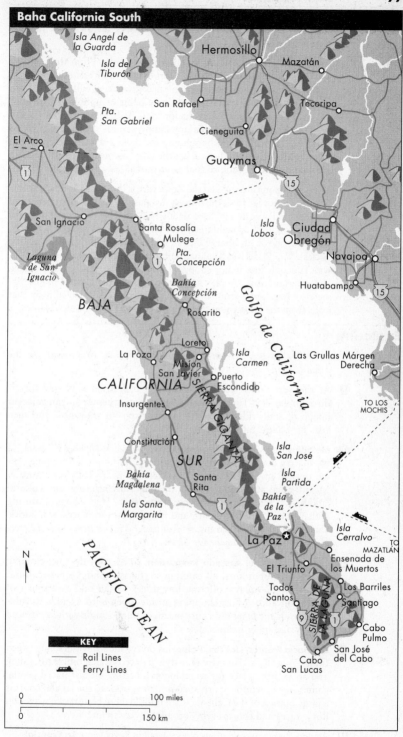

Baha California South

Isla Angel de la Guarda

Isla del Tiburón

Hermosillo

Mazatán

San Rafael

Pta. San Gabriel

Tecoripa

Cieneguita

El Arco

Guaymas

15

San Ignacio

Santa Rosalía

Mulege

Isla Lobos

Ciudad Obregón

Pta. Concepción

Navajoa

Laguna de San Ignacio

1

BAJA

Bahía Concepción

Huatabampo

15

Rosarito

Loreto

Isla Carmen

Las Grullas Márgen Derecha

La Poza

Misión San Javier

Puerto Escondido

CALIFORNIA

Insurgentes

SIERRA GIGANTA

TO LOS MOCHIS

Constitución

SUR

Isla San José

Bahía Magdalena

Santa Rita

Isla Partida

Golfo de California

Isla Santa Margarita

1

Bahía de la Paz

N

La Paz

Isla Cerralvo

TO MAZATLÁN

El Triunfo

Ensenada de los Muertos

PACIFIC OCEAN

Todos Santos

Los Barriles

Santiago

19

SIERRA DE LA LAGUNA

1

Cabo Pulmo

KEY

Cabo San Lucas

San José del Cabo

Rail Lines

Ferry Lines

0   100 miles

0   150 km

popular musicians and dancers perform at the Cultural Center; and there are an extraordinary number of places in town that provide good food and drinks.

Shopping is one of Tijuana's other main draws. From the moment you cross the border, people will approach you or call out and insist that you look at their wares. If you drive, workers will run out from auto-body shops to place bids on new paint or upholstery for your car. All along Avenida Revolución and its side streets, shops sell everything from tequila to Tiffany lamps; serious shoppers can spend a full day searching and bargaining for their items of choice. If you intend to buy food in Mexico, get the U.S. customs list of articles that are illegal to bring back so that your purchases won't be confiscated.

The Río Tijuana area, called the Zona Río, is the city's glamorous zone. The area is not far from the border, just past the usually dry riverbed of the Tijuana River along Paseo de los Héroes. This boulevard is one of the city's main thoroughfares, with large statues of historical figures, including one of Abraham Lincoln, in the center of the *glorietas* (traffic circles). The Plaza Río Tijuana, built on Paseo de los Héroes in 1982, was Tijuana's first major shopping center. Pueblo Amigo, a shopping and entertainment complex at the north end of the Zona Río, just 300 meters (328 yards) from the border, has a pedestrian walkway that leads from the border and through the plaza to Paseo de los Héroes.

Exploring

Numbers in the margin correspond to points of interest on the Tijuana map.

① At the **San Ysidro Border Crossing**, a pedestrian walkway travels through the Viva Tijuana dining and shopping center and an adjacent lineup of stalls filled with the full spectrum of souvenirs, and then goes up Calle 2 into the center of town.

② **Mexitlán** (Av. Ocampo between Calles 2 and 3, ☎ 66/38–41–01), a fascinating combination of museum and entertainment/shopping center, opened in 1991. Designed by architect Pedro Ramírez Vásquez, Mexitlán has scale models of all the major architectural and cultural landmarks throughout Mexico; restaurants and shops featuring authentic cuisine and folk art; and frequent performances by folkloric dancers and musical groups. ☛ *Adults $3.25; children under 12 free.* ☉ *Tues.–Fri. 10–6, weekends 12–8.*

③ Calle 2 intersects **Avenida Revolución**, lined with designer-clothing shops and restaurants, all catering to tourists. Shopkeepers call out from their doorways, offering low prices for an odd assortment of garish souvenirs. Many shopping arcades open onto Avenida Revolución; inside the front doors are mazes of small stands with low-priced pottery and other handicrafts.

④ **El Palacio Frontón (Jai Alai Palace)** is on Avenida Revolución between Calles 7a and 8a. The Moorish-style palace is a magnificent building and an exciting place for watching and betting on fast-paced jai alai games (*see* Spectator Sports, *below*). Next door to the jai alai court is a large branch of the Caliente Race Book, where bettors can wager on horse races and sports events broadcast via satellite TV.

TIME OUT Among the many restaurants along Avenida Revolución, **La Especial** (Av. Revolución 718, ☎ 66/85–66–54) is a favorite for Mexican food that hasn't been fancied up for the tourists.

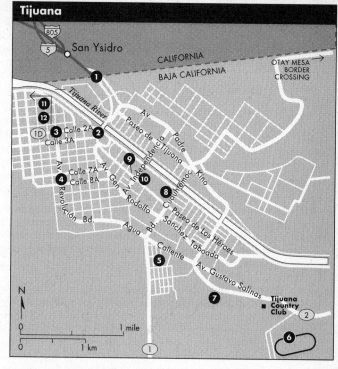

At Calle 11a, Avenida Revolución becomes Boulevard Agua Caliente

5 and passes by **El Toreo de Tijuana,** where bullfights are held from May through September (*see* Spectator Sports, *below*). A five-minute drive

6 away is the **Hipódromo de Agua Caliente,** or Agua Caliente Racetrack. In the Foreign Book area, bettors can wager on races televised via satellite from California. En route to the track you'll see the two

7 gleaming, mirrored towers of the **Gran Hotel**—Tijuana's glamour spot.

8 Between Boulevard Agua Caliente and the border is the **Río Tijuana** area, which runs parallel to the river. With its impressive Cultural Center and shopping complex, this section of town, along Avenida Paseo de los Héroes, is fast becoming Tijuana's Zona Rosa.

Mundo Divertido is a popular family attraction in the Río zone. The amusement park includes a miniature golf course, batting cages, an exciting roller coaster, and a video game parlor with more than 130 games. The park has a food court with hot dogs and burgers along with tacos and corn on the cob. *Paseo de los Héroes at Calle Rodriguez, no ☎. ⊙ Weekdays 11–10, weekends 11–11.*

9 The **Cultural Center** was designed by architects Manuel Rosen and Pedro Ramírez Vásquez, who also created Mexico City's famous Museum of Anthropology. The Cultural Center's exhibits of Mexican history are a good introduction for the thousands of visitors whose first taste of Mexico is at the border. The Omnimax Theater, with its curving 180-degree screen, features *El Pueblo del Sol (People of the Sun),* a cinematic tour of Mexico that's become somewhat outdated. Guest artists appear at the Cultural Center regularly. The center's bookstore has an excellent selection on Mexican history, culture, and arts in both Spanish and English. It's about a 20-minute walk from Avenida Revolución to the Cultural Center, and you must cross some very busy thoroughfares. You're best off taking a taxi. *Paseo de los Héroes and Av. Independencia,* ☎ *66/84–11–11.* ☛ *Museum: $1.60; museum and Omnimax Theater: $5.50 for English-language shows, $2.30 for Spanish.* ☉ *Daily 11–7; English-language version of the film* El Pueblo del Sol *presented daily at 2 PM.*

⑩ Plaza Río Tijuana, the area's largest shopping complex, is across the street from the Cultural Center on Paseo de los Héroes. It is enormous, with good restaurants, department stores, and hundreds of shops. The plaza has become a central square of sorts, where holiday fiestas are held. This stretch of Paseo de los Héroes has been landscaped with shade trees and flowers, and there are long, wide sidewalks leading from the shopping complex to the Cultural Center.

TIME OUT The restaurant inside the Cultural Center serves fairly good Mexican food throughout the week. It's a good place for just sitting to relax and absorb all you've seen. **Panadería Suzette,** in the Plaza Río shopping center, has an array of Mexican and French pastries; coffee is free with your selection.

⑪ Playas Tijuana along the oceanfront is a mix of modest and expensive residential neighborhoods, with a few restaurants and hotels. The **⑫** long, isolated beaches are visited mostly by locals. **Plaza de Toros Monumental,** the "Bullring by the Sea," is at the northwest corner of the beach area, right by the border. Bullfights are held here on alternate Sunday afternoons from May through September. Admission to bullfights varies, depending on the fame of the matador and the location of your seat.

Shopping

The traditional shopping strip is Avenida Revolución, between Calles 1 and 8. The avenue is lined with shops and arcades that display a wide range of crafts and curios. Bargaining is expected on the streets and in the arcades, but not in the finer shops. **Sanborns** (Av. Revolución at Calle 8, ☎ 66/88–14–62) has beautiful crafts from throughout Mexico, an excellent bakery, and chocolates from Mexico City. The finest folk art store in Tijuana, **Tolan** (Av. Revolución between Calles 7 and 8, ☎ 66/88–36–37) carries everything from antique carved wooden doors to tiny ceramic miniature village scenes. **La Piel** (Av. Revolución between Calle 4 and 5, ☎ 66/87–23–98), a recommended leather shop, offers dependable quality in jackets, backpacks, and luggage. **Ralph Lauren Polo Outlet** (Viva Tijuana Center, ☎ 66/88–76–98) is a licensed outlet for the designer's sportswear. **Sara's** (Av. Revolución at Calle 4, ☎ 66/88–29–32), one of the best department stores, features imported perfumes and fine clothing.

The Avenida Revolución shopping area spreads down Calle 1 to the pedestrian walkway leading from the border. The shops in **Plaza Revolución,** at the corner of Calle 1 and Avenida Revolución, stock quality crafts. Begin shopping at the stands along the border-crossing walkway, comparing prices as you travel toward Avenida Revolución. You may find that the best bargains are closer to the border; you can pick up your piñatas and serapes on your way out of town. The **Mercado Hidalgo** (Av. Independencia at Av. Sanchez Taboada, two blocks south of Paseo de los Héroes) is Tijuana's municipal market, with rows of fresh produce, grains, and herbs, some souvenirs, and the best selection of piñatas in Baja.

Shopping Centers

Plaza Río Tijuana on Paseo de los Héroes is described in Exploring, *above,* as is **Mexitlán** on Avenida Ocampo, which stocks high-quality folk art from throughout Mexico. **Pueblo Amigo** on Paseo de los Héroes is a fanciful pseudopueblo with colonial-style adobe buildings painted in bright blues, greens, and yellows; **Ley,** a gourmet grocery that sells salad by the pint and hard-to-find Mexican delicacies such as fresh mole sauce and pickled carrots and cauliflower, is one of the center's best shops. **Plaza Fiesta,** on Paseo de los Héroes across from Plaza Río Tijuana, has a collection of boutiques, jewelry stores, and stained-glass shops. Next door, the **Plaza de los Zapatos** gathers together more than a dozen stores selling designer shoes imported from throughout the world.

Participant Sports

Golf

The **Tijuana Country Club** (Blvd. Agua Caliente, east of downtown, ☎ 66/81–78–55) is open to guests of some hotels. It provides rental clubs, electric and hand carts, and caddies for the 18-hole course. Opened in 1993, the **Real del Mar Golf Club** (12 mi south of the border on the Ensenada toll road, ☎ 66/13–34–01) has 18 holes overlooking the ocean.

Spectator Sports

Bullfights

Bullfights, considered artistic spectacles, not sporting events, feature skilled matadors from throughout Mexico and Spain. They are held at **El Toreo de Tijuana** (Av. Agua Caliente just outside downtown, ☎ 66/85–22–10) on Sunday at 4, May through September. In July and August you can also see fights at the **Plaza de Toros Monumental** (Playas Tijuana area, Ensenada Hwy., ☎ 66/85–22–10 in San Diego) on Sunday at 4.

Greyhound Races

At the **Hipódromo de Agua Caliente,** horse racing was phased out in 1993, but greyhounds race nightly at 7:45, and afternoons at 2 on weekends. In the Foreign Book area, gamblers can bet on races taking place in California and shown at Caliente on TV monitors. *Blvd. Agua Caliente at Salinas,* ☎ *66/81–78–11; in San Diego,* ☎ *619/231–1919.*

Jai Alai

This ancient Basque sport, in some ways similar to handball but using a large, scooped-out paddle called a *frontón,* is played in the Moorish-style Palacio Frontón, or **Jai Alai Palace.** *Av. Revolución and Calle 8,* ☎ *66/88–01–25 or 619/231–1919 in San Diego.* ☛ *$3–$5.*

Dining

There is no shortage of good eating in Tijuana, from *taquerías* (taco stands) to gourmet and Continental restaurants; Avenida Revolución resembles one long food court with places for every taste and budget. A few of the best restaurants from the '20s and '30s still attract a steady clientele with their excellent international cuisine and reasonable prices. On an even more moderate scale, there are scores of seafood restaurants and kitchens that serve great Mexican food, unadulterated for foreign tastes. At night the street life often becomes rowdy, with tourists demonstrating the effects of potent Mexican margaritas.

Beef and pork are excellent, both grilled and marinated. Pheasant, quail, rabbit, and duck are popular in the more expensive places. And the seafood is unbeatable. Grilled lobster and shrimp served with beans, rice, and tortillas are fixtures in casual restaurants modeled after those at the popular seaside fishing village of Puerto Nuevo south of Rosarito.

Dress is casual, and reservations are not required unless otherwise noted. Some restaurants add a 15% service charge to the bill.

CATEGORY	COST*
$$$	$15–$20
$$	$8–$15
$	under $8

*per person for a three-course meal, excluding drinks and service

$$$ **El Taurino.** Walk a few blocks west of Avenida Revolución and you're in the true downtown Tijuana, where residents work, shop, and eat. One of their favorite spots is this cozy steak house, where the host greets his guests in Spanish or English, recognizing regular patrons from both sides of the border. Request a menu in English and zero in on the beef selections, especially the New York steak, called *cabrería.* Shrimp and lobster are also good choices, and all come with soup or salad. ✕ *Calle 6 No. 7531,* ☎ *66/85–70–75. MC, V.*

$$$ **Pedrin's.** One of Tijuana's best seafood restaurants overlooks the Jai Alai Palace from a second-story garden room. Meals include deep-fried fish appetizers, fish chowder, salad, an entrée, and a sweet after-dinner drink of Kahlua and cream. Recommended dishes include *rajas shrimp,* covered with melted cheese and green chilies, and grilled lobster. ✕ *Av. Revolución 1115,* ☎ *66/85–40–52. AE, MC, V.*

$$ **El Faro de Mazatlán.** Fresh fish simply prepared is the hallmark of one of Tijuana's best seafood restaurants. This is the place to try ceviche, abalone, squid, and lobster without spending a fortune. Meals start with a savory soup and crusty rolls. The dining room, frequented by professionals from nearby offices, is a peaceful spot for a long, leisurely lunch. ✕ *Blvd. Sanchez Taboada 9542,* ☎ *66/84–88–22. MC, V.*

$$ **La Fonda Roberto's.** Roberto's is by far the best restaurant in Tijuana for traditional cuisine from the many culinary regions of Mexico. Try the *chiles en nogada* (chilies stuffed with raisins and meat and topped with cream and pomegranate seeds), meats with spicy achiote sauce, and many varieties of mole. Portions are small, so order liberally and share samples of many dishes. ✕ *Old Ensenada Hwy. (also called Calle 16 de Septiembre), near Blvd. Agua Caliente in the Siesta Motel,* ☎ *66/86–16–01. MC, V.*

$$ **La Leña.** The sparkling clean, white dining room in La Leña faces an open kitchen where chefs grill unusual beef dishes, such as *Gaonera,* a tender fillet of beef stuffed with cheese and guacamole. The owner often visits with his guests, asking their opinion on the menu and offering samples of tripe—only for the strong of stomach. ✕ *Blvd. Agua Caliente 4560,* ☎ *66/86–47–52; also at Av. Revolución between Calles 4 and 5. AE, MC, V.*

$$ **La Taberna Española.** The mainstay of Plaza Fiesta's multi-ethnic cafés, this Spanish tapas bar attracts a youthful, sophisticated crowd. The tapa (appetizer) menu is printed in Spanish, but with a bit of imagination you should be able to select a representative sampling, including octopus in its own ink, a plate of spicy sausages, a wedge of Spanish tortilla with potatoes and eggs, and a bowl of fava beans.

The interior café is smoky, fragrant, and invariably crowded; sit at the outdoor tables for a better view of the crowd waiting in line. ✗ *Plaza Fiesta, Paseo de los Héroes 10001,* ☎ *66/84–75–62. No credit cards.*

$$ Tía Juana Tilly's. Popular with both tourists and locals looking for revelry and generous portions of Mexican specialties, this is one of the few places where you can get *cochinita píbil* (a Yucatecan specialty made of roast pig, red onions, and bitter oranges) or the traditionally bitter and savory chicken mole. Part of the same chain is Tilly's Fifth Ave., catercorner to the original on Avenida Revolución. ✗ *Av. Revolución at Calle 7,* ☎ *66/85–60–24. AE, MC, V.*

$ Carnitas Uruapan. At this large, noisy restaurant, patrons mingle at long wood tables, toasting one another with chilled *cervezas* (beer). The main attraction here is *carnitas* (marinated pork), sold by weight and served with homemade tortillas, salsa, cilantro, guacamole, and onions. ✗ *Blvd. Díaz Ordaz 550,* ☎ *66/81–61–81; also at Paseo de los Héroes at Av. Rodríguez, no ☎. No credit cards.*

$ La Especial. Located at the foot of the stairs leading to an under-
★ ground shopping arcade, this restaurant attracts diners in search of home-style Mexican cooking at low prices. There's nothing fancy about the seemingly endless basement room—which is never empty. ✗ *Av. Revolución 718,* ☎ *66/85–66–54. No credit cards.*

$ Señor Frog's. Heaping plates of barbecued chicken and ribs and buckets of ice-cold bottles of cerveza are the mainstay at this fun and festive formula eatery, one of many in the Carlos Anderson chain. The loud music and laughter make for a raucous atmosphere, and the food is consistently good. ✗ *In the Pueblo Amigo Center, Paseo Tijuana,* ☎ *66/85–36–98. AE, MC, V.*

Lodging

Tijuana's hotels are clustered downtown, along Avenida Revolución; near the country club on Boulevard Agua Caliente; and in the Río Tijuana area on Paseo de los Héroes. There are ample accommodations for all price levels. **Baja Information** can reserve hotel rooms (*see* Important Addresses and Numbers *in* Tijuana Essentials, *below*).

CATEGORY	COST*
$$$$	over $90
$$$	$60–$90
$$	$25–$60
$	under $25

*All prices are for a standard double room, excluding service charge and sales tax (10%).

$$$$ Gran Hotel. The two mirrored towers of the hotel are Tijuana's most
★ ostentatious landmarks, signs of prosperity and faith in the economic potential of this lucrative border town. The Gran Hotel often hosts receptions and parties for Tijuana's elite and is considered by many to be the city's most glamorous place for a drink or meal. The rooms on the club floors are particularly extravagant, with separate seating areas, king-size beds, and astounding views of Tijuana's sprawl. ▣ *Blvd. Agua Caliente 4558, 22420,* ☎ *66/81–70–00 or 800/472–6385,* ⒻⒶⓍ *66/81–70–16. 422 rooms with bath. Restaurant, pool, tennis courts, health club, nightclub, travel services. MC, V.*

$$$ Holiday Inn Pueblo Amigo. Finally there is a thoroughly modern hotel right in the center of Tijuana's tourist zone. Opened in early 1995 at Pueblo Amigo in the Zona Río near the border and Avenida Revolución, the bright, white Holiday Inn has several sizes of rooms, from standard to presidential suites; all are elegantly decorated in green, beige, and peach, with cable TV, minibars, and direct-dial long-distance telephones. The indoor pool, sauna, and gym are especially popular with business travelers, who also have use of meeting facilities and a business center. The hotel's Alcazar restaurant is quickly becoming a favorite luncheon meeting spot for executives from the businesses in the Zona Rio district. ☎ *Via Oriente 9211 at Pueblo Amigo, 22450,* ☎ *66/83–50–30 or 800/998–6968,* FAX *66/83–50–32. 108 rooms and suites. Restaurant, indoor pool, beauty salon, sauna, exercise room. AE, MC, V.*

$$$ **Lucerna.** Once one of the most charming hotels in Tijuana, the Lucerna has become run-down, and the rooms are in need of renovation. Still, the lovely gardens, large swimming pool surrounded by palms, touches of tile work, and folk art lend Mexican character to the hotel. The Lucerna's travel agency is particularly helpful with planning trips into Mexico. ☎ *Paseo de los Héroes 10902, and Av. Rodríguez, 22320,* ☎ *66/34–20–00 or 800/LUCERNA,* FAX *66/34–24–00. 170 rooms with bath, 9 suites. Restaurant, coffee shop, pool, nightclub, travel services. MC, V.*

$$$ **Otay Bugambilias.** There is finally a tourist hotel near the Tijuana airport that's clean and comfortable. The pink, three-story Bugambilias was an instant hit with travelers and those who do business in the Otay Mesa industrial area. The motel-like rooms feature kitchenettes; suites have separate seating areas. Extras include a small gym, sauna, and swimming pool. ☎ *Blvd. Industrial at Carretera Aeropuerto, 22450,* ☎ *66/23–84–11 or 800/472–1153,* FAX *66/23–76–00. 129 rooms. Restaurant, bar, pool, exercise room, meeting rooms. MC, V.*

$$ **Corona Plaza.** Though the exterior of this hotel resembles that of a nondescript office building, the interior is surprisingly pleasant. Rooms, furnished in handsome bleached wood, overlook an atrium lobby and restaurant. For less noise and more air, ask for a second- or third-floor room near the pool. The bullring is within walking distance; other attractions are just a short cab ride away. ☎ *Blvd. Agua Caliente 1426, 22450,* ☎ *66/81–81–83,* FAX *66/81–81–85. Restaurant, pool. MC, V.*

$$ **La Mesa Inn.** This Best Western hotel/motel has a small, shaded pool and rooms you could find anywhere, with tan walls, brown carpet, earth-tone decor, and no charm; stay away from those by the street and pool. Though the rooms are nothing special, the hotel books up quickly. Try to make reservations in advance. ☎ *Blvd. Díaz Ordaz 50, 22440,* ☎ *66/81–65–22 or 800/528– 1234,* FAX *66/81–28–71. 125 rooms. Bar, coffee shop, pool. MC, V.*

$$ **La Villa de Zaragoza.** La Villa is a well-maintained, brown stucco motel with a good location—near the Jai Alai Palace and one block from Revolución. It has the nicest rooms downtown in this price range. ☎ *Av. Madero 1120, 22000,* ☎ *66/85–18–32. 42 rooms. Restaurant. MC, V.*

$ **Villas Juvenil Youth Hostel.** The hostel is set in a quiet, peaceful park and is part of a sports complex. The 20 beds are in same-sex dorms, and there is a cafeteria. ☎ *Av. Padre Kino, 22320,* ☎ *66/84–25–23 or 66/84–75–10. No credit cards.*

The Arts and Nightlife

Tijuana has toned down its Sin City image; much of the action now takes place at the **Jai Alai Palace** and the racetrack. Several hotels, especially the **Lucerna** and **Gran Hotel,** feature live entertainment. **Iguanas** (Blvd. Paseo de los Héroes, ☎ 66/82–49–67), at the Pueblo Amigo shopping center, is an 18-and-over club; appearances by New

Wave and rock artists draw as many patrons from San Diego as from Tijuana. Cover charge varies with the group. Tickets to some performances at Iguanas are available through TicketMaster (☎ 619/220–8497 in San Diego).

The Hard Rock Cafe (Av. Revolución 520 between Calles 1 and 2, ☎ 66/85–02–06) has the same menu and decor as other branches of the famous London club and is popular with both families and singles. **OH! Laser Club** (Paseo de los Héroes 56, ☎ 66/84–02–67) is one of the oldest discos in town, popular with the sophisticated set. **Heaven & Hell** (Paseo de los Héroes 10501, ☎ 66/84–84–84) is less formal than most and extremely frenetic. **Baby Rock** (Calle Diego Rivera 1482, ☎ 66/84–94–38), an offshoot of a popular Acapulco disco, attracts a young, hip crowd. Tijuana's discos are elegant and sophisticated, and usually have strict dress codes, with no T-shirts, jeans, or sandals allowed.

Tijuana Essentials

Arriving and Departing

BY PLANE

Mexicana (☎ 800/531–7921), **Aeromexico** (☎ 800/237–6639), and **Aero California** (☎ 800/237–6225) serve many cities in Mexico from Tijuana, with fares that are often lower than those for flights from the United States. **Air LA** (☎ 800/933–5952) flies from Los Angeles to Tijuana. The airport is located on the eastern edge of the city, near the Otay Mesa border crossing. The cab fare from the San Ysidro border or from the Otay Mesa border is about $10 per person. Shuttle services operate Volkswagen vans (*combis*) from the airport to downtown and the borders.

BY CAR

U.S.-5 and I-805 end at the border crossing in San Ysidro; Highway 905 leads from I-5 and I-805 to the border crossing at Otay Mesa, near the Tijuana airport. Day-trippers often prefer to park their cars on the U.S. side and walk across the border. There are acres of parking lots by the border, charging from $8 to $15 per day. Park at a guarded lot, since break-ins are common. Those driving into Tijuana should purchase Mexican auto insurance, available at many stands along the last exit before the border crossing. On holidays and weekends there can be a wait at the border when traveling into Mexico. The wait to get back into the United States can be as long as two hours, though lines are usually shorter at the Otay Mesa crossing.

Many car-rental companies do not allow their cars to be driven into Mexico. **Avis** (☎ 800/331–1212) permits its cars to go from San Diego, CA, into Baja as far as 450 miles south of the border. Cars must be returned by the renter to San Diego, and Mexican auto insurance is mandatory. Cars leased from **Courtesy Rentals** (2975 Pacific Hwy., San Diego, 92101, ☎ 619/497–4800 or 800/252–9756) may be taken as far as Ensenada and San Felipe. **M&M Jeeps** (2200 El Cajon Blvd., San Diego, 92104, ☎ 619/297–1615 or 800/464–5724) rents two- and four-wheel-drive vehicles with packages covering tours of the entire Baja California Peninsula.

BY TROLLEY

The **San Diego Trolley** (☎ 619/233–3004) travels from the Santa Fe Depot, at Kettner Boulevard and Broadway, to within 100 feet of the border every 15 minutes from 5 AM to midnight. The 45-minute trip costs $1.75.

Greyhound (☎ 619/239–1288 or 800/231–2222) serves Tijuana from San Diego several times daily; the Greyhound terminal in Tijuana is at Av. Mexico at Madero (☎ 66/86–06–95). **Mexicoach** (☎ 619/232–5049) has bus service from the trolley depot on the U.S. side of the border to Avenida Revolución in Tijuana. **Baja California Tours** (6986 La Jolla Blvd., No. 204, La Jolla, CA 92037, ☎ 619/454–7166, FAX 619/454–2703) has daily bus tours to Tijuana and on to Rosarito, Ensenada, and San Felipe. **Autotransportes de Baja California** (☎ 66/85–84–72) links Tijuana with other points in Baja; **Tres Estrellas de Oro** (☎ 66/86–91–86) travels into mainland Mexico; and **Autotransportes del Pacífico** (☎ 66/86–90–45) has service to the Pacific coast. The Tijuana Central Bus Station is at Calzada Lázaro Cárdenas and Boulevard Arroyo Alamar (☎ 66/26–17–01).

Getting Around

Although all border stations are often open and new crossings are under consideration, there are still long lines to reenter the United States, so those who plan to spend just a day in Tijuana are advised to park on the U.S. side of the border and walk across. There is a large lot with scores of taxis on the Tijuana side of the border; from there you can reach the airport, the Cultural Center, the Río area, or Avenida Revolución for under $10. The 2-kilometer (1¼-mile) walk to Avenida Revolución is an easy one through Viva Tijuana, an open-air shopping mall completed in 1991. A walkway leads from the border to the Zona Río; follow the signs to Pueblo Amigo on your immediate right after you cross the border.

BY CAR

The combination of overpopulation, lack of infrastructure, and heavy winter rains make many of Tijuana's streets difficult to navigate. It's always best to stick to the main thoroughfares. Plenty of signs at the border will lead you to the main highways and to downtown, but once you hit the streets, Tijuana can be very confusing. There are parking lots along Avenida Revolución and at most major attractions; as noted above, it is advisable to leave your car in a guarded lot. If you park on the street, pay attention to the signs. Your license plates will be removed if you park illegally.

The larger U.S. rental agencies have offices at the Tijuana International Airport. Offices in town include **Avis** (Av. Agua Caliente 3310, ☎ 66/86–40–04), **Budget** (Paseo de los Héroes 77, ☎ 66/34–33–03), and **National** (Av. Agua Caliente 5000, ☎ 66/86–21–03).

BY TAXI

Taxis in Tijuana are both plentiful and inexpensive, with fares to all parts of the city running less than $10 per person. Be sure to agree on the price before the car starts moving.

BY BUS

The downtown bus station is at Calle 1a and Avenida Madero (☎ 66/86–95–15). Most city buses at the border will take you downtown; the bus to the border from downtown departs from Calle Benito Juárez, also called Calle 2a, between Avenidas Revolución and Constitución. All buses marked "Centro Camionera" go through downtown.

Guided Tours

San Diego Mini-Tours (1726 Wilson Ave., National City, CA 91950, ☎ 619/477–8687 or 800/235–5393, FAX 619/477–0705) has frequent departures throughout the day from San Diego hotels to Avenida

Revolución in Tijuana and back, and connections with a Mexican-operated trolley tour of Tijuana. **Baja California Tours** (6986 La Jolla Blvd., No. 204, La Jolla, CA 92037, ☎ 619/454–7166, FAX 619/454–2703) offers specialized Tijuana excursions, including visits to private homes and tours of art galleries and artists' studios.

Important Addresses and Numbers

EMERGENCIES
Police (☎ 134), **Red Cross** (☎ 132), **Fire** (☎ 136), **U.S. Consulate** (☎ 66/81–74–00).

VISITOR INFORMATION
The **Tijuana Chamber of Commerce** is the best source of tourist information. *Av. Revolución and Calle 1,* ☎ 66/85–84–72. ⊙ *Daily 9–7.*

The Attorney General for the Protection of Tourists Hot Line (☎ 66/88–05–55) takes calls weekdays to help with tourist complaints and problems.

Baja Information (7860 Mission Center Court, Suite 202, San Diego, CA 92108, ☎ 619/298–4105 or 619/299–8518; 800/225–2786 in the U.S.; 800/522–1516 in CA, AZ, and NV; FAX 619/294–7366) handles reservations for many Baja hotels and arranges a variety of package deals.

There is a **tourism office** (☎ 66/83–13–10) at Av. Revolución and Calle 1a with maps, newspapers, and English-speaking clerks; it's open daily 9–5. Tourist information booths are located just inside the border and at the airport. The State Secretary of Tourism Office (☎ 66/81–94–92, FAX 66/81–95–79) is in the Plaza Patria at Blvd. Diaz Ordaz and Av. Las Americas; it's more administrative than tourist oriented.

ROSARITO BEACH

Not long ago, Playas de Rosarito (Rosarito Beach) was a small seaside community with virtually no tourist trade. Part of the municipality of Tijuana, it was an overlooked suburb on the way to the port city of Ensenada. But as the roads improved, and particularly after Baja's Transpeninsular Highway was completed in 1973, Rosarito Beach began to flower. Vacation suites were added along the beach, and time-share and condo units were put up, although as recently as 1980, the Rosarito Beach Hotel was the only major resort in the area.

The '80s brought an amazing building boom to Rosarito. The main street, alternately known as the Old Ensenada Highway and Boulevard Benito Juárez, is now packed with restaurants, bars, and shops. Rosarito's population, about 100,000, is growing steadily.

Still, it is a relaxing place to visit. Southern Californians have practically made Rosarito a weekend suburb. Surfers, swimmers, and sunbathers come here to enjoy the beach, one of the longest in northern Baja: It's an uninterrupted stretch of sand from the power plant at the far north end of town to below the Rosarito Beach Hotel, about 8 kilometers (5 miles) south. Horseback riding, jogging, and strolling are popular along this strand. Whales pass not far from shore on their winter migration; dolphins and sea lions sun on rocks jutting out from the sea. Rosarito has always attracted a varied crowd, and today's group is no exception—an assemblage of prosperous young Californians building villas in vacation developments, retired Americans and Canadians homesteading in trailer parks, and travelers of all ages from all over the world.

Hedonism and health get equal billing in Rosarito. One of the area's major draws is its seafood, especially lobster, shrimp, and abalone. The visiting Americans act as if they've been dry for months—margaritas and beer are the favored thirst quenchers. People throw off their inhibitions here, at least to the degree permitted by the local constables. A typical Rosarito day might begin with a breakfast of eggs, refried beans, and tortillas, followed by a few hours of horseback riding on the beach. Lying in the sun or strolling through the shops takes care of midday. Siestas are imperative and are usually followed by more shopping, strolling, or sunbathing before dinner, dancing, and sleep.

Several hotels, restaurants, and campgrounds line the coastline south of Rosarito. Some places have been around for years and have a dedicated following; others are in the planning and development stages. This region is expected to boom over the next few years. Bajamar, about 48 kilometers (30 miles) south of Rosarito, is the largest development, with a hotel, several housing compounds, and an 18-hole golf course; future plans include a marina.

Exploring

Rosarito Beach has few historic or cultural attractions, beaches and bars being the main draws. Sightseeing consists of strolling along the 8-kilometer (5-mile) beach or down Boulevard Benito Juárez. Note: Street numbers and addresses are changing along Juárez. To reduce confusion, ask for landmarks when getting directions.

An immense PEMEX gasoline installation and electric plant anchor the northern end of Boulevard Juárez, which then runs along a collection of new shopping arcades, restaurants, and motels. The eight-story **La Quinta del Mar** hotel is the first major landmark, followed by the **Quinta Plaza** shopping center, which has a car wash, pharmacy, bakery, specialty shops, and restaurants, as well as the **tourism office** and the **Centro de Convenciones,** a 1,000-seat convention center. The **Festival Plaza** hotel and shopping center, with its distinctive roller coaster-like facade, sits a bit farther south on Boulevard Juárez, just before the Rosarito Beach Hotel.

TIME OUT   The long glassed-in bar that sits on a little hill between the pool and the beach at the **Rosarito Beach Hotel** (☎ 661/2–01–44) is the best place for absorbing the hotel's ambience. The margaritas are a potent reminder that you're in Mexico, and the nachos are fairly good. Have Sunday brunch ($15) in the dining room, overlooking the pool.

Off the Beaten Track

The most popular side trip from Rosarito Beach is **Puerto Nuevo** (Newport) at Kilometer 44 on the old highway. A few years ago the only way you could tell you'd reached this fishing community was by the huge painting of a 7-Up bottle on the side of a building. You'd drive down the rutted dirt road to a row of restaurants where you were served the classic Newport meal: grilled lobster, refried beans, rice, homemade tortillas, butter, salsa, and lime. The meal became a legend, and now at least 30 restaurants have the identical menu. Try one of the family-run places, like Ponderosa (see Dining, below).

Shopping

The two major resort hotels have shopping arcades equipped with laundromats, taco stands, and some good crafts stores. The **Calimax** grocery store on Boulevard Juárez is a good place to stock up on necessities.

Rosarito is a great place to shop for pottery and wood furniture. Curio stands and open-air artisans' markets line Boulevard Juárez both north and south of town, with the best pottery stands on the highway to the south. Another cluster of stands appear at Puerto Nuevo, where diners sated on lobster and beer bargain for cotton blankets, seashell lamps, and piñatas. Within Rosarito proper, **Casa Torres** (Rosarito Beach Hotel Shopping Center, ☎ 661/2–10–08) carries a wide array of imported perfumes. **Margarita's** (Rosarito Beach Hotel Shopping Center, no ☎) has a great selection of Guatemalan textiles and clothing. **Oradia Imports** (Quinta Plaza Center, ☎ 661/2–16–37) focuses on imported perfumes and crystal. **Casa del Arte y La Madera** (Quinta del Mar Plaza, ☎ 661/2–13–00) always has an irresistible selection of Mexican folk art with a fish and sea theme, and creatively painted furnishings. The shelves of **Taxco Curios** (Quinta del Mar Plaza, ☎ 661/2–18–77) are filled with handblown glassware. **Casa la Carreta** (Km 29 Ensenada Hwy., ☎ 661/2–05–02), one of Rosarito's best furniture shops, is worth a visit just to see the woodcarvers create elaborate desks, dining tables, and armoires. **Rangel** (Blvd. Juárez 151-A, ☎ 661/2–14–26) specializes in rattan and wood furnishings. **La Hacienda** (Blvd. Juárez 97, ☎ 661/2–07–21) has a good selection of painted tiles. **Tony's Surf Shop** (Blvd. Juárez 312, ☎ 661/2–11–92) offers surfing gear for sale or rent.

Sports and Outdoor Activities

Fishing

There is a small fishing pier at Kilometer 33 on the Old Ensenada Highway; surf casting is allowed on the beach. There is no place in Rosarito that issues fishing licenses, but tourism officials say licenses are not necessary if you fish from shore. Unfortunately, the ocean tends to be polluted, especially in residential areas—it is not a good idea to eat fish caught close to shore.

Golf

Two golf courses have opened in the Rosarito area, and more are in the planning stages. **Bajamar** (Km 77.5 Ensenada Hwy., ☎ 615/5–01–51 or 800/342–2644), a 1976 course revamped and reopened in late 1993, will be joined by a second resort course; the first nine holes are scheduled to open by the end of 1995. **Real del Mar** (☎ 661/3–34–01) has an 18-hole course in the center of a planned golf community; it's located at Kilometer 19.2 on the toll highway Ensenada Cuota, 12 miles south of the border and 6 miles north of Rosarito. Golf packages are available at some Rosarito Beach hotels.

Horseback Riding

Horses can be rented at the north and south ends of Juárez and on the beach for $10 per hour. Check the horses carefully; some are pathetically thin. The number of horses on the beach is now restricted, and the horses are better cared for.

Surfing

The waves are particularly good at **Popotla**, Kilometer 33, **Calafia**, Kilometer 35.5, and **Costa Baja**, Kilometer 36, on the Old Ensenada Highway.

Dining

Nearly all of Rosarito's restaurants feature the same items—lobster, shrimp, fresh fish, and steak—at nearly the same prices: about $15 to $18 for dinner. Some restaurants tack a 15% service charge onto your bill. Dress is casual and reservations are not required unless otherwise noted.

CATEGORY	COST*
$$$	$15–$20
$$	$8–$15
$	under $8

per person, excluding drinks and service

Rosarito Beach

$$$ Dragon del Mar. A miniature waterfall greets guests in the marble foyer of this elegant Chinese restaurant, which features a pianist playing relaxing music. Carved wooden partitions in the expansive dining room help create an intimate dining experience. The food is well prepared and appealing to the eye as well as the palate. ✕ *Blvd. Juárez 283,* ☏ *661/2–06–04. MC, V.*

$$$ La Casa de la Langosta. You needn't drive to Puerto Nuevo for lobster; just visit this branch of one of that area's best restaurants. The traditional lobster dinner is the house specialty, of course, but you can also get grilled fish and shrimp. The second-story dining room and kitchen are impeccably clean and the food dependable, though not overly exciting. ✕ *Quinta Plaza,* ☏ *661/2–09–24. MC, V.*

$$$ La Leña. The cornerstone restaurant of the Quinta Plaza shopping
★ center, La Leña sits on such a high-rise that you can see the ocean from the window tables. The dining room is spacious, with the tables spread far enough apart for privacy. Try any of the beef dishes, especially the tender *carne asada* (grilled strips of beef) with tortillas and guacamole. There's a branch of the Caliente Race Book wagering center on the premises. ✕ *Quinta Plaza,* ☏ *661/2–08–26. MC, V.*

$$ Azteca. The enormous dining room at the Rosarito Beach Hotel has a view of the pool and beach area. Many visitors come here exclusively for the lavish Sunday brunch, where margaritas are the drink of choice. Both Mexican and American dishes are offered, and the size of the portions makes up for the erratic quality of the food. The hotel offers a Mexican buffet and fiesta here on Friday nights. ✕ *Rosarito Beach Hotel, Blvd. Juárez,* ☏ *661/2–01–44. MC, V.*

$$ El Nido. A dark, wood-paneled restaurant with leather booths and a large central fireplace, this is one of the oldest eateries in Rosarito. Diners unimpressed with the newer, fancier establishments come here for the good mesquite-grilled steaks. ✕ *Blvd. Juárez 67,* ☏ *661/2–14–30. MC, V.*

$$ Mariscos de Rosarito Vince's. This seafood restaurant and deli is pop-
★ ular with expatriate Americans—they swear that Vince's has the best lobster in town. Mariachis add to the nightly festivities. ✕ *Blvd. Juárez 77,* ☏ *661/2–12–53. No credit cards.*

$$ René's. One of the oldest restaurants in Rosarito (1924), René's features *chorizo* (Mexican sausage), quail, frogs' legs, and lobster. There's an ocean view from the dining room, a lively bar, and mariachi music. ✕ *Blvd. Juárez south of the Rosarito Beach Hotel,* ☏ *661/2–10–20. MC, V.*

$ Juice 'n Juice. Rosarito's Mexican/health-food restaurant is a no-frills lunch counter with lots of salads, juices, yogurt, and granola. Good cheese enchiladas and other meatless Mexican dishes give vegetarians a chance to sample the local fare. Beef burgers and burritos are also served. ✗ *Blvd. Juárez 98,* ☎ *661/2–03–38. No credit cards.*

$ **La Flor de Michoacán.** Carnitas (marinated pork roasted over an open pit) Michoacán-style, served with homemade tortillas, guacamole, and salsa, are the house specialty. The tacos *tortas* (marinated pork kebabs roasted on skewers) and tostadas are great. The surroundings are simple but clean. Takeout is available. ✗ *Blvd. Juárez 291,* ☎ *661/2–18–58. No credit cards. Closed Wed.*

$ **Los Arcos.** Next to the Rosarito Beach Hotel, this café serves home-style Mexican food and offers open-air dining in summer. ✗ *Blvd. Juárez 29,* ☎ *661/2–04–91. No credit cards.*

$ **Rosarito Village Cafe.** Inexpensive margaritas, mariachis, and takeout Mexican food make this restaurant a popular watering hole; it's also a good place for U.S.-style breakfasts. ✗ *Next to Rosarito Beach Hotel, Blvd. Juárez 777,* ☎ *661/2–86–54. MC, V.*

South of Rosarito Beach

$$$ **Calafia.** The owners of this restaurant and trailer park are in the process of transforming their establishment into a cultural center, with a museum devoted to historical artifacts from the region. Still, most visitors are drawn to Calafia's restaurant, where tables are scattered on small terraces down the cliffside to the crashing sea. The food is standard Mexican fare, but it all tastes great when combined with the fresh salt air and sea breezes. Calafia has an outdoor dance floor at the base of the cliffs, where live bands sometimes perform. Trailers are available for rent on a nightly or weekly basis at the top of the cliffs. ✗ *Km 35.5 Old Ensenada Hwy.,* ☎ *661/2–15–81 or 800/ CALAFIA. MC, V.*

$$$ **La Fonda.** At this popular restaurant, you can sit on an outdoor patio ★ overlooking the beach and sip potent margaritas served with greasy nachos and hot salsa. Fresh lobster, grilled steaks, prime rib, and traditional Mexican dishes are accompanied by a delicious black-bean soup. The bar is usually crowded, and the patrons boisterous. ✗ *Km 59 Old Ensenada Hwy., no* ☎. *No credit cards.*

$$ **Puerto Nuevo.** Newport is a village of 25 to 30 restaurants that serve the same dishes—grilled or deep-fried lobster or shrimp, Spanish rice, refried beans, and homemade tortillas with melted butter, lime, and hot sauce. Some places have full bars; others serve only wine and beer. **Ortega's,** with four branches in Newport and two in Rosarito, is the most crowded; **Ponderosa** is smaller and quieter and is run by a gracious family; **Costa Brava** is newer and more elegant, with tablecloths and an ocean view; and **La Casa de la Langosta** serves grilled fish along with lobster and shrimp. Lobsters in most places are priced as small, medium, and large—medium is about $15. The lobster served in Newport comes from local waters during lobster season (October through March) and is imported from Australia the rest of the year. There is some concern that the waters close to shore have become polluted, but the fishermen say they catch the lobsters a mile or so offshore, where the waters are safe. ✗ *Km 44 Old Ensenada Hwy., no* ☎. *Most places are open for lunch and dinner on a first-come, first-served basis. Some take credit cards.*

Lodging

The Rosarito area has nearly 2,000 hotel rooms—and more in the planning stages. You can usually get a room without advance reservations, except during holiday periods, when the town fills up completely. Several agencies in the United States book reservations at Rosarito hotels and at nearby condo and time-share resorts, which may actually cost less than hotel rooms if you are traveling with a group of four or more. For details, contact **Baja Information** (7860 Mission Center Court, Suite 202, San Diego, CA 92108, ☎ 619/298–4105; in the U.S., 800/ 225–2786; in CA, NV, and AZ, 800/522–1516) or **Baja California Tours** (6986 La Jolla Blvd., No. 204, La Jolla, CA 92037, ☎ 619/454– 7166, FAX 619/454–2703). Reservations are a must on holiday weekends. Many hotels require a minimum two-night stay for a confirmed reservation, and inexpensive rooms are hard to find.

CATEGORY	COST*
$$$	$60–$90
$$	$25–$60
$	under $25

All prices are for standard double room, excluding service charge and sales tax (10%).

Rosarito Beach

$$$ **Brisas del Mar.** A modern motel (built in 1992), the Brisas del Mar is especially good for families, since the large pastel rooms comfortably accommodate four persons. A few of the rooms on the second story have hot tubs and views of the ocean; all have air-conditioning and TV. ⊞ *Blvd. Juárez 22, ☎ and FAX 661/2–25–47; reservations in the U.S. Box 1867, Chula Vista, CA 91912, ☎ 619/685–1246 or 800/ 697–5223. 66 rooms. Bar, coffee shop. MC, V.*

$$$ **Rosarito Beach Hotel.** Dating from the Prohibition era, this venerable
★ hotel continues to be Rosarito's centerpiece. Several buildings have been added over the years, and there always seems to be some sort of renovation going on to preserve the hotel's character while modernizing its services. It's still a charmer, with huge ballrooms, tiled public rest rooms, and a glassed-in pool deck overlooking a long beach. Rooms and suites in the low-rise buildings and tower facing the beach are modern, though somewhat sterile; more characterful accommodations in the original building surrounding the swimming pool have been overhauled. Midweek reduced rates are often available; oceanview rooms exceed the upper limit of the expensive ($$$) category. A 1930s mansion next door to the hotel has been refurbished as the Casa Playa Spa, a full-service European facility with massage, beauty treatments, exercise equipment, saunas and hot tubs, and a restaurant. ⊞ *Blvd. Juárez at the south end of town, ☎ 661/2–01–44 or 800/343– 8582, FAX 661/2–11–76; reservations: Box 430145, San Diego, CA 92143. 275 rooms and suites. 2 restaurants, bar, 2 pools, spa, health club, beach, tennis courts, convention center. MC, V.*

$$ **Baja Village.** This motel is on Rosarito's main drag, which is very noisy during the day; the advantage is that restaurants, stores, and the beach are all within walking distance. Rooms are carpeted, and some have color TV. ⊞ *Blvd. Juárez 228 at Via Las Olas, ☎ and FAX 661/ 2–00–50. U.S. mailing address: Box 309, San Ysidro, CA 92073. 21 rooms, 3 suites. Restaurant, bar. MC, V.*

$$ **Festival Plaza.** Designed with unrestrained fun in mind, Festival Plaza is definitely geared toward a youthful crowd. The motel-like rooms are in an eight-story building with a unique facade meant to resemble a roller coaster. Several rowdy bars front the hotel on Boulevard Juárez, and the central courtyard serves as a concert stage, children's playground, and party headquarters. Some suites have hot tubs; most rooms are similar to what you'd find in a U.S. motel. Noise is a definite factor; stay elsewhere unless you want to join the festivities. ⊞ *Blvd. Juárez 11, 22710, ☎ 661/2–08–42 or 800/453–8606, FAX 661/*

2–01–24. 114 rooms. 2 restaurants, 3 bars, pool, disco, playground. AE, MC, V.

$$ **Los Pelicanos Hotel.** Completed in 1990, this hotel—one of the few situated directly on the beach—has prices that vary depending on the location of the rooms and the presence or absence of a balcony with an ocean view. The second-story restaurant and bar are popular sunset-watching spots. ☎ *Calle Cedros 115, ☎ 661/2–04–45, ℻ 661/2–17–57; U.S. mailing address: Box 3871, San Ysidro, CA 92073. 39 rooms. Restaurant, bar. MC, V.*

$ **Cupalas del Mar.** Opened in 1991, this small hotel between Boulevard Juárez and the beach is quieter than most, with sunny, clean rooms and satellite TV. ☎ *Calle Guadalupe Victoria 9, 22710, ☎ 661/2–24–90, ℻ 661/2–24–94. 39 rooms. Pool, hot tub. No credit cards.*

$ **Motel Quinta Chica.** This motel at the south end of town has little character but comfortable beds. Rooms in the front face the free road and enjoy ocean breezes; those in the back have the constant roar of traffic on the toll road. ☎ *Km 26.8 Old Ensenada Hwy., 22710, ☎ 661/2–13–00, ℻ 661/2–12–15. 90 rooms. MC, V.*

South of Rosarito Beach

$$$ **Grand Baja Resort.** A good value for families and groups, this resort offers beachfront condo rentals with daily and long-term rates; split the cost of a suite or studio between two couples and you'll be in the moderate ($$) range. The units come in a variety of sizes, from studios to two-bedroom oceanfront condos; most have kitchens. The Grand Baja is a block away from the cluster of Puerto Nuevo lobster restaurants. ☎ *Km 44.5 Old Ensenada Hwy., ☎ 661/4–14–84, ℻ 661/4–11–42; reservations in the U.S., 3549 Camino del Rio South, San Diego, CA 92108. 150 units. Pool, tennis courts. MC, V.*

$$$ **Hacienda Las Glorias.** Located on the grounds of the Bajamar golf resort, which lies about halfway between Rosarito and Ensenada (*see* Sports and Outdoor Activities, *above*), the Hacienda Las Glorias is one of the prettiest hotels on the coast. Designed like a Mexican hacienda surrounding a central courtyard, it features rooms with French doors leading to landscaped patios, tables, and chairs by the windows. The pool, clubhouse, and restaurant are a few yards away from the hotel rooms. Private homes and condos edge the golf course and the cliffs overlooking the ocean. An equestrian center is in the planning stages, and there are tennis courts on the property. ☎ *Km 77.5 Ensenada Hwy., Ensenada, 22800, ☎ 615/5–01–51, reservations in the U.S. 800/ 342-2644, ℻ 615/5–01–50. 80 rooms. Restaurant, bar, pool, golf, tennis. AE, MC, V.*

$$$ **La Fonda.** A longtime favorite with beachgoers, La Fonda has a few
★ well-worn rooms, decorated with carved-wood furniture and folk art, with great views of the ocean. The restaurant and bar are immensely popular; if you plan on getting any sleep, ask for a room as far away from them as possible. The hotel does not have a phone, and reservations can be made only by mail. Allow two weeks to receive your confirmation. ☎ *Km 59 Old Ensenada Hwy., no ☎; reservations in the U.S.: Box 268, San Ysidro, CA 92073. 18 rooms. Restaurant, bar, beach. No credit cards.*

$$$ **Las Rocas.** An elegant addition to the strip of older hotels perched on
★ cliffs above the ocean, this hotel is terraced up a hillside, giving all the rooms ocean views. The white building, with blue-and-purple trim, stands out vividly against the surroundings. Some suites have fireplaces, coffeemakers, and microwaves. The pool and whirlpool seem to spill over the cliffs into the ocean. ☎ *Km 37 Old Ensenada Hwy., ☎ and ℻ 661/2–21–40; reservations in the U.S.: Box 8851, Chula*

Vista, CA 91912, ☎ *619/425–2682; or 800/733–6394 outside CA. 74 rooms and suites. Restaurant, bar, hot tub, beach. AE, MC, V.*

$$ Oasis Resort. This full-scale resort on a long, perfect beach has become incredibly popular since it opened in 1992. The hotel section has one-bedroom, ocean-view suites with heat, air-conditioning, cable TVs, and minibars. RVs with full kitchens and maid service are also available. Though not especially peaceful, the Oasis is a fun spot where guests quickly become friends and end up booking return visits together. ⌦ *Km 40 Old Ensenada Hwy., 22710,* ☎ *661/3–32–55,* ⅢX *661/3–32–52; reservations in the U.S., 800/462–7472. 100 suites, 12 RVs, 55 RV spaces. Restaurant, bar, 2 pools, wading pool, hot tub, sauna, exercise room, miniature golf, tennis courts, recreation room. MC, V.*

Nightlife

The many restaurants in Rosarito Beach keep customers entertained with live music, piano bars, or *folklórico* (folk music and dance) shows; the bar scene is also active. Drinking-and-driving laws are stiff—the police will fine you no matter how little you've had. If you plan to drink, take a cab or assign a designated driver.

There's a lot going on at night at **Rosarito Beach Hotel** (Blvd. Juárez, ☎ 661/2–01–44): live music at the ocean-view Beachcomber Bar and Hugo's; a Mexican Fiesta on Friday nights; and a live band at the cavernous disco. The Festival Plaza (*see* Lodging, *above*) has become party central for Rosarito's youthful crowd and presents live concerts on the hotel's courtyard stage most weekends. Dedicated to the art of drinking tequila, **El Museo Sal y Limón** (Festival Plaza, ☎ 661/2–08–42) offers more than 130 brands of the fiery drink. **Rock & Roll Taco** (Festival Plaza, ☎ 661/2–08–42) is just what its name suggests— a taco stand and boisterous bar all in one. **Papas and Beer** (Blvd. Juárez near the Rosarito Beach Hotel, ☎ 661/2–03–43) draws a young, energetic crowd. **Rene's** (Blvd. Juárez south of town, ☎ 661/ 2–10–61) often has live bands or mariachis; crowds fill the bar to watch sports events on satellite TV. **Calafia** (Km 35 Ensenada Hwy., ☎ 661/2–15–81) is alternately rowdy and subdued, depending on what type of band is playing by the dance floor.

Rosarito Beach Essentials

Arriving and Departing

Rosarito Beach is 29 kilometers (18 miles) south of Tijuana, on the Pacific coast. There is no airport, but **Tres Estrellas de Oro** (☎ 66/ 86–91–86 in Tijuana) has bus service between Tijuana and Ensenada, stopping at the terminal in Rosarito on Avenida Benito Juárez across from the Rosarito Beach Hotel.

The easiest way to get to Rosarito Beach is to drive. Once you cross the border, follow the signs for Ensenada Cuota, the toll road that runs south along the coast. Take the Rosarito exit, which leads to what is alternately called the Old Ensenada Highway and Boulevard Juárez in Rosarito. The tolls from Tijuana to Rosarito run about $7. Rest rooms are available near the toll booths. Although the alternate free road—Ensenada Libre—has been vastly improved, it is difficult for the first-timer to navigate, but here are directions if you want to try: In Tijuana, drive south on Avenida Revolución to Boulevard Fundadores and bear right. You'll discover that the free road and the toll road merge just north of Rosarito. Drive slowly on both roads, and keep an eye out for road work ahead—usually marked by a row of large rocks placed across a lane. These rock barriers can appear out of nowhere and are a major driving hazard.

Getting Around

Most of Rosarito proper can be explored on foot, which is a good idea on weekends, when Boulevard Juárez has bumper-to-bumper traffic. To reach Puerto Nuevo and points south, continue on Boulevard Juárez (also called Old Ensenada Highway and Ensenada Libre) through town and head south. There is a tremendous amount of construction taking place along this stretch of road, incidentally, with time-share communities and resorts popping up side by side along the oceanfront cliffs. Taxis travel this stretch regularly. Settle the fare before departing. Buses from Tijuana and Ensenada stop across the street from the Rosarito Beach Hotel; if you wish to get off at other beach areas along the way, take a local rather than an express bus.

Important Addresses and Numbers

EMERGENCIES

Police (☎ 134), **Fire** (☎ 136), **Red Cross** (☎ 132).

GUIDED TOURS

Baja California Tours (☎ 619/454–7166, FAX 619/454–2703) conducts bus tours from San Diego to Rosarito Beach, including overnight accommodations.

VISITOR INFORMATION

The **tourist information office** (Blvd. Juárez, on 2nd floor of Quinta Plaza shopping center, ☎ 661/2–03–96 or 661/2–30–78) has brochures from several hotels and restaurants and copies of the *Baja Times,* a handy, tourist-oriented, English-language newspaper. The staff speaks English and is extremely helpful. The **Rosarito Convention and Visitors Bureau** offers brochures and information packets through its toll-free number in the United States (☎ 800/962–BAJA).

ENSENADA

Ensenada is a major port 104 kilometers (65 miles) south of Tijuana on Bahía de Todos Santos. The paved highway (Mexico Route 1) between the two cities often cuts a path between low mountains and high oceanside cliffs; exits lead to rural roads, oceanfront campgrounds, and an ever-increasing number of resort communities. The small fishing communities of San Miguel and El Sauzal sit off the highway to the north of town, and the Coronado Islands can be clearly seen off the coast.

Juan Rodríguez Cabrillo first discovered Ensenada in 1542. Sebastián Vizcaino named the region Ensenada–Bahía de Todos Santos (All Saints' Bay) in 1602. Since then the town has drawn a steady stream of "discoverers" and developers. First ranchers made their homes on large spreads along the coast and up into the mountains. Gold miners followed, turning the area into a boomtown during the late 1800s. After the mines were depleted, the area settled back into a pastoral state for a while, but the harbor gradually grew into a major port for shipping agricultural goods from the surrounding ranches and farms. Now it is one of Mexico's largest seaports and has a thriving fishing fleet and fish-processing industry. The smell of fish from the canneries lining the highway can be overpowering at times.

Ensenada is a popular weekend destination for southern Californians. There are no beaches in Ensenada proper, but beaches north and south of town are satisfactory for swimming, sunning, surfing, and camping. During the week Ensenada is just a normal, relatively calm port city, with a population nearing 300,000.

For decades most hotels and bars have catered to groups of young people intent on drinking and carousing. The beachside strip between San Miguel and Ensenada has long been a haven of moderately priced oceanfront motels and trailer parks. But now there is a concerted effort to attract conventioneers and business travelers. A group of civic boosters has renovated the Riviera del Pacifico, the grand old gambling hall–turned–civic center that is Ensenada's most stately edifice. The waterfront area has been razed and rebuilt, with taco stands replaced by shopping centers, hotels, and the massive Plaza Marina, opened in 1992. Several strip malls have opened in town, and cruise ships regularly anchor offshore.

Marina Coral, a pleasure-boat marina and large hotel complex, is under construction north of town, with completion projected for late 1995. Plans are also underway to move the cruise ship pier to the waterfront across the street from Riviera del Pacifico.

Highway 3 runs east from Ensenada to San Felipe through the foothills of the Sierra Pedro San Martir. The same highway runs north from Ensenada to Tecate through the Guadalupe Valley where many of the area's vineyards and wineries are located. If you are traveling south, Ensenada is the last major city you'll see for hundreds of miles on Mexico Highway 1 or the Transpeninsular Highway. **San Quintín,** 184 kilometers (115 miles) south of Ensenada, is an agricultural community said to be the windiest spot in Baja. Sportfishing is particularly good here, and tourism is increasing. Many of San Quintín's visitors arrive in RVs towing boats, but a few small hotels are doing a healthy business. Farther south are turnoffs for a dirt road to **San Felipe** and a paved road to **Bahía de los Angeles.** At the end of the northern section of Baja, 595 kilometers (372 miles) from Ensenada, stands a steel monument in the form of an eagle, 42 meters (138 feet) high. It marks the border between the states of Baja Norte and Baja Sur. The time changes from Pacific to Mountain as you cross the 28th parallel. **Guerrero Negro,** Baja Sur's northernmost town, with hotels and gas stations, is 2 kilometers (1½ miles) south.

Exploring

Numbers in the margin correspond to points of interest on the Ensenada map.

The city of Ensenada, the third largest in Baja, hugs the harbor of **Bahía de Todos Santos.** If you have access to a car, begin your tour of Ensenada by driving north up Calle 2 or east on the Mexico Highway 1 bypass around town into the Chapultepec Hills to **El Mirador** (The Lookout). From here you can see the entire Bahía de Todos Santos, from the canneries of San Miguel south to the towns of Punta Banda and La Bufadora.

To tour the waterfront and downtown, you'll be better off on foot. As Alternate Highway 1 leads into town from the north, it becomes Boulevard Costero, running past shipyards filled with massive freighters. To the right, between the water and the street, the massive Plaza Marina is completed but far from filled with the expected restaurants and shops. At the northernmost point at the water's edge sits an indoor-outdoor **Fish Market,** where row after row of counters display piles of shrimp as well as tuna, dorado, marlin, snapper, and

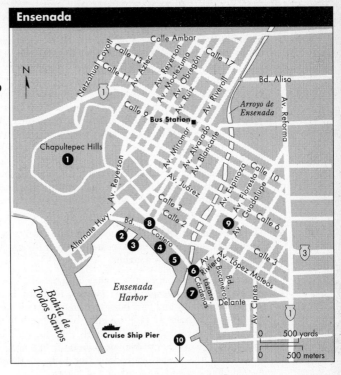

dozens of other species of fish caught off Baja's coasts. Outside, stands sell grilled or smoked fish, seafood cocktails, and fish tacos. Browsers can pick up some standard souvenirs, eat well for very little money, and take some great photographs. The hot-pink Plaza de Mariscos, which blocks the view of the traditional fish market from the street, is a comfortable place in which to eat.

TIME OUT You can't visit the fish market without trying at least one fish taco. Strips of fresh snapper, halibut, or other freshly caught fish are dipped in batter and deep-fried, then wrapped in fresh corn tortillas. Choose your topping—cilantro, salsa, tomatoes, onions, pickled carrots—from an array of dishes set out on the counter.

Boulevard Costero runs along the waterfront from the market and the **Sportfishing Pier,** where fishing and whale-watching tours depart. A large branch of the Caliente Foreign Book chain sits next door, blocking much of the waterfront view. Caliente offers wagering on sports events and horse races shown on satellite TV. At the intersection of Boulevard Costero and Avenida Riveroll is the **Plaza Cívica,** with sculptures of Benito Juárez, Miguel Hidalgo, and Venustiano Carranza. Cruise ships dock offshore from here, and passengers are ferried to the pier, where they can walk to the **Centro Artesenal de Ensenada** shopping center. This small shopping center has never really been a success, but it does house Ensenada's best shop, the Galería de Pérez Meillón (*see* Shopping, *below*). Ensenada's waterfront is scheduled for a long-overdue cleanup and restoration, with the commercial ships moved to the north end, away from the tourist zone. Plans include a new cruise ship pier across from Riviera del Pacifico (*see below*).

❻ Boulevard Costero becomes Boulevard Lázaro Cárdenas at Avenida Riviera, site of the **Riviera del Pacífico.** This rambling, white adobe hacienda-style mansion was built in the 1920s with money raised on both sides of the border. An enormous gambling palace, hotel, restaurant and bar, the glamorous Riviera was frequented by wealthy U.S. citizens and Mexicans, particularly during Prohibition. When gambling was outlawed in Mexico and Prohibition ended in the United States, the palace lost its raison d'être. In 1977 the Tourism and Convention Bureau began refurbishing the palace and its lavish gardens. During daylight visitors can now tour the elegant ballrooms and halls, which host occasional art shows and civic events. Riviera del Pacífico is now officially called the Centro Social, Cívico y Cultural de Ensenada (Social, Civic and Cultural Center of Ensenada), and there are plans to include it in a major convention-center complex along the waterfront. *Blvd. Costero and Av. Riviera,* ☎ *617/6–43–10.* ☞ *Free.* ☉ *Daily 9–5.*

❼ The **State Tourist Office** (*see* Important Addresses and Numbers *in* Ensenada Essentials, *below*) is located south of Riviera del Pacifico, a short walk from the tourist zone.

❽ Ensenada's traditional tourist zone is centered one block east of the waterfront along **Avenida López Mateos.** High-rise hotels, souvenir shops, restaurants, and bars line the avenue from its beginning at the foot of the Chapultepec Hills for eight blocks south to the dry channel of the Arroyo de Ensenada. Locals shop for furniture, clothing, **❾** and other necessities on **Avenida Juárez** in Ensenada's downtown area. The city's largest cathedral, **Our Lady of Guadalupe,** is at Avenida Floresta and the south end of Juárez.

❿ About 30 minutes south of Ensenada by car, **La Bufadora** is an impressive blowhole in the coastal cliffs at Punta Banda. Water splashes up to 75 feet in the air with startling power, spraying sightseers standing nearby. The blowhole has long been a natural attraction, but the area around it had become littered with trash and rundown buildings. State officials have begun a major restoration of the area, and a paved parking lot, permanent artisans' stands, rest rooms, and restaurants are under construction. To reach La Bufadora drive south on Highway 1 to Maneadero, then turn right on Highway 23, a narrow two-lane road down the point.

Shopping

Most of the tourist shops are located along Avenida López Mateos beside the hotels and restaurants. There are several two-story shopping arcades, many with empty shops. Dozens of curio shops line the street, all selling similar selections of pottery, woven blankets and serapes, embroidered dresses, and onyx chess sets.

Artes de Quijote (Av. López Mateos 503, ☎ 617/6–94–76) has an impressive high-quality selection of carved-wood doors, huge terracotta pots, crafts from Oaxaca, and large brass fish and birds. **Los Castillo** (Av. López Mateos 815, ☎ 617/6–11–87) and **Artesanías Castillo** (Av. López Mateos 656, ☎ 617/6–11–87) both have extensive displays of silver jewelry from Taxco. **Girasoles** (Av. López Mateos, no phone), opened in 1994, displays a great selection of dolls, pine-needle baskets, and pottery made by the Tarahumara Indians from the Copper Canyon. **Xuchitl** (Av. López Mateos at Alvarado, ☎ 617/4–09–76) is one of the best shops in town for wooden masks, tin mirrors and frames, and hand-painted pottery. **La Mina de Salomón** (Av. López

Mateos 1000, ☎ 617/8–28–36) carries elaborate jewelry by artist Sergio Bustamante in a tiny gallery next to El Rey Sol restaurant.

Centro Artesenal de Ensenada, a shopping center on the waterfront, caters to cruise-ship visitors. The best shop by far is the **Galería de Pérez Meillón** (Blvd. Costera 1094–39, ☎ 617/4–03–94), which carries museum-quality pottery and varied folk art by the indigenous peoples of northern Mexico.

Sports and Outdoor Activities

Golf
The **Baja Country Club** (Hwy. 1 south of Ensenada at Maneadero, ☎ 617/3–03–03) has a secluded 18-hole course in a resort development. *See* Sports and Outdoor Activities *in* Rosarito Beach, *above,* for details on **Bajamar Golf Resort,** some 32 kilometers (20 miles) north of Ensenada.

Sportfishing
Fishing boats leave the **Ensenada Sportfishing Pier** regularly. The best angling is from April through November, with bottom fishing good in the winter. Charter vessels and party boats are available from several outfitters along Avenida López Mateos, Boulevard Costero, and off the sportfishing pier. Trips on group boats cost about $50 per day. You can book sportfishing packages including transportation, accommodations, and fishing through **Baja California Tours** (☎ 619/454–7166 in CA). Licenses are available at the tourist office or from charter companies.

Ensenada Clipper Fleet (pier, ☎ 617/8–21–85) has charter and group boats.

Gordo's Sportfishing (*see* Guided Tours *in* Ensenada Essentials, *below*), one of the oldest sportfishing companies in Ensenada, has charter boats, group boats, and a smokehouse.

Tennis
Bajamar and the **Baja Country Club** (*see* Golf, *above*) have courts open to members and guests.

Beaches

Since the waterfront in Ensenada proper is taken up by fishing boats, the best swimming beaches are south of town. **Estero Beach** is long and clean, with mild waves. Surfers populate the beaches off Highway 1 north and south of Ensenada, particularly at **San Miguel, California, Tres Marías,** and **La Joya** beaches; scuba divers prefer **Punta Banda,** by La Bufadora. Lifeguards are rare; swimmers should be cautious. The tourist office in Ensenada has a map that shows safe diving and surfing beaches.

Dining

Some restaurants add a service charge of 10% to 15% to your bill in addition to the 15% tax. Dress is casual, and no reservations are necessary unless otherwise indicated.

CATEGORY	COST*
$$$	$15–$20
$$	$8–$15
$	under $8

per person for a three-course meal, excluding drinks and service

$$$ **El Rey Sol.** A family-owned French restaurant more than 40 years old,
★ El Rey Sol is in a charming building with stained-glass windows and
is decorated with wrought-iron chandeliers and heavy oak tables and
chairs. Specialties include French and Mexican presentations of fresh
fish, poultry, and vegetables grown at the owner's farm in the Santo
Tomás Valley. Appetizers come with the meal; the excellent pastries
are baked on the premises. ✗ *Av. López Mateos 1000,* ☎ *617/
8–17–33. Reservations recommended. AE, MC, V.*

$$$ **La Embotelladora Vieja.** The most exciting new restaurant Ensenada
★ has seen in years is set in a converted wine-aging room at the Santo
Tomás winery. The decor is classic country-French, with wine bins
stacked floor-to-ceiling under brick arches and crystal goblets glistening on candlelit tables. The so-called Baja French menu includes
appetizers of smoked tuna and French pâté; among the most sublime
entrées are the grilled lobster in cabernet sauvignon sauce and beef
Montpellier with green peppercorns. Teetotalers, note: Nearly every
dish is prepared with wine, though you can order some without alco-
hol-laden sauces. All of Baja's wineries are represented on the impressive wine list. The restaurant is so outstanding that southern
Californians drive to Ensenada for long lunches here. ✗ *Av. Miramar
666,* ☎ *617/4–08–07. MC, V.*

$$ **Bronco's Steak House.** A great find near the San Nicolas Hotel,
Bronco's serves exceptional steaks and Mexican specialties. Try the
Boca del Rio, a New York steak stuffed with grilled onions and fiery
serrano chiles. Tripe appears frequently on the menu, satisfying the
cravings of local diners gathered at many of the wood tables. Brick
walls, wood plank floors, and hanging spurs and chaps give the place
a Wild West feel, but the mood is subdued and relaxed. ✗ *Av. López
Mateos 1525,* ☎ *617/6–49–00. MC, V.*

$$ **Casamar.** A long-standing, dependable restaurant, Casamar is known
for its wide variety of excellent seafood. Lobster and shrimp are pre-
pared in several ways but seem freshest when grilled *con mojo y ajo*
(with butter and garlic). The upstairs bar has live jazz on weekend
nights. ✗ *Blvd. Lázaro Cárdenas 987,* ☎ *617/4–04–17. MC, V.*

$$ **El Charro.** You can get rotisserie chicken, beans, rice, and tortillas far
more cheaply at other places in downtown, but El Charro still attracts
a steady stream of locals and tourists. Part of the draw is the location,
not far from Hussong's and other watering holes, and the food is con-
sistently good. Hungry patrons hover over platters of chiles rellenos,
enchiladas, and fresh chips and guacamole at heavy wooden picnic
tables under a ceiling of charred wooden beams. Plump chickens
slowly circle over a wood fire by the front window, and the aroma of
grilled beef and simmering beans fills the air. ✗ *Av. López Mateos 475,*
☎ *617/8–38–81. MC, V.*

$ **Plaza Mariscos.** Several taco stands fill this bright pink plaza in front
of the fish market. One way to choose your dining spot is by check-
ing out the bowls of condiments arrayed on picnic tables between the
stands—if the salsa, onions, cilantro, and pickled vegetables look
good, you're bound to like the tacos as well. ✗ *Blvd. Costero, no* ☎.
No credit cards.

$ **Plaza Mexico.** You can eat in or take out your meals at this brightly
lit café, where mariachis add to the festive ambience on Friday and
Saturday nights. Thick grilled steaks and marinated carne asada are
the best dinner bets; the tacos are good for inexpensive meals or
snacks. Margaritas and beer are available. ✗ *Av. López Mateos 2184,*
☎ *617/7–21–51. No credit cards.*

Lodging

Ensenada has a glut of hotel rooms at the moment, and package deals abound. Most rooms are least expensive during midweek and in the winter, when Ensenada can be chilly and breezy. Several companies can book rooms in Ensenada and throughout Baja. For information contact: **IMPA/Mexico Information** (7860 Mission Center Ct., Suite 202, San Diego CA 92108, ☎ 619/298–4105 or 800/522–1516, FAX 619/294–7366); **Baja California Tours** (6986 La Jolla Blvd. No. 204, La Jolla, CA 92037, ☎ 619/454–7166, FAX 619/454–2703); and **Mexico Resorts International** (Box 120637, Chula Vista, CA 91912, ☎ 619/422–6900 or 800/336–5454, FAX 619/422–6910). Unless otherwise indicated, the postal code for the Ensenada lodgings listed is 22800.

CATEGORY	COST*
$$$$	over $90
$$$	$60–$90
$$	$25–$60
$	under $25

All prices are for a standard double room, excluding service charge and tax (10%).

$$$$ **Las Rosas.** This elegant pink palace just north of town is by far the
★ most modern hotel in the area; the atrium lobby features marble floors, mint-green-and-pink upholstered couches facing the sea, and a green-glass ceiling that glows at night. All rooms face the ocean and pool; some have fireplaces and Jacuzzis, and even the least expensive accommodations are lovely. The hotel is booked solid most weekends; make reservations far in advance. ☎ *Mexico Hwy. 1, north of town,* ☎ *617/4–43–20,* FAX *617/4–45–95. 32 rooms and suites. Restaurant, bar, pool, hot tub. AE, MC, V.*

$$$ **Punta Morro.** For seclusion and the sound of crashing surf, you can't beat this all-suites hotel beside the university campus. The three-story tan building faces the north end of the bay; the restaurant sits on rock pilings above the waves. All accommodations have terraces facing the ocean, kitchenettes, and seating areas; some also feature fireplaces. Stairs lead down to a rocky beach, but the surf is usually too rough for swimming. ☎ *Mexico Hwy. 1, 2 mi north of town, Box 2891,* ☎ *617/8–35–07 or 800/726–6426,* FAX *617/4–44–90; reservations in the U.S.: Box 43-4263, San Ysidro, CA 92143. 30 suites. Restaurant, bar, pool, hot tub, beach. MC, V.*

$$$ **San Nicolás.** Hidden behind cement walls painted with Indian
★ murals, this massive resort doesn't look like much from the street. The San Nicolás was built in the early 1970s, but much of it has been refurbished. The suites boast tiled hot tubs; living rooms with deep green carpeting, mauve furnishings, and beveled-glass doors; and mirrored ceilings in the bedrooms. The less extravagant rooms are comfortable and decorated with folk art. A waterfall cascades into the pool, and a good restaurant overlooks the gardens. An indoor swimming pool (the only one in an Ensenada hotel) opened in 1994, and there is a branch of Caliente Sports Book on the premises. ☎ *Av. López Mateos (also called Calle 1) and Av. Guadalupe, Box 19,* ☎ *617/6–40–70,* FAX *617/6–49–30; reservations in the U.S.: Box 43706, San Diego, CA 92143. 150 rooms and suites. Restaurants, bar, 2 pools, hot tub, disco, convention center. AE, MC, V.*

$$$ **Villa Marina.** At 12 stories, the blue-and-white Villa Marina is the tallest hotel in town, though not necessarily the most luxurious. Rooms face either the waterfront or downtown and have small balconies, blue carpeting and walls, bathtubs with showers, and sinks

outside the bathroom. The nightclub on top of the hotel has a spectacular view of the region, but noise from live bands on weekends makes rooms on the floor below less desirable. A small shopping plaza fronts the hotel on the main shopping and dining street. ⌗ *Av. López Mateos at Balancarte,* ☎ *617/8–33–21,* ⸬ *617/8–33–51; reservations in the U.S.: Box 727, Bonita, CA 91908. Restaurant, bar, pool, nightclub. MC, V.*

$$ Quintas Papagayo. A bungalow and low-rise seaside establishment opened in 1947, Quintas Papagayo is a place where couples honeymoon and come back each year for their anniversaries. The accommodations are rustic, but you feel as if you've discovered a special hideaway where everyone remembers your name. Fireplaces, kitchens, patios, and decks are available. A new marina and high-rise hotel are under construction next door. ⌗ *Mexico Hwy. 1, north of town,* ☎ *617/4–41–55 or 617/4–45–75; reservations: Box 150, Ensenada, BC or* ☎ *619/491–0682 in the U.S. 50 rooms. Restaurant, bar, pool, beach, tennis courts. MC, V.*

$$ Villa Fontana. An architectural oddity in a town full of Spanish tiled roofs, this peak gabled hotel has a New England look. The rooms are decorated in pastels; choose one at the back, away from street noise. There is enclosed parking—a major plus in downtown Ensenada. ⌗ *Av. López Mateos 1050,* ☎ *and* ⸬ *617/8–34–34; reservations in the U.S.: 800/DAYS–INN. 60 rooms. Pool, travel services. MC, V.*

$ Joker Hotel. A bizarre, brightly colored mishmash of styles makes it hard to miss this hotel, conveniently located for those traveling south of Ensenada. Spacious rooms have private balconies, satellite TV, and phones. ⌗ *Mexico Hwy. 1, Km 12.5,* ☎ *and* ⸬ *617/6–72–01; reservations in the U.S.: 800/22–JOKER. 40 rooms. Pool, hot tub. MC, V.*

Nightlife

Ensenada is a party town for college students, surfers, and other young tourists. **Hussong's Cantina** (Av. Ruíz 113, ☎ 617/8–32–10) has been an Ensenada landmark since 1892, and has changed little since then. A security guard stands by the front door to handle the often-rowdy crowd, a mix of locals and tourists of all ages over 18. The noise is usually deafening, pierced by mariachi and ranchera musicians and whoops and hollers from the inebriated. **Papas and Beer** (Av. Ruíz at López Mateos, ☎ 617/8–42–31) is oriented toward the college set, who hang out the second-story windows shouting at their friends.

Hotel Villa Marina (Av. López Mateos at Balancarte, ☎ 617/8–33–21) opened a night club on the 11th floor in late 1994. The views from the tallest building downtown are staggering, as is the noise of recorded disco music. Live dance bands play Thursday through Saturday nights.

Ensenada Essentials

Arriving and Departing

BY PLANE

Ensenada's **Aeropuerto el Cipres** (☎ 617/6–63–03) was expanded in 1993 and in 1994 began receiving flights from Los Angeles on **Air LA** (☎ 800/933–5952). Service was cancelled in late 1994, but may have started up again by the time you travel.

BY BUS

Ensenada can be reached by bus from Tijuana, Mexicali, and Mexico City. **Autotransportes de Baja California** and **Tres Estrellas de Oro** travel throughout Baja, linking all the major cities. The bus station is at Avenida Riveroll between Calles 10 and 11 (☎ 617/8–67–70).

BY SHIP

Ensenada is a year-round port for **Starlite Cruises** (☎ 800/488–7827), which features one-day cruises from San Diego, with gambling on board ship.

BY CAR

Most people who visit Ensenada drive. Tourist cards are required only if you are traveling south of Ensenada or staying longer than 72 hours.

Mexico Highway 1, called Ensenada Cuota, is a toll road that runs along the coast from the Tijuana border to Ensenada. The toll booths along the road accept U.S. and Mexican currency; tolls are usually about $2.50. The road is excellent, though it has some hair-raising curves atop the cliffs and is best driven in daylight (the stretch from Rosarito Beach to Ensenada is one of the most scenic drives in Baja). The free road, called Ensenada Libre, runs parallel to the toll road off and on, cutting east of the low hills along the coast. Although free, the road doubles your traveling time and is very rough in spots.

Getting Around

Most of Ensenada's attractions are situated within five blocks of the waterfront; it is easy to take a long walking tour of the city. A car is necessary to reach La Bufadora, the Chapultepec Hills, and most of the beaches. Buses travel the route from Ensenada through Guerrero Negro at the border between Baja California and Baja Sur and continue down to the southernmost tip of Baja.

BY BUS

Tres Estrellas de Oro and **Autotransportes de Baja California** cover the entire Baja route and connect in Mexicali with buses to Guadalajara and Mexico City.

BY TAXI

There is a *sitio* (central taxi stand) on Avenida López Mateos by the Bahía Hotel (☎ 617/8–34–75). Be sure to set the price before the taxi starts moving. Destinations within the city should cost less than $10.

BY CAR

Ensenada is an easy city to navigate in that most of the streets are marked. If you are traveling south, you can bypass downtown Ensenada on the Highway 1 truck route down Calle 10. To reach the hotel and waterfront area, stay with Alternate Highway 1 as it travels along the fishing pier and becomes Boulevard Costero, also known as Lázaro Cárdenas and Carretera Transpeninsular. This road ends at Calle Agustín Sangines, also called Calle Delante, which leads out to Highway 1 traveling south. The parking meters along Ensenada's main streets are patrolled regularly; parking tickets come in the form of either a boot on the car's tires or confiscated license plates. Parking has become horrendous as new shopping centers spring up on former parking lots. The paid parking at the new Plaza Marina at the beginning of Boulevard Costero may be your best option.

Ensenada Rent-a-Car (☎ 617/8–18–96) has an office on Avenida Alvarado between Lázaro Cárdenas and López Mateos.

Guided Tours

Baja California Tours (6986 La Jolla Blvd., No. 204, La Jolla, CA 92037, ☎ 619/454–7166, FAX 619/454–2703) offers comfortable, informative bus trips throughout Baja and can arrange special-interest tours, including whale-watching and fishing trips and tours to the wineries and La Bufadora. Vans depart daily from San Diego to Ensenada; midweek transportation and hotel packages are a real bargain.

Las Bodegas de Santo Tomás (Av. Miramar 666, ☎ 617/8–33–33), Baja's oldest winery, gives tours and tastings Monday through Saturday at 11 AM, 1 PM, and 3 PM, and Sunday at 11 AM and 1 PM. The cost is $1.50. **Cavas Valmar Winery** (Calle Ambar 810, ☎ 617/8–64–05) offers winery tours by appointment.

Gordo's Sportfishing (Sportfishing Pier, ☎ 617/8–21–90) operates whale-watching trips from December through February. The half-day trip goes to La Bufadora and Isla Todos Santos and costs $35 per person.

Important Addresses and Numbers

EMERGENCIES

Police (Ortíz Rubio and Libertad, ☎ 134), **Hospital of the Americas** (Av. Arenas 151, ☎ 617/6–03–01), **Red Cross** (☎ 132).

LANGUAGE CLASSES

A great way to get to know Ensenada and simultaneously improve your Spanish is to attend weekend or week-long classes at the **International Spanish Institute of Ensenada** (☎ 617/6–1–09 or 619/472–0600 in CA).

VISITOR INFORMATION

The **State Tourist Commission** office (Blvd. Costera 1477, ☎ 617/2–30–22, FAX 617/2–30–81) is open weekdays 9–7, Saturday 10–3, Sunday 10–2; there's always an English-speaking clerk on hand to assist travelers. The **Convention and Visitors Bureau** (☎ 617/8–24–11) has a stand with pamphlets and brochures on Boulevard Costero at the waterfront.

NORTHEAST BAJA: MEXICALI, TECATE, AND SAN FELIPE

Mexicali, with a current population estimated at 850,000, shares the Imperial Valley farmland and the border crossing with Calexico, a small California city. The capital of Baja California, Mexicali sees a great deal of government activity and a steady growth of *maquiladoras* (foreign manufacturing plants). Though water is scarce in these largely desert lands, the Mexicali area is blessed with some of the world's richest topsoil, and agriculture is a primary source of income in this section of Mexico. Mexicali is not a tourist destination but rather a place where politicians and bureaucrats meet. A train that reaches points throughout Mexico originates in Mexicali, which is also a point of entry for travelers to the beaches of San Felipe.

At the end of Highway 5, which travels 200 kilometers (125 miles) south of Mexicali along solitary stretches of desert and salt marshes, lies the fishing village of **San Felipe** (population 18,000) on the Sea of Cortés. Not until 1948, when the first paved road from the northern capital was completed, did San Felipe become a town of permanent residence. Now it is home to an impressive fishing and shrimping fleet. A hurricane nearly destroyed San Felipe in 1967, but residents rebuilt most of the town, and since then it has grown steadily.

Bahía San Felipe has dramatic changes in its tides. The tides crest at 6 meters (20 feet), and since the beach is so shallow, the waterline can move in and out up to 1 kilometer (about ½ mile). The local fishermen are well aware of the peculiarities of this section of the Sea of Cortés. Many of them visit the shrine of the Cerro de la Virgen (Virgin of Guadalupe), which sits high on a hill at the north end of the bay, before setting sail.

A popular getaway spot for years, San Felipe used to be a place where only hardy travelers in recreational vehicles and campers hid out for weeks on end. Now there are at least two dozen campgrounds and a dozen hotels in town and on the coastline both north and south of town, which fill up quickly during the winter and spring holidays. A new resort complex and marina are under construction just south of town, with a 60-room hotel now open. Dune buggies, motorcycles, and off-road vehicles abound. On weekends San Felipe can be boisterous. The town also draws many sportfishermen, especially in the spring; launches, bait, and supplies are readily available.

Tecate is about 144 kilometers (90 miles) west of Mexicali on Highway 2. It is a quiet community, a typical small Mexican town (population about 100,000) that happens to be on the border. So incidental is the border to local life that its gates are closed from midnight until 6 AM. Tecate beer, one of the most popular brands in Mexico, is brewed here. Maquiladoras and agriculture are the other main industries. Tecate's primary tourist draw is Rancho la Puerta, a fitness resort that caters to well-heeled southern Californians. A bit farther south, the valleys of Guadalupe and Calafía boast some of Mexico's lushest vineyards. Olives and grain are also grown in profusion here.

Exploring

Most visitors come to **Mexicali** on business, and the city's sights are few and far between. A tourist-oriented strip of curio shops and sleazy bars is located along Avenida Francisco Madero, one block south of the border. The **Regional Museum**, administered by the Autonomous University of Baja California (UABC), provides a comprehensive introduction to the natural and cultural history of Baja. *Av. Reforma 1998, near Calle L,* ☎ *65/52–57–17.* ☛ *Free.* ☾ *Tues.–Fri. 9–6, weekends 10–4.*

Parque Obregón at Avenida Reforma and Calle Irigoyen and **Parque Constitución** at Avenida México and Zuazua are the only two parks in downtown Mexicali. The **Mexicali Zoo** is in the City Park, **Bosque de la Ciudad,** south of town; the entrance is at the south end of Calle Victoria, between Cárdenas and Avenida Independencia.

If you allocate an hour for exploring **Tecate,** you'll be hard put to fill your time. **Parque Hidalgo,** in the center of town, is a typical Mexican village plaza, with a small gazebo and a few wrought-iron benches. **Parque López Mateos,** on Highway 3 south of town, is the site for dance and band concerts on summer evenings.

San Felipe is the quintessential dusty fishing village, with one main street (two if you count the highway into town). The *malecón* (waterfront boardwalk) runs along a broad beach with a swimming area in the middle and public changing rooms at the north end. Taco stands, bars, and restaurants line the sidewalk across the street from the beach. The only landmark in town is the **shrine of the Virgin of Guadalupe,** at the north end of the malecón on a hill overlooking the Sea of Cortés and San Felipe Bay.

Shopping

In Mexicali, **Baldini Importers** (Calle 7 and Av. Reforma, ☎ 65/61–23–10) offers a nice selection of imported items. In San Felipe, **Curios Merida** (Av. Mar de Cortez, no ☎) has a better-than-average selection of sombreros, sundresses, and T-shirts, and a large supply of fireworks.

Sports and Outdoor Activities

Mexicali

GOLF

You can play golf at the **Mexicali Campestre Golf Course** (Km 11.5 on Hwy. 5 south of town, ☎ 65/61–71–30).

San Felipe

FISHING AND WATERSPORTS

The Sea of Cortés offers plentiful sea bass, snapper, corbina, halibut, and other game fish. Clamming is good here as well. Several companies offer sportfishing trips; among the most established are **Alex Sportfishing** (☎ 657/7–10–52), **Pelicanos** (☎ 657/7–11–88), and **San Felipe Sportfishing** (☎ 657/7–10–55). **Del Mar Cortés Charters** (Box 9, San Felipe, 21850, ☎ 657/7–13–03) conducts fishing trips, full- and half-day Trimaran tours of the Sea of Cortés, and boat charters. It can also arrange kayak and Hobie Cat rentals through the El Dorado private community north of town. **Enchanted Island Excursions** (233 Paulin #8512, Calexico, CA 92231, ☎ 657/7–14–31 in San Felipe) offers off-road, dune-buggy tours and boat excursions.

Dining

Northeast Baja is not known for fine dining, but there are several good Chinese restaurants in Mexicali. (The construction of the Imperial Canal in 1902 brought an influx of Chinese residents to the region.) Your best bet in San Felipe is seafood, especially fresh shrimp. Dress is casual and reservations are not required.

CATEGORY	COST*
$$$	$15–$20
$$	$8–$15
$	under $8

per person for a three-course meal, excluding drinks and service

Mexicali

$$$ **La Misión Dragón.** With its eclectic landscape, this restaurant resem-
★ bles a combination mission house and Chinese palace. Behind its gates are fountains, a garden, and Asian and Mexican artifacts. The locals hold large dinner celebrations here, and the Chinese food is top-notch. ✕ *Av. Lázaro Cárdenas 555, ☎ 65/66–43–20 or 65/66–44–51. MC, V.*

$$ **Cenaduría Selecta.** This charming restaurant has been serving traditional Mexican food since 1945. Service is formal and efficient, the menus come in wooden folders, and the rows of booths always seem to be filled with locals enjoying themselves. ✕ *Av. Arista and Calle C 1510, ☎ 65/62–40–47. MC, V.*

$ **Las Cazuelas.** A nice, clean restaurant, Las Cazuelas serves traditional Mexican dishes and good combination meals. ✕ *Av. Benito Juárez 56, ☎ 65/64–06–49. No credit cards.*

San Felipe

$$ George's. A favorite with resident Americans, George's has comfy padded red Naugahyde booths, powerful margaritas, and very good chiles rellenos, carne asada, and seafood. ✕ *Av. Mar de Cortés 336,* ☎ *657/7–10–57. MC, V.*

$$ Juan's Place. A family-run operation two blocks east of the waterfront, Juan's offers consistently excellent home-style cooking at reasonable prices. The catch of the day and grilled meats come with boiled vegetables—ask for beans, rice, and the delicious homemade tortillas instead. ✕ *Calle de Ensenada, no* ☎. *No credit cards.*

$ Tony's Tacos. The most popular of the many taco stands along the waterfront, Tony's is a simple spot with sidewalk picnic tables and a counter lined with condiments for the house specialty—cheap, delicious fish tacos. ✕ *Malecón at Av. Chetumal, no* ☎. *No credit cards.*

$ El Toro. Open only for breakfast, El Toro is renowned among locals and San Felipe regulars for its *chorizo, machaca* (shredded beef), *huevos rancheros,* and American-style breakfasts. The parking lot fills with trailers hauling dune buggies and motorcycles as large groups gather to fuel up before a long day on the dunes. ✕ *Hwy. 5, north of town,* ☎ *657/7–10–32. No credit cards.*

Tecate

$$ El Passetto. The best Italian restaurant in Tecate, El Passetto has superb garlic bread and homemade pasta. The proprietor makes his own wines, which are pretty good. There's live music on weekends. *Callejón Libertad 200,* ☎ *665/4–1361. MC, V.*

$ Panadería El Mejor. The best bakery in the Tecate area, El Mejor is open 24 hours daily. The fresh breads and pastries are legendary, and free coffee comes with your purchase. ✕ *Av. Juárez 331,* ☎ *665/4–00–40. No credit cards.*

$ Plaza Jardín. The setting is plain and the food simple Mexican fare, but the café tables outside offer a gratifying view of the plaza. ✕ *Andador Libertad 274,* ☎ *665/4–34–54. No credit cards.*

Lodging

Hotels are abundant in Mexicali but scarce in San Felipe and Tecate. Accommodations, as a rule, are modest and plain. **IMPA/Mexico Information** (7860 Mission Center Ct., Suite 202, San Diego, CA 92108, ☎ 619/298–4105 or 800/522–1516 in CA, AZ, and NV; 800/225–2786 elsewhere in the U.S., ℻ 619/294–7366) handles hotel reservations for the area.

CATEGORY	COST*
$$$$	over $90
$$$	$60–$90
$$	$25–$60
$	under $25

*All prices are for a standard double room, excluding service charge and sales tax (10%).

Mexicali

$$$ Holiday Inn. This is the perennial favorite of those doing business in the city, with standard rooms and services and no surprises. Holiday Inn also operates a Crowne Plaza hotel in Mexicali, in the very expensive (**$$$$**) price range. ▣ *Av. Benito Juárez 2220, 21270,* ☎ *65/66–38–01* ℻ *65/57–05–55; reservations in the U.S.: 800/465–4329. 173 rooms. Restaurant, bar, coffee shop, pool. AE, MC, V.*

$$$ **La Lucerna.** The prettiest hotel in Mexicali, La Lucerna has lots of
★ palms and fountains around the pool. ☎ *Av. Benito Juárez 2151,*
21270, ☎ *65/66–10–00 or 800/582–3762,* FAX *65/66–47–06. 200*
rooms. Restaurant, coffee shop, bar, pool. MC, V.

San Felipe

$$$$ **San Felipe Marina Resort.** This full-scale resort will eventually include
a 100-slip marina along with resort homes and hotels. At present, a
terra-cotta color building facing the sea has 60 units available as hotel
rooms, time-share units, or private condos. Most rooms have
kitchens with microwaves, coffeemakers, and refrigerators; woven
rugs on white-tile floors and folk art decorations; and balconies or
patios with sea views. The pool sits above the beach next to a palapa
bar; a second indoor pool is a delight on cold winter days. The resort
is a five-minute drive south of town on the water and has an RV
campground next door. ☎ *Km 4.5 Carretera San Felipe Aeropuerto,*
21850, ☎ *657/7–15–68, 619/558–0295 or 800/777–1700 in the*
U.S., FAX *657/7–14–55. Restaurant, bar, indoor and outdoor pools,*
exercise room, camping, tennis courts. MC, V.

$$$ **Costa Azul.** Opened in 1994, the Costa Azul is the largest hotel right in
town, at the south end of the malecón. Several three-story buildings
frame a parking lot and pool area, and the restaurant and bar are in a
two-story building on the beach. The rooms are far from spectacular
and look like they may not hold up well, but the location can't be beat.
Monday through Wednesday, room rates are almost 20% lower. ☎
Av. Mar de Cortés at Calle Ensenada, 21850, ☎ *657/1–15–48,* FAX
657/7–15–49; reservations in the U.S.: 233 Pauline Ave., No. 6252,
Calexico, CA 92231. 140 rooms. Restaurant, bar, pool. MC, V.

$$$ **El Cortez.** Easily the most popular hotel in San Felipe, the El Cortez has
several types of accommodations, from moderately priced bungalows
to expensive hotel rooms with white walls, pastel bedspreads and
drapes, and white-tile floors; some have two bedrooms. The hotel's
beachfront and second-story bars are both enduringly popular, and the
restaurant is the nicest water-view dining spot in town. The hotel is a
five-minute walk from the malecón. ☎ *Av. Mar de Cortez s/n, 21850,*
☎ *657/7–10–56,* FAX *657/7–10–55; reservations in the U.S.: Box 1227,*
Calexico, CA 92232. 102 rooms. Restaurant, bar, pool. MC, V.

$$$ **Las Misiones.** A pretty oasis of blue pools and green palms by the
beach, this resort is popular with group tours. Las Misiones is a good
choice for travelers who want to get away from it all, but you'll need
a car or cab to get to town. A new building just down the street from
the hotel contains suites with kitchens. ☎ *Av. Misión de Loreto 130,*
21850, ☎ *657/7–12–80 or 800/336–5454,* FAX *657/7–12–83. 241*
rooms, 20 suites. Restaurant, bar, 3 pools, tennis courts. MC, V.

Tecate

$$$ **Hacienda Santa Veronica.** Billed as an off-road and dirt-racing country
club, the Hacienda is a pretty countryside resort featuring rooms fur-
nished with Mexican colonial beds, bureaus, and fireplaces. The off-
road raceway is set far enough away from the rooms to keep the noise
of revving engines from disturbing the guests, and a number of trails for
horseback riding traverse the property. ☎ *Hwy. 2, 2 mi east of Tecate,*
21275, no ☎*; reservations in the U.S.,* ☎ *619/298–4105 or 800/*
522–1516. 87 rooms. Restaurant, bar, pool, horseback riding, tennis
courts. MC, V.

Health Spa

Tecate

$$$$ Rancho la Puerta. For those who can afford $1,500 or more a week, Rancho la Puerta is a peaceful, isolated health spa and resort just west of Tecate. Spanish-style buildings with red-tiled roofs and modern glass-and-wood structures are spread throughout the sprawling ranch. Hiking trails lead off into scrub-pine hills surrounding the resort, and a large bright-blue pool is a central gathering spot. Guests stay in luxurious private cottages and usually check in for a week or more, taking advantage of the special diet and exercise regimen to lose weight and shape up. ☒ *Hwy. 2, 3 mi west of Tecate, 21275* ☏ *65/4–11–55 or 619/744–4222 in CA, 800/443–7565,* FAX *65/4–11–08. 80 rooms. Restaurant, pool, hair salon, massage, health club, tennis courts. AE, MC, V.*

The Arts and Nightlife

Mexicali

Teatro del Estado (☏ 65/64–07–57), on Calle López Mateos near the government center, often presents stage hits from Mexico City; dance troupes and musical groups, both classical and modern, are frequently featured as well.

San Felipe

There's not much nightlife in San Felipe, but the bar at the **El Cortés Hotel** (☏ 657/7–10–56) is always crowded.

Northeast Baja Essentials

Arriving and Departing

BY PLANE

Mexicana (☏ 800/531–7921) has daily flights between Mexicali and Guadalajara and Mexicali and Mexico City.

There were no commercial airlines flying to San Felipe's international airport at press time. **Air LA** (☏ 800/933–5952) cancelled service to San Felipe in 1994; check to see if its service has started up again.

BY CAR

Mexicali is located on the border, opposite Calexico, California, approximately 184 kilometers (115 miles) east of San Diego and 88 kilometers (55 miles) west of Yuma, Arizona. Tecate lies on the border between Tijuana and Mexicali on Highway 2. A new toll road between Tijuana and Tecate opened in 1994, and another is under construction between Tecate and Mexicali. The 134-kilometer (84-mile) journey from Tecate east to Mexicali on La Rumorosa, as the road is known, is as exciting as a roller-coaster ride, with the highway twisting and turning down steep mountain grades and over flat, barren desert. San Felipe lies on the coast, 200 kilometers (125 miles) south of Mexicali via Highway 5. Visitors in this area will not need tourist cards but should purchase Mexican car insurance at agencies near the border.

BY BUS

Four Mexican bus lines run out of the Mexicali station. **Tres Estrellas de Oro** goes through Tecate on its way to Tijuana; **Transportes del Pacífico** goes to Mexico City and other points on the mainland; **Transportes Norte de Sonora** frequents border towns in Baja and on the mainland; and **Autotransportes de Baja California** goes to San Felipe, Tijuana, and Ensenada. It is possible to purchase reserved seats the day before departure, but only at the bus station (Centro Cívico, Av. Independencia, ☎ 65/57–24–22 or 65/57–24–23).

Mexicali: Central Bus Station (Centro Cívico, Av. Independencia, ☎ 65/57–24–22).

San Felipe: Central Bus Station/Autotransportes de Baja California (Av. Mar Caribe at Av. Manzanillo, ☎ 657/7–15–16).

Tecate: Central Bus Station (Av. Benito Juárez and Calle Abelardo Rodríguez, ☎ 665/4–12–21).

BY TRAIN

Although there is no train service available through Baja, **El Tren del Pacífico** (Estación de Ferrocarril, Box 3–182, Mexicali, Baja California, Mexico, ☎ 65/57–2101 or 65/57–23–86) runs from Mexicali to points south in the mainland interior. The station is located at the south end of Calle Ulises Irigoyen, a few blocks north of the intersection of Avenida López Mateos and Avenida Independencia. Trains leave twice daily.

Getting Around

BY CAR

The ideal way to see the northeastern part of Baja is to drive your own car or rent one in Mexicali. Most U.S. car-rental agencies do not allow their cars to be taken into Mexico. (*See* Getting Around by Car in the Tijuana section, *above,* for those that do.) Be sure to buy Mexican auto insurance before driving into Baja.

Two major rental agencies operate out of the Mexicali airport: **Budget** (☎ 800/527–0700) and **Hertz** (☎ 800/654–3131).

BY TAXI

Taxis are easy to find in Mexicali, Tecate, and San Felipe. Negotiate your fare before you start the trip.

Guided Tours

Baja California Tours (6986 La Jolla Blvd., No. 204, La Jolla, CA 92037, ☎ 619/454–7166, ℻ 619/454–2703) offers comfortable, informative bus trips daily from San Diego to San Felipe; midweek transportation and hotel packages are a real bargain.

Important Addresses and Numbers

EMERGENCIES

Mexicali: Police (Centro Cívico, ☎ 65/52–44–43); **Hospital** (Durango and Salina Cruz, ☎ 657/57–16–66).

San Felipe: Police (Ortiz Rubio and Libertad, ☎ 657/7–13–50 or 657/7–10–21); **Hospital** (☎ 657/7–10–06 or 657/7–15–44).

Tecate: Police (Libertad Alley, ☎ 665/4–11–76 or 134); **Red Cross** (☎ 132); **Fire** (☎ 136).

VISITOR INFORMATION

In Mexicali, information is available at the **Mexicali Convention and Tourism Bureau** office (Calz. López Mateos at Calle Compresora, ☎ 65/52–23–76) and the **State Secretary of Tourism Office** (Calle Calafia at Calz. Independencia, ☎ 65/56–10–72). The posted hours of both tourism offices are weekdays 9–7 and weekends 9–2, but you may arrive to find their doors closed, especially on weekdays during lunch. In Tecate, the **State Tourism Office** (1305 Libertad Alley, ☎ 665/4–10–95) has a full array of pamphlets and an English-speaking clerk; the office is open weekdays 9–7 and weekends 10–3. The **San**

Felipe State Tourism Office (Av. Mar de Cortés, ☎ 657/7–11–55) is open weekdays 9–7 and weekends 10–2.

GUERRERO NEGRO AND SCAMMON'S LAGOON

Humans aren't the only travelers who migrate below the border for warmth in the winter months. Every winter thousands of great gray whales swim south from the Bering Sea off Alaska to the tip of the Baja Peninsula. From January through March up to 6,000 stop close to the shore at several spots along the Baja coast, including Scammon's Lagoon—at the 28th parallel, just over the state line between Baja California and Baja Sur—to give birth to their calves. Far from diminutive, the newborns weigh about one-half ton and drink nearly 50 gallons of milk each day.

If it weren't for the whales, and the Transpeninsular Highway, which runs near town, few travelers would venture to **Guerrero Negro,** a town of 10,000 located some 720 kilometers (450 miles) south of Tijuana; the name Guerrero Negro, which means Black Warrior, was derived from a whaling ship that ran aground in nearby Scammon's Lagoon in 1858. Near the Vizcaíno desert, on the Pacific Ocean, the area is best known for its salt mines, which provide work for much of the town's population and produce one-third of the world's salt supply. Salt water collects in more than 780 square kilometers (300 square miles) of sea-level ponds and evaporates quickly in the desert heat, leaving huge blocks of pure white salt.

Scammon's Lagoon is about 27 kilometers (17 miles) south, down a passable but rough sand road that crosses the salt flats. The lagoon got its name from U.S. explorer Charles Melville Scammon of Maine, who discovered it off the coast of Baja in the mid-1800s. The whales and calves that visited these waters were a much easier and more plentiful prey for the whalers than the great leviathans swimming in the open sea. On his first expedition to the lagoon, Scammon and his crew collected more than 700 barrels of valuable whale oil, and the whale rush was on. Within 10 years, nearly all the whales in the lagoon had been killed, and it took almost a century for the whale population to increase to what it had been before Scammon arrived. It wasn't until the 1940s that the U.S. and Mexican governments took measures to protect the whales and banned the whalers from the lagoon.

Today whale-watching boats must have permission from the Mexican government to enter Scammon's Lagoon, known in Mexico as Laguna Ojo de Liebre (Hare's Eye Lagoon). The area around the lagoon is now a national park, Parque Natural de Ojo de Liebre (Hare's Eye Natural Park). Whale-watching from the shores of the lagoon can be disappointing without binoculars. But it is still an impressive sight to see the huge mammals spouting water high into the air, their 12-foot-wide tails striking the water.

Many of the whale-watching tour operators offer expeditions to Scammon's Lagoon, either by boat or motorcoach from California. The other major whale-watching spots are farther south at **Laguna San Ignacio** and **Bahía Magdalena,** both on the Pacific coast. If traveling on your own, you can reach Laguna San Ignacio from the town of San Ignacio; Magdalena Bay (called "Mag Bay" by regulars) is about a four-hour drive across the peninsula from La Paz. Fishermen will take you out in their boats to get closer to the whales at both places. But for a better view, and an easier stay in this rugged country, travel with an outfitter who will arrange your travel, your accommodations, and your time on the water. The whales will come close to your boat, rising majestically from the water, and sometimes swim close enough to be petted on their crusted backs.

Dining

The best restaurant in town, specializing in seafood, is **Malarrimo,** on Boulevard Zapata near the entrance to town. Though the prices have climbed to the high-moderate range, the food is still worth the cost. Try **Mario's,** on Boulevard Zapata by the El Morro hotel, for seafood and Mexican dishes. The small, pretty **Puerto Viejo** on Boulevard Zapata also offers good standard Mexican dishes and seafood, but prices here are higher.

Lodging

There are several hotels in Guerrero Negro, none of which is worth visiting as a destination unto itself. Double-occupancy rooms cost from about $25 to $70 per day; rates tend to increase during the peak whale-watching season from January through March. None of the hotels has heat, and winter nights can be downright frigid. Credit cards are not normally accepted, but the hotels do take traveler's checks.

El Morro. A small motel operated by the owners of one of the largest hotels in Santa Rosalia, the El Morro is serviceable; the air-conditioned rooms have private baths and hot showers. ☎ *Blvd. Zapata,* ☎ *115/7–04–14. 32 rooms.*

La Pinta. A few kilometers outside of town and looking like an oasis of palms in the desert, La Pinta is the largest hotel in town. The clean, functional rooms are dependable, and the setting more attractive than that of other local lodgings, but the rates are very high for the area. Package deals are sometimes available for travelers using the La Pinta hotels throughout the peninsula. ☎ *Reservations in the U.S.:* ☎ *800/ 336–5454. 26 rooms. Coffee shop.*

Malarrimo. This popular trailer park and restaurant has an eight-room motel, with private baths and TV. It fills up quickly and is one of the best deals in town. ☎ *Blvd. Zapata,* ☎ *115/7–02–50.*

Guerrero Negro Essentials

Arriving and Departing

BY PLANE

The nearest international airport to Guerrero Negro is in La Paz, 800 kilometers (500 miles) southeast; the airport at Loreto, though closer, receives only one flight a day, from Los Angeles. There is a small airstrip in town.

BY CAR AND BUS

Guerrero Negro is just south of the Baja California–Baja Sur state line, about 720 kilometers (450 miles) from the Tijuana border. **Tres Estrellas de Oro** (☎ 112/2–64–76 in La Paz) has buses to Guerrero Negro from La Paz.

Guided Tours

The best way to see the whales is with a tour company that's familiar with the area. **Baja Expeditions** (2625 Garnet Ave., San Diego, CA 92109, ☎ 619/581–3311, 800/843–6967 in the U.S. and Canada), the premier Baja adventure operator in the United States, has whale-watching trips on boats and kayaks. **Baja Discovery** (Box 152527,

San Diego, CA 92195, ☎ 619/262–0700 or 800/829–BAJA) operates a whale-watching camp at Laguna San Ignacio south of Guerrero Negro, with tent camping on an island in the lagoon and boat trips among the whales. **Baja California Tours** (6986 La Jolla Blvd., No. 204, La Jolla, CA 92037, ☎ 619/454–7166, ℻ 619/454–2703) has information and makes reservations with several companies offering whale-watching tours. **Eco-Tours Malarrimo** (Blvd. Zapata at the entrance to Guerrero Negro, ☎ 115/7–02–50) conducts guided tours from Guerrero Negro to Scammon's Lagoon; two hours in a small boat watching the whales runs $40 per person.

LORETO

On the Sea of Cortés, some 1,200 kilometers (750 miles) south of the U.S. border in California, Loreto's setting is truly spectacular. The gold and green hills of the Sierra Gigante seem to tumble into the cobalt sea. Rain is rare. According to the local promoters, the skies are clear 360 days of the year. There aren't even any bugs—or at least very few—to plague vacationers. The dry, desert climate is not one in which insects thrive.

Loreto was the site of the first California mission. Jesuit priests Eusebio Kino and Juan María Salvatierra settled the area in the 1680s, and work began on the mission buildings in 1697. It was from Loreto that Father Junípero Serra, a Franciscan monk from Mallorca, Spain, set out in 1769 to found missions from San Diego to San Francisco—in the land then known as Alta California.

Mexico won its independence from Spain in 1821, and the missions were gradually abandoned. The priests, who were often from Spain, were ordered to return home. Loreto had been the administrative as well as the religious center of the Californias, but with the withering of the mission and the 1829 hurricane that virtually destroyed the settlement, the capital of the Californias was moved to La Paz. A severe earthquake struck the Loreto area in 1877, further destroying the town.

For a century the village languished. The U.S. fishermen who rediscovered the town were a hearty breed who flew down in their own aircraft and went after marlin and sailfish in open launches. Loreto's several small hotels were built to serve this rough-and-ready set; most of the properties were built before 1960, when no highway came down this far and there was no airport worthy of the name.

In 1976, when the coffers were filled with oil revenue, the government tapped the Loreto area for development. Streets were paved in the dusty little village, and telephone service, electricity, potable water, and sewage systems were installed in both the town and the surrounding area. The town even got an international airport. A luxury hotel and championship tennis center were opened in Nopolo, about 8 kilometers (5 miles) south of town. Then the money dried up, investors could no longer be found, and everything came to a halt. A second surge of development occurred in the early 1990s, when the government invested in an 18-hole golf course at the edge of the sea in Nopolo. But the course has not drawn the anticipated crowds and is empty much of the time.

Today Loreto, with a population of 15,000, is a good place to escape the crowds, relax, and go fishing. The fears of sports enthusiasts that the town would be spoiled have thus far been largely unfounded, though the residential trailer parks are filling up and private homes are clustered in secluded enclaves. Loreto is much the way it was decades ago, except that now it is more accessible.

All that may change if the plans of Fonatur, the government tourism-development agency, go through. Its projects take in some 24 kilometers (15 miles) of coastline. A large marina has gone up at Puerto Escondido, but planned hotels are awaiting construction. Loreto is slated as a bedroom community for the people who will work at the hotels, shops, and restaurants that have yet to be built.

Exploring

One could allocate 15 minutes for a tour of downtown Loreto and still have time left over. The renovated malecón, built in 1991, has turned the waterfront into a pleasant place for a stroll: A marina houses the panga fleet and private yachts; the adjoining beach is a popular gathering spot for locals, especially on Sunday afternoons; and the beach playground has a great assortment of play equipment for children. The small **zócalo** and town center is one block west on Calle Salvatierra. The only historic sight is **La Misión de Nuestra Señora de Loreto,** the first of the California missions. Founded in 1697 by Jesuit Father Juan María Salvatierra, the church was the beginning of a chain of missions that eventually stretched as far as San Francisco and Sonoma in what is now the United States. The carved stone walls, wood-beam ceilings, gilded altar, and primitive-style portraits of the priests who have served there are worth seeing. Next door, the **Museum of Anthropology and History,** also called **El Museo de los Misiones** (☎ 113/5–05–41, ☯ Wed.–Fri. 9–4, weekends 9–2), contains religious relics, tooled leather saddles used in the 19th century, and displays of Baja's history. Adjacent to the church is a shopping complex with boutiques that sell fine silver and crafts.

Nopoló, an area being developed for luxury resorts, is about 8 kilometers (5 miles) south of town. The five-star Stouffer Presidente closed in 1992; part of the hotel has since reopened as the Loreto Inn. The nine-court tennis complex across the way is still in operation. Between the highway and Nopoló Bay, the first nine holes of a spectacular 18-hole golf course opened in 1991 after years of construction. Though there are plans for more hotels, condos, and private homes in the area, for now, sidewalks and concrete foundation slabs run through fields of weeds and shrubs.

More progress has been made 16 kilometers (10 miles) down the road in **Puerto Escondido,** where the marina contains more than 100 boat slips. A recreational vehicle park, **Tripui,** has a good restaurant, a few motel rooms, a snack shop, a bar, stores, showers, a laundry, a pool, and tennis courts. A boat ramp has been completed at the marina; the port captain's offices (☎ 113/5–06–56, 𝔽𝔸𝕏 113/5–04–65, ☯ Weekdays 8–3) are located just south of the ramp. Boaters must pay a fee to launch at the ramp. **Isla Danzante,** 5 kilometers (3 miles) southeast of Puerto Escondido, has good diving and reefs.

Picnic trips to nearby **Coronado Island,** inhabited only by sea lions, may be arranged in Loreto at Nopoló or in Puerto Escondido. Snorkeling and scuba-diving opportunities are excellent.

Off the Beaten Track

Go north on Highway 1 for 134 kilometers (84 miles) to reach **Mulege,** an old mission settlement and now a charming tropical town set beside a river flowing into the Sea of Cortés. Mulege has become a popular destination for travelers who are interested in exploring the nearby mountains and for kayakers drawn to Bahía Concepción, the largest protected bay in Baja.

Well worth an hour's stroll is **Santa Rosalia,** 64 kilometers (40 miles) north, a dusty mining town with a mix of French, Mexican, and American Old West–style architecture. It's known for its **Iglesia Santa Barbara,** a prefabricated iron church designed by Alexandre-Gustave Eiffel, creator of the Eiffel Tower. Be sure to stop by **El Boleo** (Av. Obregon at Calle 4), the best-known bakery in Baja, where fresh breads bring a lineup of eager customers weekday mornings at 10 AM.

Shopping

There are few opportunities for shopping in Loreto. Curios and T-shirts are available at shops at the hotels and downtown. **El Alacran,** which is in the small shopping complex behind the church on Calle Salvatierra, has a remarkable selection of folk art, jewelry, and sportswear. Groceries and ice are available on Calle Salvatierra at **El Pescador,** the town's only remaining supermarket.

Sports and Outdoor Activities

Fishing

Fishing put Loreto on the map, especially for the American sports enthusiast. Cabrillo and snapper are caught year-round; yellowtail in the spring; and dorado, marlin, and sailfish in the summer. Visitors who plan to fish should bring tackle with them because top-notch gear can be difficult to find, though some sportfishing fleets do update their equipment regularly. All Loreto-area hotels can arrange fishing, and many own skiffs; the local fishermen congregate with their small boats on the beach at the north and south ends of town. **Alfredo's Sportfishing** (Blvd. Mateos at Juárez, across from the marina, ☎ 113/5–01–65, FAX 113/5–05–90) has good guides for anglers. **Arturo's Fishing Fleet** (Calle Juárez and Callejón 2, one block from the marina, ☎ 113/5–04–09 or 800/777–2664) has several types of boats and fishing packages. **Sportsman's Tours** (201 Oak Ave., Carlsbad, CA 92008, ☎ 619/630–BAJA or 800/234–0618, FAX 619/434–1328) organizes fishing trips to Loreto and other spots in Baja.

Golf

The first nine holes of the 18-hole Loreto Campo de Golf (☎ 113/5–07–88), located along Nopoló Bay at the south side of Fonatur's resort development, opened in 1991. Several hotels in Loreto offer golf packages and reduced or free greens fees.

Kayaking

Kayakers who have heard the tales of Baja's gorgeous undeveloped coastline are flocking to the peninsula by the dozens, in groups arranged through outfitters that include **Baja Expeditions** (2625 Garnet Ave., San Diego, CA 92109, ☎ 619/581–3311; 800/843–6967 in the U.S. and Canada). Mulege and Bahia Concepción are especially popular for paddling. **Baja Tropicales** (Box 60, Mulege, BCS 23900, ☎ and FAX 115/3–01–90) offers rentals of kayaks, wet suits, and other gear as well as whale-watching trips on the Pacific coast and several types of kayaking tours, including day trips and overnighters in the area of Mulege. In Loreto, **Deportes Blazer** (Hidalgo 18, ☎ 113/5–09–11) rents kayaks.

Scuba Diving

The coral reefs off Coronado and Carmen islands are an undersea adventure. **Deportes Blazer** (Hidalgo 18, ☎ 113/5–09–11) rents scuba gear and has an air compressor. **Arturo's** (*see* Fishing, *above*) runs dive trips to the nearby islands and has scuba gear available for rent.

Tennis

The **Loreto Tennis Center** (☎ 113/5–07–00), 8 kilometers (5 miles) south of Loreto, is open to the public.

Beaches

Most Loreto-area hotels are on the water, but the rock-filled beaches that front them are disappointing.

Dining

There aren't many restaurants in Loreto, but the seafood is excellent no matter where you go. Reservations are not required, and the dress is casual.

CATEGORY	COST*
$$	$8–$15
$	under $8

per person for a three-course meal, excluding drinks and service

$$ **The Embarcadero.** This restaurant's open-air deck looking out to the marina and beach is the perfect spot for catching up on the local fishing news. Alfredo's sportfishing is next door, and anglers with their own boats in the marina often stop by for lunch. Fish tacos and grilled-fish dinners are the best choices. ✕ *Blvd. Mateos at Juárez,* ☎ *113/5–01–65. No credit cards.*

$$ **El Super Burro.** This large, palapa-covered restaurant a half-block from the waterfront is as popular with locals as tourists. Meats are grilled at the front of the dining room, where cooks juggle take-out and dine-in orders. The Mexican combination plate isn't outstanding, but it is plentiful; a better choice is the fresh fish. Those on a budget can fill up on tacos or baked potatoes stuffed with cheese and meat. ✕ *Paseo Hidalgo between Madero and the malecón, no* ☎. *No credit cards.*

$ **Café Olé.** The best taquería in town also offers good burgers, ice-cream cones, chocolate shakes, and french fries. ✕ *Calle Francisco Madero,* ☎ *113/5–04–96. No credit cards.*

Lodging

The choices are good, but limited. The postal code for Loreto is 23880; for Mulege, 23900.

CATEGORY	COST*
$$$	$60–$90
$$	$25–$60
$	under $25

All prices are for a standard double room, excluding service charge and sales tax (10%).

Loreto

$$$ **La Pinta.** Part of a chain of Baja California hotels, the La Pinta is a collection of plain brick buildings housing spacious, air-conditioned rooms with satellite TVs. ▨ *Blvd. Misión de Loreto,* ☎ *113/5–00–25,* FAX *113/5–00–26; reservations in the U.S.,* ☎ *800/336–5454. 48 rooms. Restaurant, bar, pool, fishing, 2 tennis courts. MC, V.*

$$$ Oasis. This is one of the original fishing camps and a favorite with those who want to spend as much time as possible on the water. Many of the rooms, set amid a tropical oasis of palms, have a view of the water. The hotel has its own fleet of skiffs. ⊠ *Calle de la Playa at Zaragoza, Box 17,* ☎ *113/5–01–12,* FAX *113/5–07–95; reservations in the U.S., 800/777–2664. Pool, boating, fishing, tennis court. MC, V.*

$$ Misión. This is an old favorite, with one of the most popular swimming pools and second-story bars in town. The rooms and public spaces are in desperate need of renovation, but that doesn't deter the diehard anglers who enjoy being across the street from the marina. ⊠ *Blvd. Mateos at Calle de la Playa, Box 49,* ☎ *113/5–00–48,* FAX *113/5–06–48; reservations in the U.S., 800/777–2664. 54 rooms. Restaurant, bar, pool, fishing. MC, V.*

$$ Plaza Loreto. Since its opening in 1992, the Plaza Loreto has garnered ★ a loyal following of Loreto regulars who appreciate the comfortable rooms and prime downtown location. Located near the old mission, the two-story hotel has an upstairs bar overlooking the street; 18 rooms have been completed, and another section and pool are under construction. The rooms are by far the best in town, with TVs, coffeemakers, and huge showers. ⊠ *Paseo Hidalgo,* ☎ *and* FAX *113/5–08–55; reservations in the U.S., 800/777–2664. 18 rooms. Bar. MC, V.*

$$ Villas de Loreto. New owners took over this long defunct property in 1994 and created one of Loreto's nicest hideaways just south of town. Four large rooms with separate kitchenettes and front porches have already opened, and four more are near completion. The owners are refurbishing the old swimming pool and palapa bar and have great plans for the property. A large RV and tent campground is located behind the hotel buildings. To get here, turn right off Salvatierra onto Madero and drive across the dry riverbed to signs for the hotel. ⊠ *Antonio Mijares at the beach,* ☎ *and* FAX *113/5–05–86. 4 rooms. Pool, camping. No credit cards.*

Mulege

$$ Serenidad. Some 128 kilometers (80 miles) north of Loreto, this hotel is worth the trip. The rooms have fireplaces (nights can be chilly), and the Saturday barbecue is a Baja institution. ⊠ *Mulege,* ☎ *115/3–01–11,* FAX *115/3–03–11. 48 rooms. Restaurant, pool, private airstrip. MC, V.*

$ Hacienda. French-Canadian Jean-Pierre bought this historic Mulege hacienda in 1992 and is gradually restoring its rooms, including a large ballroom with fireplace. Guests read and lounge in rocking chairs by the pool or at stools along the bar, where snacks and meals are served throughout the day. Special festivities include paella nights, pig roasts, and trips to the nearby cave paintings in the mountains. Even when other hotels in the area are nearly empty, the Hacienda is filled with European travelers attracted by the ambience and incredibly low (by Baja standards) room rates. ⊠ *Calle Madero, Mulege,* ☎ *and* FAX *115/3–00–21. 18 rooms. Restaurant, bar, pool, travel services. No credit cards.*

Nightlife

After-dark entertainment is pretty much limited to hotel lobby bars; the fisherfolk drawn to the Loreto area turn in early.

Loreto Essentials

Arriving and Departing

BY PLANE
Aero California (☎ 800/237–6225, 113/5–00–50 or 113/5–05–66 in Loreto) has daily flights from Los Angeles and La Paz to Loreto's airport, which is 7 kilometers (4 miles) southwest of town.

BY CAR AND BUS
Loreto is 1,200 kilometers (750 miles) south of the U.S. border via Highway 1. Early starts are recommended to avoid nighttime driving. **Tres Estrellas de Oro** and **Aguila** provide service along this route. The Loreto bus terminal (☎ 113/5–07–67) is on Salvatierra and Tamaral at the entrance to town.

BY FERRY
The **Sematur ferry** travels from Guaymas on the mainland Pacific coast to Santa Rosalia on the Baja California peninsula. Currently, the ferry departs for the 12-hour trip to the mainland at 8 AM on Wednesday and Sunday and arrives in Santa Rosalia on Tuesday and Friday at 3 PM. Advance tickets are available at the Santa Rosalia ferry terminal (☎ 115/2–00–14, FAX 115/2–00–13), just south of town on the highway to Loreto, but schedules are often erratic.

Getting Around

BY TAXI
Taxis are in good supply, and fares are inexpensive. It is wise to establish the fare in advance.

BY RENTAL CAR
The only car-rental franchise in Loreto closed in 1993. Check at the hotels and airport to see if another has opened by the time you visit. There are two gas stations in Loreto; be sure to fill your tank before heading out on any long jaunts.

Guided Tours
Picnic cruises to Isla Coronado, excursions into the mountains to visit the San Javier Mission and view prehistoric rock paintings, and day trips to Mulege can be arranged through hotels. **Alfredo's Sportfishing** (on the malecón, Box 39, Loreto BCS 23880, ☎ 113/5–01–65, FAX 113/5–05–90) can arrange tours as well as fishing excursions and is a good source of general information on the area.

Visitor Information
The **Fonatur Tourist Information Office** (on the east side of the highway just after the turnoff into Loreto, no ☎; closed weekends) is the only information center in town that's open at this time. Hotel tour desks may be better sources for basic facts. **Police** (☎ 113/5–00–35) may not speak English.

LA PAZ

La Paz is one of those cities that make you wish you'd been here 20 years ago. In the slowest of times, in late summer when the heat is oppressive, you can easily see how it must have been when it was a quiet place, living up to its name—"Peace." Today the city has a population of 170,000, with a large contingent of retirees from the United States and Canada. Travelers use La Paz as both a destination in itself and a stopping-off point en route to Los Cabos. Sportfishing is a major lure, though some enjoy La Paz as the most Mexican city on the peninsula, with the feel of a mainland community that has adapted to tourism while retaining its character.

It was commerce that first attracted Hernán Cortés and his soldiers in 1535: The beautiful bay was rich with oysters and pearls. In 1720 the Jesuits arrived to civilize and convert the Indians. Instead, the missionaries inadvertently decimated the local populace by introducing smallpox. Within 30 years, there was no one left to convert.

While the rest of Mexico was being torn apart by revolution, a permanent settlement was established in 1811. La Paz became a refuge for those who wished to escape the mainland wars. In 1829, after then-capital Loreto was leveled by a hurricane, La Paz became the capital of the Californias. Troops from the United States occasionally invaded, but sent word to Washington that the Baja Peninsula was not worth fighting for. In 1853 a different group of invaders arrived from the United States. Led by William Walker, these southerners were intent on making La Paz a slave state but were quickly banished by the Mexicans. Peace reigned for the next century. In 1940, disease wiped out the oyster beds, and with the pearls gone, La Paz no longer attracted prospectors and was left tranquil.

La Paz officially became the capital of Baja California Sur in 1974 and is now the state's largest settlement. It is the site of the power plant for all the state, a fleet of cruise ships, the ferry to Mazatlán, the state bureaucracy, the governor's home, and the state jail. It is the stop-off for fishermen and divers headed for Cerralvo, La Partida, and Espiritu Santo islands, where parrot fish, manta rays, neons, and angels blur the clear waters by the shore, and marlin, dorado, and yellowtail leap out of the deep, dark sea.

Exploring

Numbers in the margin correspond to points of interest on the La Paz map.

The Malecón

❶ The **malecón** is La Paz's sea wall, tourist zone, and main drag rolled into one. As you enter town from the southwest, Paseo Alvaro Obregón becomes the malecón (waterfront walkway) at a cluster of high-rise condos. Construction continues at the west entrance to town, where a marina and hotel are scheduled to open by the end of ❷ 1995 at the 500-acre **Fidepaz Marina,** 10 blocks north of the current ❸ center of activity. The **State Secretary of Tourism office** is a few blocks from the marina.

❹ La Paz's only true colonial Mexican hotel is **Los Arcos** (*see* Lodging, *below*). The center courtyard has a fountain surrounded by flowers and is a pleasant place for a short respite, if no one is playing Ping-Pong nearby.

❺ La Terraza, the streetside restaurant at the **La Perla Hotel** (Paseo Obregón 1570, ☎ 112/2–07–77), has the best seats on the malecón for watching the steady stream of teens cruising through town in their cars, red and yellow lights twinkling around their license plates and the latest U.S. hits blaring on their radios.

❻ A two-story white gazebo is the focus of the **Malecón Plaza,** a small cement square where musicians sometimes appear on weekend nights. The tourist information center sits beside the gazebo. Across the street, Calle 16 de Septiembre leads inland to the city center.

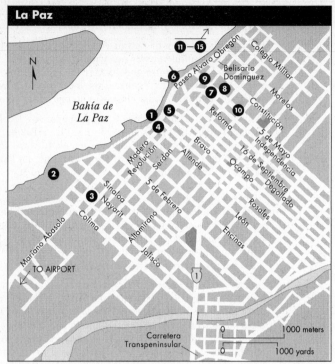

Central La Paz

This downtown district is the busiest in all Baja Sur, with shops crammed together on narrow crowded streets. Browse through **Dorian's,** a large department-store chain at the corner of Avenidas Septiembre and Agosto, for any sundries you might need.

7 **La Catedral de Nuestra Señora de La Paz** (Our Lady of La Paz Cathedral) is downtown's big attraction. It was built in 1860 near the site of La Paz's first mission, which was established in 1860 by Jesuit
8 Jaime Bravo. It faces the zócalo, which also goes by the names **Plaza Constitución** and **Jardín Velazco.**

9 On the opposite end of the plaza is the **Biblioteca de las Californias,** a library specializing in the history of Baja California, with reproductions of the local prehistoric cave paintings, oil paintings of the missions, and the best collection of historical documents on the peninsula. Films and lectures are sometimes presented in the evening. Check the bulletin board outside the library or ask the librarian for information. *Madero at Cinco de Mayo,* ☎ *112/2–26–40.* ☉ *Weekdays 8–6.*

One gets an excellent sense of La Paz's culture and heritage at the
10 **Museum of Anthropology,** constructed in 1983 at the corner of Altamirano and Cinco de Mayo. Exhibits include re-creations of Comondo and Las Palmas Indian villages, photos of cave paintings found in Baja, and copies of Cortés's writings on first sighting La Paz. Many of the exhibit descriptions are written only in Spanish, but the museum's staff will help translate for you. *Ignacio and Cinco de Mayo,* ☎ *112/2–01–62.* ☛ *Free.* ☉ *Weekdays 8–6, Sat. 9–2.*

Pichilingue

South of town, Paseo Alvaro Obregón, or the malecón, becomes what is commonly known as the Pichilingue Road, which curves north along the bay about 16 kilometers (10 miles) to the terminals where the ferries from Mazatlán and Topolobampo arrive and many of the sportfishing boats depart. Just outside town the road divides, with outgoing traffic climbing up a steep cliff overlooking deserted beaches.

⑪ A few kilometers south is the most deluxe resort in town, La Concha. Next door is the **Government House,** surrounded by guards and gates. Home of the governor of Baja California Sur, the house has an impressive view of the curving bay and city lights. The scenery **⑫** becomes less inviting as you pass the **Ferry Terminal,** where warehouses serve as waiting rooms. Roadside stands serving oysters and grilled fish line the highway across the street from the terminal.

⑬ Since the time of pirate ships and Spanish invaders, **Pichilingue** was known for its preponderance of oysters bearing black pearls. In 1940 an unknown disease killed off all of them, leaving the beach deserted. Now Pichilingue is a pleasant place for sunbathing and watching the sportfishing boats bring in their haul.

TIME OUT Two large palapas, open from sunrise to sunset, serve cold beer and oysters *diablo* (raw oysters steeped in a fiery hot sauce), as well as some of the freshest and least expensive grilled fish in town—a full meal with drinks won't cost more than $10. Any taxi driver will know what you're talking about if you say you want oysters diablo in Pichilingue.

⑭ Paved roads to La Paz's most beautiful beaches were completed in 1992. Off a dirt road just past Pichilingue, **Playa Tecolote** is a small, crystal-blue cove with a clean beach and no facilities. The larger **⑮** **Playa Coyote** has a restaurant, water-sports equipment rentals, and palapas for shade. Overnight camping is currently allowed at both beaches.

Off the Beaten Track

The workshop of weaver **Fortunato Silva** (Abasolo 3315, ☏ 112/2-45–75) sits on a dirt lot just outside town, on the way to the airport. Silva, an elderly gentleman who speaks no English, demonstrates his craft in a large workroom filled with looms and spinning wheels. His siblings and offspring (some of whom speak English) weave the yarn into simple rugs, place mats, and tablecloths that are sold in a small shop out front.

Shopping

Shops carrying a predictable assortment of sombreros, onyx chess sets, and painted plaster curios are scattered along Avenida Obregón across from the malecón. **Artesanías la Antigua California** (Av. Obregón 220, ☏ 112/5–52–30) has the nicest selection of Mexican folk art in La Paz, including wooden masks and lacquered boxes from Guerrero, along with a good supply of English-language books on Baja. At **México Lindo** (Av. Obregón at Calle Bravo, ☏ 114/2–18–90) you'll find a good display of handblown glassware. **La Tiendita,** in the lobby of the Los Arcos Hotel (Av. Obregón 498, ☏ 114/2–27–44), has embroidered guayabera shirts and dresses, tin ornaments and picture frames, and some black pottery from Oaxaca.

Sports and Outdoor Activities

Diving
Popular diving spots include the white coral banks off Isla Espíritu Santo, the sea lion colony off Isla Partida, and the seamount 14 kilometers (9 miles) farther north.

Scuba Aguilar (Independencia 107, Box 179-B, ☎ 112/2–18–26, FAX 112/2–86–44) gives windsurfing and sailing lessons, rents equipment, and operates dives and excursion tours to Espíritu Santo and the wreck of the *Salvatierra,* a sunken ferry boat. Two-tank dive trips run $65.
Baja Expeditions (Sonora 586, ☎ 112/5–38–28, FAX 112/5–38–29; for reservations in the U.S.: 2625 Garnet Ave., San Diego, CA 92109, ☎ 619/581–3311 or 800/843–6967, FAX 619/581–6542) offers hotel and diving packages and live-aboard dive boat trips to the islands, seamount, and wrecks; it's best to make reservations in the United States before traveling to La Paz.

Fishing and Boating
The considerable fleet of private boats in La Paz now has more room for docking at three marinas, the **Fidepaz** at the north end of town and the **Marina Palmira** and **Marina La Paz** south of town. Several U.S. and Mexican companies run long-range and one-day fishing charters from La Paz, and most hotels have fishing operations. The **Dorado Velez Fleet** (Box 402, La Paz 23000, ☎ 112/2–27–44, ext. 608), operated by Jack Velez in the Los Arcos hotel, has cabin cruisers that can be chartered starting at about $240 per day. **La Paz Fishing** (Box 417, Palm Springs, CA 92263, ☎ 112/2–13–13) runs trips for anglers out of the Las Arenas area south of La Paz. **Sportsman's Tours** (201 Oak Ave., Carlsbad, CA 92008, ☎ 619/630–BAJA or 800/234–0618, FAX 619/434–1328) operates fishing trips to La Paz and other spots in Baja.

Spectator Sports
Fishing tournaments are held in August and November, and the Baja 1,600-kilometer (1,000-mile) road race in November creates a mighty roar.

Beaches

Swimming and snorkeling are best south of town, on the way to Pichilingue. Near the La Concha resort is **Playa Camancito,** once part of the government house compound. There's a U-turn just north of the beach that will lead you back to the entrance.

Playa de Pichilingue, between the ferry landing and the end of the point, has plenty of private space and two palapa restaurants that serve cold drinks and fish. Beyond the palapas, off a dirt road, is **Punta Balandra,** with scores of secluded coves and the popular **Playa Tecolote** and **El Coyote,** where locals and travelers crowd the clean beaches on summer weekends.

Dining

Some restaurants, particularly in the hotels, add a service charge of 10%–15% to your bill. Dress is casual, and no reservations are necessary unless otherwise indicated.

CATEGORY	COST*
$$$	$15–$20
$$	$8–$15
$	under $8

per person for a three-course meal, excluding drinks and service

$$$ **El Bismark.** You've got to wander a bit out of your way to reach El Bis-
★ mark, where locals go for good, homestyle Mexican food. Specialties
include the *cochinita píbil* (marinated pork chunks) served with home-
made tortillas; carne asada served with beans, guacamole, and tor-
tillas; and enormous grilled lobsters. You'll see families settle down for
hours at long wood tables, while waitresses divide their attention
between the patrons and the soap operas on the TV above the bar. ✕
Santos Degollado and Av. Altamirano, ☎ *112/2–48–54. MC, V.*

$$$ **Restaurant Bermejo.** The most upscale, elegant restaurant in town
has a faithful following of locals and tourists in search of comfortable
booths, candles, and courteous waiters. The menu is primarily Italian
these days. There are a few moderately priced dishes here, and the
steaks are worth splurging on. ✕ *Paseo Obregón 498,* ☎ *112/2–
27–44. Reservations recommended. AE, MC, V.*

$$ **Trattoria La Pazta.** Trendy and sleek, La Pazta is furnished with black
lacquered tables and chairs set against white walls and tiled floors.
Local and imported ingredients are blended with homemade pastas;
try the pasta with squid in a wine and cream sauce, or curried
chicken. Those craving an espresso or cappuccino will be more than
pleased with the café's selection of coffees. ✕ *Allende 36-B,* ☎ *112/
5–11–95. No credit cards.*

$$ **La Paz-Lapa.** The noise level here is deafening, but this is a fun place,
with a wide-screen TV in the bar and waiters so jolly you expect them
to break into song. The food—your basic beef, chicken, fish, and
Mexican selections—is tasty and plentiful. Also referred to as Carlos
'n' Charlie's, La Paz-Lapa is a member of the popular Carlos Anderson restaurant chain. The restaurant moved to a new location in
1994; it's still on the malecón but now at the corner of Calle 16 de
Septiembre. Live bands appear on weekend evenings on the back
patio. ✕ *Paseo Obregón,* ☎ *112/2–92–90. MC, V.*

$$ **La Terraza.** The open-air restaurant at the Hotel Perla is the best peo-
ple-watching spot in town, with sidewalk-level tables facing the
malecón. The menu includes everything from French toast to pasta—
with decent enchiladas, huevos rancheros, and fresh fish. La Terraza
is a good hangout for morning coffee and afternoon and evening
snacks. ✕ *Paseo Obregón,* ☎ *112/2–07–77. MC, V.*

$ **El Quinto Sol Restaurante Vegetariano.** El Quinto's bright green exte-
rior walls are painted with Indian snake symbols and smiling suns.
The back room is a natural-foods store stocked with grains, soaps,
lotions, oils, and books. The restaurant serves yogurt with bananas
and wheat germ, ceviche tostadas, and a nonmeat version of *machaca,*
a marinated shredded beef dish. ✕ *Belisario Domínguez and Indepen-
dencia,* ☎ *112/2–16–92. No credit cards.*

$ **Taco Hermanos Gonzalez.** La Paz has many great taco stands, but the
Gonzalez brothers still corner the market with their hunks of fresh
fish wrapped in corn tortillas. Bowls of condiments line the small
stand, and customers jam the sidewalk while munching on the best
fast food in town. ✕ *Corner of Mutualismo and Esquerro, no* ☎. *No
credit cards.*

Lodging

La Paz has hotels clustered along the malecón, with a few of the more
expensive places outside town on the road to Pichilingue and the road
to the airport. If you're interested in sunbathing and relaxing on the
beach, stay outside town.

CATEGORY	COST*
$$$	$60–$90
$$	$25–$60
$	under $25

All prices are for a standard double room, excluding service charge and sales tax (10%).

$$$ Club El Moro. A vacation-ownership resort with suite rentals on a nightly and weekly basis, El Moro boasts a garden of lush palms and a densely landscaped pool area with one of the few hot tubs in town. You can recognize the building by its stark-white turrets and domes; rooms are Mediterranean in style and decor, with arched windows, Mexican tiles, and private balconies. The restaurant is excellent and elegant. ⊞ *Km 2 Carretera a Pichilingue, Box 357, 23010,* ☎ *and* FAX *112/2–40–84 or 112/2–70–10. 17 suites. Restaurant, bar, pool, travel services. AE, MC, V.*

$$$ La Concha Beach Resort. Come to La Concha for its clean, curving beach; modern, well-maintained rooms; and very good restaurant. Some rooms lack TVs, but guests gather around the large-screen TV in an upstairs lounging area, which also has tables for playing cards and games and a small selection of English-language novels. The hotel operates a free shuttle to town twice daily (taxis to town cost $10 each way). Condo units adjacent to the hotel are available on a nightly, weekly, and monthly basis. ⊞ *Km 5 Carretera a Pichilingue, 23010,* ☎ *112/2–65–44,* FAX *112/2–62–18; reservations in the U.S., 800/999–2252. 109 rooms. Restaurant, palapa and lobby bars, pool, fishing and whale-watching packages, 2 tennis courts, gift shop. AE, MC, V.*

$$$ La Posada de Englebert. For 25 years, divers have stayed in La
★ Posada's casitas, which feature wood shutters, haphazardly tiled bathrooms, fireplaces, worn couches in the living rooms, and rocking chairs on the porches. At night, miniature lights twinkle in the palm trees and guitarists stroll among the blue umbrellas on the patio while guests dine on grilled fish and lobster. Saturday-night entertainment alternates between folkloric dancing and a Hawaiian luau. ⊞ *Av. Reforma and Playa Sur, Box 152, 23000,* ☎ *112/2–40–11,* FAX *112/2–06–63. 26 suites, 4 casitas. Restaurant, palapa bar, pool, beach. MC, V.*

$$$ Los Arcos. Many say Los Arcos is the nicest hotel in La Paz, but that depends on the location of your room. Resist the waterfront view and request a room in the central courtyard, where the rush of water in the fountain drowns out the music from the street and the noise from the pool area. All rooms have balconies and TVs. The self-service coffee shop opens early so those headed out on fishing boats can have breakfast and pick up a box lunch. The Cabañas de Los Arcos next door offers several small brick cottages surrounded by gardens and a small hotel with a swimming pool. ⊞ *Paseo Obregón 498 between Rosales and Allende, 23000,* ☎ *112/2–27–44,* FAX *112/5–43–13; reservations in the U.S.: 18552 MacArthur Blvd., Suite 205, Irvine, CA 92715,* ☎ *714/476–5555 or 800/347–2252,* FAX *714/476–5560. 180 rooms at the main hotel, 30 bungalows and rooms at the Cabañas. Restaurant, coffee shop, bar, 2 pools, sauna, fishing. MC, V.*

$$ Hotel Lorimar. A favorite with annual visitors to La Paz, the Lorimar is located up a slight hill behind the Los Arcos Hotel, within easy walking distance of the malecón. The rooms are well maintained, with double beds and tiled bathrooms. Guests congregate on the back patio or at the second-story restaurant, which has a view of the waterfront. ☎ *Bravo 110, La 23000,* ☏ *112/5–38–22,* FAX *112/5–63–87. 20 rooms. Restaurant. No credit cards.*

$$ **Hotel Mediterrane.** Situated behind Trattoria La Pazta, the Mediterrane has five cool white rooms with air-brushed blue ceilings, pale wood furnishings, and king-size beds. Two rooms are air-conditioned; large windows and fans provide sufficient breeze for the rest. A second-story terrace at the front of the building offers a view of the water; a bar for the terrace is in the planning stages. ☎ *Allende 36-B, 23000,* ☏ *and* FAX *112/5–11–95. 5 rooms. Restaurant. No credit cards.*

$ **Pension California.** This run-down hacienda, offering clean blue-and-white rooms with baths and a courtyard with picnic tables and a TV, draws backpackers and low-budget travelers. A laid-back, friendly camaraderie prevails. ☎ *Av. Degollado 209, 23000,* ☏ *112/2–28–96. 25 rooms. No credit cards.*

The Arts and Nightlife

El Teatro de la Ciudad (Av. Navarro 700, ☏ 112/5–00–04) is La Paz's cultural center. The theater seats 1,500 and is used for stage shows by visiting performers as well as local ensembles.

La Paz-Lapa (*see* Dining, *above*) has live bands on weekend nights and a lively crowd throughout the week. You can dance to recorded music at **Laser Disco** (Paseo Obregón at Degollado, ☏ 112/2–31–33) Friday through Sunday nights; there are also occasional appearances by live bands.

La Paz Essentials

Arriving and Departing

BY PLANE
The La Paz airport, about 16 kilometers (10 miles) north of town, is served by **Aero California** (☏ 112/5–10–23 or 800/237–6225) from Tijuana and Loreto and **Aeromexico** (☏ 112/2–00–91 or 800/237–6639) from Los Angeles, Tucson, Tijuana, Mexico City, and other cities within Mexico.

BY CAR
La Paz is 1,474 kilometers (921 miles) south of the U.S. border at Tijuana on the Transpeninsular Highway and 211 kilometers (132 miles) north of Los Cabos at the southern tip of the peninsula. The city of La Paz curves along the bay of La Paz and faces the sea in a northwesterly rather than an easterly direction. When you approach the city on Highway 1 from the north, you'll enter from the southwest.

BY BUS
Tres Estrellas de Oro (☏ 112/2–64–76) and **Aguila** (☏ 112/2–70–94) operate buses along the Transpeninsular Highway to the border and Los Cabos.

BY FERRY
The ferry system connecting Baja to mainland Mexico has been privatized and is constantly undergoing changes in rates and schedules. Currently there are Sematur ferries from La Paz to Mazatlán and La Paz to Topolobampo. Tickets are available at the ferry office at the dock on the road to Pichilingue (☏ 112/2–94–85, FAX 112/5–65–88) and at the downtown Sematur office (Av. 5 de Mayo 502, ☏ 112/5–38–33, FAX 112/5–46–66). Purchase your ticket personally in advance of your trip—and expect confusion. Travelers planning to take cars and motor homes on the ferry to the mainland must obtain a vehicle permit before

boarding the ferry. Tourism officials in La Paz strongly suggest that you obtain the permit when crossing the border into Baja; though permits are not needed in Baja, offices at the border are better equipped to handle the paperwork than those in La Paz. Everyone crossing to the mainland needs a tourist card, also available at the border.

Getting Around

BY RENTAL CAR

A car is not necessary if you plan to stay in town, since taxis are readily available. But if you'd like to explore the more remote beaches, wheels are a must. Rental is about $70 per day for a Volkswagen Beetle, with insurance and unlimited mileage. If you want a sedan or air-conditioning, call ahead to reserve a car. Rental agencies include **Budget** (Paseo Obregón at Hidalgo, ☎ 112/2–10–97); **Hertz** (☎ 112/2–09–19) and **Avis** (☎ 112/2–26–51), both at the airport; and **Servitur Autorento** (5 de Febrero at Abasolo, ☎ 112/2–14–48).

BY TAXI

Taxis are inexpensive, but be sure to set the price with your driver before the cab gets going.

Guided Tours

Travel agencies in the hotels and along Paseo Obregón offer tours of the city, day-long trips to Los Cabos, sportfishing, and boating excursions.

Important Addresses and Numbers

EMERGENCIES

Police (112/2–66–10), **Fire** (112/2–00–54), **Red Cross** (112/2–11–11). **Clínica La Paz** (Revolución 461, ☎ 112/2–06–85 or 112/2–28–00) has English-speaking doctors on staff.

VISITOR INFORMATION

The **State Secretary of Tourism office** is located west of downtown on the highway (☎ 112/4–01–00, FAX 112/4–07–22). The **tourist information center** is on the malecón near Calle 16 de Septiembre (☎ 112/2–59–39) and is open weekdays 8–8.

LOS CABOS

At the southern tip of the 1,600-kilometer (1,000-mile) Baja California Peninsula, the land ends in a rocky point called El Arco (The Arch), a place of stark and mysterious beauty. The waters of the Sea of Cortés swirl into the Pacific Ocean's rugged surf as marlin and sailfish leap above the waves. The desert ends in sand coves, with cactus standing at their entrances like sentries under the soaring palm trees.

Pirates found the capes at the tip of the peninsula an ideal lookout for spotting Spanish galleons traveling from the Philippines to Spain's empire in central Mexico. Missionaries soon followed, seeking to save the souls of the few thousand local Indians who lived off the sea. The good fathers established the missions of San José del Cabo and Cabo San Lucas in the mid-1700s, but their colonies did not last long. The missionaries had brought syphilis and smallpox along with their preachings, and by the end of the century the indigenous population had been nearly wiped out.

A different sort of native, the massive gamefish that appeared to be trapped in the swirl of surf where the ocean meets the sea, brought the explorers back. In the 1940s and 1950s the capes became a haven for millionaires, who built lodges on rocky gray cliffs overlooking secluded coves and bays. By the 1960s, lavish resorts had begun to rise in the barren landscape.

Connected by a 20-mile stretch of highway called the Corridor, the two towns that grew around the Spanish missions, Cabo San Lucas and San José del Cabo, were distinct until the late 1970s, when the Mexican government's office of tourism development (Fonatur) targeted the southern tip of Baja as a major resort and dubbed the area Los Cabos.

Fonatur's initial target for development, San José del Cabo is the municipal headquarters for the two towns. A hotel zone was cleared along the long stretch of waterfront on the Sea of Cortés, and an 18-hole golf course and private residential community were constructed south of the town center. But a picturesque downtown, with colored lights in the fountains along the main street, still maintains the languid pace of a Mexican village. Despite the development, San José remains the more peaceful of the two towns and is the one that travelers seeking a quiet escape prefer.

Many of the legendary fishing lodges and exclusive resorts built before the government stepped in were on the Corridor between the two towns. Since the mid-1980s, the area has seen the completion of several private communities and large-scale resorts; three championship golf courses are now open on the Corridor; and at least two more are under construction, along with several hotels and resort compounds. The highway between the two towns has been widened to four lanes.

Cabo San Lucas, once an unsightly fishing town with dusty streets and smelly canneries, has become the center of tourism activity for the area. The sportfishing fleet is headquartered here, and cruise ships anchored off the marina disperse passengers into town. Trendy restaurants and bars line the streets, and massive hotels have risen on every available plot of waterfront turf; a five-story condo-hotel complex along the bay blocks the view from the town's older hotels. Cabo San Lucas has become an in spot for travelers seeking fun, rowdy nightlife, and extensive dining and shopping options.

You need only drive a few miles north of Los Cabos into the desert or along the two coastlines to understand the magnitude of the development that has taken place at the peninsula's tip. Electricity and telephone service are still nonexistent in some communities outside Los Cabos: Settlements consist of lone ranches, farms battered by wind and sun, outposts of rugged retirees in rusted motor homes, and isolated hotels operating on their own generators. The true Baja appears in waves of unmitigated heat, clouds of dust, and vistas of desert and sky broken only by thorny cacti and the sight of hawks in flight.

Exploring

You needn't worry about reserving lots of time for sightseeing here—each town can easily be toured in an hour or so. Only a few streets are named, but the towns are small enough for you to find what you're looking for without wandering very far.

Cabo San Lucas and **San José del Cabo** are about 32 kilometers (20 miles) apart on Mexico Highway 1. Some hotels in each offer tours to the other town, which is a good way to see the sights; or you can take a taxi between the towns. If you want to check out the lavish fishing resorts or the beaches, you're better off renting a car and stopping off for lunch or a swim along the way.

Numbers in the margin correspond to points of interest on the Los Cabos Coast, San José del Cabo, and Cabo San Lucas maps.

San José del Cabo, the larger of the two towns, has about 25,000
❶ inhabitants. The main street is **Boulevard Mijares.** The south end of
❷ the boulevard has been designated the tourist zone, with the **Los Cabos Club de Golf** as its centerpiece. Fonatur owns 4,000 acres along this
❸ stretch and has built a **Commercial and Cultural Center** in the middle. A few reasonably priced hotels are situated along this strip, on a beautiful long beach where the surf, unfortunately, is too dangerous for swimming. At the end of the strip, on Paseo San José by the Hotel
❹ Presidente Inter-Continental, is the **Estero de San José,** where the freshwater Río San José flows into the sea. The estuary is now a natural preserve closed to boats. Wildlife is gradually reappearing; over 200 species of birds can be spotted here. A building at the edge of the estuary is being refurbished as a cultural center with exhibits on Baja's indigenous people.

Take Boulevard Mijares north into town, through a stretch of restau-
❺ rants and shops. **City Hall** is on your left near Avenida Zaragoza, where Boulevard Mijares ends—a spot marked by a long fountain illuminated at night by colored lights. There is a small, shaded plaza here with a few café tables in front of small restaurants.

❻ One block east on Avenida Zaragoza is a large central **plaza** with a white wrought-iron gazebo and green benches set in the shade. The
❼ town's church, the **Iglesia San José,** looms above the plaza. Be sure to walk up to the front and see the tile mural of a captured priest being dragged toward a fire by Indians.

The bus station, hospital, market, and pharmacies are all located on the next few streets south of Zaragoza, and most of the town's souvenir shops and restaurants are clustered in the surrounding streets.

As you drive south on Mexico Highway 1 toward Cabo San Lucas,
❽ ❾ you'll first pass **Costa Azul,** a good surfing beach, and **Playa Palmilla,** San José's best swimming beach. Above the beach is the **Hotel Palmilla,** a rambling, hacienda-style resort with its own small white adobe chapel. Intensive construction is underway at the Palmilla, including a 27-hole golf course designed by Jack Nicklaus and a resort enclave of more than 1,000 homes and condos. The Cabo Real project a few miles south includes another golf course and the Meliá Cabo Real and Westin Regina hotels. Still farther south are beaches for swimming and snorkeling, and some spectacular hotels; most worth visiting are the
❿ ⓫ **Bahía Chileno** at the **Hotel Cabo San Lucas** and the **Bahía Santa María** at the **Twin Dolphin** hotel. The beaches at both bays have white sand, clear blue water, and schools of fish just offshore.

Highway 1 leads into the center of **Cabo San Lucas,** ending at Kilometer 1 on the Transpeninsular Highway. The main downtown street,
⓬ Avenida Lázaro Cárdenas, passes the pretty **Plaza San Lucas** with its white wrought-iron gazebo. Buildings around the plaza are gradually being refurbished to house galleries and restaurants. Most of the shops, services, and restaurants are located between Avenida Cárdenas and the waterfront.

TIME OUT When the sun's heat has exhausted your energy, stop at the nearest branch of **Helados Bing,** a pink-and-white-striped ice-cream stand that serves delectable cones, shakes, and floats. One is on Boulevard Mijares in San José, and another is located on Highway 1 just north of Cabo San Lucas.

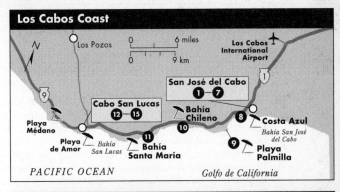

Los Cabos Coast

Boulevard
Mijares, **1**

City Hall, **5**

Commercial
and Cultural
Center, **3**

Estero de San
José, **4**

Iglesia San
José, **7**

Los Cabos
Club de Golf, **2**

Plaza, **6**

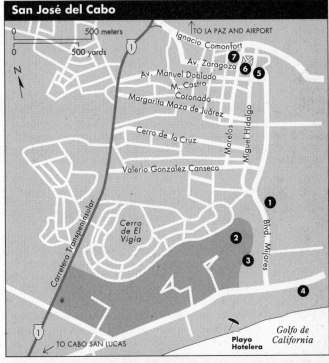

San José del Cabo

Bahía de Cabo
San Lucas, **14**

El Arco, **15**

Handicrafts
Market, **13**

Plaza San
Lucas, **12**

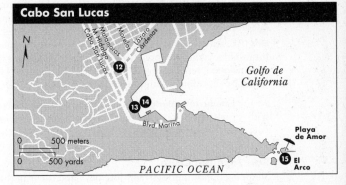

Cabo San Lucas

Boulevard Marina has been transformed from a dusty main drag into a busy thoroughfare lined with hotels and cafés. Paved walkways now run from here to the hotels and beaches on the east end of town and west to the **Handicrafts Market** at the Cabo San Lucas marina.

⓭

⓮ The sportfishing fleet is docked in the **Bahía de Cabo San Lucas,** and there are glass-bottom boats available at the water's edge.

⓯ The most spectacular sight in Cabo San Lucas is **El Arco.** The natural rock arch is visible from the marina and from some of the hotels but is more impressive from the water. A little farther on, and visible from the water, is **El Faro de Cabo Falso** (Lighthouse of the False Cape). You need a four-wheel-drive vehicle to reach the lighthouse by land. If you don't take at least a short boat ride out to the arch and **Playa de Amor,** the beach underneath, you haven't fully appreciated Cabo.

Shopping

Shopping may be beating out fishing as the sport of choice in Los Cabos these days. The selection of handicrafts and sportswear in the towns is excellent.

Cabo San Lucas

Some of the nicest shops in Cabo San Lucas are located in **Plaza Bonita** on the waterfront at the beginning of Boulevard Marina. **Cartes** (Plaza Bonita, ☎ 114/2–17–70) is the best of the many interior design stores in Los Cabos, with an irresistible array of hand-painted pottery and tableware, pewter frames, handblown glass and carved furniture. **Libros** (Plaza Bonita, ☎ 114/3–17–70) carries a vast number of English-language novels and magazines. **Dos Lunas** (Plaza Bonita, ☎ 114/3–19–69) offers a trendy selection of colorful sportswear. **Francisco's Cafe del Mundo** (Plaza Bonita, no ☎) is the place to take a break for an espresso or cappuccino.

Boulevard Marina and the side streets between the waterfront and the main plaza are filled with an ever-changing parade of small shops. **Necri** (Blvd. Marina between Madero and Ocampo, ☎ 114/3–02–83) has an excellent selection of folk art and furnishings. **Galería El Dorado** (Blvd. Marina between Guerrero and Madero, ☎ 114/3–08–17) displays paintings and sculpture by local artists in the front room and various curios in the back. **Faces of Mexico** (Hidalgo at Zapata, no ☎) has moved several times in the past few years but seems settled at this bright blue building next to Pancho's restaurant. The owner collects wooden masks and religious statues and always has a fascinating display. **Cuca's Blanket Factory** (Cardenas at Matamoros, ☎ 114/3–19–13) sells the typical array of serapes and cotton blankets with a twist—you can design your own and have it ready the next day. **Mama Eli's** (Av. San Lucas, ☎ 114/3–16–16) is a three-story gallery with fine furnishings, ceramics, appliquéd clothing, and children's toys. **Galeria Gatemelatta** (on the dirt road to the Hotel Hacienda, ☎ 114/3–11–66) specializes in colonial furniture and antiques.

At the **Handicrafts Market** in the marina you can pose for a photo with an iguana, plan a ride in a glass-bottomed boat, or browse to your heart's content through stalls packed with blankets, sombreros, and pottery.

San José del Cabo

Shopping opportunities in San José del Cabo occur in the few streets around the main plaza and City Hall. Across Boulevard Mijares from City Hall is **Almacenes Goncanseco** (Blvd. Mijares 18, ☎ 114/2–09–12), where you can get film, postcards, groceries, and liquor. **ADD**

(Av. Zaragoza at Hidalgo, ☎ 114/2–27–27), an interior design shop, sells gorgeous hand-painted dishes from Guanajuato and carved-wood furniture from Michoacan. The great selection of English-language magazines, books, and newspapers at **La Botica** (Blvd. Mijares 33, ☎ 114/2–35–66) includes the *Los Angeles Times* and *USA Today*. **La Casa Vieja Boutique** (Blvd. Mijares, ☎ 114/2–02–70) carries gauze dresses, accessories, and guayabera shirts for men. **Copal** (Zaragoza 20, ☎ 114/2–30–70) has a nice array of carved animals from Oaxaca, masks from Guerrero, and heavy wooden furnishings. For fresh produce, flowers, meat, fish, and a sampling of local life in San José, visit the **Mercado Municipal** off Calle Doblado.

Sports and Outdoor Activities

Diving

El Arco is a prime diving and snorkeling area, as are several rocky points off the coast. Most hotels offer diving trips and equipment rental. Companies serving divers in Cabo San Lucas include **Amigos del Mar** (near the sportfishing docks at the harbor, ☎ 114/3–05–05, FAX 114/3–08–87); **Palmilla Divers** (Hotel Palmilla, ☎ 114/2–05–82); and **Tio Watersports** (at the Melia San Lucas, ☎ 114/3–10–00). In San Jose, **Killer Hook Surf Shop** (Av. Hidalgo, ☎ 114/2–24–30) sells and rents snorkeling gear, along with surfboards and boogie boards. The *Solmar V* (at the Solmar Hotel and the marina, ☎ 114/3–00–22 or 800/344–3349, FAX 310/454–1686), a live-aboard dive and fishing boat, takes weeklong trips to the islands of Socorro, San Benedicto, and Clarion, and the coral reefs at Cabo Pulmo. It has 12 cabins with private baths (maximum: 24 passengers).

Fishing

There are more than 800 species of fish in the waters off Los Cabos. Most of the hotels will arrange fishing charters, which include a captain and mate, tackle, bait, licenses, and drinks. Prices start at $250 per day for a 25-foot cruiser. Some charters provide lunch, and most can arrange to have your catch mounted, frozen, or smoked. Most of the boats leave from the sportfishing docks in the Cabo San Lucas marina. Usually there are a fair number of pangas for rent at about $25 per hour with a five-hour minimum. Dependable companies include **Hotel Palmilla Sportfishing** (Hotel Palmilla in San José del Cabo, ☎ 114/2–05–82 or 800/637–2226), the **Solmar Fleet** (*see* Solmar V *in* Diving, *above*) and **Pisces Sportfishing Fleet** (at the marina, ☎ 114/3–12–88 or 800/946–2252), **Gaviota Fleet** (at the marina, ☎ 114/3–04–30 or 800/932–5599), and **Minerva's** (at the marina and on Madero between Blvd. Marina and Guerrero, ☎ 114/3–12–82, FAX 114/3–04–40).

Golf

The public, nine-hole **Los Cabos Club de Golf** (Blvd. Mijares, ☎ 114/2–09–05) in San José was built in 1988 and for many years was the only golf course in Los Cabos. Today there are several championship courses open for play and more under construction as developers bank on Los Cabos's prominence as a golf destination. Several of the new courses will eventually be closed to the public, but for now avid duffers should be able to gain access to most courses. Among the most spectacular is the 27-hole Jack Nicklaus–designed course at the **Palmilla Golf Club** (Palmilla Resort, ☎ 114/2–17–01 or 114/2–17–08). A second Nicklaus course is underway at **Cabo del Sol** (☎ 114/2–17–01), a resort development in the Corridor. The Robert Trent Jones–designed **Cabo Real Golf Club** (at the Melia Cabo Real Hotel in the Corridor, ☎ 114/2–90–00, ext. 9205) has 18 of its 36 holes open for play. **Campo de Carlos,** a planned golf resort community in the Corridor close to Cabo San Lucas, is slated to have two 18-hole courses.

Tennis
The **Los Cabos Campo de Golf** (☎ 114/2–09–05) has lighted tennis courts that are open to the public; fees are $8 per hour during the day and $12 per hour at night.

Beaches

Cabo San Lucas
Playa Médano, just north of Cabo San Lucas, is the most popular stretch in Los Cabos (and possibly in all Baja) for sunbathing and people-watching. The 3-kilometer (2-mile) span of white sand is always crowded, especially on weekends.

Playa Hacienda, in the inner harbor by the Hacienda Hotel, has the calmest waters of any beach in town and good snorkeling around the rocky point. **Playa Solmar,** fringing the Solmar Hotel, is a beautiful wide beach at the base of the mountains leading into the Pacific, but it has dangerous surf with a swift undertow. Stick to sunbathing here.

Playa de Amor consists of a secluded cove at the very end of the peninsula, with the Sea of Cortés on one side and the Pacific Ocean on the other. The difference between the peaceful, azure cove on the Sea of Cortés and the pounding white surf of the Pacific is dramatic.

San José del Cabo
Playa Hotelera is the stretch of beach that most of the finer hotels use. It's beautiful, but the current is dangerously rough, and swimming is not advised. At the east end of the beach, near the Hotel Presidente Inter-Continental, there is a freshwater lagoon filled with tropical birds and plants. If you plan to spend time here, be sure to douse yourself with insect repellent. The best swimming beach near San José is **Playa Palmilla,** which is protected by a rocky point just south of town. The northern part of the beach is cluttered with boats and shacks, but if you walk south you'll reach the Hotel Palmilla beach, a long stretch of white sand and calm sea.

Los Cabos
Some of the finest resorts in Los Cabos are situated off the highway between the two towns, and they're set on some of the area's finest beaches. **Playa Bahía Santa Maria,** by the Twin Dolphins Hotel, is a picture-perfect white-sand cove protected by towering brown cliffs. The snorkeling here is superb, with hundreds of colorful fish swarming through chunks of white coral. Just north of the hotel there is a public access trail to the beach. **Bahía Chileno,** by the Hotel Cabo San Lucas, an underwater preserve teeming with marine life, is a great place for snorkeling and diving. Rocky in parts, the beach is smoothest in front of the hotel.

Dining

Fresh fish, lobster, and shrimp are the dining draws here, along with abalone and quail. Prices in Los Cabos have risen dramatically, and inexpensive restaurants are hard to find. Some restaurants add a service charge of 10%–15% to your total. Unless otherwise noted, dress is casual and reservations are not necessary.

CATEGORY	COST*
$$$	$25–$35
$$	$15–$25
$	under $15

per person for a three-course meal, excluding drinks and service

Cabo San Lucas

$$$ **El Galeón.** Considered the most distinguished restaurant in town, El Galeón is located across from the marina. The choice seats are on the outside terraces facing the water; the inside is decorated with lots of heavy wood furniture. Traditional Italian, Mexican, and American dishes are prepared expertly, with an emphasis on thick, tender cuts of beef. The piano bar is a nice setting for a late-night brandy. ✗ *Across from the marina by the road to the Finesterra Hotel,* ☎ *114/3–04–43. AE, MC, V.*

$$$ **Mi Casa.** One of Cabo's best restaurants is in an eye-catching, cobalt-
★ blue building painted with a mural of a burro, just across the street from the main plaza. Mexican cuisine reaches gourmet status here with fresh tuna and dorado served with tomatillo salsa or Yucatecan *achiote;* or with such sophisticated dishes as *chili en nogada,* a meat-stuffed pepper topped with walnut sauce and pomegranate seeds. The restaurant quickly outgrew its small dining room and has spread into a large back courtyard. It's especially nice at night, illuminated by candlelight and the moon. ✗ *Av. Cabo San Lucas,* ☎ *114/3–19–33. MC, V.*

$$$ **Peacocks.** The ubiquitous fresh-fish dinner achieves gustatory emi-
★ nence when prepared by chef Bernard Voll. His dorado is coated with a crust of chopped pecans, his shrimp masterfully tossed with spinach fettuccine. This chef is known for his incredible desserts—if you miss dinner, be sure to stop by for a cappuccino and tequila mousse. ✗ *Paseo Pescador near Playa Médano,* ☎ *114/3–18–58. AE, MC, V.*

$$ **El Delfin.** Other restaurants on Playa Médano seem to attract larger crowds, but El Delfin serves the best food. The grilled lobster receives high grades and is reasonably priced to boot; the glassed-in dining room provides a cool and comfortable respite from the beach sun. ✗ *Playa Médano,* ☎ *114/3–09–01. MC, V.*

$$ **El Rey Sol.** By far one of the best and most authentically Mexican restaurants in Cabo San Lucas, El Rey Sol is a bit out of the way, on the road to Playa Médano. The abalone is succulent, and the seafood combination—lobster, oysters, crab, and fish—incredibly generous and outrageously good, though expensive. The spicy *7-Mares* soup, with seven varieties of seafood from octopus to clams, is guaranteed to *levantar muertos* (raise the dead) or, at the very least, cure tequila hangovers. This large brick restaurant is warm and cozy, and the Mexican breakfasts are popular with both townsfolk and tourists. ✗ *On the road to Playa Médano,* ☎ *114/3–11–17. AE, MC, V.*

$$ **The Fish Company.** Opened in 1994, this small seafood restaurant was an instant success. Nine tables covered with blue-and-white cloths sit just in from the sidewalk in the narrow dining room, and the aroma of fresh grilled fish fills the air. Breakfast specialties include a great chorizo-and-cheese omelette; lunch and dinner choices include shrimp with oyster sauce and fresh fish smothered in garlic. You can bring your catch here and have it prepared in a low-cost feast. ⊞ *Av. Guerrero between Blvd. Marina and Zapata,* ☎ *114/3–14–05. No credit cards.*

$$ **Rio Grill.** The prettiest restaurant on the waterfront, the Rio Grill alternates between being soothing and romantic and downright rowdy. Soft music plays during candlelit steak or lobster dinners, but

when the live music starts at 9:30 PM, the place really rocks. ✗ *Blvd. Marina 31,* ☎ *114/3–13–35. MC, V.*

$ **Tacos Chidos.** Taco stands are beginning to appear all over Cabo San Lucas. Chidos has been around for a long time and serves one of the cheapest breakfasts in town: Eggs dishes served with beans, rice, tortillas, and coffee run well under $5. Tostados, tamales, and torta sandwiches fill out the menu, along with the requisite fish, beef, and pork tacos. Best of all, Chidos will deliver your order to your hotel. ✗ *Av. Zapata at Guerrero,* ☎ *114/3–05–51. No credit cards.*

$ **Taquería San Lucas.** Longtime Cabo devotees know this simple restaurant as the Broken Surfboard; by any name, it's the best budget place in town. A few rickety wooden tables and chairs sit next to the sidewalk, where there's always someone lounging about ready to share fishing tales and surfing lore. The menu sticks with such basic Mexican and American fare as tacos, burgers, and burritos. Breakfast is an especially good deal. ✗ *Av. Hidalgo between Madero and Zapata, no* ☎*. No credit cards.*

San José del Cabo

$$$ **Damiana.** For a special night out, visit this small hacienda tucked
★ beside the plaza, past the center of town. The lounge area has overstuffed couches where you can unwind before claiming your table on the patio. Fuchsia bougainvillea wraps around the tall pines shading the wrought-iron tables, and the pink adobe walls glow in the candlelight. Start with fiery oysters diablo, then move on to the tender chateaubriand or charbroiled lobster. You'll find the setting so relaxing and charming that you will want to linger well into the night. ✗ *Blvd. Mijares 8,* ☎ *114/2–04–99. AE, MC, V. No lunch.*

$$$ **La Paloma.** This restaurant, with an upstairs patio overlooking the
★ Hotel Palmilla's pool and gardens as well as the sea, offers both a sublime setting and unparalleled food. The Continental menu has taken a turn toward lighter, healthier fare. The Sunday brunch is still the most lavish in the area, and worth a few hours of your time, followed by a long siesta. Have at least one meal here. ✗ *Hotel Palmilla, Hwy. 1 just north of San José,* ☎ *114/2–05–82. AE, MC, V.*

$$ **Tropicana Bar and Grill.** Start the day with coffee and French toast at the sidewalk tables in front of this enduringly popular restaurant. Later, as the temperature rises, it's more comfortable to sit inside the large, air-conditioned bar over an ice-cold lemonade, watching sporting events and music videos on TV. In the evening, the back patio quickly fills with a loyal clientele who enjoy the garden setting and reliable cooking. The menu has grown over the years to include U.S. cuts of beef along with fajitas, chiles rellenos, and lobster, always in demand. The nightly dinner special is usually a good deal. ✗ *Blvd. Mijares 30,* ☎ *114/2–09–07. MC, V.*

$ **Las Hornillas.** Chicken roasted on a spit over an open fire is the specialty at this casual eatery, more popular with locals than tourists. The half chicken with rice, beans, and tortillas is more than sufficient for a ravenous diner, and the chicken fajitas come on a platter loaded with grilled onions, green peppers, and white meat. ✗ *Calle Manuel Doblado 610,* ☎ *114/2–23–24. No credit cards.*

$ **Pescadería del Mar.** Seafood doesn't get any better than at this small fish market and café on the highway just outside downtown San José. A brick smoker stoked with mesquite sits in one corner of the patio restaurant, and the aroma of smoking dorado, marlin, and wahoo fills the air. Budget diners can fill up on fish tacos or chiles stuffed with smoked fish, but may find themselves splurging on giant shrimp cocktails followed by grilled lobster or a whole fried fish. If you've caught a few big ones on a sportfishing trip, consider having them smoked here for a tasty souvenir. ✕ *Blvd. Mauricio Castro 1110,* ☎ *114/2–32–66. No credit cards. Closed Tues.*

Lodging

The accommodations in Los Cabos are mostly expensive and exclusive. Some of the hotels offer the American Plan (AP) with three meals. A few of the resorts do not accept credit cards and often add a 10%–20% service charge to your bill. Most properties also raise their rates for the December–April high season. Rates here are based on high-season standards. Expect to pay 25% less during the off-season. The postal code for Cabo San Lucas is 23410; for San José del Cabo, 23400.

CATEGORY	COST*
$$$$	over $160
$$$	$90–$160
$$	$40–$90
$	under $40

All prices are for a standard double room, excluding service charge and sales tax (10%).

Cabo San Lucas

$$$$ **Meliá San Lucas.** From the moment you enter the Meliá and spot El
★ Arco framed by the lobby's arches, you know you're at a hotel where details are important. The blue walls and linens in the rooms complement the views of the aquamarine sea; the outer adobe walls of the terraced hotel buildings glow orange and gold with the changing sunlight. The Meliá has a long beach with calm waters, a spacious hot tub under the palms, and all the equipment you could need for playing on and in the water. ⌸ *Playa Medano,* ☎ *114/3–10–00 or 114/3-10–60,* ℻ *114/3–04–18; reservations in the U.S.: 800/336–3542. 161 rooms and suites. 3 restaurants, 2 pools, hot tub, beach, meeting rooms. AE, MC, V.*

$$$ **Finisterra.** One of the oldest hotels in Cabo, the Finisterra is now also one of the most modern, thanks to a new eight-story tower rising directly from the beach. A second tower should be completed by the end of 1995. A three-story-high palapa covers the restaurant and bar on the beach next to two free-form swimming pools. The rooms in the new building, with oceanfront balconies, are by far the nicest; some have king-size beds. The older section of the hotel is favored by long-time guests who like the fishing lodge feel of the stone buildings. The restaurant is only fair, but the Whale Watcher bar atop a high cliff has the best view in town. ⌸ *Blvd. Marina,* ☎ *114/3–00–00,* ℻ *114/ 3–05–90; reservations in the U.S.: 18552 MacArthur Blvd., Suite 205, Irvine, CA 92715,* ☎ *714/476–5555 or 800/347–2252,* ℻ *714/ 476–5560. 197 rooms. 2 restaurants, bar, 3 pools, travel services. AE, MC, V.*

$$$ **Hacienda.** Set on the tip of a tree-filled point jutting into San Lucas Bay, the Hacienda resembles a Spanish colonial inn with its white arches and bell towers, stone fountains, and statues of Indian gods set amid scarlet hibiscus and bougainvillea. The white rooms have red-tile floors, tile baths, and folk art hanging on the walls; the bar is a veritable museum of Indian artifacts. ⌸ *Playa Medano,* ☎ *114/3–01–22; reservations in the U.S.: Box 48088, Los Angeles, CA 90048,* ☎ *800/733–2226. 112 rooms, suites, and beachfront cabanas. Restaurant, bar, pool, beach, dive shop. MC, V.*

$$$ **Solmar Suites.** From afar, the Solmar looks like a space colony, set
★   against granite cliffs at the tip of Land's End, facing the wild Pacific. In
1992 the rooms were completely redone as suites with tiled baths and
separate seating areas, decorated in Mexico–Santa Fe style. A few of
the adjacent time-share units with kitchenettes and a private pool area
are available on a nightly basis. The surf here is far too dangerous for
swimming, but don't miss a stroll along the wide strip of beach. Most
visitors hang out around the pool and swim-up bar, joining in with the
ever-present musicians. The Solmar's sportfishing fleet is first-rate. ☎
Blvd. Marina, Box 8, ☎ *114/3–35–35,* ℻ *114/3–04–10; reservations
in the U.S.: Box 383, Pacific Palisades, CA 90272,* ☎ *310/459–9861
or 800/344–3349,* ℻ *310/454–1686. 66 rooms, 4 suites, 68 condos.
Restaurant, bar, pool, beach, dive shop, tennis court. AE, MC, V.*

$$ **Mar de Cortés.** A favorite among die-hard fishers, this small, casual
inn has seen better days. Still, it is quiet (though some early risers can
be noisy as they leave for the sea at dawn), cool, and reasonably
priced. The oldest rooms have brick ceilings, tiled floors and colonial-
style furnishings. Newer rooms are brighter, but lack character. Some
rooms have patios by the swimming pool. ☎ *Av. Cárdenas,* ☎ *114/3–
00–32,* ℻ *114/3–02–32; reservations in the U.S.: 17561 Vierra Can-
uon Rd., No. 99, Salinas, CA 93907,* ☎ *408/663–5803 or 800/347–
8821,* ℻ *408/663–1904. 16 rooms. Restaurant, pool. MC, V.*

$ **Las Villas Turismo Juvenil.** Cabo's youth hostel is about 10 blocks
from the waterfront in a quiet neighborhood. Two dormitory rooms
have bunk beds and shelves, and there are several private rooms with
shared baths. In the courtyard, guests can use sinks and counters to
wash their clothes and fix meals. Reservations are suggested, especially from November through February. ☎ *Av. de la Juventud,* ☎
114/3–01–48. 2 dorms, 11 private rooms. No credit cards.

$ **Siesta Suites.** You'll have to forego air-conditioning to stay in the inex-
pensive range, but you'll get a large, immaculately clean room with
kitchenette. The three-story hotel sits on a fairly quiet side street just
two blocks from the marina, and the proprietors are the friendliest in
town. Opened in 1994, the hotel quickly garnered a loyal following;
reservations are a must in the winter season. ☎ *Calle Zapata, Box
310,* ☎ *and* ℻ *114/3–27–73; reservations in the U.S.:* ☎ *909/
945–5940. 15 rooms. Kitchenettes. No credit cards.*

Between the Capes

$$$$ **Palmilla.** Just outside San José, the Palmilla is a gracious, sprawling
★   hacienda-style resort. Tiled stairways lead up from flower-lined paths
to large apartments with hand-carved furniture, French doors opening
onto private patios, and tiled baths. The buildings are spread along a
hillside overlooking the beach, with fountains and bougainvillea-
draped statues throughout. The service is delightfully personalized,
and the hotel's La Paloma restaurant (*see Dining, above*) is excellent.
Construction is underway on a large-scale resort development surrounding the hotel; a 27-hole, Jack Nicklaus–designed golf course
was completed in 1993. The rooms are being remodeled in 1995. ☎
Carretera Transpeninsular, 1 about 8 km (5 mi) from San José, ☎
114/2–05–82, ℻ *114/2–05–83; reservations in the U.S.: 4343 Von
Karman Ave., Newport Beach, CA 92660,* ☎ *800/637–2226. 62
rooms, 7 suites, 2 villas. Restaurant, bar, pool, beach, golf privileges,
tennis court, private airstrip. AE, MC, V.*

$$$$ **Twin Dolphin.** Sleek and Japanese-modernistic with an austere air, the
Twin Dolphin has been a hideaway for the rich and famous since
1977. Guest rooms are in low-lying casitas along a seaside cliff and
are furnished in minimalist style. The hotel is worth a visit if only for

the reproductions of Baja's cave paintings on the lobby wall. ⚅ *Km 12, Carretera Transpeninsular, Cabo San Lucas,* ☎ *114/3–18–03,* FAX *114/3–18–04; reservations in the U.S.: 1625 W. Olympic Blvd., Suite 1005, Los Angeles, CA 90015,* ☎ *800/421–8925,* FAX *213/380–1302. 44 rooms, 6 suites. Restaurant, bar, pool, beach, fishing, putting green, tennis court. MC, V.*

$$$$ **Westin Regina Resort.** Opened in 1994, the Westin is architecturally astounding, if a bit intimidating in size. It's a long walk from the parking lot and lobby to the rooms and pool, set on a cliff atop a man-made beach. The luxurious rooms are among the best in Los Cabos, with satellite TV, in-room safes, hair dryers, bathtubs and separate walk-in showers, and both air-conditioning and ceiling fans—a boon to those who prefer open windows and sea breezes. Two of the corridor's best golf courses are nearby, and the hotel is designed to keep its guests happy without them ever having to leave the grounds. ⚅ *Km 22.5 Carretera Transpeninsular, Box 145, San José del Cabo,* ☎ *114/2–90–00 or 800/228–3000,* FAX *114/2–90–10. 243 rooms. 3 restaurants, 3 pools, exercise room, beach, tennis courts. AE, MC, V.*

$$$ **Meliá Cabo Real.** Even if you're staying elsewhere, stop here for a glimpse of the future. This Meliá is incredibly huge and opulent, spread over a hilltop with a meandering crystal-blue pool, fountains, waterfalls, white canopies shading rest areas, and a private beach created by a small jetty jutting from the rocky hillside. Maya carvings and bas reliefs adorn the walls in the rooms, which all have landscaped terraces. The Cabo Real resort development around the hotel is still ongoing, with an 18-hole golf course now open. Meliá guests can use it for a fee. ⚅ *Km 19.5 Carretera Transpeninsular, Cabo San Lucas,* ☎ *114/3–09–67,* FAX *114/3–10–03; reservations in the U.S.:* ☎ *800/336–3542,* FAX *305/854–0660. 299 rooms. 2 restaurants, café, room service, pool, exercise room, beach, dive shop, fishing, tennis courts. AE, MC, V.*

San José del Cabo

$$$ **Hotel Presidente Inter-Continental Los Cabos.** By far the nicest hotel in San José, this property sits at the end of the hotel zone, next to the estuary. It resembles a pueblo set amid beachside cactus gardens. The buildings curve around an enormous blue pool; the rooms have shaded patios, minibars, king-size beds, deep bathtubs, and couches, tables, and chairs that face the sliding glass doors. The Presidente runs a low-cost shuttle service to beaches along the corridor and to Cabo San Lucas twice daily. ⚅ *Paseo San José, at the end of the hotel zone,* ☎ *114/2–00–38, reservations in the U.S.:* ☎ *800/327–0200,* FAX *114/2–02–32. 250 rooms, including 6 suites. 2 restaurants, bar, pool, beach, fishing, horseback riding, tennis courts. AE, MC, V.*

$$ **Tropicana Inn.** This small hotel is a great option for those who aren't desperate to be on a beach. The stucco buildings frame a pool and palapa bar in a quiet enclave behind San José's main boulevard. The rooms are air-conditioned, have satellite TV, and are maintained to look brand-new. ⚅ *Blvd. Mijares 30,* ☎ *114/2–15–80,* FAX *114/2–15–90. 40 rooms. Restaurant, bar, pool. MC, V.*

$ **Hotel San José Inn.** This small hotel, built in 1991, is about a five-minute walk from town and offers simple rooms with concrete floors, showers, and pastel furnishings. The rates are the lowest in town, and the proprietress is very accommodating. ⚅ *Calle Obregón 2 at Calle Degollado,* ☎ *114/2–14–91,* FAX *114/2–14–28. 20 rooms. Snack bar. No credit cards.*

$ **Posada Terranova.** San José's best budget hotel added 15 new rooms in 1993, greatly improving your chances of finding one available when you call for reservations (a must during holiday periods). The large rooms are painted a clean, bright white and have two double beds and tiled bathrooms. Despite the expansion, the hotel still feels like a friendly home where guests congregate at the front patio tables or in the restaurant to compare their days. ⊞ *Calle Degollado at Zaragoza,* ☎ *114/2–05–34,* FAX *114/2–09–02. 20 rooms. Restaurant, bar. MC, V.*

Nightlife

The nightlife in Cabo San Lucas took a definite upturn when members of the rock band Van Halen opened **Cabo Wabo** (Calle Guerrero, ☎ 114/3–11–88). The latest U.S. bands play over an excellent sound system, but the real highlight is the impromptu jam sessions with appearances by Van Halen's many friends in the music business. **Squid Roe** (Av. Cárdenas, ☎ 114/3–06–55) is the rowdiest spot in town, packed with young foreigners who work in the local tourist industry and know how to party. **Giggling Marlin** (Blvd. Marina, ☎ 114/3–06–06) seems like it's been around forever as the favorite watering hole for fishermen and their girlfriends. **Rio Grill** (Blvd. Marina, ☎ 114/3–13–35) absolutely booms with rock 'n' roll and reggae except when the live bands give way to the karaoke contingent. **El Galeón** (Blvd. Marina, ☎ 114/3–04–43) is about the only refuge for the quieter crowd who sip brandy by the piano bar.

In San José del Cabo the hottest nightspot is **Bones Disco** at the Hotel Presidente Inter-Continental (Paseo San José, ☎ 114/2–00–38). **Iguana Bar** (Blvd. Mijares 24, ☎ 114/2–02–66) is a local hangout, with live rock 'n' roll on weekend nights during the high season.

Los Cabos Essentials

Arriving and Departing

BY PLANE

The **Los Cabos International Airport** (☎ 114/2–03–41) is about 11 kilometers (7 miles) north of San José del Cabo and about 48 kilometers (30 miles) from Cabo San Lucas. **Aero California** (☎ 114/2–09–43 or 800/237–6225) flies to Los Cabos from Los Angeles, Tijuana, and Phoenix; **Mexicana** (☎ 114/2–09–60 or 800/531–7921) from Guadalajara, Mexico City, Mazatlán, Puerto Vallarta, Denver, and Los Angeles; **Alaska Airlines** (☎ 114/2–09–59 or 800/426–0333) from Anchorage, Fairbanks, Portland, Phoenix, San Francisco, San Diego, Los Angeles, and Seattle. **United** (☎ 800/241–6652) flies from New York and Chicago, connecting in Los Angeles, from December through June.

Vans shuttle passengers from the airport to the hotels in both towns but don't run from the hotels back to the airport. Many of the hotels have sign-up sheets for guests who wish to share a cab and the $30 or so fare to the airport.

BY CAR

Mexico Highway 1, also known as the Transpeninsular Highway, runs the entire 1,600 kilometers (1,000 miles) from Tijuana to Cabo San Lucas. The highway's condition varies depending on the weather and intervals between road repairs. It should not be driven at high speeds or at night. The road between San José del Cabo and Cabo San Lucas was widened to four lanes in 1993 and is in good condition, though dips and bridges become flooded in heavy rains.

Tres Estrellas de Oro (☎ 114/2–02–00) travels from Tijuana to Los Cabos and between San José and Cabo San Lucas daily. The peninsula-long trip takes about 22 hours.

BY BOAT

Several cruise lines—including **Carnival** (☎ 800/327–9501), **Princess** (☎ 800/421–0522), and **Royal Caribbean** (☎ 800/327–0271)—use Cabo San Lucas as a port of call; there is a handicrafts market at the marina designed to accommodate cruise-ship passengers.

Getting Around

BY CAR

The best way to see the sights is on foot. The downtown areas of San José and Cabo San Lucas are compact, with the plaza, church, shops, and restaurants within a few blocks of one another. If you want to travel frequently between the two towns or to remote beaches and coves, you will need a car.

Most hotels and resorts have car-rental desks; the cost of a Volkswagen Beetle or a Jeep averages $60 per day, including tax and insurance, plus 18¢ per kilometer. The following car-rental agencies all have desks at the airport and in one or both towns: **Amca** (☎ 114/3–25–15); **Avis** (☎ 114/2–06–80); **Budget** (☎ 114/3–02–41); **Dollar** (☎ 114/2–06–71); **Hertz** (☎ 114/3–02–11); **National** (☎ 114/3–60–00); and **Thrifty** (☎ 114/2–16–71). **M&M Jeeps** (at the Hotel Presidente Inter-Continental, ☎ 114/2–11–81; or in San Diego, CA, ☎ 619/297–1615 or 800/464–5724), which rents two- and four-wheel-drive vehicles, offers a package option. Travelers can rent the vehicles for a one-way trip from San Diego to Los Cabos without a drop-off fee and arrange their own accommodations or they can purchase an all-inclusive self-guided tour package.

BY TAXI

Cab fares are standardized by the government, but you should confirm the price before you get into the car. The fare between the two towns is about $25.

Guided Tours

With the water as the main attraction, most tours involve getting into a boat and diving or fishing. Nearly everyone takes a ride to El Arco, the natural rock arches at Land's End, and Playa de Amor (Lover's Beach), where the Sea of Cortés blends into the Pacific. Nearly all hotels have frequent boat trips to El Arco; the fare depends on how far your hotel is from the point. Tour boats dock by the arts-and-crafts market in the Cabo San Lucas marina, and the sidewalk along the water is lined with salesmen offering boat rides. Check out the boat before you pay, and make sure there are life jackets on board.

Contactours (Hotel Finisterra, ☎ 114/3–33–33; and at several other hotels) and **TourCabos** (Plaza los Cabos, Paseo San José, ☎ 114/2–09–82, FAX 114/2–20–50) offer tours of the region, boat trips, horseback riding and information on water sports. **Baja Travel Adventures** (☎ 114/3–19–34) runs trips to Todos Santos and La Paz and individually designed tours; ask at the hotel tour desks if there's no answer when you phone.

Pez Gato (on the marina near the Plaza Las Glorias hotel, ☎ 114/3–37–97) has sailing and sunset cruises on a 46-foot catamaran, with live music and free drinks ($50 per person), as well as snorkeling and sailing tours ($30 per person). All trips depart from the marina in

Cabo San Lucas; call or stop by the booth at the marina for further information.

Important Addresses and Numbers

EMERGENCIES

Police: Cabo San Lucas (☎ 114/3–39–77), San José del Cabo (☎ 114/2–03–61); **Hospital:** Cabo San Lucas (☎ 114/3–01–02); San José del Cabo (☎ 114/2–00–13).

VISITOR INFORMATION

In San José del Cabo a **tourist information office** opened in 1994 at the old post office building on Zaragoza at Mijares (no ☎). The office is supposed to be open weekdays 9–2 and 4–7, but was still getting established at press time. In Cabo San Lucas, a **tourist information office** opened in late 1994 on Av. Hidalgo at Guerrero (☎ 114/3–41–80, FAX 114/3–22–11; ⊙ Weekdays 9–2 and 4–7, Sat. 9–1).

4 Sonora

Rancheros *continue to ride the range in Mexican cowboy country, but beef has been upstaged by beaches in this northwestern state's economy. Along with relatively unspoiled (and inexpensive) coastal towns such as Kino Bay and Guaymas, Sonora's lures include colonial Alamos, an immaculate former silver mining center, and a sprinkling of Spanish missions.*

By Dan Goss
Anderson

SONORA, MEXICO'S second-largest, second-richest state, is a vacationland with its own band of devoted followers, many from Arizona, for whom the beaches of Sonora are closer, cheaper, and more interesting than those of southern California. This stretch of the Mexican northwest is reminiscent of the old Wild West in the United States. Cowboys ride the range, and ranchero ballads not unlike country-and-western songs blare from saloons and radios. Irrigated ranchlands feed Mexico's finest beef cattle, and rivers flowing westward from the Sierra Madre are diverted by giant dams to water the once-barren land that now produces cotton, sugarcane, and vegetables. Hermosillo, Sonora's capital, bustles with commerce in the midst of the fertile lands that turn barren again toward the coast.

Mexico Highway 15 begins at the border town of Nogales, adjacent to the U.S. town of Nogales, Arizona. It passes southward through Hermosillo and reaches the Gulf of California (also called the Sea of Cortés) at Guaymas, 418 kilometers (261 miles) from the Arizona border. The Sonoran desert dominates the landscape through northern Sonora, as it does in southern Arizona. Long stretches of flat scrub are punctuated by brown hills and mountains, towering saguaros, and organpipe cacti. Highway 15 continues southward after Guaymas, as the landscape gradually takes on a more tropical aspect, and finally enters the state of Sinoloa just north of the city of Los Mochis. Except in the mountains, the entire region is uncomfortably warm between May and late September, with afternoon temperatures sometimes exceeding 120°F.

In 1540 Francisco Vázquez de Coronado, governor of the provinces to the south, became the first Spanish leader to walk the plains of Sonora. More than a century later, Fray Eusebio Francisco Kino led a missionary expedition to Sonora and what is now southern Arizona, founding several towns there. Although Alamos, in the south of Sonora, boomed with silver-mining wealth in the late 17th century, no one paid much attention to the northern part of the region for the next three centuries; it was not part of the Mexican territory ceded to the American flag after the War of 1847. Sonora became a haven for Arizona outlaws, and international squabbles bloomed and faded over the next decades as officials argued over issues such as the right to pursue criminals across the border. During the last quarter of the 19th century, Porfirio Díaz, dictator of Mexico for three decades, finally moved to secure the state by settling it.

For Don Porfirio, however, developing Sonora may have been a mistake: The revolutionaries who later overthrew him came from here. In fact, Mexico was ruled by the Sonora dynasty for nearly a quarter of a century and, until the tragic 1994 assassination of Sonora native son Luis Donaldo Colosio, the ruling party candidate for president, it appeared likely that a Sonoran would soon control the destiny of the country again. The Mexican Revolution brought prosperity to the state, and it continues to thrive. Its inhabitants have adopted modern farming techniques that allow them to grow enough wheat not only for Mexico but for export as well.

Mexico Highway 2 enters Sonora's far northwest from Baja California, paralleling the U.S. border. There are several crossing points, but most people entering from the United States do so at Nogales, which is also a point of entry for winter fruit and vegetables exported to the United States.

EXPLORING

Numbers in the margin correspond to points of interest on the Sonora map.

❶ A bustling town, **Nogales** can become fairly rowdy on weekend evenings, when underage Tucsonans head south of the border to drink. It has some good restaurants, however, and visitors can find fine-quality crafts and furnishings in addition to the usual border schlock. If you're just coming for the day, it's best to park on the Arizona side of the border (you'll see many guarded lots that cost about $4 for the day) and walk across. Practically all the good shopping is within easy strolling distance of the border.

The shopping area centers mainly on Avenida Obregón, which begins a few blocks west of the border entrance and runs north–south; just follow the crowds. Most of the good restaurants near the border are also on Obregón. Take Obregón as far south as you like; you'll know you have entered workaday Mexico when the shops are no longer fronted by smiling, English-speaking hucksters trying to hustle you in the door ("Take a look! Good prices!").

❷ Set at the northern end of the Sea of Cortés, **Puerto Peñasco** is a popular wintering spot for American RVers and retirees, and a favorite weekend getaway for beach-seeking Arizonans—especially college kids during school breaks. It was dubbed "Rocky Point" by British explorers in the 18th century, and that's the name by which most Americans still know it today. Puerto Peñasco is 104 kilometers (65 miles) south of the Arizona border on Mexico Highway 8, which links to U.S. Highway 85 at the Lukeville, Arizona–Sonoyta, Sonora, border crossing. The Mexican immigration laws are relaxed for tourists crossing in this so-called "free zone"; simply drive through (but don't neglect to get Mexican auto insurance—crucial in case of an accident).

The town itself, built in the early 1960s, is rather faceless, but the "old town" area has a number of interesting shopping stalls and restaurants. The real draw, however, is the miles of sandy beaches, often punctuated by stretches of black, volcanic rock that get inundated at high tide. Rocky Point boasts one of the largest tide changes in the world—as much as 23 feet, depending on the season. At low tide the rocky stretches of coastline are great for poking among countless shallow tide pools inhabited by such local marine life as octopus, shrimp, and starfish. This coastline will probably change very soon, however; the construction of the $150 million Marina Peñasco—a complex that will eventually include a shopping center, luxury hotel, condos and villas, a yacht club, and a 200-slip marina—is designed to attract a more upscale U.S. clientele, and other developers are waiting in the wings.

The northern Gulf area forms a desert-coast ecosystem unmatched in the Western Hemisphere, and scientists from both the United States and Mexico conduct active research programs at the **Desert and Ocean Studies Center** (known as CEDO, its acronym in Spanish), on the eastern edge of town. You can tour the facility to learn about its history and current projects, or come by to pick up a tide calendar—useful if you're planning beach activities. *Turn east at the municipal building and follow signs for Caborca Rd., where there will be signs for Las Conchas Beach and CEDO.* ☎ 638/3–54–03. *Tour hrs are posted on the door.*

144

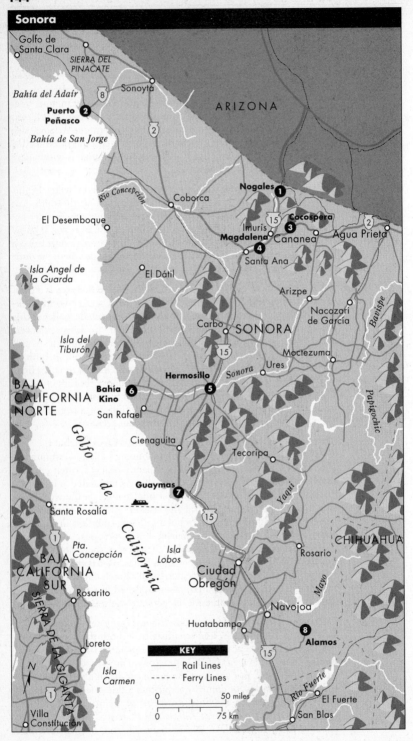

Sonora

3 About 65 miles southeast of Nogales, between Imuris and Cananea (take Highway 15 Libre to Highway 2), you can visit the ruins of **Cocospera,** one of the two dozen churches established in the state of Sonora and Arizona by Father Eusebio Francisco Kino between 1687 and 1711; the crumbling adobe mission sits on a bluff above an oak forest and farmlands in a mountain pass in the Sierra Madre Occidental.

4 Go back to Highway 15 Libre and continue south from Imuris some 23 kilometers (14 miles) to reach **Magdalena,** where the grave of Father Kino was discovered in 1966. His remains are in a mausoleum across the plaza from Santa Maria Magdalena de Buquivaba, another of the missions he founded. A $1 million monument to the memory of this pioneer priest also stands here. A number of shops surround the plaza, selling curios, blankets, and religious artifacts; stop in at the bakery for some excellent sweet rolls and bread. Magdalena is now also known as the final resting place of its beloved native son, slain presidential candidate Luis Donaldo Colosio.

If you're really interested in Spanish missions and in rural Mexican life as it has been lived for centuries, drive just a few kilometers north of Magdalena to **San Ignacio,** another of Father Kino's churches, still in use in a tiny Mexican farming village.

5 About 185 kilometers (115 miles) from Magdalena on Highway 15, **Hermosillo** (population about 600,000) is the capital of Sonora, a status it has held on and off since 1831. It is the seat of the state university and benefits from that institution's cultural activities. Although the city's name sounds to those who know a bit of Spanish as if it means "little beauty," it actually honors José Mariá González Hermosillo, one of the leaders in Mexico's War of Independence. Settled in 1742 by Captain Augustín de Vildosola and a contingent of 50 soldiers, Hermosillo was originally called Pitic, the Pima Indian name for "the place where two rivers meet." The city's most prestigious neighborhood, home of the governor and U.S. consul, among other prominent citizens, still bears the name Pitic. Located immediately north of the highway into town and just behind the Hotel Bugambilia, the area is worth an hour's stroll to view the creative handling of concrete, tile, and other materials in the homes of Hermosillo's more affluent residents.

A business center for the state of Sonora, Hermosillo is largely modern, but some lovely plazas and parks hark back to a more graceful postcolonial past. Although Hermosillo is usually just considered a jumping-off point for Bahía Kino or Guaymas, it has a number of attractions in its own right, as well as the best accommodations and restaurants until you reach Guaymas. The city's main boulevard is lined with monuments to Sonora's famous sons: Adolfo de la Huerta, Alvaro Obregón, Plutarco Elías Calles, and Abelardo Rodríguez (after whom the boulevard is named), all presidents of the country after the revolution (Rodríguez also served as governor of Sonora). At the center of town, the **Plaza Zaragoza** boasts the impressive **Catedral de San Agustín** (1878), recently regilded at great expense. Across from the cathedral is the **Palacio de Gobierno del Estado,** its graceful courtyard surrounded by somewhat disjunctive modern murals depicting Sonoran history, and between the two buildings sits an ornate Victorian gazebo. On the south edge of town, the **Plaza de los Tres Pueblos** marks the original settlement.

Two museums are worth a visit. Overlooking the city, on the Cerro la Campana (Hill of Bells), the **Museo de Sonora,** a former penitentiary, now hosts a variety of regional history displays; you can also tour the tiny, dark prison cells. The **Museo de la Universidad de Sonora** (on Blvds. Luis Encinas and Rosales) has interesting exhibits of pre-Columbian artifacts. On the highway south of town, stop at the **Centro Ecologico,** a zoo modeled after the Arizona-Sonora Desert Museum in Tucson. (It's best visited November through March because of summer heat.) If you don't feel like walking through the entire zoo, which is rather spread out, consider arranging for a golf cart by calling the office of tourism. *Museums and Centro Ecologico open Wed.–Sun. 9–3.*

Some 104 kilometers (65 miles) west of Hermosillo, on the shore of the Sea of Cortés, lies **Bahía Kino** (Kino Bay). Highway 16 from Hermosillo is excellent, and the beaches are the prettiest in northwest Mexico. For many years, Bahía Kino was undiscovered except by RV owners and other aficionados of the unspoiled, but a great change has taken place in the last decade, when Arizonans began to build condos here. Bahía Kino itself is divided into Kino Viejo (Old Kino), the Mexican village, and Kino Nuevo (New Kino), where the condos, RV sites, and other typical tourist facilities are.

Consider taking a run across the narrow channel to Isla del Tiburón (Shark Island), which is being developed into one of the finest wildlife and game refuges in North America. Permission to visit Tiburón may be obtained from the Port Captain, at the end of the main street in Kino Viejo. Ask at any of the area hotels or RV parks where to find a reliable guide. Only the Seri Indians, for whom Isla del Tiburón is a traditional fishing ground, need no permit. You might see some of these Indians at Bahía Kino selling their fine ironwood carvings of animals. Turtle hunting used to be an integral part of the Seri culture, and the capture of a turtle was once the subject of a ritual observance, but these creatures are now protected by law. (Note: The Seris will request money if you take their picture. The polite way to handle this is to request permission and offer them a dollar or so before taking the photo.)

Guaymas, about 135 kilometers (83 miles) south of Hermosillo, takes its name from San José de Guaymas, a Jesuit mission founded in 1701 that is 16 kilometers (10 miles) to the north of what is now the city. In many of Mexico's ports, it can be said that the mountains come down to meet the sea, but at Guaymas, both the mountains and the desert abut the water. The clear air and the sun shining on the mountains provide panoramas of striking, ever-changing beauty.

Now one of Mexico's major seaports, Guaymas was once a quiet fishing town that drew only the hardy, adventuresome traveler; however, by the first half of this century, it had begun to emerge as an important commercial port. Its growth accelerated in the early 1980s, when Ford Motor Company put a half-billion-dollar assembly plant in nearby Hermosillo and shipped the completed products through Guaymas. The last two decades have also seen major resort development in San Carlos, 16 kilometers to the west, where hotels and restaurants now abound.

Guaymas has not one but two bays: Bacochibampo and San Carlos. San Carlos has beaches, many white adobe homes owned by retired Americans, a marina with a good number of yachts, a country club, a Club Med, and a Howard Johnson's resort. From Bacochibampo boats set out to catch marlin, yellowtail, red snapper, sea bass, and sailfish. Guaymas Marina, a port in the Sea of Cortés with security dock facilities and electricity, is upgrading and expanding its facilities. Large fishing boats can be rented for $100 to $200 a day. Smaller outboards for waterskiing, fishing, or pleasure jaunts are also available.

South of Guaymas, Route 15 continues toward Mazatlán by way of Ciudad Obregón and Navojoa, both of which are modern agricultural and industrial centers. Some 53 kilometers (32 miles) east of Navojoa and set in the foothills of the Sierra Madre Occidental is **Alamos,** the most authentic colonial-style town in Sonora and a Mexican national monument. Here the lower Sonoran desert meets the dry tropical forest. If you're interested in seeing the unusual flora and fauna of the region, inquire at a local hotel about hiring a guide.

Coronado camped here in 1540, and a Jesuit mission was established in 1630, but the town really boomed when silver was discovered in the area during the 1680s. Wealth from the mines financed Spanish expeditions to the north—as far as Los Angeles and San Francisco during the 1770s and 1780s—and the town became the capital of the state of Occidente, which combined the provinces of Sinaloa and Sonora, from 1827 to 1832. A government mint was established here in 1864. The mines closed by the end of the 19th century, and the town went into decline, but today Alamos, with many houses beautifully restored by Americans who have settled here, serves as a showcase of its glorious past. A British visitor to the town in the early 19th century remarked on its cleanliness, and Alamos remains spotless today, with streets swept by local residents early every morning.

Points of interest include the imposing **cathedral** in the central Plaza las Armas, begun in 1787 on the site of a 17th-century Jesuit adobe church and completed in 1894. It is fronted by an ornate Moorish-style wrought-iron gazebo, brought from Mazatlán in 1904. To the west of the square, on Guadalupe Hill, is the Alamos **jail,** built around the turn of the century; visitors may tour the structure on certain days, and the shop by the prison entrance sells items such as bola ties, belts, and key chains made by the inmates. Tours of the many beautiful **restored colonial homes** in town are also offered; the tourist office and all the local hotels have listings of the times and rates.

Not to be missed, the **Museo Costumbrista de Sonora** gives an excellent overview of the cultural history of the entire state of Sonora. The numerous well-marked (but only in Spanish) displays include artifacts from the nearby silver mines and coins from the mints of Alamos and Hermosillo, as well as typical examples of the clothing and furnishings of prominent local families. *Calle Guadalupe Victoria 1 (on Plaza las Armas),* ☎ *642/8–00–53.* ⊙ *Wed.–Sat. 9–1 and 3–6, Sun. 9–6.* ☛ *Free; donation suggested.*

About 8 kilometers (5 miles) to the west of Alamos is **Aduana,** formerly the site of one of the richest mines in the district. There's not much to see here now except the church of Nuestra Señora de Balvanere. A cactus that grows out from one of its walls is said to mark the spot where the Virgin appeared to the Yaqui Indians in the late 17th century, an event that is celebrated by a procession every November 21.

Off the Beaten Track

Midway between Puerto Peñasco and the border is **Sierra del Pinacate,** a Biosphere Reserve International Park most notable for its rock formations and craters, so moonlike that they were used for training the Apollo astronauts. The diversity of the lava flows makes Pinacate unique, as does the striking combination of Sonoran desert and volcanic field. Highlights of the area include Santa Clara peak, a little more than 4,000 feet high and 2.5 million years old, and El Elegante crater, 1 mile across and 750 feet deep, created by a giant steam eruption

150,000 years ago. There are no facilities of any kind at Pinacate; you'll need to bring your own water, food, and extra gasoline, as well as a good map; you can get one in Arizona at Si Como No bookstore in Ajo or at Tucson's Map and Flag Center, or in Mexico at CEDO (*see* Puerto Peñasco *in* Exploring, *above*). A high-clearance vehicle is strongly advised, and four-wheel drive is recommended. Camping is allowed with a permit obtainable from the Oficina Sierra del Pinacate in Sonoyta, a block south of the border crossing on the west side of the street. Summer temperatures can be blistering; the best time to visit is between November and March, when daytime temperatures hover between 60 and 90 degrees. Tours can be arranged through the tourism office in Puerto Peñasco (*see* Sonora Essentials, *below*); an excellent naturalist-led tour in English is also available from **Ajo Stage Lines** (100 Estrella, Ajo, AZ 85321, ☎ 602/387–6559 or 800/942–1981). As with protected wilderness areas in the United States, no animals, plants, or archaeological artifacts may be removed.

SHOPPING

Nogales

Nogales is one of Sonora's best shopping areas, with a wide selection of handicrafts, furnishings, and jewelry. At the more informal shops, bargaining is not only acceptable, but expected. The following shops, however, tend to have fixed prices: **El Sarape** (Av. Obregón 161, ☎ 613/2–03–09) specializes in sterling silver jewelry from Taxco and designer clothing for women. **Mickey & CIA** (Av. Obregón 128–130, ☎ 613/2–22–99) has two floors of handcrafted Mexican treasures, *equipale* (pigskin) furniture, Talavera ceramic dishes, pottery, glassware, and liquors. **Firenze** (Av. Obregón 111, ☎ 613/2–22–52) features gifts, fine perfumes and beauty products, and crafts. East of the railroad tracks and off the beaten tourist path, **El Changarro** (Calle Elias 93, ☎ 613/2–05–45) carries high-quality furniture, antiques, pottery, and handwoven rugs.

Hermosillo

In the downtown markets of Hermosillo, particularly along Avenidas Serdán and Monterrey, you can buy anything from blankets and candles to wedding attire, as well as a variety of *charro* (Mexican cowboy) items; the variety of goods concentrated in this area equals what you'll find in Nogales, and the prices are better.

Guaymas/San Carlos

Plaza el Vigía, a huge shopping center on the main road from the north into Guaymas, has everything from groceries, film, toiletries, and clothes to household wares. Also in Guaymas, visit the **Casa de las Conchas** (Calle 23 and Av. Serdán, across from Plaza de los Tres Presidentes, ☎ 622/2–01–99) and sample beautiful handicrafts, as well as 400 to 500 types of seashells; right next door is a great little ice cream parlor. In San Carlos, **Lourdes Gift Shop** (Plaza Comercial San Carlos 16, ☎ 622/6–00–22), next to the Plaza Las Glorias Hotel, offers an extensive selection of folk art, glassware, and clothing. **Sagitario's Gift Shop** (Carretera San Carlos 132, ☎ 622/6–00–90), across from the entrance to the San Carlos Country Club, features clothing and a variety of crafts, including wood carvings, baskets, and Talavera tile.

Alamos

Small stores lining the Alameda (northwest of the central plaza) in Alamos sell Mexican sweets, fabrics, belts, and hats, among other items; for traditional crafts (but not local ones), try the gift shops in the **Casa de los Tesoros** (*see* Lodging, *below*) and **La Mansion** hotels.

SPORTS

Diving

San Carlos Diving Center (Apdo. 655, San Carlos, ☎ 622/6–00–49), on the main street of San Carlos, has diving excursions in the Sea of Cortés. There are also two large boats available for scuba diving; inquire about these at any hotel or at the marina.

Fishing

Manny's Beach Club (Av. Coahuila and Blvd. Matamoros, Puerto Peñasco, ☎ 628/3–36–05) offers an all-day fishing trip in the Gulf for $40, as well as day and sunset cruises for $15. **Cortez Explorers** (Carreterra Bahía, across from Marina San Carlos, ☎ 622/6–08–08 or 520/885–9848 in Tucson; Howard Johnson's, ☎ 622/6–07–94) runs deep-sea fishing trips as well as sunset cruises and diving charters. The company also rents Jet Skis and ski boats. Other smaller outfitters have boats for rent in the bay.

Golf

Most hotels in the Guaymas/San Carlos area can arrange for temporary membership at the **San Carlos Country Club,** which has an 18-hole golf course.

Hunting

Hunting for birds (duck, dove, and pigeon) and deer draws an increasing number of Americans to Sonora every winter. The bird season is October through March, and deer season is during November and December. Hunting is not permitted without a Mexican guide; a reliable one in Hermosillo is Alberto Noriega at **Sonora Outfitters** (Aguascalientes 132, ☎ 62/14–10–01, 62/16–47–01, or 62/14–82–52). In Guaymas, contact **Solimar Hunting Adventures** (622/4–00–15).

BEACHES

All the main beaches of the state have paved access roads. There are hotels and restaurants near the beaches in San Carlos, Guaymas, Puerto Peñasco, and Bahía Kino. Miles and miles of more secluded beaches run along the Sea of Cortés, but access is difficult and there are no facilities.

DINING

There are no five-star restaurants in Sonora, but shrimp aficionados will find plenty to like here, as will those drawn to traditional Mexican dishes such as enchiladas, burritos, and *carne asada* (grilled meat); indeed, the style of Mexican cooking with which most Americans are familiar derives from this region. Casual dress (but not beachwear) is always acceptable, and reservations are rarely needed.

CATEGORY	COST*
$$$$	over $35
$$$	$25–$35
$$	$15–$25
$	under $15

per person, excluding drinks, service, and tax

Alamos

$ **Asadero Los Sabinos.** This small, unpretentious café, with indoor and outdoor seating, offers house specials of beef tips and ranch-style shrimp, along with several types of tacos and hamburgers. It's two blocks west of the Hotel Casa de los Tesoros, across the arroyo. ✕ *2 de Abríl No. 5, no ☎ . No reservations. No credit cards.*

$ **Casa de Café.** This American-run coffeehouse in the Mansión de la Condesa Magdalena caters to the town's expats, who enjoy good cappuccino, café latte, pastries, and scones in the lushly landscaped courtyard of a 1685 mansion. Bring a newspaper and sit for a while. ✕ *Calle Obregón 2,* ☎ *642/8–02–21. No reservations. No credit cards.* ☉ *7 AM–noon.*

$ **Restaurante Doctor Alfonso Ortíz Tirado.** Named after an Alamos singer who earned fame in Mexico City, this place is off the tourist track: It's north of the plaza, past the convent and up the hill through the barrio (take a left at the fork). There's no sign or number, but you'll see five arches and some outdoor tables. Come for local flavor and for fresh tostadas, tacos, gorditas, and soups; you can easily fill up for $4 or less. ✕ *Calle Matamoros 28, no ☎ . No reservations. No credit cards. BYOB. No lunch.*

Guaymas/San Carlos

$$ **Del Mar.** On the main street of town, this place does surf-and-turf Guaymas-style. A series of small dining rooms with beamed ceilings and tiled floors are separated by bricked arches, from which hang fishing nets and assorted flotsam and jetsam. The fish Santo Domingo (broiled local bass with mushrooms, green peppers, and melted cheese) is popular, as is the mixed seafood grill. ✕ *Av. Serdán and Calle 17, Guaymas,* ☎ *622/4–02–25. Reservations accepted. AE, MC, V.*

$$ **Los Barcos.** Across the street from the harbor, Los Barcos offers a predictable seafood and steak menu. The main room is large and pseudo-beach casual, with picnic tables and overhead palm fronds and nets; there are also two smaller, more traditional dining rooms. Especially good is the house special seafood plate, which includes calamari, octopus, and shrimp in a white wine sauce. ✕ *Malecón Malpica between Calles 21 and 22, Guaymas,* ☎ *622/2–76–50. No reservations. MC, V.*

$-$$ **Rosa's Cantina.** Picnic tables fill two large dining rooms where diners feast on ample breakfasts of eggs with *chorizo* or *huevos rancheros.* The tortilla soup is great for lunch or dinner. ✕ *On the main road through San Carlos,* ☎ *622/6–03–07. No reservations. MC, V.*

$$ **Bananas.** American food (BLTs, burgers, fries) and Mexican fare—try the fish tacos—are served in a single large room with a peaked ceiling lined with palm fronds; there are a few seats in the entrance patio as well. A copy of Charlie Chaplin's 1924 carriage license hangs on the wall by the rest rooms. ✕ *On the main road through San Carlos, no ☎ . No reservations. MC, V.*

Hermosillo

$$$$ **La Siesta.** This family-run inn, located in the Siesta Motel, is best known for its fine cuts of Sonoran beef. ✕ *Blvd. Kino Norte and 1° de Mayo,* ☎ *62/14–39–89. No reservations. MC, V.*

$$$$ **Xochimilco.** This large and friendly place is deeply shaded by large fiddle-leaf figs and yucateca trees on a narrow side street in the southern part of town (from Rosales, follow the sign near the Oxxo store). Popular with locals and regulars from across the border, Xochimilco serves well-prepared typical Sonoran dishes. ✕ *Av. Obregón 5,* ☎ *62/50–40–89. Reservations for groups. AE, MC, V.*

$$ **El Chalet de la Guitarra.** This small, immaculate restaurant specializes in pastas and other Italian dishes, served in ample portions. There's

live music nightly. ✕ *Just off Blvd. Kino, at Villareal, across from B.F. Goodrich,* ☎ *62/14–91–41. Reservations accepted. MC, V.*

$$ **Hotel Bugambilia Restaurant.** A small dining room with beamed ceilings and red-checked tablecloths and curtains, this cheerful place serves excellent tortilla soup and Mexican-style veal cutlets. For breakfast, try the *chilaquiles con huevos* (chopped tortillas, cooked in a red chile sauce, topped with scrambled or fried eggs), a specialty of the house. ✕ *Blvd. Kino 712,* ☎ *62/14–50–50. No reservations. AE, MC, V.*

Kino Bay

$$$ **El Pargo Rojo.** As befits a restaurant near the sea, this plain but friendly dining room has a nautical motif. Entrées include an excellent *sopa de marisco* (seafood soup) and fresh flounder stuffed with clams, scallops, and shrimp. There's live music on weekend nights. ✕ *Av. Mar de Cortés 1426,* ☎ *624/2–02–05. Reservations accepted. AE, MC, V.*

Nogales

$$ **El Cid.** The menu here offers a wide selection—everything from sandwiches and burgers to fresh seafood. There's candlelight dining and dancing with live music on Friday and Saturday nights and mariachi music on Sunday evenings. ✕ *Av. Obregón 124,* ☎ *631/2–64–00. Reservations accepted. AE, MC, V.*

$$ ★ **El Greco.** As its name suggests, this place has a distinctly Mediterranean ambience, but with a Mexican colonial twist. You can choose from excellent Greek salads, Alaskan king crab, or typical American and Mexican fare. Free margaritas come with lunch and dinner. ✕ *Av. Obregón 152,* ☎ *62/2–42–59. Reservations accepted. AE, MC, V.*

$ **Elvira.** The free shot of tequila that comes with each meal will whet your appetite for Elvira's fine fish dishes, chicken mole, or chile rellenos. This large, friendly restaurant (divided into more intimate dining areas) is at the very end of Av. Obregón next to the border and popular with frequent visitors to Nogales. ✕ *Av. Obregón 1,* ☎ *631/2–47–73. No reservations. DC, MC, V.*

Puerto Peñasco

$$$ ★ **Puesta del Sol.** A bit formal inside, but with plenty of outdoor seating on a patio overlooking the beach, Puesta del Sol offers many seafood dishes and soups, with appetizers for the American palate. The fish mornay (with a creamy cheese sauce) is good, as is the grilled lobster, and the margaritas are to die for. ✕ *Hotel Playa Bonita, Paseo Balboa,* ☎ *638/3–25–86. Reservations accepted. MC, V.*

$$–$$$ **Costa Brava.** This small, split-level restaurant has excellent service and a great view overlooking the Gulf. For four, try the excellent *marinera de la casa,* a seafood combination featuring octopus, shrimp, sea snails, and clams. The Shrimp Carlos V—broiled fish and shrimp stuffed with cheese and wrapped in bacon—is also very tasty. Hundreds of business cards on the wall testify to this place's popularity with Americans. ✕ *Blvd. Kino and 1° de Junio,* ☎ *638/3–31–30. MC, V.*

$$ **La Curva.** This family restaurant, featuring great quesadillas, tostadas, and chile rellenos, is easy to spot if you look for the mermaid on the sign. Turn east where the railroad tracks cross the main road into town. ✕ *Blvd. Kino and Comonfort,* ☎ *638/3–34–70. Reservations advised for dinner in winter and on holiday weekends. MC, V.*

$ **Manny's Beach Club.** Manny's is the place for those who don't want to put too much distance between the water's edge and their next margarita; it's right on the beach and sports signs like "No shoes, no shirt, no problem." Neither the burgers and fries nor the tacos are anything special; still, as the quintessential beach hangout for all ages, Manny's is not to be missed in Puerto Peñasco. ✕ *Av. Coahuila and Blvd. Matamoros,* ☏ *638/3–36–05. No reservations. No credit cards.*

LODGING

Lodging in Sonora is no longer the bargain it once was, but prices are still lower here than for comparable accommodations in the better-known vacation spots in other parts of Mexico.

CATEGORY	COST*
$$$$	over $90
$$$	$60–$90
$$	$25–$60
$	under $25

All prices are for a standard double room, excluding tax.

Alamos

$$$ **Casa de los Tesoros.** This hotel, the House of Treasures, is a picturesque and romantic converted 18th-century convent. Recently renovated and redecorated, the rooms are former nuns' cells and have fireplaces, tiled baths, antique furnishings, and high-quality handicrafts on the walls. Room rates include breakfast. ☎ *Av. Obregón 10, Box 12, 85760,* ☏ *642/8–00–10,* ☏ *642/8–04–00. 14 rooms. Restaurant, bar, pool. MC, V.*

$$$ **Casa Encantada.** Set just off the main square, this lovely bed-and-breakfast owned by a California couple is the converted 250-year-old mansion of one of Alamos's former Spanish mine owners. Rooms retain a colonial character, with high-beamed ceilings, fireplaces, and carved-wood furnishings, but all have tiled private baths and good lighting. The copious breakfast, served on a plant-filled patio overlooking a small pool, might include frittatas, fresh fruit, and homebaked breads. ☎ *Calle Juárez 20, 85760,* ☏ *642/8–04–82 or 800/422–5485,* ☏ *714/752–2331. 9 rooms. Pool, bicycles, meeting room. MC, V.*

$$$ **Casa Obregón Dieciocho.** It would be hard to find more charming ac-
★ commodations at a better price ($48 a night) than those in this 275-year-old mansion owned by artist and chef Roberto Bloor. Each of the inn's three suites has a bedroom, sitting room, fireplace, coffeemaker, bath, and private patio. Guests can sit out in a lovely, lush garden; colorful crafts and paintings abound throughout the house. Write away for reservations or (at a slightly extra expense) book through Casa de Los Tesoros (*see above*). ☎ *Av. Obregón 18, 85760, no* ☏ *. 3 suites. No credit cards.*

Guaymas/San Carlos

$$$$ **Club Med Sonora Bay.** Although San Carlos is expanding rapidly in its direction, this Club Med is still secluded from the main tourist area, its verdant 42-acre complex spread behind a large gate fronted by saguaro cactus. Accommodations are characteristically charming but plain, and the range of available activities is as great as one would expect from the chain. All meals, drinks, and tips—and many sports, such as sailing and scuba diving—are included. It's worth paying extra for the dawn horseback ride to the foothills of the nearby Sierra Madre. ☎ *Playa de los Algodones, San Carlos 85400,* ☏ *622/6–01–66, for U.S. reservations 800/CLUB-MED,* ☏ *622/6–00–70. 375 rooms. Restaurant, bar, pool, 2 saunas, beach, windsurfing, boating, golf course, horseback riding, 31 tennis courts. AE, MC, V. Closed Oct. 27–Mar. 12.*

$$$$ **Howard Johnson's.** Forget the familiar orange roofs: This huge structure, rising from San Carlos Bay en route to Club Med, is thoroughly,

strikingly, pink. Opened in 1992, this is the most luxurious hotel in Sonora, with an impressive marble-floor atrium lobby that opens out onto a large pool and beach. Rooms are done in an attractive contemporary style, with pastel-patterned bedspreads and drapes, rattan-style wood furnishings, faux-burnished copper lamps, and beige carpeting. All have safes and minibars, and rooms on the first two floors have balconies. ⊡ *Mar Barmejo, 4, Los Algodones, Box 441, San Carlos 85506,* ☎ *622/6–07–94, for U.S. reservations 800/654–2000,* FAX *622/6–07–77. 148 rooms, 25 suites. 2 restaurants, snack bar, 2 bars, 2 pools, hot tub, exercise room, volleyball, horseback riding, 2 tennis courts, car rental, travel services. AE, MC, V.*

$$$ **Playas de Cortés.** This fine, older hotel, built in the colonial style, is set amid lush gardens that lead down to the sea. The rooms are furnished with handcarved antiques and many have fireplaces; unfortunately, accommodations are not as well maintained as they might be. To reach this hotel from the highway, take the turnoff for Colonia Miramar. ⊡ *Bahía Bacochibampo, San Carlos 85506,* ☎ *622/1–12–24 or 622/1–10–48,* FAX *622/1–01–35. 120 rooms. Restaurant, bar, pool, beach, tennis. AE, DC, MC, V.*

$$$ **Plaza Las Glorias.** This condo-hotel complex, opened in 1994, overlooks the San Carlos marina. It's smaller than Howard Johnson's, but nearly as impressive, and also caters to American tastes. Subtle pastels set a tasteful tone in the comfortable modern rooms. Most accommodations offer a tiny kitchenette; a few feature private Jacuzzis. ⊡ *Plaza Comercial San Carlos 10, Planta Baja, San Carlos 85006,* ☎ *622/6–10–21 through 6–10–34,* FAX *622/6–10–35. 87 rooms, 18 suites. Restaurant, snack bar, 3 pools, golf, baby-sitting, travel services, car rental. AE, MC, V.*

$$-$$$ **Hotel Armida.** Close to the shops and restaurants of downtown Guaymas, this sand-colored, Mediterranean-style hotel features a large, well-kept pool; a good coffee shop where locals gather for power breakfasts; and an excellent steak house, El Oeste. Rooms in the hotel's old section are dark, with ill-matched furnishings. The larger, brighter accommodations in the newest section, done in light wood, are worth the higher rates; many have balconies overlooking the pool. ⊡ *Carretera Internacional, Box 296, Guaymas 85420,* ☎ *622/4–30–35, for U.S. reservations 800/732–0780,* FAX *622/2–04–48. 80 rooms, 45 suites. 2 restaurants, coffee shop, bar, room service, pool, disco, laundry service, car rental, airport shuttle. AE, MC, V.*

$$ **Fiesta San Carlos.** This small hotel on the bay has mismatched furnishings but is clean and comfortable. Accommodations with kitchens are available. Breakfast is included in the room rate. ⊡ *San Carlos Bay, San Carlos 85006,* ☎ *622/6–02–29,* FAX *622/6–37–33. 33 rooms. Restaurant, bar, pool. MC, V.*

$$ **Las Playitas.** The best deal in town, this combination trailer park/motel
★ on Guaymas Bay has plain but characterful rooms—with tinwork mirrors and beamed ceilings—opening out onto a cobblestoned, bougainvillea-lined path. Even if you don't sleep here, come for the lively, eclectically decorated restaurant and bar. The food is good and inexpensive, but if you'd rather eat what you caught that day, you can get it cooked up with trimmings added for a small price. ⊡ *Carretera al Varadero Nacional, Guaymas 85420,* ☎ *622/1–52–27 or 622/1–51–96. 29 bungalows with shower, 93 RV spaces. Restaurant, bar, pool. MC, V.*

Hermosillo

$$$ **Fiesta Americana.** This full-service property is the largest in town and popular among business travelers. The decor is predictable, but some

rooms have excellent views, and the beds are large and firm. ⛏ *369 Blvd. Kino, 83010,* ☎ *62/15–18–20, for U.S. reservations 800/ FIESTA–1,* ℻ *62/15–37–31 or 62/15–14–90. 222 rooms. Restaurant, cafeteria, lobby bar, pool, hot tub, tennis courts, disco, travel services. AE, MC, V.*

$$$ **Holiday Inn Hermosillo.** Two-thirds of the attractive rooms in this contemporary Spanish-style hotel look out on extensive, well-kept gardens and a good-size pool. The staff is geared toward accommodating the many Mexican business travelers who stay here. ⛏ *Blvd. Kino and Roman Corral, 83010,* ☎ *62/14–45–70. 144 rooms with shower. Restaurant, bar, pool, nightclub, travel services. AE, MC, V.*

Kino Bay

$$ **Posada del Mar.** The most pleasant property in Bahía Kino, the Posada is decorated mission-style, with folk art on the brick walls in the rooms and pretty gardens by the pool. ⛏ *Blvd. Mar de Cortéz and Creta, Box 132, 83340,* ☎ *62/42–01–55; in Hermosillo,* ☎ *62/18–12–21. 48 rooms. Restaurant, bar, pool, beach. MC, V.*

$$ **Posada Santa Gemma.** A good place for families, this hotel consists of two-story bungalows, each with a fireplace, full kitchen, and upstairs balcony overlooking the sea. ⛏ *Blvd. Mar de Cortéz, 83340,* ☎ *62/42–00–26. 14 bungalows, each with 2 bedrooms. Beach. MC, V.*

Puerto Peñasco

$$$–$$$$ **Plaza Las Glorias.** Scheduled to open in early 1995 but still closed at press time (spring 1995), this posh condo-hotel overlooking the harbor is the first step of what may become a billion-dollar investment by Mexican and American developers; a marina, yacht club, and health club eventually will be built here. Rooms (including some with small kitchenettes) will be geared toward American tastes; all have views of the sea. ⛏ *Paseo Las Glorias, Las Explanadas 83550,* ☎ *800/544– 4686, 210 rooms. Restaurant, pool. AE, MC, V.*

$$$ **Fiesta de Cortés.** These two-bedroom suites with kitchenettes are very popular with families and senior citizens. The place has its own pool, and the beach is a three-minute walk away. ⛏ *Apdo. 151, Puerto Peñasco 83550, or Box 441, Lukeville, AZ 85341,* ☎ *638/3–34–24. 27 rooms. Pool. MC, V.*

$$$ **Playa Bonita.** Playa Bonita offers clean, comfortable rooms; ask for one facing the hotel's broad, sandy beach. This place is very popular with Americans, who also enjoy the Puesta del Sol restaurant (*see* Dining, *above*). ⛏ *Paseo Balboa 100, 83550,* ☎ *638/3–25–86 or 602/994– 4475; in the U.S., 800/569–1797. 76 rooms, 2 suites, RV park. Restaurant, bar, beach. MC, V.*

$$ **Costa Brava.** All the rooms in this small downtown hotel overlook the Gulf. Right down the street are the fish markets, popular with those who like to bring the catch of the day back across the border. ⛏ *Malecón Kino and 1° de Julio, 83550,* ☎ *638/3–41–00 or 638/3–41–01,* ℻ *638/3–36–21. 25 rooms. Bar. MC, V.*

NIGHTLIFE

Guaymas/San Carlos

Gathering spots in the area include **Xanadu,** a Guaymas disco at Malecón Malpica; **Bar El Yate,** a sports bar at the Marina San Carlos; **Casanova Discoteque** at the Hotel Armida; **Charles Baby,** for the younger set, at Avenidas Serdán and Malecón; the bar at the **Las Play-**

itas motel on weekends; and **Pappas Tappas** or **Rana's & Rana's bar at the Neptuno Restaurant,** both on the main San Carlos highway.

Hermosillo

Hermosillo is home to several lively night spots: **Bar Ali Baba** at the Plaza Pitic (Boulevards Kino and Roman Yocupicio); and **Blocky'O Disco,** Rodríguez at Aguascalientes, for the younger set.

Puerto Peñasco

Nightlife tends to be spontaneous and informal in Puerto Peñasco, although the Playa Bonita hotel offers live music that attracts an older crowd. A younger group tends to congregate along the beaches near Manny's, where recorded music is always blaring.

SONORA ESSENTIALS

Arriving and Departing

By Plane

Aeromexico (☎ 800/237–6639) has daily flights to Hermosillo and Guaymas from Tucson and flights from Los Angeles to Hermosillo via Tijuana. **Arizona Airways** (☎ 800/274–0662) flies from Tucson and Phoenix to Hermosillo (3 flights a day), Guaymas (1 flight a day), and Ciudad Obregon (3 flights a day). Aeromexico has direct flights to Hermosillo from many cities in Mexico—including Mexico City, Chihuahua, and Guadalajara—and from La Paz and Mexico City to Guaymas; connections to other U.S. cities can be made from these points.

By Car

Many visitors to Sonora travel by car from Tucson via I-19 to the border in Nogales, Arizona, and then pick up Mexico 15, which begins in Nogales, Sonora. Highway 15 is now a divided four-lane highway, making the ride much quicker and easier than it used to be. This convenience, however, doesn't come cheap: Tolls on the road through the state, already high, were raised even more in early 1993 to pay for the highway improvement. Drivers heading down to Alamos can now expect to pay approximately $30 in fees. The alternative "Libre" (Free) routes are much slower and often poorly maintained.

There are two points of entry into Nogales. Most drivers take U.S. I-19 all the way to the end and then follow the signs to the border crossing. This route, however, will take you through the busiest streets of Nogales. It's better to take the Mariposa exit west from I-19, which leads to the international truck crossing and joins a small periphery highway that connects with Highway 15 after skirting the worst of Nogales traffic.

The official checkpoint for entering Mexico is 21 kilometers (13 miles) south of Nogales. It is here that you have to buy insurance and complete the paperwork to bring in your car if you haven't already done so in Tucson at either **Sanborn's Mexico Insurance** (2900 E. Broadway, ☎ 602/327–1255) or **The Arizona Automobile Association** (8204 E. Broadway, ☎ 602/296–7461; or 6950 N. Oracle Rd., ☎ 602/885–0694). *See* Driving *under* Smart Travel Tips *in* The Gold Guide, regarding the requirements for driving into Mexico.

By Train

As we went to press, first-class train service from the U.S. border into Sonora was nonexistent. For the most current information, contact **Mexico by Train** (☎ and FAX 210/725–3659 or 800/321–1699).

By Bus

Elite runs a deluxe air-conditioned coach from Nogales to Hermosillo for around $12. Frequent buses travel to Hermosillo and Guaymas from Nogales, Tijuana, and Mexicali via **Tres Estrellas de Oro** and **Transportes de Sonora.**

By Ferry

Ferries run from Guaymas to Santa Rosalia on the Baja coast; the crossing takes about 12 hours. At press time, the management of the ferry was changing and schedules were erratic. Check with the Guaymas tourist office (*see* Important Addresses and Numbers, *below*) for the latest information and schedules. Cars can be shipped on the ferry; reserve at least three days in advance.

Getting Around

By far the easiest way to get around is by automobile; Guaymas and San Carlos are particularly spread out. Most hotels have car-rental agencies. Buses between towns are frequent and inexpensive.

By Rental Car

GUAYMAS

Here the agencies to contact are **Budget** (☎ 622/2–14–50) and **Hertz** (☎ 622/2–10–00), both on the main highway.

HERMOSILLO

Rental agencies include **Hertz** (Blvds. Rodríguez and Tamaulipas, ☎ 62/14–81–00) and, across the street, **Budget** (☎ 62/14–08–85).

Important Addresses and Numbers

Note: In addition to the tourism offices listed below—better to visit than to try to reach by phone—the Sonora Department of Tourism has an excellent Travel Fax line that operates out of Arizona: If you dial 602/930–4815 from a fax phone, a recorded menu will allow you to receive information about Puerto Penasco, Hermosillo, Guaymas, or Kino Bay. Those who don't have a fax can phone 602/930–4871 to receive an information packet by mail.

Alamos

The tourist information office, located on the main plaza (Calle Juárez 6, ☎ 642/8–04–50), is open weekdays 9–2 and 4–6, Saturday 9–2.

Guaymas

The tourist office can be found at Avenida Serdán 441, between Calles 12 and 13, 2nd floor (☎ 622/2–56–67 or 622/4–29–32).

EMERGENCIES

Police (☎ 622/2–00–30), **Red Cross** (☎ 622/2–08–79), **hospital** (☎ 622/2–01–22).

Hermosillo

There is a tourist information office at the Palacio Administrativo (Calles Tehuántapec and Comonfort, ☎ 62/14–63–04, FAX 62/17–00–60; from the U.S., 800/4–SONORA).

EMERGENCIES

Police (☎ 62/16–15–64), **Red Cross** (☎ 62/14–07–69), **hospital** (☎ 62/12–18–70). **The Green Angels**, a very helpful state-run road service for travelers, can be reached at 62/14–63–04.

U.S. CONSULATE
The consulate is on Calle Monterrey, in back of the Hotel Calinda near downtown (☎ 62/17–26–13; for emergencies, 62/17–23–75).

Kino Bay

EMERGENCIES

Rescue One (☎ 62/42–01–51), a volunteer search-and-rescue unit, can help with both land and sea emergencies. Notify the group if you're planning a trip over water or into isolated desert regions; if you're very late in returning, Rescue One will go looking for you.

Puerto Peñasco

The tourism office is at Boulevards Juárez and V. Estrella (☎ 638/3–41–29 or 638/3–25–55).

5 The Copper Canyon: From Los Mochis to Chihuahua City

The Copper Canyon is actually a series of gorges, some of them deeper than the United States' Grand Canyon; they are home to the Tarahumara Indians, renowned for their running ability. A train trip through this magnificent, largely uncharted region usually begins or ends in Chihuahua, a lively mid-sized city with a museum devoted to Pancho Villa.

By Edie Jarolim

Updated by
Chris
Humphrey

THE MAGNIFICENT series of gorges known collectively as the Copper Canyon (in Spanish, *Barranca del Cobre*) is the real hidden treasure of the Sierra Madre. Inaccessible to the casual visitor until 30 years ago and still largely uncharted, the canyons may now be explored by taking one of the most breathtaking rides in North America: The *Chihuahua al Pacífico* railroad whistles down 661 kilometers (410 miles) of track, crossing 86 tunnels and 35 bridges through rugged country as rich in history and culture as in physical beauty.

The barrancas of the Sierra Tarahumara, as this portion of the Sierra Madre Occidental is known, are on the western edge of the Pacific "Ring of Fire." Formed by seismic and volcanic activity, which at the same time hurled a good quantity of the earth's buried mineral wealth to the surface, the canyons were carved throughout the millennia by the Urique, Serpentrión, Batopilas, and Chínipas rivers and further defined by wind erosion. Totaling more than 1,452 kilometers (900 miles) in length and capable of enveloping four of the Arizona Grand Canyons, the gorges are nearly a mile deep and wide in places; the average height of the peaks is 8,000 feet, and some rise to more than 12,000 feet. Four of the major barrancas—Copper, Urique, Sinforosa, and Batopilas—descend deeper than the Grand Canyon, Urique by nearly 1,500 feet.

The idea of building a rail line to cross this region was first conceived in 1872 by Albert C. Owen, an idealistic American socialist. Owen met with some success initially. More than 1,500 people came from the states to join him in Topolobampo, his utopian colony on the Mexican west coast, and in 1881 he obtained a concession from Mexican president General Manuel Gonzáles to build the railroad. Construction on the flat stretches near Los Mochis and Chihuahua presented no difficulties, but eventually the huge Sierra Madre mountains got in the way of Owen's dream, along with the scourge of typhoid and disillusionment within the community.

After Owen abandoned the project in 1893, it was taken up in 1900 by American railroad magnate and spiritualist Edward Arthur Stilwell. One of Stilwell's contractors in western Chihuahua was Pancho Villa, who ended up tearing up his own work during the Mexican Revolution in order to impede the movement of government troops. By 1910, when the Mexican Revolution started, the Mexican government had taken charge of building the railroad line, but progress was very slow until 1940, when surveying of the difficult Sierra Madre stretch finally began in earnest. Some 90 years and more than $100 million after it started, the Ferrocarril Chihuahua al Pacífico was dedicated on November 23, 1961.

The rail line no longer starts at Topolobambo but at nearby Los Mochis. Chihuahua City, at the other end of the line, was established in 1709. Today Chihuahua, the capital of the state of that name and a prosperous economic center, derives its wealth from mining—the Spanish discovered silver in the region as early as 1649—as well as from ranching, agriculture, and lumber.

The Tarahumara Indians, who once occupied the entire state of Chihuahua, were not unaffected by the foreign activity in the area: They were forced to serve in the mines by the Spanish and on the railroad by the Mexicans and the Americans. The threat of slavery and the series of wars that began in the 1600s and continued until the 20th century forced them to retreat deeper and deeper into the canyons. Semi-nomadic, many roam the high plateaus of the Sierra Madre in summer and move down to the canyon floor in winter to live in stone cliff dwellings or hidden wooden houses. The Tarahumara population, ravaged by disease and poverty, is now estimated at approximately 50,000.

EXPLORING

Imagine visiting the Grand Canyon in the days before it was tamed by tourist facilities, and you'll have some sense of what a trip through the Copper Canyon will be like—for better and for worse. That is, with the opportunity to encounter a relatively untouched natural site come some of the attendant discomforts of the rustic experience. But if you are careful in your choice of time to visit and are properly prepared, the trip's myriad rewards should far outstrip any temporary inconveniences.

You'll see some beautiful scenery if you just ride the railroad, including a panoramic look at Copper Canyon during a 15-minute stop at Divisadero, but you'll experience only a fraction of what the canyons have to offer if you don't get off the train. If possible, plan on a night in Cerocahui (Bahuichivo stop), one at Posado Barrancas or Divisadero (the train stations are five minutes apart), and one or two at Creel.

About 60% of the people who visit the Copper Canyon come via Los Mochis, which is the easiest route if you're traveling from California or Arizona. It's also by far the most desirable route if you come in winter, because some of the best scenery is to be seen at the western end of the ride and you're likely to miss it if you approach Los Mochis in the evening. Your choice of route matters less in the extended daylight hours of summer.

Unless you are planning to head down deep into the barrancas, winter—December through February—is not the best time to come; many of the hotels in the region are inadequately prepared for the cold, and the minor rainy season in January renders some of the roads for side excursions impassable. The warm months are May through September; the rainy season, June through September, brings precipitation for a short period every day, but this shouldn't interfere with your enjoyment in any way. It's temperate in the highlands during the summer; if you're planning to hike down into the canyons, however, remember that the deeper you go, the hotter it will get. The best months to visit are October and November, when the weather is still warm and rains have brought out all the colors in the Sierra Tarahumara.

Many people visit during Christmas and Easter, specifically to see the Tarahumara celebrations of those holidays. Closely related to the Pima Indians of southern Arizona, the Tarahumara are renowned for their running ability. (*Tarahumara* is a Spanish corruption of *Rarámuri,* which means "running people" in their language; it is said that in earlier times they survived as hunters by chasing deer to the point of collapse.) Around Christmas, Easter, and other religious feast days, the Tarahumara compete in races that can last up to three days. The men run in small groups, kicking a wooden ball for a distance of 161 kilometers (100 miles) or more. On these and other feast days, tribal elders consume peyote or *tesguino,* a sacred fermented corn liquor.

Numbers in the margin correspond to points of interest on the Copper Canyon map.

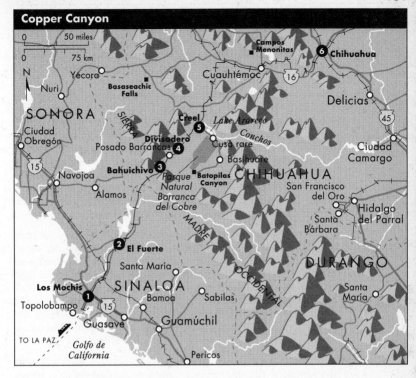

❶ The first stop on the western end of the rail line, **Los Mochis** (population about 300,000) is an agricultural boomtown; its location near the harbor at Topolobampo and the railroad makes it the export center of the state of Sinaloa, which produces many of Mexico's basic crops. Visitors can tour Benjamin Johnston's sugar refinery, the Ingenio Azucarero, around which the town grew. Near Johnston's estate you can still see the American colony, the group of brick bungalows that housed his associates, as well as a workers' hostel and the country club. Not far away, on Calles Obregón and Mina, the Museo Regional del Valle del Fuerte has rotating exhibits of paintings and crafts by local artists, and the public library next door displays pictures of the early days of the city. Labels are in Spanish only. ☎ *681/2–46–92.* ☛ *$1.60.* ☾ *Tues.–Sun. 10–1 and 4–7.*

Cottonwood trees and bougainvillea line the highway from Los Mochis to **Topolobampo;** on both sides of the road are fields planted with crops ranging from sugarcane to marigolds and mangos (36 varieties are produced here). Once the site of Albert Owen's utopian colony and the center of the railroad building activity in the area, Topolobampo is now considered a suburb of Los Mochis, 15 minutes away. A huge tuna-packing factory sits at the entrance to the bay, and local fisherman—90% of the population—ply the harbor in small shrimp boats; they compete for their catch with the many dolphins that cavort in the bay. Isla El Farallón, just off the coast, is a breeding ground for the sea lions that gave the town its name: In the language of the Mayo Indians who once dominated the area, Topolobampo means "watering place of the sea lions."

❷ Eighty kilometers (50 miles) east of Los Mochis, **El Fuerte** is a small colonial town, named after the 17th-century fort built by the Spaniards to protect against attacks by the local Mayo, Sinaloa, Zuaque, and Tehueco Indians. Originally called San Juan de Carapoa, it was founded in 1564 by Spanish conquistador Don Francisco de Ibarra and a small group of soldiers. Located on the central El Camino Real route, El Fuerte was at one time the frontier outpost from which the Spanish set out to explore and settle New Mexico and California. For three centuries, it was also a major trading post for gold and silver miners from the nearby Sierras and the most important commercial and farming center of the area; it was chosen as Sinaloa's capital in 1824 and remained so for several years. There are intact colonial mansions in what is now a rather sleepy town of 25,000; one of the best is the Hotel Posada Hidalgo (*see* Lodging, *below*). Most of El Fuerte's historic houses are set off the cobblestoned streets leading from the central plaza; a number of them have been converted into government offices.

If you want to catch an extra hour and a half of sleep, spend the night at El Fuerte and board the train at 7:30 AM. As the train ascends almost 5,906 feet into the mountains from here to Bahuichivo, it passes through 54 tunnels and over 24 bridges, including the longest and highest ones of the rail system. The scenery shifts from Sinaloan thorn forest, with cactus and scrublike vegetation, to the pools, cascades, and tropical trees of the Rio Serpentrión canyon, to the oak and pine forest that begins to take over past Temoris, where a plaque marks the dedication of the railroad by President López Mateos in 1961.

❸ From the train station at **Bahuichivo,** two hotels have buses that make the 45-minute ride up the bumpy, unpaved road to the quiet mountain village of **Cerocahui.** This is a good place to get a sense of how people live in the canyon area. Next door to the Hotel Misión is a Jesuit mission, established around 1690 by Juan María de Salvatierra, who proselytized widely in the region; it is said that because the Tarahumara were the most difficult Indians to convert, he considered this mission his favorite among the many he founded. Nearby, the church operates a boarding school for Tarahumara children. Visitors can hike or ride horses to two nearby waterfalls and to a silver mine (closed since 1988), but the prime reason to come to Cerocahui is its accessibility to Urique Canyon. It's a kidney-crunching ride to the Cerro del Gallego lookout point, where amid mountains spread against the horizon, you can make out the Urique River and the town of Urique, a slim thread and a dot on the distant canyon bottom. On the way up you'll pass a Tarahumara cave where Indian women sell baskets; nearby, a shrine to the Virgin is strikingly set against a spring in the mountainside surrounded by tropical foliage. From Cerro del Gallego the road continues down the canyon into the old mining town of Urique, which has a few basic hotels and restaurants. A public bus makes the trip from Cerocahui a few times a week, but many visitors opt for the round-trip, full-day tours offered by the local hotels (*see* Lodging, *below*).

For the most comfort in the most spectacular setting on the route, get off at the Posada Barrancas stop or, five minutes away, at the Di-
❹ visadero stop. There's little to do in **Divisadero,** a postage stamp of a place on the Continental Divide, but it's impossible to remain unastounded by the vistas of the Copper Canyon, said to have derived its name from the facts that copper used to be mined in the area and that the canyon turns copper-colored at sunset. You can also glimpse a bit of the distant Urique and Tararechua canyons from here. A popular excursion that takes about four hours round-trip, whether you're trav-

eling on two feet or on horseback, is a visit to Bacajipare, a Tarahumara village.

⑤ Nestled in pine-covered mountains, **Creel** is a rugged mining and logging town that grew up around the railroad station. The largest settlement in the area, it's a gathering place for Tarahumara Indians seeking supplies and markets for their crafts. It's easy to imagine American frontier towns at the turn of the century looking like Creel—without, of course, the backpacking contingent that makes this town its base. A cluster of small hotels here offer tours to the many points of interest in the area. It's 19 kilometers (12 miles) from Creel to Cusárare, an Indian village that hosts a 300-year-old mission built by the Jesuits for the Tarahumara. En route, you'll pass limpid-blue Lake Arareco and the Valley of the Mushrooms, with its strange volcanic-rock formations. An impressive waterfall can be reached by an easy 4-kilometer (2½-mile) hike from Cusárare through a lovely piñon forest. If the unpaved roads are passable, consider taking the longer trips to the Recohuata Hot Springs, a fairly strenuous hike down from the rim of the Tararecua Canyon, and to El Tejaban, a spectacular overlook at the Copper Canyon. It's a five-hour drive along rough roads to Basaseachic Falls, and you'll have to stay overnight if you want to visit Batopilas (*see* Off the Beaten Track, *below*), but several worthwhile day trips en route to the latter include Basihuare, where huge vertical outcroppings of rock are crossed with wide horizontal bands of color; the Urique Canyon overlook, affording a perspective of that barranca that differs from the one at Cerocahui; and La Bufa, site of a former Spanish silver mine.

⑥ After the peaceful Copper Canyon, the sprawling city of **Chihuahua,** with nearly 1 million inhabitants, may come as a bit of a jolt. Two of the most famous figures in Mexico's revolutionary wars are closely tied to the city. Father Miguel Hidalgo, the father of Mexican independence, and his coconspirators were executed by the Spanish here in 1811. And Chihuahua was home to General Pancho Villa, whose revolutionary army, the División del Norte (Army of the North), was decisive in overthrowing dictator Porfirio Díaz in 1910 and securing victory in the ensuing civil war. In addition, Benito Juárez, known as the Abraham Lincoln of Mexico, made Chihuahua his base in 1865 during the French invasion of the country.

Whatever you do, don't miss a visit to the Museo Histórico de la Revolución en el Estado de Chihuahua, better known as **Pancho Villa's House.** Villa lived in this home, completed in 1909, with his second wife, Luz Corral (he had three wives, none of whom he divorced). She stayed here until her death on June 6, 1981, willing the residence to the government, which restored it as a national museum. The 50 small rooms that used to board Villa's bodyguards have been converted into exhibition rooms displaying artifacts of Chihuahua's cultural and revolutionary history. Parked outside in the museum's courtyard is the bullet-ridden 1919 Dodge in which Villa was assassinated in 1923 at the age of 45. *Calle Décima 3014,* ☎ *14/16–29–58.* 🖝 *Less than $1.* 🕒 *Daily 9–1 and 3–7.*

Another must-see is the **Catedral** on the central Plaza de la Constitución. Construction on this beautiful Baroque structure was started by the Jesuits in 1726, but not completed until 1825 because of Indian uprisings in the area. The exterior is made of the pinkish limestone quarried in this region; inside, the opulent church has altars made of Carrara marble, a 24-karat solid gold ceiling, a beautiful cedar-and-brass carved depiction of St. Peter and St. Paul, and a huge German-made organ. In the back of the cathedral, the Museum of Sacred Art displays the work of seven local artists of the 18th-century Mexican Baroque tradition, as well as commemorations of the 1990 visit of Pope John Paul II. ☛ *50¢.* ☾ *Weekdays 10–2 and 4–6.*

At the nearby Plaza Hidalgo, the **Palacio del Gobierno** (State Capitol) was built by the Jesuits as a convent in 1882. Converted into government offices in 1891, it was destroyed by a fire in the early 1940s and rebuilt in 1947. Murals around the patio by artist Pino Mora depict famous episodes from the history of the state of Chihuahua; a plaque commemorates the spot where Father Hidalgo was executed on the morning of July 30, 1811. ☎ *14/10–63–24.* ☾ *Daily 8–11 AM.*

Around the corner from the entrance to the Palacio del Gobierno, on Calle Libertad, the **Palacio Federal** (Federal Building) houses the city's main post office and telegraph office, as well as the dungeon where Hidalgo was imprisoned before he was executed by the Spanish; his pistols, traveler's trunk, crucifix, and reproductions of his letters are on display here. ☾ *Daily 9–7.*

Also connected to the history of Father Hidalgo is the **Iglesia de San Francisco** (San Francisco Church), located on Avenida Libertad at Calle 15. It's the oldest (1721) church built in Chihuahua that is still standing. Hidalgo's decapitated body was interred in the chapel of this simple church from 1811 to 1827, when it was sent to Mexico City; his head was publicly displayed for 10 years by Spanish Royalists in Guanajuato on the Alhóndiga de Granaditas (*see* Guanajuato *in* Chapter 8, The Heartland of Mexico).

Slightly outside the center of town but well worth a visit is the Cultural Museum of the University of Chihuahua, known as **Quinta Gameros.** This Art Nouveau mansion, with beautiful stained-glass windows, ornate carved wooden staircases, and Italian blown-glass chandeliers, was built in 1910 by Julio Corredor, a Columbian architect, for Manuel Gameros, a wealthy mining engineer. An eclectic collection includes European art from the 18th and 19th centuries, pottery of the local Paquime Indians, and artifacts of the nearby Mennonite community. Concerts, lectures, and exhibitions of local artists are also held here. *Calle Bolívar 401,* ☎ *14/16–66–84.* ☛ *$2.* ☾ *Tues.–Sun. 10–2 and 4–7.*

A restoration project has made the site of the town's original settlement, **Santa Eulalia,** particularly appealing. The 20-minute drive southeast of town is compensated by the colonial architecture and cobblestoned streets of this small town; the religious artwork in the 18th-century cathedral is noteworthy, and the Mesón de Santa Eulalia Restaurant has a lovely spot.

Off the Beaten Track

Seventy-three kilometers (45 miles) northeast of Creel but reached via an unpaved, winding road, the 806-foot **Basaseachic Falls** are among the highest cascades in Mexico and a most impressive sight.

A remote village of about 600 people, **Batopilas** was once one of the wealthiest towns in Mexico because of the nearby veins of silver mined on and off from the time of the conquistadores; at one point it was the only place in the country besides Mexico City that had electricity. The 80-kilometer (48-mile) ride down dusty, unpaved roads to the now-sleepy town at the bottom of Batopilas Canyon takes about 5½ hours from Creel (closer to 8 hours on the local bus, which runs about three times a week). Sights in this lush, flower-filled oasis include the ruined hacienda of Alexander Shepherd, built in the late 1800s by one of the town's wealthiest mine owners; the original aqueduct, which still services the town (it's set along the Camino Real); and a triple-domed 17th-century cathedral, mysteriously isolated in the Satevo Valley and reached via a scenic 6.4-kilometer (4-mile) hike from town. You'll need to stay overnight at one of Batopilas's modest posadas or at the Riverside Lodge (*see* Lodging, *below*).

A rather anomalous experience in Mexico is a visit to the large **Mennonite community** (Campos Menonitas) in the town of Cuauhtémoc, about 105 kilometers (65 miles) west of Chihuahua. Approximately 20,000 Mennonites came to the San Antonio Valley in 1922 at the invitation of President Alvaro Obregón, who gave them the right to live freely and autonomously in return for farming the 100,000 hectares (247,000 acres) of land they purchased. Tours can be arranged either in Chihuahua (*see* Guided Tours *in* Copper Canyon Essentials, *below*) or at the Tarahumara Inn in Cuauhtémoc.

SHOPPING

Tarahumara crafts, which provide the Indians with their only cash income, include lovely handwoven baskets made from palm leaves and pine bark; carved wooden dolls; crude pottery; brightly colored belts and sashes woven using backstrap looms; and wooden fiddles, sometimes with mask faces, from which the men produce haunting music. The Tarahumara, who are generally shy about talking with tourists, sell their wares throughout the Copper Canyon area; their prices are fair, so bargaining is unnecessary (as well as inappropriate). Baskets run from $1 for the smallest to about $15 for the largest. Tarahumara wares are sold at the market outside the train station at Divisadero and at a number of shops in Creel, the best one of which is **Artesanías Misión,** right off the central plaza.

In Chihuahua, **Mercado de Artesanías** (Calle Victoria 506 across from the cathedral, ☎ 14/16−27−16) sells everything from jewelry, candy, and T-shirts to crafts from all over the region. The small **gift shop at the Museo de Arte Popular** (Calle Reforma 5, no ☎) has a good selection of items from all over Mexico, including many that are made by the Tarahumara. In addition to selling gems and geodes from the area, the **Rock Shop** (Calle Décima, directly across from Pancho Villa's home, ☎ 14/15−28−82) offers a wide variety of crafts.

SPORTS AND OUTDOOR ACTIVITIES

Hiking

Mexico's Copper Canyon Country, by M. John Fayhee, is a good source of information about hiking the barrancas, but even the most experienced trekkers should enlist the help of local guides, who can be contacted through all the hotels in the area or through travel agents in Los Mochis and Chihuahua. Few adequate maps are available for even the so-called marked trails, and many of the better-worn routes into the canyon are made by the Tarahumara, whose prime concern is getting from one habitable area to the next rather than getting to the bottom.

Urique Canyon is most easily reached from Cerocahui (Bahuichivo stop). The Copper Canyon is most accessible from Divisadero; trails range from easy rim walks to a 27-kilometer (17-mile) descent to the bottom, which takes seven or eight hours. If you're in Creel, a gentle and rewarding hike is the 5-kilometer (3-mile) walk from the Copper Canyon Lodge to the Cusárare Falls. More difficult but equally scenic are the treks down to Recohauta Hot Springs and to the base of Basaseachic Falls; both are about three hours round-trip. The descent into Batopilas Canyon from Creel requires an overnight stay.

Horseback Riding

All hotels in the canyon area can arrange for local guides with gentle horses. Most trips are not for couch potatoes, however. The trails into the canyon are badly defined and can be rocky as well as slippery if the weather is icy or wet; at rough spots you might be asked to dismount and walk part of the way. A fairly easy and inexpensive ride is to Wicochic Falls at Cerocahui, about two hours round-trip, including a half-hour hike at the end, where the trail is too narrow for the horses. From Divisadero, the trip to Bacajipare, a Tarahumara village in the Copper Canyon, affords stunning vistas; it's an exciting four-hour ride round-trip, but it's not for the faint of heart.

DINING AND LODGING

Dining

Along the Copper Canyon trail you'll encounter rustic areas where there are few eateries besides those connected with lodges, as well as sophisticated culinary centers like Chihuahua.

In Los Mochis and Topolobampo your best bet is seafood. Restaurants tend to be inexpensive. At the hotels in Cerocahui, Divisadero, and Posada Barrancas, food is included in the price of the room. Don't even think about dieting here: You'll get three freshly cooked, hearty meals a day, often with meat courses and dessert at both lunch and dinner. There are a few more dining options in Creel, where, in addition to the hotel dining rooms, there are a number of inns along the town's main street, Avenida López Mateos; **La Cabana, El Caballo Bayo,** and **Lupita** all offer good, inexpensive Mexican fare.

You'll have the most choice in Chihuahua. The state is a large producer of beef, so upscale steakhouses and places serving *carne asada* (char-broiled strips of marinated beef) abound, but a variety of Mexican specialties and seafood flown in from the coast is also available. Many of Chihuahua's well-appointed international restaurants are located in the Zona Dorada, on Calle Juárez starting from its intersection with Calle Colón.

Dress is casual everywhere except at a few of the more upscale restaurants in Chihuahua. Unless otherwise indicated, reservations are not necessary.

CATEGORY	COST*
$$$$	over $20
$$$	$15–$20
$$	$8–$15
$	under $8

per person, excluding drinks, service, and sales tax (10%)

Lodging

Accommodations in this area tend to fall into two categories: comfortable but characterless in the large cities and charming but to varying degrees rustic in the small ones. In Cerocahui, Divisadero-Posada Barrancas, and Creel, all the hotels send buses or cars to meet the train; if you don't have a reservation, you'll have to make a quick decision and then hop on a vehicle sent out by the hotel of your choice. During the summer and around Christmas and Easter, it's important to book in advance. Where indicated, rates for hotels include meals. Note: Although Posada Barrancas and Divisadero are only five minutes apart, lodgings in these two places are listed separately so as to clarify the stop where you should get off the train.

The postal code for Los Mochis is 82000. The postal code for all the listed hotels in Chihuahua is 31000.

CATEGORY	COST*
$$$$	over $90
$$$	$60–$90
$$	$25–$60
$	under $25

All prices are for a standard double room, excluding 10% tax.

Batopilas

DINING AND LODGING

$$$$ **Riverside Lodge.** A restored late-19th-century hacienda, this lodging is quirkily charming. Each of the high-ceilinged rooms is individually decorated—one with a prayer niche, for example, another with vintage Elizabeth Taylor posters—but all have spacious private baths and huge, soft feather duvets. Only partially wired for electricity, the accommodations have an odd mix of kerosene reading lamps and electrical outlets for hair dryers. The home-cooked meals are excellent, and guests are free to raid the refrigerator and liquor cabinet (just sign the book; you'll be billed later). The lodge must be booked as part of a six-night package with the Copper Canyon Lodge in Creel (*see below*), which has the same owner. ☒ *Batopilas; contact Copper Canyon Lodges, 2741 Paldan, Auburn Hills, MI 48326,* ☎ *810/340–7230 or 800/776–3942. 15 rooms. Library, hiking. MC, V.*

Cerocahui

DINING AND LODGING

$$$$ **Hotel Misión.** Part of the Balderrama chain—the Copper Canyon's equivalent of the Grand Canyon's Fred Harvey hotel empire—this is the only tourist accommodation in town. The main house, which looks like a combination ski lodge and hacienda, contains the hotel's office, small shops, dining room, bar, and lounge. In winter, guests huddle for warmth around two large fireplaces, the prime sources of heat and light: Cerocahui isn't wired for electricity, and the hotel uses its generator for only a few hours, generally from 7 to 9 in the morning and 7 to 11 in the evening. The plain but characterful rooms, with beamed ceilings and Spanish Colonial-style furnishings, are a pyromaniac's dream: They're equipped with fuel and matches for guests to light the wood-burning stove and a kerosene lamp for light. ☒ *Cerocahui (train stop: Bahuichivo; mailing address: Santa Anita Hotel, Box 159, Los Mochis, Sinaloa),* ☎ *681/8–70–46, ext. 432,* ☒ *681/2–00–46. 30 rooms with bath. Restaurant, bar. AE, MC, V.*

$$$$ **Paraíso del Oso Lodge.** Opened in 1990, this lodge near Cerocahui offers plain rooms with simple wooden furniture handmade by locals. Guests must stoke the stove for heat at night, since there is no elec-

tricity here. A huge window-filled lobby affords excellent views of the cliffs above the lodge, and a gift shop carries local crafts as well as wares from other parts of Mexico. ⊠ *3 mi outside of Cerocahui; contact Columbus Travel, Rte. 12, Box 382B, New Braunfels, TX, 78132,* ☎ *210/885–2000 or 800/843–1060 for reservations. 16 rooms with bath. Dining room. MC, V in U.S.; cash or personal checks only on premises.*

Chihuahua

DINING

$$$ La Mansión del Gourmet. If you dine at this stately 1950s mansion, just across the canal from downtown, you'll feel as though you're at a private party; the effect is enhanced by the piano in the center of the dining room, played each afternoon and evening. A variety of international fare is available, including a large selection of steaks, the house specialty. For visual as well as culinary excitement, try a sizzling *platillo flameado* with either beef or shrimp. ✕ *Avenida Universidad,* ☎ *14/14–38–78. Reservations accepted. AE, DC, MC, V.*

$$ Club de Los Parados. Thirty-seven years of Chihuahua's history have
★ passed through the doors of this landmark restaurant, set in an adobe-style house that would seem more at home in New Mexico. It was started by Tony Vega, a wealthy cattle rancher who died in 1991, as a place for him to come with his fellow ranchers. The story goes that when they went out drinking, the one who sat (or fell) down first had to pick up the tab; Los Parados means "the standing ones." Excellently grilled steaks and chicken as well as tasty Mexican specialties are served in a large room, decorated in muted southwestern colors, with a wood-burning kiva fireplace; the *carne asada* (charbroiled strips of marinated beef) with guacamole is particularly good. A private dining room is lined with photographs of Tony Vega and all the important people in town, including native Chihuahuan Anthony Quinn. ✕ *Av. Juárez 3901,* ☎ *14/15–35–09 or 14/10–53–35. Reservations accepted. AE, MC, V.*

$$ La Calesa. A large, dimly lit room with wood paneling and red tablecloths and curtains, this looks like the classic steakhouse it is. The onion soup and chile with *aserdo* (a local cheese) make good appetizers. The filet mignon and rib eye steaks from the area are particularly recommended as entrées; try the former cooked in garlic with shrimp and mushrooms. The clubby bar has a good selection of wines and liquors. ✕ *Av. Juárez 3300,* ☎ *14/10–10–38 or 14/16–02–22. Reservations recommended for large groups. AE, MC, V.*

$ El Taquito. Three blocks south of the Palacio del Gobierno, this modest restaurant specializes in tacos and other typical Mexican dishes, although the dining room, with vines and black-and-white etchings of local scenes on the wall, looks somewhat Mediterranean. The chiles rellenos, enchiladas suizas, and chicken burritos with mole sauce are all good choices; you can get a bottle of sangria to accompany your meal for about $6. ✕ *Venustiano Carranza 1818,* ☎ *14/10–21–44. No reservations. No credit cards.*

$ La Parilla. A good place to take a break from downtown sightseeing, this fast-food eatery across the street from the Hotel San Francisco will delight dedicated carnivores. After the waiter hands you an order form/menu on which you mark your choice, he'll come over with a tray bearing the cuts of meat being offered that day. A strolling guitarist makes the rounds of this plain, white-walled room with plastic tables and chairs and an open grill in the back. The *menu turístico* includes steak with mashed potatoes, soup, and salad for about $6.50; you'll get your own grill if you order the house special, *parillados,* a sirloin platter served with guacamole and chile sauces as well as potatoes. ✕ *Victoria 420,* ☎ *14/15–58–56. No reservations. AE, MC, V.*

LODGING

$$$$ **Villa Suites.** This appealing property combines comfort, style, and
★ convenience: Ten minutes from the downtown sights but set off in a quiet area, it is the first all-suite hotel in Chihuahua. Each of the rooms, tastefully decorated in contemporary style with a green or blue and beige color scheme, has a kitchenette with stove, dishwasher, and coffeemaker, as well as a VCR and an exercycle. A complimentary Continental breakfast buffet is served at the Clubhouse, which also houses the hotel's indoor pool, Jacuzzi, and exercise equipment. Eager to accommodate the many American business travelers who stay here, the English-speaking staff is friendly and helpful. ⌨ *Escudero 702,* ☎ *14/14–33–50,* ☏ *14/14–33–13. 72 suites. Restaurant, room service, indoor and outdoor pools, spa, health club, Ping-Pong, basketball. AE, DC, MC, V.*

$$$ **Hotel San Francisco.** A favorite of Mexican business travelers, this modern four-story hotel has a prime location right next to the Catedral and Plaza de Armas. It's clean and comfortable if somewhat bland rooms are equipped with color televisions and telephones. The lobby, somewhat gloomy during the day, is lively at night. ⌨ *Victoria 409,* ☎ *14/16–75–50, toll-free in the U.S. 800/847–2546, toll-free in Mexico 91–800/1–41–07,* ☏ *14/15–35–38. 111 rooms, 20 suites. Restaurant-bar, travel services. AE, MC, V.*

$$ **Posada Tierra Blanca.** Across the street from the Palacio del Sol but considerably less expensive, this modern motel-style property is convenient to the downtown sights. Rooms, decorated in red and black with pseudo-antique furnishings, are large and well heated in winter; all have TVs. The striking *Stages of Man* mural in the lobby was painted by Pina Mora, the same artist who decorated the courtyard of the Palacio del Gobierno (*see* Exploring, *above*). ⌨ *Niños Heroes 100,* ☎ *14/15–00–00. 103 rooms with bath. Restaurant, piano bar, pool. AE, MC, V.*

Creel

DINING

$$ **The Steak House.** The restaurant of the Hotel Cascada, this is a fun place to have dinner; taped music and a good bar draw both locals and tourists in the evening. As the name suggests, steak is the focus of the menu, but there are tasty seafood dishes, all reasonably priced, as well. ✕ *Av. López Mateos 49,* ☎ *145/6–01–51. No reservations. AE, MC, V.*

$ **Veronica's.** This clean, unpretentious little eatery on the main street is popular with locals and tourists alike, and it's easy to see why: a wide selection of Mexican standards prepared simply but with care and at very reasonable prices. *Comida corridas*—set meals with soup, main course, and dessert—are available, or you can order à la carte off the menu. Try the excellent *sopa de verduras* (vegetable soup). ✕ *Av. López Mateos, no* ☎. *No reservations. No credit cards.*

DINING AND LODGING

$$$$ **Copper Canyon Lodge.** About 24 kilometers (15 miles) from the train
★ station, near Cusárare Falls and overlooking a piñon forest, this rustic hotel couldn't have a nicer setting. The pine-walled rooms, with their light-wood, Spanish-style furnishings and tiled modern baths, are very attractive, and the lodge where hearty meals are served family style is cozy and appealing. The only catch is that there's no electricity. The kerosene lamps are fine for light year-round. This place must be booked

as part of a package with the Riverside Lodge in Batopilas (*see above*). ☒ *Copper Canyon Lodges, 2741 Paldan, Auburn Hills, MI 48326,* ☎ *810/340–7230 or 800/776–3942. 23 rooms. Restaurant, bar.*

LODGING

$$ **Parador de la Montaña Motel/The Little Resort.** Built 20 years ago, the Parador is considered the fanciest hotel in town, but it's showing its age. The furniture is dark, as is the lighting. Recently remodeled rooms still have the same cheerless decorating scheme, but the hotel is used by many tour operators and is frequently booked up, so its bar and restaurant are often lively in the evening. ☒ *Av. López Mateos 44,* ☎ *145/6–00–75,* FAX *145/6–00–85. Reservations: Allende 114, Chihuahua, Chih.* ☎ *14/10–45–80,* FAX *14/15–34–68. 50 rooms with shower. Restaurant, bar. AE, MC, V.*

$–$$ **La Posada de Creel.** This hotel, the oldest in Creel, was recently renovated and turned into a bed-and-breakfast with 10 private rooms and 11 rooms that sleep four. Right off the train tracks and two blocks from the station, the inn provides simple but clean accommodations. ☒ *Apdo. 7, Creel,* ☎ *145/6–01–42; reservations in the U.S., Box 3, Cleburne, TX 76033,* ☎ *817/558–9979 or 817/641–9979,* FAX *817/641–9979. 21 rooms. Restaurant. No credit cards.*

$ **Margarita's.** If a small boy at the train station offers to take you to
★ Margarita's, go with him. Otherwise you might miss one of the best deals in town: There's no sign on the door, and even if you follow directions (right off the main town plaza, between the two churches perpendicular to each other), you're likely to think you're walking into a private kitchen when you open the door. At this gathering spot for backpackers, you can get anything from a bunk bed in the dorm ($5) to a double room with two beds (around $8 per person); all prices include a tasty home-cooked breakfast and dinner. The rooms, with wrought-iron lamps, light-wood furnishings, and clean, modern baths, are as pleasant as anything you'll find for twice or three times the price. Last year owner Margarita opened up a new, more upscale place with a proper restaurant near the Parador de la Montaña Motel; room rates there are still a bargain at $27 for a double, including dinner. ☒ *Av. López Mateos y Parroquia 11,* ☎ *145/6–00–45, 145/6–02–45 (new hotel), 21 rooms, most with private bath. Restaurant. No credit cards.*

Divisadero

DINING AND LODGING

$$$$ **Hotel Cabanas Divisadero-Barrancas.** This property sits right on the edge of the Copper Canyon; the dining room and rooms 1 through 10 in the old section and 35 through 52 in the new section all enjoy panoramic views. The old rooms, with dark furnishings, have decks, while the new ones, somewhat farther from the dining room but lighter in decor, have balconies. Food and service get mixed reviews from the international visitors who sign the guest log, but you're not likely to notice what you're eating when you look out of the dining-room window. ☒ *Reservations: Av. Mirador 4516, Box 31238, Colonia Residencial Campestre, Chihuahua, Chih.,* ☎ *14/16–51–36,* FAX *14/15–65–75. 52 rooms with shower. Restaurant, bar. AE, MC, V.*

El Fuerte

DINING AND LODGING

$$$ **Hotel Posada Hidalgo.** You'll be transported back to a more gracious
★ era at this lovely restored hacienda, with its lush tropical gardens and cobblestoned paths. Designated a Historic Landmark in 1913, it was built in 1895 by Rafael Almada, a rancher and the richest man in nearby

Alamos; he had furniture shipped from as far as San Francisco for his lavish home, where he entertained the local elite. It's difficult to choose between the larger rooms with balconies, set off of a lobby filled with period artifacts, and the ones that open out onto the gardens; all are decorated with rough-hewn handcrafted furniture in Spanish Colonial style. *Langostino* (crayfish) is a specialty of the hotel dining room. ☎ *Hidalgo 101,* ☎ *681/3–0242; reservations: Hotel Santa Anita, Box 159, Los Mochis, Sin.,* ☎ *681/8–70–46,* FAX *681/2–00–46. 40 rooms with bath. Dining room-bar, pool, disco. AE, MC, V.*

Los Mochis
DINING

$$ **El Farallón.** With its nautical decor and murals, the dining room of this simple restaurant sets the tone for the excellent fish served here. ✕ *Obregón 593, corner Angel Flores,* ☎ *681/2–14–28. No reservations. MC, V.*

$$ **Restaurante España.** This slightly upscale restaurant in downtown Los Mochis is popular with the local business crowd. Good seafood and Spanish dishes are served around an intriguing-looking indoor fountain. ✕ *Obregón 526,* ☎ *681/2–22–21 or 681/2–23–35. Reservations accepted. AE, MC, V.*

$ **El Taquito.** Located in the very center of Los Mochis, this diner-style restaurant offers well-prepared and reasonably priced Mexican standards 24 hours a day, every day. For a hearty meal try the *Tampiqueña,* a tasty steak with enchiladas, guacamole, and *frijoles* (beans) on the side. ✕ *Calle Leyva between Hidalgo and Independencia,* ☎ *681/2–81–19. No reservations. MC, V.*

LODGING

$$$ **Hotel Santa Anita.** The central reservations link of the Balderrama chain, this downtown hotel is also an informal information center for what's happening along the *Chihuahua al Pacífico* route, as well as the place to book tours. Built in 1959, the property has been renovated continually; rooms are large and tastefully furnished in muted pastels, with comfortable modern furniture. All have cable TV, and many have hair dryers, unusual for this part of the country. ☎ *Leyva and Hidalgo, Apdo. 159, Los Mochis, Sin.,* ☎ *681/8–70–46,* FAX *681/2–00–46. 133 rooms with bath. Restaurant, bar, travel services. AE, DC, MC, V.*

$$ **El Dorado.** On the main street of town and, as a result, noisy as well as convenient to restaurants and shops, this modest but clean motel/hotel is a good value. Rooms are light-filled and have TVs; a small pool is set among palm trees in the back. ☎ *525 N. Leyva, corner Valdez,* ☎ *681/5–11–11,* FAX *681/2–01–79. 93 rooms with bath. Coffee shop, bar, pool, travel services. AE, MC, V.*

Posada Barrancas
DINING AND LODGING

$$$$ **Hotel Mansion Tarahumara.** It's a bit disconcerting to come across a red-turreted, medieval-style castle out here in barranca country, but somehow this whimsical property works. All the rooms (15 of them in individual cabins) have light-pine furniture beautifully designed in Spanish contemporary style. The newest units have pine-log walls; the older rooms feature gray cobblestoned walls that match the castle's exterior. The large dining room with its high-vaulted ceiling is hard to keep warm in winter but has wonderful views of the Sierra Madre. ☎ *Av. Juárez 1602, 1-A, Colonia Centro, Chihuahua, Chih.,* ☎ *and* FAX *14/16–54–44. 46 rooms with bath and fireplace. Restaurant, bar, disco. AE, MC, V.*

$$$$ **Hotel Posada Barrancas.** A good base from which to explore the Barranca del Cobre, this hotel added an annex in 1992. The rooms in this section, done in light wood, are your best bet; the older accommodations have undistinguished dark, contemporary-style furnishings, pseudo-stucco walls, and linoleum-tile floors. From the vertical beams in the main lodge/dining room hang strings of butterfly cocoons used in Tarahumara ceremonial dances, sometimes performed at the hotel in the evening. ☎ *Posada Barrancas; reservations: Hotel Santa Anita, Box 159, Los Mochis, Sin.,* ☎ *681/8–70–46,* ꜰᴀx *681/2–00–46. 78 rooms with bath. Restaurant, bar, exercise room. AE, DC, MC, V.*

$$$$ **Hotel Posada Barrancas Mirador.** Opened in mid-1993, this bright pink
★   hotel—the latest link in the Balderrama chain—is perched on the edge of the Copper Canyon, facing Balancing Rock. The dining room and all the guest rooms have spectacular views; balconies seem to hang right over the abyss. Accommodations are light and bright, with custom-made furniture and individually controlled air-conditioning and heat, and meals are copious and tasty. ☎ *Posada Barrancas; reservations: Hotel Santa Anita, Box 159, Los Mochis, Sin.,* ☎ *681/8–70–46,* ꜰᴀx *681/2–00–46. 36 rooms. Restaurant, bar, meeting room. AE, DC, MC, V.*

Topolobampo
DINING

$ **Yacht Hotel.** Open to cool breezes from Topolobampo Bay, this hotel restaurant is a pleasant place for enjoying well-prepared Mexican dishes as well as the fresh seafood caught in the small fishing boats that sail by. Note: This restaurant is going to close in October 1995 when the hotel undergoes renovation; it's due to reopen in January 1996. The phone number will change, but when we went to press, the new one was not available. ✗ *Yacht Hotel, on the waterfront,* ☎ *681/2–00–88 or 681/2–03–08. No reservations. MC, V.*

NIGHTLIFE

Sitting around and chatting with fellow guests in your lodge is about the extent of nighttime activity in the heart of Sierra Madre country, though occasionally one of the hotels in Divisadero or Posada Barrancas will have performances in the evening by Tarahumara dancers. In Creel, head to **The Steak House** or the **Parador de La Montaña Motel** (*see* Dining and Lodging, *above*) for an after-dinner drink; there's often a sports match on TV at **El Caballo Bayo** (Av. Lopez Mateos, at the west end of town, no ☎). Things are a bit more lively in Los Mochis, where locals kick up their heels at **Fantasy** (Hotel Plaza Inn, Leyva and Cardenas, ☎ 681/5–80–20) and **Morocco** (Leyva and Rendon, ☎ 681/2–13–88), two downtown discos, but Chihuahua has the most nightlife options in the area. **La Reggae** (Blvd. Ortiz Mena and Bosque de la Reina, ☎ 14/15–47–55) draws a crowd with dancing feet for its rock-and-roll bands. At **Chihuahua Charlie** (Av. Juárez 3329, ☎ 14/17–70–65), DJs spin discs nightly; come early for dinner—the food is as good as the music. The popular **La Puerta de Alcalá** (Revolución 1608, ☎ 14/15–83–93) disco sometimes has live music. The bar at the **Hotel San Francisco** features a good lounge singer, and the lobby bar at the **Hotel Sicomoro** also has live entertainment nightly (*see* Dining and Lodging, *above*, for both).

COPPER CANYON ESSENTIALS

Arriving and Departing

By Plane
LOS MOCHIS
AeroCalifornia (☎ 800/237–6225) has daily flights from Los Angeles to Los Mochis and also flies from Tijuana, Mexico City, and Guadalajara every day. On **Aeromexico** (☎ 800/237–6639) you can get to Los Mochis from Tucson, Mexico City, and La Paz every day. **Leo López** (☎ 915/778–1022) departs from El Paso to Los Mochis via Chihuahua Monday through Friday.

CHIHUAHUA
Leo López flies to Chihuahua from El Paso twice a day Monday through Friday and in the morning on Saturday and Sunday. **Aeromexico** has a daily direct flight to Chihuahua from Los Angeles, as well as daily flights from Tucson (with a plane change at Hermosillo) and from San Antonio (with a connection in Monterrey). Within Mexico, the airline has four daily flights to Chihuahua from Mexico City, two from Monterrey, one from Guadalajara, and one from Tijuana.

By Car
LOS MOCHIS
Drive down to Los Mochis from Nogales on the Arizona border. Mexico Highway 15, four lanes much of the way, will take you all the way there, a distance of 763 kilometers (474 miles).

CHIHUAHUA
Most U.S. visitors drive to Chihuahua via Mexico Highway 45 from the El Paso–Ciudad Juárez border, a distance of 375 kilometers (233 miles), or up from Mexico City, 1,440 kilometers (895 miles).

COPPER CANYON
Paved roads now connect Chihuahua to Creel: Take Mexico Highway 16 west to San Pedro, then State Highway 127 south to Creel. The 300-kilometer (186-mile) trip takes 3½ to 4 hours if the weather is good. This drive, through the pine forests of the Sierra Madre foothills, is more scenic than the railroad route via the plains area. Driving is a good option if you have an all-terrain vehicle, because there are many worthwhile, if difficult, excursions into the canyons from Creel. A new road from Chihuahua to Bahuichivo via Divisadero has recently been finished, but it is not recommended. It's full of potholes and especially dangerous during rain or snow, even with a four-wheel-drive vehicle. A route to Urique Canyon is also planned.

By Train
LOS MOCHIS
At present, there is no first-class service from any U.S. border city to either Los Mochis or Chihuahua. For the most current information, contact **Mexico by Train** (☎ and FAX 210/725–3659 or 800/321–1699).

COPPER CANYON
Sierra Madre Express of Tucson (Box 26381, Tucson, AZ 85726, ☎ 520/747–0346 or 800/666–0346) runs its own deluxe trains (with dome car, dining car, and Pullman) to the Copper Canyon from Tucson, offering eight-day, seven-night trips approximately four times a year. Two other tour operators, **Tauck Tours** (Box 5027, Westport, CT 06881, ☎ 800/468–2825) and **RFD Travel** (5201 Johnson Dr., Mission, KS 66205, ☎ 800/365–5389), charter the trains and their personnel for similar excursions the rest of the time. The newest deluxe excursions into the

area are offered by **DRC Rail Tours** (16800 Greenspoint Park Dr., Suite 245 N, Houston, TX 77060, ☎ 800/659–7602); they depart from El Paso. Prices start from $1,300 (per person, based on double occupancy) for a five-day trip and can run as high as $4,300 for an eight-day trip, though DRC offers a nine-day excursion for $2,400.

By Bus

LOS MOCHIS

The **Tres Estrellas de Oro, Transportes del Pacífico,** and **Transport Norte de Sonora** bus lines all leave every hour from Nogales to Los Mochis; with luck, the trip should take about 12 hours. The cost is approximately $30.

CHIHUAHUA

The **Transportes de Norte** (☎ 14/29–02–42 or 14/29–02–40), **Chihuahuenses** (☎ 14/29–02–42 or 14/29–02–40), and **Omnibus de México** (☎ 14/10–30–90) lines run clean, air-conditioned buses from Ciudad Juárez to Chihuahua; these leave approximately every 15 minutes from 7 AM to 8 PM. The cost of the trip, which takes about 4½ hours, is approximately $17 for first class, $22 for the new Ejectivo luxury coaches. Buses shuttle between El Paso and Ciudad Juárez every two hours; the price is $5.

By Boat

The Baja Express catamaran from La Paz to Topolobampo is no longer running; the only service provided for passengers is via **car ferry,** which takes eight to nine hours and is not always available. In Los Mochis, contact Viajes Paotan (Serapio Rendon 517 Pte., ☎ 681/5–19–14) for information and reservations; in Topolobampo, contact Grupo Sematur de California (☎ 681/2–01–04 or 800/6–96–96, ℻ 681/2–00–34).

Getting Around

By Car

LOS MOCHIS

Car companies in town include **Budget** (Leyva and Angel Flores, behind the Santa Anita Hotel, ☎ 681/5–83–00, ℻ 681/5–84–00); **National** (Leyva 127 Nte., ☎ 681/2–65–52); and **Aga** (Leyva and Callejón Municipal, ☎ 681/2–53–60).

CHIHUAHUA

Avis (Av. Universidad 1703, ☎ 14/14–19–99), **Hertz** (Av. Revolución 514, ☎ 14/16–64–73), and **Dollar** (Hotel Sicomoro, Ortiz Mena 405, ☎ 14/14–21–71) all have offices at the airport also.

By Taxi

LOS MOCHIS

Taxis are readily available but not very cheap for long distances. It costs about $17 to get to the airport from downtown Los Mochis.

CHIHUAHUA

Easy to find, taxis can be engaged at your hotel or hailed on the street. Since fares are negotiable, always agree on a price before entering the cab. You'll usually pay less if you speak Spanish.

By Train

COPPER CANYON

The Ferrocarril Chihuahua al Pacífico line runs a first-class and a second-class train daily in each direction from Chihuahua and Los Mochis. *El Tren Estrella,* the first-class train, departs from Los Mochis at 6 AM and arrives in Chihuahua 12 hours later; westbound, it departs from Chihuahua at 7 AM and arrives in Los Mochis around 7 PM (most of the time, but problems with the weather or other difficulties may cause long or short delays). Tickets can be purchased through almost any hotel in Los Mochis or Chihuahua or directly at the train station. The price is about $40 each way, but there's a 15% charge for any stopovers en route. These should be arranged at the time of ticket purchase. Reservations (☎ 14/15–77–56 in Chihuahua, ☎ 681/5–77–75 in Los Mochis) should be made at least a week in advance during the busy months of July and August and around Christmas and Easter. It's best to book through a hotel, tour company, or travel agency (*see* Arriving and Departing by Train, *above*), as the phones in the local train stations are rarely answered. Note: Once the pride of the Mexican rail system, *El Tren Estella* has become run-down in recent years. It's the scenery, not the vehicle, that continues to draw passengers. We've also had reports of tourist robberies on the Chihuahua al Pacifico train. Exercise caution by carrying passports and cash in a money belt and leaving your jewelry at home.

The second-class train, *La Tarahuamara,* leaves an hour later from each terminus but makes many stops and is scheduled to arrive 3½ hours later in both directions than the first-class train. Though it is less comfortable, this train is a good way to meet the locals. No reservations are needed; prices are approximately $12 each way. There are no dining cars on either train; it's best to bring your own food and water. Soda, beer, snacks, and ham-and-cheese sandwiches are available on the first-class train.

It's possible to ship your car on the train, but it's not worth the expense or the bother. If you're driving down to Los Mochis, you're better off leaving your car there and taking the train round-trip. If you're coming via Chihuahua, however, you should consider driving to Creel and doing a round-trip from there (*see* Arriving and Departing by Car, *above*).

Guided Tours

Almost all of the large hotels in Los Mochis and Chihuahua have in-house travel agencies that can arrange both city tours and tours of the Copper Canyon area, as well as hiking, hunting, and fishing expeditions. In Los Mochis, the Santa Anita and La Colinas hotels (*see* Lodging, *above*) offer city tours for about $17 per person; these take approximately 3½ to 4 hours and include a boat trip around Topolobampo Bay. In Chihuahua, independent travel agents include **Quezada Tours** (Calle Aldama 316–3, ☎ 14/15–75–13 or 14/15–70–19, FAX 14/15–75–44); the American Express agent **Rojo y Casavantes** (Calle Vincent Guerrero 1207, ☎ 14/15–58–58 or 14/15–74–70, FAX 14/15–53–80); and, particularly recommended, **Turismo Al Mar** (Av. Reforma 400, ☎ 14/16–65–89 or 14/16–59–50, FAX 14/16–65–89). Half-day city tours for a minimum of two people average $16 per person; full-day van trips into Mennonite country run about $40 per person, with a minimum of four needed.

From the United States, the oldest and most reliable operator in the area is **Pan American Tours** (Box 9401, El Paso, TX 79984, ☎ 915/778–5395 or 800/876–3942). Prices for tours between Los Mochis and Chihuahua, based on double occupancy and including train but not airfare, range from about $200 to $500 per person, depending on length of stay and number of stops made; some meals and all transfers are covered. **Columbus Travel** (Rte. 12, Box 382B, New Braunfels, TX 78132, ☎ 210/885–2000 or 800/843–1060, FAX 210/885–2010) offers daily departures to the Copper Canyon from Presidio or El Paso, Texas, as well as from Tuscon and Los Angeles. Trips range from $680 for a five-night trip to $2,000 for a 12-day excursion including a stay in Batopilas. The company has agents in Divisidero, Cerocahui, and Alamos who arrange day hikes. **California Native** (6701 W. 87th Pl., Los Angeles, CA 90045, ☎ 800/926–1140) offers a seven-day escorted trip through the Copper Canyon every month for $1,400, which includes round-trip airfare from Los Angeles, transportation, lodging, meals, and tips. It also offers a nine-day backpacking trip into the area for about $700. This rate includes train fare from Los Mochis or Chihuahua into the canyons, three nights' lodgings, a guide for the five-day hike, much of the food for the hike, and burros to carry food and cooking supplies. Hikers carry their own packs.

Important Addresses and Numbers

Emergencies

LOS MOCHIS

Police (☎ 681/2–00–33); **Cruz Roja** (Red Cross; Guillermo Prieto and Tenochtitlan, ☎ 681/5–08–08).

CHIHUAHUA

Police (☎ 14/81–19–00); **Cruz Roja** (☎ 14/11–14–84 or 14/11–22–11); **Bomberos** (Fire Department; ☎ 14/10–07–70). Two facilities for handling the injured or sick are **Clínica del Parque** (Calle de la Llave and Leal Rodriguez, ☎ 14/15–74–11 or 14/15–90–87) and **Hospital del Centro del Estado** (Calle 33 and Rosales, ☎ 14/15–47–20).

Late-Night Pharmacies

Farmacia San Jorge (Ave. Independencia and Angel Flores, ☎ 681/5–74–74) in Los Mochis is open 24 hours a day.

Chihuahua has an abundance of pharmacies in the center of the city that provide late-night service. **Farmacia Mendoza** (Calle Aldama 1901, ☎ 14/16–44–14 or 14/10–27–96) is open 24 hours.

Money Exchange

Be sure to change money before you get into real barranca country: There are no banks in Cerocahui, Divisadero, or Posada Barrancas, and no guarantee that the hotels in those places will have enough cash to accommodate you. A bank in the main plaza at Creel transacts foreign exchanges only from 10:30 to noon. Even in Los Mochis, banking hours are, for the most part, limited to weekdays between 9 and 1; some banks reopen at 3 and a few are open on Saturday morning. In Chihuahua banks are open weekdays from 9 to 1:30 and from 3:30 to 7:30, and Saturday from 9 to 1:30; the **Casa de Cambio Rachasa** (Av. Ocampo and Niños Heroes, ☎ 14/10–03–33; ☉ Mon.–Sat. 9–9, Sun. 9–2) and **Rubarza** (Aldama 202A, ☎ 14/16–60–44; ☉ weekdays 9–7, Sat. 10–1) both offer good exchange rates and quick service. In general, you're best off getting your pesos at the hotels in Los Mochis and Chihuahua; the exchange rate is slightly lower, but no commission is charged, and you won't have to spend a confusing half hour or more switching lines at the bank.

Visitor Information

LOS MOCHIS

The **Oficina de Turismo** (☎ 681/2–66–40 or 681/2–76–10, ext. 131), located on Allende and Ordoñez (inside the Unidad Administrativa del Gobierno del Estado building, on the first floor in the back), can provide travelers with a variety of information.

CHIHUAHUA

The **Government Tourist Office** (Av. Libertad and Calle 13, 1st Floor, ☎ 14/16–21–06 or 14/15–91–24, ext. 4511 or 4512) has many informative brochures and a helpful, English-speaking staff. ⊘ *Weekdays 8–1:30 and 3:30–6.*

There is also an **Oficina de Información** (☎ 14/15–91–24, ext. 4515) in the central patio of the Palacio del Gobierno in Plaza Hidalgo. ⊘ *Mon.–Sat. 9–7 and Sun. 9–4.*

6 Pacific Coast Resorts

Hollywood introduced us to two of the Mexican Riviera's most popular towns: Liz Taylor and Richard Burton's sleepy, steamy Puerta Vallarta in Night of the Iguana, *and the sparkling Manzanillo coast that served as the backdrop to Bo Derek in* 10. *These days both places are prime cruise ship destinations, as is Mazatlán, a bustling port that attracts sportsfishing enthusiasts and surfers.*

By Maribeth
Mellin

Updated by
Wendy Luft

A **CROSS THE GULF** of California from the Baja California Peninsula lies Mazatlán, Mexico's largest Pacific port and the closest major Mexican resort to the United States, some 1,200 kilometers (750 miles) south of the Arizona border. This is the beginning of what cruise-ship operators now call the Mexican Riviera, or the Gold Coast. The coastline for the next 1,400 kilometers (900 miles) is Mexico's tropical paradise. The Gulf of California, or the Sea of Cortés, as it is also called, ends just below the Tropic of Cancer, leaving the Pacific coastline open to fresh sea breezes. The Mexican Riviera resorts—Mazatlán, Puerto Vallarta, Manzanillo, Ixtapa, Zihuatanejo, and Acapulco—are therefore less muggy than gulf towns to the north. The temperature of the water is a bit lower, however, and waves can get very rough.

The Pacific coast doesn't have the rich cultural heritage of Mexico's inland colonial villages and silver cities, and the history is sketchy at best. This is not an area for touring ruins, museums, and cathedrals, but rather a gathering spot for sun worshipers, sportfishermen, surfers, and swimmers. Not far from the resort regions are jungle streams and ocean coves, but the majority of visitors never venture to these isolated sites, preferring instead to immerse themselves in the simultaneously bustling and restful resort lifestyle, where great dining, shopping, and sunbathing are the major draws.

Mazatlán is first and foremost a busy commercial center, thanks to an excellent port and the fertility of the surrounding countryside. More than 600,000 acres of farmland near Mazatlán produce tomatoes, melons, cantaloupes, wheat, and cotton, much of which is shipped to the United States. And nearly all the 150,000 tons of shrimp that are hauled in annually are processed and frozen for the American and Japanese markets.

Sportfishing accounts for Mazatlán's resort status. The port sits at the juncture of the Pacific and the Sea of Cortés, forming what has been called the world's greatest natural fish trap. But fishing is not the only attraction. Hunters are drawn to the quail, duck, and dove that thrive in the hillsides, and surfers find great waves on nearby beaches. Another draw is the relatively low price of accommodations—about half the going rate of accommodations in Cancún.

Tepic, capital of the state of Nayarit, lies between Mazatlán and Puerto Vallarta. It's the jumping-off point to these destinations for train travelers, who can catch public buses to the coast. Budget travelers and those who eschew the bustle of the megaresorts often head straight for San Blas, a small seaside village some 37 kilometers (23 miles) northwest of Tepic through the jungle.

Some 323 kilometers (200 miles) south of Mazatlán is Puerto Vallarta, by far the best-known resort on the upper Pacific coast. The late film director (and sometime resident) John Huston put the town on the map when he filmed Tennessee Williams's *The Night of the Iguana* on the outskirts of the village in 1964. The gossip about stars Richard Burton and Elizabeth Taylor—both married at the time, but not to each other—brought this quaint Mexican fishing village with its cobblestoned lanes and whitewashed, tile-roofed houses to the public's attention. Before long, travel agents were deluged with queries about Puerto Vallarta, a place many had never heard of before.

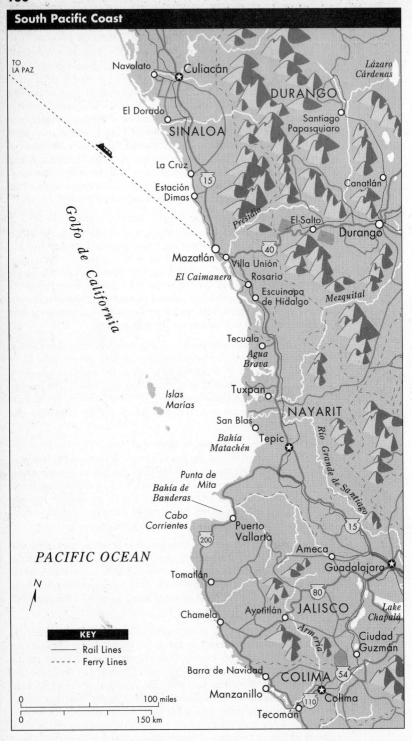

TO
LA PAZ

Navolato   Culiacán

Lázaro Cárdenas

DURANGO

El Dorado

SINALOA

Santiago Papasquiaro

La Cruz

Canatlán

(15)

Estación Dimas

Presidio

El-Salto

Durango

(40)

Mazatlán   Villa Unión

El Caimanero   Rosario

Escuinapa de Hidalgo

Mezquital

Golfo de California

Tecuala

Agua Brava

Tuxpan

Islas Marías

NAYARIT

San Blas

Bahía Matachén   Tepic

Río Grande de Santiago

Punta de Mita

Bahía de Banderas

Cabo Corrientes

(15)

PACIFIC OCEAN

Puerto Vallarta

(200)

Ameca

Guadalajara

N

Tomatlán

(80)

Chamela   Ayotitlán   **JALISCO**

Lake Chapalá

Armería

Ciudad Guzmán

KEY
—— Rail Lines
----- Ferry Lines

Barra de Navidad

COLIMA

(54)

0   100 miles

Manzanillo

(110)   Colima

0   150 km

Tecomán

More than 250,000 people live in Puerto Vallarta today, and upwards of 700,000 tourists arrive each year. The fabled cobblestoned streets are clogged with bumper-to-bumper traffic during the holiday season, and the sounds of construction often drown out the pounding surf. Elizabeth Taylor's and Richard Burton's adjoining homes are now a bed-and-breakfast. Despite its resort status, parts of Puerto Vallarta are still picturesque. For a sense of the Eden that once was, travel out of town to the lush green mountains where the Río Tomatlán tumbles over boulders into the sea.

Manzanillo, at the south end of the central Pacific coast, had more of a storybook start than did Puerto Vallarta. Conquistador Hernán Cortés envisioned the area as a gateway to the Orient: From these shores, Spanish galleons would bring in the riches of Cathay to be trekked across the continent to Veracruz, where they would be off-loaded to vessels headed for Spain. But Acapulco, not Manzanillo, became the port of call for the Manila galleons that arrived each year with riches from beyond the seas. Pirates are said to have staked out Manzanillo during the colonial era, and chests of loot are rumored to be buried beneath the sands.

With the coming of the railroads, Manzanillo became a major port of entry, albeit not a pretty one. Forty or 50 years ago, a few seaside hotels opened up on the outskirts of town, which vacationers reached by train. The jet age, however, seemed to doom the port as a sunny vacation spot. Then Bolivian tin magnate Antenor Patiño built Las Hadas (The Fairies), a lavish Moorish-style resort complex, inaugurated in 1974. It attracted the beautiful people, and for a while Las Hadas was better known than Manzanillo itself. The film *10* made a star of the resort as well as household names of its stars, Bo Derek and Dudley Moore.

In recent years, there's been a push to turn Manzanillo and coastal villages to the north, such as Barra de Navidad, Melaque, Tenacatita, and Costa de Careyes, into a tourist zone. A four-lane toll road now cuts the driving time between Manzanillo and Guadalajara, Mexico's second-largest city, to three hours. Older hotels have been spruced up and all-inclusive resorts constructed. On the drawing board are plans to build a $50 million marina complex in downtown Manzanillo, with 240 slips, hotels, restaurants, shops, and a pedestrian walkway along the shore.

MAZATLÁN

Mazatlán is the Aztec word for "place of the deer," and long ago its islands and shores sheltered far more deer than humans. Today it is a city of some 400,000 residents and draws more than 500,000 foreign tourists a year. Sunning, surfing, and sailing have caught on here, and in the winter months visitors from inland Mexico, the United States, and Canada flock to Mazatlán for a break in the sun. From November through April, the temperature range is 21°–27°C (70°–80°F), and the summer months are not nearly as warm as in the more popular tourist areas farther south. Hotel and restaurant prices are lower than elsewhere on the coast, and the ambience is more that of a fishing town than a tourist haven.

Upscale resorts and ritzy restaurants are not part of Mazatlán's repertoire, though there is a fair dose of luxury at El Cid, Camino Real, and Pueblo Bonito resorts. Work is underway on two adjacent marinas on the estuary that stretches north from the El Cid golf course to the Camina Real Hotel. The El Cid Resort complex is being expanded, and Mexico's leading development company, Grupo Situr, is building a residential resort community that calls for an 18-hole golf course, a large marina, villas, condos, and a Bel-Air hotel.

Hunting and fishing were the original draw for visitors. At one time, duck, quail, pheasant, and other wildfowl fed in the lagoons; and jaguars, mountain lions, rabbits, and coyotes roamed the surrounding hills. Hunters have to search a little harder and farther for their prey these days, but there's still plenty of wildlife near Mazatlán. The city is the base for Mexico's largest sportfishing fleet; fishermen haul the biggest catches (in size and number) on the coast. The average annual haul is 10,000 sailfish and 5,000 marlin; a record 973-pound marlin and 203-pound sailfish were pulled from these waters.

The Spaniards settled in the Mazatlán region in 1531 and used the indigenous people as a labor force to create the port and village. The center of Mazatlán gradually moved north, so that the original site is now 32 kilometers (20 miles) southeast of the harbor.

The port has a history of blockades. In 1847 during the Mexican War, U.S. forces marched down from the border through northeast Mexico and closed the port. In 1864, the French bombarded the city and then controlled it for several years. Mexico's own internal warring factions took over from time to time. And after the Civil War in the United States, a group of southerners tried to turn Mazatlán into a slave city.

Today Mazatlán has the largest shrimping fleet in Mexico. Sinaloa, one of Mexico's richest states, uses Mazatlán's port to ship its agricultural products.

Exploring

Numbers in the margin correspond to points of interest on the Mazatlán map.

The **Zona Dorada** (Golden Zone) is the tourist region, and it is from this point that most visitors begin touring the city. Unfortunately, Mazatlán's highlights are spread far and wide, and walking from one section of town to the other can take hours. The best way to travel is via pulmonías, so you can sunbathe and take pictures as you cruise along, although you won't be able to roll up any windows to protect yourself from automobile fumes. If you choose to rent a car and drive, you can tour at your own pace. There are no traffic jams in Mazatlán, except near the market in downtown, where parking can also be a major problem.

1 The Zona Dorada begins on Avenida Camarón Sábalo at **Punta Camarón** (Shrimp Point), the rocky outcropping on which Valentino's Disco sits, resembling a Moorish palace perched above the sea. Going north, Avenida Camarón Sábalo forms the eastern border of the zone, while Avenida Loaiza runs closer to the beach. In this four-block pocket are most of the hotels, shops, and restaurants, and the majority of non-residents intent on having a good time sunning, shopping, and partying. Head here to souvenir-shop, hit the discos, and check out the hotel bars.

2 A stroll through the **Mazatlán Arts and Crafts Center** (Av. Loaiza 417, ☎ 69/13–50–22) will give you a good sampling of the souvenir selection—onyx chess sets, straw sombreros, leather jackets, and Mickey Mouse piñatas. Some of the shops in the center close for siesta from 2 to 4 PM.

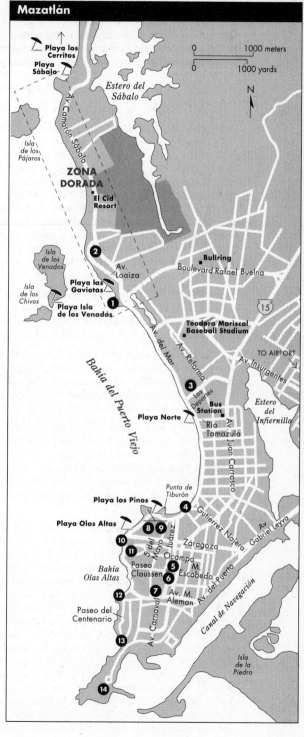

No Name Café (☎ 69/13–20–31), right in the Arts and Crafts Center, is a good spot for a beer or *agua mineral* (mineral water) and lime. Mexico's version of Baskin-Robbins, **Helados Bing** (no ☎), has good hot-fudge sundaes and ice cream cones. It's at the corner of Avenida Camarón Sábalo and Avenida Gaviotas. **Panadería Panamá** (☎ 69/13–69–77), also on Camerón Sábalo across from the Las Palmas hotel, is a bakery that has tables where you can sit and enjoy fragrant cinnamon-flavored coffee.

Traveling north, Avenida Loaiza merges into Avenida Sábalo at Avenida Gaviotas, and Avenida Sábalo continues along the coast, past El Cid Resort, one of the largest tourist developments in Mexico. Along the beach side of Avenida Sábalo are some of Mazatlán's largest, most luxurious, and priciest hotels; opposite the beach are many of the better low-cost motels. Along this route there is a good view of Mazatlán's three Pacific islands—**Isla de los Pájaros** (Bird Island), **Isla de los Venados** (Deer Island), and **Isla de los Chivos** (Goat Island). Just past the Camino Real resort, Avenida Camarón Sábalo becomes Avenida Sábalo Cerritos and crosses over the Estero del Sábalo, a long lagoon popular with bird-watchers. The area north of here will someday be an exclusive touring and resort area; towering condos are already being built.

South of Valentino's, this main road changes names frequently in its 15-mile length. At Punta Camarón it becomes Avenida del Mar, which leads toward Old Mazatlán. The 10-mile **malecón,** Mazatlán's version of a main highway and beachfront boardwalk, begins here.

❸ **Acuario Mazatlán** (Mazatlán's aquarium) is a few blocks south, down Avenida de los Deportes. The aquarium, with its tanks of sharks, sea horses, eels, lobsters, and multicolored salt- and freshwater fish, is a must-see. A fanciful bronze fountain and sculpture of two boys feeding a dolphin marks the aquarium's entrance. *Av. de los Deportes 111,* ☎ *69/81–78–15.* ☛ *About $5 adults, $2.50 children.* ☉ *Daily 9:30–6:30.*

Avenida del Mar continues south past beaches popular with the locals and travelers staying at the budget hotels across the street. The **Monumento al Pescador** (Fisherman's Monument) is Avenida del Mar's main landmark, and it is a strange sight. An enormous, voluptuous, nude woman reclines on an anchor, her hand extended toward a nude fisherman dragging his nets.

❹ Calle Juárez and Calle Cinco de Mayo intersect with Avenida del Mar and lead to Mazatlán's real downtown, where the streets are filled with buses and locals rushing to and from work and the market. Many travelers never see this part of Mazatlán, but it's worth a visit. Head for the blue-and-gold spires of the **Mazatlán Catedral,** at Calles Juárez and Ocampo, and you'll be in the heart of the city. The cathedral, built in 1890 and made a basilica in 1935, has a gilded and ornate triple altar, with murals of angels overhead and many small altars along the sides. A sign at the entrance requests that visitors be appropriately attired (no shorts or tank tops inside). The **zócalo,** called **Plaza Revolución,** just across the street, has one of the most fascinating gazebos in Mexico—what looks like a '50s diner inside the lower level and a wrought-iron bandstand on top. The green-and-orange tile on the walls, ancient jukebox, and soda fountain serving shakes, burgers, and hot dogs couldn't make a more surprising sight. On the streets facing the zócalo are the City Hall, banks, post office, and telegraph office.

❼ The **Teatro Angela Peralta,** built in 1860 and now beautifully restored, is at Sixto Osuna and Carnaval, about three blocks from the zócalo. It was declared a historic monument in 1990.

Back along the waterfront, Avenida del Mar turns into Paseo
❽ Claussen as it heads south, passing by **El Fuerte Carranza,** an old
❾ Spanish fort built to defend the city against the French, and **Casa del Marino,** a shelter for sailors. Playa los Piños, a popular surfing beach,
❿ stretches along this road. **High-Divers Park,** where young men climb to a white platform and plunge into the sea, is located nearby; at night, when the divers leap carrying flaming torches, it's spectacular. Some of Mazatlán's best surfing beaches are along this strip.

⓫ The malecón continues past **Cerro de la Nevería** (Icebox Hill). Wealthy landowners in Mazatlán imported ice from San Francisco in the late 1800s and stored it in underground tunnels in this hill. The next land-
⓬ mark is the statue of **La Mazatleca,** a bronze nymph rising from a giant wave. Across the street is a small bronze deer, Mazatlán's mascot.

Paseo Claussen leads into Olas Altas, site of Old Mazatlán, the center for tourism in the 1940s. Olas Altas (which means high waves) ends at a small traffic circle. A plaque at the circle bears the state symbol of Sinaloa.

⓭ Above Olas Altas is **Cerro de Vigía** (Lookout Hill), with a lookout point, weather station, and rusty cannon. The view from this windy hill is fantastic, overlooking both sides of Mazatlán, its harbor, and the Pacific. It's a steep climb up and is better done by taxi than on foot. The **Centenario Pérgola,** at the top of the hill, was once used by the Spaniards as a place to watch for pirates.

At the end of the malecón, the road becomes Paseo del Centenario
⓮ and continues south to the tip of the peninsula. At the tip is **Cerro del Crestón** (Summit Hill) and **El Faro,** said to be the second-highest light-house in the world after Gibraltar, with a range of 36 nautical miles. It takes about 30 minutes to hike up to the lighthouse, but you get a great view of the harbor and sea. This side of the peninsula is devoted to boats, and the road running along the many docks and military installations is called Avenida del Puerto. The sportfishing fleet is anchored at the base of Cerro del Crestón; the next docks north are used by cruise ships and merchant vessels. Launches for **Isla de la Piedra** leave from a small dock by the military base.

TIME OUT Many of the small *palapas* (beach shacks) set up along the sportfishing docks serve a tasty smoked marlin. The palapas near the launches to Isla de la Piedra sell sugarcane sticks, which look like bamboo and are good for quenching your thirst.

What to See and Do with Children

The **Acuario Mazatlán** (*see* Exploring, *above*), with its tanks of salt- and freshwater fish, sharks, and films about sea life, is a perfect child-pleaser. On Sundays in particular, it is packed with families. At the large playground next door, skateboarders practice their tricks while the little ones play on the slides and swings. A small zoo sits amid the trees in the botanical garden beside the aquarium; the most interest-ing animals are the crocodiles.

Shopping

In the **Zona Dorada,** particularly along Avenida Camarón Sábalo and Avenida Rodolfo T. Loaiza, you can buy everything from piñatas to designer clothing. The best place for browsing is the **Mazatlán Arts and Crafts Center** (*see* Exploring, *above*), originally designed as a place to view artisans at work and buy their wares. Now the center is filled with shops and boutiques, and the only craft you see is the fine art of bartering. **Madonna** (Las Garzas, Zona Dorada, ☏ 69/14–23–89) displays an extensive collection of silver and gold jewelry as well as masks and papier mâché items. Dealers Ron and Teresa Tammekand represent a number of top artists at **Mazatlán Art Gallery** (Plaza Balboa on Av. Camarón Sábalo, ☏ 69/14–36–12), and hold one-person shows during the winter season. **Evolución** (Av. R. T. Loaiza 204, ☏ 69/16–08–39) is a new-age bookstore with a fine collection of English-language books.

For sportswear, visit **Aca Joe** (Av. Camarón Sábalo and Av. Gaviotas, ☏ 69/13–33–00), whose line of well-designed casual clothes for men is popular throughout Mexico and the United States. The well-advertised colors of **Benetton** (Av. Camarón Sábalo 1000, ☏ 69/14–84–11), as well as its hip clothing, draw shoppers into the Italian sportswear chain. Both are in the Zona Dorada. In the same area, **Sea Shell City** (Av. R. T. Loaiza 4077, ☏ 69/13–13–01) is a must-see; it has two floors packed with shells from around the world that have been glued, strung, and molded into every imaginable shape from lamps to necklaces. Check out the enormous fountain upstairs, covered with thousands of shells. **Designer's Bazaar** (Av. R. T. Loaiza 7, ☏ 69/83–60–39) a two-story shop near Los Sábalos Hotel, has probably the best selection of high-quality folk art, leather wallets and belts, hand-embroidered clothing, and a good sampling of fashionable swimsuits. Leather shops are clustered along the southern end of the Zona Dorada.

The **Mercado Central,** downtown between Calle Juárez and Serdán, is a gigantic place filled with produce, meat, fish, and handicrafts that are sold at the lowest prices in town. It takes more searching to find good-quality handicrafts, but that's part of the fun. Browse through the stalls along the street outside the market for the best crafts.

Sports and Fitness

Fishing

More than a dozen sportfishing fleets operate from the docks south of the lighthouse. Hotels can arrange charters, or you can contact the companies directly. Charters include a full day of fishing, lunch, bait, and tackle. Prices range from $60 per person on a party boat to $300 to charter an entire boat. Charter companies to contact include **Bill Heimpel's Star Fleet** (☏ 69/82–26–65), **Flota Faro** (☏ 69/81–28–24), **Estrella** (☏ 69/82–38–78), **Flota Bibi** (☏ 69/81–36–40), and **De Oro** (☏ 69/82–31–30).

Golf

The spectacular 27-hole course at **El Cid** (☏ 69/13–33–33), designed by Robert Trent Jones, is reserved for members of the resort, hotel guests, and their guests. There is a nine-hole course at the **Club Campestre de Mazatlán** (☏ 69/80–02–02), on the outskirts of town on Route 15.

Hunting

Several species of duck and white-wing doves, mourning doves, and quail abound in the Mazatlán area. The season runs from September through March. **Aviles Brothers** (Box 221, ☏ 69/81–37–28) is the most experienced outfitter, arranging licenses and the rental of firearms. The cost of a six-hour hunt is $175, including transportation, retriever, and English-speaking guide. Nonhunters can go along for $50.

Tennis

Many of the hotels have courts, some of which are open to the public. There are a few public courts not connected to the hotels. Call in advance for reservations at **El Cid Resort,** 13 courts (☎ 69/13–33–33); **Racket Club,** 6 courts (☎ 69/13–59–39); and **Club de Tenis Reforma,** 8 courts (☎ 69/86–43–56).

Water Sports

Jet Skis, Hobie Cats, and Windsurfers are available for rent at most hotels, and parasailing is very popular along the Zona Dorada. Scuba diving and snorkeling are catching on, but there are no really great diving spots. The best is around Isla de los Venados. For rentals and trips, contact the following operators: **Caravelle Beach Club** (Av. Camarón Sábalo, ☎ 69/13–02–00), **El Cid Resort Aqua Sport Center** (Av. Camarón Sábalo, ☎ 69/13–33–33), **Los Sábalos** (Av. Camarón Sábalo, ☎ 69/83–53–33), and **Ocean Sports Center** (Punta de Sábalo, ☎ 69/13–11–11).

Spectator Sports

Baseball

The people of Mazatlán loyally support their team, Los Venados, a Pacific League Triple A team. Games are played at the Teodoro Mariscal Stadium (Av. Deportes) from October through April.

Bullfights

Spectacles are held most Sunday afternoons between December and Easter at the bullring on Boulevard Rafael Buelna. Tickets are available at the bullring, through most hotels, and from **Valentino's** (☎ 69/84–17–77).

Beaches

Playa Los Cerritos

The northernmost beach on the outskirts of town, which runs from Camino Real Resort to Punta Cerritos, is also the cleanest and least populated. The waves can be too rough for swimming, but they're great for surfing.

Playa Sábalo and Playa las Gaviotas

Mazatlán's two most popular beaches are along the Zona Dorada. There are as many vendors selling blankets, pottery, lace tablecloths, and silver jewelry as there are sunbathers. Boats, Windsurfers, and parasailers line the shores. The beach is protected from heavy surf by the three islands—Venados, Pájaros, and Chivas. You can safely stroll these beaches until midnight and eavesdrop on the social action in the hotels while enjoying a few solitary, romantic moments sans vendors and crowds.

Playa Norte

This strand begins at Punta Camarón (Valentino's is a landmark) along Avenida del Mar and the malecón and runs to the Fisherman's Monument. The dark brown sand is dirty and rocky at some points, but clean at others, and is popular with those staying at hotels without beach access. Palapas selling cold drinks, tacos, and fresh fish line the beach; be sure to try the fresh coconut milk.

Playa Olas Altas

This beach, whose name means "high waves," was the first tourist beach in Mazatlán, running south along the malecón from the Fisherman's Monument. Surfers congregate here during the summer months, when the waves are at their highest.

Playa Isla de los Venados

Boats make frequent departures from the Zona Dorada hotels for this beach on Deer Island. It's only a 10-minute ride, but the difference in ambience is striking; the beach is pretty, uncluttered, and clean, and you can hike around the southern point of the island to small, secluded coves covered with shells.

Playa Isla de la Piedra

The locals head here on weekends. Entire families, bearing toys, rafts, and picnic lunches, ride over to the island on *pangas* (small, open boats) from the dock near the train tracks. Sixteen kilometers (10 miles) of unspoiled beaches here allow enough room for all visitors to spread out and claim their own space; this won't be the case for long, however, if work resumes on a tourist megadevelopment, which would see the surrender of 900 acres of the island to a host of hotels, villas, two golf clubs, and tennis and riding clubs. Small shacks and palapas sell drinks and fresh fish, and on Sundays the island looks like a small village, with lots of music and fun.

Dining

The emphasis in Mazatlán is on casual, bountiful dining, and the prices are reasonable. Shrimp and fresh fish are the highlights; be sure to have a seafood cocktail along the beach. Dress is casual in Mazatlán, although shorts are frowned upon for dinner and most restaurants require footwear at all meals. Chic resortwear is not out of place in establishments like Sr. Peppers, La Concha, and Casa Loma. When you check your bill, be aware that some restaurants, particularly in the hotels, add a service charge of 10% to 15% to your total, as well as 10% tax.

CATEGORY	COST*
$$$$	over $35
$$$	$25–$35
$$	$15–$25
$	under $15

per person, excluding drinks, service, and sales tax (10%)

$$$$ **Casa Loma.** An out-of-the-way, elegant restaurant in a converted villa, Casa Loma serves international specialties such as chateaubriand, duck à l'orange, and osso buco. Lunch on the patio is less formal. Have a martini made by an expert, and save room for the fine pastries. ✗ *Av. Gaviotas 104,* ☎ *69/13–53–98.* ☉ *Oct.–mid-May. MC, V.*

$$$$ **La Concha.** Certainly the prettiest waterside dining spot, La Concha is
★ a large enclosed palapa with three levels of seating at tables spread far apart, a spacious dance floor decked with twinkling lights, and outdoor tables by the sand. Adventurous types might attempt the stingray with black butter or calamari in its ink. The more conservative can try a thick filet mignon cooked to perfection. During the winter season, a singer croons Las Vegas–style ballads as couples dance. La Concha is also open for breakfast. ✗ *El Cid Resort, Av. Camarón Sábalo,* ☎ *69/13–33–33. AE, DC, MC, V.*

$$$ Sr. Peppers. Elegant yet unpretentious, with ceiling fans, lush foliage, and candlelit tables, Sr. Peppers serves choice steaks and lobsters cooked over a mesquite grill. Enjoy the dance floor and live music. ✕ *Av. Camarón Sábalo, across from the Camino Real hotel,* ☎ 69/ 14–01–20. *AE, MC, V. No lunch.*

$$ El Mirador. A real find on the top of Cerro de Vigía, this unassuming
★ restaurant has some of the freshest, most flavorful fish around. The ceviche is made with fresh shrimp, chopped and marinated in lime juice with tomatoes, onions, cilantro, and peppers. The salsa and chips are homemade and delicious, and meals include soup, salad, and dessert. Stick with the shrimp and fish, and you'll be delighted. The strong wind atop the lookout tends to whip through the open windows, which can be quite invigorating. ✕ *Atop Cerro de Vigía,* ☎ 69/81–37–40. *MC, V.*

$$ El Paraíso Tres Islas. A wonderful palapa on the beach, across from
★ the Seashell Museum, Tres Islas is a favorite with families who spend all Sunday afternoon feasting on fresh fish. Try smoked marlin, oysters diablo, octopus, or the seafood platter. The setting is the nicest in town, close to the water with a good view of the three islands. The waiters are friendly and eager to help. ✕ *Av. R. T. Loaiza 404,* ☎ 69/ 14–28–12. *MC, V.*

$$ El Shrimp Bucket. In Old Mazatlán, under forest-green awnings, is an establishment that was the original Carlos 'n Charlie's. The garden patio restaurant is much quieter than its successors—some would call it respectable. Best bets are fried shrimp served in clay buckets and barbecued ribs. Portions are plentiful. Breakfast is also served. It's the place to see where all the Carlos 'n Charlie's action began. ✕ *Olas Altas 11-126,* ☎ 69/81–63–50. *AE, MC, V.*

$$ Señor Frog. Another member of the Carlos Anderson chain, Señor Frog is as noisy and entertaining as the rest. Bandidos carry tequila bottles and shot glasses in their bandoliers, leather belts that held ammunition in the old westerns. Barbecued ribs and chicken, served with corn on the cob, and heaping portions of standard Mexican dishes are the specialty, and the drinking, dancing, and carousing go on well into the night. The tortilla soup is excellent. ✕ *Av. del Mar 225,* ☎ 69/82–19–25. *AE, MC, V.*

$ Doney. This big downtown hacienda has been serving great Mexican
★ meals since 1959. The large dining room has old photos of Mazatlán, a high brick ceiling, and embroidered tablecloths, all of which give you the feeling that you're sitting in someone's home. The Doney is named after a restaurant in Rome, though there is nothing Italian about the menu. Try the *chilaquiles* (casserole of tortillas and chile sauce), mole, or fried chicken. The meringue and fruit pies are excellent. ✕ *Mariano Escobedo at Calle Cinco de Mayo,* ☎ 69/81–26–51. *AE, MC, V.*

$ Jungle Juice. As you might suspect, the specialties here are unusual fruit-juice concoctions with names like King Kong and Tarzan. But it's the good food—fish, chicken, and ribs—the satellite TV dish that captures major sports events, and the classic rock and roll that make this a favorite gathering spot. ✕ *Av. de las Garzas and Laguna,* ☎ 69/ 13–33–15. *MC, V.*

$ Karnes en Su Jugo. A small family-run café on the malecón, with a
★ few outdoor tables and a large indoor restaurant, this establishment specializes in *karnes en su jugo,* literally, "beef in its juice," a Mexican stew with chopped beef, onions, beans, and bacon. It's a satisfying meal, especially when eaten with a basket of homemade tortillas. ✕ *Av. del Mar 550,* ☎ 69/82–13–22. *AE, MC, V.*

$ Mucho Taco. This bright blue taco stand in the heart of the Zona Dorada is open 24 hours—a blessing for those who stay out at the discos until the wee hours. The tacos are fresh and tasty, and you can eat at the small sidewalk tables or take your feast back to your room. ✕ *Av. Camarón Sábalo, no ☎. No credit cards.*

Lodging

Most of Mazatlán's hotels are in the Zona Dorada, along the beaches. Less expensive places are in Old Mazatlán, the original tourist zone along the malecón—on the south side of downtown. Most hotels raise their rates for the November–April high season; rates are lowest in the summer, during the rainy season. Price categories are based on high-season rates—expect to pay 25% less during the off-season. The postal code for Mazatlán is 82110.

CATEGORY	COST*
$$$$	over $160
$$$	$90–$160
$$	$40–$90
$	under $40

All prices are for a standard double room, excluding 10% tax.

$$$ Pueblo Bonito. By far the most beautiful property in Mazatlán, this all-
★ suite hotel and time-share resort has an enormous lobby with chandeliers, beveled glass doors, and gleaming red-and-white tiled floors. The pink terra-cotta rooms have domed ceilings. An arched doorway leads from the tiled kitchen into the elegant seating area, which is furnished with pale pink and beige couches and glass tables. Pink flamingos stroll on the manicured lawns, golden *koi* (carp) swim in small ponds, and bronzed sunbathers repose on padded white lounge chairs by the crystal-blue pool. This is as elegant as Mazatlán gets. ⊡ *Av. Camarón Sábalo 2121, ☎ 69/14–37–00; reservations in the U.S., 800/442–5300. 250 suites. 2 restaurants, bar, 2 pools, beach. AE, MC, V.*

$$$ Westin Camino Real. Location is the big plus at this property, which is far from the frenzy of the Golden Zone, past a rocky point at the northernmost edge of town. The beach is a bit of a hike from the hotel rooms, through the densely landscaped grounds and down a small hill. The hotel, one of the first in Mazatlán, has undergone drastic renovation, and a blue, green, and pink color scheme now prevails. If you're more interested in relaxing in peace than in carousing, this is your best bet. ⊡ *Av. Camarón Sábalo, ☎ 69/13–11–11; reservations in the U.S., 800/7–CAMINO. 169 rooms. 2 restaurants, bar, pool, beach, 2 tennis courts. AE, DC, MC, V.*

$$ El Cid. The largest resort in Mazatlán, and perhaps in Mexico, El Cid has
★ 1,100 rooms spread over 900 acres. A 100-slip marina began operating in 1994, and the Marina El Cid and Yacht Club, a 192-suite hotel, opened in 1995. A mega-travel service, with its own deep-sea fishing fleet, sightseeing and cultural tours, sailing, snorkeling, sunset cruises, bass fishing, and hunting, is also planned, as is an additional 18-hole golf course. The spacious hotel rooms overlook the pool and beach (one of the longest and cleanest in the area), and the hotel is popular with convention groups as well as lone travelers. The glass-enclosed arcade has nice boutiques, and La Concha (*see Dining, above*) is one of the most romantic spots on the beach. ⊡ *Av. Camarón Sábalo, ☎ 69/13–33–33; reservations in the U.S., 800/525–1925. 1,100 air-conditioned rooms, suites, and villas. 12 restaurants, 4 bars, 6 pools, 27-hole golf course, 13 tennis courts, shops, disco. AE, DC, MC, V.*

$$ Holiday Inn. A consistently good hotel, the Holiday Inn is a long walk from the Zona Dorada, and little traffic runs by. Tour and convention groups fill the rooms and keep the party mood going by the pool and on the beach. Children have a small play area with swings and a wading pool, and there is live, upbeat music in the lobby. All of the rooms are done in whites and pastels, and there are large sliding glass doors that open to a pretty view of the islands. ▦ *Av. Camarón Sábalo 696, ☎ 69/13–22–22. 183 rooms. Restaurant, 2 bars, air-conditioning, pool, beach. AE, DC, MC, V.*

$$ Los Sábalos. A white high-rise in the center of the Zona Dorada, Los Sábalos has a great location, a long clean beach, and lots of action. You feel as though you're a part of things, amid the flight attendants who lay over here, and it's only a short walk to Valentino's, the best disco in town. ▦ *Av. Loaiza 100, ☎ 69/83–53–33; reservations in the U.S., 800/528–8760. 185 rooms. 2 restaurants, 3 bars, pool, health club, beach, 2 tennis courts. AE, DC, MC, V.*

$$ Playa Mazatlán. Palapas are set up on the patios by the rooms in this
★ casual hotel, which is popular with Mexican families and laid-back singles more concerned with comfort than style. The bright, sunny rooms have tiled headboards over the beds and tiled tables by the windows. There's a volleyball net on the beach, and two small stands sell good, inexpensive snacks. ▦ *Av. Loaiza 202, ☎ 69/13–44–44; reservations in the U.S., 800/222–4466. 425 rooms. Restaurant, bar, air-conditioning, pool, beach. AE, DC, MC, V.*

$ Azteca Inn. This pink-and-white bargain, across the street from El Sábalo beach, is a great find for budget travelers who like to be in the center of things. The color scheme of the interior isn't carried over into the rooms, which are decorated in reds and yellows, but most of the accommodations have two double beds, and all have cable TV. The staff couldn't be friendlier. ▦ *Av. Loaiza 307, ☎ 69/13–44–77 or 69/13–44–25. 74 rooms. Restaurant, bar, pool, hot tub. AE, DC, MC, V.*

$ Bungalows Mar Sol. This older motel has clean, cluttered rooms furnished in a mishmash of colors and styles. A long garden area fronts the parking lot, and there are lounge chairs, a small fountain, and a palapa-covered Ping-Pong table, but no pool. The beach is across the street, and though the motel is north of town, buses do stop close by frequently. ▦ *Av. Camarón Sábalo 1001, ☎ 69/14–01–08. 16 bungalows. MC, V.*

$ Sands. This is a beachfront hotel with many of the amenities of the larger and more expensive resort hotels, but at a fraction of the price. It is popular with retirees and wanderers who want to stay put for a while. All of the rooms are air-conditioned and have color TVs with some U.S. channels. ▦ *Av. del Mar 1910, ☎ 69/82–06–00. 86 rooms. Restaurant, bar, pool. AE, MC, V.*

Nightlife

Caracol Tango Palace (☎ 69/13–33–33) at El Cid is Mazatlán's premier nightspot. **Fandango's** (☎ 69/13–73–63), in the Las Palmas shopping center, is also popular, and **Valentino's** (☎ 69/83–62–12) still draws a glitzy crowd. Its stark white towers rise on Punta Camarón at the beginning of the Zona Dorada. Enjoy easy listening or romantic music here, or opt for rock around the clock on the dance floor.

Also at the Valentino's complex is **Bora Bora** (☎ 69/86–49–49), a casual palapa bar on the beach that stays alive with music and dancing from 8 PM to 4 AM. **Sheik** (☎ 69/86–28–48), a restaurant extravaganza, is also located here, but it needs a lot of improvement in the food and service departments. Still, don't miss it—stop in during early evening for a drink at least.

One of the **Mexican fiestas** at the Playa Mazatlán or the Oceano Palace is also a good entertainment bet; the fiesta at the Plaza Maya offers a buffet and a two-hour show that includes a performance of the Flying Indians of Papantla. Almost all hotel travel desks can provide you with information on days and times.

Mazatlán Essentials

Arriving and Departing

BY PLANE

Airport and Airlines. Mazatlán's Rafael Buelna International Airport is serviced by several airlines. **Aeromexico** (☎ 800/237–6639) has flights from Tucson. **Alaska Airlines** (☎ 800/426–0333) flies in from San Francisco, San Jose, and Los Angeles; **Delta** (☎ 800/241–4141) from Los Angeles; and **Mexicana** (☎ 800/531–7921) from Denver, Los Angeles, and several Mexican cities.

Between the Airport and Hotels. The airport is a good 40-minute drive from town. **Autotransportes Aeropuerto** (☎ 69/82–70–08) provides shuttles using Volkswagen vans. They charge $6 per person for *colectivo* service, $21 for a private car.

BY CAR

Mazatlán is 1,212 kilometers (751 miles) from the border city of Nogales, Arizona, via Mexico Route 15. An overnight stop is recommended, as driving at night in Mexico can be hazardous.

BY TRAIN

The Mexican train system is in a state of flux, with schedules changing constantly. Contact **Mexico by Train** (☎ and FAX 210/725–3659 or 800/321–1699) for the most current information about trains to Mazatlán. The train depot is located south of town. Tickets may be purchased at the train station in the neighborhood of Col. Esperanza (☎ 69/84–66–04).

BY BUS

Transportes Norte de Sonora has service to Mazatlán from Nogales, Sonora; other companies connect the coast with inland Mexico. The bus terminal is on Carretera Internacional 1203 (☎ 69/81–38–46).

BY FERRY

Ferry service between La Paz and Mazatlán was privatized a few years back and the service is now fairly reliable. The ferry departs daily from Mazatlán's Playa Sur terminal at 3 PM and takes about 18 hours to reach La Paz. The fare is $20 for regular passage and $60 per person for a private cabin for two with bed and bath (☎ 69/81–70–21).

BY SHIP

Cruise ships from the **Commodore, Carnival,** and **Princess** lines, among others, include Mazatlán on their winter itineraries.

Getting Around

Most tourist hotels are located in the Zona Dorada, about 3 kilometers (5 miles) north of downtown, but taxis and buses cruise the strip regularly. A fun way to get around is on the *pulmonías* (open-air jitneys, literally "pneumonias"). The fare, for up to three passengers, starts at about $2 and increases according to the length of the trip. Complaints have been registered, however, about one's susceptibility to fumes from other vehicles.

BY CAR

A car is not necessary in town since public transportation is good, but you might want one for a self-guided tour of the area. Rentals usually include free mileage. A Volkswagen Beetle costs about $65 per day with insurance; a sedan with air-conditioning and automatic transmission is about $117 per day. The following rental firms have desks at the airport: **Hertz** (Av. Camarón Sábalo 314, ☎ 69/13–60–60), **Budget** (Av. Camarón Sábalo 402, ☎ 69/13–20–00), and **National** (Av. Camarón Sábalo in the Plaza el Camarón, ☎ 69/13–60–00).

Guided Tours

Tour agencies have offices in most hotels and along the Zona Dorada. **Marlin Tours** (Calle Laguna 300, ☎ 69/14–26–90) and **Viajes el Sábalo** (at the Los Sábalos hotel, ☎ 69/14–30–09, with branches at the Camino Real and Vidafel hotels; *see* Lodging, *above*) offer a full range of tours with pickup service. Note: Formerly ubiquitous sidewalk stands staffed by persuasive individuals offering free tours of the area along with free drinks and meals—whose true goal is to sell time-shares and condos—have been limited to areas in front of these properties.

The three-hour **City Tour,** which should cost around $15, is a good way to get the lay of the land, particularly downtown, which can be a bit confusing.

Cruises aboard the *Yate Fiesta* (☎ 69/85–22–37) cost about $15 and navigate the bay and the harbor, past the islands and sportfishing fleet; these and other harbor cruises generally last about three hours and feature music and dancing. Viajes El Sábalo runs a five-hour tour to **Isla de la Piedra** (Stone Island), with time for lunch and a swim. The cost is about $30.

Also available are all-day country tours, which go to **Concordia,** known for its furniture makers (a huge wood chair marks the entrance to the small town), and on to **Copala,** a scenic colonial mining town (cost: about $35). **Marlin Tours** runs a trip to Teacapan, an ecological reserve. The 8-hour excursion costs $45 and includes Continental breakfast served on the bus, a stop at Rosario, and a seafood lunch at the almost deserted beach. Jungle tours take you to **San Blas** and the **Río Tovara** (in the state of Nayarit), where boats travel upriver through mangrove jungle to a small spring-fed pond. The tour companies also offer individual guided tours and sportfishing outings.

Important Addresses and Numbers

CONSULATES

United States (R. T. Loaiza 202, ☎ 69/16–58–89); **Canada** (Hotel Playa Mazatlán, ☎ 69/13–73–20).

EMERGENCIES

The **Public Tourism Ministry** (☎ 69/14–32–22) is an agency of the police department instituted specifically for tourists. **Red Cross** (☎ 69/81–36–90), **Sharp Hospital** (☉ 24 hrs, ☎ 69/83–92–03).

VISITOR INFORMATION

Information on Mazatlán and city tours is available at the hotels. Another source of information, the **City Tourism Bureau,** is at Paseo Olas Altas 1300, in the Bank of Mexico Building. ☎ 69/85–12–21. ☉ *Weekdays 9–7, Sat. 9–1.*

PUERTO VALLARTA

On the edge of the Sierra Madre range sits one of the most popular vacation spots in Mexico. When Puerto Vallarta first entered the public's consciousness, with John Huston's 1964 movie, *The Night of the Iguana,* it seemed an almost mythical tropical paradise. Indeed, at the time it was a quiet fishing and farming community in an exquisite setting.

Puerto Vallarta's Bahía de Banderas (Bay of Flags) attracted pirates and explorers as early as the 1500s; it was used as a stopover on long sailings, as a place for the crew to relax (or maybe plunder and pillage). Sir Francis Drake apparently stopped here. In the mid-1850s, Don Guadalupe Sánchez Carrillo developed the bay as a port for the silver mines by the Río Cuale. Then it was known as Puerto de Peñas and had about 1,500 inhabitants. It remained a village until 1918, when it was made a municipality by the state of Jalisco and named after Ignacio L. Vallarta, a governor of Jalisco.

In the 1950s, Puerto Vallarta was essentially a pretty hideaway for those in the know—the wealthy and some hardy escapists. After the publicity brought on by *The Night of the Iguana,* tourism began to boom. PV—as the former fishing village is called these days—is now a city with more than 150,000 residents and an additional 100,000 in the surrounding countryside. Airports, hotels, and highways have supplanted palm groves and fishing shacks. About 700,000 tourists visit each year, and from November through April cobblestoned streets are clogged with pedestrians and cars. There are now about 9,000 hotel rooms in Puerto Vallarta.

Despite the transformation, every attempt has been made to keep the town's character and image intact. Even the parking lot at the local Gigante supermarket is cobblestoned, and by law any house built in town must be painted white. Visitors still see houses with red-tile roofs on palm-covered hills overlooking glistening blue water. Pack mules clomp down the steep cobblestoned streets. Within 16 kilometers (10 miles) of town are peaceful coves, rivers rushing to the sea, and steep mountain roads that curve and twist through jungles of pines and palms.

In the high season, from December through April, the temperature is in the 70s and 80s, the water temperature in the 60s and low 70s. The off-season brings rain: light afternoon showers in the early summer and major rainstorms in the late summer and fall. You miss out on constant sunshine in the off-season; it's humid and the temperatures are high (in the 80s and 90s), and the mosquitoes can be a nuisance; but you enjoy emptier beaches, warmer water (well into the 70s), and less-crowded streets. You also benefit from a 25% to 30% reduction in room rates and the opportunity to do a little bargaining on rental-car costs.

Exploring

Orientation

Central Puerto Vallarta has three major parts: the northern hotel and resort region, the downtown area (also called Old Town), and the Río Cuale and Playa de los Muertos. A rental car or cab is necessary to explore the hotel zone, which is basically a long stretch of shopping centers, restaurants, and hotels, but you don't want to have a car downtown and in the Río Cuale area. Most of the interesting sights can be covered on foot—just be sure you wear comfortable shoes for the cobblestone streets.

Numbers in the margin correspond to points of interest on the Puerto Vallarta map.

The Hotel Zone

① The big attraction in the north is the **Marina Vallarta** area, which is practically a town unto itself with a marina, hundreds of condominiums, several major hotels, shopping centers, an 18-hole golf course, and the Royal Pacific Yacht Club. Nuevo Vallarta, just over the Jalisco state line in Nayarit, at the mouth of the Río Ameca, is a beautiful new community with beachfront houses and condos on canals with direct access to the bay. In addition, the area is home to three all-inclusive resorts, Jack Tar village, the Radisson Plaza, and the Diamond Resort Puerta Vallarta.

Seven miles farther north, on still another beautiful beach, is the town of Bucerias. From there, you follow the bend of Banderas Bay past several small and pristine beaches—including Cruz de Huanacaxtle and Anclote—to **Punta Mita,** on the northern tip of the Bahía de Banderas. Punta Mita features blue bay water that's perfect for swimming and, around the bend, waves for surfing. Here, the views of the bay and of the Sierra Madre mountains are fantastic, and this is definitely a prime spot to view a sunset. Scuba divers like the fairly clear waters around the Isla Marietas, offshore.

Downtown and the Río Cuale

When you start seeing cobblestoned streets, you're in the downtown area also known as Old Town. This is the heart of PV, a vestige of old **②** Puerto Vallarta. The **malecón** begins at Díaz Ordáz. A seawall and sidewalk run along the bay, and restaurants, cafés, and shops are across the street. The malecón is downtown's main drag, a nice place to rest on a white wrought-iron bench. There are some interesting sculptures along the walkway, including the bronze sea horse that has become Puerto Vallarta's trademark.

③ The main zócalo, **Plaza de Armas,** is just after Díaz Ordáz and merges **④** with Morelos at Zaragoza Street. The **City Hall** is on the north side of the plaza. This building is home to a colorful mural, painted in 1981 by Puerto Vallarta's most famous artist, Mañuel Lepe. The mural (above the stairs on the second floor) depicts Puerto Vallarta as a fanciful seaside fishing and farming village. The tourism office is on the first floor.

⑤ Dominating the square from a block east is **La Iglesia de Nuestra Señora de Guadalupe** (Church of Our Lady of Guadalupe), topped by an ornate crown; it's a replica of the one worn by Carlota, the empress of Mexico in the late 1860s. There are signs posted at the entrances asking that you not visit the church wearing shorts or sleeveless T-shirts.

⑥ The **Mercado Municipal** is located at Miramar and Rodríguez, at the foot of the old bridge over Río Cuale. The market is small enough to tour quickly.

⑦ The stretch above town along the river is called **Gringo Gulch,** named after the thousands of expatriates from the United States who settled here in the 1950s. Elizabeth Taylor's home, Casa Kimberly, was sold in 1990 and has been converted into a bed-and-breakfast (*see* Lodging, *below*).

TIME OUT Dining and drinking are the malecón's big attractions, from early morning till just before dawn. If you're there in the morning, have breakfast at

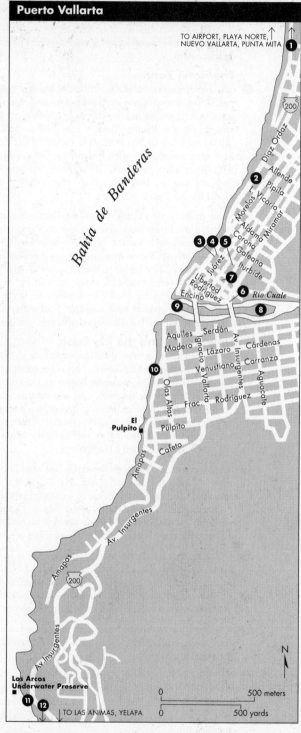

Puerto Vallarta

TO AIRPORT, PLAYA NORTE,
NUEVO VALLARTA, PUNTA MITA

Bahía de Banderas

Díaz Ordaz
Allende
Pipila
I. Vicario
Morelos
Aldama   Miramar
Corona
Galeana
Iturbide
Juárez
Libertad
Rodríguez
Río Cuale
Encino

Aquiles
Serdán
Madero
Ignacio Vallarta
Lázaro
Av. Insurgentes
Cárdenas
Venustiano
Carranza
Olas Altas
Frac. Rodríguez
Aguacate

El
Pulpito
Púlpito
Cafeto

Amapas

Av. Insurgentes

Amapas

200

Av. Insurgentes

N

Las Arcos
Underwater Preserve

TO LAS ANIMAS, YELAPA

0   500 meters
0   500 yards

Las Palomas; evening happy hours are boisterous and fun at **Carlos O'Brian's,** where a six-pack of Corona beer in a silver pail is the favored drink.

Río Cuale Island and Playa de los Muertos

8 The Río Cuale runs into the bay just past Plaza de Armas. **Río Cuale Island** is in the middle of the river. There are steps leading under the two bridges that cross the river, then a long park and walkway from Avenida Insurgentes to the waterfront. The island has an outdoor marketplace with boutiques, souvenir stands, trendy restaurants, and

9 inexpensive cafés. The **Museo Arqueológico** at the western tip of the island has a nice collection of pre-Columbian figures and Indian artifacts. The museum director lectures in English Tuesdays at 1 PM. *No* ☎. ☉ *10–2 and 4–6.*

TIME OUT On the east end of Río Cuale Island, **Le Bistro Café** is a beautiful spot to enjoy a light breakfast, lunch, or dinner or to simply relax at the bar with a drink and some good taped jazz.

10 **Playa de los Muertos,** the beach on the south side of the Río Cuale, has long been the budget traveler's domain, though it has some of the more expensive restaurants and shops. It is the most popular and most crowded beach in Puerto Vallarta. Parasailers lift off while sunbathers recline on the sand. Beach toys for rent include everything from rubber inner tubes to Windsurfers. Vendors stroll the beach, hawking lace tablecloths, wood statues, kites, and grilled fish on a stick. Plaza Lázaro Cárdenas is a pretty spot at the north end of the beach. To the south, Playa de los Muertos ends at a rocky point called El Púlpito. PV's tourism promoters have given up trying to change the name of Playa de los Muertos (Beach of the Dead Ones) to Playa del Sol (Beach of the Sun). If you see an address for the latter, head for the former.

TIME OUT Eating grilled fish on a stick at Playa de los Muertos is like having a hot dog at Coney Island: it's what you *do*. Buy it from one of the stands at the south end of the beach, then stroll along and watch the show. For a sit-down break, get a beer and tacos or enchiladas at **El Dorado** at the north end.

Mismaloya and Boca de Tomatlán

11 A visit to Puerto Vallarta without a side trip to **Playa Mismaloya** is nearly unthinkable, since this is where "the movie" was made. The 13-kilometer (8-mile) drive south on Route 200 passes by spectacular houses, some of PV's oldest and quietest resorts, and a slew of condo and time-sharing developments. A pretty cove, somewhat spoiled by La Jolla de Mismaloya, a huge hotel complex built on its shores, Mismaloya is backed by rugged, rocky hills and affords a good view of Los Arcos, a rock formation in the water. Motor launches leave from Boca de Tomatlán for Los Arcos and the more secluded beaches of Las Animas, Quimixto, and Yelapa; the cost is from $3 to $6 per person, per hour.

12 **Boca de Tomatlán** is a small village at the mouth of the Tomatlán River. It's a beautiful spot where you can wade in freshwater pools. Just before you reach the dirt road to the beach, there are several large palapa restaurants. Chee Chee's, a massive restaurant, shopping, and swimming-pool complex, spreads down a steep hillside like a small village. Farther along the main road, through Boca, is Chico's Paradise, a large restaurant set amid giant boulders and surrounded by pools and small waterfalls.

Shopping

Puerto Vallarta can get into a shopper's blood. Chain stores line the main streets, selling designer-label clothing at prices comparable to, if not higher than, those at home. Prices in the shops are fixed, and American dollars and credit cards are accepted. Bargaining is expected in the markets and by the vendors on the beach, who also freely accept American money. Most stores are open from 10 AM to 8 PM. A few close for siesta at 1 or 2, then reopen at 4.

Art

The late Mañuel Lepe is perhaps Puerto Vallarta's most famous artist. His primitive style can be seen in the prints and posters that are still available at several of the galleries and shops around town. Sergio Bustamante, the creator of life-size brass, copper, and papier-mâché animals, has his own gallery, **Sergio Bustamante** (Juárez 275, ☎ 322/2-11-29; Paseo Díaz Ordaz 700 A, ☎ 322/3-14-07; and Paseo Díaz Ordaz 542, ☎ 322/2-54-80). **Galería Uno** (Morelos 561, ☎ 322/2-09-08), specializes in art from all over Mexico, but owner Jan Lavender is especially enthusiastic about promoting local talent. Contemporary art and sculpture are displayed in one of Mexico's finest galleries, **Galería Pacífico** (Insurgentes 109, ☎ 322/2-19-82). In addition to paintings, **Galería Vallarta** (Juárez 263, ☎ 322/2-02-90) carries jewelry and glass sculptures produced by owners Gene and Barbara Peters.

Clothing

Most of the brand-name sportswear shops are located along the malecón and down its side streets. Many of these stores also have branches in the shopping centers or along Carretera Aeropuerto. **Aca Joe** (Díaz Ordáz 588, ☎ 322/3-04-24) offers excellent quality pants, T-shirts, shorts, jackets, and sweats in smashing colors, all neatly displayed. **Guess** (Paseo Díaz Ordaz 2660, ☎ 322/2-64-70) carries its own line of well-designed quality sportswear. As the store's name suggests, the attractive sports and casual wear sold at **Nautica** (Plaza Marina 46A, ☎ 322/1-02-01) have a nautical influence.

More elegant, dressier clothes, made of soft flowing fabrics in tropical prints, can be found at **Sucesos Boutique** (Libertad and Hidalgo, ☎ 322/2-10-02, and Los Arcos hotel, ☎ 322/2-15-83), which features handpainted fabrics and fashionable gauze resortwear that is sold in exclusive boutiques throughout Mexico. **Valenciana** (Corona 160, ☎ 322/3-04-18) offers hand-painted straw hats; cotton fashions for women by Tipicano, Opus I, and Dunas; and some imaginative accessories. **María de Guadalajara** (in the Puesta del Sol codominiums in Marina Vallarta, ☎ 322/1-02-62, ext. 1015; at Morelos 550, ☎ 322/2-23-87; and at Plaza Malecón and Paseo Díaz Ordáz, ☎ 322/2-47-35) carries easy-to-wear clothing for women in gauzy cotton fabrics dyed in luscious colors.

Folk Art

Few cities in Mexico have a collection of the country's fine folk arts that is as representative as the one in Puerto Vallarta. Masks, pottery, lacquerware, clothing, mirrors, glass dishes, windows and lamps, carved-wood animals and doors, antiques and modern art, hand-dyed woven rugs and embroidered clothing are all available in the markets and from vendors. **Nevaj** (Morelos 223, ☎ 322/2-69-59) carries high-quality folk art from Central and South America, including primitive and sublime weavings, bags, shawls, and dresses. **Olinalá** (Lázaro Cárdenas 274, ☎ 322/2-49-95) is a two-story gallery and shop filled with masks from all over Mexico, as well as lacquered boxes and trays from Michoacán. **Arte Mágico Huichol** (Calle Corona 179, ☎ 322/2–30–77) features beaded tapestries and weavings from the Huichol Indians of Nayarit. **La Rosa de Cristal** (Insurgentes 272, ☎ 322/2–56–98) carries a full line of blown-glass items made in their Tlaquepaque workshop. **Querubines** (Juárez and Galeana, ☎ 322/2–34–75) displays crafts, including ceramics, glassware, and jewelry, from all over Mexico, as well as a wearable collection of intricately embroidered native clothing made from hand-loomed cloth.

Jewelry

There is a good selection of Mexican silver in Puerto Vallarta, but watch out for fake silver made with alloys. Real silver carries the 925 silver stamp required by the government. It is best to visit a reputable jeweler, such as **Ric Taxco** (Pueblo Viejo shopping center, ☎ 322/3–01–43, and Villa Vallarta shopping center (☎ 322/4–45–98), where much of the sterling silver and gold jewelry was inspired by pre-Hispanic designs. **Joyas Finas Suneson** (Morelos 593, ☎ 322/2–57–15) specializes in fine silver jewelry and objets d'art by some of Mexico's finest designers.

Markets

The **Mercado Municipal,** at Avenida Miramar and Libertad, is a typical market plopped down in the busiest part of town. Flowers, piñatas, produce, and plastics are all shoved together in indoor and outdoor stands that cover a full city block. The strip of **shops along Rio Cuale Island** is an outdoor market of sorts, with souvenir stands and exclusive boutiques interspersed with restaurants and cafés. Bargaining at the stalls in the market and on the island is expected.

Shopping Centers

The highway on the north side of town is lined with small arcades and large shopping centers that are occupied by handicrafts and sportswear shops. The best selections are at **Plaza Malecón,** at the beginning of Díaz Ordáz; **Plaza Marina,** by the airport; the **Gigante Plaza,** by the Fiesta Americana hotel; and **Villa Vallarta,** by the Plaza las Glorias hotel.

Sports

Swimming, sailing, windsurfing, and parasailing are popular sports at the beachfront hotels. The hotels have stands on the beach offering boat trips and equipment, and you need not be a guest to buy these services.

Fishing

Sportfishing is good off Puerto Vallarta most of the year, particularly for billfish, roosterfish, dorado, yellowtail, and bonito. The marlin season begins in November. The Progreso Fishermen's Cooperative has a shack on the north end of the malecón and offers a variety of options for fishing trips; most hotels can arrange your reservations. Large group boats cost about $60 per person for a day's fishing; other cruisers may be chartered for prices ranging from from $150 to $350 a day, depending on the size of the boat and the length of the trip. Charters include a skipper, license, bait, and tackle; some also include lunch.

Golf

Los Flamingos Country Club (☎ 322/7–15–15) has an 18-hole golf course. Reservations should be made through your hotel a day in advance. The country club is about 12 kilometers (8 miles) north of the airport, and transportation is provided with your reservations.

There is another, Joe Finger–designed, 18-hole course at the Marina Vallarta complex (☎ 322/1–01–71).

Tennis

Most of the larger hotels have tennis courts. Nonmembers may also play at the **John Newcombe Tennis Club** (☎ 322/4–01–23), **Los Tules** (☎ 322/4–45–60), and **Los Flamingos Country Club** (☎ 322/7–15–15).

Water Sports

Snorkeling and diving are best at Los Arcos, a natural underwater preserve on the way to Mismaloya. Punta Mita, about 80 kilometers (50 miles) north of Puerto Vallarta, has some good diving spots, as does Quimixto Bay, about 32 kilometers (20 miles) south and accessible only by boat. Experienced divers prefer Las Tres Marietas, a group of three islands off the coast.

Some of the hotels have snorkeling and diving equipment for rent and offer short courses on diving at their pools. For dive trips and rentals, contact the following shops: **Chico's Dive Shop** (Díaz Ordáz 772, ☎ 322/2–18–95) and **Paradise Divers** (Continental Plaza Vallarta, ☎ 322/4–44–48; Marriott, ☎ 322/1–00–04; Jack Tar Village, ☎ 329/ 7–01–00; Pueblito Paraíso Nuevo Vallarta, ☎ 329/7–03–44).

Beaches

Beaches in Mexico are federal property and are not owned by the hotels; some hotels try to keep their beaches exclusive by roping off an area where the hotel's lounge chairs must be kept.

Playa Norte

Also known as **Playa de Oro,** this is the northernmost beach, stretching from the marina and cruise-ship terminal to downtown. The beach changes a bit with the character of each hotel it fronts; it is particularly nice by the Fiesta Americana and the Krystal hotels.

Playa de los Muertos

Long ago, this beach was the site of a battle between pirates and Indians. The town's boosters tried for years to change the name to Playa del Sol (Beach of the Sun), but they weren't successful. The budget travelers hang out here, and vendors selling kites, blankets, and jewelry seem as abundant as the sunbathers.

Playa las Animas and Yelapa

These secluded fishing villages are accessible only by boat. Both villages have small communities of hardy isolationists; of late, Yelapa has attracted more and more foreigners who settle in for good. At Yelapa, take a 20-minute hike from the beach into the jungle to see the waterfalls. Tour groups visit the beaches daily.

Dining

Puerto Vallarta has many fine restaurants, some with spectacular views, others hidden in the small, romantic patios of former homes, and still others—especially those on the malecón—as popular for people-watching as they are for their great seafood. Dining prices are comparable to those in the United States, and there are few real bargains. Dress is casual in Puerto Vallarta, even at the most glamorous spots, though shorts are frowned upon at dinner.

CATEGORY	COST*
$$$$	over $35
$$$	$25–$35
$$	$15–$25
$	under $15

*per person, excluding drinks, service, and sales tax (10%)

$$$$ **La Perla.** This restaurant and its chef are famous for their sublime
★ Mexican haute cuisine, service, and ambience. The best dish by far is
the veal stuffed with squash flowers, though the chicken in red wine
and the beef fillet with stuffed chili, rice, and beans are also superb.
The chef really shows his worth with the pastries, which are
renowned throughout PV—and by all means try the flaming crêpes
prepared here. There is a separate lounge in the restaurant for after-
dinner drinks, coffee, and dessert. The restaurant is decorated in
vibrant Mexican colors. ✕ *Hotel Camino Real, Playa Las Estacas,* ☎
322/3–01–23. Reservations advised. AE, DC, MC, V. No lunch.

$$$ **Chef Roger.** The cozy patio of a typical Puerto Vallarta house is the
★ unpretentious setting for one of the best restaurants in town. Roger
Docier, the Swiss owner and chef, combines his European training
with Mexican ingredients, and the results are superb. Don't leave
town without trying the fillet of fish served with shrimp in a lobster
sauce. ✕ *Augustín Rodríguez 267,* ☎ *322/2–59–00. Reservations
required. AE, DC, MC, V. No lunch.*

$$$ **Chez Elena.** This restaurant is among the town's best. Located up a
★ steep street behind Vallarta's famous crown-topped church, Chez
Elena is especially agreeable for an early dinner after enjoying the
sunset and a delightful tropical drink on the rooftop El Nido bar. The
shrimp dishes are excellent, as are the Mexican dishes, especially the
cochinita pibil (pork prepared in a spicy pumpkin seed–based Yucatecan sauce), the *pollo en chipotle* (chicken served with a chipotle chili
sauce), and the chicken mole. Top it all off with a perfect brownie and
café mulatto. ✕ *Matamoros 520,* ☎ *322/2–01–61. Reservations
advised. AE, MC, V. No lunch.*

$$$ **Le Bistro.** By far the classiest restaurant along Río Cuale, Le Bistro has
a black-and-white tiled bar, gray-and-white striped tablecloths, and
handsome waiters. The taped jazz is played at just the right level so
that it doesn't intrude on conversation. Try the brochette Brubeck,
made of grilled giant shrimp and generous hunks of tenderloin. The
mango and lemon pie is a must. ✕ *Río Cuale Island,* ☎ *322/2–02–83.
No reservations. AE, MC, V. Closed Sun.*

$$$ **Señor Chico's.** On the Alta Vista hill overlooking all of Puerto Val-
larta, Señor Chico's is a magnificent spot from sunset into night-
time. The Caesar salad is good, as is any seafood choice, but it's the
view that really makes the place. Enjoy live music from 8 to 11 PM.
✕ *Púlpito 377,* ☎ *322/2–35–70. Reservations advised. AE, DC,
MC, V. No lunch.*

$$ **Andale.** A Playa de los Muertos hangout and a good spot for an after-
★ noon beer with the locals, this restaurant serves good fettuccine with
scallops, great garlic bread, and an unusual chicken *Mestizo* with
white wine, pineapple juice, and jalapeño peppers. ✕ *Paseo de
Velasco 425,* ☎ *322/2–10–54. AE, D, MC, V.*

$$ **Brazz.** A big, airy place decorated with brightly colored piñatas, Brazz
is a branch of the Guadalajara chain, known for its generous steaks
and prime rib and good Mexican dishes. The salad bar is the best in
town. Mariachi music plays continuously. ✕ *Morelos at Galleana,* ☎
322/2–03–24. Reservations advised. AE, DC, MC, V. No lunch.

$$ El Dorado. A must for at least one lunch, this Playa de los Muertos palapa is popular with American expatriates. The eclectic menu includes spaghetti, burgers, and crepes, but stick with such specialties as dorado-style fish, broiled with a thick layer of melted cheese. ✕ *Amapas and Púlpito,* ☎ *322/2–15–11. AE, DC, MC, V.*

$$ La Fuente del Puente. Located just across from the market, above the riverbank, this outdoor café is popular with budget travelers. The bright pink-and-blue neon along the ceiling is an unusual touch for PV. The prices are low, the food good, and the crowd amiable. ✕ *Av. Miramar at the old bridge,* ☎ *322/2–11–41. MC, V.*

$$ Las Palomas. Breakfast at this malecón café is a daily ritual for many and a place for the reunion of Puerto Vallarta regulars upon their return to town. Have *jugo de lima* (similar to lemonade but made with the region's tart limes). Homesick? Have hot oatmeal with cinnamon and sugar; otherwise, stick with the *huevos con chorizo* (eggs with spicy sausage) and coffee spiced with cinnamon. The people in the mural on one of the walls are all well-known characters in Puerto Vallarta. Stick around town long enough and you'll probably run into a few of them. ✕ *Díaz Ordáz at Aldama,* ☎ *322/2–36–75. No reservations. AE, MC, V.*

$ The Pancake House and the Diner. This is the town's most popular spot for breakfast, serving 12 varieties of pancakes, waffles, eggs, French toast, and great coffee. ✕ *Basilo Badillo 289,* ☎ *322/2–62–72. No reservations. No credit cards.*

$ Rito Baci's. This popular deli and pizza parlor delivers to homes and hotels. All the pastas are made on the premises. The crispy-crusted pizza is excellent, and the sausage spicy and flavorful. Try the sausage sandwich as well. ✕ *Calle Ortiz de Domínguez 181,* ☎ *322/2–64–48. MC, V.*

$ Tutifruti. Sample great fresh-squeezed juices at a small stand in the downtown shopping area; choose your desired combination of mango, papaya, melon, and pineapple. Filling *tortas* (sandwiches) cost about $2. ✕ *Morelos 552 and Corona,* ☎ *322/2–10–68. No credit cards. Closed Sun.*

Lodging

Most of PV's deluxe resorts are located to the north; south of downtown and the Río Cuale, in the Playa de los Muertos and Olas Altas areas, the rates are lower. Some of the nicest, older hotels are a few miles south of town. Budget hotels maintain the same rates year-round, but rates at the pricier places usually go down 25% to 30% just after Easter week through December 15. Reservations are a must at Christmas, New Year's, and Easter. The postal code for Puerto Vallarta is 48300.

CATEGORY	COST*
$$$$	over $160
$$$	$90–$160
$$	$40–$90
$	under $40

All prices are for a standard double room, excluding 10% tax.

$$$$ Fiesta Americana. A seven-story palapa covers the lobby and a large
★ round bar. The dramatically designed terra-cotta building rises above a deep blue pool that flows under bridges, palm oases, and palapa restaurants set on platforms over the water. The rooms have a modern blue, pink, and lavender color scheme; each has white marble floors, tiled bath with powerful shower, and balcony. The beach bustles with activity—parasailing, windsurfing, boat tours, snorkeling,

and, of course, sunbathing. The restaurants are excellent, especially the breakfast buffet by the pool. Of all the full-service resorts, Fiesta Americana has the most tropical and luxurious feel. ⚏ *Carretera Aeropuerto,* ☎ *322/4–20–10 or 800/FIESTA–1. 291 rooms with bath. 4 restaurants, 3 bars, karaoke bar, pool, hair salon, beach, travel services. AE, DC, MC, V.*

$$$$ **La Jolla de Mismaloya.** Despite the fact that the overpowering design of this hotel has ruined the view of beautiful Mismaloya Bay, the lucky guests here literally have half of the bay (this is where the movie *The Night of the Iguana* was filmed) to themselves, as well as a fabulous view of Puerto Vallarta's famous arches (rock formations jutting out of the sea). The southern half of the bay is crowded with beachfront restaurants and motor launches that go to even more remote beaches. The hotel's one- and two-bedroom suites have terraces and kitchenettes. Though somewhat out of the way, this is a hotel that consistently gets high marks from its guests. ⚏ *Off Hwy. 200 at Mismaloya Bay,* ☎ *322/8–06–60; reservations in the U.S., 800/329–2344. 303 suites. Restaurant, bar, 3 pools, exercise room, beach, tennis courts, disco. AE, DC, MC, V.*

$$$$ **Marriott Casa Magna.** Located in Marina Vallarta, with El Salado beach to the front and the Marina's 18-hole, Joe Finger–designed golf course to the rear, the Marriott Casa Magna is one of Vallarta's newest, largest, and most glamorous hotels. The vast, plant-filled, marble lobbies that open onto the huge pool area are hung with chandeliers. The rooms are decorated with light woods and soft colors. All overlook the bay. And if the water sports, tennis, restaurants, night clubs, and other amenities of the hotel aren't enough, guests have access to the facilities of the Marina Vallarta complex, including a huge shopping center, a yacht club, and yet more restaurants. Rate includes a buffet breakfast. ⚏ *Marina Vallarta,* ☎ *322/1–00–04 or 800/228–9290. 433 rooms and suites with bath. 3 restaurants, bars, pool, beach, tennis, disco. AE, DC, MC, V.*

$$$ **Bel-Air.** Reminiscent of a Palm Springs estate, this pale pink mansion
★ with white columns is simply but elegantly decorated. Fresh flowers and plants, antiques, and original works of art by Sergio Bustamante grace the rooms and corridors of this spacious property. Built in 1990 as the Villas Quinta Real, this property includes 50 suites and 25 villas that command views of the golf course of the Marina Vallarta complex. Though the hotel is not directly on the beach, its amenities are many, and its location between the first and 18th holes of the Marina Vallarta Golf Course makes it ideal for golfers. Transportation is provided to and from the airport and within the Marina complex. ⚏ *Marina Vallarta, Pelicanos 311,* ☎ *322/1–08–00 or 800/457–7676. 50 suites and 25 1- to 3-bedroom villas. Restaurant, bar, room service, pool, spa, golf course. AE, MC, V.*

$$$ **Camino Real.** One of PV's first hotels, this property sits on a lovely small bay south of town. The rooms have cool marble floors with white furniture and bright pink, yellow, and purple highlights against stark white walls. The hotel has all the five-star touches—from plush robes in the rooms and the feel of an established, comfortable resort to the palapas on the beach and the fragrant white jasmine blooming along the natural waterfall. A newer 11-story tower houses the Royal Beach Club, which also has a convention/banquet center. ⚏ *Playa Las Estacas,* ☎ *322/1–50–00; reservations in the U.S., 800/7-CAMINO. 337 rooms (93 in new tower). 5 restaurants and bars, 2 pools, wading pool, beach, 2 tennis courts. AE, DC, MC, V.*

$$$ **Continental Plaza Puerto Vallarta.** Ideal for tennis buffs, this Mediterranean-style complex features the John Newcombe Tennis Club, which has eight courts and offers daily tennis clinics. The resort has a shopping plaza, several restaurants and bars, a large swimming pool, and a nice beach. ☒ *Carretera Aeropuerto,* ☎ *322/4–01–23; reservations in the U.S.,* 800/88–CONTI. *424 rooms with bath. Restaurants, bars, pool, beach, 8 tennis courts. AE, DC, MC, V.*

$$$ **Krystal Vallarta.** A full-service resort that sprawls over acreage
★ equivalent to that of a small town, the Krystal has 460 rooms, including 48 villas, each with a private pool. There are six restaurants, including Tango, which serves Argentine *churrasco* (barbecue), and Kamakura, which serves Japanese food. Not all rooms are by the ocean, but the secluded beach can accommodate all sunseekers. Christine's disco has a knock'em-dead light show. ☒ *Carretera Aeropuerto,* ☎ *322/4–02–02 or 800/231–9860. 412 rooms with bath, 48 villas. 6 restaurants, bars, pools, beach, 2 tennis courts, disco, travel services. AE, DC, MC, V.*

$$$ **Qualton Club & Spa.** The Qualton hotel is a spa, with a fitness center and state-of-the-art machines, a jogging trail running through the hotel grounds, beauty treatments from hydromassage to herbal wraps, nutritional analysis, and computerized exercise and diet regimes. You don't have to be a fitness freak to stay here, though. The rooms in the two wings and main 14-story tower are done in peaceful mauves and blues; deluxe rooms have ocean-view balconies. Meals, drinks, and most sports activities and spa services are included in the room rate, and a "dine-around" program allows guests to sample restaurants in other areas. ☒ *Carretera Aeropuerto,* ☎ *322/4 44 46. 219 rooms. 3 restaurants, bar, 2 pools, hot tub, spa, beach. AE, DC, MC, V.*

$$ **Buenaventura.** This hotel's location is ideal, on the edge of down-
★ town, within walking distance (10 blocks or so) of the Río Cuale and, in the opposite direction, of the shops, hotels, and restaurants on the airport highway. From the street it looks rather austere, but just inside the door is an enormous five-story open lobby and bar. The bright, cheerful rooms in yellows and whites have beamed ceilings and pale wood furnishings. ☒ *Av. México 1301,* ☎ *322/2–37–37; reservations in the U.S.,* 800/878–4111. *209 rooms with bath, 4 suites. 2 restaurants, 2 bars, pool, beach. AE, DC, MC, V.*

$$ **Casa Kimberly.** The former homes of Elizabeth Taylor and Richard Burton, located on opposite sides of the street but joined by a footbridge (in a part of town now called Gringo Gulch), have been converted into a bed-and-breakfast. Both houses are surprisingly unpretentious; only Liz's had a pool. The owner, naturally enough, exploits the Liz and Dick legend; tour groups visit in the mornings. Lavender (supposedly Elizabeth's favorite color, at least during her Puerto Vallarta days) prevails, and tables and walls are adorned with photos of the famous lovers. The rate includes a full breakfast. ☒ *Calle Zaragoza 445,* ☎ *322/2–13–36. 8 suites. Pool. AE, MC, V.*

$$ **Las Palmas.** The palapa entrance to Las Palmas is unique—four bam-
★ boo bridges suspended from the ceiling and parrots screeching under the palms. The rooms have shared balconies and brown spreads and drapes. The accommodations are first-rate for this price category. ☒ *Cerrada las Palmas 50,* ☎ *322/4–06–50; reservations in the U.S.,* 800/995–8584. *114 rooms with bath. Restaurant, bar, pool. AE, DC, MC, V.*

$$ **Los Cuatro Vientos.** The most charming small hotel in PV, Cuatro Vientos (meaning Four Winds) is located up a steep hill behind town, tucked among the red-tile-roofed cottages. Its 16 rooms are often booked a year in advance by repeat guests. The simple rooms with arched brick ceilings have colorful flowers stenciled on the walls and folk-art knickknacks. The restaurant, Chez Elena (*see* Dining, *above*), is among PV's best, and there's a pleasant rooftop bar open in high season. ☎ *Matamoros 520,* ☎ *322/2–01–61. 16 rooms with bath. Restaurant, bar. MC, V.*

$$ Mar Elena. These suites on the north side of town are a good bargain for travelers who want a kitchen and living-room setup. The building is rather plain, but the kitchens and bathrooms are beautifully tiled and some of the rooms have cable TV. The pool is on the roof; the beach is a block away. ☎ *Carretera Aeropuerto Km 2,* ☎ *322/4–44–25. 30 suites. Pool. MC, V.*

$$ Molino de Agua. This hotel's bungalows are spread out along the riverbed amid lush trees and flowers. Stone pathways wind under willows, past caged parrots and monkeys, and lead to cottages with wood shutters and redbrick walls. However, the din emanating from the bar area after 5 PM can be disturbing, and none of the cottages have telephones. ☎ *Vallarta 130,* ☎ *322/2–19–07. 62 rooms with bath. Restaurant, snack bar, 2 pools, hot tub, beach. AE, MC, V.*

$$ Playa Los Arcos. By far the most popular hotel on the beach by the Río Cuale, Los Arcos has a pretty central courtyard and pool and a friendly air. A glass elevator rises by the pool to the rooms, which have bright orange furnishings and small balconies. ☎ *Olas Altas 380,* ☎ *322/2–05–83. 140 rooms with bath. Restaurant, bar, pool, beach. AE, DC, MC, V.*

$ Posada de Roger. One of the least expensive hotels, the Posada de
★ Roger is in many ways the most enjoyable, if you like the company of Europeans and Canadians who are savvy about budget traveling. The showers are hot, the beds comfortable, and the pool an international meeting spot. You can have your mail held there, and the desk clerks are knowledgeable about other budget hotels and restaurants. ☎ *Basilio Badillo 237,* ☎ *322/2–08–36. 56 rooms with bath. Restaurant, bar, pool. AE, MC, V.*

$ Posada Río Cuale. This small, friendly inn on the south side of Río
★ Cuale has one of the best gourmet restaurants in town (aptly named Le Gourmet) and a nice sense of serenity. The beds are big and cozy; flowers are placed on each nightstand; and with only 21 rooms, the place rarely becomes noisy. ☎ *Calle Aquiles Serdán 242,* ☎ *322/2–04–50. 21 rooms with bath. Restaurant, bar, pool. AE, MC, V.*

Nightlife

Puerto Vallarta is a party town, where the discos open at 10 PM and stay open until 3 or 4 AM. A minimum $7 cover charge is common in the popular discos, many of which are at the hotels. The Krystal has **Christine's,** which features a spectacular light show set to music from disco to classic rock nightly at 11:30. **Sixties,** at the Marriott, features music for almost all ages, and **Friday López,** at the Fiesta Americana, has karaoke and dancing. Tables start to disappear from the lower level of the **Hard Rock Café** (☎ 322/2–55–32), downtown on the malecón, at about 10:30 PM, and by 11 PM the live music starts and there is dancing everywhere. **La Pachanga** (Av. México 918, ☎ 322/3–10–95) is a popular new place with live entertainment, mariachis, and a folk ballet. **El Panorama** (☎ 322/2–18–18), at the Hotel La Siesta, is a real nightclub with a floor show and live music during the high season. A guitarist plays romantic tunes at **El Nido,** the bar at Los Cuatro Vientos, known for its sunset view. **Iggy's,** at the La Jolla Mismaloya Hotel, is the perfect drinking and dancing spot for those who like to converse without shouting. Everything its name implies and more, **Collage** (☎ 322/

1–05–05), on the highway at the Marina Vallarta complex, hosts several restaurants, a bowling alley, a large-screen video golf game, billiards, two bars, shuffleboard, a video arcade, and a disco.

Mexican fiestas are popular at the hotels and can be lavish affairs with buffet dinners, folk dances, and fireworks. Reservations may be made with the hotels or travel agencies. Some of the more spectacular shows are at La Iguana Tourist Center, the Krystal, the Sheraton, and the Westin Regina. On Thursday, the Meliá hosts a flamenco night with Spanish buffet.

Excursion to Manzanillo

The coastline south of Puerto Vallarta is sprinkled with some of the Mexican Riviera's most exclusive and secluded one-of-a-kind resorts. But you'll never see them from the highway when you take 200 south—a rugged, twisting road through a tropical forest of pines and palms. Most of the resorts are reached by unpaved roads (though the coast is only a short distance from Highway 200). Guests usually fly to Puerto Vallarta or Manzanillo (one hour south) and take a taxi or hotel van to the resort. Once there, they stay put for a week or more, leaving only for the requisite shopping spree in PV. As you travel south, the best resorts are in Mismaloya, Tecuán, Careyes, and Tenacatita.

Lodging

$$$$ **Fiesta Americana Los Angeles Locos.** Canadians come here by the charter-jet load, drawn to the amiable surroundings, the all-inclusive drinks and meals, and the chance to relax with friends. The hotel's design is similar to that of other Fiesta Americana properties, with the large, comfortable rooms clustered in a horseshoe-shaped terra-cotta building around the bay. Tours to Puerto Vallarta and Manzanillo are available through the Tlaloc Travel Agency on the premises. ☎ *Hwy. 200 in Tenacatita,* ☎ *335/1–50–05; reservations in the U.S., 800/ FIESTA–1. 201 rooms and suites. Restaurant, bar, pool, beach, horseback riding, disco, travel services. AE, DC, MC, V.*

$$$$ **Las Alamandas.** One of Mexico's most exclusive—and expensive—
★ resorts, Las Alamandas is low key rather than glitzy. Surrounded by a natural preserve that hosts abundant wildlife, the property's villas and casitas are decorated with folk art and traditional Mexican furnishings (some offer TVs and VCRs). Among the various outdoor activities are horseback riding, fishing, and boat rides along the San Nocolas River. Many guests fly into the hotel's private helipad; others take the hotel's air-conditioned limo from either the Puerto Vallarta (1 hour, 45 minutes) or Manzanillo (1½ hours) airports. There's a two-night-stay minimum; meal packages are available. ☎ *Apt. Postal 201, San Patricio, Melaque, Jalisco 48980,* ☎ *328/5–55–00,* FAX *328/5–50–27; reservations in the U.S.: 3525 Sage Rd., Houston, TX 77056,* ☎ *713/ 961–3117 or 800/223–6510,* FAX *713/961–3411. 1 casita and 4 villas (including 9 suites). Restaurant, in-room VCRs, pool, Ping-Pong, croquet, exercise room, volleyball, beach, mountain bikes, tennis court. No credit cards.*

$$$$ **Playa Blanca.** This Club Med has all the services the pioneer all-inclusive chain is known for—diving, fishing, pool bars, horseback riding, and even a trapeze and circus school. The food, usually served buffet style, is ample and good, and there are two restaurants where you can be served by waiters. The guests tend to be young and active, and the resort is far from having a feeling of isolation: With 300 rooms, a disco, and aerobic classes, the ambience is more celebratory than somnolent. ☎ *Off Hwy. 200, next door to Bel-Air hotel,* ☎ *335/*

1–00–01; *reservations in the U.S., 800/CLUB-MED. 300 rooms. 2 restaurants, bar, dining rooms, pool, beach, horseback riding, tennis court. AE, DC, MC, V.*

$$$ **Bel-Air.** The Costa Careyes hotel, a secluded playground for the rich and famous located on one of the most breathtaking coves on Mexico's Pacific coast, had gotten a bit shabby by the time it was taken over by the Bel-Air group of California. Yet the results of its major remodeling, unveiled in late 1993, are stunning. While freshening up the facilities, the new owners have maintained the best of the former hotel—the feeling of seclusion, the unpretentiousness, the warm Mediterranean colors, and, of course, the spectacular setting. The rooms—each with a terrace, some with a pool—have an understated elegance. The small beach, however, is disappointing, and the resort has opened an office to sell time shares. ▣ *96 km (57½ mi) north of the Manzanillo airport. Box 24, Cihuatlan 48970, Jalisco, ☎ 335/1–00–00; reservations in the U.S., 800/648–4097. 60 units, suites, casitas, and private homes. 2 restaurants, 2 bars, pool, spa, hot tub, paddle tennis, polo fields, horseback riding, tennis courts. AE, MC, V.*

$$$ **Costa Azul Adventure Resort.** This environment-friendly resort, some 30 miles north of Puerto Vallarta, was designed by a group of southern California surfers, so you know water sports are going to be big here. But horseback riding and mountain biking through an ecological preserve are also featured. Rooms in this intimate, friendly place are simply but attractively decorated, and the adventure package, including all meals and activities, is very reasonably priced. ▣ *San Francisco, Nayarit; for reservations contact DFW Tours, ☎ 800/527– 2589, ext. 171. 28 units. Restaurant, bar, boating, snorkeling, surfing, horseback riding. MC, V.*

$$ **El Tecuán.** Small and economical, this beachfront hotel has all the facilities of larger resorts, including its own lagoon and two tennis courts. ▣ *Km. 33.5 Carretera Barra de Navidad–Puerto Vallarta, ☎ 335/ 1–50–18. 40 rooms. Restaurant, bar, pool, beach, tennis courts. AE, MC, V.*

Puerto Vallarta Essentials

Arriving and Departing

BY PLANE

Airport and Airlines. Puerto Vallarta's **Gustavo Díaz Ordáz International Airport** is 6½ kilometers (4 miles) north of town, not far from the major resorts. The Mexican airlines have daily flights from Mexico City and Guadalajara; flights from Los Cabos Thursday and Saturday; and from Mazatlán on Monday, Friday, and Sunday. **Mexicana** (☎ 800/531– 7921) has service from Chicago, Los Angeles, San Francisco, San Antonio, and Denver; **Aeromexico** (☎ 800/237–6639) from Los Angeles. Several American carriers also serve Puerto Vallarta, including **Alaska Airlines** (☎ 800/426–0333), **American** (☎ 800/433–7300), **Continental** (☎ 800/821–2100), and **Delta** (☎ 800/221–1212).

Between the Airport and Hotels. Volkswagen vans provide economical transportation from the airport to hotels, and all the car-rental agencies have desks in the airport.

BY CAR

Puerto Vallarta is about 1,900 kilometers (1,200 miles) from Nogales, Arizona, at the United States–Mexico border, 354 kilometers (220 miles) from Guadalajara, and 167 kilometers (104 miles) from Tepic. Driving to Puerto Vallarta is not difficult, but driving in the city can be horrid. From December through April—peak tourist season—traffic clogs the small cobblestoned streets; during the rainy season from July through October, the streets become flooded and the hills are muddy and slippery.

BY TRAIN

Trains run daily from Mexicali, Nogales, and Guadalajara to Tepic; from Tepic, it is a three-hour bus ride to Puerto Vallarta. The train is unreliable, crowded, and slow, and is best left to those with plenty of time and patience.

BY BUS

There is no central bus station in Puerto Vallarta, but most of the carriers are located on Avenida Insurgentes between the Río Cuale and Calle Serdán: **Transportes del Pacífico** (Av. Insurgentes 100, ☎ 329/2–10–15) and **Elite** (Basilio Badillo 11, ☎ 322/3–11–17), which incorporates three lines: Estrella Blanca, Tres Estrellas de Oro, and Norte de Sonora. Elite offers excellent first-class service (reclining seats, air-conditioning, refreshment service, functioning bathroom) to Guadalajara, Aguascalientes, and Mexico City.

BY SHIP

Several cruise lines, including Carnival, Bermuda Star, Princess, Royal Caribbean, Holland-America, Norwegian, and Seaborn, sail to Puerto Vallarta from Los Angeles during the winter months.

Getting Around

BY BUS

City buses and *combis* (Volkswagen vans) serve downtown, the northern hotel zone, and the southern beaches. Bus stops—marked by a blue-and-white sign with a drawing of a bus—are located every two or three blocks along the highway (Carretera Aeropuerto) and in town. To take a combi to Mismaloya or other points south, go to the Combi Terminal on Calle Piño Suárez or the bus stop at Plaza Lázaro Cárdenas just south of Los Arcos Hotel.

BY TAXI

Many hotels post fares to common destinations; be sure to agree on a fare before the cab takes off. The ride from the northside hotels to downtown costs about $4.50, plus $1.10 to cross the bridge.

BY RENTAL CAR

There are several agencies in Puerto Vallarta that rent Jeeps, open-air Volkswagen Beetles, and automatic-transmission sedans. During the high season, rentals start at $60 per day, including insurance and mileage; off-season, they start at $45 per day. Be certain to ask about special promotions, even during the high season. All the car-rental agencies below have desks at the airport; some have offices along the highway, but they are spread out, so compare prices at the airport or call from your hotel. Agencies to contact include **Avis** (Carretera Aeropuerto Km 2.5, ☎ 322/1–11–12), **Budget** (Carretera Aeropuerto Km 5, ☎ 322/1–18–88), **Hertz** (Paseo de las Palmas 1602, ☎ 322/2–00–24), **National** (Carretera Aeropuerto Km 1.5, ☎ 322/2–11–07), and **Dollar** (Paseo de las Palmas 1728, ☎ 322/3–13–54).

Guided Tours

The three-hour city tour is a good way to get the lay of the land, from Gringo Gulch and the Río Cuale to Mismaloya Beach. Almost everyone goes on at least one daytime or sunset cruise around the bay, sighting pretty isolated coves and barren beaches from the deck of a sailboat or yacht. A full-day excursion to Yelapa or Las Animas, seaside communities that can be reached only by boat, gives you a feeling of what life is like in a secluded tropical paradise.

Tropical tours visit mango and banana plantations in Nayarit and include stops in Nayarit's capital, Tepic, and the small seaside town of San Blas. Other trips head south to Boca de Tomatlán, the mouth of the river that flows from the mountains into the sea. Horseback riding is available at ranches in the mountains—three hours are spent riding, and time is taken for lunch and a swim in a mountain stream or lake.

Tours may be arranged through your hotel or one of the many tour operators with offices at hotels and in town. Reliable tour operators include **American Express** (Morelos 660, ☎ 322/3–29–55) and **Intermar Vallarta** (Paseo de la Marina s/n, Condominio via Golf, ☎ 329/1–07–34). City tours run about $18; tours to Yelapa also run about $18; and tours to Las Animas and Quimixto cost from $36 to $41. It's worth the few extra dollars to go on a private tour (small groups) in a Volkswagen van rather than with a large group on a tour bus.

Important Addresses and Numbers

CONSULATES
U.S. Consul (Parian del Puente 12A, ☎ 322/2–00–69, ☉ Weekdays 9–1); **Canadian Consul** (Av. Hidalgo 226, ☎ 322/2–53–98; ☉ Weekdays 10–2).

EMERGENCIES
Police (City Hall on Av. Juárez, ☎ 322/2–01–23), **Red Cross** (Río de la Plata and Río Balsas, ☎ 322/2–15–33), **Hospital** (Basilio Badillo 365, ☎ 322/2–35–72).

VISITOR INFORMATION
The **State Tourism Office**, sadly, is no longer one of the best in Mexico. *City Hall on Av. Juárez, by the zócalo,* ☎ 322/2–02–42. ☉ *Weekdays 9–9, Sat. 9–1.*

MANZANILLO

Nature is undoubtedly Manzanillo's best attraction. Its twin *bahías* (bays), Manzanillo and Santiago, where crystal blue waters lap white-sand shores, have caught outsiders' eyes since Cortés conquered Mexico. In the July–September rainy season, rivers and lagoons swell, forming waterfalls and ponds. White herons and pink flamingos flock to the fertile waters, and white butterflies flutter above the flowers in the chamomile fields (*manzanillo* is Spanish for chamomile).

Santiago Peninsula, which divides Bahía Santiago and Bahía Manzanillo, is the site of Las Hadas (The Fairies) resort. From the water or points above the beach, the resort seems a mirage, a sea of white domes and peaks that radiate in the midday heat. When Bolivian tin magnate Antenor Patiño conceived of this white palace in the early 1960s, Manzanillo was easier to reach by sea than land, a rugged, primitive port that attracted the hardy who didn't mind creating their own tropical paradise. In 1974, when Señor Patiño's retreat was complete, the international social set began to visit Manzanillo, thus putting the city in magazines and on television screens around the world. Even then, Manzanillo remained essentially a port city with only a few tourist attractions.

Manzanillo is still relatively undeveloped, a sleeper compared with other Pacific coast resorts. Investors have plenty of land to divvy up for their financially rewarding havens, and existing resorts are spread out. Many shops and hotel desks close for afternoon siesta, and on Sundays most businesses are shut (including restaurants) and everyone heads for the beach.

Exploring

A vacation in Manzanillo is not spent shopping and sightseeing. You stay put, relax on the beach, and maybe take a few hours' break from the sun and sand to survey the local scene casually.

The **Santiago** area is tourist-oriented, with clusters of shops and restaurants by the beach. Work hasn't yet started on the marina project, announced in late 1992, which calls for public and private developers to invest $50 million to create a downtown pier complex that will have a cruise-ship dock, a shopping center, a heliport, and gardens. The next area to the east, **Salahua,** is a settlement with homes, a baseball field, and restaurants. **Las Brisas** beach is farther south, past the traffic circle and Avenida Morelos, the road to town. Some of the more reasonably priced hotels are located here.

Downtown is busy and jam-packed. At the beginning of the harbor, Route 200 jogs around downtown and intersects with Highway 110 to Colima. Avenida Morelos leads past the shipyards and into town. Just before you reach the port, stop at **Laguna de San Pedrito,** where graceful white herons and vivid pink flamingos assemble at sunset. The **zócalo,** or **Jardín de Obregón,** is right on the main road by the waterfront. It's a small square, quite lively in the evening.

Shopping

Most of the hotels offer a small selection of folk art and beachwear, but, in general, shops selling items that might interest tourists don't fare well in Manzanillo, probably because most visitors are more interested in activities involving the sun and sea. There are some fairly uninteresting shops around Manzanillo's main square, hardly worth the trip downtown. About the best bet for handcrafted folk art is **Centro Artesenal Las Primaveras** (Juárez 40 in Santiago, ☎ 333/3–16–99). Most of the shops are closed from 2 to 4; many are open Sunday from 10 to 2.

Sports

Fishing
Manzanillo claims to be the sailfishing capital of the world; the season runs from mid-October through March, with an international sailfish tournament held every November. Blue marlin and dorado are also abundant. Sportfishing charters are available at the major hotels and tour agencies.

Golf
La Mantarraya (☎ 333/4–00–00), the 18-hole golf course at Las Hadas, designed by Roy Dye, has been rated among the world's 100 best courses by *Golf Digest*. **Club Santiago** (☎ 333/5–04–10) has a nine-hole course designed by Larry Hughes.

Tennis
Most of the resort hotels have tennis courts.

Water Sports
The rocky points off Manzanillo's peninsulas and coves make good spots for snorkeling and scuba diving. Small boats called *pangas* can be rented on some beaches so you can reach the better spots.

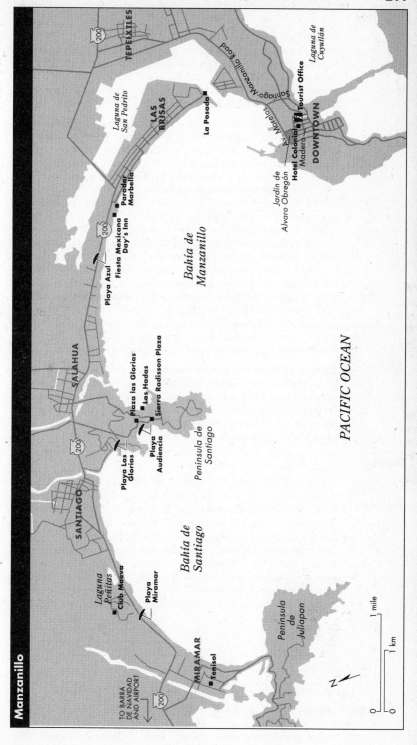

Manzanillo

TEPEIXTLES

Laguna de San Pedrito

LAS BRISAS

La Posada

Santiago-Manzanillo Road

AV. Morelos

Laguna de Cuyutlán

Hotel Colonial Tourist Office
Madera
Jardín de Alvaro Obregón
DOWNTOWN

Parador Marbella

Fiesta Mexicana
Day's Inn

Playa Azul

Bahía de Manzanillo

SALAHUA

Plaza las Glorias
Las Hadas
Sierra Radisson Plaza
Playa Las Glorias
Playa Audiencia

Península de Santiago

PACIFIC OCEAN

SANTIAGO

Bahía de Santiago

Laguna Peñitas
Club Maeva
Playa Miramar

MIRAMAR
Tenisol

Península de Juliapan

TO BARRA DE NAVIDAD AND AIRPORT

1 mile
1 km

Beaches

In Manzanillo, every day is a beach day, and Sundays are downright festive, with half the town gathered to play onshore. Windsurfing has become quite popular, and Jet Skis roar about, but there isn't much in the way of parasailing. The sand is a mix of black, white, and brown, with the southernmost beaches the blackest. Most beaches post warning flags if the conditions are dangerous or jellyfish have been sighted.

Playa Miramar, at the north end of Santiago Bay, is populated by windsurfers and boogie-boarders. The beach in front of Club Santiago, once the favored hangout for locals, is now accessible only by walking north along the beach from the highway or by passing the guards at the club gates. The main stretch of beach is across the highway from Club Maeva. **Playa Audiencia,** in a cove along the north side of Santiago Peninsula, is a small beach between two rock outcroppings—it's a good spot for snorkeling. (The local Indians supposedly granted Cortés an audience on the beach—thus the name.) The Sierra Radisson Plaza hotel is located in the middle of the beach, making public access limited. **Playa Azul,** also called Playa Santiago, is a long strand that runs from Santiago along Manzanillo Bay to Playa Las Brisas. The surf gets rough along the north end; swimming is better toward Las Brisas. South of town is **Playa Cuyutlán,** a black-sand beach on the open sea. Legend has it that the great *ola verde* (green wave) rises some 30 feet each spring during the full moon. In reality, the surf is high in spring but not quite as big as the original ola verde, which took the tiny town of Cuyutlán by surprise in 1959.

Barra de Navidad and **San Patricio Melaque,** to the north, have popular beaches that are good for surfing in the fall months. Palapa restaurants along the beach serve fresh fish. In Barra there are panga trips to a small island just offshore, where unbroken seashells are abundant. When the tide is low, it is possible to walk along the beach from Barra to Melaque, a distance of about 6 kilometers (almost 4 miles).

Dining

Manzanillo has some good restaurants, several with scenic views of the jungle and water that compensate for their lack of culinary excitement. As more shops appear along the Santiago–Manzanillo Road, so do restaurants that are geared toward tourists. Dress is usually casual but not sloppy (no bathing suits or bare feet), even in the more expensive restaurants, although in L'Récif and Legazpi women and men usually wear chic resortwear. Reservations are almost never necessary, but we have indicated those places that do accept them. Be aware that some restaurants, particularly in the hotels, add a 10%–15% service charge to your tab, as well as 10% tax.

CATEGORY	COST*
$$$$	over $35
$$$	$25–$35
$$	$15–$25
$	under $15

*per person, excluding drinks, service, and sales tax (10%)

$$$$ ★ Legazpi. Manzanillo's only gourmet restaurant is at Las Hadas, and it is beautiful. The service is white-gloved perfection, but friendly rather than pretentious, and the food is decidedly elegant. The emphasis is on caviar and smoked salmon, consommés and bisques, seafood and steaks with French sauces, and wonderful pastries. ✕

Las Hadas, ☎ *333/4–00–00. Reservations accepted. AE, DC, MC, V. Closed Wed., Fri., and Sun. No lunch.*

$$$ **El Vaquero.** The setting is reminiscent of a cowboys' saloon, and the emphasis is on beef, marinated and seasoned as *carne asada* or grilled as good old American steaks. Some steaks are served and priced by weight to satisfy the healthiest appetite. ✕ *Crucero Las Brisas,* ☎ *333/3–16–54. Reservations advised. MC, V.*

$$$ **L'Récif.** Situated in a fantastic cliff-top setting far from town, L'Récif
★ has a breathtaking view and a swimming pool—you can go for lunch, spend the afternoon sunning and swimming, then stay for dinner. The restaurant's owner is French, and the menu includes pâté with Armagnac, quail with muscat, and mango mousse. The Sunday brunch (served only in winter) is a must. ✕ *Off the Santiago–Manzanillo Rd., north of Santiago, at the sign for Vida del Mar,* ☎ *333/ 5–06–80. Reservations accepted. AE, MC, V.*

$$ **Manolo's.** The lobster and shrimp are reasonably priced, and the Mexican dishes are tasty at this longtime favorite for great seafood dinners and steaks. ✕ *Santiago–Manzanillo Rd.,* ☎ *333/3–21–40. Reservations accepted. AE, MC, V. Closed Sun. No lunch.*

$$ **Osteria Bugatti.** The most popular dinner spot near downtown, Bugatti's has a loyal following of locals and tourists who crave seafood prepared in the Italian manner and oysters Rockefeller. ✕ *Santiago–Manzanillo Rd., near Las Brisas,* ☎ *333/3–29–99. Reservations advised. DC, MC, V. Closed Sun. No lunch.*

$$ **Willy's.** Some people have been known to dine at Willy's every night of
★ their stay in Manzanillo. The food is that good, and the owner, Jean François, is that personable and gracious. Michelle, Jean's wife, prepares delicious onion soup, a sublime bordelaise sauce, and decadent desserts. A guitarist enlivens the informal beachfront setting of wooden chairs and tables under a wooden roof. ✕ *Crucero Las Brisas,* ☎ *333/ 3–17–94. Reservations advised. MC, V. No lunch.*

$ **Juanito's.** This gringo hangout is owned by an American who married a local girl and settled in Manzanillo. It specializes in great burgers and fries, American breakfasts, barbecued ribs, and fried chicken. ✕ *Blvd. Costero M. de la Madrid 14,* ☎ *333/3–13–88. No reservations. AE, MC, V.*

$ **La Posada.** Breakfast here is an integral part of any Manzanillo experience. Pancakes, French toast, fried eggs, and bacon are made to order and served in the large *sala* (living room) facing the sea. The mood is casual. Sandwiches and drinks are served in the afternoon, but breakfast is your best bet. ✕ *La Posada, Las Brisas,* ☎ *333/ 3–18–99. No reservations. MC, V.*

$ **Pancho's.** A popular spot packed with seashells, caged parrots, and beer-drinking merrymakers, it serves fresh fish that pulls people in and keeps them coming back. ✕ *Av. Miguel López de Legazpi, No. 53,* ☎ *333/7–01–76. Reservations accepted. MC, V.*

Lodging

Lodging in Manzanillo was at one time a bargain, but no more. The hotels you might once have booked for $10 or so a night now cost $25 or more, and budget travelers usually either stay in downtown's few remaining hotels or head to the towns of Barra de Navidad and Melaque. As with the rest of the Pacific Coast, Manzanillo is undergoing a building boom. The resorts are spread out along the Santiago–Manzanillo Road. The postal code for Manzanillo is 28200.

CATEGORY	COST*
$$$$	over $160
$$$	$90–$160
$$	$40–$90
$	under $40

All prices are for a standard double room, excluding 10% tax.

$$$$ **Club Maeva.** Families love the playgrounds and children's pools, small theater, tennis courts, and disco at this all-inclusive resort. The blue-and-white bungalows (with kitchenettes) are spread over a high hillside across the highway from the beach; a bridge crosses over the road to the water. ⊞ *Santiago–Manzanillo Rd., at Playa Miramar,* ☎ *333/5-05-93 or 800/GO-MAEVA. 514 rooms with bath. 4 restaurants, 2 pools, beach, water slide (Super Maeva Splash), 12 tennis courts, disco. AE, MC, V.*

$$$$ **Las Hadas.** Though its creator, Antenor Patiño, is long gone, Las Hadas is still something to marvel at. A member of the Leading Hotels of the World, Las Hadas was for many years Manzanillo's premier resort, the kind of place where vacationers were content to check in and stay put. The setting and grounds are still beautiful, but some of the rooms and furnishings and—even more important—the once impeccable service have been severely neglected lately. ⊞ *Santiago Peninsula, off the Santiago–Manzanillo Rd.,* ☎ *333/4-00-00 or 800/228-3000. 220 rooms with bath, 41 suites. 4 restaurants, 5 bars, pools, hair salon, massage, beach, golf course, 10 tennis courts. AE, DC, MC, V.*

$$$$ **Sierra Radisson Plaza.** Manzanillo's newest hotel is a 19-story giant
★ with white stucco walls and a red tile roof. Most of the 350 inviting rooms and suites have private balconies and a view of the bay. A large free-form pool, four tennis courts, and several bars and restaurants round out the property. Light wood and pastel colors dominate the pleasant decor. ⊞ *Avenida de la Audiencia 1,* ☎ *333/3-20-00 or 800/333-3333. 350 rooms and suites. 3 restaurants, 4 bars, pool, beach, 4 tennis courts. AE, DC, MC, V.*

$$$ **Fiesta Mexicana Days Inn.** This bright white five-story hotel stands out
★ on the highway. It has a lovely central courtyard with a large swimming pool. The rooms have pretty wood-frame windows and comfortable bentwood lounges; those on the ocean side are the most quiet. ⊞ *Santiago–Manzanillo Rd., in Playa Azul,* ☎ *333/3-21-80 or 800/633-1414. 186 rooms with bath. Restaurant, bar, piano bar, disco, travel services. AE, MC, V.*

$$$ **Plaza Las Glorias.** Situated in the center of the Santiago Peninsula,
★ Las Glorias has a lovely setting above the golf course. Rooms are spacious and comfortable, with pale green and blue couches and chairs, firm mattresses, and glass-and-wood tables and dining chairs. ⊞ *Av. Tesoro off the Las Hadas Rd.,* ☎ *333/3-04-40; reservations in the U.S., 800/342-AMIGO. 85 1-bedroom villas. Restaurant, bar, pool, beach, golf privileges, tennis courts. AE, MC, V.*

$$ **La Posada.** This "passionate pink" hotel has been a hangout for North
★ Americans since 1957. With only 24 rooms, most guests get to know each other well, mingling in the *sala,* a large living/dining room with a communal coffee pot. Rooms are comfortable and simple; old iron keys work the antique locks. Tipping of individual employees is discouraged; the proprietor suggests that you leave a sum equal to 10% of your final tab in the tip box by the coffee urn. The room rate includes a complete breakfast. ⊞ *Las Brisas,* ☎ *333/3-18-99. 24 rooms with bath. Bar, snack bar, pool, beach. MC, V.*

$$ **Parador Marbella.** This hotel is one of the few reasonably priced places on the beach. The best rooms are on the ocean; each has a tiny balcony under the palms. The accommodations are now color-coordinated and offer air-conditioning and TV. ⊡ *Santiago–Manzanillo Rd., Km 9.5,* ☎ *333/3–11–03. 94 rooms with bath. Restaurant, bar, pool. MC, V.*

$$ **Tenisol.** This condominium complex features villas, apartments, and studios in a neighborhood setting. The view toward Santiago Peninsula and Manzanillo is lovely at night, and the beach, one of the most popular, is active all day. ⊡ *Playa Miramar,* ☎ *333/5–04–13 or 303/841–7099. 60 rooms with bath. Restaurant, bar, beach, 9-hole golf course. AE, MC, V.*

$ **Hotel Colonial.** This was once the grandest hotel in Manzanillo. Although the Colonial has gone downhill since its heyday, it's still the best place to stay in downtown, a block away from the noise of the plaza. Only some of the units have air-conditioning. ⊡ *Av. México 100,* ☎ *333/2–10–80. 38 rooms with bath. Restaurant, bar. MC, V.*

Nightlife

During the high season, there is nightlife at two discos on the Santiago–Manzanillo Road—**Oui** (☎ 333/3–23–33) and **Enjoy** (☎ 333/3–28–39)—and at **Boom Boom** (☎ 333/3–21–80) at the Fiesta Mexicana. The **Legazpi** (☎ 333/4–00–00) piano bar at Las Hadas is also a good spot for a nightcap. At **Bugatti's** (☎ 333/3–29–29) there's a piano bar and dancing that goes on until the wee hours. **VOG** (☎ 333/3–18–75) is another popular place to boogie.

Manzanillo Essentials

Arriving and Departing

BY PLANE

Airport and Airlines. Manzanillo's **Aeropuerto Internacional Playa de Oro** is 32 kilometers (20 miles) north of town, on the way to Barra de Navidad. **Aeromexico** (☎ 800/237–6639) and **Mexicana** (☎ 800/531–7921) offer service from Los Angeles to Manzanillo, with connections in Tijuana and Guadalajara, respectively. The majority of both airlines' flights to Manzanillo leave from Mexico City.

From the Airport. Volkswagen vans transport passengers from the airport to the major resorts; these shuttle services are less expensive than taxis.

BY CAR

The trip south from the Arizona border to Manzanillo is about 2,419 kilometers (1,500 miles); from Guadalajara, it is 332 kilometers (200 miles); from Puerto Vallarta, 242 kilometers (150 miles). Highway 200 runs along the coast from Tepic, Nayarit, to Manzanillo. Hazardous conditions and unexpected, drastic detours are common, especially during the rainy season.

BY TRAIN

Second-class trains run to Manzanillo from Guadalajara—an adventure for some, but for most it is a tedious trip, lasting a minimum of eight hours and ending at the ship and freight yards outside town.

BY BUS

Tres Estrellas de Oro (☎ 333/2–01–35) travels to Manzanillo from Tijuana, from Mexico City and Guadalajara, and from the coastal towns. Many of the area's resorts are located 1 to 2 kilometers (½ to 1 mile) from the bus stop on the highway.

Getting Around

BY CAR

Cars are almost essential for exploring the area on your own. The highway from Santiago to Manzanillo is commonly called Carretera Santiago–Manzanillo, Manzanillo–Aeropuerto, Salahua–Santiago, or any number of things depending on the closest landmark. It's called the Santiago–Manzanillo Road throughout this chapter to lessen confusion. Route 200 runs north along the coast past Manzanillo and Santiago bays to Barra de Navidad and Melaque; Route 110 goes east to Colima.

Avenida Morelos, the main drag in town, runs from Manzanillo Bay past the port and shipyards to the plaza. If you plan to explore the downtown, park along the waterfront across from the plaza and walk—all the shops and hotels are within a few blocks. **Avis** (☎ 333/3–01–90), **Budget** (☎ 333/3–14–45), and **National** (☎ 333/3–06–11) have offices in the airport, and most big hotels have at least one company represented. Rates vary depending on where you rent your car, but rentals are generally costly ($50–$90 per day, including insurance). Most offer 300 kilometers (186 miles) free, which should give you enough roaming for one day.

Guided Tours

The best way to see Manzanillo is with a tour guide. Operators will arrange special-interest or private tours as well as sportfishing trips, sunset cruises, and horseback outings. Most agencies have offices along the highway that encircle Santiago and Manzanillo bays, and most hotels offer at least one agency's services. Agencies include **Bahías Gemelas Agencia de Viajes** (Sierra Radisson Plaza hotel, ☎ 333/3–20–00; Blvd. Costero M. de la Madrid 2556, ☎ 333/3–21–00) and **Aeroviajes Manzanillo** (Plaza Las Glorias hotel, ☎ 333/3–04–40; Av. México 69, ☎ 333/2–25–65).

Important Addresses and Numbers

Street addresses are not often used in Manzanillo; instead, locations are designated by neighborhood—the Las Brisas area, Santiago Peninsula (also known as the Las Hadas Rd.), and so on. Maps with actual street names are rare (or inaccurate).

EMERGENCIES

Police (☎ 333/2–10–04), **Hospital** (☎ 333/2–00–29).

VISITOR INFORMATION

Information on Manzanillo is scanty at best and rarely consistent. The **State Tourism Office** (Blvd. Costero Miguel de la Madrid Km 9.5, ☎ 333/3–22–77) is supposed to be open weekdays 9–3 and weekends 10–1, but call first to be sure. More accurate information is available from tour operators and hotels.

7 Guadalajara

The colonial architecture that dates to Guadalajara's heyday as a silver lode for the Spanish is among the lures of Mexico's second-largest city; Guadalajara also introduced the world to mariachis and tequila. Some of the best arts and crafts in the country can be found at Tlaquepaque, on the outskirts of town, and Tonalá, about 10 minutes away.

Updated by
Chris
Humphrey

TRADITIONS ARE preserved and customs perpetuated in Guadalajara; it's a place where the siesta is an institution and the fiesta an art form. The city is the birthplace of *el jarabe tapatío* (the Mexican hat dance), *charreadas* (rodeos), mariachis, and tequila.

Mexico's second-largest city, Guadalajara is engaged in a struggle to retain its provincial ambience and colonial charm as its population approaches 6 million. Emigrés from Mexico City after the devastating 1985 earthquake and staggering numbers of the rural poor seeking employment have created a population explosion that strains the capacity of public services and the city's often outdated infrastructure. Visitors to the city can enjoy the tree-lined boulevards, parks, plazas, and stately Churrigueresque architecture, but recent years have brought traffic jams and occasional heavy pollution, coming from the industrial zone outside of the city, to the downtown area.

Guadalajara has always been one of the most socially traditional and politically conservative cities in Mexico. It has also been the seat of Christian fundamentalism and was one of the strategic areas of the *Cristeros,* a movement of right-wing Catholic zealots in western Mexico in the 1920s. *Tapatíos,* as the city's residents are called (the name comes from *tlapatíotl,* three units or purses of cacao or tortillas used as currency by the Indians of the state of Jalisco), even seem to take a certain amount of pride in their straight and narrow outlook. The International Gay and Lesbian Association (ILGA) wanted to hold its 1991 annual conference here, but such a public outcry ensued—protests ranging from mass marches to death-threatening graffiti to indignant newspaper editorials—that the municipal and state government refused permission. At the last minute, the convention found a home in Acapulco.

Still, Tapatíos are historically accustomed to challenge and change. Within 10 years of its founding in 1532, the location of the city changed three times. In 1542 the City Council followed the advice of Doña Beatriz Hernández to build the city in the center of the Atemajac Valley, where it could expand. Thus Guadalajara was placed on a mile-high plain of the Sierra Madre, bounded on three sides by rugged cliffs and on the fourth by the spectacular Barranca de Oblatos (Oblatos Canyon). A near-perfect semitropical climate and proximity to the Pacific Ocean (240 kilometers, or 150 miles, away) ensure warm, sunny days with just a hint of humidity and cool, clear nights.

Geographically remote from the rest of the republic during the nearly 300 years of Spanish rule, the city cultivated and maintained a political and cultural autonomy. By the end of the 16th century, tons of silver were flowing into Guadalajara from area mines, creating the first millionaires of what was then known as New Galicia. Under orders from Spain, much of the wealth was lavished on magnificent churches, residences, and monuments. Many of these reminders of the golden era still stand in a series of contiguous plazas in downtown Guadalajara. The imposing 16th-century cathedral is the symbol of the city and an ideal starting point for a leisurely day or two of exploration.

The city also has numerous modern attractions and activities, including a zoo, a planetarium, and the immense Parque Agua Azul, which has carnival rides, a minitrain, swimming pool, and Sunday concerts. There are exhibitions of contemporary art at the Instituto Cultural Cabañas and in private galleries throughout the city, and tours of

Museo Orozco, the former home and studio of Guadalajara's most famous muralist, José Clemente Orozco.

Guadalajara is also a great place for shopping. The Mercado Libertad, Latin America's largest enclosed market, and El Baratillo, the world's largest flea market, offer a seemingly endless variety of merchandise and the opportunity to bargain with vendors. The Plaza del Sol, Latin America's biggest shopping mall, and Calle Esteban Alatorre, encompassing eight city blocks with more than 60 shoe stores, sell products you could buy at home, but usually with much lower price tags.

The suburbs of San Pedro Tlaquepaque (Tla-kay-*pah*-kay) and Tonalá (Toe-na-*la*) produce some of Mexico's finest and most popular traditional crafts and folk art, including intricate blown-glass miniatures, jewelry, silver and copperware, leather and handcarved wood furniture, and handwoven clothing. In Tlaquepaque, located on the southeastern fringe of Guadalajara, more than 300 shops line pedestrian malls and plazas. This charming town, which gained international acclaim for its ceramics, is also the birthplace of mariachi music.

Tonalá is 8 kilometers (5 miles) east of and centuries removed from its commercial neighbor. One of Mexico's oldest pueblos, Tonalá is a quiet village with dusty, cobblestoned streets and adobe houses. Only in the past few years have craftspeople—primarily ceramicists—welcomed tourists into their homes and workshops.

Perhaps it is the Mexican arts and culture, perhaps the favorable exchange rate, perhaps the springlike climate; whatever the reason, more than 25,000 U.S. and Canadian citizens have retired in the Guadalajara area. The majority reside along the shores of Lake Chapala, Mexico's largest inland body of water. In the towns of Chapala (45 kilometers, or 28 miles, south of Guadalajara) and nearby Ajijic (Ah-he-*heek*), residents enjoy most of the amenities and services they were accustomed to north of the border.

EXPLORING

Beginning around 1960, 20th-century architecture started to threaten the historical integrity of this provincial state capital. In the early 1980s, city fathers declared a 30-square-block area in the heart of the city a cultural sanctuary. The 16th-century buildings here are connected by a series of large Spanish-style plazas where today's inhabitants enjoy life: Young children chase gaily colored balloons, young lovers cuddle on tree-shaded park benches, and grandparents stroll hand in hand past vendors and marble fountains. At nearby Mariachi Plaza the nostalgic songs and music of costumed troubadors can be heard. The downtown walking tour (Tour 1) visits the churches, monuments, and museums of colonial Guadalajara.

The second tour focuses on the traditional arts and crafts of Tlaquepaque and Tonalá, two towns that are a 20-minute drive from downtown Guadalajara. The third tour covers the lakeside towns of Chapala and Ajijic, 45 kilometers (28 miles) south of Guadalajara. This scenic area is a weekend retreat for wealthy Tapatíos and a retirement haven for *norte-americanos*.

Tour 1: Colonial Guadalajara

Numbers in the margin correspond to points of interest on the Downtown Guadalajara map.

220

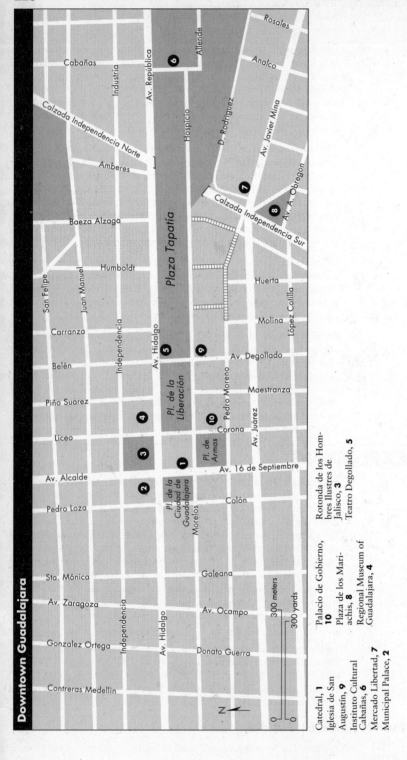

Downtown Guadalajara

Catedral, **1**
Iglesia de San
Augustín, **9**
Instituto Cultural
Cabañas, **6**
Mercado Libertad, **7**
Municipal Palace, **2**

Palacio de Gobierno,
10
Plaza de los Mari-
achis, **8**
Regional Museum of
Guadalajara, **4**

Rotonda de los Hom-
bres Ilustres de
Jalisco, **3**
Teatro Degollado, **5**

★ ❶ The focal point of downtown is the **catedral,** consecrated in 1618. It is an intriguing mélange of architectural styles, the result of design and structural modifications during the 60 years of construction. Its emblematic twin towers replaced the original, much shorter ones, which were toppled in the devastating earthquake of 1818. The interior contains fine examples of 16th- to 18th-century Spanish art and decor. Ten of the silver-and-gilt altars were gifts of King Fernando VII (in appreciation of Guadalajara's financial support of Spain during the Napoleonic Wars); the 11th, of sculpted white marble, was carved in Italy in 1863. The altar and statue dedicated to Our Lady of the Rose are exquisite. The statue, carved from a single piece of balsa wood, was a gift from King Charles V in the 16th century. The image and remains of Saint Innocence, brought here from the catacombs of Rome, are on the left side of the main altar. On the walls of the cathedral hang some of the world's most beautiful *retablos* (altarpieces); above the sacristy is the priceless 17th-century painting of Bartolomé Esteban Murillo, *The Assumption of the Virgin.* The sign near the front door requests that visitors be appropriately attired. *Av. Alcalde between Av. Hidalgo and Calle Morelos.* ⊘ *Daily 7 AM–9 PM.*

The main entrance to the cathedral overlooks the **Plaza de la Ciudad de Guadalajara,** a spacious square that is ideal for serious people-watching, since Tapatíos use it as a shortcut. Walk across Avenida Hidalgo from the north side of the plaza (to your left as you face the

❷ cathedral) to the **Municipal Palace** (City Hall). Though this building has a colonial facade, it was not built until 1952. You may wish to stop in to see the mural by Gabriel Flores—a prominent and prolific Tapatío—on the center stairwell (you may *have* to visit the palace to pay a 50¢ fine to retrieve your front license plate—traffic police remove them from illegally parked cars).

Directly across Avenida Alcalde, on the north side of the cathedral, is

❸ the **Rotonda de los Hombres Ilustres de Jalisco** (Monument to the Illustrious Men of Jalisco). A tree-shaded rotunda encircled by 17 Doric columns, it is actually a mausoleum containing the remains of 11 of Jalisco's favorite sons. Surrounding the monument are brass sculptures representing those who are buried inside.

From the east side of the monument, walk across Calle Liceo to the

★ ❹ **Regional Museum of Guadalajara** (also known as the State Museum). Constructed at the end of the 17th century, this distinguished Baroque and colonial building served as a seminary until 1918. Since then, it has housed the art, archaeology, and history museum. The first-floor galleries, which surround a courtyard of Roman arches and tropical gardens, contain artifacts and memorabilia that trace the history of western Mexico from prehistoric times through the Spanish conquest. In the main gallery are the royal carriages of Emperor Maximilian and President Juárez. On the second floor is an impressive collection of works by European and Mexican artists, including Bartolomé Esteban Murillo and Diego Rivera. *Av. Hidalgo between Calle Liceo and Pino Suárez,* ☎ *3/613–2670.* ☛ *About $4.50; free on Sun.* ⊘ *Tues.–Sat. 9–3, Sun. 10–3.*

Occupying the next block to the left on Avenida Hidalgo is the **Palacio de Legisladores** (Legislative Palace). Over the past 300 years this building has been a customs house, tobacco warehouse, and *posada* (inn). On the next block, across Calle Belén, is the **Palacio de Justicia** (Hall of Justice), the state courthouse. This colonial building was originally part of the city's first convent.

★ ❺   Directly across Avenida Hidalgo is the famous **Teatro Degollado,** Guadalajara's opera house. Inaugurated in 1866, the magnificent structure was modeled after Milan's La Scala. Above the Corinthian columns gracing the entranceway is a relief depicting Apollo and the seven Muses. Inside, red and gold balconies ascend to a multitiered dome adorned with Gerardo Suárez's depiction of Dante's *Divine Comedy.* The theater is the permanent home for the Guadalajara Philharmonic and the Ballet Folklórico. ☎ *3/614–4773.* ☉ *During performances* (see *The Arts and Nightlife,* below, *for information) and 4–6 when there are no afternoon performances.*

Walk around to the rear to **Founders Square.** According to tradition, this is the spot on which the city was founded; the sculpted frieze of the theater's rear wall depicts the ceremony with 60 of the founding fathers.

You are now at the head of the **Plaza Tapatía,** a five-block-long pedestrian mall lined with stores and galleries and filled with trees, fountains, and whimsical sculptures.

TIME OUT   An outlet of the city's most popular ice-cream franchise, **Helados Bing** is located two blocks east of the Teatro Degollado on the north side of the plaza, just east of the Children's Fountain. For natives, a stop at Helados Bing is a custom (if not an obsession); for tourists, it is a welcome respite from an afternoon of sightseeing. Choose from 30 flavors of pasteurized ice cream and find a shaded bench where you can take in the activity.

★ ❻   On the east end of the plaza is the **Instituto Cultural Cabañas,** the city's cultural center. Bishop Juan Cruz Ruíz Cabañas founded an orphanage in this building in 1810; it was home for 400 orphans and indigent children until the 1970s. The rooms, which surround 23 flower-filled patios, contain permanent and revolving art exhibits. The central dome of the main chapel displays a series of murals painted by José Clemente Orozco in 1938–39. *The Man of Fire,* which depicts a man enveloped in flames who is ascending toward infinity and yet not consumed by the fire, represents the spirit of mankind. It is generally considered to be his finest work. There is a permanent exhibit of Orozco's paintings, cartoons, and drawings in Room 189. Ask the attendant at the front desk for an English-speaking guide. *Calle Cabañas 8 at the Plaza Tapatía,* ☎ *3/617– 4322 or 3/617–4440.* ☞ *About $2.50.* ☉ *Tues.–Sat. 10–6, Sun. 10–3. Closed Mon.*

As you leave the Instituto, walk back west through the Plaza Tapatía to the **Quetzalcóatl Fountain** at the center of the plaza; turn left and
❼   walk down the stairs to get to the **Mercado Libertad** (Liberty Market). Inside this modern three-story building is Latin America's largest enclosed market. Within a three-square-block area you can browse through more than 1,000 privately owned stalls selling everything that is grown, manufactured, or handmade in Mexico.

Turn left as you leave the market and cross Avenida Javier Mina (we recommend that you use the pedestrian overpass to avoid the constant flow of traffic) to **Iglesia de San Juan de Díos** (San Juan de Díos Church). In front of the church, you will see a line of colorful calandrias, each behind a patient, motionless horse. Next to the church is
❽   the **Plaza de los Mariachis,** a picturesque little plaza where mariachi groups perform. While the action and ambience are best during the evening, you might enjoy a break from sightseeing in one of the cafés. A mariachi serenade is $5 a song.

From the intersection in front of the church, turn right on Calzada Independencia; walk two blocks and then go back up the stairs to Plaza Tapatía. Turn left as you enter the mall and continue west for four blocks (giving you the opportunity to see the stores on this side of the plaza) to the oldest church in the city, **Iglesia de San Augustín** (St. Augustine Church), at Avenida Degollado and Calle Morelos. Though this venerable building has been remodeled many times since its consecration in 1574, the sacristy has been preserved in its original form. The building to the left of the church, originally a cloister of the Augustinian monks, is now the School of Music of the University of Guadalajara. This is a good place to hear street musicians.

As you leave the church, turn left and continue down Calle Morelos to Avenida Corona, turn left again and walk a half block to the main entrance of the **Palacio de Gobierno** (Governor's Palace). A Churrigueresque and neoclassical structure built in 1643, it is the residence of the governor of the state of Jalisco and the site of some of Orozco's most imaginative and passionate murals. As you enter the palace, on the stairwell to your right is a dramatic mural depicting Father Hidalgo and the Mexican people's struggle for freedom. Its inspiration was Father Hidalgo's 1810 proclamation abolishing slavery in Mexico. ⊙ *Weekdays 9–8.*

As you leave the palace, cross Avenida Corona to the **Plaza de Armas.** Trees and benches in this lovely square surround an ornately sculpted kiosk, a gift from France in 1910.

Tour 2: Tlaquepaque and Tonalá

Tlaquepaque is known throughout the country as an arts-and-crafts center. The distinctive hand-painted pottery, sold in stores throughout the town, was first fashioned here by Tonaltecan Indians in the mid-16th century. The small village remained virtually isolated until June 13, 1821, when the Mexican Treaty of Independence was signed here. Soon after, the wealthy residents of Guadalajara, who had used the village as a weekend retreat, began to build palatial mansions in which to spend the summers. Many of these magnificent buildings have been restored, and today they house shops and restaurants.

During this period, according to one legend, a growing French colony living in the area was (inadvertently) responsible for naming one of Mexico's most renowned musical institutions. French aristocrats hired groups of street singers and musicians to entertain at weddings. The French word *mariage* was soon transformed into *mariachi.*

In 1870 the art of glass-blowing was introduced from Europe. As people started coming to purchase the pottery and intricate glass creations, more artisans—weavers, jewelers, and wood-carvers—arrived and built workshops. A new tradition was born.

In 1973 downtown Tlaquepaque underwent a major renovation, the highlight of which was the creation of a wide pedestrian mall. Twentieth-century commercialism had arrived. You can spend the day browsing in the shops and boutiques and stop at lunch to listen to the lively songs of the mariachis.

The village of Tonalá, 10 minutes by car from Tlaquepaque, is one of the oldest pueblos in Mexico. It was both the pre-Hispanic capital of the Indians of the Atemajac Valley and the capital of New Spain when Captain Juan de Oñate moved the city of Guadalajara here in 1532. Within three years, however, unfriendly Indians and a lack of water had forced the Spaniards to abandon the location.

Over the past 400 years, the village has existed in contented seclusion. The simple adobe houses and dusty streets belie the artistic refinement of Tonalá's residents. It is in this small pueblo that most of the ceramics and pottery sold in Tlaquepaque (and in many other parts of the world) are made. Behind the tall gray walls, families create the lovely ceramics, cobalt-blue glassware, and playful animals with the same material and techniques their ancestors used centuries ago. On Thursdays and Sundays, this merchandise is sold at bargain prices at one of the best *tianguis* (markets) in all of Mexico. Most of the stores in Tlaquepaque and Tonalá are open weekdays 10–2 and 4–7, Saturday 10–6.

Numbers in the margin correspond to points of interest on the Tlaquepaque map.

The 20-minute ride from downtown Guadalajara to **Tlaquepaque** will cost about $7 in a cab. If you're driving, take Avenida Revolución southeast from the city; at the Plaza de la Bandera (at the intersection of Calzada del Ejército), jog to your right onto Boulevard Tlaquepaque and into the town. When you reach the *glorieta* (traffic circle), follow the circle around to Avenida Niños Héroes. The first intersection is Calzada Independencia (the pedestrian mall), where you'll begin your

★ ❶ tour on foot. Turn left and walk one block to the **Museo Regional de la Cerámica** (Regional Museum of Ceramics). Exhibits in the museum, housed in a colonial mansion, trace the evolution of ceramics in the Atemajac Valley during the past century. There is also an exhibit of Indian folk art from the area and prize-winning entries from the national ceramics competition. *Calle Independencia 237,* ☎ *3/635–5404.* ☛ *Free.* ☺ *Tues.–Sat. 10–4, Sun. 10–1.*

❷ Walk across the street to the **Sergio Bustamante Gallery,** devoted to an artist whose work is found in galleries throughout the world. You can purchase one of Bustamante's whimsical sculptures for considerably less here. Silver- and gold-plated jewelry and bronze sculptures are on display in this modern gallery; the flamingos under the waterfall in the rear are real. *Calle Independencia 236,* ☎ *3/657–8354.* ☺ *Mon.–Sat. 10–7.*

❸ Next door is Tlaquepaque's oldest blown-glass factory, **Artmex la Rosa de Cristal.** The store contains a large variety of hand-blown glass objects and figures; the intricate miniatures are surprisingly inexpensive. Plan to arrive before lunch so you can go into the factory (open weekdays 10–1:30, Sat. 10–noon) and watch the craftsmen shove long tubes into a white-hot fire, retrieve a bubbling glob, and in a few minutes create one of the pieces you saw in front. *Calle Independencia 232,* ☎ *3/639–7180.* ☺ *Mon.–Sat. 10–6:30, Sun. 10–2.*

❹ On the next block east is **Bazar Hecht,** a 12-room hacienda filled with handcarved furniture, antiques, and designer fashions. The Hecht family is known throughout Mexico for its high-quality, ornately sculpted tables and chairs. Part of the fun is wandering through this beautiful building, wondering what it would have been like to grow up in the colonial ambience of 19th-century Tlaquepaque. *Calle Independencia 158,* ☎ *3/635–22–41.* ☺ *Mon.–Sat. 10–2:30 and 3:30–6:30.*

Turn left as you leave Bazar Hecht and left again at the next corner (Prisciliano Sánchez); walk one block along Calle Morelos, which, with Calle Guillermo Prieto, forms an L-shaped arcade. In the center of the

❺ arcade is the **Templo Parroquial de San Pedro** (Parish Church of St. Peter). Franciscan friars founded the church during the Spanish conquest, naming it in honor of San Pedro de Analco. According to custom, the town was named after the principal church, and in 1915 the

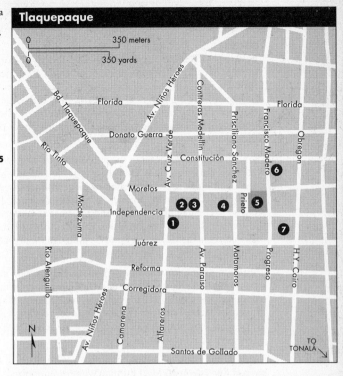

Tlaquepaque

name was officially changed to San Pedro Tlaquepaque. The altars of Our Lady of Guadalupe and Saint Joseph are intricately carved in silver and gilt; the chapel of the Daughters of Mary contains the moving oil painting of *La Purísima*. ⊙ *Daily 7 AM–9 PM.*

TIME OUT Turn right as you leave the church and walk through the arcade; when you reach Constitución, make another right. At the next intersection, ★ with Madero, turn right yet again and walk a half block to the **Restaurant with No Name** (Francisco Madero 80, ☎ 3/635–4520 or 3/635–9677), considered by food critics and patrons to be one of Mexico's best culinary establishments. There are tables both indoors and on the patio of this 17th-century colonial mansion. High adobe walls surround the hacienda and the extensive gardens, which are filled with orchids and exotic birds. The restaurant serves Spanish nouvelle cuisine, a combination of pre-Hispanic and modern recipes. Daily entertainment includes *suave* jazz and traditional Mexican music.

6 The next door to the left is the **Ken Edwards Gallery.** In 1959 Mr. Edwards developed a technique to transform the fragile Tonalá pottery into a lustrous, hardened, glazed stoneware. The store is filled with brightly colored, hand-painted plates, cups, and vases. Prices are much lower than you would pay outside Mexico; ask to see the seconds, some real bargains. *Madero 70,* ☎ *3/618–0313.* ⊙ *Mon.–Sat. 10–6:30.*

7 One block south of the gallery is **El Parián,** a square block of outdoor cafés frequented by mariachis eager to perform. El Parián (named after the Chinese section of Manila, with which the conquistadors traded) is the heart of Tlaquepaque. The atmosphere is festive, if not boisterous, on weekends. The shops in the arcades around El Parián should be used only to compare prices; do your shopping in the galleries and boutiques on Calzada Independencia or another main street.

Tonalá

The village of **Tonalá** is a 10-minute ride (about $7 for a cab) from Tlaquepaque. If you're driving, take Avenida Revolución south to Carretera Tonalá and make a left on the Carretera into Tonalá. Follow Avenida Tonalá (the same street you were on) to the main square in the center of the village. Follow Avenida Juárez one block away from the plaza to reach **La Iglesia Parroquial** (the parish church) built in 1533. Inside is a sculpture of Pope Pius IX.

From the northwest corner of the plaza, at Calles Hidalgo and Zapata, walk west (left) one block on Calle Zapata to Avenida Morelos, then right a half block to the **workshop of Jorge Wilmot** (Av. Morelos 76–88, no ☎). This factory produces intricately designed, hand-painted stoneware ceramic plates, cups, and figurines that are sold throughout the world. Unfortunately, the opening hours of this shop, like many others in the village, vary greatly, although the artist lists his hours as weekdays 10–6 and Saturday 10–1.

Turn right as you leave the workshop, and right again at the next intersection, to the **Museo Nacional de la Cerámica** (National Ceramics Museum). On exhibit are the ceramics and pottery of several Mexican states dating from pre-Columbian times to the present. There is also a workshop and a small store. *Constitución 110,* ☎ *373/3–04–94.* ☛ *Free.* ☼ *Tues.–Sat. 10–4, Sun. 10–2.*

Turn left and continue a half block on Avenida Morelos to the **workshop of Ken Edwards.** Meet the man who revolutionized the centuries-old technique of firing ceramics. Either Edwards or his wife is usually on hand to show visitors their facilities. *Av. Morelos 184,* ☎ *373/3–23–13.* ☼ *Weekdays 10–6:30.*

★ The Thursday and Sunday *tianguis* (markets) have expanded to all-day affairs that cover dozens of blocks. Under low-slung tarps you will find blue glassware, ceramics, leather goods, and odd icons and figurines at incredibly low prices.

Tour 3: Lake Chapala and Ajijic

This tour visits the lakeside communities of Chapala and Ajijic. Unfortunately, Lake Chapala—Mexico's largest inland body of water—is polluted, and water levels have been so low in the past few years that some Mexican ecologists predict there will be no lake at all in a few years' time. It does, however, provide a setting for spectacular sunsets, afford enough humidity to keep the abundant bougainvillea blooming, and ensure that there are no drastic temperature fluctuations.

The town of Chapala is 45 kilometers (28 miles) south of Guadalajara, on the northwest shore of the lake. With its proximity to the large city and its comfortable climate, it is surprising that tourists did not frequent the area until the late 19th century. Then-President Porfirio Díaz heard that aristocrats had discovered the ideal place for weekend getaways. The president began spending holidays here in 1904. Soon summer homes were built, and in 1910 the Chapala Yacht Club opened. Word of the town, with its lavish lawn parties and magnificent estates, spread quickly to the United States and Europe.

Nowadays this town of 35,000 attracts a less influential but equally fun-loving assortment of visitors. On weekends the streets are filled with Mexican families. During the week American and Canadian retirees stroll along the lakeside promenade, play golf, and relax on the verandas of downtown restaurants.

Five miles west of Chapala, along the Carretera Chapala-Jocotepec, is the village of Ajijic, featuring several blocks of art galleries and crafts shops. Despite this commercial influence, its small-town ambience is still defined by its narrow cobblestoned streets, whitewashed buildings, and gentle pace.

Lake Chapala

Numbers in the margins correspond to points of interest on the Lake Chapala Area map.

From downtown Guadalajara take Calzada del Federalismo south to Calzada Lázaro Cárdenas (the Sports Stadium is on the corner); turn left on Calzada Cárdenas and continue south. Follow the signs as Calzada Cárdenas converges with the newly expanded and resurfaced Highway 23 to Mexico City; the trip takes 50 minutes. There is also frequent bus service to Chapala from Guadalajara's old bus station on the corner of Calles Analco and Cinco de Febrero. From the Chapala bus station there are buses every hour to Ajijic.

After you pass the turnoff to Ajijic, the highway becomes Avenida Madero as you enter Chapala. Follow Avenida Madero down to the
① **San Francisco Church,** two blocks north of the lake, and park your car. Easy to spot by the blue neon crosses on its twin steeples, the church was built in 1528 and reconstructed in 1580. In 1538 Franciscan friar Miguel de Bolonio founded the town and began to convert the Taltica Indians to Christianity. Their chief was named Chapalah, from which the name Chapala originated.

② Walk across the street to the **Hotel Nido** (Av. Madero 202, ☎ 376/5–21–16), the oldest hotel on the lake. It was built in the beginning of the century to accommodate President Porfirio Díaz and his entourage during their frequent visits. In the 1940s Mexican film star Maria Felix spent the first of her numerous honeymoons at the Nido, and the dark high-ceilinged lobby still feels like the scene of a melodrama waiting to happen. There are pictures of turn-of-the-century Chapala on the walls and a picturesque patio and garden in the rear. (The hotel has 30 rooms with bath, a restaurant and bar, and an outdoor swimming pool. There are no ☎ s or TVs in the rooms.)

Turn right as you leave the hotel and walk two blocks to the lake. On the corner of Avenida Madero and Paseo Ramón Corona is the **Cazadores Restaurant** (☎ 376/5–21–62, closed Mon.), once the summer home of the Braniff family (owners of the now defunct airline) and now an ideal place to enjoy a cool liquid refreshment and watch the action along the *malecón* (lakeside promenade). Walking left down the Paseo Ramón Corona as you leave the restaurant, you will pass a number of open-air cafés featuring *pescado blanco* (white fish). Because of the pollution of the lake, we do not recommend that you partake of this regional delicacy. There is a small **handicrafts market** at the end of the Paseo Ramón Corona (two blocks from Avenida Madero).

Walk back to Avenida Madero and then to the end of the pier, where *marineros* (sailors) rent boats that will take you for a tour of the lake
③ or its islands. The most popular trip is to **Isla de los Alacránes** (Scorpion Island) to enjoy a meal in one of the tiny restaurants there. The price for a round-trip cruise is between $20 and $35 (for the launch, with a capacity of six adults).

Lake Chapala Area

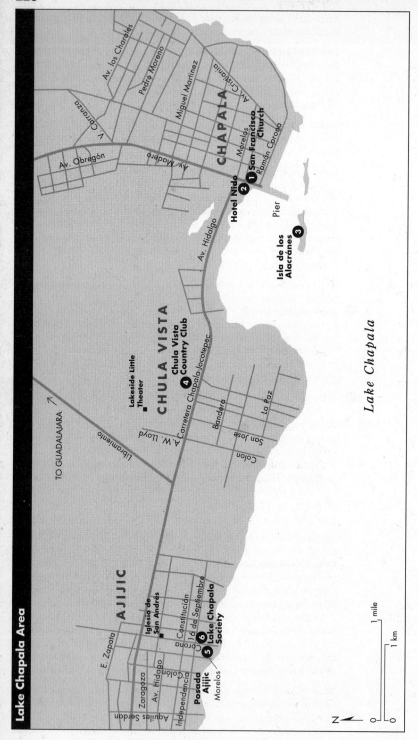

Lake Chapala

TO GUADALAJARA

AJIJIC

E. Zapata
Zaragoza
Av. Hidalgo
Independencia
Constitución
Colón
Corona
16 de Septiembre
Aquiles Serdán
Morelos

Iglesia de
San Andrés

5 Posada Ajijic
6 Lake Chapala Society

CHULA VISTA

Libramiento

A. W. Lloyd

Lakeside Little
Theater

4 Chula Vista
Country Club

Carretera Chapala-Jocotepec

Bandera
San José
La Paz
Colón

CHAPALA

Av. los Charales
Pedro Moreno
Miguel Martínez
V. Carranza
Av. Obregón
Av. Madero
Av. Cristóbal
Av. Hidalgo

Morelos
Ramón Corona
1 San Francisco
Church
2 Hotel Nido
Pier
3
Isla de los
Alacránes

N

0   1 mile
0   1 km

Return to your car and take a right at the traffic light (the only one in town) onto Avenida Hidalgo. You will be heading west to the village of Ajijic. Three kilometers (2 miles) from Chapala is the community of **Chula Vista,** the most American colony in Mexico. On the hillside north of the road, there are dozens of condos. Among them is the **Chula Vista Country Club** (Paseo de Golfo No. 1, ☏ 376/5–22–81), a favorite of the local *norteamericano* community. The "billygoat" golf course here affords the golfer great vistas of the lake as well as a workout, since the rugged terrain cannot be negotiated by golf cart. Just west of the Chapala suburb, above the PAL Trailer Park (and next to the Oak High School), is the 120-seat **Lakeside Little Theater** (☏ 376/5–23–68), which stages English-language musicals and plays throughout the year. There is a small cafeteria in the trailer park. The **Lake Chapala Department of Tourism** is 2 kilometers (1 mile) west of the trailer park. *Auditorio Ribera de Chapala,* ☏ *376/5–31–41.* ⊙ *Weekdays 9–3, Sat. 9–1.*

Ajijic

As you enter Ajijic, turn left onto Avenida Colón and continue two blocks until you reach the plaza and the **Iglesia de San Andrés** (Church of St. Andrew). Weekly events and festivities take place on this lovely plaza.

Park your car at the plaza and walk down Morelos toward the lake; along the way you can stop in at the many stores and boutiques that sell everything from designer fashions to traditional arts and crafts.

⑤ Where Calle Morelos meets the lake, you'll find the **Posada Ajijic,** a hacienda-style building that is the social, commercial, and political convocation center for Ajijic residents. Many people come to the restaurant and bar, under sculpted wood archways, for the daily happy hour and stay to watch the spectacular sunsets. For the past few years, members of the Huichol Indian tribe have set up shop in a corner of the lush gardens, where they weave their colorful serapes. *16 de Septiembre No. 2, Frente al Lago, esquina Morelos,* ☏ *376/6–07–44 or 376/6–04–30.*

⑥ Backtrack to 16 de Septiembre to find the headquarters of **Lake Chapala Society,** a nonprofit organization that can answer your questions about the area. *16 de Septiembre No. 16A, no* ☏. ⊙ *Mon.–Sat. 10–1.*

TIME OUT For a cold beer and—unlikely as it may sound—some good, fresh-cooked Italian food, stop in at **Salvador's Restaurant** (Avenida Hidalgo 17, no ☏, no credit cards accepted). A favorite watering hole for local *norteamericanos,* this spot has a bar with a large-screen television often tuned to American sports. For a hearty meal try the *spaghetti siciliano,* with mushrooms, green peppers, and onions. The frozen margaritas are renowned.

If you're looking to spend a night in this tranquil area, the **Nueva Posada** (Donato Guerra No. 9 Apdo. 30, 45920, ☏ 376/6–14–44, ☏ and FAX 376/6–13–44) is a favorite of honeymooners and other vacationers. The landscaping draws you to the lakeside, framed in bougainvillea. Seventeen spacious, airy, and well-lit rooms have colonial furniture and original watercolors. The hotel also provides fine entertainment each night, typically an American jazz trio or tropical music, and chef Lorraine Rousseau's eclectic menu is very popular with expatriates.

Museums in Guadalajara

Many of Guadalajara's museums are free, and the rest charge a nominal fee.

Museo de la Ciudad de Guadalajara opened in 1992 to commemorate the 450th anniversary of the founding of the city. The building was once a hacienda; now it houses collections of artwork, artifacts, and reproductions of documents that provide extensive information about the city's development. *Av. Independencia 684, between Barcenas and Medellin,* ☎ *3/658–2531.* ☛ *$1.* ۞ *Tues.–Sat. 10–5, Sun. 10–3.*

Museo de Arqueología de Occidente de México (Archaeological Museum of Western Mexico) houses artifacts from the states of Colima, Jalisco, and Nayarit. *Calzada Independencia and Calzada del Campesino, in front of Parque Agua Azul, no* ☎ . ☛ *35¢.* ۞ *Daily 10–2 and 4–7.*

El Museo Orozco. The artist's workshop was converted into a museum after his death in 1949. It contains a large collection of his paintings and frescoes. *Aurelio Aceves 27, just west of Los Arcos,* ☎ *3/616–8329.* ☛ *35¢.* ۞ *Tues.–Sun. 10–2.*

What to See and Do with Children

Parque Agua Azul is Guadalajara's largest and most popular park. Amid acres of trees and flowers are carnival rides, tropical birds in cages, a geodesic dome filled with butterflies, and a swimming pool. *Calzada Independencia Sur and Calzada Gonzales Gallo.* ☛ *$4.* ۞ *7–6:30.*

Planetario Severo Díaz Galindo. A modern facility with astronomy shows and aeronautical displays, the planetarium also features exhibits that allow children to test the forces and laws of nature. *Av. Ricardo Flores Magón 599,* ☎ *3/674–4106 or 3/674–0397.* ☛ *Museum 35¢, tour and museum 75¢, movie 85¢.* ۞ *Mon.–Sat. 9:30–6.*

Zoológico Guadalajara (Guadalajara Zoo). Located in the Barranca Huentitán (Huentitán Canyon), the zoo has 1,800 animals representing 250 species. For 50¢ a train provides guided tours. The adjacent *Selva Mágica* (Magic Jungle) amusement park has carnival rides and attractions. *Paseo del Zoológico 600 next to the Planetarium,* ☎ *3/638–4312.* ☛ *About $2 adults, $1.15 children.* ۞ *Tues.–Sun. 10–6.*

Off the Beaten Track

Many of the activities at the **Rancho Río Caliente** health resort and vegetarian, alcohol-free spa are literally in hot water—therapeutic hot mineral water. You can steam away your mental tensions and body toxins in front of the 20-foot-high wall of volcanic rock and then dip into one of the mineral-water–filled swimming pools. The resort offers sparse but comfortable accommodations, facials and massages, T'ai Chi instruction, hiking, horseback riding, and classes in yoga and body awareness. *Apdo. 1187, Guadalajara, Jalisco,* ☎ *3/615–7800 (answering service) or 415/615–9543 in the U.S. The spa is 30 km (19 mi) from Minerva Fountain on Hwy. 15.*

Ten kilometers (6 miles) northeast of downtown Guadalajara via Calzada Independencia is a spectacular 2,000-foot-deep gorge called **Barranca de Oblatos** (Oblatos Canyon). The view from the top of the canyon is impressive.

The **Basilica of the Virgin of Zapopan** (Calzada Avila and Av. Las Américas, 6 mi northeast of downtown), with an ornate Plateresque facade and Mudejar tiled dome, was consecrated in 1730. It is known throughout Mexico as the home of La Zapopanita, Our Lady of Zapopan. The 10-inch-high statue is venerated as the source of many miracles in and around Guadalajara. Every year on October 12, more than

1 million people crowd the streets leading to Zapopan as the Virgin is returned to the basilica after a five-month absence during which she visits every church in the city.

Centuries ago the Tiquilas, a small Nahuatl-speaking tribe, established a settlement 56 kilometers (35 miles) northwest of Guadalajara in **Tequila** in the picturesque Jaliscan countryside. The Tiquilas discovered that the heart of the maguey cactus exuded *mezcal* (a kind of honey). When fermented, it produced the intoxicating drink for which Mexico is now well known. You can tour the famous Sauza Distillery or one of the other modern tequila distilleries in town. Follow the signs, and plan to arrive between 10 AM and 1 PM.

The modern administration building of the **Universidad de Guadalajara** houses the first murals painted by Orozco after he returned to Guadalajara at age 53. In addition to these two powerful works—located behind the stage and in the dome of the auditorium—there are beautiful murals by Amado de la Cueva and David Alfaro Siqueiros. *Av. Juárez at Tolsa, 3 km (2 mi) west of downtown,* ☎ *3/625–8888.* ⊗ *8 AM–9 PM.*

Behind the university building is the **Templo Expiatorio** (Tolsa and Av. Francisco Madero). Though this church is nearly a century old, construction is still underway, albeit at a leisurely pace. The church is modeled after the Cathedral of Orvieto in Italy, and it is an outstanding example of unadulterated Gothic architecture.

SHOPPING

Shoppers in Guadalajara can choose from a broad variety of high-quality merchandise at low prices. Of course, you will also find low-quality products at high prices; *caveat emptor.* Store hours are generally Monday–Saturday 9–9, Sunday 10–1. The major areas for shopping in the city are outlined below; those interested in traditional arts and crafts should visit Tlaquepaque and Tonalá (*see* Tour 2 *in* Exploring, *above*).

Malls

In Guadalajara, as in all major cities, shopping malls are springing up everywhere; the city now has 24 of them.

Plaza del Sol. The city's largest mall has 500,000 square feet of commercial space, enough room for 300 businesses and services and parking for 500 cars. *Av. López Mateos and Mariano Otero (across from the Hyatt Hotel),* ☎ *3/121–5950.* ⊗ *Weekdays 10–8, weekends 10–6.*

Plaza México. There are 100 commercial establishments in the city's second most popular shopping mall. *Av. México 3300, at the corner of Calle Yaquis, on the city's west side,* ☎ *3/647–0098.* ⊗ *Weekdays 10–8, weekends 10–6.*

Plaza Galería del Calzado. The 60 stores in this recently built mall all sell shoes. Guadalajara is one of Mexico's leading shoe centers, and high-quality footwear and accessories are available here, many at lower prices than in the States. *Av. México and Calle Yaquis, next to the Plaza México,* ☎ *3/647–6422.* ⊗ *Weekdays 10:30–8:30, weekends 10–4.*

Markets

In **Mercado Libertad,** Latin America's largest enclosed market, more than 1,000 vendors sell everything from clothing to crafts to live animals and gold watches. *Calzada Independencia and Av. Javier Mina.* ☉ *Daily 10–8.*

El Baratillo is the world's largest flea market. Thirty city blocks are lined with stalls, tents, and blankets piled high with new, used, and antique merchandise. *On Calle Juan Zavala, east of Mercado Libertad.* ☉ *Sun. 7–3.*

SPORTS

Spectator Sports

Bullfights

Corridas begin at 4:30 PM at **Plaza Nuevo Progreso;** they're usually held on Sunday. You can buy tickets for either the *sol* (sunny) or *sombra* (shady) side of the bullring. Since the action does not begin until just before sunset, opt for the cheaper seats on the sunny side. *Calzada Independencia across from the Estadio Jalisco,* ☎ *3/637–9982 or 3/626–2369.* ☛ *$6–$22.*

Charreadas

The Mexican rodeo takes place at **Lienzo Charros de Jalisco** every Sunday at noon. The *charros* (cowboys) compete in 10 events; mariachis perform during breaks in the action. *Campo Charro Jalisco, Dr. R. Michel, 577, next to Agua Azul Park,* ☎ *3/619–7771.* ☛ *About $3.*

Soccer

Estadio Jalisco. Professional soccer matches are on Saturday at 8:45 PM and sometimes on Sunday at 2 PM. *North end of Calzada Independencia, near bullring,* ☎ *3/637–0563.* ☛ *75¢–$7.*

Participant Sports

Fitness Clubs

The **Hyatt** and **Holiday Inn** fitness clubs are open to nonmembers. At **Gold's Gym** (Chimalhuacán 3574, off Av. López Mateos Sur, ☎ 3/647–8594) guest passes are available for about $7 per day.

Golf

Golf clubs that admit foreign travelers include **Atlas Golf Club** (Carretera Guadalajara-Chapala, in front of Montenegro Park, ☎ 3/689–0085), the **San Isidro Golf Club** (highway to Zacatecas, Km 14.5, ☎ 3/633–2814 or 3/633–2728), and the **Chula Vista Country Club** (☎ 376/5–22–81). If you have credentials from a U.S. golf club, you can play at the **Guadalajara Country Club** on weekdays (☎ 3/641–4045 or 3/641–4002).

Tennis

The **Holiday Inn** (☎ 3/634–1034) allows nonguests to use its courts for a fee. There are municipal courts at **Parque Avila Comancho** (Av. Plaza Patria, no ☎).

DINING

The quality and variety of Guadalajara's restaurants have improved to accommodate the tastes and budgets of the international business community. While native restaurateurs and chefs continue to present traditional and classic Mexican dishes, a new breed of immigrant *cuisinier* has introduced such ethnic delicacies as French Creole *chicken sauté Louisiane,* classic Japanese *shabu shabu,* and Spanish *paella.* A bit oddly for a landlocked city, many restaurants offer extensive seafood selections. Many restaurants close early, so if you are accustomed to dining after 9 PM, it's advisable to call first to check if the establishment remains open. Generally, you will feel comfortable wearing casual-chic clothes at establishments in the moderate ($$) and inexpensive ($) categories, but Guadalajara is a big, business-oriented city, which means diners tend to dress up a bit. Still, Maximino's is the only restaurant where men are likely to feel out of place without a jacket.

CATEGORY	COST*
$$$$	over $35
$$$	$25–$35
$$	$15–$25
$	under $15

per person excluding drinks, service, and sales tax (10%)

$$$ **Maximino's.** A favorite with the upper crust of Guadalajara, Maximino's is located in a beautiful two-story mansion in a quiet neighborhood near the university; some consider it to be the best restaurant in town. The interior—dominated by the sweeping staircase—is elegantly decorated, and tables are set up on both floors as well as on the back patio (in season). The international menu has strong French influences, and the seafood choices are extensive, including Norwegian salmon and Dutch sole. Try the shrimp thermidor, prepared with paprika and hollandaise sauce. Soft strains of a jazz trio play during most meals. ✕ *Lerdo de Tejada 2043,* ☎ *3/615–3424, 3/615–3435, or 3/625–0076. Reservations advised. AE, DC, MC, V.*

$$$ **Moravia.** Both Tapatios and tourists come to enjoy the elegant ambience and superb Continental cuisine. A full-length stained-glass window in the rear of the main room overlooks manicured gardens. Appetizers include oysters Rockefeller (eight choice oysters on the half-shell lightly breaded and covered with a rich mornay sauce) and piñon crème with spinach soup, a Moravian specialty. Entrées include fish fillet Florentina (in a tangy white-wine sauce served on a bed of spinach) and *filete pimienta* (steak in a green peppercorn and cream sauce). ✕ *López Mateos N. 1143 on cnr of Colomos,* ☎ *3/641–8487. Reservations advised weekends. AE, MC, V. Closed Sun. and national holidays.*

$$$ **Sí Como No.** Classical Mexican elegance pervades this intimate bi-level
★ room overlooking a neat, lush garden; cobalt-blue water glasses provide a charming accent to the white-on-white decor. Chef Salvador Rodriguez masterfully combines traditional native recipes with New Orleans Creole. The extensive dinner menu changes monthly. Some of the chef's specialties are crabmeat crepes in a rich hollandaise sauce, a spicy shrimp Creole in a tangy tomato sauce, and mignonettes of veal Normandy. ✕ *Av. Chapalita 120,* ☎ *3/121–7823. Reservations advised. AE, DC, MC, V.*

$$ **Copenhagen.** The decorative tilework of Tonalá artisan Jorge Wilmot
★ covers the walls of this restaurant, which bills itself as the Paella Place. Since 1952 the Copenhagen has featured the famous dish of Valencia, Spain. The secret of a great paella lies in the texture of the rice. The grain in both presentations, *Copenhagen* (in white wine) and *à la marinera* (with seafood), is loose and dry but still tender. The menu also features beef and seafood entrées. Copenhagen is also the unofficial headquarters for Guadalajara's jazz aficionados; it show-

cases some of the city's best jazz musicians, who entertain each evening at 8. ✗ *López Cotilla and Marcos Castellanos,* ☎ *3/625–2803. Reservations advised weekends. AE, DC, MC, V. Closed May 1 and Dec. 25.*

$$ Guadalajara Grill. Fun and revelry share top billing with the food at this Carlos 'n Charlie's affiliate. The large, tri-level room is decorated with Mexican knickknacks and antique street lamps; turn-of-the-century photographs of Guadalajara are displayed in the foyer and on the back wall. The tender barbecued baby ribs are by far the favorite of both natives and tourists. Shrimp lovers will be happy to find the crustaceans grilled, baked, boiled, or served in a casserole. There is live entertainment every evening. ✗ *Av. López Mateos 3771,* ☎ *3/631–5622. Reservations advised. AE, MC, V. Closed national holidays.*

$$ La Copa de Leche. This downtown, family-owned and -operated restaurant is an institution in Guadalajara. You can choose from two distinct dining areas: El Balcon, an open-air terrace overlooking Avenida Juárez, or the main dining room with traditional Mexican decor, a 40-foot ceiling, and an antique fireplace. Specialties include *pescado California* (California whitefish sautéed with avocados and oranges) and *pierna de cerdo* (pork shank baked in a tangy port wine sauce); for dessert try one of the flambés. ✗ *Av. Juárez 414-B,* ☎ *3/614–9435 or 3/614–9437. Reservations advised weekends. AE, MC, V. Closed national holidays.*

$$ La Pianola. The entrance—through what looks like an open-air kitchen where costumed women are making tortillas—is a little off-putting, but inside La Pianola is a proper restaurant, with hundreds of items on a huge menu. Specialties include *pozole* (thick pork and hominy soup), chili, and menudo. The signature player-piano music accompanies your meal. ✗ *Av. México 3220,* ☎ *3/813–1385 or 3/813–2412. Reservations advised. AE, DC, MC, V.*

$$ La Rinconada. This enclosed patio of a restored colonial mansion houses hanging plants, stone pillars, handcarved doors with frosted glass windows, and a piano and bass duo plucking out American standards. La Rinconada exudes an old-plantation graciousness in a centrally located position on Calle Morelos between the Teatro Degollado and the Instituto Cultural Cabañas. Specialties of the house include shrimp scampi and the *Plato Mexicano Arrachera* (a flank steak served with guacamole, enchiladas, and beans and rice). ✗ *Calle Morelos 86,* ☎ *3/613–9914. Reservations accepted. AE, DC, MC, V.*

$ ★ Dainzu. Named after the centuries-old Mixtec ruin just outside of Oaxaca City, this 12-table restaurant has white-plaster walls and a red-tiled ceiling, with regional posters and ornamentation on the walls. Generous portions are brought to you on hefty white ceramic plates. Featured among the Oaxacan specialties are tender beef, pork, and chicken dishes prepared in a tangy green or black mole sauce and *pollo almendro* (chicken smothered in onions). Complete the Oaxacan experience with a mug of *chocolate caliente* (hot chocolate) and sweet *pan de Oaxaca.* Tell your cabdriver to take Calle Mariano Otero to the *Chocolate Ibarra* (chocolate factory), and then turn east to Avenida Diamante (between the Plaza del Sol and the Plaza Arboledas). ✗ *Av. Diamante 2598,* ☎ *3/647–5086. No reservations. No credit cards. Closed Mon.*

$ La Chata. Dark-toned beams and brick archways are offset by Day-Glo plaid tablecloths in this popular Jaliscan restaurant. One of the best of chef Martina's special soups is *caldo Halpeña,* a thick stew of chicken, avocado, rice, and cheese. Specials include such spicy roasted meat dishes as *carne tampiqueña,* served with rice, beans, and enchiladas. A good complement to this is a cool, sweet *horchata,* a drink made from rice and brown sugar simmered in milk and then chilled. There is another La Chata downtown, with the same authentic feel and the same gaudy yet distinctive tablecloths. ✕ *Av. López Mateo Sur, across from Holiday Inn,* ☎ *3/632–4532. No reservations. AE, MC, V. Closed national holidays.*

$ La Hacienda de Jazo. Since the early 1970s, a regular stream of Tapatíos as well as tourists have been coming through the doors of this well-known eatery near the university to sample straightforward but well-prepared food. The restaurant is laid out in a hacienda style, and a piano-bass-sax trio performs most afternoons. The menu covers Mexican standards, with an emphasis on steaks, including filet mignon and T-bone. ✕ *Justo Serrano 2022,* ☎ *3/616–8280 or 3/616–6342. No reservations. MC, V.*

$ La Trattoria. Michelli Primucci's Italian eatery has swiftly become the favorite of the city's American and Canadian communities. Under the vigilant eye of Michelli's brother-in-law Alberto, this unpretentious, squeaky-clean restaurant churns out superb Italian dishes that are reasonably priced. The *combination la trattoria* is lasagna, fettuccine, and spaghetti in a zingy house sauce. In addition to pasta plates, the restaurant offers a limited selection of beef and seafood entrées. All meals come with a trip to the salad bar. The popularity of La Trattoria is increasing to include a large contingent of young locals—especially for Saturday-night dates. ✕ *Av. Niños Héroes 3051,* ☎ *3/122–1817. No reservations. AE, MC, V. Closed Dec. 25.*

$ Oui El Cafe. Dark wood, stained glass, and Tiffany lamps set the trendy
★ tone at this pleasant café, where plates of small *tacos de carnes* (meat tacos) and *tortasa humada* (buns filled with smoked meat) appear on the table to tempt your appetite even before you order. The tender barbecue ribs, a specialty, are served with a full plate of baked or french fried potatoes, rice, and steamed vegetables. The copious meal ends with a complimentary small brandy snifter of Ron Pope, a rich eggnog sprinkled with nutmeg. ✕ *Plaza Vallarta,* ☎ *3/630–0188 or 3/630–2204. No reservations. AE, MC, V.*

$ Saint Michel. This is a unique addition to Guadalajara's growing register of restaurants. You would expect to find the front dining room, with its stone walls and arches, in a French castle; the room to the rear has a contemporary Mexican flair, with beige walls, beamed ceilings, and a pleasant view of the patio and gardens. Saint Michel serves more than 50 varieties of crepes, half of which are desserts. Crepe specialties include *Azteca* (with chicken and cheese), beef Stroganoff, *Scissy* (with strawberries, cheese, and cream), and *Gran Amirante* (with shrimp in a thick white-wine sauce). Meals include a trip to the salad bar. ✕ *Av. Vallarta 1700,* ☎ *3/630–1820. Reservations advised. AE, DC, MC, V. Closed national holidays.*

LODGING

Until 20 years ago, most of Guadalajara's hotels were in the downtown area. As commercial interest in the city grew and businesses began springing up throughout the metropolitan area, hotels were constructed on Avenida López Mateos, a 10-mile strip extending from Minerva Fountain to the Plaza del Sol shopping center. Expo-Guadalajara (Latin America's largest convention center) opened in 1987, and the city's hotels immediately began major remodeling projects to accommodate the convention business.

Guadalajara today offers a fine variety of hotels in all price ranges. Hotels in this city follow the tradition initiated by the hotels in resort areas of raising prices every year on December 15. An excellent time to visit Guadalajara is from the beginning of October (during the *Fiestas de Octubre*) until mid-December.

Call ahead if you're apprehensive about noise levels outside your hotel room. Many hotels are located on busy intersections, and you'd be well advised to consult the reservation clerk on the matter of a room away from the hubbub.

The rates given are based on the year-round or peak-season price; off-peak (summer) rates may be slightly lower. You can expect hotels in the expensive ($$$) and very expensive ($$$$) categories to have purified-water systems and English-language TV channels.

CATEGORY	COST*
$$$$	over $160
$$$	$90–$160
$$	$40–$90
$	under $40

*All prices are for a standard double room, excluding 10% tax.

$$$$ **Hyatt Regency.** This imposing pyramidal structure dominates the hotel strip. Opened in 1983, the Hyatt is popular with vacation charter groups and business travelers seeking the comfortable uniformity the hotel chain affords. Street-level escalators lift you past cascading waterfalls to the plush 12-story atrium lobby; two glass-enclosed elevators whisk you up to your floor. Spacious rooms feature hypoallergenic carpets and queen- or king-size orthopedic mattresses. The hotel's indoor Polaris Ice Skating Rink (the only such facility in the city) is open to nonguests. The Hyatt succeeds in integrating varied restaurant, club, and common areas and providing all with consistently good service by an attentive staff. For the best city view, request a room on an upper floor facing the bustling Plaza del Sol shopping center. ⌂ *Av. López Mateos Sur and Moctezuma, 45050,* ☎ *3/678–1234 or 800/228–9000,* FAX *3/678–1222. 317 rooms with bath, 29 suites. 2 restaurants, bar, pool, health club. AE, DC, MC, V.*

$$$$ **Quinta Real.** Stone and brick walls, colonial arches, and objets d'art
★   highlight the classical Mexican architecture in all public areas of this luxury hotel, located in a quiet residential neighborhood on the city's west side. Suites are plush and intimate, with select neocolonial furnishings, including glass-topped writing tables with carved-stone pedestals, fireplaces with marble mantelpieces, and original art. Tiled baths feature marble sinks and bronze fixtures (some suites have sunken tubs with Jacuzzis). Deluxe accommodations, located in the recently completed tower, are more lavish, though removed from the gardens below. ⌂ *Av. México 2727, 44680,* ☎ *3/615–0000 or 800/445–4565 in the U.S., 800/3–62–15 in Mexico,* FAX *3/630–1302. 78 suites. Restaurant, piano bar, pool. AE, DC, MC, V.*

$$$ **Camino Real.** A 15-minute cab ride from downtown will bring you to this sprawling resort located 3 kilometers (2 miles) west of Minerva Fountain. By day, you can relax in the shade of rubber and jacaranda trees; by night, you can enjoy the turn-of-the-century Aquellos Tiempos restaurant or live entertainment in La Diligencia lounge. The rooms are in two-story wings surrounding manicured lawns and tropical gardens. They are large and have placid pastel color schemes, matching bedspreads and curtains, and modern furniture. Those in the rear wing face busy, noisy Avenida Vallarta. ⌂ *Av. Vallarta 5005, 45050,* ☎ *3/647–8000 or 800/228–3000,* FAX *3/121–7936. 205 rooms. 2 restaurants, bar, coffee shop, 5 pools, tennis court, playground, babysitting. AE, DC, MC, V.*

$$$ Carlton. The only first-class property in downtown Guadalajara, this modern 20-story tower hotel was totally remodeled in 1988. The oversize rooms with light beige walls and ceilings have matching dark-blue curtains and bedspreads. Public areas are well maintained but sparsely decorated; the rear gardens and fountain are surrounded by ivy-draped walls. Though the hotel is convenient for tourists, it caters to the business traveler. The upper floors offer a spectacular view of the city and a retreat from the horrendous street noise. Service, though friendly, has been less than efficient of late. ☎ *Av. Niños Héroes 105, at corner of Av. 16 de Septiembre, 44100, ☎ 3/614–7272 or 800/36–200 in Mexico, FAX 3/613–5539. 217 rooms, 5 suites. Restaurant, 2 bars, pool, health club, disco. AE, MC, V.*

$$$ Fiesta Americana. The dramatic glass facade of this luxury high-rise
★ faces the Minerva Circle. The location, warm contemporary Mexican ambience, and excellent service make this hotel a popular choice for both business travelers and tourists. Four glass-enclosed elevators ascend above the 11-story atrium lobby and adjoining Lobby Bar (one of Guadalajara's most popular night spots). The ample rooms have a pastel color scheme, modern furnishings (including molded seating and desk areas), and panoramic city views. The hotel presents a German Café Night (Thursday), an Italian Fiesta (Friday), and an International Buffet (every day in the Chula Vista cafeteria). The best rooms are on the upper floors, well away from the revelers down in the Lobby Bar. ☎ *Aurelio Aceves 225, 45050, ☎ 3/825–3434 or 800/223–2332, FAX 3/630–3725. 353 rooms, 38 suites. 2 restaurants, cafeteria, 2 bars, pool, exercise room, 2 tennis courts. AE, DC, MC, V.*

$$$ Holiday Inn. Those who come to Guadalajara for its eternally springlike climate will enjoy the Holiday Inn. There are expansive, well-tended gardens; jacaranda, tulip, and rubber trees providing shade; and a large pool and sunbathing area to take full advantage of the outdoors. Indoors, everything is just as well tended, and the staff is efficient and bilingual. The rooms feature marble baths, upholstered furniture, carpeting, and lots of natural light. Choose a room in the tower for a view of the mountains or one adjacent to the courtyard and its parklike greenery. ☎ *Av. Lopez Mateos Sur 2500, 45050, ☎ 3/634–1034, or toll free 800/0–09–99, 800/3–65–55 in Mexico, FAX 3/631–9393. 289 rooms, 4 suites. 2 restaurants, cafeteria, bar, pool, health club, tennis courts, playground, car rental. AE, DC, MC, V.*

$$$ Plaza Del Sol. Location and price make families and young adults head for this hotel's two towers rising over the south end of the Plaza del Sol shopping center. The intimate Solaris Restaurant and the Bar Sol provide enjoyable and romantic evenings. Public areas and rooms feature glossy white walls trimmed in aquamarine or mauve. The accommodations have modern furniture and wall-to-wall carpeting. Rooms in the newer tower are a bit larger and have a view of the shopping center below. ☎ *Av. López Mateos and Calle Mariano Otero, 45050, ☎ 3/647–8790, FAX 3/122–9865. 341 rooms with bath, 14 suites. Restaurant, cafeteria, bar, pool, nightclub. AE, DC, MC, V.*

$$ De Mendoza. Mature travelers and tour groups from the United States and Canada often choose this downtown hotel because of its convenient location (on a quiet side street just one block from the Teatro Degollado) and charming postcolonial architecture and ambience. Beamed ceilings, handsculpted wood furniture and doors, and wrought-iron railings decorate public areas and rooms. The staff is bilingual and will be glad to direct you on a tour of nearby historical sites. ☎ *Venustiano Carranza 16, 44100, ☎ 3/613–4646 or 3/614–2621, FAX 3/613–7310. 93 rooms with bath, 17 suites. Restaurant, pool. AE, DC, MC, V.*

$$ **Diana.** Mexican and European tourists favor this six-story hotel, located two blocks from Minerva Fountain. The white-stucco lobby adjoins a small lounge and busy restaurant. Standard-size rooms have white-on-white walls and ceilings with brightly patterned curtains and bedspreads; all have desks and window air conditioners. The best rooms are on the upper floors in the rear, away from the activity and traffic on Yáñez; suites have private saunas. ☎ *Circunvalacíon Agustín Yáñez 2760, 44100, ☎ 3/615–5510. 155 rooms with bath, 4 suites. Restaurant, cafeteria, bar, pool. AE, DC, MC, V.*

$$ **Fénix.** This mid-rise hotel caters to business travelers and national tourists. The lobby is active and busy and the staff efficient. The location, just off a principal downtown intersection, makes this hotel an ideal choice for the short-term visitor. The comfortable standard-size rooms have simple appointments and furnishings. The Co-Co Bar is one of Guadalajara's livelier venues, and guests are allowed free admission. ☎ *Av. Corona 160, 44100, ☎ 3/614–5714, FAX 3/613–4005. 240 rooms with bath, 19 suites. Restaurant, bar, disco, nightclub. AE, DC, MC, V.*

$$ **Frances.** The brothers Oliveros carefully renovated Guadalajara's oldest hotel (1610), preserving and restoring its original architecture and charm. During reopening ceremonies in 1981, the four-story downtown hotel was designated a national monument. The venerable Frances has a three-story enclosed atrium lobby with stone columns and colonial arches surrounding a polished marble fountain and cut crystal-and-gilt chandelier. Even if you're not a guest, you may enjoy a ride in the antique cage elevator that holds three adults. Though room sizes vary, all share a colonial ambience, with rose-colored stucco walls, polished wood floors, and high-beamed ceilings. For the best city views, ask for a room facing Calle Maestranza. The Frances is ideal for travelers willing to exchange the amenities of a modern hotel for the hospitality of Guadalajara's grande dame. ☎ *Calle Maestranza 35, 45050, ☎ 3/613–1190, FAX 3/658–2831. 60 rooms with bath. 2 restaurants, bar. AE, DC, MC, V.*

$$ **Posada Guadalajara.** Rooms in this colonial-style hotel's four contiguous six-story towers open onto airy, wrought-iron railed hallways overlooking the small patio and circular pool. The unassuming accommodations are clean and comfortable, with traditional appointments. In addition to a loyal cadre of international patrons, the Posada welcomes visiting sports teams. Depending on your disposition (and the age and inclinations of your fellow guests), you will find the evenings here to be either festive or raucous. The hotel is just south of Calzada Lázaro Cárdenas (arterial access to downtown). ☎ *Av. López Mateos Sur 1280, 45050, ☎ 3/121–2022. 162 rooms with bath, 18 suites. Restaurant, pool. AE, DC, MC, V.*

THE ARTS AND NIGHTLIFE

Guadalajara has a reputation as a cultural and performing arts center. During the past 20 years, the active U.S. and Canadian communities have developed a schedule of English-language cultural events. You can attend a performance, an exhibition, or a recital almost any day of the year.

The Arts

Ballet

Ballet Folklórico of the University of Guadalajara (☎ 3/617–4440 or 3/618–9914) offers traditional Mexican folkloric dances and music in the Teatro Degollado every Sunday at 10 AM.

Performance Venues

Teatro Degollado (Degollado and Belén, ☎ 3/614–4773), a magnificent theater built in 1886 and totally remodeled in 1988, presents nationally and internationally famous artists for performances throughout the year. The refurbished velvet seats are comfortable, the acoustics are excellent, and the central air-conditioning is a treat.

Concha Acústica, the outdoor theater in Parque Agua Azul, presents festivals of music and dance every Sunday at 5 PM.

Instituto Cultural Cabañas (Calle Cabañas 8 at the Plaza Tapatía, ☎ 3/617–4322 or 3/617–4440), built in 1810, has 23 flowered patios and permanent and revolving art exhibits. Theater, dance, and musical performances take place on an open-air stage within the institute. The Instituto also has a movie theater.

Plaza de Armas is host to the **State Band of Jalisco** every Tuesday, Thursday, and Saturday evening at 6:30. On Wednesday evening, the **Municipal Band of Guadalajara** performs at 6:30.

Symphony

Filarmónico Jalisco (☎ 3/613–2024), conducted by Maestro Guadalupe Flores, performs Sundays and Fridays at the Teatro Degollado.

Nightlife

Guadalajara is not known for its nightlife. The nightclubs in major hotels provide good local entertainment and, occasionally, internationally known recording artists. The best hotel clubs are the **Lobby Bar,** in the Hotel Fiesta Americana; **Memories,** in the El Tapatío; **La Diligencia,** in the Camino Real; and **La Fiesta,** in the Holiday Inn. As in the coffeehouses of the 1960s, patrons sit around a small stage at **Peña Cuicacalli** (Av. Niños Héroes 1988, ☎ 3/625–4690) and listen to jazz, blues, and folk, or Latin American music; performances are Tuesday through Thursday at 8 PM.

Discos

You can dance all night at **Oz** (Av. Mariano Otero and Av. López Mateos) and **Daddy-O** (Av. López Mateos and Atzayacatl). A good downtown choice is **Maxim's** (Calle Maestranza 35). Hotel discos include **the Factory,** in the Hotel Aranzazú.

GUADALAJARA ESSENTIALS

Arriving and Departing

By Plane

AIRPORT AND AIRLINES

Libertador Miguel Hidalgo International Airport (☎ 3/688–5248 or 3/688–5127) is 16.6 kilometers (11 miles) south of Guadalajara. Unfortunately, Guadalajara's only commercial airport is frequently unable to meet the demands of the increased air service to the city. A new international terminal is planned in the next decade.

Aeromexico (☎ 800/237–6639, 3/669–0202 in Guadalajara) has nonstop service to Guadalajara from Los Angeles and San Francisco; **Mexicana** (☎ 800/531–7921, 3/647–2222 in Guadalajara) offers direct flights from Los Angeles. Through Dallas, **American Airlines** (☎ 800/433–7300, 3/616–4090 in Guadalajara) provides service to Guadalajara from all cities in its system. **Continental Airlines** (☎ 800/525–0280, 3/647–4446 in Guadalajara) provides the same service through Houston. **Delta Airlines** (☎ 800/221–1212, 3/630–3530 in Guadalajara) flies direct from Los Angeles.

By van. **Autotransportes Terrestre de Aeropuerto** (☎ 3/619–02–13) is a *combi* (VW minibus) service to city hotels and other destinations in the Guadalajara area. Fares, based on distance from the airport, are between $10 and $15 per person.

By Taxi. Taxis charge between $12 and $18 to city hotels. You can bargain with drivers, but make sure you both agree on the fare before you enter the cab.

By Limousine. Royal Limousines (Hotel Quinta Real, Avenida Mexico 2727, ☎ 3/616–3932 or 3/615–0000, ext. 121) has chauffeur-driven stretch limousines to downtown Guadalajara for $55.

By Car. The Chapala Highway 23, a well-paved four-lane thoroughfare, stretches north from the airport to the city. The 30-minute trip can be delayed by slow-moving caravans of trucks and weekend recreational traffic. To reach downtown hotels, just past El Tapatío Resort, turn left from the highway onto Calzada Gonzales Gallo and then right onto Avenida 16 de Septiembre at Parque Agua Azul; to hotels on Avenida López Mateos Sur, just past El Tapatío Resort, turn left from the highway onto Calzada de las Torres, which turns into Calzada Lázaro Cárdenas.

Most international and domestic car-rental agencies have booths at the airport in both the domestic and international terminals.

By Train

The Mexican train system, which had been improving for a while, is currently in a state of flux. At press time, the only first-class rail service to Guadalajara from near the U.S. border was via *El Pacífico,* which departs from Mexicali (across from Calexico, CA). The *Tapatío,* departing from Mexico City at 8:30 PM, arrives at Guadalajara at 8 AM; it departs Guadalajara at 9 PM, arriving in Mexico City at 8:30 AM. The round-trip fare (no meals, only snacks available) is $40 first-class coach, $100 Pullman. Information about current schedules and fares can be obtained from **Mexico by Train** (☎ and FAX 210/725–3659 or 800/321–1699). The Estación de Ferrocarril (train station, ☎ 3/650–0826 or 3/650–0314) is located at the south end of Avenida 16 de Septiembre, near Parque Agua Azul.

By Bus

First-class, air-conditioned buses with rest rooms provide daily service to Guadalajara from most major cities on the border. **Greyhound** (☎ 800/237–8211) has lists of the telephone numbers of bus terminals in border cities served by Mexican bus lines. English-speaking representatives of the Mexican carriers will give you schedule and fare information. The **Nueva Central Camionera** (New Central Bus Station ☎ 3/657–4353) is located 10 kilometers (6 miles) southeast of downtown Guadalajara on the highway to Zapotlanejo.

Getting Around

Guadalajara's major attractions are best seen on foot. For points of interest outside the city center, Guadalajara has an inexpensive, well-organized public transportation system.

By Bus

This is without a doubt the most economical and efficient but least comfortable means of traversing the city. Buses run every few minutes between 6 AM and 10:30 PM from the center of the city to all local attractions, including Tlaquepaque and Zapopan. The 25¢ fare makes buses the preferred mode of transportation for Guadalajara natives, so expect to stand during daylight hours. The new Tur III buses, which run on some of the main routes through the city—including out to Tlaquepaque and Tonalá—cost $1. Consequently, they are much less crowded than the smaller, older buses.

By Tram

The *tren ligero* (light train) runs along Avenida Federalismo from the Periférico (city beltway) Sur to Periférico Norte, near the Benito Juárez Auditorium. The system, which is clean, safe, and efficient, has 16 trains running at five-minute intervals between 19 stations and costs about 40¢. A second line, running east–west along Av. Juarez, is under construction.

By Taxi

Taxis are readily available and reasonably economical. Tell the driver where you are going and agree on a fare *before* you enter the cab. Fare schedules, listing prices to downtown and all major attractions, are posted in the lobby of all hotels. *Sitios* (cab stands) are located near all hotels and attractions.

Guided Tours

City Tours

Copenhagen Tours (Blvd. de las Cordilleras 152, ☎ 3/629–7957 or 3/629–4758) has several city tours, with admission to attractions included in the price. **Panoramex** (Calzada Federalismo Sur 948, ☎ 3/610–5109 or 3/610–5005), Guadalajara's largest tour company, provides city tours and day-long excursions to Tequila, Lake Chapala, and Tlaquepaque for about $30, including lunch. Air-conditioned buses with bilingual guides depart from Los Arcos and Parque San Francisco each morning. **Royal Limousines** (Miguel de Cervantes 382, Sector Juárez, ☎ 3/616–3939) offers a variety of city and area tour packages in a stretch limousine with bilingual guide; domestic liquor is included in all tours. Limousines can also be rented for $40 per hour for self-guided tours.

Personal Guides

The **Sindicato de Guias de Turistos** (Roberto Arellano Deyran, secretary, ☎ 3/657–8376) maintains a list of licensed bilingual guides. These guides charge $12 per hour for orientation or special-interest tours in their own automobiles. Most hotels have a list of guides available on short notice.

Calandrias

You can hire a horse-drawn carriage in front of the Museo Regional, the Mercado Libertad, or Parque San Francisco. The charge is about $10 for a half-hour tour and about $17 for a full hour, for up to four passengers. Few drivers speak English.

Opening and Closing Times

Banks hours vary widely: Branches of Bancomer are open weekdays 9–5 and Saturday 10–1; Banamex hours are weekdays 9–2.

Museums are open Tuesday–Sunday 9–4 generally, but hours may vary.

Stores in downtown Guadalajara and in shopping malls are open Monday–Saturday 9–9 and Sunday 10–1; supermarkets keep similar hours but are open Sunday 9–9.

Important Addresses and Numbers

Consulates

United States (Progreso 175, near the intersection of Av. Chapultepec and Av. La Paz, ☎ 3/825–2700 or 3/825–2998, ⅁X 3/826–6549, after-hours emergency ☎ 3/825–5553).

Canada (Aurelio Aceves 225, in Fiesta Americana hotel, ☎ 3/625–3434, ext. 3005, or 3/616–5642).

Emergencies

City police (☎ 3/617–6060); **state police** (☎ 3/622–3886); **highway patrol** (☎ 06); **fire department** (☎ 3/619–5241 and 3/623–0833); **Cruz Roja** (Red Cross; ☎ 3/613–1550), and **Cruz Verde** (Green Cross; ☎ 3/643–7190).

HOSPITALS

Hospital del Carmen (Tarascos 3435, near the Plaza México, ☎ 3/647–1048 or 3/647–6313), **Hospital México-Americano** (Colomos 2110, ☎ 3/641–0089 or 3/642–4279), and **Hospital Santa María Chapalita** (Niño Obrero 1666, in the Chapalita neighborhood, ☎ 3/621–1224 or 3/621–4373).

DOCTORS

The U.S. Consulate (*see* Consulates, *above*) maintains a list of English-speaking doctors. All major hotels have the names of doctors who are on 24-hour call.

LATE-NIGHT PHARMACIES

Farmacias Guadalajara has several branches that are open 24 hours. *Avenida Las Americas 2*, ☎ 3/615–8516; *Av. Javier Mina 221*, ☎ 3/617–8555.

English-Language Bookstores

Sandi Bookstore features a variety of newspapers, magazines, and books. *Tepeyac 718 in the Chapalita neighborhood*, ☎ 3/121–0863. ⊙ *Weekdays 9:30–2:30 and 3:30–7, Sat. 9:30–2.*

PUBLICATION

The weekly *Colony Reporter* newspaper is the best of a mixed lot of English-language periodicals. Its stories and community and cultural listings provide a great deal of information otherwise unavailable. It is sold for $1 at newsstands and hotels.

Travel Agencies

Many of the city's 150 travel agencies are in the two hotel zones, El Centro (downtown) and on Avenida López Mateos Sur (on the southwest side of the city). There is an American Express office at Avenida Vallarta 2440, near Los Arcos (☎ 3/615–8712 or 3/615–8910).

Telephones

All major hotels have telephones in the lobbies from which guests can make local calls at no charge.

Visitor Information

The main office is well stocked with timely information on area hotels, restaurants, and attractions, and has a helpful, bilingual staff. *Calle*

Morelos 102, in the Plaza Tapatía, ☎ *3/652–2222.* ⊘ *Weekdays 9–8, weekends 9–1.*

Branch offices are located in **Tlaquepaque** (Guillermo Prieto 80, near the main entrance to El Templo Parroquial de San Pedro, the parish church, ☎ 3/635–1503) and **Zapopan** (Vicente Guerrero 233, ☎ 3/633–0571). *Both offices are open weekdays 9–8:30, Sat. 9–1.*

8 The Heartland of Mexico

Rich with the history of Mexico's revolution, the heartland is a treasure of colonial towns—Zacatecas, Guanajuato, Querétaro, Morelia, and Pátzcuaro—whose residents now lead quiet, largely traditional lives. Even in San Miguel de Allende, an American art colony and home to a well-known language institute, women wash their clothes and gossip at the local lavanderia *as they have for hundreds of years.*

By Laura Anne
Broadwell

Updated by
Chris
Humphrey

MEXICO'S HEARTLAND, so named for its central location, has neither the beaches of the west coast nor the ruins of Yucatán. Rather, this fertile farmland along with the surrounding mountains is known for its leading role in Mexican history, particularly during the War of Independence, and for its especially well-preserved examples of colonial architecture. The Bajío (ba-*hee*-o), as it is also called, corresponds roughly to the states of Guanajuato and parts of Querétaro and Michoacán. In the hills surrounding the cities of Guanajuato, Zacatecas, Querétaro, and San Miguel de Allende, the Spaniards found silver in the 1500s, leading them to colonize the area heavily.

Three centuries later, wealthy Creoles (Mexicans of Spanish descent) in Querétaro and San Miguel took the first audacious steps toward independence from Spain. When their clandestine efforts were discovered, two of the early insurgents, Ignacio Allende and Father Miguel Hidalgo, began in earnest the 12-year War of Independence. One of the bloodiest skirmishes was fought in the Alhóndiga de Granaditas, a mammoth grain-storage facility in Guanajuato that is now a state museum.

When Allende and Hidalgo were executed in 1811, another native son, José María Morelos, picked up the independence banner. This mestizo priest-turned-soldier, with his army of 9,000, came close to gaining control of the land before he was killed in 1815. Thirteen years later, the city of Valladolid was renamed Morelia in his honor.

Long after the War of Independence ended in 1821, the cities of the Bajío continued to play a prominent role in Mexico's history. Three major events took place in Querétaro alone: In 1848 the Mexican-American War ended with the signing of the Treaty of Guadalupe Hidalgo; in 1867 Austrian Maximilian of Hapsburg, crowned emperor of Mexico by Napoléon III of France, was executed in the hills north of town; 50 years later the Mexican Constitution was signed here.

Many travelers barrel past the Bajío to points north or west of Mexico City. But there are many reasons others make it their destination. Some stop for a few days to browse in the shops of San Miguel or Guanajuato for bargains in silver and other local crafts. Others venture to the state of Michoacán, renowned for its folklore and folk crafts, especially ceramics and lacquerware.

For those who stay longer, the rewards are ample, as each of these colonial cities has a wealth of architectural styles. La Parroquia, the Gothic-style parish church of San Miguel de Allende, designed by an Indian mason, puts a Gallic touch on an otherwise very Mexican skyline; Guanajuato boasts a 17th-century Baroque centerpiece, the Basílica Colegiata de Nuestra Señora; Zacatecas, a national monument city, has the best example in Mexico of a Baroque cathedral; in Morelia, the 200-foot Baroque towers of the central cathedral are among the tallest in Mexico; and in Pátzcuaro and Querétaro, the ornate 16th-century colonial mansions surrounding the city squares have been converted into hotels and government offices.

Driving through the Bajío, especially scenic Michoacán, is recommended. Within hours the landscape can change from lakeside pine forests to lush subtropical terrain. Day-trippers from Pátzcuaro can explore the crater of an extinct volcano in San Juan Parangaricútiro or the ruins of an ancient Tarascan Indian capital, Tzintzuntzán. Harried

Heartland

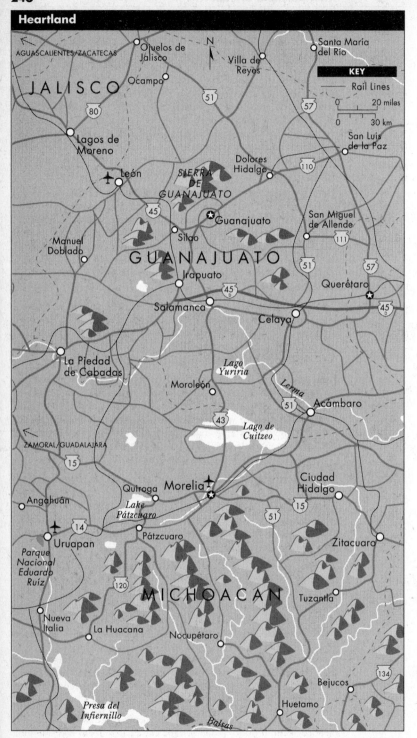

N

JALISCO

Ojuelos de Jalisco

Ocampo

Villa de Reyes

Santa María del Río

KEY

Rail Lines

0   20 miles

0   30 km

San Luis de la Paz

51

57

80

Lagos de Moreno

León

SIERRA DE GUANAJUATO

Dolores Hidalgo

110

45

Guanajuato

San Miguel de Allende

111

Manuel Doblado

Silao

GUANAJUATO

51

57

Irapuato

45 D

Querétaro

45 D

Salamanca

Celaya

La Piedad de Cabadas

Lago Yuriria

Moroleón

Lerma

51

Acámbaro

43

Lago de Cuitzeo

ZAMORA/GUADALAJARA

15

Quiroga

Morelia

Ciudad Hidalgo

Angahuán

Lake Pátzcuaro

15

14

Pátzcuaro

51

Uruapan

Zitacuaro

Parque Nacional Eduardo Ruíz

120

MICHOACÁN

Tuzantla

Nueva Italia

La Huacana

Nocupétaro

134

Presa del Infiernillo

Bejucos

Huetamo

Balsas

city dwellers often head to the state of Querétaro for the weekend, where they unwind in the thermal springs of San Juan del Río and Tequisquiapan. Though the restorative powers of these springs have never been proved scientifically, the waters are said to ease arthritis pain, cure insomnia, and improve digestion.

The heartland also honors the events and people that helped to shape modern Mexico. In ornate cathedrals or bucolic plazas, down narrow alleyways or high atop hillsides, the traveler will discover monuments—and remnants—of a heroic past. During numerous fiestas, the visitor can savor the region's historic spirit. On a night filled with fireworks, off-key music, and tireless celebrants, it's hard not to be caught up in the vital expression of national pride.

Tourism is welcomed in the heartland, especially in these hard economic times, and tourists are treated naturally by residents, who go about their lives in an ordinary fashion. Families visit parks for Sunday picnics, youngsters tussle in school courtyards, old men chat in shaded plazas, and Tarascan women in traditional garb sell their wares in crowded *mercados* (markets). Though a tour operator or vendor may attempt to persuade foreign passersby to part with their money, rarely is the overture less than good-natured. Unlike areas where attractions have been specifically designed for tourism, the Bajío relies on its historic ties and the architectural integrity of its cities to appeal to the traveler.

SAN MIGUEL DE ALLENDE

San Miguel de Allende first began luring foreigners in the late 1930s when Stirling Dickinson, an American, and prominent locals founded an art school in this mountainous settlement. The school, now called the Instituto Allende, has grown in stature over the years—as has the city's reputation as a writers' and artists' colony. Walk down any cobblestoned street and you're likely to see residents of a variety of national origins. Some come to study at the Instituto Allende or the Academia Hispano-Americana, some to escape the harsh northern winters, and still others to retire.

Cultural offerings in this town of about 110,000 reflect its large American community. There are literary readings, art shows, a lending library, and aerobics classes. Nevertheless, San Miguel, declared a national monument in 1926, retains its Mexican characteristics. Wandering down streets lined with 18th-century mansions, you'll also discover fountains, monuments, and churches, all reminders of the city's illustrious—and sometimes notorious—past. The onetime headquarters of the Spanish Inquisition in New Spain, for example, is located at the corner of Calles Hernández Macías and Pila Seca; the former Inquisition jail stands across the way.

Exploring

Numbers in the margin correspond to points of interest on the San Miguel de Allende map.

Most of San Miguel's historic sights are clustered in the downtown area and can be seen in a couple of hours. Begin at the main plaza, commonly called **El Jardín** (the garden). Seated on one of its gray wrought-iron benches, you'll quickly get a feel for the town: Old men with canes exchange tales, youngsters in school uniform bustle by, fruit vendors hawk their wares, and bells from the nearby La Parroquia pierce the thin mountain air at each quarter hour.

248

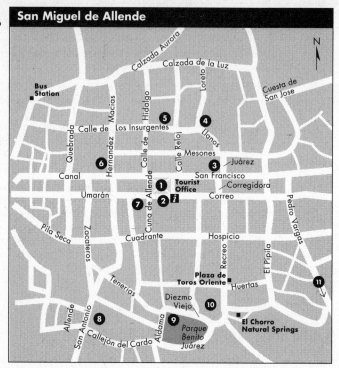

San Miguel de Allende

2️⃣ Leaving El Jardín, cross Calle del Correo to reach **La Parroquia** on the south side of the plaza. This imposing pink Gothic-style parish church, made of local *cantera* sandstone, was designed in the late 19th century by self-trained Indian mason Ceferino Gutiérrez, who sketched his designs in the sand with a stick. Gutiérrez was purportedly inspired by postcards of European Gothic cathedrals. Since the postcards gave no hint of what the back of those cathedrals looked like, the posterior of La Parroquia was done in quintessential Mexican style.

La Parroquia still functions as a house of worship, though its interior has been changed over the years. Gilded wood altars, for example, were replaced with neoclassical stone altars. The original bell, cast in 1732, still calls parishioners to mass several times daily.

3️⃣ Three blocks from La Parroquia, the **Iglesia de San Francisco,** on Calle Juárez, has one of the finest Churrigueresque facades in the state of Guanajuato. (José Churriguera, a 17th-century Spanish architect, was noted for his extravagantly decorative Baroque style.) Built in the late 18th century, the church was financed by donations from wealthy patrons and by revenue from bullfights. Topping the elaborately carved exterior is the image of Saint Francis of Assisi; below are sculptures of Saint John and Our Lady of Sorrows, as well as a crucifix.

Continue a few steps north on Calle Juárez until you reach Calle Mesones and the colorful **Mercado Ignacio Ramírez,** which occupies the small plaza directly in front of the Oratorio de San Felipe Neri and spills over onto the surrounding streets (for about six blocks). This market is particularly active on Sundays, when country folk come to town with pigs, chickens, and other livestock, along with succulent produce. During the week, rows of fresh fruits and vegetables are supplemented by racks of cheaply made clothing, inexpensive American toys, and blaring Mexican-made tapes and records. The dome of the **Oratorio de San Felipe Neri** is visible just beyond the market. This church, located across the market plaza on Calle de los Insurgentes, was built by local Indians in 1712. The pink stone of the eastern facade (with its figure of Our Lady of Solitude) is a remnant of the original chapel; its newer southern front was built in an ornate Baroque style. In 1734 the wealthy Count of Canal paid for an addition to the Oratorio. His **Templo de Santa Casa de Loreto,** dedicated to the Virgin of Loreto, is just behind the Oratorio; its main entrance, now blocked by a grille, is in the left rear of the Oratorio. Peer through the grille to see the heavily gilded altars and effigies of the count and his wife, under which they are buried.

⑤ Continue down Calle de los Insurgentes for another block to **La Biblioteca Pública** (☎ 415/2–04–35). Posted on the bulletin board in the entranceway to the library are many notices (mostly in English) about events such as literary readings or yoga and aerobics classes. Inside are the offices of the English-language newspaper, *Atención San Miguel*, as well as a reading room with back issues of popular publications and English books—it's a great place to take a breather from sightseeing. On Sundays the library offers a two-hour house-and-garden tour of San Miguel that departs at noon. Tickets cost about $9, with all proceeds going to the library. *Calle de los Insurgentes 25, ☎ 415/2–02–93 or 415/2–37–70. ☉ Weekdays 10–2 and 4–7, Sat. 10–2.*

From the library, walk two blocks west to Calle Hernández Macías and then head south. At No. 75, across the street from the building
⑥ that houses the U.S. Consulate, is the **Bellas Artes** cultural center. This impressive cloister, once the Royal Convent of the Conception, is now an institute for the study of music, dance, and the visual arts. Several murals, including one by the famed Mexican painter David Siqueiros, are on exhibit. There's also a cafeteria inside. ☎ *415/2–08–89. ☉ Daily 10–2 and 4–6:30.*

Directly behind Bellas Artes, the **Iglesia de la Concepción** touts one of the largest domes in Mexico. The two-story roof, completed in 1891, boasts both elegant Corinthian columns and ornamental pilasters and is said to have been inspired by the dome of Les Invalides in Paris. Ceferino Gutiérrez (of La Parroquia fame) is credited with its design.

Take Hernandez Macias south for a block and turn left on Umará to
⑦ reach the **Casa de Ignacio Allende.** Now housing a museum and gallery, this is the birthplace of Ignacio Allende, one of Mexico's great independence heroes. Allende was a Creole aristocrat who, along with Father Miguel Hidalgo, plotted in the early 1800s to overthrow the Spanish regime. At clandestine meetings held in San Miguel and nearby Querétaro, the two discussed strategies, organized an army, gathered weapons, and enlisted the support of clerics for the struggle ahead.

Spanish Royalists learned of their plot and began arresting conspirators in Querétaro on September 13, 1810. Allende and Hidalgo received word of these actions and hastened their plans. At dawn on September 16, they rang out the cry for independence, and the fighting began. Allende was the military leader of the insurrection and was captured and executed by the Royalists the following year. As a tribute to his brave efforts, San Miguel El Grande became San Miguel de Allende in the 20th century. *Calle Cuna de Allende 1, ☎ 415/2–24–99. ☛ Free. ☉ Tues.–Sun. 10–4.*

TIME OUT On the southwest corner of the Plaza is **Cafe del Jardín** (Portal Allende 2, ☎ 415/2–06–50). This unassuming little café has excellent coffee, cappuccino, hot chocolate, and snack food; breakfasts are tasty and inexpensive. There's friendly service and best of all—it's that American influence—two cups of coffee for the price of one!

After exploring downtown, take a leisurely stroll to sights in San Miguel's outlying neighborhoods. From the south side of the plaza (the side with La Parroquia), head west four blocks on Calle de Umarán until you reach Calle Zacateros. Turn south on this narrow cobblestoned street to reach some of the town's most interesting crafts shops—stocked with everything from silver jewelry to Mexican ceremonial masks. Keep in mind that many stores close for siesta from 2 to 4 PM.

Past the shops, Calle Zacateros becomes Ancha de San Antonio. On **8** your left at No. 20 is the entrance to the celebrated **Instituto Allende** (☎ 415/2–01–90, FAX 415/2–45–38). The school is set in the former hacienda of the Count of Canal. Since its founding in 1951, thousands of students from around the world have come to learn Spanish and to take classes in social studies and the arts. Courses last from a couple of weeks to a month or longer. Lush with bougainvillea, rose bushes, and ivy vines, the grounds provide a quiet refuge for students and visitors alike.

From the institute, continue south on Ancha de San Antonio until you reach Callejón del Cardo on your left. This road, unlike so many in town, is wide and paved, looking as though it might lead to a private estate. Continue past St. Paul's Episcopal Church, where many Americans worship, until you arrive at the cobblestoned Calle Aldama on your left.

Heading downhill, walk briefly through a neighborhood of white-**9** washed houses before reaching the north entrance to **Parque Benito Juárez,** a favorite of joggers, sweethearts, and children. The five-acre park—the largest in San Miguel—is a shaded labyrinth of evergreens, palm trees, and gardens. Take a few minutes to stroll around, or find a bench and observe the activity around you.

Return to the north rim of the park, where Calle Diezmo Viejo turns off Calle Aldama. Follow Calle Diezmo Viejo until the imposing terra-cotta-colored La Huerta Santa Elena is in front of you. From here turn **10** left and walk one block uphill to reach the **Lavandería,** one of San Miguel's most endearing places. At this outdoor public laundry—a collection of cement tubs set above Juárez Park—local women gather daily to wash clothes and gossip as their predecessors have done for centuries. Though some women claim to have more efficient washing facilities at home, the lure of the spring-fed troughs—not to mention the chance to catch up on the news—brings them daily to this shaded courtyard.

Calle de Recreo, the road above the Lavandería, heads north back toward the plaza. At times narrow and dusty, it leads uphill past quiet pastel-colored residences and lovely views of the surrounding mountains. To return to town, follow Recreo north for several blocks until you reach Calle del Correo. Make a left, and in three blocks you'll be back at the main plaza.

11 For energetic exploration, consider a climb to **El Mirador** ("the lookout"). One block before town, turn right off Recreo onto Calle Hospicio. Follow Hospicio for three blocks until you reach Calle Pedro Vargas, a narrow, busy two-way street. Make a right and head uphill. Soon you'll notice a statue of Ignacio Allende on your left; a panorama of the city, mountains, and reservoir will be below on your right. The vista is most commanding at sunset, and chances are you won't be alone, as El Mirador is popular with both locals and tourists.

The walk back to town is an approximately 15-minute downhill trek. (Calle Pedro Vargas hits Calle del Correo, which takes you back to the plaza.) Taxis are usually available and the trip back should cost no more than $1.50.

Off the Beaten Track

Roughly 50 kilometers (30 miles) north of San Miguel via Route 51 is the town of **Dolores Hidalgo,** which played an important role in the fight for independence. It was here, before dawn on September 16, 1810, that Father Miguel Hidalgo—the local priest—gave an impassioned sermon to his clergy that ended with the cry, "Mexicanos, Viva México!" At 11 PM on September 15, politicians throughout the land repeat the "grito," signaling the start of Independence Day celebrations. On September 16 (and only on this day), the bell in Hidalgo's parish church is rung.

Casa Hidalgo, the house where the patriot lived, is now a museum. It contains copies of important letters Hidalgo sent or received and other independence memorabilia. *Calle Morelos 1,* ☎ *468/2–01–71.* ☺ *Tues.–Sat. 9–2 and 4–6, Sun. 10–2.* ☛ *About $4.*

The town is also known for its output of handpainted ceramics, most prominently tiles and tableware. Dolores Hidalgo can be reached easily by bus from San Miguel de Allende. Buses depart frequently from the Central de Autobuses; travel time is about one hour.

Shopping

For centuries San Miguel's artisans have been creating a wide variety of crafts ranging from straw products to metalwork. Though some boutiques in town may be a bit pricey, there are good buys on silver, brass, tin, woven cotton goods, and folk art. Opening and closing hours are erratic; a number of stores open at 9 AM, but many others don't start conducting business until 11; some shut their doors for traditional afternoon siesta (2 through 4 or 5). Closing hour tends to be around 7 or 8 PM and most (but not all) shops are closed on Sunday. Most San Miguel shops accept MC and V.

Brass and Tinware
Several stores in town sell locally crafted metal objects, such as plates and trays, chests, mirrors, and decorative animals and birds.

Casa Cohen (Reloj 12, ☎ 415/2–14–34) carries furniture and metalware in all shapes and sizes. **Casa Canal** (Calle de Canal 3, ☎ 415/2–04–79), set in a beautiful old hacienda, sells new furniture, though much of it is made in traditional styles.

Designer Clothing
Benetton (Mesones 80, ☎ 415/2–08–30) carries the colorful modern fashions you'd expect—though what they're doing in San Miguel is anyone's guess. **Sidell** (Quebrada 117, ☎ 415/2–04–86) markets one-of-a-kind clothing (mostly for women) designed and made by the owners. The pieces are all hand-dyed and silk-screened.

Folk Art
For handpainted masks, ceremonial art objects, and other regional handicrafts, try the following:

Artes de México (Aurora 47 at Dolores Hidalgo exit, ☎ 415/2–07–64) has been producing and selling traditional crafts, including furniture, metalwork, and ceramics, for more than 40 years. **Casa Maxwell** (Calle de Canal 14, ☎ 415/2–02–47) is ideal for one-stop shoppers: This seemingly endless building offers folk art, ceramics, jewelry, furniture, glassware, metalware, modern clothing, and a lot more. **El Pegaso** (Corregidora 6, ☎ 415/2–13–51), a combined art shop and restaurant, sells traditional art from Mexico and Guatemala, including some rare pieces on the second floor. **La Calaca** (Mesones 93, no ☎) also focuses on folk art from the Americas, mainly Mexico, Guatemala, and Peru. **Tonatiu Metzli** (Las Flores 27, ☎ 415/2–08–69) features a colorful selection of work from Mexico, China, Africa, and elsewhere. **Veryka** (Zacateros 6-A, ☎ 415/2–21–14), whose emphasis is on Latin American folk art, has a particularly fine selection of *muertos* (skeleton figurines for the Day of the Dead) from Puebla.

Jewelry

Established in 1963, **Joyería David** (Calle Zacateros 53, ☎ 415/2–00–56) has an extensive selection of gold, silver, copper, and brass jewelry, all made on the premises. A number of pieces contain Mexican opals, amethysts, topaz, malachite, and turquoise. The extremely reputable **Beckmann Joyería** (Calle Hernández Macías 115, ☎ 415/2–16–13) designs its own gold and silver pieces. **Platería Cerro Blanco** (Calle de Canal 17, ☎ 415/2–05–02) also creates and crafts its own silver and gold jewelry and will arrange a visit to its *taller* (workshop) on request. **Platería y Joyería Julio** (Calle del Correo 8, ☎ 415/2–02–48) sells silver pieces made by San Miguel artists and carries a large selection of religious jewelry—crucifixes, medallions of the Virgin, and the like.

Sports

Participant Sports

Travelers who enjoy the sporting life will find good facilities for swimming, tennis, horseback riding, and golf at deluxe and first-class hotels situated near the Instituto Allende or on the outskirts of town. (The San Miguel tourist office can provide a list of these properties.) The **Hotel Hacienda Taboada** (Km 8 on the Dolores Hidalgo Hwy., ☎ 415/2–08–88, FAX 415/2–17–98) has simmering thermal pools that are open to the public for a nominal fee. The **Club de Golf Malanquin** (Km 3 on the Celaya Hwy., ☎ 415/2–05–16) features a heated pool, steam baths, tennis courts, and nine holes of golf, all of which are open to the public.

Spectator Sports

Visitors who want to witness the pageantry of a traditional Mexican bullfight can do so at the **Plaza de Toros Oriente** (situated off Calle de Recreo) several times a year. The most important contest takes place during the last week of September when the town's patron saint San Miguel (known in English as St. Michael the Archangel) is commemorated. Posters announcing fights are set up in El Jardín in the center of town and at the Fonda La Mesa del Matador restaurant at Calle Hernández Macías 76.

Dining

For its size, San Miguel has a surprising number of international restaurants (about 170 at last count). The recent influx of Americans has given rise to new Tex-Mex and health-food establishments; a European influence has contributed to nearly authentic French, Italian, and Spanish cuisines. Regional Mexican food is available in a variety of price ranges. Much of this fare is made from pork, chicken, or ground beef and often broiled, fried, or covered with a bread-crumb batter. Dishes are prepared with onions or garlic and served with a red or green chile sauce. Unless otherwise indicated, dress is casual.

CATEGORY	COST*
$$$$	over $20
$$$	$15–$20
$$	$8–$15
$	under $8

per person, excluding drinks and service

$$$$ **La Vendimia.** One of San Miguel's best restaurants, La Vendimia offers cuisine described by proprietors Jack Jesse and Federico Escovar as Continental with a touch of southern California. In a setting designed and furnished by a local Mexican artist, you'll be served such dishes as fresh tuna and julienne mushrooms in a Japanese sauce, and, for the homesick, a meat loaf almost like Grandma used to make (except Grandma never added chorizo), with spinach and mashed potatoes. The happy hour on the patio from 6 to 8 PM Monday–Saturday features flamenco and other lively guitar music; Sundays, December through March, there's jazz from 8 to 10 PM. ✗ *Hidalgo 12,* ☎ *415/2–26–45. Reservations advised. MC, V.*

$$$ **La Antigua Restaurant y Tapa Bar.** A cheerful room with fewer than a dozen tables (each with a baby-blue tablecloth and a vase of orange carnations) and a polished wood bar that can seat up to 15 people, La Antigua puts its clientele in the mood for a large variety of tapas with its European café furniture and Spanish bolero music. Among its specialties are *queso antiguo* (baked cheese with chilies), *chisterra* (a sliced and fried Spanish-style sausage), *camarones con tocineta* (jumbo shrimp fried with bacon), and *pulpo antiguo* (squid sautéed in garlic and herbs). All dishes are served with bread or tortillas. ✗ *Calle Canal 9,* ☎ *415/2–25–86. Reservations accepted. AE, MC, V.*

$$$ **La Princesa.** More upscale restaurants have opened in San Miguel recently, but La Princesa is still *the* place to go for intimate dining. The romantic ambience is enhanced by cloth-covered tables, dark wood paneling, lazily turning ceiling fans, a large wine selection, and musicians who entertain from 8 PM to 3 AM. The Executive Menu, served daily 1–8 PM, includes soup, one of eight entrées (ranging from fillet of red snapper to Mexican-style stuffed peppers), dessert, coffee or tea, and a complimentary margarita. After 8 PM the menu features steak dishes, including chateaubriand for two, and the prices climb. ✗ *Calle de Recreo 5,* ☎ *415/2–14–03. Reservations not accepted. AE, MC, V.*

$$ **Fonda Meson de San José.** On a tree-shaded cobblestoned patio inside a complex of small shops, this well-established restaurant offers German as well as Mexican cuisines. Owner-chef Angela Merkel is enthusiastic about her roulade, potato pancakes, and German chocolate cake and once a month invites other local chefs to display their talents. The German buffet, originally offered for Oktoberfest, is in great demand. ✗ *Mesones 38,* ☎ *415/2–38–48. Reservations not accepted. No credit cards.*

$$ **Mamá Mía.** It might seem odd to order Italian food in Mexico, but Mamá Mía has a satisfying assortment of pastas and pizzas, as well as a decent fettuccine bolognese and spaghetti parmesana. House specials include fettuccine Alex (with white wine, ham, cream, and mushrooms) and fettuccine à la Mexicana (with ground sausage, peppers, onions, and tomatoes). Folk musicians entertain on the lush outdoor patio come

dusk. ✕ *Calle de Umarán 8,* ☎ *415/2–20–63. Reservations not accepted. MC, V.*

$$ **Rincon Español.** The soft pink walls of this pleasant Spanish restaurant are covered with reproductions of the works of famous Spanish artists—Joan Miró, Picasso, and Salvador Dalí—and its nickname, La Casa de la Paella, reveals the dining room's specialty. Not a little of the charm of this place derives from the evening guitar music and flamenco dancing, pleasing adjuncts to dessert. ✕ *Correo 29,* ☎ *415/2–29–84. Reservations not accepted. MC, V.*

Lodging

San Miguel has a wide selection of hotels ranging from cozy bed-and-breakfasts to elegant all-suite properties. Rooms fill up quickly during summer and winter seasons, when northern tourists migrate here in droves. Make reservations several months in advance if you plan to visit at these times.

CATEGORY	COST*
$$$$	over $90
$$$	$60–$90
$$	$25–$60
$	under $25

*All prices are for a standard double room, excluding 10% tax.

$$$–$$$$ **Casa de Sierra Nevada.** Once the home of the archbishop of Guana-
★ juato and the marquise of Sierra Nevada, this elegant country-style inn (built in 1850) hosted George Bush in 1981 and continues to attract ambassadors, diplomats, heads of state, film stars, and bullfighters. Its complex of four colonial buildings, on either side of a cobblestoned street a few blocks from La Parroquia, contains 18 individually decorated suites and five standard rooms. Lace curtains, handwoven rugs, chandeliers, and prints by artist Diego Rivera adorn some rooms; fireplaces, cozy private terraces, and skylights enhance others. From the terrace of room No. 1, there's an excellent view of La Parroquia. 🏨 *Calle Hospicio 35, 37700,* ☎ *415/2–04–15 or 415/2–18–95. 20 rooms with bath. Restaurant, spa. AE, MC, V.*

$$$ **Villa Jacaranda.** An all-suite hotel located near the Parque Benito Juárez, the Villa Jacaranda boasts a full range of amenities. Rooms, though unimaginatively decorated, have space heaters and cable TVs (with channels from the United States). The hotel's Cine/Bar shows American movies Tuesday–Saturday at 7:30 PM and live sports events on a giant screen. The price of admission—roughly $3—includes a drink. 🏨 *Calle Aldama 53, 37700,* ☎ *415/2–10–15 or 415/2–08–11,* ᴲᴬᵡ *415/2–08–83. 15 suites. Restaurant, pool, hot tub. AE, MC, V.*

$$$ **Casa Carmen.** Run by a very friendly long-time San Miguel family, this pension is an oasis of peace in the center of town. Set in a 200-year-old hacienda just two blocks from the Plaza, it features large, immaculate rooms tastefully decorated with antiques and other wooden furnishings. Two of the double rooms in the front have an upstairs loft for the bed, and the two small patios are ideal places to relax with a good book after walking around San Miguel. 🏨 *Correo 31, 37700,* ☎ *415/2–08–44. 11 rooms. Breakfast and lunch included in room rates. No credit cards.*

$$ **La Mansión del Bosque.** Located on a quiet side street across from the
★ Parque Benito Juárez, this renovated hacienda opened as a guest house and restaurant in 1968. Its American owners, George and Ruth Hyba, cater to long-term guests in the winter and more transient visitors in the off-season. The hotel, which operates on a Modified American Plan

that includes breakfast and dinner, has guest rooms with such homey touches as handwoven cotton spreads, locally made throw rugs and artifacts, and bookshelves. Many rooms feature working fireplaces as well as private, plant-filled terraces. The lounge off the foyer has books and magazines, a telephone for long-distance calls, and a house cat that watches over the premises. ⊡ *Calle Aldama 65, 37700,* ☎ *415/2–02–77. 23 rooms with bath. Restaurant, bar. No credit cards.*

$$ Posada de las Monjas. This 19th-century structure has been operating as a hotel for more than 50 years. It caters to long-term visitors, mainly students from the Instituto Allende or Academia Hispano-Americana, but welcomes guests for shorter stays. Rooms are furnished in a colonial style, with some furniture in the old wing looking worn enough to be authentically 17th century. The rooftop public terrace has tables and lounge chairs and offers commanding views of mountains and city. Some rooms have fireplaces, and there's a communal television in the lobby. ⊡ *Calle de Canal 37, 37700,* ☎ *415/2–01–71. 65 rooms with bath; 37 are in a new wing. Restaurant, bar, laundry service. AE, DC, MC, V.*

$$ Posada de San Francisco. This colonial-style property, located on the main plaza downtown, resembles an old Spanish monastery—a crucifix hangs in the lobby beneath a stone archway, and some rooms have crosses over the beds. Rooms on the plaza will appeal to people-watchers, but on weekends and during the busy season these quarters can be rather noisy. For a quieter setting, request a room on the second or third floor (some overlook nearby mountains and churches) or one inside, facing the bougainvillea-draped courtyard. ⊡ *Plaza Principal 2, 37700,* ☎ *and* FAX *415/2–14–66, 415/2–00–72, or 415/2–24–25. 52 rooms, suites, and junior suites with bath. Restaurant, bar. MC, V.*

$$ Villa Mirasol. Each of this lodging's seven rooms is decorated with original prints, oil paintings, pastels, and small sculptures; most of the rooms are flooded with sunlight during the day. All have either a private or shared terrace; the ones facing Calle Pila Seca have beautiful vistas of the surrounding hills. Located on a quiet and secluded street no more than a 10-minute walk from the principal plaza, Villa Mirasol includes in its price a rich breakfast, such as *chilaquiles* (baked tortillas with cheese and chicken) or Mexican-style scrambled eggs with chilies, tomatoes, and onions, as well as coffee and pastries in the afternoon. The hotel was a private house until 1983 and today its cozy and intimate atmosphere affords visitors a welcome distinction from the larger, less personal hotels in the area. It also offers its guests use of the Club de Golf free of charge. ⊡ *Pila Seca 35, 37700,* ☎ *415/2–15–64. 7 rooms with bath. MC, V.*

The Arts and Nightlife

San Miguel, long known as an artists' colony, continues to nurture that image today. Galleries, museums, and art shops line the streets near El Jardín, and two government-run salons—at **Bellas Artes** (Calle Hernández Macías 75) and the **Instituto Allende** (Ancha de San Antonio 20)—showcase the work of a variety of Mexican artists. For a sampling of regional talent, visit the **Galería San Miguel** (Plaza Principal 14, ☎ 415/2–04–54), **Galería Atenea** (Calle Cuna de Allende 15, ☎ 415/2–07–85), and the **Klingerman Gallery** (Calle de Umarán 6, ☎ 415/2–09–51). If a rather large painting or photograph strikes your fancy, don't despair: Some gallery owners will ship your newfound treasure back to the States for you.

Nightlife in San Miguel is also plentiful. On most evenings you can readily satisfy a whim for a literary reading, an American movie, a theatrical production, or a turn on a disco dance floor. The most up-to-date listings of events can be found in the English paper *Atención San Miguel,* published every Friday. The bulletin board at the public library (Calle de los Insurgentes 25) is also a good source of current events.

La Taberna de los Reyes (Hidalgo 3, no ☎) features dance music from 9 PM until 2 AM Thursday through Sunday, with dinner/theater on Wednesday at 9:30 PM. Other places that feature live music include **Pancho and Lefty's** (Calle Mesones 99, ☎ 415/2–19–58), with rock, jazz, and blues bands, depending on the night. **La Fragua** (Calle Cuna de Allende 3, ☎ 415/2–11–44), located just a couple of doors off the Plaza, often has traditional Mexican bands. At **Mamá Mía** (Calle de Umarán 8, ☎ 415/2–20–63) you can hear Peruvian folk music and classical guitar. **El Jardín** (San Francisco 4, ☎ 415/2–17–06), though more of a restaurant than a club, has a piano bar. **Laberintos Disco** (Calle Ancha de San Antonio 7, ☎ 415/2–03–62), across from the Instituto Allende outside the center of town, is often hopping until the early morning hours. **El Ring Disco Club** (Calle de Hidalgo 25, ☎ 415/2–19–98) hasn't been around for very long, but invariably attracts a good crowd on the weekends.

San Miguel de Allende Essentials

Arriving and Departing

BY PLANE

Continental (☎ 800/525–0280), **Mexicana** (☎ 800/531–7921), and **Aeromexico** (☎ 800/237–6639) all offer international service to Leon International Airport, which is about two hours from San Miguel. In the United States, Continental has direct flights from Houston; Mexicana flies from Chicago, San Antonio, and Los Angeles; and Aeromexico leaves nonstop from Los Angeles only. Taxis from the airport to downtown cost about $25.

BY CAR

Driving time from Mexico City to San Miguel is roughly four hours via Route 57 (to Querétaro) and Route 111 (Querétaro to San Miguel). The freeway saves a half hour in travel time by bypassing Querétero. Cars can be rented at various outlets in Mexico City; in San Miguel, **Renta de Autos Gama** (Calle de Hidalgo 3, ☎ 415/2–08–15) has a limited selection of standard-shift compacts available.

BY TRAIN

The *Aztec* leaves Mexico City for San Miguel de Allende at 9 AM, arriving in San Miguel at 2 PM; it departs San Miguel at 2 PM and arrives in Mexico City at 7 PM. The first-class round-trip fare is $11. The train from Monterrey to Mexico City also stops at San Miguel. For current schedules and fares, contact **Mexico by Train** (☎ and FAX 210/725–3659 or 800/321–1699).

The San Miguel train station (☎ 415/2–00–07) is located on La Calzada de Estación (Station Highway).

BY BUS

Direct bus service is available daily between the Central del Norte (North Bus Station) in Mexico City and the new Central de Autobuses in San Miguel. Several major lines—including **Flecha Amarilla, Herradura de Plata, Primera Plus,** and **Tres Estrellas de Oro**—offer frequent service; travel time is about four hours. Inexpensive, second-class bus service is also available from San Miguel to other area cities.

Getting Around

San Miguel de Allende is best negotiated on foot, keeping in mind two pieces of advice. The city is more than a mile above sea level, so visitors not accustomed to high altitudes may tire quickly during their first few days there. Streets are paved with rugged cobblestone, and some of them do not have sidewalks. Sturdy footwear, such as athletic or other rubber-soled shoes, is therefore highly recommended.

BY TAXI

Taxis can easily be hailed on the street or found at taxi stands such as **Sitio Allende** in the main plaza (☎ 415/2–05–50 or 415/2–01–92), **Sitio San Francisco** on Calle Mesones (no ☎), or **Sitio San Felipe** on Calle Juárez (no ☎). Flat rates to the bus terminal, train station, and other parts of the city apply.

Important Addresses and Numbers

CONSULATE

The U.S. Consular agent is Colonel Phil Maher. *Calle Hernández Macías 72,* ☎ *415/2–23–57 during office hours;* ☎ *415/2–00–68 or 415/2–00–99 for emergencies.* ⊙ *Mon. and Wed. 9–1 and 4–7; Tues. and Thurs. 4–7.*

EMERGENCIES

Police (☎ 415/2–00–23). **Ambulance-Red Cross** (☎ 415/4–82–92 or 415/4–82–96). **Fire Department** (415/2–08–77 or 415/2–01–64).

Hospital. The staff at **Union Médica** (Calle de San Francisco 50, ☎ 415/2–22–33 and 415/2–17–61) can refer you to an English-speaking doctor.

Pharmacies. San Miguel has many pharmacies, but American residents recommend **Botica Agundis,** where English speakers are often on hand. *Calle de Canal 26,* ☎ *415/2–11–98.* ⊙ *Daily 10–midnight.*

MONEY EXCHANGE

Banks will change dollars or traveler's checks at certain hours of the day, usually in the morning. Lines, however, are often long and move slowly. A better bet is the **Deal Casa de Cambio.** *San Francisco 4,* ☎ *415/2–29–32.* ⊙ *Weekdays 9–2 and 4–6, Sat. 9–2.*

ENGLISH-LANGUAGE BOOKSTORES

El Colibrí (Sollana 30, ☎ 415/2–07–51) has a good selection of novels, magazines, and a few art supplies. **Lagundi.** (Umaran 17, ☎ 415/2–08–30) has a large selection of magazines, but no books. Its emphasis these days is on having the most art supplies in town.

TRAVEL AGENCIES

Major agencies are **Viajes Vértiz** (American Express representative at Calle de Hidalgo 1A, ☎ 415/2–18–56 or 415/2–16–95, FAX 415/2–04–99) and **Viajes San Miguel** (Sollana 4, ☎ 415/2–25–37 or 415/2–28–32, FAX 415/2–25–38).

BUSINESS SERVICES

La Conexion (Aldama 1, ☎ and FAX 415/2–16–87 or 415/2–15–99) offers 24-hour answering and fax service, a Mexico address for receiving mail, lockboxes, a Macintosh computer center, and other services. ⊙ *Weekdays 8–6, Sat. 8–3, Sun. 10–2.*

VISITOR INFORMATION

The **Delegación de Turismo** is located in the center of town on the southeast corner of Plaza Principal (also called El Jardín) to the left of La Parroquia (parish church). Climb the steps of the outdoor restaurant La Terraza and turn right; the tourist office is next to the pizza stand.

Most of the brochures here are in Spanish, but an English-speaking staff member can help with basic information. You can also pick up a good map of the city that locates major hotels, restaurants, and historic attractions. *Plaza Principal s/n,* ☎ *415/2–17–47.* ⊘ *Mon.–Sat. 10–3 and 5–7:30.*

GUANAJUATO

Once Mexico's most prominent silver-mining city, Guanajuato is a colonial gem, tucked into the mountains at 6,700 feet. This provincial state capital is distinguished by twisting cobblestoned alleyways, pastel-walled houses, 15 shaded plazas, and a vast subterranean roadway (where a rushing river once flowed). In the center of town is Alhóndiga de Granaditas—an 18th-century grain-storage facility that was the site of the first battle in Mexico's War of Independence from Spain.

The city comes alive in mid-October with the International Cervantes Festival, a two-week-long celebration of the arts. Day-to-day affairs, however, continue as usual. Students still rush to class with books tucked under their arms, women eye fresh produce at the Mercado Hidalgo, and old men utter greetings from behind white-washed doorways. On weekend nights, *estudiantinas* (student minstrels dressed as medieval troubadours) serenade the public in the city squares.

At first Guanajuato's underground roadways and poorly marked streets may seem daunting. Armed with a good map and a sense of adventure, however, you can enjoy exploring the city's hidden passages. If you do get lost, just remember that the top of the Alhóndiga (which can be seen from many spots in town) points north, and the spires of the Basílica Colegiata Nuestra Señora de Guanajuato, at the Plaza de la Paz, point south.

Exploring

Numbers in the margin correspond to points of interest on the Guanajuato map.

Although many of Guanajuato's major attractions are within walking distance of one another, the fact that the downtown is shaped like an oblong loop makes this a confusing city to get around. The map that you'll pick up at the tourist office (Plaza de la Paz 14) probably won't make things too much clearer. It's difficult to notate on maps the frequent changes of street names—or the fact that many of the streets don't have signs.

❶ Still, the tourist office is a good place to begin a walking tour. Turn right and walk up Avenida Juárez to reach **Jardín Unión,** the tree-lined, wedge-shaped plaza that is Guanajuato's central square. Two sides of the wedge are pedestrian walkways; the third is Avenida Juárez. On Thursday and Sunday evenings, musical performances take place in the bandshell here; at other times, groups of musicians break into impromptu song along the plaza's shaded tile walkways.

❷ The ornate **Teatro Juárez** is just past the Jardín to your right on Calle de Sopeña. Adorned with bronze lion sculptures and a line of large Greek muses looming over the Jardín from the roof, the theater was inaugurated by Mexican dictator Porfirio Díaz in 1903 with a performance of *Aïda.* It now serves as the principal venue of the annual International Cervantes Festival (*see* The Arts and Nightlife, *below*). A brief tour of the Art Deco interior is available for a nominal fee. ☎ *473/2–01–83.* ⊘ *Tues.–Sat. 9–2 and 5:15–7:45, Sun. 10–2.*

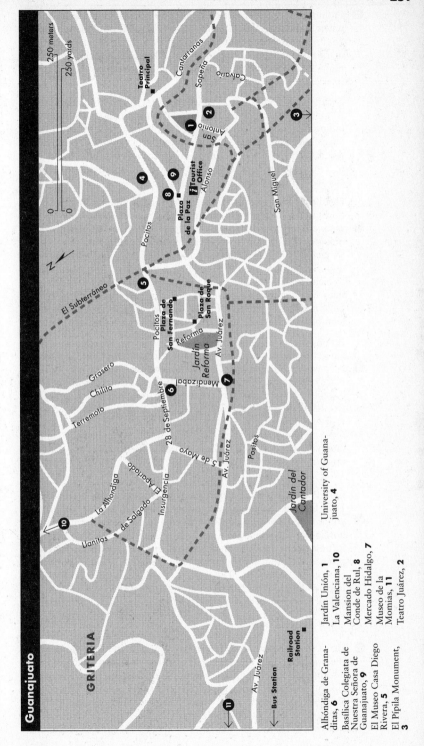

Guanajuato

GRITERIA

Teatro Principal ■

Cantarranas

Sopeña

Calvario

1

2

3

San Antonio

Alonso

San Miguel

4

9

8 ■

ℹ Tourist Office

Plaza de la Paz ■

Pocitos

5

El Subterráneo

Pocitos

Plaza de San Fernando

Plaza de San Roque ■

Reforma

Av. Juárez

Jardín Reforma

Mendizábal

7

Grasero

Chilito

Terremoto

6

28 de Septiembre

5 de Mayo

Av. Juárez

Pocitos

La Alhóndiga

El Apartado

Insurgencia

de Salgado

Llanitos

10

Jardín del Contador

Av. Juárez

Av. Juárez

◄ Bus Station

Railroad Station ■

11

250 meters

250 yards

0

0

N

Alhóndiga de Granaditas, **6**

Basílica Colegiata de Nuestra Señora de Guanajuato, **9**

El Museo Casa Diego Rivera, **5**

El Pípila Monument, **3**

Jardín Unión, **1**

La Valenciana, **10**

Mansión del Conde de Rul, **8**

Mercado Hidalgo, **7**

Museo de la Momias, **11**

Teatro Juárez, **2**

University of Guanajuato, **4**

❸ From the Teatro Juárez it's an hour's steep climb to **El Pípila,** a monument to José Barajas, a young martyr of the War of Independence of 1810. Bear right on Calle de Sopeña just past the theater, and a sign marked El Pípila will direct you onto Callejón de Calvario, which eventually leads to the hillside memorial. It's easier to take a taxi or bus (marked Pípila) from the Jardín.

Nicknamed El Pípila, Barajas was a young miner who crept into the Alhóndiga de Granaditas (*see below*), where Spanish Royalists were hiding. With a stone shield strapped to his back, he set the front door ablaze. He died, but the Spanish troops were captured by Father Hidalgo's army in this early battle, giving the independence forces their first major military victory. There's a splendid panoramic view of the city from the monument.

Head back into town via Calle Cantarranas, a main street that winds down the hill and around the Jardín Unión. Just before Calle Cantar-
❹ ranas changes its name to Calle Pocitos, you'll see the **University of Guanajuato** (☎ 473/2–41–50), an institution founded in 1732 as a Jesuit seminary. The original Baroque church, La Compañia, still stands next door. The current university building, built in the 1950s, was designed to blend in with the town's architecture, but the modern interior is at odds with the colonial facade. If you do wander inside, check out the bulletin boards for notices of cultural events in town. (Also check bulletin boards along the pedestrian walkways of the Jardín.)

Among the school's most famous alumni is Diego Rivera, one of Mexico's great muralists. A short way down from where Calle Cantarranas
❺ becomes Calle Pocitos, you'll see **El Museo Casa Diego Rivera,** the birthplace of the artist. On view are 97 works by the master, among them his studies for the controversial mural commissioned for New York City's Rockefeller Center. Completed in 1933, the painting contained a portrait of Russian revolutionary Vladimir Lenin, which caused it to be removed immediately after it was displayed. The museum also contains family portraits, as well as the bed in which Rivera slept as a child and other family furniture. *Calle Pocitos 47,* ☎ *473/2–11–97.* ⓢ *Tues.–Sat. 10–2 and 4–6, Sun. 10–3.*

Calle Pocitos weaves past more residences and eventually becomes Calle 28 de Septiembre. On the left, just past the junction with Mendizabal,
❻ you'll find **Alhóndiga de Granaditas,** a massive stone structure with horizontal slit windows. This 18th-century grain-storage facility, a fortress during the War of Independence and the site of El Pípila's courageous act, is now a state museum with exhibits on local history, archaeology, and crafts. The hooks on which the Spanish Royalists impaled the heads of Father Hidalgo, Ignacio Allende, and two other independence leaders still hang on the exterior. *Calle 28 de Septiembre 6,* ☎ *473/2–11–12.* ☛ *About $4; free on Sun.* ⓢ *Tues.–Sat. 10–2 and 4–6, Sun. 10–3.*

❼ Head one block south to return to Avenida Juárez and the **Mercado Hidalgo.** You can't miss the 1910 cast-iron-and-glass structure, reminiscent of Victorian England's train stations and markets. Though the balcony stalls are filled with T-shirts and cheap plastic toys, the lower level offers authentic local wares, including fresh produce, peanuts, honey-drenched nut candies, and colorful basketry. Vendors line the sidewalk in front of the market, hawking flowers and local crafts.

Turn right on Juárez as you leave the market and continue on until the road splits near the Jardín Reforma. Leaving crowded Juárez, which veers to the right, keep to the left and cut down Calle Reforma, a short alleyway lined with shops. Bear right at the end of the street and you'll come to two pleasant courtyards: Plaza San Roque, which hosts outdoor performances during the Cervantes Festival, and Plaza San Fernando, a shady square where many book fairs are held.

This short detour will return you to Avenida Juárez, where it's a slight climb up to **Plaza de la Paz.** Built from 1895 to 1898, this square is surrounded by some of the city's finest colonial buildings. Chief among them is the 18th-century **Mansion del Conde de Rul,** residence of the count of Rul and Valenciana, who owned what was then the country's richest silver mine (*see below*). The two-story structure, located at the corner of Avenida Juárez and Callejón del Estudiante, was designed by famed Mexican architect Eduardo Tresguerras.

⑨ Dominating the plaza is the imposing **Basílica Colegiata de Nuestra Señora de Guanajuato,** a 17th-century Baroque church painted a striking yellow. Inside is the oldest Christian statue in Mexico, a bejeweled 8th-century statue of the Virgin. The highly venerated figure was a gift from King Philip II of Spain in 1557. On the Friday preceding Good Friday, miners, accompanied by floats and mariachi bands, parade to the basilica to pay homage to the Lady of Guanajuato.

Continuing up Avenida Juárez about half a block past the plaza, you'll pass the tourist office again and arrive back at the Jardín Unión, thus completing a circular tour of the city's main attractions.

TIME OUT For alfresco dining at the Jardín, try the terrace at the **Hotel Museo Posada Santa Fe** (Jardín Unión 12, ☎ 473/2–00–84). The menu includes such pricey specialties as broiled trout and chicken with mole, but you can just order a cappuccino and a slice of cake. Another outdoor café, **El Agora** (El Agora del Baratillo, ☎ 473/2–33–00), located down an alley off the plaza's southeast corner, has less expensive offerings. A four-course lunch, including soup, rice, entrée, and dessert, runs about $4.

⑩ There are two other sights worth exploring around Guanajuato. A few miles north of town on Highway 110 is the **Iglesia de San Cayetano,** known all over Guanajuato as **La Valenciana.** Constructed over 20 years in the latter part of the 18th century, it is one of the best-known colonial churches in all of Mexico. The pink stone facade is brilliantly, baroquely ornate. Inside are three altars, each handcarved in wood and covered in gilt, in separate styles: Plateresque, Chiaroscuro, and Baroque. There are also fine examples of religious painting from the viceregal period. The silver mine near the church, also called La Valenciana, is said to have produced one-fourth of all the silver in the world from the mid-1500s to the early 1800s. It's still in operation today. Although you can't descend into the 1,650-foot-deep mine shaft, if the caretaker is around, he'll usually let you take a peek down. La Valenciana is included in any guided tour of the city, and there are also frequent buses (marked La Valenciana) from the center.

⑪ For a macabre thrill, take a taxi from town to the **Museo de las Momias,** located at the municipal cemetery off Calzada del Panteon, at the north end of town. In the museum, mummified human corpses—once buried in the cemetery—are on display. Until the law was amended in 1958, if a gravesite had not yet been paid for, the corpse was removed after five years to make room for new arrivals. Because of the mineral properties of the local soil, these cadavers (the oldest is about 100 years old) were in astonishingly good condition upon exhumation. The most gruesome are exhibited in glass cases. *Panteon Municipal,* ☎ *473/2–06–39.* ☛ *About $1.50.* ☼ *Daily 9–6.*

Dining

Guanajuato's better restaurants are located in hotels near the Jardín la Unión and on the highway to Dolores Hidalgo. For simpler fare, private establishments around town offer a good variety of Mexican and international dishes. Dress tends to be casual in this provincial university town.

CATEGORY	COST*
$$$$	over $20
$$$	$15–$20
$$	$8–$15
$	under $8

per person, excluding drinks and service

$$$$ **El Comedor Real.** Continental cuisine served in a medieval environment
★ defines El Comedor Real. The bright, whitewashed, and brick-domed restaurant in the Hotel Castillo Santa Cecilia serves such specialties as *filete pimiente* (steak with peppercorns), breaded trout with tartar sauce, and fish soup with vegetables. Troubadours perform every Friday and Saturday at 10:30 PM at La Cava, the bar next door. ✕ *Carretera a la Valenciana s/n,* ☎ *473/2–04–85. Reservations advised on weekends. AE, DC, MC, V.*

$$ **El Retiro.** This traditional Mexican restaurant up the street from the Teatro Juárez lives up to its name, the Retreat. Though it is often crowded for the main midday meal, at other times you can relax with a steaming cappuccino and listen to classical music. A full *comida corrida* runs about $5; for more substantial fare, try the mole poblano with chicken, broiled steak with mushroom sauce, or a Spanish omelet. ✕ *Calle de Sopeña 12,* ☎ *473/2–06–22. Reservations not accepted. MC, V.*

$$ **Tasca de Los Santos.** This cozy restaurant, located across the street from
★ the Basílica, specializes in Spanish and international cuisines. Recommended dishes include the *sopa de mariscos* (shellfish soup with shrimp, clams, and crabs), and *filete parrilla* (grilled beef with baked potatoes and spinach). *Huevos Reina* is a delicious light dish consisting of eggs and mushrooms baked in a cheese and wine sauce. Dine indoors or outside under white umbrellas on the plaza, with a view of the fountain. A variety of music, ranging from French to Russian, enhances the cosmopolitan mood. ✕ *Plaza de la Paz 28,* ☎ *473/2–23–20. Reservations not accepted. MC, V.*

$ **El Pingüis Cafeteria.** Cheap and plentiful food attracts the university crowd to this spartan eatery. A midday meal, consisting of soup, Mexican rice, a chicken or beef dish, dessert and coffee, costs about $3. The *café americano* is excellent, as is the *consume de verduras* (vegetable soup). The service can be slow, but vibrant music and a lively crowd will keep you entertained. While you wait, note the posters of Mexican art on the walls. ✕ *Jardín la Unión at Allende 3,* ☎ *473/2–14–14. Reservations not accepted. No credit cards.*

$ **El Unicorno Azul.** Those growing weary of heavy meat dishes might want to stop by this food counter just behind Jardín la Unión: It offers fruit drinks, yogurt, and vegetarian hamburgers and sandwiches. Next store is a health food store under the same ownership. ✕ *Agora del Baratillo,* ☎ *473/2–07–00. No credit cards.*

$ **Restaurant Valadez.** Dark wood-paneled walls give way to large windows overlooking the Teatro Juárez at this downtown restaurant. House dishes include *filete à la Tampiqueña* (beefsteak served with guacamole, cheese enchiladas, and beans), hamburger Valadez (topped with cheese and bacon), and crepes with tequila and blackberries. The bar serves Campari, Dubonnet, and tequila drinks for less than $2.

✕ *Jardín la Unión 3,* ☎ *473/2–11–57. Reservations not accepted. AE, DC, MC, V.*

Lodging

Guanajuato's less expensive hotels are located near the bus station, along Avenida Juárez and Calle de la Alhóndiga. Moderately priced and upscale properties are near the Jardín la Unión and on the outskirts of town. It's best to secure reservations at least six months in advance if you plan to attend the Cervantes Festival, which usually runs from mid- to late October.

CATEGORY	COST*
$$$	$60–$90
$$	$25–$60
$	under $25

All prices are for a standard double room, excluding 10% tax.

$$$ **Hotel Museo Posada Santa Fe.** This colonial-style property, located at the Jardín la Unión, has been in operation since 1862. Large historic paintings by local artist Don Manuel Leal hang in the wood-paneled lobby; a sweeping carpeted stairway leads to second-floor quarters. Each room, decorated in warm, autumnal colors, has a wood minibar, color TV, and telephone. Rooms facing the plaza can be noisy; quieter rooms face narrow alleyways. ⊡ *Plaza Principal at Jardín la Unión 12, 36000,* ☎ *473/2–00–84 or 2–02–07,* ℻ *473/2–46–53. 47 rooms with bath. Restaurant, bar, outdoor hot tub. AE, MC, V.*

$$$ **Parador San Javier.** This immaculately restored hacienda was converted
★ into a hotel in 1971. In fact, a safe from the Hacienda San Javier and old wood trunks still decorate the large, plant-laden lobby. The rooms are clean and have attractive appointments: lace curtains, crisp coverlets, and blue-and-white-tiled baths. The 16 rooms reached via a stone archway have some rugged colonial details. A word of caution: Large convention groups sometimes use the facility. ⊡ *Plaza Aldama 92, 36000,* ☎ *473/2–06–26,* ℻ *473/2–31–14. 115 rooms with bath. 2 restaurants, bar, café, outdoor pool, disco. AE, MC, V.*

$$–$$$ **Hostería del Frayle.** Just a half block off Jardín la Unión, this quiet, four-story lodging was once the *Casa de Moneda,* where ore was taken to be refined after it was brought out of the mines. Built in 1673 and turned into a hotel in the mid-1960s, it features whitewashed plaster and wood-beamed rooms arranged around a small maze of stairways, landings, and courtyards; all have TVs and telephones, and some have excellent views of the Pípila, Teatro Juárez, and Jardín la Unión. The staff is extremely friendly and helpful. ⊡ *Calle Sopeña 3,* ☎ *473/2–11–79,* ℻ *473/2–11–79, ext. 138. 37 rooms with bath. Restaurant-bar. MC, V.*

$ **Hotel Socavón.** One of Guanajuato's newer hotels, this modest five-story property was built in 1981. Don't be put off by the gloomy, tunnel-like entrance: Open-air walkways, with views of surrounding mountains, lead to guest quarters. Each room has a wood-beamed ceiling, is simply furnished with a bed, desk, and television, and has a modern bath. Fourth-floor corner rooms offer some good views. ⊡ *Calle de la Alhóndiga 41A, 36000,* ☎ *473/2–48–85 or 473/2–66–66. 37 rooms with bath. Restaurant. AE, MC, V.*

The Arts and Nightlife

Guanajuato, on most nights a somnolent provincial capital, awakens each fall for the **International Cervantes Festival.** During two weeks in

October world-renowned actors, musicians, and dance troupes (which have included the Bolshoi Ballet) perform nightly at the Teatro Juárez and at other venues in town. The Plaza San Roque, a small square near the Jardín Reforma, hosts a series of *Entremeses Cervantinos*—swashbuckling one-act farces by classical Spanish writers. Grandstand seats require advance tickets, but crowds often gather by the edge of the plaza for free. If you plan to be in Guanajuato for the festival, contact the Festival Internacional Cervantino office in Mexico City (Alvaro Obregón 273, piso 3, Colonia Roma, 06700, ☎ 5/533–4123) or Ticketmaster (☎ 5/325–9000 in Mexico City) at least six months in advance for top-billed events.

At other times of the year, nightlife in Guanajuato is mostly relegated to dramatic, dance, and musical performances at the **Teatro Juárez** (Calle de Sopeña, ☎ 473/2–01–83) and the **Teatro Principal** (Calle Hidalgo, ☎ 473/2–15–23), which has begun showing American movies several times a week. Some hotels, including the Parador San Javier and the Castillo Santa Cecilia, provide evening musical entertainment. There are also several nightclubs located in or near the downtown area, including **Discoteque El Pequeño Juan** (Panorámica Al Pípila at Callejón de Guadalupe, ☎ 473/2–23–08), whose panoramic view of the city at night is stunning, and the small but lively **Discoteque La Fragua** (Calle Tepetapa 45, ☎ 473/2–27–15).

Excursion to León

León, 56 kilometers (35 miles) northwest of Guanajuato, is best known as the shoemaking capital of Mexico. It is also an important center for industry and commerce. With more than 1 million people, it is the state's most populous urban area.

If you know footwear and have the time (and patience) to browse through the downtown shops, you may find some good buys in León. First try the Plaza de Zapatos, a mall with 70 stores located on Boulevard Adolfo López Mateos roughly one block from the bus station. From here take a taxi west (about a 10-minute ride) to the Zona Peatonal, a pedestrian zone with several shoe stores. On Calle Praxedis Guerrero there are various artisans' stands selling leather goods.

Flecha Amarilla buses leave Guanajuato's Central Camionera every 15 minutes for León; the ride takes about 45 minutes and costs less than $1. Pick up a map of León at the tourist office in Guanajuato.

Guanajuato Essentials

Arriving and Departing
BY PLANE

Mexicana (☎ 800/531–7921) has flights to **Leon International Airport,** 56 kilometers (35 miles) north of Guanajuato, from Los Angeles, San Antonio, and Chicago. **Aeromexico** (☎ 800/237–6639) flies directly from Los Angeles; **Continental** (☎ 800/525–0280) offers service from Houston. The one-hour taxi ride from the airport to town costs about $25.

BY CAR

Guanajuato is 432 kilometers (268 miles) northwest of Mexico City via Route 57 (to Querétaro) and Route 45 (through Celaya and Irapuato), approximately a five-hour drive.

BY BUS

Direct bus service is available between the Central del Norte (North Bus Station) in Mexico City and Guanajuato's Central Camionera (☎ 473/3–13–29); taxis to downtown from the Camionera cost $3 to $4. Several lines—including **Flecha Amarilla** and **Estrella Blanca**—offer hourly service; travel time is about five hours. Frequent inexpensive bus service is available from Guanajuato to other Bajío cities.

Getting Around

Don't bother with a car in Guanajuato. Many of the attractions are within strolling distance of one another and located between Avenida Juárez and Calle Pocitos, the city's two major north-south arteries. The twisting subterranean roadway—El Subterráneo—also has a primarily north-south orientation.

BY TAXI

Nonmetered taxis can be hailed on the street or found at *sitios* (taxi stands) near the Jardín la Unión, Plaza de la Paz, and Mercado Hidalgo. Set a price before you get into the cab.

Guided Tours

Transporte Exclusivo de Turismo (Av. Juárez and Calle 5 de Mayo, ☎ 473/2–59–68) is a kiosk that offers several tours of Guanajuato and its environs. A 3½-hour tour, with an English-speaking guide, of the Museum of Mummies, the church and mines of Valenciana, the monument to Pípila, the Panoramic Highway, subterranean streets, and residential neighborhoods costs $18 per person, minimum six people. A five-hour evening tour of the Pípila monument and one or two nightclubs, including one drink, is about $20 per person, minimum six people. *Estudiantinas* perform during the weekend tours.

Important Addresses and Numbers

EMERGENCIES

Police (☎ 473/2–02–66). **Ambulance-Red Cross** (☎ 473/2–04–87). **Hospital General** (☎ 473/2–08–59 or 473/2–08–50). Since few people in Guanajuato have a good command of English, in an emergency it's best to contact your hotel manager or the tourist office.

PHARMACY

A recommended pharmacy is **El Fenix** (Juárez 104, ☎ 473/2–61–40), open Mon.–Sat. 7:45 AM–9:45 PM, Sun. 8:45 AM–9 PM.

TRAVEL AGENCIES

Viajes Georama, the American Express representative, is at Plaza de la Paz 34 (☎ 473/2–59–09, 473/2–19–54, or 473/2–51–01, FAX 473/2–35–97). **Viajes Mandel** is at Plaza de la Paz 62 (☎ 473/2–60–37 or 473/2–71–95, FAX 473/2–60–89).

VISITOR INFORMATION

The **Guanajuato tourist office** is at Plaza de la Paz 14, at the back of a courtyard (☎ 473/2–15–74, 473/2–00–86, or 473/2–19–82, FAX 473/2–42–51; ☉ Weekdays 8:30–7:30, weekends 10–2). There is also a tourist information kiosk at the Central Camionera bus station. Maps and brochures (mostly in Spanish) are available at both locations.

ZACATECAS

In colonial days Zacatecas was the largest silver-producing city in the world and sent great treasures of the precious metal to the king of Spain. Still a large silver-mining center, with factories producing silver jewelry and trade schools training apprentices in the fine art of handmade silver craft, Zacatecas is a relatively undiscovered jewel for tourists. Although it is a state capital with a population of some 300,000, it has the feel of a much smaller place; the town is kept spotlessly clean by Zacatecan pride, under a mandate by the governor of the state of Zacatecas. This destination is also famous for its historical role as the scene of one of Pancho Villa's most spectacular battles and for its 18th-century colonial architecture.

One of the town's unique charms is the *tambora,* a musical walk up and down the streets and alleyways led by a *tamborazo,* a typical local band that shatters the evening quiet with merriment. Also known as a *callejóneada* (*callejón* means "alley"), the tambora is a popular free-for-all, in which everyone along the way either joins in the procession or leans from balconies and doorways to cheer the group on. During the December *feria* (festival), the tamborazos play night and day as they serenade the Virgin of Zacatecas.

Exploring

Numbers in the margin correspond to points of interest on the Zacetecas map.

1 The elaborately carved 18th-century **cathedral** on Avenida Hidalgo is considered one of the best examples of Mexican Baroque style in the country. Each of the facades tells a different legend; according to one of them, an anticlerical governor of the state used the cathedral's silver cross and baptismal font to mint Zacatecas's first silver coins.

2 Adjoining the cathedral is the **Plaza de Armas** and the Governor's Palace, an 18th-century mansion containing flower-filled courtyards and, on the main staircase, a powerful mural depicting the history of Zacatecas.

Across the street stand two more of the town's beautiful 18th-century colonial buildings, both declared national monuments. They are built from native pink stone and have lacy ironwork balconies. One of them now houses the Paraiso Zacatecas Hotel, and the other is presently a

3 municipal building called the **Palacio de la Mala Noche** (Palace of the Bad Night). Legend has it that this was the home of a silver-mine owner who was so often called upon to help the needy that he built a hidden door from which he could enter and leave the palace undisturbed. One night a terrible storm was raging, yet a worker had the temerity to pound on the front door. He finally gained entrance with his good news: silver had been found in a mine considered exhausted. Up the hill along the side of the palace, you will find the so-called hidden door.

4 In the Plaza Santo Domingo north of the cathedral, the **Pedro Coronel Museum** was originally a Jesuit monastery and was used as a jail in the 18th century. The museum is one of a kind in Mexico and Latin America, housing the work of Zacatecan artist and sculptor Pedro Coronel and his extensive collection of the works of Picasso, Dali, Miró, Braque, and Chagall among others, as well as an abundance of art from Africa, China, Japan, India, Greece, and Egypt. ☎ 492/2-80-21. ☛ *Weekdays about $3; free on Sun.* ☉ *Mon.–Wed., Fri.–Sat. 10–2 and 4–7, Sun. 10–5, closed Thurs.*

5 The fine 17th-century **Templo de Santo Domingo** is adjacent to the museum. It has a Baroque facade, and inside are some old paintings of religious subjects in gold leaf.

TIME OUT   The **Cafe Y Neveria Acropolis** (Av. Hidalgo at Plazuela Candelario Huizar, ☎ 492/2-12-84), alongside the cathedral, is an ice cream parlor in the daytime and a coffeehouse at night. Come here for Turkish cof-

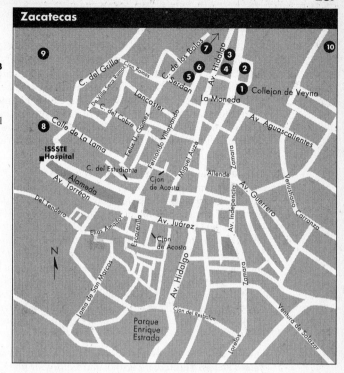

Zacatecas

fee (under $1), ice cream, and other desserts. Breakfast is served from
8:30 to 12:30.

6 Heading north on Avenida Hidalgo, you will come to **Teatro Calderon**
(☎ 492/2–86–20), opened in 1891. Restored to its former glory in 1987,
it is one of the city's many fine examples of colonial architecture.

7 Not to be confused with the Pedro Coronel Museum is the **Rafael Coronel Museum** (the men were brothers), located in the Exconvento de San
Francisco, out of the town center toward Lómas del Calvario. Its 18th-
century facade of mellowed pink tones conceals a rambling structure of
open-arched corridors, all leading through garden patios to rooms that
contain an amazing collection of some 3,700 **máscaras** (masks)—including
saints and devils, wise men and fools, animals and humans—used in regional festivals all over Mexico. There is also an outstanding display of
puppets. *Northeast of downtown, off Vergel Nuevo, between Chaveño
and Garcia Salinas.* ☞ *About $3, free on Sun.* ☺ *Mon.–Tues., Thurs.–Sat.
10–2 and 4–7, Sun. 10–5, closed Wed.*

For those interested in wandering farther afield, walk up the Alameda,
8 past the hospital to the **Eden Mine** (El Mina Eden), which functioned
from 1586 until 1960, and is now a tourist attraction. From the entrance
on Antonio Dovali off Avenida Torreon beyond the Alameda Garcia
de la Cadena, an open mine train runs down into the underground tunnels; there is a small gift shop at the entrance. The tour (there is a nominal fee) is in Spanish, but you'll have no trouble imagining what the
life of the miners was like. Be sure to wear sturdy shoes, and remember that mines are pretty dark. This one is no exception; through much
of the tour, your only light may be the guide's flashlight. Farther down

the train track there is another stop at, of all places, a discotheque! (*See* Nightlife, *below.*) ☞ *$3.* ⊙ *Daily 10–6.*

❾ From inside the mine, there's an elevator to Cerro del Grillo (Cricket Hill) on the northeast side of the city, where you can catch the **Teleferico,** the only cable car in the world that crosses an entire city (it runs from 10 to 7 daily). True, it crosses at the narrowest point, but it presents a magnificent panoramic view of the city and its many Baroque church domes and spires. At the cost of a little more than a dollar, the ride takes you up to Cerro de la Bufa—well worth it, as it's quite a climb up otherwise. The price is the same whether you ride both ways or walk one.

❿ **Cerro de la Bufa,** the trademark of the city, is the site of Pancho Villa's definitive battle against dictator Victoriano Huerta in June 1914. The spacious **Plaza de la Revolución,** paved with the three shades of pink Zacatecan stone, is crowned with three huge equestrian statues of Villa and two other heroes, Felipe Angeles and Panfilo Natera. Also on the site are the **Museo de la Toma de Zacatecas** (⊙ Tues.–Sun. 10–5, ☞ $1.50), which has nine rooms filled with historic objects such as guns, newspapers, furniture, and clothing from the days of Pancho Villa; and the **Sanctuary of the Virgin of Patrocinio,** a chapel dedicated to the patron of the city. The very tip-top of the hill has a meteorological observatory; you'll need to get special permission from the Zacatecas tourist office to visit. From Cerro de la Bufa, you can catch a taxi back into town.

Finally, since this is a silver town, you won't want to miss a visit to the **Centro Platero Zacatecas,** a school and factory for fine handmade silver jewelry and other items, housed in the 18th-century mansion of **Don Ignacio de Bernardez** (Colonia Bernardez, ☎ 492/3–10–07). It's fascinating to watch student silversmiths master this fine tradition.

Shopping

Jewelry and other silver products are for sale on the premises of the **Centro Platero Zacatecas** (Colonia Bernardez, ☎ 492/3–10–07) or in the factory's shop located downtown in **Centro Commercial El Mercado** (Calle Hidalgo, next to the cathedral), a group of boutiques in what was once a covered market. Opposite the east end of the Plaza de Armas is **La Cazzorra** (Hidalgo 713, ☎ 492/4–04–84), a collectibles shop with authentic antiques, books about Zacatecas, wood furniture, Huichol art, and ceramics. The owners—husband and wife—are a good source of information about the city.

Dining

Several of Zacatecas's better restaurants are located in hotels; another is right in El Mercado, the boutique area on Calle Hidalgo near the cathedral. Other popular restaurants can be found on Avenida Juárez, which intersects Hidalgo. Unless otherwise indicated, dress is casual.

CATEGORY	COST*
$$$$	over $20
$$$	$15–$20
$$	$8–$15
$	under $8

per person, excluding drinks and service

$$$$ **Quinta Real.** In the Quinta Real hotel, this elaborate, formal restaurant with white tablecloths and flowers on the tables serves fine Continental cuisine, with such specialties as medallion of beef in a tangy port sauce and desserts flambéed at the table. There is also a bar. ✗ *434 Av. Rayon and Gonzales Ortega,* ☎ *492/2–84–40. Reservations suggested. AE, MC, V.*

$$$ **Candiles.** This popular downtown meeting place is situated in the Paraiso Zacatecas hotel, a great place to observe the local business crowd as well as the interesting assortment of hotel guests. Candiles has cream-and-vermilion walls, arches, and soft lighting. Black lacquer slatted chairs contrast with white tablecloths and crystal. The impressive menu includes both Continental and regional dishes. Try the veal marsala or the *filete pimienta* (steak with peppercorns). ✗ *Paraiso Zacatecas Hotel, Av. Hidalgo 703,* ☎ *492/2–61–83. No reservations. AE, DC, MC, V.*

$$$ **La Cuija.** Zacatecas specialties such as an appetizer basket filled with four sweet varieties of cactus flower, peeled and juicy, are the rule here. Also try the *pollo adobada* (chicken in a rich chili sauce) or *carne a la Mexicana* (beef grilled with tomatoes, onion, and salsa). The decor approximates a wine cellar, and in addition to fine food, the restaurant serves wine from the owner's Cachola Vineyards (*see* Excursions, *below*). ✗ *Centro Commercial El Mercado,* ☎ *492/2–82–75. Reservations suggested. MC, V.*

$ **Cenaduria Los Dorados.** Enchilada lovers should be sure not to miss this quiet little restaurant, a local favorite just a few blocks northeast of the cathedral. Among the 12 different varieties available here are the excellent *enchiladas Villistas*—tortillas stacked like pancakes filled with chicken or cheese. A side order of guacamole and chips is huge and very tasty. ✗ *Plazuela de García 1314,* ☎ *492/2–57–22. Reservations accepted. No credit cards.*

$ **Rancho Viejo.** This informal ranch-style restaurant serves dishes with a Zacatecan flavor, including *huchepos* (tamales with sour cream) and enchiladas covered with vegetables and a rich red chile sauce. ✗ *Carretera Panamericana 101,* ☎ *492/2–67–47. Reservations accepted. AE, MC, V.*

Lodging

Many of Zacatecas's best lodgings are in the city's treasured historic buildings, which have been preserved in all their 18th- and 19th-century beauty. Others are situated in the surrounding mountains and have wonderful views of the picturesque city as well as the silver-mined hills.

CATEGORY	COST*
$$$$	over $90
$$$	$60–$90
$$	$25–$60
$	under $25

All prices are for a standard double room, excluding 10% tax.

$$$$ **Mesón de Jobito.** Built in the early half of the 19th century, this build-
★ ing has been a hotel for well over a hundred years, but only came to its current owners in 1992. It combines the amenities of a luxury hotel with the pleasant, relaxed ambience of a hacienda: The reception area is a tastefully decorated *sala* where the guests sit down on antique chairs to sign in. Two levels of guest rooms, painted in rich colors and dec-

orated in a modern but tasteful style, surround a narrow courtyard. The staff is extremely friendly and helpful. The pervasively restful atmosphere is enhanced by the Mesón's perfect location on a blissfully quiet little plaza just a few blocks from the cathedral. ⊞ *Jardín Juárez 143,* ☎ *and* FAX *492/4–17–22. 31 rooms with bath. Restaurant, bar. MC, V.*

$$$$ **Quinta Real.** This hotel must be one of the most unusual in the country—or any country: It is built around Mexico's oldest bullring, the second one constructed in the Western Hemisphere. Although spirited bullfight music plays softly in the background, matadors no longer face the bulls here. Instead, the terrazo-paved ring provides a unique view for the 49 guest rooms, each with a balcony overlooking the *plaza de toro.* Large and bright, the rooms are decorated in pastel fabrics that complement the dark traditional furniture. The bar occupies some of the former bull pens, and an outdoor café with bright-yellow umbrellaed tables occupies two levels of the spectator area. ⊞ *434 Av. Rayon and Gonzales Ortega, 98000,* ☎ *492/2–91–04 through 07 or 800/426–0494,* FAX *492/2–84–40. Restaurant, café, bar. AE, MC, V.*

$$$$ **Radisson Paraiso Zacatecas.** Facing the Plaza de Armas and the cathedral in the heart of the city, the Zacatecas is situated in one of Zacatecas's beautiful old colonial buildings, which has been declared a national monument. The pink-stone facade dates from the 18th century, and the more recent additions match perfectly. Rooms are decorated in cream, blue, and fuschia and furnished with copies of Spanish antiques as well as modern pieces. Those facing the plaza are susceptible to late night and early morning tamborazo music during festivals; on the other hand, from your small balcony you'll get a great view of the goings-on. The rooms facing the interior courtyard are quieter. ⊞ *Av. Hidalgo 703, Colonia Centro, 98000,* ☎ *492/2–61–83 through 87. 116 rooms with bath. Restaurant, bar, convention center. AE, DC, MC, V.*

$$–$$$ **Hotel Gallery.** One of the most modern hotels in Zacatecas, this pleasant property is located only three blocks from the historic town center. From the bay windows of its front rooms you can see over the rooftops of the whitewashed dome of the beautiful Baroque-style Templo San José. Rooms, all with satellite TV and individual climate control, are done in cool blue, green, and white; furnishings include Mexican chests painted white and lacy white ironwork headboards. Bathrooms are marble. The staff is extremely friendly and helpful. ⊞ *Blvd. Lopez Mateos y Callejón del Barro, 98000,* ☎ *492/2–33–11,* FAX *492/2–34–15; in Mexico City, 5/525–9081, 5/525–9082, or 5/525–9083. 134 rooms with bath, including 3 junior suites and a Suite Presidencial. Restaurant and coffee shop, bar, indoor pool, sauna, 2 squash courts, nightclub, meeting rooms. AE, DC, MC, V.*

$$ **Motel del Bosque.** *Bosque* means "forest" or "woods" in Spanish, and this clean and quiet motel near the greenbelt offers a superb view of Zacatecas. Close to the Teleferico station at Cerro del Grillo high above the city, yet not terribly far from the center, the motel has clean, carpeted bungalows spread along the hillside in rows and divided by cobblestoned parking areas. ⊞ *Paseo Diaz Ordaz, 98000,* ☎ *492/2–07–45, 492/2–07–46, or 492/2–07–47. 70 rooms with bath. Restaurant. AE, DC, MC, V.*

Nightlife

If only for its uniqueness, a must-visit is **El Malacate** (☎ 492/2–30–02), the discotheque in the Mina El Eden, a stop on the Eden Mine train and more than 1,000 feet underground. It's best to make reservations at this popular place, which is both crowded and noisy. At the opposite end of the height spectrum is **El Elefante Blanco** (Mina La Gallega 15, ☎ 492/2–71–04), another discotheque, but this time one with a panoramic view of the city. For some surprisingly good local blues and jazz, head to **Arcano** (Hidalgo 111, downstairs, ☎ 492/2–05–38), a small lounge-bar favored by the Zacatecas art and intellectual crowd. The band plays Thursday through Saturday until 1 AM. There's also live music in the lobby bar of the **Radisson Paraiso Zacatecas,** and the **Hotel Gallery** has a nightclub with live entertainment (*see* Lodging, *above,* for both).

Excursions to Zona Arqueológica La Quemada and Cachola Vins

Zona Arqueológica La Quemada, about 50 kilometers (30 miles) southwest of Zacatecas, is the site of an ancient city that was already a ruin before the advent of the Spaniards in the 16th century. Seven different Indian cultures built one community atop the other, and the present site rises high above the plain. The spot is totally undeveloped as a tourist attraction, making the climb quite rugged, but once you reach the top, the whole area spreads out below you. The edifices—what remains of them—appear to be constructed of thin slabs of stone wedged into place. The principal draw is a group of rose-colored ruins containing 11 large, round columns built entirely of the same small slabs of rock seen in the rest of the ruins. ☞ *$4, free on Sun.* ☺ *Tues.–Sun. 10–5.*

Located 7 kilometers (4 miles) southeast from the center of Zacatecas is the small town of **Guadalupe,** a spot not to be missed by those interested in colonial art and architecture. The centerpiece of the town is the ex-Convento de Guadalupe, founded by Franciscan monks in 1707. It currently houses the **Museo de Arte Virreinal** (*virreinal* means "viceregal," or colonial), run by the Instituto Nacional de Antropología y Historia. The convent is itself a work of art, with its Baroque-style Templo de Guadalupe and the Capilla de Nápoles, but even more impressive is the stunning collection of art under its roof. Works by Miguel Cabrera, Nicolás Rodriguez Juárez, Cristóbal de Villalpando, and Andrés López are included, among others. *Jardín Juárez s/n, Guadalupe,* ☎ *492/3–23–86.* ☞ *$4, free on Sun.* ☺ *Tues.–Sun. 10–4:30.*

Another worthwhile side trip is a jaunt to the award-winning vineyard **Cachola Vins,** in Valle de las Arsinas. The cold winters, mild springtimes, and temperate summers in the valley produced a silver medal for the vineyard's 1986 Cachola French Columbard at the VINEXPO 1991 in France. Tours of the vineyard are best arranged beforehand, especially if you would like a tasting. *Cruce de Carretera Panamericana, Km 634, Las Arsinas, Guadalupe,* ☎ *492/2–72–56.*

Zacatecas Essentials

Arriving and Departing

BY PLANE
Mexicana (☎ 800/531–7921) has direct service to Zacatecas from Chicago, Denver, and Los Angeles. In Zacatecas the Mexicana Airlines office is located on Hidalgo (☎ 492/2–74–29, 492/2–74–70, or 492/2–32–48). The airport is 29 kilometers (18 miles) north of town; Aerotransports (☎ 492/2–59–46) provides transportation. A taxi ride to town will cost about $25.

BY CAR

Zacatecas is 603 kilometers (375 miles) northwest of Mexico City via Route 57 (to Querétero and San Luis Potosi) and Route 49, approximately a 7½- to 8-hour drive.

BY BUS

Omnibus de México operates several first- and second-class buses daily from Mexico City to Zacatecas.

Getting Around

You can reach most of the town-center attractions by foot, although you will need to rent a car or hire a taxi if you want to tour a mine or take a ride on the Teleferico (cable car) to the top of Cerro de la Bufa. The city has an excellent and inexpensive bus system.

Guided Tours

Viajes Mazzoco (Enlace 313, ☎ 492/2–08–59 or 492/2–51–59; ☎ and FAX 492/2–55–59), a well established travel agency and the local American Express representative, can arrange tours of the city center, El Eden Mine, the Teleferico, and La Bufa for about $25 per person.

Important Addresses and Numbers

EMERGENCIES

Police (☎ 492/2–01–80). **Red Cross** (☎ 492/2–30–05). **Emergency Service,** dial 06. Since English is not generally spoken in Zacatecas, it's best to contact your hotel manager or the tourist office in case of an emergency.

Hospital (☎ 492/3–30–04).

Pharmacy. Farmacia Isstezac (Dr. Ignacio Hierro 522, ☎ 492/2–80–89) is open 24 hours a day.

VISITOR INFORMATION

The **Tourist Information** booth (Módulo de Información Turistica; Av. Hidalgo 629, no ☎, ⊙ daily 8–8) is located near the town cathedral. The state **Dirección Estatal de Turismo** is at Prolongación Gonzalez s/n, across from the train station (☎ 492/4–05–52 or 492/4–03–93, FAX 492/2–93–29).

QUERÉTARO

A state capital and industrial center of nearly 800,000 people, Querétaro, like other Bajío cities, has played a significant role in Mexican history. In 1810, in the home of Josefa Ortiz de Dominguez—a heroine of the independence movement known as La Corregidora—the first plans for independence were hatched. In 1848 the Mexican-American War was concluded in this city with the signing of the Treaty of Guadalupe Hidalgo. Emperor Maximilian made his last stand here in 1867 and was executed by firing squad in the Cerro de las Campañas (Hill of the Church Bells) north of town. A small memorial chapel, built by the Austrian government, marks the spot. A gigantic statue of Benito Juárez crowns a park on the crest of the hill just above it. In 1917 the Mexican Constitution, which still governs the land, was signed in this city.

Throughout Querétaro there are markers, museums, churches, and monuments that commemorate the city's heroes and historic moments. A prevailing sense of civic pride is evident in the impeccably renovated mansions, the flower-draped cobblestoned pedestrian walkways, and the hospitable plazas, which are softly lit at night. The people are among the most congenial in central Mexico and are quick to share their favorite sites and tales with travelers.

Querétaro is also renowned for opals—red, green, honey, and fire stones, as opposed to the blue Australian kind. However, visitors should beware of street vendors, who may sell opals so full of water that they crumble shortly after purchase; depend upon reputable dealers (*see* Shopping, *below*).

Though Querétaro's boundaries extend for some distance, the historic district is in the heart of town. A day or two can easily be spent here, visiting museums, admiring the architecture, and learning the local history.

Exploring

Numbers in the margin correspond to points of interest on the Querétaro map.

① The city's most noteworthy sights are near the **Plaza Independencia** or **Plaza de Armas.** Bordered by carefully restored colonial mansions, this immaculate square is especially lovely at night, when the central fountain is lit. Built in 1824, the fountain is dedicated to the Marquis de la Villa del Villar, who constructed Querétaro's elegant aqueduct and provided the city with drinking water. The old stone aqueduct with its 74 towering arches still stands at the east end of town, though it no longer brings water into the city.

The **Palacio del Gobierno del Estado,** also known as **La Casa de la Corregidora,** is on the plaza's northwest corner. Today it houses municipal government offices, but in 1810 it was the home of Querétaro's mayor-magistrate (El Corregidor) and his wife, Josefa Ortiz de Domínguez (La Corregidora). On many evenings conspirators—including Ignacio Allende and Father Miguel Hidalgo—came here under the guise of participating in La Corregidora's literary salon. When the mayor-magistrate learned that they were actually plotting the course for independence, he imprisoned his wife in her room. La Corregidora managed to whisper a warning to a coconspirator, who notified Allende and Hidalgo. A few days later, on September 16, Father Hidalgo tolled the bell of his church to signal the beginning of the fight for freedom. A replica of the bell can be seen atop the Palacio del Gobierno del Estado. ⊙ *Weekdays 9–9, weekends 9–6.*

Continue to walk around the square counterclockwise. At Plaza Independencia 4 is the Palacio de Justicia, and beside it, the **Casa de Ecala,** a Baroque palace that retains its original facade and currently houses the offices of DIF, a family services organization. As the story goes, its 18th-century owner adorned his home elaborately in order to outdo his neighbor. When the neighbor complained, City Hall stepped in and halted construction. Visitors are welcome to walk around the courtyard when the offices are open (weekdays 7 AM–9 PM, Sat. 9–3).

Just past the Casa de Ecala is Avenida Libertad Oriente, one of the city's bougainvillea-draped pedestrian walkways. Turn west here and walk two blocks to reach Calle Corregidora, named after the heroine of the revolution. Bear right again, and in the middle of a long block you'll **②** find the entrance to the **Museo Regional de Querétaro.** This bright yellow, 17th-century Franciscan monastery displays the works of colonial and European artists in addition to historic memorabilia, including early copies of the Mexican Constitution and the table on which the

Treaty of Guadalupe Hidalgo was signed. *Calle Corregidora Sur 3,* ☎ *463/12–20–31.* ☛ *About $4.* ⊘ *Tues.–Sun. 10:30–4:30.*

Cross the street to Avenida Madero, another "pedway," this one lined with shops. (Cars have use of the street between 2 and 4 PM daily.) The **Jardín Obregón,** the city's main square, will be on your right. You'll also pass a number of lapidary shops selling opals (not blue like Australian opals but beautiful nonetheless) and other locally mined gems. If you're in the market for loose stones or opal jewelry, do some comparison shopping, as you're apt to find better prices here than in the United States.

❸ One block past Avenida Juárez on the corner of Allende Sur, you'll see the former **Casa de la Marquesa** on your left at No. 41. The structure is currently being converted into a hotel, but it was once the ostentatious home of the Marquesa de la Villa del Villar, who apparently had a penchant for things Arabic. Notice the studios on the second floor, one of which is covered with Middle Eastern tiles.

❹ Across Allende, next to the Church of Santa Clara, is the neoclassical **Fountain of Neptune.** It was built in 1797 by Eduardo Tresguerras, the renowned Mexican architect and a native of the Bajío. The fountain originally stood in the orchard of the Monastery of San Antonio, but when the monks faced serious economic problems, they sold part of their land and the fountain along with it.

❺ From the fountain, make a left on Calle Allende and walk nearly one block to a fine example of Baroque architecture, the **State Museum of Art,** housed in an 18th-century Augustinian monastery. The museum's collection focuses on European and Mexican paintings from the 17th through the 20th centuries. *Calle Allende 14,* ☎ *463/12–23–57.* ☛ *About $1.50.* ⊘ *Tues.–Sun. 11–7.*

❻ Retrace your steps back to Calle Corregidora. Make a left and walk one block to Calle 16 de Septiembre. Across the street is the **Jardín de la Corregidora,** prominently marked by a statue of the heroine. Behind this monument stands the **Arbol de la Amistad** (Tree of Friendship). Planted in 1977 in a mixture of soils from around the world, the tree symbolizes Querétaro's hospitality to all travelers.

TIME OUT   At the Jardín de la Corregidora you may want to find a bench and sit for a while. This is the calmest square in town, with many choices for outdoor eating (*see* Dining, *below*).

Shopping

El Rubi (Av. Madero 3 Pte., ☎ 463/12–09–84), just off Querétaro's Plaza Principal, is a reputable dealer for opals and other gems. The owner, Señora Villalon, provides information on the mining, care, and value of opals. The store is open weekdays 10–2 and 4–5, Saturday 10–2.

Dining

Many of Querétaro's dining spots are located near the main plaza (Jardín Obregón), along Calle Corregidora, near the Teatro de la República, and particularly in the Jardín de la Corregidora. There are more upscale restaurants in hotels on the Plaza Independencia or off Route 57, north of the city. In early evenings women set up stoves in a square near the Plaza Independencia and tempt passersby with cheap and hearty fare, but for health reasons, food cooked on the street should be avoided throughout Mexico. Unless otherwise indicated, dress is casual.

CATEGORY	COST*
$$$	$15–$20
$$	$8–$15
$	under $8

per person, excluding drinks and service

$$$ **Fonda del Refugio.** Situated in the Jardín de la Corregidora, this restaurant offers intimate indoor and outdoor dining. Inside, fresh flowers adorn white-clothed tables; outside, comfortable leather chairs face the surrounding gardens. Seafood and beef fillets are a specialty; order the fillet of beef cooked in red wine, lemon, mustard, and peppers, or the scallops prepared in marsala. Cocktails are served on the terrace at night. ✗ *Jardín de la Corregidora 26,* ☎ *463/12–07–55. Reservations not accepted. AE, MC, V.*

$$$ **Restaurante Josecho.** Bullfight aficionados and other sports fans fre-
★ quent this highway road stop next to the bullring at the southwest end of town as much for the lively atmosphere as for the food. Wood-paneled walls are hung with hunting trophies, including geese, elk, bears, and leopards; waiters celebrate patrons' birthdays by banging on pewter plates and blasting a red siren. Though the place can be raucous, it does quiet down at night, when a classical guitarist performs. House specialties include *filete Josecho* (steak with cheese and mushrooms), *filete Chemita* (steak sautéed in butter and onions), and shrimp crepes smothered in a cheese and tomato sauce. ✗ *Dalia 1, next to the Plaza de Toros Santa María,* ☎ *463/16–02–29. Reservations not accepted. AE, DC, MC, V.*

$$ **El Cortijo de Don Juan.** At lunchtime businessmen and families favor this garden location, making it the busiest spot in the shaded Jardín. Vendors stroll by with a variety of wares, from homemade cheeses to large, inflatable crayons; and children sing songs for a small donation. Free snacks are served with drinks in the afternoon, or you can order from a menu that includes *pollo adobado* (chicken in a rich chile sauce), *jamón serrano* (a prosciutto-type ham), and *paella Valenciana* (rice casserole with chicken, sausage, and seafood), served on Saturdays only. The inside rooms are filled with photos of famous matadors; a bull's head is mounted prominently on the wall. A guitarist plays Thursday, Friday, and Saturday nights. ✗ *Jardín de la Corregidora 14,* ☎ *463/14–30–37. Reservations not accepted. AE, MC, V.*

$ **Comedor Vegetariano Natura.** This natural-foods kitchen, one of a chain of four in Querétaro, will be of interest to the vegetarian traveler. (A second one, not far away, is located at Juárez 47, off Plaza Obregón.) Traditional vegetarian fare, such as soy burgers with cheese, is on the menu, as are Mexican-influenced dishes, such as guayaba- or papaya-flavored yogurt and enchiladas stuffed with soy and cheese. ✗ *Vergara Sur 7,* ☎ *463/14–10–88. Reservations not accepted. No credit cards. Closed Sun.*

$ **La Mariposa.** Celebrating more than 50 years in business, La Mariposa is easily recognized by a wrought-iron butterfly (*mariposa*) over the entrance. This is the place for light Mexican lunches—enchiladas, tacos, tamales, and *tortas* (sandwiches). ✗ *Angela Peralta 7,* ☎ *463/12–11–66, 463/12–48–49, or 463/12–18–71. Reservations not accepted. No credit cards.*

Lodging

Several new properties in various price ranges have opened in Querétaro in the past 10 years. Lower-priced hotels are located near the main plaza and thus tend to be noisy; newer high-rises are near the bus station but are quiet inside; and deluxe properties, including a Holiday Inn, are on the outskirts of town.

CATEGORY	COST*
$$$$	over $90
$$$	$60–$90
$$	$25–$60
$	under $25

All prices are for a standard double room, excluding 10% tax.

$$$$ ★ **Mesón de Santa Rosa.** Located on the quiet Plaza Independencia, this elegant all-suite property occupies a restored hacienda. Rooms are clustered around a quiet courtyard. Each has a lace-hung glass door and a decor that includes warm autumn colors and wood-beamed ceilings. ☎ *Pasteur Sur 17, 76000,* ☎ *463/14–59–07 or 463/14–59–05,* FAX *463/12–55–22. 21 suites. Restaurant, bar, pool. AE, MC, V.*

$$$ **Hotel Amberes.** A modern high-rise built in 1981, Hotel Amberes faces the Alameda Hidalgo park on a rather busy street, but rooms are well insulated and fairly quiet. Standard features include beds with floral spreads, color TVs, free-standing fans, and modern baths with purified tap water. ☎ *Corregidora Sur 188, 76000,* ☎ *463/12–86–04 or 463/12–85–55,* FAX *463/12–41–51. 140 rooms with bath. Restaurant, bar. AE, MC, V.*

$$$ **Hotel Mirabel.** A favorite among business travelers and conventioneers, this modern high-rise hums with activity. Its carpeted rooms, however, are insulated and quiet and feature color TVs, telephones, wood desks, and air-conditioning. Some double rooms have views of the Alameda Hidalgo park; some single rooms overlook a soccer stadium. ☎ *Av. Constituyentes Oriente 2, 76000,* ☎ *463/14–30–99 or 463/14–34–44,* FAX *463/14–35–85. 171 rooms with bath. Restaurant, bar, convention center. AE, MC, V.*

$$ **Hotel Señorial.** Built in 1981, this sprawling four-story property has clean, modern rooms with telephones and TVs. Beds are covered with printed spreads that clash with the floral drapes. Rooms in front face a narrow, busy street, but traffic slows in the evening. There are purified-water dispensers in the hallways. ☎ *Guerrero Norte 10-A, 76000,* ☎ *463/14–37–00. 45 rooms with bath. Restaurant. MC, V.*

$ **Hotel Plaza.** This modest property, located on the main plaza, offers clean accommodations and lots of hot water. Rooms facing the principal square are extremely noisy—even at night. Inside rooms, particularly those on the second floor, are much quieter but dark. All rooms have telephones and most have TVs, but for those that do not, there is a small color TV above the soda machine in the tiled lobby. ☎ *Av. Juárez Norte 23, 76000,* ☎ *463/12–11–38 or 463/14–19–45. 29 rooms with bath. AE, MC, V.*

Nightlife

Band concerts are held in the Jardín Obregón, Querétaro's main square, every Sunday evening at 6.

Excursion to San Juan del Río and Tequisquiapan

San Juan del Río and Tequisquiapan, both within an hour's drive of Querétaro, have long been frequented by harried Mexican urbanites who come to shop for semiprecious gems and to soak in the area's thermal waters. It's best, however, to avoid Tequisquiapan, home to more than 20 volcanic spas, on weekends, when locals book up most of the hotels. The tourist office in Querétaro can supply you with brochures.

The simplest way to reach these towns is by car. Route 57, the quick, well-traveled road to Mexico City, passes by San Juan del Río 51 kilometers (32 miles) from Querétaro. Tequisquiapan is 19 kilometers (12 miles) east of San Juan, off Route 120. Buses service both towns from Querétaro, but the trip is longer. You'll probably want to do your shopping first in San Juan del Río (a center of commerce), then head to Tequisquiapan to relax at its lush resort spas.

Most of San Juan's gem shops are located near the main plaza downtown. **Lapidaria Guerrero** (Av. Juárez Poniente 4, ☎ 472/2–14–81) specializes in opal, amethyst, turquoise, and topaz jewelry. **La Guadalupana** (Calle 16 de Septiembre 5, ☎ 472/2–01–03), a cluster of shops in a large courtyard, sells opal, amethyst, topaz, and onyx jewelry, hand-embroidered blouses, brassware, and wood carvings.

Your first stop in Tequisquiapan should be the tourist office. The staff has a list of the spas in town and can tell you which hotels rent out facilities for the afternoon. There is no phone, but during the week the office of municipal government (☎ 472/3–07–57 or 472/3–00–09) may be able to answer questions. *Andador Niños Héroes at cnr of Morelos.* ⊙ *Weekdays 9–2 and 5–8, weekends 10–1.*

After visiting the spas, stop by the verdant main plaza for a beverage or snack and then head to the shops or to the Mercado de Artesanías, where woven goods, jewelry, and locally made furniture are sold. Each summer the city hosts a week-long wine and cheese festival that includes bullfights and mariachi bands.

Querétero Essentials

Arriving and Departing

BY CAR

Querétaro is 220 kilometers (136 miles) northwest of Mexico City, a three-hour drive via Route 57. Cars can be rented at various outlets in Mexico City; in Querétaro try **Budget** (Av. Constituyentes Oriente 73, ☎ 463/13–44–98, FAX 463/13–44–38), **Auto Rent** (Av. Constituyentes Oriente 24-B, ☎ 463/14–20–39 or 463/14–50–96), or **National** (Calle 13 de Septiembre 43, ☎ and FAX 463/16–52–40 or 463/16–35–44).

BY TRAIN

The *Constitucionalista* departs from Mexico City at 7 AM and arrives in Querétaro at 10 AM; the return trip leaves Querétaro at 2:40 PM and arrives in Mexico City at 6:30 PM. Tickets should be purchased one day in advance; the round-trip fare is $13. For current schedule and rate information, contact **Mexico by Train** (☎ and FAX 210/725–3659 or 800/321–1699) or call the local station (☎ 463/12–17–03 or 463/12–17–89).

BY BUS

Direct bus service is available daily between the Central del Norte (North Bus Station) in Mexico City and Querétaro's Central de Autobuses. Major lines—including **Flecha Amarilla, Omnibus de México, Tres Estrellas de Oro,** and **Transportes del Norte**—offer frequent service; travel time is about three hours. Frequent inexpensive bus service is available from Querétaro to other heartland cities.

278

Casa de la
Marquesa, **3**

Fountain
of Neptune, **4**

Jardín de la
Corregidora, **6**

Museo Re-
gional de
Querétaro, **2**

Plaza Indepen-
dencia, **1**

State Museum
of Art, **5**

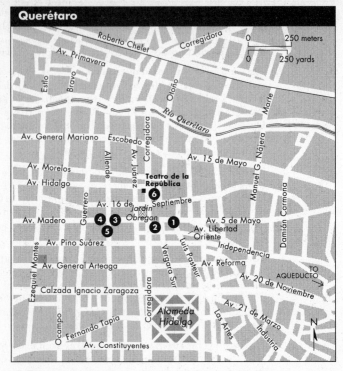

Getting Around

Many of Querétaro's historic sites are within walking distance of one another in the downtown district and can be reached by a series of walkways that are closed to automobile traffic most of the day. If you want to venture farther afield, you will find that buses and taxis run frequently along the main streets and are inexpensive.

Guided Tours

On request, the tourist office conducts a free 90-minute English-language walking tour of the city's historic landmarks. To arrange a city tour, call the office (*see* Important Addresses and Numbers, *below*) one day in advance.

Important Addresses and Numbers

EMERGENCIES

Police (☎ 463/12–30–03 or 463/12–02–66). **Ambulance-Red Cross** (☎ 463/13–28–28 or 463/13–28–04). **Fire Department** (463/12–06–27 or 463/12–39–39). **Protectur** (☎ 463/14–04–28) offers legal assistance with robberies, fraud, and detention/arrest.

Hospital. Sanatorio Alcocer Pozo (Calle Reforma 23, ☎ 463/12–01–49 or 463/12–17–87).

MONEY EXCHANGE

Casa de Cambio Acueducto (Avenida Juárez Sur 58, ☎ 463/12–93–04 or 463/14–31–89) is open weekdays 9–2 and 4–6, Sat. 9–1.

TRAVEL AGENCIES

Wagons-Lits Viajes (Centro Comercial Plaza Niza at Zaragoza y Tolsa 3, ☎ 463/14–30–20 or 463/14–33–44).

VISITOR INFORMATION
The **Dirección de Turismo del Estado** is outside the center of town at Avenida Constituyentes Oriente 102. City maps and brochures of the state of Querétaro are available, and the bilingual staff is extremely helpful. ☎ 463/13–84–83 or 463/13–85–12, 𝖥𝖠𝖷 463/13–85–11. ☉ Weekdays 9–2 and 5–8, weekends 9–3.

In addition, on the Plaza de la Independencia, right next to the Mesón de Santa Rosa, there's a tourist information booth with pamphlets on Querétero and the surrounding area. Pastuer Sur 17, no ☎. ☉ Weekdays 9–3 and 6–8, weekends 9–3.

MORELIA

Morelia, with its long, wide boulevards and earth-tone colonial mansions, is the gracious capital of the state of Michoacán. Founded in 1541 as Valladolid (after the Spanish city), it changed its name in 1828 to honor José María Morelos, the town's most famous son. The legendary mule skinner-turned-priest took up the battle for independence after its early leaders were executed in 1811.

Morelos began with an ill-equipped army of 25 but soon organized a contingent of 9,000 that nearly gained control of the country. Though he was defeated and executed in 1815, he left behind a long-standing reformist legacy that called for universal suffrage, racial equality, and the demise of the hacienda system.

The city today still pays tribute to Morelos: His former home has been turned into a museum, and his birthplace is now a library. Although Morelia's colonial heritage is preserved by its status as a national monument, the city is also forward-thinking. It's the site of a politically liberal university that often holds rallies supporting social and political causes. Look closely along Avenida Madero, and you'll see political fliers posted on buildings.

In addition, Morelia has the delicious distinction of being the candy capital of Mexico. So strong, in fact, is the sweet-eating tradition that the city houses a Mercado de Dulces, or sweets market. If you want to sample some local confections (made from candied fruit or evaporated milk), walk over to Calle Gómez Farías, three blocks west and a half block north of the main plaza.

Morelia is also the home of writers, artists, philosophers, and poets, as well as American retirees. To explore Morelia and its surrounding hillside neighborhoods thoroughly would take some time. However, if you stroll through the historic plazas and frequent the cafés (as many locals do), you will begin to feel the city's vitality.

Exploring

Numbers in the margin correspond to points of interest on the Morelia map.

Many of Morelia's points of interest are located within a few blocks ❶ of the main square, the **Plaza de Armas** or **Plaza de los Mártires.** Several rebel priests were brutally murdered on this site during the War of Independence, and the plaza is named after them. Today, however, the square belies its violent past: Sweethearts stroll along the tree-lined walks, vendors sell mounds of peanuts, placards announce cultural events, and lively recorded music blasts from a silver-domed bandshell.

❷ Slightly east of the plaza lies Morelia's famed **Catedral,** a majestic structure built between 1640 and 1744. It is known throughout Mexico for its 200-foot Baroque towers, among the tallest in the land, and for its 4,600-pipe organ, one of the finest in the world. The organ is on the balcony at the back of the cathedral. An international organ festival is held here each May.

❸ As you leave the cathedral, cross Avenida Madero and walk to the **Placio de Gobierno.** This former Tridentine Seminary, built in 1770, has had such notable graduates as independence hero José María Morelos, social reformer Melchor Ocampo, and the first emperor of Mexico, Agustín de Iturbide. Striking murals decorate the stairway and second floor. Painted by local artist Alfredo Zalce in the early 1960s, they depict dramatic, often bloody scenes from Mexico's history. From the second floor you can catch a glimpse of the cathedral's spires across the way. *Av. Madero 63,* ☎ *43/12–78–72.* ⊘ *Daily 7 AM–11 PM.*

From the palace, walk four blocks east along Avenida Madero (past a number of banks) until you reach Calle de Belisario Domínguez. Make a right and walk one block to the Church of San Francisco. To the rear of the church, in the former convent of San Francisco, is the entrance
❹ to the **Casa de las Artesanías del Estado de Michoacán.** This two-story marketplace is a virtual cornucopia of crafts from around the state. In the 16th century, Vasco de Quiroga, the bishop of Michoacán, helped the Tarascan Indians develop artistic specialties so they could be self-supporting. The rooms display the work the Tarascans still produce: copper goods from Santa Clara del Cobre, lacquerware from Uruapan, straw items and pottery from Pátzcuaro, guitars from Paracho, macabre ceramic figures from Ocumicho. At the **Museo Michoacana de las Artesanías** (☎ 43/12–24–86, ⊘ Daily 9–8) in the two main floors around the courtyard, some of these items are showcased behind glass while artists demonstrate how they are made. The store (☎ 43/12–12–48) is located in several rooms to the right of the museum entrance. Though the market offers an excellent selection of goods, prices are often better in the indigenous villages. If you plan to explore these outlying towns, you may want to do your shopping there.

Walk two blocks south on Calle Vasco de Quiroga, a street lined with vendors, until you reach Saldaña. Walk west another two blocks to
❺ Avenida Morelos Sur; the corner building on your right is the **Casa Museo de Moreles,** acquired in 1801 by the Mexican independence leader and home to generations of the Moreles family until 1934. Now a two-story museum owned by the Mexican government, it contains family portraits (including one of Morelos's mother, who, he said, "gave him constant spirit and strength"), a copy of Morelos's birth certificate, various artifacts from the independence movement (such as a camp bed used by Ignacio Allende), and the blindfold Morelos wore for his execution. The excellent free tour is in Spanish only. *Av. Morelos Sur 323,* ☎ *43/13–26–51.* ☞ *Small admission fee.* ⊘ *Daily 9–6:30.*

From the museum, walk one block north to Calle Corregidora, then
❻ one block west to Calle García Obeso. On this corner stands **Casa Natal,** Morelos's birthplace, now a library and national monument housing mostly history and literature books (as well as two murals by Alfredo Zalce). Be sure to visit the courtyard in back. It's a tranquil square, adjacent to the Church of San Agustín, with rosebushes, evergreens, and wild poinsettias; a marker and an eternal flame honor the fallen hero. *Calle Corregidora 113,* ☎ *43/12–27–93.* ☞ *Free.* ⊘ *Weekdays 9–noon and 2–8, Sat. 9:30–2 and 4–7, Sun. 9:30–2.*

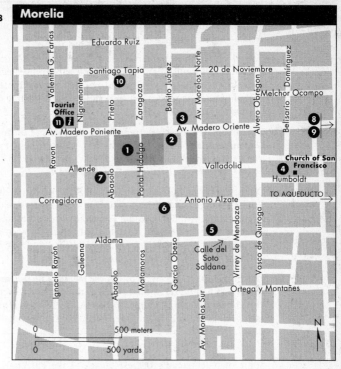

Morelia

Walk west on Calle Corregidora until you reach Calle Abasolo; head
north one block to Calle Allende, where you'll find the **Museo Michoacana.** An 18th-century former palace, the museum traces the history of Mexico from its pre-Hispanic days through the Cardenista period,
which ended in 1940. President Lázaro Cárdenas, a native of Michoacán, was one of Mexico's most popular leaders because of his nationalization of the oil industry and his support of other populist
reforms. The ground floor contains an art gallery, plus archaeological
exhibits from Michoacán and other parts of Mexico. Upstairs is an assortment of colonial objects, including furniture, weapons, and religious paintings. *Calle Allende 305,* ☎ *43/12–04–07.* ☛ *About $4.* ☉
Tues.–Sat. 9–7, Sun. 9–2.

TIME OUT   When you've finished your tour, walk across the street to the *portales.* A
number of popular sidewalk cafés are set among these colonial stone arcades. For a sandwich or a fruit cocktail, or a good selection of juices,
coffees, and teas, try **Café Catedral** (Portal Hidalgo 213, ☎ 43/12–
32–89). No one will mind if you linger over a book or newspaper for
the better part of an hour sipping an excellent *café americano* (and, in
fact, you might have to wait that long just to get the bill).

After refueling at the portales, continue east on Avenida Madero to
the **Bosque Cuauhtémoc,** Morelia's largest park. This walk should
take about 15 minutes, providing you aren't sidetracked en route by
temptations such as Helados Bing (Av. Madero 422), an ice cream shop
offering more than 20 flavors.

Avenida Madero forks as you near the park. Keep to the right, passing the **Fountain of the Tarascans** on a square to your left. Just past
the square, Morelia's mile-long **aqueduct** begins. This structure, which

consists of 250 arches, was built in 1785 and was once the city's main source of drinking water. It's particularly beautiful at night when its arches—some rising to 30 feet—are lit.

Two blocks farther (Madero is now called Avenida Acueducto) is the entrance to Bosque Cuauhtémoc. If you happen by during the week, you may encounter university students studying (or lounging) beneath the palms and evergreens; on weekends, especially Sunday, the park is filled with families on outings.

❾ Continue past the park entrance for two blocks to the **Museo de Arte Contemporáneo** on your right, where the works of contemporary Mexican and international artists are on view. *Av. Acueducto 18, ☎ 43/12– 54–04. ☛ Free. ☉ Tues.–Sun. 10–1:45 and 4–7:45.*

On the corner of Guillermo Prieto and Santiago Tapia, directly across from a small plaza with statues of Don Quiroga de Vasco and Miguel de Cervantes, is the **Museo del Estado,** a history museum in a stately mansion once the home of Augustín de Iturbide, Mexico's only native-born emperor. *Guillermo Prieto 176, ☎ 43/13–06–29. ☛ Free. ☉ Daily 9–2 and 4–8 in summer; 9–2 and 4–7 in winter.*

⓫ For those who have a sweet tooth, the **Mercado de Dulces** (candy market) is just behind the tourist office at the corner of Avenida Madero Poniente and Valentín Gómez Farías. All sorts of local sweets are for sale, such as *ate,* a candied fruit. The market is open daily 9–9.

Dining

Some of Michoacán's tastiest dishes—Lake Pátzcuaro white fish, tomato-based Tarascan soup, such corn products as *huchepos* and *corundas,* and game (rabbit and quail)—are featured at Morelia restaurants. Traditional chicken and beef fare are also available, as well as international dishes. As a rule, more upscale restaurants are located in hotels near the plaza and on the outskirts of town. Unless otherwise indicated, dress is casual.

CATEGORY	COST*
$$	$8–$15
$	under $8

per person, excluding drinks and service

$$ Boca del Rio. Large picture windows opening onto a busy intersection
★ provide lots of light for this cheerful restaurant, which claims to have fresh fish and seafood trucked in daily from Sinaloa and Veracruz. Located between the bus station and the Mercado de Dulces, it provides light snacks, such as *cocktel de camarones* (shrimp cocktail) or *sopa de mariscos* (a rich broth filled with clams, mussels, shrimp, and crab), and heartier fare, such as *pescadillos* (tostadas stuffed with lightly cooked, marinated fish and served with a salad) or *jaiba rellena* (crabs stuffed with mushrooms and cheese and liberally seasoned with garlic). ✗ *Valentín Gómez Farías 185, ☎ 43/12–99–74. Reservations accepted. AE, DC, MC, V.*

$$ El Rey Tacamba. Brightly colored decorations mark this pleasant restaurant, located on the north side of the Plaza de Armas. Among its specialties are *mixiote de carnero,* a piquant (although not spicy) mutton dish, first stewed and then steamed in banana leaves; *pollo moreliano,* chicken roasted in a rich, red chile sauce and served with enchiladas covered in vegetables; and *carne tampiqueña,* a grilled flank steak accompanied by guacamole, refried beans, and tostadas. Once completely reliable, both food and service have gotten mixed reports lately.

✕ *Portal Galeana 157,* ☎ *43/12–20–44. Reservations accepted. No credit cards.*

$$ Los Comensales. This garden restaurant, a downtown favorite among
★ the bullfight crowd, is set in an old colonial house north of the main
plaza. Tables are spaced casually around a plant-filled courtyard where
caged birds sing energetically. Regional dishes include *pollo de plaza*
(chicken with enchiladas, carrots, potatoes, and cheese) and *huchepos*
(tamales and sour cream). For breakfast, try *calabaza con leche* (baked
squash with brown sugar and milk). ✕ *Calle Zaragoza 148,* ☎ *43/12–
93–61. Reservations not accepted. No credit cards.*

$ Café del Bosque. During the week, university students frequent this
1960s-style restaurant. It's tacky—floral carpet and bright green
booths—but the food is good and fairly cheap. Most students can af-
ford sandwiches or burgers; if you feel like spending a bit more, order
pollo moreliano (chicken with enchiladas, vegetables, and french fries)
or *carne à la Mexicana* (grilled beef cooked with onions, tomatoes, lemon
juice, and salsa). There's a small but pleasant terrace for outdoor din-
ing. ✕ *Plaza Rebullones, Local C-7,* ☎ *43/13–28–13. Reservations
not accepted. AE, MC, V.*

$ El Paraíso. To jump-start your day, have a cup of the strong, rich cap-
puccino at El Paraíso. Breakfasts—the recommended meal at this
downtown eatery—run the gamut from eggs and pancakes to fresh fruit,
granola, and exotic juices (watermelon, mango, pineapple, and guayaba).
The specialty is *jamón Paraíso,* fried eggs, ham, and grated cheese. The
plain surroundings—Formica tables and blue-tiled walls—don't deter
locals. ✕ *Portal Galeana 103,* ☎ *43/12–03–74. Reservations not ac-
cepted. No credit cards.*

Lodging

Morelia offers a number of pleasant colonial-style properties both in
the downtown and outlying areas. Generally, the cheapest hotels are
located near the bus station, moderately priced selections are clustered
around the plaza (or on nearby side streets), and deluxe resort prop-
erties are in or near the Santa María hills.

CATEGORY	COST*
$$$$	over $90
$$$	$60–$90
$$	$25–$60
$	under $25

All prices are for a standard double room, excluding 10% tax.

$$$$ Villa Montana. This deluxe property, owned by French Count Philippe
★ de Reiset, has all the markings of a wealthy Mexican estate. Set high
above Morelia in the Santa María hills, its five impeccably groomed
acres are dotted with a pool, tennis court, and fanciful stone sculptures.
Each individually decorated unit has at least one piece of antique furniture and often a fireplace and private patio. A renowned restaurant
offers North American, French, and Mexican food. Guests have a
choice of either CP (Continental Plan with breakfast) or MAP (Modified American Plan with breakfast and lunch or dinner). ⌂ *Calle Pat-
zimba s/n, 58000,* ☎ *43/14–02–31 or 43/14–01–79,* ℻ *43/15–14–23.
55 rooms with bath. Restaurant, piano bar, pool, tennis court, recreation room, laundry service, convention hall. AE, MC, V.*

$$$ Hotel Posada de la Soledad. Set in a restored private mansion built in
★ the late 17th century, the Posada de la Soledad is conveniently located
one block from the Plaza de Armas. The rooms in the front of the hotel,
the oldest section, are surrounded by an elegant patio with a large foun-

tain and bougainvillea, as well as vintage carriages from the colonial era. Rooms located here have sturdy wood furnishings, elegantly hand-carved by Michoacán craftsmen. The rooms facing north on Calle Melchor Ocampo, however, should be avoided due to heavy traffic on that street. Rooms in a newer (1960s) section at the back of the hotel are smaller and less elaborately furnished but stay quiet and are comfortably appointed with earthtone carpeting and bedspreads. In the off-season, they can be had for a discount. The Posada also has an elegant restaurant and a darkly lit bar where a guitar trio plays plaintive, romantic music. ☎ *Ignacio Zaragoza 90, 58000,* ☎ *43/12–18–88,* FAX *43/12–21–11. 58 rooms with bath. Restaurant, bar. AE, DC, MC, V.*

$$ Hotel Catedral. Located in a restored colonial mansion, this three-story property began operating as a hotel some 30 years ago. Its modern rooms are clustered around a skylit courtyard; some overlook the main plaza and cathedral on Avenida Madero. Interior quarters have less dramatic views but are less noisy. All rooms have dark wood furnishings, telephones, and color TVs. ☎ *Calle Zaragoza 37, 58000,* ☎ *43/13–04–06 or 43/13–04–67,* FAX *43/13–07–83. 44 rooms with bath. Restaurant, bar, dry cleaning. AE, MC, V.*

$$ Hotel Mansion Acueducto. An elaborate wood and wrought-iron staircase leads from the elegant lobby to more modest quarters upstairs. Rooms have dark, colonial-style furniture, telephones, and black-and-white TVs. Older rooms overlook the aqueduct and nearby park; rooms in the motel-like wing have views of the garden, pool, and surrounding mountains. Student groups at times book the entire property. ☎ *Av. Acueducto 25, 58000,* ☎ *43/12–33–01 or 43/12–20–20. 36 rooms with bath. Restaurant, bar, pool. AE, MC, V.*

$ Hotel Concordia. Rooms are simply furnished at this hotel (some spreads are slightly worn), but sheets are clean and showers have hot water throughout the day. On weekends, Mexican families with young children frequent this spot and tend to rise (and wake others) early. ☎ *Valentín Gómez Farías 328, 58000,* ☎ *43/12–30–53. 51 rooms with bath. DC, MC, V.*

Morelia Essentials

Arriving and Departing

BY PLANE

There are daily flights between Francisco Mujica International Airport, 24 kilometers (15 miles) north of Morelia, and Mexico City's International Airport on **Aeromexico** (☎ 800/237–6639; 43/13–05–55 in Morelia; 5/627–0207 in Mexico City). Flights are subject to cancellation, and flight times change often and must be confirmed one day in advance. The 25-minute taxi ride from the airport to Morelia costs about $15.

BY CAR

The drive from Mexico City to Morelia (302 kilometers, or 187 miles) on Route 126 through Toluca, Atlacamulco, Contepec, and Maravatio takes about 3 hours and 45 minutes. In Morelia, **Budget** has an office at the Misión Hotel (☎ 43/13–67–28) but will pick up clients at the airport.

BY TRAIN

The *Purepecha* leaves Mexico City at 10 PM, arriving in Morelia at 6:30 AM; the return train leaves Morelia at 11 PM and arrives in Mexico City at 7:30 AM. The round-trip fare costs $21 first-class. Train schedules are subject to change without notice. For current schedules and rates, contact **Mexico by Train** (☎ and ℻ 210/725–3659 or 800/321–1699) or the local train station (☎ 43/16–16–97).

Direct bus service is available daily between the Terminal Poniente (West Terminal) in Mexico City and Morelia's Central de Autobuses (☎ 43/12–56–64). Several bus lines offer frequent service; the most direct trip (cost: $19), which takes five hours, is on Herradura de Plata (via Corta). Buses leave every hour or two around the clock. Frequent inexpensive bus service is also available from Morelia to other points in Michoacán and throughout the heartland.

Getting Around
As in many of the heartland cities, Morelia's principal sights are near the center of town and you can reach them on foot. Street names in Morelia change frequently, especially on either side of Avenida Madero, the city's main east–west artery. Taxis in Morelia can be hailed on the street or found near the main plaza. Buses run the length of Avenida Madero.

Guided Tours
The following operators conduct tours of Morelia: **Autoturismo Morelia** (Calle Colima 486, ☎ 43/14–08–26), **Michoacán Tour Guides and Conductors Association** (Calle Nigromante 79, ☎ 43/13–26–54), **Tours Lindo Michoacán** (Calzada Madera and Av. Jalisco, ☎ 43/14–99–43), **Transportación Turística Valladolid** (Antonio de Savedra 8, ☎ 43/14–73–84).

Important Addresses and Numbers
EMERGENCIES
Police (☎ 43/12–22–22). **Ambulance-Red Cross** (Cruz Rojo; ☎ 43/14–51–51 or 43/14–50–25). **Consumer Protection Office** (☎ 43/12–40–49). **Fire Department** (☎ 43/12–12–35).

Hospital Memorial (☎ 43/15–10–47 or 43/15–10–99).

MONEY EXCHANGE
Casa Cambio Valladolid (Portal Matamoros 86, ☎ 43/12–85–86) is open weekdays 9–6, Sat. 9–1:30.

TRAVEL AGENCIES
Viajes Lopsa is the American Express representative (Service Las Américas, Local 27, Artilleros del 47, ☎ 43/14–19–50, ℻ 43/14–77–16). **Servicios Establecidos Para el Turismo** is located at Portal Hidalgo 229 (☎ 43/12–36–64).

VISITOR INFORMATION
The **Secretaría Estatal de Turismo** in the Palacio Clavijero provides city maps and brochures of the state of Michoacán. Only a few of the brochures are in English, however. *Calle Nigromante 79, ☎ 43/13–26–54 or 43/12–80–81, ℻ 43/12–98–16 or 43/12–04–15. ☺ Weekdays 9–9, weekends 9–4.*

PÁTZCUARO

Pátzcuaro, the 16th-century capital of Michoacán, exists in a time warp. A bit more than an hour by car from Morelia, this beautiful lakeside community set at 7,250 feet in the Sierra Madre is home to the Tarascan Indians, who fish, farm, and ply their crafts as they have for centuries. Women, wrapped tightly in their striped wool *rebozos* (shawls), hurry to market in the chill, smoky morning air. Men, in traditional straw hats, wheel overburdened carts down crooked, dusty back streets.

The architecture, too, has remained largely unchanged throughout the years. In the 16th century, under kindly Bishop Vasco de Quiroga, Pátzcuaro underwent a building boom of sorts. After he died in 1565, the state capital was moved to Morelia, and the town became a cultural (and architectural) backwater for hundreds of years. Modern visitors will see 16th-century mansions surrounding the downtown plazas; one-story whitewashed houses with sloping tile roofs line the side streets and hills.

Despite the altitude, the weather in Pátzcuaro is temperate year-round. (Autumn and winter nights, however, are cold; sweaters and jackets are a must.) On November 1—the night preceding the Mexican Day of the Dead—the town is inundated with tourists en route to Janitzio, an island in Lake Pátzcuaro, where one of the most elaborate graveyard ceremonies in all of Mexico takes place. Unless you have hotel reservations six months in advance, don't expect to find a room anywhere near Pátzcuaro on November 1 or 2.

Exploring

Numbers in the margin correspond to points of interest on the Pátzcuaro map.

❶ Most of Pátzcuaro's sights can be visited in a few hours, but the town deserves to be explored at a leisurely pace. Begin at the **Plaza Vasco de Quiroga,** the larger of two downtown squares. A tranquil courtyard surrounded by ash trees and 16th-century mansions (since converted into hotels and shops), the plaza commemorates the bishop who restored dignity to the Tarascan people. During the Spanish conquest, Nuño de Guzmán, a lieutenant in Hernán Cortés's army, committed atrocities on the local population in his efforts to conquer western Mexico. He was eventually arrested by the Spanish authorities, and in 1537 Vasco de Quiroga was appointed bishop of Michoacán. Attempting to regain the trust of the indigenous people, he established a number of model villages in the area and promoted the development of commerce among the Tarascans. Quiroga died in 1565, and his remains were consecrated in the Basílica de Nuestra Señora de la Salud (*see below*).

❷ From the plaza, cross over to the **tourist office** at Ibarra 2 (inside the patio on the right side), where you can collect maps and brochures on the region. As you leave the office, return to the plaza and continue around it until you reach Calle Dr. José María Coss on the east side.

❸ Turn right on this street, and in less than a block you'll see a long cobblestoned walkway leading to **La Casa de los 11 Patios,** an 18th-century convent with a number of high-quality shops featuring Tarascan handiwork. As you meander through the gardens and courtyards, you'll encounter weavers producing large bolts of cloth, artists trimming black lacquerware with gold, and seamstresses embroidering blouses. Children may approach you and ask if you'd like to hear the history of the Casa. In return they expect a small donation. If you plan to shop in Pátzcuaro, this is a good place to start. You can view the selection of regional goods and begin to compare prices.

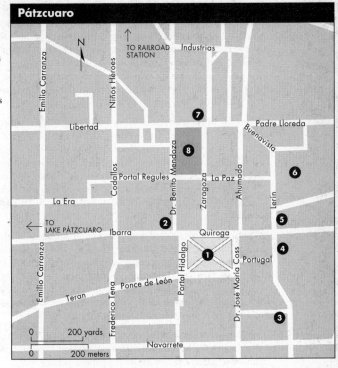

Pátzcuaro

❹ As you leave the shops, continue up a stone walkway to Calle Lerín. Its aging stone walls and whitewashed houses with sloping tile roofs have an ancient feel about them. A block to the north (past Calle Portugal) is the **Templo de la Compañía,** Michoacán's first cathedral. It was begun in 1540 by order of Vasco de Quiroga and completed in 1546. When the state capital was moved to Morelia some 20 years later, the church was taken over by the Jesuits. Today it remains much as it was in the 16th century. Moss has grown over the crumbling stone steps outside; the dank interior is planked with thick wood floors and lined with bare wood benches.

❺ Continue along Calle Lerín another half block to the **Museo de Artes Populares** on your right. Home to the Colegio de San Nicolás Obispo in the 16th century, the building today houses displays of colonial and contemporary crafts, such as ceramics, masks, lacquerware, paintings, and ex-votos in its many rooms. Behind this building is a *troje* (traditional Tarascan wood house) braced atop a stone platform. ☎ 434/2-10–29. ☛ *About $4.* ☉ *Tues.–Sat. 9–7, Sun. 9–3.*

❻ Directly down Calle Lerín and across a cobblestoned courtyard is **La Basílica de Nuestra Señora de la Salud.** Out front Tarascan women sell hot tortillas, herbal mixtures for teas, and religious objects. From this point you can glimpse Lake Pátzcuaro in the distance. The church was begun in 1554 by Vasco de Quiroga but was never completed. Throughout the centuries others—undaunted by earthquakes and fires—took up the cause and constructed a church in honor of the Virgin of Health. Near the main altar is a statue made of cornstalk paste and orchid "juice." Several masses are still held here daily; the earliest begins shortly after dawn.

❼ Continue downhill from the basilica (take Buenavista to Libertad and turn left) to reach the **Biblioteca Pública Gertrudis Bocanegra.** In the back of this library is a vast mural depicting in great detail the history of the region and of the Tarascan people. It was completed by Juan O'Gorman in 1942. If you look closely at the bottom, you may be able to make out the image of Gertrudis Bocanegra, a local heroine who was shot in 1814 for refusing to divulge the revolutionaries' secrets to the Spaniards. ☉ *Weekdays 9–7.*

From the library, continue for a half block to the large outdoor **mercado** sprawled along Calle Libertad and its side streets. At times the road is so crowded with people and their wares—fruit, vegetables, beans, rice, herbs, and sponges—that it is difficult to walk. On Friday, market day, the street is particularly packed. If you press on for about a block, you'll see an indoor market to your left, filled with more produce, large hanging slabs of meat, hot food, and a variety of cheap trinkets.

❽ When you've completed your market stroll, retrace your steps down Calle Libertad. Across the street from the library, stop in at the **Plaza Bocanegra.** This square, marked by a statue of the local heroine, is just one block north of Plaza Vasco de Quiroga, your starting point. While Bocanegra is the smaller of the two squares, it is the center of Pátzcuaro's commercial life. Bootblacks, pushcart vendors, and bus and taxi stands to Lake Pátzcuaro are all found in this plaza.

TIME OUT Before heading to the lake, sit in the shady square for a moment and enjoy a rich Michoacán ice-cream or fruit bar. Then grab a taxi or the San Bartolo/Lago bus to the *embarcadero* (wharf).

A 10-minute ride will take you to the tranquil shores of **Lake Pátzcuaro.** There are a few lakeside restaurants here that serve fresh whitefish and other local catches. Amble along the dock or peek into the waterfront crafts shops. If you have time, a boat trip to **Janitzio** (the largest of Lake Pátzcuaro's five islands) is highly recommended.

Wooden launches, with room for 25 people, depart for Janitzio daily from 9 to 6. Purchase round-trip tickets for $3 at a dockside office (where prices are controlled by the tourist department). The ride to Janitzio takes about 30 minutes and is particularly beautiful in late afternoon, when the sun is low in the sky. Once you're out on the lake, fishermen with butterfly nets may approach your boat. The nets are no longer used for fishing, but for a small donation these locals will let you take their picture.

On most days (November 2 being the exception), Janitzio is a quiet island inhabited by Tarascan Indians. It is crowned by a huge statue of independence hero José María Morelos, which is accessible by a cobblestoned stairway. Though the road twists past many souvenir stands as it ascends, don't be discouraged. The view from the summit—of the lake, the town, and the surrounding hills—is well worth the climb. Inside the statue are some remarkable murals that spiral up from the base to the tip of the monument.

Off the Beaten Track

The remains of **Tzintzuntzán,** the ancient capital of the Tarascan Indian kingdom, lie 17 kilometers (10½ miles) northeast of Pátzcuaro. When the Spanish came to colonize the region in the 16th century, some 40,000 Tarascans lived and worshiped in this lakeshore village, which they called "place of the hummingbirds." The ruins of their pyramid-shape temples, or *yacatas,* still stand today and are open to the public for a small admission charge. Visitors can also find vestiges of a 16th-century Franciscan monastery where Spanish friars attempted to convert the Indians to Christianity. Though Tzintzuntzán lost some prominence when Bishop Vasco de Quiroga moved the seat of his diocese to Pátzcuaro in 1540, the village is still well known for the straw and ceramic handicrafts made by the Tarascan Indians and sold in numerous shops along the main street of town. To reach Tzintzuntzán, take the bus marked Quiroga from Pátzcuaro's Central Camionera; travel time is about 30 minutes.

Dining

Most restaurants in Pátzcuaro specialize in seafood. In addition to whitefish (which is featured on most menus), look for *trucha* (trout) and *charales* and *boquerones* (two small, locally caught fish served as appetizers). Tarascan specialties, such as a tomato-based soup with cheese, cream, and tortillas (called *sopa tarasca*) are also common. As a rule restaurants are located around the two plazas and in hotels. Since the large meal is served at midday, many dining establishments are shuttered by 9. Unless otherwise indicated, dress is casual.

CATEGORY	COST*
$$	$8–$15
$	under $8

per person, excluding drinks and service

$$ **La Casona.** This unpretentious restaurant on Plaza Vasco de Quiroga, with whitewashed walls and white ceiling *vigas* (beams), is brightened by orange tablecloths. The house specialties include *caldo de pesca* (fish soup), and *pescado blanca* (whitefish), among other local dishes. ✕ *Plaza Vasco de Quiroga 65,* ☎ *434/2–11–79. Reservations not accepted. MC, V.*

$ ★ **El Patio.** Though this low-key restaurant features mouth-watering whitefish platters (including salsa, vegetables, and french fries), it's possible to duck in at midday for just a strong cappuccino or glass of local wine. (There are several varieties of wine; waiters can help you choose among them.) For a late-afternoon snack, a plate of quesadillas with a side order of guacamole is highly recommended, and the *sopa tarasca* is superb. ✕ *Plaza Vasco de Quiroga 19,* ☎ *434/2–04–84. DC, MC, V.*

$ **Restaurante Gran Hotel.** Though this one-room restaurant is connected to the Gran Hotel, it is independently owned and attracts a mix of locals and tourists to its midday meal. The furnishings are simple: tables covered with amber-colored cloths and set beneath wood chandeliers. The food is good and wholesome. Specialties include lightly breaded whitefish, chicken with mole sauce, and Tarascan soup. ✕ *Portal Regules 6,* ☎ *434/2–04–43. Reservations not accepted. MC, V.*

$ ★ **Restaurante Hotel Posada La Basílica.** From a corner table in this glass-enclosed restaurant, patrons have views of the mountains, the lake, and tile-roofed homes. Open for breakfast and lunch (8–4), this dining spot offers such regional specialties as broiled trout with garlic and tamales with cheese and cream Mexican-style eggs and a fresh-fruit platter are recommended morning fare. ✕ *Calle Arciga 6,* ☎ *434/2–11–08. Reservations not accepted. MC, V.*

$ **Restaurante Los Escudos.** This colonial-style restaurant, located on the Plaza Vasco de Quiroga, is frequented by foreigners who stay in the adjoining hotel. The varied menu ranges from club sandwiches to multicourse midday meals. Two particularly tempting treats are the Tarascan soup and *pollo especial Los Escudos* (chicken sautéed in tomato sauce and vegetables). Checked tablecloths and yellow chimney lamps create a cozy atmosphere. ✕ *Portal Hidalgo 74,* ☎ *434/2–01–38 or 434/2–12–90. Reservations not accepted. MC, V.*

Lodging

Though Pátzcuaro has no deluxe properties, there are an ample number of clean, moderately priced hotels. Most are located on or within a few blocks of the Plaza Vasco de Quiroga. Several more expensive properties are situated on Avenida Lázaro Cárdenas, the road to Lake Pátzcuaro. If you're planning to be in town on or near November 2, the Mexican Day of the Dead, make hotel reservations at least six months in advance.

CATEGORY	COST*
$$$	$60–$90
$$	$25–$60
$	under $25

All prices are for a standard double room, excluding 10% tax.

$$$ Hotel Posada de Don Vasco. Located several minutes out of town on the road to Lake Pátzcuaro, this sprawling resort hotel offers a wide range of indoor and outdoor amenities. Its 30 newer rooms are thickly carpeted and have either balconies or patios; the older quarters, decorated in a colonial style, are smaller and open onto a courtyard. The manicured grounds are relatively quiet despite the occasional rumbling of a passing bus or truck. ⊞ *Av. Las Americas 450, 61500,* ☎ *434/2–02–27 or 434/2–27–04,* FAX *434/2–02–62. 99 rooms with bath, 4 suites. Restaurant, pool, badminton, bowling, tennis courts, billiards. AE, DC, MC, V.*

$$ Hotel Posada La Basílica. This colonial-style inn, housed in a 17th-century building, faces the Basilica of the Virgin of Health. On some mornings strains from a postdawn mass filter softly into the hotel; in the evenings, when there's a fair across the way, louder, more resonant music is audible. Though noisy, the property deserves a positive mention for its comfortable, individually decorated rooms. Thick wood shutters cover floor-to-ceiling windows, walls are trimmed in handpainted colonial designs, and the rugs are handwoven. Some rooms have fireplaces, but check with management before attempting to use them, as not all of them are functional. ⊞ *Calle Arciga 6, 61600,* ☎ *434/2–11–08 or 434/2–11–81; reservations 434/2–06–59. 11 rooms with bath. Restaurant. MC, V.*

$$ Los Escudos. The 16th-century home of the Count de la Lama and the Marquis de Villahermosa de Alfaro on the Plaza Vasco de Quiroga is today a cozy hotel. Its courtyards brim with potted plants, and some guest rooms contain small murals of Tarascan Indian scenes. Ten rooms situated in back and shielded from street noise open onto an outdoor patio. All rooms have color TVs and telephones; five rooms offer fireplaces. ⊞ *Portal Hidalgo 73, 61600,* ☎ *434/2–01–38 or 434/2–12–90,* FAX *434/2–02–07. 30 rooms with bath. Restaurant. MC, V.*

$$ Mansión Iturbe. This hotel, housed in a 17th-century mansion, still re-
★ tains much of its colonial charm. Plant-filled courtyards are ringed by stone archways. Rooms, featuring large wood-and-glass doors, are partially carpeted and decorated with red-and-black checked spreads and drapes. The tranquil second-floor courtyard has a good view of the neighborhood. ⊞ *Portal Morelos 59, 61600,* ☎ *434/2–03–68. 12 rooms with bath. Restaurant, bicycles. MC, V.*

$$ Mesón del Gallo. Located on a fairly quiet side street near the Casa de los 11 Patios, this two-story property offers modern rooms in a garden setting; the beds have wood-and-tile headboards and magenta spreads and drapes. Suites, complete with minibars, are furnished in more subdued hues. The pool is encircled by bougainvillea, fruit trees, and a rock garden. When the second-floor banquet room is rented out for afternoon parties, the decibel level rises. ⊞ *Calle Dr. José María Coss 20, 61600,* ☎ *434/2-14-74,* ℻ *434/2-15-11. 20 rooms with bath, 5 suites. Restaurant, bar, pool. AE, MC, V.*

Nightlife

The Dance of Los Viejitos (Old Men), a widely known Mexican native dance, is performed on Wednesday and Saturday evenings at the Hotel Posada de Don Vasco (☎ 434/2-27-04). A buffet dinner with entertainment costs approximately $17.

Excursion to Uruapan

The subtropical town of **Uruapan,** located about 64 kilometers (40 miles) west of Pátzcuaro, is distinctly different from its lakeside neighbor. Some 2,000 feet lower than Pátzcuaro—though still at an elevation of 5,300 feet—it is a populous, commercial center with a warm climate and lush vegetation. The town's name is derived from the Tarascan word *urupan,* meaning "where the flowers bloom."

Uruapan can be reached from Pátzcuaro by either car or bus. Route 14 is the most direct route between the two cities. There is also frequent bus service on the Flecha Amarilla and other major lines; travel time is about 70 minutes.

You can see several points of interest within a few hours. The first, **La Huatápera,** is located off Uruapan's Plaza Principal. This 16th-century hospital has been converted into the **Museo Regional de Arte Popular.** It houses a collection of crafts from the state of Michoacán, including an excellent display of lacquerware made in Uruapan. ☎ *452/2-21-38.* ☛ *Free.* ⊙ *Weekdays 10-2 and 4-7, weekends 10-2.*

The **Mercado de Antojitos,** an immense, sprawling market, begins directly in back of the museum and extends quite a distance north along Calle Constitución. Along the road, Tarascan Indians sell large mounds of produce, fresh fish, beans, homemade cheese, and a variety of cheap manufactured goods. If you travel south along Calle Constitución, you'll come to a courtyard where vendors sell hot food.

For good *carne asada* (charbroiled beef served with grilled scallions, avocado, and *frijoles charro*—beans in broth), try **Parilla Tarasca** (Calle Alvaro Obregón 4, no ☎), a two-level restaurant specializing in grilled meat.

Head over to the **Parque Nacional Eduardo Ruiz,** located about a half mile from the Plaza Principal off Calle Independencia. Stroll through the verdant acreage to the source of the River Cupatitzio and abundant fountains, waterfalls, and springs.

Eleven kilometers (7 miles) south along the river is the magnificent waterfall at **Tzaráracua.** At this point the Cupatitzio plunges 150 feet off a sheer rock cliff into a riverbed below; a rainbow seems to hang perpetually over the site. Buses marked Tzaráracua leave sporadically from the Plaza Principal in Uruapan. You can also take a taxi or drive there via Avenida Lázaro Cárdenas.

Farther afield, about 32 kilometers (20 miles) north of Uruapan, lies the dormant **Paricutín volcano.** Its initial burst of lava and ashes wiped out the nearby village of San Juan Parangaricutiro in 1943. Today travelers can visit this buried site by hiring gentle mountain ponies and a Tarascan guide in the town of Angahuan. To reach Angahuan, take the Los Reyes bus from Uruapan's Central Camionera or go by car via the Uruapan-Carapan highway.

Pátzcuaro Essentials

Arriving and Departing

BY CAR

Driving time from Mexico City to Pátzcuaro is about seven hours. From Morelia, two roads lead to Pátzcuaro: The newer passes through Tiripetio; the older passes through Quiroga and Tzintzuntzán. Cars can be rented at locations in Mexico City or Morelia; there are no rental outlets in Pátzcuaro.

BY TRAIN

Train service between Mexico City and Pátzcuaro is available daily on the Mexican National Railways. The *Purepecha* departs Mexico City at 10 PM and arrives in Pátzcuaro at 7:30 AM; the return trip leaves Pátzcuaro at 10 PM and arrives in Mexico City at 7:30 AM. The roundtrip fare is $24. There are no sleeping cars, but train seats do recline. Train schedules are subject to change without notice. For current schedules and rates, contact **Mexico by Train** (☎ and FAX 210/725–3659 or 800/321–1699) or the local train station (☎ 434/2–08–03).

BY BUS

Direct bus service is available daily between the Terminal Poniente (West Terminal) in Mexico City and Pátzcuaro's Central Camionera. Several bus lines offer frequent service; the most direct trip, which takes six hours, is on **Herradura de Plata** (via Corta). Frequent inexpensive bus service is available from Pátzcuaro to other points in Michoacán and throughout the heartland.

Getting Around

Many of Pátzcuaro's principal sights are located near the Plaza Vasco de Quiroga and Plaza Bocanegra in the center of town. Taxis and buses to the lake can also be found at these main squares. If you want to visit surrounding villages, taxi drivers will drive you for a reasonable rate. Be sure to agree on a fee before setting out.

Important Addresses and Numbers

EMERGENCIES

Police (☎ 434/2–05–65 or 434/2–00–04).

Clinic. Centro Médico Quirúrgico (Portal Hidalgo 76, ☎ 434/2–19–98); **Hospital Civil** (☎ 434/2–02–85).

Pharmacy. Farmacia La Paz (at the corner of La Paz and Bocanegra in the Plaza Bocanegra, ☎ 434/2–08–10).

MONEY EXCHANGE

Banca Promex (Portal Regules 9, ☎ 434/2–24–66), **Banamex** (Portal Juárez 32, ☎ 434/2–15–50 or 434/2–10–31), **Bancomer** (Zaragoza 23, ☎ 434/2–03–34 or 434/2–09–52). A **Banamex Caja Permanente ATM** is located on Dr. Benito Mendoza, between the two plazas. Note:

Many Pátzcuaro restaurants and hotels do not accept traveler's checks, though some will take major credit cards.

VISITOR INFORMATION

The **Delegación de Turismo** distributes city maps and brochures (in Spanish). *Ibarra 2, Interior 4, off the Plaza Vasco de Quiroga,* ☎ *434/2–12–14.* ☉ *Mon.–Sat. 9–2 and 4–7, Sun. 9–2.*

9 Acapulco

If Acapulco no longer tops the glitterati top-ten list, it remains both a sentimental favorite and a party-hearty resort town, boasting some of the glitziest discos this side of the Pacific. The cobblestoned streets of nearby Taxco, the silver city, are lined with master jewelers, while Ixtapa and Zihuatanejo, a few hours away, juxtapose modern shopping malls with pristine beaches.

FOR SUN LOVERS, beach bums, and other hedonists, Acapulco is the ideal holiday resort. Don't expect high culture, historic monuments, or haute cuisine. Anyone who ventures to this Pacific resort 433 kilometers (260 miles) south of Mexico City does so to relax. Translate that as swimming, shopping, and nightlife. Everything takes place against a staggeringly beautiful natural backdrop. Acapulco Bay is one of the world's best natural harbors, and it is the city's centerpiece. By day the water looks clean and temptingly deep blue; at night it flashes and sparkles with the city lights.

By Anya Schiffrin

Updated by Wendy Luft

The weather is Acapulco's major draw—warm waters, almost constant sunshine, and year-round temperatures in the 80s. It comes as no surprise, then, that most people plan their day around laying their towel on some part of Acapulco's many miles of beach. Both tame and wild water sports are available—everything from waterskiing to snorkeling, diving, and the thrill of parasailing. Less strenuous possibilities are motorboat rides and fishing trips. Championship golf courses, tennis courts, and the food and crafts markets also occasionally lure some visitors away from the beach, but not out of the sun.

Most people rouse themselves from their hammocks, deck chairs, or towels only when it is feeding time. Eating is one of Acapulco's great pleasures. In addition to the glitzy places, there are many good no-frills, down-home Mexican restaurants. Eating at one of these spots gives you a glimpse into the real Mexico: office workers breaking for lunch, groups of men socializing over a cup of coffee.

At night Acapulco is transformed as the city rouses itself from the day's torpor and prepares for the long hours ahead. Even though Acapulco's heyday is past, its nightlife is legendary. This is true despite the fact that many of the discos along the main drag still look as if they were designed in the early '70s by an architect who bought mirrors and strobe lights wholesale. Perpetually crowded, the discos are grouped in twos and threes, so most people go to several places in one night.

Acapulco was originally an important port for the Spanish, who used it to trade with countries in the Far East. The Spanish built Fuerte de San Diego (Fort San Diego) to protect the city from pirates, and today the fort houses a historical museum. The name of the late Teddy Stauffer, an entrepreneurial Swiss, is practically synonymous with that of modern Acapulco. He hired the first cliff divers at La Quebrada in Old Acapulco and founded the Boom Boom Room, the town's first dance hall, and Tequila A Go-Go, its first discotheque. The Hotel Mirador at La Quebrada and the area stretching from Caleta to Hornos beaches, near today's Old Acapulco, were the center of activity in the 1950s, when Acapulco was a town of 20,000 with an economy based largely on fishing.

Former President Miguel Alemán Valdés bought up miles of the coast just before the road and the airport were built. The Avenida Costera Miguel Alemán bears his name today. Since the late 1940s, Acapulco has expanded eastward so that today it is one of Mexico's largest cities, with a population of approximately 2 million. Currently under development are a 3,000-acre expanse known as Acapulco Diamante and the areas known as Punta Diamante and Playa Diamante.

EXPLORING

Acapulco is a city that is easily understood, easily explored. During the day the focus for most visitors is the beach and the myriad activities that happen on and off it—sunbathing, swimming, waterskiing, parasailing, snorkeling, deep-sea fishing, and so on. At night the attention shifts to the restaurants and discos. The Costera Miguel Alemán, the wide boulevard that hugs Acapulco Bay from the Scenic Highway to Caleta Beach (about 8 kilometers, or 5 miles), is central to both day and night diversions. All the major beaches, big hotels—minus the more exclusive East Bay properties, such as Las Brisas, Sheraton, Camino Real, Pierre Marqués, and the Princess—and shopping malls are off the Costera. Hence most of the shopping, dining, and clubbing takes place within a few blocks of the Costera, and many an address is listed only as "Costera Miguel Alemán." Because street addresses are not often used and streets have no logical pattern, directions are usually given from a major landmark, such as CiCi or the zócalo.

Old Acapulco, the colonial part of town, is where the Mexicans go to run their errands: mail letters at the post office, buy supplies at the Mercado Municipal, and have clothes made or repaired at the tailor. Here is where you'll find the zócalo, the church, and Fort San Diego. Just up the hill from Old Acapulco is La Quebrada, where, five times a day, the cliff divers plunge into the surf 130 feet below.

The peninsula just south of Old Acapulco contains remnants of the first version of Acapulco. This primarily residential area was prey to dilapidation and abandonment for many years, but efforts were made to revitalize it—such as reopening the Caleta Hotel and opening the aquarium on Caleta Beach and the zoo on Roqueta Island—and although its past glory hasn't returned, it is now a popular area for budget travelers, especially Mexican and European. The Plaza de Toros, where bullfights are held on Sundays from Christmas to Easter, is in the center of the peninsula.

If you arrived by plane, you've had a royal introduction to Acapulco Bay. As you drive from the airport, via the Scenic Highway, the first thing you see on your left is the golf course for the Acapulco Princess. Just over the hill is your first glimpse of the entire bay, and it is truly gorgeous, day or night.

Numbers in the margin correspond to points of interest on the Acapulco map.

❶ La Base, the Mexican naval base next to Plaza Icacos, anchors the eastern terminus of the Costera. There are no tours.

❷ The **Casa de la Cultura** is on the beach side of the Costera, just past the Hyatt Regency. It includes a small archaeological museum, an exhibit of crafts from the entire state of Guerrero, and the Ixcateopan art gallery with changing exhibits. ☎ 74/84–38–14. ☛ *Free.* ☉ *Weekdays 9–2 and 5–8, Sat. 9–5.*

❸ CiCi (short for Centro Internacional para Convivencia Infantil), on the Costera, is a water-oriented theme park for children. There are dolphin and seal shows, a freshwater pool with wave-making apparatus, water slide, miniaquarium, and other attractions. ☎ 74/84–82–10. ☛ *$10 adults, $7 children.* ☉ *Daily 10–6.*

❹ About a half mile past CiCi, on the right side of the Costera, is **Centro Internacional** (the Convention Center), not really of interest unless you are attending a conference there. One exception is the **Mexican Fiesta**

held Monday, Wednesday, and Friday evenings from November 15 to April 15, and Wednesday and Friday the rest of the year. There are three options: A buffet dinner, open bar, and show costs $38; the show and open bar, without dinner, is $20; entrance to the show alone is $15. The buffet dinner begins at 7:30, the fiesta at 8:15; call 74/84–70–50 for additional information.

⑤ Continue along through the heart of the Costera until you reach **Papagayo Park,** one of the top municipal parks in the country. Named for the hotel that formerly occupied the grounds, Papagayo sits on 52 acres of prime real estate on the Costera, just after the underpass at the end of this strip. Youngsters enjoy the life-size model of a Spanish galleon like the ones that once sailed into Acapulco when it was Mexico's capital of trade with the Orient. There is an aviary, a roller-skating rink, a racetrack with mite-size race cars, a replica of the space shuttle *Columbia,* bumper boats in a lagoon, and other rides. ☎ 74/85–96–23. ☛ *Small fee to enter; rides cost about $1 to $2.30.* ⊙ *Daily 10–8.*

⑥ The sprawling **Mercado Municipal,** a few blocks west of the Costera, is Acapulco at its most authentic. Locals come to purchase their everyday needs, from fresh vegetables and candles to plastic buckets and love potions. Go between 10 AM and 1 PM and ask to be dropped off near the *flores* (flower stand) closest to the souvenir and crafts section. If you've driven to the mercado, locals may volunteer to watch your car; be sure to lock your trunk and tip about 35¢.

The stalls within the mercado are densely packed together but luckily are awning-covered, so things stay quite cool despite the lack of air-conditioning. From the flower stall, as you face the ceramic stand, turn right and head into the market. There are hundreds of souvenirs to choose from: woven blankets, puppets, colorful wooden toys and plates, leather goods, baskets, hammocks, and handmade wooden furniture including child-size chairs. There is even a stand offering charms, amulets and talismans, bones, herbs, fish eyes, sharks' teeth, lotions, candles, and soaps said to help one find or keep a mate, increase virility or fertility, bring peace to the home, or ward off the evil eye. You can also find some kitschy gems: Acapulco ashtrays and boxes covered with tiny shells or enormous framed pictures of the Virgin of Guadalupe. There are also silver jewelry vendors, but unless you really have a good eye for quality, it's best to buy silver only from a reputable dealer (*see* Shopping, *below*).

⑦ Built in the 18th century to protect the city from pirates, **El Fuerte de San Diego** is on the hill overlooking the harbor next to the army barracks in Old Acapulco. (The original fort, destroyed in an earthquake, was built in 1616.) The fort now houses the **Museo Historico de Acapulco,** under the auspices of Mexico City's prestigious Museum of Anthropology. The exhibits portray the city from prehistoric times through Mexico's independence from Spain in 1821. Especially noteworthy are the displays touching on the Christian missionaries sent from Mexico to the Far East and the cultural interchange that resulted. ☎ 74/82–38–28. ☛ *$4.20, Sun. free.* ⊙ *Tues.–Sun. 10:30–5.*

⑧ Acapulco is still a lively commercial port and fishing center. If you stroll along the **waterfront,** you'll see all these activities at the commercial docks. The cruise ships dock here, and at night Mexican parents bring their children to play on the small treelined promenade. Farther west, by the zócalo, are the docks for the sightseeing yachts and smaller fishing boats. It's a good spot to join the Mexicans in people-watching.

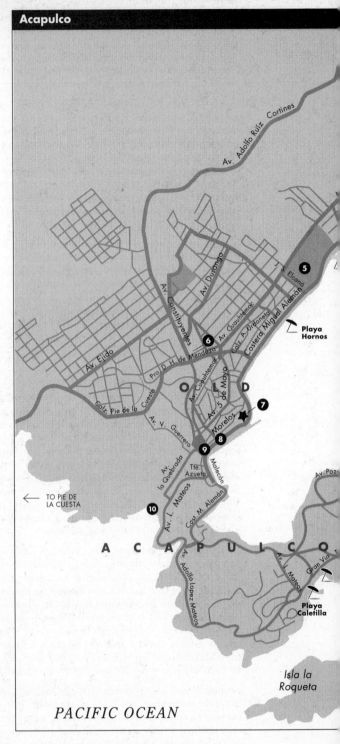

Av. Rancho Acapulco

Paseo del Farallón

Av. Cuauhtémoc

Av. W. Masieu

Av. Almirante Cristóbal Colón

Av. Horacio Nelson

Magallanes

Golf Course

Lobo Solitario

④

③

②

①

Diana Glorieta

Costera Miguel Alemán

Costera Miguel Alemán

Playa Condesa

Playa Icacos

Playa Hornitos

Punta Guitarrón

Bahía de Acapulco

Carretera Escénica

E A S T

B A Y

TO AIRPORT →

zo del Rey

Tropical

Playa Caleta

Bahía de Puerto Marqués

Punta Bruja

Playa Roqueta

TO PUNTA DIAMANTE →
AND BARRA VIEJA

N

| 0 | 880 yards |
| 0 | 800 meters |

❾ The **zócalo** is the center of Old Acapulco, a shaded plaza in front of **Nuestra Señora de la Soledad,** the town's modern but unusual church, with its stark-white exterior and bulb-shaped blue and yellow spires. Overgrown with dense trees, the zócalo is the hub of downtown. All day it's filled with vendors, shoeshine men, and people lining up to use the pay phones. After siesta, they drift here to meet and greet. On Sunday evenings there's music in the bandstand. There are several cafés and news agents selling the English-language *Mexico City News,* so tourists lodging in the area are drawn here, too. Just off the zócalo, Sanborns attracts locals and tourists alike; many linger for hours over the newspaper and a cup of coffee. Around the zócalo are several souvenir shops, and on the side streets you can get hefty, fruity milk shakes for about $1. The flea market, inexpensive tailor shops, and Woolworth's (*see* Shopping, *below*) are nearby.

TIME OUT   The café at 45 Cinco de Mayo, below the German restaurant, serves *churros* every afternoon beginning at 4. This Spanish treat of fried dough dusted with sugar and dipped in hot chocolate is popular at *merienda,* which means "snack."

❿ A 10-minute walk up the hill from the zócalo brings you to **La Quebrada.** It's home to the Mirador Hotel, *the* place for tourists in the 1940s; it still retains some sheen from its glory days. But these days, most visitors eventually make the trip here because this is where the famous cliff divers jump from a height of 130 feet daily at 1 PM and evenings at 7:30, 8:30, 9:30, and 10:30. The dives are thrilling, so be sure to arrive early. Before they dive, the brave divers say a prayer at a small shrine near the jumping-off point. Sometimes they dive in pairs; often they carry torches. There's an admission fee (about $1.50), paid at a booth outside the hotel before you enter the viewing area; when you exit, some of the divers may also be waiting to greet you—and to ask for tips.

What to See and Do with Children

CiCi and **Papagayo Park** (*see above*).

Children might also like to see **Magico Mundo Marina,** the aquarium on Caleta beach, where there is also a sea lion show, swimming pools, a toboggan, scuba diving, and (for rent) Jet Skis, inner tubes, bananas (inflatable rubber tubes pulled along the beach by motorboats), and kayaks—not to mention clean rest rooms. From here you can take the glass-bottom boat to Roqueta Island for a visit to the small zoo. Palao's restaurant on Roqueta Island has a sandy cove for swimming, a pony, and a cage of monkeys that entertain youngsters. ☛ *Aquarium: $6.50 adults, $4.40 children. Ferry service to Roqueta Island, including zoo: $6.50. Glass-bottomed boat: $6.50.*

SHOPPING

Commerce, in general, has been going through hard times in Acapulco, although you wouldn't know it by seeing the number of T-shirt shops and boutiques along the Costera. The fact is that this is a buyer's market and the abundance of air-conditioned shopping malls and boutiques make picking up gifts and souvenirs all the more pleasurable. Also pleasurable—but dangerous insofar as loosening your purse strings—is a custom practiced in many shops: giving free margaritas, beers, or soft drinks to browsers. Except for the markets, most places

Reality check. Call home.

—— *AT&T USADirect® and World Connect® The fast, easy way to call most anywhere.* ——

Take out AT&T Calling Card or your local calling card.** Lift phone. Dial AT&T Access Number
for country you're calling from. Connect to English-speaking operator or voice prompt.
Reach the States or over 200 countries. Talk. Say goodbye. Hang up. Resume vacation.

Argentina♦	001-800-200-1111	**Guyana***††	165
Belize♦	555	Honduras †	123
Bolivia*	0-800-1112	**Mexico**◊◊◊■	95-800-462-4240
Brazil	000-8010	Nicaragua	174
Chile	1-23-0-0311	**Panama**■	109
Colombia	980-11-0010	Paraguay (Asuncion City)†	0081-800
Costa Rica*■	0-800-0-114-114	**Peru**†	171
Ecuador*	999-119	**Suriname**†	156
El Salvador*■	190	Uruguay	00-0410
Guatemala*	190	**Venezuela***■	80-011-120

AT&T
Your True Choice

For a free wallet sized card of all AT&T Access Numbers, call: 1-800-241-5555.

All the best trips start with **Fodor's**.

close for siesta. The typical hours of business are 10–1 and then 4–7, though these hours vary slightly. Most shops close on Sunday.

The flea markets in Acapulco carry what seems to be an inexhaustible supply of inexpensive collectibles and souvenirs, including serapes, ceramics, straw hats, shell sculptures, carved walking canes, and wooden toys. The selections of archaeological artifact replicas, bamboo wind chimes, painted wooden birds (from $5 to $100 each), shell earrings, and embroidered clothes begin to look identical. Prices at the flea markets are often quite low, but it's a good idea to compare prices of items you're interested in with prices in the shops, and bargaining is essential. It's best to buy articles described as being made from semiprecious stones or silver in reputable establishments. If you don't, you may find that the beautiful jade or lapis lazuli that was such a bargain was really cleverly painted paste, or that the silver was simply a facsimile called *alpaca*. There are a couple of fashionable boutiques that sell designer clothes, but the majority of shops stock cotton sportswear and casual resort clothes. Made-to-order clothes are well made and especially reasonable. Otherwise be careful, since quality is not high and many goods self-destruct a few months after you get back home. Note: Although you'll find price tags on all the merchandise in the tony-looking boutiques, they're not always written in stone; that is, although bargaining may be subtle at the posher stores, if something catches your fancy, it never hurts to indicate that you might want to buy it if only the price were a bit lower.

Shopping Districts

The main shopping strip is on Costera Miguel Alemán from the Acapulco Plaza to the El Presidente Hotel. Here you can find Benetton, Peer, Aca Joe, Look, Polo Ralph Lauren, and other fashionable sportswear boutiques. Downtown (Old) Acapulco doesn't have many name shops, but this is where you'll find the inexpensive tailors patronized by the Mexicans, lots of little souvenir shops, and the flea market with crafts made for tourists. Most of the tailors are on Calle Benito Juárez, just west of the zócalo. Also downtown are Woolworth's and Sanborns.

Food and Flea Markets

The **Mercado Municipal,** the best place to shop for crafts, is described in Exploring, *above.*

El Mercado de Artesanías is a 20-minute walk from the zócalo. Turn left as you leave Woolworth's and head straight until you reach the Multibanco Comermex. Turn right for one block and then turn left. When you reach the Banamex, the market is on your right. The market itself is a conglomeration of every souvenir in town: fake tribal masks, the ever-present onyx chessboards, the $25 hand-embroidered dresses, imitation silver, hammocks, ceramics, even skin cream made from turtles (don't buy it, because turtles are endangered and you won't get it through U.S. Customs). The market is open daily 9–9.

Two blocks west of the zócalo is **Calle José M. Iglesia,** home to a row of little souvenir shops that have a smaller selection than the big markets but many more T-shirts and more shell sculptures, shell ashtrays, and shell key chains than you ever imagined possible.

Art

Contemporary Art Gallery (Hyatt Regency, Costera Miguel Alemán 1, ☎ 74/84–28–88) carries the work of contemporary Mexican artists, including Leonardo Nierman.

Galería Rudic (on the Costera across from the Continental Plaza, ☎ 74/86–68–06) is one of the best galleries in town, with a good collection of top contemporary Mexican artists, including Armando Amaya, Leonardo Nierman, Norma Goldberg, Trinidad Osorio, and José David Alfaro Siqueiros.

The sculptor **Pal Kepenyes** continues to receive good press. His jewelry is available in the Hyatt Regency arcade. It's also on display in his workshop at Guitarrón 140. Good luck with his perennially busy phone number, ☎ 74/84–37–38.

Sergio Bustamente's whimsical painted papier-mâché and giant ceramic sculptures can be seen at the Princess Hotel shopping arcade and at his own gallery (scheduled to move at press time; ask at your hotel for its new location).

Boutiques

Whereas the majority of hotels and restaurants have managed to survive the ups and downs of Acapulco's popularity, recent economic woes have taken their toll on boutiques, many of which have closed branches or shut down completely. The mall section (*see below*) lists mostly clothing shops, but several places strung along the Costera, mainly between the El Presidente and Fiesta American hotels, also sell casual wear; **Aca Joe, Peer, Polo Ralph Lauren,** and **Look** are among the survivors of the town's retail crisis. There are also a few high-fashion boutiques that will make clothes to order, and many can alter clothes to suit you, so it is always worth asking.

Nautica, (Plaza Bahía, ☎ 74/85–75–11; smaller shop at Las Brisas hotel, ☎ 74/84–15–80) is a boutique stocked with stylish casual clothing for men.

COS (Costera Miguel Alemán, outside entrance to the Fiesta Americana Condesa del Mar hotel, ☎ 74/81–24–34; and at the Acapulco Plaza Hotel, ☎ 74/85–25–15) carries a sensational line of swimsuits for equally sensational bodies.

Pit (Princess arcade, ☎ 74/69–10–00) offers a smashing line of beach cover-ups and hand-painted straw hats, as well as bathing suits and light dresses.

Custom-Made Clothes

Esteban's (Costera Miguel Alemán 2010, across from the Club de Golf, ☎ 74/84–30–84) is the most glamorous shop in Acapulco, boasting a clientele of international celebrities and many of the important local families. Esteban's made-to-order clothes are formal and fashionable; his opulent evening dresses range from $200 to $3,000, though daytime dresses average $120. If you scour the racks, you can find something for $100. The real bargains are on the second floor, where some items are marked down as much as 80%. Esteban has a back room filled with designer clothes.

Benny (Costera Miguel Alemán 114, across from the Torres Gemelas Condominium, ☎ 74/84–15–47, and downtown at Ignacio de la Llave

2, local 10, ☎ 74/82–22–28), known for years for his custom-designed resort wear for men, now caters to women as well.

Jewelry

Antoinette (Acapulco Princess shopping arcade, ☎ 74/69–10–00) has gold jewelry of impeccable design, set with precious and semiprecious stones, that you wouldn't be surprised to find on Fifth Avenue. It's worth going to window shop, even if you know you won't buy anything. Surprisingly, their display of silver items is uninspired.

Suzette's (Hyatt Regency hotel, ☎ 74/69–12–34), a tony shop that's been around for years, has a very laudable selection of gold jewelry.

Silver

Many people come to Mexico to buy silver. Taxco, three hours away, is one of the silver capitals of the world (*see* Excursions from Acapulco, *below*). Prices in Acapulco are lower than those in the United States but not dirt-cheap by any means. Bangles start at $8 and go up to $20; bracelets range from $20 to $250. Just look for the .925 sterling silver hallmark, or buy the more inexpensive silver plate that is dipped in several coats (*baños*) of silver. **Miguel Pineda** and **Los Castillo** are two of the more famous design names. Designs range from traditional bulky necklaces (often made with turquoise) to streamlined bangles and chunky earrings.

Tane (Hyatt Regency hotel, ☎ 74/84–63–48; Camino Real hotel, ☎ 74/66–10–10; and Las Brisas hotel, ☎ 74/81–08–16) carries small selections of the exquisite flatware, jewelry, and objets d'art created by one of Mexico's most prestigious (and expensive) silversmiths.

Joyeria La Mina (Costera Miguel Alemán 182, across from Acapulco Plaza, ☎ 74/84–63–02) carries an interesting collection of silver and gold jewelry.

Malls

Malls in Acapulco range from the lavish air-conditioned shopping arcade at the Princess to rather gloomy collections of shops that sell cheap jewelry and embroidered dresses. Malls are listed below from east to west.

The cool arcade of the **Princess** is one of Acapulco's classiest, most comfortable malls. Serious shopping takes place here. Best bets are quality jewelry, clothes, leather, accessories, and artwork. Even if you are staying on the Costera, it is worth the cab ride out here just to see the shops.

On the Costera, across from the Fiesta Americana Condesa Hotel is the **Plaza Condesa,** which offers a cold-drink stand, an Italian restaurant, a gym and weight-training center, and a greater concentration of silver shops than you'll find anywhere else in Acapulco. The multilevel **Marbella Mall,** at the Diana Glorieta, has **Martí,** a well-stocked sporting goods store, and Bing's Ice Cream, as well as several restaurants. **Aca Mall,** which is on the other side of the Diana Glorieta, is all white and marble. Here you'll find Polo Ralph Lauren, Ferrioni, Aca Joe, and Martí.

Plaza Bahía, next to the Acapulco Plaza, is a huge, completely enclosed and air-conditioned mall where you could easily spend an entire day. Here you'll find Dockers, Benetton, Nautica, and Ferrioni, for chic casual wear for men and women; Ragazza, which carries an exquisite line of fine lingerie; Aspasia, which carries a line of locally designed glitzy evening dresses and chunky diamanté jewelry; Bally for shoes; restaurants and snack bars; and a video-games arcade.

Department Stores

Sanborns is the most un-Mexican of the big shops. It sells English-language newspapers, magazines, and books, as well as a line of high-priced souvenirs, but its Mexican glassware and ceramics cannot be found anywhere else in town. This is a useful place to come for post-cards, cosmetics, and medicines. Sanborns's restaurants are recommended for glorified coffee-shop food. The Estrella del Mar branch (Costera Miguel Alemán 1226, ☎ 74/84–44–13) and the downtown branch (Costera Miguel Alemán 209, ☎ 74/82–61–67) are both open from 7 AM to midnight during the high season, and from 7 AM to 11 PM during the low season.

Supermarkets have fared much better than boutiques. Branches of **Aurrerá, Gigante,** and **Price Club,** and Acapulco's original supermarket, fittingly called **Super Super,** all on the Costera, sell everything from light bulbs and newspapers to bottles of tequila and postcards. If you are missing anything at all, you should be able to pick it up at either of these stores or at the **Comercial Mexicana,** which has three branches: one near the Diana at Av. Farallón 216, another downtown at Costera Miguel Alemán 243, and a third at Av. Ruiz Cortines 13.

Woolworth's, at Escudero 250 in Old Acapulco, is much like the five-and-dime stores found all over the United States but with a Mexican feel.

SPORTS AND THE OUTDOORS

Participant Sports and Fitness

Acapulco has lots for sports lovers to enjoy. Most hotels have pools, and there are several tennis courts on the Costera. The weight-training craze has caught on, and gyms are opening. You'll find one at Plaza Condesa across from the Fiesta Americana Condesa Hotel.

Fishing

Sailfish, marlin, shark, and mahimahi are the usual catches. Head down to the docks near the zócalo and see just how many people offer to take you out for $30 to $40 a day. It is safer to stick with one of the reliable companies whose boats and equipment are in good condition.

Fishing trips can be arranged through your hotel, downtown at the Pesca Deportiva near the *muelle* (dock) across from the zócalo, or through travel agents. Boats accommodating 4 to 10 people cost $180–$500 a day, $45 to $60 by the chair. Excursions usually leave about 7 AM and return at 1 or 2 PM. You are required to get a license ($8) from the Secretaría de Pesca above the central post office downtown, but most fishing outfits take care of this. Don't show up during siesta, between 2 and 4 in the afternoon. For deep-sea fishing, **Divers de México** (*see* Scuba Diving, *below*) has well-maintained boats for 4 to 10 passengers for $200 to $400. They also offer private yacht charters. Small boats for freshwater fishing can be rented at **Cadena's** and **Tres Marías** at Coyuca lagoon.

Fitness and Swimming

Acapulco weather is like August in the warmest parts of the United States. This means that you should cut back on your workouts and maintain proper hydration by drinking plenty of water.

Acapulco Princess Hotel (Carretera Escénica, Km 17, ☎ 74/69–10–00) offers the best fitness facilities, with six pools (including one saltwater pool), 11 tennis courts, two basketball courts, and a gym with stationary bikes, Universal machines, and free weights. Because the Princess is about 15 kilometers (9 miles) from the city center, you can even swim in the ocean here, avoiding the pollution of Acapulco Bay. Beware: The waves are rough and the undertow is strong.

Villa Vera Spa and Fitness Center (Lomas del Mar 35, ☎ 74/84–03–33) has a modern spa and fitness center and is equipped with exercise machines (including step machines), free weights, and benches. Masseuses and cosmetologists give facials and massages inside or by the pool, as you wish. Both the beauty center and the gym are open to nonguests.

Westin Las Brisas (Carretera Escénica 5255, ☎ 74/84–15–80) is where you should stay if you like to swim but don't like company or competition. Individual casitas come with private, or semiprivate, pools; the beach club has two saltwater pools, a Home Fitness System, and workout machines.

Most of the major hotels in town along the Costera Miguel Alemán also have pools.

Golf

There are two 18-hole championship golf courses shared by the Princess and Pierre Marqués hotels. Reservations should be made in advance (☎ 74/84–31–00). Greens fees are $67 for guests and $89 for nonguests. There is also a public golf course at the Club de Golf (☎ 74/84–07–81) on the Costera across from the Acapulco Malibú hotel. Greens fees are $24 for nine holes, $35 for 18 holes.

Jogging

If you don't like beach jogging, the only real venue for running in the downtown area is along the sidewalk next to the Costera Miguel Alemán at the seafront, but you'll have to go very early, before traffic fumes set in. Away from the city center, the best area for running is out at the Acapulco Princess Hotel, on the airport road. A 2-kilometer (1-mile) loop is laid out along a lightly traveled road, and in the early morning you can also run along the asphalt trails on the golf course.

Scuba Diving

Divers de México (downtown near the Fiesta and Bonanza yachts, ☎ 74/82–13–98), owned by a helpful and efficient American woman, provides English-speaking captains and comfortable American-built yachts. A three- to four-hour scuba-diving excursion, including equipment, lessons in a pool for beginners, and drinks, costs about $52 per person. If you are a certified diver, the excursion is $45.

Arnold Brothers (Costera Miguel Alemán 205, ☎ 74/82–18–77) also runs daily scuba-diving excursions and snorkeling trips. The scuba trips cost $40 and last for 2 to 2½ hours.

Tennis

Court fees range from about $7 to $25 an hour during the day and are 15% more in the evening. At the hotel courts, nonguests pay about $5 more per hour. Lessons, with English-speaking instructors, are about $35 an hour; ball boys get a $2 tip.

Acapulco Plaza, three hard-surface courts, two lighted for evening play (☎ 74/69–00–00). **Acapulco Princess,** two indoor courts, nine outdoor (☎ 74/69–10–00). **Club de Tennis and Golf,** across from Hotel Malibu, Costera Miguel Alemán (☎ 74/84–07–81). **Hyatt Regency,** five lighted courts (☎ 74/69–12–34). **Pierre Marqués,** five courts (☎ 74/66–10–00). **Tiffany's Racquet Club,** Avenue Villa Vera 120, five courts (☎ 74/84–79–49). **Villa Vera Hotel,** three outdoor lighted clay courts (☎ 74/84–03–33).

Water Sports

Waterskiing, broncos (one-person motorboats), and parasailing can all be arranged on the beach. Parasailing is an Acapulco highlight and looks terrifying until you actually try it. Most people who do it love the view and go back again and again. An eight-minute trip costs $22. Waterskiing is about $44 an hour; broncos cost $29 an hour. Windsurfing can be arranged at Caleta and most of the beaches along the Costera but is especially good at Puerto Marqués. At Coyuca Lagoon, you can try your hand (or feet) at barefoot waterskiing. The main surfing beach is Revolcadero.

Spectator Sports

Bullfights

The season runs from Christmas to Easter, and *corridas* are held on Sunday at 5:30. Tickets are available through your hotel or at the Plaza de Toros ticket window (Av. Circunvalación, across from Caleta Beach, ☎ 74/82–11–81; ☉ Mon.–Sat. 10–2 and Sun. 10:30–5). Tickets cost from $23 to $30, and a $28 to $30 seat in the first four rows—in the shade (*sombra*)—is worth the extra cost. Preceding the fight are live folk music, Mexican snacks, beer, and soft drinks. At 5:30 the *corrida* will begin with three instead of the usual four bulls, followed by an *escarramuza charra* (an exhibition of riding skills performed by colorfully garbed women riders).

Beaches

The lure of sun and sand in Acapulco is legendary. Every sport is available, and you can eat in a beach restaurant, dance, and sleep in a *hamaca* (hammock) without leaving the water's edge. If you want to avoid the crowds, there are also plenty of quiet and even isolated beaches within reach. However, some of these, such as Revolcadero and Pie de la Cuesta, have very strong undertows and surfs, so swimming is not advised. Despite an enticing appearance and claims that officials are cleaning up the bay, it remains polluted. In addition, although vending on the beach has been officially outlawed, you'll still find yourself approached frequently by souvenir hawkers. If these things bother you, we suggest that you follow the lead of the Mexican cognoscenti and take the waters at your hotel pool.

Beaches in Mexico are public, even those that seem to belong to a big hotel. The list below moves from east to west.

Barra Vieja

About 27 kilometers (16 miles) east of Acapulco, between Laguna de Tres Palos and the Pacific, this magnificent beach is even more inviting than Pie de la Cuesta (*see below*) because you're not bothered by itinerant peddlers and beggars; the drive there is also more pleasant.

Revolcadero

A wide, sprawling beach next to the Pierre Marqués and Princess hotels, its water is shallow and its waves are fairly rough. People come here to surf and ride horses.

Puerto Marqués

Tucked below the airport highway, this strand is popular with Mexican tourists, so it tends to get crowded on weekends.

Icacos

Stretching from the naval base to El Presidente, this beach is less populated than others on the Castera. The morning waves are especially calm.

Condesa

Facing the middle of Acapulco Bay, this stretch of sand has more than its share of tourists, especially singles. The beachside restaurants are convenient for bites between parasailing flights.

Hornos and Hornitos

Running from the Paraíso Radisson to Las Hamacas hotel, these beaches are packed shoulder to shoulder with Mexican tourists. These tourists know a good thing: Graceful palms shade the sand, and there are scads of casual eateries within walking distance.

Caleta and Caletilla

On the peninsula in Old Acapulco, these two beaches once rivaled La Quebrada as the main tourist area in Acapulco's heyday. Now they attract families. Motorboats to Roqueta leave from here.

Roqueta Island

A ferry costs about $6.50 round-trip, including entrance to the zoo; the trip takes 10 minutes each way. Acapulqueños consider Roqueta Island their day-trip spot.

Pie de la Cuesta

You'll need a car or cab to reach this relatively unpopulated spot, about 15 minutes west of town. A few rustic restaurants border the wide beach, and straw palapas provide shade.

DINING

Dining in Acapulco is more than just eating out—it is the most popular leisure activity in town. Every night the restaurants fill up, and every night the adventurous diner can sample a different cuisine: Italian, German, Japanese, American, Tex-Mex, and, of course, plain old Mex. The variety of styles matches the range of cuisines: from greasy spoons that serve regional specialties to rooftop gourmet restaurants with gorgeous views of Acapulco Bay. Most restaurants fall somewhere in the middle, and on the Costera there are dozens of beachside restaurants, roofed with palapa (palm frond), as well as wildly decorated rib and hamburger joints popular with visitors under 30. Loud music blares from many Costera restaurants, and proprietors will aggressively try to hustle you inside with offers of drink specials. If you're looking for a hassle-free evening, it's best either to avoid this area or decide in advance precisely where you want to dine.

One plus for Acapulco dining is that the food is garden fresh. Each morning the Mercado Municipal is abuzz with restaurant managers and locals buying up the vegetables that will appear on plates that evening. Although some top-quality beef is now being produced in the states of Sonora and Chihuahua, many of the more expensive restaurants claim that they import their beef from the States. Whether or not they're telling the truth, the beef is excellent in most places. Establishments that cater to tourists purify their drinking water and use it to cook vegetables. In smaller restaurants, ask for bottled water with or without bubbles (*con* or *sin gas*).

The top restaurants in Acapulco can be fun for a splurge and provide very good value. Even at the best places in town, dinner rarely exceeds $60 per person, and the atmosphere and views are fantastic. Ties and jackets are out of place, but so are shorts or jeans. Unless stated otherwise, all restaurants are open daily from 6:30 or 7 PM until the last diner leaves. Several restaurants have two seatings: 6:30 for the *gringos* and 9 for the Mexican crowd, who wisely head directly for the discos after dinner to dance off the calories.

CATEGORY	COST*
$$$$	over $35
$$$	$25–$35
$$	$15–$25
$	under $15

per person, excluding drinks, service, and sales tax (10%)

American

$$$ **Embarcadero.** A nautical motif pervades Embarcadero, which is well loved by both Acapulco regulars and resident Americans. It is designed to look like a wharf with the bar as the loading office. Wooden bridges lead past a fountain to the thatched eating area, piled high with wooden packing crates and maps. The food is American with a Polynesian touch. You can have deep-fried shrimp with garlic sauce, tempura, chicken, or steak. The "salad barge" is enormous. ✕ *Costera Miguel Alemán, southeast of CiCi Park,* ☎ *74/84–87–87. No reservations. AE, DC, MC, V. Closed Mon. off-season.*

$$ **Carlos 'n' Charlie's.** This is without a doubt the most popular restau-
★ rant in town; a line forms well before the 6:30 PM opening. Part of the Anderson group (with restaurants in the United States and Spain as well as Mexico), Carlos 'n' Charlie's cultivates an atmosphere of controlled craziness. Prankster waiters, a jokester menu, and eclectic decor—everything from antique bullfight photos to a tool chest of painted gadgets hanging from the ceiling—add to the chaos. The crowd is mostly young and relaxed, which is what you need to be to put up with the rush-hour traffic noise that filters up to the covered balcony where people dine. The menu straddles the border, with ribs, stuffed shrimp, and oysters among the best offerings. ✕ *Costera Miguel Alemán 999,* ☎ *74/84–12–85 or 84–00–39. No reservations. AE, DC, MC, V.*

$$ **Hard Rock Cafe.** A bar, restaurant, and dance hall filled with rock
★ memorabilia, this link in the international Hard Rock chain is one of the most popular spots in Acapulco, and with good reason. The southern-style food—fried chicken, ribs, hamburgers—is very well-prepared and the portions are more than ample. The taped rock music begins at noon, and a live group starts playing at 11 PM (except Tuesday). There's always a line at the small boutique on the premises where you can buy sports clothes and accessories bearing the Hard Rock label. ✕ *Costera Miguel Alemán 37,* ☎ *74/84–66–80. No reservations. AE, MC, V.*

Continental

$$$$ Bella Vista. This alfresco restaurant in the exclusive Las Brisas area has fantastic sunset views of Acapulco. Its large menu offers a wide variety of dishes that range from Asian appetizers to Italian and seafood entrées. Try the delicious (and spicy!) Thai shrimp, sautéed in sesame oil, ginger, Thai chili, and hoisin sauce, or the red snapper Etouffée, cooked in chardonnay, tomato, herbs, basil and oyster sauce. ✗ *Carretera Escéncia 5255,* ☎ *74/84–15–80, ext. 500. Reservations required. AE, DC, MC, V.*

$$$$ Coyuca 22. This is possibly the most expensive restaurant in Aca-
★ pulco; it is certainly one of the most beautiful. Diners eat on terraces that overlook the bay from the west, on a hilltop in Old Acapulco. The understated decor consists of Doric pillars, sculptures, and large onyx flower stands near the entrance. Diners gaze down on an enormous illuminated obelisk and a small pool. The effect is that of eating in a partially restored Greek ruin sans dust. Diners can choose from two fixed menus or order à la carte. Seafood and prime ribs are house specialties. ✗ *Avenida Coyuca 22 (a 10-minute taxi ride from the zócalo),* ☎ *74/82–34–68 or 74/83–50–30. Reservations required. AE, DC, MC, V. Closed Apr. 30–Nov. 1.*

$$$ Madeiras. Vying with its neighbor, Miramar *(see below),* for most
★ chichi place in Acapulco, Madeiras is very difficult to get into, especially on weekends and during the Christmas and Easter holidays; many people make reservations by letter before they arrive. The bar-reception area features Art Nouveau–style chairs and startling coffee tables made of glass resting on wooden animals, the dishes and flatwear were created by silversmiths in nearby Taxco, and all the tables have a view of Acapulco glittering at night. Dinner is served from a four-course, prix fixe menu and costs about $32 without wine. Entrées include the delicious Spanish dish of red snapper in sea salt, tasty chilled soups, stuffed red snapper, and a choice of steaks and other seafood, as well as the *crepas de huitlacoche* (huitlacoche, or cuitlacoche, is a corn fungus that was a delicacy to the Aztecs). Desserts are competently prepared but have no special flair. There are seatings every 30 minutes from 7 to 10:30 PM. ✗ *Scenic Hwy. just past La Vista shopping center,* ☎ *74/84–69–21. Reservations required. No children under 8. AE, DC, MC, V.*

French

$$$$ El Olvido. One of Acapulco's newest establishments, it is also one of the most romantic, with a beachside setting and Mediterranean decor. French chef Daniel Janny blends the techniques of his native land with Mexican ingredients, which results in creations such as salmon roll with mango vinaigrette and quail in a honey, pineapple and *pasilla* chili sauce. ✗ *Plaza Marbella,* ☎ *74/81–02–14. Reservations advised. AE, DC, MC, V.*

$$$$ Le Gourmet. Although its food is somewhat inconsistent, this restaurant is thought by many to be one of Acapulco's premier establishments. Many people staying down on the Costera brave the 15-minute taxi ride to partake of a tranquil meal in a plush setting. The French menu has all the classics: vichyssoise, steak au poivre sautéed in cognac, and such Acapulco favorites as lobster and red snapper fillets. The atmosphere is luxurious and genteel, with roomy, comfortable chairs, silent waiters, and air-conditioning. ✗ *Acapulco Princess Hotel,* ☎ *74/69–10–00. Reservations advised. AE, DC, MC, V.* ☉ *Dec. 15–Apr. 15.*

310

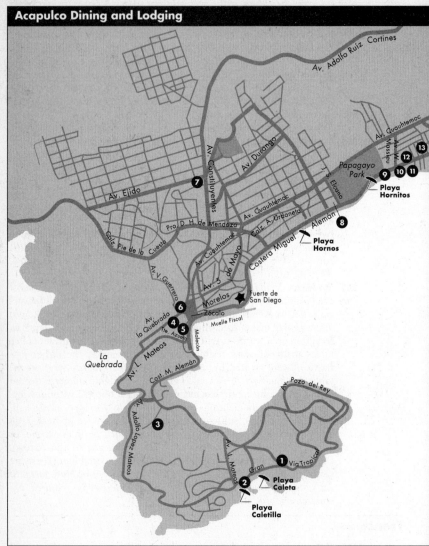

Dining

Acapulco Fat Farm, **5**
Bella Vista, **37**
Beto's, **19**
Blackbeard's, **18**
Carlos 'n' Charlie's, **21**
Casa Nova, **38**
Coyuca 22, **3**
El Cabrito, **27**
El Olvido, **28**
Embarcadero, **29**
Hard Rock Cafe, **26**

Le Gourmet, **41**
Los Rancheros, **33**
Madeiras, **36**
Miramar, **34**
100% Natural, **13**
Paradise, **17**
Sirocco, **8**
Suntory, **30**
Tlaquepaque, **7**
Villa Fiore, **24**
Zapata, Villa y Cia., **32**
Zorrito's, **11**

Lodging

Acapulco Plaza, **15**
Acapulco Princess, **39**
Autotel Ritz, **12**
Boca Chica, **2**
Camino Real Acapulco Diamante, **42**
Copacabana, **31**
Fiesta Americana Condesa Acapulco, **22**
Gran Motel Acapulco, **16**

Hotel Acapulco Tortuga, **20**
Hotel Misión, **4**
Hyatt Regency Acapulco, **32**
Las Brisas, **37**
Maralisa Hotel and Beach Club, **14**
Pierre Marqués, **40**
Plaza las Glorias El Mirador, **6**
Plaza las Glorias Paraíso, **9**
Ritz, **10**

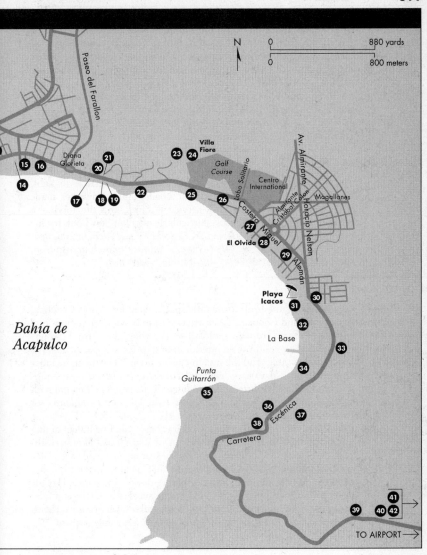

Bahía de
Acapulco

TO AIRPORT →

$$$ **Miramar.** Light-wood furniture and a fountain provide the decoration
★   for this understated place, but the real glamour comes from the view of
     the bay and the flickering lights of Acapulco. Traditional dishes, such as
     pâté and lobster thermidor, are served alongside classics with a new
     twist: ceviche with a hint of coconut and red snapper papillote. Smoked
     salmon, smoked oyster mousse, and duck are all specialties. Miramar is
     not as intimate as its neighbor, Madeiras, and many large groups from
     the Princess book long tables, so the noise level is rather high. ✕ *Scenic
     Hwy. at La Vista shopping center,* ☎ *74/84–78–74. Reservations
     advised. AE, MC, V. Closed Sept.–Oct.*

Health Food

$ **100% Natural.** Six family-operated restaurants specialize in light,
★   healthful food—yogurt shakes, fruit salads, and sandwiches made
     with whole-wheat bread. The service is quick and the food is a
     refreshing alternative to tacos, particularly on a hot day. Look for the
     green signs with white lettering. ✕ *Costera Miguel Alemán 200, near
     the Acapulco Plaza,* ☎ *74/85–39–82. Another branch across from
     Casa de la Cultura,* ☎ *74/81–08–44. No credit cards.*

Italian

$$$$ **Casa Nova.** Another ultraromantic spot created by Arturo Cordova,
★   the man behind Coyuca 22 (*see above*), Casa Nova is carved out of a
     cliff that rises up from Acapulco Bay. The views, both from the ter-
     race and the air-conditioned interior dining room, are spectacular, the
     service impeccable, and the Italian cuisine divine. The menu includes
     antipasto, fresh pastas, a delightful *cotolette de vittello* (veal chops
     with mushrooms), lobster tail, and *linguini alle vongole* (linguini with
     clams, tomato, and garlic). ✕ *Scenic Hwy., just past Madeiras,* ☎
     74/84–68–19. Reservations required. AE, DC, MC, V.

$$$ **Villa Fiore.** Here, the owners of Madeiras bring you fine Italian dining
     under the stars in the candlelit garden of what looks like an 18th-
     century Venetian villa (there's also indoor seating in case of rain). Din-
     ers can choose from two fixed menus that include appetizer, soup,
     main course (chicken, fish, meat, or pasta), dessert and coffee. Opt for
     the *calamari fritti* (fried squid in marinara sauce) as a starter, and fillet
     of stuffed sea bass with crab or ravioli for entrées. Service is excellent.
     ✕ *Avenida del Prado 6,* ☎ *74/84–20–40. Reservations advised. AE,
     DC, MC, V. Closed Wed.*

Japanese

$$$$ **Suntory.** At this traditional Japanese restaurant you can dine either in
     a blessedly air-conditioned interior room or in the delightful Oriental-
     style garden. It's one of the few Japanese restaurants in Acapulco and
     also one of the only deluxe restaurants that is open for lunch. Spe-
     cialties are the sushi and the teppan-yaki, prepared at your table by
     skilled chefs. ✕ *Costera Miguel Alemán 36, across from the La
     Palapa hotel,* ☎ *74/84–80–88. Reservations advised for dinner. AE,
     DC, MC, V.*

Mexican

$$$ **Zapata, Villa y Cia.** This is a Mexican version of the Hard Rock Café,
     where the music and food (excellent) are strictly Mexican and the
     memorabilia is Mexican Revolution, with guns, hats, and pho-
     tographs of Pancho Villa. The definite highlight of an evening here is
     a visit from a sombrero-wearing baby burro, so be sure to bring your

camera. ✗ *Hyatt Regency, Costera Miguel Alemán 1,* ☎ *74/84–28–88. Reservations advised. AE, DC, MC, V.*

$$ Los Rancheros. With a view of the water in the posh East Bay, here's dining at about half what you'd pay at Madeiras or Miramar. The decor is colorful, folksy Mexican with paper streamers, checked tablecloths, and lopsided mannequins in local dress. Specials include *carne tampiqueña* (fillet of beef broiled with lemon juice), chicken enchiladas, and *queso fundido* (melted cheese served as a side dish with chips). There is live music daily, noon to midnight. ✗ *Scenic Hwy. just before Extasis disco (on left as you head toward airport),* ☎ *74/84–19–08. AE, MC, V. Closed Tues.*

$$ Tlaquepaque. As hard to find as it is to pronounce, this is one of the
★ best restaurants in Acapulco. It's well worth the 15-minute cab ride into the northwestern residential section of Acapulco (tell your driver it is around the corner from where the Oficina de Tránsito used to be). Owner-chef José Arreola was a chef at the Pierre Marqués for 15 years and he takes his job very seriously. Don't insult him by asking if the water is purified or if the vegetables are safe. The menu is 100% Mexican, excellent and authentic. If your party numbers four or more, Señor Arreola likes nothing better than to select a family-style meal, which can include quail liver tostadas, deep-fried tortillas, and chiles rellenos. The alfresco dining area sits on a stone terrace bordered by pink flowering bushes and an abandoned well. The outside tables have a perfect view of the kitchen filled with locally made pots. Thursday is *pozole* day, when a thick soup of hominy and pork is served. ✗ *Calle Uno, Lote 7, Colonia Vista Alegre,* ☎ *74/85–70–55. Reservations advised Thurs. (pozole day). No credit cards. Closed Mon.*

$$ Zorrito's. The old Zorrito's, a rather dingy but popular café, is no
★ longer, but a new, very clean restaurant of the same name is now attracting tourists. The menu features a host of steak and beef dishes, and the special, *filete tampiqueña,* comes with tacos, enchiladas, guacamole, and frijoles. ✗ *Costera Miguel Alemán and Anton de Alaminos, next to Banamex,* ☎ *74/85–37–35. No reservations. AE, MC, V.* ☉ *2 PM–6 AM. Closed Tues.*

$ El Cabrito. This is a local favorite for true Mexican cuisine and ambience. The name of the restaurant—"The Goat"—is also its specialty. In addition, you can choose among mole; jerky with egg, fish, and seafood; and other Mexican dishes. ✗ *Costera Miguel Alemán, between Nina's and Hard Rock,* ☎ *74/84–77–11. No reservations. MC, V.*

Mexican/American

$ Acapulco Fat Farm. A cozy place in the center of town, this casual restaurant offers specialties including ice cream made with all natural ingredients, U.S.-style cakes and pies, sandwiches, hamburgers, seafood, and good Mexican food as well. The background music is classical, which is unusual for Acapulco, and there's an exhibition of paintings as well as a book exchange. ✗ *Juárez 10,* ☎ *74/83–53–39. No reservations. No credit cards.*

Seafood

$$$$ Blackbeard's. Dark, with a pirate-ship motif, Blackbeard's has maps covering the tables in the cozy booths, and the walls are adorned with wooden figureheads. Every movie star, from Bing Crosby to Liz Taylor, who ever set foot here has his or her photo posted in the lounge. Jumbo portions of shrimp, steak, and lobster keep customers satisfied. A disco on the premises starts throbbing at 10:30 PM. ✗ *Costera*

Miguel Alemán, on Condesa Beach near the Fiesta Americana Condesa, ☏ *74/84–25–49. Reservations advised. AE, MC, V.*

$$$ **Paradise.** This is the leading beach-party restaurant. T-shirted waiters drop leis over your head as you arrive, hand roses to the ladies, teach dance steps, and sing tropical songs. The menu (primarily seafood) has the same number of dishes as drinks, a pretty good indicator of what this place is like. Paradise has one of the biggest dance floors in Acapulco and live music day and night. Chaos reigns at lunchtime (from 2 to 5), and the mood picks up again from 8:30 to 10:30. Expect a young crowd. ✗ *Costera Miguel Alemán 107, next to Mimi's Chili Saloon,* ☏ *74/84–59–88. No reservations. AE, DC, MC, V.*

$$ **Beto's.** By day you can eat right on the beach and enjoy live music; by
★ night this palapa-roofed restaurant is transformed into a dim and romantic dining area lighted by candles and paper lanterns. Whole red snapper, lobster, and ceviche are recommended. There is a second branch next door and a third—where the specialty is *pescado a la talla* (fish spread with chili and other spices and then grilled over hot coals)—at Barra Vieja Beach. Beto's Safari turns into a disco on Fridays and Saturdays after 10. ✗ *Beto's, Costera Miguel Alemán at Condesa Beach,* ☏ *74/84–04–73. Beto's Safari, Costera Miguel Alemán, next to Beto's,* ☏ *74/84–47–62. Beto's Barra Vieja, Barra Vieja Beach, no* ☏. *AE, MC, V.*

Spanish

$$ **Sirocco.** This beachside eatery is numero uno for those who crave Spanish food in Acapulco. The tiled floors and heavy wooden furniture give it a Mediterranean feel. Specialties include *pulpo en su tinta* (octopus in its own ink) and other types of seafood. Order paella (there are 10 varieties) when you arrive at the beach—it takes a half hour to prepare. ✗ *Costera Miguel Alemán, across from Aurrerá,* ☏ *74/85–23–86 or 74/85–94–90. Reservations not required. AE, MC, V.* ☉ *1:30–11 PM.*

LODGING

Accommodations in Acapulco run the gamut from sprawling, big-name complexes with nonstop amenities to small, family-run inns where hot water is a luxury. Wherever you stay, however, prices will be reasonable compared with those in the United States, and service is generally good, since Acapulqueños have been catering to tourists for more than 40 years. Accommodations above $90 (double) are air-conditioned (but you can find air-conditioned hotels for less) and include a minibar, TV, and a view of the bay. There is usually a range of in-house restaurants and bars, as well as a pool. Exceptions exist, such as Las Brisas, which, in the name of peace and quiet, has banned TVs from all rooms. So if such extras are important to you, be sure to ask ahead. If you can't afford air-conditioning, don't panic. Even the cheapest hotels have cooling ceiling fans.

Although Acapulco has been an important port since colonial times, it lacks the converted monasteries and old mansions found in Mexico City. But the Costera is chockablock with new luxury high rises and local franchises of such major U.S. hotel chains as Hyatt and Howard Johnson. Since these hotels tend to be characterless, your choice will depend on location and what facilities are available. All major hotels can make water-sports arrangements.

In Acapulco geography is price, so where you stay determines what you pay. The most exclusive area is the Acapulco Diamante, home to some of the most expensive hotels in Mexico—so lush and well equipped that most guests don't budge from the minute they arrive. The minuses: Revolcadero Beach is too rough for swimming (though great for surfing), and the East Bay is a 15-minute (expensive) taxi ride from the heart of Acapulco. There is also very little to do in this area except play golf at the Acapulco Princess, dine at three of Acapulco's better restaurants (Madeiras, Casa Nova, and Miramar), and dance at the glamorous Extravaganzza, Palladium, and Fantasy discos.

Americans tend to stay on Costera Miguel Alemán, where the majority of large hotels, discos, American-style restaurants, and airline offices may be found, along with Acapulco's most popular beaches. All the Costera hotels have freshwater pools and sundecks, and most have restaurants and/or bars overlooking the beach, if not on the sand itself. Hotels across the street are almost always less expensive than those directly on the beach; because there are no private beaches in Acapulco, all you have to do is cross the road to enjoy the sand.

Moving west along the Costera leads you to downtown Acapulco, where the fishing and tour boats depart and the locals go about their business. The central post office, Woolworth's, and the Mercado Municipal are here, along with countless restaurants where a complete meal can cost as little as $5. The beaches here are popular with Mexican vacationers, and the dozens of little hotels attract Canadian and European bargain hunters.

Note: Most hotels are booked solid Christmas and Easter week, so if you plan to visit then, it's wise to make reservations months in advance.

CATEGORY	COST*
$$$$	over $160
$$$	$90–$160
$$	$40–$90
$	under $40

*All prices are for a standard double room, excluding 10% sales (called IVA) tax.

Acapulco Diamante

$$$$ **Acapulco Princess.** This is the first hotel you'll see as you leave the air-
★ port. A pyramid-shaped building flanked by two towers, the Princess has the largest capacity of any hotel in Acapulco. The hotel's fact sheet makes fascinating reading: 50 chocolate cakes are consumed daily and 2,500 staff meals are served. The Princess is one of those megahotels that are always holding at least three conventions, with an ever-present horde in the lobby checking in and greeting their fellow dentists or club members. But more rooms equals more facilities. The Princess has seven restaurants, seven bars (several of which close during the low season—April through October), a disco, tennis, golf, and great shopping in a cool arcade. The pool near the reception desk is sensational—fantastic tropical ponds with little waterfalls and a slatted bridge leading into a swimming-sunning area. Rooms are light and airy, with cane furniture and rugs and curtains in colorful tropical prints. Guests can also use the facilities of the hotel's smaller sibling, the Pierre Marqués; a free shuttle bus provides transport. Accommodations include breakfast and dinner (in high season). ⊠ *Box 1351 Playa Revolcadero, 39300,* ☎ *74/69–10–00 or 800/223–1818,* FAX *74/69–10–16. 1,019 balconied rooms with bath. 7 restau-*

rants, 7 bars, banquet rooms, 6 pools, 2 18-hole golf courses, 11 ten-nis courts, dance club. AE, DC, MC, V.

$$$$ **Las Brisas.** Set high on a hillside and across the bay from most of the
★ other main hotels, Westin's Las Brisas hotel remains distinct in Aca-pulco for the secluded haven it provides its guests. This self-contained luxury complex covers 110 acres and has accommodations that range from one-bedroom units to deluxe private casitas, complete with pri-vate pools that are small yet swimmable. All have beautiful bay views. Most of the facilities are open only to guests, though outsiders with a reservation may dine at the El Mexicano restaurant. Everything at Las Brisas is splashed with pink, from the staff uniforms to the stripe up the middle of the road. Attention to detail is Las Brisas's claim to fame: Minibars are stocked with cigarettes, liquor, and snacks, and fresh hibiscus blossoms are set afloat in the pools each day. Hotel registra-tion takes place in a comfortable lounge to avoid lines, and guests are served tropical mixed drinks to sip. There are almost three employees per guest during the winter season. Transportation is by white-and-pink Jeep. You can rent one for $75 a day, including tax, gas, and insurance; or, if you don't mind a wait, the staff will do the driving. And transport is necessary—it is a good 15-minute walk to the beach restaurant, and all the facilities are far from the rooms. There is an art gallery and a few other stores. On Thursday there is a Jeep ranch safari, and Friday night is Cantina Night. Tipping is not allowed, but a service charge of $20 a day is added to the bill. The rate includes Continental breakfast and temporary membership in the La Concha Beach Club. ☎ *Carretera Escénica 5255, 39868,* ☎ *74/84–15–80 or 800/228–3000,* 𝔽𝔸𝕏 *74/84–22–69. 300 rooms with bath. 4 restaurants, 2 bars, 3 pools (2 saltwater), hot tub, sauna, 5 tennis courts, exercise room, beach, 2 meeting rooms. AE, DC, MC, V.*

$$$$ **Pierre Marqués.** This hotel is doubly blessed: It is closer to the beach
★ than any of the other East Bay hotels, and guests have access to all the Princess's facilities without the crowds. In addition, it has three pools and five tennis courts illuminated for nighttime play. Rooms are fur-nished identically to those at the Princess (but no TVs here) but villas and duplex bungalows with private patios are available. Many people stay here to relax, then hit the Princess's restaurants and discos at night—the shuttle bus runs about every 10 minutes 24 hours a day. Accommodations include mandatory breakfast (breakfast and dinner during Christmas week). ☎ *Box 1351, Playa Revolcadero, 39907,* ☎ *74/66–10–00 or 800/223–1818,* 𝔽𝔸𝕏 *74/66–10–46. 344 rooms with bath. 2 restaurants, bar, 3 pools, 2 18-hole golf courses, 5 tennis courts.* ☾ *Winter season only. AE, DC, MC, V.*

$$$ **Camino Real Acapulco Diamante.** Opened in May 1993, Acapulco's newest hotel is set at the foot of a lush tropical hillside on exclusive Pichilingue beach, far from the madding crowd. All rooms are done in luscious pastels, with tiled floors, balcony or terrace, luxurious baths, ceiling fans, and air-conditioning. Each has a view of peaceful Puerto Marqués bay. Rates include a buffet breakfast. ☎ *Playa Pichilingue, 39867,* ☎ *74/66–10–10 or 800/7–CAMINO,* 𝔽𝔸𝕏 *74/66–11–11. 156 rooms. 2 restaurants, 2 bars, 2 pools, tennis courts, exer-cise room. AE, DC, MC, V.*

$$$ **Sheraton Acapulco.** Perfect for those who want to enjoy the sun and the sand but don't have to be in the center of everything, this Shera-ton is isolated from all the hubbub of the Costera and is rather small in comparison with the chain's other properties in Mexico. The spa-cious, attractively decorated rooms and suites—all with private bal-conies, and many with sweeping views of the entire bay—are distributed among 13 villas that are set on a hillside on secluded Guitarrón Beach 10 kilometers (6 miles) east of Acapulco proper. In order to reach your room, however, it's necessary to wait for a staff-operated funicular—a slow, sometimes frustrating procedure. The hotel's romantic fine-dining room, La Bahia, serves excellent Continental cuisine. ☎ *Costera Guitarrón 110, 39359, ☎ 74/81–22–22 or 800/325–3535, FAX 74/84–37–60. 185 rooms with bath, 15 suites. 3 restaurants, 3 bars, 2 pools. AE, DC, MC, V.*

The Costera

$$$$ Hyatt Regency Acapulco. Another megahotel that you never have to leave, this property is popular with business travelers and convention-eers. (Ex-President López Portillo used to stay in—what else?—the Presidential Suite.) All the rooms are decorated in soft pastels and were refurbished in 1994. Five tennis courts, five restaurants (including a beachside seafood place and a Mexican dining room), five bars, and a lavish shopping area provide the action. The Hyatt is a little out of the way, a plus for those who seek quiet. Rooms on the west side of the hotel are preferable for those who want to avoid the noise of the maneuvers at the neighboring naval base. ☎ *Costera Miguel Alemán 1, 39869, ☎ 74/69–12–34 or 800/223–1234, FAX 74/84–30–87. 690 rooms with bath. 4 restaurants, 5 bars, pool, massage, sauna, 5 tennis courts, 6 meeting rooms, parking. AE, DC, MC, V.*

$$$$ Royal El Cano. One of Acapulco's traditional favorites has been com-
★ pletely remodeled, while still (thankfully) maintaining its '50s flavor. The interior decorators get an A+: The rooms are snappily done in white and navy blue, with white tiled floors and beautiful modern bathrooms. The only exception is the lobby, which is excruciatingly blue. There's a delightful outdoor restaurant, a more elegant indoor one, and a pool that seems to float above the bay with whirlpools built into the corners. ☎ *Costera Miguel Alemán 75, 39690, ☎ 74/84–19–50, FAX 74/84–86–37. 180 rooms with bath. 2 restaurants, bar, pool. AE, DC, MC, V.*

$$$ Acapulco Plaza. This Fiesta Americana resort is the largest and one of the newest hotels on the Costera. Like the Princess, the Plaza has more facilities than many Mexican towns: seven bars and five restaurants, four tennis courts, steam baths, and two pools. The Plaza Bahía next to the hotel is the largest shopping mall in town. The lobby bar is most extraordinary—a wooden hut, suspended by a cable from the roof, reached by a gangplank from the second floor of the lobby and over-looking a garden full of flamingos and other exotic birds. Guest rooms tell the same old story: pastels and blond wood replacing passé dark greens and browns. People rave about the accommodations and facili-ties, especially the time-share rooms, and there has been some improve-ment in service under the new management. ☎ *Costera Miguel Alemán 123, 39670, ☎ 74/69–00–00 or 800/FIESTA-1, FAX 74/85–97–00. 1,008 rooms with bath. 5 restaurants, 7 bars, pools, sauna, 4 tennis courts, health club, meeting rooms. AE, DC, MC, V.*

$$$ Copacabana. Here's a good buy if you yearn for a modern hotel in the center of things. The staff is efficient and helpful, the ambience relaxed and festive. The lobby and pool (with a swim-up bar) are always crowded with people enjoying themselves. The psychedelic pseudo-Mexican lemon-and-lime hues pervade the halls and bed-rooms. ☎ *Tabachines 2, 39670, ☎ 74/84–32–60 or 800/221–6509, FAX 74/84–62–68. 422 rooms, showers only. 2 restaurants, 2 bars, pool, meeting rooms. AE, DC, MC, V.*

$$$ Fiesta Americana Condesa Acapulco. Right in the thick of the main shopping-restaurant district, the Condesa, as everyone calls it, is ever popular with tour operators. In recent years, we have had several complaints about the shabbiness of the accommodations, but all the rooms, as well as the lobby, were totally redone in 1994 in very lively and attractive modern Mexican decor. ☎ *Costera Miguel Alemán 97, 39670,* ☎ *74/84–28–28 or 800/FIESTA–1,* FAX *74/85–97–00. 500 rooms with bath. 2 restaurants, bar, 2 pools, meeting rooms. AE, DC, MC, V.*

$$$ Plaza Las Glorias Paraíso. The last of the big Costera hotels is a
★ favorite of tour groups, so the lobby is forever busy. The rooms look brighter and roomier since the management replaced the heavy Spanish-style furniture with light woods and pastels. Guests lounge by the pool or at the beachside restaurant by day. The rooftop La Fragata restaurant provides a sensational view of the bay at night. The pool area is rather small and the beach can get crowded, but the restaurants are exceptionally good and the staff couldn't be nicer. Book early for high season, which is prime time for the tour groups. ☎ *Costera Miguel Alemán 163, 39670,* ☎ *74/85–55–96 or 800/342–AMIGO,* FAX *74/82–45–64. 422 rooms with bath. 2 restaurants, bar, coffee shop, pool, sauna, 5 meeting rooms. AE, DC, MC, V.*

$$$ Villa Vera. A five-minute drive north of the Costera leads to one of
★ Acapulco's most exclusive hotels. Guests are primarily affluent American business travelers, actors, and politicians. This luxury estate, officially the Villa Vera Hotel and Racquet Club, is unequaled in the variety of its accommodations. Some of the villas, which were once private homes, have their own pools. Standard rooms, in fashionable pastels and white, are not especially large. No matter. No one spends much time in the rooms. The main pool, with its swim-up bar, is the hotel's hub. By night guests dine at the terraced restaurant, with its stunning view of the bay. There's an exercise facility, and three championship tennis courts host the annual competition for the Miguel Alemán and Teddy Stauffer cups. For guests who don't have their own cars, transportation is provided by hotel Jeep. Book well in advance; guests have been known to make reservations for the following year as they leave. ☎ *Box 560, Lomas del Mar 35, 39690,* ☎ *74/84–03–33 or 800/323–5655,* FAX *74/84–74–79. 80 rooms with bath. Restaurant, pools, beauty salon, massage, sauna, 3 tennis courts. AE, DC, MC, V.*

$$ Autotel Ritz. A good buy for its fairly central location, this hotel attracts bargain hunters and senior citizens. The uncarpeted rooms are simply decorated, but the furniture is chipped and smudged with paint. Facilities include a restaurant, a decent-size pool with a bar, and room service until 9 PM. Rooms not on the Costera are reasonably quiet. ☎ *Ave. Wilfrido Massieu, Box 886, 39670,* ☎ *74/85–80–23 or 800/448–8355,* FAX *74/85–56–47. 100 rooms with bath. Restaurant, bar, pool. AE, DC, MC, V.*

$$ Gran Motel Acapulco. This is a find for its reasonable price and central location. Bare walls and floors and blond-wood furniture give the recently redecorated rooms a monastic appeal. The small pool has a bar, and a snack bar is open during the high season. Ask to stay in the old section, where the rooms are larger and quieter and have a partial beach view. ☎ *Costera Miguel Alemán 127, 39670,* ☎ *74/85–59–92,* FAX *74/84–73–85. 88 rooms with bath. Bar, pool, 3 tennis courts, parking. MC, V.*

$$ Hotel Acapulco Tortuga. A helpful staff and prime location make the "Turtle Hotel" an appealing choice. It is also one of the few nonbeach hotels to have a garden (handkerchief-size), a beach club (in Puerto

Marqués), and a pool where most of the guests hang out. At night the activity shifts to the lobby bar, with the crowd often spilling out onto the street. The downside of this merriment is the noise factor. The best bet is a room facing west on an upper floor. All rooms have blue-green pile rugs and small tables. Breakfast is served in the lobby café; lunch and dinner can be taken in the more formal restaurant. ☎ *Costera Miguel Alemán 132, 39300,* ☎ *74/84–88–89 or 800/832–7491,* FAX *74/84–73–85. 252 rooms with bath. 2 restaurants, coffee shop, lobby lounge, pool, meeting rooms. AE, DC, MC, V.*

$$ **Maralisa Hotel and Beach Club.** Formerly the Villa Vera's sister hotel,
★ this hotel, located on the beach side of the Costera, is now a part of the Howard Johnson chain. The sundeck surrounding two small pools—palm trees and ceramic tiles—is unusual and picturesque. The rooms are light, decorated in whites and pastels. This is a small, friendly place; all rooms have TVs and balconies, and the price is right. ☎ *Box 721, Calle Alemania, 39670,* ☎ *74/85–66–77 or 800/ IGO–HOJO,* FAX *74/85–82–28. 90 rooms with bath. Restaurant, bar, 2 pools, beach. AE, DC, MC, V.*

$$ **Ritz.** From its brightly painted exterior, it's clear that the Ritz is serious
★ about vacations. The lobby is also seriously colorful. Parties are a hotel specialty; outdoor fiestas are held weekly, and Friday is Italian night in the Los Carrizos restaurant. The pink-and-rattan rooms add to the 1950s beach-party flavor. Accommodations include mandatory breakfast, tips, and tax. ☎ *Box 259, Costera Miguel Alemán and Magallanes, 39580,* ☎ *74/85–75–44 or 800/448–8355,* FAX *74/85–70–76. 252 rooms with bath. 3 restaurants, 3 bars, pools, sauna, beach, meeting rooms. AE, DC, MC, V.*

Old Acapulco

$$ **Boca Chica.** This small hotel is in a secluded area on a small peninsula,
★ and its terraced rooms overlook the bay and Roqueta Island. It's a low-key place that's a favorite of Mexico City residents in the know. There's a private beach club with a natural saltwater pool for guests and a seafood, sushi, and oyster bar. Accommodations include mandatory breakfast and dinner in high season. ☎ *Caletilla Beach, 39390,* ☎ *74/83–67–41 or 800/34–MEXICO,* FAX *74/83–95–13. 40 rooms. 2 pools. AE, DC, MC, V.*

$$ **Plaza las Glorias El Mirador.** The old El Mirador has been taken over by the Plaza las Glorias chain, which is part of the Sidek conglomerate responsible for marina and golf developments all over Mexico. Very Mexican in style—white with red tiles—the Plaza las Glorias is set high on a hill with a spectacular view of Acapulco and of the cliff divers performing at La Quebrada. ☎ *Quebrada 74, 39300,* ☎ *74/ 83–11–55 or 800/342–AMIGO,* FAX *74/82–45–64. 143 rooms with bath. 2 restaurants, 3 pools. AE, DC, MC, V.*

$$ **Suites Alba.** Situated on a quiet hillside in "Acapulco Tradicional," the Alba is a resort-style hotel that offers bargain prices. All rooms and bungalows are air-conditioned and have a kitchenette, private bath, and terrace. There is no extra charge for up to two children under 12 sharing a room with relatives, which makes it especially popular with families. Caleta and Caletilla beaches are within walking distance, but the hotel provides free shuttle service to Caleta during the winter season. ☎ *Grand Via Tropical 35, 39390,* ☎ *74/83–00–73,* FAX *74/85– 70–76. 283 rooms. 3 restaurants, bar, grocery, 3 pools, tennis court, beach. MC, V.*

$ Hotel Misión. Two minutes from the zócalo, this attractive budget hotel is the only colonial hotel in Acapulco. The English-speaking family that runs the Misión lives in a traditional house built in the 19th century. A newer structure housing the guest rooms was added in the 1950s. It surrounds a greenery-rich courtyard with an outdoor dining area. The rooms are small and by no means fancy, with bare cement floors and painted brick walls. But every room has a shower, and there is even hot water. The Misión appears in several European guidebooks, so expect a Continental clientele. The best rooms are on the second and third floors; the top-floor room is large but hot in the daytime. ⛨ *Calle Felipe Valle 12, 39300,* ☎ *74/82–36–43. 27 rooms, showers only. No credit cards.*

THE ARTS AND NIGHTLIFE

Acapulco has always been famous for its nightlife, and justifiably so. For many visitors the discos and restaurants are just as important as the sun and the sand. The minute the sun slips over the horizon, the Costera comes alive with people milling around window-shopping, deciding where to dine, and generally biding their time till the disco hour. Obviously you aren't going to find great culture here; theater efforts are few and far between and there is no classical music. But disco-hopping is high art in Acapulco. And for those who care to watch, there are live shows and folk-dance performances. The tour companies listed in Exploring, *above,* can organize evening jaunts to most of the dance and music places listed below.

Entertainment

The **Acapulco International Center** (also known as the Convention Center) has a Mexican fiesta Monday, Wednesday, and Friday from November 15 to April 15, and Wednesday and Friday the rest of the year; it features mariachi bands, singers, and the "Flying Indians" from Papantla. The show with dinner and drinks costs about $38; entrance to the show alone is $15. Performance with open bar is $20. The buffet dinner starts at 7:30, the performance at 8:15. On Friday, Cantina Night at El Mexicano restaurant in **Las Brisas** hotel, the fiesta starts off with a *tianguis* (marketplace) of handicrafts and ends with a spectacular display of fireworks.

The famous **cliff divers** at La Quebrada (*see* Exploring, *above*) give one performance in the afternoon and four performances every night. For about $27 **Divers de México** organizes sunset champagne cruises that provide a fantastic view of the spectacle from the water. For reservations, call (☎ 74/82–13–98) or stop by the office downtown near the *Fiesta* and *Bonanza* yachts. The *Fiesta* (☎ 74/83–18–03) runs cruises at 7:30 PM on Tuesday, Thursday, and Saturday for about $41, as well as a Moonlight Romantic Cruise with open bar, live and disco music, and a "Latino Tropical" show on Friday, Saturday, and Sunday from 10:30 PM to 1 AM for $18. Or you can take the *Bonanza*'s (☎ 74/83–18–03) sunset cruise with open bar (domestic drinks) for about $20. All boats leave from downtown near the zócalo. Many hotels and shops sell tickets, as do the ticket sellers on the waterfront. At the Colonial, on the Costera across from the San Diego Fort, there's a professional **water-ski show** Tuesday through Sunday at 8 PM (☎ 74/83–91–07).

Don't forget the nightly entertainment at most hotels. The big resorts have live music to accompany the early evening happy hour, and some feature big-name bands from the United States for less than you would pay at home. Many hotels sponsor theme parties—Italian Night, Beach Party Night, and similar festivities.

Dance

Nina's (on the Costera near CiCi, ☎ 74/84–24–00) is a combination dance hall and disco where the band plays salsa and other Latin rhythms. There's a live show—mostly impersonations of famous entertainers—at 12:45.

Discos

The legendary Acapulco discos are open 365 days a year from about 10:30 PM until they empty out, often not until 4 or 5 AM. Reservations are advisable for a big group, and late afternoon or after 9 PM are the best times to call. New Year's Eve requires advance planning.

Except for Pyramid Club, Palladium, Fantasy, and Extravaganzza, all the discos are on the Costera and, except for Le Dome, are in three different clusters. They are listed here roughly from east to west:

Pyramid Club, a combination disco and video bar designed to look like a 21st-century Aztec pyramid and equipped with the last word in sound systems, has replaced Tiffany, the posh disco at the Princess Hotel. *Princess Hotel, ☎ 74/69–10–00.*

Palladium, inaugurated at the end of 1993, proves that Acapulco remains the disco capital of the world. Extravaganzza creator Tony Rullán has produced another spectacle: a waterfall that cascades down the hill from the dance-floor level and makes this place hard to miss. As at Extravaganzza, the dance floor is nearly surrounded by a huge window, giving dancers a spectacular view of all Acapulco. *On the Scenic Highway to Las Brisas, ☎ 74/81–03–30.*

Extravaganzza. Vying with Palladium for first place as Acapulco's most splendiforous disco, Extravaganzza has the ultimate in light and sound. It accommodates 700 at a central bar and in comfortable booths, and a glass wall provides an unbelievably breathtaking view of Acapulco Bay. No food is served, but Los Rancheros is just a few steps away. The music (which is for all ages) starts at 10:30. *On the Scenic Hwy. to Las Brisas, ☎ 74/84–71–64.*

Fantasy is one of the most exclusive of all the discos in Acapulco. If there are any celebrities in town, they'll be here, rubbing elbows with or bumping into local fashion designers and artists—since Fantasy is quite snug, to put it nicely. This is one of the only discos where people really dress up, the men in well-cut pants and shirts and the women in racy outfits and cocktail dresses. The crowd is 25–50 and mainly in couples. Singles gravitate toward the two bars in the back. A line sometimes forms, so people come here earlier than they do to other places. By midnight the dance floor is so packed that people dance on the wide windowsills that look out over the bay. At 2 AM there is a fireworks display. A glassed-in elevator provides an interesting overview of the scene and leads upstairs to a little shop that stocks T-shirts and lingerie. *On the Scenic Hwy., next to Las Brisas, ☎ 74/84–67–27.*

D'Paradise is all black inside and has a fabulous light show each night after midnight. This is a good-size place with tables on tiers looking down at the floor, and it is one of the few discos where on weekdays you can find a fair number of Mexicans. Any day of the week, this is a good bet to catch up on the Top 10 from Mexico City, as well as the American dance hits. The atmosphere is friendly and laid-back. *Across the Costera from Baby O,* ☎ *74/84–88–15.*

Baby O is an old favorite. Even midweek it is packed to the gills. Eschewing the glitz and mirrors of most discos in Acapulco, Baby O resembles a cave in a tropical jungle. The crowd is 18–30 and mostly tourists, although many Mexicans come here, too. In fact, this is one of Acapulco's legendary pickup spots, so feel free to ask someone to dance. When the pandemonium gets to you, retreat to the little hamburger restaurant. *Costera Miguel Alemán 22,* ☎ *74/84–74–74.*

Hard Rock Cafe, filled with rock memorabilia, is part bar, part restaurant, part dance hall, and part boutique (*see* Dining, *above*).

Discobeach is Acapulco's only alfresco disco and its most informal one. The under-30 crowd sometimes even turns up in shorts. The waiters are young and friendly—some people find them overly so. One night they're all in togas carrying bunches of grapes, the next they're in pajamas. Every Wednesday, ladies' night, all the women receive flowers. "Sex on the Beach" (rum, vodka, Cointreau, fruit juice, and grenadine)—don't say you weren't warned—is the house specialty, in all senses of the word. This is a very popular place. *On Condesa Beach,* ☎ *74/84–70–64.*

News is enormous, with seating for 1,200 people in love seats and booths. There are different theme parties and competitions nightly—bikini contests on Tuesday and Carnival Night (with lambada and limbo contests and a Brazilian-style show) on Thursday. Winners walk off with a bottle of champagne or dinner for two; occasionally the prize has been a trip to Hawaii. From 10:30 (opening time) to 11:30, the music is slow and romantic; then the disco music and the light show begin, and they go on till dawn. *Costera Miguel Alemán, across from the Hyatt Regency,* ☎ *74/84–59–02.*

EXCURSIONS

Taxco, the Silver City

It's a picture-postcard look—Mexico in its Sunday best: white stucco buildings nuzzling cobblestoned streets, red-tiled roofs and geranium-filled window boxes bright in the sun. Taxco (pronounced *tahss*-co), a colonial treasure that the Mexican government declared a national monument in 1928, tumbles onto the hills of the Sierra Madre in the state of Guerrero. Its silver mines have drawn people here for centuries. Now its charm, mild temperatures, sunshine, and flowers make Taxco a popular tourist destination.

Hernán Cortés discovered Taxco's mines in 1522. The silver rush lasted until the next century, when excitement tapered off. Then in the 1700s a Frenchman, who Mexicanized his name to José de la Borda, discovered a rich lode that revitalized the town's silver industry and made him exceedingly wealthy. After Borda, however, Taxco's importance faded, until the 1930s and the arrival of William G. Spratling, a writer-architect from New Orleans. Enchanted by Taxco and convinced of its potential as a silver center, Spratling set up an apprentice shop, where his artistic talent and his fascination with pre-Columbian design combined to produce silver jewelry and other artifacts that soon earned Taxco its worldwide reputation as the Silver City. Spratling's inspiration lives on in his students and their descendants, many of whom are the city's current silversmiths.

Exploring

Numbers in the margin correspond to points of interest on the Taxco Exploring map.

❶ Begin at the **zócalo,** properly called **Plaza Borda,** heading first into the
❷ **Church of San Sebastián and Santa Prisca,** which dominates the main square. Usually just called Santa Prisca, it was built by French silver magnate José de la Borda in thanks to the Almighty for his having literally stumbled upon a rich silver vein. The style of the church—sort of Spanish Baroque meets Rococo—is known as Churrigueresque, and its pink exterior is a stunning surprise.

❸ Just a block from the zócalo, behind Santa Prisca, is the **Spratling Museum,** formerly the home of William G. Spratling (*see* Introduction, *above*). This wonderful little museum explains the working of colonial mines and displays Spratling's collection of pre-Columbian artifacts. *Porfirio Delgado and El Arco,* ☎ *762/2–16–60.* ☛ *Small entrance fee.* ☉ *Tues.–Sun. 10–5.*

❹ **Casa Humboldt,** a block away, was named for the German adventurer Alexander von Humboldt, who stayed here in 1803. The Moorish-style 18th-century house has a finely detailed facade. It now houses a museum of colonial art. *Calle Juan Ruíz Alarcón 6,* ☎ *762/2–55–01.* ☛ *Free.* ☉ *Tues.–Sun. 9–6.*

❺ Down the hill from Santa Prisca is the **Municipal Market,** which is worth a visit, especially early on Saturday or Sunday morning.

TIME OUT Around the plaza are several *neverías* where you can treat yourself to an ice cream in a delicious fruit flavor, such as coconut. **Bar Paco's,** directly across the street from Santa Prisca, is a Taxco institution; its terrace is the perfect vantage point for watching the comings and goings on the zócalo while sipping a margarita or a beer.

Off the Beaten Track

About 15 minutes northeast of Taxco are the Caves of Cacahuamilpa (Grutas de Cacahuamilpa). The largest caverns in Mexico, these 15 large chambers comprise 12 kilometers (8 miles) of geological formation. Only some caves are illuminated. A guide can be hired at the entrance to the caves.

Shopping

SILVER

Most of the people who visit Taxco come with silver in mind. Three types are available: sterling, which is always stamped .925 (925 parts in 1,000) and is the most expensive; plated silver; and the inexpensive *alpaca,* which is also known as German silver or nickel silver. Sterling pieces are usually priced by weight according to world silver prices, and of course fine workmanship will add to the cost. Work is also done with semiprecious stones; you'll find garnets, topazes, amethysts, and opals. If you plan to buy, check prices before leaving home. When comparison shopping in the more than 200 silver shops in Taxco, you will see that many carry almost identical merchandise, although a few are noted for their creativity. Among them:

Elena de los Ballesteros (Celso Muñoz 4, ☎ 762/2–37–67) is a very elegant shop with work of outstanding design.

324

Casa
Humboldt, **4**
Church of San
Sebastián and
Santa Prisca, **2**
Municipal
Market, **5**
Plaza Borda
(Zócalo), **1**
Spratling
Museum, **3**

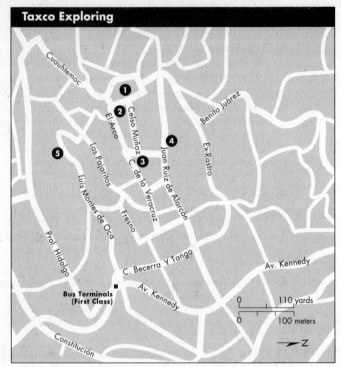

Taxco Exploring

Galería de Arte en Plata Andrés (Av. John F. Kennedy 28, ☎ 762/2-37-78) has unique designs created by the personable Andrés Mejía.

Los Castillo (Plazuela Bernal 10, ☎ 762/2-06-52) is the most famous and decidedly one of the most exciting silver shops; it's known for innovative design and for combining silver with ceramics and such other metals as copper and brass. The artisans are disciples of Spratling.

Pineda's Taxco (Plaza Borda 1, ☎ 762/2-32-33, and Av. John F. Kennedy 160, ☎ 762/2-19-32) has fine designs and fine workmanship.

Spratling Ranch (south of town on Highway 95, ☎ 762/2-00-62) is where the heirs of William Spratling turn out designs using his original molds.

LOCAL WARES

Lacquered gourds and boxes from the town of Olinalá, masks, bowls, straw baskets, bark paintings, and many other handcrafted items native to the state of Guerrero are available from strolling vendors and are displayed on the cobblestones at "sidewalk boutiques." **Arnold's** (Palma 1, ☎ 762/2-00-86) has an interesting collection of ceremonial masks; originals come with a certificate of authenticity as well as a written description of origin and use. **Gracias a Dios** (Bernal 3, ☎ 762/2-08-70) carries women's clothing, with brightly colored ribbons and appliqués, designed by Tachi Castillo, as well as a less original selection of crafts. **La Calleja** (Calle Arco 9, 2nd floor, ☎ 762/2-08-70) offers a wide and well-chosen selection of native arts and handicrafts.

Sunday is market day, which means that artisans from surrounding villages descend on the town, as do visitors from Mexico City. It can get crowded, but if you find a seat on a bench in Plaza Borda, you're set to watch the show and peruse the merchandise that will inevitably be brought to you.

Sports and Fitness

You can play golf or tennis, swim, and ride horses at various hotels around Taxco. Call to see if the facilities are open to nonguests. Bullfights are occasionally held in the small town of Acmixtla, 6 kilometers (4 miles) from Taxco. Ask at your hotel about the schedule.

Dining

Gastronomes can find everything from tagliatelle to iguana in Taxco restaurants, and meals are much less expensive than in Acapulco. Dress is casual, but less so than at the resorts.

CATEGORY	COST*
$$$$	over $20
$$$	$15–$20
$$	$8–$15
$	under $8

per person excluding drinks, service, and sales tax (10%)

$$$$ **La Ventana de Taxco.** The Italian recipes inherited from the former manager, Mario Cavagna, coupled with Mexican specialties and a fantastic view, still draw a loyal crowd to this restaurant, although it has lost some of its former sheen. ✕ *Hacienda del Solar Hotel, Hwy. 95, south of town,* ☎ *762/2–05–87. Reservations required on weekends. AE, MC, V.*

$$$$ **Pagaduría del Rey.** In the Posada Don Carlos, south of town via
★ Avenida John F. Kennedy, this restaurant has a long-standing reputation for Continental fare served in comfortable surroundings. This is definitely the best place in town. ✕ *Calle H. Colegio Militar 8 (Colonia Cerro de la Bermeja),* ☎ *762/2–34–67. Reservations not necessary. MC, V.*

$$$$ **Toni's.** Prime rib and lobster are the specialties. There's also a great view and a romantic setting. ✕ *Monte Taxco Hotel,* ☎ *762/2–13–00. Reservations accepted. AE, DC, MC, V.*

$$$ **Cielito Lindo.** This charming restaurant features a Mexican-international menu. Give the Mexican specialties a try—for example, *pollo en pipian verde,* a chicken simmered in a mild, pumpkinseed-based sauce. ✕ *Plaza Borda 14,* ☎ *762/2–06–03. No reservations. MC, V.*

$$$ **La Taberna.** This is another successful venture of the proprietors of
★ Bora Bora, Taxco's popular pizza place. The menu is varied, with the likes of pastas, beef Stroganoff, and crepes to choose from. ✕ *Benito Juárez 8,* ☎ *762/2–52–26. Reservations suggested. MC, V.*

$$ **Bora Bora.** Exceptionally good pizza is what's on the menu here. ✕
★ *Callejón de las Delícias 4, behind Paco's Bar,* ☎ *762/2–17–21. No reservations. No credit cards.*

$$ **Piccolo Mondo.** More casual than its neighbor, Toni's, this place serves pizza baked in a wood-burning brick oven and meats and chicken charcoal-broiled at your table. ✕ *Monte Taxco Hotel,* ☎ *762/2–13–00. Reservations advised. AE, MC, V. Closed Mon.–Thurs.*

$$ **Señor Costilla.** That's right. This translates as Mr. Ribs, and the whimsical name says it all. The Taxco outpost of the zany Anderson chain serves barbecued ribs and chops in a restaurant with great balcony seating. ✕ *Plaza Borda 1,* ☎ *762/2–32–15. No reservations. MC, V.*

$ **La Hacienda.** In the Hotel Agua Escondida, this charming restaurant serves Mexican and international specialties. The best buy: the daily fixed-price *comida corrida.* ✕ *Guillermo Spratling 4,* ☎ *762/2–06–63. No reservations. MC, V.*

Lodging

Whether your stay in Taxco is a one-night stopover or a few days' respite from the madness of Acapulco, there are several categories of hotel to choose from within Taxco's two types: the small inns nestled on the hills skirting the zócalo and the larger, more modern hotels on the outskirts of town.

CATEGORY	COST*
$$$$	over $90
$$$	$60–$90
$$	$25–$60
$	under $25

All prices are for standard double room, excluding 10% sales (called IVA) tax.

$$$$ **Monte Taxco.** A colonial style predominates at this hotel, which has a knockout view, funicular, and three restaurants, a disco, and nightly entertainment. ☎ *Box 84, Lomas de Taxco, 40200,* ☎ *762/2–13–00,* FAX *762/2–14–28. 156 rooms, suites, and villas with bath. 3 restaurants, 9-hole golf course, 3 tennis courts, horseback riding, dance club. AE, DC, MC, V.*

$$$ **Hacienda del Solar.** This small resort (off Hwy. 95 south of town) was once the best in town, but it's seen better days. Its restaurant, La Ventana de Taxco (*see above*), maintains many loyal patrons. ☎ *Box 96, 40200,* ☎ *762/2–03–23,* FAX *762/2–46–32. 22 rooms with bath. Restaurant, pool, tennis court. MC, V.*

$$$ **Posada de la Misión.** Laid out like a village, this hotel is close to
★ town and has dining-room murals by the noted Mexican artist Juan O'Gorman. ☎ *Box 88, Cerro de la Misión 32, 40230,* ☎ *762/2– 00–63,* FAX *762/2–21–98. 150 rooms with bath. Pool, tennis court. AE, DC, MC, V.*

$$$ **Rancho Taxco-Victoria.** This in-town hotel, in two buildings connected by a bridge over the road, is under the same management as the De la Borda (*see below*) and suffers from the same neglect. It has its rooms done in classic Mexican decor. There's also the requisite splendid view. ☎ *Box 83, Carlos J. Nibbi 5, 40200,* ☎ *762/2–02–10,* FAX *762/2–00–10. 64 rooms with bath. Restaurant, bar, pool. AE, MC, V.*

$$ **Agua Escondida.** Popular with some regular visitors to Taxco, this small hotel has simple rooms decorated with Mexican-style furnishings. ☎ *Guillermo Spratling 4, 40200,* ☎ *762/2–07–26,* FAX *762/2– 13–06. 50 rooms with bath. Restaurant, café-bar, pool. MC, V.*

$$ **De la Borda.** Long a Taxco favorite, De la Borda is a bit worn, but the rooms are large and comfortable and the staff couldn't be more hospitable. Ask for a room overlooking town. There's a restaurant with occasional entertainment, and many bus tours en route from Mexico City to Acapulco stay here overnight. ☎ *Box 6, Cerro del Pedregal 2, 40200,* ☎ *762/2–00–25,* FAX *762/2–06–17. 95 rooms with bath. Restaurant, pool. AE, MC, V.*

$$ **Loma Linda.** This is a basic motel on the highway just east of town. ☎ *Av. John F. Kennedy 52, 40200,* ☎ *762/2–02–06,* FAX *762/2–51–45. 55 units. Restaurant, bar, pool. AE, MC, V.*

$$ **Los Arcos.** For those seeking lodgings in central Taxco, Los Arcos offers basic accommodations around a pleasant patio. ☎ *Calle Juan Ruíz de Alarcón 12, 40200,* ☎ *762/2–18–36,* FAX *762/2–32–11. 25 rooms with bath. MC, V.*

$$ **Posada de los Castillo.** This in-town inn is straightforward, clean, and good for the price. ☎ *Juan Ruíz de Alarcón 7, 40200,* ☎ *762/2– 13–96,* FAX *762/2–34–71. 15 rooms. DC, MC, V.*

$$ Santa Prisca. The patio with fountains is a plus at this colonial-style hotel. ▦ *Cena Obscuras 1, 40200,* ☎ *and* FAX *762/2-00-80. 40 rooms. Restaurant, bar. AE, MC, V.*

The Arts and Nightlife

THE ARTS

Taxco has no abundance of cultural events, but it's noted for its festivals, which are an integral part of the town's character. These fiestas provide an opportunity to honor almost every saint in heaven with music, dancing, marvelous fireworks, and lots of fun. The people of Taxco demonstrate their pyrotechnical skills with set pieces—wondrous blazing "castles" made of bamboo. (Note: Expect high occupancy at local hotels and inns during fiestas.)

January 18, the feast of Santa Prisca and San Sebastián, the town's patron saints, is celebrated with music and fireworks.

Holy Week, from Palm Sunday to Easter Sunday, brings processions and events that blend Christian and Indian traditions, the dramas involving hundreds of participants, images of Christ, and, for one particular procession, black-hooded penitents. Most events are centered on Plaza Borda and the Santa Prisca Church.

September 29, Saint Michael's Day (Dia de San Miguel), is celebrated with regional dances and pilgrimages to the Chapel of Saint Michael the Archangel.

In **early November,** on the Monday following the Day of the Dead celebrations on November 1 and 2, the entire town takes off to a nearby hill for the Fiesta de los Jumiles. The *jumil* is a crawling insect that is said to taste strongly of iodine and is considered a great delicacy. Purists eat them alive, but others prefer them stewed, fried, or combined with chili in a hot sauce.

In **late November or early December,** the National Silver Fair (Feria Nacional de la Plata) draws hundreds of artisans from around the world for a variety of displays, concerts, exhibitions, and contests held around the city.

NIGHTLIFE

Travelers should satisfy their appetite for fun after dark in Acapulco. Although Taxco has one or two discos, a couple of piano bars, and some entertainment, the range is limited.

Still, you might enjoy spending an evening perched on a chair on a balcony or in one of the cafés surrounding the Plaza Borda. Two traditional favorites are the **Bar Paco** (Plaza Borda 12, ☎ 762/2-00-63) and **Bertha's** (Plaza Borda 9, ☎ 762/2-01-72), where a tequila, lime, and club-soda concoction called a Bertha is the house specialty.

Or immerse yourself in the thick of things, especially on Sunday evening, by settling in on a wrought-iron bench on the zócalo to watch children, lovers, and fellow people-watchers.

Most of Taxco's nighttime activity is at the Monte Taxco hotel, either at the **Windows** discotheque or at **Tony's Bar,** where there's a performance of the Papantla fliers ($6) nightly except Sunday. On Saturday nights at the hotel's El Taxqueño restaurant there's a buffet and a terrific fireworks display (Taxco is Mexico's fireworks capital), and at Windows, a show put on by the hotel's employees.

Some of the best restaurants, including La Ventana de Taxco, have music.

Taxco Essentials

GETTING THERE

By Car. There are several ways to travel to Taxco from Acapulco, and all involve ground transport.It takes about 3 hours to make the drive from Acapulco to Taxco, using the new—and very expensive—toll road. It is common practice to hire a chauffeured car or a taxi. Check with your hotel for references and prices.

By Bus. First-class **Estrella de Oro** buses leave Acapulco several times a day from the Terminal Central de Autobuses de Primera Clase (Av. Cuauhtémoc 1490, ☎ 74/85–87–05). The cost for the approximately four-hour ride is about $14 one way for deluxe service. The Taxco terminal is at Avenida John F. Kennedy 126 (☎ 762/2–06–48). First-class **Flecha Roja** buses depart Acapulco several times a day from the Terminal de Autobuses (Ejido 47, ☎ 74/69–20–29). The one-way ticket is about $12 for first-class service. The Taxco terminal for this line is at Avenida John F. Kennedy 104 (☎ 762/2–01–31).

GETTING AROUND

Unless you're used to byways, alleys, and tiny streets, maneuvering anything bigger than your two feet through Taxco will be difficult. Fortunately, almost everything of interest is within walking distance of the zócalo. Minibuses travel along preset routes and charge only a few cents, and Volkswagen "bugs" provide inexpensive (average $2) taxi transportation. Remember that Taxco's altitude is 5,800 feet. Wear sensible shoes for negotiating the hilly streets, and if you have come from sea level, take it easy on your first day.

Ixtapa and Zihuatanejo

In Ixtapa/Zihuatanejo, 3½ hours by car (250 kilometers/150 miles) up the coast from Acapulco, you can enjoy two distinct lifestyles for the price of one—double value for your money.

Ixtapa/Zihuatanejo is a complete change of pace from hectic Acapulco. The water is comfortably warm for swimming, and the waves are gentle. The temperature averages 78°F year-round. During the mid-December–Easter high season, the weather is sunny and dry, and in the June–October rainy season the short, heavy showers usually fall at night.

Ixtapa (pronounced eeks-*tah*-pa), where most Americans stay—probably because they can't pronounce Zihuatanejo (see-wha-tah-*nay*-ho)—is big, modern, and young, established in 1976. Exclusively a vacation resort, it was invented and planned, as was Cancún, by Fonatur, Mexico's National Fund for Tourism Development. Large world-class hotels cluster in the Hotel Zone around Palmar Bay, where conditions are ideal for swimming and water sports, and just across the street are a couple of football fields' worth of shopping malls. The hotels are well spaced; there's always plenty of room on the beach, which is lighted for strolling at night; and the pace is leisurely.

Zihuatanejo, which means "land of women" in Purepecha, the language of the Tarascan Indians, lies 7 kilometers (3 miles) to the southeast. According to legend, Caltzontzin, a Tarascan king, chose this bay as his royal retreat and enclosed it with a long protective breakwater, which is known today as Las Gatas. Zihuatanejo is an old fishing village that has managed to retain its charm; but it's also the area's municipal center, and its *malecón* (waterfront) and brick streets are lined with hotels, restaurants, and boutiques.

Exploring

No matter where you go in Ixtapa/Zihuatanejo, you get the fresh-air, great-outdoors feeling of a place in the making, with plenty of room to spare.

Zihuatanejo is a tropical charmer. The seaside promenade overlooks the town dock and cruise-ship pier; tiny bars and restaurants invite you to linger longer. From town the road soars up a hill that has a handful of restaurants and hotels perched on breezy spots overlooking the bay. Another sprinkling of hotels surround pancake-flat **Madera Beach. La Ropa,** farther along, is Zihuatanejo's most popular beach and the location of one of Mexico's best small hotels, Villa del Sol. **Las Gatas** beach, beyond, lined with dive shops and tiny restaurants, is also popular but is accessible only by water.

At the opposite end of the area, about five minutes beyond the Ixtapa Hotel Zone, is pretty **Playa Quieta,** a small beach used by Club Med. From here you can take a boat ride to **Isla Ixtapa,** about $2, and spend a wonderful day in the sun far from other people. Once the boat lands, take the path to the other side of the island for better sunning and swimming.

Shopping

At last count there were seven shopping malls in Ixtapa. La Puerta, the first one built, is now flanked by terra-cotta-colored Ixpamar, colonial-style Los Patios, and bright white Las Fuentes. The ubiquitous **Aca Joe** (☎ 753/3–03–02) and **Polo Ralph Lauren** (☎ 753/3–12–72) are in Las Fuentes, as is **Africán** (☎ 753/3–24–15), which carries 100%-cotton safari-style clothing for men and women. **El Baul** (no ☎), with handicrafts from the state of Guerrero, is in La Puerta; **Tanga Boutique** (☎ 753/3–05–98), offering a stunning selection of Mexican and imported beachwear, and **La Fuente** (☎ 753/3–08–12), which sells clothes with native-inspired designs, are in Los Patios. **El Huizteco** (no ☎), which sells some of the best folk art in the state, is in Ixpamar. Don't let the modern facades and sparkling decor fool you: Most prices are within everyone's range. There is sometimes free live entertainment on the patio at Ixpamar. Downtown Zihuatanejo has a municipal minimarket and a host of tiny stores. You must go inside to discover bargains in souvenirs and decorations, T-shirts, and embroidered dresses. On Calle Vicente Guerrero is one of the best handicrafts shops in all of Mexico—**Coco Cabaña** (☎ 753/4–25–18) which is owned by the same people who run Coconuts restaurant. **Alberto's,** at Cuauhtémoc 15 (☎ 753/4–21–61), and **Ruby's,** just a few steps down at Cuauhtémoc 7 (☎ 753/4–39–90), have the town's best selection of silver jewelry, and at **La Zapoteca** (☎ 753/4–23–73), on the waterfront, you'll find handloomed woolen rugs, wall hangings, and hammocks. The owners have another shop at Calles 5 de Mayo and Juan N. Alvarez (same ☎). On Calle Juan N. Alvarez, Indians sell baskets and other handmade wares that they bring from the surrounding areas.

Sports and Fitness

Although several hotels have tennis courts and there are two beautiful championship golf courses in Ixtapa, most of the outdoor activities in Ixtapa/Zihuatanejo center on the water. At the **water-sports center** in front of Villa del Sol on La Ropa you can arrange for waterskiing, snorkeling, diving, and windsurfing.

DEEP-SEA FISHING

Boats with captain and crew can be hired at the **Cooperativa de Lanchas de Recreo and Pesca Deportiva** (Av. Ruíz Cortines 40 at the Zihuatanejo pier, ☎ 753/4–20–56) or through **Turismo Caleta** (La Puerta shopping center in Ixtapa, ☎ 753/3–04–44). The cost for seven hours is $170 for a 25- to 26-foot boat, $270 for a 32- to 36-footer. Rates include seven sodas, seven beers, and an instructor.

GOLF AND TENNIS

The **Ixtapa Golf Club** (☎ 753/3–10–62) is open to the public. The greens fee is $50; tennis costs $8 an hour in the daytime, $10 at night. Caddies cost $18 a round and carts go for $33. A second 18-hole golf course is located at Marina Ixtapa (☎ 753/3–14–10), where the greens fee is $55, including the cart, and caddies cost $20 for 18 holes. Marina Ixtapa has a special offer of $135 for three days of golf, including cart rental. Most of the hotels in Ixtapa and a few in Zihuatanejo have tennis courts; nonguests can usually play for a fee.

HORSEBACK RIDING

You can rent horses at La Manzanilla Ranch, near Playa La Ropa, and at Playa Linda.

PARASAILING

You can try this scary-looking sport on the beach in the Ixtapa Hotel Zone. A 10-minute ride will cost about $20.

SAILING

Hobie Cats and larger sailboats are available for rent at La Ropa Beach for $25–$70 per hour.

SCUBA DIVING

The **Zihuatanejo Scuba Center,** at Calle Cuauhtémoc 3 (☎ 753/4–21–47), is operated by marine biologist Juan Barnard Avila. The staff, which includes some expatriate Americans, is enthusiastic and knowledgeable. The single-tank dive costs $45 ($40 if you have your own gear); the double-tank dive costs $70 ($60 without equipment) and includes two separate dives and lunch at Puerto Mío. This outfit also offers night dives, including lights and batteries, for $55, and a five-day certification course for $350. Divers can have their underwater adventures videotaped for an additional $40.

WINDSURFING

This popular activity can be arranged at Las Gatas and La Ropa beaches for about $18 per hour—$28 per hour with lessons.

Dining

Meals are generally less expensive in downtown Zihuatanejo than in Ixtapa or in the restaurants up in the hills, and even the most expensive ones will cost considerably less than those in Acapulco. The restaurants will fall at the lower end of our price categories, verging on the category below, and casual dress is acceptable everywhere.

CATEGORY	COST*
$$$$	over $35
$$$	$25–$35
$$	$15–$25
$	under $15

per person excluding drinks, service, and sales tax (10%)

IXTAPA

$$$ **Bogart's.** This restaurant is romantic and elegant, with Moorish-Arabic decor and an international menu. The *Crepas Persas* (Persian crepes)

filled with cheese are topped with sour cream and caviar. Or try *Suprema Casablanca:* chicken breasts stuffed with lobster and then breaded and fried. ✗ *Hotel Krystal, Playa Palmar,* ☎ *753/3–03–33. Reservations required. AE, DC, MC, V.*

$$$ Carlos 'n' Charlie's. Hidden away at the end of the beach, this outpost of the famous Anderson's chain serves pork, seafood, and chicken in a Polynesian setting almost on the sand. ✗ *Next to Posada Real Hotel,* ☎ *753/3–00–85. No reservations. AE, MC, V.*

$$$ El Faro. El Faro sits atop a hill next to the funicular that goes up to the Club Pacífica complex. It has an extensive menu that includes *camarones en salsa de albahaca* (shrimp in a basil sauce). Another draw is the spectacular view. ✗ *Playa Vista Hermosa,* ☎ *753/3– 10–27. Reservations advised. AE, MC, V.*

$$$ El Sombrero. This popular place serves Mexican food, seafood, and international dishes. The potpourri Mexicana, with chicken in mole sauce, an enchilada, and a spicy sausage, is a good introduction to real Mexican cookery. ✗ *Los Patios shopping center,* ☎ *753/3– 04–39. Reservations advised. MC, V. Closed Sun.*

$$$ Las Esferas. This place in the Westin Brisas Ixtapa is a complex of two
★ restaurants and a bar. **Portofino** specializes in Italian cuisine and is decorated with multicolored pastas and scenes of Italy. In **El Mexicano** the specialties are naturally Mexican, as is the decor—bright pink tablecloths, Puebla jugs, a huge tree of life, antique wood carvings, and blown glass. ✗ *Playa Vista Hermosa,* ☎ *753/3–21–21, ext. 3444. Reservations necessary at Portofino, advised at El Mexicano. AE, DC, MC, V.*

$$$ Villa de la Selva. Just past the Westin Ixtapa, this restaurant has tables set up on multilevel terraces under the stars. Excellent international dishes, grilled steaks, and seafood are served in a romantic setting, and special lighting after dark illuminates the sea and the rocks below. ✗ *Paseo de la Roca,* ☎ *753/3–03–62. Reservations advised. AE, MC, V. No lunch.*

$$ Da Baffone. The atmosphere is easy and informal at this well-run Italian restaurant with two dining areas; you can choose the air-conditioned dining room or the open-air porch. Try the spaghetti *siubeco,* prepared with cream, peppers, shrimp, and wine. ✗ *La Puerta shopping mall,* ☎ *753/3–11–22. Reservations advised. AE, MC, V.*

$ Café Onyx. Mexican and international dishes are served under an awning at this alfresco eatery. ✗ *Across from the Holiday Inn, in the Ixtapa Plaza shopping mall,* ☎ *753/3–03–46. No reservations. MC, V.*

$ Nueva Zelanda. This is a fast-moving cafeteria with good food that
★ you order by numbers. Chicken enchiladas with green sauce, *sincronizadas* (flour tortillas filled with ham and cheese), and the *licuados* (milk shakes with fresh fruit) are all tasty. Families with young children gather here, and there is usually a line on weekends. Dinner for two can cost less than $10. ✗ *Behind the bandstand,* ☎ *753/ 3–08–38. No reservations. No credit cards.*

ZIHUATANEJO

$$$$ La Casa Que Canta. Sheltered under a thatched roof and set on a cliff
★ overlooking Zihuatanejo Bay, this appealing restaurant was created by Ercolino Crugnale, executive chef at the Stouffer Stanford Court in San Francisco. His innovative menu includes Continental, Mexican, and seafood selections. Breads and cakes are baked each day on the premises. ✗ *La Casa Que Canta hotel, Camino Escénico a Playa La Ropa,* ☎ *753/4–27–22. Dinner only for nonguests. No children under 16. Reservations required. AE, MC, V.*

$$$ **Coconuts.** Excellent seafood and salads are served in elegant surroundings. ✕ *Calle Agustín Ramírez 1,* ☎ *753/4–25–18. Reservations required. DC, MC, V. Closed Sept.–Oct.*

$$$
★ **Villa del Sol.** This restaurant, in the hotel that bears the same name, has earned a worldwide reputation for excellent quality and service. The international menu is prepared by Swiss, German, and Mexican chefs. ✕ *Hotel Villa del Sol, Playa La Ropa,* ☎ *753/4–22–39. Dinner reservations advised. AE, MC, V.*

$$ **Casa Elvira.** Elvira Reyes, the owner, claims that this is the oldest restaurant in town—it's been around since 1956. It's quaint and clean, decorated with Talavera tiles and handicrafts from Pátzcuaro, and the prices are reasonable. There's a fairly large selection of fish and seafood, including an excellent *parrillada de mariscos* (seafood grill), as well as such traditional Mexican dishes as poblano peppers stuffed with cheese and *puntas de filete albañil* (a kind of stew). ✕ *Paseo del Pescador 8, between the dock and the basketball court,* ☎ *753/4–20–61. Reservations advised. MC, V.*

$$ **La Bocana.** This restaurant is a favorite with locals as well as visitors. The service is good and the seafood is a treat. You can eat three meals a day here. Musicians sometimes stroll through. ✕ *Calle Juan N. Alvarez 13,* ☎ *753/4–35–45. MC, V.*

$$ **La Gaviota.** At this mini-beach club you can spend an afternoon swimming and sunning after having a seafood lunch. Lots of locals like this one, and the bar is pleasant. ✕ *On Playa La Ropa,* ☎ *753/ 4–38–16. No reservations. MC, V.*

$$
★ **Taboga.** *Pescado Yugoslavia* (fillet of fish prepared with cheese, potatoes, and vegetables) is just one of the tasty seafood dishes served in this quaint, recently renovated place across from the Aeromexico office. ✕ *Calle Juan N. Alvarez and Cinco de Mayo,* ☎ *753/4–26–37. No reservations. MC, V.*

$ **Garrobos.** This delightful restaurant specializes in seafood and Mexican cuisine. Try the seafood brochettes. ✕ *Calle Juan N. Alvarez 52, near the church and museum,* ☎ *753/4–29–77. Reservations advised. MC, V.*

$ **La Perla.** At Doña Raquel's popular seaside restaurant and video sports bar, the hands-down favorite is *Filete La Perla,* a fish fillet baked in aluminum foil with cheese, garlic, onion, and tomato. ✕ *Playa La Ropa,* ☎ *753/4–27–00. MC, V.*

$ **La Sirena Gorda.** The specialty here is seafood tacos (try the shrimp-and-bacon combo); meals are served in rustic yet pleasant surroundings. ✕ *Paseo del Pescador 20-A,* ☎ *753/4–26–87. MC, V.* ☉ *Thurs.–Tues. 7 AM–10 PM.*

$
★ **Nueva Zelanda.** From breakfast through dinner everybody drops in to this little coffee shop-style eatery, which serves *tortas* (Mexican sandwiches on crusty rolls), tacos, and enchiladas. ✕ *Calle Cuauhtémoc 23,* ☎ *753/4–23–40. No reservations. No credit cards.*

$ **Puntarenas.** This plain place serves Mexican food and great breakfasts. It's a favorite with those in the know and there's often a line, but it's worth the wait. ✕ *Across the bridge at end of Calle Juan N. Alvarez, no* ☎*. No reservations. No credit cards.* ☉ *High season only.*

Lodging

Ixtapa/Zihuatanejo hotel rates vary widely, and after Easter they drop 30%–40% and sometimes more. Most of the budget accommodations are in Zihuatanejo, where the best hotels are on or overlooking La Madera or La Ropa Beach and the least expensive are downtown.

CATEGORY	COST*
$$$$	over $160
$$$	$90–$160
$$	$40–$90
$	under $40

*All prices are for a standard double room, excluding 10% sales (called IVA) tax.

IXTAPA

$$$$ **Krystal Ixtapa.** This attractive beachfront property is part of a Mexi-
★ can chain. Home to Christine's, Ixtapa's most popular disco, and Bogart's (*see* Dining, *above*), the Krystal is one of the liveliest spots in town. ☎ *Blvd. Ixtapa, 40880,* ☎ *753/3–03–33 or 800/231–9860,* FAX *753/3–02–16. 254 rooms and suites with bath. 2 restaurants, coffee shop, pool, 2 tennis courts, dance club. AE, DC, MC, V.*

$$$$ **Presidente Ixtapa Forum Resort.** This is a beautifully landscaped resort that was among Ixtapa's first beachfront properties. The rooms are divided between colonial-style villas that line winding paths through the grounds and a tower with a glass elevator that provides a sensational view of Ixtapa. Room rates include all meals and beverages. ☎ *Playa Palmar, 40880,* ☎ *753/3–00–18 or 800/327–0200,* FAX *753/3–23–12. 401 rooms with bath. 3 restaurants, bar, 2 pools, wading pool, 2 tennis courts. AE, DC, MC, V.*

$$$$ **Westin Brisas Ixtapa.** This is a pyramid-shaped hotel whose rooms
★ (all with private balconies) seem to cascade down the hill to secluded Vista Hermosa beach. It is one of Ixtapa's largest hotels and is noted for excellent service. ☎ *Playa Vista Hermosa, Box 97, 40880,* ☎ *753/3–21–21 or 800/228–3000,* FAX *753/3–07–51. 428 rooms with bath. 3 restaurants, 2 bars, 3 pools, wading pool, 4 tennis courts. AE, DC, MC, V.*

$$$ **Dorado Pacífico.** A high-rise located on the beach in the center of Ixtapa, this hotel is noted for its spectacular atrium lobby, with fountains and panoramic elevators, and a large pool. The rooms are spacious and very well kept. ☎ *Playa Palmar, 40880,* ☎ *753/3–20–25 or 800/448–8355,* FAX *753/3–01–26. 285 rooms with bath. 3 restaurants, bar, pool, 2 tennis courts. AE, DC, MC, V.*

$$ **Casa de la Tortuga.** Those seeking seclusion and inexpensive lodgings in the Ixtapa/Zihuatanejo area might venture some 30 minutes northwest (up the coast) to the tiny village of Trocones. A main house offers clean, simply furnished rooms (some with private baths) with a kitchen and garden; the entire house can be rented for a reasonable rate. Farther along the beach and owned by the same proprietors are six rooms right on the shore, each with private bath, king-size bed, private porch, and hammock; there's a restaurant and kitchen facilities on the premises. Continental breakfast is included in the room rates for both facilities. ☎ *Trocones beach, Apdo. 277, Zihuatanejo, Guerrero 40880,* ☎ *and* FAX *753/4–32–96. 6 rooms, 6 bungalows. Restaurant, hiking. No credit cards.*

$$ **Posada Real.** Smaller and more intimate than most of the other Ixtapa hotels, this colonial-style member of the Best Western chain sits on Palmar Beach, has lots of charm, and offers good value. ☎ *Playa Palmar, 40880,* ☎ *753/3–16–85, 753/3–17–45, or 800/526–1234,* FAX *753/3–18–05. 108 rooms with bath. 3 restaurants, 2 bars, 2 pools, wading pool, dance club. AE, DC, MC, V.*

ZIHUATANEJO

$$$$ **La Casa Que Canta.** Resembling a thatched-roof pueblo village, the "House That Sings" is perched on a cliff overlooking La Ropa Beach. All of the individually decorated suites feature ceiling fans as well as

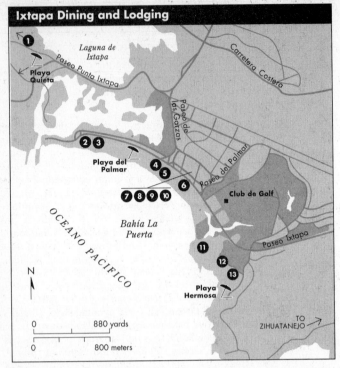

Ixtapa Dining and Lodging

air-conditioning, luxurious bathrooms, hand-painted and -crafted furniture, and unique Mexican handicrafts. Two have private pools. The on-premises restaurant is excellent (*see* Dining, *above*). Children under 16 are not accepted. ⊞ *Camino Escénico a Playa La Ropa, 40880,* ☎ *753/4–27–22 or 800/525–4800,* 🖷 *753/4–20–06. 18 suites. Restaurant, pools. AE, DC, MC, V.*

$$$$ Puerto Mío. This small hotel overlooking Zihuatanejo Bay is part of a marina and residential development. The suites, distributed among several Mediterranean-style villas, are tastefully furnished, and the decor makes wonderful use of the bright colors associated with Mexico. ⊞ *Playa del Almacen, Bahía de Zihuatanejo, 40880,* ☎ *753/4–37–45,* 🖷 *753/4–36–24. 26 suites. Restaurant, bar, pool, 2 tennis courts. AE, DC, MC, V.*

$$$$ Villa del Sol. A small hotel with a reputation as one of the finest in
★ Mexico, the Villa del Sol is set on the best beach in Zihuatanejo. Although the hotel has all the amenities of a large resort, it retains an intimate feeling. Rates include breakfast and dinner; children under 14 are not accepted in high season. ⊞ *Playa La Ropa, Box 84, 40880,* ☎ *753/4–29–95 or 800/525–4800,* 🖷 *753/4–40–66. 59 suites (1 and 2 bedrooms). Restaurant, air-conditioning, pool, tennis court, beach. AE, MC, V.*

$$$ Irma. Simple and clean, this hotel on a bluff overlooking Playa La Madera (and accessible by a stairway) gets lots of repeat visitors. Guests may use the beach club at the Fiesta Mexicana. ⊞ *Playa la Madera, Box 4, 40880,* ☎ *753/4–20–25 or 800/336–5454,* 🖷 *753/ 4–37–38. 75 rooms with bath. Restaurant, bar, 2 pools, tennis. AE, DC, MC, V.*

$$ Avila. Downtown and close to all the pier activity, the Avila has large clean rooms (all are air-conditioned), TVs, and ceiling fans. ⊞ *Calle*

Dining
Casa Elvira, **7**
Coconuts, **9**
Garrobos, **2**
La Bocana, **3**
La Casa
Que Canta, **17**
La Gaviota, **16**
La Perla, **20**
La Sirena
Gorda, **4**
Nueva
Zelanda, **8**
Puntarenas, **5**
Taboga, **10**
Villa del Sol, **18**

Lodging
Avila, **6**
Bungalows
Pacíficos,**11**
Catalina-
Sotovento, **14**
Fiesta Mexi-
cana, **15**
Irma, **13**
La Casa
Que Canta, **17**
Puerto Mío, **1**
Villa del Sol, **18**
Villas las
Urracas, **19**
Villas
Miramar, **12**

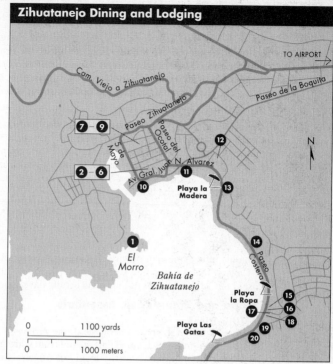

Zihuatanejo Dining and Lodging

Juan N. Alvarez 8, 40880, ☎ *753/4–20–10. 27 rooms with bath. AE, MC, V.*

$$ **Bungalows Pacíficos.** Each of these bungalows features two spacious, well-ventilated rooms (sleeping four between them), a kitchen, and a large terrace. ☎ *Playa la Madera, 40880,* ☎ *753/4–21–12. 6 bungalows. No credit cards.*

$$ **Catalina-Sotovento.** Really two hotels in one, this oldie-but-goodie sits on a cliff overlooking the beach, to which you descend on stairs. The rooms are large and decorated in Mexican colonial style, with ceiling fans. All the rooms were recently renovated, and 30 suites with large terraces overlooking the beach were added. ☎ *Playa La Ropa, Box 2, 40880,* ☎ *753/4–20–32 through 42 (10 lines),* FAX *753/4–29–75. 154 rooms with bath. 2 restaurants, 2 bars. AE, DC, MC, V.*

$$ **Fiesta Mexicana.** The pretty Mediterranean-style rooms are surrounded by inviting palm-shaded gardens. Make reservations well in advance, especially for the winter season. ☎ *Playa la Ropa, Box 4, 40880,* ☎ *753/4–37–76 or 800/336–5454,* FAX *753/4–36–36. 61 rooms with bath. Restaurant, bar, pool. AE, DC, MC, V.*

$$ **Villas Miramar.** Overlooking La Madera beach, the pretty stucco
★   rooms are nicely decorated and have tiled showers, air-conditioning, and ceiling fans. This hotel is a good value, but you need to book three months in advance (at least six months for Christmas and Easter). ☎ *Playa La Madera, Box 211, 40880,* ☎ *753/4–21–06,* FAX *753/4–21–49. 17 rooms, 1 suite. Restaurant, bar. AE, MC, V.*

$$ **Villas las Urracas.** Each of the units has a porch in a shaded garden, a kitchen, and a stove. Bungalows las Urracas is a great bargain— and lots of people know it, which places it in great demand. ☎ *Playa La Ropa, Box 141, 40880,* ☎ *753/4–20–49. 16 bungalows. No credit cards.*

The Arts and Nightlife

A good way to start an evening is at a happy hour in one of Ixtapa's hotels. Drinks are two for the price of one, and there is no cover charge to enjoy the live music—and, of course, the sunset. **The Bay Club,** on the road to Playa La Ropa, has a marvelous ocean view. The **Tropical Bar** at Coconuts is a lively spot in Zihuatanejo. **Benji-Pio Bar,** in the El Portal shopping center, and **Le Club,** at the Westin Ixtapa, are also popular.

Christine's at the Krystal in Ixtapa is the town's liveliest disco. **Magic Circus,** a disco in the Galerías shopping mall across from the Ixtapa Palace hotel, attracts a spirited young crowd (it's open only during the high season). **Euforia** is a spectacular disco across from the Posada Real hotel. Every night **Carlos 'n' Charlie's** has a dance party on a raised platform on the beach.

On Friday night during the high season, the **Sheraton Ixtapa** and the **Villa del Sol** hotel in Zihuatanejo stage lively Mexican Fiestas that are lots of fun.

The only movie house in the area is **Cinema Paraíso,** in Zihuatanejo at Calles Nicolás Bravo and Cuauhtémoc (☎ 753/4–23–18). Tickets cost about $1.50. Movies in English generally have Spanish subtitles.

Ixtapa and Zihuatanejo Essentials

GETTING THERE

By Plane. You can fly to Ixtapa on **Mexicana Airlines** from San Francisco and Los Angeles via Guadalajara, and from Chicago via Mexico City. **Delta** flies to Ixtapa nonstop from Los Angeles. Both **Mexicana** and **Aeromexico** have daily nonstop service from Mexico City and most other major cities in Mexico, but there is no direct air service from Acapulco. **Taesa** (☎ 5/227–0700, in Mexico City) has nonstop service from Mexico City Monday, Friday, and Sunday. **SARO** (☎ 5/273–1766, in Mexico City) connects Mexico City and Ixtapa Monday, Thursday, Friday, and Sunday.

By Car. The trip from Acapulco is a 3½-hour drive over a good road that passes through small towns and coconut groves and has some quite spectacular ocean views for the last third of the way. There is a chance that you may be stopped by soldiers checking for drugs and arms. They generally only look into the car and wave you on.

By Bus. Estrella de Oro and Flecha Roja offer deluxe service (which means that the air-conditioning and toilets are likely to be functioning) between Acapulco and Zihuatanejo. The trip takes about four hours and costs $10. You must reserve and pick up your ticket one day in advance and get to the terminal at least a half hour before departure. Estrella de Oro buses leave from the Terminal Central de Autobuses de Primera Clase (Av. Cuauhtémoc 1490, ☎ 74/85–87–05). The Flecha Roja buses leave from the Terminal de Autobuses (Ejido 47, ☎ 74/69–20–29).

GETTING AROUND

Unless you plan to travel great distances or visit remote beaches, taxis and buses are by far the best way to get around. Rental cars (automatic shift and air-conditioning) cost about $100 per day; Jeeps about the same.

Taxis are plentiful, and fares are reasonable. The average fare from the Ixtapa Hotel Zone to Zihuatanejo, Playa La Ropa, or Playa Quieta is about $5. There's no problem getting cabs, and there are taxi stands in front of most hotels.

The **buses** that operate between the hotels and from the Hotel Zone to downtown Zihuatanejo run approximately every 20 minutes and charge about 20¢.

Scooters can be rented at **Ola Renta Motos** (in the Los Patios shopping center, across from the Dorado Pacífico hotel, no ☎) for $15–$20 an hour, depending on the size.

Pedicabs (*cucarachas*) decorated with balloons can be rented at Ola Renta Motos for $15 per hour. Bikes also cost $15 per hour. A bicycle for two runs $18 per hour. The rental tent is open daily 9–8.

Rental-car offices in Zihuatanejo: **Budget** at Los Patios shopping center (☎ 753/3–21–62), **Dollar** at the Hotel Krystal (☎ 753/3–03–33, ext. 1110), and **Hertz** (Calle Nicolás Bravo 10, ☎ 753/4–30–50 or 753/4–22–55). In Ixtapa: **Avis's** only office is in the airport (☎ 753/4–22–48), and the other companies have branches there. Jeeps can be rented at the airport from **Dollar** (☎ 753/4–23–14).

GUIDED TOURS
Most Acapulco-based travel agencies can set up one-day tours to Ixtapa/Zihuatanejo for about $150, for a minimum of 4 people, including guide, transportation (car, minibus, or bus), and lunch. If your hotel travel desk can't make these arrangements for you, contact **Turismo Caleta** (Calle Andrea Dória 2, ☎ 74/84–65–70) or **Acuario Tours** (Costera Miguel Alemán 186, opposite the Acapulco Plaza Hotel, ☎ 74/85–61–00).

For another perspective, take a six-hour cruise for $55 on **Yates del Sol's** 12-passenger trimaran *Tri-Star* (☎ 753/4–35–89) or on the *Las Brisas*, operated by **Sailboats of the Sun** (☎ 753/4–20–91). Both set sail from the Puerto Mío marina in Zihuatanejo and include open bar (domestic drinks), live music, dancing, and a fresh-fish lunch at Ixtapa Island. Both the *Tri-Star* and *Las Brisas* have two-hour sunset cruises of Zihuatanejo Bay. For $45 the *Tristar* also operates a four-hour sail and snorkel cruise to Playa Manzanillo beach for snorkeling, swimming, and shell collecting; it ends with a ride on their 2400-square-foot spinnaker at Playa La Ropa. Included are open bar and snacks. Snorkel equipment is available for rent from both outfits.

ACAPULCO ESSENTIALS

Arriving and Departing

By Plane
AIRPORT AND AIRLINES
From the United States: **American** (☎ 800/433–7300) has nonstop flights from Dallas; connections from Chicago and New York through Dallas. **Continental** (☎ 800/821–2100) has nonstop service from Houston. **Delta's** (☎ 800/241–4141) nonstop service is from Los Angeles. **Mexicana** (☎ 800/531–7921) has one-stop service from Chicago, New York, and Los Angeles, and connecting service from Miami, San Antonio, San Francisco, and San Jose, California, all via Mexico City. **Aeromexico's** (☎ 800/237–6639) flight from New York to Acapulco stops in Mexico City. Other major carriers, including **United, Canadian, Alaska, Lufthansa, KLM,** and **Iberia,** fly into Mexico City, where you can make a connection to Acapulco.

From New York via Dallas, flying time is 4½ hours; from Chicago, 4¼ hours; from Los Angeles, 3½ hours.

Private taxis are not permitted to carry passengers from the airport to town, so most people rely on **Transportes Aeropuerto** (☎ 73/66–99–88), a special airport taxi service. The system looks confusing, but there are dozens of helpful English-speaking staff to help you figure out which taxi to take.

Look for the name of your hotel and the number of its zone on the overhead sign on the walkway in front of the terminal. Go to the desk for your zone and buy a ticket for an airport taxi that goes to your zone. The ride from the airport to the hotel zone on the trip costs about $5 per person for the *colectivo,* $34 for a nonshared cab. The drivers are usually helpful and will often take you to hotels that aren't on their list. Tips are optional. The journey into town takes 20 to 30 minutes.

By Car
The trip to Acapulco from Mexico City on the old road takes about six hours. A new, privately built and run four-lane toll road connecting Mexico City with Acapulco is expensive (about $86 one-way) but well maintained, and it cuts driving time between the two cities from six hours to 3½ hours. Many people opt for going via Taxco, which can be reached from either road.

By Ship
Many cruises include Acapulco as part of their itinerary. Most originate from Los Angeles. Cruise operators include **Carnival Cruise Lines** (☎ 800/327–9501); **Clipper Cruise Line** (☎ 800/325–0010); **Cunard Line** (☎ 800/5–CUNARD); **Holland America Lines** (☎ 800/628–4855); **Krystal Cruises** (☎ 800/446–6645); **Princess Cruises** (☎ 800/421–0522); **Royal Caribbean Cruise Line** (☎ 800/327–6700); **Royal Cruise Line** (☎ 800/227–4534); **Royal Viking Line** (☎ 800/422–8000); and **Seaborn Cruise Line** (☎ 800/929–9595). Bookings are generally handled through a travel agent.

By Train and Bus
There is no train service to Acapulco from anywhere in the United States or Canada. Buses to Acapulco can be boarded on the U.S. side of the border, but the trip is not recommended; even the most experienced travelers find the journey exhausting and uncomfortable. Bus service from Mexico City to Acapulco, however, is excellent. First-class buses are comfortable and in good condition, and the trip takes 5½ hours. They leave every hour on the half-hour from the Tasqueña station. A first-class ticket costs about $20, one way. There is also deluxe service, called *Servicio Diamante,* with airplanelike reclining seats, refreshments, rest rooms, air-conditioning, movies, and hostess service. The deluxe buses leave four times a day, also from the Tasqueña station, and cost about $32. *Futura* service (regular reclining seats, air-conditioning, and a rest room) costs $23.

Getting Around

Getting around in Acapulco is quite simple. You can walk to many places and the bus costs only 30¢. Taxis cost less than they do in the United States, so most tourists quickly become avid taxi takers.

By Bus
The buses tourists use the most are those that go from Puerto Marqués to Caleta and stop at the fairly conspicuous metal bus stops along the way. If you want to go from the zócalo to the Costera, catch the bus that says "La Base" (the naval base near the Hyatt Regency). This bus detours through Old Acapulco and returns to the Costera

just east of the Ritz Hotel. If you want to follow the Costera for the entire route, take the bus marked "Hornos." Buses to Pie de la Cuesta or Puerto Marqués say so on the front. The Puerto Marqués bus runs about every half hour and is always crowded. If you are headed anywhere along the Costera Miguel Alemán, it's best to go by the Aca Tur bus. For 60¢ you can ride in deluxe, air-conditioned buses that travel up and down the main drag from the Hyatt to the Caleta hotels every 10 minutes.

By Taxi
How much you pay depends on what type of taxi you get. The most expensive are hotel taxis. A price list that all drivers adhere to is posted in hotel lobbies. Fares in town are usually about $2 to $5; to go from downtown to the Princess Hotel or Caleta beach is about $10 to $16. Hotel taxis are by far the plushest and are kept in the best condition.

Cabs that cruise with their roof light off occasionally carry a price list but usually charge by zone. You need to reach an agreement with these drivers, but the fare should be less than it would be at a hotel. There is a minimum charge of $1.50. Some taxis that cruise have hotel or restaurant names stenciled on the side but are not affiliated with an establishment. Before you go anywhere by cab, find out what the price should be and agree with the driver on a price.

The cheapest taxis are the little Volkswagens. Officially there is a $1.50 minimum charge, but many cab drivers don't stick to it. A normal—i.e., Mexican-priced—fare is about $2 to go from the zócalo to the Elcano hotel, but lots of luck getting a taxi driver to accept that from a tourist. Rates are about 50% higher at night, and though tipping is not expected, Mexicans usually leave small change.

You can also hire a taxi by the hour or the day. Prices vary from about $18 an hour for a hotel taxi to $13 an hour for a street taxi. Never let a taxi driver decide where you should eat or shop, since many get kickbacks from some of the smaller stores and restaurants.

By Horse and Carriage
Buggy rides up and down the Costera are available evenings. There are two routes: from Papagayo Park to the zócalo and from Condesa Beach to the Naval base. Each costs about $10.

Guided Tours

Orientation Tours
There are organized tours everywhere in Acapulco, from the red-light district to the lagoon. Tours to Mexican fiestas in the evenings or the markets in the daytime are easy to arrange. Tour operators have offices around town and desks in many of the large hotels. If your hotel can't arrange a tour, contact **Consejeros de Viajes** at the Torre de Acapulco, Costera Miguel Alemán 1252, ☎ 74/84–74–00, or **Acuario**, Costera Miguel Alemán, opposite the Plaza Hotel, ☎ 74/85–61–00.

Important Addresses and Numbers

Consulates
United States (Club del Sol Hotel, ☎ 74/85–72–07); **Canada** (Club del Sol Hotel, ☎ 74/85–66–21).

Emergencies
Police, ☎ 74/85–06–50. The **Red Cross** can be reached at ☎ 74/85–41–00. Two reliable hospitals are **Hospital Privado Magallanes**, Wil-

frido Massiue 2, ☎ 74/85–65–44, and **Hospital Centro Médico,** J. Arevalo 99, ☎ 74/82–46–92.

Doctors and Dentists

Your hotel and the Secretaría de Turismo can locate an English-speaking doctor. But English-speaking doctors don't come cheap—house calls are about $150. The U.S. consular representative has a list of doctors and dentists, but it's against their policy to recommend anyone in particular.

English-Language Bookstores

English-language books and periodicals can be found at **Sanborns,** a reputable American-style department-store chain, and at the newsstands in some of the larger hotels. Many small newsstands and the Super-Super carry the *Mexico City News,* an English-language daily newspaper that occasionally carries articles about Acapulco.

Travel Agencies

American Express, at La Gran Plaza shopping center, Costera Miguel Alemán 1628 (locals 7, 8, and 9), ☎ 74/69–11–00 to 09, and **Viajes Wagon-Lits,** at Scenic Highway 5255 (lobby of Las Brisas Hotel), ☎ 74/84–16–50, ext. 392.

Visitor Information

The **State of Guerrero Department of Tourism (SEFOTUR;** Costera Miguel Alemán 187, across from Bodegas Aurrerá, ☎ 74/86–91–64 or 74/86–91–71) is open Monday–Saturday 9–2 and 4–7. The staff speaks English, has brochures and maps on other parts of Mexico, and can help you find a hotel room.

10 Oaxaca

The geographic, ethnic, and culinary diversity of Oaxaca has made the state a favorite of Mexico aficionados. Descendents of the Mixtec and Zapotec Indians, who built the Monte Albán and Mitla complexes near Oaxaca City, comprise the majority of residents; their handicrafts and festivals are extremely colorful. Although less exotic, the state's coastal developments of Puerto Escondido and Bahías de Huatulco are beloved by surfers and beach bums.

Updated by
Patricia Alisau

THE CITY OF OAXACA (Wah-*hah*-kah), one of Mexico's colonial treasures, sits on the vast, fertile, mile-high plateau of the Oaxaca Valley, encircled by the majestic Sierra Madre del Sur mountain range. It is located in the geographic center of the state of Oaxaca, of which it is the capital.

The state, Mexico's fifth largest, is situated in the country's southernmost section, bordered by the states of Chiapas to the east, Veracruz and Puebla to the north, and Guerrero (whose touristic claims to fame are Acapulco and Ixtapa) to the west. The south of Oaxaca State spans 509 kilometers (316 miles) of lush tropical Pacific coastline with magnificent beaches. Until recently, the beaches of Oaxaca have been relatively unknown and unexploited, except for the long-established small fishing town and seaside hideaway of Puerto Escondido and the even smaller town of Puerto Angel. But now Huatulco, 125 kilometers (75 miles) west of Puerto Escondido, is beginning to appear on maps as the government works to turn it into a world-class resort.

Oaxaca is endowed with a vast geographic and ethnic diversity. Together with neighboring Chiapas, Oaxaca has the largest Indian population of the region, which explains its richness and variety in handicrafts, folklore, culture, and gastronomy. Most are descendants of the Mixtec or Zapotec Indians, whose villages dot the valleys, mountainsides, and coastal lowlands. Today two out of every three Oaxaqueños are Indians and come from one of 16 distinct groups within the Mixtecs and Zapotecs. They speak 52 dialects of eight distinct languages and for the most part can barely understand one another. If they speak Spanish, it is a second language to them.

The Zapotecs and Mixtecs flourished in the area thousands of years ago. The archaeological ruins of Monte Albán, Mitla, and Yagul are among the vivid reminders of their splendid legacies. Within a 40-kilometer (25-mile) radius of the city of Oaxaca, they all bear witness to highly religious, creative, advanced civilizations that were knowledgeable in astronomy and had a system of writing that may be one of the oldest in North America.

Their civilizations were conquered by the Aztecs, who in the 15th century gave Oaxaca its name: *Huaxyaca*. In the Náhuatl language it probably means "by the acacia grove," referring to the location of the Aztec military base. Then came the Spanish conquest in 1528. The Spanish monarch, Charles V, gave Cortés the title of Marqués del Valle de Oaxaca as a reward for his conquest of Mexico. Cortés preferred to live elsewhere, so an estate was never built on the lands conferred with the title, but Cortés's descendants kept the property until Mexico's bloody 1910 Revolution.

Oaxaca's gift to Mexican politics was Presidents Benito Juárez and Porfirio Díaz, two of the country's most important leaders. Juárez, a Zapotec, was a sheepherder from San Pablo Gelatao, a settlement about 64 kilometers (40 miles) north of Oaxaca. As a child he spoke only his native Zapotec tongue. Often referred to as Mexico's Abraham Lincoln, Juárez was trained for the clergy but later studied law and entered politics. He was elected governor of the state (1847), chief justice of the Supreme Court of Mexico (1857), and then president (1859–1872), defeating efforts to convert the country into a monarchy under Maximilian. Porfirio Díaz, one of Juárez's generals, seized the presidency by coup in 1877 and held office until overthrown by the Mexican Revolution in 1910.

Today the capital—officially, Oaxaca de Juárez—is still the state's major attraction, with a population of about 180,000 and more than 2 million visitors a year. The city is traditionally Indian, but cosmopolitan touches are everywhere. Women and children sell woven bracelets and men offer shoeshines around the city's many parks and squares while painters and weavers display their wares on grassy lawns. Stark-white galleries exhibit the pottery, textiles, and fanciful wooden animals, called *alebrijes,* that have drawn international attention to Oaxaca's artisans. Mariachis blare in the streets; salsa, rock, and jazz bands percolate in intimate clubs.

The large, lively, and Victorian-looking zócalo draws both visitors and locals to its shaded walks, commodious park benches, and, in its center, an ornate bandstand. Closed to motor-vehicle traffic, the zócalo still bustles at all hours of the day.

Oaxaca celebrates Mexican holidays and its own state's fiestas with an intensity of color, tradition, and talent that attracts visitors in hordes. Hotels are usually booked solid around the Day of the Dead and Christmas, but the tourist office (*see* Important Addresses and Numbers *in* Oaxaca City Essentials, *below*) can often help. *El Día de Muertos* begins with graveyard celebrations in the nearby villages of Xoxo and Atzompa on October 31 and ends in the cemeteries on November 2, when families partake in the favorite food of the dead; in between, the city, and especially the zócalo, are abuzz with activity. On December 23, the *Noche de Rabanos* (Night of the Radishes), the zócalo is packed with growers and artists displaying their hybrid radishes carved and arranged in tableaux that depict everything from Nativity scenes to space travel. Prizes are awarded for the biggest and the best, and the competition is fierce. Other arrangements are made with *flores immortales* (small dried flowers) or *totomoxtl* (corn husks). Bring plenty of film.

Oaxaca's other major celebration is the *Guelaguetza* (Zapotec for "offering" or "gift"), held on the last two Mondays in July. Dancers from all the various mountain and coastal communities converge on the city bearing tropical fruits, baskets, weavings, and pottery. They perform elaborate dances in authentic costumes from early morning until late at night at the Guelaguetza Auditorium, often shown on maps as *Lunes del Cerro* (Monday of the Hill). Various hotels in town offer mini-Guelaguetzas at night; the best is at the Hotel Camino Real Oaxaca on Wednesday and Friday.

EXPLORING OAXACA CITY

Numbers in the margin correspond to points of interest on the Oaxaca City map.

The colonial heart of Oaxaca is laid out in a simple grid, with all major attractions within walking distance of one another. Most explorations of the town begin at the shady **zócalo,** the heart of the city and its pedestrian-only main square. On the south side of the ❶ zócalo is the splendid 19th-century neoclassical **Palacio de Gobierno** (State Capitol). The fascinating murals inside depict the history and cultures of Oaxaca.

❷ On the zócalo's northwest corner is the **Catedral Metropolitana de Oaxaca.** Begun in 1544, it was partially destroyed by earthquakes

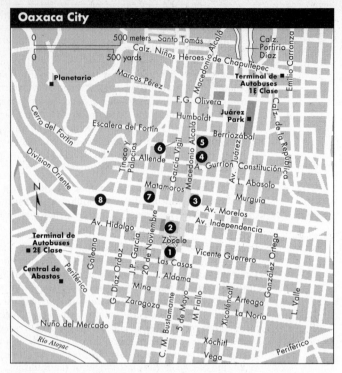

and not finished until 1733. The facade is Baroque, with a wood-cogged clock presented to the city by the king of Spain. *Av. Indepen-dencia 50,* ☎ *951/6–55–80.* ☉ *Daily 7 AM–9 PM.*

From the northeast corner of the zócalo, head up the pedestrian mall on Calle Macedonio Alcalá. Pastel, restored colonial mansions and some of Oaxaca's best galleries, shops, and restaurants line this street. It is also lively and well-lit at night, and there are frequent outdoor arts-and-crafts exhibits. Of particular note is the **Museo de Oaxaca** (also known as the **Museo de Arte Contemporaneo de Oaxaca**), housed in a former colonial residence. (The building is often erroneously called the "Casa de Cortes" but, in fact, the conqueror never built a home for himself in Oaxaca.) Inside are exhibits featuring the crafts and art-works of local artists in a variety of media. Be sure to check out what remains of the frescoes in the second-floor gallery at the front of the building. *Calle Macedonio Alcalá 202,* ☎ *951/6–84–99.* ☛ *Donations appreciated.* ☉ *Wed.–Mon. 10:30–8, closed Tues.*

A few blocks farther on you will come to the **Iglesia y Ex-Convento de Santo Domingo,** the church and ex-monastery of Santo Domingo. It is one of the most brilliantly decorated churches in Oaxaca, a city renowned for its many churches. The 16th century monastery has an ornate carved facade between two high bell towers. The interior is a profusion of white and gold, typical of the energy with which Mex-ico seized on the Baroque style and made of it something unique. *Calle Macedonio Alcalá and A. Gurrión,* ☎ *951/6–3720.* ☉ *Daily 7–1 and 4–8.*

Part of the old convent alongside the church houses the **Museo Regional de Oaxaca,** or state museum, which is laid out in a series of galleries around the cloister. This ethnological collection focuses on the various Indian groups within Oaxaca. The centerpiece of the collection is the gold and jade treasures taken from the tombs at Monte Albán, the Mixtec and Zapotec ruin just outside Oaxaca. There is also a large collection of ceremonial masks and costumes from the different tribes of the valley; some of the Indian women who come into town for the market still wear traditional costumes, and with a bit of study here at the museum, you will be able to identify their home villages. The other part of the old convent next to the church, a military barracks until January 1994, is being converted into a Museum of Colonial Art and already has some pieces on display. ☎ *951/6–29–91.* ☛ *Both museums $3, free on Sun. and national holidays.* ☉ *Tues.–Fri. 10–6, weekends 10–5. Closed Mon.*

As you leave the church and enter the wide Santo Domingo Plaza, you are likely to be accosted by Indian boys selling rough sketches on bark (they make an easy-to-carry gift) and a variety of other crafts. From the front of the plaza, walk west on Calle Allende one block to Calle **❻** García Vigil. Turn right and proceed a block and a half to the **Museo Casa de Benito Juárez** (the Juárez House Museum). Memorabilia of the Mexican hero is displayed in this 19th-century colonial house where he was a servant during his youth. *Calle García Vigil 609,* ☎ *951/6–18–60.* ☛ *$1, free on Sun. and holidays.* ☉ *Tues.–Sun. 9–7.*

Backtracking toward the zócalo, take García Vigil south to Morelos and **❼** head west on Morelos to the **Museo de Arte Prehispánico "Rufino Tamayo"** (Tamayo Museum of Pre-Hispanic Art). This old, carefully restored colonial mansion with interior courtyard has a small but excellent collection of pre-Hispanic pottery and sculpture. It was originally the private collection of the late painter-muralist Rufino Tamayo, who presented it to his hometown in 1979. There are exhibits from all over the country, arranged geographically and chronologically. Perhaps the most delightful item is the model of a ball court for sacred Indian games with figurines representing the participants and spectators. *Av. Morelos 503,* ☎ *951/6–47–50.* ☛ *$2.* ☉ *Mon. and Wed.–Sat. 10–2 and 4–7, Sun. 10–3. Closed Tues.*

When you leave the museum, turn right and walk three blocks until **❽** you reach the Baroque **Basílica de la Soledad,** the Basilica of Our Lady of Solitude. This 1682 structure houses the statue of the Virgin, Oaxaca's patron saint. She stands in a gilded shrine and wears a magnificent robe of jewel-studded black velvet. She was found in the pack of a stray mule that had died. This event was construed by the faithful as a miracle, and the church was built to commemorate it. Believed to have supernatural healing powers, the statue remains the object of fervent piety for the devout populace. *Av. Independencia 107 at Galeana,* ☎ *951/6–7566.* ☉ *Daily 6 AM–8 PM.*

Excursions from Oaxaca

The onetime holy city of more than 40,000 Zapotecs, **Monte Albán** is among the most interesting and well-preserved archaeological ruins in the country. Experts estimate that a mere 10% of the site is uncovered; excavations are constantly taking place to unearth more knowledge about the fascinating Zapotec culture. Monte Albán overlooks the Oaxaca Valley from a flattened mountaintop 9 kilometers (5½ miles) southwest of Oaxaca. The Zapotecs leveled the area in about 600 BC. They arranged the buildings along a perfect north–south axis, with the exception of one structure thought to have been an observatory that is more closely aligned with the stars than with the earth's poles. The oldest of the four temples is the **Temple of the Dancers,** so named because of the remains of elaborately carved stone figures that once covered the building. The figures are nude and, because of their distorted positions, have since come to be thought of not as dancers but as patients in what might have been a hospital or school of medicine. Another major point of interest is the ball court, site of a complicated game—part basketball, part soccer. The players' objective was to navigate the ball into a lowered area in the opponents' court with only their hips and elbows. There is some speculation that the captain of the losing team was sacrificed, but this is dubious. About 1,000 years ago, the Zapotecs were conquered by the Mixtecs. The Mixtecs never lived in Monte Albán but used it as a city of the dead, a massive cemetery of lavish tombs. More than 160 have been discovered, and in 1932 **Tomb 7** yielded a treasure unequaled in North America. Inside were more than 500 priceless Mixtec objects, including gold breastplates; jade, pearl, ivory, and gold jewelry; and fans, masks, and belt buckles of precious stones and metals. All are now on view at the Regional Museum of Oaxaca.

There are special tourist buses to Monte Albán from the Mesón del Angel hotel running every hour or so from 8:30 to 3:30; the last bus back is at 5:30. The fare is about $2 round-trip. A taxi from the zócalo should run $4 or $5. ☛ $3, Sun. and holidays free. ۞ Daily 8–5.

Some 40 kilometers (25 miles) southeast of Oaxaca is **Mitla,** another complex of ceremonial structures started by the Zapotecs but taken over and heavily influenced by the Mixtecs. The name, from the Aztec word *mictlan,* means "place of the dead." The architecture here is totally different from that of any of the other ruins in the area. The stone walls are inlaid with smaller stones cut into geometric patterns, forming a mosaic that is sometimes almost Grecian in appearance. Unlike other ancient buildings in North America, there are no human figures or mythological events represented—only abstract designs. A trip here can be nicely combined with a stop at the Tule Tree (*see* Off the Beaten Track, *below*); the colonial church of Mitla, built against the walls of other Mixtec ruins; and the large open-air crafts market by the ruins. ☛ $2, Sun. and holidays free. ۞ Archaeological zone: daily 8:30–6.

About 30 kilometers (19 miles) southeast of Oaxaca on the road to Mitla is **Yagul,** another group of ruins. Not as elaborate as Monte Albán, but set in a lovely spot on top of a hill, Yagul is certainly beautiful and interesting enough to make it worth the trip. This city is predominantly a fortress that is set slightly above a group of palaces and temples; it includes a ball court and more than 30 uncovered underground tombs. ☛ $1.75, Sun. and holidays free. ۞ Archaeological zone: daily 8–6.

Off the Beaten Track

No trip to Oaxaca would be complete without visiting at least some of the dozen or more villages surrounding the city. Many are known for the skills of their artisans, who use both ancient and modern techniques to create their folk-art pieces; they often live among generations of families who have their own special designs for pottery, woven rugs, and wood carvings. A trip to a few of these towns can be combined with a visit to at least one archaeological site, a colonial church or two, and a regional market.

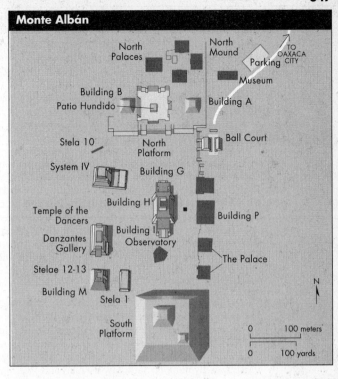

Monte Albán

North Palaces · North Mound · Parking · TO OAXACA CITY · Museum · Building B · Patio Hundido · Building A · Stela 10 · North Platform · Ball Court · System IV · Building G · Building H · Temple of the Dancers · Building I · Observatory · Building P · Danzantes Gallery · The Palace · Stelae 12-13 · Building M · Stela 1 · South Platform · N · 0 100 meters · 0 100 yards

A west-to-south counterclockwise route from the city takes in **Atzompa,** where the descendants of Teodora Blanca create fanciful *muñecas* (dolls) from clay and other potters make the region's traditional green-glazed plates, bowls, and cups, all in array on Tuesday market day. In **Arrazola,** artists carve *alebrijes,* grand dragons and snakes from copal wood, then paint them with surrealistic designs in vivid colors. On Thursdays, **Zaachila** has the most authentic livestock and food market in the area, while **Etla's** Wednesday market is famous for its cheeses, mole, and chocolate. The southern route goes to **San Bartolo Coyotepec,** the center for glossy black pottery sold in people's yards and from a multistalled building on the side of the road. In **Santo Tomás Jalietza,** women work on small, backstrap looms in the center of town, weaving elaborate belts and table runners from pastel cotton. Friday's market in **Ocotlan** is known for its handicrafts, especially woven baskets, and for its handcrafted machetes and knives, famous throughout Mexico. Some of the machetes are inscribed with colorful local sayings.

An eastward route includes **Teotitlán del Valle,** where giant rug looms sit in front of many houses; **Santa Ana del Valle,** where Lucio Aquino is famous for his rugs; and **Tlacolula,** where the Sunday market spreads for blocks around a Baroque 16th-century chapel. On Sundays it seems that all of Oaxaca take this route, starting at the Tule Tree (*see below*), moving to the ruins of Mitla, and then on to the crafts centers and market. The markets on other routes are held on special days throughout the week, and you can easily fill a week with tours and never see the same sight twice. If you have to budget your time, use tour guides for these trips so you don't miss out on the fascinating details.

Standing 6½ kilometers (4 miles) east of Oaxaca in Santa María del Tule is the **Tule Tree** (located on Tehuantepec Highway en route to Mitla), a huge ahuehuete cypress that is estimated to be more than 2,000 years old. One of the biggest in the world, it is some 140 feet high with roots buried more than 60 feet in the earth; it takes 35 adults with their arms outstretched to embrace it. The tree is the traditional center of the town of Santa María and is larger than the church behind it.

SHOPPING

Oaxaca City was and remains the focus of Indian life, mostly that of Zapotecs and Mixtecs who live in the valley and nearby mountains. They come to town to buy and sell, especially on Saturdays. Although the market is no longer as colorful as it was in D. H. Lawrence's day (see his *Mornings in Mexico*), it remains an authentic exotic spectacle. This is the largest Indian market in all of Mexico, and only Michoacán and Chiapas can rival Oaxaca in the variety and quality of crafts. Expect hectic activity and bright colors. (It might come as a surprise not to hear much Spanish spoken at the markets but rather the singsong Zapotec and Mixtec languages in which changes in the pitch of the voice change the meaning of the word.)

The Saturday market is held at the **Central de Abastos** (Supply Center) on the southern edge of the town center. Late Friday and early Saturday, Indians stream to this site, spreading their wares over blocks and blocks of empty lots and through an enormous central warehouse. By noon on Saturday, the market is swarming with thousands of sellers and shoppers, and the experience can be quite overwhelming. Don't burden yourself with a lot of camera equipment or purses and bags; you'll have a hard enough time keeping track of companions in the jostling, bumping crowd. If you see something you really want, purchase it on the spot—you'll never find your way back. The market is active during the rest of the week, too; if you go then, you can check out the mounds of multicolored chilies and herbs, the piles of tropical fruit, the aisles of baskets, rugs, and jewelry. Some sections are filled with plastic household products, others with automotive and electronic gadgets. But it's on Saturday that you see the best handicrafts: *huipiles* (embroidered blouses) that vary with the village of origin; *rebozos* (shawls) of cotton and silk; pottery shaped without a wheel; colorful woven baskets; wooden and tin toys; machetes with leather sheaths. Bargaining is expected.

The several market areas in Oaxaca are active daily, though Saturday is the busiest day. **Mercado Benito Juárez** and **Mercado 20 de Noviembre** are two blocks south of the zócalo between Calle las Cases and Calle Mina. This two-block area has some crafts, but most tempting are the food stalls, which serve simple meals for locals and budget travelers alike. Two blocks farther south is **Mercado de Artesanías,** at the corner of Calles José P. García and Ignacio Zaragoza, which features mostly textiles. While they tend their stands, Trique Indian women and children weave wall hangings with simple backstrap looms.

Prospective folk-art buyers in Oaxaca City and surrounding villages should heed one major caveat, or risk being saddled with more than they expected. It is not too difficult to ship your purchases home from many of the city's shops and shipping services, provided you have a receipt showing that you paid the 10% sales tax on all items purchased. Many of the artisans have begun giving out official government tax receipts; but if you buy from one who does not, you may have a hard time finding someone to ship your wares for you, and when you do, it will be very expensive. Ask for receipts, and for referrals to shipping agents. Also, check out the displays at the shops in town and learn about quality and design before you start spending lots of pesos.

Besides having a mother lode of markets, Oaxaca also has some spectacular shops and galleries, most near the zócalo. The huge, sprawling **Fonart** store (Manuel M. Bravo 116 at García Vigil, ☎ 951/6–57–64) has a representative selection of arts and crafts, not only from Oaxaca but also from other regions of the country. Several gallery-style shops feature the true masters of the folk arts. The prices can be quite high, but as your eye becomes adjusted to the differences in quality and technique, you can appreciate the talent involved. **Artesanías "Chimalli"** (García Vigil 513–A, ☎ 951/4–21–01) has shelves and shelves of *alebrijes*—bright pink, orange, and purple carved copal-wood cats, dogs, tigers, rabbits, and snakes with comical expressions and fantasy shapes. The shop's inventory also includes decorative tin picture frames and wooden chairs painted with a likeness of Pancho Villa. **La Mano Mágica** (Macedonio Alcalá 203, ☎ 951/6–42–75) is a large gallery inside a hacienda, with rotating shows from Oaxaca's premier artists, working on-site in either pottery, textiles, wood or paint. Such folk art as life-size papier mâché skeletons and devils add a macabre touch to the scene, while vats of boiling dye steam in the open patio. Prices tend to be a little high here. **Yalalag** (Macedonio Alcalá 104, ☎ 951/6–21–08) has delicately woven huipiles and a courtyard filled with tons of black Oaxacan pottery plus miniature ceramic chapels and Spanish dolls. **Artesanías de Oaxaca** (A. Gurrión, corner of Macedonia Alcalá, ☎ 951/4–32–01) has a more eccentric selection than most of its neighbors; the Mestas family is happy to guide you through their treasure of masks, traditional costumes, antique hobby horses, and other unusual wood crafts. **Oro de Monte Albán** (Macedonia Alcala 307, ☎ 951/6–18–12) is one of several branches of the store selling gold and silver reproductions of pre-Colombian jewelry found in the tombs of royalty at the Monte Albán archaeological site. Ten different pieces, including Xipe, the god of Spring, are beautifully reproduced. Leading local artists exhibit and sell their paintings and sculptures at **Galería Arte de Oaxaca** (Trujano 102, ☎ 951/4–09–10).

Several shops specialize in gold and silver jewelry designed in the style of the jewels found at Monte Albán. You'll find a number of them along Calle Macedonia Alcalá and A. Gurrión. Most shops close from 2 to 4 in the afternoon; many are closed Sunday.

DINING

Though you can dine on overpriced Continental food, one of the highlights of visiting Oaxaca is the opportunity to enjoy its traditional cuisine, one of the finest and most elaborate in all Mexico. Oaxaca is known as "the land of seven moles" because of its seven distinct kinds of multispiced mole sauces. Only one of them is made with chocolate, rivaling that of Puebla (mole poblano) in thickness and flavor because of the outstanding quality of the local chocolate. Tamales stuffed with cheese and chicken or pork are another treat. The home- and factory-produced mezcal differs in flavor with its maker and can be as high as 80 proof, so be careful when you imbibe. One variety, slightly sweet, is flavored with oranges; others are sold in festive ceramic containers. The open-air cafés surrounding the zócalo are good for drinks, snacks, and people-watching, with the scene changing from peaceful serenity over early-morning coffee to pulsating frenzy in late evening. If you want to join the crowds at these restaurants, the *comida corrida* (set menu served at midday) makes an economical choice.

Except at restaurants in the expensive ($$$) category, dress tends to be casual.

CATEGORY	COST*
$$$	$25–$35
$$	$15–$25
$	under $15

per person, excluding drinks and tip

$$$ **El Refectorio.** The dining room at the Hotel Camino Real does not disappoint. The best meal is the Sunday champagne brunch, served from 1 to 6. The regular menu offers high-end versions of local dishes such as chicken in mole, Oaxacan (mole-filled) tamales, and fish fillet baked in banana leaf. Choose a table overlooking the garden courtyard, and linger over your meal in this 16th-century convent. ✗ *Hotel Presidente Oaxaca, Cinco de Mayo 300,* ☎ *951/6–06–11. AE, DC, MC, V.*

$$$ **El Tule.** On a hill above town, the Hotel Victoria's prime location is enhanced by this veranda dining room that serves international fare in addition to such Oaxacan specialties as chicken in mole and *queso asadero,* Oaxacan cheese baked to a crisp crust on the outside and creamy on the inside. The restaurant overlooks the hotel gardens and the valley below. ✗ *Hotel Victoria, Km 545 of Rte. 190,* ☎ *951/5–26–33. AE, MC, V.* ◷ *Daily 7 AM–10:30 PM.*

$$ **Catedral.** This local favorite calls itself the House of Fillets. It offers six meat fillet entrées, as well as regional dishes, hamburgers, sandwiches, and a variety of soups. The most pleasant place to dine is by the fountain in the courtyard. ✗ *1 block north of the Catedral, at the corner of Calle García Vigil and Av. Morelos,* ☎ *951/6–32–85. MC, V.*

$$ **El Asador Vasco.** Basque (*vasco*) cuisine is featured here along with an
★   outstanding Oaxacan version of mole sauce—steamy, black, and marvelous on chicken or turkey—and a sumptuous gratiné of oysters in chipotle sauce. The tables overlooking the zócalo are in great demand. Live serenading by the *tuna* student minstrels evokes medieval Spain (Thurs.–Sat. evenings starting at 8:30). ✗ *On the west side of the zócalo, upstairs, Portal de Flores 10-A,* ☎ *951/6–97–19. AE, DC, MC, V.*

$$ **La Casita.** Many in the know consider this the best place to enjoy the cuisine of Oaxaca. The actual dishes are displayed on a counter by the door, so you can see what your food will look like before you order. This eatery is especially famous for *chapulines* (grasshoppers, in season in the fall months), but there are also more conventional dishes, such as enchiladas with chicken and spicy mole sauce. Try to get a table by the window (it's on the second floor), so you can watch the activity in the park below while you dine. ✗ *Av. Hidalgo 612 (south of Alameda de León),* ☎ *951/6–29–17. AE, MC, V.* ◷ *Daily noon–7.*

$$ **La Morsa.** The name means "walrus," the informal palapa setting is tastefully tropical amid gardens and fountains, and super-fresh seafood is the specialty. Try the *platón de mariscos* (shellfish platter) with oysters, shrimp, squid, and octopus; or fish fillet *a la veracruzana* (with tomato sauce), *a la mexicana* (with green chile sauce), or with a creamy chipotle sauce. The oyster dishes are a bargain. ✗ *Calzada (not Calle)*

Porfirio Díaz 240, Col. Reforma, ☎ *951/5–22–13. Reservations recommended. AE, MC, V.* ⊙ *Tues.–Sun. noon–8. Closed Mon.*

$$ **Nuu-Luu.** The name in Mixtec, "picturesque place," couldn't be more
★ appropriate. Located in a pretty suburb in the northern part of town (just 8 minutes from the zócalo), this delightful open-air restaurant, which just enlarged its dining space to 30 tables, overlooks a large country garden lush with exotic fruit trees. Renowned chef-owner Guadalupe Salinas prepares a changing array of Oaxacan specialties, including a spectacular mole made with seven kinds of chiles; it's served with turkey, chicken, or pork. The cost of a meal that allows you to sample nearly everything on the menu is extremely reasonable. ✗ *Iturbide 100, San Felipe del Agua,* ☎ *951/5–31–87. Reservations recommended, especially on weekends. (Private transportation is provided from and to your hotel.) AE, MC, V.* ⊙ *Daily 8–6.*

$ **Del Jardín.** Everybody seems to wind up at this place, the happening café on the zócalo from 8 till late. The Oaxacan tamales (with chicken and mole) and piquant chile rellenos are good, as are many of the sandwiches, soups, tacos, and more substantial pork and seafood dishes on the menu. ✗ *Portal de Flores 10 (west side of zócalo),* ☎ *951/6–26–29. AE, MC, V.*

$ **El Biche Pobre "2."** This place is a bit of a hike from the city center, but your bill for the fine *botana surtida* (sampler plate)—with tamales, *sopas* (soups), chile rellenos, croquettes, and other treats— will be astonishingly low. You can walk the meal off afterward in nearby Juárez Park. ✗ *Calz. de la República 600 at Calle Hidalgo,* ☎ *951/3–46–36. AE, MC, V.* ⊙ *Daily 1–6.*

$ **El Mesón.** The spanking-clean dining room and open-air kitchen in
★ this restaurant right off the zócalo make it a favorite for locals and visitors, who stop by for a snack or full meal from the long paper menu, where you check off your items of choice. Try the *cebollitas* (grilled whole green onions) as a side dish with your *cecina enchilada* (grilled strips of pork covered with chile powder) and fresh corn tortillas made at the tortilleria at the entrance. For an intense sugar fix, have a cup of rich Oaxacan chocolate and a slice of nut or cheese pie. ✗ *Av. Hidalgo 805, at Valdivieso,* ☎ *951/6–27–29. MC, V.* ⊙ *Daily 8 AM–midnight.*

LODGING

Oaxaca has no luxury resorts, but it does have some magnificently restored properties and dozens of smaller, moderately priced accommodations, most in downtown locations.

CATEGORY	COST*
$$$	$90–$160
$$	$40–$90
$	under $40

All prices are for a standard double room, excluding 10% tax.

$$$ **Hotel Camino Real Oaxaca.** A monastic air lingers in the breezy patios
★ and small enclosed gardens of this beautifully restored former convent (1576), designated a National Monument; it became part of the Camino Real hotel chain in September 1994. One of the hotel's three courtyards, the one with the large stone basin in the center, is still called *La Lavenderia* (the laundry); it is where the nuns of the convent used to wash their clothes. The rooms, of course, are far from austere; all have deluxe conveniences and are undergoing a million-dollar remodeling for further soundproofing (it should be finished by 1997).

Stop in for a drink and look around even if you don't stay here. ☎ *Cinco de Mayo 300, 06800, ☎ 951/6–06–11 or 800/7–CAMINO, ⅢX 951/6–07–32. 91 rooms. Restaurant, 2 bars, pool, travel services. AE, DC, MC, V.*

$$ Mesón de Angel. This large hotel near the markets is a favorite with Mexican families, groups, and traveling salesmen. There is a big pool in the hotel garden and attractive newly remodeled rooms with terraces, orthopedic mattresses, desk fans, and TVs (channels in Spanish only). Tourist buses to Monte Albán and Mitla leave from here. ☎ *F. J. Mina 518, 68000, ☎ 951/6–66–66, ⅢX 951/4–54–05. 50 rooms. Restaurant, pool, travel services. No credit cards.*

$$ Misión de los Angeles. Though this resort-style hotel is a long way from the zócalo, its peaceful gardens and relaxed ambience make it a good choice. The hotel is near Plaza Juárez, a central park and plaza frequented more by locals than by tourists, and the commodious dining room is popular with tour groups. ☎ *Calzada Porfirio Díaz 102, 68000, ☎ 951/5–15–00, ⅢX 951/5–16–80. 173 rooms. 2 restaurants, 2 bars, jogging, pool, disco, tennis court, recreation room. AE, MC, V.*

$$ Victoria.
★ Surrounded by terraced grounds and well-kept gardens, this sprawling salmon-color complex is perched on a hill overlooking the city. Draw back your curtains at dawn and catch your breath at the view: Oaxaca awakening under the Sierra Madre. The hotel has a good restaurant, tennis court, heated pool, and disco, and the property is strewn with picture-perfect bougainvillea. Rooms, bungalows, and suites are available; be sure to request one with a view. ☎ *Km 545 of Mexico 190, 06800, ☎ 951/5–26–33, ⅢX 951/5–24–11. 149 rooms, suites, and bungalows. Restaurant, bar, pool, tennis court. AE, MC, V.*

$ Fortin Plaza. This modern six-story hotel, with beautifully landscaped gardens overlooking town and the surrounding mountains, is just downhill from the Victoria. Its rather modest exterior is offset by an exquisitely designed interior that makes lavish use of marble, wood, glass, and stone. Front balconied rooms offer the best views, but if you're looking for a good night's sleep, choose the quieter rear rooms. The hotel has a pool, but it's small and is sandwiched between the highway and the building. ☎ *Av. Venus 118, 68000, ☎ 951/5–77–77, ⅢX 951/5–13–28. 93 rooms. Restaurant, bar, pool. AE, DC, MC, V.*

$ Las Rosas. This small second-floor hotel half a block off the zócalo offers clean, basic rooms around a central courtyard at a price that's hard to beat. The owners are pleasant, and there are pretty mountain views from the little roof garden. ☎ *Trujano 112, ☎ 951/4–22–17. 19 rooms. MC, V.*

$ Marqués del Valle. Right on the zócalo and in the middle of things, the property's restaurant serves a good breakfast, from bananas and cream to hotcakes. The hallways can act like echo chambers for the cathedral bells from next door. ☎ *Portal de Clavería s/n, 68000, ☎ 951/6–32–95, ⅢX 951/6–99–61. 95 rooms. Restaurant, travel services. AE, DC, MC, V.*

$ Principal. This popular budget hotel—one of the best of the group—fills up quickly, but the owners can refer you to other hotels in the area as well as provide insider touring tips. Rooms in this colonial house face a bare central courtyard ringed by potted geranium plants. Each room has small folk-art touches, and the whole place has a friendly, homey feeling. ☎ *Cinco de Mayo 208, 68000, ☎ and ⅢX 951/6–25–35. 16 rooms. No credit cards.*

$ Villa Maria. Popular with Americans, Europeans, and Japanese, this compound is sprinkled with one-, two-, and three-bedroom furnished apartments overlooking a spacious patio. Friendly, bilingual hostess Maria Garcia makes her guests feel as though they're part of a family. Linens and dishes come with the units (which have suitable touches of Mexican decor), but phones, cable TV, and maid service are extra. It's a small hike to the main square from here, but taxis and buses run frequently. Rentals are by the week or month, with rates starting at $350 a month for a one-bedroom unit; advance reservations are advised. ⊞ *Arteaga 410, 6800,* ☎ *951/6–50–56,* FAX *951/4–25–62. 14 apartments. No credit cards.*

OAXACA CITY ESSENTIALS

Arriving and Departing

BY PLANE

Mexicana (☎ 800/531–7921, 951/6–73–52 in Oaxaca) offers service from Chicago to Oaxaca City with a stop in Mexico City to pick up more passengers. Otherwise, flights from the United States require travelers to change planes in Mexico City for either an **Aeromexico** (☎ 800/237–6639, 951/6–71–01 in Oaxaca) or **Mexicana** nonstop to Oaxaca City's **Benito Juárez Airport,** about 8 kilometers (5 miles) south of town. There is also service for triangle flight itineraries, including the Oaxacan coastal resorts of Huatulco or Puerto Escondido. Local domestic airlines serving Oaxaca are: **Aviacsa** (☎ 951/3–18–09) from Tuxtla Gutiérrez, Villahermosa, Mérida, and Cancún; **Aero Vega** (☎ 951/6–27–77) from Puerto Escondido; and **Aeromorelos** (☎ 951/6–30–10) from Puerto Escondido and Huatulco. Taxis are plentiful, and microbuses are available from the airport to hotels in town.

BY CAR

From Mexico City, you can take Mexico 190 (Pan American Highway) south and east through Puebla and Izúcar de Matamoros to Oaxaca—a distance of 546 kilometers (338 miles) along a rather curvy road. This route takes about six hours. Better is the new toll road (in operation since December 1994), which connects Mexico City to Oaxaca City via Tehuacan; it cuts down on curves and on driving time by about an hour and a half.

BY BUS

There are direct bus trips from Mexico City to Oaxaca, with innumerable stops in between. The first-class bus terminal is at Calzada Niños Héroes de Chapultepec at Emilio Carranza, ☎ 951/6–22–70. **ADO** (☎ 951/5–17–73) and **Cristóbal Colon** (☎ 951/5–12–14) both provide first-class service; Cristóbal Colon also offers deluxe-class service. The second-class bus station is on the Periferico at Las Casas, ☎ 951/6–57–76. Several other bus lines serve the surrounding states and have desks at one or both terminals. Most routes are tortuous and grueling, going through narrow mountain roads.

Guided Tours

Unless you're on a strict budget, take advantage of the many tour companies that offer guided trips to the archaeological sites, colonial churches and monasteries, outlying towns (some of which have weekly market days), and the folk-art centers. Each tour is different in character and color; prices start at $10. There are licensed individual guides as well, available through the tourism office and the various agencies for up to $17 per hour for a minimum of three persons. **Turismo El Convento de Oaxaca** (Calle Cinco de Mayo 300, in the Hotel Camino Real Oaxaca, ☎ 951/6–28–48), **Viajes Turísticos Mitla** (F. J. Mina 518, in the Hotel Mesón de Angel, ☎ 951/6–53–27 or 951/4–31–61), and **Agencia Marqués del Valle** (Portal de Clavería s/n, ☎ 951/4–69–70, 951/4–69–62, or 951/6–62–94) are among the most established agencies.

Important Addresses and Numbers

Consulate
The U.S. consular representative is at Macedonio Alcalá 201, int. 204 (☎ and ⛶ FAX 951/4–30–54). ☉ *Weekdays 9–2.*

Emergencies
Dial 06 locally for all emergencies, including police and hospital. The **police** direct line is ☎ 6–11–55 or 6–32–18; **hospital** (Red Cross) is ☎ 6–44–55 or 6–78–28.

Visitor Information
The English-speaking staff at the local tourist office can help plan your stay in the city as well as any excursions you might want to make to nearby ruins, such as Monte Albán, Mitla, and Yagul. *Cinco de Mayo 200 (corner of Morelos),* ☎ *951/6–48–28.* ☉ *Daily 8–8. (There is also a small branch at Independencia and García Vigil, no* ☎*,* ☉ *Daily 9–3 and 4–8.)*

THE OAXACA COAST

Oaxaca's 520-kilometer (322-mile) coastline is mainland Mexico's last Pacific frontier. Huatulco, 291 kilometers (180 miles) from the capital, is the newest project of Fonatur, the Mexican government's tourism developers. The Bahías de Huatulco, as the area is being called, covers 51,900 acres of mountain lowlands and coastal stretches, the vast majority of which have never been developed. The focal point of the master-planned development is a string of nine sheltered bays (bahías) swathed in golden sand beaches that stretch across 23 miles of the Pacific coastline.

Today Huatulco's beauty can best be seen from a boat (*see* Guided Tours *in* Oaxaca Coast Essentials, *below*), since most of the bays are inaccessible by road. Tangolunda Bay is the site of the area's major hotels. The towns of Santa Cruz de Huatulco and La Crucecita are being developed as well. The town of Santa María Huatulco, for which the tourism destination is named, is 18 kilometers (11 miles) from the bays and is largely ignored by developers.

Puerto Escondido, 111 kilometers (69 miles) west of Huatulco, has long been prime territory for international surfers. The town has the coast's first airport (not international) and is in many ways better developed for travelers than Huatulco. Puerto Angel, midway between the two airports, is the budget traveler's destination, with a ragtag selection of hotels and bungalows spread into the hills overlooking the bay and, incongruously, a military installation smack in its center.

Exploring

Numbers in the margin correspond to points of interest on the Oaxaca Coast map.

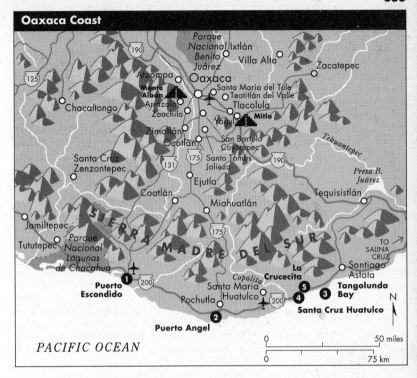

Oaxaca Coast

PACIFIC OCEAN

❶ **Puerto Escondido** is the first coastal town in Oaxaca south of Acapulco on Highway 200. The airport is on the northern edge of town,
as are the hotels favored by charter groups. **Playa Bacocho,** just south
of the airport, is a new housing-and-hotel development, and some
inviting bars, discos, and restaurants have opened in this area.

The main intersection in Puerto Escondido is at Highway 200 and
Avenida Alfonso Pérez Gasga, which travels south into the tourist
zone. On the north side of the highway this street is called Avenida
Oaxaca. Traveling down a steep hill, Avenue Gasga passes many of
the tourist hotels; at the bottom, traffic is prohibited and the street
becomes a four-block-long pedestrian mall lined with shops, restaurants, and lodgings that spread to the sands of the main beach. The
town market, **Mercado Benito Juárez,** is a long walk from most of the
tourist hotels, but it's more vibrant and entertaining than anything
along the tourist strip. The panga fleet is at the north end of this
beach, where the water is calm albeit polluted. **Laguna Agua Dulce** is
at the south end of the tourist strip, followed by **Marinero Beach,** then
a sharp outcropping of rocks, and, finally, the most famous beach of
all, **Zicatela.**

One of the top 10 surfing beaches in the world, Zicatela is a long
stretch of cream-color sand battered by the **Mexican Pipeline,** as this
stretch of mighty surf is called. In August and November international surfing championships are held here, and the town fills with
sun-bleached blonds of both sexes intent on serious surfing and hard
partying. Do not swim in these waters unless you can withstand
deadly undertows and rip currents. Instead, watch the surfers at sun-

set from the palapa restaurant at the Hotel Santa Fe, surely the prettiest hotel in town.

② **Puerto Angel,** about 81 kilometers (50 miles) southeast of Puerto Escondido, is a dusty village on a beautiful bay that, sadly, shows signs of pollution these days. The central town beach has been taken over by the navy, and the most popular swimming-and-sunning territory is at **Playa Panteón,** just past the oceanfront cemetery (*panteón* means cemetery). Other good (and less populated) swimming and snorkeling beaches are nearby. Six kilometers (about 4 miles) west of town is **Zipolite,** a bay known for its nude sunbathing; it's a favorite with surfers, aging hippies, and travelers who are content with a hammock on the beach and little else in the way of creature comforts. The undertow is extremely dangerous here—*zipolite* means killer, and several dozen foolish swimmers die in these waters every year.

The newly opened **Museum of the Sea Turtle** in Mazunte makes an interesting side trip from Puerto Angel. The popularity of turtle hunting once put the sea creatures, who come to this coastal area to lay eggs each year, in danger of extinction; Mazunte even had its own slaughter house for their meat. The carnage stopped with the 1990 government ban on turtle hunting, and now Mazunte is devoted to protecting the species. A dozen aquariums are filled with turtle specimens that once again flourish in the nearby ocean. To get here from Puerto Angel, take Highway 200 toward San Pedro Pochutla; about 15 kilometers (9 miles) past the town, follow the turnoff marked SAN AGUSTIN. A few miles down the road, you'll come to a sign for PLAYA MUZUNTE; ask for directions to the "museo," which is on the beach. *Playa Mazunte, no* ☎. ☛ *$2.* ☉ *Tues.–Sun. 9–4.*

Bahías de Huatulco, the Fonatur development, is still suffering growing pains. The vast majority of Huatulco's tourists rarely leave the bars, restaurants, and beaches of their respective resorts. The Hua-

③ tulco of the future is most evident at **Tangolunda Bay,** where the major hotels are in full swing, and parasailers glide over fleets of sightseeing boats. A small shopping/restaurant center is located across from the entrance to the Sheraton, but most of the shopping and dining take place in the towns of Santa Cruz and La Crucecita, each about 10 min-

④ utes from the hotels by taxi. **Santa Cruz** is located on the bay of the same name, where glass-bottom boats and sightseeing tours are available. The waterfront is lined with bright blue, pink, and orange shacks offering a disappointing selection of crafts and souvenirs for sale. A central zócalo with a wrought-iron gazebo has been built nearby, and tourists and locals alike mingle in the grassy plaza.

⑤ **La Crucecita,** just off Highway 200, is more developed, with a few condominium complexes and a central park. Modern buildings with arches and balconies are going up along the streets by the park, and this is becoming the place for hanging out at sidewalk cafés and shopping in boutiques. The bus station and long-distance telephone office are here, along with a smattering of budget rooms.

Dining

Unfortunately, Oaxacan cuisine—the cheeses, mole sauces, and meats that make dining in the capital memorable—is in short supply along the coast. Seafood is your best bet. Huatulco's restaurants are getting better, and some of the places in Puerto Escondido are very good. With a few exceptions, the cooking in Puerto Angel is mediocre; the palapa restaurants along the Playa Panteón are distinguished mainly for their high prices, bad service, and aggressive young sidewalk hawkers. Dress is casual at all restaurants except where noted, and reservations are not necessary.

CATEGORY	COST*
$$$	over $25
$$	$15–$25
$	under $15

per person, excluding drinks and tip

Huatulco

$$$ **Casa Real.** Your only choice for glamorous dining thus far is in the Sheraton Hotel. The menu emphasizes northern Italian dishes—any of the pastas is a good choice—and the ambience is decidedly upscale, with heavy polished tables and chairs, stained-glass doors, and elaborate floral arrangements. It's very romantic at night when flickering candles grace the tables. Try the hotel's Mexican restaurant as well. ✕ *Sheraton Hotel, Blvd. Benito Juárez, Tangolunda Bay,* ☎ *958/1–00–55. AE, MC, V. No lunch.*

$$ **½ Carlos 'n' Charlie's.** The odd name refers to the size of this closet-like addition to the Carlos 'n' Charlie's chain, with all the trappings of the famous franchise packed in meager space. ½ has dependable food—barbecued ribs, tortilla soup, burgers, fries, and platters of fresh oysters—and fun for those who like downing shots of tequila and beer. ✕ *Ave. Flamboyan and Calle Carrizal, Crucecita,* ☎ *958/7–00–05.* ◔ *4 PM–1 AM. MC, V.*

$$ **Restaurante María Sabina.** This is a great place for sitting at a sidewalk table and watching the locals and tourists mingle in Crucecita's pretty plaza. No mystery exists here about how your food is prepared, since the grill is on the sidewalk, and the cook will chat with you as he chars your steak or fish. ✕ *West side of plaza, Crucecita,* ☎ *958/7–02–19. No credit cards.*

Puerto Angel

$ **Posada Rancho Cerro Largo.** Feeling adventurous? Take a cab from town, or a bus to Zipolite and a cab from there, to this simple inn with a spectacular view. You can take the path down to the beach, or just relax in a hammock while the proprietor, Mario Corella, whips up an excellent lunch of local fish or, if you're vegetarian, produce. If you *really* want to get away from it all, you can rent one of his four pretty palapa cabins overlooking the water (no plumbing, but jugs of clean, fresh water) and let him cook three meals a day for you. ✕ *Above Playa Aragon, off the hwy. west of Zipolite and before San Augustín and Mazunte (AP 121, Pochutla, 70900 Oax.), no* ☎. *No credit cards.*

Puerto Escondido

$$$ **Santa Fe.** By all means treat yourself to at least one meal here. The
★ menu is divided between seafood, vegetarian, and traditional Mexican dishes. The fruit salad is a pyramid of papaya, pineapple, and melon; the avocado cocktail is perfectly spiced; and if you like flan, the coconut version here is heaven. The tables overlooking the surf are wonderful at dawn and sunset, and in the noonday heat it's nice to relax in the shade under a whirring fan. ✕ *Hotel Santa Fe, Calle del Morro s/n,* ☎ *958/2–01–70. MC, V.*

$$ **Bananas.** This happening place under a palapa roof features seafood and fish platters along with hamburgers and nachos. Whenever football, baseball, and other U.S. sports events are on TV, Bananas fills up fast. ✕ *Av. Gasga,* ☎ *958/2–00–05. MC, V.*

$ Art 'n' Harry's. This surfer hangout overlooking the Pipeline is the place to relax with a drink and watch videos or zone out on heavy-metal CDs. The menu offers all types of stir-fry, salad, spaghetti dishes, and seafood. ✗ *South end of Zicatela Beach, no ☎. No credit cards.*

$ Cafeteria Cappuccino. In this small restaurant and coffeehouse, locals play backgammon in the shade at tiny wrought-iron tables. The menu is pretty much the same as everywhere else. Try the lime mousse or *crepas con cajeta* (crepes with caramel sauce) for dessert, or some yogurt and fruit for breakfast. ✗ *Av. Gasga, ☎ 958/2–0334. No credit cards.*

$ Mario's Pizzaland. The proprietor is a courtly, generous Italian who produces pizzas with all sorts of exotic toppings, including seafood. Even better are the gigantic green salads made with vegetables washed in purified water—a precaution one cannot rely on at other restaurants. ✗ *Av. Gasga just past the tourist zone, ☎ 958/2–05–70. No credit cards.*

$ La Gota de Vida. This small vegetarian café and health-food store on the bottom of the Gasga hill has all sorts of salads made from vegetables washed in purified water; *licuados* (milk shakes) made with yogurt, papaya, and mango; vegetable soups; and fresh carrot juice—all for under $5. ✗ *Av. Gasga, no ☎. No credit cards.*

$ La Patisserie (a.k.a. **Carmen's Bakery**). This little place, on a small road that connects the main highway with Playa Marinero, sells great breads, croissants, and sandwiches; it's also good for a breakfast of fruit salad with yogurt and granola. *No ☎. No credit cards.*

$ La Perla. Because it's in the "real" town uphill from the tourist zone, this excellent seafood restaurant has some of the best prices in town. *Pulpo* (octopus) is wonderfully tender; the excellent ceviche comes in a spicy cocktail sauce. It's a bit of a walk but a short, cheap cab ride. ✗ *Av. Rafael Ortega Velarde s/n, ☎ 958/2–04–61. MC, V. ☉ Daily 10–10.*

$ Perla Flameante. The fresh dorado, shark, tuna, and pompano come with teriyaki, Cajun, or garlic seasonings at this second-story bamboo restaurant overlooking the beach. The deep-fried onion rings and zucchini are terrific. They're open for breakfast. ✗ *Av. Gasga, near end of tourist strip, ☎ 958/2–01–67. No credit cards.*

Lodging

Hotel rates vary considerably in this area. Although almost all the hotels in Puerto Escondido fall into the moderate ($$) or inexpensive ($) price range, those in Huatulco are considerably pricier, with the Omni Zaashila topping the scale. The high season along the coast runs from mid-December to mid-April; rates increase by 20% during this time. Budget accommodations are scarce in Huatulco, although more moderately priced rooms are becoming available.

CATEGORY	COST*
$$$$	over $160
$$$	$90–$160
$$	$40–$90
$	under $40

All prices are for a standard double room, excluding 10% tax.

Huatulco

$$$$ **Omni Zaashila.** Huatulco's newest showpiece is a contemporary stucco
★ Mexican-cum-Mediterranean palace overlooking a secluded lagoon with its own private beach. The resort has been landscaped with 27 acres of gardens, fountains, and waterfalls; a third of the rooms have

their own private pools. The rates are high, and unlike those at most of the high-end properties here, they aren't all-inclusive. ⌕ *Playa Rincón Sabroso s/n, Tangolunda Bay, 70989,* ☎ *958/1–04–60, reservations in the U.S., 800/843–6664,* ⅷ *958/1–04–61. 128 rooms, 32 1-bedroom suites, 32 2-bedroom suites. 3 restaurants, bar, 100-meter pool, tennis court.*

$$$$ **Royal Maeva.** This all-inclusive resort caters to charter groups and Mexican families as well as lone travelers. The emphasis is on fun, fun, fun, and if you're not a fan of loud music, stay in a room that's away from the pool area. The rooms are spacious, colorful, and adorned with heavy blue-and-peach fabric and light-wood furniture. There are plenty of activities, from talent shows to sports demonstrations. ⌕ *Tangolunda Bay, Blvd. Benito Juárez 227, 70989,* ☎ *958/ 1–00–00, reservations in the U.S., 800/431–2822,* ⅷ *958/1–02–20. 300 rooms. 3 restaurants, 5 bars, pool, exercise room, beach, 5 tennis courts. AE, MC, V.*

$$$–$$$$ **Club Med.** The club's biggest compound in Mexico sprawls over a sloping hillside overlooking Tangolunda Bay. The 500 rooms are spread out in lavender-and-blue clusters with giant color-coded towers on top to help guests find their way home. There are three beaches, and the list of amenities is endless. The idea is to keep the guests so absorbed in Club Med's goings-on that they never leave the grounds. Week-long fitness programs are particularly popular. Packages with airfare included are usually available. Advance booking is mandatory. ⌕ *Tangolunda Bay, 70989,* ☎ *958/1–00–33,* ⅷ *958/1–01–01. Reservations: 40 W. 57th St., New York, NY 10019,* ☎ *800/CLUB–MED. 500 rooms. 5 restaurants, 3 pools, exercise room, 3 beaches, 12 tennis courts. AE, MC, V.*

$$$–$$$$ **Holiday Inn Crowne Plaza.** This all-suite hotel consists of 10 buildings built in a series of tiers separated by banks of steps. It is set on 2½ acres of landscaped gardens. Rooms are large, with private terraces, and have regional furnishings complemented by bright Mexican color schemes. All rooms have minibars, and the 32 master suites have whirlpool baths. Although the hotel is not on the water, it offers free transportation to its beach club next to the Sheraton. You can opt for either all-inclusive or standard room rates. ⌕ *Tangolunda Bay, Blvd. Benito Juárez 8, 70989,* ☎ *958/1–00–44, reservations in U.S.,* ☎ *800/ HOLIDAY,* ⅷ *958/1–02–21. 135 suites. 3 restaurants, 3 bars, 2 pools, steam room, exercise room, beach, tennis court, 18-hole golf course. AE, D, DC, MC, V.*

$$$–$$$$ **Sheraton.** Now offering all-inclusive as well as standard room tariffs, the Sheraton is the most user-friendly of the upscale hotels on Tangolunda Bay, with boutiques, a travel agency, and a selection of restaurants. The rooms are done in soft peaches and pinks, with blessedly powerful air-conditioning, heavy drapes to block the sun, and bathtubs—a real luxury in these parts. ⌕ *Tangolunda Bay, Blvd. Benito Juárez, 70989,* ☎ *958/1–00–55, reservations in the U.S. 800/ 325–3535,* ⅷ *958/1–01–13. 347 rooms. 3 restaurants, 3 bars, 2 pools, exercise room, beach, 4 tennis courts, shopping arcade. AE, DC, MC, V.*

$$ **Hotel Castillo Huatulco.** The closest accommodations to the plaza and Santa Cruz Bay are the newly remodeled rooms at the Castillo, which overlook the Santa Cruz Marina. This hotel resembles a motel from the front but looks like a quasi-resort inside. It's a good choice if you want to be near rental boats, close to the luxury hotels, and away from the business bustle of Crucecita. There's free transportation to the hotel's beach club on Chahue Bay. ⌕ *Blvd. Bahía Santa Cruz,*

Crucecita, 70989, ☎ *958/7–00–51,* FAX *958/7–01–31. 107 rooms. Restaurant, bar, pool, beach. AE, D, MC, V.*

$$ Posada Binniguenda. The first hotel in Santa Cruz, the Binniguenda is not on the beach but stands close to the marina, in the center of the town's developing hotel-restaurant-shopping scene. The dusty-pink adobe, red-tile-roof building forms a "U" around the courtyard and pool. The rooms have heavy colonial furnishings, commodious showers, satellite color TV, and wood-and-glass French doors leading to small wrought-iron balconies. ☎ *Blvd. Benito Juárez 5, Box 44, Santa Cruz, 70989,* ☎ *958/7–00–77, reservations in the U.S. 800/ 262–2656,* FAX *958/7–02–84. 74 rooms. 2 restaurants, bar, pool, car rental. AE, MC, V.*

$ Hotel Griffer. This is the least expensive place to stay in Huatulco and thus fills up quickly. Located on a busy in-town corner, the hotel offers simple, serviceable rooms and no frills. The restaurant is operated separately from the hotel and is a good spot for down-home breakfasts and lunch with the locals. ☎ *Av. Guamuchil at Carrizal, Crucecita, 70989,* ☎ *and* FAX *958/7–00–48. 18 rooms. Restaurant, bar. MC, V.*

Puerto Angel

$ La Buena Vista. This pretty hotel offers clean, simple rooms—some with balconies, some with hammocks just outside, but only four with hot water—and a third-floor restaurant that has a superb view (hence the name) and one of the most dependable kitchens in town. Don't be put off by the approach, which is up a narrow alley off a dirt road just west of the bridge on Avenida Principal, the town's main road. ✕ *Apdo. 48, Puerto Angel, 70902 Oax.,* ☎ *and* FAX *958/4–31–04. 15 rooms with bath. No credit cards.*

$ La Cabaña de Puerto Angel. Just across from Playa Panteón, this is the best-located hotel in town. The accommodating proprietors keep a big pot of coffee at the front desk for early risers, along with a library of paperback novels and maps of Mexico. The rooms have louvered windows with screens and ceiling fans; some have small balconies. ☎ *Across from Playa Panteón, 70902,* ☎ *958/4–31–05 or 958/4–00–76. 23 rooms. MC, V.*

$ Posada Cañon Devata. California comes to Puerto Angel in this ecological hideaway carved into a forested hillside. The greenness of the place in winter, when the rest of the coastal landscape dries to brown, attests to the owners' ingenuity. The simple bungalows on the hill offer private retreats; at the top is El Cielo ("heaven"), where guests gather to take in the sunset. The restaurant below, open to nonguests (you must reserve in the morning for dinner), is a find for vegetarians. Like the town itself, this is a comfortable place for single women. ☎ *Past the cemetery, off Blvd. Virgilio Uribe,* ☎ *and* FAX *958/4–30–48. Reservations: Apdo. 10, Puerto Angel, 70902 Oax. 10 inn rooms, 6 bungalows. Restaurant, snorkeling. No credit cards. Closed May–June.*

Puerto Escondido

$–$$$$ Fiesta Mexicana. This hotel on the Playa Bacocho out near the airport is decorated with bold, sunny colors, thatch, and nautical designs. It has a warm ambience and a helpful staff. Rooms are large and simply furnished. Twenty-two more rooms were added in 1995. ☎ *Blvd. Benito Juárez, Puerto Escondido, 71980,* ☎ *958/2–01–50,* FAX *958/2– 01–15. 86 rooms. 2 restaurants, bar, pool, tennis, disco, travel services. AE, MC, V.*

$$–$$$ **Hotel Santa Fe.** Your room here will have colonial furnishings, a tiled
★ bath, drapes and spreads of heavy woven Mexican cloth in soothing
lavenders and blues, a telephone, air-conditioning and a ceiling fan,
and maybe a balcony overlooking the pool. Five rooms were recently
added to the property. The hotel also manages the eight one-bedroom
Bungalows Santa Cruz next door. The newest adjunct is the **Studios El
Tabachin:** six splendid apartments with kitchens, satellite TV, stunning ocean views—and monthly rates, if you're lucky enough to be
staying that long. The owners also operate a small country inn about
two hours away, in the pine forests of the Oaxaca mountains, amid
coffee plantations and crystal-clear rivers. 🖾 *Calle del Morro by
Zicatela Beach, Apdo. 96, Puerto Escondido, Oax., 71980,* ☎ *958/
2–01–70,* FAX *958/2–02–60. (El Tabachin reservations by mail only,
same address c/o Paul Nunn Cleaver). 44 rooms, 8 bungalows, 6
apartments. Restaurant, bar, pool, travel services. AE, MC, V.*

$$ **Paraíso Escondido.** This colonial-style hotel perches on the hillside
overlooking Avenida Gasga and has splendid coastal vistas and a
friendly aura that encourages mingling. No two rooms are alike, and
all are furnished with a folkloric mixture of wood dressers, tin mir-
rors, and brightly colored drapes and spreads. The hotel and the
grounds are an ongoing, lovingly crafted art project. 🖾 *Calle Union
10, 71980,* ☎ *958/2–04–44. 20 rooms. Restaurant, bar, pool. No
credit cards.*

$ **Casas de Playa Acali.** You can choose from five sizes and styles of
accommodations at this cluster of cabanas by the main beach. The
least expensive rooms are in small bungalows without air-conditioning
or patios; the most expensive, though still a bargain, are four new bun-
galows offering terraces, kitchens, and a dining area. This is a good
choice for groups of four or six surfers who want to share expenses
and prepare their own meals. 🖾 *Calle del Morro, 71980,* ☎ *958/2–
07–54. 10 cabanas. Kitchenettes, pool. No credit cards.*

$ **Castillo del Reyes.** Proprietor Don Fernando runs an amiable show in
his small, immaculately clean establishment. It has no pool or restau-
rant, so the clients tend to congregate around the front desk, drinking
their own sodas and beer. The simple rooms have clean white walls
and powerful showers with plenty of hot water. 🖾 *Av. Gasga, 71980,*
☎ *958/2–04–42. 17 rooms. No credit cards.*

$ **Hotel Arcoiris.** This three-story, colonial-style hotel is on Zicatela
Beach, south of the Santa Fe, and is a good choice for those who want
privacy and security but cannot afford the Santa Fe. Most rooms
overlook the beach and have ceiling fans, fairly firm double beds, and
private balconies with hammocks. Eight of the rooms have kitch-
enettes. The third-floor restaurant is a great spot for sunset-watching.
🖾 *Calle del Morro, Zicatela Beach, Apdo. 105, 71980,* ☎ *and* FAX
958/2–04–32. 24 rooms. Restaurant, bar, pool. MC, V.

$ **Jardín Escondido.** The cabanas here have hammocks hanging out
front, mosquito nets over the beds, tile baths and showers, and white
brick walls. Weekly and monthly rates are available. 🖾 *Calle del
Morro 300, Box 97, 71980,* ☎ *958/2–03–48. 8 bungalows. Pool. No
credit cards.*

$ **Villas Los Delfines.** An enterprising couple from the capital have cre-
★ ated this solitary paradise atop a hill overlooking the coast, with eight
first-class cabanas spread along the hillside. The cabanas have full
kitchens, separate bedrooms, and hammocks hanging outside. The
husband is an architect with a fine eye for classical Mexican design.
The cool blue pool sits in the middle of the compound, beside a palapa
restaurant. 🖾 *Cerro de la Iguana, Carretera Costera del Pacifico Km*

71, Box 150, 71980, ☎ and FAX 958/2–04–67. 8 cabanas. Restaurant, bar, pool. MC, V.

Oaxaca Coast Essentials

Arriving and Departing

BY PLANE

Puerto Escondido has a national airport with daily service from Oaxaca on **Aeromorelos** (☎ 958/2–06–53) and on tiny Cessnas run by **Aero Vega** (☎ 958/2–01–51). **Mexicana** (at the airport, ☎ 958/2–03–00) flies to Puerto Escondido daily from Mexico City, and also from Los Angeles (via Mexico City).

Aeropuerto Bahías de Huatulco, is about 16 kilometers (10 miles) from town on Highway 200. **Mexicana** (☎ 958/1–02–28) flies to Huatulco from Mexico City, Guadalajara, Acapulco, Monterrey, and several other Mexican and U.S. gateways. **Aeromorelos** and private charters connect Huatulco with Oaxaca City and other destinations. Make reservations at the airport or through travel agencies, and be sure to confirm them 24 hours before your flight.

Estrella del Valle has recently begun deluxe Marco Polo bus service from Oaxaca City to Puerto Escondido and Huatulco. The trip to the coast, which is supposed to take seven hours, leaves from the bus station on the Periferico at Las Casas.

BY BUS AND CAR

Don't attempt to take the second-class bus from Oaxaca to Puerto Escondido or Huatulco unless you have an iron-clad stomach and lots of time. The twisting, jarring ride through the mountains takes about 10 hours. The 370-kilometer (230-mile) trip from Acapulco is less strenuous, and buses run hourly. The bus station in Puerto Escondido is on Avenida Oaxaca (☎ 958/2–04–27). Huatulco's bus station is in La Crucecita, on Avenue Gardenias at Calle Ocotillo (☎ 958/7–02–61; *see* Getting Around By Bus, *below*).

The drive from Oaxaca City to the coast on Highway 175 or 190 is rough, and although the scenery through the mountains is superb, all your attention will be focused on the twisting, roughly paved road. Do not attempt this drive at night. Plan on taking 10 hours or so, and leave early enough to be at your destination before dark.

Note: We received one report of a violent abduction of two tourists on Highway 200 between Salina Cruz and Puerto Angel at noon, so be careful even in daylight.

Getting Around

BY BUS

There are direct buses stringing together Puerto Escondido, Puerto Angel, and Huatulco, but you must stop at Pochutla, just off the highway near Puerto Angel, where buses leave off and pick up passengers. If you are going to Huatulco, be sure to specify that your final destination is the bus terminal in La Crucecita, which is closest to the bays.

BY CAR

The drive on Highway 200 from Puerto Escondido to Huatulco should be relatively hassle-free (but *see* Note, *above*), and having a car allows you to turn off the main road onto unmarked dirt roads leading to secluded beaches. But rental cars are expensive (starting at $50 per day, including insurance and unlimited mileage, for a Volkswagen beetle), and there is an additional drop-off fee if you don't return the car where you picked it up. **Budget** has franchises in Huatulco (☎ 958/7–00–10) and Puerto Escondido (☎ 958/2–03–12); nonaffiliated local firms often quote lower rates, but their vehicles may be in questionable condition.

Guided Tours

In **Puerto Escondido** the most exciting tours are run by ornithologist Michael Malone, who offers dawn and sunset excursions (Dec.–Apr.) into the Manialtepec Lagoon, a prime bird-watching area. Tours are $34 per person and can be arranged through your hotel or through **Turismo Rodimar** (Av. Gasga 905, ☎ 958/2–07–34 or 958/2–07–37), the most reliable and comprehensive agency in town. The agency also has a day tour to Puerto Angel, which includes the new Museum of the Sea Turtle (*see* Exploring, *above*).

The safest swimming and snorkeling beaches in Puerto Escondido are **Puerto Angelito** and **Carrizalillo;** both are complicated to reach by foot, but they're 10 minutes by boat from the town beach. Transportation is available from the many fishermen who park their *pangas* (small boats) on the sand near town and use them as water taxis. The ride should cost a few dollars.

In **Huatulco** you can't possibly grasp the beauty of the bays without touring them by boat. The venture takes four to six hours, with stops at Bahía San Augustín or El Maguey (where fishermen grill their catch over open fires) and at one of several secluded beaches for swimming and snorkeling. Bay cruises leave from and return to the beach in front of the Sheraton Hotel and cost about $20 a person. You can also catch one at the marina at Santa Cruz, where the local cooperative charges a couple of dollars less.

Bahías Plus, with offices in the Royal Maeva hotel (☎ 958/1–00–00) and in Santa Cruz at the Posada Binniguenda (☎ 958/7–09–32, ⅏ 958/7–02–16) is one of the most comprehensive travel agencies in Huatulco and has suburban van or bus tours to Puerto Angel and Puerto Escondido (van tours start at $30 per person in a group of six), as well as plane tours to Oaxaca ($337 per person). Most of the major hotels also have travel agencies.

Important Addresses and Numbers

VISITOR INFORMATION

Information is scanty at best in this area. The **Puerto Escondido tourism office** (☎ 958/2–01–75) has a new location on Blvd. Benito Juárez, about a block from the Aldea del Bazar Hotel at the Playa Bacocho development. The office is open weekdays 9–1 and 5–8, and Sat. 9–2, but don't count on finding anyone there who can speak English. Your hotel or the local tourism agencies (*see* Guided Tours, *above*) are a better bet. In Huatulco the **Fonatur** office (☎ 958/7–00–90 or 958/7–00–30) is on Av. Chahue, about a five-minute drive from the Sheraton Hotel in Tangolunda Bay. Hours are erratic, information scarce, and there is no state tourism office yet. You're better off using the travel agents in the hotels.

11 Chiapas and Tabasco

Much in the news these days because of the rebellion of its indigenous peoples, the state of Chiapas has always been an off-the-beaten-path destination, a gateway to Guatemala best known for the colonial town of San Cristóbal and for the jungle-covered ruins of Palenque, considered by many to be the most interesting in Mexico.

By Erica
Meltzer

Updated by
Patricia Alisau

KNOWN TO MOST foreigners until recently only as gateways to Guatemala and home to the ruins of Palenque and the colonial town of San Cristóbal de Las Casas, Chiapas and Tabasco were never prime destinations for first-time visitors to Mexico. And the world attention drawn to Chiapas in early 1994 and 1995 as the site of a native uprising has cast a pall over tourism, although the conflict is very localized and has not involved any negative incidents concerning visitors. But for those looking for an outstanding travel experience, a well-planned trip to this area can be very satisfying, particularly if you arrange for your visit to coincide with a local festival. Unlike beach resorts such as Cancún and Acapulco, this area is not one that visitors can jet to in a few hours from major U.S. gateways. Substantial ground transportation, either by bus or car, is absolutely necessary. People working in the tourist industry often don't speak English but are becoming more professional in dealing with tourists. Tourist information can be more difficult to obtain in Tabasco than in Chiapas.

The less touristic nature of these states has its own appeal. In Chiapas, at least, the locals are less self-conscious, less sophisticated, and they seem less out to make a quick buck. And though gringos are hardly a novelty, it can be refreshing to be noticed as an outsider rather than ignored as one more anonymous face in an ongoing "invasion."

The Indians' wariness of strangers has a historic basis. A bloody past of exploitation by and fierce confrontation with outsiders remains vividly present, as already impoverished indigenous communities in Chiapas are forced to compete for their lands with developers and new settlers. Most of eastern Chiapas borders on Guatemala, and during the past 20 years it has been overrun, first by the landless poor relocated from other parts of Mexico, and then by tens of thousands of Guatemalan refugees (most of whom have been repatriated to their native country through an amnesty program that went into effect in 1993). Because of its isolation, Chiapas has been at the margin of the nation's development. It is one of the poorest states in Mexico, with appallingly high rates of alcoholism, violence, illiteracy, and death due to unhygienic conditions. Land distribution, too, is skewed: 1% of the landowners hold 15% of the territory, keeping the colonial system nearly intact, and repression is rampant. The indifference of the Mexican government to their plight helped bring the anger of the indigenous people to a boil in early 1994, leading to an armed uprising by a group calling themselves the Zapatista National Liberation Army. The willingness of the government to negotiate with the rebels—and international interest in their plight—bodes well for the possibility of change in the region. Zapatista spokesman Subcomandante Marcos has become a cult figure in Mexico, his ski-masked image appearing on everything from magazine covers to children's toys.

Although it was nominally made rich half a century ago with the discovery of oil in the gulf, Tabasco also has a bloody past. During the 1920s and 1930s, Tomás Garrido Canabal, a vehemently anticlerical governor, outlawed priests and had all the churches either torn down or converted to other uses. Riots, deportations, and property confiscations were common. When British writer Graham Greene visited Tabasco in 1938, he called it "the Godless state." No wonder he found people voicing "the rather wild dream . . . of a rising which will separate Chiapas, Tabasco, Yucatán, and Quintana Roo from the rest of

Mexico and of an alliance with Catholic Guatemala"! Yet to the visitor, Tabasco's turbulent past is barely evident today; a wholly different spirit prevails here than in Chiapas.

Although the events of 1994 and 1995 may well delay some plans, Chiapas is not likely to remain off the tourist track for long. It is an important segment of the Mundo Maya travel circuit created by the Mexican government in the early 1990s to showcase its splendid Maya ruins and colonial cities in the name of regional development and preservation. The Lacondon jungle is already disappearing, its Indian inhabitants being driven to live in a smaller portion of their ancestral lands. Massive erosion and deforestation are taking their toll as the new settlers burn the forest and exhaust the soil by raising cattle.

For the present, however, travelers threading their way along tortuous mountain roads—full of dramatic hairpin turns along the edges of desolate ravines—will come upon remote clusters of huts and cornfields planted on near-vertical hillsides. They will pass Indian women wrapped in deep blue shawls and coarsely woven wool skirts, and Indian children selling fruit and flowers by the roadside. Chiapas has nine separate Indian groups, primarily the highland-dwelling Maya Tzeltals and Tzotzils, many of whom do not speak Spanish.

Tabasco is of interest primarily as a gateway to the Maya ruins at Palenque in Chiapas and to "green" tourists, lured by lakes, lagoons, and caves and by the wild rivers surging through the jungle. Travelers will find Villahermosa's CICOM museum of pre-Columbian archaeology and the collection of Olmec heads at Parque La Venta a good introduction to the Indian heritage of Tabasco, so evident also in Chiapas. (And no, Tabasco sauce does not come from here or from anywhere else in Mexico; it originated in Louisiana.)

The highlights of a trip to Chiapas and Tabasco are still the ruins of Palenque and the town of San Cristóbal de las Casas. The latter can be reached by car or bus from either Tuxtla (*Tus*-tla) Gutiérrez, a convenient point of departure because of its airport and access to San Cristóbal, or Villahermosa, which also has a major airport. A sample itinerary might begin in Tuxtla, then head east to San Cristóbal for a few nights. From here move on to Toniná, Agua Azul, and Palenque, and finally on to Villahermosa. From Palenque or San Cristóbal you can arrange an excursion to the Maya ruins of Bonampak and Yaxchilán (Yas-chee-*lan*) near the Guatemalan border (although the Mexican government has temporarily suspended permission to visit there because it falls within rebel-held territory). A popular day trip from San Cristóbal is to the Lagunas de Montebello (Lakes of Montebello).

Note: As of this writing (spring 1995), travel to Chiapas was safe. The Mexican Government Tourist Office in New York City can give you updated information. Or contact the U.S. State Department for any traveler's advisories at the time you are planning to visit.

SAN CRISTÓBAL DE LAS CASAS

San Cristóbal, the chief city of the Chiapas highlands, is a pretty town of about 120,000 situated in a valley of pine forests and orchards. Native Mexican women are as common a sight as young and aging hippies, who come because the place is inexpensive and relatively unfettered by tourism. More Europeans than Americans visit San Cristóbal, and it is the preferred stopping point for those venturing north to Palenque or south to Guatemala.

Chiapas and Tabasco

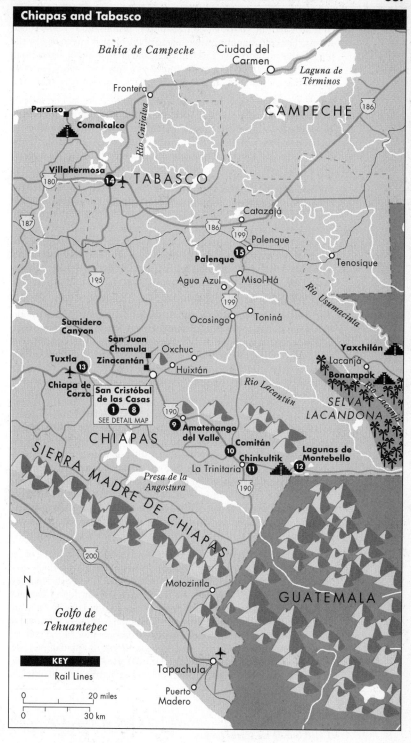

Bahía de Campeche

Ciudad del Carmen

Laguna de Términos

Frontera

Paraíso

Comalcalco

CAMPECHE

186

Villahermosa

180

TABASCO

14

187

186

199

Catazajá

Palenque

195

Palenque

15

Tenosique

Agua Azul

Misol-Há

Río Usumacinta

199

Ocosingo

Toniná

Sumidero Canyon

San Juan Chamula

Zinacantán

Oxchuc

Yaxchilán

Tuxtla

13

Huixtán

Lacanjá

Chiapa de Corzo

San Cristóbal de las Casas

1 — 8

SEE DETAIL MAP

Río Lacantún

Bonampak

SELVA LACANDONA

190

9

Amatenango del Valle

CHIAPAS

Comitán

10

Lagunas de Montebello

Chinkultik

La Trinitaria

11

12

SIERRA

Presa de la Angostura

190

MADRE

DE

CHIAPAS

200

N

Motozintla

GUATEMALA

Golfo de Tehuantepec

KEY

—— Rail Lines

Tapachula

0   20 miles

0   30 km

Puerto Madero

San Cristóbal is also among the finest colonial towns in Mexico: It has churches, red-tile roofs, elegant Spanish mansions, and cobblestoned streets. The cold, haunting atmosphere of the place is intensified by the remarkable quality of the early morning and late-afternoon light. Small enough to be seen on foot in the course of a day, San Cristóbal is also captivating enough to invite a stay of three days, a week, or even a month.

In addition to viewing the monuments from the colonial era, visitors usually plan an early morning visit to see the Indians gather at the *mercado* (market), browse for local handicrafts, or explore one of the indigenous villages in the vicinity. Just soaking up the ambience in one of San Cristóbal's little cafés or unpretentious restaurants is a pleasure.

In 1524, the Spaniards under Diego de Mazariegos decisively defeated the Chiapan Indians at a battle outside town. Mazariegos founded the city, which was called Villareal de Chiapa de los Españoles, in 1528. For most of the viceroyalty, or colonial era, Chiapas, with its capital at San Cristóbal, was a province of Guatemala. It was of greater strategic than economic importance to the Spaniards, lacking the gold and silver of the north. Instead, the state's agricultural resources became entrenched in the *encomienda* system, tantamount to slavery. "In this life all men suffer," lamented a Spanish friar in 1691, "but the Indians suffer most of all."

The situation improved only slightly through the efforts of Bartolomé de las Casas, the eponymous bishop of San Cristóbal who in the mid-1500s protested the colonials' torture and massacre of the Indians. The Indians protested in another way, murdering priests and other *ladinos* (whites) in infamous uprisings. (Chiapans still refer to whites as either ladinos or *Españoles*—Spaniards—whether they are "pure-blooded" or mestizo.)

Mexico, Guatemala, and the rest of New Spain declared independence in 1821. For a brief two years, Chiapas remained part of Guatemala, electing by plebescite to join Mexico on September 14, 1824, the *día de la mexicanidad* of Chiapas (the day is still celebrated in San Cristóbal and all over Chiapas). In 1892, because of San Cristóbal's allegiance to the Royalists during the War of Independence, the capital was moved to Tuxtla Gutiérrez; with it went all hope that the town would keep pace with the rest of Mexico. It was not until the 1950s that the roads into town were paved and the first automobiles arrived. Modern times came late to San Cristóbal, for which most visitors are thankful.

It is worthwhile to try to schedule your visit to coincide with one of the local festivals. Major festival dates in the area (check with the tourist office for a broader sampling) are: January 20–22, San Sebastian festival in Zinacantán; Carnival and Easter Week in San Juan Chamula, Zinacantán, and other villages; every Friday during Lent in Zinacantán; June 22–24, San Juan festival in Chamula; July 24–25, festival of the patron saint of San Cristóbal; August 9–10, celebration of San Lorenzo in Zinacantán; December 12, feast of the Virgin of Guadalupe (celebrated for a week in Tuxtla Gutiérrez); and December 31 in several indigenous highland villages, celebrations to install the new civil officials.

Exploring

Numbers in the margin correspond to points of interest on the San Cristóbal de las Casas map.

San Cristóbal is laid out in a grid pattern and centered around the zócalo, with street names changing on either side of the square. For example,

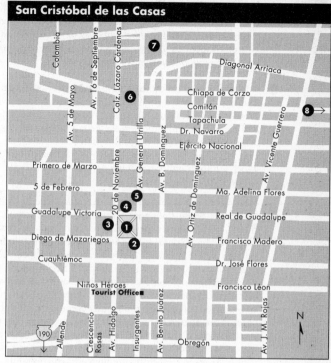

San Cristóbal de las Casas

Francisco Madero to the east of the square becomes Calle Diego de Mazariegos to the west.

1 The heart of San Cristóbal is small and can be seen on foot in two hours or less. Begin at the **zócalo,** around which the Spaniards built all their colonial cities. In its center stands the gazebo, which is used by musicians on festive occasions. Surrounding the square are a number of 16th-century buildings, many former mansions of the conquistadores. Tile roofs and wood-beamed ceilings adorn corridors flanking central patios, which are surrounded by arched columns and filled with huge potted plants. (Don't be afraid to go into buildings whose doors are open.)

2 Perhaps the most famous mansion is the so-called **Casa de Diego de Mazariegos,** opposite the square on the southeast corner of Calle Diego de Mazariegos. One of the most exquisite specimens of colonial architecture in Mexico, the Casa is now the Hotel Santa Clara. The stone mermaid and lions outside it are typical of the period's Plateresque style, as ornate and busy as the work of a silversmith.

3 Continue in a northwesterly direction around the zócalo to the **Palacio Municipal,** which was the seat of the state government until 1892, when Tuxtla Gutiérrez became the capital.

4 Perpendicular to the Palacio Municipal, on the north side of the zócalo, is **La Catedral,** built in 1528, then demolished and rebuilt in 1693, with subsequent additions during the 18th and 19th centuries. Noteworthy attractions in the cathedral include the painting of Our Lady of Sorrows, to the left of the altar; the gold-plated *retablo de los Reyes* (altarpiece); the Chapel of Guadalupe; and the gold-encrusted pulpit. ☺ *Daily 10:30–8.*

TIME OUT   The cozy and relaxing **Los Amorosos (The Lovers) Cafe** (Calle Dr. José
Flores 12A, corner of Av. Belisario Domínguez), in the Jaime Sabines
cultural center, is the favorite haunt of local intellectuals and poets who
dine on Mexican specialties or drink their way through seven different
kinds of cappuccino until midnight.

⑤ A block north of the cathedral, the **Museo del Ambar** (Amber Museum)
is a must for those intrigued by this prehistoric resin, which produces
some of the most beautiful ornamental jewelry around. José Luis Coria
and his wife, Guadalupe, are the proud owners of this immense collection of pieces carved by local artisans. Many items contain fossilized
insects and plant life and others are shaped into pre-Hispanic figures,
which are absolutely fascinating. *Av. General Utrilla 10, ☎ 967/8−35−
07. ☛ Free. ۞ Sun.−Fri. 10−8.*

Head north about four blocks on Avenida General Utrilla toward the
⑥ **Templo de Santo Domingo,** a three-block-long complex housing the
church, former convent, regional history museum, and Templo de la Caridad. The church dates from 1547−1569, and the two-headed eagle—
emblem of the Hapsburg dynasty that once ruled Spain and its American
dominions—broods over its pediment. The pink stone facade, carved
in an intensely ornamental style known as Baroque Solomonic, was clearly
influenced by the church of Antigua, Guatemala: Saints' figures, angels,
and grooved columns overlaid with vegetation motifs abound. The interior is dominated by lavish altarpieces; an exquisitely fashioned pulpit; a sculpture of the Holy Trinity; and wall panels of carved cedar,
one of the precious woods of Chiapas that centuries later lured the woods-
men of Tabasco to the obscure highlands surrounding San Cristóbal.
At the southeast corner of the church park lies the tiny **Templo de la
Caridad,** built in 1711 to venerate the Immaculate Conception. Its highlight is the finely carved altarpiece. The **ex-Convento de Santo Domingo,**
immediately adjacent to the church, now houses San Jolobil, an Indian
cooperative selling rather expensive local weavings and a good selection of colorful postcards (open daily 9−2 and 4−7). The small regional
history museum, also part of the Templo de Santo Domingo complex,
is open Tuesday−Sunday 9−6.

⑦ The municipal **mercado** occupies an eight-block area to the northeast
of Santo Domingo. Best visited early in the morning—especially on the
busiest day, Saturday—the market is the social and commercial center for the Indians from surrounding villages. Stalls overflow with
local produce such as turkeys, medicinal herbs, flowers, firewood, and
wool, as well as huaraches, grinding stones, and candied fruit. The market is open daily, but it is most colorful on Saturdays. Be very discreet
about taking photographs.

Visitors who are interested in the culture and history of the Indians,
particularly the Lacandones, should set aside an afternoon to tour the
⑧ **Centro de Estudios Científicos Na-Bolom,** a handsome former colonial
building built in 1891 on the outskirts of town. Na-Bolom (House of
the Jaguar) began as the residence of Franz and Gertrude Blom, who
purchased the 22-room house in 1950. Together they founded an institute dedicated to ethnological and ecological research on the region.
The property is blissfully isolated from the rest of San Cristóbal, notably because of its extensive garden of firs, fruit trees, vegetables, and
flowers.

Na-Bolom features the Bloms' collection of religious treasures that had
been hoarded in attics during the anticlerical 1920s and 1930s. A museum houses Franz Blom's findings from the classic Maya site of

Moxviquil (mosh-vee-*keel*), found in the outskirts of San Cristóbal, and there is a room full of objects from the daily life of the Lacandones, a tribe descended from the ancient Maya; the Bloms documented their traditions and helped ensure their survival. A library holds more than 18,000 volumes on Chiapas and the Maya. Na-Bolom is also a guest house, and revenues from guests, tours, and the bookshop go to support the work of the institute (*see* Lodging, *below*). Arrange for a meal at Na-Bolom at the very least, even if you are not staying there.

Na-Bolom is dedicated to reforestation of the surrounding area, planting 35,000 trees each year. Trudi Blom, who was born in 1901, received the United Nations' 500 Global Roll of Honor award in 1991 for her lifelong work on the preservation of the environment. She died in 1993, but the nonprofit, private institute is being run by a carefully selected board of directors. *Av. Vicente Guerrero 31 between Comitán and Chiapa de Corzo,* ☎ *967/8–14–18.* ☛ *$1, including library.* ☉ *Tues.–Sun. 9–1:30; tours (about $3) Tues.–Sun.*

Those interested in regional ethnic apparel might consider a visit to the **Museo Sergio Castro.** It's a private gallery run by the anthropologist/agronomist for whom the museum is named, so you must call ahead for an appointment. *Guadalupe Victoria 47,* ☎ *967/8–42–89.* ☛ *$3.*

Off the Beaten Track

After an early morning venture to San Cristóbal's market, head four blocks south to the little **plaza at Calle Dr. Navarro and Avenida B. Domínguez.** When the sun edges in over the red-tile roofs, the square is bathed in golden light and is wonderfully cozy and private.

San Cristóbal is divided into several **barrios** (neighborhoods) that are within easy walking range. The barrios originated in colonial times, when the Indian allies of the triumphant Spaniards were moved onto lands on the outskirts of the nascent city. Each barrio was dedicated to a different occupation. There were Mexican weavers, Tlaxcala fireworks manufacturers, and pig butchers from Cuxhtali. Although these divisions no longer exist, other customs have been kept alive. For example, each Saturday certain houses downtown will put out red lamps, to indicate that fresh homemade tamales are for sale. The San Cristóbal tourist office can provide more details and arrange trips to the barrios.

Surrounding San Cristóbal are many small and seldom-visited Indian villages that are celebrated for the exquisite colors and embroidery work of their inhabitants' costumes. Huixtán (Hwees-*tan*) and Oxchuc (Os-*chuc*) are about 28 and 43 kilometers (17 and 26 miles) respectively, on the road to Ocosingo; Chenalhó lies 32 kilometers (20 miles) along the paved road beyond Chamula. *Colectivos* and taxis are available. The Sunday market and weavers' cooperative in Tenejapa (27 kilometers, or 17 miles, northeast of San Cristóbal) are worth seeing. Tenejapa has a small pensión.

Shopping

The artisans of San Cristóbal and Chiapas produce some of the most striking indigenous folk art of Mexico. Best are the blouses, tunics, and caps, bedspreads and tablecloths finely embroidered with native designs; brightly colored *fajas* (sashes); and leather goods, such as belts and purses. Lacandon bows and arrows, and the beribboned hats worn by local men, also make good souvenirs. San Cristóbal is also known for its quality wrought-iron work, especially its crosses. There are no department stores in San Cristóbal. The market, while picturesque, sells more produce than handicrafts.

The market is flooded with goods from Guatemala and not always those of the highest quality. Always ask if an item comes from Guatemala. If the answer is yes—you'll be lucky to encounter such honesty—bargain fiercely: Guatemalan goods are priced several times higher in San Cristóbal than they would be if purchased in Guatemala. Guatemalan cloth is easily recognizable: Most of it is rough, dark blue cotton with multicolor cotton needlepoint or trim.

Among its excellent selection of wares, **San Jolobil** (in the ex-Convento de Santo Domingo, 20 de Noviembre, ☎ 967/8–26–46), the regional crafts cooperative, sells hand-dyed woolen sweaters and men's tunics, embroided pillow covers, and pre-Hispanic design wall hangings. At a workshop across the street, you can watch Indian weavers working on the traditional backstrap loom. **La Galeria** (Hidalgo 3, ☎ 967/8–15–47) offers exclusive designs by Kiki Oberstenfeld, who imbues her dolls, posters, woodcuts, and children's books with primitive and folk art motifs. The store also carries hand-painted tiles and winsome weavings from Teneapa and appealing items from other regions of Mexico. Among the smart shops clustered along Real de Guadalupe is **Citlali** (Real de Guadalupe 27, ☎ 967/8–40–85), which specializes in attractive amber jewelry mixed with silver. Although the prices are higher than in other shops, the designs are more sophisticated. **Ropa Tipica y Artesanias** (Real de Guadalupe 64B, no ☎) sells embroidered blouses, jackets, and children's clothing, all with indigenous designs. The government-run **Casa de las Artesaniás** (Calle Niños Heroes and Av. Hidalgo, ☎ 967/8–1–80) has wooden toys, ceramic jugs, embroidered blouses, bags and handwoven textiles for sale by the yard, and a tiny ethnographic museum with indigenous costumes in back.

An unusual shop in an old colonial home, **Taller Lenateros** (Flavio A. Paniagua 54, ☎ 967/8–51–74) carries handmade books, boxes, postcards, and writing paper fashioned on the premises out of recycled flower petals, plants, and bark. Owner Amber Past from Minneapolis conducts tours of the workshop ($1), which employs about two dozen Mayas.

Shops in town are generally open 9–2 and 4–8. Indian women and children often accost visitors on the streets with their wares, mostly textiles, but their selections are not as varied as those in the shops, and prices will not necessarily be any better. You can be assured, though, that the proceeds go directly to the craftspersons themselves.

Sports

Horseback Riding
A ride into the neighboring indigenous villages can exercise the mind as well as the body. Most hotels can arrange for rentals of horses. Guides working through the tourist office and travel agencies can also hire horses and accompany tourists. Allow a minimum of six hours for a satisfying trip.

Dining

San Cristóbal's restaurants offer an ample choice of Mexican and international cuisines and can be rated the best in the state (although they're not outstanding compared to those in other regions of Mexico). Chiapas has regional specialties but borrows heavily from Yucatán and Oaxaca. Adventurous palates should try *atole* (cornmeal drink), tamales, candied fruit, and any dishes that contain the tasty herbs *chipilín* and *herba santa*. Although the region raises cattle, the best beef is exported. Prices, however, are quite reasonable: A filling dinner (helped out by tortillas in one of their myriad forms) with beer rarely costs more than $10 per person. The town closes down early, so unlike in other parts of Mexico, it is a fairly common practice to eat dinner before 8. There is no dress code to speak of in this part of Mexico, and no reservations are necessary.

CATEGORY	COST*
$$	$8–$15
$	under $8

per person, excluding drinks, service, and sales tax (10%)

$$ **Casa del Pan Cantante.** Organically grown fruits, vegetables, and coffee get top billing at this hip vegetarian restaurant that even has meat-lovers changing their eating habits. Menu offerings include tamales *Chiapanecos* with local *chipilín* and *santa herba* spices in a cheese filling, hot bean soup, curried vegetable *empanadas* (turnovers), and vegetable pizza served on a flaky strudel crust. Chocolate brownies (not to be found elsewhere in Chiapas) and cheese-fruit pie are house favorites for dessert. A small bakery sells homemade breads, chocolate chip and oatmeal cookies, fruit preserves, and empanadas—as well as Celtic flute music cassettes. Musical groups with repertoires from jazz to pop perform 8–11 PM weekends. ✗ *Av. Belisario Domínguez and Dr. Navarro,* ☏ *967/8–04–68. MC, V.*

$$ **Fogón de Jovel.** Owned by A.T.C., one of the largest travel agencies in town, this restaurant has a crafts shop, a marimba band, and costumed waiters. A cover charge is in effect when folkloric dances are performed. The menu leans toward southeast Mexican cooking and the variety is impressive. Warning: Fogón de Jovel caters mainly to tourists. ✗ *Av. 16 de Septiembre 11,* ☏ *967/8–11–53 or 967/8–25–57,* ℻ *967/8–31–45. MC, V.*

$$ **La Parilla.** A new meat-eaters enclave, opened in 1994, with a menu chock full of charcoal-grilled steak, sausage, ribs, brochettes, plus smoked chicken prepared *à la Mexicana,* with beans and piping hot tortillas on the side. Wooden beams, beribboned hats hanging from the ceiling, and bright Mexican colors add a cheerful touch to this otherwise somber-looking eatery. ✗ *Av. Belisario Domínguez 32 A,* ☏ *967/8–22–20. MC, V.*

$$ **Restaurante del Teatro.** Decorated with both European and local artwork, this popular French/Italian restaurant across from the Hotel Flamboyant Español specializes in Chateaubriand, crepes, fresh pasta dishes, and chocolate mousse. The French owner keeps the atmosphere relaxed and unhurried. ✗ *Av. 1 de Marzo 8,* ☏ *967/8–31–49. AE, MC, V.*

Lodging

San Cristóbal is sufficiently small to place almost any hotel within walking distance of the major attractions. Most of the hotels listed are colonial, either architecturally or decoratively, in keeping with the rest of town. All rooms in hotels listed have baths; air-conditioning is not necessary at this high altitude and in fact, fireplaces are welcome. Hotels are open year-round. The postal code for San Cristóbal is 29200.

CATEGORY	COST*
$$$$	over $90
$$$	$60–$90
$$	$25–$60
$	under $25

All prices are for a standard double room, excluding 10% tax.

$$$ **Flamboyant Español.** Opened in 1907, the hotel is a sister to the Flamboyant in Tuxtla Gutiérrez. The colonial charm of the former Hotel Español, with its fireplaces and bougainvillea-filled courtyard, blue-tiled seats, and fountain, has been retained. The older section, a restored colonial house, has rooms with fireplaces. We have received reports, however, of room reservations not being honored and deposits not being returned. ⊞ *1 de Marzo 15,* ☎ *967/8–00–45 or 967/8–06–23,* ℻ *967/8–05–14. 52 rooms. Restaurant, bar, meeting room, travel services. AE, MC, V.*

$$$ **Hotel Casa Mexicana.** This new, beautifully designed hotel in a restored
★ colonial mansion is colorful, clean, bright, and friendly. Large rooms, good beds, beamed ceilings, a lovely garden, attractive artwork, and a Swiss chef in the hotel restaurant all help make this an outstanding hostelry. All the accommodations have telephones and TV, and the two junior suites offer Jacuzzis. ⊞ *28 de Agosto 1,* ☎ *967/8–06–98, 967/8–06–83, or 967/8–13–41,* ℻ *967/8–26–27. 23 rooms, 2 junior suites, 3 villas. Restaurant, bar, room service, sauna, massage, tennis, baby-sitting, travel services. AE, DC, MC, V.*

$$$ **Hotel Casavieja.** Three blocks east of the zócalo and close to many of
★ the town's attractions, this new (opened late 1993) hotel is built around a centuries-old house and replicates the colonial architecture of that structure. Each spacious, comfortable room has large windows looking out onto one of the three charming interior courtyards; in addition to the telephones and TVs found in all the accommodations, the suites boast Jacuzzis. The Espinosa family, who run and own the hotel, are extremely warm and knowledgeable hosts. ⊞ *Ma. Adelina Flores 27,* ☎ *967/8–03–85,* ℻ *967/8–52–23. 38 rooms, 2 suites. Restaurant, bar, parking. MC, V.*

$$$ **Posada Diego de Mazariegos.** This hotel is in two sections that face each other across the street. Rooms on the second floor of the older and quieter half, a 200-year-old mansion that also houses the restaurant, have wrought-iron window frames, oak balustrades, red-tile floors, and wood-beamed ceilings; some rooms have fireplaces. The newer section is covered with a giant fiberglass dome that keeps out rain but seals in noise. Many consider this to be San Cristóbal's most elegant property, but others feel that it has become tacky and pretentious. ⊞ *5 de Febrero 1,* ☎ *967/8–06–21 or 967/8–07–28,* ℻ *967/8–08–27. 77 rooms. Restaurant-bar, cafeteria, travel services, car rental. AE, DC, V.*

$$ **Hotel Posada El Paraíso de Eden.** One of San Cristóbal's newer inns (opened 1993), this charming colonial home has 13 guest rooms with beamed ceilings; some have lofts and carpeting, but there are no TVs or phones. Comfortable leatherback chairs in the guest lounge overlook a sunny patio. The bar/restaurant offers piped-in classical music and the personal attention of owners Daniel and Teresa Suter, who met in Switzerland—thus the presence of Swiss dishes such as raclette (melted cheese and potatoes) on the otherwise Mexican menu. Choose a room away from the street and lounge for more solitude. ⊞ *Av. 5 de Febrero 19,* ☎ *and* ℻ *967/8–00–85. 13 rooms. Restaurant-bar. MC, V.*

$$ Hotel Santa Clara. In the historic Casa de Diego Mazariegos on the zócalo, this clean, quiet, and appealing hotel is convenient to all town-center attractions. During daylight hours, two brilliantly colored guacamaya birds entertain guests in the lovely indoor patio. ⛴ *Insurgentes 1,* ☎ *967/8–08–71 or 967/8–11–40,* FAX *967/8–10–41. 53 rooms. Restaurant, bar, cafeteria, pool, travel services. AE, DC, MC, V.*

$$ Mansión del Valle. A few blocks from the zócalo, this 19th-century property has been converted into a hotel with tasteful Spanish colonial design details such as wrought-iron banisters, terrazzo floors, and a large inner atrium filled with greenery. Rooms are spacious; seven have patios overlooking a park. ⛴ *Calle Diego de Mazariegos 39, 29240,* ☎ *967/8–25–82 or 967/8–25–83,* FAX *967/8–25–81. 45 rooms. Restaurant-bar, cafeteria. AE, MC, V.*

$$ Na-Bolom. A dozen guest rooms are available at this center for the study
★ and preservation of the Lacandon Indians and the rain forest (*see* Exploring, *above*). Each of the rustic but cozy rooms is decorated with the accoutrements of a specific indigenous community—crafts, photographs, and books—and contains what might be the only bathtubs in San Cristóbal hostelries. Guests staying at Na Bolom receive a free tour of the house, free entrance to a documentary presentation, access to the library, and information about the area. Book well in advance; ask for a garden view. Guests share the dining room with staff and volunteers at a separate charge. ⛴ *Av. Vicente Guerrero 33,* ☎ *967/8–14–18. 15 rooms. V.*

$ Rincón del Arco. Near Na-Bolom, this hotel has charming touches, especially each room's fireplace, quilts, and the clay stoves shaped like bulls and jaguars. The best room is No. 11. The dining room has two fireplaces, wrought-iron wagon-wheel chandeliers, and other regional touches. ⛴ *Calle Ejército Nacional 66,* ☎ *967/8–13–13,* FAX *967/8–15–68. 36 rooms. Restaurant, bar. AE, MC, V.*

$ Villa Real. This is a plain but functional property, with a small restaurant. ⛴ *Av. Benito Juárez 8,* ☎ *967/8–29–30. 24 rooms. V.*

The Arts and Nightlife

San Cristóbal has only a modest offering of cultural events. Inquire at the tourist office and bookshops about upcoming lectures on regional ethnography and the selva. **Na-Bolom** occasionally sponsors talks and audiovisual presentations. Although San Cristóbal has one disco—frequented mostly by young locals—nightlife is not one of the city's main draws. Dinner is eaten early by Mexican standards—about 8. While a few of the restaurants and hotels that cater to gringos provide some form of musical entertainment (and the usual spectacle available at bars), the best diversion can be found in front of a fireplace. Bring along one of B. Traven's jungle novels.

Excursions from San Cristóbal

Caves of San Cristóbal

The spectacular limestone stalactites and stalagmites are illuminated for one entire kilometer (more than half a mile) inside these labyrinthine caves, which were discovered in 1960 and were fully explored only a few years ago. The park surrounding the caves has a picnic area. A Spanish-speaking guide is usually available for a small fee. Horses can be rented on weekends. The caves are located in the San Cristóbal Recreational Park, in the midst of a pine forest. *11 km (7 mi) southeast of town off Rte. 190.* ☛ *$1.* ☉ *Check with the San Cristóbal tourist office to see if caves are open; they have an erratic schedule. When open, hrs are 9–5.*

San Juan Chamula

The spiritual and administrative center of the Chamula Indians is justly celebrated, as much for its rich past as for its turbulent present. The Chamula are a Tzotzil-speaking Maya group of nearly 52,000 individuals (out of a total of 300,000 Tzotzils) who live in hamlets scattered throughout the highlands; there are several thousand of them in San Juan Chamula.

The Chamula are fiercely religious, a trait that has played an important role in their history. The Chamula uprising of 1869 started when some tribesmen were imprisoned for crucifying a boy in the belief that they should have their own Christ. Some 13,000 Chamula then rose up to demand their leaders' release and massacred scores of ladino villagers in the process. More recently, the infiltration of Protestant evangelists into the community led to the expulsion of the Indian converts by Chamula authorities. In the last 20 years, more than 20,000 have been forced to abandon their ancestral lands and now live on the outskirts of San Cristóbal de las Casas, dressing in conventional clothing and usually found selling handicrafts in San Cristóbal's street markets. The Human Rights Commission is trying to mediate their return to the Chamula community.

San Juan Chamula is 12 kilometers (7½ miles) northwest of San Cristóbal. Head west on Guadalupe Victoria, which forks to the right onto Ramón Larrainzar. Continue 4 kilometers (2½ miles) until you reach the entrance to the village. Most of these roads are paved and they are far more interesting than the alternate route, which is to take the main road to Tuxtla 8 kilometers (5 miles) and then turn right when you see signs. You can catch one of the colectivos that run regularly from the market in San Cristóbal, or you can hire a taxi or ride horseback (*see* Sports *in* San Cristóbal de las Casas, *above*). To get permission to enter the church, go first to the tourist office on the main square. Admission to the church is about 60¢.

Physically and spiritually, life in San Juan Chamula revolves around the church, a white-stucco building with red, blue, and yellow trim. Extreme care must be exercised in entering the church. A "guardian" inside the church, dressed in a wool tunic and carrying a big club, will tell you that taking photographs is absolutely prohibited.

There are no pews in the church, the floor of which is strewn with fragrant pine needles. The Indians sit chanting while facing colorfully attired saints' statues that are so highly polished they resemble porcelain dolls. For the most part, worshipers appear oblivious to intruders, continuing with their rituals: They burn candles of various colors, drink Coca-Cola, and may have a live chicken or eggs with them for healing the sick. They "pass" the illness to the chicken or egg, which then gets disposed of outside the church. The church is named after St. John the Baptist, the main god of the universe, according to Chamulan belief—which also relegates Jesus Christ to the position of a minor saint.

Outside the church there is no taboo against photography, but adults prefer not to be photographed. Flocks of children will pester you to buy small trinkets from them and will allow you to photograph them in exchange for a small fee (about 30¢ a shot). The best time to visit San Juan Chamula is on Sunday, when the market is in full swing and more formal religious rites are performed. Some male market vendors can act surly at times, so be prepared.

Zinacantán

The village of Zinacantán (Place of the Bats) is even smaller than San Juan Chamula and is reached by taking a paved road west just outside San Juan Chamula. Here photography is totally forbidden, except for the row of village weavers on view along the main street (a recent attraction added by the government-sponsored Family Institute). It is the scenery en route to Zinacantán—terraced hillsides with cornfields and orchards—that draws visitors. Aside from a new museum, *Museo Ik'al Ojov* (open 8–5; free), which shows off Zinacatlan costumes down through the ages, there isn't much to see in the village itself except on Sundays, when people gather from the surrounding parishes, or during religious festivals. The men wear bright pink *serapes* (ponchos); the women cover themselves with bright pink *rebozos* (shawls). Watch for the plethora of crosses around the springs and mountains on the way to Zinacantán: They mark a Chamula cemetery of Christian origin. Zinacantán is 4 kilometers (2½ miles) west of Chamula. From Chamula, follow signs along a paved road. From San Cristóbal, take the Tuxtla road about 8 kilometers (5 miles) and look for the turnoff on your right. Colectivos depart for the village from the San Cristóbal market.

San Cristóbal de las Casas Essentials

Arriving and Departing

BY PLANE

Airports and Airlines. The closest major airport is in Tuxtla Gutiérrez, 85 kilometers (53 miles) west. There are three daily flights from Mexico City on **Mexicana** (☎ 800/531–7921; airport, ☎ 961/3–49–21; in Tuxtla, 961/2–20–32 and 961/1–14–90). **Aviación de Chiapas** (Aviacsa, ☎ 961/2–80–81 or 961/3–50–29; Mexico City, ☎ 5/590–9522) also has daily flights between Tuxtla and Mexico City. For charter flights to the ruins of Bonampak and Yaxchilán, contact **Montes Azules** (☎ 961/3–22–56 or 961/3–22–93), a new air charter company in Tuxtla Gutiérrez or **Viajes Miramar** (☎ 961/7–77–77, ext. 7230, or 961/2–39–83, FAX 961/5–59–25 or 961/2–39–30), a travel agency in Tuxtla. San Cristóbal's new airport started receiving local flights in 1995.

Between the Airport and Center City. The easiest way to get from Tuxtla to San Cristóbal is by taxi. The two-hour ride costs about $50 for one to four persons. Many travel agencies in both cities provide private taxi service. By car, follow Route 190. First-class bus service on **Cristóbal Colon** costs under $4. You can catch a *colectivo* (shared taxi service in a van or minibus) to San Cristóbal at either of the two airports in Tuxtla Gutiérrez: From the Mexicana airport, it costs about $10 per person; from the Aviasca airport, $9 per person.

BY CAR

From Tuxtla, Route 190 goes east through Chiapa de Corzo to San Cristóbal. Route 190 continues southeast to Comitán and the Guatemalan border. Route 199 is the preferred route from San Cristóbal to Villahermosa via Toniná, Agua Azul, and Palenque. Route 195 is a more circuitous route between San Cristóbal and Villahermosa and entails hours upon hours of hairpin curves; it's only for the stalwart and absolutely not to be traveled at night because of seasonal fog as well as a lack of reflectors, illumination, and other cars to help in case of emergency. Though very expensive, car rentals are available at the Tuxtla and Villahermosa airports as well as in San Cristóbal.

Omnibus Cristóbal Colon (Av. 2 Norte Pte., ☎ 961/2–16–39 or 961/2–26–24) offers deluxe Plus and first- and second-class bus service between Tuxtla and San Cristóbal. The **Cristóbal Colon** terminal is at Avenida Insurgentes and Pan American Highway, Route 190. In San Cristóbal, second-class service to Tuxtla and Guatemala departs from the terminal at Allende and Pan American Highway. **Transportes Tuxtla** (Panamerican Highway at Allende) runs second-class buses northeast along the Ocosingo to Palenque.

Getting Around

The most enjoyable and thorough way to explore San Cristóbal, as with many other colonial Mexican towns, is on foot. Trying to maneuver a car on its narrow, cobblestoned streets filled with pedestrians is a needless test of patience. If you do come to town with a car, leave it in the hotel garage except for excursions outside San Cristóbal. Taxis can be found at the *sitio* (taxi stand) next to the cathedral (☎ 967/8–03–96), and there is colectivo service to outlying villages, departing from and returning to the market. **Budget Rent-a-Car** has offices at Calle Diego de Mazariegos 36 in San Cristóbal (☎ 967/8–18–71 or 967/8–31–00).

Guided Tours

The best travel agencies are **A.T.C.** (Av. 5 de Febrero 15; ☎ 967/8–25–50, 967/8–25–57, 967/8–18–75, 967/8–25–88), **Viajes Pakal** (Calle Cuauhtémoc, No. 6A, ☎ 967/8–28–18 or 967/8–42–93, FAX 967/8–28–19), and **Lacantún** (Calle Madero 18–21, ☎ 967/8–25–87 or 967/8–25–88). Most tour operators transport passengers in minibuses and can arrange hotel pickup.

ORIENTATION TOURS

A.T.C. runs full-day city tours that also cover Na-Bolom, San Juan Chamula, and the San Cristóbal Caves. Five-hour horseback tours to outlying villages can also be arranged.

REGIONAL TOURS

A.T.C., Pakal, and **Lacantún** organize tours to Bonampak, Yaxchilán, Palenque, Agua Azul, Lagunas de Montebello, Amatenango, Belize, Chincultik, Comitán, Guatemala, Sumidero Canyon, Tuxtla Gutiérrez, and Yucatán. Special-interest tours and treks—Lacandon Indians, birdwatching, flora and fauna, river trips, rain-forest excursions—are also available. You can also arrange your trip from the United States through **Ceiba Adventures** (Box 2274, Flagstaff, AZ 86003, ☎ 602/527–0171, FAX 602/527–8127), which offers guided adventure trips to Palenque, Bonampak, and Yaxchilan, including cave explorations plus river rafting along several Chiapan waterways sunk deep in the jungle.

PERSONAL GUIDES

The tourist office can put you in touch with licensed English-speaking guides who leads tours to San Juan Chamula, Zinacantán, and the area ruins.

Important Addresses and Numbers

EMERGENCIES

Municipal police (☎ 967/8–05–54). **Federal Highway Police** (☎ 967/8–64–66). **Cruz Roja (Red Cross;** Prolongación Ignacio Allende, ☎ 967/8–07–72). The **Hospital Regional** is located at Insurgentes 26 (☎ 967/8–07–70). The **Social Security Clinic** is outside of town on Calle Tabasco and Diagonal Centenario (☎ 967/8–07–68).

Soluna (Calle Real de Guadalupe 13B) has a good selection of archaeology and travel books in English.

The **San Cristóbal tourist office** (☎ 967/8-65-70, ℻ 967/8-08-65) is on Insurgentes Sur s/n next to San Francisco Plaza. (It was scheduled to move in 1995; check at the Insurgentes Sur locale for the new address.) Check the bulletin board here upon arrival for information on tours and side trips. ⊘ *Mon.–Sat. 8–8, Sun. 8–2.*

LAGUNAS DE MONTEBELLO

Numbers in the margin correspond to points of interest on the Chiapas and Tabasco map.

East of San Cristóbal lies one of the least explored and most exotic regions of Chiapas: the selva lacandona. Incursions of developers, land-hungry settlers, and refugees from neighboring Guatemala are transforming Mexico's last frontier, which for centuries has been the homeland of the Lacandones, a small tribe descended from the ancient Maya. This trip can be done in a day, as the lakes themselves are 155 kilometers (96 miles) or about 3 hours by car from San Cristóbal. If you are driving during the rainy season, however, the trip may take longer. For extended exploration of the lakes, we suggest an overnight stay in Comitán. The itinerary can be covered by car or tour, but a car is highly preferable because of the freedom it allows for exploration on one's own. Tour agencies in San Cristóbal booking the Montebello Lakes are **A.T.C.** (5 de Febrero 15, ☎ 967/8-25-50, 967/8-18-75, or 967/8-25-88), **Viajes Pakal** (Calle Cuauhtemoc 6A, ☎ 967/8-28-18 or 967/8-42-93), or **Lacantun** (Calle Madero 18-21, ☎ 967/8-25-87, 967/8-25-88).

⑨ Head south 35 kilometers (22 miles) on Route 190 to **Amatenango del Valle,** a small village known for its handsome, primitive pottery. By the side of the road, women sell ocher, black, and brown clay flowerpots and animal figurines that have been fired on open kilns. The rugged foothills and pine groves surrounding San Cristóbal subside into a low plain along the next stretch of the road; the mountains appear to have been sliced in two, revealing their rust-red innards, sad artifacts of the devastating erosion caused by the clearing of the forests.

⑩ **Comitán** is at the halfway point to the lakes, and though the city has few attractions, it is one of the few places on the way to Guatemala that offer lodgings and restaurants. From the zócalo there are fine views of the hills. Comitán's tourist office (☎ 963/2-23-03 through 963/2-23-07, ext. 138 or 139, on the ground floor of the Municipal Palace, facing the zócalo) is open Monday–Saturday 9–8:30, Sunday 9–2.

Many of the Mexicans who work at the few remaining Guatemalan refugee camps in Chiapas live in Comitán. Beginning in 1981, some 46,000 Guatemalan peasants fled a wave of political repression by crossing the border into ramshackle camps, only to be hunted down by the Guatemalan army. Mexico eventually moved more than half of the refugees to safer, more distant camps, but many Guatemalans preferred to remain in Chiapas, and there are still camps near Comitán at Las Margaritas and La Trinitaria. However, most of these refugees have headed home under an amnesty program put into effect in 1993. Comitán, whose original Maya name was Balún-Canán, or "Nine Stars," flourished early on as a major center linking the lowland temperate plains to the edge of the Maya empire on the Pacific. Even today, it serves as the principal trading point for the Tzeltal Indians and such Guatemalan goods as sugarcane liquor and orchids. The present city was built by the Spaniards, but few traces of the colonial era remain. Notable exceptions are two churches, Santo Domingo de Guzmán and San Sebastián, in which part of Chiapas's struggle for independence from Spain took place.

The **Casa-Museo Dr. Belisario Domínguez,** former home of a martyr of the revolution, opened as a museum in 1985 and re-creates that turbulent era with an array of documents and photographs. *Av. Dr. Belisario Domínguez Sur 17.* ☞ *About 35¢.* ☉ *Tues.–Sat. 10–6:45, Sun. 9–12:45.*

⓫ The small, late-classic Maya site of **Chincultik** will interest only hardcore archaeology buffs, although it has a lovely forest location, a view of the Montebello Lakes, and a large *cenote* (sacred well). From Comitán, continue south 15 kilometers (9 miles) on Route 190 until you see a very small turnoff for the lakes (marked only by a green-and-white sign depicting a tree) outside of La Trinitaria. After 39 kilometers (24 miles), there is a dirt road on the left that leads to the ruins, which are another 5 kilometers (3 miles) off the highway; a 10-minute hike is then required. The ruins, which are only partially restored, include a ball court, pyramid, cenote, and stelae. ☞ *About $2.50.* ☉ *Daily 8–4.*

Other small Maya sites newly uncovered include **Tenan Puente** and **Junchavin,** ceremonial centers built at around the same time as Chincultik. Located on the outskirts of Comitán, they are open to the public, though no restoration has been started on them.

At Km 22 is the **Museo Parador Santa Maria** (no ☎), a modest lodging built around the remains of an old hacienda, with seven rooms and a restaurant. These are adequate, inexpensive accommodations.

⓬ Ample signs and guardposts mark the entrance to the **Lagunas de Montebello** (Montebello Lakes), 9 kilometers (5½ miles) away. Together, the 60-odd lakes and surrounding selva constitute a 2,437-acre national park. A different color permeates each lake, whose waters glow with vivid emerald, turquoise, amethyst, azure, and steel-gray tints, caused by various oxides. The setting is serene and majestic, with clusters of oak, pine, and sweet gum. Practically the only denizens of the more accessible part of the forest are the clamorous goldfinch, mockingbirds, and the rare quetzal bird. To the east, wild animals roam: pumas and jaguars, deer and bears.

At the park entrance, the road forks. The left leads to the Lagunas Coloradas (Colored Lakes). At **Laguna Bosque Azul,** the last lake along that road, there are picnic tables, rest rooms, and, at the end of the road, a shabby but serviceable café. In this area, you may encounter local guides who run 10-day walking tours into the jungle, including a visit to the Lacandon village of Lacanjá (near the ruins of Bonampak). This can be a fascinating excursion with someone who knows the area, but make sure you're getting a fair deal. The right fork at the park entrance continues along dirt roads for 14 kilometers (9 miles) before dwindling into a footpath. If you walk down the right fork, you will see some of the more beautiful lakes. The largest, **Tziscao,** forms the border between Mexico and Guatemala and is the site of the Tziscao Lodge and the Hospedaje La Orquidia hostelries, both of which are dirt-cheap and very basic (no hot water), but offer food service, horses, boats, and excellent fishing. Buses leave infrequently from Comitán (2 Av. Poniente Sur 17–B, ☎ 963/2–08–75) to Laguna Bosque Azul and Tziscao. There is also colectivo service.

TUXTLA GUTIÉRREZ

Tuxtla Gutiérrez is the thriving capital city of the state of Chiapas. In 1939 Graham Greene characterized it as "not a place for foreigners—the new ugly capital of Chiapas, without attractions . . . It is like an unnecessary postscript to Chiapas, which should be all wild mountain and old churches and swallowed ruins and the Indians plodding by." That bleak description is slowly changing, as new luxury buildings like the Camino Real Hotel add sparkle to the city. Nonetheless, Tuxtla Gutiérrez is a city through which most visitors to Chiapas will pass, and it is of vital economic and political importance. It is the state's transportation hub, and it does have what is probably the most exciting zoo in Latin America, along with a comprehensive archaeology museum. It is also convenient for its proximity to Chiapa de Corzo and the Sumidero Canyon, which have little in the way of accommodations.

The state capital since 1892, Tuxtla's first name derives from the Nahuatl word *tochtlan,* meaning "abundance of rabbits." Its second name, Gutiérrez, honors Joaquín Miguel Gutiérrez, who fought for the state's independence and incorporation into Mexico.

Exploring

⓭ The highway into town is endless. **Tuxtla** (population 525,000) does not have many conveniences for tourists, and it can be difficult to get your bearings. If you stay on the main drag you will run smack into the zócalo, known locally as the *parque central,* which is fronted by huge government buildings. The Tuxtla tourist office is on the ground floor of Edificio Plaza de las Instituciones (Blvd. Dr. Belisario Domínguez 950, ☎ 961/2–55–09 or 961/2–45–35). It is open weekdays 9–3 and 6–9.

Only the most obstinate animal-hater would fail to be captivated by the free-roaming inmates of the **Tuxtla Zoomat,** all native Chiapans. The 100-plus species on display include black widows, jaguars, marsupials, iguanas, quetzal birds, boa constrictors, tapirs, eagles, and monkeys. *Southeast of town off Libramiento Sur.* ☛ *Free but donation appreciated.* ⊘ *Tues.–Sun. 8:30–5.*

Amateur archaeologists and botanists should head for **Parque Madero,** which includes the Regional Museum of Chiapas (⊘ Tues.–Sun. 9–4), the Botanical Garden (⊘ Tues.–Sun. 8–6), and the orchid house (⊘ Tues.–Sun. 10–1). One of the largest collections of Maya artifacts worldwide is on the ground floor of the museum, an innovative structure of glass, brick, and marble. On the upper floor are displays of colonial pieces and regional handicrafts and costumes. *Northeast of downtown, between 5a Av. Norte and 11a Calle Oriente.* ☛ *Free.*

A fine small museum of indigenous Indian cultures throughout Chiapas opened in 1993 at the government-run **Casa de Las Artesanías,** which also has a good selection of regional handicrafts. Amber from Chiapas (one of the few places in the world with amber mines) fashioned into necklaces, earrings, and pendants, as well as hand-embroidered and brocaded table mats and leather bags, gold filigree jewelry, and lacquerware are among the local specialties. *Blvd. Dr. Belisario Domínguez Km 1083,* ☎ *961/2–22–75.* ☛ *Free.* ⊘ *Daily 9–2 and 5–8.*

As its name suggests, **Parque de Las Marimbas** (Centro and 8 Pte.) hosts marimba bands Thursday through Sunday at 7 PM.

Dining

For price categories, *see* Dining *in* San Cristóbal, *above*.

$$$ Montebello. Lobster and prime rib headline the menu at this classy new specialty restaurant at the Camino Real Hotel. This intimate (only 16 tables) place is most romantic at night when the city lights shimmer into view. The elegance of the earth-tone decor is set off by an unusual white mural of the Sumidero cliffs sculpted into a wall. The chef at the chain's Las Hadas resort in Manzanillo has been shipped to Tuxtla to oversee the kitchen and make a gourmet restaurant out of Montebello. ✕ *Blvd. Dr. Belisario Domínguez 1195,* ☎ *961/7–77–77. Reservations advised for dinner. AE, MC, V. Closed Mon.*

$$ La Selva. Specialties from Chiapas such as a mixed *Chiapaneco* platter with *mole,* rice, beans, and grilled beef top a menu that satisfies multiple tastes with a broad sampling of international dishes. A tropical atmosphere sizzles with marimba music. It's open from 8 AM to midnight. ✕ *Blvd. Dr. Belisario Domínguez 1360,* ☎ *961/5–07–18. MC, V.*

$ Las Pichanchas. This restaurant, open for breakfast, lunch, and dinner, features an outstanding variety of regional dishes, as well as live
★ marimba music and nightly folkloric dances. ✕ *Central Oriente 837,* ☎ *961/2–53–51. AE, MC, V.*

Lodging

Lodgings are plentiful in Tuxtla. For prices, *see* Lodging *in* San Cristóbal, *above*.

$$$$ Camino Real. A new star appeared on the hotel horizon in 1994 with the opening of this hilltop oasis of luxury and comfort. It has already been dubbed "The Chiapanecan Dream" by locals who have never seen anything so fairy-tale beautiful in the state capital. Rooms surround a huge open-air pool and bar area with exotic vegetation; the sounds of jazz emanate at night. A concierge floor, business center with computer rentals, and meeting facilities draw many business travelers, who entertain clients in the Azulejos restaurant, enclosed in a sky-blue glass dome (there's a champagne brunch on Sundays), or at the upscale Montebello (*see* Dining, *above*). All rooms have a view of the mountains, remote-control satellite color TV, room safes, minibars, phones, and full bathroom amenities. ☏ *Blvd. Dr. Belisario Domínguez 1195, 29060,* ☎ *961/7–77–77 or 800/7–CAMINO,* ℻ *961/7–77–71. 210 rooms and suites. 2 restaurants, bar, pool, health club, tennis courts, travel agency, car rental. AE, MC, V.*

$$$$ Hotel Flamboyant. If you want something with Moorish touches and
★ a restful atmosphere, try one of the guest rooms in this luxury hotel. Accommodations are set off long hallways with wide archways; all are air-conditioned and have TVs. Twenty-four rooms face the large garden, while a dozen are located off a smaller and extremely tranquil inner garden. Capacious is the byword: the pool is huge, and so are the public areas. The restaurant is light and airy, but the bar is dark and tacky. A disadvantage is the location—a 10-minute drive west of town—but there's a pretty shopping mall next door. ☏ *Blvd. Dr. Belisario Domínguez Km 1081, 29000,* ☎ *961/5–08–88 or 961/5–09–99,* ℻ *961/5–00–87. 118 rooms. Restaurant, bar, disco, travel agency, car rental. AE, MC, V.*

$$$ Bonampak. A Best Western hotel that has recently been completely and tastefully redone, Bonampak has small rooms and a pool set in lush gardens, which have been whittled down to make way for a shopping mall going up next door. The cafeteria and restaurant have a well-deserved reputation for good regional cooking, steaks, and soups. ☎ *Blvd. Dr. Belisario Domínguez 180, 29030,* ☎ *961/3–20–50 or 800/528–1234,* FAX *961/2–77–37. 70 rooms. Restaurant, cafeteria, bar, pool, tennis, travel agency, car rental. AE, MC, V.*

$$ **Gran Hotel Humberto.** Close to the main square, this hotel has small, functional but air-conditioned rooms, all with TVs (local stations only). The elevators in this eight-story property are old and the hall-ways are dismal, but proximity to downtown is an advantage. ☎ *Central Poniente 180, 29030,* ☎ *961/2–20–80 or 961/2–20–44,* FAX *961/2–97–71. 112 rooms. Restaurant. AE, MC, V.*

Excursions from Tuxtla Gutiérrez

Some 12 kilometers (8 miles) southeast of Tuxtla, on the road to San Cristobal, **Chiapa de Corzo** was founded in 1528 by Diego de Mazarie-gos, who one month later fled the mosquitoes and transported all the settlers to San Cristóbal (then called Chiapa de los Españoles, to dis-tinguish it from Chiapa de los Indios, as Chiapa de Corzo was origi-nally known).

Life in this small, dusty town on the banks of the Grijalva revolves, inevitably, around the zócalo, lorded over by a bizarre 16th-century Mozarabic fountain modeled after Isabella's crown. The interior is dec-orated with stories of the Indians.

Chiapa's lacquerware museum, facing the plaza, contains a modest col-lection of delicately carved and painted *jícaras* (gourds). ("The sky is no more than an immense blue jícara, the beloved firmament in the form of a cosmic jícara," explains the *Popul Vuh*, a 16th-century chronicle of the Quiché Maya.) The lacquerware on display is both local and imported, coming from Michoacán, Guerrero, Chiapas, and Asia. The museum is open Tuesday–Saturday 9–2 and 4–6, Sunday 9–1. A workshop behind the museum is open during the week and gener-ally keeps the same hours as the museum.

TIME OUT On the opposite side of the square from the museum, the **Jardines de Chiapa** (Portal Oriente s/n) serves an excellent and inexpensive variety of regional cuisines in a lovely patio setting. Try the *tasajo* (sun-dried beef served with pumpkin-seed sauce) and the *chipilín con bolita* soup, made with balls of ground corn paste cooked in a creamy herbal sauce and topped with Chiapas's famous cheese.

Several handicraft shops line the square, selling huarches, ceramics, lac-querware, the famous Parachico masks, and regional costumes. Just outside of town, behind the Nestlé plant, are some nearly unnotice-able Maya-Olmec ruins dating from 1450 BC.

The next stop—18 kilometers (11 miles) north of Tuxtla—is the **Sum-idero Canyon,** whose gaping, almost vertical walls descend 4,000 feet for some 15 kilometers (9 miles). It lends itself to comparison with the Grand Canyon; it was formed about 12 million years ago, and the Gri-jalva River slices through it, erupting in waterfalls and coursing through caves. Ducks, pelicans, herons, raccoons, iguanas, and butterflies live at the base, which can be viewed from five lookout points off the high-way; the two-hour trip via colectivo costs $8 per person for a mini-mum of 12 persons. As you visit the canyon, think about the fate of the Chiapa Indians, who jumped into it rather than face slavery at the hands of the Spaniards. Boat trips to the hydroelectric dam in Chicoasen and back depart daily between 7 AM and 4 PM from the tiny island of

Cahuaré and the dock at Chiapa de Corzo; they take approximately two hours and cost about $11 per person (there's a four-person minimum). You can rent your own boat for about $63.

Tuxtla Gutiérrez Essentials

Arriving and Departing

BY PLANE

Mexicana (Belisario Dominguez 1934 L/3, ☏ 961/2–00–20 or 961/1–14–90, FAX 961/2–20–53; at the airport, ☏ 961/3–49–21) flies nonstop to Mexico City from the Tuxtla airport, which is in the town of Ocozocoautla, 22 kilometers (14 miles) west. **Aviacsa** (in Tuxtla, ☏ 961/2–80–81, FAX 961/3–50–29; at the airport, ☏ and FAX 961/5–10–11; in Mexico City, ☏ 5/559–9522) also operates daily flights to Mexico City. *Note:* Mexicana uses the Tuxtla airport, which is frequently fogged in; Aviacsa flies into Aeropuerto Fco. Sarabia, which is not. In 1994, Mexicana got permission to use Aviacsa's airport in foggy weather.

BY CAR

Route 190 goes from San Cristóbal to Tuxtla and west into Oaxaca. If you are skipping Palenque, an alternative road to or from Villahermosa is via Pichucalco, on Route 195. Although it's paved and rushes past beautiful scenery, the road is a nightmare of endless miles of hairpin curves. The trip takes 6 hours, so leave early enough to arrive at your destination before the sun goes down. Driving this road at night is dangerous.

BY BUS

Omnibus Cristóbal Colón (Av. 2 Norte Pte., ☏ 961/2–16–39 or 961/2–26–24) offers deluxe *plus* and first- and second-class bus service between Tuxtla and Oaxaca, Palenque, Villahermosa, Tapachula, and Mérida.

Guided Tours

Viajes Miramar (1A Oriente Norte 310, ☏ 961/2–39–83, 961/2–39–30; or Hotel Camino Real, local 2, ☏ 961/7–77–77, ext. 7230, FAX 961/5–5925), run by the Fernandez sisters, offers city tours of Tuxtla Gutiérrez, plus excursions to Chiapa de Corzo and Sumidero Canyon.

VILLAHERMOSA AND TABASCO

Graham Greene's succinct summation of Tabasco as a "tropical state of river and swamp and banana grove" captures its essence. Though the state played an important role in the early history of Mexico, its past is rarely on view; instead, it is Tabasco's modern-day status as a supplier of oil that overwhelms the visitor. Set on a humid coastal plain and crisscrossed by abundant rivers, low hills, and unexplored jungles, the landscape is marred by shantytowns and refineries reeking of sulfur. The capital city of **Villahermosa** epitomizes the mercurial development of Tabasco (the airplane was here before the automobile). Though the city has cramped and ugly neighborhoods, the newer areas are spacious and have beautiful buildings and landscaping. Villahermosa is the home of a fine archaeology museum, and it is also the place to see the giant stone heads carved by Tabasco's ancient inhabitants, the Olmecs.

This is not to say that the rest of Tabasco has nothing to offer the visitor. There are beaches, but the tourist infrastructure is minimal, and in some places strollers might come away with tar on their feet. The fired-brick Maya ruins of Comalcalco attest to the influence of Palenque. Probably the most interesting region is the one to the south and east of Villahermosa, where rivers and canyons are home to jaguars, deer, and alligators; this was where the English pirate Sir Francis Drake hid from the Spaniards.

Tabasco—specifically the mouth of the River Grijalva—lay along the route of the Spanish explorations of Mexico in 1518–19. At that time, the state's rivers and waterways, along which the Olmecs and their descendants lived, served as a trade route between the peoples of the north and those of the south. When the Spaniards came to Tabasco, they had to bridge 50 rivers and contend with swarms of mosquitoes, beetles, and ants, as well as with almost unbearable heat, but the region was so lush that one early chronicler termed it a Garden of Eden.

The Spanish conquest was facilitated by the state of almost constant tribal warfare between the Tabascans and their Aztec overlords. Among the 20 slave women turned over to the victors was a Chiapan named Malintzín, or Malinche, who was singled out by the Spaniards for her beauty and her ability to speak both the Maya and the Nahuatl languages. Called Marina by the Spaniards, she learned Spanish and became not only Cortés's mistress and the mother of his illegitimate son but also the willing interpreter of Indian customs. Marina's cooperation helped the conquistador trounce both Moctezuma and Cuauhtémoc, the last Aztec emperors.

Until the early 20th century Tabasco slumbered; it did not become a state until 1824. After the American Civil War, traders from the southern United States began operating in the region and on its rivers, hauling the precious mahogany trees upstream from Chiapas and shipping them north from the small Tabascan port of Frontera. This was Tabasco's most prosperous era until the discovery of oil 50 years ago and the oil boom of the 1980s. Now the city is about to enter another era of prosperity with the relocation of PEMEX (the government-run oil monopoly) research offices to Villahermosa.

Exploring

Downtown Villahermosa contains a pedestrian shopping mall, a museum of popular culture, and a folk-art shop, but the **CICOM Museum of Anthropology** should be seen first. Located on the right bank of the Grijalva, the museum is part of a huge cultural complex dedicated to research on the Olmec and Maya (which is what the Spanish acronym CICOM stands for) and provides one of the last tranquil vistas of Villahermosa as it might have looked 50 years ago. Although most of the explanations are in Spanish, that should not detract from the visual pleasure of the displays. The entire ground floor is devoted to Tabasco and the Olmec, or "inhabitants of the land of rubber," who flourished in Tabasco as early as 1800 BC and disappeared about 1,600 years later. The Olmecs have long been honored as the mother culture of Mesoamerica and as inventors of the numerical and calendrical systems that spread throughout the region, though recent research suggests that the Olmecs might actually have been influenced by the Maya, rather than the other way around.

Some of the most interesting artifacts of the Olmec, other than the giant stone heads on view at Parque La Venta (*see below*), are the remnants of their jaguar cult, which are displayed in the museum. The jaguar symbolized the earth fertilized by rain, and many Olmec sculptures portray werejaguars (half-human, half-jaguar, similar to a werewolf) or jaguar babies. Other sculptures portray human heads emerging from the mouth of a jaguar, bat gods, bird-headed humans, and female fertility figurines. The collection of recently discovered burial urns, found in the Tapijulapa caves west of Palenque, is outstanding. All of Mexico's ancient cultures are represented on the upper two floors, from the red-clay dogs of Colima and the nose rings of Nayarit to the huge burial urns of the Chontal Maya, who built Comalcalco. Don't miss the vivid reproductions of the Maya murals from Bonampak. CICOM also houses a handicrafts shop, restaurant, library, and theater. *Carlos Pellicer 511, an extension of the malecón,* ☎ 93/12–95–21. ☛ *About $3.* ☉ *Daily 9–8.*

TIME OUT   Stop off for a beer and a plate of fresh shrimp at the **Capitán Beulo** (Paseo Malecón Madrazo and Zaragoza), a small riverboat restaurant that also runs 90-minute cruises along the Grijalva. There's no admission charge for the cruise, but passengers must order food (no minimum). The cruise departs at 1:30, 3:30, and 9 PM every day except Monday.

The giant stone heads carved by the Olmec and salvaged from the oil fields of La Venta, on the western edge of Tabasco near the state of Veracruz, are on display in **Parque La Venta,** situated west of CICOM in a tropical garden on the beautiful Lago de las Ilusiones (Lake of Illusions). These six-foot-tall, baby-faced Negroid heads, weighing upwards of 20 tons, have sparked endless scholarly debate. It has been theorized that they depict ancient Phoenician slaves who wound up on the coasts of Mexico, that they were meant to represent space invaders, and that because of the obesity and short limbs of the figures, they are proof of endocrine deficiencies among the ancient Olmec. More likely, they simply celebrate the earth's fecundity. La Venta contains 30 sculptures, not all of them heads. There are also were jaguars, priests, monsters, stelae, and stone altars oddly reminiscent of ancient Mesopotamian art. The park also has a tiny zoo with creatures such as Tabascan river crocodiles and wild parrots. A small natural history museum, the **Museo del Historia Natural,** recently opened just outside the entrance to the park, to the left of the admission booths. It's filled with attractive displays of Tabasco's native plants and animal species, which are now under the protection of the government's new conservation policies. *Blvd. Ruiz Cortines near Paseo Tabasco,* ☎ 93/5–22–28. ☛ *Museum, zoo, and park: about $1.50; park only: 90¢.* ☉ *Daily 9–4.*

Dining

For price categories, *see* Dining *in* San Cristóbal, *above.*

$$ **El Mesón del Duende.** This restaurant, which translates as the House of the Elf, serves Spanish cuisine, including a savory Galician broth, veal, goat, paella, and seafood. The modest decor is in keeping with the family-style atmosphere. ✕ *Gregorio Méndez 1703,* ☎ 93/5–13–24. *MC, V.* ☉ *Until 1 AM. Closed Wed.*

$$ **Los Tulipanes.** Next door to the CICOM Museum, the spacious Los
★   Tulipanes specializes in steaks and seafood and has a tranquil view of the river. Try the stuffed crab, shrimp, or the Tabasco specialty, *pejelagarto,* a fish that resembles a small alligator but is a succulent treat. ✕ *Carlos Pellicer 511,* ☎ 93/2–92–09 or 93/2–92–17. *AE, MC, V.*

$ **Leo.** This is a very popular spot for tasty beef and pork tacos with a large menu and a spacious dining area. ✕ *Paseo Tabasco 429,* ☎ 93/12–44–63. *MC, V.* ☉ *Daily till 1 AM.*

Lodging

Villahermosa hotels are relatively expensive, especially when compared with those in San Cristóbal. Generally speaking, the newer, American-style hotels are away from the city center, near Tabasco 2000 and Parque La Venta, and the older and more modest hotels are downtown. For price categories, *see* Lodging *in* San Cristóbal, *above*.

$$$$ **Holiday Inn.** Situated across from La Choca Park, this inviting nine-story resort property offers air-conditioned rooms with cable TV, minibars, and room service. The rambling lobby, with attractive niches and corners and rattan furniture, eventually leads to the Tabasco 2000 shopping mall, which has the largest number of upscale stores in Villahermosa. A restaurant below the hotel lobby has floor-to-ceiling windows shaded by bamboo curtains and a lovely garden view. There's live nightly entertainment in the Jaguar Lounge. ☎ *Paseo Tabasco 1407, 86030,* ☎ *93/16–44–00 or 800/HOLIDAY,* ☎ *93/16–45–69. 190 rooms. Restaurant, bar, pool. AE, DC, MC, V.*

$$$$ **Hyatt Regency Villahermosa.** This American-style luxury hotel built in 1983 offers the amenities of the worldwide Hyatt chain: air-conditioned rooms with cable TV, voice mail, and minibars, plus two executive floors with concierge service. The coffee shop has been newly remodeled with pleasing tropical decor, and the popular El Plataforma video bar in the lobby is decked out like the inside of an offshore oil platform with photos of oilmen at work. The Snob disco attracts the young and restless, especially on weekends. ☎ *Av. Juarez 106, Zona Hotelera, 86050,* ☎ *93/13–44–44, 93/15–12–34 or 800/228–9000,* ☎ *93/15–58–08 or 93/15–12–35. 206 rooms. 2 restaurants, 3 bars, pool, 2 tennis courts, disco, travel services, car rental. AE, DC, MC, V.*

$$$ **Calinda Viva Villahermosa.** This hotel has an attractive whitewashed exterior reminiscent of a hacienda and a spacious lobby decorated in earth tones that has an Old Mexico feeling about it. The hotel's restaurant, in fact, is named La Hacienda and features many regional dishes like tamales with *chipílin* herb and cream of *cha-ya* (a spinachlike plant) soup. The staff is friendly and very helpful. All of the 241 rooms have air-conditioning, FM stereos, color TVs, and phones; many have balconies. ☎ *Paseo Tabasco 1201, 86050,* ☎ *93/15–00–00,* ☎ *93/5–30–73. Restaurant, 2 bars, coffee shop, pool, disco. AE, DC, MC, V.*

$$$ **Cencali.** This colonial-style hotel in the new hotel zone is situated in a park and surrounded by lakes and lush greenery; it definitely has the best view in town. All the cheerfully decorated rooms have lots of light and vistas of either the lakes or the lagoon; 30 of the best also have balconies looking out over coconut palm, guava, and almond trees. All the accommodations are air-conditioned. ☎ *Juárez and Paseo Tabasco, 86040,* ☎ *93/5–19–94 through 93/5–19–99,* ☎ *93/5–66–00. 116 rooms, 3 suites. Restaurant, bar, pool. AE, DC, MC, V.*

$$$ **Maya Tabasco Best Western.** The Maya Tabasco has 156 rooms with air-conditioning, TVs, and phones, a rather plain lobby, a gift shop, and a dazed-looking staff. This is the best hotel in the neighborhood near the crowded downtown area, and will do if all other hotels listed are full (which happens quite often). ☎ *Ruiz Cortines 907, 86000,* ☎ *93/14–44–66, 93/14–03–60 or 800/528–1234,* ☎ *93/12–10–97. MC, V.*

$$ **Don Carlos.** Formerly the Manzur, this downtown hotel has always been popular for its unpretentious atmosphere and good service. TVs and phones are available in every room. ☎ *Av. Madero 422, 86000,* ☎ *93/2–*

24–99, FAX *93/2–46–22. 102 rooms, 14 suites. Restaurant, bar, lounge. AE, MC, V.*

Excursions from Villahermosa

The most important Maya site in Tabasco is **Comalcalco,** about 60 kilometers (37 miles) northwest of Villahermosa off Route 187. The abundant cocoa plants in the region provided food and livelihood for a booming population during the late classic period (AD 600–900), when Comalcalco was built; the site marks the westernmost reach of the Maya. Descendants of the Chontal Maya, who constructed Comalcalco, still live in the vicinity. This site is unique among Mayan cities for its use of fired brick, as the Tabasco swamplands lacked the stone for building that was found elsewhere in the Mayan empire. The bricks were apparently inscribed and painted with enigmatic "anonymous messages" before being covered with stucco. The major pyramid, on the Great Eastern Acropolis, is decorated with large stucco masks and carvings, and the museum houses many of the artifacts that were uncovered there. ☞ *About $1.50.* ☉ *Daily 9–4:30.*

If not seeing the Gulf of Mexico will leave you feeling deprived, continue 19 kilometers (12 miles) to **Paraíso.** Bear in mind, however, that Tabasco is not known for its beaches: For the most part, they are dirty and almost totally lacking in tourist infrastructure. There is one hotel on the beach and others in the town of Paraíso, a few kilometers inland.

Villahermosa and Tabasco Essentials

Arriving and Departing

BY PLANE

Aeromexico has daily nonstop service from Mexico City. **Mexicana** has three daily nonstop flights from Mexico City, and both airlines offer connecting flights to other Mexican cities. Travel agencies book charter flights to Palenque and Bonampak.

BY CAR

Take Route 186 from Palenque and points east (Campeche, Chetumal, Mérida), Route 195 from Tuxtla (it's very curvy), or Route 180 from Coatzacoalcos and Veracruz.

BY BUS

There is frequent first- and second-class service to Campeche, Chetumal, Mérida, Mexico City, Palenque, San Cristóbal, Tapachula, Tuxtla Gutiérrez, Veracruz, and elsewhere. Buses arrive and depart from **Centro de Autobuses de Tabasco** (Carretera del Golfo s/n, ☎ 93/2–29–77). Deluxe and first-class service is available to the above cities, also on **ADO** (Calle F.J. Mina 297, ☎ 93/12–14–46 or 93/12–76–92).

Getting Around

Villahermosa—population 500,000—is surrounded by three rivers but oriented toward the River Grijalva to the east, which is bordered by the *malecón* (boardwalk). The city is huge, and driving can be tricky. The main road through town is almost a highway; exit ramps are about 1 kilometer (½ mile) apart, and tourist destinations are not clearly marked. Nevertheless, driving is the best way to get around. Most taxi service is collective and runs along fixed routes; information about city buses, on the other hand, can be difficult to find.

BY RENTAL CAR

Several major car rental companies, including Avis, Dollar, Hertz, and National, have offices in Villahermosa and at the airport. Reliable local companies include **Tabasco Auto Rent** (Blvd. Ruíz Cortines 1201, ☎ 93/2–80–03 or 93/2–34–69) and **Rentauto Usumacinta** (Hotel Cencali, ☎ 93/5–18–21 or 93/5–19–99), which also has an office at the Aeropuerto Internacional.

Important Addresses and Numbers

TRAVEL AGENCIES

Agencia de Viajes Tabasco (Madero 718, ☎ 93/2–53–18, 93/2–50–96, FAX 93/4–27–80, or Galeria Tabasco 2000, ☎ 93/6–40–88, FAX 93/16–64–37) and **Turismo Grijalva** (Zaragoza 911, ☎ 93/2–43–94, or 93/4–42–05, FAX 93/12–25–96) offer a range of excursions from the city.

VISITOR INFORMATION

The main tourist office is located in the huge Tabasco 2000 complex, opposite the municipal palace. *Paseo Tabasco 1504, Tabasco 2000 complex,* ☎ *93/6–36–33, 93/6–28–89, or 93/6–28–91.* ☉ *Weekdays 9–3 and 6–8. An auxiliary office at Parque La Venta is open daily 9–4.*

PALENQUE

⑮ The ruins of **Palenque** are to many people the most beautiful in all Mexico. Chichén Itzá may be more expansive, and Teotihuacan more monumental, but Palenque possesses a mesmerizing quality, perhaps because of its intimacy. It is, after all, just a cluster of ocher buildings intermingled with grassy mounds and tall palm groves set in a rain forest. But in the early morning or late afternoon, sunlight illuminates the structures in a hazy, iridescent glow; there are the eerie shrill calls of birds, and the local Indians, descendants of the Maya, wander about collecting banana leaves, oranges, and avocados. Whether or not visitors are archaeology fans, they cannot fail to be moved by the sanctity of Palenque.

A Spanish priest was led to the site by some local Indians in 1773, and in 1785 a royal Spanish expedition made its way to Palenque. In about 1833 an eccentric German count set up house with his mistress for three years in a building known as the Templo del Conde (Temple of the Count). American explorers John Lloyd Stephens and Frederick Catherwood lived briefly in the palace during their 1840 expedition. In 1923 serious excavations began under the direction of Franz Blom, cofounder of Na-Bolom in San Cristóbal. Work continued intermittently until 1952, when Alberto Ruz Lhuillier, a Mexican archaeologist, uncovered the tomb of the 7th-century King Pacal beneath the Temple of the Inscriptions.

Seeing Palenque, one can understand why archaeologist Sylvanus Morley honored the Maya as the "Greeks of the New World." The most important buildings of the site date from the mid- to late-classic period (6th–9th centuries), although it was inhabited as early as 1500 BC. Palenque marks the architectural apogee of the western Maya empire.

Since the early 1980s, groundbreaking work has been done on the Maya by archaeologists, linguists, and astronomers. The deciphering of 98% of Palenque's hieroglyphics in 1988 has revolutionized scholars' understanding of both the Maya and the bloody history of Palenque. For example, the glyphs have revealed the complex history of the Palenque dynasties and shown how prevalent self-mutilation was. It is now hypothesized that Palenque reached its peak during a period of transition for Maya civilization, when the rulers—Pacal in particular—were bent on expanding the city-state's power over rival city-states. The site was abandoned around AD 800 for reasons still hotly disputed, making it one of the earliest Maya sites to be deserted in a west-to-east extinction pattern. In its heyday, Palenque encompassed nearly 25 square miles; the excavated portions of the ruins cover only a half mile.

Exploring

The ruins are open daily 8–5, and there is an admission charge of about $1.50. Since no formal guides are available, we suggest that you buy a guidebook in town.

Temple of the Inscriptions

On your right as you enter the site is a 75-foot pyramid. Reaching the tomb inside involves a relatively easy, if slow, climb. The pyramid is dedicated to Pacal, the "Mesoamerican Charlemagne," who took Palenque to its most glorious heights during his 70-year reign, which ended circa AD 692.

Once at the summit, take a good, long look around you, particularly at the imposing palace to your right, which fills the field of vision. This is the best view of Palenque, and it provides an excellent orientation to the other buildings. Atop this temple and the smaller surrounding temples are vestiges of roof combs—delicate vertical extensions that resemble ornamental hair combs worn by Spanish women—one of the most distinctive architectural features of the southern Mayas. Then descend 80 feet down a steep, damp flight of stairs into the tomb, one of the first crypts ever found inside a Mexican pyramid. (This is not for claustrophobes, particularly on very warm days and when the site is crowded.) Pacal's diadem and majestic jade, shell, and obsidian mask are in Mexico City's Museum of Anthropology. The intricately carved sarcophagus lid, weighing some 5 tons and measuring 10 by 7 feet, however, remains. A "psychoduct," or hollow stone tube through which Pacal's soul was thought to have passed to the netherworld, leads up to the temple. It can be difficult to make out the carvings on the slab, but they depict Pacal, prostrate beneath a sacred ceiba tree. The lords of the nine underworlds are carved into stucco reliefs on the walls around him; his more earthly companions were several youths, whose remains were uncovered in an antechamber of the sepulcher. ☉ *Tomb: daily 10:30–4.*

Temple 13

In 1994, this small and unassuming temple attached to the Temple of the Inscriptions revealed a royal tomb hidden in its depths. The tomb, which probably belonged to Pacal's mother or grandmother is under investigation at this writing but will be on view in the site's museum in the future.

Palace

Built at different times, the palace is a complex of patios, galleries, and other buildings set on a 30-foot-high platform. Stucco work adorns the pillars of the galleries and the inner courtyards. There are numerous friezes and masks inside, most of them depicting Pacal and his dynasty. Remarkably well preserved, their style is sinuous and linear, stylized but restrained. Steam baths in the Southwestern Patio suggest that priests once dwelled in the adjoining cellars and that the galleries were probably used for religious ceremonies.

Group of the Cross

To the right of the palace you'll cross the tiny Otulum River, which in ancient times was roofed over to form a nine-foot-high vaulted causeway, or aqueduct. Tombs were discovered beneath the largest, the

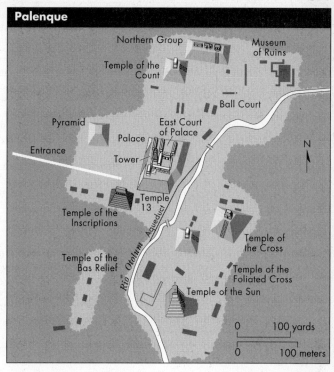

Palenque

Temple of the Cross, and the most exquisite roof combs are found on these buildings.

Northern Group

To reach this cluster, walk north along the river (little more than a creek), passing the palace and then the unexcavated ball court on your left. This group includes five buildings in varying states of disrepair, of which the largest and best preserved is the Temple of the Count.

Complex "C"

A short hike northwest of the Northern Group lies a recently opened area containing remains of the homes of Maya nobles and a few small temples completely shrouded in jungle. In order to maintain the natural setting in which the ruins were found, minimal restoration is being done. Early explorers like John L. Stephens cut pathways through the area, which can still be followed down through a meandering river today.

Museum

A new museum includes fine stelae, hieroglyphs, and, especially noteworthy, the stucco fragments of handsome Maya faces. There are also maps of the Maya zone and of Palenque itself. The museum, just outside the parking lot entrance to the ruins along the highway, is open daily 9–5.

Off the Beaten Track

Just 18 kilometers (11 miles) from Palenque is the waterfall of **Misol-Ha,** 2 kilometers (1 mile) to the right off Route 199; swimming is permitted in the pool formed by the 100-foot cascade. The much larger and faster falls of **Agua Azul** are another 22 kilometers (14 miles) toward Ocosingo (4 more kilometers—2½ miles—off the highway);

swimming is permitted. Both of these cataracts are surrounded by giant palm fronds and tropical flowers; monkeys and toucans frolic in the vicinity. There are restaurants, camping facilities, and rest rooms.

Between San Cristóbal and Palenque, on a dirt road running along the Jatate River in the midst of the steamy jungle, is the archaeological site of **Toniná.** Currently under exploration, this site is closely linked to Palenque: Recent excavations indicate that the vanquished rulers of Palenque and Yaxchilán were brought here as prisoners for execution. To date, several ball courts and the main pyramid platform, taller than those of Tikal and Teotihuacán, have been uncovered. As one of the last major ceremonial centers to flourish before the Maya decline in this area, Toniná, with its monumental architecture and noteworthy sculptures, is rapidly adding to our knowledge of Maya civilization. Toniná can be reached by following the dirt road from Ocosingo, off Route 199.

Dining

Generally speaking, the food served in Palenque town is modest in both quality and price. On the other hand, most of the restaurants are open-air, which is where you want to be in this part of Mexico (except when it rains, and then the thatched roofs are welcome). Try **El Paraíso,** 2 kilometers (1 mile) from the ruins; **La Selva,** next door to the Hotel La Cañada, Merle Green 14; or the **Calinda Nututún Viva,** at the hotel of the same name. Don't expect to use credit cards.

Lodging

For prices, *see* Lodging *in* San Cristóbal, *above.*

$$$$ **Misión Palenque.** This motel-style resort is the town's only luxury hotel. Located on the north side of town off Route 199, it has a free shuttle bus to the ruins. All rooms are air-conditioned and have a terrace, minibar, and phone. ☒ *Rancho San Martín de Porres, 29960,* ☎ *934/5–00–66 or 934/5–04–44,* ☒ *934/5–03–00. 144 rooms. Restaurant-bar, pool, tennis court. AE, DC, MC, V.*

$$$ **Chan Kah.** Four kilometers (2½ miles) from the ruins in a paradisiacal ★ jungle setting, this property has a stone-lined pool, a resident spider monkey, aromatic jasmine bushes, and a stream flowing around the back. The restaurant is overpriced, and meals are accompanied by Muzak and movie soundtracks, but the 14 bungalows feature mahogany furnishings and have ceiling fans (surprisingly adequate, despite the humidity); bungalows 6 through 10 offer views of both the pool and the stream. ☒ *Km 3 Carr. Ruinas 29960,* ☎ *934/5–11–00, 934/5–07–62, 934/5–08–26, or 934/5–09–74,* ☒ *934/5–08–20. 38 units. Restaurant-bar, lagoon-style pool. MC, V.*

$$ **Nututún Viva Palenque.** This property has 60 air-conditioned rooms, restaurant/bar, disco, natural pool, and trailer park. ☒ *Apdo. 74, Carretera Ocosingo Km. 3.5, 29960,* ☎ *934/5–01–00 or 934/5–01–61,* ☒ *934/5–06–33. AE, DC, MC, V.*

Excursions from Palenque

Because access is difficult, only the most devoted fans of the Maya will attempt the trip to the ruins of **Bonampak** and **Yaxchilán** (Yasche-*lan*), 183 and 133 kilometers (114 and 83 miles), respectively, southeast of Palenque. Bonampak is renowned for its vivid murals of ancient Maya life, though some segments of them are sadly deteriorated; they are under constant restoration because the high humidity in the area eats away at the colors. (The reproductions at the archaeological museums in Mexico City and Villahermosa are better.) Recent excavations at Yaxchilán, on the other hand, have uncovered captivating temples and carvings in a superb jungle setting.

Bonampak, a contemporary of Yaxchilán, was built on the banks of the Lacanjá River during the 7th and 8th centuries and remained undiscovered until 1946. Explorer Jacques Soustelle called it "a pictorial encyclopedia of a Mayan city." Indeed, the scenes portrayed in the three rooms of the Templo de las Pinturas graphically recall subjects such as life at court and the prelude and aftermath of battle with unusual realism.

Yaxchilán, which means "place of green stones," is a contemporary of Bonampak. It is dominated by two acropolises containing a palace, temples with finely carved lintels, and great staircases. Until very recently, the Lacandon, who live in the vicinity, made pilgrimages to this site in the heart of the jungle, leaving behind "god pots" (incense-filled ceramic bowls) in honor of ancient deities. They were particularly awed by the headless sculpture of Xachtun (Washa-*tun*) at the entrance to the temple (called structure 33) and believe that the world will end when its head is replaced on its torso.

Yaxchilán was situated on the trade route between Palenque and Tikal; the site was recently threatened with destruction by plans for a huge dam to be built by Mexico and Guatemala. The plans have been put on hold due to lack of funds, though they may yet come to fruition.

Arriving and Departing
Both sites can be reached by making arrangements for a small chartered plane in Palenque or San Cristóbal. In San Cristóbal, contact **A.T.C.** (5 de Febrero 15, ☎ 967/82–5–50, 967/8–18–75, or 967/8–25–88). The six-hour, round-trip tour costs about $300 (possibly less, with a minimum of four people) and includes lunch. In Palenque, contact **Viajes Shivalva** (Calle Merle Green 1A or Apartado 237, ☎ 934/5–04–11, ℻ 934/5–03–92); in the U.S., contact **Ceiba Adventures** (Box 2274, Flagstaff, AZ 86003, ☎ 602/527–0171, ℻ 602/527–8127). The trip takes five hours and costs the same as the trip from San Cristóbal. Some trips add the Lacandon village of Lacanjá. (For other tours to the ruins, *see* San Cristóbal, *above*). A road that will connect Yaxchilán with Bonampak is under consideration. In any case, wear sturdy shoes, carry insect repellent, and protect yourself from mosquitoes, ticks, sandflies, and undergrowth.

Palenque Essentials
Arriving and Departing
BY PLANE
Chartered flights are available through travel agencies in Tuxtla Gutiérrez, San Cristóbal, and Villahermosa; many of them continue on to the ruins of Bonampak and Yaxchilán.

BY CAR
The 90-minute, 143-kilometer (89-mile) trip from Villahermosa on Route 186 to Catazajá, then on Route 199 to Palenque, is easy; most of the way the roads are straight and paved. It takes about four hours to drive from Palenque to San Cristóbal on scenic Routes 199 and 190. Exercise caution during the rainy season (June through October), when the roads are slick.

Daily trains from Mexico City take at least 24 hours and are very uncomfortable. First-class service from Mérida takes 11 hours; second-class service makes more stops and takes 16 hours. The train station is 10 kilometers (6 miles) from town.

First- and second-class service is available from Villahermosa (2½ hours), San Cristóbal (6 hours), Mexico City (14 hours), Mérida (8 hours), Campeche (6 hours), and Tuxtla Gutiérrez (9 hours).

Getting Around

The town of Palenque, some 8 kilometers (5 miles) east of the ruins, is dusty, unsightly, and commercial, providing only the most basic dining and lodging facilities. Shops on the main street have an adequate selection of regional crafts, though there are much better offerings in San Cristóbal. The tourist office (Av. Juárez and Abasolo at the Plaza de las Artesanias, ☎ 934/5–07–60, 934/5–08–28, FAX 934/5–01–41, 934/5–02–39) is open weekdays 9–3 and 6–9.

Visitors with a car will have the easiest time reaching both Palenque and its surrounding attractions, but colectivo service is available from the town center to the ruins and the neighboring waterfalls.

12 Northeastern Mexico and Veracruz

Many winter Texans get their first taste of Mexico in the northeastern border towns of Nueva Laredo, Reynosa, and Matamoros; those who venture farther down to Monterrey are rewarded with the far more sophisticated dining and shopping of the country's third-largest city. The little-explored pyramids of El Tajín and the raffish charm of Veracruz, the first European city established on the North American mainland, are among the many reasons to continue south.

IF THE NORTHEASTERNMOST Mexican states of Nuevo Leon and Tamalipaus are not, for the most part, the Mexico touted in glossy color brochures and full-page magazine ads, they are by no means bereft of attractions. A hybrid of Mexican and U.S. culture, the three border cities of Nuevo Laredo, Reynosa, and Matamoros are good places to pick up handicrafts and sample authentic Mexican dishes at relatively low prices. Improved roads have also led more people to take advantage of the opportunity to visit Monterrey, Mexico's third-largest city and the region's highlight, offering cultural attractions, five-star hotels and restaurants, and, of course, shops. In Monterrey, you can arrange horseback rides and treks into the pine forests of the nearby Sierra Madre mountains. And just north of the border between the states of Veracruz and Tamaulipas, the port of Tampico bustles with New Orleans–style atmosphere.

Those who venture down into the state of Veracruz will be well rewarded for their efforts. The area is rich in culture and history: Visitors can explore El Tajín, one of Mexico's most fascinating and least visited archaeological sites; wander the venerable port of Veracruz, where the Spanish first landed in 1519; witness the fascinating ritual of the *volodores* of Papantla; and enjoy an archaeological museum second only to the one in Mexico City. They can also stroll the plazas of quaint mountain villages, laze on sandy beaches, and dine on some of the best seafood in Mexico, prepared in the famous Veracruz style.

NORTHEASTERN MEXICO

Updated by
Jessica Blatt
and "Mexico"
Mike Nelson

Few travelers go out of their way to visit northeastern Mexico, an arid area that's becoming increasingly industrial as more and more multinational companies establish *maquiladoras* (foreign-owned factories in duty-free zones) along the border. But day- and weekend-trippers from Texas enjoy the foreign color and cuisine of border towns like Nuevo Laredo, Matamoros, and Reynosa. And only 230 km (143 miles) from the border is Monterrey, a fast-paced city that's home to Mexico's major brewery, some good museums, and one of Latin America's finest universities.

Nature lovers can enjoy the Parque Nacional Cumbres de Monterrey, northwest of the city, with its impressive Cola de Caballo (Horsetail Falls). Also near Monterrey are the dramatic Barranca de Huasteca (Huasteca Canyon) and Grutas García, caves with an underground lake and a stalactite and stalagmite forest. Many sports enthusiasts are lured farther down into the area by the magnificent hunting and fishing at Lake Vincente Guerrero, not far from Ciudad Victoria. Those seeking salt-water attractions will find plenty by the sea near Tampico, which also boasts many interesting architectural sights.

Exploring

Numbers in the margin correspond to points of interest on the Northeastern Mexico map.

1 Two bridges connect **Nuevo Laredo** with Laredo, Texas. However, tourists must use either International Bridge 1 or the Columbia Bridge, 42 kilometers (26 miles) northwest of Laredo, the only ones with facilities for clearing people and vehicles for travel to the interior of Mexico. For brief excursions across the border, consider leaving

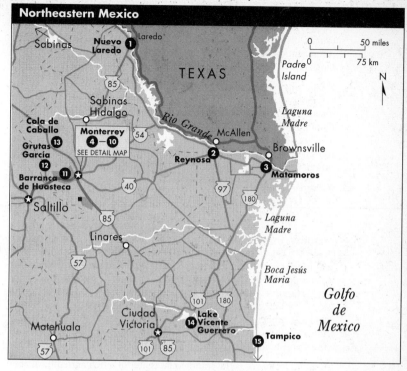

Northeastern Mexico

your car in Laredo and walking over. This eliminates the long wait—often a half hour or more—to bring a car back into the United States.

Of all the eastern border towns, Nuevo Laredo receives the largest onslaught of American souvenir-seekers. Shopping is the primary pursuit here, and you'll find a warren of stalls and shops concentrated on Avenida Guerrero in a seven-block stretch that extends from the International Bridge to the main plaza. In addition to the standard border town schlock, Nuevo Laredo shops stock a good selection of high-quality handicrafts imported from all over Mexico, at somewhat inflated prices. Wander a few blocks off the main drag in any direction for better prices and smaller crowds. There's also a large crafts market on the east side of Avenida Guerrero, just north of the plaza.

Nuevo Laredo was founded after the Treaty of Guadalupe Hidalgo in 1848, which ended the Mexican-American War. The treaty established the Río Bravo (or Rio Grande) as the border between the two countries, and forced Mexico to give up a substantial amount of territory. Many of Laredo's Mexican residents, who suddenly found themselves living in the United States, crossed the river and founded Nuevo Laredo on what had been the outskirts of town. Today, Nuevo Laredo's economy depends greatly on gringos who head south for a few days of drunken revelry, returning home with a bottle of tequila, suitcases full of souvenirs, and a mean hangover.

2 Because of its manageable size and mellow attitude, **Reynosa,** across the border from McAllen, Texas, is one of the most pleasant points of entry into Mexico and a convenient starting point if you're bound for Mexico City, Monterrey, or the Bajío. That said, Reynosa is still an industrial border town of limited charm, driven economically by the petrochemical industry, agriculture, and the ever-present tourist trade. As you enter town, you'll see the Zona Rosa (Pink Zone) tourist district, with a few curio shops and a couple of bars and restaurants. The heart of the city, around Plaza Principal, is about five blocks from the International Bridge.

Plaza Principal is in many ways a typical Mexican town center, but its original colonial church has been joined like a Siamese twin to an ultramodern newer addition with arches and stained-glass windows. Hidalgo Street, a colorful pedestrian mall of shops and street vendors, leads off from the plaza. Many Texans save money by having their teeth fixed south of the Rio Grande—which explains the many dental offices you'll see in this area.

③ Matamoros, across from Brownsville, Texas (the southernmost point in the continental United States), is the most historic of the border towns, dating from the 18th century. It is named H. Matamoros, or Heroic Matamoros, for one of the many rebellious priests who was executed by the Spaniards during the War of Independence (1810–1821). The first major battle of the Mexican-American War was fought here when guns in Matamoros began shelling Fort Brown on the north side of the river. Shortly afterward, troops of Zachary Taylor occupied Matamoros and began their march south. During the U.S. Civil War, nearby Bagdad became a major port for Confederate blockade runners. A wild and wicked place, Bagdad was destroyed by a hurricane a century ago; treasure hunters often discover bits and pieces of it among the dunes on the beach.

Today Matamoros is the commercial center of a rich agricultural area and a manufacturing center for Mexico's in-bond industry. Some 20 years ago, Avenida Alvaro Obregón, which leads from the main bridge, was spruced up to "dignify" the Mexican side of the border, but the area has not been maintained and has reverted to typical border-town shabbiness. Nonetheless, this is where you'll find some of the best shops, restaurants, and accommodations. Also of interest is the **Casa Mata Museum** in the remains of Fort Mata, built in 1845 to defend the city against American invasion. The fortress wasn't completed in time, and Zachary Taylor's troops were able to capture Matamoros easily. Casa Mata now displays photos and artifacts, mostly from the Mexican Revolution. *Corner of Guatemala and Santos Degollado,* ☎ *88/13–59–29.* ☛ *Free.* ☺ *Tues.–Sun. 9:30–5:30.*

Mexico's third-largest city and the capital of the state of Nuevo León, **Monterrey** is an industrial center, a brewer of beer and forger of steel, with nothing in the way of a laid-back lifestyle. Still, it is a favorite with weekenders and "winter Texans" from the Rio Grande Valley who find Monterrey so near—a three-hour drive from the border or a short flight from Dallas, Houston, or San Antonio—and yet so foreign. The top hotels are clustered close together downtown, and several streets, including Avenida Morelos—the main drag—are now pedestrian malls.

The new Monterrey metro, which runs along elevated tracks across the city, is modern and efficient. There are only two lines, but a third is in the works. Magnetic cards are used to enter the station; buy them from station vending machines in units of one, three, or five rides; each ride costs less than 50¢. The metro runs every day from 4:45 AM to 11:45 PM.

Numbers in the margin correspond to points of interest on the Monterrey map.

The impressive **Gran Plaza,** which covers 100 acres and was completed in 1985 as part of an urban renewal project, is within walking distance of downtown hotels; better known as Macroplaza, it's one of the world's largest public squares. The plaza extends from the new

4 and modernistic **Palacio Municipal** (City Hall) several blocks past the cathedral, the old City Hall, and the Legislative Palace to the neo-

5 classical **Palacio de Gobierno** (State Palace). Towering above it is a concrete slab topped by the Lighthouse of Commerce, a laser beam that flashes from 8 to 11 nightly. Handsome Saddle Mountain and the craggy Sierra Madre provide a majestic backdrop.

6 Gran Plaza now has a new art museum, the **Museo de Arte Contemporaneo (MARCO),** to brag about as well. The focus is on the contemporary art of Mexico and Latin America, but the 14 galleries also include work from other parts of the world. You can listen to live music on a beautiful water-filled marble patio on Wednesday and Sunday afternoons (5:30–7:30) and watch the candlelit tables fill up with arts types, sipping coffee and nibbling on pieces of pie. *Gran Plaza, corner of Zuazua and Ocampo,* ☎ *8/342–4871.* ☛ *About $3, free on Wed.* ◷ *Tues. and Thurs.–Sat. 11–7, Wed. and Sun. 11–9.*

Monterrey dates from 1596, although for the first couple of centuries

7 it was little more than an outpost. Construction of the **cathedral**—on the Gran Plaza a block or so from Palacio Municipal—began in 1600

8 but took some 250 years to finish. The **Obispado** (Bishop's House) is the only landmark to be completed in the colonial era (1788). About 1.5 kilometers (a mile) from the city center along Avenida Padre Mier, and built on a hilltop as a home for retired prelates, the Obispado was used as a fort during the Mexican-American War (1847), the French Intervention (1862), and again during the Mexican Revolution (1915). Today it houses the **Regional Museum of Nuevo León.** It has exhibits that focus on the history of the area, but the major appeal is its splendid view of Monterrey. *Far west end of Av. Padre Mier.* ☛ *Small fee.* ◷ *Tues.–Sat. 10–6., Sun. 10–5.*

In recent years, Mexican beer has taken the world by storm. Monter-

9 rey is where all this started when the **Cuauhtémoc Brewery** opened a century ago. Named after a famous Aztec chief, the brewery is the heart of an industrial empire producing Carta Blanca and Tecate beer. Today the brewery complex includes the **Mexican Baseball Hall of Fame,** a sports museum, an art gallery, and a beer garden with free beer (the biggest draw). *Av. Universidad 2202,* ☎ *8/375–7847.* ☛ *Free.* ◷ *Tues.–Sun. 9:30–9. Brewery tours weekdays 9–1 and 3–6, but call (*☎ *8/375–2200) to confirm.*

The brewery spawned a glass factory for bottles, a steel mill for caps, a carton factory, and eventually several industrial conglomerates, one

10 of which, Alfa, gave Monterrey the **Alfa Cultural Center,** probably the best museum of science and technology in the country. The museum has many hands-on exhibits and an IMAX theater. Free buses to the museum run from the downtown *alameda* (main square) every half hour, returning on the hour from the museum. *Av. Gómez Morín at Roberto Garza Sada,* ☎ *8/356–5696.* ☛ *About $3.50.* ◷ *Tues.–Fri. 3–9; Sat. 2–9; Sun. 1–9:30.*

Numbers in the margin correspond to points of interest on the Northeastern Mexico map.

400

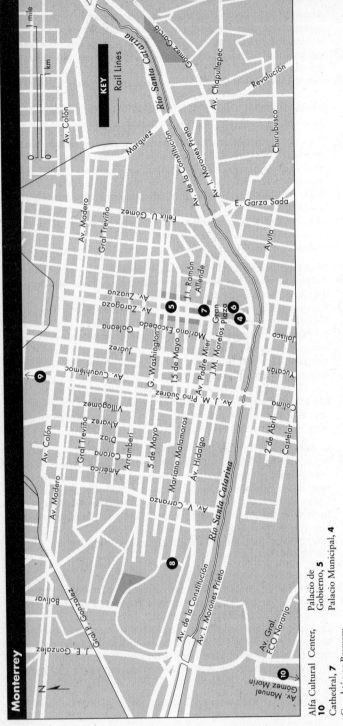

Monterrey

KEY

— Rail Lines

Alfa Cultural Center, **10**

Cathedral, **7**

Cuauhtémoc Brewery, **9**

Museo de Arte Contemporaneo, **6**

Obispado, **8**

Palacio de Gobierno, **5**

Palacio Municipal, **4**

⓫ Mexico's Highway 40 leads to scenic **Barranca de Huasteca** (Huasteca Canyon) in the western suburb of Santa Caterina. The canyon is about 2 miles down a paved road to the south of the village; ⓬ the drive through the 1,000-foot-deep gorge is spectacular. The **Grutas García** (Garcia Caves) are farther northwest, about 40 kilometers (25 miles) from downtown Monterrey off Highway 40. A swaying funicular leads to the caves, where guides lead the way through a mile of underground grottoes. This site is far less commercialized than are similar attractions north of the border. ☛ *Caves (including funicular): about $6.65 adults, $4 children.* ⊙ *Daily 9–5.*

North of the caves, in the Sierra Madre mountains just off Highway 85, is the **Parque Nacional Cumbres de Monterrey.** One of the high-⓭ lights of a trip here is a view of **La Cascada Cola de Caballo** (Horse Tail Falls), a dramatic waterfall that tumbles down from the pine-forested heights. The waterfall is about half a mile from the park's entrance, up a cobblestone road; you can rent a docile horse for about $3 from the local kids who hang out by the ticket booth, or hop on a horse-pulled carriage for $2.50. Entrance to the falls (open daily 8–7) is $3.

Go back through Monterrey and continue south on Mexico 85 until you come to Ciudad Victoria, capital of Tamaulipas state. From here, head a short distance northeast on Highway 101 to reach the man-⓮ made **Lake Vicente Guerrero,** a favorite with American bass fishermen year-round and, during the winter months, an excellent place to hunt duck and white-wing dove. Several camps in the area, such as El Tejon and El Sargento lodges, cater to American sports enthusiasts. For information, contact Sunbelt Hunting and Fishing (Box 3009, Brownsville, TX 78520, ☎ 210/546–9101 or 800/876–4868, ⅢX 210/544–4731).

If you continue on Highway 85 just past Ciudad Valles, you can pick ⓯ up Highway 80 to **Tampico,** a picturesque if raffish port adjoining Ciudad Madero, an oil-refining center. Because of its relative proximity to the border, Tampico gets a smattering of tourists and is a fascinating place in which to wander around for a spell; it has a bit of the feel of a run-down New Orleans French Quarter. Plaza Libertad, near the harbor, is shaggy and unkempt—very much the tropical waterfront. A block away is the regal Plaza de Armas, with its majestic City Hall guarded by towering palms. The cathedral here, started in 1823, was completed with funds donated by Edward L. Doheny, an oil magnate implicated in the Teapot Dome scandal of the 1920s.

Shortly after the Spanish conquest, the Franciscans established a mission in the area near a Huastec fishing village, but the settlement was constantly battered by hurricanes and pirate attacks. In 1828 the Spaniards attempted to reconquer then-independent Mexico by landing troops at Tampico, but they were soundly defeated. With later invasions by the Americans and then the French, the port languished until oil was discovered in the region at the turn of the 20th century. The British and Americans developed the industry until a strike in 1938 led to its nationalization. Petroleum helped Tampico prosper but didn't do much to enhance tourism in the area. Río Pánuco is so polluted that it no longer attracts tarpon fishermen, although the big ocean freighters are an impressive sight. Except for Aerolitoral flights from McAllen and San Antonio, Texas, Tampico airport now handles only domestic flights, and the hotel chains have returned their properties to local owners.

Shopping

Matamoros

The most appealing shops are on Calle Obregón, the street that leads from the border bridge to the center of town. **Garcia's** (Obregón 82, ☎ 88/12–39–29, 88/13–18–33, or 88/12–00–22) is a restaurant with a huge gift shop that carries a nice selection of craft items. Across from Garcia's, **Bob's Azteca Gift Shop** (77 Obregón, ☎ 88/12–88–19) offers rugs and crafts at discount prices. **Barbara** (Obregón 37, ☎ 891/6–54–56) has an attractive assortment of quality handicrafts, carved wood, home furnishings, and even good costume jewelry and imported cosmetics.

Matamoros Market, downtown, is the place to haggle for bargains; you get what you pay for.

Nuevo Laredo

International Bridge 1 leads into Avenida Guerrero, where you'll find most of Nuevo Laredo's shops—classy and junky alike. **Granada** (Guerrero #504, ☎ 87/12–86–44) has better quality items than many of the other vendors, including lead crystal and serapes. In addition, a number of artisan shops are located in the **Nuevo Mercardo de la Reforma** mall, three blocks south of the bridge. The **Ma Cristina** mall, one-half block north of the square, houses about two dozen curio outlets. Most stores remain open until 8 PM.

Reynosa

Trevino's (Calle Los Virreys, ☎ 89/22–14–44) has a good selection of Mexican arts and crafts, sculpture, papier mâché, perfumes, liquors, and clothing, with a cocktail lounge in the rear.

Monterrey

Top-quality shops center on Plaza Hidalgo, near the major hotels, with leather and cowboy boots as the local specialties. **Carapan** (Hidalgo #305 Ote, ☎ 8/345–4422) has the most interesting collector's items and fine crafts in the city, rivalling stores anywhere in the country. **Sanborns** (Escobedo No. 920, just off Plaza Hidalgo, ☎ 8/342–1441 or 8/343–1824) offers an excellent selection of silver, onyx, and other Mexican craft items. **Casa de las Artisanias de Nuevo Leon** (corner of Allende and Dr. Coss, ☎ 8/345–5877 or 8/345–5817) carries quality shawls, embroidered clothing, pottery, and silver services, among other crafts. Take a taxi from your hotel to seek out the superb lead crystal made by **Krystaluxus** (José María Vigil 400, ☎ 8/354–6396 or 8/351–9100, ext. 112); there are showrooms in town, but their prices are higher. Guided tours of the factory are given Monday through Saturday at 10:30 AM. The **Mercado Indio** (Bolivar Norte 1150), with dozens of stalls, is a favorite with souvenir hunters.

Sports

Fishing

Tarpon and snapper fishing is popular at **Chairel Lagoon,** with boats and equipment available for rent. **Lake Vicente Guerrero,** near Ciudad Victoria, has some of the best bass fishing and duck hunting in the country, while some very good angling is available at **La Pesca** on the Tamaulipas coast between Matamoros and Tampico east of Ciudad Victoria and Soto La Marina.

Golf

Hotels can arrange temporary memberships in one of **Monterrey's** three golf courses. In **Tampico,** Lagunas de Miralta Country Club (☎ 12/23–87–27) sells day passes at Centro Comercial Tres Arcos on

Hidalgo for its golf course at Km 26.1 on the Carretera Tampico–Altamira. Ask at your hotel about passes or special discounts at other local clubs.

Beaches

Matamoros

About 30 kilometers (18 miles) from downtown Matamoros is **Playa Bagdad,** the site of the Confederacy's only open harbor during the U.S. Civil War. Freighters skirting the Union naval blockade unloaded their war supplies and loaded up with Confederate cotton destined for Europe. Today, palapas run the length of the shore, and dozens of restaurants offer fresh seafood at reasonable prices.

Tampico

Playa Miramar, about 5 kilometers (3 miles) from town, is a favorite with locals. Lounge chairs, towels and showers are available for rent from the hotels and restaurants along the beach. Public transportation is available from Tampico for about 35¢.

Dining

Although Northeastern Mexico isn't especially renowned for its cuisine, a nice variety of dishes from around the country is available here. Among the regional specialties are *cabrito* (roast kid), *huachinango* (red snapper), and *café de olla,* a delicious blend of coffee, chocolate, cinnamon, and other spices brewed in a clay pot. With the exception of Monterrey's Residence, where a jacket and tie are necessary, restaurants are generally casual.

CATEGORY	COST*
$$$	over $25
$$	$15–$25
$	under $15

per person, excluding drinks, service, and tax

Border Towns

MATAMOROS

$$$ **The Drive Inn.** In spite of the name, this is a formal restaurant with crystal chandeliers, linen tablecloths, and a dance floor. Expect a romantic evening, and stick with steak and seafood specialties. ✕ *Av. Hidalgo at Calle 6a,* ☎ *88/12–00–22. No reservations. MC, V.*

$$ **Los Nortenos.** A goat slow-roasting over hot coals in the window is the not-so-subtle advertisement for the best cabrito in town. A dozen plain tables with plastic tablecloths are the setting for an equally spare menu—goat, guacamole, and quesadillas. ✕ *Calle 9a and Abosolo (across from market), no* ☎. *No reservations. No credit cards.*

$$ **Garcia's.** Rebuilt and redecorated over its own parking garage, this is
★ a romantic place for dancing and dining on lobster or steak. An elevator from the garage leads up to a gift shop with wares from all over Mexico as well as to the restaurant and a bar. ✕ *Calle Alvaro Obregón,* ☎ *88/3–15–66, 88/3–18–33, or 88/3–44–04. Reservations advised. AE, DC, MC, V.*

NUEVO LAREDO

$$$ **Winery (La Vinteria).** This Mexican version of a Continental wine bar
★ serves such regional specialties as *tampiqueña* steak and *queso fundido* (melted cheese), often served in a bowl with *chorizo* (spicy sausage) to be spread on tortillas. It has the best selection of Mexican wines in town. ✕ *Matamoros 308, corner of Victoria,* ☎ *87/12–08–95. No reservations. AE, DC, MC, V.*

$$ **El Dorado.** Dating from the Prohibition era, this spot is a favorite with the Texas crowd—a hangout better known for its atmosphere than for its cuisine. ✕ *Ocampo at Belden,* ☎ *87/12–08–95. No reservations. AE, DC, MC, V.*

$$ **Mexico Tipico.** This establishment offers both indoor and outdoor patio dining, with mariachis coming in off the street to entertain patrons. The patio, partially covered, features a waterfall. Specialties are *carne asada* (grilled meat) and cabrito. True to its name, Mexico Tipico serves the typical Mexican plate of beef, chicken, or cheese enchiladas with rice and refried beans. ✕ *Guerrero 934,* ☎ *87/ 12–15–25. No reservations. MC, V.*

REYNOSA

$$ **Sam's.** Wild game and seafood are the specialties here. In winter, Sam's is frequented by Americans from the Rio Grande Valley and snowbirds from Minnesota. ✕ *Allende 990, Reynosa,* ☎ *89/22– 00–34 or 89/22–34–34. No reservations. MC, V.*

$ **La Majada.** Like all good cabrito restaurants, this is one is simple and to the point: roast kid, guacamole, and quesadillas are pretty much what you'll find. Don't come for the atmosphere but for the a local specialty at its best. ✕ *Av. Miguel Aleman (½ block from bridge), no* ☎. *No reservations. MC, V.*

Monterrey

$$$ **Luisiana.** Perhaps the most elegant dining room downtown, this is a
★ taste of how New Orleans is imagined in Mexico. There are no Cajun specialties on the menu, but the deepwater crawfish are divine. Wonderfully prepared steak and seafood dishes make this one of the best restaurants in the country. ✕ *Hidalgo Ote. 530,* ☎ *8/340–5040 or 8/345–5418. Reservations advised. AE, DC, MC, V.*

$$$ **Residence.** A clubby meeting place for Monterrey's high-power
★ industrialists and executives, Residence has a menu featuring both Mexican specialties and Continental dishes. ✕ *Degollado and Mata-moros,* ☎ *8/345–5418, 8/345–5040, or 8/345–5478. Lunch reserva-tions advised. AE, DC, MC, V.*

$$ **El Rey de Cabrito.** The restaurant's name ("King of Cabrito") is no lie: This is *the* place to try the regional specialty dish, probably the best roast kid you'll ever eat. The owner keeps his own goat herds, and cabrito is the only dish that's served. ✕ *817 Constitución,* ☎ *8/345– 3232 or 8/345–3292. No reservations. MC, V.*

$$ **Sanborns.** Part of a national chain that is a Mexican institution, this is the place for hamburgers and malts as well as tacos and enchiladas. ✕ *Just off Plaza Hidalgo,* ☎ *8/343–1834. No reservations. AE, MC, V.*

Tampico

$$ **Diligencias.** Stuffed crabs are the specialty at this well-known seafood cafe. It's easy to find: the facade is covered with a colorful mural depicting denizens of the deep. ✕ *Ayuntamiento 2702,* ☎ *12/13– 76–42. AE, MC, V.*

$ **Cafe y Nevería Elite.** A popular gathering spot for breakfast, coffee, and ice-cream treats as well as other short-order meals. Don't be put off by the noise and the rather worn Formica tables; it's all part of the local color. ✕ *Av. Díaz Mirón 211 Ote.,* ☎ *12/12–03–64. No credit cards.*

Lodging

Catering mostly to business travelers and short-term tourists, the hotels in the border towns are what you'd expect—no great bargains, but mostly well-kept. Monterrey affords more choices in all price ranges, from luxury to bottom of the line.

CATEGORY	COST*
$$$$	over $160
$$$	$90–$160
$$	$50–$90
$	under $50

All prices are for a standard double room, excluding tax.

Border Towns

MATAMOROS

$$ Gran Hotel Residencial. A pleasant low rise built along Spanish Colonial lines with a large pool in the patio, this is the center of activity for much of Matamoros. All rooms have been remodeled and are bright and modern. ⛛ *Alvaro Obregón at Amapolas (6 blocks from new bridge), Matamoros, Tamps. 87330,* ☎ *88/3–94–40. 120 rooms. Restaurant, bar, pool. AE, MC, V.*

NUEVO LAREDO

$$$ El Rio. A modern white structure spread out on large landscaped grounds, this motel has a spacious lobby and large guest rooms. Those in Section 200 have been redecorated; other rooms still have dark Spanish Colonial furniture. All units include shower and telephone. ⛛ *5 km (3 mi) south on Hwy. 85, Nuevo Laredo, Tamps. 88000,* ☎ *87/14–36–66. 149 rooms. Dining room, bar, 2 pools. AE, MC, V.*

$ Hotel Posada Mina. This is a good bet for those who are seeking budget accommodations, not luxury. A remodeled old yellow brick building about six blocks west of the new bridge, the Mina has very small rooms, but they are clean with good beds, individual A/C and heat, color TVs, and private baths. ⛛ *Mina 35, Nuevo Laredo, Tamps. 88000,* ☎ *87/13–14–73. 5 rooms. No credit cards.*

$ Hotel Reforma. An older hotel just a half block south of Plaza Hidalgo, Reforma has a restaurant opening both off the lobby and the street, and secure parking in back a block away. Rooms in the older section, although somewhat small and rather nondescript, are comfortable; junior suites in the new section are spacious and modern. All units come with shower, TV, and telephone. ⛛ *Guerrero 822, Nuevo Laredo, Tamps. 88000,* ☎ *87/12–62–50,* ⸬ *87/12–67–14. 38 rooms. Restaurant, bar. MC, V.*

REYNOSA

$$$ Motel Virrey. On the Monterrey highway, 10 kilometers (6 miles) from town, this comfortable modern lodging is a good bet for those who got a late start driving to Monterrey or want to avoid the congestion of downtown. Good service, a pool, and lots of parking draw repeat customers. ⛛ *Blvd. Hidalgo at Praxedis Balboa, Reynosa, Tamps. 88500,* ☎ *89/23–10–50,* ⸬ *89/23–88–67. 160 rooms. Restaurant, pool. MC, V.*

$ Astromundo. Downtown and handy to the market and the few good local restaurants, this popular hotel gets a lot of traffic from weekending winter Texans. ⛛ *Juárez at Guerrero, Reynosa, Tamps. 88500,* ☎ *and* ⸬ *89/22–56–25. 106 rooms. Restaurant, bar, pool. MC, V.*

$ San Carlos. This five-story hotel on the square has air-conditioned rooms with cable TV. Business travelers and tourists appreciate its central location, close to the square and shopping center. ⛛ *Hidalgo 970, Reynosa, Tamps. 88500,* ☎ *89/22–12–80,* ⸬ *89/22–26–20. 65 rooms. Restaurant. AE, MC, V.*

Monterrey

$$$$ Ambassador. The best hotel in this part of Mexico, this downtown landmark ★ was restored several years ago as a Westin/Camino Real. It offers spacious, comfortable rooms, a piano bar in the lobby, and a health club, among other facilities. ☎ *Hidalgo at Emilio Carranza, Monterrey, NL 64000,* ☎ *8/340–6390 or 8/342–2040,* 𝔽𝔸𝕏 *8/342–1904 or 800/7– CAMINO. 241 rooms and suites. 2 restaurants, 3 lounges, pool, racquetball, 2 tennis courts, travel services. AE, DC, MC, V.*

$$$$ **Ancira Radisson Plaza Hotel Monterrey.** Built in 1912 but kept like new,
★   the property is reminiscent of the grand hotels of Europe. It features good dining, a popular bar, and large, comfortable rooms. ☎ *Hidalgo at Escobedo, Monterrey, NL 64000,* ☎ *8/345–7575 or 800/333–3333,* 𝔽𝔸𝕏 *8/344–5226. 240 rooms and suites. Pool. AE, DC, MC, V.*

$$$$ **Hotel Monterrey.** This large remodeled and modernized hotel has three convenient entrances into a grand marble and mirror-filled lobby: one facing the Gran Plaza, another off the Morelos pedestrian mall, and the third opening onto the small green Plaza de la Corregidora across from Sanborn's. Rooms are a nice size, decorated in pleasant pastels, and the hotel has a romantic dancing lounge. ☎ *Morelos 574, Monterrey, NL 64000,* ☎ *8/343–5120 through 5129, or 800/432–9605,* 𝔽𝔸𝕏 *8/344–7378. 197 rooms. Restaurant, bar. AE, MC, V.*

$$$ **Chipinque.** This hilltop resort property overlooking the city is won-
★   derful if you have a car. The view from the restaurant is extraordinary, especially at night. ☎ *Meseta de Chipinque, Monterrey, NL 66297,* ☎ *8/378–1100,* 𝔽𝔸𝕏 *8/378–1338. 43 rooms. Restaurant-bar, pool, tennis court. AE, MC, V.*

$$ **Colonial.** This moderately priced downtown hotel is well kept up. It's not for light sleepers, however; the nightclub next door often keeps the noise level high until late. ☎ *Hidalgo 475, Monterrey, NL 64000,* ☎ *8/343–6791,* ☎ *and* 𝔽𝔸𝕏 *8/343–6792. 85 rooms. MC, V.*

$$ **Motel Dorado.** A good buy, this motel is quiet and offers a pool as well as clean, air-conditioned rooms. The staff is friendly and helpful. ☎ *Carretera Laredo No. 901 Nte., Monterrey, NL 64000,* ☎ *8/352–4050, 8/ 352–4058,* 𝔽𝔸𝕏 *ext. 119. 65 rooms. Restaurant. MC, V.*

$$ **Royalty.** Good location and lower than usual prices for this expensive city are the main attractions here. ☎ *Hidalgo Oriente 402,* ☎ *8/340– 2800,* 𝔽𝔸𝕏 *8/340–5812. 66 rooms. Restaurant, bar, exercise room. MC, V.*

Tampico

$$$ **Camino Real.** Attractively decorated, this low-rise property 20 minutes from the city center comes close to being a resort (in spite of the name, it's not part of the Camino Real chain). ☎ *Hidalgo 2000, Tampico, Tamps. 89640,* ☎ *12/13–88–11 or 800/5–70–00 in Mexico,* 𝔽𝔸𝕏 *12/ 13–92–26. 102 rooms. Restaurant, bar, pool. AE, DC, MC, V.*

$$ **Hotel Colonial.** This hotel, touting a new image with added services, also has a fresh look. White walls make the rather small rooms seem larger, and deep red drapes complement the dark-toned furniture. ☎ *Madera 210 Ote., Tampico, Tamps. 89000,* ☎ *12/12–76–76. 138 rooms. Restaurant, bar, travel services. AE, MC, V.*

$ **Hotel Plaza.** This centrally located budget hotel is clean and comfortable, if a little drab. Rooms are small but air-conditioned, and all have phones and TVs. ☎ *Madero 204, Tampico, Tamps. 89000,* ☎ *12/14–16–78 or 12/14–17–84. 40 rooms. Restaurant. MC, V.*

Nightlife

Border Towns

In Nuevo Laredo, **Victoria's,** three blocks from Bridge 1, is a noisy favorite; **The Winery** and **El Dorado** are somewhat more sedate, and **Quintana Rock** is the local disco. **Garcia's** and the **Gran Hotel Residencial** are where the action is in Matamoros. In Reynosa, the **Impe-**

rial offers quiet, slow-dance music with a combo or strolling trio, depending on the night; the older clientele is well-dressed. The Zona Rosa has several discos and **Trevino's,** with a piano bar.

Monterrey

Fashionable folk, residents, and visitors alike flock to the downtown hotels for after-dark action. The **Crowne Plaza Lobby Bar** is loud enough to dismay guests who turn in early, but it delights the young-at-heart crowd. At the **Ambassador,** the pianist is more reserved. **El Cid,** at the Hotel Monterrey, features cheek-to-cheek dance music, and **Bar 1900** (Gran Ancira Radisson Plaza), a classic but upscale Mexican cantina, has flamenco dancers every Friday night. **Baccarat** (Rio Grijalva and Mississippi) is a top disco, reached by taxi. **Cows Disco** (Av. Garza Sada 4502) is also popular.

Tampico

Eclipse (Universidad 2004, ☎ 12/13–14–95) has dancing on Thursday only; the rest of the week, it's a video bar. **Byblos** (Byblos 1, ☎ 12/13–08–27) is another popular disco. The bar at the **Camino Real Hotel** (Hidalgo 2000, ☎ 12/13–88–11) offers music and dancing in the evening.

Northeastern Mexico Essentials

Arriving and Departing

BY PLANE

From Mexico City, **Aeromexico** (☎ 800/AEROMEX) has service to Matamoros and Reynosa; **Mexicana** (☎ 800/531–7921) flies to Nuevo Laredo.

Mexicana has flights from Chicago and San Antonio to Monterrey; **Aeromexico** has service from Houston, New York, and Los Angeles. **Continental** (☎ 800/525–0280) flies from Chicago, Las Vegas, Los Angeles, Miami, and New York, with a nonstop flight from Houston. **American** (☎ 800/433–7300) has five flights a day to Monterrey from Dallas. **Aerolitoral** (U.S. reservations handled by Aeromexico, ☎ 800/AEROMEX) has service from McAllen, Laredo, and San Antonio, Texas.

Monterey's **Aeropuerto Internacional Mariano Escobedo** (☎ 8/345–4432), equipped with luggage storage ($4 a day) and a money exchange booth, is 6 kilometers (4 miles) northeast of downtown. The only way to get here is by taxi, which will cost about $12.

Aerolitoral has direct flights between San Antonio and McAllen, Texas and Tampico. Both **Aeromexico** and **Mexicana** offer flights between Tampico and Mexico City, and Mexicana also has Tampico–Monterrey service.

BY CAR

With unleaded gasoline now more widely available, an increasing number of American motorists are exploring Mexican highways. A car trip is not without its red tape, however. For details about driving into Mexico, *see* Driving *in* The Gold Guide's Smart Travel Tips A to Z. **Sanborn's Mexican Insurance** (2009 S. 10th St., McAllen, TX ☎ 800/222–0158, ℻ 210/686–0732) can help you complete the paperwork in advance—for free if you buy insurance there, otherwise for a fee.

Distances are deceiving in this part of Mexico because of mountainous driving in the Sierra Madre Oriente. It generally takes three hours to drive from the border to Monterrey; from Monterrey to Ciudad Victoria it's another four hours; Ciudad Victoria to Pachuca (a mountainous route with hairpin turns) takes approximately six hours; and the trip from Pachuca to Mexico City runs about two hours.

Border Towns. Downtown Nuevo Laredo is reached by two bridges, International Bridge 1 and the Columbia–Laredo Bridge (42 kilometers/26 miles northwest of Laredo), both points of entry required for vehicles heading to the interior. The New Bridge is the best route from downtown Brownsville to downtown Matamoros. U.S. 281 leads down to Hidalgo, Texas, and the bridge crossing into Reynosa.

From Matamoros, Mexico 180 runs down the Gulf Coast to Tampico, Veracruz, and beyond. A turnoff on Mexico 101 leads to the hunting and fishing camps at Lake Vicente Guerrero. Mexico 97 leads from Reynosa into Mexico 101/180, which meet up for a bit. From Reynosa, you can drive the free routes Mexico 40 to Mexico 35 to Linares; here Mexico 58 will lead you across to San Roberto (and Mexico 57) via a spectacular road with a most unusual mural by Ferderico Cantu chiseled out of the side of a mountain.

Monterrey. From Laredo, the old Pan-American Highway, Mexico 85 Libre (free), and the now completed four-lane Mexico 85 Cuota (toll) both lead to Monterrey, some 242 kilometers (150 miles) south; the latter road, which ends in Monterrey, is a much better one, although the toll is expensive (about $27). It's exactly the same price to take the toll road Mexico 40 to Monterrey from Reynosa; while the Laredo route is more scenic, traversing some nice mountains, Laredo itself is more congested to get through than Reynosa. The Reynosa road, while flat and dull, is more convenient to downtown Monterrey.

Tampico. The port is roughly a seven-hour drive from Matamoros on Mexico 180, or eight hours from Monterrey via Mexico 85, which connects with Mexico 80.

BY TRAIN
The train system in Mexico is in a state of flux. Currently, there is no first-class train service from the border to Monterrey or Tampico, although the first-class **El Regiomontano,** with seats and sleeping berths, runs from Monterrey to Saltillo, San Luis Potosí, and Mexico City. For the most up-to-date information about schedules and prices, contact **Mexico by Train** in Laredo (☎ and FAX 210/725–3659 or 800/ 321–1699).

BY BUS
Northeastern Mexico is well connected by buses, which are becoming downright luxurious while fares remain low. Information on Mexican bus service is available from terminals in Laredo (Valley Transit, ☎ 210/723–4324), McAllen (Valley Transit, ☎ 210/686–5479), and Brownsville (Valley Transit, ☎ 210/546–7171). **Transportes del Norte** (☎ 8/318–3745 in Monterrey), in conjunction with **Greyhound,** goes from San Antonio, Dallas, and Houston to Monterrey.

Guided Tours
Several U.S. tour operators, including **Sanborn's Viva Tours** (2015 S. 10th St., McAllen, TX ☎ 210/682–9872 and 800/395–VIVA), run shopping and sightseeing tours to the border towns and coach excursions into the interior. **Viva** has also inaugurated a four-day tour to El Tajín (*see* Veracruz, *below*). **Osetur Tours** (☎ 8/347–1533, 8/347– 1599 or 8/347–1614) in Monterrey provides sightseeing excursions in the areas.

Important Addresses and Numbers

CONSULATES

Matamoros. The **U.S. Consulate** is at Calle 1 No. 2002 and Azaleas (☎ 88/12–44–02). ☉ Weekdays 8–10 and 1–4.

Monterrey. Canada: Edificio Kalos, Zaragoza 1300 Sur, Suite 108 (☎ 8/344–3200). ☉ Weekdays 9–5:30. **United States:** Constitución 411 Poniente (☎ 8/343–0650 or 8/345–2120). ☉ Weekdays 8–2.

EMERGENCIES

Matamoros. Police: González and Calle Venteuno (☎ 88/2–07–32 and 88/2–03–22) **Cruz Roja (Red Cross) Hospital:** Garcia and L. Caballero (☎ 88/2–00–44 and 891/6–65–62).

Nuevo Laredo. Police: Maclovio Herréra and Ocampo (☎ 87/12–21–46 or 87/12–30–25); **Cruz Roja (Red Cross):** Independencia 1619 at San Antonio (☎ 87/12–09–49 or 87/12–09–89).

Reynosa. Police: Morales between Veracruz and Nayarit (☎ 89/23–56–55, 89/23–01–95) **Hospital Santander:** Alvaro Obregón #101 (☎ 89/22–96–22).

Monterrey. Police: Gonzalitos and Lincoln (☎ 8/343–2576) **Cruz Roja (Red Cross) Hospital:** Universidad and Camelo (☎ 8/375–1212).

Tampico. Police: Sor Juana Ines de la Cruz and Tamaulipas (☎ 12/12–10–32) **Cruz Roja (Red Cross) Hospital:** Tamaulipas and Colegio Militar, Zona Centro (☎ 12/12–13–33).

ENGLISH-LANGUAGE BOOKSTORE

In Monterrey, the **American Bookstore** (Garza Sada 2404-A, near the Pemex station, ☎ 8/387–0838) has a great selection of books in English.

VISITOR INFORMATION

The best information about this part of Mexico is found in Texas border towns, especially at places that sell Mexican automobile insurance (which is mandatory in Mexico). This list will give you a head start in searching out such sources: **Sanborn's Viva Tours,** 2015 S. 10th St., McAllen, ☎ 210/682–9872 or 800/395–8482; **Sanborn's Mexican Insurance,** 2009 S. 10th St., McAllen, ☎ 800/222–0158, FAX 210/686–0732; **Bravo Insurance,** 2212 Santa Ursula, Laredo, ☎ 210/723–3657, FAX 210/723–0000; **Johnny Ginn's Travel,** 1845 Expressway 77, Brownsville, ☎ 210/542–5457, FAX 210/504–2919.

The **Brownsville Chamber of Commerce** (1600 E. Elizabeth, ☎ 210/542–4341), one block from the International Bridge, has excellent street maps of Brownsville and Matamoros. ☉ Daily 9–5.

A few blocks from the International Bridge in **Matamoros** is a small white building marked Tours-Transport (Tamaulipas and Obregón, ☎ 88/12–21–18), where friendly older men answer questions and try to sell you a two-hour tour of Matamoros (it's not worth it). ☉ Daily 8–6.

In **Nuevo Laredo,** the tourist office (Puente Internacional s/n, ☎ 87/12–01–04), near the International Bridge on Guerrero, is open daily 8:30–8. The pleasant folks here aren't very helpful, but they've got maps of the city.

The tourism office in **Reynosa** (Oaxaca 360, ☎ 89/2–11–89 or 89/2–24–49) is generally open during the week from 9–3.

In **Monterrey, Infotour** (Zaragoza, at Matamoros, ☎ 8/345–0870, 8/345–7007, or toll-free 800/235–2438 in the U.S., 95/800/83–222 in

Mexico), at the Gran Plaza, is one of Mexico's best tourist offices. In addition to its great brochures and maps, the office has a helpful English-speaking staff. ⊙ Daily 10–5.

The local tourism office in **Tampico** is well hidden one flight up in a building at the corner of Olmos and Carranza (☎ 12/12–26–78); the stairs are at Olmos 101 between a newsstand and a fast food stand. However, the place has so little information that the walk up is rarely worth the effort. ⊙ Weekdays 9–7.

VERACRUZ

By Jessica Blatt and Ariana Mohit

The state of Veracruz, a long, skinny crescent of land bordering the Gulf of Mexico, is often ignored by travelers, many of whom do no more than glimpse the state through the window of a bus barreling toward the Yucatán Peninsula. But while Veracruz's ruins and beaches can't compare with those on the Yucatán, the state is popular with vacationing Mexicans, drawn to the cool hill towns of the Sierra de Los Tuxtlas and the liveliness of Veracruz city.

Descending from the volcanic Sierra, the Veracruz coast consists of flat lowlands characterized by terrible heat and swamps and pockmarked by noisome oil refineries. As you head inland a ways—Veracruz is only 140 kilometers across at its widest point—the land rises to meet the Sierra Madre Oriental range, with its 5,610-meter Pico de Orizaba (also called Citlaltépetl), Mexico's highest mountain. In the foothills of this range, you'll find the university town and state capital of Jalapa, where students share the colonial streets with local farmers who have come to town to market their crops. The state does have some good beaches along the coast, particularly around the northern city of Tuxpán, but the real reasons to come are the atmosphere, the history, and the people. All of these are to be found at their best in the city of Veracruz, a working port with so many marimba bands in the *zócalo* (main square) on weekend evenings that they must compete to be heard.

Olmec civilization thrived in Veracruz long before the rise of the Maya. The state's best-preserved ruins, at El Tajín near Papantla, are thought to have been the work of yet another civilization, which had its heyday later, between AD 550 and AD 1100. By the time Hernán Cortés landed in Veracruz in 1519, the Aztecs held sway, but within a very short time the Indian population was decimated by disease and war. To meet their labor needs, the Spanish then brought a large number of Africans to Veracruz as slaves, and their presence has had a profound influence on the character of the place. In modern times, the discovery of oil here prompted a population explosion that saw the number of Veracruzanos go from about 1 million at the beginning of the century to more than 6 million today. For most foreign travelers, the sulfurous stench of a coastal oil refinery is an unpleasant intrusion on their tropical reverie, but for many of the state's residents, it's their lifeblood.

Exploring

Numbers in the margin correspond to points of interest on the Veracruz and East Central Mexico map.

❶ **Veracruz** was Mexico's premier seaside resort and the port of entry for most foreign visitors until a few decades ago; travelers arrived by ship, then boarded a train to Mexico City, often looking wistfully back. Today relatively few foreigners find their way to Veracruz's beaches, but domestic vacationers are lured into the fun-loving but

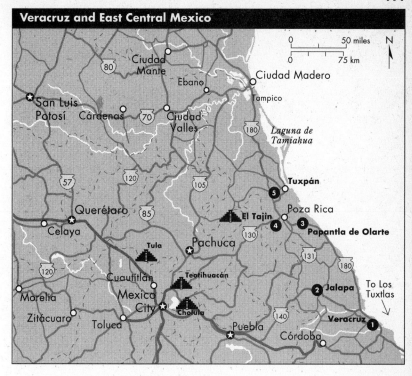

Veracruz and East Central Mexico

not particularly sophisticated town by prices that are far lower than those found in Acapulco, Puerto Vallarta, or Cancún. The best time of all, for many, to visit is the week before Ash Wednesday when *Carnaval,* Mexico's version of Mardi Gras, takes place. It's wild, merry, and far less self-conscious than the better-known celebrations in Rio or New Orleans. The biggest problem at such times is finding a room, but the local tourist office can usually come up with acceptable accommodations. The same is true during Christmas and Easter week, when all of Mexico goes on vacation and heads for the beach.

Veracruz was the first European city to be established on the North American mainland and the major gateway for Spanish settlement of Mexico, although the spot where Cortés landed in 1519 is likely about 50 kilometers (30 miles) north of town. What is professed to be his home, a rustic compound now in a state of decay, is located on the northern edge of the city and is worth seeing if only for its crumbling, roofless masonry, taken over by clinging vines and massive tree roots.

If this is your first visit, a good place to get oriented is the **Museo de la Ciudad.** The region's history is narrated via artifacts and displays, and scale models of the city help you get the lay of the land. Also exhibited are copies of pre-Columbian statues and contemporary indigenous art. A $1 donation pays for a guided tour by a bilingual student. *Zaragoza at Morelos, no ☏. ☎ $3. ☉ Mon.–Sat. 9–4.*

During the viceregal era, Veracruz was the only east-coast port permitted to operate in New Spain. As a result, it was frequently attacked by pirates. The great **Fort of San Juan de Ulúa,** built shortly after the conquest and the last territory in Mexico to be held by the Spanish Royalists, is a monument to that swashbuckling era. A miniature city

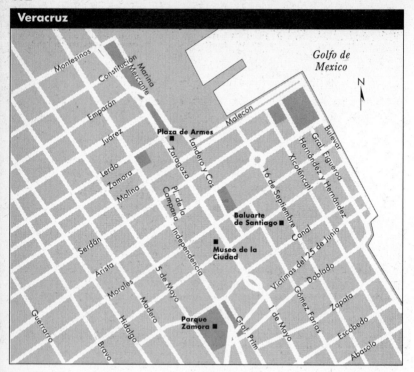

in itself, the island fort is a maze of moats, ramparts, and drawbridges smack in the middle of the busy port area (it's now connected to the mainland by a causeway). Fortification of the island began in 1535 under the direction of Antonio de Mendoza, the first viceroy of New Spain. Ground coral, sand, and oyster shells were used for the original walls. A few centuries later, the fort was used as a prison, housing such figures as Benito Juárez, who was held prisoner here by conservative dictator Santa Anna before being exiled to Louisiana in 1853. After independence, it was used in unsuccessful attempts to fight off first the invading French, the Americans, then the French again and, in 1914, the Americans. *Reached via causeway from downtown Veracruz. No* ☎. ☛ *$4.50, free Sun. and holidays.* ☉ *Tues.–Sun. 9–4.*

Also of interest is **Baluarte de Santiago,** a fortress and museum. It's all that's left of old city walls and was also built (in 1636) as a defense against pirates. The colonial bulwark is impressively solid from the outside and romantically lit at night. Inside is a small museum that displays temporary art exhibits—not really worth the admission fee. Come on Sunday when it's free. *Canal at 16 de Septiembre, no* ☎. ☛ *$4.50, free Sun.* ☉ *Tues.–Sun. 10–4:30.*

Since 1993, Veracruz has been the home of one of the three most important aquariums in the world, the state-of-the-art **Acuario de Veracruz;** in addition to its public displays, this impressive complex also houses a marine research center. Located in a shopping plaza on Playa de Hornos, a quick cab ride from the center, the aquarium is extremely popular with locals, who flock here on weekends. It contains a round tank with 3,000 different species of marine life native to the Gulf of Mexico, including nurse sharks, manta rays, barracudas, and sea turtles. Shark movies, of the make-you-never-want-to-set-foot-in-the-ocean-again variety, are shown near the exit. If that doesn't do the trick, check out the enormous shark-shaped outline on the far wall, above the caption: This is the actual size of a great white shark caught off the coast of Tuxpán, Veracruz. *Plaza Acuario in Malecón del Puerto de Veracruz,* ☎ *29/34–79–84.* ☞ *$5 adults, $1.75 children 2–12.* ⊙ *Mon.–Thurs. 10–7, Fri.–Sun. 10–7:30.*

Those who haven't been discouraged away from the shore head for the beaches, which begin on the southern edge of town and extend to Mocambo, about 7 kilometers (4 miles) farther. Beyond Mocambo is the fishing village of Boca del Río, where a little Atoyac river meets the sea and every other house seems to be a restaurant. Many are modest, but serve some of the best seafood in Mexico. Most of these cafés feature live musical entertainment, but customers are expected to pay for the songs they order.

Veracruz itself is famed as a musical city, hometown of La Bamba and its own special brand of song played by lively trios outfitted all in white and slapping away at tiny guitars and portable harps. In the evening, mariachis entertain outside the sidewalk cafés around the main plaza. Whether at night or during the day, a stop at one of the town's cafés is de rigeur; the original Café de la Parroquia, facing a corner of the plaza, is known internationally for its atmosphere and its fantastic coffee (*see* Dining, *below*).

② Some 100 kilometers (62 miles) to the northwest of Veracruz city, **Jalapa** is perched on the side of a mountain, between the coastal lowlands of Veracruz and the high central plateau. A little more than 1,400 meters above sea level, the city has an enviable climate that will come as a pleasant surprise to perspiration-soaked escapees from the coast. The capital of the state of Veracruz and a university town, Jalapa boasts a diverse population; you are as likely to see long-haired young people sitting around in cafés as you are wizened campesinos walking to work. The town is also home to a symphony orchestra and a state theater that attracts big-name performers. Its hills pose intriguing engineering problems—in some places you'll find the twisting, cobblestone streets bordered by six-foot high sidewalks built to compensate for sudden, sharp inclines. (Note: You'll often see the name of the city spelled "Xalapa"; Jalapa is the Hispanicized version of the latter, a Nahuatl word.)

The town's prime cultural attraction is the **Museo de Antropologia de Jalapa;** with more than 29,000 pieces on display, it is second only to Mexico City's archaeological museum. The building is divided into three sections focusing on the Huastec, Totonac, and Olmec cultures of the state of Veracruz. Highlights include stone Olmec heads and a burial mound complete with bones, ritually deformed skulls, and ceremonial statuettes. There is also an exhibit on the contemporary clothing and customs of the Indians of Veracruz state. Guided tours by English-speaking students are available Tuesday–Sunday 11 AM–4 PM, but you may want to call in advance and make an appointment, as the tour schedule is unpredictable. *Av. Jalapa s/n,* ☎ *28/15–49–52.* ☞ *$3, students $2.* ⊙ *Tues.–Sun. 10–5.*

TIME OUT   Jalapa's health-conscious student population supports a number of juice bars around the city center, such as **Jugos California** on Enríquez, where you can snack on a tropical fruit-and-yogurt smoothie or fruit salad.

③ Some 250 kilometers (150 miles) northwest of Veracruz on Highway 180, **Papantla de Olarte** sits amid tropical hills, the center of a vanilla-producing region. A distinctive mix of Spanish colonial and indigenous influence can be seen here: Totonac men in flowing white pants lead their donkeys through the crowded streets and palm trees shade the traditional, tiled zócalo. The town is best known for its *voladores* (fliers), who dive off a 25-meter pole next to Papantla's ornate cathedral. This ritual was originally performed as a tribute to the god of sun and rain—the tree or pole used in the ceremony was meant to bring the participants closer to him. The four fliers begin the dance on a platform at the top of the ceremonial pole, each facing one of the cardinal directions. They begin their descent from the side of the platform facing east—where the sun rises and the world awakes—twisting left for 13 full rotations each. Between them, the four fliers circle the pole 52 times, once for each year of the cycle of the Totonac calendar. A fifth man, the prayer giver, sits atop the pole, playing a small flute while keeping rhythm on a drum as the fliers descend. Originally, the ceremony was held on the vernal equinox, but now the voladores fly for the crowds every Saturday and Sunday at 12:45 PM and give special performances during Corpus Christi.

4 Just 15 minutes outside Papantla lie the extensive ruins of **El Tajín** (a Totonac word meaning "thunder"); take an unnumbered (but signed) road 13 kilometers (8 miles) west. Although much of the site has been restored, many structures are still hidden under thick jungle growth; some archaeologists speculate that hundreds of buildings remain to be excavated. Little is known for certain about this complex, not who built it, when, nor why. It is thought to have been a religious complex that thrived from about AD 600 to 1200. By some accounts, it was the most influential center in Mexico for a period; it was a source of cacao beans, which were used as money in pre-Hispanic times. Early theories attributed the complex to a settlement of either Totonacs or Huastecas, the two most important cultures of the Veracruz area. Given the immense size and unique architecture and art that characterizes the complex, however, scholars are now talking about a distinct El Tajín cultural group. The city remained hidden until 1785, when it was discovered by a Spanish engineer.

Evidence suggests that the southern half of the uncovered ruins—the area around the lower plaza—was reserved for ceremonial purposes. Its centerpiece is the 60-foot-high **Pyramid of the Niches,** an impressive six-level structure with 365 indentations—one for each day of the year—which may once have contained small altars. Just south of the pyramid, a dumbbell-shaped **ball court** was the site of a sacred ball game; some say that this game, played throughout Mesoamerica, may have originated at El Tajín. Similar in some ways to soccer—players used a hard rubber ball that could not be touched with the hands, and suited up in knee pads and body protectors—it was far more deadly: Intricate carvings at this and other complexes indicate that the games ended with human sacrifice. It's still a subject of debate whether the sacrificial victim was the winner or loser of the match. **El Tajín Chico,** to the north, is thought to have been the secular part of the city, administrative and residential. The most important structure here is the **Building of the Columns.** The columns once held up stone ceilings, but early home builders from Papantla removed the ceiling stones to construct the first houses in the town.

Guided tours of the El Tajín are not available: The plaque at the entrance tells some of what little is known about the site in Spanish, English, and French, but the rest is up to your imagination. The entrance is lined with fondas that sell cheap eats and mountains of tacky souvenirs, and there's a large, cafeteria-style restaurant at the site. If the "killer beast" exhibit in the museum at the entrance doesn't dissuade you, and you're prepared to work your way through the thick jungle, you can see some more recent finds along the dirt paths that lead over the nearby ridges. ☞ *$4.50, free Sun.* ☯ *Tues.–Sun. 9–6.*

Note: In early 1994, the most important archaeological find in the Veracruz area in more than 200 years ago was announced: Another ancient site was discovered some 40 miles from El Tajín, near the coastal village of El Pital. Covered by jungle, this seaport, which likely thrived between AD 100 and 600, extended more than 40 square miles and was occupied by thousands of people. Research is still at very preliminary stages and excavation has barely begun, but it is believed that El Pital may shed much light on the history of pre-Hispanic culture, and perhaps even provide a missing link between the Olmec and Maya civilizations.

❺ About an hour northeast of Papantla (take Mexico 130 to the coast), **Tuxpán** is a peaceful riverside town with winding streets. Juárez, the main street, runs parallel to **Río Tuxpán,** and is lined with diners, hotels, and shops. The **Parque Reforma** is the center of social activity in town, with more than a hundred tables set around a hub of cafés and fruit stands, and the river is clean enough for swimming. *Lanchas* (flat-bottom boats) shuttle passengers across the river to the **Casa de Fidel Castro,** where Castro lived for a time while planning the overthrow of Fulgencio Batista. A replica of the *Granma,* the ship that carried Fidel's men from Tuxpán to Cuba, moulders outside. Inside, the casa is bare save some black-and-white photos of Fidel and Mexican President Lázaro Cárdenas. But Tuxpán's main draw is the untouristed miles of beaches that begin just 7 kilometers (4 miles) to the east of town. The surf at **Playa Tuxpán** isn't huge, but there's enough action to warrant breaking out your surf- or boogieboard. Landlubbers can groove to the tropical tunes that drift out of the seafood and beer stands in the pine grove behind the beach.

TIME OUT Of the palapas on Playa Tuxpán, the most established is **Restaurant Miramar,** which has an extensive menu and also provides umbrellaed beach chairs for customers. Farther down, try **El Tigre Costeño,** run by a friendly family whose male members moonlight weaving palm-frond hats to sell on the beach.

Sports

You won't really want to see what's under the water near most of the beaches around the port of Veracruz, but there are some nice places to submerge in the Tuxpán area. You can rent underwater gear from **Aquasport** (☎ 783/7–02–59), just before Playa Tuxpán. They can also arrange trips to Isla Lobos ($100 a day) that include all permits, scuba gear, food, and transportation. No scuba classes are offered, however, so non-experts must stick with snorkeling.

Shopping

Veracruz
There are many seashells and dried and varnished frogs, iguanas, and armadillos heaped in stacks at the stands lining the waterfront, and at the mercado on Insurgentes you'll find all sorts of goods, including leather and jewelry. Independencia, the main shopping street, has little to interest tourists.

Beaches

Veracruz City's beaches are much less inviting than you might expect: Most are somewhat dirty, and the water is fairly polluted. The beach begins on the southern edge of the city at **Villa del Mar** but is at its best down toward **Mocambo,** about 7 kilometers (4 miles) from downtown Veracruz. Better beaches are farther from town: About 4 kilometers (2½ miles) south of Playa Mocambo is **Boca del Río,** a small fishing village at the mouth of the Río Jamapa that is quickly getting sucked into greater Veracruz.

Playa Tuxpán is the most accessible beach in the Tuxpán area, about 7 kilometers (4 miles) from downtown. For scuba diving, head to **Tamiaula,** a small village just north of Tuxpán, where you can hire a fishing boat for the 45-minute journey to the prime diving around **Isla Lobos** (Wolf Island). There are a military outpost and a lighthouse on the island. In the shallow water offshore you'll find a few shipwrecks and colorful reefs that are home to a large variety of sealife, including pufferfish, parrotfish, damselfish, and barracuda.

Dining

Very little in the state of Veracruz is truly formal. Even in the city of **Veracruz,** reservations are almost never necessary, and a jacket and tie would look out of place almost anywhere (except perhaps at La Mansión). The emphasis, as befits this hot, breezy port town, is on casual comfort and simple, fresh food; mostly *pescado* (fish) and *mariscos* (shellfish). Veracruz is famous for its signature dish, known throughout Mexico as *pescado a la veracruzana* (Veracruz-style fish) and known here as *huachinango a la veracruzana* (Veracruz-style snapper). The basic dish consists of red snapper cooked in tomatoes, onions, capers, peppers, and herbs. Leaving Veracruz without sampling this would be both a shame and a bit of a feat, as every chef has his own special version, which he will insist you try.

It's also easy to eat well in **Jalapa,** where most restaurants are informal, family-style affairs, and the emphasis is on flavorful, home-style meals. It's not uncommon to hear the pat-pat of tortillas being hand-formed as you eat, and beans, onions, chiles (this is, after all, the hometown of the jalapeño), and meat form the base of most dishes. You can eat cheaply and heartily in **Papantla,** but with little variation. And to say that dress is casual here would be an understatement: Shorts and a T-shirt won't get you a second glance even in Restaurant Enrique, the town's fanciest dining room. Just as **Tuxpán's** best attractions are its pretty river and nearby beaches, the best places to eat here are the small, family-run seafood stands and palapas lining the beach as well as the river as it makes its way to the Gulf at Playa Tuxpán. If you ask for the *platillo del día* (daily dish), most likely you'll be treated to a cold shrimp, calamari, or crab cocktail, or a plate of fried fish or shrimp with Spanish rice and tortillas.

CATEGORY	COST*
$$$$	over $20
$$$	$15–20
$$	$8–$15
$	under $8

per person, excluding drinks, service, and tax

Jalapa

$$$ El Molino del Quijote. This small, family eatery specializes in Spanish cuisine and seasonal seafood. Among the starters are some excellent soups, most notably a pungent garlic broth and a satisfying *caldo marinero* (fisherman's soup). Entree specialties include lobster—steamed, grilled, or prepared with whiskey or butter—and a rich paella, thick with tomato, shrimp, and shellfish. The restaurant is lively and informal, with efficient, casual service. ✗ *Miguel Aleman 136,* ☎ *28/15–33–08. MC, V.*

$$ La Casa de Mama. This pleasant restaurant is on a noisy thoroughfare just east of the center of town. The dark, antique furnishings and lazy ceiling fan almost succeed in giving this place the feel of a northern Mexican hacienda, but the incessant street noise reminds you that you're in a busy capital city. Never mind; you'll be focussing on the generous portions of meats, shrimp, and fish, served with rich sauces and simple accompaniments such as plain white rice or mashed potato. ✗ *Avila Camacho 113,* ☎ *28/17–31–44 or 28/17–62–32. AE, MC, V. No dinner Sun. and Mon.*

$$ La Pérgola. ★ Designed in the early 1960s by Enrique Murillo, the attractive Pérgola is a relaxing place for an afternoon or evening meal. The menu concentrates on steaks and shrimp, painstakingly prepared and imaginatively presented. For dessert, try the *plátanos flameados con brandy* (plantains flambéed in brandy) or an order of crêpes suzette. Umbrella-shaded tables on the patio offer a view of the leafy entrance to the Universidad Veracruzana and its enormous sports stadium. ✗ *Av. Universidad, at Calle Pérgola, Lomas del Estadio,* ☎ *28/ 17–53–53. AE, MC, V.*

$$ 1-2-3. ★ This midsize restaurant, located on a busy thoroughfare in the northern part of the city, looks unpromising from the street. The interior, however, comes as a pleasant surprise. Painted in muted, contrasting shades of green and purple, the dining-room walls are lined with the work of local artists, and modern sculpture is scattered about the room. The food, a combination of Mexican and international dishes, is more than reasonably priced. Mexican entrées include sirloin tips with chipotle chiles and *crepas de huitlacoche* (crepes filled with a special corn fungus and bathed in cream sauce). International choices such as Waldorf salad, curried chicken, and steak tartare are knowledgeably prepared. Adjoining the dining rooms is a quiet, casual bar that opens onto the restaurant's simple courtyard. ✗ *Ruíz Cortines 857,* ☎ *28/14–71–22. AE, MC, V. No dinner Sun.*

$ El Balcón de la Agora. This small café, part of the Agora de la Ciudad cultural center in Parque Juárez, is popular with students who come to study over a strong cup of coffee or an inexpensive sandwich. Open-air balcony seating provides an excellent view of the green city below and, in the distance, the Pico de Orizaba mountain. Order at the cash register as you enter, then present your receipt at the counter as you repeat your order. ✗ *Bajos del Parque Juárez,* ☎ *28/18– 57–30. No credit cards. Breakfast and lunch only.*

$ La Fonda. ★ The entrance to this charming, traditional restaurant is hidden on a small pedestrian walkway off the busy Calle Enríquez, a block from Parque Juárez. Brightly colored streamers, baskets, dried and fresh flowers, and murals adorn the walls and ceiling, and the warm corn tortillas served with every meal are made before your eyes. The food is well-prepared, hearty northern Veracruzan fare: Beef or chicken, and beans, *nopales* (cactus strips), and/or chile are essential elements of almost every dish. ✗ *Antonio M. de Rivera 1 (also known as the Callejon del Diamante), at Enríquez,* ☎ *28/18–45–20. AE, MC, V. Closed Sun.*

Papantla

$$ **Restaurant Enrique.** This restaurant, on the bottom floor of the Hotel Premier, is the most expensive in town (you can expect to pay about $10 per person). Tables are covered in blue-and-white linens, and stuffed sea creatures adorn the walls, but the attempt at elegance is effectively defeated by the roar of the TV and the even-louder air-conditioning. Still, this is your best bet if you've had all the meat and fried food you can stomach: The menu includes a number of fish dishes, as well as delicacies such as crawfish (in stew, steamed, or grilled) and octopus. There's also a full bar. ✕ *Enríquez 103,* ☎ *784/ 2–00–80. MC, V.*

$ **Plaza Pardo.** Oddly enough, the Pardo specializes in burgers 'n' fries and malts. It's clean, inexpensive, and fun, with an open storefront that looks directly out onto the square. Basic Mexican dishes and breakfasts are also available. ✕ *Enríquez 105,* ☎ *784/2–00–59. No credit cards.*

$ **Restaurante Sorrento.** The Sorrento is the most popular restaurant in
★ Papantla, crowded at mealtimes with locals who come to enjoy the cheap regional seafood and to catch a few minutes of the *telenovela* (soap opera) on the corner set. The dining room, painted entirely lavender and lined with colorful tilework, is staffed by a young, all-female staff. ✕ *Enríquez 104, no* ☎. *No credit cards.*

$ **Restaurant Tajín.** The Hotel Tajín's sunny restaurant is comparatively elegant and hardly more expensive than the storefont eateries near the second-class bus station. House specialties include a fillet of fish stuffed with shellfish, *jaibas rellenas* (stuffed crab), rabbit marinated in chile, and Yucatecan *pollo píbil* (chicken in a spicy, pumpkin seed-and-chile sauce). Don't be alarmed by the misleading bilingual menu—the *tasajo cerdo* is not, in fact, "steak porpoise," but marinated pork. ✕ *Hotel Tajín, Nuñez y Domínguez 104,* ☎ *784/2–17–34. MC, V.*

Tuxpán

$$ **Antonio's.** Next to the Hotel Reforma on Juárez and serving as its restaurant, Antonio's is a quiet, comparatively elegant eatery with a varied menu. The *azuela de mariscos* (shellfish stew) is excellent, as are the prawns, served grilled or in garlic sauce. A number of beef dishes and sandwiches are also available, as well as cocktails from the full bar. ✕ *Juárez s/n at Garizurieta,* ☎ *783/4–16–02 AE, DC, MC, V. Breakfast, lunch, and dinner.*

$$ **Charlôt.** For anything other than seafood or tacos, the best place in Tuxpán is undoubtedly Charlôt. Opened just a few years ago, this French and international restaurant is a favorite of local businesspeople, and it's not uncommon to find an entire corner of the restaurant taken over by an expansive lunch meeting. The pretty dining room is decorated with ceramics and other *artesanía*. The house specialty is medallions of beef in mushroom sauce, but simple steaks as well as some fish dishes and pizzas are also featured. Service is good and there's a full bar. ✕ *Reyes Heroles 35, at Zozimo Pérez,* ☎ *783/ 4–40–28. MC, V. Closed Mon.*

$$ **El Volador.** The restaurant in the Hotel Tajín, across the river from central Tuxpán, is bright and airy, with a semicircular wall of windows overlooking the Río Tuxpán. Homemade corn chips and fresh salsa with plenty of cilantro arrive at your table as soon as you order. Dishes run the gamut from local favorites such as *camarones al mojo de ajo* (shrimp in garlic sauce) and pescado a la veracruzana to American-style offerings such as T-bone steaks and hamburgers. It's nothing to make a special trip for, but come if you happen to be on this side of the river visiting the Casa de Fidel Castro (still a taxi ride away from here, however) or just want an excuse to make the pleasant skiff crossing. ✗ *In Hotel Tajín, Km 2.5 Carretera a Cobos,* ☎ *783/4–22–60. AE, DC, MC, V.*

$ **Cafetería El Mante.** Ask any Tuxpán resident where to get a good, inexpensive breakfast, and you'll be sent to this place. It's loud, with plastic chairs, plastic tablecloths, and cheap, greasy, salty—and, oh yes, tasty—food. The most popular breakfast dish is *bocoles con huevo* (basically, fried egg dumplings). The El Mante is open daily until midnight, making it a dependable, central stop for a cholesterol-laden snack at almost any hour. ✗ *Piplan 8, at Juárez,* ☎ *783/ 4–57–36. No credit cards.*

Veracruz

$$$$ **La Mansión.** This elegant restaurant is part of an expansive nation-wide chain specializing in grilled meats. The Veracruz branch, on the boulevard just east of downtown, features attractive Southwestern decor in subdued greens and peaches, as well as brisk and efficient service. A few soups and salads are served, but the menu is dominated by thick cuts of steak. The extensive wine selection consists almost exclusively of domestic, Spanish, and French reds. ✗ *Ruíz Cortines s/n, across from Blue Ocean disco,* ☎ *29/37–13–63 or 29/37–13–38. AE, MC, V. Closed Mon.*

$$$$ **Mariscos Villa Rica.** This casual, seafront palapa restaurant is worth
★ the small effort required to find it. Hidden on a small street that runs parallel to Playa Mocambo, the Villa Rica is a favorite with locals and visitors in the know, but sees almost no casual tourists. The menu consists entirely of seafood. Specialties include sea bass, snapper, prawns, and lobster, prepared as you wish. There is a small, reason-ably priced wine list, but the beverage of choice among loyal patrons is cold Corona with lime. Live music is featured daily, from 2:30 PM on. ✗ *Calle Mocambo s/n, Boca del Río,* ☎ *29/37–76–80. MC, V.*

$$$ **La Fragata.** Those who are not staying at the romantic 1930s Hotel Mocambo can visit its restaurant for an evening meal and see the place at its best—when the breezes off the water blow in at night and the ter-raced gardens are illuminated. For the full effect, request an outdoor table. Dinner offerings range from filet mignon to huachinango stuffed with shrimp and calamari, but there's nothing in the way of lighter fare beyond a few disappointing salads. The restaurant is rarely crowded, and service is casual and very friendly. ✗ *In Hotel Mocambo, Ruíz Cortines s/n, on Playa Mocambo in Boca del Río,* ☎ *29/22–02–05. AE, MC, V.*

$$$ **Restaurant Albatros.** This unlikely establishment, tucked away in a residential neighborhood a few blocks from the waterfront, has the feel of a semi-exclusive men's club. It's furnished in dark woods, and waiters in bow ties scurry about to the sound of live piano music. The menu includes some unusual dishes, such as *filete de res Azteca* (steak in corn fungus sauce) and the slightly oversalty *crema de flor de cal-abaza* (cream of squash-flower soup). The real attraction, however, is the fresh seafood, which the accommodating chef will prepare to your specifications. ✗ *16 de Septiembre 1480 at Azueta,* ☎ *29/31–25–85. MC, V.*

$$ **La Bamba.** This casual eatery sits just off the malecón, suspended on
★ stilts above the water. Seats on the terrace enjoy a cooling sea breeze, and Mexican ballads play over the sound system. The management prides itself in its innovative seafood dishes; these include *pámpano Bamba* (the house special sea bass), which comes smothered in shrimp, calamari, and shellfish, all sautéed in garlic. The menu also features not-too-expensive lobster, as well as a number of beef and poultry dishes. A modest selection of wines, most of them Mexican,

and cocktails complement the food. ✕ *Avila Camacho at Zapata,* ☎ *29/32–53–55. AE, MC, V. Closed Mon.*

$$ **Pardiño's.** In Boca del Río, about 10 kilometers (6 miles) south of downtown Veracruz, this modest eatery is a star in a village of seafood restaurants. Plain tables in a storefront on Boca del Río's main square belie the elegant preparation of such dishes as crabs *salpicón* (finely chopped with cilantro, onion, and lime), grilled sea bass, and, of course, huachinango a la veracruzana, here served with sweet *plátanos fritos* (fried plantains). Also delicious are the simple, fresh appetizers, such as shrimp cocktail with generous chunks of ripe avocado. Pardiño's has another location in downtown Veracruz, but it lacks the charm of the Boca del Río restaurant. ✕ *Boca del Río: Zamora 40,* ☎ *29/86–01–35; Veracruz: Landero y Coss 146 at the malecón,* ☎ *29/31–48–81. MC, V.*

$ **Café Catedral.** This sizable café, crowded with simple, bare wooden tables, has at least a few patrons at any hour of the day. Customers are almost exclusively locals, drawn by the vigorous ceiling fans, the exceptionally efficient service, and the enormous portions of basic, hearty *cocina veracruzana* (Veracruz cuisine). The huge menu offers a number of egg dishes and sandwiches, as well as more substantial entrées (including, of course, the ubiquitous huachinango a la veracruzana). ✕ *Ocampo 202, 1 block from Parque Zamora,* ☎ *29/32–52–06. No credit cards.*

$ **Café de la Parroquia.** One of the most famous sidewalk cafés in Mex★ ico, the Parroquia is an indispensable stop for a *café lechero* (coffee with hot milk). It is lively at all times of the day: Crowds of guayabera-clad functionaries from the nearby civil offices tap their glasses with spoons to call a refill-bearing waiter, and marimba or mariachi music competes with the pitches of street vendors. The menu features a wide selection of egg dishes, such as Spanish-style omelets (called tortillas) as well as soups, sandwiches, a traditional version of huachinango a la veracruzana, and hearty steak and chicken entrées—but the coffee is the real draw. A second location, the Gran Café de la Parroquia (on the malecón at Insurgentes Veracruzanos 340) tends to draw lots of local families. ✕ *Independencia 105, across from the cathedral,* ☎ *29/32–25–84. No credit cards.*

$ **Tortas Koy Koy.** This unpretentious sandwich joint, set right on the verdant Parque Zamora, is a favorite date spot for young *jarochos* (as natives of Veracruz are known). It specializes in excellent sandwiches of house-roasted chicken, pork, or beef served with beans, cheese, tomato, and avocado, and accompanied by a plate of spicy pickled vegetables. Burgers and fries are also on the menu, along with traditional Mexican offerings such as tacos and tamales. Don't miss such fresh beverages as *horchata* (a sweetish drink made with rice, milk, water, and cinnamon)—they're served in enormous goblets and cost hardly anything. ✕ *Manuel Doblado s/n,* ☎ *329/1–50–49. No credit cards.*

Lodging

Veracruz's tourist industry is less well-developed than one might expect, and it has no truly world-class hotels. The port of **Veracruz** does offer a number of inexpensive hotels with plenty of atmosphere, and the moderately priced and more expensive places offer good value for your money, especially in comparison with their counterparts in areas that see more foreign tourism. The area along the water south of downtown (toward Boca del Río), especially along Playa Mocambo, is showing signs of turning into a mini *zona hotelera* (tourist strip). It is here that you will find the better beaches, as well as most of the fancier hotels and resorts.

While there are plenty of clean, comfortable budget options in downtown **Jalapa,** more upscale options are limited. The nicer hotels, located a bit out of town, can be inconvenient if you don't have a car, because local bus service is infrequent, and Jalapa's many cultural offerings are concentrated in the zona centro. Many people choose to see Tajín as a day trip from the more developed city of Tuxpán, only briefly passing through Papantla. If you decide to spend a night or two here, your options are limited. **Papantla** has few hotels, and none is exceptional, though the Premier is well-equipped. Fortunately, they are concentrated in a five-block radius and almost never fill up, so you can simply walk around town once you arrive and decide which suits you best. For now, **Tuxpán** lacks a five-star hotel, though a fancy establishment called Hotel May Palace was under construction on the Parque Reforma at press time. It is, however, easy to find a safe, comfortable, reasonably priced room. Tuxpán sees very little foreign tourism, and aside from Semana Santa (Easter week) and August, when middle-class Mexicans head en masse for the beach, its hotels are usually empty.

CATEGORY	COST*
$$$$	over $110
$$$	$70–$110
$$	$40–$70
$	under $40

All prices are for a standard double room, excluding tax.

Jalapa

$$$ **Posada Coatepec.** In the coffee- and orchid-growing town of Coate-
★ pec, approximately 15 minutes' drive from Xalapa, the Posada Coatepec is a member of the prestigious Small Grand Hotels of Mexico group. This hotel, which specializes in personalized service and fine food, is a villa comprising 24 beautifully decorated suites, each with color satellite-TV and a minibar. ☎ *Hidalgo 9, Coatepec, 91501,* ☎ *28/16–05–44,* FAX *28/16–00–40. Restaurant, pool. AE, MC, V.*

$$$ **Fiesta Inn Xalapa.** This hotel has the sterile feel of a chain hotel and is also a bit out of the way, in a primarily residential neighborhood, 10 minute's drive from the center of town. However, if you have a car and are looking for a comfortable, quiet, secure, and well-equipped base, the Fiesta Inn is a good bet. Guest rooms in the two-story, colonial-style structure are decorated in cool blues and grays and have color satellite-TVs, telephones, air-conditioning, bathtubs, and plenty of morning sunlight. Flawless English is spoken at the reception desk. ☎ *Km 2.5 Carretera Xalapa–Veracruz, Fracc. Las Animas, 91000,* ☎ *28/12–79–20 or 800/FIESTA–1,* FAX *28/12–79–46. 116 rooms, 4 suites. Restaurant, bar, pool, business services. AE, MC, V.*

$$ **Maria Victoria.** This pink-and-beige high-rise looms over Calle Zaragoza, just one block from Parque Juárez. The building can only be described as ugly, but the location can't be beat, and you won't find better rooms for the price. Many of them have nice views; all are spacious and well-furnished, with TVs (local stations only), telephones, and purified water on tap. ☎ *Zaragoza 6, 91000,* ☎ *28/18–60–11 or 91/800/2–60–08 (toll-free in Mexico),* FAX *28/18–05–01. 96 rooms, 18 suites. Restaurant, bar, pool. AE, MC, V.*

$$ **Hotel Xalapa.** The Hotel Xalapa is the best-equipped downtown hotel, with all the amenities of a much more expensive establishment: a bar, restaurant, and gift shop; air-conditioning, telephones, color satellite-TV, bathtubs, and minibars in every room; and free, covered parking for guests. The building itself—another 1960s-style institutional behemoth—is not particularly attractive, but the rooms are large, sunny, and very quiet. ☎ *Esq. Victoria y Bustamante, Zona Centro, 91000,* ☎ *28/*

18–22–22 or 28/17–70–64, FAX *28/18–94–24. 170 rooms, 30 suites. AE, MC, V.*

$ Hotel Citlalli. A 10-minute walk uphill from Parque Juárez, the Citlalli is a great bargain. The public areas are spotless and well-lit, and every room is spacious, with a large, clean private bath, phone, and TV that receives local stations. Some rooms have balconies. Free, covered parking is provided for guests. ☎ *Clavijero 43, 91000,* ☎ *28/18–34–58. 42 rooms. No credit cards.*

$ Hotel Salmones. Once a high-class establishment, the Hotel Salmones
★ has clearly seen better days. Still, vestiges of its lost glory remain—the high ceilings, sweeping staircases, dark-wood fixtures, and big, beautiful windows are untouched by time. The very clean rooms lack air-conditioning (hardly necessary in this cloudy city) but are tastefully and simply decorated. All have televisions (local stations only) and telephones; some offer small balconies. ☎ *Zaragoza 24, 91000,* ☎ *28/17–54–31. 60 rooms. Restaurant, bar. MC, V.*

Papantla

$$ Hotel Premier. Right on Papantla's pretty, lively zócalo, the Premier is the town's swankiest hotel. The lobby is lined with mirrors and furnished with small, purple chairs that were once dedicated to the no-longer-functional bar. The rooms themselves are spotless and good-size and have tiny balconies overlooking the square. Amenities include bedside lamps still encased in plastic, tiled bathrooms, air-conditioning, telephones, and color satellite TVs. ☎ *Enríquez 103, 93400,* ☎ *784/2–00–80. 20 rooms. Restaurant. MC, V.*

$ Hotel Pulido. The cheapest acceptable hotel around, the Pulido has plenty of street noise and no air-conditioning, but each room offers a ceiling fan, serviceable beds, and a private bath with hot water. Ask for a room on the second floor, which is somewhat quieter. ☎ *Enríquez 205, 93400,* ☎ *784/2–00–36. 23 rooms. No credit cards.*

$ Hotel Tajín. Under the same management as the Hotel Premier, the Tajín is less expensive than its slightly more central cousin. The televisions offer local stations only, some rooms have ceiling fans instead of air-conditioning, and the telephones don't always work, but, all in all, the Tajín isn't a bad deal. Its hillside perch makes for nice views, and the rooms, while fairly small and decorated in a startling pink and green, are spotless and comfortable. ☎ *Nuñez y Domínguez 104, 93400,* ☎ *784/2–06–44. 60 rooms. Restaurant. MC, V.*

$ Hotel Totonacapan. This slightly gloomy hotel is located a few blocks from the center, near the second-class bus station. It's acceptable, but only should be an option if you don't want to pay for the Premier and the Tajín is full. The rooms are big and bare, with large windows that don't quite dispel a sense of claustrophobia. Still, the staff is extremely friendly and the rooms have air-conditioning, color TVs (local stations only), and telephones. Coolers in the hall dispense purified water, and a diner-style restaurant downstairs serves standard breakfast. ☎ *20 de Noviembre (at Olivo), 93400,* ☎ *784/2–12–16. 36 rooms. No credit cards.*

Tuxpán

$$ Hotel Reforma. The Reforma is a lovely building located a block from the waterfront in the heart of downtown. It lacks a lobby, but has a central courtyard with a number of skylights, a fountain, and a few wrought-iron tables where guests often congregate in the afternoon. Rooms are somewhat dark, but clean and comfortable, with phones, air-conditioning, color satellite-TVs, good-size bathrooms, and some antique furnishings. Street noise can be a problem on the first floor. ☎

Juárez 25, 92801, ☎ *783/4–02–10 or 783/4–04–60,* ⓕⓧ *783/4–06–25. 98 rooms. AE, DC, MC, V.*

$$ **Hotel Tajín.** This place looks like a first-class resort from the outside, but once you enter, you'll be reminded of nothing so much as a college dorm: Long beige hallways with faded blue carpets lead past scores of identical, bland rooms with almost no decorative touches. However, the Tajín's location on the banks of the river, a bit east of and across from the center, means that almost every room overlooks the water and the green city of Tuxpán. It also means that the traffic noise of downtown is replaced by the sounds of river birds at night. The hotel is easy to reach by car (just cross the bridge and drive east for about 5 minutes), but there is no bus service. Pedestrians must take either a longish taxi ride from the center or catch a beach-bound bus to the Paso de Esquifes La Peñita, where a small motorboat shuttles passengers across the river. From the skiff landing, the hotel is a three-minute (if often muddy) walk away. ⌖ *Km 2.5 Carretera a Cobos, 92801,* ☎ *783/4–22–60 or 783/4–25–72,* ⓕⓧ *783/4–51–84. 140 rooms. Restaurant, bar, pool, dance club, chapel. AE, DC, MC, V.*

$ **Hotel y Restaurante Café e Arte.** This rather pretentiously named little beach dive had barely opened its doors at press time, but the owners have big plans—air-conditioned rooms, a pool, and a restaurant with a full bar. For now, rooms are bare but serviceable, with private bathrooms and screens to let in the breezes and keep out the bugs. ⌖ *Playa Tuxpán, Barra Norte, 92801, no* ☎. *5 rooms. No credit cards.*

$ **El Huasteco.** This place falls into the cheapest-of-the-cheap category and is popular among budget travelers. The management takes no reservations, so if you're looking for a truly inexpensive room, your best bet is to show up here early in the day. The rooms are basic but clean, and all have bathrooms and air-conditioning. (The latter is a necessity in humid, tropical Tuxpán.) ⌖ *Morelos 41 (just inland from Parque Reforma), 92801,* ☎ *783/4–18–59. 40 rooms. No credit cards.*

$ **Hotel Florida.** Don't be deceived by the dark lobby or the cramped
★ elevator: The Hotel Florida is the best hotel deal in downtown Tuxpán. The rooms are decorated in bright pastels and offer ample light and space, as well as large, immaculate bathrooms. Basic rooms have telephones and vigorous ceiling fans; slightly more expensive rooms have phones, TVs (local stations only), and air-conditioning. Terraces on each floor enjoy views of the cathedral and waterfront. ⌖ *Juárez 23 (catercorner to cathedral), 92801,* ☎ *783/4–02–22 or 783/4–06–02. 78 rooms. Restaurant, cafeteria. MC, V.*

$ **Playa Azul.** Outside of pitching a tent or renting a hammock, staying in this motel-style establishment is the cheapest way to spend the night on Playa Tuxpán. Rooms are small, run-down, cement-box affairs with two beds, a small TV (local stations only), a ceiling fan, and a private bathroom with hot and cold running water. ⌖ *Km 2.5 Carretera a la Termo, Barra Norte, 92801, no* ☎. *15 rooms. Restaurant. No credit cards.*

Veracruz

$$$$ **Continental Plaza Veracruz.** Opened in early 1994, this is the Veracruz–Boca del Río area's newest and best-equipped luxury hotel, specifically geared toward business travelers. It has a complete business center staffed by bilingual secretaries and sits atop a 3000-person capacity convention center. The amply furnished rooms, decorated in a bright, tropical motif, have climate control, satellite TVs, minibars, and taps spouting potable water. One- or two-bedroom suites, some with Jacuzzis, are also available, and accommodations on an executive floor entitle guests to exclusive concierge service and complimentary

Continental breakfast. ☎ *Ruíz Cortines 3501, Boca del Río, 94260,* ☎ *29/85–05–05 or 91/800/9–02–29 (in Mexico) or 800/882–6684 (U.S.),* FAX *29/85–05–01. 212 rooms, 23 suites. Restaurant, bar, indoor pool, exercise room, baby-sitting. AE, MC, V.*

$$$$ **Torremar.** Established in 1980 as part of the Hyatt chain, this deluxe, high-rise resort on Playa Mocambo has been independent since 1982. The rooms, somewhat excessively decorated in pastels, contain all the amenities, including minibars. Suites feature small balconies with fantastic views of the Gulf of Mexico. An executive floor, with special concierge service and complimentary breakfast, is also available. Kids will like the cascading poolside fountain and the organized activities in the children's play area. ☎ *Ruíz Cortines 4300, Boca del Río, 94260,* ☎ *29/31–34–66 or 91/800/29–900 (toll-free in Mexico). 232 rooms. Bars, exercise room. AE, MC, V.*

$$$ **Emporio.** This large, business-oriented hotel is fun and well-situated—right on the malecón. While the decor is modern and unremarkable, the rooms are the brightest and cheeriest to be found downtown. Some have sea views, and all have marbled bathrooms with bathtubs (those in the suites are Jacuzzis). Dine in the popular restaurant, or in the shade of an umbrella at any of the hotel's three pools (one is equipped with a waterfall and a number of slides). ☎ *Insurgentes Veracruzanos 210, 91700,* ☎ *29/32–00–20 or 91/800/2–95–20 (toll-free in Mexico),* FAX *29/31–22–61. 202 rooms, 40 suites. Restaurant, 3 pools. AE, MC, V.*

$$$ **Hotel Mocambo.** When the Mocambo was built in 1934, it was Mex-
★ ico's only Gulf Coast resort. Newly remodeled, it remains the prettiest and most romantic hotel in the Veracruz area. The guest rooms, while spacious and air-conditioned, are somewhat bare, and some of the facilities (such as the tennis courts) are showing their age, but the Mocambo is nevertheless a delight. Its sprawling, terraced gardens lead down towards the palm-lined Playa Mocambo. Dark wood fixtures, art-deco touches (such as a set of flowerlike pillars around the indoor pool), and attentive service all add to the feeling that the Mocambo belongs in another, more decorous age. ☎ *Ruíz Cortines s/n, on Playa Mocambo in Boca del Río, 94260,* ☎ *29/22–02–05 or 91/800/2–90–01 (toll-free in Mexico),* FAX *29/22–02–12. 123 rooms. Restaurant, bar, cafeteria, pool, exercise room. AE, MC, V.*

$$ **Hotel Colonial.** A comfortable but bland establishment, the Hotel Colonial is right on the zócalo, two blocks from the waterfront. All rooms have TVs, phones, air-conditioning, and small balconies; those in the old wing are smaller, but have a bit more character, with wooden fixtures and colored tiles. A pretty, tiled terrace on the fifth floor overlooks the greenery of the main square, and a lookout patio on the sixth floor provides a panoramic view of the city center. The helpful staff at the reception desk speak some English. ☎ *Miguel Lerdo 117, 91700,* ☎ *29/32–01–93,* FAX *29/32–24–65. 182 rooms, 21 suites. Indoor pool. MC, V.*

$$ **Hotel Ruiz Milan.** This multistory waterfront hotel is an excellent value for the price. Guest rooms, though on the small side, are clean, comfortable, and modern. All have color satellite-TVs, telephones, balconies, ample closet space, and sizable bathrooms; you have to request air-conditioning. The pleasantly cool lobby is always crowded with Mexican businesspeople, and the hotel itself has all the amenities of a much more expensive establishment, including an indoor pool with a bar, a lobby bar, a comfortable restaurant, and free covered parking. ☎ *Paseo del Malecón 432, 91700,* ☎ *29/32–27–72 or 29/32–37–77,* FAX *ext. 106. 88 rooms. MC, V.*

$$ **Hotel Villa Florencia.** This comfortable, quiet hotel is tucked away on an affluent residential street paralleling one of the prettier stretches of Playa Mocambo. Large, standard motel-style rooms are brightened by splashes of tilework; all have two beds, televisions, and sliding-glass doors that open onto patios overlooking the attractive pool area. None of the rooms, however, has a phone. ☎ *Calcada Mocambo 207, Boca del Río, 94260, ☎ 29/21–02–44. 27 rooms. Restaurant. AE, MC, V.*

$$ **Villa del Mar.** This unassuming hotel, just across from one of the nicer
★ sections of downtown beach, is an ideal place to bring kids. The standard, motel-style rooms are spacious and comfortable, and surround a large, pretty garden with a tennis court, pool, and small playground. All the accommodations have color TVs, telephones, and air-conditioning. The staff is very helpful, and English is spoken at the reception desk. A number of bungalows (accommodating up to five people) are also available: These are a bit gloomy and lack air-conditioning, but some have kitchenettes. ☎ *Avila Camacho s/n, at Bartolomé de las Casas, 91700, ☎ 29/31–15–90 or 29/31–33–66, FAX 29/ 32–71–35. 90 rooms, 15 bungalows. AE, MC, V.*

$ **Hotel Concha Dorada.** The basically characterless Concha Dorada has the cheapest rooms on the zócalo. Accommodations are cramped but clean, and all have color TVs (local stations only) and telephones; some are air-conditioned. The downstairs restaurant–sidewalk café serves simple fare and is especially popular (noisy) at lunchtime. ☎ *Lerdo 77, near Zaragoza, 91700, ☎ 29/31–32–46, FAX 29/31–31–21. 36 rooms. MC, V.*

$ **Gran Hotel Diligencias.** Founded as a luxury hotel in 1850, the Gran Hotel Diligencias was thoroughly remodeled in the 1960s—and appears to have been sliding downhill ever since. Still, it's not bad for the price. Rooms are large enough, and all are clean and have TVs, telephones, air-conditioning, and balconies. The location—just opposite the zócalo and a block from the venerable Gran Café de la Parroquia—is ideal for anyone who wants to see the city on foot. ☎ *Independencia 1115, 91700, ☎ 29/31–21–16, FAX 29/31–31–57. 106 rooms, 12 suites. Restaurant. AE, DC, MC, V.*

$ **Hotel Santander.** Once known as the Hotel Vigo, the Santander is a true budget hotel, only two blocks from the zócalo. Rooms are slightly musty and lack air-conditioning, but all are comfortably furnished, with working ceiling fans and color TVs (local stations only). Ask for an upstairs rooms: These cost no more and have telephones and small balconies with views of the city. ☎ *Landero y Coss 123, at Mario Molina, 91700, ☎ 29/32–45–29 or 29/32–86–59. 42 rooms. No credit cards.*

Nightlife

Jalapa

The **Ágora** (Parque Juárez) cultural center stages art exhibits and the occasional folk-music performance, and shows classic and avant-garde films in its cinema club. Stop by during the day to see what's planned. The **Teatro del Estado** (Ignacio de la Llave s/n, ☎ 28/ 17–41–77, ext. 38) is the big, modern, state theater of Veracruz. The Orquesta Sinfónica de Jalapa performs here, often giving free concerts during off-season (early June to mid-August). Check *El Diario de Jalapa* (the Jalapa city newspaper, available at newsstands) for dates and times of performances, or stop by the Ágora.

Such other nightlife as there is in this student town is generally youth oriented. **Video Bar Terraza,** above the restaurant/bar Terraza Jardín, is a crowded lounge popular with students and young professionals. The upscale **Café El Escorial** purveys beer, coffee, and live music to a well-heeled crowd. **La 7a Estación** (20 de Noviembre, near Central Camionera) is packed with salsa dancers on Wednesday nights; Thursday–Saturday, rock and alternative music are featured. **Tortilla Flats** (Díaz Mirón 23, off Parque Los Berros), a small restaurant near the university, offers rock music on Saturday nights, starting about 9.

Veracruz

Every Tuesday and Friday night after 8, the Plaza de Armas is the scene of open-air dances, with a dressed-up crowd and live marimba music. Sunday nights, the dancing moves to Parque Zamora.

Discos and video bars are plentiful along the malecón. Both **Ocean** (Ruíz Cortines 8, at Ávila Camacho, ☎ 29/37–63–27), a flashy, modern discotheque, and **Blue Ocean** (Ávila Camacho 9, ☎ 29/22–03–66), a video bar with a light show, are packed on Friday and Saturday nights with a young, largely local crowd.

Excursion to Las Tuxtlas

Some 140 kilometers (84 miles) south of Veracruz, a small volcanic mountain range, the Sierra de Los Tuxtlas, meets the sea. Simply known as **Los Tuxtlas,** this area has lakes, waterfalls, rivers, mineral springs, and access to beaches, making it a popular stopover for travelers heading east from Mexico City to the Yucatán. The region's three principal towns—Santiago Tuxtla, San Andrés Tuxtla, and Catemaco—are carved into the mountainsides more than 200 meters above sea level, lending them a coolness even in summer that's the envy of the perspiring masses on the coastal plain. The Tuxtlas gain an air of mystery from the cool, gray fog that slips over the mountains and lakes and the whisperings among the townspeople about the *brujos* (witches), also called *curanderos* (healers), who read tarot cards, prescribe herbal remedies, and cast spells here.

While much of the architecture here is of the 1960s school of looming cement, all three towns are laid out in the colonial style around a main plaza and a church, and all have a certain amount of charm; Santiago Tuxtla has managed to retain more of its colonial character than the other two Tuxtla towns. The region was also a center of Olmec culture, and Olmec artifacts and small ruins abound. A huge stone Olmec head dominates the zócalo at Santiago Tuxtla, and 21 kilometers (13 miles) east are the ruins of **Tres Zapotes,** now decidedly unspectacular, but once an important Olmec ceremonial center believed to have been occupied as early as AD 100.

Today, the economic life of Los Tuxtlas depends on cigar manufacturing and tourism. The largest of the three towns is San Andrés, which is also the local transport hub. With plenty of hotels, it serves as a good base from which to explore the entire region. From Santiago, you can check out the ruins at Tres Zapotes; the town also has an informative museum where you can learn about the region's indigenous heritage and contemporary local cultures. **Lake Catemaco** is popular among Mexicans as a summer and Christmas resort and is also the place to go for a *consulta* (consulation) with a brujo or curandero, should you have any problems or questions that require some spiritual clarity or supernatural intervention.

Veracruz Essentials

Arriving and Departing

BY PLANE

Continental (☎ 800/231–0856) has direct flights to the city of Veracruz from Houston. Both **Mexicana** and **Aeromexico** provide nonstop service from Mexico City. No city bus serves the airport, and a cab to the city center costs $12. A minivan ($10) also runs between the airport and the downtown office of **Transportación Terrestre Aeropuerto** (Hidalgo 826, bet. Canal and Morales, ☎ 29/32–32–50).

BY CAR

The city of Veracruz can be reached within about eight hours by traveling south from Tampico via Mexico 180, or within six hours from Mexico City via Mexico 150. The roads throughout the state, paved and kept up with oil money, are generally very good.

Jalapa. Viajes Herlu (Av. Orizaba 125, ☎ 28/15–51–81, FAX 28/15–45–53) can arrange car rentals.

Tuxpán. If you enjoy tooling along the coast, you can rent a car from **Diversion y Viajes** (Juárez s/n, at Humboldt, ☎ 783/4–21–50), which has an office by the water.

Veracruz. Avis has an office at the Veracruz airport (☎ 29/31–15–80 or 800/331–1084 for international reservations). You'll find **Hertz** (Aquiles Serdan 14, ☎ 29/32–40–21 or 800/654–3001) downtown, behind the Emporio Hotel.

BY BUS

Veracruz. The main bus terminal (Díaz Mirón 1698, ☎ 29/37–57–44) is about 4 kilometers (2½ miles) south of the zócalo. The main bus company is **Autobuses del Oriente (ADO)** (☎ 29/37–57–88), with daily service to Jalapa and round-the-clock departures for Mexico City. ADO also offers first- and second-class service to Reynosa, on the Texas border. For those headed south, **Cristobal Colón** (☎ 29/35–03–17) and **Cuenca** (☎ 29/35–54–05) go to Oaxaca and Chiapas. **Autobuses Unidos** (☎ 29/37–57–32) and **Transportes Los Tuxtlas** (☎ 29/37–28–78) operate from another station on the same block and offer frequent second-class service to Jalapa and Los Tuxtlas.

Guided Tours

Operadora Terrestre de Veracruz (Pedro de Alvarado 223, Fracc. Reforma, ☎ 29/37–66–19 or 29/37–06–61) offers city tours as well as tours of Tajín and Papantla, Los Tuxtlas, and Jalapa. Diving and fishing trips are available, too. There's also a tour desk at the Hotel Torremar.

Boat tours of the bay depart from the malecón daily 7–7. Boats leave whenever they're full, and the $4, half-hour ride includes a (Spanish-language) talk on Veracruz history. Longer trips to nearby **Isla Verde** (Green Island) and **Isla de Enmedio** (Middle Island) leave daily from the shack marked PASEO EN LANCHITA near the Plaza Acuario. Boats leave whenever they're full, so it's best to come in a big group. The cost should be about $5–$7 per person, but feel free to bargain.

Important Addresses and Numbers

CONSULATE

Veracruz. United States Consulate: Víctimas del 25 del Julio 384, bet. Gómez Farias and 16 de Septiembre, ☎ 29/31–58–21; ⊙ Weekdays 9–1.

CURRENCY EXCHANGE

Jalapa. One block from Parque Juárez, **Casa de Cambio Jalapa** (Zamora 36, ☎ 28/18–68–60) offers good rates. You can also change money in the mornings at several banks on Parque Juárez.

Papantla. The **Banamex** (Enríquez 102), just past Andy's Cadillac Bar, changes both cash and traveler's checks weekdays 9–noon and has an ATM that accepts Cirrus, Plus, Visa, and MasterCard.

Tuxpán. Bancomer (Juárez, at Escuela Médico Militar, ☎ 783/4–00–09) changes cash and traveler's checks weekdays 9:30–noon.

Veracruz. The best rates in town are available at **Bancomer** (Juárez, at Independencia), but money-changing hours are limited (weekdays 9 AM–11:30 AM) so you'll have to arrive early to make it through the lines. For later hours, try **Casa de Cambio Puebla** (Juárez 112, ☎ 29/31–24–50), open weekdays 9–6, or use the ATM at **Banamex** (also on Juárez, at Independencia).

EMERGENCIES

Jalapa. The number for the **police** is 28/17–63–10. For an ambulance, call the **Cruz Roja** (☎ 28/14–45–00).

Papantla. Police (☎ 784/2–01–93); **Cruz Roja** (☎ 784/2–01–01).

Tuxpán. Police (☎ 783/4–02–52); **Cruz Roja** (☎ 783/4–01–58).

Veracruz. Oficinas Para La Seguridad del Turista (☎ 91/800/9–03–92) operates a 24-hour toll-free hot line to provide legal and medical help for tourists in Veracruz. **Police:** Playa Linda 222, ☎ 29/38–06–64 or 29/38–06–93. **Hospital Regional de Veracruz:** 20th Nov. s/n, ☎ 29/32–27–05 or 29/32–36–90, and **Cruz Roja (Red Cross),** ☎ 29/37–55–00.

PHARMACIES

Jalapa. Calle Enríquez is lined with pharmacies. For 24-hour service, the pharmacy in **Super Tiendas Ramón** (Revolución 171, at Sagayo, ☎ 28/18–09–35) is your best option.

Papantla. Farmacia Médico (Gutierrez Zamora 3, ☎ 784/2–19–41), open daily 7:30 AM–10 PM, is the largest pharmacy in town. The staff doesn't speak English but is good at charades.

Veracruz. Benavides (Independencia 1291, at Serdán ☎ 29/31–89–29) is a big, convenient drugstore downtown, but it closes at 10 PM daily. For 24-hour service, try **Farmacia San Francisco** (5 De Mayo 1634, ☎ 29/32–27–88).

VISITOR INFORMATION

Jalapa. You can get information (in Spanish only) as well as maps and pamphlets from the helpful folks at the **municipal tourist office** (Ávila Camacho 191, ☎ 28/18–70–75). ☉ Weekdays 9–4.

Papantla. The **tourist office** (Palacio Municipal, on the zócalo, ☎ 784/2–01–77) has an attentive staff, but you'll have a hard time getting information if you don't speak Spanish. ☉ Weekdays 9–3, Sat. 9–1.

Tuxpán. The staff at the small **tourist office** (Juárez 65, ☎ 783/4–01–77) across the street from the cathedral is friendly but only speaks Spanish, and maps are in chronic short supply. ☉ Daily 10–3 and 5–7.

Veracruz. The bilingual staff at the **Subdelegación Federal de Turismo** (Palacio Municipal, on zócalo, ☎ 29/32–19–99) has some helpful pamphlets and a lot of enthusiasm. ☉ Daily 9–9.

13 The Yucatán Peninsula

Mexico's most visited region, the Yucatán has something for everyone: the high-profile sparkle of Cancún; the spectacular snorkeling of Cozumel; the laid-back beachcombing of Isla Mujeres; the fascinating Spanish–Maya mix of Mérida; and the evocative Maya ruins of Tulum, Chichén Itzá, and Uxmal. The region is an ecotourist's dream, too, from the huge Sian Ka'an Biosphere Reserve on the Caribbean Coast to Río Lagartos National Park on the Gulf of Mexico, migration ground for thousands of flamingos and other birds.

WHEN ASKED what attracts them to Mexico, most visitors will mention beaches and ruins—and some of the best of each are found on the Yucatán Peninsula.

Yucatán comprises Mexico's most popular tourist destination, Cancún, and some of the country's most celebrated ruins, the pre-Columbian cities of the Maya. While much of the peninsula is vast, scrubby desert—"one living rock," as an early Spanish priest put it—with a smattering of jungles and hills, its eastern coastline on the clear, turquoise waters of the Caribbean has superb natural endowments. In addition to a semi-tropical climate, the Caribbean coast offers unbroken stretches of beach and the world's fifth-longest barrier reef, which lies just off the island of Cozumel. Also part of the Yucatán is the diminutive Isla Mujeres (Isle of Women) and, on the west side of the peninsula, Mérida, a city that deserves more tourists than it gets. Mérida was one of the first cities built by the Spaniards, and it retains its colonial ambience and charm.

The peninsula's spectrum of attractions is matched by an equal range of accommodations, from the never-leave-the-site resorts of Cancún to more modest properties near the ruins and humble but adequate beach shacks. Yucatán therefore appeals to travelers of all budgets and inclinations, from package tour–takers to backpackers and travelers who prefer to rent a car. It offers bird-watching, water sports, archaeology, handicrafts, and the savory Yucatecan cuisine. Above all, however, there are the *Yucatecos* themselves: Veteran travelers to Mexico often remark on the openness and friendliness of these people who, like their Maya ancestors, are short and swarthy, with prominent cheekbones and aquiline noses.

The peninsula encompasses the states of Yucatán, Campeche, Quintana Roo (until 1974 a Mexican territory), Belize, and a part of Guatemala, and covers 113,000 square kilometers (43,630 square miles). International airports at Cancún and Cozumel provide nonstop service from several North American cities; the Mérida airport handles primarily domestic flights. Cruise ships call at Cozumel and Playa del Carmen, and other harbor facilities are being developed at Progreso on the north coast off the Gulf of Mexico.

CANCÚN

Updated by
Melissa Rivers

Flying into Cancún, Mexico's most popular destination, all you see are green treetops for miles. It's clear from the air that this resort was literally carved out of the jungle. When development began here in 1974, the beaches were deserted except for their iguana inhabitants. Now, luxury hotels line the oceanfront, and nearly 2 million visitors a year come for the white sand beaches and crystalline Caribbean waters. They also come for the sizzling nightlife and, in some cases, for proximity to the Yucatán ruins. Although the resort is too glitzy and tourist-oriented for some, it draws thousands of repeat visitors.

Cancún City is on the mainland, but the hotel zone is on a 22½-kilometer (14-mile) barrier island off the Yucatán peninsula. The resort is designed to please American tastes; most people speak English, and devotees of cable TV and Pizza Hut will not be disappointed. Dedicated beach bums will cherish the cool, white, porous limestone sand and clear blue waters here, and the sun shines an average of 240 days a year, reputedly more than at almost any other Caribbean spot. Temperatures linger appealingly at about 80°F. You can sample Yucatecan foods and watch folkloric dance demonstrations as well as knock back tequila slammers at the myriad night spots.

But there can be more to the resort than plopping down under a *palapa* (pre-Hispanic thatched roof). For divers and snorkelers, the reefs off Cancún, nearby Cozumel, and Isla Mujeres are among the best in the world. Cancún also provides a relaxing home base for visiting the stupendous ruins of Chichén Itzá, Tulum, and Cobá on the mainland—remnants of the area's rich Maya heritage—as well as the Yucatán coast and its lagoons.

Cancún has gone through the life cycle typical of any tourist destination. At its inception, the resort drew the jet set; lately, it has attracted increasing numbers of less affluent tourists, primarily package tour–takers and college students, particularly during spring break when hordes of flawless, tanned young bodies people the beaches and restaurants.

As for the island's history, not much was written about it before its birth as a resort. The island does not appear on the early navigators' maps and little is known about the Maya who lived here; apparently Cancún's marshy terrain discouraged development. It is recorded that Maya settled the area during the preclassical era, in about AD 200, and remained until about the 14th or 15th century. In the mid-19th century, minor Maya ruins were sighted; however, they were not studied by archaeologists until the 1950s and mid-1970s. In 1970 then-President Luis Echeverría first visited the site that had been chosen to retrieve the state of Quintana Roo from obscurity and abject poverty.

Exploring

Cancún is divided into two zones: the hotel zone, which is shaped roughly like the numeral 7, and Cancún City or downtown Cancún, known as *el centro*, 4 kilometers (2½ miles) west of the hotel zone on the mainland.

Paseo Kukulcán is the main drag in the hotel zone, and because most of the 7 is less than a kilometer wide, both the Caribbean and the lagoons can be seen from either side of it. Regularly placed kilometer markers on the roadside help indicate where you are; they go from Km 1 on the mainland, near downtown, to Km 20 at Punta Nizuc. The hotel zone consists entirely of hotels, restaurants and shopping complexes, marinas, and time-share condominiums; there are no residential areas as such. It's not the sort of place you can get to know by walking. Paseo Kukulcán is punctuated by driveways with steep inclines turning into the hotels, most of which are set at least 100 yards from the road. The lagoon side of the boulevard consists of scrubby stretches of land, many of them covered with construction cranes, alternating with marinas, shopping centers, and restaurants. What is most scenic about Cancún is the dramatic contrast between the vivid turquoise-and-violet sea and the blinding alabaster-white sands.

Numbers in the margin correspond to points of interest on the Cancún map.

Cancún's scenery consists mostly of its beautiful beaches and crystal-clear waters. There are also a few intriguing sites tucked away among the modern hotels. Heading north from Punta Nizuc and keeping your eye on the seaside, you can see as many as eight hotels within the space of 1 kilometer, one right after the next, with barely any distance between them.

① The small **Ruinas del Rey** are located on the lagoon side at Km 17, roughly opposite El Pueblito and Playa de Oro. Large signs point out the site, which is now incorporated into the Caesar Park Resort complex. First mentioned in a 16th-century travelogue and then in 1842, when they were sighted by American explorer John Lloyd Stephens and his draftsman, Frederick Catherwood, the ruins were finally explored by archaeologists in 1910, though excavations did not begin until 1954. In 1975 archaeologists, along with the Mexican government, began the restoration of Del Rey and San Miguelito (a nearby ruin that is now inaccessible; *see below*).

Del Rey may not be particularly impressive when compared to major archaeological sites such as Tulum or Chichén Itzá, but it is the largest ruin in Cancún and definitely worth a look. The ruin is notable for its unusual architecture: two main plazas bounded by two streets. Most of the other Maya cities, which were not in any sense planned but had developed over centuries, contained one plaza with a number of ceremonial satellites and few streets. The pyramid here is topped by a platform, and inside its vault are stucco paintings. Skeletons found buried both at the apex and at the base indicate that the site may have been a royal burial ground. Originally named Kin Ich Ahau Bonil, Maya for "King of the Solar Countenance," the 2nd–3rd-century BC site was linked to astronomical practices in the ancient Maya culture. No 🍽. ☛ *About $3, free on Sun.* ☉ *Daily 8–5.*

② About half a kilometer away from Del Rey—between Km 16 and 17—but on the east side of Kukulcán, is another Maya site: **San Miguelito,** a very small stone building (about the size of a shack) with a number of columns about 4 feet high. At press time, this site was fenced off and not accessible to the public, but this may change with further development of the Caesar Park Resort.

③ Another ruin, **Yamil Lu'um** (meaning "hilly land"), stands on the highest point of Cancún and is situated at Km 12, to the left of the Sheraton. A small sign at the hotel will direct you to the dirt path leading to the site. Although it comprises two structures—one probably a temple, the other probably a lighthouse—this is the smallest of Cancún's ruins. Discovered in 1842 by John Lloyd Stephens, the remains date from the late 13th or early 14th century.

Just after Km 12, near the Melia Turquesa, Sheraton, and Radisson hotels, you'll come in sight of Laguna Bojórquez on your left; buildings span nearly the entire length of the spit of land that encloses the lagoon. On the far side of that spit, along the road that forks to the left **④** (between Km 6 and Km 7), is **Pok-Ta-Pok** golf course, whose Maya name means "ball game." Situated on the 12th hole is yet another Maya ruin, consisting of two platforms and vestiges of other buildings.

Approaching the northern tip of the vertical leg of the 7—Punta Can- **⑤** cún—you'll pass **Playa Chac Mool** at Km 10, one of the few public beaches on Cancún, with restaurants and changing areas. At the tip of Punta Cancún, look for the fourth Maya ruin, a tiny shrine that is fairly insignificant except that it's been cleverly incorporated into the architecture of the Hotel Camino Real. When you round the corner, you'll be on the bay side (Bahía de Mujeres) of the island, where calmer waters prevail than on the sea side.

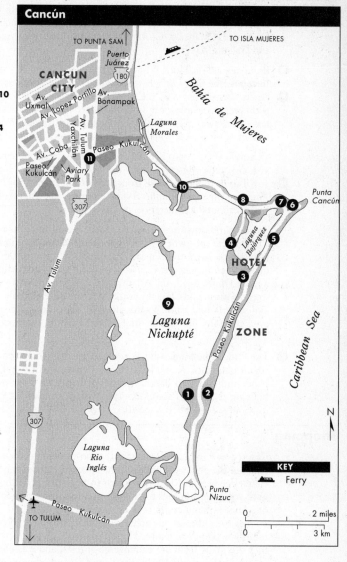

At Km 9, you'll come upon a traffic circle, where the **Inter Plaza** and the **Cancún Convention Center** (☎ 98/83–01–99), a large venue for cultural events, are located. In addition to the convention center, the Inter Plaza complex contains 15 restaurants, 21 boutiques, a bank, and several airline offices. At press time, a 525-foot observation tower was still under construction. Originally scheduled for completion in late 1994, and now set for 1996, it will feature the highest viewing platform in Latin America. The **National Institute of Anthropology and History,** the small museum on the ground floor of the convention center, traces Maya culture by showcasing a fascinating collection of 1,000–1,500-year-old artifacts collected throughout Quintana Roo. ☎ 98/83–03–05. ☛ About $3, free on Sun. ⊘ Tues.–Sun. 9–7. Guided tours available in English, French, German, and Spanish.

❼ Between the convention center and the Hotel Presidente Inter-Continental is a half-mile-long string of **shopping malls,** including Plaza Caracol, La Mansión–Costa Blanca, Plaza Lagunas, Plaza Terramar, and Galería Mayfair.

❽ Right beyond the Hotel Presidente Inter-Continental, at Km 7, is **Playa Tortugas,** the other beach where guests of the beachless downtown **❾** hotels are welcome. To the south, on your left, you'll reach **Laguna Nichupté,** the center for most of the water-sports activities. Also in the lagoon are swampy areas that host mangrove trees and more than 200 species of birds. Ask your hotel to arrange for a boat and guide.

Continue along Paseo Kukulcán past the numerous hotels. Just before you cross the causeway onto the mainland, at the Hotel Calinda, **❿** you'll come to **Playa Linda,** from which ferries depart for Isla Mujeres. The less expensive public ferries leave for the island from Puerto Juárez, about 9 kilometers (6 miles) farther north.

As you enter downtown Cancún, Paseo Kukulcán turns into Avenida Cobá at the spot where it meets **Avenida Tulum,** the main thoroughfare and the location of many restaurants and shops. Life-size reproductions of ancient Mexican art, including the Aztec calendar stone, a giant Olmec head, the Atlantids of Tula, and the Maya chac mool (reclining rain god), line the grassy strip dividing Tulum's northbound and southbound lanes. Visitors looking for shopping bargains, however, generally find better prices if they stick to the parallel Avenida Yaxchilán.

⓫ The Cancún **bullring,** a block south of the Pemex station, hosts year-round bullfights. A matador, *charos* (Mexican cowboys), a mariachi band, and flamenco dancers entertain during the hour preceding the bullfight (2:30 PM). *Paseo Kukulcán at Av. Bonampak,* ☎ *98/84–54–65 or 98/84–82–48.* ☛ *About $40.* ☉ *Fights held Wed. at 3:30 PM.*

Shopping

Resort wear and handicrafts are the most popular purchases in Cancún, but the prices are high and the selection standard; if you're traveling elsewhere in Mexico, it's best to postpone your shopping spree until you reach another town. Still, you can find a respectable variety of Mexican handicrafts ranging from blown glass and hand-woven textiles to leather goods and jewelry made from local coral and tortoiseshell. (Don't be tempted by the tortoiseshell products: The turtles they are made from are endangered species, and it is illegal to bring tortoiseshell into the United States and several other countries.)

Caveat emptor applies as much to Cancún as it does to the "bargain" electronics stores on Fifth Avenue in New York City or in Hong Kong. Throughout Mexico you will often get better prices by paying with cash (pesos or dollars) or traveler's checks. This is because Mexican merchants are averse to the commissions charged by credit-card companies and frequently tack that commission—6% or more—onto your bill. If you can do without the plastic, you may even get the 10% sales tax lopped off.

Bargaining is expected in Cancún, but mostly in the market. Suggest half the asking price and slowly come up, but do not pay more than 70% of the quoted price. Shopping around is a good idea, too, because the crafts market is very competitive. But closely examine the merchandise you want to purchase: Some "authentic" items—particularly jewelry—may actually be shoddy imitations.

In Cancún, shopping hours are generally weekdays 10–1 and 4–7, although more and more stores are staying open throughout the day rather than closing for siesta between 1 and 4 PM. Many shops keep Saturday morning hours, and some are now open Sunday until 1 PM. Shops in the malls tend to be open weekdays from 9 or 10 AM to 8 or 10 PM.

Downtown

The wide variety of shops downtown along Avenida Tulum (between Avenidas Cobá and Uxmal) includes **Fama** (Av. Tulum 105, ☎ 98/84–65–86), a department store offering clothing, English reading matter, sports gear, toiletries, liquor, and *latería* (crafts made of tin). Also on Tulum is the oldest and largest of Cancún's crafts markets, **Ki Huic** (Av. Tulum 17, between Bancomer and Banco Atlantico, ☎ 98/84–33–47), which is open daily from 9 AM to 10 PM and houses about 100 vendors.

Hotel Zone

Fully air-conditioned malls (known as *centros comerciales*), as streamlined and well-kept as any in the United States or Canada, sell everything from fashion clothing, beachwear, and sportswear to jewelry, household items, video games, and leather goods.

The newest mall on the scene is **Kukulcán Plaza** (Paseo Kukulc´n Km 13), with about 45 shops (including Izod, Benetton, and Harley Davidson boutiques), 12 restaurants, a bar, a liquor store, a bank, a cinema, bowling lanes, and a video arcade.

Flamingo Plaza (Paseo Kukulcán Km 11.5, across from the Hotel Flamingo) includes a full-service gym, exchange booth, some designer emporiums and duty-free stores, several sportswear shops, two boutiques selling Guatemalan imports, a drug store, and a Planet Hollywood boutique. At the food court, in addition to the usual McDonald's and fried-chicken concessions, you'll find Chicándole, offering what might be the only fast-food mole enchiladas around.

Just across from the convention center site, **Plaza Caracol** (Paseo Kukulcán Km 8.5) is the largest and most contemporary mall in Cancún, with about 200 shops and boutiques, including two pharmacies, art galleries, a currency exchange, and folk art and jewelry shops, as well as cafés and restaurants. Fashion boutiques include Benetton, Bally, Gucci, and Ralph Lauren; in all these stores, prices are lower than in their U.S. counterparts. One drawback here: Aside from formal restaurants, there are no places where shoppers can rest their feet.

To the back of—and virtually connected to—Plaza Caracol are two outdoor shopping complexes: The pink stucco **La Mansion–Costa Blanca** specializes in designer clothing and has several restaurants, art galleries, a bank, and a liquor store; **Plaza Lagunas** is dedicated primarily to sportswear shops, such as Ellesse and Ocean Pacific. Also near Plaza Caracol, **Plaza Terramar** (opposite the Hotel Fiesta Americana) sells beachwear, souvenirs, and folk art, and has a restaurant and a pharmacy.

Plaza Nautilus (Paseo Kukulc´n Km 3.5, lagoon side), the mall closest to downtown and a favorite of American shoppers, has a bookstore, liquor store, art gallery, perfumery, folk art shop, and Super Deli, as well as about 65 other shops.

Specialty Shops
GALLERIES

Orbe (Plaza Caracol, ☎ 98/83–15–71) specializes in sculptures and paintings by contemporary Mexican artists. **La Galería** (La Mansíon–Costa Blanca mall, ☎ 98/83–39–94) is both the showroom and studio of Gilberto Silva, a sculptor who employs Maya techniques on local limestone. **Mayart** (La Mansíon–Costa Blanca mall, ☎ 98/84–12–72 or 98/84–15–69), displays replicas of Maya art, temple rubbings, and contemporary painting and sculpture. The **Galería de Sergio Bustamante** (Hyatt Cancún Caribe, ☎ 98/83–00–04), displays and sells the work of the popular Mexican artist.

Sports and Fitness

Golf

The main course is at **Pok-Ta-Pok** (Paseo Kukulcán between Km 6 and Km 7, ☎ 98/83–08–71), a club with fine views of both sea and lagoon, whose 18 holes were designed by Robert Trent Jones, Sr. The club also has a practice green, a swimming pool, tennis courts, and a restaurant. The greens fees are $66 ($51 after 2 PM); electric cart, $30; clubs, $15; caddies, $20; and golf clinics, $25 per hour. Playing hours are 6 AM–6 PM (last tee-off is at 4 PM). There is a new 18-hole championship golf course at the **Caesar Park Cancún** (Paseo Kukulcán Km 17, ☎98/81–80–00); greens fees are $90 ($70 for hotel guests), carts cost $20, and club rentals run $15–$25. The **Hotel Melia Cancún** (Paseo Kukulcán Km 12, ☎ 98/85–11–60) has an 18-hole course, as well.

Health Clubs

Most of the deluxe hotels have their own health clubs, although few of them are very large. There are, however, two gyms in Cancún: Both **Gold's Gym** (Plaza Flamingo, ☎ 98/83–29–33 or 98/83–29–66) and **Michel's Gym** (Av. Sayil 66, ☎ 98/84–23–94) feature modern equipment and exercise facilities.

Jogging

Although to some people the idea of jogging in the intense heat of Cancún sounds like a form of masochism, fanatics should know that there is a 14-kilometer (9-mile) track extending along half the island, running parallel to Paseo Kukulcán from the Punta Cancún area into Cancún City.

Water Sports

Water sports—particularly snorkeling, scuba diving, and deep-sea fishing—are popular pastimes in Cancún, because some 500 species of tropical fish, including sailfish, bluefin, marlin, barracuda, and red snapper, live in the adjacent waters. Snorkeling gear can be rented for $10 per day. Sailboards are available for about $50 an hour; classes go for about $35 an hour. Parasailing costs $35 for eight minutes; waterskiing, $70 per hour; jet skiing, $70 per hour, or $60 for Wave Runners (double-seated Jet Skis). Paddle boats, kayaks, catamarans, and banana boats are also readily available. **Aqua Tours** (Paseo Kukulcán Km 6.25, ☎ 98/83–04–00, FAX 98/83–04–03) and **Aqua-World** (Paseo Kukulcán Km 15.2, ☎ 98/85–22–88, FAX 98/85–22–99) maintain large fleets of water toys.

FISHING

Deep-sea fishing boats and other gear may be chartered from outfitters for about $350 for four hours, $450 for six hours, and $550 for eight hours. Charters generally include a captain, a first mate, gear, bait, and beverages. **Aqua Tours, AquaWorld,** and the **Royal Yacht**

Club (Paseo Kukulcán Km 16, ☎ 98/85–29–30 or 98/85–32–60) are just a few of the companies that operate large fishing fleets.

SAILBOARDING

Although some people sailboard on the ocean side in the summer, activity is limited primarily to the bay between Cancún and Isla Mujeres. If you visit the island in July, don't miss the National Wind-surfing Tournament (☎ 98/84–32–12), in which athletes test their mettle. The **International Windsurfer Sailing School** (☎ 98/84–20–23), at Playa Tortugas, rents equipment and gives lessons.

SNORKELING AND SCUBA DIVING

Snorkeling is best at Punta Nizuc, Punta Cancún, and Playa Tortugas, although you should be especially careful of the strong currents at the latter. Some charter-fishing companies offer a two-tank scuba dive for about $100. As the name implies, **Scuba Cancún** (☎ 98/83–10–11) specializes in diving trips and offers NAUI, CMAS, and PADI instruction. **Aqua Tours Dive Center and Marina** (☎ 98/83–04–00 or 98/83–02–27) offers scuba tours and a resort course, as well as snorkeling trips. **Aqua-World** (☎ 98/85–22–88, FAX 98/85–22–99) runs snorkeling trips from its artificial island off Punta Nizuc. If you've brought your own snorkeling gear and want to save money, just take a city bus down to Club Med and walk along the resort's beach for about a mile until you get to Punta Nizuc.

Dining

At last count, there were more than 1,200 restaurants in Cancún, but—according to one profiting restaurateur—only about 100 are worth their salt, so to speak. Finding the right restaurant in Cancún is not easy. The downtown restaurants that line the noisy Avenida Tulum often have tables spilling onto pedestrian-laden sidewalks; however, gas fumes and gawking tourists tend to detract from the romantic outdoor-café ambience. Many of the hotel-zone restaurants, on the other hand, cater to what they assume is a tourist preference for bland, not-too-foreign-tasting food.

One key to good dining in Cancún is to find the haunts—mostly in the downtown area—where locals go for Yucatán-style food prepared by the experts. Many menus are highlighted by seafood made with fresh lime juice and other authentic Mexican specialties, but it takes more to make a Cancún dining experience: Look for a place where the waiters artistically prepare meals at tableside or where cocktails are served flaming. Fish caught from the waters around the island, then grilled and seasoned with lime juice, is a sure bet. Grilled pork and chicken prepared with spices used in Maya cooking, such as *achiote,* are other local specialties.

Generally speaking, dress is casual here, but many restaurants will not admit diners with bare feet, short shorts, or no shirts. Unless otherwise stated, restaurants serve lunch and dinner daily.

CATEGORY	COST*
$$$$	over $35
$$$	$25–$35
$$	$15–$25
$	under $15

per person, excluding drinks, service, and tax

Hotel Zone

Hotel zone restaurants are located on the Cancún Hotel Zone Dining and Lodging map.

$$$$ Bogart's. Whether you consider it amusingly elaborate or merely pretentious, it's hard to be neutral about Bogart's, probably the most expensive and talked-about restaurant in town. Taking off from the film *Casablanca,* the place is decorated with Persian rugs, fans, velvet-cushioned banquettes, and fountains; waiters wear fezzes and white suits. A menu as eclectic as the patrons of Rick's Cafe features many seafood and Mediterranean dishes. The food is okay, but don't expect large portions; servings are nouvelle style. ✕ *Paseo Kukulcán, Hotel Krystal,* ☎ *98/83–11–33. Reservations required; seatings at 7 and 9:30. AE, MC, V. No lunch.*

$$$$ The Club Grill. A prime choice for that romantic, special occasion din-
★   ner, the Ritz-Carlton's fine dining room is divided into intimate chambers; one of them has a dance floor and a small stage for live music in the evening. Walls are trimmed with rich wood, fresh flower arrangements abound, and tall windows look out onto a bubbling courtyard fountain and the Caribbean beyond. European grill with a Mexican spin is the house specialty. White bean soup, lobster ravioli, and blackened rib eye with Yucatecan spices are popular menu choices. Service is attentive and discreet. ✕ *Paseo Kukulcán (Retorno del Rey 36),* ☎ *98/85–08–08. Reservations advised. AE, DC, MC, V.*

$$$ El Mexicano. One of Cancún's largest and most popular restaurants seats 300 for a folkloric dinner show in a room resembling the patio of a hacienda. Details such as elaborately hand-carved chairs and numerous regional dishes convey a feeling of authenticity. But this is a touristy spot, and the dancing-girl show is not a window into Yucatecan culture. Granted that, try the *empanxonostle* (steamed lobster, shrimp, fish, and herbs); it promises to be as extravagant as El Mexicano's surroundings. ✕ *La Mansión–Costa Blanca Shopping Center,* ☎ *98/83–22–20 and 98/83–22–20. Reservations advised; folkloric ballet at 8 PM. AE, MC, V.*

$$$ Hacienda El Mortero. Pampering waiters, strolling mariachis, lush hanging plants, fig trees, and candlelight make this reproduction plantation home a very popular spot to dine. The menu offers a selection of country cooking, and the steaks and ribs are first class. ✕ *Paseo Kukulcán, Hotel Krystal,* ☎ *98/83–11–33. Reservations required for the 7 and 9:30 PM seatings. AE, MC, V. No lunch.*

$$$ La Fisheria. Excellent wood-oven pizzas are offered in addition to
★   seafood standards such as New England clam chowder, steamed mussels, smoked salmon, and lobster in this ultramodern (polished stone floors, galvanized steel stairs, and glass walls) establishment. There is often live entertainment in the evenings. ✕ *Plaza Caracol,* ☎ *98/83–13–95. Reservations accepted. AE, MC, V.*

$$ Captain's Cove. Both waterfront locations feature popular breakfast buffets served under palapa roofs. The decor is decidedly nautical, with rigging draped on the walls and chandeliers in the shape of ships' steering wheels. The restaurant near the Casa Maya Hotel overlooks the Caribbean Sea toward Isla Mujeres; the other is situated beside the Nichupté Lagoon. Both present lunch and dinner menus filled with seafood dishes and charbroiled steak and chicken. Parents appreciate the lower-priced children's menu, an unusual feature in Cancún. ✕ *Paseo Kukulcán 16.5, lagoonside across from the Royal Mayan Hotel,* ☎ *98/85–00–16; beachside, next to Casa Maya Hotel,* ☎ *98/83–06–69. No reservations. AE, MC, V.*

Dining
Bogart's, **9**
Captain's Cove, **2, 17**
Carlos 'n Charlie's, **4**
Casa Rolandi, **7**
The Club Grill, **13**
El Mexicano, **6**
Hacienda
El Mortero, **9**
La Fisheria, **7**
Lorenzillos, **11**
100% Natural, **12**
Splash, **12**

Lodging
Caesar Park Beach,
Golf Resort **19**
Calinda Viva Cancún,
5
Days Inn El Pueblito, **18**
Fiesta Americana Condesa, **16**
Fiesta Americana Coral
Beach Cancún, **8**
Hyatt Regency Cancún,
10
Marriott Casa Magna,
14
Meliá Cancún, **15**
Ritz-Carlton
Cancún, **13**
Villa Deportiva
Juvenil Cancún, **1**
Villas Tacul, **3**
Westin Regina Resort
Cancún, **20**

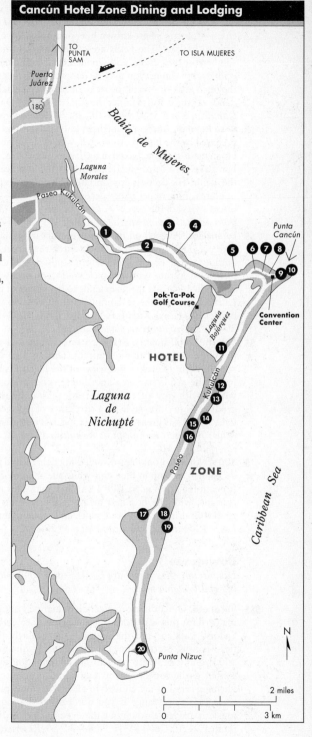

Cancún Hotel Zone Dining and Lodging

$$ **Carlos 'n Charlie's.** A lively atmosphere, a terrific view of the lagoon, and good food make this restaurant—part of the popular Anderson chain—Cancún's best-known hot spot. You'll never run out of bric-a-brac to look at: The walls are catchalls, with tons of photos, while sombreros, bird cages, and wooden birds and animals hang from the ceilings. For dinner you may be tempted by barbecued ribs sizzling on the open grill, or one of the steak or seafood specials. After your meal, dance off the calories under the stars at the Pier Dance Club. ✕ *Paseo Kukulcán Km 5.5,* ☎ *98/83–08–46. No reservations. AE, MC, V.*

$$ **Casa Rolandi.** Authentic northern Italian and Swiss dishes are skillfully prepared by the Italian owner-chef, who grew up near the Swiss border. Homemade lasagna, baked in the large stucco oven, and an ample salad bar make for a satisfying dinner. Many fish and beef dishes are also on the menu. The decor is appropriately Mediterranean—white walls, lots of plants, and copper plates decorating the tables—and the back room offers a view of the beach. ✕ *Plaza Caracol,* ☎ *98/83–18–17. Reservations advised during high season. AE, MC, V.*

$$ **Lorenzillos.** Perched on its own peninsula in the lagoon, this nautical spot provides a pleasant place to watch the sunset, sip a drink on the outdoor patio, or sample excellent seafood. Specialties include grilled or broiled lobster (you can pick your own) and whole fish Veracruz-style. The seafaring theme extends to the names of the dishes (like Jean Lafitte beef) and the restaurant itself (Lorenzillo was a 17th-century pirate). ✕ *Paseo Kukulcán Km 10.5,* ☎ *98/83–12–54 and 98/83–30–73. Reservations accepted. AE, MC, V.*

$$ **Splash.** Good-quality Art Deco furnishings and neon lights add to
★ the sleek design of this restaurant. During high season, the outside terrace with its peek-a-boo view of the lagoon is usually full. Never mind: the inside bar area and dining room are cooler. You can't go wrong with any of the homemade pastas or the charcoal-grilled grouper Bora Bora–style (in a rich sauce of peaches and clarified butter). Splash has great happy hour specials and all-you-can-eat dinner deals. ✕ *Paseo Kukulcán at Kukulcán Plaza,* ☎ *98/85–30–01. No reservations. MC, V.*

$ **100% Natural.** Looking for something light? Head to the cheery open-
★ air eatery done up in blue-and-white tile and colorful tropical murals beneath the green neon 100% NATURAL sign. This is *the* place for vegetarians, with the broadest array of soups, fruit and veggie salads, fresh fruit drinks (39 at last count), and other nonmeat menu items. ✕ *Paseo Kukulcán at Kukulcán Plaza,* ☎ *98/85–29–04. No reservations. MC, V.*

Downtown

Downtown restaurants are located on the Downtown Cancún Dining and Lodging map.

$$$ **Bucanero.** Quiet dining in a candlelit marine atmosphere is the drawing card for this seafood restaurant, built to resemble the interior of a Spanish galleon, and the seafood—particularly the lobster specialties—is tops. Start the meal with lobster bisque or black bean soup, and round it out with the seafood combination, which includes lobster in garlic sauce, shrimp and squid brochette, and a fish fillet. Heaping servings are enough to feed two, which puts this in the moderate ($$) price range if you don't mind sharing your meal. Piano music is played throughout the evening and waiters are dressed as pirates. ✕ *Av. Cobá 88,* ☎ *98/84–22–80. Reservations accepted. AE, MC, V. No lunch.*

Dining

Bucanero, **2**
El Pescador, **8**
Grill D'Leo, **4**
La Dolce Vita, **1**
La Habichuela, **12**
La Parrilla, **9**
Rosa Mexicano, **6**

Lodging

Antillano, **5**
Holiday Inn Centro Cancún, **3**
María del Lourdes, **10**
Plaza Carrillo's, **7**
Plaza del Sol, **11**

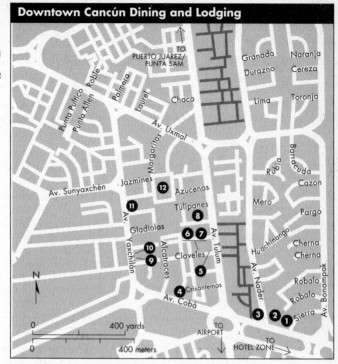

Downtown Cancún Dining and Lodging

$$\textbf{\$\$\$}$$ ★ **La Dolce Vita.** This appealing restaurant has a strong and well-deserved local following. White stucco walls and columns, lots of hanging plants, and candlelit tables with lace cloths give the dining room a romantic appeal. Favorites from the excellent Northern Italian and Continental menu include seafood antipasto, *bouquinete dolce vita* (a local white fish stuffed with shrimp and mushrooms and baked in puff pastry), and creamy tiramisù. ✕ *Av. Cobá 87,* ☎ *98/84–04–61 and 98/84–13–84. Reservations advised. AE, MC, V. No weekend lunch.*

$$\textbf{\$\$\$}$$ ★ **La Habichuela.** This charmer—once an elegant home—is perfect for anyone looking for a relaxed, private atmosphere. The candlelit garden exudes peacefulness, while a statue of Pakal, the Maya god of astronomy and culture, surveys all. Try the *cocobichuela*—lobster and shrimp in a light Indian sauce served on a bed of rice inside a coconut—a specialty of the house. ✕ *Margaritas 25,* ☎ *98/84–31–58. Reservations advised. MC, V. No lunch during low season.*

$$\textbf{\$\$}$$ ★ **El Pescador.** It's first-come, first-served here, with long lines, especially during high season. But people still flood into this rustic Mexican-style restaurant with nautical touches; the open-air patio is particularly popular. Heavy hitters on the menu include red snapper broiled with garlic and freshly caught lobster specials. For dessert, consider sharing the cake filled with ice cream and covered with peaches and strawberry marmalade. La Mesa Del Pescador, a new offshoot in Plaza Kukulcán, is not usually as crowded as this place. ✕ *Tulipanes 28,* ☎ *98/84–26–73; Plaza Kukulcán,* ☎ *98/85–05–05. No reservations. AE, MC, V.*

$$\textbf{\$\$}$$ **La Parrilla.** If you're looking for the place where local Mexicans—young and old—hang out, you've found it in this popular downtown spot, an old classic by Cancún standards (it opened in 1975). Everything from the food to the bougainvillea and palapa roof is authentic.

Popular dishes include the grilled beef with garlic sauce and the tacos *al pastor* (tacos with pork, pineapple, coriander, onion, and salsa). ✕ *Av. Yaxchilán 51,* ☎ *98/84–53–98. No reservations. AE, MC, V. Closed Dec. 25. No lunch.*

\$\$ ★ **Rosa Mexicano.** One of Cancún's prettiest Mexican colonial–style restaurants presents waiters dressed as *charros* (Mexican cowboys), pottery and embroidered wall hangings, floor tiles with floral designs, and a cozy, softly lighted atmosphere. For extra romance, make a reservation for the candlelit patio. Savory appetizers include *nopalitos* (cactus strips sautéed with corn, cilantro, and cheese). Specialties are *filete Rosa* (beef and onions in a tequila-orange sauce) and *camarones al ajillo* (shrimp sautéed in olive oil and garlic, with chili peppers). ✕ *Calle Claveles 4,* ☎ *98/84–63–13. Reservations advised. AE, MC, V. No lunch.*

\$ ★ **Grill D' Leo.** There's a long grill stretched along one wall of this red-tile-roof, open-air diner, so you can let your attention drift from the straw hats dangling from the ceiling to watch the cooks whip up tacos, quesadillas, sopas, enchiladas, and homemade tortillas. Another option is to grill your own beef, chicken, pork, sausage, and onions right at your table (not recommended on a hot day). Salad, rice, and beans come with all entreés. ✕ *Av. Cobá 11 (across from hospital),* ☎ *98/84–13–82. No reservations. No credit cards. No lunch before 2* PM.

Lodging

The most important buildings in Cancún are its hotels, which presently number more than 110. Choosing from this variety can be bewildering, because most hotel brochures sound—and look—alike. Many properties were built during the island's first development phase in the mid-1970s by international hotel chains known for their streamlined, standardized versions of hospitality, and some were substantially renovated following the damage wrought by Hurricane Gilbert in 1988. Hotels here tend to favor "neo-Maya" architecture (palapa roofs, massive pyramidal stone structures, and stucco walls interspersed with red tile roofs and quasi-Mediterranean Moorish arches), bland contemporary-style furniture, and pastel hues.

For the most part, the hotels in the downtown area don't offer anything near the luxury or amenities of the hotel zone properties. They do, however, afford visitors the opportunity to stay in a popular resort without paying resort prices, and many offer free shuttle service to the beach. Expect minibars, satellite TV, laundry and room service, private safes, and bathroom hairdryers in hotels in the very expensive (\$\$\$\$) category; in addition, almost every major hotel has suites, rooms for nonsmokers and guests with disabilities, an in-house travel agency and/or a car-rental concession, guest parking, water-sports facilities, and a daily schedule of games and activities for guests. Unless otherwise noted, all hotels have air-conditioning and private baths. All Cancún hotels are within the 77500 postal code. Rates quoted refer to the peak winter season, from December to early May.

CATEGORY	COST*
\$\$\$\$	over \$175
\$\$\$	\$120–\$175
\$\$	\$50–\$120
\$	under \$50

All prices are for a standard double room, excluding 10% tax.

Hotel Zone

Hotel zone properties are located on the Cancún Hotel Zone Dining and Lodging map.

$$$$ Caesar Park Beach & Golf Resort. Liberal use of Mérida marble, Mexican tile murals, and colorful oil paintings give this appealing Westin property, one of Cancún's newest luxury resorts, a distinctly Mexican flavor. Rooms, too, carry out the theme, with tile floors, rattan furniture, and local artwork; all have a private balcony with a view of the ocean, and a few can also see the resort's championship 18-hole golf course across Paseo Kukulcán. Lavish interconnecting pools (seven!) and streams wind through palm-dotted lawns. The next few years should see the addition of two malls, a marina, more restaurants, and 80 beach villas. ☎ *Paseo Kukulcán Km 17 (Box 1810),* ☎ *98/81–80–00 or 800/228–3000,* ☒ *98/81–80–80. 325 rooms. 2 restaurants, 2 bars, 7 pools, 2 saunas, aerobics, exercise room, golf course, 2 tennis courts. AE, DC, MC, V.*

$$$$ Fiesta Americana Coral Beach Cancún. The newest of the Cancún Fiesta properties, this all-suite hotel lies just in front of the convention center and shopping malls. The large salmon-colored structure—built in Mediterranean style with blue wrought-iron balconies—houses a lobby with marble-tiled floors, potted palms, and a stained-glass skylight. The ample-size rooms have oceanfront balconies, marble floors, rounded doorways, and stained-glass windows. As for outdoor activities, choose between the 1,000-foot beach and the 660-foot pool. This is Cancún's largest convention hotel; expect the clientele and occasional slow service to match. ☎ *Paseo Kukulcán, Lote 6 (Box 14),* ☎ *98/83–29–00 or 800/FIESTA–1,* ☒ *98/83–31–73. 602 suites. 4 restaurants, 5 bars, pool, health club, 3 tennis courts. AE, DC, MC, V.*

$$$$ Marriott CasaMagna. The six-story Marriott is rather eclectically designed: In the lobby, modern furnishings are set in an atrium with Mediterranean-style arches, crystal chandeliers, and hanging vines. Three restaurants overlook the handsome pool area and the ocean. The rooms, decorated in contemporary Mexican style, have tile floors and ceiling fans and follow a soft rose, mauve, and earth-tone color scheme. You can learn to prepare Mexican dishes if you attend cooking lessons (one of many guest activities), or you can sit back and watch the chef do the work at Mikado (*see* Dining, *above*), the hotel's fine Japanese steakhouse. ☎ *Paseo Kukulcán (Retorno Chac L-41),* ☎ *98/85–20–00 or 800/228–9290,* ☒ *98/85–13–85. 412 rooms, 38 suites. 4 restaurants, bar, sauna, health club, 2 tennis courts, nightclub. AE, DC, MC, V.*

$$$$ Meliá Cancún. The Meliá Cancún is a boldly modern version of a Maya temple, fronted by a sheer black marble wall and a sleek waterfall. Public spaces exude elegance; the boutiques could not be more chic. Ivory, dusty-pink, and light-blue hues softly brighten the rooms (all with private balcony or terrace); white-lacquered furniture and wall-to-wall carpeting create a luxurious ambience. An upscale spa, with modern cardiovascular and strength training equipment and an array of pampering and rejuvenating body treatments, was added in early 1995. The Meliá Turquesa, a 408-room sister property across the street from Flamingo Plaza, is not as glitzy, but has a more intimate, friendlier atmosphere. ☎ *Paseo Kukulcán Km 16,* ☎ *98/85–11–60 or 800/336–3542,* ☒ *98/85–12–63. 450 rooms. 5 restaurants, 3 bars, 2 pools, spa, 18-hole golf course, 3 tennis courts. AE, DC, MC, V.*

$$$$ Ritz-Carlton Cancún.
★ When it opened in 1993, this ultra-posh, peach-color property set new standards for luxury and service in Cancún. The air-conditioned lobby and public areas are richly appointed with

fine European and American antiques and thick carpets; the atrium is topped by a massive stained-glass dome. Stylish rooms, done in comfortable shades of blue, beige, and peach, offer all the amenities—wall-to-wall carpeting, travertine marble bathrooms with telephones, separate tub and shower, plush terry robes, and large balconies overlooking the Caribbean. The hotel's elegant restaurants, especially the Club Grill (*see* Dining, *above*) and the new Fantino (serving Northern Italian dinner fare), are standouts. ☎ *Paseo Kukulcán, Retorno del Rey 36,* ☎ *98/85–08–08 or 800/241–3333,* FAX *98/85–10–15. 370 rooms and suites. 3 restaurants, 2 bars, 3 pools, 2 spas, exercise room, 3 tennis courts, pro shop, library. AE, DC, MC, V.*

$$$$ **Villas Tacul.** The accommodations in this large complex (23 villas situated on 5 acres), set on its own stretch of beach en route to downtown, are appointed with red-tile floors and authentic Mexican colonial–style furniture, wagon-wheel chandeliers, and tin-work mirrors. Each villa has a kitchen and from two to five bedrooms, making this a good place for families and couples traveling together. An individual housekeeper keeps each unit spotless and serves private breakfasts for an extra charge. There are a few modestly priced studio rooms without kitchen facilities, as well. The grounds are beautifully landscaped, with well-trimmed lawns and islands of palm trees in the pool. ☎ *Paseo Kukulcán Km 5.5,* ☎ *98/83–00–00, 98/83–00–80, or 800/842–0193,* FAX *98/83–03–49. 23 villas. Restaurant, bar, pool, basketball, 2 tennis courts. AE, DC, MC, V.*

$$$$ **Westin Regina Resort Cancún.** This luxury property, at the southern end of the island, is one of the few hotels with direct access to both a 1,600-foot beach and Laguna Nichupté, which it shares with Club Med. The low-rise, postmodern-style hotel was designed and decorated by one of Latin America's leading architects. In the public areas, stark white stucco walls contrast with brilliant pink or blue recessed areas that frame an array of sculptures and other artwork; from the lobby, you can look down on a stylish restaurant with stunning ocean views. In the spacious guest rooms, handsome rustic furnishings and colorful Mexican folk art stand out against white walls and pale marble floors. ☎ *Paseo Kukulcán Km 20 (Box 1808),* ☎ *98/85–00–86, 98/85–05–37, or 800/228–3000,* FAX *98/85–00–74. 391 rooms. 4 restaurants, 3 bars, 5 pools, exercise room, 2 tennis courts. AE, DC, MC, V.*

$$$ **Fiesta Americana Condesa.** Casual elegance and luxurious amenities are hallmarks of this sprawling, friendly hotel. Situated toward the southern end of the hotel zone, the Condesa has a Mediterranean-style facade featuring balconies, rounded arches, and alternating ocher, salmon, and sand-color walls. But it's the huge palapa fronting the structure that makes it hard to miss. Three seven-story towers overlook a tranquil inner courtyard with hanging plants and falling water. The rooms, highlighted by dusty-pink stucco walls and gray-blue carpets, offer the same tranquility. Balconies are shared by three standard rooms; costlier rooms have their own balconies. Oceanfront suites have a private hot tub on the terrace. ☎ *Paseo Kukulcán Km 16.5 (Box 5478),* ☎ *98/85–10–00 or 800/FIESTA–1,* FAX *98/85–18–00. 502 rooms. 5 restaurants, 2 bars, health club, 3 tennis courts. AE, DC, MC, V.*

$$$ **Hyatt Regency Cancún.** A cylindrical 14-story tower with the Hyatt trademark—a striking central atrium filled with tropical greenery and topped by a skylit dome—affords a 360° view of the sea and the lagoon. Soothing blue, green, and beige tones prevail in the rooms, which also feature contemporary Mexican furniture and striking green marble vanities. This hotel, much larger and livelier than its sister property, boasts an enormous two-level pool with a waterfall. The

breakfast buffet in the hotel's pretty waterfront dining room, Cilantro, is good. The Punta Cancún location is convenient to the convention center and several shopping malls. ☎ *Paseo Kukulcán (Box 1201),* ☎ *98/83–09–66, 98/83–12–34, or 800/233–1234,* FAX *98/83–13–49. 300 rooms. 2 restaurants, 4 bars, pool, exercise room, recreation room. AE, DC, MC, V.*

$$ Calinda Viva Cancún. This beige stucco 8-story building—part of the Quality hotel chain—is not one of the most attractive in town, but it makes a reliable standby and is in a good location, on the north beach near many malls. Redecorated in late 1994, the functional, moderate-size rooms have marble floors and contemporary pastel decor; half have private balconies and ocean views. The property also features a small garden, a beach, a marina, a water sports center, and a Mexican restaurant. ☎ *Paseo Kukulcán Km 8.5 (Box 673),* ☎ *98/83–08–00 or 800/344–5049. 216 rooms. Restaurant, bar, pool, 2 tennis courts. AE, DC, MC, V.*

$$ El Pueblito Beach Hotel. El Pueblito, meaning little town, is an apt
★ name for this property, which consists of clusters of guest rooms in terraced trilevel units that invoke Old Mexico. Interconnecting pathways lined with tropical foliage lead to intriguing terrace pools with waterfalls and stone archways; there's even a long waterslide for kids. Rooms, which are large for the price, feature marble floors and simple rattan furnishings; a few have kitchenettes. ☎ *Paseo Kukulcán Km 17.5,* ☎ *98/85–06–72,* FAX *98/85–07–31. 239 rooms. 2 restaurants, 2 bars, 5 pools, tennis court, travel services. AE, DC, MC, V.*

$ Villa Deportiva Juvenil Cancún. This government-run youth hostel on the beach has glass walls, a cable TV room, a congenial lounge, a pool, and dormitory beds (separate rooms for men and women). There is also an area for camping. ☎ *Paseo Kukulcán Km 3,* ☎ *98/83–13–37. 33 rooms (300 beds) with shared baths. Basketball, volleyball, Ping-Pong. No credit cards.*

Downtown

Downtown properties are located on the Downtown Cancún Dining and Lodging map.

$$$ Holiday Inn Centro Cancún. The place to stay if you want to be down-
★ town and have all the amenities, this is the newest (built 1990) and most upscale hotel in the area. It's less expensive than similar properties in the hotel zone and provides free transportation to the beach of the Crown Princess Club. The attractive pink four-story structure, with a Spanish tile roof, affords easy access to restaurants and shops. Rooms are somewhat generic motel modern but have appealing Mexican touches. ☎ *Av. Nader 1, S.M. 2,* ☎ *98/87–44–55 or 800/HOLI-DAY,* FAX *98/84–79–54. 246 rooms. Restaurant, 2 bars, pool, tennis court, exercise room, nightclub, coin laundry. AE, DC, MC, V.*

$$ Antillano. This old but prettily appointed property features wood fur-
★ nishings, a cozy little lobby bar, and a tiny pool. Extras such as tiled bathroom sinks and air-conditioning in the halls and rooms make this hotel stand out a bit from others in its league. Suites with kitchenettes are available. ☎ *Av. Tulum at Calle Claveles,* ☎ *98/84–15–32 or 98/84–11–32,* FAX *98/84–18–78. 48 rooms. Pool, bar. AE, DC, MC, V.*

$$ María del Lourdes. The María del Lourdes has some nice touches
★ throughout, such as the colonial-style restaurant with rust-and-white stucco walls and the garden surrounding a small pool in the back. The rooms are bright, with sparse, functional decor. ☎ *Av. Yaxchilán 80,* ☎ *98/84–47–44,* FAX *98/84–12–42. 81 rooms. Restaurant, bar, pool, coin laundry. AE, MC, V.*

$$ Plaza Carrillo's. One of the first hotels to be built in Cancún City, this one is conveniently located in the heart of the downtown area next to the Plaza Carrillo shopping arcade and Carrillo's restaurant (*see* Dining, *above*), which are under the same ownership. The rooms are simply furnished but clean and well maintained. 🏨 *Calle Claveles 35,* 🕾 *98/84–12–27 or 98/84–48–33,* 🖷 *98/84–23–71. 43 rooms. Restaurant, pool. AE, MC, V.*

$$ Plaza del Sol. This three-story Spanish colonial–style hotel, a block south of the Margarita Cancún, was closed and under floor-to-ceiling renovation at press time, but should be reopened by late 1995. Long popular with students, Europeans, and Canadians, it's worth checking out. 🏨 *Av. Yaxchilán 31,* 🕾 *98/84–38–88 or 800/446–4656,* 🖷 *98/84–92–09. 87 rooms. Restaurant, 2 bars, pool, laundry service, travel services, car rental. AE, DC, MC, V.*

The Arts and Nightlife

Two new entertainment complexes offer one-stop shopping for nightlife in Cancún. Garishly colored **Mexico Magico** (Paseo Kukulcán Km 12, 🕾 98/834–9802) features dinner shows (Italian, Mexican, Caribbean, and Spanish), international boutiques, video bars, strolling musicians, and an open-air disco with live music. At press time, business was not exactly booming; by the time you read this, the place might have folded. The multi-story **Party Center** (Paseo Kukulcán Km 9, 🕾 98/83–03–51), next to the convention center, hosts several clubs, a sports bar, and two discos (Tequila Rock and Baja Beach Club), as well as numerous restaurants, specialty boutiques, and a money exchange.

Film

Local movie theaters showing American and Mexican films include **Espectáculos del Caribe** (Av. Tulum 44, 🕾 98/84–04–49), **Cines Cancún 1 and 2** (Av. Cobá 112, 🕾 98/84–16–46), and **Telecines Kukulcán** (🕾 98/85–30–21) in Plaza Kukulcán.

Festivals

Cancún's **Jazz Festival** (🕾 800/542–8953) premiered in 1991 and featured Wynton Marsalis and Gato Barbieri. Sponsored by the Cancún Office of Special Events, the jazz fest is now joined by Country Western Fest in July and Rockfest in October. At press time, the 1996 schedule was not yet available.

Performances

The **ballet folklórico** dinner show (Hotel Continental Villas Plaza, Paseo Kukulcán Km 11, 🕾 98/83–10–95) consists of stylized performances of regional Mexican dances including the hat dance and *la bamba*. By comparison with the renowned Ballet Nacional Folklórico of Mexico City, this troupe suffers, but if it's all you're able to see of the brilliant Mexican dance traditions, which blend pre-Hispanic and Iberian motifs, then go for it. An admission price of about $50 includes the buffet—a sampling of regional Mexican cooking, the show, and one drink. Performances are held Monday through Saturday; dinner is at 7, the show at 8:30.

Similar Mexican fiesta dinner shows are held once a week at the **Westin Regina** (🕾 98/85–00–86) and the **Meliá Turquesa** (🕾 98/83–25–44). Both include folkloric ballet, mariachi music, a Mexican buffet, and drinks. Call for dates, prices, and reservations.

Discos

Cancún wouldn't be Cancún without its glittering discos, which generally start jumping about 10:30 PM. **Azucar** (Camino Real Hotel, ☎ 98/83–04–41) sizzles to a salsa beat nightly; the beautiful people don't turn up here until *really* late. **Dady'O** (Paseo Kukulcán Km 9.5, ☎ 98/83–31–34 or 98/83–33–33) has been around for a while but is still a very "in" place, especially with the younger set. **Christine** (Krystal Cancún hotel, ☎ 98/83–11–33) attracts a slightly older, elegantly attired crowd and features an incredible light show. **La Boom** (Paseo Kukulcán Km 3.5, ☎ 98/83–14–58) includes a video bar with a light show and is not always crowded, although it can squeeze in 1,200 people.

Music

Batacha (Hotel Miramar Misión, ☎ 98/83–17–55), a small Caribbean nightclub, is a low-key spot to enjoy some Latin sounds. Visit the **Hard Rock Cafe** (Plaza Lagunas, Paseo Kukulcán, ☎ 98/83–20–24) for live rock bands (generally six nights a week) and molto music nostalgia. You can hear Caribbean beat dance music (marimba, mariachi, reggae, etc.) at **Jalapeños** (Paseo Kukulcán Km 7, ☎ 98/832–8960) nightly from 8. **La Palapa** (Club Lagoon Hotel, ☎ 98/83–11–11), offering dancing on a pier over the lagoon, inspires romance. The place to go for hot live reggae is **Mango Tango** (Paseo Kukulcán Km 14.2, ☎ 98/85–03–03), which sits lagoonside across the street from the Ritz-Carlton. **Planet Hollywood** (Flamingo Plaza, Paseo Kukulcán Km 11.5, ☎ 98/85–07–23) is currently the ticket in town; crowds push their way in for the Hollywood memorabilia—and hope to catch a glimpse of such stars as Demi Moore and Arnold Schwarzenegger, who occasionally check in on their investment. **Reflejos** (Hyatt Regency, ☎ 98/83–09–66) has a chic lounge with a small dance floor.

Cancún Essentials

Arriving and Departing

BY PLANE

Cancún International Airport is 16 kilometers (9 miles) southwest of the heart of Cancún City, 10 kilometers (6 miles) from the southernmost point of the hotel zone. **Aeromexico** (☎ 800/237–6639, ☎ 98/84–10–97 and 98/84–35–71 in Cancún) flies nonstop from Houston and New York. **American** (☎ 800/433–7300, ☎ 98/86–00–55 or 98/86–00–86 in Cancún or toll free in Mexico 800/9–04–60) has nonstop service from Dallas, Raleigh/Durham, and Miami. **Continental** (☎ 800/231–0856, ☎ 98/86–00–40 in Cancún) offers daily direct service from Houston. **Mexicana** (☎ 800/531–7921, ☎ 98/87–44–44 or 98/86–01–20 in Cancún) nonstop flights depart from Chicago, Los Angeles, Miami, and New York. In Cancún, Mexicana subsidiaries **Aerocaribe** (☎ 98/84–20–00 [downtown], 98/86–00–83 [airport]) and **Aerocozumel** (☎ 98/84–20–00 [downtown], 98/86–01–62 [airport]) offer flights to Cozumel, the ruins at Chichén Itzá, Mérida, and other Mexican destinations.

Between the Airport and Hotels. A counter at the airport exit sells tickets for buses (called *colectivos*) and taxis; prices for the latter range from $15 to $25, depending on the exact destination. Buses, which cost about $8, are air-conditioned and vend soft drinks and beer on board, but may be slow if they're carrying a lot of passengers and need to stop at many hotels.

BY CAR

Cancún is at the end of Route 180, which goes from Matamoros on the Texas border to Campeche, Mérida, and Valladolid. The road trip from Texas to Cancún can take up to three days. Cancún can also be reached from the south via Route 307, which passes through Chetumal and Belize. There are few gas stations on these roads, so try to keep your tank filled.

BY BUS

The bus terminal (Av. Tulum and Av. Uxmal, ☎ 98/84–13–78 or 98/84–39–48) downtown serves first-class buses making the trip from Mexico City and first- and second-class buses arriving in Cancún from Puerto Morelos, Playa del Carmen, Tulum, Chetumal, Cobá, Valladolid, Chichén Itzá, and Mérida. Public buses (Route 8) make the trip out to Puerto Juárez and Punta Sam for the ferries to Isla Mujeres.

Getting Around

Motorized transport of some sort is necessary, since the island is somewhat spread out. Public bus service is good and taxis are relatively inexpensive.

When you first visit Cancún City (downtown), you may be confused by the layout. There are four principal avenues: Tulum and Yaxchilán, which run north–south; and Uxmal and Cobá, which go east–west. Streets bounded by those avenues and running perpendicular to them are actually horseshoe-shaped, so you will find two parallel streets named *Tulipanes,* for instance. However, street numbers or even street names are not of much use in Cancún; the proximity to landmarks, such as specific hotels, is the preferred way of giving directions.

BY BUS

Public buses operate between the hotel zone and downtown from 6 AM to midnight; the cost is 45¢. There are designated bus stops, but drivers can also be flagged down along Paseo Kukulcán. Although the service is a bit erratic, buses run frequently and can save you considerable money on taxis, especially if you're staying at the southern end of the hotel zone.

BY CAR AND MOPED

Renting a car for your stay in Cancún is probably an unnecessary expense, entailing tips for valet parking, as well as gasoline and rather costly rental rates (on a par with those in any major resort area around the world). What's more, driving here can be harrowing when you don't know your way around. Downtown streets, being cobblestoned to give the area an "Old Mexico" look, are frequently clogged with traffic. However, if you plan to do some exploring, using Cancún as a base, the roads are excellent within a 100-kilometer (62-mile) radius.

Car Rentals. Rental cars are available at the airport or from any of a dozen agencies in town, and most are standard-shift subcompacts and Jeeps; air-conditioned cars with automatic transmissions should be reserved in advance. Rental agencies include **Avis** (☎ 98/86–02–22 at the airport, 98/83–08–00 at Hotel Calinda Viva, or 98/83–08–03 at Mayfair Plaza); **Budget** (☎ 98/84–41–01 at Av. Tulum 214); **Econo-Rent** (☎ 98/84–21–47 at the airport, 98/84–18–26 or 98/84–14–35 at Calle Tulipanes 16); **National** (☎ 98/86–01–53 at the airport or 98/84–00–97 at Av. Uxmal 12); or **Hertz** (9 locations, ☎ 98/86–01–50 at the airport or 98/87–66–44 at Reno 35). The **Car Rental Association**

(☎ 98/84–20–39) can help you arrange a rental as well. Rates average about $45 per day.

Moped Rentals. Mopeds and scooters are also available throughout the island. While fun, they are risky, and there is no insurance available for the driver or the vehicle. The accident rate is high, especially downtown, which is considered too congested for novice moped users. Rates start at about $25 per day.

BY TAXI
Taxis to the ferries at Punta Sam or Puerto Juárez cost $15–$20 or more; between the hotel zone and downtown, $8 and up; and within the hotel zone, $5–$7. All prices depend on the distance, your negotiating skills, and whether you pick up the taxi in front of the hotel or go onto the avenue to hail a green city cab (the latter will be cheaper). Since taxi rates fluctuate according to gasoline taxes and the drivers' whims, check with your hotel. Most list rates at the door; confirm the price with your driver before you set out. If you lose something in a taxi or have questions or a complaint, call the **Sindicato de Taxistas** (☎ 98/83–18–40 or 98/88–69–90).

BY SHIP
Boats leave Puerto Juárez and Punta Sam (both north of Cancún City) for Isla Mujeres every half hour or so; *see* Isla Mujeres, *below,* for details.

Guided Tours
There are no guided tours of Cancún per se, because other than several tiny Maya ruins, there is virtually no sightseeing to do on the island. Most popular are tours to the surrounding islands, the beaches along the Cancún–Tulum corridor (Akumal is the best known), or the Maya ruins on the mainland—Chichén Itzá, Cobá, and Tulum (these trips usually include a stop at the lagoons at Xel-Ha or Xcaret).

CRUISES
Dinner Cruises. A lobster-dinner cruise on board the 62-foot vessel *Columbus* (☎ 98/83–14–88 or 98/83–32–68) includes a full lobster or steak dinner, open bar, and dancing for $70; the boat departs the Royal Mayan Yacht Club Monday–Saturday, and sails at 4 and 7:30. The *Cancún Queen* (☎ 98/85–22–88), a paddlewheeler departing from the AquaWorld Marina (Paseo Kukulcán Km 15.2), offers a similar excursion for $65. **Expocancún** (☎ 98/84–80–92 or 98/84–82–20) offers "Caribbean Carnival Night," an Isla Mujeres beach-party excursion aboard a 100-foot motorized catamaran that sails from Playa Tortuga. Nightly trips last from 5:30 to 11, cost under $65, and include a buffet dinner, open bar, limbo and other beach contests, live music, and a colorful floor show.

Day Cruises. Also popular are the day cruises to Isla Mujeres, which include snorkeling in El Garrafó, time for shopping downtown, as well as Continental breakfast, open-bar buffet lunch, and music. Expocancún books the "Fiesta Maya Cruise," which is particularly popular with locals; it departs at 10 from the pier next to Grimonds, returns at 5, and costs about $55.

Submarine Cruises. Nautibus (☎ 98/83–10–04 or 98/83–21–19), or the "floating submarine," has a 1½-hour Caribbean-reef cruise that departs the Playa Linda marina six times daily. The $30 price includes music and drinks. Comparable tours aboard one of the **Sub See Explorer** (☎ 98/85–22–88), or the "yellow submarines," depart from AquaWorld in the central hotel zone and can be combined with snorkeling for a full day's outing; the cost with snorkeling is about $40, $35 without. Latest to join the underwater ranks is **Atlantis** (☎ 98/83–30–21), Cancún's first true submarine (the others float on the surface and have window seats below). Tours, available every hour from 10 to 3, include an hour-long cruise from Playa Linda to and from the submarine site, and 50 minutes dive time in the sub. The basic price is $80 (half that for children 4–12); add $10 and more time if you want to include lunch (not advised if you're prone to motion sickness).

AIR TOURS

A 10-minute, $35-per-person ultralight plane ride over the lagoons and Caribbean reefs departs from **Pelican Pier** (Paseo Kukulcán Km 5.5, ☎ 98/83–03–15 or 98/83–19–35), across from the Casa Maya; a 20-minute ride, covering the whole island, costs about $90. Cessna 206 air taxis are also available for charters; the cost is $440 per hour (a maximum of five passengers can split the price).

Aeroquetzal (Plaza México, Av. Tulum 200, ☎ 98/87–13–53 or 98/84–39–38), a small Guatemalan carrier, flies between Cancún and Guatemala City, continuing on to Flores and the ruins at Tikal, for $270 round-trip.

JEEP TOURS

Intermar Caribe (☎ 98/84–42–66) leads daily Jeep tours through the jungle to unexcavated ruins. The $50 price includes lunch.

Important Addresses and Numbers

CONSULATES

United States (Av. Nader 40, S.M. 2A, Edificio Marruecos 31, ☎ 98/84–24–11 or 98/84–63–99) is open daily 9–2 and 3–6.

Canada (Plaza México Local 312, upper floor, ☎ 98/84–37–16) is open daily 11 AM–1 PM. For emergencies outside office hours, call the Canadian Embassy in Mexico City (☎ 5/254–3288).

EMERGENCIES

Police (☎ 98/84–19–13); **Red Cross** (Av. Xcaret and Labná, S.M. 21, ☎ 98/84–16–16); **Highway Patrol** (☎ 98/84–11–07).

Hospital Americano (Calle Viento 15, ☎ 98/84–61–33) and **Total Assist** (Claveles 5, ☎ 98/84–10–92 or 98/84–81–16), both with English-speakers on staff, provide emergency medical care.

ENGLISH-LANGUAGE BOOKSTORES

Fama (Av. Tulum 105, ☎ 98/84–65–86) specializes in books on the Yucatán and offers a large selection of English-language magazines. **La Surtidora** (Av. Tulum 17, ☎ 98/84–11–03) sells a variety of English-and Spanish-language books.

LATE-NIGHT PHARMACIES

Farmacia Turística (Plaza Caracol, ☎ 98/83–18–94) and **Farmacia Extra** (Plaza Caracol, ☎ 98/83–28–27) deliver to hotels 9 AM–10 PM. **Farmacia Paris** (Av. Yaxchilán, in the Marrufo Bldg., ☎ 98/84–01–64) also fills prescriptions.

VISITOR INFORMATION

The **state tourist office** (Av. Tulum 26, ☎ 98/84–80–73), next to Multibanco Comermex, is open daily 9–9. At this office, at the airport, and at many hotels, you can pick up a copy of **Cancún Tips,** a free pocket-size guide to hotels, restaurants, shopping, and recreation that usually contains a discount card for use at various establishments. The magazine staff also runs a number of information centers around town, including one at Plaza Caracol (☎ 98/83–27–45) that is open daily 10–10.

ISLA MUJERES

Updated by
Melissa Rivers

A tiny fish-shaped island just 8 kilometers (5 miles) off Cancún, Isla Mujeres (*ees*-lah moo-*hair*-es) is a tranquil alternative to its bustling western neighbor. Only about 5 miles long by ½ mile wide, Isla has flat sandy beaches on its northern end and steep rocky bluffs to the south. Because of its proximity to Cancún, it has turned into a small-scale tourist destination, but it is still a peaceful island retreat with a rich history and culture centered on the sea.

Part of that history is blessed by the presence of Isla's first known inhabitants, the ancient Maya. Their legacy lies in the names, features, and language of their descendants here, but not, unfortunately, in the observatory they built on the Southern tip—Hurricane Gilbert obliterated the well-preserved ruin in 1988; restoration efforts are ongoing. The Spanish conquistadores followed: After setting sail from Cuba in 1517, Hernández de Córdoba's ship blew here accidentally in a storm. Credited with "discovering" the island, he and his crew dubbed their find "Isle of Women." One explanation of the name's origin is that Córdoba and company came upon wooden idols of Maya goddesses. Another theory claims the Spaniards found only women when they arrived—the men were out fishing.

For the next several centuries, Isla, like many Caribbean islands, became a haven for pirates and smugglers, then settled into life as a quiet fishing village. In this century, it started out as a vacation destination for Mexicans; the '60s witnessed a hippie influx; since the late '70s, day-trippers from Cancún increasingly disembark here, and Isla's hotel, restaurant, and shop owners are seeing more activity than ever.

Exploring

Numbers in the margin correspond to points of interest on the Isla Mujeres map.

We start our itinerary in the island's only town, known simply as *el pueblo,* which extends the full width of Isla's northern "tail." The village is sandwiched between sand and sea to the north, south, and east; no high-rises block the view. Activity centers around the waterfront ❶ **piers** and on the coastal main drag, Avenida Rueda Medina. Two blocks inland, you'll find the other spot where everyone gathers—the ❷ **main square,** *la placita* or *el parque,* bounded by avenidas Morelos, Bravo, Guerrero, and Hidalgo. This is an ideal place to take in the daily life of the town.

Two of the island's finest and most popular beaches are on the northwest part of the island: Follow any of the north–south streets in town ❸ to **Playa Cocoteros** (Cocos), and walk east along the pretty strip of ❹ white sand to **Playa Norte.** At both, you can wade far out in the placid waters. Hurricane Gilbert's only good deed, according to isleños, was to widen these and other leeward-side beaches by blowing sand over from Cancún. At both beaches you can sit at congenial palapa bars for drinks and snacks; Cocos has lots of stands where you can rent snorkel gear, Jet-Skis, floats, sailboards, and sometimes parasails. At the northernmost end of Playa Norte, you'll find Punta Norte and come upon an abandoned hotel on its own private islet. A wood-planked bridge leads to the property, which has changed hands several times and for a long time was supposed to open as an all-inclusive resort called the Costa Club; those plans have been dropped indefinitely. The other building you'll see jutting out on a rocky point is a private home.

❺ On the road parallel to Playa Cocoteros (Lopez Mateos), you'll find Isla's **cemetery,** with its 100-year-old gravestones. Among the lovingly decorated tombs, many in memory of children, is that of Fermín Mundaca (*see* Hacienda Mundaca, *below*). A notorious 19th-century slave trader (often billed more glamorously as a pirate), Mundaca is said to have carved his own tombstone with a skull and crossbones. On one side of the tomb an inscription reads in Spanish: "As You Are, I Once Was"; the other side warns, "As I Am, So Shall You Be." Mundaca's grave is empty, however; his remains lie in Mérida where he died. The monument is not easy to find—ask a local to point out the unidentified marker.

❻ To explore the rest of the island, you'll need to take a moped or taxi south along Avenida Rueda Medina, which leads out of town. The first landmark you'll pass after the piers is the **Mexican naval base,** which is closed to the public. From the road, however, you can see (but *not* photograph) the modest flag-raising and -lowering ceremonies at sunrise and sunset. Continuing southward, the *salinas* (salt **❼** marshes) will be on your left, and on your right you'll see the **Laguna Makax,** where pirates are said to have anchored their ships as they lay in wait for the hapless vessels plying Spanish Main (the geographical area in which Spanish treasure ships trafficked).

❽ Continue along the main road until you come to the "S" curve at the end of Laguna Makax; you'll see a dirt drive and stone archway to the left marking the entrance to the remains of the **Hacienda Mundaca,** built by Fermín Mundaca de Marechaja, the 19th-century slave trader–cum-pirate mentioned above. When the British navy began cracking down on slavers, he settled on the island and built an ambitious estate with resplendent tropical gardens. The story goes that he constructed it to woo a certain island maiden who, in the end, chose another man.

What little remained of the hacienda has mysteriously vanished, except for a sorry excuse of a guardhouse, an arch, a pediment, and a well. Locals say that the government tore down the mansion, or at least neglected its upkeep. (Purportedly, the government will soon rebuild the site as a tourist attraction; however, this has been rumored for the last several years and nothing has come of it.) If you push your way through the jungle—the mosquitoes are fierce—you'll eventually come to the ruined stone archway and triangular pediment, carved with the following inscription: *Huerta de la Hacienda de Vista Alegre MDCCCLXXVI* (Orchard of the Happy View Hacienda, 1876). No ☎. ☛ *Free.*

❾ About a block southeast of the hacienda, turn right off the main road when you come to the sign that says PESCA. This smaller, unmarked side road loops back north. About ¼ mile farther on the left is the entrance to the government-run **marine biology station,** which is devoted primarily to the study and preservation of sea turtles, lobsters, and coral reefs. During working hours, visitors can examine various species. The ecologists here care for and release about 6,000 infant turtles each month during the hatching season (May to September). No ☎. ☛ *$2.* ☺ *Weekdays 9–5.*

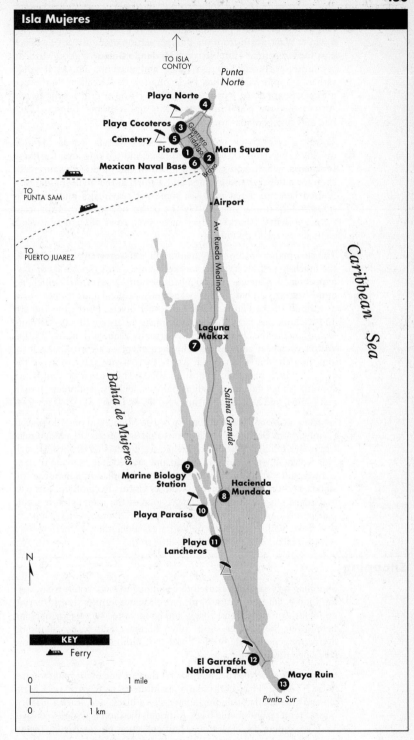

Isla Mujeres

The beach stretching to the north and south of the biology station is ⑩ **Playa Paraíso,** a very pleasant spot to have a bite to eat and relax for a while. Walk north from the biology station along the lovely beach past the Cristalmar Hotel to reach **Hacienda Gomar,** a good Mexican restaurant featuring a buffet lunch and marimba music. If you'd rather not put your shoes back on, try the excellent barbecued grouper, snapper, or barracuda at **Blacky's** open grill on the beach. Also in the area you'll find handicraft and souvenir shops, a beach bar, and small palapas for shade.

Traveling south back on the main road (Avenida Rueda Medina) ⑪ quickly brings you to the unpaved drive and parking area for **Playa Lancheros,** where you can have lunch in the modest restaurant or shop for handicrafts, souvenirs, and T-shirts at the small stands. Also housed here, in a sea pen, are some pet sea turtles and harmless *tiburón gato* (nurse sharks). On the ocean side live the carnivorous *tintorera* (female sharks), which have seven rows of teeth and weigh as much as 1,100 pounds.

⑫ The next major site along the main road is **El Garrafón National Park,** the much-hyped, overvisited snorkeling mecca for thousands of day-trippers from Cancún. Although still beautiful, Garrafón—which lies at the bottom of a bluff—was once almost magical in its beauty. Now, as a result of the hands and fins of eager divers, Hurricane Gilbert, and anchors cast from the fleets of tourist boats continually arriving from Cancún, the coral reef here is virtually dead. Still, nearly 25,000 visitors each year are impressed by the scenery—parrotfish, angelfish, and the rich blue-green water. Arrive early if you want to avoid the crowds, which start to form around 10 AM. There are food stands and souvenir shops galore, as well as palapas, lockers, equipment rental, rest rooms, and a small aquarium. *No* ☎. ☛ *Under $2.* ☉ *Daily 9–4.*

Continuing around the southern tip of Isla Mujeres, about 1 kilometer ⑬ (⅗ mile) from Garrafón, you'll come to the sad vestiges of a **Maya ruin,** formerly a temple dedicated to Ixchel, the goddess of fertility. Though Hurricane Gilbert walloped the ruin and succeeded in blowing most of it away, restoration efforts are underway. The adjacent **lighthouse** still stands, and the keeper sometimes allows visitors to climb up. Just past that point, on the windward side, is one of the island's most scenic patches of coastline. Follow this perimeter road into town; it's a beautiful drive, with a few rocky pull-off areas along the way, perfect for a secluded picnic since this road sees little traffic.

Shopping

Shopping on Isla Mujeres used to be limited to basic resort wear, suntan lotions, and groceries. Now, more Mexican crafts shops offering good deals on silver, fabric bags, and handcrafted objects are opening here. Even the smaller shops often accept credit cards. Shopping hours are generally daily 10–1 and 4–7, although many stores now stay open through siesta.

La Loma (Av. Guerrero 6, 2nd floor, on the east side of the main square, ☎ 987/7–02–23) has a selection of exquisite crafts from all over Mexico and Guatemala, including amber, silver, black jade, leather jewelry, masks, pottery, and textile bags. Although the shop is not inexpensive, La Loma offers the biggest and best collection on the island. **Tienda Paulita** (Avs. Morelos and Hidalgo, ☎ 987/7–00–14) features a standard selection of folk art and handmade clothing in a fairly large space. **Rachat & Romero** (Av. Rueda Medina, ☎ 987/7–03–31), housed in the pink building by the dock, sells gold, silver, and gemstones. In 1991, the owners of Rachat & Romero opened **Van Cleef & Arpels** (Avs. Juárez and Morelos, ☎ 987/7–02–99), with a similarly impressive jewelry selection in a large corner shop. **Casa del Arte Mexica** (Av. Hidalgo 6, ☎ 987/7–04–59) has a good choice of clay reproductions, silver jewelry, batiks, rubbings, wood carvings, leather, and hammocks.

Sports and Fitness

Fishing

Billfish are a popular catch in spring and early summer; the rest of the year, you can fish for barracuda and tuna, as well as for shad, sailfish, grouper, red snapper, and Spanish mackerel.

Bahía Dive Shop (Av. Rueda Medina 166, across from the pier, ☎ and FAX 987/7–03–40) charges $250 for a day of deep-sea fishing, $200 a day for cast fishing (tarpon, snook, and bonefish), and $20 an hour for offshore fishing (barracuda, snapper, and smaller fish).

Snorkeling and Scuba Diving

Bahía Dive Shop (Av. Rueda Medina 166, across from the pier, ☎ and FAX 987/7–03–40) rents snorkeling and scuba equipment and runs three-hour boat and dive trips to the reefs and the Cave of the Sleeping Sharks. Snorkel gear goes for $5 a day; tanks are $45–$60, depending on the length of the dive. **Mexico Divers** (Av. Rueda Medina and Av. Medero, 1 block from the ferry, ☎ 987/7–01–31), also called **Buzos de México,** runs three-hour snorkeling tours for $15; two-tank scuba trips start at $40 for a reef dive and $60 for the shark cave dive. Rental gear is available. Dive master Carlos Gutiérrez also gives a resort course for $80 and open-water PADI certification for $350 (his prices are generally negotiable).

Dining

Dining on Isla Mujeres offers what you would expect on a small island: plenty of fresh-grilled seafood—lobster, shrimp, conch, and fish. You can also try Mexican and Yucatecan specialties like *carne asada* (broiled beef), *mole poblano* (a spicy sauce of chile, chocolate, sesame, and almonds), *pollo píbil* (chicken baked in banana leaves in a tangy sour orange sauce), and *poc chuc* (pork marinated in sour orange sauce with pickled onions). Those who crave more familiar fare can opt for pizza, steak, or shish-kebab. Generally, restaurants on the island are casual, though shirts and shoes are required at most indoor dining rooms.

CATEGORY	COST*
$$$$	over $20
$$$	$15–$20
$$	$8–$15
$	under $8

per person, excluding drinks, service, and tax

$$$ **Chez Magaly.** A very elegant establishment on the grounds of the
★ Nautibeach Condo-hotel, this mostly French restaurant is tastefully decorated with plants, leather chairs, and Chinese blinds. Seafood grills, lobster quiche, jambalaya, and tequila-flambéed mangos are among the specialties. To complement the meal, choose from an extensive wine list. ✕ *Av. Rueda Medina, Playa Norte,* ☎ *987/7–02–59 or 987/7–04–36. Reservations advised. MC, V. Closed Mon. and 2 wks in June.*

$$$ **Maria's Kan Kin.** Near El Garaffón, at the southern end of the island, this beach restaurant features gourmet seafood. Choose a live lobster or try one of the specialties, which tend to be prepared with a French twist, like lobster bisque and chocolate mousse. It's the perfect spot for a long lunch that extends to sunset. ✕ *On the main road to Garaffón,* ☎ *987/7–00–15. MC, V.*

$$ **Arriba.** Vegetarians will appreciate the fresh vegetable shish kebabs, tempura, sautés, and spaghetti whipped up and served on the open terrace of this second-floor eatery, a half block north of the plaza on Avenida Hidalgo. Well-prepared shrimp and lobster are also crowd pleasers. Cheerful planters brighten the sparsely furnished room. Fresh fruit margaritas draw a crowd to the nightly happy hour. ✕ *Av. Hidalgo (between Avs. Madero and Abasolo),* ☎ *987/7–04–58. No reservations. No credit cards. No lunch.*

$$ **El Limbo Sea House.** This restaurant—housed in the Hotel Roca Mar, which has been carved into the side of a cliff—offers a sensational view of the sea; the water laps up to the lower level windows. The decor is typical for the island—nets, seashells, and rustic wood furniture. Included on the menu are pollo píbil, pork chops, and steak, as well as many seafood specials. You have the choice of fish or shellfish broiled, breaded, fried, or in garlic, all served with rice or french fries and salad. ✕ *Av. Bravo and Av. Guerrero, at Hotel Roca Mar,* ☎ *987/7–01–01. No reservations. No credit cards.*

$$ **Pizza Rolandi.** Red tables, yellow director's chairs, and green walls and
★ window trim set an upbeat tone at this very "in" chain restaurant. Select from a broad variety of Italian food: lobster pizzas, calzones, and pastas. Grilled fresh fish and shrimp are highly recommended, and salads are excellent. Or just stop in for a drink at one of the outside tables; the margaritas, cappuccino, and espresso are the best in town. ✕ *Av. Hidalgo (between Avs. Madero and Abasolo),* ☎ *987/7–04–30. No reservations. AE, MC, V.*

$ **Lonchería La Lomita.** This simple, homestyle diner isn't much to look
★ at, but you'll find hearty servings of chicken, steak, and seafood cooked to order (grilled, fried, or sautéed) here. The octopus sautéed in butter and garlic is particularly tasty. Amazingly low-priced lunch and dinner set menus include beans, rice, and tortillas or bread; breakfast is also available. ✕ *Av. Juárez 25-B (just past Av. Allende), no* ☎. *No reservations. No credit cards.*

$ **Mirtita's, Piscis,** and **Villa del Mar.** Next to one another on Av. Rueda Medina across from the ferry dock, these are favorite local hangouts. All serve fresh seafood and Yucatecan specialties. ✕ *Av. Rueda Medina. No* ☎. *No credit cards.*

Lodging

The approximately 25 hotels (about 600 rooms) on Isla Mujeres generally fall into one of two categories: The older, more modest places are situated right in town, and the newer, more expensive properties tend to have beachfront locations around Punta Norte and, increasingly, on the peninsula near the lagoon. Most hotels have ceiling fans; some have air-conditioning, but few offer TVs or phones. All hotels share the 77400 postal code.

CATEGORY	COST*
$$$	$60–$90
$$	$25–$60
$	under $25

All prices are for a standard double room, excluding 10% tax.

$$$ **Na-Balam.** This intimate, informal hostelry set on Playa Norte will
★ fulfill all your tropical-paradise fantasies. Three corner suites with
balconies affording outstanding views of sea and sand are well worth
$80. The simple, attractive rooms have turquoise-tiled floors, carved
wood furniture, dining areas, and patios facing the beach; photos of
Mexico in its bygone days and Mexican carvings grace the walls. A
swimming pool and eight more rooms were added in 1995. ⌷ *Calle
Zazil Ha 118,* ☎ *987/7–02–79,* FAX *987/7–04–46. 26 rooms. Restau-
rant, bar, air-conditioning, pool, beach. AE, MC, V.*

$$ **Belmar.** Right in the heart of town, above Pizza Rolandi, this small
hotel shares a charming plant-filled inner courtyard with the restau-
rant, which means it can occasionally be noisy here until 11 PM. Standard rooms are pretty, with tiled baths and light-wood furniture. One
enormous suite features a private Jacuzzi on a patio, a tiled kitchenette, and a sitting area. All rooms have phones, satellite TV, and air-
conditioning. ⌷ *Av. Hidalgo 110 (between Avs. Madero and
Abasolo),* ☎ *987/7–04–30,* FAX *987/7–04–29. 11 rooms. MC, V.*

$$ **Cabañas María del Mar.** A rather mind-boggling assortment of rooms
★ are available in this unusual beachfront hotel with a unique Mexican
atmosphere. Some of the rooms are rather spare, but those in the
slightly more expensive "castle" section have hand-carved wood fur-
nishings by local artisans as well as folk art, tiled baths, and hand-
painted sinks. The hotel has a prime location on Playa Cocoteros,
and its reasonable room rates include Continental breakfast. ⌷ *Av.
Carlos Lazos 1,* ☎ *987/7–01–79,* FAX *987/7–02–13. 55 rooms, includ-
ing 12 cabañas. Restaurant-bar, air-conditioning, pool, motorbikes,
travel services. MC, V.*

$$ **Posada del Mar.** This hotel's assets include its prime location between
town and Playa Cocos and its reasonable prices. Rooms have bal-
conies overlooking a main road and beyond to the waterfront. The
simple wood furnishings appear somewhat worse for wear, although
baths are clean, with cheerful colored tiles. Inexpensive ($) private
bungalows are also available. A new bar next to the pool is as popular as the street-front palapa-roof restaurant. ⌷ *Av. Rueda Medina
15A,* ☎ *987/7–03–00, 987/7–00–44,* FAX *987/7–02–66. 40 rooms.
Restaurant, bar, pool. AE, MC, V.*

$ **Poc-Na.** The island's youth hostel, at the eastern end of town, rents
bunks or hammocks (which cost less) and has lockers and showers,
but it requires a deposit that's almost twice the cost of the accommodations. One bonus is its proximity to the beach. ⌷ *Av. Matamoros
15,* ☎ *987/7–00–90 or 987/7–00–59. Dining room. No credit cards.*

The Arts and Nightlife

The Arts

Festivals and cultural events are held on many weekends, with live
entertainment on the outdoor stage in the main square. The whole
island celebrates events like the spring regattas and the Caribbean
music festivals. (For annual celebrations, *see* Festivals and Seasonal
Events *in* Chapter 1, Destination: Mexico.) **Casa de la Cultura,** near the
youth hostel, offers folkloric dance classes year-round. The center also
operates a small public library and book exchange. *Av. Guerrero,* ☎
987/7–03–07. ☉ *Weekdays 8–8.* For English-language films visit **Cine
Blanquita** (Av. Morelos, between Avs. Guerrero and Hidalgo, no ☎).

Nightlife

Most restaurant-bars feature a happy hour from 5 to 7; the palapa bars
at Playa Cocos are an excellent place to watch the sunset. The current

hot spot is **Ya Ya's** (Av. Rueda Medina 42 near the lighthouse and Playa Cocos, no ☎), run by some good ol' boys from Dallas who serve up huge Texas steaks, chili dogs, and shrimp etouffé along with live jazz, rock, and reggae jam sessions until 2 or 3 AM. The bar at the **Posada del Mar** (Av. Rueda Medina 15, ☎ 987/7–03–00) can be subdued or hopping, depending on what's going on in town. **Buho's,** the bar-restaurant at Cabañas María del Mar (Av. Carlos Lazo 1, ☎ 987/7–01–79), is another good choice for a relaxing drink at sunset or later at night. **Restaurante La Peña** (Av. Guerrero 5, ☎ 987/7–03–09) has music and dancing on its open-air terrace overlooking the sea.

Isla Mujeres Essentials

Arriving and Departing by Boat

ARRIVING

The **Caribbean Express** and the **Caribbean Miss** (☎ 987/7–02–54 or 987/7–02–53), both air-conditioned cruisers with bar service, make several 30-minute crossings daily. They leave Puerto Juárez on the mainland for the main ferry dock in Isla Mujeres from 7:30 AM to 7:30 PM at approximately 30-minute intervals; the fare is under $4 per person. There are also three slower passenger ferries that leave at 7:30, 8:30, 9:30, 10, 10:30, and 11:30 AM, and at 12:30, 1:30, 2:30, 3:30, 4:30, 5:30, 6:30, and 7:30 PM; the schedule varies depending on the season, so check the times posted at the dock. The one-way fare is only about $1.50 and the trip takes 45 minutes, but delays and crowding are frequent.

It's also possible to hire a private *lancha,* or motorboat, which makes the crossing from Punta Sam, 5 kilometers (3 miles) north of Punta Juárez, in about 18 minutes. The fare is usually about $4 per person but varies. Water taxis charge a flat fee, about $20, divided by the number of passengers; a full load keeps the price low. Another convenient, more expensive service, the **Shuttle** (☎ 98/84–64–33, in Cancún), runs directly from the Playa Linda dock in Cancún's hotel zone at least six times a day and costs about $15 round-trip. Cars are unnecessary on Isla (*see* Getting Around, *below*), but **municipal ferries** that accommodate vehicles as well as passengers leave from Punta Sam and take about 45 minutes. Check departure times posted at the pier, but you can count on the schedule running from about 7 AM to 9 PM. The fare is under $2 per person and $10 per vehicle.

DEPARTING

The **Caribbean Express** and the **Caribbean Miss** (☎ 987/7–02–54 or 987/7–02–53) make the trip from Isla Mujeres to Puerto Juárez between 8 AM and 8 PM at approximately 30-minute intervals; the fare is under $4 per person. The slower passenger ferry departs from the main dock at Isla Mujeres to Puerto Juárez at approximately 5, 6, 6:30, 7:30, 8:15, 8:45, 9:30, 10:30, and 11:30 AM, and at 12:30, 1:30, 2:30, 3:30, 4:30, 5, 5:30, 6:30, and 7:30 PM. The first car ferry from Isla Mujeres to Punta Sam leaves at about 6 AM and the last departs at about 7:15 PM. Again, schedules vary, so you should call ahead or check the boat schedule posted at the pier.

Getting Around

BY CAR

There is little reason for tourists to bring cars to Isla Mujeres, because there are plenty of other forms of transportation that cost much less than renting and transporting a private vehicle. Moreover, though the main road is paved, speed bumps abound and some areas are poorly lighted.

BY TAXI

If your time is limited you can hire a taxi (Av. Rueda Medina, ☎ 987/7–00–66) for a private island tour at about $15 an hour. Fares run $1–$2 from the ferry or downtown to the hotels on the north end, at Playa Cocoteros. Taxis line up right by the ferry dock around the clock.

BY MOPED

The island is full of moped rental shops. Among them are **Motorent Kankin** (Av. Abasolo 15, ☎ 987/7–00–71), **Ppe's Rentadora** (Av. Hidalgo 19, ☎ 987/7–00–19 or 987/7–04–97), and **Ciro's Motorent** (Av. Guerrero N 11 at Av. Matamoros, ☎ 987/7–05–68). Rentals cost about $5 per hour, $35 per day.

BY BICYCLE

Bicycles are available for hardy cyclists, but don't underestimate the hot sun and the tricky road conditions. **Rent Me Sport Bike** (Avs. Juárez and Morelos, 1 block from the main pier, no ☎) offers five-speed cycles starting at less than $2 an hour; a full day costs about $5. You can leave your driver's license in lieu of a deposit; the place is open daily 8–6.

Moped and bicycle riders alike should watch for the many speed bumps, which can give you an unexpected jolt. Avoid riding at night; some roads have no street lights.

Guided Tours

TOUR OPERATORS

Local agencies include **Club de Yates de Isla Mujeres** (Av. Rueda Medina, ☎ 987/7–02–11 or 987/7–00–86, ☉ Daily 9–noon) and **La Isleña** (Avs. Morelos and Juárez, ☎ 987/7–05–78, ☉ Daily 7 AM–9 PM), half a block from the pier.

BOAT TOURS

Cooperativa Lanchera (waterfront, near the dock, no ☎) offers four-hour launch trips to the Virgin, the lighthouse, the turtles at Playa Lancheros, the coral reefs at Los Manchones, and El Garrafón, for about $35. **Cooperativa Isla Mujeres** (Av. Rueda Medina, ☎ 987/7–02–74), next to Mexico Divers, rents boats at $120 for a maximum of four hours and six people, and $15 per person for an island tour with lunch (minimum six people). A trip to **Isla Contoy,** 45 minutes to the north, costs $65 per person and includes a light breakfast, lunch, and drinks. It departs at 9 AM and returns at 5 PM.

Important Addresses and Numbers

EMERGENCIES

Medical Service (☎ 987/7–01–95 and 987/7–06–07); **Hospital** (☎ 987/7–00–01); **Police** (☎ 987/7–00–82); **Red Cross** (☎ 987/7–00–85).

LATE-NIGHT PHARMACIES

Farmacia Isla Mujeres (Av. Juárez, next to the Caribbean Tropic Boutique, ☎ 987/7–01–78) and **Farmacia Lily** (Avs. Madero and Hidalgo, ☎ 987/7–01–64) are open Monday–Saturday 8:30 AM–9:30 PM and Sunday 8:30 AM–3 PM.

VISITOR INFORMATION

The **tourist office** (Av. Hidalgo 6, behind the basketball court, ☎ 987/7–03–16), located on the main square, two blocks from the ferry, is open weekdays 9–2 and 7–9.

COZUMEL

Updated by
Melissa Rivers

Cozumel provides a balance between Cancún and Isla Mujeres: Though attuned to North American tourism, the island has managed to keep development to a minimum. Its expansive beaches, superb coral reefs, and copious wildlife—in the sea, on the land, and in the air—attract an active, athletic crowd. Rated one of the top destinations in the world among underwater enthusiasts, Cozumel is encircled by a garland of reefs entrancing divers and snorkelers alike. Despite the inevitable effects of docking cruise ships (shops and restaurants actively recruit customers on an increasingly populous main drag), the island's earthy charm and tranquility remain intact. The relaxing atmosphere here is typically Mexican—friendly and unpretentious. Cozumel's rich Maya heritage is reflected in the faces of 60,000 or so isleños; you'll see people who look like ancient statues come to life, and occasionally hear the Maya language spoken.

A 490-square-kilometer (189-square-mile) island 19 kilometers (12 miles) to the east of Yucatán, Cozumel is mostly flat, its interior covered by parched scrub, dense jungle, and marshy lagoons. White sandy beaches with calm waters line the island's leeward (western) side, which is fringed by a spectacular reef system, while the powerful surf and rocky strands on the windward (eastern) side, facing the Caribbean, are broken up here and there by calm bays and hidden coves. Most of Cozumel is undeveloped, with a good deal of the land and the shores set aside as national parks; a few Maya ruins provide what limited sightseeing there is aside from the island's glorious natural attractions. San Miguel is the only established town.

Exploring

Cozumel is about 53 kilometers (33 miles) long and 15 kilometers (9 miles) wide, but only a small percentage of its roads—primarily those in the southern half—are paved. Dirt roads can be explored, with care, in a four-wheel-drive vehicle. Aside from the 3% of the island that has been developed, Cozumel is made up of expanses of sandy or rocky beaches, quiet little coves, palm groves, scrubby jungles, lagoons and swamps, and a few low hills (the maximum elevation is 45 feet).

Numbers in the margin correspond to points of interest on the Cozumel map.

❶ Cozumel's principal town, **San Miguel,** serves as the hub of the island; its Avenida Rafael Melgar, along the waterfront, is the main strip of shops and restaurants. The **Plaza del Sol** is the main square, most often simply called *la plaza* or *el parque.* Directly across from the docks, it's hard to miss. A number of government buildings are here, including the large and modern convention center (used more for local functions than for formal conferences) and the **state tourist office** (☎ 987/2–09–72). The square is the heart of the town, where everyone congregates in the evenings. Heading inland (east) from the malecón takes you away from the touristy zone and toward the residential sections.

The **Museo de la Isla de Cozumel** is a good place to begin orienting yourself. Housed on two floors of what was once the island's first luxury hotel are four permanent exhibit halls of dioramas, sculptures, charts, and explanations of the island's history and ecosystem. The museum also presents temporary exhibits, guided tours, and workshops. A restaurant on the second floor of the museum offers good food and a great waterfront view. *Av. Rafael Melgar between Calles 4 and 6 N,* ☎ *987/2–14–75,* FAX *987/2–15–45.* ☛ *$3.* ☉ *Daily 10–6.*

Three thousand years of pre-Hispanic Mexican culture and art are showcased in the new **Cozumel Archaeological Park,** five minutes by cab from the pier and plaza area. Meso-American history is traced through more than 65 full-size replicas of Toltec, Mexicas, and Maya statues and stone carvings surrounded by jungle foliage. *Av. 65 S,* ☎ *987/2–09–14.* ☛ *$3.* ☉ *Daily 8–6.*

❷ Divers and snorkelers may want to take a plunge off the pier at **La Ceiba,** part of a second cluster of hotels and shops just south of town and adjacent to the international passenger terminal for cruise ships. About 100 yards offshore lie the remains of a small airplane that was placed here in 1977 during the making of a Mexican movie. An underwater trail marks various types of sea life, including sponges and enormous coral formations; visibility is excellent to about 30 meters.

❸ About a 10-minute drive south of San Miguel you will find **Chankanaab Nature Park** (the name means "small sea"), a lovely salt-water lagoon that the government has made into a wildlife sanctuary, botanical garden, and archaeological park. Underwater caves, off-shore reefs, a protected bay, and a sunken ship attract droves of snorkelers and scuba divers. Some 60-odd species of marine life, including fish, coral, turtles, and various crustaceans, reside in the lagoon; however, a major scientific study is currently under way, so swimming through the underwater tunnels from the lagoon to the bay or walking through the shallow lagoon are no longer permitted. Still, there's plenty to see in the bay, which hides crusty old cannons and anchors as well as statues of Jesus Christ and Chac Mool. An interactive educational museum, four dive shops, a restaurant, four gift shops, a snack stand, and a dressing room with lockers and showers are on the premises. *Carretera Sur, Km 9, no* ☎. ☛ *$5, children under 13 free.* ☉ *Daily 6 AM–5:30 PM.*

❹ Just south of Chankanaab, **Playa Corona,** which shares access to the Yucab reef, offers the same brilliant marine life as the park. Snorkeling equipment is available for rent, and the restaurant here serves conch and shrimp ceviche, *fajitas,* and more. The crowds that visit Chankanaab haven't yet discovered this tranquil neighbor.

❺ More southerly still lies **Playa San Francisco,** an inviting 5-kilometer (3-mile) stretch of sandy beach that's considered one of the longest and finest on Cozumel. Comprising the beaches known as Playa Maya and Santa Rosa, San Francisco gets especially crowded during high season, on weekends (with cruise-ship passengers), and on Sunday (when locals come to eat fresh fish and hear live music). The beach has two outdoor restaurants, a bar, dressing rooms, gift shops, volleyball nets, beach chairs, and a variety of water sports equipment for rent. Divers also use this beach as their jumping-off point for dives to the San Francisco reef and the Santa Rosa wall. An abundance of turtle grass in the water makes swimming less popular. Just past San **❻** Francisco, **Playa del Sol** has complete facilities, including a restaurant-bar, shops, and snorkeling and Jet Ski equipment; you can also rent horses and trot down the beach.

❼ A turnoff at Km 17.5 leads about 3 kilometers (2 miles) inland to the village and ruins of **El Cedral,** once the largest Maya site on Cozumel and the temple sighted by the original Spanish explorers in 1518. (To explore the areas off the paved road, a four-wheel-drive vehicle is

Cozumel

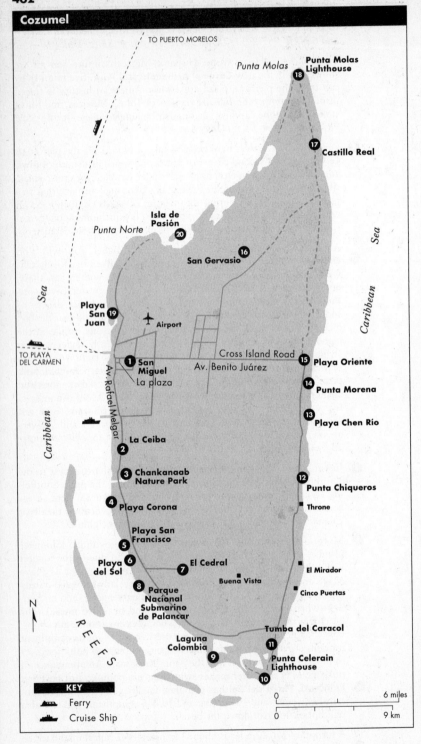

TO PUERTO MORELOS

Punta Molas

Punta Molas Lighthouse 18

Castillo Real 17

Sea

Isla de Pasión 20

Punta Norte

Sea

San Gervasio 16

Caribbean

Playa San Juan 19

Airport

TO PLAYA DEL CARMEN

Cross Island Road 15 **Playa Oriente**

Av. Benito Juárez

14 **Punta Morena**

1 **San Miguel**
La plaza

13 **Playa Chen Río**

Caribbean

La Ceiba 2

Chankanaab Nature Park 3

12 **Punta Chiqueros**

■ Throne

Playa Corona 4

Playa San Francisco 5

Playa del Sol 6

El Cedral 7

■ **El Mirador**

8 **Parque Nacional Submarino de Palancar**

■ **Buena Vista**

■ **Cinco Puertas**

N

R E E F S

Laguna Colombia

Tumba del Caracol

11

9

Punta Celerain Lighthouse

10

KEY

🚢 Ferry

🚢 Cruise Ship

0 _____ 6 miles

0 _____ 9 km

strongly recommended.) The first Mass in Mexico was reportedly celebrated at this temple, most of which was torn down by the conquistadores. All that remains is a small structure capped by jungle growth; its Maya arch, best viewed from inside, is covered by faint traces of paint and stucco. Nearby, a small green-and-white cinder-block church is typical of rural Mexico. A number of crosses are shrouded in embroidered lace, and, during religious festivals, the simple room is adorned with folk art.

8 Backtrack to the coast and continue south, and you'll come to **Parque Nacional Submarino de Palancar,** whose beach, with a gently sloping shore enlivened by palm trees, is far more deserted than San Francisco. Offshore lies the famous **Palancar Reef,** which is practically Cozumel's raison d'être. Because of the diversity of coral formations and the dramatic underwater peaks and valleys, divers rank this reef among the top five in the world. There is a water sports center and a bar-café on the beach here.

9 At the island's southern tip and most commonly reached by boat (although there is a trail) is the **Laguna Colombia,** a prime site for jungle aficionados. Fish migrate here to lay their eggs, and barracuda, baby fish, and birds show up in great numbers in season. Popular diving and snorkeling spots can be found offshore in the reefs of **Tunich, Colombia,** and **Maracaibo.**

10 If you continue east on the paved road, you'll reach the eastern Caribbean coast. Make a right turn off the paved road onto a dirt road and follow it for 4 kilometers (3 miles) south to get to the **Punta Celerain Lighthouse,** surrounded by sand dunes at the narrowest point of land. The lighthouse affords a misty, mesmerizing view of pounding waves, swamps, and scraggly jungle. The point comes to life at midday when the lighthouse keeper serves fried fish and beer, and locals and tourists gather to chat.

11 After visiting the lighthouse, backtrack on the dirt road north. The east coast of Cozumel presents a splendid succession of mostly deserted rocky coves and narrow, powdery beaches—sadly garbage-strewn in spots—posed dramatically against astoundingly turquoise water. Swimming can be treacherous here if you go too far out or if a southwestern wind is blowing, but there is nothing to prevent solitary sunbathing on any of the several beaches. When you return to the paved road, you will first pass the **Tumba del Caracol,** another Maya ruin that may have served as a lighthouse. If you didn't eat at the Punta Celerain lighthouse, stop for a snack, some cold beer, and hot reggae tunes at the nearby **Paradise Café** (no ☎), the local hang-out on **Playa Paradiso.** A couple of minuscule ruins are in this area—**El Mirador** and the **Throne.**

12 **Punta Chiqueros,** a moon-shaped cove sheltered from the sea by an offshore reef, is the next attraction en route. Part of a longer stretch of beach that most locals call Playa Bonita—it's also known as Playa San Martin or *Tortuga Desnuda* (Naked Turtle)—it has fine sand, clear water, and moderate waves. You can swim and camp here, watch the sun set and the moon rise, and dine at the Playa Bonita restaurant-bar, which has fine fresh fish. A little less than 5 kilometers **13** (3 miles) away is **Playa Chen Río,** another good spot for camping or exploring, where the waters are clear and the surf is not too strong.

14 Nearly 1 kilometer (½ mile) north of Chen Río along the main road is **Punta Morena,** where waves crash on the rocky beach and, on June nights when the moon is full, turtles come to lay their eggs.

⑮ The cross-island road meets the east coast at **Mezcalito Café** on **Playa Oriente;** here you can take the cross-island road west toward town or continue north. If you choose the latter route, you'll need a four-wheel drive vehicle to travel on a rough dirt road that deadends past Punta Molas; eventually you'll have to turn around.

⑯ If you're headed towards town, it's worth making a detour inland to view the ruins of **San Gervasio,** the largest extant Maya and Toltec site on Cozumel. To get there, take the cross-island road west to the army airfield and turn right; follow this road north for 7 kilometers (4 miles). San Gervasio was once the island's capital and probably its ceremonial center, dedicated to the fertility goddess Ixchel. The classical- and postclassical-style site was continuously occupied from AD 300 to AD 1500. What remains today are several small mounds scattered around a plaza and several broken columns and lintels that were once part of the main building or observatory. Hire one of the English-speaking guides who wait at the entry to the site to explain the unlabeled ruins. ☛ *$1 access to road, $3.50 access to ruins.* ☉ *Daily 8–5.*

⑰ The road to the ruins is a good one, but a nearly unmaneuverable dirt road leads northeast of San Gervasio back to the unpaved coast road. At the junction is a marvelously deserted beach where you can camp. Heading north along this beach, you'll come to **Castillo Real,** another Maya site, comprising a lookout tower, the base of a pyramid, and a temple with two chambers capped by a false arch.

⑱ A number of other minor ruins are spread across the northern tip of Cozumel, which terminates at the **Punta Molas Lighthouse,** an excellent spot for sunbathing, birding, and camping. As noted above, this entire area is accessible only by four-wheel-drive vehicles (or by boat), but the jagged shoreline and the open sea offer magnificent views, making it well worth the trip.

⑲ Back on the leeward side of the island, north of town, is a long expanse of sandy beach known as **Playa San Juan,** which culminates in Punta Norte. The island's northern cluster of hotels occupies the sea side of the highway here; across the way are several restaurants. Just beyond Punta Norte, smack in the middle of Abrigo Bay, you'll

⑳ find **Isla de Pasión.** The secluded beaches of this tiny island are now part of a state reserve, and fishing is permitted. There are no facilities on the island, and since so few people go, there are no scheduled tours; you'll have to bargain with a local boat owner for transportation if you want to visit.

Shopping

Cozumel has three main shopping areas: **downtown** along the waterfront, on Avenida Rafael Melgar, and on some of the side streets around the plaza (there are more than 150 shops in this area alone); at the **crafts market** (Calle 1 S, behind the plaza) in town, which sells a respectable assortment of Mexican wares; and at the cruise-ship **passenger terminal** south of town, near the Casa Del Mar, La Ceiba, and Sol Caribe hotels. There are also small clusters of shops at **Plaza del Sol** (on the east side of the main plaza), **Villa Mar** (on the north side of the main plaza), and **Plaza Maya 2000** (across from the Sol Caribe). As a general rule, the newer, trendier shops line the waterfront, while the area around Avenida 5a houses the better crafts shops. The **town market** (Calle Rosada Salas, between Avs. 20a and 25a) sells fresh produce and other essentials.

Department Stores

Pama (Av. Rafael Melgar S 9, ☎ 987/2–00–90), near the pier, features imported food, luggage, snorkeling gear, jewelry, and crystal. **Prococo** (Av. Rafael Melgar N 99, ☎ 987/2–18–75 or 987/2–19–64) offers a good selection of liquor, jewelry, and gift items. **Duty Free Mexico** (Av. Rafael Melgar at Calle 3 S, ☎ 987/2–07–96) puts a strong emphasis on top-line fragrances.

Specialty Stores

CLOTHING

Several trendy sportswear stores line Avenida Rafael Melgar (between Calles 2 and 6). Try **Aca Joe** (Av. Rafael Melgar 101, ☎ 987/2–36–77), a Mexican-based chain, for casual resort wear in the latest styles. **Explora** (Av. Rafael Melgar 49, ☎ 987/2–03–16) offers a casual line of modish cotton sports clothing. **La Fiesta Cotton Country** (Av. Rafael Melgar N 164-B, ☎ 987/2–20–32), a large store catering to the cruise ships, sells a variety of T-shirts as well as souvenirs.

JEWELRY

Jewelry on Cozumel is pricey, but it tends to be of higher quality than the jewelry you'll find in many of the other Yucatán towns. **Casablanca** (Av. Rafael Melgar N 33, ☎ 987/2–11–77) specializes in gold, silver, and gemstones, as well as expensive crafts. As its name suggests, the new **Colombian Emeralds International** (Av. Rafael Melgar 341, ☎ 987/2–12–51) features the sparkling green jewels, as well as other precious rocks and minerals. The toney **Van Cleef & Arpels** (Av. Rafael Melgar N 54, ☎ 987/2–11–43) offers a superlative collection of high-end silver and gold jewelry.

MEXICAN CRAFTS

Los Cinco Soles (Av. Rafael Melgar N 27, ☎ 987/2–01–32 or 987/2–20–40) is your best bet for one-stop shopping. The nearly block-long store features an excellent variety of well-priced, well-displayed items, including blue-rim glassware, brass and tin animals from Jalisco, Mexican fashions and silver jewelry. **Talavera** (Av. 5a S 349, ☎ 987/2–01–71) carries beautiful ceramics from all over Mexico—including tiles from the Yucatán—as well as masks from Guerrero, brightly painted wooden animals from Oaxaca, and carved chests from Guadalajara.

Sports and the Outdoors

Most people come to Cozumel to take advantage of the island's water-related sports—scuba diving, snorkeling, and fishing (*see below*) are particularly big, but jetskiing, sailboarding, waterskiing, and sailing remain popular as well. You will find services and rentals throughout the island, especially through major hotels and watersports centers such as **Del Mar Aquatics** (Carretera a Chankanaab Km 4, ☎ 987/2–16–65 or 800/877–4383, FAX 987/2–18–33) and **Aqua Safari** (Av. Rafael Melgar 429 between Calles 5 and 10 S, ☎ 987/2–01–01).

Fishing

The waters off Cozumel swarm with more than 230 species of fish, the numbers upholding the island's reputation as one of the world's best locations for trolling, deep-sea fishing, and bottom fishing. Beaky jawed billfish—including swordfish, blue marlin, white marlin, and sailfish—are plentiful here in late April through June, their migration season. World records for catches are frequently set on the island in these months.

High-speed fishing boats can be chartered for $300 for a half day or $350 for a full day, for a maximum of six people, from the **Club Naútico de Cozumel** (Puerto de Abrigo, Av. Rafael Melgar, Box 341, ☎ 987/2–01–18 or 800/253–2701, FAX 987/2–11–35), the island's headquarters for game fishing. Daily charters are easily arranged from the dock or at your hotel, but you might also try **Aquarius Fishing and Tours** (Calle 3 S, ☎ 987/2–10–92) or **Yucab Reef Diving & Fishing** (Av. Rosado Salas 85 between Av. Rafael Melgar and Av. 5 S., ☎ 987/2–41–10 or ☎ and FAX 987/2–18–42). All rates vary with the season.

Scuba Diving

With more than 30 charted reefs whose average depths range from 50 to 80 feet and a water temperature that hits about 75°F–80°F during peak diving season (June–August, when hotel rates are coincidentally at their lowest), Cozumel is far and away Mexico's number-one diving destination. The diversity of options includes deep dives, drift dives, shore dives, wall dives, and night dives, as well as theme dives focusing on ecology, archaeology, sunken ships, and photography. With all the shops to choose from, divers, especially those with less experience or who don't bring their own equipment, should look for high safety standards and documented credentials. Make sure your instructor has PADI certification (or FMAS, the Mexican equivalent) and is affiliated with the **SSS recompression chamber** (Calle 5 S 21B, between Av. Rafael Melgar and Av. 5a S, next to Discover Cozumel, ☎ 987/2–23–87 and 987/2–18–48) or the recompression chamber at the **Hospital Civil** (Av. 11 S, between Calles 10 and 15, ☎ 987/2–01–40 or 987/2–05–25).

DIVE SHOPS AND TOUR OPERATORS

Most dive shops can provide you with all the incidentals you'll need, as well as with guides and transportation. You can choose from a variety of two-tank boat trips and specialty dives ranging from $45 to $60; three-hour resort courses cost about $50–$60, and 1½-hour night dives, $30–$35. Basic certification courses, such as PADI's Discover Scuba or Naui's introductory course, are available for about $350, while advanced certification courses cost as much as $700. Equipment rental is relatively inexpensive, ranging from $6 for tanks or a lamp to about $8–$10 for a regulator and B.C. vest; underwater cameras rentals can cost as much as $35, video camera rentals run about $75, and professionally shot and edited videos of your own dive are priced at about $160.

Because dive shops tend to be competitive, it is well worth your while to shop around when choosing a dive operator. In addition to the dive shops in town, many hotels have their own operations and offer dive and hotel packages starting at about $350 for three nights, double occupancy, and two days of diving. You can also pick up a copy of the *Chart of the Reefs of Cozumel* in any dive shop. Before choosing a shop among the many choices, check credentials, look over the boats and equipment, and consult experienced divers who are familiar with the operators here. Here's a list to get you started on your search: **Aqua Safari** (Av. Rafael Melgar 429 between Calles 5 and 10 S, ☎ 987/2–01–01); **Blue Angel** (Av. Rafael Melgar, next to Hotel Villablanca, ☎ 987/2–16–31), for PADI certification; **Blue Bubble** (Av. 5a S at Calle 3 S, ☎ 987/2–18–65), for PADI instruction; **Dive Paradise** (Av. Rafael Melgar 601, ☎ and FAX 987/2–10–07; also at Calle 3 S and Av. Rafael Melgar, ☎ 987/2–27–46); **Fantasia Divers** (Av. 25 at Calle Adolfo Rosado Salas, ☎ 987/2–28–40 or 800/336–3483, FAX 987/2–12–10);

Michelle's Dive Shop (Av. 5 S. 201 at Calle Adolfo Rosado Salas, ☎ 987/2–09–47); **Ramone Zapata Divers** (Chankanaab Nature Park, ☎ 987/2–05–02); **Scuba Du** (Hotel Presidente Inter-Continental Cozumel, ☎ 987/2–03–22 or 987/2–13–79, FAX 987/2–41–30); **Studio Blue** (Calle Rosado Salas 121 between Calles 5 and 10, ☎ and FAX 987/2–43–30); **Tico's Dive Center** (Av. 5 N 121 between Calles 2 and 4, ☎ and FAX 987/2–02–76); **Yucab Reef** (Av. Rosado Salas 85 between Av. Rafael Melgar and Av. 5 S., ☎ 987/2–41–10 or ☎ and FAX 987/2–18–42).

Snorkeling

There is good snorkeling in the morning off the piers at the Hotel Presidente Inter-Continental and La Ceiba, where fish are fed. The shallow reefs in Chankanaab Bay, Playa San Francisco, and the northern beach at the Club Cozumel Caribe also provide clear views of brilliantly colored fish and sea creatures.

Tour operators that specialize in snorkeling include **Fiesta Cozumel** (☎ 987/2–07–25, 987/2–04–33, or 987/2–13–89) and **Caribe Tours** (☎ and FAX 987/2–31–00 or 987/2–31–54). As its name suggests, **Snorkozumel** (Av. Rafael E. Melgar 471, ☎ 987/2–41–66) is devoted to running snorkeling excursions. Locals say that the best snorkeling trips are aboard *El Zorro* (*see* Guided Tours *in* Cozumel Essentials, *below*), a 35-passenger, 45-foot catamaran with a huge sun deck, operated by Fiesta Cozumel. Directly off the beach, excellent snorkeling is to be had near La Ceiba, the Presidente Inter-Continental, and the Fiesta Americana Cozumel Reef, as well as at Chankanaab and Playa Corona; snorkeling equipment is available for less than $10 a day at these locations.

Dining

Dining options on Cozumel reflect the nature of the place as a whole, with some harmless pretension at times but mainly the insouciant, natural style of the tropical island. More than 80 restaurants in the downtown area alone offer a broad choice, from air-conditioned fast food outlets and Americanized places serving Continental fare and seafood in semiformal "nautical" settings to simple outdoor eateries that specialize in fish. Casual dress and no reservations are the rule in most moderate ($$) and inexpensive ($) Cozumel restaurants. In expensive ($$$) restaurants, you would not be out of place if you dressed up, and reservations are advised.

CATEGORY	COST*
$$$	$25–$35
$$	$15–25
$	under $15

per person, excluding drinks, service, and tax

$$$ ★ **Arrecife.** A well-trained staff and impeccably prepared seafood and Mediterranean fare put this hotel restaurant in a class by itself. Tall windows and excellent views of the sea complement the stylish decor—potted palms, white wicker furniture, pink walls—while musicians, who play regularly, further enhance the romantic mood. However, the restaurant is only open on a regular basis four months out of the year. ✗ *Hotel Presidente Inter-Continental Cozumel,* ☎ *987/2–03–22. AE, DC, MC, V. Closed Feb.–June and Sept.–Nov.*

$$$ **La Cabaña del Pescador.** To get to this rustic palapa-covered hut, you've got to cross a gangplank, but it's worth it if you're looking for well-prepared fresh lobster. The tails are sold by weight, and the

rest—including a delicious eggnog-type drink served at the end of the meal—is on the house. Seashells and nets hang from the walls of this small, dimly lit room, and geese stroll outside. ✕ *Carretera San Juan Km 4, across from Playa Azul Hotel north of town, no ☎. No credit cards. No lunch.*

$$ El Capi Navegante. Locals say you'll find the best seafood in town here: The captain's motto is: "The fish we serve today slept in the sea last night." Specialties like whole red snapper and stuffed squid are skillfully prepared and sometimes flambéed at your table. Highly recommended dishes include conch ceviche and deep-fried whole snapper. Nautical blue-and-white decor adds personality to this place. ✕ *Av. 10a S 312 at Calle 3, ☎ 987/2–17–30. AE, MC, V.*

$$ La Choza. Home-cooked Mexican food—primarily from the capital
★ and among the best in town—is the order of the day at this family-run establishment. Dona Elisa Espinosa's specialties include chicken mole, red snapper in sweet mustard sauce, and grilled lobster; meals come with soup (onion and tortilla are the best) and fresh tortillas. In 1993, the Espinosa family opened La Choza Grill (Carretera Chankanaab Km 3.5, across from Sol Caribe, ☎ 987/2–49–20), featuring dishes from Jamaica, Cuba, Belize, and Guatemala; and in 1994, they initiated Agua Salada (☎ 987/2–09–58), focussing entirely on seafood. It's half a block down from La Choza on Calle Rosada Salas. ✕ *Calle Rosada Salas 198 at Av. 10a S, ☎ 987/2–09–58. AE, MC, V.*

$$ Pancho's Backyard. A jungle of greenery and trickling fountains set
★ the tone at this inviting restaurant on the cool patio of Los Cincos Soles shopping center. The menu highlights local standards such as black bean soup, *carmone al carbon* (grilled prawns), and fajitas. Round out your meal with coconut ice cream in Kahlua. ✕ *Av. Rafael Melgar N 27 at Calle 8 N, ☎ 987/2–21–41. AE, MC, V. Closed Sun. No lunch Sat.*

$$ Rincón Maya. Spicy Yucatecan specialties are the order of the day in this festive, friendly eatery. Miguel Mena Mendosa serves up fresh seafood, beef, pork, and chicken prepared with *achiote* and other traditional herbs used in Maya cooking. Colorful piñatas, flags, and fish hang from the ceiling, while hats and masks line the walls. ✕ *Av. 5a S between Calles 3 and 5, ☎ 987/2–04–67. No credit cards. No lunch.*

$ Café Caribe. Coffee junkies and folks with a serious sweet tooth flock
★ to the little L-shaped Café Caribe for the mouth-watering selection of coffees, ice cream, and freshly baked cakes, pies, and muffins. It's the perfect spot for both breakfast and after-dinner coffee and dessert. ✕ *10 Av. S 215, ☎ 987/2–36–21. No credit cards. Closed Sun. No lunch.*

$ El Foco. A *taqueria* serving pork, *chorizo* (spicy Mexican sausage), and cheese-soft tacos, this eatery also does ribs and steak. Graffitied walls and plain wood tables make it a casual, fun spot to grab a bite and a *cerveza*. ✕ *Av. 5 S 13-B between Calle Rosado Salas and Calle 3, no ☎. No credit cards.*

$ Prima Pasta & Pizza Trattoria. This Northern Italian diner just off the plaza has a strong following of patrons who come for hearty, inexpensive pizzas, calzone, sandwiches, and pastas. The breezy dining area, on the second floor terrace above the kitchen, smells heavenly and has a charming Mediterranean mural painted on two walls. Business has been so good that the owner, Texan Albert Silmai, branched out in 1994, opening Rio Grande, a tiny Tex-Mex diner, just a few doors down (at Calle Rosado Salas 113). ✕ *Calle Rosado Salas 109, ☎ 987/2–42–42. MC, V.*

Lodging

Cozumel's hotels are in three main areas, all on the island's western, or leeward, side: in town, and north and south of town. Because of the proximity of the reefs, divers and snorkelers tend to congregate at the southern properties. Sailors and anglers, on the other hand, prefer the hotels to the north, where the beaches are better. Most budget hotels are in town. All hotels have air-conditioning unless otherwise noted, and all hotels share the 77600 postal code.

CATEGORY	COST*
$$$$	over $160
$$$	$90–$160
$$	$40–$90
$	under $40

All prices are for a standard double room, excluding 10% tax.

$$$$ **Meliá Mayan Peradisus.** Lush tropical foliage and spectacular sunsets over the beach combine with modern architecture and amenities to make this property north of town memorable. Large windows in the light, cheerful lobby look out onto a pool and swim-up palapa snack bar. Standard rooms are attractively decorated with colorful tropical-print bedspreads and light-wood furniture; superior rooms are larger and have balconies overlooking the water. This resort turned all-inclusive in late 1994, bringing on an international staff of entertainers and activity coordinators to keep guests happily busy. There are plans for a golf course and 25 more rooms. ☎ *Box 9, Carretera a Sta. Pilar 6,* ☎ *987/2–05–23, 987/2–04–11, or 800/336–3542,* FAX *987/2–15–99. 200 rooms. 3 restaurants, 3 bars, 2 pools, hot tub, spa, saunas, beach, dive shop, bicycles, miniature golf, horseback riding, 2 tennis courts, disco, playground. AE, MC, V.*

$$$$ **Presidente Inter-Continental Cozumel.** This hotel exudes luxury, from
★ the courteous, prompt, and efficient service to the tastefully decorated interior. The Presidente is famed not only for possessing one of the best restaurants on the island, Arrecife (*see* Dining, *above*), but also for its respectable and professional water-sports center. Located on its own broad, white beach near the end of the southern hotel zone, the property ranks among the best on the island for snorkeling. All rooms are done in bright, contemporary colors with cedar furnishings; deluxe rooms, with private terraces, are huge. Complimentary coffee is delivered to your room at the time of your wake-up call. ☎ *Carretera a Chankanaab Km 6.5,* ☎ *987/2–03–22, 987/2–15–20, or 800/327–0200,* FAX *987/2–13–20. 253 rooms. 2 restaurants, coffee shop, 3 bars, no-smoking rooms, pool, dive shop, motorbikes, 2 tennis courts, car rental. AE, DC, MC, V.*

$$$ **Fiesta Americana Cozumel Reef.** Located on the less developed southern end of the island, near the Hotel Presidente Inter-Continental and Chankanaab, the hotel's beach offers easy access to spectacular underwater scenery. The high-ceilinged lobby, with its rattan furniture and polished marble floors, hosts a glitzy silver shop featuring some unusual pieces. Standard rooms are large, with sea-green headboards and well-made light-wood furnishings; all have balconies looking out on the ocean as well as hairdryers and direct-dial phones. ☎ *Carretera a Chankanaab Km 7.5,* ☎ *987/2–26–22 or 800/FIESTA–1,* FAX *987/ 2–26–66. 162 rooms. 3 restaurants, 3 bars, no-smoking rooms, 2 pools, exercise room, jogging, dive shop, motorbikes, 2 tennis courts, car rental. AE, MC, V.*

$$$ Fiesta Inn. This three-story Spanish-roofed structure, south of town and across the street from the beach, has a comfortable lobby with a fountain and garden, brightly decorated modern rooms with Moorish archways, a large pool, and an international dining facility. Fully carpeted rooms are painted light blue, with cream-color wicker furniture and private balconies. Request a room on the third floor (the rate is the same) for an ocean view. The sing-along Laser-Karaoke Bar draws exhibitionists from all over town. We've received complaints of spotty maintenance and cleanliness, but encountered no problems on our last visit here. ☎ *Carretera a Chankanaab Km 1.7,* ☎ *987/2–28–11, 987/2–28–99, or 800/FIESTA–1,* FAX *987/2–21–54. 180 rooms. Restaurant, 2 bars, no-smoking rooms, pool, hot tub, bicycles, motorbikes, tennis court. AE, MC, V.*

$$$ Galápago Inn. This pretty white stucco hotel just south of town primarily accommodates divers; the simply-furnished, brightly tiled rooms are not sold by the night but exclusively as part of dive packages—booked in Houston—that take full advantage of the hotel's expert diving staff and advanced certification diving school. The central garden, with tiled benches and a small fountain, contributes to the inn's Mediterranean feel. The staff here are cheerful and accommodating. ☎ *Carretera a Chankanaab Km 1.5,* ☎ *987/2–06–63 or 800/847–5708. 58 rooms. Restaurant, bar, pool, beach. AE, MC, V.*

$$ Casa del Mar. Located south of town near several boutiques, sports
★ shops, and restaurants, this three-story hotel is frequented by divers. An unpretentious but tasteful lobby, which has natural wood banisters and overlooks a small garden, exemplifies the overall simplicity of the place. Cheerful rooms feature yellow-tiled headboards, nightstands, and sinks; Mexican artwork; and small balconies with views of the pool just outside or the sea across the road. The bilevel cabañas, which sleep three or four, are a very good buy at $115. ☎ *Box 129, Carretera a Chankanaab Km 4,* ☎ *987/2–19–44 or 800/877–4383,* FAX *987/2–18–55. 98 rooms, 8 cabañas. 2 restaurants, 2 bars, pool, hot tub, dive shop. AE, MC, V.*

$$ Villas Las Anclas. Conveniently located parallel to the malecón, these
★ villas are actually furnished apartments for rent by the day, week, or month. The duplexes include a downstairs sitting room, dining area, and a kitchenette; a spiral staircase leads up to a small bedroom with a large desk (but no phone or TV). Rooms are extremely attractive, with tastefully bright patterns set off against white walls. Each apartment is stocked with fresh coffee and a coffeemaker, not that you need a waker-up: The roosters next door get rather rowdy around sunrise. ☎ *Box 25, Av. 5a S 325 between Calles 3 and 5 S,* ☎ *987/2–19–55,* ☎ *and* FAX *987/2–14–03. 7 units. Kitchenettes. No credit cards.*

$ Bazar Colonial. This attractive, modern three-story hotel, located over a small cluster of shops, has pretty, red-tile floors and bougainvillea, which add splashes of color. Natural wood furniture, TVs (a recent addition), kitchenettes, bookshelves, sofa beds, and an elevator make up for the lack of other amenities, such as a restaurant and a pool. ☎ *Av. 5a S 9 near Calle 3 S,* ☎ *987/2–05–06,* FAX *987/2–05–42 or 987/2–02–11. 28 rooms. Kitchenettes. AE, MC, V.*

$ Mesón San Miguel. Situated right on the square, this hotel sees a lot
★ of action because of the accessibility of its large public bar and outdoor café, which are often filled with locals. The remodeled rooms are clean and functional, with air-conditioning, satellite TV, phones, and balconies overlooking the plaza—amenities unusual in a budget hotel, making this a good bet for your money. ☎ *Av. Juárez 2 Bis,* ☎

*987/2–03–23, 987/2–02–33, or 800/783–8384, FAX 987/2–18–20. 100
rooms. Bar, café, pool, recreation room. MC, V.*

The Arts and Nightlife

Although Cozumel doesn't have much in the way of highbrow performing arts per se, it does offer visitors an opportunity to attend performances that reflect the island's heritage, including Fiesta Mexicana
nights at the **Fiesta Americana Hotel** (☎ 987/2–26–22). The shows,
offered Thursday and Sunday from 6 to 9 PM during high season, feature folkloric dancers, mariachis, a cock fight, an open-bar buffet dinner, and tequila shots; the cost is about $70.

Bars

For a quiet drink and good people-watching, try **Video Bar Aladino** at
the Mesón San Miguel, at the northern end of the plaza. Serious bar-
hoppers like **Carlos 'n' Charlie's** (Av. Rafael Melgar 11, between
Calles 2 and 4 N, ☎ 987/2–01–91) for hang-on-the-rafters, raucous
fun; don't come here if you're the retiring type. Folks are always
spilling out over the outdoor patio (sometimes literally) at **Chilly's**
(Av. Rafael Melgar near Av. Benito Juárez, ☎ 987/2–18–32), where a
papier mâché Marilyn Monroe in a *Some Like It Hot* pose surveys a
rowdy crowd. The new **Hard Rock Cafe** (Av. Rafael Melgar 2A near
Av. Benito Juárez, no phone at press time) wasn't yet open when we
visited, but it promises to include all the nostalgic music memorabilia
that characterizes the international chain. You and your friends provide the entertainment at the sing-along **Laser-Karaoke Bar** (Fiesta
Inn, ☎ 987/2–28–11). Jock types can play video games or check out
football scores at the **Sports Page Video Bar and Restaurant** (corner
5 Av. N and Calle 2 N, ☎ 987/2–11–99).

Live Music

The piano bar in **La Gaviota** (Sol Caribe Cozumel Hotel, ☎
987/2–07–00, ext. 251), is well attended, and trios and mariachis perform nightly in the lobby bar from 5 to 11 during high season. For
romantic piano or guitar serenades, try the dining room of **Arrecife**
(Hotel Presidente Inter-Continental Cozumel, ☎ 987/2–03–22; high
season only). In addition to tasty lobster dishes, **Joe's Lobster House**
(Av. 10 S 229 between Calle Rosada Salas and Calle 3 S, ☎ 987/
2–32–75) serves up hot reggae and salsa every night at 10:30 PM; this
is *the* hot spot for live entertainment.

Cozumel Essentials

Arriving and Departing

BY PLANE

The **Cozumel Airport** (☎ 987/2–09–28) is 3 kilometers (2 miles) north
of town. **Continental** (☎ 987/2–04–87, 800/231–0856) provides nonstop service from Houston. **Mexicana** (☎ 987/2–01–57, 800/531–
7921) flies nonstop from Miami and San Francisco; **Aerocaribe** (☎
987/2–09–28) and **Aerocozumel** (☎987/2–08–77), both Mexicana subsidiaries, fly to Cancún and other destinations in Mexico, including
Chichén Itzá, Chetumal, Mérida, and Playa del Carmen. The airport
departure tax is $12.

Between the Airport and Hotels. Because of an agreement between the
taxi drivers' and the bus drivers' unions, there is no taxi service from
the airport; taxi service is available *to* the airport, however. Arriving
passengers reach their hotels via the *colectivo*, a van with a maximum
capacity of eight. Buy a ticket at the airport exit: the charge is $5 per

passenger to the hotel zones, a little under $3 into town. If you want to get to your hotel without waiting for the van to fill and for other passengers to be dropped off, you can hire an *especial*—an individual van costing a little under $20 to the hotel zones, about $8 to the city. Taxis to the airport cost about $8 from the hotel zones and approximately $5 from downtown.

BY FERRY

Passenger-only ferries depart from the dock at **Playa del Carmen** (no ☎) for the 40-minute trip to the main pier in Cozumel (*see* Exploring *in* Mexico's Caribbean Coast, *below* for details on Playa del Carmen). They leave approximately every hour between 5:15 AM and 8:45 PM and cost about $7 one way, $10 round trip. Return service to Playa operates from roughly 4 AM to 7:45 PM. Verify the regularly changing schedule. The car ferry from **Puerto Morelos** (☎ 987/2–17–22), on the mainland to the north of Playa del Carmen, is not recommended unless you *must* bring your car. The three- to four-hour trip costs about $30 depending on the size of the car or $4.50 per passenger. Again, schedules change frequently, so call ahead. Tickets can be bought up to a day in advance.

BY JETFOIL

A waterjet catamaran and two large speed boats make the trip between Cozumel (downtown pier, at the zócalo) and Playa del Carmen. This service, operated by **Aviomar** (☎ 987/2–05–88 or 987/2–04–77), costs the same as the ferry and takes almost as much time, but the vessel is considerably more comfortable and offers on-board videos and refreshments. The boats make at least ten crossings a day, leaving Playa del Carmen approximately every one to two hours between 5:15 AM and 8:45 PM and returning from Cozumel between 4 AM and 8 PM. Tickets are sold at the piers in both ports one hour before departure; call to confirm the schedule.

BY CRUISE SHIP

At least a dozen cruise lines call at Cozumel and/or Playa del Carmen, including, from Fort Lauderdale, **Costa** (☎ 800/327–2537), **Cunard/Crown** (☎ 800/221–4770), and **Princess** (☎ 800/568–3262); from Miami, **Carnival** (☎ 800/327–9501), **Chandris/Celebrity** (☎ 800/437–3111), **Dolphin/Majesty** (☎ 800/222–1003), **Norwegian** (☎ 800/327–7030), and **Royal Caribbean** (☎ 800/327–6700); from New Orleans, **Commodore** (☎ 800/327–5617); and from Tampa, **Holland America** (☎ 800/426–0327).

Getting Around

BY BUS

Because of a union agreement with taxi drivers, no public buses operate in the north and south hotel zones; local bus service runs mainly within the town of San Miguel, although there is a route from town to the airport. Service is irregular but inexpensive (under 20¢).

BY CAR

Open-air Jeeps and other rental cars, especially those with four-wheel drive, are a good way of getting down dirt roads leading to secluded beaches and small Maya ruins (although the rental insurance policy may not always cover these jaunts). The only gas station on Cozumel, at the corner of Avenida Juárez and Avenida 30a, is open daily 7 AM–midnight.

Car Rentals. Following is a list of rental firms that handle two-and four-wheel-drive vehicles (all the major hotels have rental offices): **Budget** (Av. 5a at Calle 2 N, ☎ 987/2–09–03; at the cruise-ship terminal, ☎ 987/2–17–32; and at the airport, ☎ 987/2–17–42), **Hertz** (airport, ☎ 987/2–38–88), **National Interrent** (Av. Juárez, Lote 10, near Calle 10, ☎ 987/2–32–63 or 987/2–41–01), and **Rentadora Aguilla** (Av. Rafael Melgar 685, ☎ 987/2–07–29). Rental rates start at $50 a day.

BY BIKE, MOPED, AND MOTORCYCLE

Mopeds and motorcycles are very popular here, but also extremely dangerous. Mexican law now requires all passengers to wear helmets; it's a $25 fine if you don't. For mopeds, go to **Auto Rent** (Carretera Costera S, ☎ 987/2–08–44, ext. 712), **Rentadora Caribe** (Calle Rosada Salas 3, ☎ 987/2–09–55 or 987/2–09–61), **Rentadora Chac** (Calle 1 S 101 between Av. 10 and 15, ☎ 987/2–33–25), or **Rentadora Cozumel** (Calle Rosada Salas 3 B, ☎ 987/2–14–29, and Av. 10a S at Calle 1, ☎ 987/2–11–20). Mopeds go for about $25 per day; insurance is included. Auto Rent and Rentadora Chac also rent bicycles for approximately $5–$8 per day.

BY TAXI

Taxi service is available 24 hours a day, with a 25% surcharge between midnight and 6 AM, at the main location (Calle 2 N, ☎ 987/2–00–41 or 987/2–02–36) or at the *malecón,* as the oceanside walkway is called, at the main pier in town. You can also hail taxis on the street, and there are taxis waiting at all the major hotels. Fixed rates of about $3 are charged to go between town and either hotel zone, about $8 from most hotels to the airport.

Guided Tours

ORIENTATION

Island tours are offered for about $35 by at least two of Cozumel's leading travel agencies. The **Intermar Caribe** (☎ 987/2–15–35) version includes swimming at a beach on the windward side, a visit to a "coral factory" in town, and snorkeling and lunch at Chankanaab. **Caribe Tours** (Av. Rafael Melgar at Calle 5 S, ☎ and FAX 987/2–31–00 or 987/2–31–54) sells a similar tour, focusing on the botanical gardens, archaeological replicas, and reef snorkeling at Chankanaab; the cost is about $40 and includes an open-bar lunch.

SPECIALTY TOURS

Snorkeling tours go for anywhere from $25 to $50, depending on the length, and take in the shallow reefs off Palancar, Colombia, and Yucab. Contact **Snorkozumel** (☎ 987/2–41–66 or 987/2–02–46) or **Caribe Tours** for information and reservations. **Fiesta Cozumel** (☎ 987/2–09–25 or 987/2–13–89) runs snorkeling tours from the 45-foot catamaran, *El Zorro.* Rates begin at about $50 per day and include equipment, a guide, soft drinks and beer, and a box lunch. The *Zorro* and the 60-foot catamaran *Fury* are also used for sunset cruises; the cost is under $35 for unlimited domestic drinks and live entertainment. You can book either of these sunset cruises through Caribe Tours.

Glass-bottom-boat trips provided by **Turismo Aviomar** (☎ 987/2–05–88) and Fiesta Cozumel appeal to people who don't want to get wet but do want to see the brilliant underwater life around the island. The air-conditioned semi-submarines glide over a number of reefs that host a dazzling array of fish; the tours, which cost about $30, last 1 hour and 45 minutes and include soft drinks.

Off-island tours to Tulum and Xel-Há, run by **Intermar Caribe** and **Caribe Tours,** cost about $75 and include the 30-minute ferry trip to

Playa del Carmen, the 45-minute bus ride to Tulum, 1½–2 hours at the ruins, entrance fees, guides, lunch, and a stop for snorkeling at Xel-Há lagoon.

Rancho Buenavista (☎ 987/2–15–37) offers four-hour guided horseback tours that visit three Maya ruins tucked away in Cozumel's tropical forest. The tour departs from Restaurant Acuario (Av. Rafael Melgar at Calle 11), weekdays at noon and Saturday at 11; the price ($60) includes transportation to the ranch and soft drinks or beer during the tour.

Important Addresses and Numbers

EMERGENCIES

Police (Anexo del Palacio Municipal, ☎ 987/2–00–92); **Red Cross** (Av. Rosada Salas at Av. 20a S, ☎ 987/2–10–58); **Air Ambulance** (☎ 987/2–09–12); **Recompression Chamber** (Calle 5 S 21-B, between Av. Rafael Melgar and Av. 5a S, ☎ 987/2–23–87).

ENGLISH-LANGUAGE BOOKSTORES

Publiciones Gracia (east side of the plaza, ☎ 987/2–00–31) carries a limited selection of guidebooks and English-language publications and is open Monday–Saturday 8–2 and 4–10 and Sunday 9–1 and 5–10.

LATE-NIGHT PHARMACIES

Farmacia Joaquín (plaza, ☎ 987/2–01–25) is open Monday–Saturday 8 AM–10 PM and Sunday 9–1 and 5–9.

VISITOR INFORMATION

The **state tourism office** (☎ 987/2–09–72) is upstairs in the Plaza del Sol mall, at the east end of the main square, or *la plaza,* and is open weekdays 9–2:30. A good source of information on lodgings (and many other things) is the **Cozumel Island Hotel Association** (Calle 2 N at 15a, ☎ 987/2–31–32, FAX 987/2–28–09), open weekdays 8–2 and 4–7.

MEXICO'S CARIBBEAN COAST

Updated by
Maribeth
Mellin

Above all else, beaches are what define the eastern coast of the Yucatán peninsula. White, sandy strands with offshore coral reefs, oversize tropical foliage and jungle, Maya ruins, and abundant wildlife make the coastline a marvelous destination for lovers of the outdoors. The scrubby limestone terrain is mostly flat and dry, punctuated only by sinkholes, while the shores are broken up by freshwater lagoons, underwater caves, and cliffs.

The various destinations on the coast cater to different preferences. The once laid-back town of Playa del Carmen is now host to resorts as glitzy as those found in Cancún and Cozumel, though still not quite as expensive, while the lazy fishing village of Puerto Morelos so far has been only slightly altered to accommodate foreign tourists. Rustic fishing and scuba diving lodges on the even more secluded Boca Paila and Xcalak peninsulas are gaining a well-deserved reputation for fly-fishing and superb diving on virgin reefs. The beaches, from Punta Bete to Sian Ka'an, south of Tulum, are beloved by scuba divers, snorkelers, birders, and beachcombers, and offer accommodations to suit every budget, from campsites and bungalows to condos and luxury hotels. Ecotourism is on the rise, with special programs designed to involve visitors in preserving the threatened sea-turtle population. Then, too, there are the Maya ruins at Tulum, superbly situated on a bluff overlooking the Caribbean, and, a short distance inland, at Cobá, whose towering pyramids evoke the magnificence of Tikal in Guatemala. At the Belizean border is Chetumal, a modern port and the capital of Quintana Roo; with its dilapidated clapboard houses and sultry sea air, it is more Central American than Mexican. The waters up and down the coast, littered with shipwrecks and relics from the heyday of piracy, are dotted with mangrove swamps and minuscule islands where only the birds hold sway.

Exploring

Numbers in the margin correspond to points of interest on the Mexico's Caribbean Coast map.

Our north–south exploration of the Caribbean coast takes you from Puerto Morelos to Chetumal, with brief detours inland to the ruins of Cobá and Kohunlich. **Puerto Morelos,** a small coastal town about 36 kilometers (22 miles) south of Cancún, is home to the car ferry that travels to Cozumel. The town has been left remarkably free of the large-scale development so common farther south, though each year more and more tourists stop here to take in its easygoing pace, cheap accommodations, and convenient seaside location near a superb offshore coral reef. For obvious reasons, this place is particularly attractive to divers, snorkelers, and anglers. The reef at Morelos—about 1,800 feet offshore—has claimed many ships over the centuries, and nowadays divers visit the sunken wrecks. Snorkeling gear, fishing tackle, and boats can be rented from the **Aqua Deportes** (no ☎) dive shop on the town's main beach.

About 32 kilometers (20 miles) south of Puerto Morelos is **Punta Bete,** a 6½-kilometer (4-mile) white sand beach between rocky lagoons. This point is the setting for several bungalow-style hotels that have almost become cult places for travelers who love being in or on the water. All the properties are set off from Route 307 at the end of a 2³⁄₁₀-kilometer (1²⁄₅-mile) rutted road.

A 10-minute drive farther south will take you to **Playa del Carmen,** a once-deserted beach where only a few decades ago indigenous families raised coconut palms to produce copra. Nowadays its alabaster-white beach and small offshore reefs lend themselves to excellent swimming, snorkeling, and turtle-watching, and the town has become the preferred destination of travelers who want easy access to gorgeous beaches and the archaeological sights of Yucatán.

The busiest parts of Playa are down by the **ferry pier,** around the **main plaza,** and along the **pedestrian walkway.** Take a stroll north from the pier along the beach and you'll see the essence of the town: simple restaurants roofed with palm fronds, where people sit around drinking beer for hours; a few campgrounds; and lots of hammocks. On the south side of the pier is **Playacar,** a first-class, lavish hotel that brought a sense of luxury and style to Playa del Carmen in 1991. Two more hotels, the all-inclusive **Diamond Resort** and the all-inclusive **Caribbean Village,** have opened in the Playacar complex, and the development's 18-hole championship golf course opened in 1994. If you walk away from the beach, you'll come upon the affluent section: several condominium projects and well-tended gardens and lawns that can be seen from the street. From here, only the sandy streets, the small vestiges of Maya structures, and the stunning turquoise sea on the horizon suggest you're in the tropics. The streets at both ends of town peter out into the jungle.

Six kilometers (4 miles) south of Playa is a paved road leading to **Xcaret,** a 250-acre ecological theme park on a gorgeous stretch of coastline. Maya ruins are scattered over the property, which has been lushly landscaped into a vivid green oasis set against gray limestone and the turquoise sea. On the underground river ride, visitors don life jackets and float with the cool water's currents through a series of caves. At the educational Dolphinarium, visitors can attend a dolphin workshop ($20) and even swim with the dolphins ($60); only 36 people are allowed in the water with the dolphins each day, so arrive early to sign up for your slot. The man-made beach, breakwater, and lagoons are perfect for snorkeling and swimming; instruction and water-sports equipment rentals are available. Xcaret also includes a botanical garden, a museum with reproductions of the Yucatán peninsula's main archaeological sites, stables with riding demonstrations, a dive shop, and several restaurants. Transportation is available from Cancún and Playa del Carmen on colorfully decorated buses. ☎ *in Cancún 98/83–06–54 or 98/83–07–43.* ☛ *$25.* ⊙ *Oct.–Mar., daily 8:30–5; Apr.–Sept., daily 8:30–6.*

Beachcombers and snorkelers are fond of **Paamul** (10 kilometers/6 miles south of Xcaret), a crescent-shaped lagoon with clear, placid waters sheltered by the coral reef at the lagoon's mouth. Shells, sand dollars, and even glass beads—some from the sunken pirate ships at Akumal—wash onto the sandy parts of the beach. Trailer camps, cabañas, and tent camps are scattered along the beach; a restaurant sells cold beer and fresh fish; and in the summer visitors may view one of Paamul's chief attractions: sea turtle hatchlings on the beach.

Puerto Aventuras is a 900-acre self-contained resort, which will eventually include condominiums, a 250-slip marina, a tennis club, a beach club, a dive center, an 18-hole golf course, a shopping mall, a movie theater, and five deluxe hotels with a total of 2,000 rooms. At press time, facilities in operation included several restaurants and shops, nine holes of the golf course, an excellent dive shop, the marina, and the **CEDAM underwater archaeology museum** (⊙ *Daily 10–1 and 2–6),* where old ships, coins, and nautical devices are exhibited. Accommodations including three hotels and several condo and time-share units were also open.

Nine kilometers (5½ miles) south of Paamul along a narrow path is a little fishing community called **Xpuhá,** where residents weave hammocks and harvest coconuts. Some small, overgrown pre-Hispanic ruins in the area still bear traces of paint on the inside walls.

Akumal lies about 35 kilometers (22 miles) south of Playa del Carmen and consists of three distinct areas. Half Moon Bay to the north is lined with private homes and condominiums and has some of the prettiest beaches and best snorkeling in the area. Akumal proper consists of a large resort and small Maya community with a market, laundry facilities, and pharmacy. More condos and homes and an all-inclusive resort are located at Akumal Aventuras to the south. People come here to dive or simply to walk on the deliciously long beaches filled with shells, crabs, and migrant birds.

The long curved bay and beach are rarely empty now; but although Akumal can be crowded—especially at lunchtime, when tour buses stop here en route from Tulum—it is also expansive and generally much less developed than Cancún. First and foremost, however, Akumal is famous for its diving. It's the headquarters for the Mexican Underwater Explorers Club (CEDAM); area dive shops sponsor

Mexico's Caribbean Coast

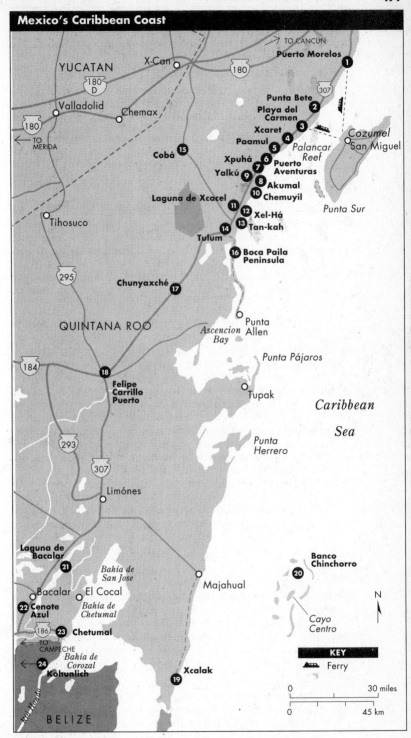

TO CANCUN

Puerto Morelos ①

YUCATAN

X-Can

180

Punta Bete ②
307

Playa del Carmen ③

Xcaret ④

Paamul ⑤

Xpuhá ⑥

Puerto Aventuras

Yalkú ⑨ ⑦

⑧ **Akumal**

⑩ **Chemuyil**

Palancar Reef

Cozumel
San Miguel

180 D

Valladolid

Chemax

180

← TO MERIDA

Cobá ⑮

Punta Sur

Laguna de Xcacel

⑪

⑫ **Xel-Há**

⑬ **Tan-kah**

⑭

Tulum

Tihosuco

⑯ **Boca Paila Peninsula**

295

Chunyaxché ⑰

QUINTANA ROO

Ascencion Bay

Punta Allen

Punta Pájaros

184

⑱

Felipe Carrillo Puerto

Tupak

Caribbean

Sea

293

Punta Herrero

307

Limónes

Laguna de Bacalar

⑳ **Banco Chinchorro**

㉑

Bahía de San Jose

Majahual

Bacalar

El Cocal

Bahía de Chetumal

㉒ **Cenote Azul**

186 ㉓ **Chetumal**

← TO CAMPECHE

Bahía de Corozal

㉔ **Kohunlich**

Cayo Centro

N

KEY

🚢 Ferry

Río Hondo

Xcalak ⑲

BELIZE

0 _____ 30 miles

0 _____ 45 km

resort courses and certification courses, and luxury hotels and condominiums offer year-round packages comprising airfare, accommodations, and diving. Deep-sea fishing for giant marlin, bonito, and sailfish is also popular.

9 Devoted snorkelers may want to walk to **Yalkú,** a practically unvisited lagoon just north of Akumal along an unmarked dirt road. Wending its way out to the sea, Yalkú hosts throngs of parrot fish in superbly clear water with visibility to 160 feet, but it has no facilities.

10 About 5 kilometers (3 miles) south of Akumal is the little cove at **Chemuyil,** where you can stop for lunch and a swim. The crescent-shaped beach is popular with tour groups and campers who pitch their tents under the few remaining palms (most were destroyed by disease and have not been replaced).

11 Continue south for a couple of kilometers along Route 307 to the **Laguna de Xcacel,** which sits on a sandy ridge overlooking yet another long white beach. The calm waters provide excellent swimming, snorkeling, diving, and fishing; birders and beachcombers like to stroll in the early morning. Camping is permitted, and a restaurant (closed on Sunday) is on the site. Tour buses full of cruise-ship passengers stop here for lunch, and the showers and dressing rooms get crowded at dusk.

12 A natural aquarium cut out of the limestone shoreline 6 kilometers (4 miles) south of Akumal, **Xel-Há** (pronounced shel-*ha*) national park consists of several interconnected lagoons where countless species of tropical fish breed; the rocky coastline curves into bays and coves in which enormous parrotfish cluster around an underwater Maya shrine. In places, you can swim fairly far out, or you can explore one of the underwater caves or the cenotes deep in the jungle. Glass-bottom boats travel to the far side of the lagoon, where stingrays and nurse sharks may be hovering beneath the surface. Lockers and dressing rooms are available, and you can rent snorkel gear ($10) and underwater cameras (the $18 fee includes a roll of film). Other park attractions include several small Maya ruins, a huge but overpriced souvenir shop, food stands, and a small museum. The enormous parking lot attests to the number of visitors who come here; try to arrive in the early morning, before all the tour-bus traffic hits. For a pleasant breakfast or lunch, you may want to try the restaurant, which serves reasonably good ceviche, fresh fish, and drinks. ☛ *$5.* ⊗ *Daily 8–5.*

13 About 9½ kilometers (6 miles) south of Xel-Há, in the depths of the jungle, stands a small grouping of pre-Hispanic structures that cover 10 square kilometers (4 square miles) and once comprised a satellite city of Tulum. **Tan-kah,** as the place is known, has still not been fully explored, and while the buildings themselves may not warrant much attention, a curious bit of more recent history does. In the 1930s an airstrip was built here; Charles Lindbergh, who was making an aerial survey of the coast, was one of the first to land on it.

14 A couple of kilometers farther south lies one of the Caribbean coast's biggest attractions: **Tulum.** The most visited Maya ruin, it is the only Maya city built on the coast and the only Maya city known to have been inhabited when the conquistadores arrived. The spectacle of its gray limestone temples against the blue-green Caribbean waters is nothing less than riveting. Visitors are no longer allowed to climb or enter Tulum's most impressive buildings (only three, described below, really merit close inspection), so you can see the ruins in two hours. You may, however, wish to allow extra time for a swim or a stroll on

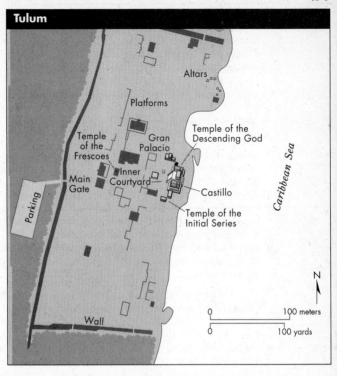

Tulum

Altars

Platforms

Temple of the Frescoes

Gran Palacio

Temple of the Descending God

Main Gate

Inner Courtyard

Parking

Castillo

Temple of the Initial Series

Caribbean Sea

Wall

N

0   100 meters

0   100 yards

the beach where it's likely that the ancient Maya beached their canoes.

The vaulted roof and corbeled arch of the two-story **Temple of the Frescoes,** to the left of the entryway, are examples of Classical Maya architecture. Faint traces of blue-green frescoes outlined in black on the inner and outer walls refer to ancient Maya beliefs. Just past the temple, the impressive **Castillo** (castle) looms at the edge of a 40-foot limestone cliff. Atop the castle, at the end of a broad stairway, sits a temple with stucco ornamentation on the outside and traces of fine frescoes inside the two chambers. The regal structure overlooks the rest of Tulum and an expanse of dense jungle to the west; the blue Caribbean blocks access from the east. To the left of the Castillo is the **Temple of the Descending God**—so called for the carving of a winged god plummeting to earth over the doorway. ☞ *$5.50, free Sun. and holidays. Parking $2. Use of video camera $8.* ⊙ *Daily 8–5.*

Tourist services are clustered at the old turnoff from Route 307 to the ruins, marked by two hotels and restaurants. The new road is a few yards farther south and is clearly marked with overhead signs. Still farther south is the turnoff for the Boca Paila Peninsula, the Sian Ka'an preserve, and several small waterfront hotels. The fourth turnoff you'll come to, about 4 kilometers (2½ miles) south of the ruins, is for the present-day village of Tulum. This small community is becoming rather unsightly and congested as its prosperity increases: markets, auto-repair shops, and other businesses continue to spring up along the road, which has been widened to four lanes.

❶ Beautiful but barely explored, **Cobá** is a 35-minute drive northwest of Tulum down a well-marked and well-paved road that leads straight through the jungle. Two tiny pueblos, Macario Gómez and Balché, with their clusters of thatched-roof white huts, are the only signs of habitation en route. Once one of the most important city-states in the entire Maya domain, Cobá now stands in solitude; the spell this remoteness is intensified by the silence at the ruins, broken occasionally by the shriek of a spider monkey or the call of a bird. Archaeologists estimate the presence of some 6,500 structures in the area, but only 5% have been uncovered, and it will take decades before the work is completed.

The city flourished from AD 400 to 1100, probably boasting a population of as many as 40,000 inhabitants. Situated on five lakes between coastal watchtowers and inland cities, its temple-pyramids towered over a vast jungle plain. Cobá (meaning "ruffled waters") exercised economic control over the region through a network of at least 16 sacbeob (wide roads), one of which, at 100 kilometers (62 miles), is the longest in the Maya world. In the elegance of its massive, soaring structures and in its sheer size—the city once covered 210 square kilometers (81 square miles)—Cobá strongly resembles Tikal in northern Guatemala, to which it apparently had close cultural and commercial ties.

The main groupings are separated by several kilometers of intense tropical vegetation, so the only way to get a sense of the immensity of the city is to scale one of the pyramids. Maps and books about the ruins are sold at the makeshift restaurants and shops that line the parking lot. None of the maps are particularly accurate, and unmarked side trails lead temptingly into the jungle. Stay on the main, marked paths unless you have a guide; several men with guide licenses congregate by the entrance and offer their services. When you go, bring plenty of bug repellent, and, if you plan to spend some time here, bring a canteen of water (you can also buy sodas and snacks at the entrance).

Cobá can be comfortably visited in a half day, but if you want to spend the night, opt for the Villa Arqueólogica Cobá (*see* Lodging, *below*), operated by Club Med and only a three-minute walk from the site along the shores of Lake Cobá. Spending the night is highly advised—the nighttime jungle sounds will lull you to sleep, and you'll be able to visit the ruins in solitude when they open at 8 AM. Even on a day trip, consider taking time out for lunch and a swim at the Villa—an oasis of French civilization—after the intense heat and mosquito-ridden humidity of the ruins. *Buses depart Cobá for Playa del Carmen and Valladolid twice daily. Check with your hotel and the clerk at the ruins for the times, which may not be exact.* ☛ *$6.50, free on Sun.* ☉ *Daily 8–5.*

Return to the coastal road heading south and continue past Tulum to the Boca Paila turnoff from Route 307. Several kilometers south, past a few bungalows and campsites, the paved road ends, and a rope over the sand marks the entrance to the **Sian Ka'an Biosphere Reserve.** The reserve includes the 1.3-million-acre **Boca Paila** ("Mouth of the River") **peninsula,** a secluded 35-kilometer (22-mile) strip of land established by the Mexican government in 1986 as one of UNESCO's internationally protected areas and named a World Heritage Site by UNESCO in 1987. The reserve constitutes 10% of the land in Quintana Roo and covers 100 kilometers (62 miles) of coast; its approximately 20 ruined sites are linked by a canal system—the only one of its kind in the Maya world.

Sian Ka'an, meaning "where the sky is born," was first settled by the Xiu tribe from Central America in the 5th century. Many species of the once-flourishing wildlife have fallen into the endangered category, but the waters here still teem with banana fish, bonefish, mojarra, snapper, shad, permit, sea bass, and alligator. Flat fishing and fly-fishing are especially popular, and the peninsula's few lodges run deep-sea fishing trips as far away as **Ascensión Bay,** two hours south of the lodges by boat. Birders take launches out to **Cajo Colibrí** (Hummingbird Cay) or to **Isla de Pájaros** to view the pelicans, frigate birds, woodpeckers, sparrow hawks, and some 350 other species of birds that roost on the mangrove roots or circle overhead. The more adventuresome travelers can explore some of the waterways' myriad caves or trek out to the tiny ruins of Chunyaxché (*see below*).

The narrow, rough dirt road down the Boca Paila peninsula is dotted with campgrounds, fishing lodges, and deserted palapas and copra farms. It ends at **Punta Allen,** a fishing village whose main catch is the spiny lobster, and the site of a small guest house. The road is filled with potholes; in the rainy season it may be completely impassable. Most fishing lodges along the way close for the rainy season in August and September, and accommodations are hard to come by. If you want to explore, start out early in the morning so you can get back to civilization before dark.

⑰ Return to Route 307 and continue south 43 kilometers (27 miles) to reach the archaeological site of **Chunyaxché,** known in ancient times as Muyil. Dating from the Late Preclassical era (300 BC–AD 200), it was connected by road to the sea and served as a port between Cobá and the Maya centers in Belize and Guatemala. Today, all that stands are the remains of a 56-foot **temple-pyramid.** From its summit you can see the Caribbean, 15 kilometers (9 miles) in the distance. Chunyaxché sits on the edge of a deep blue lagoon and is surrounded by a nearly impenetrable jungle. You can swim or fish in the lagoon. ☛ *$6.50, free on Sun. and holidays.* ☺ *Daily 8–5.*

⑱ Twenty-four kilometers (15 miles) to the south, at Km 73 on Route 307, is the town of **Felipe Carrillo Puerto,** named for a local hero who preached rebellion. In 1920 Carrillo Puerto became governor of Yucatán and instituted a series of reforms that led to his assassination. Formerly known as Chan Santa Cruz, this town also played a central role in the 19th-century War of the Castes, during which it was not only a significant political and military center but also a religious capital. It was here that what became known as the Talking Cross—interpreted as a sign for native Mexicans to attack the *dzulob* (white Christians)—first appeared. By 1904, half the local population had been annihilated in the war. Several humble hotels, some good restaurants, and a gas station may be incentives for stopping here on your southbound trek.

For devoted divers who are interested in a detour to the coast, an unremarkable 69 kilometers (43 miles) along Route 307 leads to the Majahual exit just south of Limones. The road heading toward the sea **⑲** is paved, but it turns to dirt, sand, and ruts running down to **Xcalak,** a fishing village near the tip of the Xcalak peninsula that divides Chetumal Bay from the Caribbean Sea. The landscape is lush with mangrove swamps, tropical flowers, birds, and other wildlife. The area offers some wonderfully deserted beaches, but the few small resorts here **⑳** cater mostly to divers who come to visit **Banco Chinchorro,** a 42-kilometer (26-mile) coral atoll and national park some two hours by boat from Xcalak. Littered with shipwrecks, it's an undersea explorer's dream. Fishing is not permitted here.

If you don't turn off 307 toward the coast, it's a rather monotonous 112-kilometer (69-mile) drive from Felipe Carillo Puerto until the sudden appearance of the spectacularly vast and beautiful **Laguna de Bacalar.** Also known as the Lake of the Seven Colors, this is the second largest lake in Mexico (56 kilometers or 35 miles long) and is frequented by scuba divers and other lovers of water sports. If you drive along the lake's southern shores, you'll enter the affluent section of the town of Bacalar, with elegant turn-of-the-century waterfront homes. Founded in AD 435, Bacalar appears to be the oldest settlement in Quintana Roo. On the zócalo stands the Fuerte de San Felipe, a stone fort built by the Spaniards during the 18th century to ward off marauding pirates and Indians and later used by the Maya during the War of the Castes.

Just beyond Bacalar exists the largest sinkhole in the world, the **Cenote Azul,** 607 feet in diameter, with clear blue waters that afford unusual visibility even at 200 feet below the surface. Surrounded by lush vegetation and underwater caves, the cenote attracts divers who specialize in this somewhat tricky type of dive.

Chetumal—38 kilometers (24 miles) farther along to the end of Route 307—is the last Mexican town on the southern Caribbean. It was founded in 1898 as Payo Obispo in a concerted and only partially successful effort to gain control of the lucrative traffic in the region's precious hardwoods, arms, and ammunition, and also as a base of operations against the rebellious natives. The city, which overlooks the Bay of Chetumal at the mouth of the Río Hondo, was devastated by a hurricane in 1955 and rebuilt as the capital of Quintana Roo and major port.

Overall, Chetumal feels more Central American than Mexican—not surprising, given its proximity to Belize. Run-down (but often charming) clapboard houses interspersed with low-lying ramshackle commercial establishments line the quiet streets. The mixed population includes many black Caribbeans, and the arts reflect this eclectic combination—the music includes reggae, salsa, and calypso (but little mariachi). The many Middle Eastern inhabitants have influenced the cuisine, which represents an exotic blend of Yucatecan, Mexican, and Lebanese. Although Chetumal's provisions are modest, the town presents a pleasant, extended waterfront, since the city is surrounded by the Bay of Chetumal on three sides.

The town's most attractive thoroughfare, the wide **Boulevard Bahía,** runs along the water and is a popular gathering spot at night (though on the weekend Chetumal practically shuts down). The main plaza sits between the boulevard and Avenidas Alvaro Obregón and Héroes; unremarkable modern government buildings and patriotic statues and monuments to local heroes wall in the plaza on two sides. The water lapping at the dock creates a melancholy rhythm, but if you sit at one of the sidewalk cafés by the square, you will have an appealing view of the huge, placid bay. Most of the shops are on Avenida Héroes, but the merchandise tends to be a humdrum, functional miscellany.

Sixty-eight kilometers (42 miles) west of Chetumal, off Route 186, lies **Kohunlich,** built and occupied about AD 300–600. It's renowned for the giant stucco masks on its principal pyramid, for one of the oldest ball courts in Quintana Roo, and for the remains of a great hydraulic system at the Stelae Plaza. This site is usually deserted, and in the vicinity are scores of unexcavated mounds, stelae, and thriving flora and fauna. ☛ *$4.* ☉ *Daily 8–5.*

Shopping

There aren't many high-quality crafts available along the Caribbean coast, although the shopping situation has improved in Playa del Carmen, where a few good folk-art shops are now open. **Xop** (Rincón del Sol, Av. 5 at Calle 8, no ☎) is one of the best places on the coast for handcrafted wooden masks and statues and silver jewelry set with local semi-precious stones and amber. **El Vuelo de los Niños Pájaros** (Rincón del Sol, Av. 5 at Calle 8, ☎ 987/3–04–45) has a great selection of regional music on CD and tape, along with handcrafted paper, cards, incense, and beaded baskets. The **Mercado de los Artesanías** (Tulum ruins, no ☎) contains at least 50 stalls displaying woven rugs, clay reproductions of Maya gods, and a wide array of tacky souvenirs. Several roadside artisans' markets have sprung up along Route 307; most feature a repetitive display of cotton rugs. If you drive, stock up on groceries, pharmacy items, hardware, and auto parts in Puerto Morelos, Playa del Carmen, Felipe Carrillo Puerto, or Chetumal.

Sports and the Outdoors

Water Sports

Diving, snorkeling, and fishing are among the most popular activities along the coast. The following is a brief list of outfitters. For details about where to dive, *see* Exploring, *above.*

AKUMAL

Akumal Dive Center rents equipment, runs dive trips, and has certification programs. For dive packages, including accommodations, contact Akutrame Inc. (Box 13326, El Paso, TX 79913, ☎ 915/584–3552 in TX, 800/351–1622 outside TX, 800/343–1440 in Canada).

PLAYA DEL CARMEN

The oldest shop in town, **Tank Ha** at the Maya-Bric Hotel (☎ and FAX 987/3–00–11) arranges diving and snorkeling trips to the reefs. **Wet Dreams** (Albatros Royale hotel, no ☎) has certified, bilingual instructors. Other new shops are located at the Costa del Mar hotel, Cabañas Albatros, and Playacar.

PUERTO AVENTURAS

Mike Madden's CEDAM Dive Centers (Club de Playa Hotel, ☎ 987/2–22–33 or 987/3–51–29, FAX 987/4–13–39) is a full-service dive shop with certification courses; cave and cenote diving is a specialty. There is another Mike Madden shop at the Diamond Resort in Playa del Carmen (☎ 987/3–03–40).

PUERTO MORELOS

Scuba gear is available from **Aqua Deportes** (no ☎) on the beach by the plaza.

PUNTA BETE

La Posada de Capitan Lafitte and KaiLuum (☎ 800/538–6802 for both), located on Highway 307 just north of Playa del Carmen, share an excellent, full-service dive shop and activities center called Buccaneer's Landing.

XCALAK

The **Costa de Cocos Hotel** (☎ 800/538–6802) runs deep-sea fishing and diving trips.

Dining and Lodging

Dining

Most of the restaurants along the Mexican Caribbean coast are simple beachside affairs with outdoor tables and palapa roofs. Here bargains can be found in seafood, provided it is fresh and local, such as grouper, mojarra, snapper, dorado, and sea bass. The few luxury hotels in the area have fancy restaurants offering Continental cuisine, elegant service, and of course high prices—almost as high as those in Cancún. Many of the restaurants have limited hours or close down in summer (off-season) and during the hurricane season (September). Generally, all restaurants maintain a casual dress code and do not accept reservations.

CATEGORY	COST*
$$$$	over $20
$$$	$15–$20
$$	$8–$15
$	under $8

per person excluding drinks, service, and tax

Lodging

Accommodations on the Caribbean coast run the gamut from campsites to simple palapas and bungalows to middle-range functional establishments to luxury hotels and condominiums. Many of these hotels include two or three meals in their prices. The fanciest accommodations are in Playa del Carmen, Akumal, and Puerto Aventuras, while the coastline (including the Tulum area) is sprinkled with small campgrounds and hotels on solitary beaches. Note that hotel rates drop as much as 25% in the low season (June–October).

CATEGORY	COST*
$$$$	over $90
$$$	$60–$90
$$	$25–$60
$	under $25

All prices are for a standard double room in the high season (Dec.–April), excluding 10% tax.

Akumal

DINING

$$ **La Lunita.** Locals and enterprising tourists congregate at the indoor and patio tables of this converted one-bedroom condo at Half Moon Bay for good conversation and innovative cuisine. Regulars swear by the fresh fish served with a lime and cilantro sauce or smothered in tomatoes and onions. You're sure to pick up a few tips on local events and secret beaches here. You'll need a car, a cab, or strong legs to reach this place, but it's worth it. ✕ *Go through entranceway at Club Akumal Caribe, then turn left at dirt road heading north to Half Moon Bay to Hacienda de la Tortuga,* ☎ *987/2–24–21 (condo office). No credit cards.*

DINING AND LODGING

$$$$ **Club Oasis Akumal.** An all-inclusive luxury hotel, this sprawling property started as the private preserve of millionaire Pablo Bush Romero, a friend of Jacques Cousteau. Today the beautiful beach—protected by an offshore reef—and the pier are used as the starting point for canoeing, snorkeling, diving, fishing, and windsurfing jaunts. The U-shaped building, with nautical decor, features handsome mahogany furniture and sunken blue-tile showers between Moorish arches (no doors!). All

rooms have balconies (sea view or garden view) and air-conditioning or ceiling fans (same price). The clientele consists primarily of Americans and Canadians on package deals. ☎ *For reservations: 3520 Piedmont Rd. NE, Suite 325, Atlanta, GA 30305, ☎ 800/446–2747 or 987/4–23–03, FAX 404/240–4039 or 987/3–50–51 (in Puerto Aventuras). 120 rooms. Restaurant, 2 bars, 2 pools, beach, dive shop, tennis court, recreation room, travel services, car rental. AE, MC, V.*

$$$ **Club Akumal Caribe & Villas Maya.** Accommodations at this resort, situated on the edge of a cove overlooking a small harbor, range from rustic but comfortable bungalows with red tile roofs and garden views (Villas Maya) to beachfront rooms in a modern three-story hotel building. All have air-conditioning, ceiling fans, and refrigerators. Also available are the more secluded one-, two-, and three-bedroom condominiums on Half Moon Bay and a half mile from the beach. The bungalows and hotel rooms are cheerfully furnished in rattan and dark wood. The Mediterranean-style condominium units have kitchens and balconies or terraces overlooking the pool and beach. Among the many watersports options is PADI certification. Lol Ha is the best of the three restaurants: An optional meal plan includes breakfast and dinner. ☎ *Km 104, Hwy. 307, no ☎. For reservations: Akutrame, Box 13326, El Paso, TX 79913, ☎ 915/584–3552 or 800/351–1622 outside TX, 800/343–1440 in Canada. 40 bungalows, 21 rooms, 4 villas, 5 condos. 3 restaurants, snack bar, ice cream parlor, pizzeria, bar, grocery, pool, beach, 2 dive shops. AE, MC, V.*

Bacalar
LODGING

$$$ **Rancho Encantado.** On the shores of Laguna Bacalar, 30 minutes north of Chetumal, the Rancho comprises eight private *casitas* (cottages), each with its own patio and hammocks, kitchenette, sitting area, and bathroom. The casitas and public areas feature hand-carved hardwood furnishings, woven Oaxacan rugs, and sculptures of Maya gods. Both breakfast and dinner are included in the room rate, and guests applaud the homemade breads and ice creams, curries, gumbo, lasagna, and other exotic fare (no red meat is served). You can swim and snorkel off the private dock leading into the lagoon. Adventure tours to the ruins in southern Yucatán, Campeche, and Belize are available through the U.S. office. ☎ *For reservations: Apdo. 233, Chetumal, Quintana Roo 77000, ☎ 983/8–04–27 in Bacalar. For reservations in the U.S.: Box 1644, Taos, NM 87571, ☎ 800/748–1756, FAX 505/751–0972. 8 units. Restaurant, bar. No credit cards.*

Boca Paila
LODGING

$$$$ **Caphé-Ha.** Originally built as a private home by an American archi-
★ tect, this small guest house—located between a lagoon and the ocean—is a perfect place to stay if you're interested in bonefishing and/or bird-watching. A private two-bedroom house, with a kitchen, private bath, and living room, and a two-unit bungalow (with shared baths) are your choices; though neither has fans or electricity, all the windows have screens and catch the ocean breeze. Fishing tackle and snorkeling gear are available from the property's small dock. Room rates include breakfast and dinner; advance reservations must be accompanied by a 50% deposit, and a three-day or longer stay is required during high season. ☎ *For reservations: ☎ 212/219–2198 in NY. 1 villa, 1 bungalow. Fishing. No credit cards.*

$$$$ **Casa Blanca Lodge.** Punta Pájaros, to which this remote fishing resort provides unique access, is reputed to be one of the best places in the world for light-tackle saltwater fishing. The American-managed, all-inclusive lodge—just 100 feet from the ocean—is set on a rocky out-crop covered with palm trees. The lodge's nine large, modern guest rooms provide a pleasant tropical respite at dusk. The lodge is closed September through December, but will open during that time for groups of four or more. To get here, you must take a charter flight from Cancún to the Punta Pájaros airstrip, or rent a car in Cancún and drive to Punta Allen (3 hours). From there, it's a one-hour boat trip across the bay. ⚇ *For reservations: Frontiers, Box 959, Wexford, PA 15090,* ☏ *412/935–1577 or 800/245–1950,* ⒻⒶⓍ *412/935–5388. 9 rooms. Restaurant, bar, fishing. No credit cards.*

Chetumal

DINING

$$ Emiliano's. The seafood is excellent here, as evidenced by the packed house most days at lunchtime. Try the shrimp pâté (a smooth blend of cream cheese and grilled shrimp) and the huge chili relleno stuffed with seafood. For an all-out feast for two or more, go for the seafood platter. ✗ *Av. San Salvador 557 at Calle 9,* ☏ *983/7–02–67. MC, V.*

$$ Mandinga. One of the best places in town for the freshest seafood, Mandinga is best known for its octopus and conch seafood soup, a spicy blend of the daily catch. ✗ *Av. Belice 214,* ☏ *983/2–48–24. No credit cards.*

$$ Sergio's. This popular pizza parlor is situated in a small, simply deco-rated frame house. Locals rave about the grilled steaks. ✗ *Av. Alvaro Obregón 182 at Av. 5 de Mayo,* ☏ *983/2–23–55. MC, V.*

LODGING

$$ Los Cocos. Chetumal's best hotel lacks any semblance of glamour or glitz, but it does have comfortable rooms with powerful air-condi-tioning, in-room phones, and TVs, and a pleasant garden area with a large swimming pool. The waterfront is within easy walking distance, and the hotel's travel agency is the most reliable source of informa-tion in town. ⚇ *Av. Héroes 138 at Calle Chapultepec, 77000,* ☏ *983/2–05–44,* ⒻⒶⓍ *983/2–09–20. 60 rooms. 2 restaurants, bar, pool, travel services. MC, V.*

$$ Príncipe. At the lower end of the moderate range, the Príncipe, located between the bus station and downtown, is a good deal for the price. The rooms are air-conditioned, clean, and modern, with satellite TV. ⚇ *Av. Héroes 326, 77000,* ☏ *983/2–47–99,* ⒻⒶⓍ *983/2–51–91. 52 rooms. Restaurant-bar. MC, V.*

Cobá

DINING AND LODGING

$$$ Villa Arqueólogica Cobá. This Club Med property, a three-minute ★ walk from the entrance to the Cobá ruins, overlooks one of the region's vast lakes. Tastefully done in white stucco and red paint, the hotel has a clean, airy feel. The air-conditioned rooms are small but they feel cozy, not claustrophobic. A handsome library features a large VCR and a pool table. Dining choices near the isolated Cobá ruins are quite limited, so the restaurant here is an attractive option: The food—although pricey—is very good (it's not included in the room rates as at most Club Med properties). ⚇ *For reservations:* ☏ *800/CLUB–MED. 40 rooms. Restaurant, bar, pool, tennis court. AE, MC, V.*

$ El Bocadito. Though nowhere near as lavish as the Villa, El Bocadito is a friendly, satisfactory budget alternative and only a five-minute walk from the ruins. The simple, tiled rooms fill up quickly—if you're thinking of spending the night, stop here first before visiting the ruins.

There is no hot water, and only fans to combat the heat, but the camaraderie of the clientele and staff make up for the discomforts. The restaurant is decent and clean. ☷ *On the road to the ruins, APDO 56, Valladolid, Yucatán, Mexico 97780, no ☎. 8 rooms. No credit cards.*

Felipe Carrillo Puerto

DINING AND LODGING

$ **El Faisán y El Venado.** Given the paucity of hotels in Felipe Carrillo Puerto, this centrally located one is your best bet. It's bare-bones, but you can choose between air-conditioned rooms or rooms with ceiling fans; all have color or black-and-white TVs and refrigerators. At lunchtime, the pleasant restaurant does brisk business with locals who enjoy Yucatecan specialties such as poc chuc, *bistec a la yucateca* (Yucatecan-style steak), and pollo píbil, served in a simple setting. ☷ *Av. Juárez 781, 77200, ☎ 983/4–00–43. 21 rooms. Restaurant. No credit cards.*

Paamul

DINING AND LODGING

$$ **Cabañas Paamul.** This small hostelry on a perfect white sand beach combines seclusion and comfort. Seven bungalows painted white and peach face the sea; all have two double beds, ceiling fans, and hot-water showers. A large palapa houses the restaurant, and there is a small market just off the main highway at the road to the hotel. ☷ *Km 85, Hwy. 307; reservations: Box 83, Playa del Carmen, Quintana Roo 77710, ☎ 99/25–94–22 (in Mérida). 7 rooms. Restaurant, dive shop. No credit cards.*

Playa del Carmen

DINING

$$ **La Parrilla.** The far end of the pedestrian walkway gained a social center when La Parrilla opened in 1994 at the Rincón del Sol plaza. A branch of an enduringly popular Cancún chain, the open-air restaurant sits a few feet above the street, and it's hard to resist stopping in for a beer, a platter of chicken fajitas, or the best lobster in Playa. ✗ *Av. 5 at Calle 8, no ☎. MC, V.*

$$ **Limones.** Probably the most romantic place in town, this restaurant
★ offers dining by candlelight, either alfresco in a courtyard or under the shelter of a palapa indoors. Soft guitar music adds to the amorous atmosphere. House favorites include copious entrées such as fettuccine, lasagna, and lemon-sautéed beef scaloppine. Appetizers might be home-baked pizza bread or salads. The daily dinner special is the best bargain in town. ✗ *Av. 5 at Calle 6, no ☎. MC, V.*

$$ **Máscaras.** The wood-burning brick oven here produces exceptionally
★ good thin-crusted pizzas and breads; the homemade pastas are also excellent. Be sure to try to calamari in garlic and oil, and the three-cheese pizza—the most popular item on the menu. Masks from throughout the world cover the walls; jazz plays in the background. Locals and visitors alike come here to enjoy the view of the goings-on at the zócalo. ✗ *Av. Juárez across from plaza, ☎ 987/3–01–94. MC, V.*

$ **El Tacolote.** Opened in 1992, this fanciful, colorful restaurant continues expanding, overtaking less popular restaurants. Mariachis play on most evenings in front of the sidewalk tables, where diners feast on platter of grilled meats, fajitas, or tacos with all sorts of fillings. You can eat cheaply or splurge on a multicourse feast while watching the action on the plaza from an outdoor table. ✗ *Av. Juárez across from plaza, ☎ 987/3–00–66. MC, V.*

DINING AND LODGING

$$$$ **Caribbean Village Golf and Beach Club.** Opened in 1994, this all-inclusive hotel sits on Playacar's 18-hole golf course, a few minutes from the beach. Rates include unlimited green fees and a private beach club. The deluxe rooms include both ceiling fans and air-conditioning, as well as satellite TV. Guests may also use the facilities at the hotel's sister properties in Cozumel and Cancún. ☎ *In the Playacar development,* ☎ *987/3–04–31,* FAX *987/3–03–48. For reservations: 901 Ponce de Leon Blvd., Suite 400, Coral Gables, FL 33134,* ☎ *800/858–2258,* FAX *305/444–4848. 300 rooms. Dining room, bar, 2 pools, dive shop, 3 tennis courts, car rental.*

$$$$ **Continental Plaza Playacar.** The centerpiece of an 880-acre master-planned resort, this blush-colored palace faces the sea on the south side of the ferry pier. The tropical-style rooms have ocean views and balconies or patios, marble baths, blonde wood furnishings, satellite TV, and in-room safes. The beach is one of the nicest in Playa del Carmen and is far less crowded than those to the north. The breakfast buffet is excellent. A shopping-dining-banking complex links the hotel with downtown Playa del Carmen via a pleasant pedestrian mall. There's a full-scale scuba and water-sports facility and a new 18-hole championship golf course (ask about golf packages). ☎ *Fraccionamiento Playacar, Playa del Carmen, Quintana Roo, 77710,* ☎ *987/2–15–83 or 800/882–6684. 188 rooms, 16 suites. 2 restaurants, bar, pool, dive shop, golf course, travel services. AE, MC, V.*

$$$$ **Diamond Resort.** Part of the Playacar development, this all-inclusive resort sprawls down a sloping hill to the sea. Rooms are spread out in thatch-roofed villas along winding paths; the dining room, bar, lobby, and entertainment areas are housed in a gigantic multipeaked, two-story palapa. Guests get a bit rowdy at the karaoke bar and outdoor stage, but the noise does not reach the guest rooms. Buffet-style meals are plentiful and imaginatively prepared. Playa del Carmen is a 20-minute walk or $5 cab ride north. ☎ *In the Playacar development,* ☎ *987/3–03–40,* FAX *987/3–03–48; for reservations: 901 Ponce de Leon Blvd., Suite 400, Coral Gables, FL 33134,* ☎ *800/858–2258,* FAX *305/444–4848. 296 rooms. Dining room, bar, 2 pools, dive shop, 4 tennis courts, car rental.*

$$$ **Las Palapas.** Many guests stay for 10 days or more at this get-away-
★ from-it-all destination resort. White cabañas are cheerfully blue trimmed, and duplexes feature balconies or porches, palapas, and hammocks. The beach and pool are complemented by a shuffleboard area, clubhouse, beach bar, palapa bar, and attractive palapa restaurant, where the chef prepares spectacular Mexican buffets and German specialties as well as hamburgers, tacos, and other snacks. German tour groups keep the hotel's occupancy up to 80% year-round; make reservations early. Room rates include breakfast and dinner. ☎ *Km 292 on Rte. 307, Box 116, Playa del Carmen, Quintana Roo, 77710,* ☎ *987/2–29–77. 50 cabañas. Restaurant, 2 bars, in-room safes, pool, beach. 3-night minimum stay. MC, V.*

LODGING

$$ **Albatros Royale.** One of the nicest complexes right on the beach, the
★ Royale opened in 1991 but still looks brand new. Two-story palapa-covered buildings face each other along a pathway to the sand. Hammocks hang on the balconies, where guests tend to congregate in the evenings. Large rooms are simply decorated with white walls and tile floors. Complimentary coffee and sweet rolls are set out by the front desk each morning, and a full-service dive shop opened at the hotel in 1994. ☎ *Calle 8 between the beach and Av. 5,* ☎ *987/3–00–01,* FAX

987/3–00–02. *For reservations: Turquoise Reef Group, Box 2664, Evergreen, CO 80439,* ☎ *303/674–9615 or 800/538–6802 outside CO,* FAX *303/674–8735. 31 rooms. Restaurant (at Cabañas Albatros), dive shop. MC, V.*

$$ Alejari. This two-story complex set amid lush gardens is one of the most pleasant accommodations on Playa's north beach. Some rooms have kitchenettes and fans, others provide air-conditioning. A small market and a long-distance phone booth sit on the premises. ⌖ *Calle 6N; for reservations: Box 166, Playa del Carmen, Quintana Roo, 77710,* ☎ *987/3–03–74,* FAX *987/3–00–05. 18 rooms. Kitchenettes. MC, V.*

$$ Cabañas Albatros. Recently repainted and repaired, these cabañas have the feel of the old days in Playa del Carmen, when backpackers and hippies hung out in hammocks over the sand. The comfortable and attractive cabañas all have private baths, double beds, and fans. The restaurant is a popular hangout both night and day, and is especially good for American breakfasts. ⌖ *On the beach at Calle 6,* ☎ *987/ 3–00–01,* FAX *987/3–00–02. For reservations: Turquoise Reef Group, Box 2664, Evergreen, CO 80439,* ☎ *303/674–9615 or 800/538–6802 outside CO,* FAX *303/674–8735. 23 rooms. Restaurant, dive shop. MC, V.*

$ Posada Rosa Mirador. Inexpensive lodgings are getting harder to find in Playa, once a haven for budget travelers. This small posada less than a block from the beach has the nicest rooms in its price range, spare but clean, with one or two double beds and private baths. A dorm-type room on the top floor sleeps six. ⌖ *Calle 12 at Av. 5, Playa del Carmen, Quintana Roo, 77710, no* ☎. *No credit cards.*

Puerto Aventuras

DINING

$$ ★ Papaya Republic. The loveliest restaurant on the coast, Papaya Republic is a bit of tropical paradise secluded from the nearby development. A winding jungle path leads past caged deer and monkeys on leashes to the palapa-roof restaurant set just above the beach. Gourmet dishes such as mushrooms stuffed with smoked oysters or mango flambée with brandy are prepared from the freshest ingredients available; seafood is the main attraction. Stop by for a drink at one of the plant-shrouded outdoor tables and you'll probably linger for hours. ✗ *Off the main road into Puerto Aventuras, down dirt road to the right marked by sign,* ☎ *987/3–71–50. MC, V.*

LODGING

$$$$ Club de Playa. This 30-room hotel underwent extensive renovations in 1994 and has become an all-inclusive property. The spacious rooms have stunning views of the Caribbean, and the swimming pool seems to flow right into the sea. Guests have use of a fitness room, and one of the coast's best dive shops is on the property. Guests can also enjoy the facilities and restaurants at the Club Oasis hotel on the other side of the marina. ⌖ *On beach near marina,* ☎ *987/3–51–00,* FAX *987/3–50–51. For reservations: 3520 Piedmont Rd. NE, Suite 325, Atlanta, GA 30305,* ☎ *800/446–2747,* FAX *404/240–4039. 30 rooms. Restaurant, pool, exercise room, dive shop. AE, MC, V.*

$$$$ Continental Plaza Puerto Aventuras. Situated on the marina a short distance from the beach, the Continental Plaza has a variety of rooms, many with kitchenettes. Most guest quarters are decorated in soft shades of blue and peach, and feature French doors opening onto balconies overlooking the pool. The hotel has a shuttle service to the beach; restaurants, shops, and water sports services are within walking distance. ⌖ *At marina, Puerto Aventuras, Quintana Roo, 77710,*

☎ 987/3–51–33 or 800/882–6684, FAX 987/3–51–34. 60 rooms, 40 with kitchenettes. Restaurant, bar, pool, bicycles, car rental. AE, MC, V.

Puerto Morelos

DINING

$ **Los Pelícanos.** If you're looking for good fresh fish—fried, grilled, or steamed—stop by this thatch-roofed restaurant on the beach where you can spend hours feasting on the catch of the day and watching the boats go by. ✕ On oceanfront near main plaza, ☎ 987/1–00–14. No credit cards.

DINING AND LODGING

$$$$ **Caribbean Reef Club at Villa Marina.** This gorgeous white condo
★ complex, on an isolated beach south of town, is one of the nicest hideaways along the coast. The colonial-style suites have marble floors, air-conditioning, ceiling fans, blue-tiled kitchenettes, and balconies with hammocks. The adjacent restaurant is easily the most picturesque in town, with a balcony overlooking the sea, hand-painted tile tables, and candlelight at night. A Jamaican chef prepares superb coconut shrimp, seafood gumbo, jerk chicken and other Caribbean specialties. 🏨 South of ferry dock. For reservations: Box 1526, Cancún, Quintana Roo, 77500, ☎ 987/1–01–91 or 800/3–CANCUN, FAX 987/1–01–90. 21 suites. Restaurant, bar, pool. MC, V.

LODGING

$$ **Cabañas Playa Ojo de Agua.** This dive-oriented hotel is on a lovely beach just north of town. Most of the guest rooms have kitchenettes, ceiling fans, and views of the sea or the courtyard gardens. There is a freshwater pool on the premises. 🏨 One block north of town, ☎ 987/1–00–27. For reservations: Calle 12 No. 96, Mérida, Yucatán, 97050, ☎ 99/25–02–92. 16 rooms. Pool, dive shop. No credit cards. Closed Sept. and Oct.

Punta Bete

DINING AND LODGING

$$$$ **Posada del Capitán Lafitte.** Set on an invitingly long stretch of beach
★ about 10 kilometers (6 miles) north of Playa del Carmen at Punta Bete, this lodging is known for its chummy, unpretentious atmosphere. It's no luxury resort, but a simple cluster of two-unit cabañas, each with its own private bath and ceiling fan. A duplex at the south end of the property has four two-bedroom, two-bath units, ideal for families. In the evening the European and American clientele congregates around a cozy, red-tiled pool-bar. Breakfast, dinner, tax, and tips are included in the room rate. 🏨 On a dirt road (follow signs), about 3 km (2 mi) off Rte. 307. For reservations: Turquoise Reef Group, Box 2664, Evergreen, CO 80439, ☎ 303/674–9615 or 800/538–6802 outside CO, FAX 303/674–8735. 59 rooms. Restaurant, bar, pool, beach, dive shop, car rental. AE, MC, V.

Tulum

DINING

$$ **Casa Cenote.** Don't miss this outstanding restaurant beside a large
★ cenote—this one's a mini-pool of fresh and salt water full of tropical fish, perfect for a pre-lunch dip. The beef, chicken, and cheese are imported from the United States, and the burgers, chicken fajitas, and nachos are superb. On Sunday afternoon the expats living along the coast gather at Casa Cenote for a lavish barbecue featuring ribs, chicken, beef brisket, or lobster kebabs. The restaurant operates without electricity or a generator (perishables are packed in ice cool-

ers) and closes at dark. ✕ *On a dirt road off Rte. 307, between Xel-Há and Tulum, 987/4–13–68. No reservations. No credit cards.*

DINING AND LODGING

$$ Osho Oasis. A holistic, New Age–style resort with a yoga and medita-★ tion center, Osho Oasis is the ultimate, peaceful hideaway. Fourteen super-deluxe cabañas have private baths and traditional king-size beds; the others have hammock-like mattresses suspended from the ceiling, rock floors, and mosquito nets (the windows have no screens). A generator provides electricity at night. The restaurant serves superb vegetarian meals, plus fish and lobster, and is worth visiting even if you aren't staying here. It's best to write or fax ahead for reservations. ⌨ *Along dirt road south of ruins. For reservations: Box 99, Tulum, Quintana Roo, 77780,* ☎ *987/4–27–72,* FAX *987/1–20–94, reservations in the U.S. 415/381–9861,* FAX *415/381–6746. 26 cabañas. No credit cards.*

$ Cabañas Ana y José. Several two-story buildings face the beach at this ★ small, well-loved hotel south of the ruins. All rooms have fans, tiled floors, hot water showers, and hammock hooks; those on the second floor are cooler, thanks to the sea breezes. The restaurant is one of the best along this road, and management is more than helpful. Mountain bikes are available for rent. ⌨ *On dirt road off Rte. 307 between ruins entrance and Tulum pueblo, 4 mi south of ruins, Box 15, Tulum, Quintana Roo, 77780,* ☎ *98/80–60–22 (in Cancún),* FAX *98/80–60–21 (in Cancún). 16 rooms. Restaurant. No credit cards.*

Xcalak
LODGING

$$ Costa de Cocos. For the ultimate in privacy and gorgeous scenery, you ★ can't beat the southern tip of the Xcalak peninsula, where divers and explorers congregate for trips to the famed Chinchorro Banks (weather permitting) and the nearby reefs. Costa de Cocos is one of the precious few resorts in this area (be sure to reserve in advance), and is easily the most hospitable and comfortable. Eight cleverly crafted cabañas have exquisite handcrafted mahogany furnishings, screened windows, tiled baths, and bookshelves stocked with an eclectic selection of paperbacks. Small pangas (launches) transport divers to the nearby reefs, and day trips by boat to Belize can be arranged. A restaurant was added to the resort in 1993. ⌨ *Xcalak Peninsula, 56 km (35 mi) south of Majahual. For reservations: Turquoise Reef Group, Box 2664, Evergreen, CO 80439,* ☎ *303/674–9615 or 800/538–6802 outside CO,* FAX *303/674–8735. 8 cabañas. Restaurant, dive shop, private airstrip. No credit cards.*

Xcaret
DINING

$ Restaurant Xcaret. This small palapa restaurant, its walls lined with photos from diving expeditions, serves conch ceviche, lobster, poc chuc, and french fries at prices far lower than those inside the Xcaret theme park. ✕ *Hwy. 307 at Xcaret turnoff, no* ☎. *No credit cards.*

Nightlife

There isn't much in the way of nightlife along the coast, unless you happen upon some entertainment in a luxury hotel bar. Some restaurants in Playa del Carmen have live music on weekend nights, but there are no discos or nightclubs along the coast.

Mexico's Caribbean Coast Essentials

Arriving and Departing

BY PLANE

Chetumal. The Chetumal airport is on the southwestern edge of town, along Avenida Alvaro Obregón where it turns into Route 186. **Taesa** (☎ 983/2–83–06) has daily flights from Chetumal to Cancún, Mexico City, and Mérida.

Playa del Carmen. The airstrip is near the Continental Plaza Hotel, and there is occasional shuttle service to Cozumel. At press time, a small airline called **Saab** (Playa del Carmen airstrip, ☎ 987/3–05–01) was offering charter flights to Cozumel, Mérida, Belize, and Guatemala. Check with local travel agencies to see if the airline is still running when you visit.

BY FERRY

Ferries and jetfoils—which can be picked up at the dock—run between Playa del Carmen and Cozumel about every two hours (more frequently in the early morning and evening); trips on the old ferry take about 40 minutes, those on the two enclosed hydrofoils, 30 minutes. The fee varies depending on which boat you choose, but the one-way trip costs approximately between $5 and $8.

BY CAR

The entire coast, from Punta Sam near Cancún to the main border crossing to Belize at Chetumal, is traversable on Route 307. This straight road is entirely paved and is gradually being widened to four lanes from Cancún south. Gas stations are becoming more prevalent, but it's still a good idea to fill the tank whenever you can.

BY BUS

Playa del Carmen. There is first-class service on the **ADO** line (Av. Juárez at Av. 5, ☎ 987/3–01–41) between Playa and Cancún, Valladolid, Chichén Itzá, Chetumal, Tulum, Xel-Há, Mexico City, and Mérida daily. **Autotransportes del Caribe** (Av. Juárez, no ☎) runs second-class buses to the above destinations, and express buses to Chetumal. **Autotransportes Oriente** (Av. Juárez, no ☎) has express service to Mérida eight times daily, and three buses daily to Cobá. **Playa Express** (Av. Juárez at Av. 5, no ☎) has express minibus service to Cancún every hour 6 AM–9 PM, and to Tulum four times daily; there's no space for luggage on the buses. **InterCaribe** (Av. Juárez at Av. 5, no ☎) offers deluxe service to Cancún, Chetumal, and Mérida and frequent service to the ruins at Tulum.

Chetumal. The bus station (Av. Salvador Novo 179) is served by **ADO** (☎ 983/2–06–29) and other lines. Buses run regularly to Cancún, Villahermosa, Mexico City, Mérida, Campeche, and Veracruz.

Getting Around

BY CAR

In **Playa del Carmen,** car rental agencies are beginning to appear around the ferry pier and Avenida Juárez. Rental agencies include **National** (Hotel Molcas, ☎ 987/3–00–70; for reservations, ☎ 98/86–44–90 in Cancún), **Hertz** (Hotel Diamond, ☎ 987/3–03–40; Hotel Playacar, ☎ 987/3–05–66), and **APSA** (Av. 5 between Av. Juárez and Playacar, 987/3–00–33).

Guided Tours

Mayaland Tours (Hotel America, Av. Tulum at Calle Brisa, ☎ 98/87–24–50, FAX 98/87–24–38 in Cancún, 800/235–4079 in the U.S.), runs tours to Chichén Itzá from hotels around Punta Bete, Playa del Carmen, and Akumal. Guided tours of the Sian Ka'an Reserve on the Boca Paila Peninsula can be arranged through the private, nonprofit **Amigos de Sian Ka'an** organization (Plaza América, Av. Cobá, No. 5, Suites 48–50, Cancún, QR 77500, ☎ 98/84–95–83, FAX 98/87–30–80).

Important Addresses and Numbers

EMERGENCIES

In **Chetumal: Police** (Av. Insurgentes and Av. Belice, ☎ 983/2–15–00); **Red Cross** (Av. Efraín Aguilar at Av. Madero, ☎ 983/2–05–71).

In **Playa del Carmen: Police** (Av. Juárez between Av. 15a and Av. 20a, next to the post office, ☎ 987/3–00–21); **Red Cross** (Av. Héroes de Chapultapec at Independencia, ☎ 987/3–00–45).

ENGLISH-LANGUAGE BOOKSTORES

In **Playa del Carmen,** the newsstand at the **Rincón del Sol Plaza** (Av. 5 at Calle 8, no ☎) has an excellent selection of English-language books and periodicals; used books are sold at a discount. The gift shop at the **Playacar** hotel (☎ 987/2–15–83) has a modest selection of magazines and paperbacks.

PHARMACY

In **Chetumal: Farmacia Social Mechaca** (Av. Independencia 134C, ☎ 983/2–00–44).

VISITOR INFORMATION

The **main tourist office** in **Chetumal** (Palacio del Gobierno, 2nd floor, ☎ 983/2–02–66, FAX 983/2–08–55) is open weekdays 9–2:30 and 4–7, as is the **tourist information booth** (☎ 983/2–36–63) on Avenida Héroes, just opposite Avenida Efraín Aguilar.

The unreliable tourist information booth in **Playa del Carmen** is one block from the beach on Avenida 5 (no ☎). It is supposed to be open Monday–Saturday 7–2 and 3–9 and Sunday 7–2, but it is often closed during these times.

CAMPECHE CITY

Updated by
Patricia Alisau

The city of Campeche has a run-down but lovely feel to it: No self-conscious, ultramodern tourist glitz here, just an isolated, friendly city (population 270,000) content to rest on its staid old laurels. That good-humored, lackadaisical attitude is enshrined in the Spanish adjective *campechano,* meaning easygoing, hearty, genial, cheerful. The city gets only about 20,000 tourists a year, its strongest attraction being its sense of history. You can easily imagine pirates attacking the formidable stone walls that surround the downtown, and several Maya ruins and undisturbed Maya towns are within driving distance. The city's coastline is cluttered with commercial fishing operations, and there are a few popular public beaches. It is possible to see much of Campeche City in a day or two, but you will probably want to stay longer to absorb the traditional lifestyle, whiling away the hours at a café near the plaza.

Exploring

Because it has been walled since 1676, most of historic Campeche is neatly contained in an area measuring just five blocks by nine blocks. On eight corners in the old city, or Viejo Campeche, stand *baluartes* (bastions) in various stages of disrepair or reconstruction. These were once connected by a 3-kilometer (2-mile) wall in a hexagonal fortification that helped to protect the city against the pirates who kept ransacking it. However, it was not until 1771, when Fuerte San Miguel was built on a hilltop on the outskirts of town, that the pirates were driven away for good. Only short stretches of the wall are extant, and two stone archways—one facing the sea, the other the land—are all that remain of the four gates that provided the only means of access to Campeche.

Numbers in the margin correspond to points of interest on the Campeche City map.

❶ Avenida Ruíz Cortines is Campeche's waterfront boulevard with a broad pedestrian walkway called the **malecón.** The sidewalk runs the length of the waterfront, from the Ramada Inn south to the outskirts of town, and is popular with joggers and strollers enjoying the cool sea breezes and view at sunset.

❷ One block inland on Avenida 16 de Septiembre, a modernistic building resembling a flying saucer houses the **Congreso del Estado,** the State Congress building, where government activities take place. Across Calle 8, notice the rather handsome neoclassical Municipal Palace, built in 1892 as military barracks.

❸ Continue southeast on Avenida 16 de Septiembre; on your left, where the avenue curves around and becomes Circuito Baluartes, you'll arrive at the first bastion, the **Baluarte San Carlos.** Because this one contains only scale models of the original defense system, you may prefer to save your energy for some of the more elaborate installations. The Sala de las Fortificaciones (Chamber of the Fortifications) contains the Museo de la Ciudad, or City Museum, with photographs of the city as it developed. A city tour departs from San Carlos at 4 PM during busy seasons. ☛ *Small fee.* ☉ *Daily 9–2 and 4–8.*

❹ One block east, occupying the full city block between Calles 10 and 12 and Calles 63 and 65, stands the **Ex-Templo de San José.** The Jesuits built this fine Baroque church in 1756, and today its facade stands as an exception to the rather plodding architectural style of most of the city's churches. Its immense portal is completely covered with blue Talavera tiles and crowned by seven narrow, stone finials that resemble the roofcombs on many Maya temples.

❺ One of the city's tourism offices (*see* Visitor Information *in* Campeche City Essentials, *below*) is in the **Baluarte Santa Rosa,** one of the original walls guarding the south side of the city. At present only the first-floor room housing the office is open to the public, though there are plans for further refurbishing of the building.

❻ Take Calle 10 south to Calle Bravo, where the **Iglesia de San Román** sits just outside the intramural boundary in the barrio of the same name. Though it was built earlier in the 16th century, the church became central to the lives of local native Mexicans only when an ebony image of Christ, the "Black Christ," was brought in about 1565. The legend goes that a ship that refused to carry the tradesman and his precious statue was wrecked, while the ship that did take him on board reached Campeche in record time. To this day, the Feast of San Román—when the icon is carried through the streets as part of a colorful and somber procession—is the biggest such celebration in Campeche.

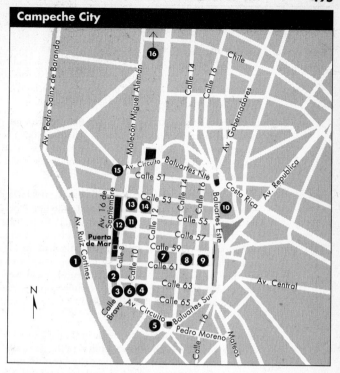

Campeche City

Now return to Avenida Circuito Baluartes and head north on Calle 12 for three blocks, then turn right onto Calle 59, where you will pass **7** the tiny **Iglesia de San Francisquito,** whose architecture and ambience do justice to the historic street's old-fashioned beauty. Behind the genteel lace curtains of some of the homes, you can glimpse equally genteel scenes of Campeche life. Along Calle 59 once stood some of Campeche's finest homes, with the ground floors serving as warehouses and the upper floors as residences.

8 One block beyond San Francisquito, at the corner of Calle 59 and Calle 14, the excellent **Museo Regional** occupies the former Casa del Teniente del Rey, or House of the King's Governor, who lived here between 1804 and 1811. The ground floor comprises the archaeological museum, which is devoted primarily to the Maya. The historical museum on the second floor covers the 18th century and includes religious art, weapons, and manuscripts. ☞ *Free.* ☺ *Tues.–Sat. 8–8, Sun. 8–1.*

9 Old Campeche ends one block east of the museum at the **Puerta de Tierra,** the only one of the four city gates that still stands with its basic structure intact. A sound-and-light show, which includes slides and a tour of the fortress, is offered every Friday at 8 PM in Spanish (price: $3). Shows in English are available for groups only; check with the tourist office for arrangements.

10 To take in the heart of a true Mexican inner city, walk north on Calle 16 for three blocks, then turn east (right) onto Calle 53, which leads to the **Mercado Municipal,** where locals congregate en masse to shop for seafood, produce, and housewares. The market is open daily from dawn to dusk. Try to arrive early, before it gets uncomfortably crowded.

After browsing through the market, walk four blocks west on Calle 55. You'll see (but won't be able to enter) a shabby-looking but impressive mansion highlighted by Moorish arcades. In 1865 Empress Carlotta, wife of the doomed Maximilian, stayed here briefly. Various shops line the street-level arcade.

⑪ Just opposite the mansion stands the **Parque Principal** or **Plaza de la Independencia,** the southern side of which—Calle 57—is lined with several agreeable cafés and hotels; the park is the focal point for the town's activities. Concerts are held on Sunday evening, when it seems all the city's residents come out for a stroll.

⑫ On the south side of the park you'll come to **Baluarte de la Soledad,** which houses the **Museo de los Estela Dr. Roman Pina Chan** in a separate section. The largest of the bastions, this one has comparatively complete parapets and embrasures that offer a sweeping view of the cathedral, the municipal buildings, and the Gulf of Mexico. Artifacts housed inside the museum, named for a renowned archaeologist from the state of Campeche, include 20 beautiful and well-proportioned Maya stelae and other pieces from various periods. This museum is a real find and not to be missed. *Calle 8 at Calle 57, no ☏. ☞ Free. ☾ Tues.–Sat. 8–8, Sun. 8–1.*

⑬ Across the street from the north side of the park—on Calle 55 between Calles 8 and 10—is another exception to the generally somber architecture rule of colonial Campeche. The **Catedral** took two centuries (from 1650 to 1850) to build and incorporates Neoclassical and Renaissance elements. Inside, the pièce de résistance is the magnificent Holy Sepulcher, carved from ebony.

⑭ Walk one block north of the cathedral to the corner of Calles 10 and 53, where you'll find the opulent, eclectic **Mansión Carvajal.** Built in the early 20th century by one of the wealthiest plantation owners in Yucatán, this structure did time as the Hotel Señorial before arriving at its present role as a government office center and headquarters for the state governor's wife and her staff. *Calle 10 s/n, between Calles 53 and 55, no ☏. ☞ Free. ☾ Mon.–Sat. 8–2:30 and 5–8:30.*

⑮ Just a short block north on Calle 8 at Calle 49 (which becomes Av. Miguel Alemán) is the **Baluarte Santiago,** the last of the bastions to be built (1704). The original bastion was demolished at the turn of the century, but it was rebuilt in the 1950s. The structure has been transformed into a botanical garden, and appropriately enough, now houses the office of ecotourism. *Calle 8 at Calle 49, ☏ 981/6–68–29. ☞ Free. ☾ Tues.–Sat. 9–1 and 4:30–8, Sun. 9–1.*

⑯ Three long blocks north, away from the city center and in a residential neighborhood, you can find the beautifully restored **Iglesia de San Francisco** (1546), the oldest church site in Campeche. Possibly more significant is that it marks the spot where, some say, the first Mass on the North American continent was said in 1517. One of Cortés's grandsons was baptized here, and the baptismal font still stands.

About 2 miles from the downtown historic district, the **Fuerte San Miguel** commands one of the grandest views in the Yucatán, overlooking the city and the Gulf of Mexico. Built in 1771, the fort was positioned to bombard enemy ships with cannon balls before they could get close enough to attack Campeche; as soon as it was completed, pirates stopped attacking the city without a fight. The fort now hosts historic displays, including Maya artifacts along with relics of Campeche's pirate past. *Carretera Escenica, no* ☎. ☞ *Free.* ☾ *Tues.– Sat. 8–8, Sun. 8–1.*

Shopping

Folk art in Campeche is typical of the rest of Yucatán's handicrafts: basketry, leather goods, embroidered cloth, and clay trinkets. With a few exceptions, most of the shops sell cheap-looking trinkets.

Visit the **municipal market** (Circuito Baluartes at Calle 53), at the eastern end of the city, for crafts and food. The new **Veleros Artesanía Boutique** (Ah-Kin-Pech shopping center, ☎ 981/1–24–46), owned by craftsman David Pérez, stocks his miniature ships, sea shells, and jewelry fashioned from sanded and polished bull's horns. Pérez's first shop, **Artesanía Típica Naval** (Calle 8 No. 259, ☎ 981/6–57–08), is still thriving but it's much smaller and more cramped than the new store. Neither store accepts credit cards.

Sports

Hunting, fishing, and birding are popular throughout the State of Campeche. Contact Don José Sansores at his office in the Hotel Castelmar (Calle 61 No. 2, ☎ 981/6–23–56, ℻ 981/1–06–24) for information regarding the regulations and best areas for each sport.

Dining

There is nothing fancy about Campeche's restaurants, but the regional cuisine is renowned throughout Mexico—particularly the fish and shellfish stews, shrimp cocktails, squid and octopus, crabs' legs, *panuchos* (tortillas stuffed with beans and topped with meat or fish), and Yucatecan specialties. Because regional produce is plentiful, most restaurants—including all those listed below—fall into the inexpensive to moderate (under $15 for a three-course meal excluding drinks and tips) price categories. Restaurants throughout Campeche have casual dress codes (no shorts) and do not require reservations.

La Ceiba. This huge place (seating 400 under two tropically inspired thatched-roof salons) specializes in lobster and shrimp plates. House favorites are *La Ceiba* lobster salad (fresh chunks mixed with diced tomato and onion) and shrimp *a la Ceiba* (cooked shrimp bathed in cream sauce). It's a little removed from the downtown area but lots of local businessmen and university students congregate here for a late breakfast or early lunch. ✕ *Av. Resurgimiento 393, near the carretera Campeche-Lerma,* ☎ 981/1–38–09. MC, V. ☾ *Daily 10 AM–7 PM.*

★ **La Pigua.** A favorite with local professionals lingering over long lunches, La Pigua is perhaps the best seafood restaurant in town, with the most pleasant ambience. The long, glass-walled dining room is surrounded by trees and plants. A truly ambitious lunch would start with a seafood cocktail or plate of cold crab claws, followed by *pescado relleno,* a fish fillet stuffed with finely diced shellfish, and then local peaches drenched in sweet liqueurs. ✕ *Av. Miguel Alemán 197-A,* ☎ 981/1–33–65. MC, V. No dinner.

Miramar. This restaurant across from Hotel Castelmar attracts locals and foreign visitors with its fabulous *huevos motuleños* (fried eggs smothered in refried beans and garnished with peas, chopped ham, shredded cheese, and tomato sauce), red snapper, shellfish, soups, and meat dishes. The wooden tables and chairs and the paintings of the coat-of-arms of the Mexican Republic give Miramar a colonial feel. ✕ *Calle 8 No. 293 A,* ☎ 981/6–28–83. MC, V.

Lodging

Most of Campeche City's hotels are old (and several are in disrepair), reflecting the city's lackadaisical attitude toward tourism. Hotels tend to be either luxury accommodations along the waterfront, with air-conditioning, restaurants, and other standard amenities, or basic downtown accommodations offering only ceiling fans and a no-credit-card policy. Those in the latter category tend to be either seedy and undesirable or oddly charming, with some architectural and regional detail unique to each.

CATEGORY	COST*
$$$	over $90
$$	$40–$90
$	under $40

All prices are for a standard double room, excluding 10% tax.

$$$ **Ramada Inn.** The luxurious Ramada has undergone major renova-
★ tions: 30 rooms and new kitchen facilities were added, and improvements were made to the swimming pool and grounds in 1994. Fairly large rooms, with all the necessary amenities, are decorated in shades of blue and have rattan furnishings; balconies overlook the pool or the bay. The lobby restaurant, El Poquito, is extremely popular with locals at breakfast and at night before the disco Atlantis opens. ⊞ *Av. Ruíz Cortines 51, along waterfront,* ☎ *981/6–22–33 or 800/228–9898,* ℻ *981/1–16–18. 149 rooms. Restaurant, coffee shop, pool, exercise room, disco, travel services. AE, MC, V.*

$$ **Alhambra.** A great choice away from the bustle of the city, the Alhambra is a modern hotel facing the waterfront near the university. A wide screen TV plays softly in the lobby; TVs in the rooms get U.S. stations, sometimes including CNN. Rooms are carpeted and clean, with king-and double-size beds. ⊞ *Av. Resurgimiento 85 between Av. Universidad and Av. Augusto Melgar,* ☎ *981/6–68–22,* ℻ *981/6–61–32. 98 rooms. Restaurant, bar, pool, tennis court. MC, V.*

$$ **Del Paseo.** Located in the quiet San Roman neighborhood, a block from the ocean, this new hotel is cheerful and well-lit. Rooms, painted in a soft rose with tasteful rattan furniture, have balconies, cable TV, and air-conditioning. A glass-roofed atrium next to the lobby is lovely with its globe lamps, park benches, and many plants. ⊞ *Calle 8 No. 215,* ☎ *981/1–00–84 or 981/1–01–00,* ℻ *981/1–00–97. 40 rooms. Restaurant, bar, room service. MC, V.*

$ **Colonial.** This building—the former home of a high-ranking army lieutenant—dates back to 1850 but was made over as a hotel in the 1940s, when its wonderful tiles were added. Pastel-colored rooms with ceiling fans are clean and functional, but the hotel's public areas have become extremely run-down. ⊞ *Calle 14 No. 122, between Calles 55 and 57,* ☎ *981/6–23–22. 30 rooms. No credit cards.*

$ **Lopez.** Cheerful pink, yellow, and white walls and an open, airy ambience make this little two-story hotel a pleasant place to stay. Standard rooms include colonial-style desks and armoires, luggage stands, and easy chairs. The restaurant serves basic Continental fare, but it's a convenient enough stop for breakfast, lunch, or dinner. ⊞ *Calle 12 No. 189, between Calles 61 and 63,* ☎ *981/6–30–21. 39 rooms. Restaurant (closed Sun.). AE, MC, V.*

Nightlife

If you're in the mood to dance, try Campeche's two discos, **Atlantis** (Ramada Inn, ☎ 981/6–22–33) and **El Dragon** (Sajuge complex on Av.

Resurgimiento, a half block from the Alhambra Hotel, ☎ 981/1–18–10 or 981/6–42–89). Both places are open Thursday to Saturday nights only. Two of Campeche's most conveniently located movie theaters, **Cine Estelar** (Av. Miguel Alemán and Calle 49-B) and **Cine Colón** (Calle 12 and Calle 59), show U.S. films with subtitles in Spanish.

Campeche City Essentials

Arriving and Departing

BY PLANE

Aeromexico (☎ 981/6–56–78 in Campeche or 800/237–6639) has one flight daily from Mexico City.

BY CAR

Campeche can be reached from Mérida in about 1½ hours along the 160-kilometer (99-mile) *via corta* (short way, Rte. 180). The alternative route, the 250-kilometer (155-mile) *via larga* (long way, Rte. 261), takes at least three hours but crosses the major Maya ruins of Uxmal, Kabah, and Sayil. From Chetumal, take Rte. 186 west to Francisco Escárcega, where you pick up Rte. 261 north; the drive takes about seven hours.

BY TRAIN

The **Mexican National Railroad** (Av. Héroes del Nacozari, s/n, ☎ 981/6–20–09 or 981/6–14–33) has routes to Campeche from Mérida and Mexico City, but the lines are not among those that have been upgraded. It may be difficult to book a sleeper on the Mexico City line (the trip is 24 hours long), so this journey is recommended only for the most stoic traveler. Two trains depart daily from Campeche, at 8 AM and 11 PM, for the 10-hour trip to Palenque.

BY BUS

There is generally a big difference between first- and second-class bus service throughout Mexico. The former is non-stop and offers more comfortable coaches; the price difference is negligible. **ADO** (Av. Gobernadores 289 at Calle 45, along Rte. 261 to Mérida, ☎ 981/6–28–02), a first-class bus line, runs service to Campeche from Coatzacoalcos, Ciudad del Carmen, and Mérida every half hour, and from Mexico City, Puebla, Tampico, Veracruz, and Villahermosa regularly, but less frequently. The deluxe **Omnibus Caribe Express** (☎ 981/1–39–73) travels between Campeche, Mérida, Villahermosa, and Cancún. Buses depart from the Plaza Ah-Kim-Pech on Av. Pedro Sainz de Baranda no. 120. There is second-class service on **Autobuses del Sur** (☎ 981/6–34–45) from Chetumal, Ciudad del Carmen, Escárcega, Mérida, Palenque, Tuxtla Gutiérrez, Villahermosa, and intermediate points throughout the Yucatán Peninsula. The second-class line **Camioneros de Campeche** (☎ 981/6–23–22) has five buses daily to Uxmal and two to Edzná.

Getting Around

BY BUS

The municipal bus system covers the entire city, but you can easily visit the major sights on foot. Public buses run along Avenida Ruíz Cortines and cost under $1.

BY CAR

There is a **Hertz** representative at the Hotel Baluartes (Av. Ruíz Cortines s/n, ☎ 981/1–18–84).

BY TAXI

Taxis can be hailed on the street, or—more reliably—commissioned from the main **taxi stand** (Calle 8 between Calles 55 and 53, ☎ 981/6–23–66 or 981/6–52–30) or at stands by the bus stations and market. Because of the scarcity of taxis, it's quite common to share them with other people headed in the same direction as you. Don't be surprised to see one already occupied slow down to where you are standing if the cab driver thinks he can pick up another fare.

Guided Tours

A three-hour walking and driving tour of the city departs daily from Baluarte San Carlos (Av. 16 de Septiembre at Circuito Baluartes) every afternoon at 4 during the months of July, August and December, as well as during Holy Week (March or April); the fee is $5. For further information contact the tourist office (*see below*).

Important Addresses and Numbers

EMERGENCIES

Police (Av. Resurgimiento s/n, a half block from the Hotel Alhambra, ☎ 981/6–23–29, or, in town, 06); **Red Cross** (Av. Resurgimiento s/n, ☎ 981/5–24–11).

LATE-NIGHT PHARMACIES

Clínica Campeche (Av. Central No. 65, near the Social Security Clinic, ☎ 981/6–56–12) is open 24 hours. The **Farmacia Alhambra** in the Hotel Alhambra (Av. Resurgimiento No. 85, between Av. Universidad and Av. Augusto Melgar, ☎ 981/1–12–46), open 7 AM–11 PM, will deliver to guests of other hotels.

VISITOR INFORMATION

The headquarters of the **State of Campeche Office of Tourism** is currently at Calle 12, No. 153 (☎ 981/6–67–67); however, it will soon be moved. Two smaller offices are located at Circuito Baluartes between Calles 12 and 14 (☎ 981/6–73–64) and Baluarte Santa Rosa (*see* Exploring, *above*). All three offices are open weekdays 9–3 and 6–9, Saturday 9–1.

MÉRIDA AND THE STATE OF YUCATÁN

Updated by
Patricia Alisau

There is a marvelous eccentricity about Mérida. Fully urban, with maddeningly slow-moving traffic, it has a self-sufficient, self-contented air that would suggest a small town more than a state capital of some 600,000 inhabitants (locals say there are 850,000). Gaily pretentious turn-of-the-century buildings have an Iberian-Moorish flair for the ornate, but most of the architecture is low-lying and although the city sprawls, it is not imposing. Grandiose colonial facades adorned with iron grillwork, carved wooden doors, and archways conceal marble tiles and lush gardens; horse-drawn carriages hark back to the city's heyday as the wealthiest capital in Mexico.

In addition to the European influence, the native Mexican presence is unmistakable: People are short and dark-skinned, with sculpted bones and almond eyes; women pad about in *huipiles* (hand-embroidered, sacklike white dresses), and craftsmen and vendors from the outlying villages come to town in their huaraches. So many centuries after the conquest, Yucatán remains one of the last great strongholds of Mexico's indigenous population. To this day, in fact, many Maya do not even speak Spanish, primarily because of the peninsula's geographic and, hence, cultural isolation from the rest of the country.

Physically, Yucatán, too, differs from the rest of the country. Its geography and wildlife have more in common with Florida and Cuba—with which it was probably once connected—than with the central Mexican plateau and mountains. A mostly flat limestone slab possessing almost no bodies of water, it is rife with underground cenotes, caves with stalactites, small hills, and intense jungle.

It is, of course, the celebrated Maya ruins—Chichén Itzá and Uxmal especially—that bring most tourists to the Yucatán, but small towns such as Valladolid, while bereft of star-quality sightseeing attractions, charm visitors with their very unpretentiousness. Rains fall heaviest here between May and November, bringing with them an uncomfortable humidity.

Exploring

Mérida's traffic and noise are frustrating, but the city is the cultural and intellectual center of the peninsula, with museums, schools, and attractions that greatly enhance the traveler's insights into the history and character of Yucatán. Consider making it one of the first stops in your travels, and make sure your visit includes a Sunday, when traffic is light and the city seems to revert to a more gracious era.

Numbers in the margin correspond to points of interest on the Mérida map.

❶ Begin at the **main square,** which the Meridanos are beginning to call the *zócalo* along with its traditional names, the Plaza Principal and Plaza de la Independencia. Ancient, geometrically pruned laurel trees and *confidenciales*—*S*-shaped benches designed for tête-à-têtes—invite lingering. The plaza was laid out in 1542 on the ruins of T'hó, the Maya city demolished to make way for Mérida, and is still the focal point around which the most important public buildings cluster.

❷ The **Casa de Montejo** sits on the south side of the plaza, on Calle 63. Montejo—father and son—conquered the peninsula and founded Mérida in 1542; they built this stately French-style palace ten years later. The property remained with the family until the late 1970s, when it was restored and converted into a bank. Step into the building weekdays between 9 and 5 to glimpse the lushly foliated inner patio.

❸ Continue around to the west side of the square, occupied by the 17th-century **Palacio Municipal** (Calle 62, between Calles 61 and 63)—the city hall—which is painted yellow and trimmed with white arcades, balustrades, and the national coat of arms.

❹ Occupying the northeast corner of the square is the **Palacio del Gobierno,** or Governor's Palace (Calle 61, between Calles 60 and 62), built in 1885 on the site of the Casa Real (Royal House). The upper floor of the Governor's Palace contains Fernando Castro Pacheco's murals of the history of Yucatán, painted in 1978.

❺ The oldest **Catedral** on the North American mainland stands cater-corner from the Palacio del Gobierno. Begun in 1561, it took several hundred Maya laborers, working with stones from the pyramids of the ravaged Maya city, 36 years to complete. Its Renaissance-style facade is stark and unadorned, with gunnery slits instead of windows, and faintly Moorish spires. Inside, the black **Cristo de las Ampollas** (Christ of the Blisters) next to the altar is a replica of the original,

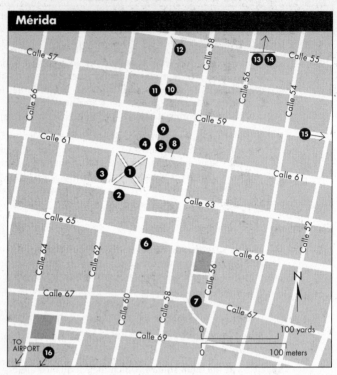

Mérida

destroyed during the Revolution. According to legend, the Christ figure was carved from a tree that had burned all night yet appeared the next morning unscathed. A later fire left the statue covered with the blisters for which it is named.

Head two blocks south from the cathedral along Calle 60 to Calle 65, Mérida's main shopping street. This bustling heart of the commercial quarter is lined with, among other businesses, banks and perfumeries.

6 Turn left to the **Mercado de Artesanías "García Rejón,"** a market where you'll find local handicrafts and souvenirs. Shops selling dry goods, straw hats, and hammocks occupy both sides of Calle 65. A block farther east, between Calles 56 and 58, stand two picturesque 19th-century edifices housing the **main post office** and **telegraph buildings.**

7 Behind them sprawls the pungent, labyrinthine **Mercado Municipal,** where almost every patch of ground is occupied by native Mexican women selling chilies, herbs, and fruit. On the second floor of the main building is the **Bazar de Artesanías Municipales,** the principal handicrafts market, where you can buy jewelry, pottery, embroidered clothes, hammocks, and straw bags.

8 History lovers should stop in at the small but informative **Museo de la Ciudad,** on Calle 61 between Calles 60 and 58, housing prints, drawings, photographs, and other displays that recount Mérida's past. *Calle 61 at Calle 58, no ☏. ☛ Free. ⊙ Tues.–Sun. 8–8.*

North of the square on Calle 60 there are many noteworthy parks and historic buildings, including, only half a block away, the small,

9 cozy **Parque Hidalgo,** or Cepeda Peraza, as it is officially known. Renovated mansions-turned-hotels and sidewalk cafés stand at two corners of the park, which comes alive at night with marimba bands and street vendors.

⑩ Just north of the park, on Calle 60 is the Italianate **Teatro Peón Contreras,** designed in 1908 along the lines of the grand European turn-of-the-century theaters and opera houses. Today, in addition to performing arts, the theater also houses temporary art exhibits and the main **Centro de Información Turistica** (☎ 99/24–91–22), which can provide information about local attractions. A new café serving cappuccino and light snacks spills out to a patio from inside the theater to the right of the Information Center.

⑪ Opposite the theater, the arabesque **Universidad Autonoma de Yucatán** plays a major role in the city's cultural and intellectual life.

⑫ Heading north on Calle 60, you'll pass the **Parque Santa Lucía** on your left, at Calle 55. The rather plain park draws crowds to its Thursday-night serenades, performed by local musicians. The small church opposite the park dates from 1575 and was built as a place of worship for the African and Caribbean slaves who lived here.

⑬ Beginning at Calle 47 and running adjacent and roughly parallel to Calle 56, the 10-block-long street known as the **Paseo de Montejo** exemplifies the Parisian airs the city took on in the late 19th century, when wealthy plantation owners were building opulent, impressive mansions. The broad boulevard, lined with tamarinds and laurels, is sometimes wistfully referred to as Mérida's Champs-Elysées. The
⑭ most compelling of the mansions, the pale peach **Palacio Cantón,** presently houses the **Museum of Anthropology and History,** dedicated to the culture and history of the Maya; it's one of the finest of its type in the country. Although bilingual legends accompany the fascinating displays, lengthier explanations are in Spanish only; private guides are available for hire. There's also an excellent bookstore. *Calle 43 at Paseo de Montejo,* ☎ *99/23–05–57.* ☛ *$4.50.* ☉ *Tues.–Sat. 9–8; Sun. 8–2; bookstore open weekdays 9–3.*

The Paseo de Montejo continues north, eventually becoming the road to Progreso. Before turning back from the museum, walk a few blocks north; you'll pass numerous restaurants and several hotels.

⑮ Several blocks east of the plaza, along Calle 59 to Calle 52, the **Museo de Arte Popular** is housed in a fine old mansion. The ground floor is devoted to Yucatecan arts and crafts, displaying weaving, straw baskets, filigree jewelry, carved wood, beautifully carved conch shells, exhibits on huipil manufacture, and the like. The second floor focuses on the popular arts of the rest of Mexico. *Calle 59, at the corner of Calle 52, no* ☎. ☛ *Free.* ☉ *Tues.–Sat. 8–8.*

⑯ At the far south of the city, about nine blocks south of the square at Calles 66 and 77, stands the **Ermita de Santa Isabel** (circa 1748), part of a Jesuit hermitage. A resting place in colonial days for travelers heading to Campeche, the restored chapel is an enchanting spot to visit at sunset. Next door there's a little garden with a waterfall and footpaths bordered with bricks and colored stones.

To Chichén Itzá and Valladolid

Numbers in the margin correspond to numbers on the State of Yucatán map.

Chichén Itzá attracts a large number of visitors who come for the famous ruins. For those traveling by car, the trip can be enhanced by

State of Yucatán

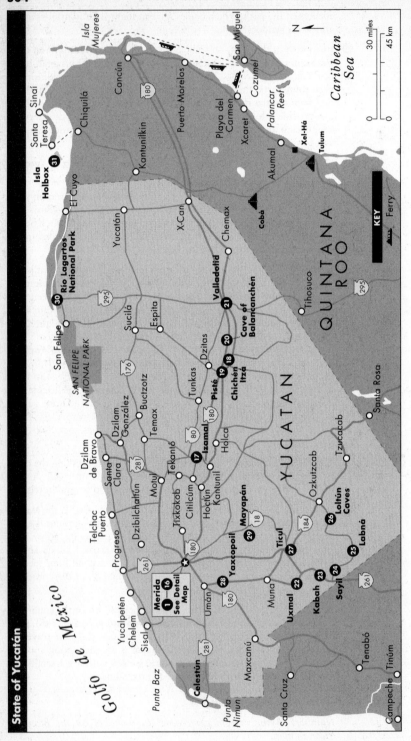

stopping at several villages on the way. Route 80 passes through **Tixkokob,** a Maya community famous for its hammock weavers. By cutting south at Tekantó and east again at Citilcúm (the road has no number, and there are few road signs), you'll reach **Izamal,** nicknamed Ciudad Amarillo (Yellow City) for the painted earth-tone-yellow buildings. In the center of town stands an enormous 16th-century **Franciscan monastery** perched on—and built from—the remains of a Maya pyramid. Another pyramid, called Kinich Kakmó, all that remains of a royal Maya city that flourished here hundreds of years ago, is a few blocks from the monastery and commands a wonderful view of the surrounding countryside.

Probably the best-known Maya ruin, **Chichén Itzá,** the Maya-Toltec center, was the most important city in Yucatán from the 10th to the 12th century. An architectural mélange, Chichén was altered by each successive wave of inhabitants, but archaeologists have yet to explain the long gaps of time when the buildings seem to have been uninhabited. The site is believed to have been first settled in AD 432, abandoned for an unknown period of time, then rediscovered in 964 by the Maya-speaking Itzás who gave the site its name; *Chichén Itzá* means "the mouth of the well of the Itzás." The Itzás also abandoned the site, and later in the 10th century it was rediscovered by the central-Mexican Toltecs, who abandoned it forever in 1224.

The majesty and enormity of this site are unforgettable. Chichén Itzá encompasses approximately 6 square kilometers (2 square miles), though only 20 to 30 buildings of the several hundred at the site have been fully explored. It's divided into two parts—Old and New—though architectural motifs from the classical period are found in both sections. A more convenient distinction is topographical, since there are two major complexes of buildings separated by a dirt path.

The martial, imperial architecture of the Toltecs and the more cerebral architectural genius and astronomical expertise of the Maya are married in the 98-foot-tall pyramid called **El Castillo** (The Castle), which dominates the site and rises above all the other buildings. Atop the castle is a temple dedicated to Kukulcán (the Maya name for Quetzalcóatl), the legendary leader-turned-deity from Tula in the Valley of Mexico who was incarnated by the plumed serpent. At the spring and fall equinoxes (March 21 and September 21), the afternoon light and shadow strike one of these balustrades in such a way as to form a shadow representation of Kukulcán undulating out of his temple and down the pyramid to bless the fertile earth. (Thousands of people travel here for to see this phenomenon; hotel reservations should be made as much as a year in advance). An excellent sound-and-light show highlights the architectural details in the Castillo and other buildings with a clarity the eye doesn't see in daylight.

A more ancient temple inside the Castillo is open to the public for only a few hours in the morning and again in the afternoon. Claustrophobes should think twice before entering: The stairs are narrow, dark, and winding, and there is often a line of tourists going both ways, making the trip somewhat frightening.

The temple rests on a massive trapezoidal square, on the west side of which is Chichén Itzá's largest **ball court,** one of seven on the site. The game played here was something like soccer (no hands were used), but it had religious as well as recreational significance. Bas-relief carvings at the court depict a player being decapitated, the blood spurting from his severed neck fertilizing the earth.

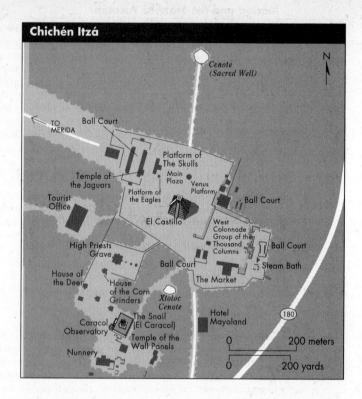

Chichén Itzá

Between the ball court and El Castillo stands a **Tzompantli,** or stone platform, carved with rows of human skulls. In ancient times it was actually covered with stakes on which the heads of enemies were impaled. The predilection for sacrifice was once believed to have come from the Toltecs, but recent research suggests that the pre-Toltec Maya had already been indulging in their own forms of the ritual. In the **Sacred Well,** a cenote 65 yards in diameter that sits half a mile north of El Castillo at the end of a 900-foot-long sacbe (road), were found skeletons of men, women, and children thrown in to placate the rain gods and water spirits. Thousands of artifacts made of gold, jade, and other precious materials, have been recovered from the brackish depths of the cenote. The well's excavation launched the field of underwater archaeology, later honed by Jacques Cousteau.

Returning to the causeway, you will see on your left the **Group of the Thousand Columns** with the famous **Temple of the Warriors,** a masterful example of the Toltec influence at Chichén Itzá. This temple so resembles Pyramid B at Tula—the Toltecs' homeland, north of Mexico City—that scholars believe the architectural plans must have been carried 1,280 kilometers (800 miles) overland. Murals of everyday village life and scenes of war can be viewed here, and an artistic representation of the defeat of the Maya can be found on the interior murals of the adjacent **Temple of the Jaguar.**

To get to the less visited cluster of structures at Chichén Itzá—often confused with Old Chichén Itzá—take the main road south from the Temple of the Jaguar past El Castillo and turn right onto a small path opposite the ball court on your left. Archaeologists are currently working in this area, restoring several buildings including the **Tomb of the High Priest,** where several tombs with skeletons and jade offerings were found. The most impressive structure within this area is the astronomical observatory called **El Caracol** (the name, meaning "snail," refers to the spiral staircase at the building's core). Built in several stages, El Caracol is possibly the sole round building constructed by the Maya. Although definitely used for observing the heavens, it also appears to have served a religious function. After leaving El Caracol, continue south several hundred yards to the beautiful **Casa de las Monjas** (Nunnery) and its annex, which have long panels carved with flowers and animals, latticework, hieroglyph-covered lintels, and Chac masks.

At Old Chichén Itzá, pure "Maya" style—with playful latticework, Chac masks, and gargoyle-like serpents on the cornices—dominates. Highlights include the **Date Group** (so named because of the complete series of hieroglyphic date inscriptions), the **House of the Phalli,** and the **Temple of the Three Lintels.** Maya guides will lead you down the path by an old narrow-gauge railroad track to even more ruins, barely unearthed, if you ask. A fairly good restaurant and great ice-cream stand are located in the entrance building, and there are refreshment stands by the cenote and on the pathway near El Caracol. ☞ *Site and museum: $6, free on Sun. and holidays. Parking: $1. Use of video camera: $8. ☉ Daily 8–5. Sound-and-light show in Spanish: $2, 7 PM; in English, $5.50, 9 PM.*

⑲ The town of **Pisté,** about 1 kilometer (³⁄₅ mile) west of the ruins on Route 180, serves mainly as a base camp for travelers to Chichén Itzá. Hotels, campgrounds, restaurants, and handicrafts shops tend to be cheaper here than south of the ruins. At the west end of town are a Pemex station and a bank.

From Chichén Itzá, drive east along Route 180 for about 4 kilometers (2½ miles), then turn left at the first dirt road you come to and con-
⑳ tinue for about ½ kilometer (³⁄₁₀ mile) to the **Cave of Balancanché.** This shrine, whose Maya name translates as "hidden throne," remained virtually undisturbed from the time of the Conquest until its discovery in 1959. Within the shrine is a large collection of artifacts—mostly vases, jars, and incense burners once filled with offerings. You'll walk past tiers of stalactites and stalagmites forming the image of sacred ceiba trees until you come to an underground lake, above which an altar to the rain god rises. In order to explore the shrine you must take one of the guided tours, which depart almost hourly, but you must be in fairly good shape, because some crawling is required; claustrophobes should skip it, and those who go should wear comfortable shoes. Also offered at the site is a sound-and-light show that fancifully recounts Maya history. *Caves can also be reached by bus or taxi from Chichén Itzá. ☞ Caves, including tour: $6, free on Sun.; show $5. ☉ Daily 9–4. Tours in English 11 AM, 1 and 3 PM; in Spanish 9 AM and noon; in French 10 AM.*

Following Route 180 east for another 40 kilometers (25 miles) will
㉑ take you to the second-largest city in the State of Yucatán, **Valladolid.** This picturesque, pleasant, and provincial town (population 50,000) is enjoying growing popularity among travelers en route to or from Chichén Itzá or Río Lagartos (*see below*) who are harried by more touristy towns. Montejo founded Valladolid in 1543 on the site of the Maya town of Zací. The city suffered during the Caste War, when it was besieged by the rebellious Maya (who killed all the Europeans they could find), and again during the Mexican Revolution.

Today, however, placidity reigns in this agricultural market town. The center is mostly colonial, although it has many 19th-century structures. The main sights are the **colonial churches,** principally the large **cathedral** on the central square and the 16th-century **San Bernardino Church and Convent** three blocks southwest. The latter were pillaged during the insurrection.

Valladolid is renowned for its cuisine, particularly its sausages. Try one of the restaurants within a block of the square, which also has two very good and reasonably priced hotels. You can also find good buys on sandals, baskets, and the local liqueur, Xtabentún, made from honey.

To Uxmal and the Puuc Route

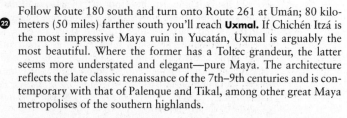

Follow Route 180 south and turn onto Route 261 at Umán; 80 kilometers (50 miles) farther south you'll reach **Uxmal.** If Chichén Itzá is the most impressive Maya ruin in Yucatán, Uxmal is arguably the most beautiful. Where the former has a Toltec grandeur, the latter seems more understated and elegant—pure Maya. The architecture reflects the late classic renaissance of the 7th–9th centuries and is contemporary with that of Palenque and Tikal, among other great Maya metropolises of the southern highlands.

The site is considered the finest and largest example of Puuc architecture, which embraces such details as ornate stone mosaics and friezes on the upper walls, intricate cornices with curled noses, rows of columns, and soaring vaulted arches. Lines are clean and uncluttered, with the horizontal—especially the parallelogram—preferred to the vertical. Many of the flat, low, elongated buildings were built on artificial platforms and laid out in quadrangles.

While most of Uxmal remains unrestored, three buildings in particular merit attention. The most prominent, the **Pyramid of the Magician,** is, at 125 feet high, the tallest structure at the site. Unlike most Maya pyramids, which are stepped and angular, it has a strangely elliptical design. Built five times, each time over the previous structure, the pyramid has a stairway on its western side that leads through a giant mask of the rain god, Chac, with its mouth wide open to two temples at the summit.

West of the pyramid lies the **Nunnery,** or Quadrangle of the Nuns considered by some to be the architectural jewel of Uxmal. You may enter the four buildings; each comprises a series of low, gracefully repetitive chambers that look onto a central patio. Elaborate decoration blankets the upper facades, in contrast with the smooth, sheer blocks that face the lower walls. The mosaics thrust into the upper facade are huge, sometimes surpassing several feet in size.

Continue walking south; you'll pass the ball court before reaching the **Palace of the Governor,** which archaeologist Victor von Hagen considered the most magnificent building ever erected in the Americas. Interestingly, the palace faces east while the rest of Uxmal faces west. Archaeologists believe this is because the palace was used to sight the planet Venus. Covering five acres and rising over an immense acropolis, the palace lies at the heart of what must have been Uxmal's administrative center. Decorating the facade are intricate friezes that required more than 20,000 individually cut stones.

First excavated in 1929 by the Danish explorer Franz Blom, the site served in 1841 as home to John Lloyd Stephens. Today a sound-and-

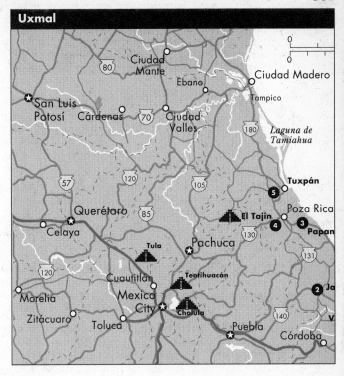

Uxmal

light show recounts Maya legends, including the kidnapping of an Uxmal princess by a king of Chichén Itzá, and focuses on the people's dependence on rain—thus the cult of Chac. The artificial colored light brings out details of carvings and mosaics that are easy to miss when the sun is shining. The show is performed nightly in English and is one of the better such productions. ☛ *Site and museum: $6, free on Sun. and holidays. Parking: $1. Use of video camera: $8.* ⊗ *Daily 8–5. Sound-and-light show in English: $4.50, 9* PM.

23 Four smaller Puuc sites near Uxmal are also worth visiting, and en route you pass through beautiful hilly jungles. **Kabah,** 23 kilometers (14 miles) south of Uxmal on Route 261, lies almost entirely in ruins; its mounded landscape has a soft, almost Grecian beauty. Linked to Uxmal by a sacbe, at the end of which looms a great independent arch, is the 151-foot-long **Palace of the Masks** (also known as **Codz-Poop** or "coiled mat"), so called because of the 250 Chac masks.

24 Five kilometers (3 miles) to the south you'll see the turnoff to **Sayil,** or "home of ants," the oldest site of the group, renowned primarily for its majestic three-story **palace** with 70 rooms. The structure recalls Palenque in its use of multiple planes, its columned porticos and sober cornices, and in the play of its long, graceful horizontal masses. ☛ *$4, free on Sun. and holidays.* ⊗ *Daily 8–5.*

25 Another 9 kilometers (6 miles) beyond Sayil, on Route 261, rests the monumental arch at **Labná.** This lovely arch, called "La Puerta" or "The Gateway," is a fanciful corbeled arch rising high into a near peak with elaborate latticework and a small chamber on each side of it. One of the true curiosities of Maya civilization is that the Maya never discovered the true, or curved, arch. ☛ *$4, free on Sun.* ⊗ *Daily 8–5.*

㉖ Continue along the road from Labná for another 18 kilometers (11 miles) to the **Loltún Caves,** a 500-meter (³/₁₀-mile) series of caverns containing Maya and stone artifacts dating from pre-Mayan times of around 2500 BC and stalactites and stalagmites. ☛ *$6, $3 on Sun.* ☉ *Tues.–Sun. 9–5; guided tours at 9:30, 11, 12:30, 2, and 3.*

㉗ From Loltún, drive 10 kilometers (6 miles) northeast to **Oxkutzcab,** where, to the left, you can pick up Route 184. An additional 17 kilometers (10½ miles) will bring you into **Ticul,** where most of the Yucatecan pottery is produced, along with huipiles and shoes. Many descendants of the Xiu dynasty, which ruled Uxmal before the Conquest, still live here. One of the larger towns in Yucatán, Ticul boasts a handsome 17th-century church.

㉘ If you wish to get back to Mérida, turn right off Route 184 at Muna onto Route 261 and follow Route 261 back to Route 180. Along Route 261, about 62 kilometers (38 miles) north of Uxmal, you may want to stop at **Yaxcopoil,** a restored 17th-century hacienda that offers a nice change of pace from the ruins. The building, with its distinctive Moorish double arch out front, has been used as a film set and is the best-known henequen plantation in the region. Visit the museum inside, which displays archaeological pieces and machinery used in the processing of henequen. *Km 33, Rte. 261.* ☛ *Free.* ☉ *Mon.–Sat. 8–sunset, Sun. 9–1.*

㉙ Those who are really enamored of Yucatán and the ancient Maya can detour at Ticul some 49 kilometers (30 miles) east on Route 18 to the ruined city of **Mayapán,** the last of the great city-states on the peninsula. There have been few excavations here, however, so archaeological evidence of past glory is limited to a few fallen statues of Kukulcán, and today the site is mainly of historical interest. *Just before Telchaquillo, Mayapán is off the road to your left; follow signs.* ☛ *$6, free on Sun.* ☉ *Daily 8–5.*

Rio Lagartos National Park and Isla Holbox

㉚ If you're a flamingo fan (flamingo season runs from April to May), take Route 295 101 kilometers (63 miles) north of Valladolid to Río Lagartos and **Río Lagartos National Park.** Actually encompassing a long estuary, not a river, the park was developed with ecotourism in mind, though the alligators for which it and the village were named have long since been hunted into extinction. In addition to flamingos, birders can spot egrets, herons, ibis, cormorants, pelicans, and even peregrine falcons flying over these murky waters; fishing is good, too, and hawksbill and green turtles lay their eggs on the beach at night. **Hotel Nefertiti,** one of five hotels in town, offers boat tours, or you can hire a boat from the docks near the hotel.

㉛ If you'd like to head even farther afield from Río Lagartos, consider a trip to **Isla Holbox,** a tiny island (25 kilometers/16 miles long) at the eastern end of the Río Lagartos estuary and just across the Quintana Roo state line. A fishing fan's heaven because of the pompano, bass, barracuda, and shark thronging its waters, the island also pleases seekers of tranquility who don't mind rudimentary accommodations (rooms and hammocks for rent) and simple palapa restaurants. Seabirds fill the air, the long sandy beach is strewn with seashells, and the swimming is good on the gulf side. To get here, take Route 176 to Kantunilkin, then head north on the unnumbered road for 44 kilometers (27 miles) to Chiquilá. Continue by ferry to the island; schedules vary, but there are two crossings (time: one hour) a day. Isla Holbox can also be reached from Valladolid.

Shopping

For the most part Mérida is the best place in Yucatán to buy local handicrafts at reasonable prices. The main products include *hamacas* (hammocks), *guayaberas* (loose dress shirts for men), *huaraches* (woven leather sandals), *huipiles* (hand-embroidered dresses), baskets, *jipis* or Panama hats, leather goods, gold and silver filigree jewelry, masks, painted gourds, vanilla, and piñatas.

On the second floor of the **central municipal market** (between Calles 65 and 56 and Calles 54 and 59) you'll find crafts, food, flowers, and live birds, among other items. If you're interested solely in handicrafts, visit the **Bazar Garcia Rejon** (corner of Calles 65 and 62), which has neat rows of indoor stalls with leather items, palm hats, hand-made guitars, and more. On Sunday starting at 9, the **Handicraft Bazaar** (in front of the Municipal Palace across from the main square) is filled with huipiles, hats and costume jewelry; also starting at 9, the **Popular Art Bazaar** (Parque Santa Lucía, at the corner of Calles 60 and 55) offers paintings, engravings, and woodcuts by local artists.

Specialty Shops

Stylish cotton dresses, skirts, and pants for women, made from traditional Yucatecan fabrics by Mérida designer Fernando Huertas, are featured at **Fernando Huertas** (Calle 59, No. 511, between Calles 60 and 62, ☎ 99/28–60–17). You might not wear a guayabera to a business meeting as some men in Mexico do, but the shirts are cool, comfortable, and attractive; for a good selection, try **Camisería Canul** (Calle 59, No. 496, between Calles 60 and 62, ☎ 99/28–35–12). Pick up jipi at **Tejidos Y Carteles Nacionales** (Calle 56, No. 530, ☎ 99/28–55–61), a hat emporium with styles for men and ladies in casual as well as dressy designs. The best place for hammocks is **Hamacas El Aguacate** (Calle 58, No. 604, at Calle 73, ☎ 99/28–64–29), a family-run establishment selling a wide variety of sizes and designs. **Casa de Artesanías** (Calle 63, No. 503, between Calles 64 and 66, ☎ 99/23–53–92) displays folk art from throughout Mexico, among them hand-painted, wooden animals from Oaxaca and hand-embroidered vests and placemats from Chiapas.

La Perla (Calle 60, No. 496-C between Calles 50 and 61, ☎ 99/28–56–12) is one of the few jewelry shops that sell difficult-to-find old-fashioned Yucatecan filigree earrings and bracelets—in silver dipped in gold. The store also stocks lots of quality silver jewelry in modern designs.

Sports

Bullfights

Bullfights are most often held from November to January, or during other holiday periods at the **bullring** (Paseo de la Reforma), near Avenida Colón. Contact the travel desk at your hotel or one of the tourist information centers; prices range from $10 to $15 for seats in the sun and from $15 to $20 for seats in the shade.

Fishing

Those interested in sportfishing for such catch as grouper, red snapper, and sea bass, among others, will be sated in **Yucalpetén,** west of Progreso. **Río Lagartos** also offers good fishing in its murky waters. In

the Parque Natural del Flamenco Mexicano in **Celestún,** you have
your choice of river or gulf fishing.

Golf

There is an 18-hole championship golf course (and restaurant, bar,
and clubhouse) at **Club Campestre de Mérida** (Calle 30, No. 500, ☎
99/44–25–55), 16 kilometers (10 miles) north of Mérida on the road
to Progreso.

Dining and Lodging

Dining

Dining out is a pleasure in Mérida. The city's 50-odd restaurants
offer a superb variety of cuisine—primarily Yucatecan, of course, but
also Lebanese, Italian, French, Chinese, and Mexican—at very reasonable prices. Generally, reservations are advised for those places
marked *$$$*, but only during the high season. Casual but neat dress is
acceptable at all Mérida restaurants.

Pisté, the village nearest to Chichén Itzá, is not a gourmand's town:
The food in most of its restaurants, which have been set up to handle
tour-bus crowds, is simple, overpriced, and only fair. The palapa-cov-
ered cafés along the main road are not bad, and the small markets
and produce stands can provide the makings for a modest picnic. The
restaurants near the ruins in Uxmal are nothing to write home about
either. The exception is Los Almendros, in Ticul, which is well worth
the 15-minute drive.

All restaurants are open for breakfast, lunch, and dinner unless other-
wise noted. People who like eating with the locals might stop in at one
of the many *loncherías* (diners) in the small towns and downtown dis-
tricts of cities for *panuchos* (cooked tortillas stuffed with beans and
topped with shredded meat or fish), *empanadas* (meat-filled
turnovers), tacos, or *salbutes* (fried tortillas smothered with diced
turkey, pickled onion, and sliced avocado).

CATEGORY	COST*
$$$$	over $20
$$$	$15–$20
$$	$8–$15
$	under $8

per person, excluding drinks, service, and tax

Lodging

Outside of Mérida you'll find that accommodations fit the low-key,
simple pace of the region. Internationally affiliated properties are the
exception rather than the rule; instead, charmingly idiosyncratic old
mansions offer visitors a base from which to explore the countryside
and Mérida itself—which merits at least a two-day stay.

In Mérida, location is very important in your choice of hotels: If you
plan to spend most of your time enjoying the city, stay in the vicinity
of the main square or along Calle 59. If you're a light sleeper, however, choose a hotel away from the plaza (traffic makes the noise level
unbearable); you're better off staying in one of the places along Paseo
de Montejo, about a 20-minute stroll from the Plaza Principal. All
hotels have air-conditioning unless otherwise noted. Properties in
Mérida have a 97000 postal code.

CATEGORY	COST*
$$$$	over $90
$$$	$60–$90
$$	$25–$60
$	under $25

All prices are for a standard double room, excluding 10% tax

Chichén Itzá

DINING AND LODGING

$$$$ **Mayaland.** The hotel closest to the ruins, this charming 1920s prop-
★ erty belongs to the Barbachano family, whose name is practically synonymous with tourism in Yucatán. In addition to a main hotel
building, there are a wing and several bungalows set in a large garden
on the 100-acre site. Colonial-style rooms in the main building feature
decorative tiles, ceiling fans, air-conditioning (except for five rooms),
and TVs; 13 bungalows also have TVs and air-conditioning. The hot
water often runs cold. Tour buses fill the road in front of the hotel, so
choose a room at the back. Light meals served poolside and at tables
overlooking the garden are a far better choice than the fixed-price
meals served in the dining room. ⊞ *Carretera Mérida–Cancún Km
120,* ☎ *in Chichén Itzá, 985/1–01–29; in Mérida, Mayaland Tours,
Av. Colón 502,* ☎ *99/46–23–31,* FAX *99/64–23–35;* ☎ *800/235–4079
in the U.S. 65 rooms. Restaurant, bar, pool. MC, V.*

$$$ **Hacienda Chichén.** A converted 17th-century hacienda, this hotel
★ once served as the home of archaeologist Edward S. Thompson and
later as the headquarters for the Carnegie archaeological expedition.
The rustic cottages have been modernized, and all rooms, which are
simply furnished in colonial Yucatecan style, have private baths and
verandas. The hotel has recently added air-conditioning to rooms and
a color satellite TV to the lobby area. An enormous old pool sits in
the midst of the landscaped gardens. Fairly good meals are served at
set hours on the patio overlooking the grounds; stick with the Yucate-
can specialties. ⊞ *Carretera Mérida–Cancún Km 120, in Chichén
Itzá* ☎ *985/1–00–45, in Mérida 99/24–88–44 or 99/24–21–50,* FAX
99/24–50–11, ☎ *800/223–4084 in the U.S. 18 rooms. Restaurant,
bar, pool. MC, V.*

$$ **Pirámide Inn Resort and RV Park.** This slightly tacky, American-
owned two-story motel in Pisté features rooms with white walls,
white tile floors, and modern furniture. The garden contains a small
Maya pyramid, a swimming pool, and a tennis court, and the restaurant is one of the best in Pisté. The RV park has been closed. ⊞ *1 km
before Chichén Itzá,* ☎ *985/6–24–62; Box 433, Mérida, Yucatán
(for reservations). 44 rooms. Restaurant, pool, tennis court, library.
MC, V.*

$ **Dolores Alba.** The best low-budget choice near the ruins is this family-
run hotel, a long-time favorite in the country south of Pisté. The rooms
are simple, clean, and comfortable; some have air-conditioning. Hammocks hang by the small pool, and breakfast and dinner are served
family-style in the main building. Free transportation to the ruins is
provided. ⊞ *Carretera Pisté–Cancún, 1½ mi south of Chichén Itzá,
reservations in Mérida Calle 63, No. 464,* ☎ *99/28–56–50,* FAX *99/28–
31–63. 28 rooms. Dining room, pool. MC, V.*

Mérida

DINING

$$$$ **Alberto's Continental Patio.** The setting—an early 18th century build-
★ ing adorned with mosaic floors from Cuba—is romantic; an inner
patio surrounded by rubber trees is ideal for starlit dining. Most of the
guests are tourists, but that need not detract from the surroundings or

the excellent food. If you order Lebanese food, your plate will be heaped with servings of shish kebab, fried kibi, cabbage rolls, hummus, eggplant, and tabbouleh, accompanied by pita bread, almond pie, and Turkish coffee. Black bean soup, enchiladas, fried bananas, and caramel custard make up the Mexican dinner; there are also a Yucatecan dinner, an Italian dinner, and à la carte appetizers and entrées. ✗ *Calle 64, No. 482, at Calle 57,* ☎ *99/28–53–67. AE, MC, V.* ☉ *Daily 11–11.*

$$$$ **La Bella Epoca.** For a truly special dinner, nothing matches the elegance
★ and style of this second-story dining room, the former ballroom of an old mansion that has been restored well beyond its original grandeur. Crystal chandeliers sparkle over tiny balcony tables overlooking Parque Hidalgo. An ambitious menu includes French, Mexican, Middle Eastern, Yucatecan, vegetarian, and unusual Maya dishes—try the *sikil-pak,* a dip with ground pumpkin seeds, charcoal-broiled tomatoes, and onions; or the succulent *pollo píbil* (chicken baked in banana leaves). Arrive for dinner before 8 PM to claim one of the small balcony tables overlooking the street. ✗ *Hotel del Parque, Calle 60, between Calles 57 and 59,* ☎ *99/28–19–28. AE, MC, V.*

$$ **La Casona.** This pretty mansion-turned-restaurant near Parque Santa Ana has an inner patio, arcade, and swirling ceiling fans; a new bar features live romantic music nightly. The accent is Yucatecan, with *poc chuc* (slices of pork marinated in sour orange juice and spices), pollo píbil, and *huachinango* (sea bass baked in banana leaf) among the recommended dishes. Some Italian offerings include homemade pasta. ✗ *Calle 60, No. 434, between Calles 47 and 49,* ☎ *99/23–99–96. AE, MC, V.* ☉ *Daily 1 PM–2 AM.*

$$ **Los Almendros.** A Mérida classic, this chain restaurant credits itself with the invention of poc chuc, and though perhaps overrated, it does know how to cater to the tourists and businesspeople who frequently fill its chairs and tables to the limit. The restaurant provides a more than passable introduction to the variety of Yucatecan cuisine, including *conchinita píbil* (pork baked in banana leaves), panuchos, *papadzules* (corn tortillas with pumpkinseed sauce), and *pollo ticuleño* (boneless, breaded chicken in tomato sauce filled with fried beans, peas, red peppers, ham, and cheese). All dishes are described in English with pictures on the paper menus. Sangria—with or without alcohol—washes it all down. ✗ *Calle 50-A, No. 493, between Calles 57 and 59,* ☎ *99/23–81–35 or 99/28–54–59, AE, DC, MC, V.*

$$ **Pórtico del Peregrino.** A red tile floor, iron grillwork, and lots of
★ plants set the tone in both the indoor and outdoor patio sections of this colonial-style restaurant with only 12 tables. The menu features lime soup, baked eggplant with chicken, shrimp, chicken píbil, shish kebab, mole enchiladas, seafood stew, chicken liver brochettes, and spaghetti. For dessert, try the coconut ice cream with Kahlua. ✗ *Calle 57, No. 501, between Calles 60 and 62,* ☎ *99/28–61–63. MC, V.*

$ **Amaro.** Formerly called Ananda Maya Ginza and strictly vegetarian, Amaro is expanding its menu to include poultry and red meats. Still, the menu is heavy on the health drinks, made mostly with local vegetables, fruit, and herbs. Regular coffee and Yucatecan beers are also served, and the salads are made with fresh local veggies washed with purified water. Recommended dishes include eggplant curry and soup made with *chaya,* a local vegetable that looks like spinach. The terrace of this old historic home provides a quiet dining atmosphere beneath a big tree. ✗ *Calle 59, No. 507, between Calles 60 and 62,* ☎ *99/28–24–51. No credit cards.* ☉ *Mon.–Sat. 9–10; closed Sun.*

$ **Santa Lucía.** Locals crowd this small dining room, a few steps below the
★ sidewalk, at lunch time, when the bountiful *comida corrida* is served.
The bargain three-course lunch usually includes such Yucatecan specialties as *sopa de lima* (lime soup) and *pollo píbil*. Before you order,
browse through the book of guests' comments to get tips on favorite
meals—the pepper steak constantly wins rave reviews. Soft tropical
music plays in the background, and the service is friendly and efficient.
There's a live band Thursday through Sunday nights. ✗ *Calle 60, No.
481, next to Parque Santa Lucía,* ☎ *99/28–59–57. MC, V.*

LODGING

$$$$ **Casa del Balam.** This very pleasant hotel on well-heeled Calle 60 has a
★ lovely courtyard ornamented with a fountain, arcades, ironwork, and a
black-and-white tile floor. The rooms are capacious and well maintained, featuring painted sinks, wrought-iron accessories, and minibars. The suites are especially agreeable, with large bathrooms, tiny
balconies, arched doorways, and mahogany bureaus. Cocktails and
light meals are served in the lobby courtyard, one of the most peaceful
places in town. ☎ *Calle 60, No. 488, Box 988,* ☎ *99/24–88–44, 99/
24–21–50, or 800/223–4084,* 🖷 *99/24–50–11. 54 rooms. Restaurant,
2 bars, minibars, pool, travel services, car rental. AE, MC, V.*

$$$$ **Fiesta Americana Mérida.** Opened in early 1995 across the street from
the Hyatt Regency, this is the newest posh hotel catering to business
travelers, groups, and conventions. With a lovely pink facade, this
low-slung building takes up a city block and features a 300-foot-high
glass-enclosed atrium. Guest rooms were not yet ready for inspection
when we visited, but all have direct-dial telephones, air-conditioning,
minibars, and color TV. ☎ *On Paseo de Montejo, corner of Av. Colón,*
☎ *99/20–21–94 or 800/FIESTA–1,* 🖷 *99/20–21–98. 350 rooms and
suites. Restaurant, bar, health club, meeting rooms, travel services.*

$$$$ **Hyatt Regency Mérida.** The first of the deluxe hotels to open on the
north end of Paseo de Montejo (in 1994), the Hyatt brought a new
level of hotel service to Mérida; at 17 stories, it's also the tallest building in the city. Guests staying on one of the two Regency Club floors
receive complimentary Continental breakfast, beverages, and snacks,
as well as concierge service. All rooms have satellite TV, direct-dial
long-distance phone service, and minibars; Club floor rooms also feature personal safes. Amenities not commonly found in Mérida include
24-hour room service and a state-of-the-art business center. ☎ *Calle
60, No. 344, at Av. Colón,* ☎ *99/42–02–02 or 800/228–9000,* 🖷 *99/
25–70–02. 299 rooms. 2 restaurants (1 with disco), bar, pool, travel
services, car rental. AE, MC, V.*

$$$ **Los Aluxes.** A good choice within walking distance of the plaza but
somewhat removed from the traffic noise, Los Aluxes is a modern, six-
story hotel with all the first-class amenities. Fountains, trees, and an
abundance of plants soften the anonymous decor, and the pool's gar-
den offers a peaceful respite. The carpeted rooms are comfortably dec-
orated in pale peach and blue. Underground parking is a major plus,
and the hotel has one of the best dining rooms in town. ☎ *Calle 60 at
Calle 49,* ☎ *99/24–21–99 or 800/782–8395,* 🖷 *99/23–38–58. 152
rooms. Restaurant, bar, pool, travel services. AE, MC, V.*

$$ **Caribe.** An old Mérida standard, the Caribe is done in typical colonial
style, including tile floors, dark wood furniture, and a large inner
courtyard with arcades. It is on Parque Hidalgo, but most of its
rooms (38 with air-conditioning) overlook the inner courtyard and
restaurant, as do the open balconies, which are lined with comfortable chairs. The rooftop sun deck and swimming pool have a great
view of the plaza and downtown. The hotel's outdoor café, El Meson,

is one of the better restaurants in Parque Hidalgo. ☎ *Calle 60, No. 500,* ☏ *99/24–90–22 or 800/826–6842,* 𝕱𝕬𝕏 *99/24–87–33. 56 rooms. Restaurant, cafeteria, pool, travel services. AE, DC, MC, V.*

$$ **Casa Mexilio.** Two partners—one Mexican, one American—have brought the best of their respective architectural and decorating traditions to bear on this choice bed-and-breakfast with eight guest rooms. Middle Eastern wall hangings, French tapestries, colorful tile floors, black pottery, tile sinks, rustic furniture, and white walls make up the eclectic decor, which reaches its pinnacle in an immensely cozy sitting room on the second floor. The price includes breakfast, and short tours to Celustun and historic haciendas are offered. This place fills up fast; reservations are required between December 15 through the end of April. ☎ *Calle 68, No. 495, between Calles 59 and 57,* ☏ *and* 𝕱𝕬𝕏 *99/ 28–25–05; for reservations* ☏ *303/674–9615 or 800/538–6802,* 𝕱𝕬𝕏 *303/674–8735. 8 rooms. Pool. AE, MC, V.*

$$ **Gran Hotel.** Cozily situated on Parque Hidalgo, this legendary 1901
★   hotel is the oldest in the city, and it still lives up to its name. The three-story neoclassical building, with an Art Nouveau courtyard, exudes charm. High ceilings in rooms drenched in cedar antique furniture provide a sense of spaciousness. Thirteen units have balconies and 24 have air-conditioning. Ask for a room overlooking the park. Porfirio Díaz and Fidel Castro stayed in sumptuous Room 17. ☎ *Calle 60, No. 496,* ☏ *99/23–69–63 or 99/24–76–32,* 𝕱𝕬𝕏 *99/24–76–22. 31 rooms. Restaurant. MC, V.*

$ **Hotel Mucuy.** While Mérida's budget hotels continue to raise their rates, the Mucuy remains one of the few good bargains around. The delightful owners make you feel like part of the family and are eager to share information about the city. The rooms, which are always immaculate, have good screens on the windows and face the patio. There's a book exchange and communal refrigerator in the lobby, and the owners live at the front of the hotel, so there's always someone around to keep things secure. ☎ *Calle 57, No. 481, between Calles 56 and 58,* ☏ *99/28–51–93,* 𝕱𝕬𝕏 *99/23–78–01. 22 rooms. No credit cards.*

Uxmal

DINING

$$ **Los Almendros.** Located in Ticul, a small town 28 kilometers (17
★   miles) east of Uxmal (turn left at Santa Elena), this restaurant offers fresher and tastier foods than do the other members of the Los Almendros chain; *poc chuc* and *cochinita píbil* are good choices. This is one place, however, where you can expect to wait in line for a table, especially during high season. ✕ *Calle 23, No. 196,* ☏ *99/24–00–21. MC, V.*

$ **Las Palapas.** A great alternative to the hotel dining rooms at Uxmal, this family-run restaurant specializes in delicious Yucatecan dishes served with homemade tortillas. When tour groups request it in advance, the owners prepare a traditional feast, roasting the chicken or pork píbil style in a pit in the ground. If you see a tour bus in the parking lot stop in—you may chance upon a memorable fiesta. ✕ *Hwy. 261, 5 km (3 mi) north of ruins, no* ☏. *No credit cards.*

LODGING

$$$$ **Hacienda Uxmal.** The oldest hotel at the site, built in 1955 and still owned and operated by the Barbachano family, this pleasant colonial-style building has lovely floor tiles, ceramics, and iron grillwork. The rooms—all with ceiling fans and air-conditioning—are tiled and decorated with worn but comfortable furniture. Inside the large courtyard are a garden and pool. Across the road and about 100 yards south you'll find the ruins. Ask about packages that include free or low-cost car rentals for the nights you spend at Uxmal and at the Mayaland hotel in Chichén Itzá. ☎ *Within walking distance of ruins,* ☎ *and* ℻ *in Uxmal 99/49–47–54 (cellular phone); in Mérida, Mayaland Tours, Av. Colón 502,* ☎ *99/46–23–31,* ℻ *99/46–23–35; in the U.S.,* ☎ *800/ 235–4079. 80 rooms. Restaurant, bar, pool. AE, DC, MC, V.*

$$ **Villa Arqueológica Uxmal.** The hotel closest to the ruins is this two-story Club Med property built around a large Mediterranean-style pool. The functional rooms have cozy niches for the beds, tiled bathrooms, and powerful air conditioners. Maya women in traditional dress serve well-prepared French cuisine in the restaurant, and large cages around the hotel contain tropical birds and monkeys. ☎ *Within walking distance of ruins,* ☎ *99/24–70–53; for reservations in the U.S.:* ☎ *800/CLUB–MED. 44 rooms. Restaurant, bar, pool, tennis court. AE, MC, V.*

Valladolid

DINING AND LODGING

$$ **El Mesón del Marqués.** This building, on the north side of the main square, is a well-preserved, very old hacienda built around a lovely courtyard. Rooms in the modern addition at the back of the hotel have air-conditioning and are attractively furnished with rustic and colonial touches; rooms in the older section have ceiling fans. Unusually large bathrooms boast bathtubs—a rarity in Mexican hotels. El Mesón also features a pool, a crafts shop, and a restaurant that serves local specialties. ☎ *Plaza Principal, Calle 39, No. 203, 97780,* ☎ *985/6–20–73,* ℻ *985/6–22–80. 26 rooms, 12 suites. Restaurant, bar, pool. MC, V.*

$ **María del Luz.** Another choice by the main plaza, this hotel is built around a small swimming pool and courtyard. The rooms have been recently renovated with new floors, fresh paint, and tiled bathrooms. Air-conditioning and televisions are being added to all the rooms. The street-side restaurant is attractively furnished with high-backed rattan chairs and linen cloths; Mexican dishes are predictable and inexpensive. ☎ *Calle 2, No. 195, 97780,* ☎ *985/6–20–71. 33 rooms. Restaurant, bar, pool. MC, V.*

The Arts and Nightlife

The Arts

MÉRIDA

Mérida enjoys an unusually active and diverse cultural life, including free government-sponsored music and dance performances nightly in local parks. For information on these and other performances, consult the tourist office, the local newspapers, or the billboards and posters at the Teatro Peón Contreras (Calle 60 at Calle 57) or Café Pop (Calle 57 between Calles 60 and 62).

Nightlife

MÉRIDA

The **Hotel Calinda Panamericana** (Calle 59, No. 455, ☎ 99/23–91–11 or 99/23–94–44) stages folkloric dances Friday and Saturday by the pool. **Tulipanes** (Calle 46, No. 462-A, ☎ 99/27–20–09), a restaurant and nightclub built over a cenote, stages a folkloric ballet and "Maya ritual" performance that ends with a "sacrifice" nightly at 8.

A number of restaurants feature live music and dancing, including **El Tucho** (Calle 60, No. 482, between Calles 55 and 57, ☎ 99/24–23–23), **Xtabay** (above El Tucho, ☎ 99/28–09–61), **Pancho's** (Calle 59 between

Calles 60 and 62, ☎ 99/23–09–42), and **Carlos 'n' Charlie's** (Prolongacion Montejo, No. 447, ☎ 99/26–02–74).

There are discos that appeal to both locals and tourists at the **Holiday Inn** (Av. Colón, No. 498, at Calle 60) and, on weekends, at the **Hotel Calinda Panamericana** (Calle 59, No. 455). Pop music mixes with salsa at **Saudaje** (Prolongacion Montejo, No. 477, ☎ 99/26–43–30 or 99/29–23–10).

STATE OF YUCATÁN

Both Chichén Itzá and Uxmal offer elaborate nighttime sound-and-light shows accompanied by narrations of Maya legends (*see* Exploring, *above*).

Mérida and Yucatán Essentials

Arriving and Departing

BY PLANE

Airport and Airlines. The Mérida airport is 7 kilometers (4 miles) west of the city's central square, about a 20-minute ride. The following airlines serve Mérida: **Aeromexico** (☎ 99/27–90–00 or 800/237–6639); **Continental** (☎ 99/46–13–59 or 800/231–0856); **Mexicana** (☎ 99/24–66–33, 99/24–67–54, or 800/531–7921); **Aerocaribe** (☎ 99/24–95–00, 99/28–67–86 in Mérida); **Aviateca** (☎ 99/46–19–16 or 99/46–13–12); and **Taesa** (☎ 99/28–69–50).

Between the Airport and City Center. A private taxi costs about $10; collective service (usually a Volkswagen minibus), about $6. For both services, pay the taxi-ticket vendor at the airport, not the driver. The irregular but inexpensive Bus 79 goes from the airport to downtown.

BY CAR

Route 180, the main road along the Gulf Coast from the Texas border to Cancún, runs into Mérida. Mexico City lies 1,550 kilometers (960 miles) to the west; Cancún, 320 kilometers (200 miles) due east. A new eight-lane toll highway, the *autopista,* now cuts the driving time between Cancún and Mérida—formerly about 4½ hours—by about one hour.

BY BUS

The **main bus station** (Calle 69, No. 544, between Calles 68 and 70, ☎ 99/24–78–68) offers frequent first- and second-class service to Akumal, Cancún, Chichén Itzá, Playa del Carmen, Puerto Morelos, Tulum, Uxmal, Valladolid, and Xel-Há. The new (opened 1994) ADO bus terminal, nearby at Calle 70 between Calles 69 and 71, can also be reached at ☎ 99/24–78–68. Several lines, such as Expreso del Oriente and Caribe Express, now offer deluxe service with air-conditioning, refreshments, and movies shown en route.

BY TRAIN

What with the uncomfortable, inadequate train service and the high incidence of robberies, not even the tourist office recommends taking trains in Yucatán. All the same, you can get second-class train service (at Calle 55 between Calles 46 and 48, ☎ 99/27–77–01 or 99/27–75–01) to Mexico City via Campeche ($20). The train to the capital takes about 36 hours—twice as long as the bus.

Getting Around

BY BUS

Mérida's municipal buses run daily from 5 AM to midnight, but service is somewhat confusing until you master the system. In the downtown area, buses go east on Calle 59 and west on Calle 61, north on Calle 60 and south on Calle 62.

BY CAR

Driving in Mérida can be frustrating because of the one-way streets and dense traffic, but having your own wheels is the best way to take excursions from the city. Prices are sometimes lower if you arrange your rental in advance through one of the large international companies. There are almost 20 car-rental agencies in town, including **Avis** (Paseo de Montejo, No. 500, ☎ 99/28–31–52 or 99/28–28–28; airport 99/84–21–34 or 99/84–21–35), **Budget** (Paseo Montejo 497, ☎ 99/24–55–69 or 99/23–36–37; airport 99/46–22–55, 99/46–13–80), **Dollar** (Hotel Mérida Misión, ☎ 99/28–67–59 or 99/23–18–55; airport 99/46–13–23), **Executive** (Calle 60, No. 446, 99/23–37–32 or 99/28–07–56; airport 99/46–13–87), and **Hertz** (Calle 55, No. 479, ☎ 99/24–28–34 or 99/24–87–66; airport 99/24–91–87).

BY TAXI

Taxis don't cruise the streets for passengers; instead, they are available at 12 taxi stands around the city, or from the main taxi office (☎ 99/28–53–24). Individual cabs cost between $4 and $5; collective service, about $1.

BY CARRIAGE

Horse-drawn *calesas* (carriages) that drive along the streets of Mérida can be hailed along Calle 60. A ride to the Paseo de Montejo and back will cost about $12.

Guided Tours

There are more than 50 tour operators in Mérida, and they generally offer the same destinations. What differs is how you go—in a private car, a van, or a bus—and whether the vehicle is air-conditioned. A two- to three-hour city tour, including museums, parks, public buildings, and monuments, will cost between $7 and $20; or you can pick up an open-air sightseeing bus at Parque Santa Lucía. A day trip to Chichén Itzá, with guide, entrance fee, and lunch, runs approximately $40. Recommended tour operators include **American Express** (Calle 56-A, No. 494, ☎ 99/28–42–22, ☏ 99/28–43–73), **Buvisa** (Paseo de Montejo, No. 475, ☎ 99/27–79–33, ☏ 99/27–74–14), **Ceiba Tours** (Calle 60, No. 495, ☎ 99/24–44–77 or 99/24–44–99, ☏ 99/24–45–88; Holiday Inn, ☎ 99/24–44–77), **Intermar Caribe** (Prolong. Paseo de Montejo 74 at Calle 30, ☎ 99/44–52–49, 99/44–52–22, ☏ 99/44–52–59), **Mayaland Tours** (Av. Colón, No. 502, ☎ 99/46–23–31 or 800/235–4079 in the U.S., ☏ 99/46–23–35; Casa del Balam hotel, Calle 60, No. 488, ☎ 99/24–49–19), **Turismo Aviomar** (Calle 58A, No. 500-C, ☎ 99/20–04–44, 99/20–04–43, ☏ 99/24–68–87), **Viajes Novedosos** (Calle 58, No. 488, ☎ 99/245996, ☏ 99/23–90–61), and **Yucatán Trails** (Calle 62, No. 482, ☎ 99/24–19–28 or 99/28–25–82, ☏ 99/24–49–19 or 99/28–59–13). **Ecoturismo Yucatán** (Calle 3, No. 235 at Col. Pensiones, ☎ 99/25–21–87, ☏ 99/25–90–47) specializes in nature tours, including bird-watching, natural history, anthropology, and the Mundo Maya.

Important Addresses and Numbers

CONSULATES

United States (Paseo de Montejo 453, ☎ 99/25–50–11, 99/25–86–77, or 99/25–54–09); **United Kingdom** (Calle 58, No. 450, at Calle 53, ☎ 99/28–61–52).

EMERGENCIES
Police (☎ 99/25–36–34); **Red Cross** (Calle 68, No. 583, at Calle 65, ☎ 99/24–98–13); **Fire** (☎ 99/24–92–42); **general emergency** (☎ 06).

ENGLISH-LANGUAGE BOOKSTORES
Librería Dante has several branches around town (Calle 59 at Calle 68; Parque Hidalgo; in the Teatro Peón Contreras, at the corner of Calles 60 and 57; and on the main square, next to Pizza Bella), all of which carry a small selection of English-language books.

LATE-NIGHT PHARMACIES
Farmacia Yza Aviación (Calle 71 at Av. Aviación, ☎ 99/23–81–16); **Farmacia Yza Tanlum** (Glorieta Tanlum, ☎ 99/25–16–46); and **Farmacia Canto** (Calle 60, No. 514, at Calle 63, ☎ 99/24–82–65).

VISITOR INFORMATION
The main **Tourist Information Center** (Teatro Peón Contreras, Calle 59, between Calle 62 and 64, ☎ 99/24–91–27) is open daily 8–8. An information kiosk, open 8–8, can be found at the airport (☎ 99/24–67–64), and there's another one next to the Palacio Municipal on Calle 62 (no ☎), open weekdays 8–2.

14 Portraits of Mexico

Mexico at a Glance: A Chronology

"Talking Mexican" by Kate Simon

"Fiesta" by Octavio Paz

More Portraits

MEXICO AT A GLANCE: A CHRONOLOGY

Pre-Columbian Mexico

c. 50,000 BC Asian nomads cross land bridge over the Bering Strait to North America, gradually migrate south

c. 5000–2,000 BC Archaic period, which marked the beginnings of agriculture and village life

c. 2,000–200 BC Formative or pre-Classic period: development of pottery, incipient political structures

c. 1500–900 BC The powerful and sophisticated Olmec civilization develops along the Gulf of Mexico in the present-day states of Veracruz and Tabasco. Olmec culture, the "mother culture" of Mexico, flourishes along gulf coast

c. 200 BC–AD 900 Classic period (Golden Age, AD 200–800): height of pre-Columbian culture. Three centers at Teotihuacan (near Mexico City), Monte Albán (Oaxaca), and Maya culture in the far south. Peaceful, priest-run city-states produce impressive art and architecture

AD 650–900 Decline of Classic cultures: fall of Teotihuacan c. 650 leads to competition among other city-states, exacerbated by migrations of northern tribes

c. 900–1521 Post-Classic period: rule passes to military; war and war gods gain prominence

c. 900–1150 Toltecs, a northern tribe, establish a flourishing culture at their capital of Tula under the legendary monarch Topiltzin-Quetzalcoatl

c. 1200 Rise of Mixtec culture at Zapotec sites of Monte Albán and Mitla; notable for production of picture codices, which include historical narratives

c. 1000–1450 Maya culture, declining in south, emerges in the Yucatán; under Toltec rule, Chichén Itzá dominates the peninsula

1111 Aztecs migrate to mainland from island home off the Nayarit coast. Vulgar and partial to human sacrifice, they are not welcomed by the peoples of central Mexico

1150–1350 Following the fall of Tula, first the Chichimecs, then the Tepanecs assert hegemony over central Mexico. The Tepanec tyrant Tezozómoc (1320–1426), like his contemporaries in Renaissance Italy, establishes his power with murder and treachery

1376 Tezozómoc grants autonomy to the Aztec city of Tenochtitlán, built in the middle of Lake Texcoco

1420–1500 Aztecs extend their rule to much of central and southern Mexico. A warrior society, they build a great city at Tenochtitlán

1502 Moctezuma II assumes throne at the height of Aztec culture and political power

1517 Spanish expedition under Francisco Hernandez de Córdoba lands on Yucatán coast

1519 Hernán Cortés lands in Cozumel, founds Veracruz, determines to conquer. Steel weapons, horses, and smallpox, coupled with a belief that Cortés was the resurrected Topiltzin-Quetzalcoatl, minimize Aztec resistance. Cortés enters Tenochtitlán and captures Moctezuma

The Colonial Period

1520–1521 Moctezuma is killed; Tenochtitlán falls to Cortés. The last Aztec emperor, Cuauhtemoc, is executed

1528 Juan de Zumarraga arrives as bishop of Mexico City, gains title of "Protector of the Indians"; native conversion to Catholicism begun

1535 First Spanish viceroy arrives in Mexico

1537 Pope Paul III issues a bull declaring that native Mexicans are indeed human and not beasts. First printing press arrives in Mexico City

1546–1548 Silver deposits discovered at Zacatecas

1547 Spanish conquest of Aztec Empire—now known as "New Spain"—completed, at enormous cost to native peoples

1553 Royal and Pontifical University of Mexico, first university in the New World, opens

1571 The Spanish Inquisition established in New Spain; it is only abolished in 1820

1609 Northern capital of New Spain established at Santa Fe (New Mexico)

1651 Birth of Sor (Sister) Juana Inés de la Cruz, greatest poet of colonial Mexico (d. 1695)

1718 Franciscan missionaries settle in Texas, which becomes part of New Spain

1765 Charles III of Spain sends José de Galvez to tour New Spain and propose reforms

1769 Franciscan Junipero Serra establishes missions in California, extending Spanish hegemony

1788 Death of Charles III; his reforms improve administration, but also raise social and political expectations among the colonial population, which are not fulfilled

1808 Napoléon invades Spain, leaving a power vacuum in New Spain

The War of Independence

1810 September 16: Father Miguel Hidalgo y Costilla preaches his *Grito de Dolores,* sparking rebellion

1811 Hidalgo is captured and executed; leadership of the movement passes to Father José Maria Morelos

1813 Morelos calls a congress at Chilpancingo which drafts a Declaration of Independence

1815 Morelos is captured and executed

The Early National Period

1821 Vicente Guerrero, a rebel leader, and Agustín de Iturbide, a Spanish colonel converted to the rebel cause, rejuvenate the Independence movement. Spain recognizes Mexican independence with the Treaty of Córdoba

1822 Iturbide is named Emperor of Mexico, which stretches from California through Central America

1823 After ten months in office, Emperor Agustín is turned out

1824 A new constitution creates a federal republic, the Estados Unidos Mexicanos; modeled on the U.S. Constitution, the Mexican version retains the privileges of the Catholic Church and gives the president extraordinary "emergency" powers

1829 President Vicente Guerrero abolishes slavery. A Spanish attempt at reconquest is halted by General Antonio López de Santa Anna, already a hero for his role in the overthrow of Emperor Agustín

1833 Santa Anna is elected president by a huge majority; he holds the office for 11 of its 36 changes of hands by 1855

1836 Although voted in as a liberal, Santa Anna abolishes the 1824 constitution. Already dismayed at the abolition of slavery, Texas—whose population is largely American—declares its independence. Santa Anna successfully besieges the Texans at the Alamo. But a month later he is captured by Sam Houston following the Battle of San Jacinto. Texas gains its independence as the Lone Star Republic

1846 The U.S. decision to annex Texas leads to war

1848 The treaty of Guadalupe Hidalgo reduces Mexico's territory by half, ceding Texas, New Mexico, and California to the United States

1853 Santa Anna agrees to the Gadsden Purchase, ceding a further 30,000 square miles to the United States

The Reform and French Intervention

1855 The Revolution of Ayutla topples Santa Anna and leads to the period of The Reform

1857 The liberal Constitution of 1857 disestablishes the Catholic Church among other measures

1858–1861 The civil War of the Reform ends in liberal victory. Benito Juárez is elected president. France, Spain, and Britain agree jointly to occupy the customs house at Veracruz to force payment of Mexico's huge foreign debt

1862 Spain and Britain withdraw their forces; the French, seeking empire, march inland. On May 5, General Porfirio Díaz repulses the French at Puebla

1863 Strengthened with reinforcements, the French occupy Mexico City. Napoléon III of France appoints Archduke Ferdinand Maximilian of Austria as Emperor of Mexico

1864 Maximilian and his empress Charlotte, known as Carlota, land at Veracruz

1867 With U.S. assistance, Juárez overthrows Mexico's second empire. Maximilian is executed; Carlota, pleading his case in France, goes mad

1872 Juárez dies in office. The Mexico City–Veracruz railway is completed, symbol of the new progressivist mood

The Porfiriato

1876 Porfirio Díaz comes to power in the Revolution of Tuxtepec; he holds office nearly continuously until 1911. With his advisors, the *cientificos,* he forces modernization and balances the budget for the first time in Mexican history. But the social cost is high

1890 José Schneider, who is of German ancestry, founds the Cerveceria Cuauhtemoc, brewer of Carta Blanca

1900 Jesús, Enrique, and Ricardo Flores Magón publish the anti-Díaz newspaper *La Regeneración.* Suppressed, the brothers move their campaign to the United States, first to San Antonio, then to St. Louis

1906 The Flores Magón group publish their Liberal Plan, a proposal for reform. Industrial unrest spreads

The Second Revolution

1910 On the centennial of the Revolution, Díaz wins yet another rigged election. Revolt breaks out

1911 Rebels under Pascual Orozco and Francisco (Pancho) Villa capture Ciudad Juárez; Díaz resigns. Francisco Madero is elected president; calling for land reform, Emiliano Zapata rejects the new regime. Violence continues

1913 Military coup; Madero is deposed and murdered. In one day Mexico has three presidents, the last being General Victoriano Huerta. Civil war rages

1914 American intervention leads to dictator Huerta's overthrow. Villa and Zapata briefly join forces at the Convention of Aguascalientes, but the Revolution goes on

1916 Villa's border raids lead to an American punitive expedition under Pershing. Villa eludes capture

1917 Under a new constitution, Venuziano Carranza, head of the Constitutionalist Army, is elected president. Zapata continues his rebellion, which is brutally suppressed

1918 CROM, the national labor union, is founded

1919 On order of Carranza, Zapata is assassinated

1920 Carranza is assassinated; Alvaro Obregón is elected president, beginning a period of reform and reconstruction. Schools are built and land is redistributed. In the next two decades, revolutionary culture finds expression in the art of Diego Rivera and José Clemente Orozco, the novels of Martin Luis Guzmán and Gregorio Lopez y Fuentes, and the music of Carlos Chavez

1923 Pancho Villa is assassinated. The United States finally recognizes the Obregón regime

1926–1928 Catholics react to government anticlericalism in the Cristero Rebellion

1934–1940 The presidency of Lázaro Cárdenas leads to the fullest implementation of revolutionary reforms

1938 Cárdenas nationalizes the oil companies, removing them from foreign control

Post-Revolutionary Mexico

1951 Mexico's segment of the Pan-American Highway is completed, confirming the industrial growth and prosperity of post-war Mexico. Culture is increasingly Americanized; writers such as Octavio Paz and Carlos Fuentes express disillusionment with the post-revolution world

1968 The Summer Olympics in Mexico City showcase Mexican prosperity, but massive demonstrations indicate underlying social unrest

1981–1982 Recession and a drop in oil prices severely damage Mexico's economy. The peso is devalued

1985 Thousands die in the Mexico City earthquake

1988 American-educated economist Carlos Salinas de Gortari is elected president; for the first time since 1940, support for the PRI, the national political party, seems to be slipping

1993 North American Free Trade Agreement (NAFTA) is signed with United States and Canada

1994 Uprising by the indigenous peoples of Chiapas, led by the Zapatistas and their charismatic ski-masked leader, Subcomandante Marcos; election reforms promised as a result

Popular PRI presidential candidate Luis Donaldo Colosio assassinated while campaigning in Tijuana. Ernesto Zedillo, generally thought to be more of a technocrat and "old boy"-style PRI politician, replaces him and wins the election

Zedillo, blaming the economic policies of his predecessor, devalues the peso in December

1995 Recession is predicted as a result of the peso devaluation. The former administration is rocked by scandals surrounding the assassinations of Colosio and another high-ranking government official; ex-President Carlos Salinas de Gortari moves to the United States

TALKING MEXICAN

MEXICANS STILL CHERISH an art once highly prized among us (think of Emerson, of Melville, of Hawthorne): conversation. They know it takes two to make a good talker—the confident speaker and the eager listener. A Mexican tête-à-tête—except among the dour mountain people, who prefer long, motionless silences—is a graceful act. The talker, carried away by his own mellifluous sounds, often repeats himself. His listener seems to find him fascinating. His eyes glow, he smiles, he melts, he frowns, he is delighted, he is appalled; he is completely immersed in the words and their passion and keeps them going with a gamut of encouragements: "*Claro, pues si*" ("Of course, obviously"), "*Qué bueno*" ("How nice"), "*Qué lindo*" ("How lovely"), "*¡No me digas!*" ("Don't tell me!"), and, as a sorrowful cadence, "*Ai lástima*" ("What a pity").

Spanish isn't absolutely essential in large centers, although all sorts of doors and amiabilities will open for the traveler who conquers a few Spanish words of greeting and politesse. The Mexican is so delighted with the "*americano*" who tries even a little that he will, with a peculiar delicate empathy, help shape the words you need. A sympathetic Mexican can make you feel that you know Spanish; it's your tongue that is stupid.

Like other languages, but more so, Spanish is heavily embroidered with diminutives. Usually endearments, they also have other uses. They serve as intensifiers of meaning: *Chico* means "small"; *chiquito,* "very small"; and *chiquitito,* "almost invisible." A diminutive also suggests doubt, skepticism. *Hay sol* means that the sun is out, but if you are in an excursion boat under a cloudy sky and the boatman hopefully says there is *solecito,* beg to be taken ashore before the descent of a storm that maddens the lake. An important early lesson in Spanish is the use of *ahora,* meaning "now," which when spoken straight out usually denotes an intention of getting something done reasonably soon. The addition of one diminutive bit—*ahorita*—stretches the distance between promise and deed; *ahoritita* carries us into improbability; *ahoritita* becomes a piece of silliness.

The curious impersonal reflexive *se* conjures up a bewildering world of small satanic forces. One doesn't break a glass. *Se me rompió*—it broke itself, no fault of mine. If you bargain with a market woman, she will not say, "I can't," but "*No se puede*"—"one (little *se*) cannot." A lost object—even my own bag—lost itself, and it wasn't *I* who caused me to be late, but that mischievous bit of fate, *se.*

This deference to unpredictable external powers may bespeak a fatalism whose reverse side is bright casualness. A Mexican will warmly, charmingly, and with—at the moment—complete sincerity declare his affection, admiration, and profound need to see you again, very soon. Unaccustomed to such quick warmth, you settle into this cozy nest of love, this having been accepted by Mexico. Time passes, nothing happens. You have been forgotten. You feel unlovely, unwelcome, the contemptible "big foot" who ate up vast Texas, responsible for all the world's messes and of course "Yankee imperialism." But it's only *se* that intervened and manipulated your friend's life in some unexpected way that was more attractive, more novel, than the prospect of another encounter with you.

A people who arrange a highly ornamented holiday for their dead and hold in awe the death dance of the bullfight are not inclined to respect precise dates, neat boxes of time. Anything is at any time likely to happen—a flat tire, a nearby fiesta, a change of mood—to be enjoyed *si Dios nos presta el tiempo* ("if God lends us the time"). Another imposing fact about the language is that the word for "to expect" (*esperar*) is identical with that for "to await" and "to hope." You might witness this miracle of linguistic transmutation at a rural train station as your assured expecting melts into vague awaiting and then vaporizes into humble hope—hope that some train that pertains to you will show up, sometime.

One of the pleasant quirks of the language is the big, baroque, generous phrase that can't mean what it says. Someone gives you his address and says, "*Esta es su casa*" or "*Aquí tiene su casa*" ("Consider this your home"), or "*Mi casa es su casa*" ("My house is your house")—obviously ridiculous and yet frequently said as proof of boundless, aristocratic generosity (a Don Quixote touch?). Clearly, the only person in Mexican history who took such statements seriously was Cortés, the conquistador who took not only the house and treasures of Moctezuma but the whole of his host's empire. Admire an object and you may be told it is yours. Smile and without making a move say, "Thank you," to which the answer may be, "To serve you" ("*A su servicio*"). "At your command" ("*A sus órdenes*") often acknowledges a formal introduction. These phrases are not servile or meant to buy favor, but express the courtliness of old Spain.

ON THE OTHER HAND, Spanish can be direct and even harsh. Observe the park signs, which say flatly, "This is yours, take care of it" ("*El parque es suyo, cuídelo*").

In other areas the touch is delicate, even elegant. One doesn't hit a man with "He is disagreeable," but, instead, one dismisses him as "little amiable." "*Venga por favor tempranito*" takes the pressure off the necessity to be absolutely on time (*temprano*). No one wants to rush you, you must understand, but try to be nice and come on time, mollified and seduced by little *ito,* the most persuasive of Mexican persuasions.

In the wide world of *amor* anything goes; the limits are wide and brilliant, painting the conversational sky with dazzling rainbows. Shelley's "I die! I faint! I fail!" are pale mutterings compared with Mexican strophes of romantic love. A woman must have quite a bit of Spanish to appreciate the flowers of words thrown at her feet. But even a little helps. Not necessarily very young or lovely, she might still have the word *guapa* ("handsome woman") wafted toward her, or if she's fair-haired, like the *Yanquis* from north of the border, she could be called *güerita* ("blondie"). Her lack of response (and there shouldn't be any unless she's ready to face the consequences) might evoke something like "Can't you even say thanks, for God's sake?" ("*¿No puedes decir gracias, por Dios?*"), and this, too, might amuse her if she happens to understand what's going on.

A knowledge of Spanish enables one to discern nuances of class in certain areas of speech. The courtliness of "*hágame el favor*" ("please do me the kindness") moves downward into the middle class with "*por favor,*" then becomes the cajoling peasant phrase "*por favorcito.*"

Perhaps most important, it lets one sample the wilder pleasures of Mexican radio, such as its ads for Pepsi-Cola. An old feeble female voice pleads, "Buy me a taco." Old feeble male voice: "Sure, they're delicious." Strong radio voice out of seemingly unrelated space: "Delicious? Pepsi-Cola is more delicious. Drink Pepsi!" This is followed by a female voice shrieking, "I can't stand it anymore. *You* pay the household bills; I can't seem to manage on the money you give me." This time the out-of-the-blue voice says gently, "Calm yourself. Have a Pepsi." Then a siren's voice, quite dulcet, with a tiny rasp of passion: "Darling, please buy me another diamond." Her lover's rich voice: "What? So that you can be even more delicious?" Voice from the blue: "More delicious? Pepsi-Cola is more delicious." Without Spanish and the radio, how could one be grateful for the sponsorship of "*Mox Foctorr de Hawlywoot, naturalmente*"?

— Kate Simon

Bronx native Kate Simon is the author of nine travel books, including Mexico: Places and Pleasures, *which remains a classic after 31 years.*

"Talking Mexican" is excerpted from her book Never Say Ahoritita Again.

FIESTA

THE SOLITARY MEXICAN loves fiestas and public gatherings. Any occasion for getting together will serve, any pretext to stop the flow of time and commemorate men and events with festivals and ceremonies. We are a ritual people, and this characteristic enriches both our imaginations and our sensibilities, which are equally sharp and alert. The art of the fiesta has been debased almost everywhere else, but not in Mexico. There are few places in the world where it is possible to take part in a spectacle like our great religious fiestas with their violent primary colors, their bizarre costumes and dances, their fireworks and ceremonies, and their inexhaustible welter of surprises: the fruit, candy, toys, and other objects sold on these days in the plazas and open-air markets.

Our calendar is crowded with fiestas. There are certain days when the whole country, from the most remote villages to the largest cities, prays, shouts, feasts, gets drunk and kills, in honor of the Virgin of Guadalupe or Benito Juárez. Each year on the fifteenth of September, at eleven o'clock at night, we celebrate the fiesta of the *Grito*[1] in all the plazas of the Republic, and the excited crowds actually shout for a whole hour . . . the better, perhaps, to remain silent for the rest of the year. During the days before and after the twelfth of December,[2] time comes to a full stop, and instead of pushing us toward a deceptive tomorrow that is always beyond our reach, offers us a complete and perfect today of dancing and revelry, of communion with the most ancient and secret Mexico. Time is no longer succession, and becomes what it originally was and is: the present, in which past and future are reconciled.

But the fiestas that the Church and State provide for the country as a whole are not enough. The life of every city and village is ruled by a patron saint whose blessing is celebrated with devout regularity. Neighborhoods and trades also have their annual fiestas, their ceremonies and fairs. And each one of us—atheist, Catholic, or merely indifferent—has his own saint's day, which he observes every year. It is impossible to calculate how many fiestas we have and how much time and money we spend on them. I remember asking the mayor of a village near Mitla, several years ago, "What is the income of the village government?" "About 3,000 pesos a year. We are very poor. But the Governor and the Federal Government always help us to meet our expenses." "And how are the 3,000 pesos spent?" "Mostly on fiestas, señor. We are a small village, but we have two patron saints."

This reply is not surprising. Our poverty can be measured by the frequency and luxuriousness of our holidays. Wealthy countries have very few: There is neither the time nor the desire for them, and they are not necessary. The people have other things to do, and when they amuse themselves they do so in small groups. The modern masses are agglomerations of solitary individuals. On great occasions in Paris or New York, when the populace gathers in the squares or stadiums, the absence of people, in the sense of a people, is remarkable: There are couples and small groups, but they never form a living community in which the individual is at once dissolved and redeemed. But how could a poor Mexican live without the annual fiestas that make up for his poverty and misery? Fiestas are our only luxury. They replace, and are perhaps better than, the theater and vacations, Anglo-Saxon weekends and cocktail parties, the bourgeois reception, the Mediterranean café.

In all of these ceremonies—national or local, trade or family—the Mexican opens out. They all give him a chance to reveal himself and to converse with God, country, friends, or relations. During these days

---

[1]*Padre Hidalgo's call-to-arms against Spain, 1810—Tr.*
[2]*Fiesta of the Virgin of Guadalupe—Tr.*

the silent Mexican whistles, shouts, sings, shoots off fireworks, discharges his pistol into the air. He discharges his soul. And his shout, like the rockets we love so much, ascends to the heavens, explodes into green, red, blue, and white lights, and falls dizzily to earth with a trail of golden sparks. This is the night when friends who have not exchanged more than the prescribed courtesies for months get drunk together, trade confidences, weep over the same troubles, discover that they are brothers, and sometimes, to prove it, kill each other. The night is full of songs and loud cries. The lover wakes up his sweetheart with an orchestra. There are jokes and conversations from balcony to balcony, sidewalk to sidewalk. Nobody talks quietly. Hats fly in the air. Laughter and curses ring like silver pesos. Guitars are brought out. Now and then, it is true, the happiness ends badly, in quarrels, insults, pistol shots, stabbings. But these too are part of the fiesta, for the Mexican does not seek amusement: He seeks to escape from himself, to leap over the wall of solitude that confines him during the rest of the year. All are possessed by violence and frenzy. Their souls explode like the colors and voices and emotions. Do they forget themselves and show their true faces? Nobody knows. The important thing is to go out, open a way, get drunk on noise, people, colors. Mexico is celebrating a fiesta. And this fiesta, shot through with lightning and delirium, is the brilliant reverse to our silence and apathy, our reticence and gloom.

According to the interpretation of French sociologists, the fiesta is an excess, an expense. By means of this squandering the community protects itself against the envy of the gods or of men. Sacrifices and offerings placate or buy off the gods and the patron saints. Wasting money and expending energy affirms the community's wealth in both. This luxury is a proof of health, a show of abundance and power. Or a magic trap. For squandering is an effort to attract abundance by contagion. Money calls to money. When life is thrown away it increases; the orgy, which is sexual expenditure, is also a ceremony of regeneration; waste gives strength. New Year celebrations, in every culture, signify something beyond the mere observance of a date on the calendar. The day is a pause: Time is stopped, is actually annihilated. The rites that celebrate its death are intended to provoke its rebirth, because they mark not only the end of an old year but also the beginning of a new. Everything attracts its opposite. The fiesta's function, then, is more utilitarian than we think: Waste attracts or promotes wealth and is an investment like any other, except that the returns on it cannot be measured or counted. What is sought is potency, life, health. In this sense the fiesta, like the gift and the offering, is one of the most ancient of economic forms.

THIS INTERPRETATION has always seemed to me to be incomplete. The fiesta is by nature sacred, literally or figuratively, and above all it is the advent of the unusual. It is governed by its own special rules that set it apart from other days, and it has a logic, an ethic, and even an economy that are often in conflict with everyday norms. It all occurs in an enchanted world: Time is transformed to a mythical past or a total present; space, the scene of the fiesta, is turned into a gaily decorated world of its own; and the persons taking part cast off all human or social rank and become, for the moment, living images. And everything takes place as if it were not so, as if it were a dream. But whatever happens, our actions have a greater lightness, a different gravity. They take on other meanings and with them we contract new obligations. We throw down our burdens of time and reason.

In certain fiestas the very notion of order disappears. Chaos comes back and license rules. Anything is permitted: the customary hierarchies vanish, along with all social, sex, caste, and trade distinctions. Men disguise themselves as women, gentlemen as slaves, the poor as the rich. The army, the clergy, and the law are ridiculed. Obligatory sacrilege, ritual profanation is committed. Love becomes promiscuity. Sometimes the fiesta becomes a Black Mass. Regulations, habits, and customs are violated. Respectable people put away the dignified expressions and conservative clothes that isolate them, dress up in gaudy colors, hide behind a mask, and escape from themselves.

Therefore the fiesta is not only an excess, a ritual squandering of the goods painfully accumulated during the rest of the year; it is also a revolt, a sudden immersion in the formless, in pure being. By means of the fiesta, society frees itself from the norms it has established. It ridicules its gods, its principles, and its laws: It denies its own self.

The fiesta is a revolution in the most literal sense of the word. In the confusion that it generates, society is dissolved, is drowned, insofar as it is an organism ruled according to certain laws and principles. But it drowns in itself, in its own original chaos or liberty. Everything is united: good and evil, day and night, the sacred and the profane. Everything merges, loses shape and individuality and returns to the primordial mass. The fiesta is a cosmic experiment, an experiment in disorder, reuniting contradictory elements and principles in order to bring about a renascence of life. Ritual death promotes a rebirth; vomiting increases the appetite; the orgy, sterile in itself, renews the fertility of the mother or of the earth. The fiesta is a return to a remote and undifferentiated state, prenatal or presocial. It is a return that is also a beginning, in accordance with the dialectic that is inherent in social processes.

The group emerges purified and strengthened from this plunge into chaos. It has immersed itself in its own origins, in the womb from which it came. To express it in another way, the fiesta denies society as an organic system of differentiated forms and principles, but affirms it as a source of creative energy. It is a true "re-creation," the opposite of the "recreation" characterizing modern vacations, which do not entail any rites or ceremonies whatever and are as individualistic and sterile as the world that invented them.

Society communes with itself during the fiesta. Its members return to original chaos and freedom. Social structures break down and new relationships, unexpected rules, capricious hierarchies are created. In the general disorder everybody forgets himself and enters into otherwise forbidden situations and places. The bounds between audience and actors, officials and servants, are erased. Everybody takes part in the fiesta, everybody is caught up in its whirlwind. Whatever its mood, its character, its meaning, the fiesta is participation, and this trait distinguishes it from all other ceremonies and social phenomena. Lay or religious, orgy or saturnalia, the fiesta is a social act based on the full participation of all its celebrants.

Thanks to the fiesta, the Mexican opens out, participates, communes with his fellows and with the values that give meaning to his religious or political existence. And it is significant that a country as sorrowful as ours should have so many and such joyous fiestas. Their frequency, their brilliance and excitement, the enthusiasm with which we take part, all suggest that without them we would explode. They free us, if only momentarily, from the thwarted impulses, the inflammable desires that we carry within us. But the Mexican fiesta is not merely a return to an original state of formless and normless liberty: The Mexican is not seeking to return, but to escape from himself, to exceed himself. Our fiestas are explosions. Life and death, joy and sorrow, music and mere noise are united, not to re-create or recognize themselves, but to swallow each other up. There is nothing so joyous as a Mexican fiesta, but there is also nothing so sorrowful. Fiesta night is also a night of mourning.

IF WE HIDE within ourselves in our daily lives, we discharge ourselves in the whirlwind of the fiesta. It is more than an opening out: We rend ourselves open. Everything—music, love, friendship—ends in tumult and violence. The frenzy of our festivals shows the extent to which our solitude closes us off from communication with the world. We are familiar with delirium, with songs and shouts, with the monologue . . . but not with the dialogue. Our fiestas, like our confidences, our loves, our attempts to reorder our society, are violent breaks with the old or the established. Each time we try to express ourselves we have to break with ourselves. And the fiesta is only one example, perhaps the most typical, of this violent break. It is not difficult to name others, equally revealing: our games, which are always a going to extremes, often mortal; our profligate spending, the reverse of our timid investments and business enterprises; our confessions. The somber Mexican, closed up in himself, suddenly explodes, tears open his breast and reveals himself, though not without a certain complacency, and not without a stopping place in the shameful or terrible mazes of his intimacy. We are not frank, but our sincerity can reach extremes that horrify a European. The explosive, dramatic, sometimes even suicidal manner in which we strip ourselves, surrender ourselves, is evidence that something inhibits and suffocates us. Something impedes us from being. And since we cannot or dare not confront our own selves, we resort to the fiesta. It fires us into the void; it is a drunken rapture that burns itself out, a pistol shot in the air, a skyrocket.

— *Octavio Paz*

Poet, essayist, and diplomat, Octavio Paz is one of Mexico's most prominent spokesmen. This essay is excerpted from his best-known work, The Labyrinth of Solitude, *originally published in 1962.*

MORE PORTRAITS

The best nonfiction on Mexico blends history, culture, commentary, and travel description. The works below are categorized, but by no means mutually exclusive. Some may be out of print and available only in libraries.

History

For decades, the standard texts written by scholars for popular audiences have been *A History of Mexico*, by Henry B. Parkes; *Many Mexicos*, by Lesley Byrd Simpson; and *A Compact History of Mexico*, an anthology published by the Colegio de México. Two journalists recently have made important contributions to the literature on historical and contemporary Mexico: Alan Riding's *Distant Neighbors: A Portrait of the Mexicans*, and Jonathan Kandell's *La Capital: The Biography of Mexico City*. Works focusing on the ancient Mexican Indian cultures include *The Maya and Mexico*, by Michael D. Coe; *The Last Lords of Palenque: The Lacandon Mayas of the Mexican Rain Forest*, by Victor Perera and Robert D. Bruce; and *The Blood of Kings: Dynasty & Ritual in Maya Art*, by Linda Schele and Mary Ellen Miller, a handsome coffee-table book that summarizes ground-breaking work in our understanding of the ancient Maya.

Culture/Ethnography

Excellent ethnographies include Oscar Lewis's classic works on the culture of poverty (*The Children of Sanchez* and *Five Families*); *Juan the Chamula*, by Ricardo Pozas, about a small village in Chiapas; *Mexico South: The Isthmus of Tehuantepec*, by Miguel Covarrubias, which discusses Indian life in the early 20th century; Gertrude Blom's *Baring Witness*, on the Lacandones of Chiapas; and *Maria Sabina: Her Life and Chants*, an autobiography of a shaman in the sate of Oaxaca.

Food

Two lushly photographed cookbooks capturing the culinary history and culture of Mexico are Patricia Quintana's *The Taste of Mexico* (Stewart, Tabori & Chang, 1993) and *Mexico the Beautiful Cookbook* (HarperCollins, 1991). Diane Kennedy's culinary works are also popular; one is *The Art of Mexican Cooking* (Bantam, 1989).

Travelogues

Two of the more straightforward accounts from the early 19th century are the letters of Frances Calderón de la Barca (*Life in Mexico*) and John Lloyd Stephens's *Incidents of Travel in Central America, Chiapas and Yucatán*. Foreign journalists have described life in Mexico during and after the revolution: John Reed (*Insurgent Mexico*); John Kenneth Turner (*Barbarous Mexico*); Aldous Huxley (*Beyond the Mexique Bay*); and Graham Greene (*The Lawless Roads*, a superbly written narrative about Tabasco and Chiapas, which served as the basis for *The Power and the Glory*). In much the same vein, but more contemporary, are works by Patrick Marnham (*So Far from God*), about Central America and Mexico, and Hugh Fleetwood, whose *A Dangerous Place* is informative despite its cantankerousness. Alice Adams' 1991 *Mexico: Some Travels and Some Travelers There*, which includes an introduction by Jan Morris, is available in paperback; James A. Michener's 1992 novel, *Mexico*, captures the history of the land and the personality of the people. Probably the finest travelogue-cum-guidebook is Kate Simon's *Mexico: Places and Pleasures*.

About the Mexican People

Poet-philosopher Octavio Paz is the reigning dean of Mexican intellectuals. His best works are *Labyrinth of Solitude*, a thoughtful, far-reaching dissection of Mexican culture, and the biography of Sor Juana Inés de la Cruz, a 17th-century nun and poet. Latin American literature is increasingly being translated into English. Among the top authors are Carlos Fuentes (*The Death of Artemio Cruz* and *The Old Gringo*), Juan Rulfo (*Pedro Páramo*), Jorge Ibarguengoitia, and Elena Poniatowska.

Recent biographies of the artist couple Frida Kahlo and Diego Rivera (by Hayden Herrera and Bertram D. Wolfe, respectively) provide glimpses into the Mexican intellectual and political life of the '20s and '30s. Laura Esquivel's novel-cum-cookbook, *Like Water for Chocolate,* captures the passions and palates of Mexico during the revolution.

Foreign Literature

D. H. Lawrence's *The Plumed Serpent* is probably the best-known foreign novel about Mexico, although its noble savage theme is considered slightly offensive today. Lawrence recorded his travels in Oaxaca in *Mornings in Mexico.* A far greater piece of literature is Malcolm Lowry's *Under the Volcano.* The mysterious recluse B. Traven, whose fame rests largely on his *Treasure of the Sierra Madre,* wrote brilliantly and passionately about Mexico in *Rebellion of the Hanged* and *The Bridge in the Jungle.* Also noteworthy is John Steinbeck's *The Sea of Cortez.*

SPANISH VOCABULARY

Note: *Mexican Spanish differs from Castilian Spanish.*

Words and Phrases

Basics

English	Spanish	Pronunciation
Yes/no	Sí/no	see/no
Please	Por favor	pore fah-*vore*
May I?	¿Me permite?	may pair-*mee*-tay
Thank you (very much)	(Muchas) gracias	(*moo*-chas) *grah*-see-as
You're welcome	De nada	day *nah*-dah
Excuse me	Con permiso	con pair-*mee*-so
Pardon me/what did you say?	¿Como?/Mánde?	ko-mo/mahn-dey
Could you tell me?	¿Podría decirme?	po-*dree*-ah deh-*seer*-meh
I'm sorry	Lo siento	lo see-*en*-toe
Good morning!	¡Buenos días!	*bway*-nohs *dee*-ahs
Good afternoon!	¡Buenas tardes!	*bway*-nahs *tar*-dess
Good evening!	¡Buenas noches!	*bway*-nahs *no*-chess
Goodbye!	¡Adiós!/¡Hasta luego!	ah-dee-*ohss*/*ah*-stah-*lwe*-go
Mr./Mrs.	Señor/Señora	sen-*yor*/sen-*yore*-ah
Miss	Señorita	sen-yo-*ree*-tah
Pleased to meet you	Mucho gusto	*moo*-cho *goose*-to
How are you?	¿Cómo está usted?	*ko*-mo es-*tah* oo-*sted*
Very well, thank you.	Muy bien, gracias.	*moo*-ee bee-*en*, grah-see-as
And you?	¿Y usted?	ee oos-*ted*
Hello (on the telephone)	Bueno	*bwen*-oh

Numbers

1	un, uno	oon, *oo*-no
2	dos	dos
3	tres	trace
4	cuatro	*kwah*-tro
5	cinco	*sink*-oh
6	seis	sace
7	siete	see-*et*-ey
8	ocho	*o*-cho
9	nueve	new-*ev*-ay
10	diez	dee-*es*
11	once	*own*-sey
12	doce	*doe*-sey
13	trece	*tray*-sey
14	catorce	kah-*tor*-sey
15	quince	*keen*-sey
16	dieciséis	dee-es-ee-*sace*
17	diecisiete	dee-*es*-ee-see-*et*-ay
18	dieciocho	dee-*es*-ee-*o*-cho
19	diecinueve	*dee-es*-ee-new-*ev*-ay
20	veinte	*bain*-tay
21	veinte y uno/veintiuno	*bain*-te-oo-no

30	treinta	*train*-tah
32	treinta y dos	train-tay-*dose*
40	cuarenta	kwah-*ren*-tah
43	cuarenta y tres	kwah-ren-tay-*trace*
50	cincuenta	seen-*kwen*-tah
54	cincuenta y cuatro	seen-*kwen*-tay *kwah*-tro
60	sesenta	sess-*en*-tah
65	sesenta y cinco	sess-*en*-tay *seen*-ko
70	setenta	set-*en*-tah
76	setenta y seis	set-*en*-tay *sace*
80	ochenta	oh-*chen*-tah
87	ochenta y siete	oh-*chen*-tay see-*yet*-ay
90	noventa	no-*ven*-tah
98	noventa y ocho	no-*ven*-tah o-cho
100	cien	see-*en*
101	ciento uno	see-en-toe *oo*-no
200	doscientos	doe-see-*en*-tohss
500	quinientos	keen-*yen*-tohss
700	setecientos	set-eh-see-*en*-tohss
900	novecientos	no-veh-see-*en*-tohss
1,000	mil	meel
2,000	dos mil	dose meel
1,000,000	un millón	oon meel-*yohn*

Colors

black	negro	*neh*-grow
blue	azul	ah-*sool*
brown	café	kah-*feh*
green	verde	*vair*-day
pink	rosa	*ro*-sah
purple	morado	mo-*rah*-doe
orange	naranja	na-*rahn*-hah
red	rojo	*roe*-hoe
white	blanco	*blahn*-koh
yellow	amarillo	ah-mah-*ree*-yoh

Days of the Week

Sunday	domingo	doe-*meen*-goh
Monday	lunes	*loo*-ness
Tuesday	martes	*mahr*-tess
Wednesday	miércoles	me-*air*-koh-less
Thursday	jueves	who-*ev*-ess
Friday	viernes	vee-*air*-ness
Saturday	sábado	*sah*-bah-doe

Months

January	enero	eh-*neh*-ro
February	febrero	feh-*brair*-oh
March	marzo	*mahr*-so
April	abril	ah-*breel*
May	mayo	*my*-oh
June	junio	*hoo*-nee-oh
July	julio	*who*-lee-yoh
August	agosto	ah-*ghost*-toe
September	septiembre	sep-tee-*em*-breh
October	octubre	oak-*too*-breh
November	noviembre	no-vee-*em*-breh
December	diciembre	dee-see-*em*-breh

Useful Phrases

Do you speak English?	¿Habla usted inglés?	*ah*-blah oos-*ted* in-*glehs*
I don't speak Spanish	No hablo español	no *ah*-blow es-pahn-*yol*
I don't understand (you)	No entiendo	no en-tee-*en*-doe
I understand (you)	Entiendo	en-tee-*en*-doe
I don't know	No sé	no *say*
I am American/ British	Soy americano(a)/ inglés(a)	soy ah-meh-ree-*kah*-no(ah)/ in-*glace*(ah)
What's your name?	¿Cómo se llama usted?	*koh*-mo say *yah*-mah oos-*ted*
My name is . . .	Me llamo . . .	may *yah*-moh
What time is it?	¿Qué hora es?	keh *o*-rah es
It is one, two, three . . . o'clock.	Es la una; son las dos, tres	es la *oo*-nah/sone lahs dose, trace
Yes, please/No, thank you	Sí, por favor/No, gracias	*see* pore fah-*vor*/no *grah*-see-us
How?	¿Cómo?	*koh*-mo
When?	¿Cuándo?	*kwahn*-doe
This/Next week	Esta semana/ la semana que entra	*es*-tah seh-*mah*-nah/lah say-*mah*-nah keh *en*-trah
This/Next month	Este mes/el próximo mes	*es*-tay mehs/el *proke*-see-mo mehs
This/Next year	Este año/el año que viene	*es*-tay *ahn*-yo/el *ahn*-yo keh vee-*yen*-ay
Yesterday/today/ tomorrow	Ayer/hoy/mañana	ah-*yair*/oy/mahn-*yah*-nah
This morning/ afternoon	Esta mañana/tarde	*es*-tah mahn-*yah*-nah/*tar*-day
Tonight	Esta noche	*es*-tah *no*-cheh
What?	¿Qué?	keh
What is it?	¿Qué es esto?	keh es *es*-toe
Why?	¿Por qué?	pore *keh*
Who?	¿Quién?	kee-*yen*
Where is . . . ?	¿Dónde está . . . ?	*dohn*-day es-*tah*
the train station?	la estación del tren?	la es-tah-see-*on* del *train*
the subway station?	la estación del Metro?	la es-ta-see-*on* del *meh*-tro
the bus stop?	la parada del autobús?	la pah-*rah*-dah del oh-toe-*boos*
the post office?	la oficina de correos?	la oh-fee-*see*-nah day koh-*reh*-os
the bank?	el banco?	el *bahn*-koh
the . . . hotel?	el hotel . . . ?	el oh-*tel*
the store?	la tienda . . . ?	la tee-*en*-dah

the cashier?	la caja?	la *kah*-hah
the . . . museum?	el museo . . . ?	el moo-*seh*-oh
the hospital?	el hospital?	el ohss-pea-*tal*
the elevator?	el ascensor?	el ah-*sen*-sore
the bathroom?	el baño?	el *bahn*-yoh
Here/there	Aquí/allá	ah-*key*/ah-*yah*
Open/closed	Abierto/cerrado	ah-be-*er*-toe/ ser-*ah*-doe
Left/right	Izquierda/derecha	iss-key-*er*-dah/ dare-*eh*-chah
Straight ahead	Derecho	der-*eh*-choh
Is it near/far?	¿Está cerca/lejos?	es-*tah sair*-kah/ *leh*-hoss
I'd like . . .	Quisiera . . .	kee-see-air-ah
a room	un cuarto/una habitación	oon *kwahr*-toe/ *oo*-nah ah-bee-tah-see-*on*
the key	la llave	lah *yah*-vay
a newspaper	un periódico	oon pear-ee-*oh*-dee-koh
a stamp	un timbre de correo	oon *team*-bray day koh-*reh*-oh
I'd like to buy . . .	Quisiera comprar . . .	kee-see-*air*-ah kohm-*prahr*
cigarettes	cigarrillo	ce-gar-*reel*-oh
matches	cerillos	ser-*ee*-ohs
a dictionary	un diccionario	oon deek-see-oh-*nah*-ree-oh
soap	jabón	hah-*bone*
a map	un mapa	oon *mah*-pah
a magazine	una revista	*oon*-ah reh-*veess*-tah
paper	papel	pah-*pel*
envelopes	sobres	*so*-brace
a postcard	una tarjeta postal	*oon*-ah tar-*het*-ah post-*ahl*
How much is it?	¿Cuánto cuesta?	*kwahn*-toe *kwes*-tah
It's expensive/ cheap	Está caro/barato	es-*tah kah*-roh/ bah-*rah*-toe
A little/a lot	Un poquito/ mucho . . .	oon poh-*kee*-toe/ *moo*-choh
More/less	Más/menos	mahss/*men*-ohss
Enough/too much/too little	Suficiente/de-masiado/muy poco	soo-fee-see-*en*-tay/ day-mah-see-*ah*-doe/moo-ee poh-koh
Telephone	Teléfono	tel-*ef*-oh-no
Telegram	Telegrama	teh-leh-*grah*-mah
I am ill/sick	Estoy enfermo(a)	es-*toy* en-*fair*-moh(ah)
Please call a doctor	Por favor llame un médico	pore fa-*vor ya*-may oon *med*-ee-koh
Help!	¡Auxilio! ¡Ayuda!	owk-*see*-lee-oh/ ah-*yoo*-dah

| Fire! | ¡Encendio! | en-*sen*-dee-oo |
| Caution!/Look out! | ¡Cuidado! | kwee-*dah*-doh |

On the Road

Highway	Carretera	car-ray-*ter*-ah
Causeway, paved highway	Calzada	cal-*za*-dah
Route	Ruta	*roo*-tah
Road	Camino	cah-*mee*-no
Street	Calle	*cah*-yeh
Avenue	Avenida	ah-ven-*ee*-dah
Broad, tree-lined boulevard	Paseo	pah-*seh*-oh
Waterfront promenade	Malecón	mal-lay-*cone*
Wharf	Embarcadero	em-bar-cah-*day*-ro

In Town

Church	Templo/Iglesia	*tem*-plo/e-*gles*-se-*ah*
Cathedral	Catedral	cah-tay-*dral*
Neighborhood	Barrio	*bar*-re-o
Foreign exchange shop	Casa de cambio	*cas*-sah day *cam*-be-o
City hall	Ayuntamiento	ah-yoon-tah-mee-*en*-toe
Main square	Zócalo	*zo*-cal-o
Traffic circle	Glorieta	glor-e-*ay*-tah
Market	Mercado (Spanish)/ Tianguis (Indian)	mer-*cah*-doe/ tee-*an*-geese
Inn	Posada	pos-*sah*-dah
Group taxi	Colectivo	co-lec-*tee*-vo
Group taxi along fixed route	Pesero	pi-*seh*-ro

Items of Clothing

Embroidered white smock	Huipil	whee-*peel*
Pleated man's shirt worn outside the pants	Guayabera	gwah-ya-*beh*-ra
Leather sandals	Huaraches	wah-*ra*-chays
Shawl	Rebozo	ray-*bozh*-o
Pancho or blanket	Serape	seh-*ra*-peh

Dining Out

| A bottle of . . . | Una botella de . . . | oo-nah bo-*tay*-yah deh |
| A cup of . . . | Una taza de . . . | oo-nah *tah*-sah deh |

A glass of . . .	Un vaso de . . .	oon *vah*-so deh
Ashtray	Un cenicero	oon sen-ee-*seh*-roh
Bill/check	La cuenta	lah *kwen*-tah
Bread	El pan	el pahn
Breakfast	El desayuno	el day-sigh-*oon*-oh
Butter	La mantequilla	lah mahn-tay-*key*-yah
Cheers!	¡Salud!	sah-*lood*
Cocktail	Un aperitivo	oon ah-pair-ee-*tee*-voh
Dinner	La cena	lah *seh*-nah
Dish	Un plato	oon *plah*-toe
Dish of the day	El platillo de hoy	el plah-*tee*-yo day oy
Enjoy!	¡Buen provecho!	bwen pro-*veh*-cho
Fixed-price menu	La comida corrida	lah koh-*me*-dah co-*ree*-dah
Fork	El tenedor	el ten-eh-*door*
Is the tip included?	¿Está incluida la propina?	es-*tah* in-clue-*ee*-dah lah pro-*pea*-nah
Knife	El cuchillo	el koo-*chee*-yo
Lunch	La comida	lah koh-*me*-dah
Menu	La carta	lah *cart*-ah
Napkin	La servilleta	lah sair-vee-*yet*-uh
Pepper	La pimienta	lah pea-me-*en*-tah
Please give me	Por favor déme	pore fah-*vor* *day*-may
Salt	La sal	lah sahl
Spoon	Una cuchara	*oo*-nah koo-*chah*-rah
Sugar	El azúcar	el ah-*sue*-car
Waiter!/Waitress!	¡Por favor Señor/Señorita!	pore fah-*vor* sen-*yor*/sen-yor-*ee*-tah

INDEX

X = *restaurant*, ▥ = *hotel*